Main Cities of Europe 2011

Contents

Contents

COUNTRIES

How to use this guide

PRACTICAL & TOURIST INFORMATION

Pages with practical information on every country and city: public transport, tourist information offices, main sites and attractions (museums, monuments, theatres, etc.).

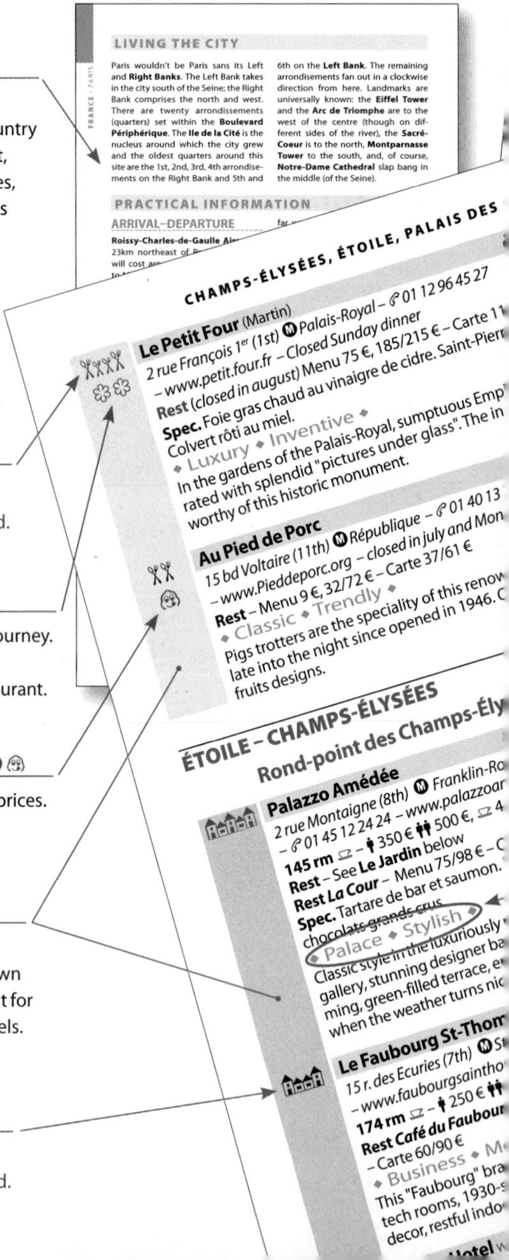

LIVING THE CITY

Paris wouldn't be Paris sans its Left and **Right Banks**. The Left Bank takes in the city south of the Seine; the Right Bank comprises the north and west. There are twenty arrondissements (quarters) set within the **Boulevard Périphérique**. The **Ile de la Cité** is the nucleus around which the city grew and the oldest quarters around this site are the 1st, 2nd, 3rd, 4th arrondisements on the Right Bank and 5th and 6th on the **Left Bank**. The remaining arrondisements fan out in a clockwise direction from here. Landmarks are universally known: the **Eiffel Tower** and the **Arc de Triomphe** are to the west of the centre (though on different sides of the river), the **Sacré-Coeur** is to the north, **Montparnasse Tower** to the south, and, of course, **Notre-Dame Cathedral** slap bang in the middle (of the Seine).

RESTAURANTS

XXXXX to X

The most pleasant : in red.

STARS

✿✿✿ Worth a special journey.
✿✿ Worth a detour.
✿ A very good restaurant.

BIB GOURMAND

Good food at moderate prices.

RESTAURANTS & HOTELS

The country is indicated by the coloured strip down the side of the page: light for restaurants, dark for hotels.

HOTELS

🏠🏠🏠🏠🏠 to 🏠

The most pleasant : in red.

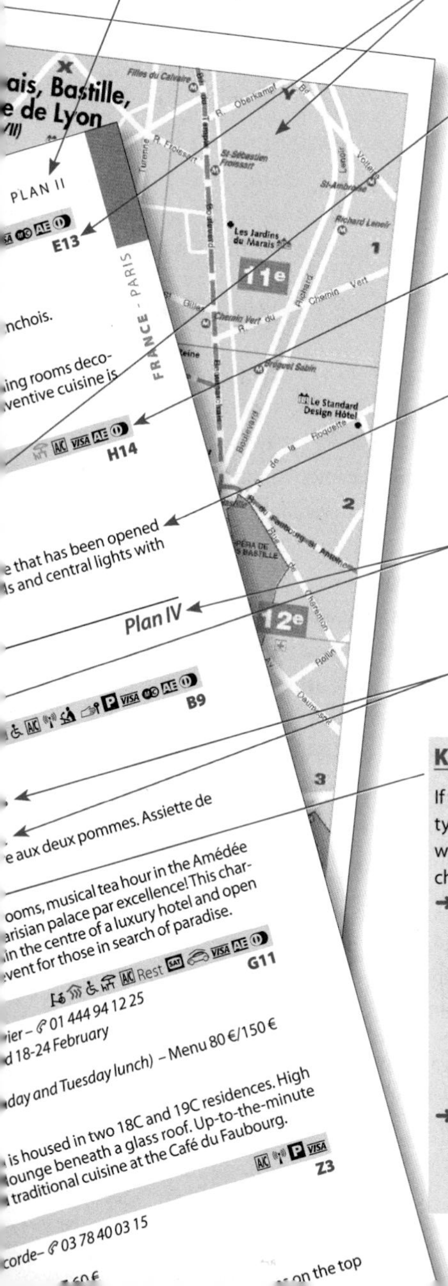

LOCATION

The country, the town, the district and the map.

LOCATING THE ESTABLISHMENT

Location and coordinates on the town plan, with principal sights.

ADDRESS

All the information you need to make a reservation and find the establishment.

FACILITIES & SERVICES

See also page 10.

DESCRIPTION OF THE ESTABLISHMENT

Atmosphere, style and character.

CLASSIFICATION BY DISTRICT

With the corresponding plan number.

PRICES

See also page 11.

KEY WORDS

If you are looking for a specific type of establishment, these key words will help you make your choice more quickly.

→ **For hotels**, the first word explains the **establishment type** (chain hotel, business, luxury, etc); the second one describes the **décor** (modern, stylish, design, etc) and sometimes a third will be used to complete the picture.

→ **For restaurants**, the first word relates to the **type of cuisine** and the second the **atmosphere**.

Commitments

"This volume was created at the turn of the century and will last at least as long".

This foreword to the very first edition of the MICHELIN Guide, written in 1900, has become famous over the years and the Guide has lived up to the prediction. It is read across the world and the key to its popularity is the consistency of its commitment to its readers, which is based on the following promises.

THE MICHELIN GUIDE'S COMMITMENTS

Anonymous inspections: our inspectors make regular and anonymous visits to hotels and restaurants to gauge the quality of products and services offered to an ordinary customer. They settle their own bill and may then introduce themselves and ask for more information about the establishment. Our readers' comments are also a valuable source of information, which we can then follow up with another visit of our own.

Independence: Our choice of establishments is a completely independent one, made for the benefit of our readers alone. The decisions to be taken are discussed around the table by the inspectors and the editor. The most important awards are decided at a European level. Inclusion in the Guide is completely free of charge.

Selection and choice: The Guide offers a selection of the best hotels and restaurants in every category of comfort and price. This is only possible because all the inspectors rigorously apply the same methods.

Annual updates: All the practical information, the classifications and awards are revised and updated every single year to give the most reliable information possible.

Consistency: The criteria for the classifications are the same in every country covered by the MICHELIN Guide.

... and our aim: to do everything possible to make travel,holidays and eating out a pleasure, as part of Michelin's ongoing commitment to improving travel and mobility.

Dear Reader

Welcome to the 30th edition of the 'Main Cities of Europe' guide.
This guide is aimed primarily at the international business traveller who regularly journeys throughout Europe but it is equally ideal for those wishing to discover the delights of some of Europe's most romantic and culturally stimulating cities for a weekend break or special occasion.

Entry in the MICHELIN Guide is completely free of charge and it continues to be compiled by our professionally trained teams of full-time inspectors from across Europe who make their assessments anonymously in order to ensure complete impartiality and independence. Their mission is to check the quality and consistency of the amenities and services provided by the hotels and restaurants throughout the year and our listings are updated annually in order to ensure the most up-to-date information.

Most of the establishments featured have been hand-picked from our other national guides and therefore our European selection is, effectively, a best-of-the-best listing.

In addition to the user-friendly layout the guide contains key thematic words which succinctly convey the style of the establishment; practical and cultural information on each country and each city; suggestions on when to go, what to see and what to eat.

Thank you for your support and please continue to send us your comments. We hope you will enjoy travelling with the 'Main Cities of Europe' guide 2011.

Consult the MICHELIN Guide at
www.ViaMichelin.com
and write to us at:
themichelinguide-europe@uk.michelin.com

Classification & Awards

CATEGORIES OF COMFORT

The MICHELIN Guide selection lists the best hotels and restaurants in each category of comfort and price. The establishments we choose are classified according to their levels of comfort and, within each category, are listed in order of preference.

🏠🏠🏠🏠🏠	XXXXX	Luxury in the traditional style
🏠🏠🏠🏠	XXXX	Top class comfort
🏠🏠🏠	XXX	Very comfortable
🏠🏠	XX	Comfortable
🏠	X	Quite comfortable
	🍺	Pubs serving good food
	🍷	Tapas bars
⌂		Other recommended accommodation
without rest.		This hotel has no restaurant
with rm		This restaurant also offers accommodation

THE AWARDS

To help you make the best choice, some exceptional establishments have been given an award in this year's Guide. They are marked ✿ or ☺ and **Rest**.

THE BEST CUISINE

Michelin stars are awarded to establishments serving cuisine, of whatever style, which is of the highest quality. The cuisine is judged on the quality of ingredients, the skill in their preparation, the combination of flavours, the levels of creativity, the value for money and the consistency of culinary standards.

✿✿✿	**Exceptional cuisine, worth a special journey** One always eats extremely well here, sometimes superbly.
✿✿	**Excellent cooking, worth a detour**
✿	**A very good restaurant in its category**

RISING STARS

These establishments, listed in red, are the best in their present category. They have the potential to rise further, and already have an element of superior quality; as soon as they produce this quality consistently, and in all aspects of their cuisine, they will be hot tips for a higher award. We've highlighted these promising restaurants so you can try them for yourselves; we think they offer a foretaste of the gastronomy of the future.

GOOD FOOD AT MODERATE PRICES

Bib Gourmand

Establishments offering good quality cuisine at reasonable prices (the actual price limit varies from country to country according to the relative costs).

PLEASANT HOTELS AND RESTAURANTS

Symbols shown in red indicate particularly pleasant or restful establishments: the character of the building, its décor, the setting, the welcome and services offered may all contribute to this special appeal.

to **Pleasant hotels**

to **Pleasant restaurants**

OTHER SPECIAL FEATURES

As well as the categories and awards given to the establishment, Michelin inspectors also make special note of other criteria which can be important when choosing an establishment.

LOCATION

If you are looking for a particularly restful establishment, or one with a special view, look out for the following symbols:

Quiet hotel

Very quiet hotel

Interesting view

Exceptional view

WINE LIST

If you are looking for an establishment with a particularly interesting wine list, look out for the following symbol:

Particularly interesting wine list
This symbol might cover the list presented by a sommelier in a luxury restaurant or that of a simple restaurant where the owner has a passion for wine. The two lists will offer something exceptional but very different, so beware of comparing them by each other's standards.

Facilities & Services

30 rm	Number of rooms
A/C	Air conditioning (in all or part of the establishment)
	Establishment with areas reserved for non-smokers
	Establishment at least partly accessible to those of restricted mobility
	Meals served in garden or on terrace
SAT	Satellite TV
	Fast internet access in bedrooms
	Wireless Internet access
Spa	Wellness centre: an extensive facility for relaxation and well-being
	Sauna – Exercise room
	Swimming pool: outdoor or indoor
	Garden
	Tennis court
	Equipped conference room
	Private dining rooms
P P	Valet parking – Garage – Car park – Enclosed parking
May-October	Dates when open, as indicated by the hotelier
M	Nearest metro station

Prices

The prices are given in the currency of the country in question. Valid for 2011 the rates shown should only vary if the cost of living changes to any great extent.

SERVICE AND TAXES

Except in Greece, Hungary, Poland and Spain, prices shown are inclusive, that is to say service and V.A.T. included. In the U.K. and Ireland, s = service included. In Italy, when not included, a percentage for service is shown after the meal prices, eg. (16 %).

MEALS

Meals 40/56	Set meal prices
Carte	'à la carte' meal prices

HOTEL

86 rm 🚹 650/750	Lowest and highest price for a comfortable single
🚹🚹 750/890	and for a double room
☕ 60/120	Prices include breakfast

BREAKFAST

☕ 20	Price of breakfast (where not included in rate)

CREDIT CARDS

	Credit cards accepted by the establishment:
AE ⓓ MC VISA	American Express – Diners Club – MasterCard – Visa

The Michelin Guide and Europe

Whether it be for business or pleasure, travellers throughout Europe know that they can rely on the Michelin Guide. For over a century, it has been their companion, first in France and then beyond the dotted borderlines printed on the Michelin maps.

Over the last hundred years, the boundaries of Europe have been extended and the circle of gold stars on the European flag has had to adjust in order to welcome other nations. The Michelin Guide has always kept abreast of these profound changes on the ground, in keeping with its goal and its motto: *serving the traveller.* Indeed, in its coverage of Europe, it has witnessed the history of the continent as it unfolded. Year after year, the guide's publication or absence from the market has reflected the great upheavals experienced during the 20th century, with its vicissitudes, crises, eras of prosperity and peace.

THE MICHELIN GUIDE: MULTILINGUAL AND INTERNATIONAL

Inspired by its success in France and encouraged by the development of the automobile industry throughout Europe, the Michelin Guide started to spread the concept to neighbouring countries: *Belgique* appeared in 1904 – the second volume in what would quickly become a true European-wide collection. The following year, a third guide – *Benelux* – was published. The collection began to adopt an approach which would include **tourist information**, with new sections covering sights and excursions not to be missed, in addition to the advice and practical information already in the guides. At the same time, the Michelin Guide collection started to espouse Michelin's international ambitions: every new title was published in the language(s) of the country, services and main facilities were indicated by **symbols** that everyone could understand, and several pages were devoted to **international regulations** useful for travellers. Consequently readers could refer to a page dedicated to «General European Traffic Rules», for example, with specific information

regarding which side of the road to drive on in every European country. It is interesting to note that, at the time, the Michelin Guide included Turkey as part of Europe, with information about traffic in that country.

MICHELIN TRAVELS ABROAD

The Michelin Guide began to expand throughout Europe and use other languages. In 1908 *The Michelin Guide to France* was published, an **adaptation in English** of the original French guide, and two years later two new titles were published: *Deutschland* und *Schweiz* and *España y Portugal*. The following year (1911) three more guides were published, expanding the collection still further: *British Isles, Alpes et Rhin*, and the exotic *Les pays du Soleil*, covering not only the Côte d'Azur, Corsica and Italy, but also North Africa and Egypt! And that same year, all of these guides were translated into English.

This unprecedented expansion marked the start of the company's desire to spread throughout Europe and North Africa. Proof of the successful formula of the Michelin Guides was summed up in an advertising poster of the era showing Bibendum – the Michelin Man – proudly demonstrating that the total number of copies of the Michelin guide collection, if piled up, would be equivalent to 60 times the height of St Paul's Cathedral in London!

Success was then interrupted in 1939, with the start of the **Second World War**. From 1940 to 1944, the absence of the guide revealed the torment which Europe was going through. When the guide finally reappeared, it was «*for official use only*», printed in Washington to accompany the officers of the Allied forces during the Normandy Landings.

FROM A EUROPEAN COLLECTION...

The 1950s brought new growth, with Michelin maps now covering all of Western Europe. But it was in the 1960s that the Michelin Guide collection really started to take on a **European dimension**, taking a step by step approach to expansion. In 1964, after a half century's absence, *Deutschland* reappeared (without the GDR and East Berlin), followed ten years later by *Great Britain & Ireland*. Meanwhile, the shorter *Paris* and *London* guides appeared on the shelves, based on information taken from the national guides, and revealing an interest in large **European capital cities**. In order to remain the indispensable companion for travellers throughout Europe, the guides would from then on follow the model of *France*: enhanced with more information, including a **rigorous selection of fine restaurants**.

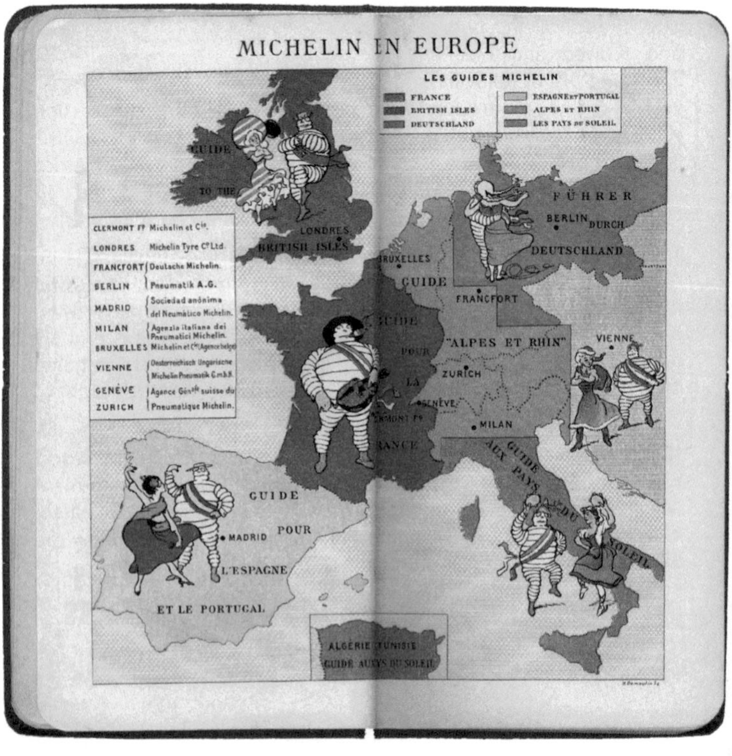

...TO A GUIDE FOR EUROPE

Means of transport were becoming more and more diversified and journey times were shortening considerably, encouraging faster travel and trips made more often and over longer distances than ever before. Michelin needed to bring tourists and business travellers alike a guide which covered the relevant areas, and at the same time crossed the borders of the new Europe to the north and to the east.

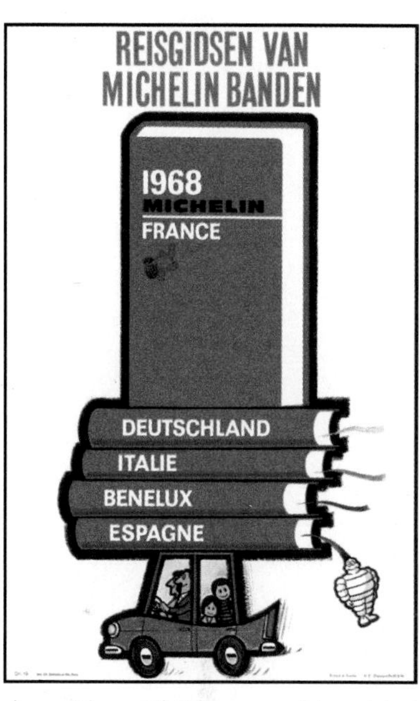

1982 saw the chance to do this. The first guide devoted to Europe was born of a **partnership** with *Times-Life Magazine* and appeared under the title *20 Cities/ Villes EUROPE*. The guide was written in English and twenty thousands copies were published. The selection of establishments adopted for the guide took the best hotel and restaurant addresses in each category from the «country» guides, following the criteria guaranteeing **a constant level of quality**, above and beyond specific national considerations.
The huge success of this first edition led the company to repeat the experience. The following year, Copenhagen and Vienna were included in the guide: until then, no guide existed which covered these cities, and the more global title *Main Cities of Europe* was adopted in 1984 with more than 50 towns and cities – some of them capitals, but also the other large influential cities in **20 countries**.

Who does not recognise the famous red cover of the Michelin Guide today? Since the beginning of the 20th century, the Guide has established itself throughout Europe thanks to quality, service and up-to-date selection. From Oslo to Athens, Lisbon to Budapest, the 24 titles in the collection (including the latest city guides to Hong Kong, Kamakura-Yokohama, Tokyo and Kobe-Kyoto-Osaka) recommend over 25 000 hotels and 16 000 restaurants, including over 1 800 starred restaurants, and 1 200 town plans. With practical information on every country and every town and city selected, the 2011 vintage of *Main Cities of EUROPE* offers you the very best. Happy reading and bon voyage with Michelin!

The world No.1 in tyres with 16.3% of the market

A business presence in over **170 countries**

A manufacturing footprint at the heart of markets

In 2009 **72** industrial sites in **19** countries produced:

- **150** million tyres
- **10** million maps and guides

Highly international **teams**

Over **109 200** employees* from all cultures on all continents including **6 000** people employed in R&D centers in Europe, the US and Asia.

*102 692 full-time equivalent staff

The Michelin Group at a glance

Michelin competes

At the end of 2009

Le Mans 24-hour race
12 consecutive years of victories

Endurance 2009
- 6 victories on 6 stages in Le Mans Series
- 12 victories on 12 stages in American Le Mans Series

Paris-Dakar
Since the beginning of the event, the Michelin group has won in all categories

Moto endurance
2009 World Champion

Trial
Every World Champion title since 1981 (except 1992)

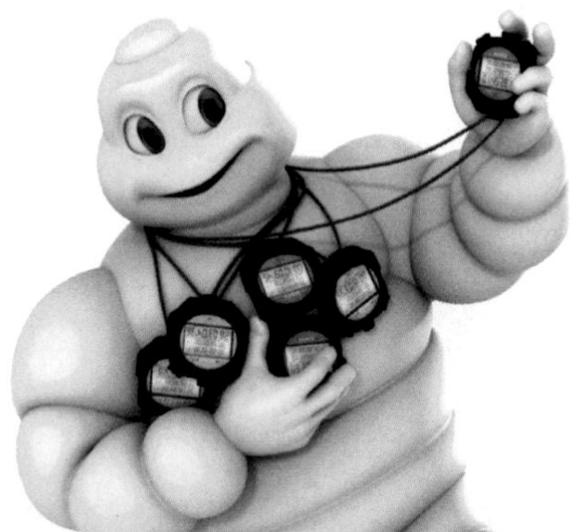

Michelin, stablished lose to its ustomers

○ 72 plants in 19 countries

- Algeria
- Brazil
- Canada
- China
- Colombia
- France
- Germany
- Hungary
- Italy
- Japan
- Mexico
- Poland
- Romania
- Russia
- Serbia
- Spain
- Thailand
- UK
- USA

● A Technology Centre spread over 3 continents

- Asia
- Europe
- North America

● Natural rubber plantations

- Brazil

Our mission

To make a sustainable contribution to progress in the mobility of goods and people by enhancing freedom of movement, safety, efficiency and the pleasure of travelling.

Michelin: committed to environmental-friendliness

ichelin, vorld leader n low rolling esistance tyres, ctively reduces uel consumption and ehicle gas emission.

For its products, Michelin develops state-of-the-art technologies in order to:

- Reduce fuel consumption, while improving overall tyre performance.
- Increase life cycle to reduce the number of tyres to be processed at the end of their useful lives;
- Use raw materials which have a low impact on the environment.

Furthermore, at the end of 2008, 99.5% of tyre production in volume was carried out in ISO 14001* certified plants.

Michelin is committed to implementing recycling channels for end-of-life tyres.

*environmental certification

Passenger Car
Light Truck

Truck

Michelin
a key mobility enabler

Earthmover

Aircraft

Agricultural

Two-wheel

Distribution

Partnered with vehicle manufacturers, in tune with users, active in competition and in all the distribution channels, Michelin is continually innovating to promote mobility today and to invent that of tomorrow.

Maps and Guides

ViaMichelin, travel assistance services

Michelin Lifestyle, for your travel accessories

MICHELIN plays on balanced performance

- **Long tyre life**
- **Fuel savings**
- **Safety on the road**

... MICHELIN tyres provide you with the best performance, without making a single sacrifice.

1 Tread
A thick layer of rubber provides contact with the ground. It has to channel water away and last as long as possible.

2 Crown plies
This double or triple reinforced belt has both vertical flexibility and high lateral rigidity. It provides the steering capacity.

3 Sidewalls
These cover and protect the textile casing whose role is to attach the tyre tread to the wheel rim.

4 Bead area for attachment to the rim
Its internal bead wire clamps the tyre firmly against the wheel rim.

5 Inner liner
This makes the tyre almost totally impermeable and maintains the correct inflation pressure.

AUSTRIA
ÖSTERREICH

PROFILE

→ **Area:**
83 853 km²
(32 376 sq mi).

→ **Population:**
8 150 000 inhabitants (est. 2005), density = 97 per km².

→ **Capital:**
Vienna (conurbation 1 892 000 inhabitants).

→ **Currency:**
Euro (€); rate of exchange: € 1 = US$ 1.37 (Dec. 2010).

→ **Government:**
Parliamentary republic and federal state (since 1955). Member of European Union since 1995.

→ **Language:**
German.

→ **Specific public holidays:**
Epiphany (6 January); Corpus Christi (late May/June); National Day (26 October); Immaculate Conception (8 December); St. Stephen's Day (26 December).

→ **Local Time:**
GMT + 1 hour in winter and GMT + 2 hours in summer.

→ **Climate:**
Temperate continental with cold winters – high snow levels – and warm summers (Vienna: January: 0°C, July: 20°C).

→ **International dialling Code:**
00 43 followed by area code without initial 0 and then the local number.

→ **Emergency:**
Police: ✆ **133**;
Medical Assistance: ✆ **144**;
Fire Brigade: ✆ **122.**

→ **Electricity:**
220 volts AC, 50Hz; 2-pin round-shaped continental plugs

→ **Formalities**
Travellers from the European Union (EU), Switzerland, Iceland and the main countries of North and South America need a national identity card or passport (America: passport required) to visit Austria for less than three months (tourism or business purpose). For visitors from other countries a visa may be required, in addition to a passport, especially for those wishing to stay for longer than three months. We advise you to check with your embassy before travelling.

VIENNA

WIEN

Population: 1 705 080 (conurbation 1 983 836) – Altitude: 156m.

ReSeandra/Fotolia.com

Beethoven, Brahms, Mozart, Haydn, Strauss...not a bad list of former residents, by any stretch of the imagination. One and all, they succumbed to the opulent aura of Vienna, a city where an appreciation of the arts is as conspicuous as its famed big cream cakes. Sumptuous architecture and a refined air reflect the city's historical position as the seat of the powerful Habsburg dynasty and former epicentre of the Austro-Hungarian Empire. This is a city where the words rococo and baroque could have been invented.

Despite its grand image, Vienna is propelling itself into the twenty-first century with a handful of seriously innovative hotspots, most notably the MuseumsQuartier cultural complex, a stone's throw from the mighty Hofburg Imperial Palace. This is not a big city, although its vivid image gives that impression. The compact centre teems with elegant shops, fashionable coffee-houses and grand avenues, and the empire's awesome nineteenth-century remnants keep visitors' eyes fixed forever upwards.

LIVING THE CITY

Many towns and cities are defined by their ring roads, but Vienna can boast a truly upmarket version: the **Ringstrasse**, a showpiece boulevard that cradles the inner city and the riches that lie therein. Just outside here – to the southwest - are the districts of **Neubau** and **Spittelberg**, both of which have taken on a quirky, modernistic feel, exemplified by the outstanding **MuseumsQuartier**, and a buzzing coterie of hip galleries and bars. To the east of town in the Leopoldstadt quarter lies **Prater,** the green lung of Vienna, and home to some of the world's oldest merry-go-rounds. Further out, southwest of the city, lies the suburban area utterly enhanced by the grandeur of the Schönbrunn palace. Where in all this is the blue Danube? Surprisingly enough, the great river of waltzing legend plays less of a role than many other city waterways as it flows some way out to the northeast of the city. Of more 'strategic' relevance to visitors is the Danube Canal, which divides the centre from the northern and eastern suburbs.

PRACTICAL INFORMATION

ARRIVAL-DEPARTURE

Wien-Schwechat Airport is 19km from the city centre. The City Airport Express train to Wien Mitte takes 16min and leaves every 30min. A taxi will cost around €30 and take 30min.

TRANSPORT

The Vienna Card, which allows unlimited travel on the whole of the city's public transport network for 72hr and offers a discount to sights, cafes, restaurants and shops, can be bought from the Tourist Office, at your hotel or from ticket offices of the Vienna Transport Authority. You can also purchase Rover tickets for 24hr or 72hr. The city's buses, trams and metro are renowned for their excellent efficiency.

There are around eighty bus routes around the city. Night buses run every half-hour throughout the small hours. The trams run every five to ten minutes, and there are timetables at every stop. You can bet your Sachertorte on them arriving exactly on time!

This is not a drivers' city. With its profusion of one-way streets, tramways and difficult-to-find parking spots, Vienna is most definitely somewhere to discover by foot or by public transport.

EXPLORING VIENNA

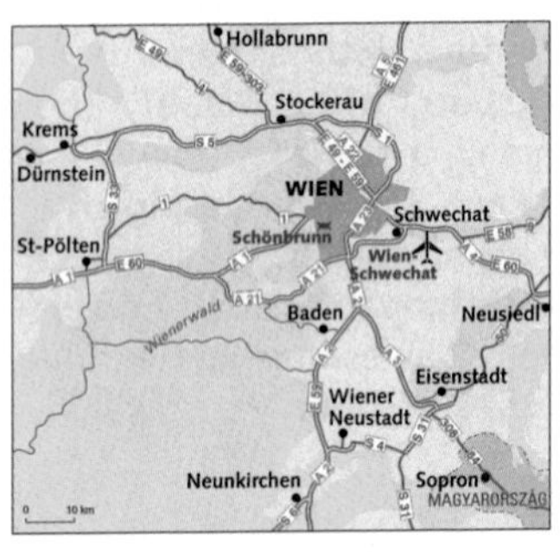

Take a ruling dynasty, give it six hundred years of power and influence, and what have you got? Answer: a city bursting with imperial pomp and palaces, a high-brow concoction set fair to impose and overawe. You've got Vienna. This is Europe's *grand dame*, where former royal palaces burst with treasure troves of art, white stallions trot daintily amongst visitors and classical concerts are performed in streets crammed with regal delights. The era of the Habsburgs came crashing to an uncomfortable end at the climax of World War I, but you only have to stroll around the old town, embraced by the Ringstrasse, to come face-to-face with its former glories. One location sums it all up: the **Hofburg**, or Imperial Palace. It dominates this famous area, and is a small town in itself, an immense palace complex with extensions and add-ons depending on the whim of successive Habsburg rulers. Two of the city's most famous institutions are based here: the **Vienna Boys' Choir** and the **Spanish Riding School**. You could spend all your time at the Hofburg, wandering around the Imperial Apartments, decked out with Biedermeier portraits and Bohemian crystal chandeliers, or following the melodramatic events of Empress Elisabeth's life in the Sisi Museum.

→ TOWERING GLORY

In time, though, you'll more than likely want to stroll the quarter-mile north to Vienna's second great visitor magnet, **St Stephen's Cathedral**, towering over Stephansplatz Square. Its chevron style mosaic roof and skeletal spires are iconic landmarks, and its near-450ft. tower (completed in 1433) means it can be seen from all over the city. Climb its 343 steps and you can return the favour. Your bird's eye view will take in a whole holiday's worth of museums and galleries, so cherry-pick the best, and your footsteps will invariably lead you to the **Art History Museum** on Maria-Theresien Platz. It's stacked with centuries of Habsburg-acquired artistic gems: the Picture Gallery is hung with 16C and 17C masters such as Titian, Caravaggio and Rubens, and there are other superb collections, including those of Roman and Egyptian antiquity.

→ QUIRKY QUARTIER

Anyone who knew Vienna before 2001 will wonder what's happened to the imperial stables, just over the road from the Art History Museum. These days, you won't see any horses, but you will find the impressively trendy **MuseumsQuartier.** This is now one of the biggest cultural complexes in the world, and its irresistible quirkiness draws visitors twenty-four hours a day (the courtyards and alleyways here never close; its cafés and bars think along much the same lines). The MQ is home to an awesome array of artists and art spaces, galleries and museums. Its defining attraction is a massive white cube – the Leopold Museum – which has five floors of 19C and 20C art, the highlights being Austria's 'dynamic duo' Klimt and Schiele: the latter's world-famous Reclining Woman is here.

Find your way out of the MQ, head east along the Ringstrasse, and before you can say Don Giovanni you're at the **Staatsoper**, or State Opera House. This is possibly the most cherished building of them all to locals, and has had a special place in Viennese hearts since it opened to the strains of Mozart in 1869. Designed in grandiose Italian Renaissance style, there's an invariable throng of people getting in line for their cheap standing-room tickets. If you can't make it to a concert here, then try the Musikverein further east. Also built in the 1860s, it matches the Opera House in terms of popularity, not least because its acoustics are second-to-none, its décor is sumptuous, and it's home to the globally renowned Vienna Philharmonic. When the play's the thing, the Viennese head back west along the Ringstrasse to the Burgtheater. You can't miss it: it's right opposite the grand neo-Gothic City Hall. Some go to the Burgtheater just to clap eyes on the sumptuously decorated staircases that define the place. Others go for the city's finest drama productions.

→ BEL-EPOQUE

Just when you think this box of treasures has given up all its golden contents, along comes a palace that even outdoes the Hofburg. The **Belvedere** is southeast of the centre, and its two superb Baroque mansions, atop a sweeping garden, offer wonderful vistas of central Vienna. One of these imposing buildings (the grander of the two, the Upper Belvedere,) houses the wondrous Austrian Art Gallery, which boasts an impressive collection of works by Klimt, plus a notable selection by Schiele. Great paintings by Van Gogh and Monet are here, too. Not to be totally outdone, the Lower Belvedere showcases treasures with a medieval, baroque and Golden Age hue.

→ THE AVANT GARDE

To be honest, the area of Leopoldstadt, to the east of the city, isn't going to win any tourism awards. On the whole, it's pretty suburban, and pretty uninteresting, save for two shining lights. The Hundertwasserhaus, by the Danube Canal, is a fifty-apartment housing complex. In 1983, avant-garde architect Friedensreich Hundertwasser took it by the scruff of the neck and converted it into an eyeball-popping explosion of colour and wavy lines, a higgledy-piggledy jumble of textures that draws tourists united by one common denominator – the dropped jaw. Meanwhile, across the canal, the more conservative Prater is a traditional magnet for suburban dwellers and visiting hordes alike; this vast park has been welcoming all comers for nearly two hundred and fifty years. It's a vast place, with a funfair, tracts of woodland, a miniature railway and a planetarium. Its giant Ferris wheel lifts you above the skyline in rickety red gondolas, and on high you can see right across to St Stephen's Cathedral. If you love the aroma of candyfloss and the twinkling tinkle of the merry-go-round, then you might want to forget the more *fin-de-siècle* attractions of Vienna, and hang round the Prater instead.

One little quarter even the most devout Prater lover would not wish to miss out on lies just beyond the MuseumsQuartier. It's called Spittelberg, and it comprises half a dozen parallel, narrow cobbled streets that have retained their eighteenth-century appeal, a taste of Old Vienna beyond the Ringstrasse. There's a modern twist here: this charming district now has a new lease of life, enhanced by a string of bars, cafés and stylish art galleries, smartly entwined with the Baroque and Biedermeier houses that have been carefully restored to their former glory.

CALENDAR HIGHLIGHTS

Vienna's cultural highlights, not to anyone's great surprise, have a predominantly musical flavour, kicking off in January with the world-famous New Year's Day Concert at the Musikverein; almost as fancy are the balls which waltz through the city in deepest winter. Two of the more glitzy are the Practitioners' Ball (January) and the Opera Ball (February), when pink carnations and *The Blue Danube* are obligatory. Springtime is heralded with April's City Festival, and free musical concerts are the backbone here. A couple of cultural biggies hit town in June. The Vienna Festival is a huge event with music and theatrical highlights being shared out, while the Danube Island Festival is a three-day extravaganza of free concerts

VIENNA IN…

→ ONE DAY

A tram ride round the Ringstrasse (two and a half miles), St Stephen's Cathedral, a section of the Hofburg Palace, cream cakes at a smart café

→ TWO DAYS

MuseumsQuartier, Spittelberg, Hundertwasserhaus, Prater

→ THREE DAYS

A day at the Belvedere, a night at the opera

by bands from far and wide with the added allure of it all happening on the river's dinky islands. Later in the month and into July the vibe changes with the Vienna Jazz Festival, which spreads itself to hip venues across the city, while later in the summer the mood changes once again with KlangBogen, a chance to catch top opera and classical performers in a widely-renowned series of concerts. November brings the Wien Modern festival, which succeeds in adding a cutting edge to contemporary classical music. It's not all batons, bass and big beats in this city – September's Literature Festival lasts for twenty four hours and features Austria's leading authors reading from their works non-stop around the clock – an "adventure in the head" - while the Viennale in October is Austria's biggest festival of film.

EATING OUT

Vienna is the spiritual home of the café ; the landing stage of Europe's first coffee bean (or so legend has it). Austrians drink nearly twice as much coffee as beer, astonishingly over a pint a day per head of population. A sweet tooth characterises the city: chunky mounds of glistening cream cakes enhance the window displays of most eateries. Is there a visitor to Vienna who hasn't succumbed to the sponge of the Sachertorte? Reflecting its empire days, the city's restaurants are many-pronged, so if you wish to eat your way around the globe, you shouldn't have a problem here. Viennese food is essentially the food of Bohemia, which means that meat has a strong presence on the plate. Beef, veal, pork, alongside potatoes, dumplings or cabbage, gives you pretty much the picture - be sure to try traditional boiled beef or the ubiquitous Wiener Schnitzel, deep-fried breaded veal. Also worth experiencing are the Heurigen, the traditional Austrian wine taverns which are found in Grinzing, Heiligenstadt, Neustift and Nussdorf. Elsewhere, there are snug cafés and sushi bars, tasty trattorias and tapas bars. MuseumsQuartier and Spittelberg are great places to head for to get good food and avoid the tourist centre scrum. If you want to eat on the hoof, the place to go is Naschmarkt, Vienna's best market, where the ethnic range of stalls spills over into the vibrant little restaurants dishing up everything from a plateful of noodles to a steaming, spicy curry. When it comes to tipping, if you're in the more relaxed, local pubs and wine taverns, just round up the bill, otherwise add on ten per cent.

→ UNDERGROUND SPY NETWORK

Much of cinema's iconic The Third Man was filmed in Vienna – and in particular, the sewers. Harry Lime spent an unforgettable period scurrying round beneath *strasse* level. He had a lot of sewer to choose from: there are about three thousand miles' worth in the city. About half can be walked, and you can sample them for yourself on various tours.

→ HOLIDAYING HAPSBURGS

Where did the Hapsburgs go for summer retreat? Answer: the grandiose **Schönbrunn Palace** three miles southwest of the centre. It's Austria's answer to Versailles, boasting a seventy foot high Palm House and a Hall of Mirrors where Mozart played. The whole complex is a symmetrical masterwork of 1500 rooms that in its day would have housed more than a thousand servants. Nowadays it welcomes over six and a half million visitors a year.

Palais Coburg

rm,

Coburgbastei 4 ✉ 1010 – Ⓜ Stubentor – ✆ (01) 51 81 80 – www.palais-coburg.com **E2**

35 suites – 670/2700 € 670/2700 €

Rest – Menu 42/64 € – Carte 34/54 €

♦ Grand Luxury ♦ Historic ♦ Modern ♦

Established in 1840 this magnificent building presents its guests with an impressive structure. Guests, who are housed in maisonettes or comfortable, luxurious suites, receive excellent service. This restaurant consists of a light and airy garden pavilion, a wine bar and a pretty bastion garden.

Imperial

Kärntner Ring 16 ✉ 1015 – Ⓜ Karlsplatz – ✆ (01) 50 11 00 – www.luxurycollection.com/imperial **E3**

138 rm – 359/819 € 359/819 €, 39 € – 35 suites

Rest *Imperial* – *(dinner only) (booking advisable)* Carte 53/83 €

Rest *Café Imperial* – Carte 35/59 €

♦ Palace ♦ Grand Luxury ♦ Historic ♦

The truly majestic atmosphere of this grand old hotel, opened in 1873, reflects the glittering era of the Kaiser. Its stylish lobby, magnificent function rooms and elegant guestrooms and suites are truly impressive. A restaurant offering a refined and exclusive ambience. The Café Imperial offers all the flair of a Viennese coffee house.

Grand Hotel

Kärntner Ring 9 ✉ 1010 – Ⓜ Karlsplatz – ✆ (01) 51 58 00 – www.grandhotelwien.com **E3**

205 rm – 370/470 € 420/520 €, 31 € – 11 suites

Rest *Le Ciel* – see below

Rest *Unkai* – *✆ (01) 5 15 80 91 10 (closed Monday lunch)* Menu 38/130 € – Carte 22/52 €

Rest *Grand Café* – *✆ (01) 5 15 80 91 20* – Carte 28/53 €

♦ Grand Luxury ♦ Classic ♦

The Grand Hotel offers classical and elegant rooms luxuriously decorated with a historical flair. There is a sushi bar inside the hotel. The Unkai features Japanese cuisine.

Sacher

Philharmonikerstr. 4 ✉ 1010 – Ⓜ Karlsplatz – ✆ (01) 51 45 60 – www.sacher.com **D3**

152 rm – 400/695 € 400/695 €, 32 € – 7 suites

Rest *Anna Sacher* – see below

Rest *Rote Bar* – Carte 33/69 €

♦ Luxury ♦ Classic ♦ Personalised ♦

Throughout this stylish hotel in the heart of Vienna you can feel the tradition that has been maintained since its opening in 1876. The rooms and suites are individual, and furnished in classic styles. The service is very attentive. The Rote Bar is sumptuously bedecked in red velvet. It serves delicious, traditional cuisine.

Bristol

Kärntner Ring 1 ✉ 1015 – Ⓜ Karlsplatz – ✆ (01) 51 51 60 – www.luxurycollection.com/bristol **D3**

140 rm – 229/529 € 259/589 €, 35 € – 10 suites

Rest *Korso* – Menu 38/58 € – Carte 36/70 €

♦ Luxury ♦ Traditional ♦ Classic ♦

This attentively run, traditional hotel boasts typical Viennese charm and period lounges which are characteristic of the beautiful interior. You will love the service and the classical elegance of the rooms. The Korso restaurant boasts a stylish atmosphere.

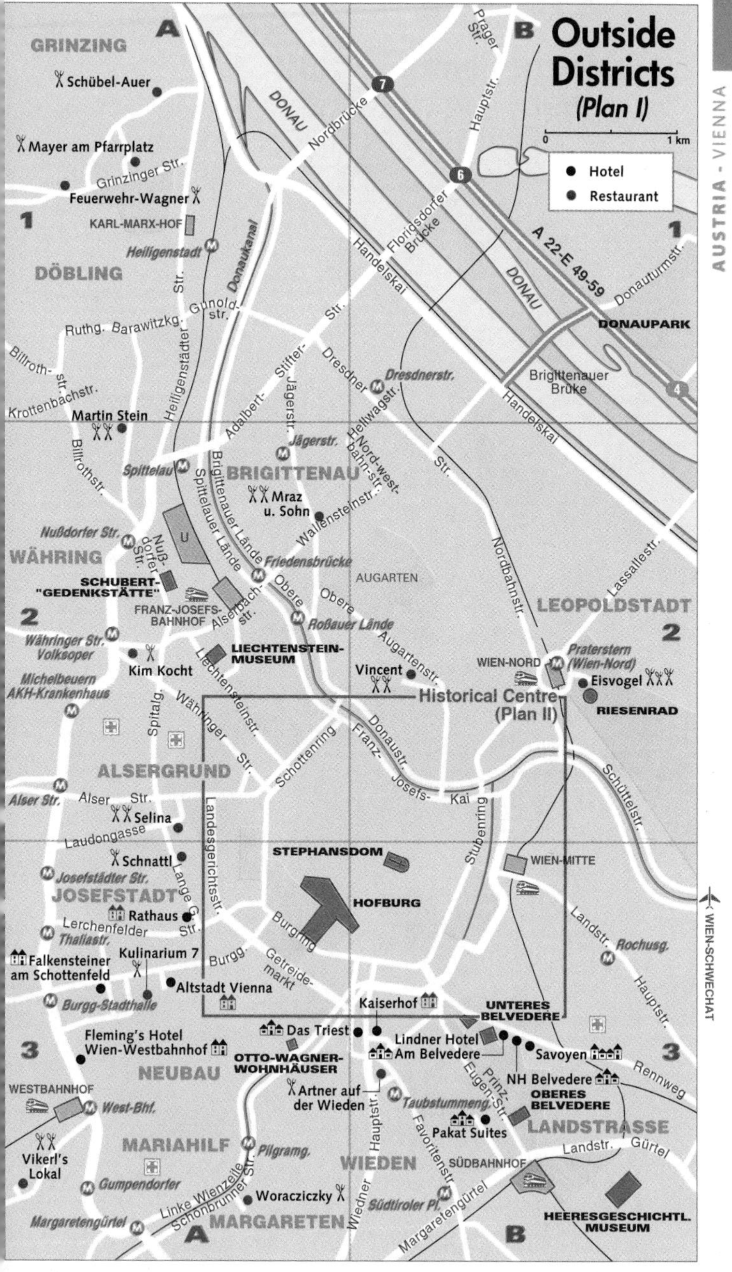

Outside Districts
(Plan I)
0
1 km
Hotel
Restaurant
GRINZING
Schübel-Auer
Mayer am Pfarrplatz
Grinzinger Str.
Feuerwehr-Wagner
KARL-MARX-HOF
Heiligenstadt
DÖBLING
Donaukanal
DONAU
Nordbrücke
Prager Str.
Hauptstr.
Floridsdorfer Brücke
Handelskai
A 22-E 49-59
Donauturmstr.
DONAUPARK
Brigittenauer Brüke
Dresdnerstr.
Gunoldstr.
Ruthg.
Barawitzkg.
Billroth-str.
Krottenbachstr.
Heiligenstädter Str.
Adalbert-Stifter-Str.
Jägerstr.
Dresdner Str.
Hellwagstr.
Nord-west-bahn-str.
Martin Stein
Billrothstr.
Spittelau
BRIGITTENAU
Mraz u. Sohn
Wallensteinstr.
Brigittenauer Lände
Spittelauer Lände
Nordbahnstr.
Lassallestr.
Nußdorfer Str.
Nuß-dorfer Str.
WÄHRING
Friedensbrücke
AUGARTEN
SCHUBERT-"GEDENKSTÄTTE"
FRANZ-JOSEFS-BAHNHOF
Alserbach-str.
Obere
Roßauer Lände
Augartenstr.
LEOPOLDSTADT
Währinger Str. Volksoper
LIECHTENSTEIN-MUSEUM
Kim Kocht
Vincent
WIEN-NORD
Praterstern (Wien-Nord)
Eisvogel
Michelbeuern AKH-Krankenhaus
Liechtensteinstr.
Historical Centre (Plan II)
RIESENRAD
Spitalg.
Währinger Str.
Schottenring
Franz-Josefs-Kai
Donaustr.
ALSERGRUND
Schüttelstr.
Alser Str.
Selina
Laudongasse
Landesgerichtsstr.
Stubenring
STEPHANSDOM
Schnattl
WIEN-MITTE
Josefstädter Str.
JOSEFSTADT
Lange G.
HOFBURG
Rathaus
Lerchenfelder Str.
Thaliastr.
Burgring
Landstr.
Rochusg.
Falkensteiner am Schottenfeld
Kulinarium 7
Burgg.
Getreidemarkt
Altstadt Vienna
Burgg-Stadthalle
Kaiserhof
UNTERES BELVEDERE
Hauptstr.
WIEN-SCHWECHAT
Das Triest
Fleming's Hotel Wien-Westbahnhof
Lindner Hotel Am Belvedere
Savoyen
OTTO-WAGNER-WOHNHÄUSER
NEUBAU
Rennweg
Prinz-Eugen-Str.
NH Belvedere
WESTBAHNHOF
West-Bhf.
Artner auf der Wieden
Taubstummeng.
OBERES BELVEDERE
Pakat Suites
LANDSTRASSE
MARIAHILF
Pilgramg.
Hauptstr.
Favoritenstr.
Landstr. Gürtel
Vikerl's Lokal
WIEDEN
SÜDBAHNHOF
Gumpendorfer
Woracziczky
Südtiroler Pl.
Linke Wienzeile
Schönbrunner Str.
Wiedner
Margaretengürtel
Margaretengürtel
MARGARETEN
HEERESGESCHICHTL. MUSEUM
A
B
1
2
3

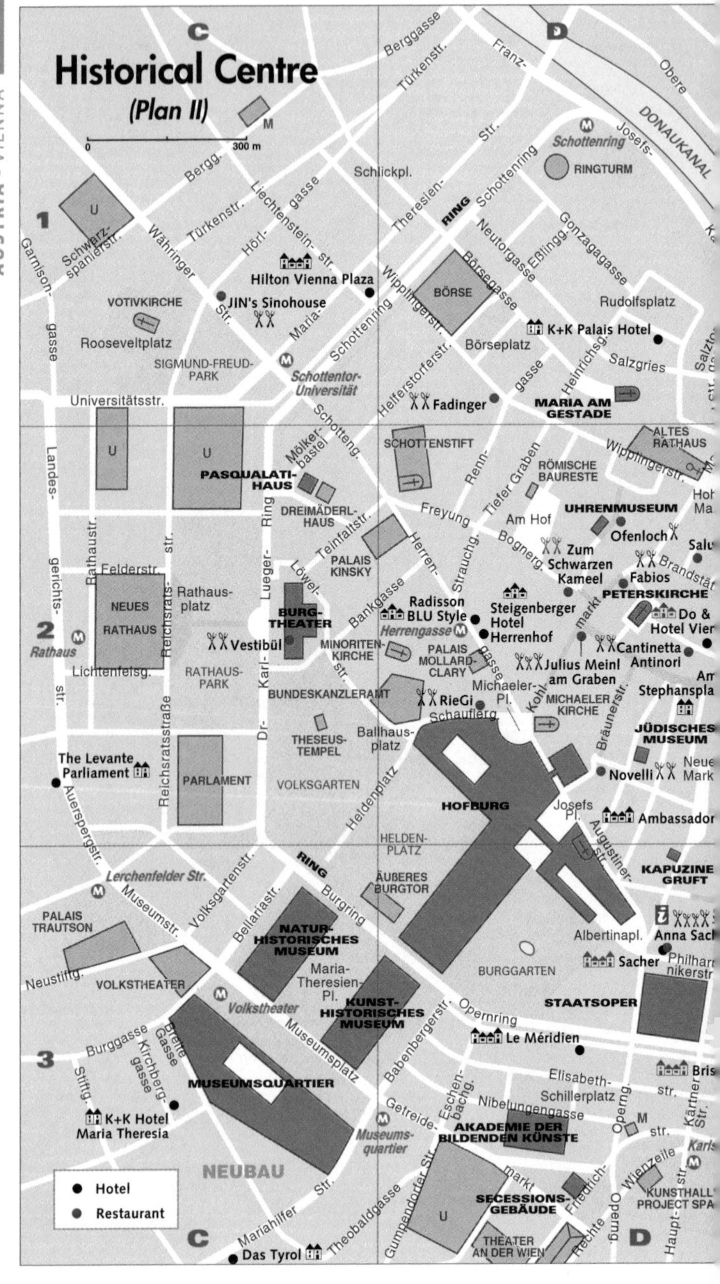
Historical Centre
(Plan II)
0
300 m
C
D
1
2
3
Hilton Vienna Plaza
JIN's Sinohouse
VOTIVKIRCHE
Rooseveltplatz
SIGMUND-FREUD-PARK
Schottentor-Universität
Schottenring
RINGTURM
BÖRSE
Börseplatz
K+K Palais Hotel
Rudolfsplatz
Salzgries
Fadinger
MARIA AM GESTADE
SCHOTTENSTIFT
ALTES RATHAUS
RÖMISCHE BAURESTE
UHRENMUSEUM
Am Hof
Ofenloch
Zum Schwarzen Kameel
Fabios
PETERSKIRCHE
PASQUALATI-HAUS
DREIMÄDERL-HAUS
PALAIS KINSKY
Radisson BLU Style
Steigenberger Hotel Herrenhof
Herrengasse
BURG-THEATER
Vestibül
MINORITEN-KIRCHE
PALAIS MOLLARD-CLARY
Julius Meinl am Graben
Cantinetta Antinori
Do & Co Hotel Vienna
Stephansplatz
NEUES RATHAUS
Rathaus
Rathausplatz
RATHAUS-PARK
BUNDESKANZLERAMT
RieGi
Michaeler-Pl.
MICHAELER KIRCHE
JÜDISCHES MUSEUM
THESEUS-TEMPEL
Ballhausplatz
The Levante Parliament
PARLAMENT
VOLKSGARTEN
HOFBURG
Novelli
Josefsplatz
Ambassador
HELDEN-PLATZ
ÄUßERES BURGTOR
KAPUZINERGRUFT
Lerchenfelder Str.
PALAIS TRAUTSON
NATURHISTORISCHES MUSEUM
Maria-Theresien-Pl.
KUNSTHISTORISCHES MUSEUM
Albertinapl.
Anna Sacher
Sacher
BURGGARTEN
STAATSOPER
VOLKSTHEATER
Volkstheater
Le Méridien
MUSEUMSQUARTIER
K+K Hotel Maria Theresia
Museumsquartier
AKADEMIE DER BILDENDEN KÜNSTE
Schillerplatz
SECESSIONSGEBÄUDE
KUNSTHALLE PROJECT SPACE
THEATER AN DER WIEN
NEUBAU
Das Tyrol
Hotel
Restaurant

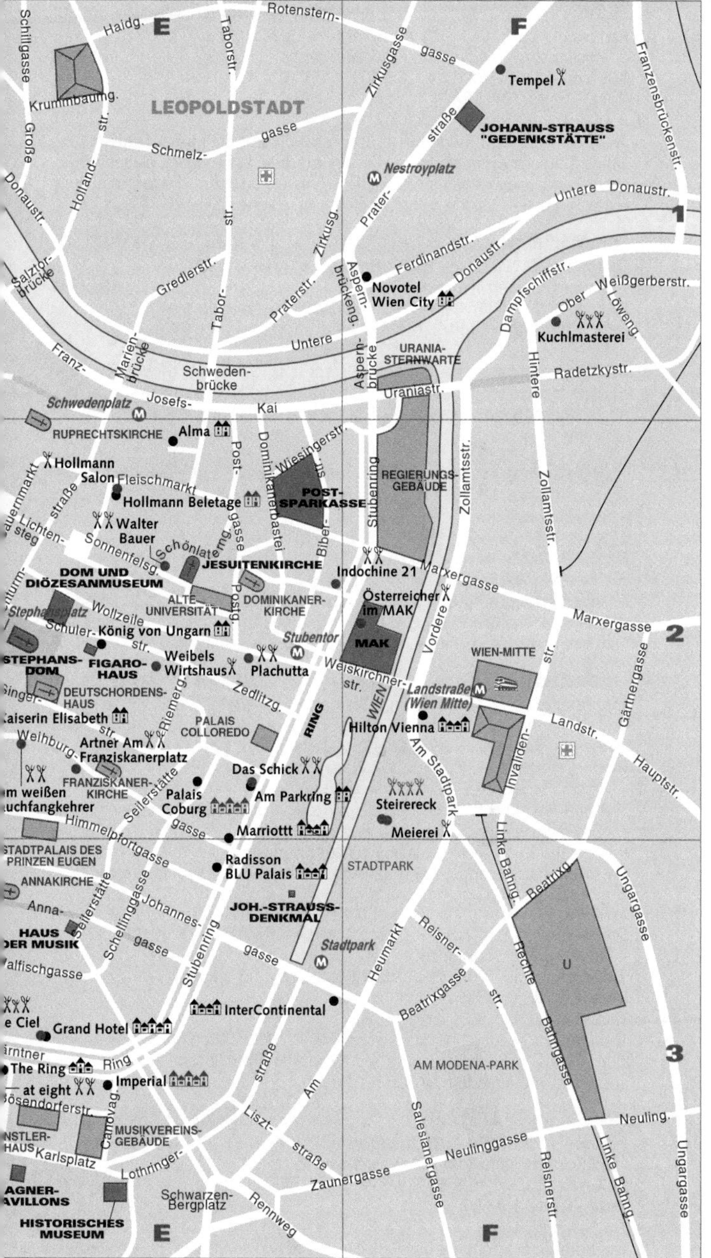
LEOPOLDSTADT
E
F
1
2
3
Tempel
JOHANN-STRAUSS "GEDENKSTÄTTE"
Nestroyplatz
Novotel Wien City
Kuchlmasterei
URANIA-STERNWARTE
Schwedenplatz
RUPRECHTSKIRCHE
Alma
Hollmann Salon
Hollmann Beletage
POST-SPARKASSE
REGIERUNGS-GEBÄUDE
Walter Bauer
JESUITENKIRCHE
DOM UND DIÖZESANMUSEUM
Indochine 21
ALTE UNIVERSITÄT
DOMINIKANER-KIRCHE
Österreicher im MAK
MAK
Stubentor
König von Ungarn
STEPHANS-DOM
FIGARO-HAUS
Weibels Wirtshaus
Plachutta
WIEN-MITTE
Landstraße (Wien Mitte)
DEUTSCHORDENS-HAUS
Kaiserin Elisabeth
PALAIS COLLOREDO
RING
Hilton Vienna
Artner Am Franziskanerplatz
FRANZISKANER-KIRCHE
Das Schick
Palais Coburg
Am Parkring
Steirereck
Meierei
Marriott
STADTPALAIS DES PRINZEN EUGEN
Radisson BLU Palais
STADTPARK
ANNAKIRCHE
JOH.-STRAUSS-DENKMAL
HAUS DER MUSIK
Stadtpark
InterContinental
Grand Hotel
The Ring
at eight
Imperial
AM MODENA-PARK
MUSIKVEREINS-GEBÄUDE
Karlsplatz
Schwarzen-Bergplatz
HISTORISCHES MUSEUM

Savoyen

Rennweg 16 ✉ 1030 – Ⓜ Karlsplatz – ✆ (01) 20 63 30 – www.austria-trend.at/hotel-savoyen-vienna Plan I **B3**

309 rm – 🛉108/300 € 🛉🛉128/350 €, ☕ 19 € – 43 suites

Rest – Carte 32/51 €

♦ Luxury ♦ Contemporary ♦

This hotel is located inside the imposing building of the former State Printing Office. The lobby is in an impressive atrium. There is a modern, elegant atmosphere and good conference facilities. This restaurant is divided into three rooms, accessible via the atrium. International cuisine is served.

Le Méridien

Opernring 13 ✉ 1010 – Ⓜ Karlsplatz – ✆ (01) 58 89 00 – www.lemeridienvienna.com **D3**

294 rm – 🛉179/355 € 🛉🛉179/355 €, ☕ 29 € – 17 suites

Rest *Shambala* – Carte 38/59 €

♦ Chain hotel ♦ Business ♦ Modern ♦

Behind its classical façade, this hotel is surprising, with its well thought out, thoroughly modern room designs. There is a lot of art on display and a special lighting concept. The distinctive design of the hotel is also present in the Shambala restaurant.

Hilton Vienna

Am Stadtpark 1 ✉ 1030 – Ⓜ Landstraße – ✆ (01) 71 70 00 – www.hilton.at/wien **F2**

579 rm – 🛉159/499 € 🛉🛉179/529 €, ☕ 29 €

Rest *S'PARKS* – Carte 32/55 €

♦ Chain hotel ♦ Luxury ♦ Modern ♦

A large conference hotel in a central location with an atrium hall and modern guestrooms. The executive level on the 15th floor has a beautiful roof terrace with wonderful views. Restaurant features a contemporary style.

InterContinental

Johannesgasse 28 ✉ 1037 – Ⓜ Stadtpark – ✆ (01) 71 12 20 – www.vienna.intercontinental.com **E3**

458 rm – 🛉189/289 € 🛉🛉219/319 €, ☕ 29 € – 32 suites

Rest – *(dinner only)* Carte 32/52 €

♦ Chain hotel ♦ Business ♦ Classic ♦

This business hotel is located by the city park. It boasts a lavish interior with a sophisticated, elegant hall and contemporary rooms, including the impressive Presidential Suite. There are many conference possibilities. There is a touch of the Mediterranean about this restaurant with its open kitchen and veranda.

Hilton Vienna Plaza

Schottenring 11 ✉ 1010 – Ⓜ Schottentor-Universität – ✆ (01) 31 39 00 – www.hilton.at/wienplaza **C1**

222 rm – 🛉159/499 € 🛉🛉179/529 €, ☕ 29 € – 13 suites

Rest – Carte 11/19 €

♦ Chain hotel ♦ Functional ♦

This grand city centre building is a sophisticatedly furnished hotel. It offers spacious rooms, including executive rooms on the upper floors. "Austrian tapas" are served in the modern NASCH restaurant.

Radisson BLU Palais

Parkring 16 ✉ 1010 – Ⓜ Stadtpark – ✆ (01) 51 51 70 – www.radissonblu.com/palaishotel-vienna **E3**

247 rm – 🛉159/349 € 🛉🛉179/349 €, ☕ 25 € – 9 suites

Rest – Carte 45/67 €

♦ Chain hotel ♦ Luxury ♦ Classic ♦

This hotel across from the City Park consists of two connected 19C palace buildings. Stylish appointments fit the historical setting. This restaurant serves international cuisine

Ambassador

Kärntner Str. 22 ✉ 1010 – Ⓜ Stephansdom – ✆ (01) 96 16 10 – www.ambassador.at **D2**

86 rm – †254/466 € ††322/584 €, ☕ 25 €

Rest – *(dinner only)* Carte 34/61 €

♦ Business ♦ Classic ♦

A successful combination of traditional and modern characterises the stylish, technically well-equipped rooms. The themed rooms are named after famous people. Modern-style restaurant.

Marriott

Parkring 12a ✉ 1010 – Ⓜ Stubentor – ✆ (01) 51 51 80 – www.viennamarriott.com **E3**

323 rm – †199/300 € ††199/300 €, ☕ 27 € – 6 suites

Rest – Carte 25/65 €

♦ Business ♦ Functional ♦

This centrally located comfortable hotel in the Stadtpark quarter boasts a spacious atrium-style lobby and well-appointed rooms decorated in warm colours. There is an executive lounge on the 8th floor. The "Garten Café" which forms part of the spacious hotel lobby offers international cuisine.

The Ring

Kärntner Ring 8 ✉ 1010 – Ⓜ Karlsplatz – ✆ (01) 22 12 20 – www.theringhotel.com **E3**

68 rm – †370/430 € ††420/480 €, ☕ 23 €

Rest *at eight* – see below

♦ Townhouse ♦ Modern ♦

This modern, well-run business hotel is housed in a historic townhouse. It has a luxurious touch and a pleasant, informal atmosphere. The heritage protected lift is not to be missed.

Do & Co Hotel Vienna

Stephansplatz 12 (6 th floor) ✉ 1010 – Ⓜ Stephansplatz – ✆ (01) 2 41 88 – www.doco.com **D2**

43 rm – †225/370 € ††225/370 €, ☕ 29 € – 2 suites

Rest – Menu 55/75 € – Carte 31/56 €

♦ Business ♦ Design ♦ Stylish ♦

This special designer hotel is directly opposite the Stephansdom. It offers modern, highly functional and yet comfortable rooms. It is a fashionable hotel with possibly the most popular bar in Vienna. European and Asian dishes are served from the visible kitchen on the seventh floor. Pleasant views can be enjoyed from the restaurant and terrace.

Radisson BLU Style

Herrengasse 12 ✉ 1010 – Ⓜ Herrengasse – ✆ (01) 2 27 80 – www.radissonblu.com/stylehotel-vienna **D2**

78 rm – †165/395 € ††165/395 €, ☕ 28 € – 6 suites

Rest *Sapori* – *(closed July - August, Saturday - Sunday and Bank Holidays)* Carte 25/40 €

♦ Townhouse ♦ Historic ♦ Design ♦

This is a stylish hotel from top to bottom. It has high quality furnishings, which despite their modernity, present a warm and personal atmosphere. The Sapori restaurant offers an international range of dishes.

Steigenberger Hotel Herrenhof

Herrengasse 10 ✉ 1010 – Ⓜ Herrengasse – ✆ (01) 53 40 40 – www.steigenberger.com/wien **D2**

196 rm – †209/289 € ††229/309 €, ☕ 28 €

Rest – *(closed Saturday lunch, Sunday)* Menu 49/59 € – Carte 35/63 €

♦ Townhouse ♦ Historic ♦ Modern ♦

Established in 1913, this grand building has neo-Classic façades. Find a tasteful modern interior in pleasant colours. The colour violet provides striking accents in the restaurant. The cuisine is Viennese with international dishes.

Das Triest

Wiedner Hauptstr. 12 ✉ *1040 – Ⓜ Karlsplatz – ☏ (01) 58 91 80 – www.dastriest.at* *Plan I* **B3**

72 rm – 226/293 € 293/358 € – 5 suites

Rest – *(closed 1 - 14 August, Saturday lunch, Sunday and Bank Holidays)* Menu 49 € – Carte 32/47 €

♦ Business ♦ Design ♦

The clean-cut lines of this designer hotel, with its homely rooms, are the work of Sir Terence Conran. The hotel is a former post station on the Vienna-Trieste run. This modern restaurant serves Italian cuisine in an attractive interior courtyard.

Lindner Hotel Am Belvedere

Rennweg 12 ✉ *1030 – Ⓜ Karlsplatz – ☏ (01) 79 47 70 – www.lindnerhotels.at* *Plan I* **B3**

219 rm – 89/279 € 109/299 €, 20 €

Rest *Taste it!* – *(closed Sunday, Monday dinner)* Menu 29/69 € – Carte 27/45 €

Rest *Heuriger Am Belvedere* – *(dinner only)* Carte 25/50 €

♦ Business ♦ Modern ♦

This modern, good-value city hotel has technically well-equipped rooms. From the leisure area on the seventh-floor there is a lovely view over the Belvedere castle. Taste it! serves Euro-Asian cuisine. Traditional Viennese food and wines.

NH Belvedere without rest

Rennweg 12a ✉ *1030 – Ⓜ Karlsplatz – ☏ (01) 2 06 11 – www.nh-hotels.com* *Plan I* **B3**

114 rm – 89/280 € 89/280 €, 17 €

♦ Chain hotel ♦ Modern ♦

This hotel in the classicist building of the former State Printing Office offers modern rooms, some with views over the Botanical Gardens. Bistro with snacks.

The Levante Parliament

Auerspergstr. 9 ✉ *1080 – Ⓜ Rathaus – ☏ (01) 22 82 80 – www.thelevante.com* **C2**

67 rm – 145/220 € 170/310 €

Rest *nemtoi* – *(closed Sunday)* Carte 25/42 €

♦ Townhouse ♦ Design ♦ Modern ♦

This boutique hotel offers excellent service and sophisticated, stylish rooms, equipped with modern technology. It is in a convenient location, and adorned with glass works by Ioan Nemtoi and Curt Themessl photographs. The restaurant offers international cuisine.

Kaiserhof without rest

Frankenberggasse 10 ✉ *1040 – Ⓜ Karlsplatz – ☏ (01) 5 05 17 01 – www.hotel-kaiserhof.at* *Plan I* **B3**

76 rm – 125/160 € 145/280 € – 4 suites

♦ Traditional ♦ Art Deco ♦ Modern ♦

Remarkable friendly service, Viennese charm, and a tasteful juxtaposition of modern and classic features characterise this beautiful 1896 hotel. There is a lovely breakfast room with a buffet service. Snack menu in the bar.

Novotel Wien City

Aspernbrückengasse 1 ✉ *1020 – Ⓜ Nestroyplatz – ☏ (01) 9 03 03 – www.novotel.com* **F1**

124 rm – 119/243 € 119/243 €, 17 € – 1 suite

Rest – Carte 25/42 €

♦ Chain hotel ♦ Modern ♦

This business hotel is right beside the Aspern Bridge and has a very contemporary and rather colourful decoration. It is a good low-cost location for families. The atmosphere in the restaurant is friendly and fashionable.

Fleming's Hotel Wien-Westbahnhof

Neubaugürtel 26 ✉ 1070 – Ⓜ West-Bahnhof – ✆ (01) 22 73 70 – www.flemings-hotels.com Plan I **A3**

173 rm – 99/239 € 125/265 € – 2 suites

Rest – Carte 21/41 €

♦ Business ♦ Modern ♦

The business hotel close to the west railway station has been maintained in a thoroughly modern style. All the rooms possess glassed-in bathrooms. Restaurant with a brasserie-style atmosphere.

Hollmann Beletage

Köllnerhofgasse 6 ✉ 1010 – Ⓜ Stephansplatz – ✆ (01) 9 61 19 60 – www.hollmann-beletage.at **E2**

25 rm – 140/170 € 150/200 €

Rest *Hollmann Salon* – see below

♦ Townhouse ♦ Design ♦ Modern ♦

This hotel, with its personal and pleasant atmosphere, is run in a sympathetic and professional manner. With an eye for style, modern features have been integrated in this classical Vienna townhouse. It has a small cinema and a lovely interior court.

K+K Hotel Maria Theresia without rest

Kirchberggasse 6 ✉ 1070 – Ⓜ Volkstheater – ✆ (01) 5 21 23 – www.kkhotels.com **C3**

123 rm – 195/220 € 270/295 €

♦ Business ♦ Modern ♦

This hotel is located in the artists' quarter of Spittelberg. It has modern rooms decorated in warm shades, some with views over Vienna. In the spacious lobby there is a bar with a snack menu.

Rathaus without rest

Lange Gasse 13 ✉ 1080 – Ⓜ Rathaus – ✆ (01) 4 00 11 22 – www.hotel-rathaus-wien.at – Closed 22 - 27 December Plan I **A3**

40 rm – 118/138 € 148/198 €, 17 € – 1 suite

♦ Townhouse ♦ Historic ♦ Design ♦

This charming historic townhouse has a modern interior. The rooms are dedicated to Austrian winegrowers, and the mini bar is stocked accordingly. Enjoy a high quality breakfast (also in the lovely interior court), as well as a wine bar with around 450 Austrian wines.

Falkensteiner Am Schottenfeld without rest

Schottenfeldgasse 74 ✉ 1070 – Ⓜ Burggasse Stadthalle – ✆ (01) 5 26 51 81 – www.schottenfeld.falkensteiner.com Plan I **A3**

144 rm – 100/170 € 100/210 €, 15 € – 1 suite

♦ Business ♦ Contemporary ♦

This business hotel offers light, modern and functional rooms. The former factory building houses modern loft rooms furnished with beautiful shades of colour.

Altstadt Vienna without rest

Kirchengasse 41 ✉ 1070 – Ⓜ Volkstheater – ✆ (01) 5 22 66 66 – www.altstadt.at Plan I **A3**

42 rm – 119/169 € 139/199 € – 8 suites

♦ Historic ♦ Design ♦ Personalised ♦

This modern hotel has the atmosphere of a historic patrician house. The unique atmosphere is pervasive. Some of the cosy rooms have particularly unusual designs by Matteo Thun. Various art objects adorn the hotel.

König von Ungarn

Schulerstr. 10 ✉ 1010 – Ⓜ Stephansplatz – ✆ (01) 51 58 40 – www.kvu.at **E2**

44 rm – ♦135/175 € ♦♦185/220 € – 1 suite

Rest – *(dinner only)* Carte 24/51 €

♦ Traditional ♦ Classic ♦

Located behind the Stephansdom, this 16C building unites a sense of classic tradition with the modern style of some very habitable designer rooms. Don't miss the attractive interior courtyard. Part of the restaurant is located in the 'Figaro House' once occupied by Mozart.

Kaiserin Elisabeth without rest

Weihburggasse 3 ✉ 1010 – Ⓜ Stephansplatz – ✆ (01) 51 52 60 – www.kaiserinelisabeth.at **E2**

63 rm – ♦126/134 € ♦♦195/245 €

♦ Traditional ♦ Classic ♦

This traditionally managed and furnished hotel with generously proportioned common areas and cosy rooms has been welcoming guests for more than 200 years. Pretty covered interior courtyard.

Das Tyrol without rest

Mariahilfer Str. 15 ✉ 1060 – Ⓜ Museumsquartier – ✆ (01) 5 87 54 15 – www.das-tyrol.at **C3**

30 rm – ♦109/229 € ♦♦149/299 €

♦ Family ♦ Modern ♦

In this lovingly restored corner building find stylish, modern guestrooms. There is a good breakfast buffet, and pieces of contemporary art accompany you throughout the hotel.

Am Parkring

Parkring 12 ✉ 1010 – Ⓜ Stubentor – ✆ (01) 51 48 00 – www.schick-hotels.com **E2**

58 rm – ♦98/172 € ♦♦122/247 €, 19 € – 8 suites

Rest *Das Schick* – see below

♦ Business ♦ Functional ♦

Opposite the Stadtpark, on the top floor of the 'Gartenbauhochhaus', are modern rooms with fabulous views over Vienna. Request one of the rooms with a balcony.

K+K Palais Hotel without rest

Rudolfsplatz 11 ✉ 1010 – Ⓜ Schwedenplatz – ✆ (01) 5 33 13 53 – www.kkhotels.com **D1**

66 rm – ♦150/195 € ♦♦175/270 €

♦ Traditional ♦ Contemporary ♦ Cosy ♦

This historic town palace is close to the city centre. It offers cosy and functionally equipped guestrooms with clean lines and warm colours.

Alma without rest

Hafnersteig 7 ✉ 1010 – Ⓜ Schwedenplatz – ✆ (01) 5 33 29 61 – www.hotel-alma.com **E2**

26 rm – ♦91/133 € ♦♦134/197 €

♦ Business ♦ Modern ♦

This attractive and resolutely modern hotel lies in a small side street near the city centre and the Danube Canal.

XXXX ✿✿ **Steirereck** (Heinz Reitbauer)

Am Heumarkt 2a (at Stadtpark) ✉ 1030 – Ⓜ Stadtpark – ☎ (01) 7 13 31 68 – www.steirereck.at – Closed Saturday - Sunday
Rest ***Meierei*** – see below **F2**
Rest – *(booking essential)* Menu 55 € (lunch)/118 € – Carte 65/103 €
Spec. Beta Sweet-Karotte mit Apfel-Rohkost-Marmelade, Basilikum und Erdnussöl. Auf dem Salzstein gegarte Äsche mit Poveraden, Eiskristallsalat und Schildampfer. Rehbock mit Waldaromen.
♦ Inventive ♦ Design ♦ Formal ♦
At this city centre restaurant close to the Stadtpark chef Heinz Reitbauer transforms predominantly local products into creative and beautifully presented dishes with a highly personal touch. The dining experience is completed by the attentive service.

XXXX **Anna Sacher** – Hotel Sacher

Philharmonikerstr. 4 ✉ 1010 – Ⓜ Karlsplatz – ☎ (01) 51 45 68 40 – www.sacher.com/de-anna-sacher.htm – Closed July - August and Monday **D3**
Rest – Menu 62/84 € – Carte 56/76 €
♦ Classic ♦ Luxury ♦
Fine classic cuisine is served with interesting desserts in the luxurious, stylish and elegant restaurant of this traditional building. There is a lower-priced lunchtime menu.

XXX **Le Ciel** – Grand Hotel

Kärntner Ring 9 (7th floor) ✉ 1010 – Ⓜ Karlsplatz – ☎ (01) 5 15 80 91 00 – www.grandhotelwien.com – Closed Sunday **E3**
Rest – Menu 38 € (lunch)/68 € – Carte 49/81 €
♦ Classic ♦ Elegant ♦
Le Ciel is an elegant restaurant on the seventh-floor with spacious dining rooms, elegant table service and a beautiful roof terrace. Exciting cuisine with a fair priced lunch menu.

XXX **Eisvogel**

Riesenradplatz 5 (Prater) ✉ 1022 – Ⓜ Praterstern – ☎ (01) 9 08 11 87 – www.stadtgasthaus-eisvogel.at Plan I **B2**
Rest – Menu 44/64 € – Carte 32/48 €
♦ Austrian ♦ Elegant ♦
This elegant city tavern has high quality interiors in bright, warm tones and friendly well-trained staff. The Austrian cooking on offer is delicious and fresh. There is a lovely terrace in front of the Ferris wheel.

XXX **Julius Meinl am Graben**

Graben 19 (1st floor) ✉ 1010 – Ⓜ Stephansplatz – ☎ (01) 5 32 33 34 60 00 – www.meinlamgraben.at – Closed Sunday and Bank Holidays **D2**
Rest – *(booking essential)* Menu 45/59 € – Carte 39/70 €
♦ Classic ♦ Formal ♦
There is a very lively atmosphere in this restaurant, which shares the building with a delicatessen that is rich in tradition. Exciting food is prepared using the best quality products.

XXX **Kuchlmasterei** with rm

Obere Weissgerberstr. 6 ✉ 1030 – ☎ (01) 7 12 90 00 – www.kuchlmasterei.at – Closed Sunday and Bank Holidays **F1**
8 suites – †247 € ††300 €, ☕ 13 € **Rest** – Carte 31/74 €
♦ International ♦ Cosy ♦ Elegant ♦
This very special restaurant has diverse, richly decorated rooms. International cuisine is served with a regional flavour. There is a beautiful, intricate wine cellar. Overnight guests enjoy individual, exclusive suites and an amazing roof terrace.

XX ✿

Novelli

Bräunerstr. 11 ✉ 1010 – Ⓜ Herrengasse – ✆ (01) 51 34 20 00 – www.novelli.at – Closed over Christmas and Sunday **D2**

Rest – *(booking advisable)* Menu 58/105 € – Carte 44/88 €

Spec. Eingelegter Gewürzkürbis mit Melone, Kräutersorbet und Rapsölvinaigrette. Kaninchen und Oktopus mit Erbsen. Taube mit Pfirsich, Fichtenwipfelsirup und Oliven-Taleggio-Gnocchi.

♦ Inventive ♦ Fashionable ♦

This restaurant brings an attentive service team and fine creative cuisine with a strong Mediterranean touch to your table. There is a modern, elegant atmosphere with strong, warm colours.

XX ✿

Mraz & Sohn

Wallensteinstr. 59 ✉ 1200 – Ⓜ Friedensbrücke – ✆ (01) 3 30 45 94 – www.mraz-sohn.at – Closed 24 December - early January, 18 - 25, April, 8 - 26 August, Saturday - Sunday and Bank Holidays *Plan I* **A2**

Rest – *(booking advisable)* Menu 38/89 € – Carte 56/70 €

Spec. Kürbis flüssig mit Ingwer, Shrimps, Baumtomaten und Büffelmozzarella. Hecht mit Blutwurst-Apfel-Landbrot. Rote Rüben Sirup und Borschtsch. Rehrücken und gebackenes Rehgulasch mit Kohlsprossencreme.

♦ Inventive ♦ Individual ♦ Fashionable ♦

Three generations of the Mraz family have applied themselves energetically to this restaurant. The food, service and atmosphere are marked by a personal approach, which with its modern and creative dishes, make this a unique venue. The wine cellar is worth a visit.

XX

Selina

Laudongasse 13 ✉ 1080 – Ⓜ Rathaus – ✆ (01) 4 05 64 04 – www.selina.at

Rest – Menu 58/81 € – Carte 26/51 € *Plan I* **A2**

♦ International ♦ Friendly ♦ Elegant ♦

This elegant restaurant has a clear southern feel and serves Mediterranean-inspired international cuisine.

XX ✿

Walter Bauer

Sonnenfelsgasse 17 ✉ 1010 – Ⓜ Stubentor – ✆ (01) 5 12 98 71 – Closed 25 July - 19 August, Saturday - Monday lunch and Bank Holidays

Rest – *(booking advisable)* Menu 79 € – Carte 45/66 € **E2**

Spec. Gänseleber mit Himbeerstreusel. Steinbut mit Spareribs und Majoranjus. Lammrücken mit Kapernaioli.

♦ Classic ♦ Cosy ♦ Family ♦

Find this restaurant in a small alley in the old town. A dedicated family, with a tradition stretching back more than 20 years, runs it. They offer fine, traditional dishes with a modern interpretation that has been creatively influenced. The cross-vaulted ceiling completes the ambience.

XX

Vestibül

Dr. Karl-Lueger-Ring 2 (at Burgtheater) ✉ 1010 – Ⓜ Herrengasse – ✆ (01) 5 32 49 99 – www.vestibuel.at – Closed 1 - 6 January, 30 July - 21 August, Saturday lunch, Sunday and Bank Holidays **C2**

Rest – Menu 49/75 € – Carte 31/75 €

♦ International ♦ Classic ♦ Brasserie ♦

You will be looked after by a coordinated team in this classic, stylish restaurant in the wings of the historic Burgtheater. The tasty, regional cuisine has a French influence and the personal touch of Christian Domschitz.

XX

Indochine 21

Stubenring 18 ✉ 1010 – Ⓜ Stubentor – ✆ (01) 5 13 76 60 – www.indochine.at – Closed Saturday lunch **E2**

Rest – Menu 38/68 € – Carte 33/54 €

♦ Fusion ♦ Exotic ♦ Cosy ♦

This attentively run restaurant offers adventurous and authentic cuisine with a strong southeast Asian accent. There is a small attractive terrace in front of the restaurant.

XX

Zum weißen Rauchfangkehrer

Weihburggasse 4 ✉ 1010 – Ⓜ Stephansplatz – ✆ (01) 5 12 34 71
– www.weisser-rauchfangkehrer.at
– Closed Sunday - Monday **E2**

Rest – *(booking advisable)* Menu 39 € – Carte 33/63 €

♦ Viennese cuisine ♦ Traditional ♦ Formal ♦

Established in 1848, this traditional inn is a family-run business bringing Viennese cuisine to your table. In the evening there is live piano played. Fantastic and extensive wine selection.

XX

Artner am Franziskanerplatz

Franziskanerplatz 5 ✉ 1010 – Ⓜ Stephansplatz – ✆ (01) 5 03 50 34
– www.artner.co.at
– Closed Saturday lunch, Sunday lunch **E2**

Rest – Menu 48/68 € – Carte 34/66 €

♦ Modern ♦ Trendy ♦

This fashionable restaurant in a historic building is in front of the Franciscan church. The contemporary cuisine offers brasserie-style dishes and additional, creative 'Massive' menus in the evening.

XX

Fabios

Tuchlauben 6 ✉ 1010 – Ⓜ Stephansplatz – ✆ (01) 5 32 22 22
– www.fabios.at
– Closed Sunday **D2**

Rest – *(booking essential)* Carte 46/75 €

♦ Mediterranean ♦ Trendy ♦

The atmosphere in this modern restaurant is lively and cosmopolitan. The restaurant is located at the end of the pedestrian zone and serves creative Mediterranean cuisine.

XX

Zum Schwarzen Kameel

Bognergasse 5 ✉ 1010 – Ⓜ Herrengasse – ✆ (01) 5 33 81 25
– www.kameel.at
– Closed Sunday and Bank Holidays **D2**

Rest – *(booking essential)* Menu 33 € (lunch)/87 € – Carte 38/72 €

♦ Traditional ♦ Cosy ♦ Friendly ♦

This traditional building has kept the same name since it opened in 1618. The former spice shop developed into a beautiful Art Nouveau restaurant with a pleasant coffee house atmosphere. It serves delicious traditional and contemporary dishes, and has a delicatessen.

XX

RieGi

Schauflergasse 6 ✉ 1010 – Ⓜ Herrengasse – ✆ (01) 5 32 91 26
– www.riegi.at
– Closed 1 week early January, 2 weeks early August, Sunday - Monday and Bank Holidays **D2**

Rest – Menu 58/92 € – Carte 47/69 €

♦ Classic ♦ Friendly ♦ Elegant ♦

This elegant and friendly restaurant close to the Hofburg boasts two menus, "Innovation" and "Evolution", and a good selection of wines. Shorter lunchtime menu.

XX

Vincent

Große Pfarrgasse 7 ✉ 1020 – Ⓜ Nestroyplatz – ✆ (01) 2 14 15 16
– www.restaurant-vincent.at
– Closed end July - mid August and Sunday *Plan I* **B2**

Rest – *(dinner only)* Carte 45/60 €

♦ Classic ♦ Individual ♦

This restaurant located in a side street serves contemporary seasonal cuisine. One of the three individual dining rooms is a modern winter garden.

XX

Das Schick – Hotel Am Parkring

Parkring 12 ✉ 1010 – Ⓜ Stubentor – ✆ (01) 51 48 00 – www.schick-hotels.com **E2**

Rest – Menu 32/52 € – Carte 30/47 €

◆ Seasonal cuisine ◆ Friendly ◆

This modern restaurant is located on the 12th floor with lovely views. The service is very friendly and the food largely seasonal.

XX

Cantinetta Antinori

Jasomirgottstr. 3 ✉ 1010 – Ⓜ Stephansplatz – ✆ (01) 5 33 77 22 – www.antinori.it **D2**

Rest – *(booking advisable)* Carte 35/62 €

◆ Italian ◆ Bistro ◆

This Viennese offshoot of the Florentine original, offers a classic Tuscan cuisine in a stylish and lively ambience. There is a wide selection of Antinori wines, also by the glass.

XX

at eight – Hotel The Ring

Kärntner Ring 8 ✉ 1010 – Ⓜ Karlsplatz – ✆ (01) 2 21 22 38 30 – www.theringhotel.com **E3**

Rest – Menu 41/58 € – Carte 31/52 €

◆ Modern ◆ Fashionable ◆

Boasting its own unique culinary concept, this designer restaurant with its clean-cut lines serves contemporary seasonal cuisine close to the city's pedestrian zone.

XX

JIN's Sinohouse

Währinger Str. 6 ✉ 1090 – Ⓜ Schottentor-Universität – ✆ (01) 3 19 10 16 – www.jins-sinohouse.at – Closed mid July - early August and Sunday **C1**

Rest – Menu 98 € – Carte 31/57 €

◆ Asian ◆ Fashionable ◆

This modern restaurant, decked out in friendly yellows and reds, serves Southeast Asian cuisine and offers a good wine menu. The restaurant is not far from the university.

XX

Fadinger

Wipplingerstr. 29 ✉ 1010 – Ⓜ Schottentor-Universität – ✆ (01) 5 33 43 41 – www.fadinger.at – Closed Saturday lunch, Sunday and Bank Holidays **D1**

Rest – *(booking advisable)* Menu 24/58 € – Carte 29/59 €

◆ International ◆ Friendly ◆

This attractive location near the stock exchange has an extremely lively atmosphere. The tasty menu is both international and regional with a good selection of wines.

XX

Plachutta

Wollzeile 38 ✉ 1010 – Ⓜ Stubentor – ✆ (01) 5 12 15 77 – www.plachutta.at

Rest – *(booking advisable)* Carte 25/48 € **E2**

◆ Viennese cuisine ◆ Traditional ◆ Inn ◆

For years, the Plachutta family has been committed to Viennese tradition. They serve beef in many forms in the green panelled dining room or on the large terrace.

X

Kim kocht

Lustkandlgasse 4 ✉ 1090 – Ⓜ Währinger Str. - Volksoper – ✆ (01) 3 19 02 42 – www.kimkocht.at – Closed 24 December - 10 January, mid July - end August, Saturday - Monday and Bank Holidays

Rest – *(booking essential)* Menu 45/65 € *Plan I* **A2**

◆ Asian ◆ Design ◆ Rustic ◆

In the show kitchen of this chic, designer restaurant, Soyhi'Kim creates exciting Korean dishes adding her personal note. She brings her menu to the table herself: 6-8pm with three courses, after 8pm with four or five courses. A small lunchtime menu.

Kulinarium7

Sigmundsgasse 1 ✉ 1070 – Ⓜ Burgg-Stadthalle – ✆ (01) 5 22 33 77 – www.kulinarium7.at
– Closed 24 December - 7 January, 19 July - 31 August, Sunday - Monday and Bank Holidays Plan I **A3**
Rest – *(dinner only)* Menu 44/66 € – Carte 34/58 €
♦ Inventive ♦ Wine bar ♦ Trendy ♦
Enjoy delicious, ambitious and creative cuisine with a regional and international influence in this restaurant. It has a modern furnishing concept that includes high stools. There is a winery in the lowest of the three cellars.

Salut

Wildpretmarkt 3 ✉ 1010 – Ⓜ Stephansplatz – ✆ (01) 5 33 13 22 – www.restaurant-salut.at
– Closed 1 week early January, August, Sunday - Monday and Bank Holidays
Rest – *(dinner only)* Carte 32/56 € **D2**
♦ French ♦ Cosy ♦ Family ♦
There is a pleasantly relaxed and casual atmosphere in this restaurant near to Stephansplatz, not least because of the friendly service offered by its proprietress. The good spicy cuisine has traditional French roots.

Schnattl

Lange Gasse 40 ✉ 1080 – Ⓜ Rathaus – ✆ (01) 4 05 34 00 – www.schnattl.com
– Closed 2 weeks after Easter, 2 weeks end August, Saturday - Sunday and Bank Holidays Plan I **A3**
Rest – *(dinner only)* Menu 38/56 € – Carte 36/54 €
♦ Regional ♦ Cosy ♦
This personally run restaurant offers regional dishes in a cosy ambience and inviting interior courtyard.

Meierei – Restaurant Steirereck

Am Heumarkt 2a (at Stadtpark) ✉ 1030 – Ⓜ Stadtpark – ✆ (01) 7 13 31 68 – www.steirereck.at
– Closed Bank Holidays **F2**
Rest – Carte 28/41 €
♦ Regional ♦ Friendly ♦
The Steirerecks milk and cheese bar is pleasantly lit and decorated all in white with fresh green colour accents. The dishes on offer are regional, and on the menu also find a typical selection of pastries.

Artner auf der Wieden

Floragasse 6 ✉ 1040 – Ⓜ Taubstummengasse – ✆ (01) 5 03 50 33 – www.artner.co.at
– Closed Saturday lunch, Sunday lunch Plan I **B3**
Rest – Menu 26/58 € – Carte 24/45 €
♦ Regional ♦ Fashionable ♦ Minimalist ♦
This simple, modern restaurant has a friendly atmosphere and tasty, contemporary, seasonal dishes on the menu. The good value lunch menu is popular.

Ofenloch

Kurrentgasse 8 ✉ 1010 – Ⓜ Stephansplatz – ✆ (01) 5 33 88 44 – www.restaurant-ofenloch.at
– Closed Sunday **D2**
Rest – *(booking advisable)* Menu 14 € (lunch)/38 € – Carte 24/41 €
♦ International ♦ Traditional ♦ Rustic ♦
This 1704 guesthouse on a lovely alley in the old town is a comfortable venue with a Viennese atmosphere. Traditional and international food is served in several rooms, and on the terraces in front of the building.

Österreicher im MAK

Stubenring 5 (at Museum MAK) ✉ 1010 – Ⓜ Stubentor – ✆ (01) 7 14 01 21 – www.oesterreicherimmak.at **F2**

Rest – Carte 25/48 €

♦ Austrian ♦ Minimalist ♦

This restaurant is in the historic building of the Museum for Applied Arts. Regional dishes are served in a modern decor with clean lines. Outdoor dining area.

Weibels Wirtshaus

Kumpfgasse 2 ✉ 1010 – Ⓜ Stubentor – ✆ (01) 5 12 39 86 – www.weibel.at **E2**

Rest – *(booking advisable)* Menu 25/27 € – Carte 25/42 €

♦ Viennese cuisine ♦ Cosy ♦

This cosy, traditional restaurant is located in the city center. Friendly service and Viennese cuisine are served in the restaurant as well as on the outdoor terrace.

Tempel

Praterstr. 56 ✉ 1020 – Ⓜ Nestroyplatz – ✆ (01) 2 14 01 79 – www.restaurant-tempel.at – Closed 23 December - 4 January, Saturday lunch and Sunday - Monday

Rest – Menu 16 € (lunch)/47 € – Carte 29/43 € **F1**

♦ Regional ♦ Bistro ♦

This cosy, bistro-style restaurant in a courtyard offers regional cuisine with international influences, which can also be enjoyed on the lovely terrace. There is a reasonably priced lunchtime menu.

Hollmann Salon – Hotel Hollmann Beletage

Grashofgasse 3 (at Heiligenkreuzerhof) ✉ 1010 – Ⓜ Stephansplatz – ✆ (01) 9 61 19 60 40 – www.hollmann-salon.at – Closed 1 - 9 January, Sunday and Bank Holidays **E2**

Rest – Menu 33/43 € – Carte 31/50 €

♦ Regional ♦ Rustic ♦

This restaurant serves regional dishes in the Heiligenkreuzerhof, a beautiful Baroque interior courtyard in the old town. There is a special lunch concept: for your business lunch you pay whatever you consider it is worth.

OUTER DISTRICTS *Plan I*

Kahlenberg Suite Hotel

Am Kahlenberg 2 (by Heiligenstädter Straße **A1***) ✉ 1190 – ✆ (01) 32 81 50 09 00 – www.kahlenberg.eu*

20 rm – †129/149 € ††149/199 € **Rest** – Carte 22/46 €

♦ Conference hotel ♦ Modern ♦

Its location is on Vienna's local mountain. The amazing views, as well as the spacious, high quality, very modern rooms with panoramic windows, makes this a very unique hotel. This restaurant with a simple, elegant style has a wonderful terrace.

Courtyard by Marriott Wien Messe

Trabrennstr. 4 (by Handelskai **B2***) ✉ 1020 – Ⓜ Praterstern – ✆ (01) 7 27 30 – www.cy-wien-messe.at*

251 rm – †116/253 € ††134/271 €, ☕ 18 € – 7 suites

Rest – Carte 28/43 €

♦ Conference hotel ♦ Modern ♦

This hotel is near the Prater and exhibition hall. Its simply designed rooms are very cosy and functional. There is a conference area with modern technical facilities. The modern bistro is decorated in a fresh green colour.

Pakat Suites without rest

Mommsengasse 5 ✉ 1040 – Ⓜ Südtiroler Platz – ☎ (01) 50 46 69 00
– www.pakatsuites.com **B3**

52 rm – 109/209 € 109/209 €, ☐ 15 €

◆ Business ◆ Design ◆

This comfortable boutique hotel is located in the embassy district. It is decorated, from the lobby through to the spacious guestrooms, in a clean-lined, modern style. There is also a pretty interior courtyard.

Landhaus Fuhrgassl-Huber without rest

Rathstr. 24 (by Krottenbachstr. **A1**) *✉ 1190*
– ☎ (01) 4 40 30 33 – www.fuhrgassl-huber.at

38 rm ☐ – 77/85 € 115/138 €

◆ Family ◆ Country house ◆ Cosy ◆

This family-run establishment in the Heurigen quarter offers homely, attractively furnished rooms in a country house atmosphere. In summer, enjoy breakfast from the extensive buffet in the lovely inner courtyard.

roomz vienna

Paragonstr. 1 (by Landstr. Gürtel **B3**) *✉ 1110 – ☎ (01) 7 43 17 77*
– www.roomz-vienna.com

152 rm – 59/115 € 69/125 €, ☐ 15 €

Rest – Carte 21/40 €

◆ Business ◆ Design ◆

This well-run and practically equipped hotel has a young, colourful design. The underground station is a 10min journey from the Dom. Handy, nearby underground car park. The lobby with its open restaurant is also fashionable.

Vikerl's Lokal

Würffelgasse 4 ✉ 1150 – Ⓜ Westbahnhof – ☎ (01) 8 94 34 30
– www.vikerls.at
– Closed 1 week early January, 1 - 15 August and Sunday dinner - Monday

Rest – *(weekdays dinner only) (booking advisable)* Menu 35/49 € – Carte 23/46 € **A3**

◆ Mediterranean ◆ Traditional ◆ Friendly ◆

The attentive hosts offer good regional cuisine with a Mediterranean accent in their restaurant on the edge of the town centre. Allow yourself to be pampered in this friendly wood-panelled restaurant.

Martin Stein

Döblinger Hauptstr. 59 (Döblinger) ✉ 1190 – Ⓜ Spittelau
– ☎ (01) 3 67 01 30 – www.martin-stein.at
– Closed August, Saturday - Sunday and Bank Holidays **A2**

Rest – Menu 55/65 € – Carte 32/52 €

◆ Seasonal cuisine ◆ Friendly ◆

A friendly husband-and-wife team run this light and airy restaurant in Döbling which offers fresh and flavoursome seasonal cuisine. There is a tram stop on the doorstep.

Eckel

Sieveringer Str. 46 (by Billrothstraße **A1**) *✉ 1190 – ☎ (01) 3 20 32 18*
– www.restauranteckel.at
– Closed 24 December - mid January, 7 - 22 August and Sunday - Monday

Rest – Carte 22/54 €

◆ Regional ◆ Family ◆ Traditional ◆

This country house features beautiful rooms, some with wood paneling. Traditional cuisine served. Beautiful terrace.

Kutschker 44

*Kutschkergasse 44 (by Währinger Straße **A2**)* ✉ *1180 – ✆ (01) 4 70 20 47 – www.kutschker44.at*
– Closed 1 - 10 January, 22 - 25 April, 26 July - 15 August, Sunday - Monday and Bank Holidays
Rest – *(dinner only)* Menu 30/39 € – Carte 22/46 €
♦ Seasonal cuisine ♦ Fashionable ♦
An unusual feature of this modern restaurant is the show kitchen, integrated into the bar, where a large proportion of the modern, international and regional dishes are prepared.

Freyenstein

*Thimiggasse 11 (by Währinger Straße **A2**)* ✉ *1180 – ✆ (0664) 4 39 08 37 – www.freyenstein.at*
– Closed 7 - 12 February, 16 - 26 April and Monday, November - May: Monday and Sunday lunch
Rest – *(weekdays dinner only) (booking advisable)* Menu 32 €
♦ Seasonal cuisine ♦ Family ♦ Individual ♦
This pleasant restaurant has a wonderful atmosphere and serves good food at a fair price. The delicious dishes are seasonal and are offered as a five-course menu, which is changed daily. There is a very beautiful garden.

Woracziczky

Spengergasse 52 ✉ *1050 – Ⓜ Pilgramgasse – ✆ (0699) 11 22 95 30 – www.woracziczky.at*
– Closed 24 December - 16 January, 10 - 23 August, Saturday - Sunday and Bank Holidays **A3**
Rest – Carte 27/44 €
♦ Viennese cuisine ♦ Neighbourhood ♦ Family ♦
This is a simple but pleasant tavern. The bright little rooms have a comfortable family feel. Viennese and international food is on offer.

Schübel-Auer

Kahlenberger Str. 22 (Döbling) ✉ *1190 – ✆ (01) 3 70 22 22 – www.schuebel-auer.at*
– Closed 1 January - 8 February and Sunday - Monday **A1**
Rest – *(open from 4pm)* Carte 14/24 €
♦ Buffet ♦ Wine bar ♦ Cosy ♦
Built in 1642 as a winegrower's house with a functioning mill, this carefully renovated building and its secluded interior courtyard, is a lovingly furnished restaurant.

Feuerwehr-Wagner

Grinzingerstr. 53 (Heiligenstadt) ✉ *1190 – ✆ (01) 3 20 24 42 – www.feuerwehrwagner.at*
– Closed Christmas and New Year **A1**
Rest – *(open from 4pm)* Carte 11/25 €
♦ Buffet ♦ Wine bar ♦ Rustic ♦
This typical, traditional Austrian wine tavern is greatly appreciated by regulars. Find a cosy, rustic decor with dark wood and simple tables. The terraced garden is particularly nice.

Mayer am Pfarrplatz

Pfarrplatz 2 (Heiligenstadt) ✉ *1190 – ✆ (01) 3 70 12 87 – www.pfarrplatz.at*
– Closed 1 - 6 January **A1**
Rest – *(open Monday – Friday from 4pm)* Carte 20/33 € *(buffet)*
♦ Buffet ♦ Wine bar ♦
A textbook traditional Austrian wine tavern: rustic furnishings, traditional Viennese folk music, and an attractive courtyard terrace. Of note: Beethoven lived here in 1817.

AT THE AIRPORT

NH Vienna Airport

rest, A/C SAT P VISA AE

Einfahrtsstr. 1 ✉ 1300 – ☎ (01) 70 15 10 – www.nh-hotels.com

500 rm – †100/340 € ††100/340 €, ☕ 19 €

Rest – Menu 59 € – Carte 35/63 €

◆ Business ◆ Modern ◆ Personalised ◆

This hotel is located opposite the arrivals hall. It has a spacious lobby and offers practical, standard rooms, contemporary designed business rooms, as well as rooms in a classic style. This bright and openly laid out restaurant offers international dishes.

SALZBURG

SALZBURG

Population: 148 330 – Altitude: 424m.

ėrald Schléwitz/Fotolia.com

Small but perfectly formed, Salzburg is a chocolate-box treasure, gift-wrapped in stunning Alpine surroundings. It's immortalised as the birthplace and inspiration of one of classical music's greatest stars, and shows itself off as northern Europe's grandest exhibitor of baroque style. Little wonder that in the height of summer its population rockets, and the sound of music wafts from hotel rooms and festival hall windows during rehearsals for the Festspiele.

In less frenzied times of the year, Salzburgers enjoy a leisurely and relaxed pace of life. Their love of music and the arts is renowned. They enjoy the outdoors, too, making the most of the surrounding mountains and lakes; on return, they'll ease into a coffee house or tavern, and indulge in the joys of goulash with dumplings, Wiener Schnitzel and apple strudel, or the richly tempting local speciality Nockerln. Meanwhile, the paths which run along the river Salzach and zig-zag through the wooded confines of Mönchsberg and the grounds of Hellbrunn are often a blur of cyclists and runners.

Salzburg made its name through salt mining and salt trading over two thousand years ago – for many decades now it's traded in culture and tourism, but it's not totally wedded to the classical world: in 2008 it hosted the first-ever conference on heavy metal music. What would Wolfgang Amadeus have made of that?

LIVING THE CITY

The dramatic natural setting of Salzburg means you're never likely to get lost. Rising above the left bank (the Old Town) is the **Mönchsberg** mountain and its fortress (the **Festung Hohensalzburg**), while the right bank (the New Town, this being a relative term) is guarded by the even taller **Kapuzinerberg**; slicing its way between them both is the Salzach river. Immediately to the east of the fortress is the quiet **Nonntal** area overlooked by the Nuns' Mountain. Over the river in the New Town stands the Mozart family home, while the graceful gardens of the **Schloss Mirabell** draw most of the right bank crowds.

PRACTICAL INFORMATION

ARRIVAL-DEPARTURE

The Hauptbahnhof (railway station) is centrally located on the right bank and is served by trains from all Europe's major locations. Meanwhile, the city's most famous icon might have been surprised to learn that he'd given his name to the local flight hub, but Wolfgang Amadeus Mozart airport is just west of the centre, and can be reached from there by cab in a quarter of an hour. For a slightly longer ride, take bus no.2 which connects the airport with the Hauptbahnhof.

TRANSPORT

Salzburg boasts a very efficient bus system. You can buy your ticket from the driver or get it in advance from tobacconists, or the ticket office of the bus terminal at the Hauptbahnhof (it's cheaper to buy it in advance). There are two main bus departure points on the left bank (Mozartsteg bridge and Hanuschplatz) and two on the right (Hauptbahnhof and Mirabellplatz). You can buy tickets in three ways: blocks of five singles, for a day's duration, or for a week.

If you take your sightseeing seriously, then get a Salzburg Card. Apart from free travel on public transport, it also gives you reduced admission to many tourist attractions, including the Museum der Moderne and the fortress. Choose your card for 24, 48 or 72 hours.

EXPLORING SALZBURG

Wandering round Salzburg is a bit like being in a Hänsel and Gretel storybook. The narrow streets and stunning mountain surroundings see to that. But the city that's been dubbed the 'Rome of the North' for its baroque style is more usually associated with two musical landmarks: Mozart was born here in 1756, and The Sound of Music was filmed here over two hundred years later. That said, very few Austrians have seen the movie, whereas the city is awash with the image of its favourite son.

The forest-clad mountains that guard over Salzburg have names that lay bare a rich monastic past: Monks' Mountain, Nuns' Mountain, and Capuchin Monks' Mountain. Before even getting to the city, all eyes are transfixed on the first of these (Mönchsberg in German), because sitting on its summit is an ancient fortress called the Festung Hohensalzburg, begun in 1077 and visible for miles around. The Altstadt (Old Town), which lies below this thousand-year old landmark, is a delight to stroll around: it's a compact area of church spires and baroque structures, built from the 16C to the 18C by the independent bishops who ran Salzburg. For over a decade, the **Altstadt** has been recognised as a UNESCO World Heritage Site.

Altstadt's star turn is its **Cathedral,** commonly regarded as the finest baroque structure in northern Europe. It's a mighty edifice, big enough to seat 10,000 people, and was first begun in 767. One of its most impressive sights is its majestic organ, guarded by carved angels; there are four others, all played by Mozart when he was the concert director here. Close by is St Peter's Abbey, the oldest monastery in the country. The ancient iron crosses that line the cemetery imbue a spooky, timeless atmosphere, and the view through the arched entrance up to the fortress above is breathtaking.

→ FESTIVE SPIRIT

Not far to the west the atmosphere changes as you arrive at the **Festival** district. In summer, the population of the city mushrooms by upwards of 200,000 for the Festspiele, a cultural extravaganza, and this area's three interlinked concert halls are where most of them head. The halls were once used as stables and the original facades are still intact. But a horse hasn't been seen around these parts for many years: the interiors have been opulently restyled to house one of the world's most famous music festivals.

You can't squeeze everyone into the festival district, of course, so if the old town feels like it's full to bursting, then you can always take refuge in a gallery or two; Salzburg has a handy selection on offer. Near the festival halls you'll find the **Rupertinum**, home to an absorbing collection of modern art, while up the same street (Wiener-Philharmoniker-Gasse) is **Artmosphere**, specialising in pop art. The more adventurous can escape to the top of Mönchsberg, where the **Museum der Moderne** offers Klimt and a range of avant-garde artists in a white stone building enhanced by glistening marble, glass ceilings and brilliant light.

→ WOLF'S CALL

Many people come to celebrate Mozart. Not only was he born here, he lived and worked here too, until restlessness caused him to pick up his clavier and disappear for good to Vienna at the age of 25. His birthplace (**Mozarts Geburtshaus**) can be found on **Getreidegasse**, which is also the Altstadt's main shopping street. Open to the public, the house includes a stage-set (reproduction), and young Wolfgang's violin (the real thing). Further east is **Mozartplatz**, a square dominated by the great man's statue, unveiled 50 years after his death – unfortunately, it doesn't look very much like him, and he's holding a pencil, even though these weren't invented until 20 years after his death! Meanwhile, across the river in **Makartplatz** stands Mozarts Wohnhaus, which is the larger premises the family moved to in 1773, and where Wolfgang composed most of his Salzburg works. Around the city, of course, there's much 'Mozartalia' to negotiate your way past in the shape of tacky souvenirs – your best bet for something to take home might be a box of Mozartkugeln, pistachio and praline sweets covered in chocolate and sold everywhere.

Just west of Mozartplatz is the most impressive square in the city: **Residenzplatz** bustles with transient life, the only ever-present here being a magnificent 17C 50ft. baroque fountain, the largest and most beautiful of its kind outside Italy. Fronting onto the square is the **Residenz Palace**, former home of the prince archbishops who ran the city for hundreds of years, the 15 state apartments resplendent with rich red silk wall coverings and fine works of art. And yes, there is a Mozart connection: he performed here as a member of the Salzburg court music ensemble.

→ LANDE CRUISING

Cross the Salzach river and you're in the 'new' town, so called because many of its medieval houses were rebuilt after a fire in 1818. It has a more open feel than the Altstadt, and there are fewer crowds. As on the left bank, there's a mountain (the Kapuzinerberg) cradling the whole area, tempting you up to its 16C Capuchin monastery and peaceful woods. Down below, the Makartplatz main square is one of the artistic treasure troves of Salzburg. On one side is Mozart's Residence, while on the other is the **Landestheater**, the city's landmark space for performances throughout the year; beyond this is the **Mozarteum**, a major destination that acts as a powerhouse for music and art displays – try catching free events staged by students from the eponymous music school.

Next to the Landestheater are the **Mirabell Gardens** - the immaculate grounds of the Schloss Mirabell - built by Archbishop Wolf Dietrich for his mistress 400 years ago. The gardens are a delight, and you needn't fork out even one euro to walk around them. There's an orangery, a rose garden and geometrically designed flowerbeds – along with strangely wonderful dwarf figures made of marble. No wonder Julie Andrews and co. burst into song when they visited here in The Sound of Music! Regarding the actual schloss itself, these days it's where the Mayor of Salzburg has his offices, so there's only one room you can visit - the Marble Hall - and you can peek too at the marble staircase. If you've been knocked out by all the baroque architecture in the city, then you might want to pay a visit to the Barockmuseum, also in the gardens. It's full of preparatory sketches and models by artists of the 17C and 18C.

→ FLYING HIGH

Despite appearances, Salzburg isn't all about the architecture of the past. Out by the airport is **Hangar 7**, a glass and steel construction shaped like an aircraft wing and completed in 2003. Fittingly for its location, it houses an interesting assortment of vintage aircraft, while Formula 1 cars from the Red Bull team add a modern contrast to the exhibits.

CALENDAR HIGHLIGHTS

Salzburg still exudes a religious air (with over a hundred churches open on a Sunday), so don't expect this to be a city where the party people hang out. Having said that, its cultural calendar is full and no event is

SALZBURG IN...

→ ONE DAY

Festung Hohensalzburg, Museum der Moderne, Cathedral, Residenzplatz

→ TWO DAYS

Mozart's birthplace, Nonntal, Kapuzinerberg, Mirabell Gardens, concert at Mozarteum

→ THREE DAYS

Mozart's residence, Hangar 7, Hellbrunn Palace (17C summer residence just south of the centre), concert at Landestheater

more fabulous than the Festspiele, from the end of July to the end of August, when great music and great theatre take over the city. The classical world is much to the fore at other times of the year as well. Mozartwoche (Mozart Week) celebrates Wolfgang's birthday at the end of January with 10 days of opera and concerts, while more contemporary composers are featured during Aspekte Salzburg in February. April comes alive with Osterfestspiele (Easter Festival) which has hosted a celebration of music and dance for over 40 years. In May, the spotlight falls on baroque music during Pfingstfestspiele (Whitsun Festival), with Bach a major focus. To whet the appetite before Festspiele, June's Sommer Szene blasts in with modern choreography and performing arts. In October, a nice contrast settles over Salzburg: the Kulturtage (Culture Days) flags up another wave of classical music and opera, while the Autumn Jazz Festival heralds a whole different sound in the city. The traditional picture is back in focus on New Year's Eve – Residenzplatz welcomes waltzers!

EATING OUT

Salzburg is well known for its excellent regional cuisine. Alongside Vienna, it's the culinary hotspot of Austria. The region beyond the city boasts a whole range of picturesque inns and tranquil beer gardens, each one typically set upon an idyllic lakeside. The old town itself, with its numerous little lanes, throngs with visitors searching out that elusive smart eatery hidden round the corner. Salzburg's cuisine takes much of its influence from the days of the Austro-Hungarian Empire, which means it's hearty and it's meaty, typified by dumplings and broths; Bavarian elements add to the rich mix. In the city's top restaurants, a regional emphasis is still very important; here the meals are prepared with a lighter, more modern touch. The quality in these establishments has improved a lot over the last decade, so that the number of restaurants with a Michelin Star or Bib Gourmand has increased greatly in Salzburg and its environs. Over the centuries, the region's cuisine has been characterised by substantial pastry and egg dishes, to fill the stomachs of local salt mine workers. There are lots of meals which feature dumplings: Pinzgauer Nocken are made of potato pastry filled with minced pork, while another favourite is Gröstl, a filling meal of 'leftovers', including potatoes, dumplings, sausages, smoked meat mixed and roasted in a pan, and served with salad. Salzburg's sweet tooth comes to the fore with its speciality Salzburger Nockerl, a soufflé omelette made with fruit and soft meringue. Be warned: it's very rich! If you want to snack in Salzburg, then Jausen is for you. Very popular in Austria generally, they are cold meals with bread and sausage, cheese, dumpling, bacon etc, followed by – if your appetite can take it – an Obstler, made from distilled fruit.

Sheraton

Auerspergstr. 4 ✉ 5020 – ✆ (0662) 88 99 90 – www.sheraton.com/salzburg **A1**

166 rm – ♦145/295 € ♦♦160/310 €, ☕ 28 € – 8 suites

Rest *Mirabell* – *(dinner only)* Carte 32/51 €

♦ Chain hotel ♦ Functional ♦

This smart hotel with comfortably furnished rooms is situated between the Congress Centre and Mirabelle Gardens. A highlight is the elegant, modern Sky Suite on seventh-floor. Mirabell offers classic cuisine and a garden-facing terrace. Small regional dishes are offered in the bistro.

Schloss Mönchstein

rest,

Mönchsberg Park 26 ✉ 5020 – ✆ (0662) 8 48 55 50 – www.monchstein.at – Closed February, 1 - 24 November **A1**

24 rm ☕ – ♦224/345 € ♦♦280/445 € – 3 suites

Rest – *(closed Tuesday, except festival period)* Menu 60 € – Carte 47/63 €

♦ Historic ♦ Personalised ♦

This 14C castle has been converted into a classy hotel set in 14,000m² of parkland. It offers elegant rooms and modern spa facilities as well as wonderful panoramic views over Salzburg. This restaurant offers classic contemporary food, some traditional dishes and a good wine list. Terrace with fine city views.

Crowne Plaza - The Pitter

Rainerstr. 6 ✉ 5020 – ✆ (0662) 88 97 80 – www.imlauer.com **B1**

199 rm – ♦89/189 € ♦♦109/199 €, ☕ 15 € – 3 suites

Rest *Imlauer* – *(closed Sunday and Monday, except festival period)* Menu 24 € (lunch)/65 € – Carte 32/65 €

Rest *Pitter-Keller* – Auerspergstr. 23 – Carte 23/39 €

♦ Chain hotel ♦ Functional ♦

Find comfortably furnished rooms with good technical facilities in this hotel from 1864. It has a central location, and an exclusive Salzburg Suite. Imlauer has an elegant dining room with Swiss pine panelling. It serves a traditional, classic menu. Find regional fare in the Pitter-Keller.

Castellani Parkhotel

Alpenstr. 6 (by Rudolfskai **B2***) ✉ 5020 – ✆ (0662) 2 06 00 – www.hotel-castellani.com*

151 rm ☕ – ♦99/190 € ♦♦129/230 € – 6 suites **Rest** – Carte 25/42 €

♦ Business ♦ Classic ♦

This hotel combines the classic and the modern. In both the listed main building and the newly built annexe, there are agelessly furnished rooms and junior suites with balconies. Restaurant with attractive inner courtyard terrace.

Altstadthotel Wolf-Dietrich without rest

Wolf-Dietrich-Str. 7 ✉ 5020 – ✆ (0662) 87 12 75 – www.salzburg-hotel.at **B1**

40 rm ☕ – ♦80/130 € ♦♦100/190 € – 6 suites

♦ Townhouse ♦ Cosy ♦

This city hotel has sophisticated rooms and some unusually designed theme suites. It also offers an organic breakfast and a tasteful terrace. There is a modern spa with an indoor pool, sauna and massage.

Auersperg without rest

Auerspergstr. 61 ✉ 5020 – ✆ (0662) 88 94 40 – www.auersperg.at

55 rm ☕ – ♦109/175 € ♦♦150/195 € – 1 suite **B1**

♦ Townhouse ♦ Contemporary ♦

A tasteful combination of the historic and modern, one of the two buildings is a listed Villa from 1892. There is a beautiful sauna area in the upper storey.

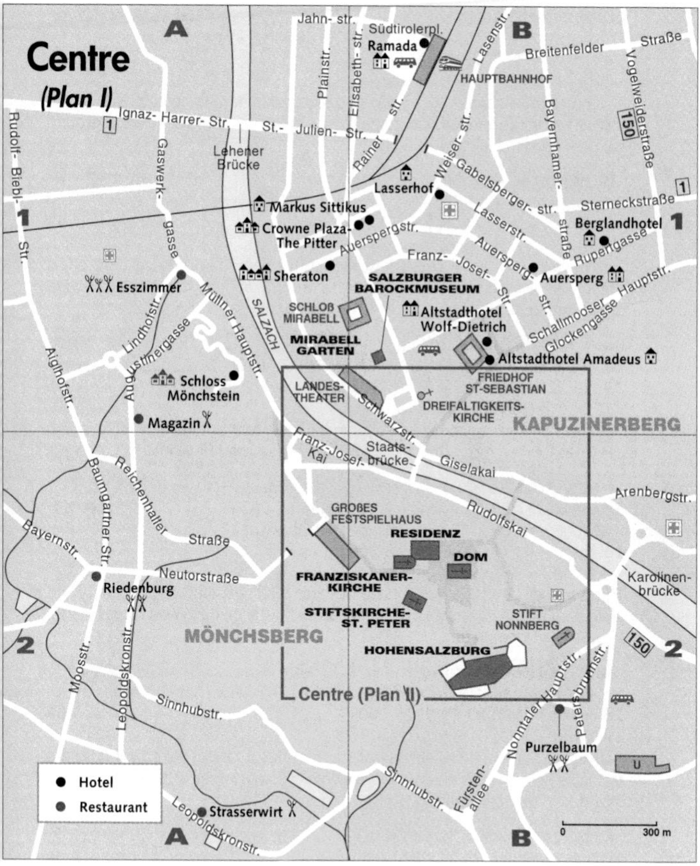

Centre (Plan I)

Zur Post without rest (with guesthouses)

Maxglaner Hauptstr. 45 (by Neutorstraße **A2***)*
5020 – (0662) 8 32 33 90
– www.stadthotel-salzburg.at
37 rm – 60/120 € 80/138 €
◆ Inn ◆ Functional ◆

This friendly, well-kept hotel has comfortable rooms with all amenities and modern bathrooms. There are newer rooms in one of the guesthouses.

Ramada without rest

Südtiroler Platz 13 5020 – (0662) 2 28 50
– www.ramada.de **B1**
120 rm – 79/140 € 99/160 €, 16 €
◆ Business ◆ Functional ◆

Ideally situated for business travellers close to the railway station, this hotel offers modern rooms and a breakfast room with a view over the castle. "Business kit" available.

Lasserhof without rest

Lasserstr. 47 ✉ 5020 – ✆ (0662) 87 33 88 – www.lasserhof.com
32 rm – 50/300 € 65/300 € **B1**
◆ Townhouse ◆ Functional ◆
This hotel offers contemporary rooms decorated in homely colours, with breakfast served in the vaulted Panorama room. Guests can park in the underground car park opposite for a reduced fee.

Berglandhotel without rest

Rupertgasse 15 ✉ 5020 – ✆ (0662) 87 23 81 – www.berglandhotel.at
18 rm – 68/83 € 98/112 € **B1**
◆ Family ◆ Historic ◆
This privately run hotel which has been in the same family since 1912 offers friendly service and individually furnished rooms, some with parquet flooring or antique furniture. There is a small terrace to the rear of the hotel.

Markus Sittikus without rest

Markus-Sittikus-Str. 20 ✉ 5020 – ✆ (0662) 87 11 21 – www.markus-sittikus.at
39 rm – 70/105 € 105/165 € **B1**
◆ Townhouse ◆ Functional ◆
This pleasantly run city hotel is located in the town centre. It has individual rooms, as well as themed rooms that peacefully face onto a lovely little interior courtyard.

Haus Arenberg without rest

Blumensteinstr. 8 (by Arenbergstraße **B2***) ✉ 5020 – ✆ (0662) 64 00 97 – www.arenberg-salzburg.at*
16 rm – 79/105 € 128/165 €
◆ Family ◆ Cosy ◆
This is a small hotel in a quiet residential area with beautiful views, a library and a pleasant breakfast terrace opening onto the lovely garden. Most rooms have a view of the Untersberg.

Altstadthotel Amadeus without rest

Linzer Gasse 43 ✉ 5020 – ✆ (0662) 87 14 01 – www.hotelamadeus.at
26 rm – 76/92 € 125/200 € **B1**
◆ Townhouse ◆ Personalised ◆
Both the guestrooms and breakfast room in this 500-year-old townhouse are tastefully furnished in warm and welcoming colours. Free afternoon coffee is included in the room price.

Esszimmer (Andreas Kaiblinger)

Müllner Hauptstr. 33 ✉ 5020 – ✆ (0662) 87 08 99 – www.esszimmer.com – Closed 1 week early January, 2 weeks early July and Sunday – Monday, except festival period, December: Sunday **A1**
Rest – *(booking advisable)* Menu 28 € (lunch)/81 € – Carte 53/79 €
Spec. Geräuchetes Rinderherz und Langostinotatar mit Zitronenöl. Heilbutt aus dem Dampf mit Blumenkohl und Trüffel. Kalbstafelspitz mit geschmolzener Gänseleber und Schalottenconfit.
◆ Classic ◆ Fashionable ◆ Elegant ◆
In this elegant, modern restaurant, which has a small rear courtyard terrace, choose between four menus (as well as a vegetarian and a fish menu) with suitable wines. Through a glass window in the floor you can see the Alm canal passing under the building.

Gasthof Auerhahn with rm

Bahnhofstr. 15 (by Plainstraße **A1***) ✉ 5020 – ✆ (0662) 45 10 52 – www.auerhahn-salzburg.at – Closed 1 week January, 3 weeks June and Sunday dinner - Monday, except festival period*
12 rm – 48/56 € 78/88 € **Rest** – Menu 37/48 € – Carte 22/41 €
◆ Regional ◆ Friendly ◆ Cosy ◆
Find good food in the cosy, rustic dining room or in the modern, open fireplace room of this restaurant. The food on offer is a both regional and international. The terrace under the trees is lovely. Losy bedrooms, near facing are quieter.

Riedenburg

Neutorstr. 31 ✉ 5020 – ✆ (0662) 83 08 15 – www.riedenburg.at
– Closed Sunday - Monday, except festival period **A2**
Rest – (booking advisable) Menu 53/89 € – Carte 50/74 €
Spec. Königskrabben und Jakobsmuscheln mit Mangomayonnaise und Brandade. Entrecôte mit Schneckenkrapferl und Leinölstaub. Exotische Salzburger Nockerl mit Muscovado-Karamelleis.
♦ Classic ♦ Cosy ♦
This restaurant consists of friendly rooms with a charming rural tone and a guest garden where you can relax under the chestnut trees. Modern dishes with a classic basis are served here.

Purzelbaum

Zugallistr. 7 ✉ 5020 – ✆ (0662) 84 88 43 – www.purzelbaum.at
– Closed Sunday - Monday lunch, except festival period **B2**
Rest – Menu 18 € (lunch)/60 € – Carte 39/62 €
♦ Seasonal cuisine ♦ Cosy ♦
This pretty wood-panelled restaurant is located among the trees at the edge of the city centre. It offers a well-furnished table of traditional, seasonal fare. There is a good value lunchtime menu.

Magazin

Augustinergasse 13 ✉ 5020 – ✆ (0662) 8 41 58 40 – www.magazin.co.at
– Closed Sunday, except festival period **A1**
Rest – (booking advisable) Menu 29/77 € – Carte 42/66 €
Spec. Gänseleber mit Quitte und Rosen. Seezunge im Schweinsnetz mit Tomate und Spinat. Wildentenbrust mit Rieslingkraut und Kürbis.
♦ Seasonal cuisine ♦ Fashionable ♦ Minimalist ♦
Contemporary seasonal cuisine prepared using high-quality ingredients and served in a stylish vaulted dining room. Shorter lunchtime menu. Appealing selection of wines. The restaurant also boasts a glass-panelled non-smoking section, leafy interior courtyard, wine and cookery shop and delicatessen.

Strasserwirt

Leopoldskronstr. 39 ✉ 5020 – ✆ (0662) 82 63 91 – www.zumstrasserwirt.at
– Closed 1 week mid January, 1 week end September - early October and Monday, October - April : Monday and Tuesday **A2**
Rest – Carte 24/46 €
♦ Home cooking ♦ Rurally ♦
This guesthouse from 1856 houses a classically decorated restaurant with high quality cherry wood-panelling and a conservatory on the terrace. It serves a regional city menu.

Pomodoro

Eichstr. 54 (by Sterneckstraße **B1**) ✉ 5020 – ✆ (0662) 64 04 38
– Closed August, over Christmas and Monday - Wednesday
Rest – (booking advisable) Carte 26/40 €
♦ Italian ♦ Family ♦ Rustic ♦
A piece of Italy is on offer in this pleasantly decorated little restaurant. Herr Tomassetti cooks a typical Cucina Casalinga, which is delicious, while Frau Lercher pays friendly attention to her guests.

HISTORICAL CENTRE — *Plan II*

Sacher

Schwarzstr. 5 ✉ 5020 – ✆ (0662) 88 97 70 – www.sacher.com
113 rm – 🚹195/330 € 🚹🚹230/636 €, ☕ 31 € – 6 suites **C1**
Rest *Zirbelzimmer* – Menu 47/85 € – Carte 42/62 €
Rest *Salzachgrill* – Carte 25/54 €
♦ Traditional ♦ Historic ♦
This grand hotel on the banks of the river Salzach is luxurious and elegant. Enjoy the beautiful rooms and individual suites. Some of the rooms are astonishing with their special view of the river. The specialty of the café is Viennese Sacher torte. The Zirbelzimmer is elegantly rustic. This Salzach-grill restaurant has a glorious terrace on the Salzach.

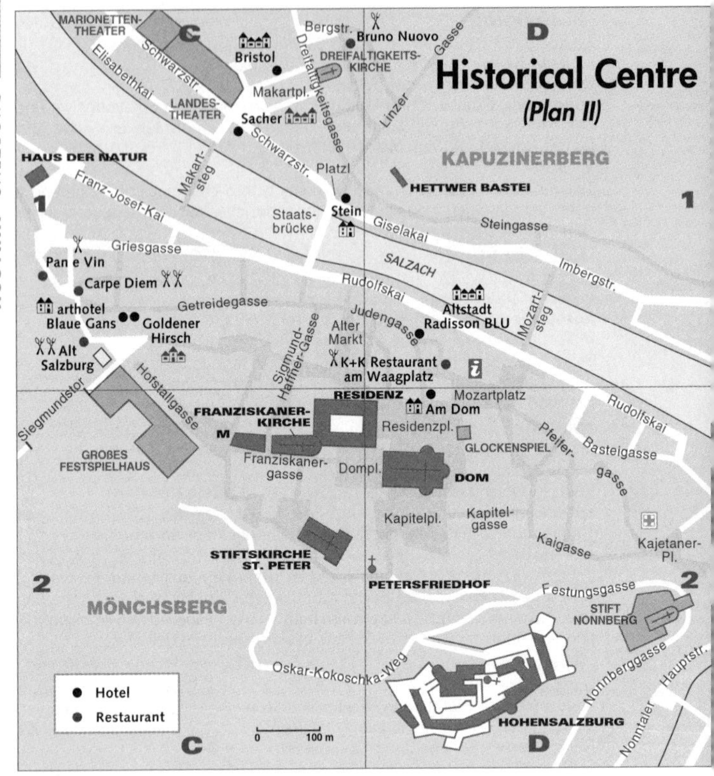

Bristol

Makartplatz 4 ✉ 5020
– ✆ (0662) 87 35 57 – www.bristol-salzburg.at
– Closed 1 February - 15 April **C1**
60 rm – 200/355 € 225/380 € – 8 suites
Rest – Carte 26/49 €
♦ Traditional ♦ Classic ♦

Built in 1892, this stylish, historic hotel is located in the city centre. It offers tasteful, comfortable guestrooms with various designs. Classic cuisine with a traditional influence is served in the pretty restaurant.

Altstadt Radisson BLU

Judengasse 15 (Rudolfskai 28)
✉ 5020 – ✆ (0662) 8 48 57 10
– www.austria-trend.at/hotel-altstadt-salzburg **D1**
62 rm – 190/500 € 220/530 €, 22 € – 13 suites
Rest – *(closed Monday, except festival period)* Carte 30/55 €
♦ Townhouse ♦ Personalised ♦

Behind historical walls, not far from Mozartplatz, find the beautiful rooms of this hotel with their classic, elegant style. The executive room and suites are spacious. This international restaurant has a conservatory on the Salzach river, and a terrace in the interior court.

Goldener Hirsch

Getreidegasse 37 ✉ 5020 – ☎ (0662) 8 08 40 – www.luxurycollection.com/goldenerhirsch **C1**

69 rm – ♦125/360 € ♦♦140/410 €, ☕ 32 € – 4 suites

Rest – Carte 37/70 €

♦ Townhouse ♦ Historic ♦

A historic atmosphere surrounds the guests in this 1407 patrician house, which watches over its cosy rooms that are full of charm and atmosphere. This restaurant serves international cuisine but with a traditional Austrian influence. A more rustic approach is found in the 'Herzl'.

arthotel Blaue Gans

Getreidegasse 41 ✉ 5020 – ☎ (0662) 8 42 49 10 – www.blauegans.at

37 rm ☕ – ♦125/155 € ♦♦145/245 € – 3 suites **C1**

Rest – *(closed Sunday and Bank Holidays, except festival period)* Carte 32/53 €

♦ Townhouse ♦ Modern ♦

This 650 year-old Salzburg guesthouse is right in the centre of the city. It houses bright, modern rooms including the special, chic 'Artelierzimmer', as well as displaying contemporary art. Pleasant, bright restaurant with attractive vaulted ceiling and a nice terrace.

Stein without rest

Giselakai 3 ✉ 5020 – ☎ (0662) 8 74 34 60 – www.hotelstein.at

56 rm ☕ – ♦79/149 € ♦♦159/199 € – 9 suites **C1**

♦ Townhouse ♦ Modern ♦

Enjoy modern living in this famous old hotel from 1399, right by the Staatsbrücke. The view from the roof terrace with its café and bar is astounding.

Am Dom without rest

Goldgasse 17 ✉ 5020 – ☎ (0662) 84 27 65 – www.hotelamdom.at

15 rm ☕ – ♦100/160 € ♦♦130/280 € **D2**

♦ Historic ♦ Design ♦

This small boutique hotel has friendly staff and high-quality designer rooms. Each floor has a name such as Sissi and Karajan. It offers convenient underground parking in the Old City.

Pan e Vin

Gstättengasse 1 (1st floor) ✉ 5020 – ☎ (0662) 84 46 66 – www.panevin.at – Closed 2 weeks early September and Sunday, except festival period

Rest – Menu 68 € – Carte 35/65 € **C1**

Rest *Trattoria* – Carte 29/47 €

♦ Mediterranean ♦ Cosy ♦

Mediterranean flavoured cuisine awaits guests in this 600 year-old building comfortably decorated in warm tones. The wine menu offers a good international selection. On the ground floor, the Trattoria serves pure Italian cuisine with a starter buffet.

Carpe Diem

Getreidegasse 50 (1st floor) ✉ 5020 – ☎ (0662) 84 88 00 – www.carpediemfinestfingerfood.com – Closed 6 - 20 February **C1**

Rest – *(closed Sunday, except festival periods)* Menu 65/90 € – Carte 45/74 €

Rest *Carpe Diem Finest Fingerfood* – Menu 18/39 €

Spec. Hummer in Zitronenvelouté mit Ravioli und Avocado. Steinbutt auf zweierlei Spinat und Trüffel. Rehrücken mit Waldpilzen und Topfen-Erdäpfelnudeln.

♦ International ♦ Fashionable ♦ Design ♦

This corner building in the inner city houses a friendly and modern designed restaurant. International cuisine with a traditional basis is offered. On the ground floor there is a bistro where you will be served refined finger food in cones.

XX **Alt Salzburg**

Bürgerspitalgasse 2 ✉ 5020 – ☎ (0662) 84 14 76 – www.altsalzburg.at – Closed 27 February - 7 March, Sunday and Monday lunch, except festival period **C1**

Rest – *(booking essential at dinner)* Menu 42/50 € – Carte 29/54 €

♦ Austrian ♦ Traditional ♦

For many years the Kögl family have operated this small, elegantly decorated restaurant in the former servants' quarters of the town hospital. The cuisine is predominantly regional in nature.

X **K+K Restaurant am Waagplatz**

Waagplatz 2 (1st floor) ✉ 5020 – ☎ (0662) 84 21 56 – www.kkhotels.com – Closed February **D1**

Rest – *(booking advisable)* Menu 55 € – Carte 26/46 €

♦ Regional ♦ Rustic ♦

This Salzburg institution is located near the city centre. It is a cosy, traditional restaurant with various rooms and a terrace in front. For groups, there is the mediaeval Freysauff cellar.

X **Bruno Nuovo**

Priesterhausgasse 20 ✉ 5020 – ☎ (0662) 87 08 11 – www.brunonuovo.at – Closed September - July: Sunday and Bank Holidays **C1**

Rest – Menu 14 € (lunch)/55 € – Carte 44/64 €

♦ Regional ♦ Family ♦

The Plotegher family serve tasty seasonal food, including a good-value lunch-time menu, in their Altstadt restaurant within walking distance of the Mirabell Palace.

ENVIRONS OF SALZBURG AND AIRPORT

AT SALZBURG-AIGEN South-East: 6 km by Giselakai B2

Doktorwirt rm,

Glaser Str. 9 ✉ 5026 – ☎ (0662) 6 22 97 30 – www.doktorwirt.at – Closed 3 weeks February, mid October - end November

41 rm – †70/125 € ††110/145 €

Rest – *(closed Sunday dinner and Monday, except festival period: Monday)* Menu 14 € (lunch)/39 € – Carte 15/43 €

♦ Inn ♦ Rustic ♦

The Schnöll family run this cosy 12C tavern. There is a spacious spa area and a lovely garden, as well as beautiful tower rooms with small bay windows. Regional cuisine is served in very comfortable rooms or on the terraces in front and behind of the building. There is a wine cellar.

Rosenvilla without rest

Höfelgasse 4 ✉ 5020 – ☎ (0662) 62 17 65 – www.rosenvilla.com – Closed 2 weeks February

15 rm – †79/125 € ††128/159 €

♦ Family ♦ Modern ♦

The extremely pleasant atmosphere in this hotel reflects the dedication of Stefanie Fleischhaker. Namely: impeccable care of the guests, tasteful modern furnishings, and a beautiful terrace on which to take breakfast in summer. There are also comfortable junior suites.

XX **Gasthof Schloss Aigen**

Schwarzenbergpromenade 37 ✉ 5026 – ☎ (0662) 62 12 84 – www.schloss-aigen.at – Closed Tuesday - Thursday lunch, except festival period

Rest – Menu 40/50 € – Carte 27/52 €

♦ Regional ♦ Inn ♦ Friendly ♦

In this former manor guesthouse with its tasteful, rustically furnished rooms, beef dishes are a speciality. A romantic terrace has been laid out under the chestnut trees of the interior courtyard.

AT SALZBURG-LEOPOLDSKRON South-West: 4 km by Moosstraße A2

Blobergerhof

Hammerauerstr. 4 ✉ 5020 – ✆ (0662) 83 02 27 – www.blobergerhof.at
– Closed over Christmas
21 rm – 55/65 € 75/95 €
Rest – *(closed Sunday) (dinner only for residents)* Carte 17/42 €
◆ Inn ◆ Cosy ◆
This family-run guesthouse was once a small farmhouse. Today it offers comfortable rooms, some with a view of the Untersberg, and many with a balcony. For families maisonettes and apartments are available.

AT SALZBURG-LIEFERING North-West: 4 km by Ignaz-Harrer-Straße A1

Brandstätter

Münchner Bundesstr. 69 ✉ 5020 – ✆ (0662) 43 45 35
– www.hotel-brandstaetter.com
– Closed 23 - 26 December
35 rm – 85/140 € 110/210 €
Rest – *(closed Sunday, except festival period, December: Sunday) (booking advisable)* Carte 24/68 €
◆ Family ◆ Cosy ◆
The Brandstätter family offer beautiful, country house-style rooms, some of which face the garden. The sauna area is welcoming. The delicious cuisine is regional and traditional. One of the cosiest rustic dining rooms is the 'Zirbenstube' with its tiled stove.

AT SALZBURG-PARSCH East: 5 km by Giselakai B2

Villa Pace without rest

Sonnleitenweg 9 ✉ 5020 – ✆ (0662) 64 40 77
– www.villapace.at
– Closed November - March
12 rm – 78/104 € 132/195 €
◆ Family ◆ Classic ◆
First-class service and beautiful, individual decoration are very important to the dedicated hostess, Claudia Bürkle. In a quiet area above the town, start your day in the chic breakfast room or on the terrace with a view over the castle.

Schmederer

Kreuzbergpromenade 2 (Schmedererplatz) ✉ 5020 – ✆ (0662) 64 82 63
– www.schmederer.at
– Closed Monday
Rest – *(booking essential for dinner)* Carte 28/56 €
◆ Seasonal cuisine ◆ Design ◆
This modern restaurant located in the upmarket residential district of Parsch is easily accessible by bus (Line 6). The flavoursome food is a happy marriage of the traditional and the contemporary, accompanied by a good selection of wines. Pretty terrace and stylish bar with humidor.

ON THE GAISBERG East: 5 km by Sterneckstraße B1

Die Gersberg Alm

Gersberg 37 ✉ 5020 – ✆ (0662) 64 12 57
– www.gersbergalm.at
44 rm – 95/125 € 137/295 € – 3 suites
Rest – *(booking advisable)* Menu 44 € – Carte 27/51 €
◆ Inn ◆ Rustic ◆
This is a unique and wonderful 19C mountain guesthouse at around 800m. The service is friendly and the rooms are cosy, with some of them having elegant, modern furnishings. This pleasant, cosy restaurant has a romantic garden terrace serving seasonal dishes.

AT THE EXHIBITION CENTRE North-West: 3 km by Ignaz-Harrer-Straße A1

EB-Hotel without rest

Aribonenstr. 20 ✉ 5020 – ✆ (0662) 23 06 48 – www.ebhotel.at
15 rm – 68/90 € 116/156 €
♦ Business ♦ Modern ♦
This friendly hotel with its characteristic orange façade offers immaculately kept, contemporary yet comfortable rooms and includes a number of quiet rooms at the back. Good breakfast. Bus stop on the doorstep.

NEAR AIRPORT South-West: 5 km by Rudolf-Biebl-Straße A1

Airporthotel

rm,

Dr.-M.-Laireiter-Str. 9 ✉ 5020 Salzburg-Loig – ✆ (0662) 85 00 20 – www.airporthotel.at
36 rm – 95/155 € 125/185 € **Rest** – *(dinner only for residents)*
♦ Inn ♦ Cosy ♦
This hotel is across from the airport, and consists of two connected hotel buildings, which are typical of the region. Functional rooms, some with air-conditioning.

Ikarus (Roland Trettel)

Wilhelm-Spazier-Str. 7a (Hangar-7, 1st floor) ✉ 5020 – ✆ (0662) 21 97 – www.hangar-7.com – Closed 22 December - 4 January
Rest – *(booking essential)* Menu 95/140 € – Carte 59/112 €
♦ Inventive ♦ Fashionable ♦ Elegant ♦
Every month a different guest chef presents his cuisine in this imposing, modern glass building. Right at the top are two bars with views of the aircraft and racing cars on display in the exhibition hall. There is a café on the ground floor.

AT BERGHEIM North: 7,5 km by Vogelweiderstraße B1

Plainlinde

Plainbergweg 30 ✉ 5101 – ✆ (0662) 45 85 57 – www.plainlinde.at – Closed Monday - Tuesday, except festival period
Rest – *(booking advisable)* Menu 23 € (lunch)/62 € – Carte 34/61 €
♦ Regional ♦ Cosy ♦ Rurally ♦
This pleasant, rustic-style restaurant offers classic regional fare and a reasonably priced wine list. It has an attractive terrace in the shade of two sweet chestnut trees and lies within walking distance of the Maria Plain basilica.

AT HALLWANG North-East: 6,5 km by Sterneckstraße B1

Pfefferschiff (Vigne, Jürgen)

Söllheim 3 ✉ 5300 – ✆ (0662) 66 12 42 – www.pfefferschiff.at – Closed 2 weeks February - March, 2 weeks September and Sunday - Monday, except festival period
Rest – *(Tuesday - Friday dinner only, except festival period) (booking advisable)* Menu 59/75 € – Carte 49/76 €
Spec. Beef Tatar mit Sauerrahmgelee, Eierschwammerl-Rührei und Nußbutterschaum. Seesaibling in Holunderöl gegart mit Paprikarisotto. Rosa gebratener Rehrücken mit Weingartenpfirsich und Steinpilztascherl.
♦ Regional ♦ Elegant ♦ Cosy ♦
This charming 17C manse sits amid greenery in the village of Söllheim just 6km outside Salzburg. The traditionally costumed staff serve meticulously prepared regional cuisine with a seasonal twist. Good range of wines. Tree-covered terrace.

AT HOF BEI SALZBURG North-East: 18 km by Sterneckstraße B1

Schloss Fuschl

Schlossstr. 19 ✉ 5322 – ✆ (06229) 2 25 30 – www.luxurycollection.com/schlossfuschl – Closed November - April
110 rm – 280/700 € 330/970 € – 19 suites
Rest *Schloss Restaurant* – Carte 42/77 €
♦ Luxury ♦ Classic ♦
First mentioned in 1461, this idyll on a small peninsula in the Fuschlsee is an exquisite residence. A collection of old masters adorns the whole hotel. There is also a lido with a bathing platform. The Schloss restaurant has a terrace with views over the lake and classic international cuisine.

BELGIUM
BELGIQUE - BELGIË

PROFILE

→ **Area:**
30 528 km^2
(11 781 sq mi)

→ **Population:**
10 757 356 inhabitants (1/01/2010), nearly 55% Flemish, 33% Walloons and about 10% foreigners. Density = 351 per km^2.

→ **Capital:**
Brussels (1 116 716 inhabitants).

→ **Currency:**
Euro (€); rate of exchange: € 1 = US$ 1.37 (Dec. 2010).

→ **Government:**
Constitutional parliamentary monarchy (since 1830) and a federal state (since 1994). Member of European Union since 1957 (one of the 6 founding countries).

→ **Languages:**
French (Wallonia), Flemish (Flanders), German (Eastern cantons); most Belgians also speak English.

→ **Specific public holidays:**
National Day (21 July), Armistice Day 1918 (11 November).

→ **Local Time:**
GMT + 1 hour in winter and GMT + 2 hours in summer.

→ **Climate:**
Temperate maritime with cool winters and mild summers (Brussels: January: 2°C, July: 18°C); more continental towards the Ardennes. Rainfall evenly distributed throughout the year.

→ **International dialling Code:**
00 32 followed by local number without the initial **0**. Electronic directories: www.skynet.be, www.belgacom.be

→ **Emergency:**
Police: ✆ **101**; Medical Assistance and Fire Brigade: ✆ **100**; Police or Medical Assistance from cellular phones : ✆ **112**.

→ **Electricity:**
220 volts AC, 50Hz; 2-pin round-shaped continental plugs.

→ **Formalities**
Travellers from the European Union (EU), Switzerland, Iceland and the main countries of North and South America need a national identity card or passport (America: passport required) to visit Belgium for less than three months (tourism or business purpose). For visitors from other countries a visa may be required, in addition to a passport, especially for those wishing to stay for longer than three months. We advise you to check with your embassy before travelling.

697

BRUSSELS

BRUXELLES/BRUSSEL

Population: 1 116 716 – Altitude: approx 100m

Guitain/Fotolia.com

It's not every city where you can employ a 16C century map and accurately navigate your way around. Or where there are enough restaurants to dine somewhere new every day for five years. Or where you'll find a museum dedicated to the comic strip. But then every city is not Brussels. Unfortunately tagged a 'grey' capital because of its associations with the suited hordes of the European Union, those who've actually visited the place know it to be, by contrast, a buzzing town, the home of art nouveau, with a wonderful maze of medieval alleys and great places to eat.

The city is warm and friendly, with a cosmopolitan outgoing feel, due in no small part to its turbulent history, which has seen it under frequent occupation. The idea of multiculturalism has long been part and parcel of life for the Bruxellois, who believe, generally speaking, that you shouldn't take things too seriously. They have a soft spot for street music and puppets, Tintin and majorettes. They do their laundry in communal places like the Wash Club, and have restaurants with names such as 'L'Idiot du Village' and 'Mort Subite' (Sudden Death). Not so grey, after all...

LIVING THE CITY

The area where all visitors wend is the area that historically belonged to the poorer elements of Brussels, the Lower Town, and in particular the **Grand Place**. Its northwest and southern quarters (Ste-Catherine and The Marolles) are of particular interest. To the east, higher up an escarpment, lies the Upper Town, which, literally and symbolically, has always had a penchant for looking down at its westerly neighbour. This is the traditional home of the aristocracy, and it encircles the landmark Parc de Bruxelles. Further east in the Upper Town is the **European Parliament** area, which is saved from itself by two rather lovely parks. Two suburbs of interest are St.Gilles, to the southwest, and Ixelles, to the southeast, where trendy bars and Art Nouveau are the order of the day.

PRACTICAL INFORMATION

ARRIVAL-DEPARTURE

Brussels-National Airport is 14km northeast of the city centre. Take the Airport City Express train which runs every 20min and takes 25min. A taxi will cost approximately €30. Eurostar trains run from Brussels-Midi, which is a 20min walk from the city centre or else take the Metro, Lines 4, 55 or 56.

TRANSPORT

Buses, trams and metro all run efficiently in Brussels. You can buy a single short distance ticket, or if you're in the city for a while, 5-10 journey cards and one-day travelcards. These are available from metro stations, travel authority (STIB/MIVB) offices, tourist information centres and newsagents.

Remember to stamp your ticket before each journey. Machines are on every metro station concourse and every tram or bus. The ticket is valid for an hour, and you can hop on and off all forms of public transport as often as you like. Roving inspectors impose heavy on-the-spot fines for anyone caught without a valid ticket.

EXPLORING BRUSSELS

Brussels is a rollicking city, living up to its Brueghelesque depictions, albeit without the medieval accoutrements.

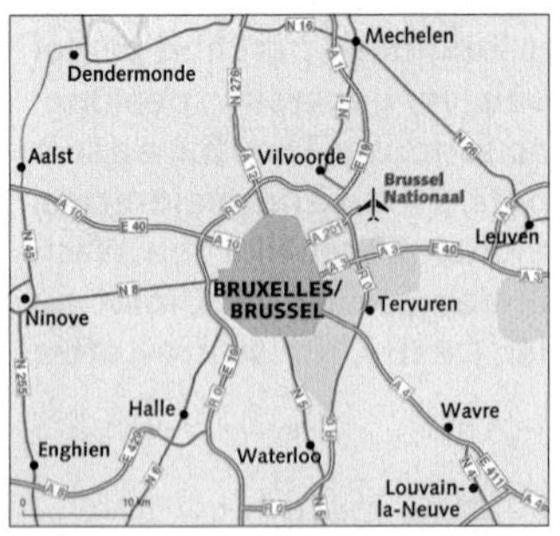

It's somewhere that's fun just to wander around, buoyed up by frites and chocolate, two 'delicacies' which announce themselves practically every step of the way. There's no better place to get a feel for Brussels than at its Lower Town heart, the Grand Place, whose Baroque magnificence makes it the world's most uniformly satisfying square. The awesomely Gothic, 15C **Town Hall** engenders enough import to take up a whole side; powerful trade guilds took up the cudgels in the late 17C and created superbly harmonious buildings in Flemish Renaissance style to complete the magical whole. No wonder Victor Hugo famously described it as "La plus belle place du monde". Around and about the Grand Place is a mix of ancient cobbled lanes; most of the thoroughfares tumbling into the main hub have a time scale that ranges from the Middle Ages up to the 18C.

The **Lower Town** is at its most magical going northwest from the Grand Place. This is a cobweb of spidery lanes topped off by dinky squares. The one that draws most visitors is Place Ste Catherine: some come for its eponymous church with curvaceous Baroque belfry, but most are seduced by its fashionable aura, inspired by a plethora of great seafood restaurants. Around here are to be found an intriguing assemblage of late 19C bourgeois houses: they're a mix of the elegant and the run-down, giving the quarter its slightly battered charm. Just up the way from here is one of the city's finest churches, St-Jean-Baptiste-au-Beguinage, decked out in fanciful Flemish Baroque detail.

➔ SOUTHERN COMFORT

If you're after a feel of old working class life, then head to the **Marolles** quarter at the southern extremity of the Lower Town. The former stronghold of Flemish weavers and craftsmen, it possesses its own (dying out) fruity dialect, the city's best daily flea market, and a neat collection of antique and suitably 21C interior design shops. Step a little way east from here, and you're on the ridge of the Upper Town, the posh side of the city with its pre-planned wide boulevards and squares. Those very same workmen from the Marolles would have crossed this 'border' to beaver away and create the elegant town houses which give the Place du Grand Sablon its abidingly popular air. Riding up the slope of the escarpment that slices Brussels in two, this is a wealthy and smart area where Art Nouveau meets grand Neoclassical. The trendy bars here act as a magnet for al fresco people-watchers in the summer months.

➔ ART ATTACK

In spite of a history spanning over a thousand years, it's fair to say Brussels doesn't boast the best museum scene in Europe. There are certainly a good number of them, but only a few seem to have any great confidence in themselves; others lean towards the mundane. So make sure you choose a good one, and chief amongst these is the **Museum of Ancient Art**, allied to the Museum of Modern Art, near the Place Royale in the Upper Town. Together they make up the Musées Royaux des Beaux Arts. Pay your money, take your choice: will you settle for the finest collection of Flemish art in the world, with many Old Masters such as Rubens, Brueghel the Elder and van Dyck (Ancient), or will you shell out your euros on a comprehensive eight floors of 20C art featuring Magritte, Monet and Gauguin (Modern)? Either way you can't lose, but don't try to do justice to both in one day: you'll never manage it.

➔ MUSIC TO YOUR EYES

The two-buses-together scenario applies to Brussels' museums. You've only just recovered from the glories of the Beaux Arts, when along comes another spellbinder, just across Place Royale. The Musical Instrument Museum is housed in a wonderful Art Nouveau building of glass and wrought-iron that was once home to the Old England company (whose name still adorns the eye-catching black façade). Inside, over three floors, the collection of instruments is breathtaking, having grown steadily from its humble nineteenth century origins. If it emits a sound, then it's probably here, from a medieval Cornemuse to a Tibetan temple trumpet, via every kind of international and European music making vessel imaginable. What's more, there's a top-floor restaurant which rewards you with superb views.

You don't have to travel much further to find somewhere to actually go and hear some music: the **Palais des Beaux-Arts** is Brussels' top cultural venue, with the city's largest classical music auditorium, home to the Belgian National Orchestra. If your taste is more operatic, then across in the Lower Town is the nineteenth century **La Monnaie**, one of the best opera venues in Europe. It has a rousing claim to fame: in 1830, a nationalistic aria sung here provoked the audience to take to the streets and rebel against their Dutch rulers, setting Belgium on its path to independence. Most productions here are sold out months in advance. Concertgoers remain as rapt as ever by the music, though these days they have a tendency to remain in their seats till the end.

→ PARKING FINE

It would appear that the life of the Bruxellois was so bound up in medieval urban intrigue and revelry that they forgot about the addition of parkland. Not quite true: there is the **Parc de Bruxelles** in the heart of the Upper Town, but it's often seen as little more than a quick shortcut to the metro rather than a green oasis to stop and linger. The best park in the city is way over to the east in Euroland: the **Parc du Cinquantenaire** has a grand arch based on the Arc de Triomphe, a fine collection of old cars housed in a palace, a renowned museum for decorative arts and ancient civilisations, and wonderful walks watched over by old elms and plane trees. Close by is another park worth a meander: Parc Leopold, which has a lake to sit by, and a lot of politicians to bypass.

Many people come to Brussels for a close encounter with **Art Nouveau**. This is the city where architecturally it all started, led by local architect Victor Horta in the late nineteenth century. In the 1890s, over two thousand new houses were built in the style. The bad news is that many have been demolished, or are in use as private houses or offices. The good news is that just about every Brussels street retains details of Art Nouveau, and Horta's house, down south on the borderline between Ixelles and St Gilles, is an absorbing museum containing many artefacts from his time spent there. Stick around these two southern suburbs for the best array of Art Nouveau buildings. Both are pretty hot, too, for their café and street life scenes. Ixelles, in particular, boasts an arty, bohemian feel – certainly enough for the likes of Marx, Dumas and Rodin, who all lived here awhile.

BRUSSELS IN...

→ ONE DAY

Grand Place, Place Ste Catherine, Musees Royaux des Beaux Arts, fish restaurant at Ste-Catherine

→ TWO DAYS

Marolles, Place du Grand Sablon, Musical Instrument Museum, concert at
Palais des Beaux-Arts or La Monnaie

→ THREE DAYS

Parc du Cinquantenaire, Horta's house, a tour of St Gilles and Ixelles

CALENDAR HIGHLIGHTS

Important festivals kick off early in the New Year in Brussels. Pleasingly, with the iffy weather outside, they take place indoors. January sees Europe's first big film festival of the year, the Brussels festival, and a month later the imposing Palais des Beaux-Arts hosts the engrossing Antiques Fair. At the same time, the city's comic strip heritage comes to the fore at the International Comic Strip and Cartoon Festival. And staying with the world of publishing, the Brussels Book Fair engrosses hundreds of visitors, also in February. March and April boast a real highlight with Ars Musica, a well-renowned celebration of contemporary music. May's Kunsten Festival des Arts is a showcase for exciting new names in dance and theatre, while classical lovers feed their fixation at the Queen Elisabeth Music Contest, also in May, during which Europe's top student musicians gather to play. If you want to know what people got up to in Renaissance times, go to July's famed Ommegang, in which two thousand participants take to the Grand Place dressed as nobles, soldiers and jesters (book well in advance for this one). Don't book, but drive up to the Drive-In Movies, every July to September at Esplanade du Cinquantenaire: blockbusters are shown on weekend evenings. Back on the musical front, there are classical shows all over the city in the Brussels Summer Festival (July and August) and gyrating hips aplenty on the Place du Chatelain for the Fiesta Latina, also in August. Finally, September's Lucky Town Festival is a very cool event indeed, with trendy cafes hosting a range of concerts.

EATING OUT

As long as your appetite hasn't been sated at the chocolatiers, or you haven't had your hand in a cone full of frites from a street stall, then you'll relish the dining experience in Brussels: this is a city where it's almost impossible to eat badly. In fact, food is one of the best reasons for visiting. Some say that the EU decamped here en masse because of the wealth of fine restaurants. As long as you stay off the main tourist drag (ie, Rue des Bouchers) then you're guaranteed somewhere good to eat within a short strolling distance and that doesn't just mean Moules Frites, which is so popular that some restaurants serve it all year but it really should be enjoyed from August until March. There are lots of places to enjoy Belgian dishes such as lobster from Ostend, eels served with green herbs, and waterzooi (chicken or fish stew simmered in water and served with vegetables). Wherever you're eating, at whatever price range, food is invariably well cooked, often bursting with innovative touches, and served with pride, albeit mixed with a slice of self-deprecating Belgian humour. As a rule of thumb, the Lower Town has the best places to eat, with the Ste-Catherine quarter's fish and seafood establishments the pick of the bunch. You'll also find a mini Chinatown here. Because of the city's cosmopolitan character, there are dozens of international restaurants, ranging from the expected cluster of French and Italian dining spots, to the more unusual Moroccan, Tunisian and Congolese destinations. Belgium beers are famous the world over and come served in special glasses but it is not just found in the taverns; you can also discover a few dishes involving the use of beer.

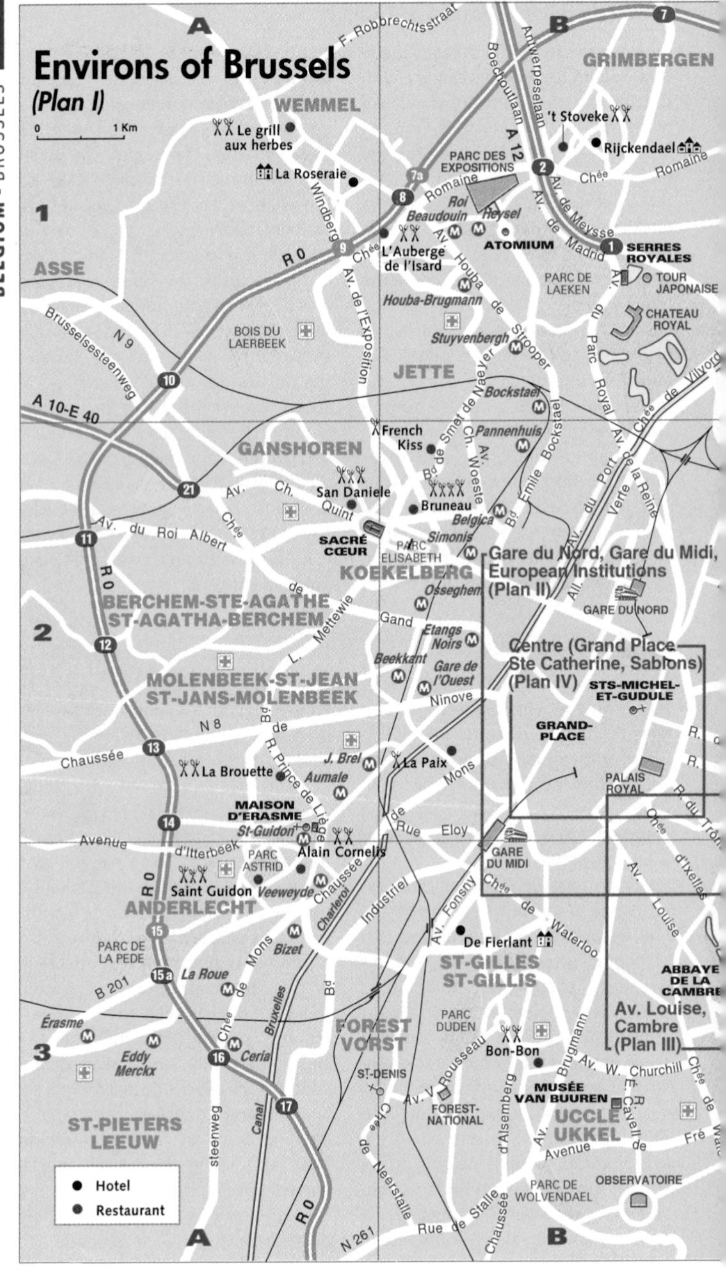
Environs of Brussels
(Plan I)
0 1 Km
WEMMEL
GRIMBERGEN
ASSE
JETTE
GANSHOREN
KOEKELBERG
BERCHEM-STE-AGATHE
ST-AGATHA-BERCHEM
MOLENBEEK-ST-JEAN
ST-JANS-MOLENBEEK
ANDERLECHT
ST-GILLES
ST-GILLIS
FOREST
VORST
UCCLE
UKKEL
ST-PIETERS
LEEUW
Le grill aux herbes
La Roseraie
L'Auberge de l'Isard
't Stoveke
Rijckendael
French Kiss
San Daniele
Bruneau
La Brouette
La Paix
Alain Cornelis
Saint Guidon
De Fierlant
Bon-Bon
PARC DES EXPOSITIONS
ATOMIUM
SERRES ROYALES
TOUR JAPONAISE
PARC DE LAEKEN
CHATEAU ROYAL
BOIS DU LAERBEEK
SACRÉ CŒUR
PARC ELISABETH
Gare du Nord, Gare du Midi, European Institutions (Plan II)
GARE DU NORD
Centre (Grand Place Ste Catherine, Sablons) (Plan IV)
STS-MICHEL-ET-GUDULE
GRAND-PLACE
PALAIS ROYAL
MAISON D'ERASME
PARC ASTRID
GARE DU MIDI
ABBAYE DE LA CAMBRE
Av. Louise, Cambre (Plan III)
PARC DE LA PEDE
PARC DUDEN
ST-DENIS
FOREST-NATIONAL
MUSÉE VAN BUUREN
PARC DE WOLVENDAEL
OBSERVATOIRE
Hotel
Restaurant

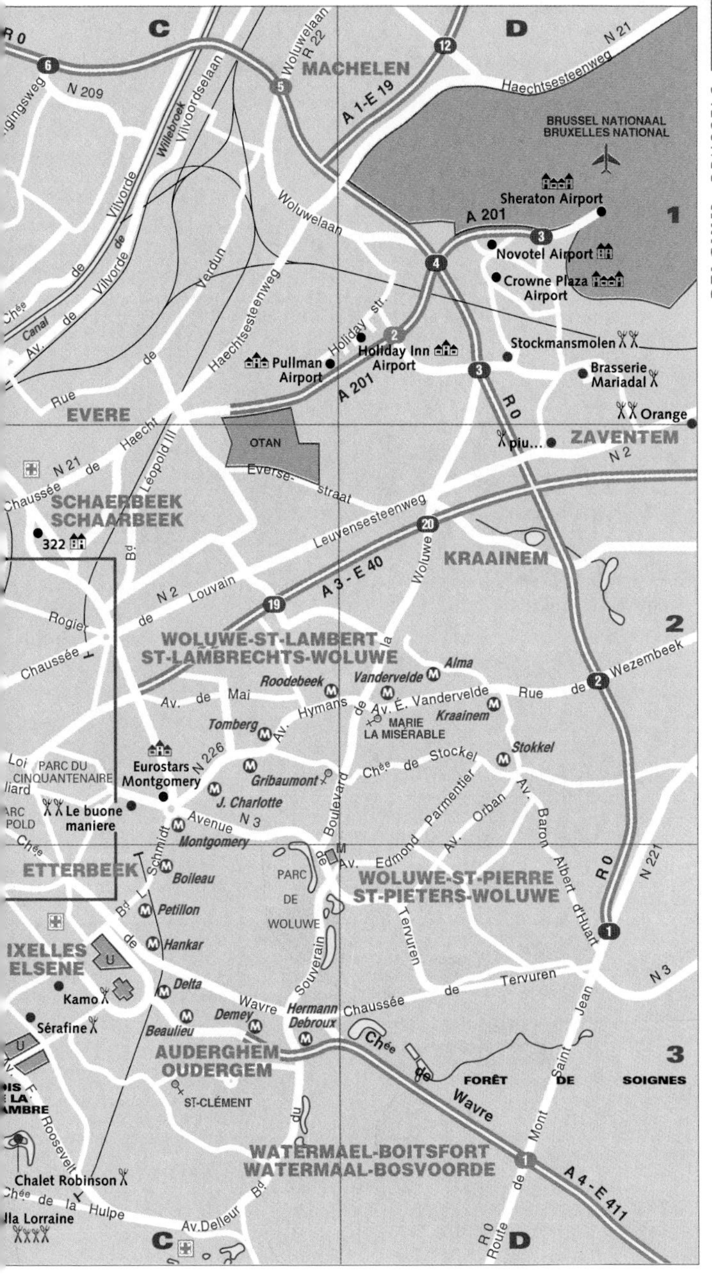
C
D
MACHELEN
BRUSSEL NATIONAAL
BRUXELLES NATIONAL
Sheraton Airport
Novotel Airport
Crowne Plaza Airport
Stockmansmolen
Brasserie Mariadal
Orange
Pullman Airport
Holiday Inn Airport
piu...
ZAVENTEM
EVERE
OTAN
SCHAERBEEK
SCHAARBEEK
322
KRAAINEM
WOLUWE-ST-LAMBERT
ST-LAMBRECHTS-WOLUWE
Alma
Vandervelde
Roodebeek
Kraainem
Tomberg
MARIE LA MISÉRABLE
Stokkel
Gribaumont
J. Charlotte
Montgomery
Eurostars Montgomery
PARC DU CINQUANTENAIRE
Le buone maniere
ETTERBEEK
Boileau
Petillon
Hankar
PARC DE WOLUWE
WOLUWE-ST-PIERRE
ST-PIETERS-WOLUWE
IXELLES
ELSENE
Kamo
Sérafine
Delta
Demey
Beaulieu
Hermann Debroux
AUDERGHEM
OUDERGEM
ST-CLÉMENT
FORÊT DE SOIGNES
WATERMAEL-BOITSFORT
WATERMAAL-BOSVOORDE
Chalet Robinson
A 1-E 19
A 201
A 3 - E 40
A 4 - E 411
R 0
N 2
N 3
N 21
N 209
N 221
N 226
Woluwelaan
Haechtsesteenweg
Leuvensesteenweg
Chaussée de Louvain
Chaussée de Haecht
Rue de Wezembeek
Av. de Mai
Av. Hymans
Av. É. Vandervelde
Chée de Stockel
Av. Edmond Parmentier
Av. Orban
Av. Baron Albert d'Huart
Av. de Tervuren
Chaussée de Wavre
Chée de Wavre
Bd. du Souverain
Chaussée de Tervuren
Av. Deleur
Chée de la Hulpe
Route de Mont Saint Jean
Av. de Vilvorde
Vilvoordselaan
Everse-straat
1
2
3

Gare du Nord, Gare du Midi, European Institutions (Plan II)

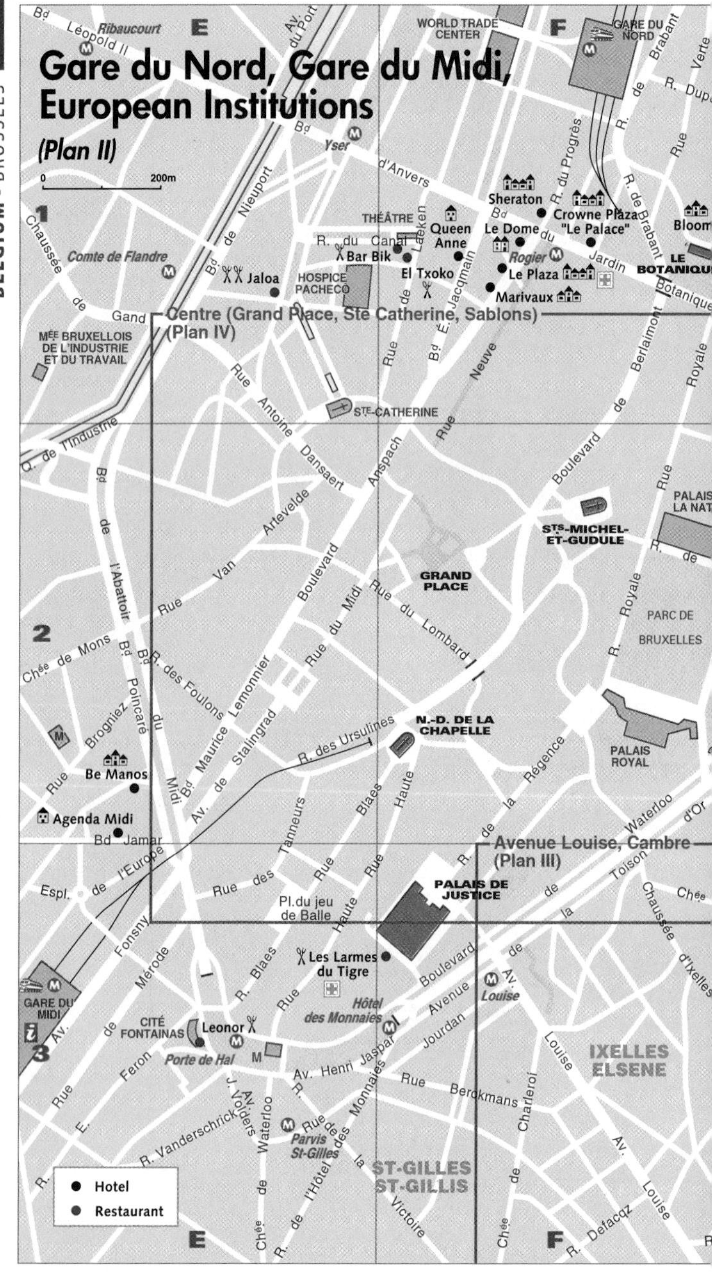

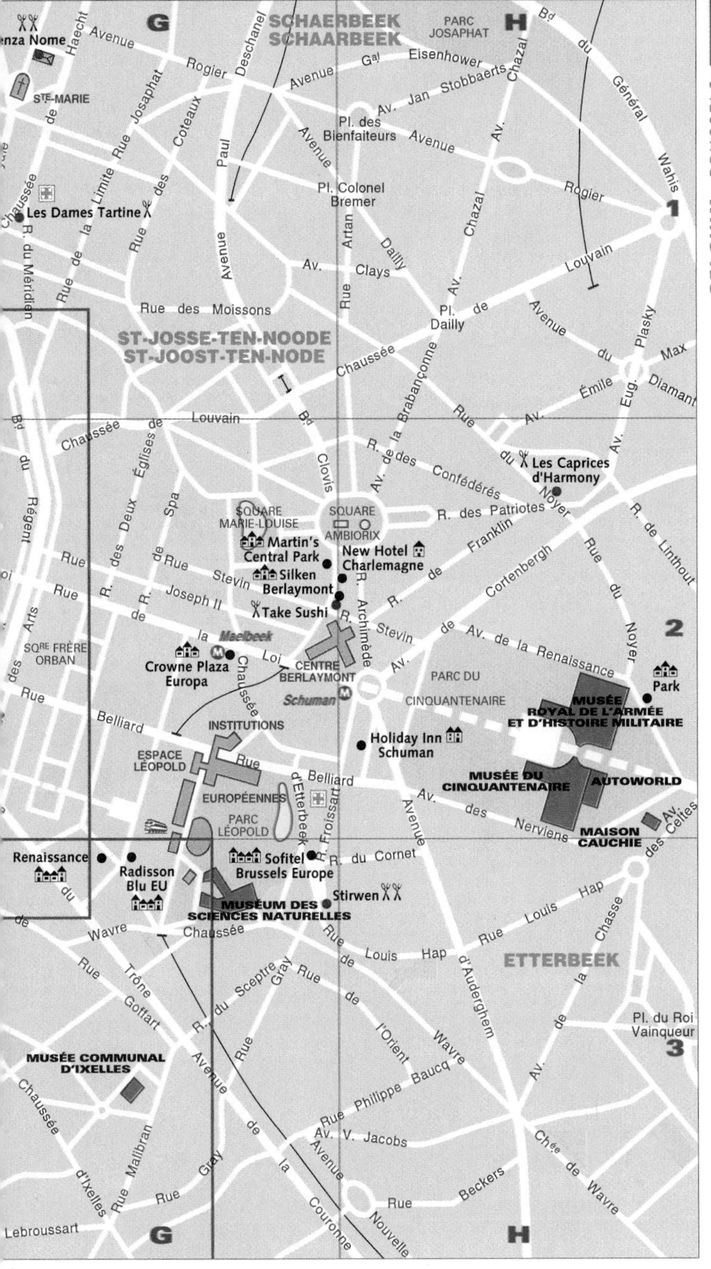
SCHAERBEEK
SCHAARBEEK
PARC JOSAPHAT
ST-JOSSE-TEN-NOODE
ST-JOOST-TEN-NODE
ETTERBEEK
Les Dames Tartine
Les Caprices d'Harmony
Martin's Central Park
New Hotel Charlemagne
Silken Berlaymont
Take Sushi
Crowne Plaza Europa
CENTRE BERLAYMONT
Schuman
Maelbeek
PARC DU CINQUANTENAIRE
MUSÉE ROYAL DE L'ARMÉE ET D'HISTOIRE MILITAIRE
Park
Holiday Inn Schuman
MUSÉE DU CINQUANTENAIRE
AUTOWORLD
MAISON CAUCHIE
INSTITUTIONS EUROPÉENNES
ESPACE LÉOPOLD
PARC LÉOPOLD
Renaissance
Radisson Blu EU
Sofitel Brussels Europe
Stirwen
MUSÉUM DES SCIENCES NATURELLES
MUSÉE COMMUNAL D'IXELLES
SQUARE MARIE-LOUISE
SQUARE AMBIORIX
SQRE FRÈRE ORBAN
STE-MARIE
Pl. des Bienfaiteurs
Pl. Colonel Bremer
Pl. Dailly
Pl. du Roi Vainqueur
G
H
1
2
3

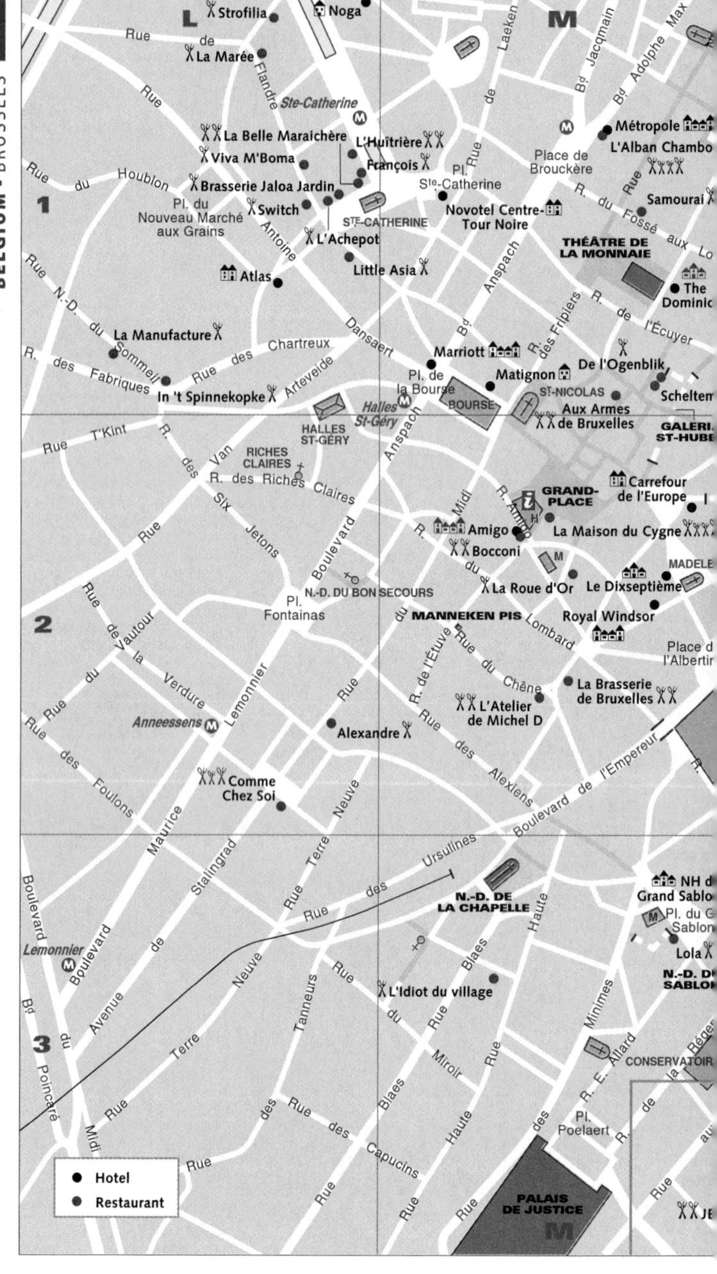
Strofilia
Noga
La Marée
Ste-Catherine
La Belle Maraichère
L'Huîtrière
Viva M'Boma
François
Brasserie Jaloa Jardin
Switch
L'Achepot
Little Asia
Atlas
La Manufacture
In 't Spinnekopke
Pl. du Nouveau Marché aux Grains
STE-CATHERINE
Pl. Ste-Catherine
Novotel Centre-Tour Noire
Place de Brouckère
Métropole
L'Alban Chambo
Samourai
THÉATRE DE LA MONNAIE
The Dominic
Marriott
Matignon
De l'Ogenblik
Pl. de la Bourse
BOURSE
ST-NICOLAS
Aux Armes de Bruxelles
Scheltem
GALERI. ST-HUBE
Halles St-Géry
HALLES ST-GÉRY
RICHES CLAIRES
R. des Riches Claires
GRAND-PLACE
Carrefour de l'Europe
Amigo
La Maison du Cygne
Bocconi
La Roue d'Or
Le Dixseptième
MADELE
N.-D. DU BON SECOURS
Pl. Fontainas
MANNEKEN PIS
Royal Windsor
Place de l'Albertin
La Brasserie de Bruxelles
L'Atelier de Michel D
Anneessens
Alexandre
Comme Chez Soi
Boulevard de l'Empereur
N.-D. DE LA CHAPELLE
NH du Grand Sablo
Pl. du G Sablon
Lola
N.-D. DU SABLO
Lemonnier
L'Idiot du village
CONSERVATOIR
Pl. Poelaert
PALAIS DE JUSTICE
Hotel
Restaurant
L
M
1
2
3

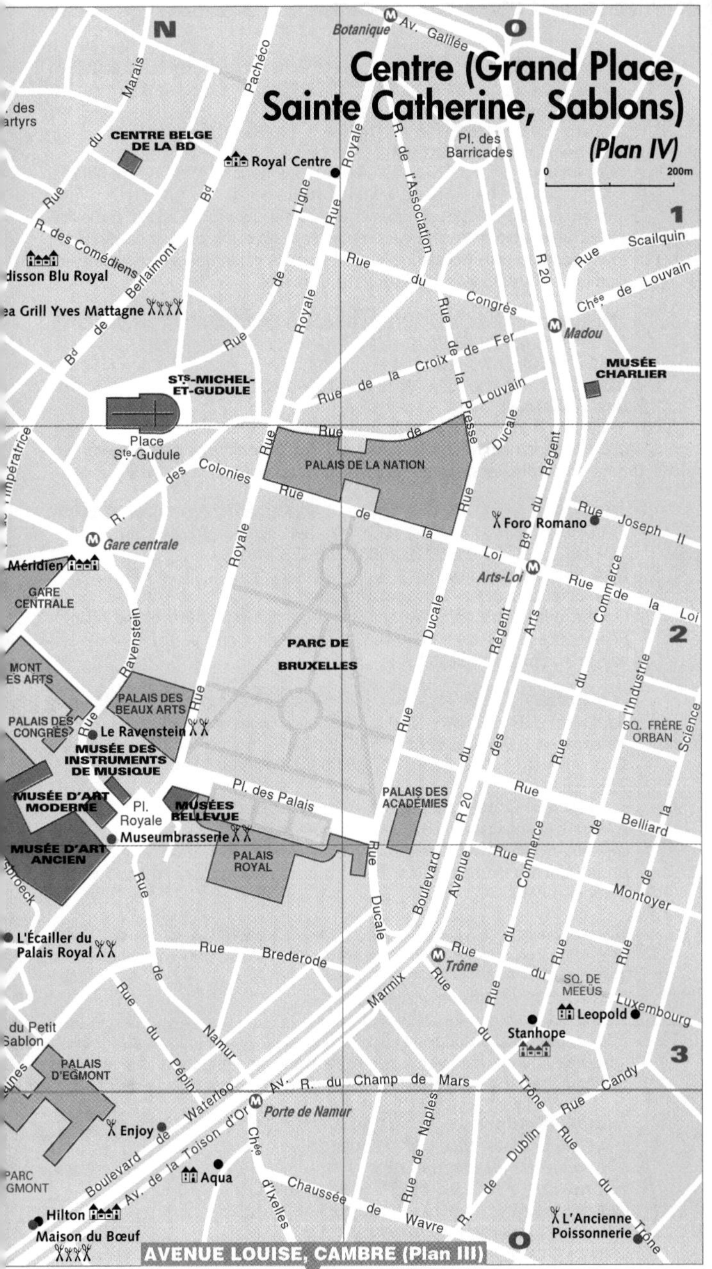
Centre (Grand Place, Sainte Catherine, Sablons)
(Plan IV)
0
200m
N
O
1
2
3
Botanique
Av. Galilée
Pl. des Barricades
Marais
Pacheco
du
Rue
R. des Comédiens
CENTRE BELGE DE LA BD
Royal Centre
Royale
Rue
Ligne
R. de l'Association
Rue du Congrès
R 20
Rue Scailquin
Chée de Louvain
Madou
MUSÉE CHARLIER
disson Blu Royal
ea Grill Yves Mattagne
Bd de Berlaimont
Rue de Royale
Rue de la Croix de Fer
Rue de la Presse
Rue de Louvain
STS-MICHEL-ET-GUDULE
Place Ste-Gudule
Rue des Colonies
PALAIS DE LA NATION
Rue Ducale
Bd du Régent
Foro Romano
Rue Joseph II
Rue de la Loi
Arts-Loi
Rue de la Loi
Rue du Commerce
Gare centrale
Méridien
GARE CENTRALE
Ravenstein
Royale
PARC DE BRUXELLES
Ducale
Régent
Arts
Rue de l'Industrie
Science
SQ. FRÈRE ORBAN
MONT DES ARTS
PALAIS DES BEAUX ARTS
PALAIS DES CONGRÈS
Le Ravenstein
MUSÉE DES INSTRUMENTS DE MUSIQUE
MUSÉE D'ART MODERNE
Pl. Royale
MUSÉES BELLEVUE
Pl. des Palais
PALAIS DES ACADÉMIES
Rue Belliard
Museumbrasserie
MUSÉE D'ART ANCIEN
PALAIS ROYAL
Rue Ducale
Boulevard
Avenue
Rue de Montoyer
L'Écailler du Palais Royal
Rue Brederode
Trône
Marnix
Rue du Trône
Rue du Luxembourg
SQ. DE MEEÛS
Leopold
Stanhope
du Petit Sablon
Rue de Namur
Rue du Pépin
PALAIS D'EGMONT
R. du Champ de Mars
Porte de Namur
Rue de Naples
Rue de Dublin
Rue Candy
Enjoy
Boulevard de Waterloo
Av. de la Toison d'Or
Chée d'Ixelles
Aqua
Chaussée de Wavre
PARC D'EGMONT
Hilton
Maison du Bœuf
L'Ancienne Poissonnerie
AVENUE LOUISE, CAMBRE (Plan III)

CENTRE (Grand Place, Sainte-Catherine, Sablons) *Plan IV*

Radisson Blu Royal

r. Fossé-aux-Loups 47 ✉ 1000 – ✆ 0 2 219 28 28 – www.radissonblu.com/royalhotel-brussels **N1**
272 rm – †495/1450 € ††495/1450 €, ☕ 30 € – 9 suites
Rest *Sea Grill Yves Mattagne* – see below
Rest *Atrium* – *✆ 0 2 227 31 70* – Menu 22 € (lunch)/35 € – Carte 35/53 €
♦ Chain hotel ♦ Palace ♦ Personalised ♦
Impressive modern glass atrium, remains of the city's fortifications, and extremely comfortable suites and guestrooms. Bar with comic book decor. Breakfast room adorned with wooden railway sleepers. A contemporary style brasserie illuminated by natural light through the glass roof.

Hilton

bd de Waterloo 38 ✉ 1000 – ✆ 0 2 504 11 11 – www.brussels.hilton.com **N3**
429 rm ☕ – †129/369 € ††129/369 € – 4 suites
Rest *Maison du Bœuf* – see below
♦ Chain hotel ♦ Grand Luxury ♦ Functional ♦
This imposing high-rise chain hotel, located between the upper and lower sections of the city, is a popular choice for international business travellers.

Amigo

r. Amigo 1 ✉ 1000 – ✆ 0 2 547 47 47 – www.roccofortecollection.com
154 rm – †199/640 € ††199/660 €, ☕ 35 € – 19 suites **M2**
Rest *Bocconi* – see below
♦ Grand Luxury ♦ Personalised ♦
Once a prison, this attractive building has retained a touch of the Spanish Renaissance. A collection of artwork, chic modern rooms and impeccable service for its upmarket clientele.

Le Plaza

bd A. Max 118 ✉ 1000 – ✆ 0 2 278 01 00 – www.leplaza.be
184 rm – †100/450 € ††100/450 €, ☕ 25 € – 6 suites *Plan II* **F1**
Rest – *(closed Saturday, Sunday and bank holidays)* Menu 20 € (lunch)/ 27 € – Carte 44/58 €
♦ Palace ♦ Grand Luxury ♦ Personalised ♦
A 1930s building imitating the George V hotel in Paris. Classic public areas, large cosy guestrooms and a superb Baroque theatre used for receptions and events. An elegant bar and restaurant beneath an attractive dome painted with a trompe l'œil sky.

Métropole

pl. de Brouckère 31 ✉ 1000 – ✆ 0 2 217 23 00 – www.metropolehotel.com
283 rm ☕ – †359/389 € ††389/419 € – 5 suites **M1**
Rest *L'Alban Chambon* – see below
♦ Grand Luxury ♦ Personalised ♦
A 19C luxury hotel overlooking Place de Brouckère. Period lobby and lounges, a retro-style lounge bar with columns, a piano and frescoes, and luxurious bedrooms and suites. Breakfast is served to a backdrop of colonial decor.

Royal Windsor

r. Duquesnoy 5 ✉ 1000 – ✆ 0 2 505 55 55 – www.royalwindsorbrussels.com **M2**
260 rm ☕ – †90/269 € ††90/269 € – 7 suites
Rest – Menu 14 € (lunch) – Carte 29/52 €
♦ Grand Luxury ♦ Personalised ♦
Luxury, comfort and refinement are the hallmarks of this hotel, which has undergone recent refurbishment. Superb service. A varied choice of traditional dishes, bistro cuisine and Belgian specialities.

Marriott

r. A. Orts 7 (opposite stock exchange) ✉ 1000 – ☎ 0 2 516 90 90 – www.marriottbrussels.com **M1**

214 rm – †99/399 € ††99/399 €, ☕ 25 € – 5 suites

Rest – *(closed Sunday dinner)* Menu 16 € (lunch)/25 €

◆ Luxury ◆ Personalised ◆

A famous piece of local folklore (The Marriage of Mademoiselle Beulemans) was conceived behind the 1900 façade adjoining the Stock Exchange. Chic public areas and bedrooms boasting every creature comfort. A brasserie with an open kitchen serving grilled dishes and American-style cuisine. Lunch buffet.

Le Méridien

Carrefour de l'Europe 3 ✉ 1000 – ☎ 0 2 548 42 11 – www.lemeridien.com/brussels **N2**

223 rm – †149/450 € ††149/450 €, ☕ 29 € – 1 suite

Rest *L'Épicerie* – ☎ 0 2 548 42 16 *(closed Easter holidays, July-August, 24, 25 and 31 December-1st January, Saturday lunch and Sunday)* Menu 38 € (lunch)/75 € – Carte 55/66 €

◆ Luxury ◆ Personalised ◆

Built in the 1990s opposite the central station, the Méridien's curved façade is palatial in style. Elegant lobby, varying categories of guestroom, and excellent seminar facilities. The focus in the traditional dining room is on refined cuisine, including a few typically Belgian dishes. Brunch on Sundays.

The Dominican

r. Léopold 9 ✉ 1000 – ☎ 0 2 203 08 08 – www.thedominican.be

146 rm – †125/425 € ††125/425 €, ☕ 27 € – 4 suites **M1**

Rest *The Grand Lounge* – Menu 27 € (lunch) – Carte 51/67 €

◆ Luxury ◆ Business ◆ Personalised ◆

A designer-inspired luxury hotel on the site of a former Dominican convent. Open spaces, elegant furniture and modern comforts which benefit from maximum attention to detail. The Grand Lounge takes full advantage of the natural light from the patio. A modern menu and non-stop service, including the popular "after-work" drinks on Thursdays.

Le Dixseptième without rest

r. Madeleine 25 ✉ 1000 – ☎ 0 2 517 17 17 – www.ledixseptieme.be

20 rm ☕ – †100/200 € ††150/400 € – 4 suites **M2**

◆ Luxury ◆ Stylish ◆

This townhouse dating from the 17C was once the official residence of the Spanish ambassador in the city. Elegant lounges, attractive inner courtyard, and guestrooms embellished with furniture of varying styles.

NH du Grand Sablon

rest,

r. Bodenbroek 2 ✉ 1000 – ☎ 0 2 518 11 00 – www.nh-hotels.com **M3**

190 rm – †80/220 € ††80/220 €, ☕ 25 € – 6 suites

Rest – *(closed Sunday and bank holidays)* Menu 17 € (lunch)/25 € – Carte 36/51 €

◆ Chain hotel ◆ Business ◆ Personalised ◆

This establishment is well located in the antiques district, close to the city's prestigious royal museums. There is a marble adorned lobby, comfortable guestrooms, and facilities for business meetings. The hotel's restaurant specialises in Italian cuisine.

Royal Centre without rest

r. Royale 160 ✉ 1000 – ☎ 0 2 219 00 65 – www.royalcentre.be

73 rm ☕ – †79/350 € ††89/390 € **N1**

◆ Chain hotel ◆ Business ◆ Functional ◆

This hotel is at the heart of the European institutions district. The modern guestrooms are of varying sizes and spread across eight floors. Marble lobby-entrance hall and comfortable lounge.

Marivaux

bd Adolphe Max 98 ✉ 1000 – ✆ 0 2 227 03 00 – www.marivaux.be
131 rm – 100/375 € 100/375 € – 4 suites *Plan II* **F1**
Rest – *(closed Saturday lunch and Sunday)* Menu 13 € (lunch), 25/50 € – Carte 30/46 €
♦ Business ♦ Functional ♦ Modern ♦
This hotel occupies several adjoining houses in the city centre. Revamped public areas, plus a conference centre which has taken over the old Marivaux cinema. New guestrooms and a gastronomic restaurant are also planned. Brasserie cuisine served amid a contemporary decor.

Carrefour de l'Europe without rest

r. Marché-aux-Herbes 110 ✉ 1000 – ✆ 0 2 504 94 00 – www.carrefourhotel.be **M2**
59 rm – 99/229 € 99/249 € – 6 suites
♦ Business ♦ Functional ♦
This hotel built a decade or so ago is situated between the Grand Place and the central train station on the edge of the Ilot Sacré. Reasonably sized, functional guestrooms which are brighter in appearance following their upgrade in 2009.

Novotel Centre - Tour Noire

r. Vierge Noire 32 ✉ 1000 – ✆ 0 2 505 50 50 – www.novotel.com **M1**
217 rm – 85/300 € 85/300 €, 18 €
Rest – Menu 23 € (lunch) – Carte 36/49 €
♦ Chain hotel ♦ Business ♦ Functional ♦
A modern chain hotel incorporating remains of the city's first wall, including a restored tower. Large bedrooms, meeting rooms, aqua-centre, fitness room and sauna. A contemporary, brasserie-style restaurant.

Atlas without rest

r. Vieux Marché-aux-Grains 30 ✉ 1000 – ✆ 0 2 502 60 06 – www.atlas.be
88 rm – 75/225 € 85/250 € **L1**
♦ Family ♦ Functional ♦
This extensively modernised 18C townhouse is situated in a lively part of the city renowned for its Belgian fashion boutiques. The majority of the hotel's rooms overlook the courtyard.

Noga without rest

r. Béguinage 38 ✉ 1000 – ✆ 0 2 218 67 63 – www.nogahotel.com
19 rm – 70/110 € 85/135 € **L1**
♦ Family ♦ Classic ♦
This welcoming mansion located in a quiet part of the city offers a cosy lounge, nautically themed bar, and comfortable, traditional guestrooms. Portraits of the Belgian royal family line the stairwell.

Queen Anne without rest

bd E. Jacqmain 110 ✉ 1000 – ✆ 0 2 217 16 00 – www.queen-anne.be
60 rm – 60/150 € 65/170 € *Plan II* **F1**
♦ Family ♦ Modern ♦
Recognisable by its glass-fronted façade, this hotel is located close to the city centre. Guestrooms and apartments offering a bright minimalist feel and discreet designer touches.

Matignon without rest

r. Bourse 10 ✉ 1000 – ✆ 0 2 511 08 88 – www.hotelmatignon.be
37 rm – 90/120 € 105/150 € **M1**
♦ Family ♦ Functional ♦
This hotel close to the city's stock exchange has been run by the same family for two decades. Well-maintained guestrooms, including nine junior suites.

XXXX ✿✿

Sea Grill Yves Mattagne – Hôtel Radisson Blu Royal

r. Fossé-aux-Loups 47 ✉ 1000 – ☎ 0 2 212 08 00 – www.seagrill.be – Closed 16-25 April, 21 July-15 August, 29 October-1st November, 1-9 January, Saturday, Sunday and bank holidays **N1**

Rest – Menu 65 € (lunch), 120/245 € bi – Carte 113/170 €

Spec. Crabe de la Mer des Glaces cuit sur gros sel, poivre et algues. Ris de veau de lait et homard, béarnaise au jus de presse, cèpes et artichauts. Turbot rôti à l'arête, béarnaise d'huîtres.

◆ Seafood ◆ Elegant ◆

The interior has been given a facelift: soft colours, luxurious, contemporary comfort and an ambitious fish and seafood menu. There is an efficient team in the kitchen and prestigious bottles on the wine list. The Sea Grill is still navigating on course!

XXXX

La Maison du Cygne

r. Charles Buls 2 (1st floor) ✉ 1000 – ☎ 0 2 511 82 44 – www.lamaisonducygne.be – Closed Christmas-New Year, Saturday lunch and Sunday **M2**

Rest – Menu 40 € (lunch)/65 € – Carte 70/91 €

Rest *L'Ommegang* – *(closed Christmas-New Year and Sunday)* Carte 30/55 €

◆ Traditional ◆ Elegant ◆

This prestigious 17C building on the Grand Place was once home to the city's butchers' guild. Varied traditional cuisine and an opulent decor. The Ommegang downstairs is a brasserie with character offering a more democratic alternative to the pomp on the upper floor. Menu and specials.

XXXX

Maison du Bœuf – Hôtel Hilton (1st Floor)

bd de Waterloo 38 ✉ 1000 – ☎ 0 2 504 13 34 – www.brussels.hilton.com – Closed Saturday lunch and Sunday **N3**

Rest – Menu 39 € (lunch), 60/95 € bi – Carte 56/94 €

◆ Classic ◆ Elegant ◆

A chic, traditional setting provides the backdrop for an appetising menu, which includes a choice of beef dishes, such as the famous rib of beef, which is carved at your table. The tables facing the park are preferable.

XXXX ✿

Bruneau (Jean-Pierre Bruneau)

(dinner)

av. Broustin 75 ✉ 1083 – ☎ 0 2 421 70 70 – www.bruneau.be – Closed mid June-mid July, 3-12 January, holiday Thursdays, Tuesday and Wednesday *Plan I* **B2**

Rest – Menu 35 € (lunch), 55/95 € – Carte 73/293 €

Spec. Coussinet de raie au king crabe. Noix de ris de veau en habit de dentelles. Blanc de coucou de Malines demi-deuil.

◆ Contemporary ◆ Elegant ◆

A renowned restaurant offering a perfect balance between the traditional and the innovative, while at the same time showcasing regional cuisine. Impressive wine list. Outdoor terrace for summer dining.

XXXX

L'Alban Chambon – Hôtel Métropole

pl. de Brouckère 31 ✉ 1000 – ☎ 0 2 217 23 00 – www.albanchambon.com – Closed 17 July-16 August, Saturday lunch, Sunday, Monday and bank holidays **M1**

Rest – Menu 30 € (lunch), 66/117 € bi

◆ Contemporary ◆ Elegant ◆ Luxury ◆

The name of the Métropole's restaurant pays homage to its architect. Classic cuisine in an old Baroque-style ballroom.

XXX ✿✿

Comme Chez Soi (Lionel Rigolet)

✉ 1000 – ✆ 0 2 512 29 21 – www.commechezsoi.be
– Closed 8 March, 12 April, 17 July-16 August, 1st November, 25 December-10 January, Wednesday lunch, Sunday and Monday **L2**

Rest – (pre-book) Menu 55 € (lunch), 84/191 € – Carte 93/193 €

Spec. Salade parmentière à l'homard et truffes noires. Suprêmes de pigeon à la cardamome verte, cannelloni de ramonache au chou chinois. Soufflé au citron vert, granité au parfum de mojito.

♦ Contemporary ♦ Formal ♦

This Brussels institution was founded in 1926. The menu features specialities that have held their own over four generations, complemented by new creations by Lionel Rigolet. It has all the comfort of a bistro, Horta-inspired decor and comfortable tables in the kitchen itself, from where you can watch the chefs in action.

XXX ✿

San Daniele (Franco Spinelli)

av. Charles-Quint 6 ✉ 1083 – ✆ 0 2 426 79 23 – www.san-daniele.be
– Closed mid July-mid August, Sunday and Monday Plan I **A2**

Rest – Menu 80 € (lunch), 51/92 € – Carte 51/92 €

Spec. Vitello tonato façon "Gualtiero Marchesi". Bar de ligne grillé au thym. Ravioli au noir de seiche, homard et courgettes, jus de crustacés.

♦ Italian ♦ Elegant ♦

An attractive dining room serving typical Italian cuisine accompanied by an enticing Italian wine list. Friendly, attentive service from the Spinelli family.

XX

Aux Armes de Bruxelles

r. Bouchers 13 ✉ 1000 – ✆ 0 2 511 55 98 – www.auxarmesdebruxelles.be

Rest – Menu 23 € bi (lunch), 35/47 € – Carte 30/80 € **M1**

♦ Traditional ♦ Brasserie ♦

This veritable Brussels institution in the Ilot Sacré district has been honouring Belgian culinary traditions since 1921. Contrasting dining rooms and a lively atmosphere.

XX

Le Ravenstein

r. Ravenstein 1 ✉ 1000 – ✆ 0 2 512 77 68 – www.leravenstein.be
– Closed 15 July-15 August, late December-early January, Saturday lunch and Sunday **N2**

Rest – Menu 22 € (lunch), 30/60 € – Carte 46/70 €

♦ Contemporary ♦ Rustic ♦

Alain Bohné presides over this restaurant housed in a listed building (15C) near the Mont des Arts area. There are two distinct ambiences: contemporary and minimalist, or positively stately. Classic cuisine.

XX

L'Atelier de Michel D

pl. de la Vieille Halle aux Blés 31 ✉ 1000 – ✆ 0 2 512 57 00
– www.ateliermicheld.be
– Closed Wednesday dinner, Saturday lunch and Sunday except bank holidays

Rest – Menu 19 € (lunch), 30/45 € bi – Carte 53/62 € **M2**

♦ Contemporary ♦ Formal ♦

A touch of the Mediterranean in the heart of Brussels. Friendly service, seasonal à la carte choices and a set "menu du marché". Fake snakeskin banquette and an open-view kitchen where this famous chef's talents come to the fore.

XX

Museumbrasserie

pl. Royale 3 ✉ 1000 – ✆ 0 2 508 35 80 – www.museumfood.be
– Closed 2 weeks in August, late December, Sunday dinner, Monday and bank holidays **N2**

Rest – Menu 20 € (lunch), 30/36 € – Carte 45/63 €

♦ Brasserie ♦ Fashionable ♦

Cooking meets art in this resolutely patriotic brasserie inside the Musées Royaux des Beaux-Arts. A new team is now in charge at this restaurant, where the highlight is the simply named Belgian menu. The icing on the cake is the decor designed by Antoine Pinto.

XX

Bocconi – Hôtel Amigo

r. Amigo 1 ✉ 1000 – ☎ 0 2 547 47 15 – www.ristorantebocconi.com
– Closed Saturday lunch **M2**

Rest – Menu 18 € (lunch)/34 € – Carte 43/73 €

♦ Italian ♦ Brasserie ♦ Elegant ♦

This renowned Italian restaurant occupies a luxury hotel near the Grand Place. Modern brasserie-style decor provides the backdrop for enticing Italian cuisine.

XX

La Belle Maraîchère

pl. Ste-Catherine 11 ✉ 1000 – ☎ 0 2 512 97 59
– www.labellemaraichere.com
– Closed 2 weeks carnival, late July-early August, Wednesday and Thursday

Rest – *(booking advisable)* Menu 36/58 € – Carte 46/99 € **L1**

♦ Seafood ♦ Bistro ♦

This welcoming, family-run restaurant is a popular choice for locals with charmingly nostalgic decor in the dining room. Enticing traditional cuisine, including fish, seafood and game depending on the season, as well as high quality sauces. Attractive set menus.

XX

JB

r. Grand Cerf 24 ✉ 1000 – ☎ 0 2 512 04 84 – www.restaurantjb.be
– Closed 21 July-15 August, Saturday lunch and Sunday **M3**

Rest – Menu 26/36 € – Carte 50/63 €

♦ Contemporary ♦ Friendly ♦ Family ♦

A family affair founded in 1979. The owner is also a sauce chef with many strings to his bow; he offers refined dishes at affordable prices. The restaurant has Lloyd Loom chairs, an Italian chandelier and yellow patina on the walls.

XX

L'Écailler du Palais Royal

r. Bodenbroek 18 ✉ 1000 – ☎ 0 2 512 87 51
– www.lecaillerdupalaisroyal.be
– Closed August, late December, bank holidays and Sunday **N3**

Rest – Carte 62/137 €

♦ Seafood ♦ Cosy ♦

An elegant and cosy oyster bar frequented by diplomats and top business executives for the past 40 years. Choose from banquette seating and a convivial counter-bar downstairs or round tables upstairs. Refined fish and seafood.

XX

La Brasserie de Bruxelles

pl. de la Vieille Halle aux Blés 39 ✉ 1000 – ☎ 0 25 13 98 12
– Closed Monday **M2**

Rest – *(open until 11 pm)* Menu 20 € (lunch)/35 € – Carte 31/60 €

♦ Traditional ♦ Brasserie ♦ Formal ♦

Laurent Veulemans left his previous restaurant (Aux Armes de Bruxelles) in 2008 for this brasserie located in the lively Vieille-Halle-aux-Blés area. Traditional Brussels cuisine.

XX

Jaloa

quai aux Barques 4 ✉ 1000 – ☎ 0 2 513 19 92 – www.jaloa.com
– Closed 1-15 August, All Saints' week, 1-7 January, Monday lunch, Saturday lunch and Sunday *Plan II* **E1**

Rest – *(set menu only)* Menu 30 € (lunch), 58/95 €

♦ Contemporary ♦ Fashionable ♦

This restaurant is housed in one of the oldest buildings in "Vismet" (17C). The innovative food – served in a single set menu – is in stark contrast with the historical setting.

XX

Lola

pl. du Grand Sablon 33 ✉ 1000 – ☎ 0 2 514 24 60 – www.restolola.be

Rest – Carte 33/62 € **M3**

♦ Italian ♦ Brasserie ♦

Friendly brasserie with a contemporary decor serving Italian dishes based on the freshest ingredients. The pleasant counter is perfect for a meal on the hoof.

L'Huîtrière

quai aux Briques 20 ✉ 1000 – ☎ 0 2 512 08 66 – www.lhuitriere.eu
Rest – Menu 17 €, 25/47 € – Carte 38/72 € **L1**
◆ Seafood ◆ Inn ◆ Rustic ◆
Fish and seafood are to the fore here, to a backdrop of old Brussels, including wood panelling and Bruegel-inspired murals. Popular with celebrities, although the star turn here is the house speciality: lobster with sea urchin butter.

La Manufacture

r. Notre-Dame du Sommeil 12 ✉ 1000 – ☎ 0 2 502 25 25 – www.manufacture.be – Closed Saturday lunch and Sunday
Rest – *(open until 11pm)* Menu 15 €, 35/50 € – Carte 32/51 € **L1**
◆ Contemporary ◆ Brasserie ◆
Metals, wood, leather and granite provide the decor in this lively, trendy brasserie in the former workshop of a famous Belgian luggage maker. Contemporary cuisine.

Alexandre (Alexandre Dionisio)

r. Midi 164 ✉ 1000 – ☎ 0 2 502 40 55 – www.alexandre-restaurant.be – Closed Saturday, Sunday and Monday **L2**
Rest – *(booking essential)* Menu 25 € (lunch)/65 € bi – Carte 43/73 €
Spec. Rouget juste saisi aux croûtons, couvert d'un nuage de noisettes et lardons. Turbotin à la mousseline d'artichauts et émulsion de coquillages. Structures de café.
◆ Contemporary ◆ Bistro ◆ Minimalist ◆
Having reached the finals of a television programme, the young chef capitalised on his moment of fame and opened his own restaurant. His cooking shows a real knowledge of ingredients and a sense of innovation.

Scheltema

r. Dominicains 7 ✉ 1000 – ☎ 0 2 512 20 84 – www.scheltema.be – Closed 24 and 25 December and Sunday **M1**
Rest – *(open until 11.30 pm)* Menu 18 € (lunch), 32/71 € bi – Carte 42/88 €
◆ Seafood ◆ Brasserie ◆
An attractive old brasserie located in the city's Ilot Sacré district. Traditional dishes and daily specials with fish and seafood specialities. A lively atmosphere and a pleasant retro-style wooden decor.

De l'Ogenblik

Galerie des Princes 1 ✉ 1000 – ☎ 0 2 511 61 51 – www.ogenblik.be – Closed Sunday **M1**
Rest – *(open until midnight)* Menu 51/58 € – Carte 48/68 €
◆ Traditional ◆ Bistro ◆
This restaurant popular with the city's business crowd has the appearance of an old café. Traditional cuisine including typical bistro dishes. The same chef has been working here since 1975.

La Roue d'Or

r. Chapeliers 26 ✉ 1000 – ☎ 0 2 514 25 54n – Closed 17 July-16 August
Rest – *(open until 11.30 pm)* Menu 13 € (lunch), 38/56 € – Carte 38/56 € **M2**
◆ Bistro ◆ Brasserie ◆
This typical old Brussels café with a friendly atmosphere mixes traditional brasserie-style dishes with a handful of Belgian specialities. Decor includes Magritte-style murals and a superb clock in the dining room.

Samourai

r. Fossé-aux-Loups 28 ✉ 1000 – ☎ 0 2 217 56 39 – www.samourai-restaurant.be – Closed 1-21 August, 24 December-6 January, Sunday lunch, Tuesday and bank holidays **M1**
Rest – Menu 27 €, 65/100 € – Carte 47/60 €
◆ Japanese ◆ Minimalist ◆
A Japanese restaurant which opened in 1975 near the Théâtre de la Monnaie. Dining rooms on three floors with a Japanese decorative theme. Top-notch cuisine based around quality products and adapted to Western tastes.

Brasserie Jaloa Jardin

pl. Ste-Catherine 5 ✉ 1000 – ✆ 0 2 512 18 31 – www.jaloa.com
Rest – *(open until 11 pm)* Menu 34 € – Carte 37/60 € **L1**
♦ Brasserie ♦ Friendly ♦ Design ♦
Typical Belgian brasserie fare is served in two bright and elegant dining rooms or on the charming and secluded courtyard terrace.

François

quai aux Briques 2 ✉ 1000 – ✆ 25 11 60 89 – www.restaurantfrancois.be – Closed 26 April-7 May, 16 August-6 September, Sunday and Monday
Rest – Menu 27 € (lunch), 35/55 € – Carte 40/105 € **L1**
♦ Seafood ♦ Brasserie ♦
Fish and seafood take pride of place in this restaurant run by the same family since the 1930s. Maritime-inspired decor including photos from the past. Fishmonger's next door.

La Marée

r. Flandre 99 ✉ 1000 – ✆ 0 2 511 00 40 – www.lamaree-sa.com – Closed 20 June-15 July, Christmas, New Year, Sunday and Monday
Rest – Carte 25/67 € **L1**
♦ Seafood ♦ Bistro ♦
A convivial restaurant with simple decor and uncomplicated cuisine, with an emphasis on fish and seafood and Portuguese dishes (on request). Open kitchen and summer terrace.

Switch

r. Flandre 6 ✉ 1000 – ✆ 0 2 503 14 80 – www.switchrestofood.be – Closed Monday lunch, Saturday lunch and Sunday **L1**
Rest – Menu 17 € (lunch), 35/46 € bi – Carte 41/53 €
♦ Contemporary ♦ Bistro ♦
Friendly staff, a contemporary bistro feel, and top-notch dishes, including a reasonably priced lunch and a flexible 'switch' menu. Traditional cuisine with experimental touches.

Viva M'Boma

r. Flandre 17 ✉ 1000 – ✆ 0 2 512 15 93 – Closed dinner Monday and Tuesday, Wednesday and Sunday **L1**
Rest – Carte 26/39 €
♦ Bistro ♦ Family ♦
This elegant canteen-style restaurant has closely packed tables and tiled walls reminiscent of a Parisian métro station. It is popular with fans of offal and old Brussels specialities (cow's udder, *choesels* (sweetbreads), marrowbone, ox cheek).

Little Asia

r. Ste-Catherine 8 ✉ 1000 – ✆ 0 2 502 88 36 – www.littleasia.be – Closed Wednesday, Sunday and bank holidays **L1**
Rest – *(open until 11 pm)* Menu 20 € (lunch), 45/60 € – Carte 36/70 €
♦ Vietnamese ♦ Fashionable ♦
A restaurant known for its well-prepared Vietnamese specialities, modern decor and smiling waitresses, overseen by a charming female owner.

L'Idiot du village

r. Notre Seigneur 19 ✉ 1000 – ✆ 0 2 502 55 82 – Closed 25-30 April, 27 July-15 August, 23 December-2 January, Saturday and Sunday **M3**
Rest – *(open until 11 pm)* Menu 15 € (lunch) – Carte 37/68 €
♦ Contemporary ♦ Bistro ♦
A neighbourhood restaurant with friendly staff, charmingly kitsch decor, an intimate ambience, and bistro-style cuisine with a contemporary flourish based around fresh ingredients. Very popular with locals.

Les Larmes du Tigre

r. Wynants 21 ✉ 1000 – ☎ 0 2 512 18 77 – www.leslarmesdutigre.be
– Closed Saturday lunch and Monday Plan II **F3**
Rest – Menu 12 € (lunch), 25/38 € – Carte 32/42 €
♦ Thai ♦ Exotic ♦
This exotic restaurant behind the Palais de Justice has been serving delicious Thai cuisine since 1985 beneath the umbrella-adorned ceiling or outdoors in fine weather. Sunday lunch and dinner buffet.

In 't Spinnekopke

pl. du Jardin aux Fleurs 1 ✉ 1000 – ☎ 0 2 511 86 95
– www.spinnekopke.be
– Closed Saturday lunch and Sunday **L1**
Rest – Menu 10 € (lunch), 42 € bi/55 € bi – Carte 30/58 €
♦ Brasserie ♦ Bistro ♦
A charming inn so typical of Brussels, with a bistro-style ambience and a menu that pays homage to the traditions of Belgian brasseries. Terrace on the square.

Bar Bik

quai aux Pierres de Taille 3 ✉ 1000 – ☎ 0 2 219 75 00
– Closed mid July-mid August, Saturday and Sunday Plan II **F1**
Rest – *(booking advisable)* Carte 28/46 €
♦ Bistro ♦ Friendly ♦
The Bar Bik (Brussels International Kitchen) menu offers simple but tasty local dishes with influences from far and wide. Friendly, down-to-earth service and minimalist decor.

El Txoko

r. Laeken 122 ✉ 1000 – ☎ 0 22 03 10 22 – www.eltxoko.be
– Closed Saturday lunch, Sunday and Monday Plan II **F1**
Rest – Menu 12 € (lunch), 16/40 € bi – Carte 27/48 €
♦ Basque cuisine ♦ Fashionable ♦ Tapas bar ♦
This excellent Basque tapas bar has a minimalist interior and is located in a trendy area. Assortment of *pintxos* and an appealing and varied array of Spanish wines. The nearby KVS (Theâtre Royal Flamand) draws in a culture loving crowd but everyone is welcome!

Strofilia

r. Marché-aux-Porcs 11 ✉ 1000 – ☎ 0 2 512 32 93 – www.strofilia.be
– Closed Saturday lunch and Sunday **L1**
Rest – *(open until 11 pm)* Menu 13 € (lunch), 30 € bi/50 € bi
– Carte 23/41 €
♦ Greek ♦ Trendy ♦
Located close to the trendy Dansaert district, this typical "ouzeri" serves guests in its large loft-style dining rooms and vaulted cellar. A choice of Greek mezze, main courses and wines. The name comes from the attractive grape press on display ("strofilia" in Greek).

L'Achepot

pl. Ste-Catherine 1 ✉ 1000 – ☎ 0 2 511 62 21
– Closed Sunday and Monday **L1**
Rest – Menu 16 € (lunch)/29 € – Carte 34/61 €
♦ Classic ♦ Bistro ♦
An elegant and welcoming neo-bistro on the lively Place Sainte-Catherine. The menu board highlights a mix of local and southern French dishes.

Leonor

av. de la Porte de Hal 19 ✉ 1060 – ☎ 0 2 537 51 56 – www.leonor.be
– Closed August, Wednesday, Sunday and bank holidays Plan II **E3**
Rest – Menu 12 € (lunch)/35 € – Carte 36/46 €
♦ Spanish ♦ Family ♦
Welcome to Spain: here, colours abound, as do tapas and Iberian nouvelle cuisine (*chipirones a la plancha* and ink sauce). Convivial atmosphere.

Enjoy

bd de Waterloo 22 ✉ 1000 – ✆ 0 2 641 57 90 – www.enjoybrussels.be
– Closed Sunday and bank holidays **N3**

Rest – Carte 32/47 €

♦ Contemporary ♦ Brasserie ♦

For those who can't choose between lunch and a BMW. This contemporary brasserie is housed in the showroom of the famous car manufacturer.

Orphyse Chaussette

r. Charles Hanssens 5 ✉ 1000 – ✆ 0 2 502 75 81
– Closed Sunday and Monday **M3**

Rest – Menu 16 €, 42/49 € – Carte 39/61 €

♦ Bistro ♦ Wine bar ♦ Neighbourhood ♦

Trompe-l'œil library, crystal chandelier and old tiling: this restaurant in the Sablon area may be small, but it has plenty of charm! Tasty cooking from the South of France.

QUARTIER LOUISE-CAMBRE *Plan III*

Conrad

av. Louise 71 ✉ 1050 – ✆ 0 2 542 42 42 – www.conradhotels.com

253 rm – 🚹199/695 € 🚹🚹229/725 €, ☕ 38 € – 14 suites **J1**

Rest *Café Wiltcher's* – *✆ 0 2 542 48 50* – Menu 20 € (lunch)/50 € – Carte 65/88 €

♦ Chain hotel ♦ Grand Luxury ♦ Personalised ♦

The Conrad offers modern luxury within the walls of an historic building dating from 1918. Attractive and stylish guestrooms, excellent leisure and spa options, as well as extensive conference facilities. A chic brasserie offering a buffet-style lunch. For afternoon tea, head for the Loui bar.

Bristol Stephanie

rest,

av. Louise 91 ✉ 1050 – ✆ 0 2 543 33 11
– www.bristol.be **J1**

139 rm – 🚹180/425 € 🚹🚹200/450 €, ☕ 25 € – 3 suites

Rest – *(closed July-August, Saturday and Sunday)* Menu 20 € (lunch), 50/78 € – Carte 40/80 €

♦ Luxury ♦ Business ♦ Personalised ♦

A luxury hotel with attractive guestrooms (49 of which have been renovated) spread between two interconnecting buildings. Superb, Norwegian-style suites. A modern brasserie with the typical decor of a leading hotel.

Sofitel Le Louise

av. de la Toison d'Or 40 ✉ 1050 – ✆ 0 2 514 22 00 – www.sofitel.com

159 rm – 🚹430/530 € 🚹🚹430/530 €, ☕ 29 € – 10 suites **J1**

Rest *Crystal Lounge* – Menu 25 € (lunch) – Carte 46/68 €

♦ Chain hotel ♦ Business ♦ Modern ♦

An escalator skirting an unusual lace mural leads to the chandelier crowned lobby of this hotel. It has been refurbished by interior designer Antoine Pinto and has attractive guestrooms. This restaurant has an ever-changing ambience and is a must for dedicated gourmets. Find an attractive menu, sophisticated decor, as well as the cocktail bar with a display of Val Saint-Lambert crystal carafes.

Le Châtelain

r. Châtelain 17 ✉ 1000 – ✆ 0 2 646 00 55 – www.le-chatelain.net

90 rm – 🚹89/650 € 🚹🚹125/650 €, ☕ 15 € – 15 suites **J2**

Rest – *(closed Sunday lunch, Friday dinner and Saturday)* Carte 33/60 €

♦ Luxury ♦ Business ♦ Personalised ♦

An opulent hotel offering well-appointed large guestrooms with an Internet connection, satellite TV and air-conditioning. Meeting rooms and a fitness centre. Belgian and French gastronomy influenced by Asian cuisine is to the fore in the Le Châtelain restaurant.

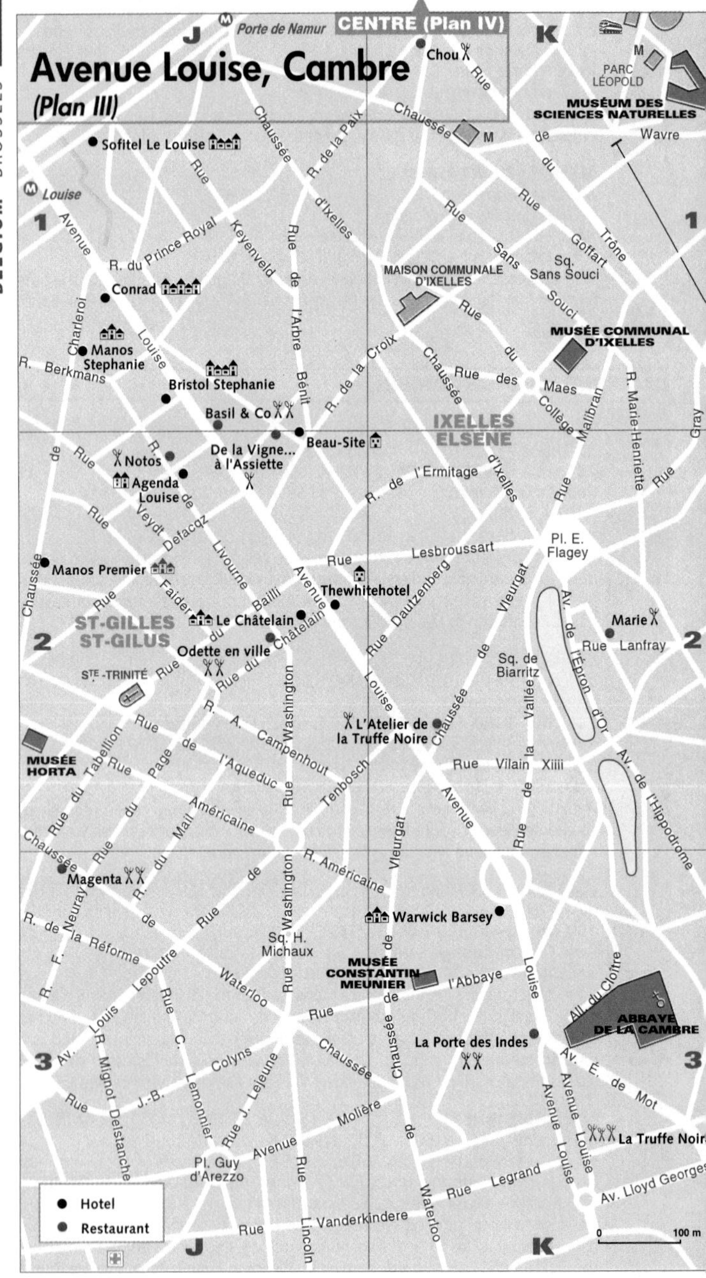

Avenue Louise, Cambre
(Plan III)
CENTRE (Plan IV)
Porte de Namur
Louise
PARC LÉOPOLD
MUSÉUM DES SCIENCES NATURELLES
Sofitel Le Louise
Conrad
Manos Stephanie
Bristol Stephanie
Basil & Co
Chou
MAISON COMMUNALE D'IXELLES
MUSÉE COMMUNAL D'IXELLES
Sq. Sans Souci
Beau-Site
De la Vigne... à l'Assiette
Notos
Agenda Louise
IXELLES ELSENE
Manos Premier
Thewhitehotel
Le Châtelain
Odette en ville
ST-GILLES ST-GILUS
STE-TRINITÉ
Pl. E. Flagey
Marie
Sq. de Biarritz
MUSÉE HORTA
L'Atelier de la Truffe Noire
Magenta
Warwick Barsey
Sq. H. Michaux
MUSÉE CONSTANTIN MEUNIER
ABBAYE DE LA CAMBRE
La Porte des Indes
La Truffe Noire
Pl. Guy d'Arezzo
Hotel
Restaurant
100 m

Warwick Barsey

av. Louise 381 ✉ *1050 – ✆ 0 2 649 98 00 – www.warwickbarsey.com*
98 rm – 115/430 € 115/430 €, ☕ 27 € – 1 suite **K3**
Rest – *(closed Saturday lunch and Sunday)* Menu 20 € (lunch)/28 € – Carte 33/73 €

♦ Luxury ♦ Business ♦ Stylish ♦

An elegant hotel teeming with Second Empire character near the Bois de la Cambre. Warm tones and a cosy atmosphere in the guestrooms. An elegant restaurant whose decor bears the signature of Jacques Garcia.

Manos Premier

(dinner)

chaussée de Charleroi 102 ✉ *1060 – ✆ 0 2 537 96 82 – www.manoshotel.com* **J2**
47 rm ☕ – 165/195 € 195/225 € – 3 suites
Rest *Kolya* – *✆ 0 2 533 18 30 (closed 24 December-4 January, Saturday lunch and Sunday)* Menu 18 € (lunch), 45/55 € – Carte 46/61 €

♦ Luxury ♦ Business ♦ Stylish ♦

The Manos Premier has the grace of a late-19C townhouse with its rich Louis XV and Louis XVI furnishings. If possible, book a room overlooking the garden. Authentic oriental hammam in the basement. Stylish restaurant, veranda and lounge bar. Chic and elegant decor, plus a charming patio.

Manos Stéphanie without rest

chaussée de Charleroi 28 ✉ *1060 – ✆ 0 2 539 02 50 – www.manoshotel.com* **J1**
50 rm ☕ – 295 € 325 €

♦ Luxury ♦ Stylish ♦

A townhouse with warm, classically styled guestrooms with a contemporary feel and light wood furnishings. Cupola above the breakfast room.

Agenda Louise without rest

r. Florence 6 ✉ *1000 – ✆ 0 2 539 00 31 – www.hotel-agenda.com*
37 rm ☕ – 70/145 € 80/160 € **J2**

♦ Business ♦ Family ♦ Functional ♦

Spacious modern guestrooms and friendly, attentive staff are the main selling points of this hotel near the Avenue Louise. Buffet breakfast. Small garden.

Aqua without rest

✉ *1050 – ✆ 0 2 213 01 01 – www.aqua-hotel.be* *Plan IV* **N3**
97 rm ☕ – 75/200 € 80/200 €

♦ Business ♦ Modern ♦

Minimalist decor embellished with a blue wood "wave" sculpture, created by contemporary artist Arne Quinze. It offers pared-down rooms with walls painted white and blue and parquet flooring. A calm environment.

Thewhitehotel without rest

av. Louise 212 ✉ *1050 – ✆ 0 2 644 29 29 – www.thewhitehotel.be*
53 rm ☕ – 85/185 € 85/185 € **J2**

♦ Business ♦ Family ♦ Design ♦

This designer hotel has a name that says it all! In addition to the white decor, the hotel displays works by Belgian artists and designers. Obliging staff and large, immaculate guestrooms.

Beau-Site without rest

r. Longue Haie 76 ✉ *1050 – ✆ 0 2 640 88 89 – www.beausitebrussels.com* **J1-2**
38 rm ☕ – 65/199 € 75/209 €

♦ Family ♦ Classical ♦

A sober, functional, but friendly family-run hotel occupying a small corner building just 100m from one of Brussels' most select streets. Reasonably spacious bedrooms.

XXXX

Villa Lorraine

av. du Vivier d'Oie 75 ✉ *1000 – ☎ 0 2 374 31 63 – www.villalorraine.be – Closed last 3 weeks July, Sunday and Monday* *Plan I* **C3**

Rest – Menu 45 € (lunch), 85/100 € – Carte 75/120 €

Rest ***Le Diptyque*** – *(open until 11 pm)* Carte 32/58 €

♦ Traditional ♦ Elegant ♦

Another institution opened in 1953 on the edge of the Bois de la Cambre. Superb setting for a gastronomic experience or a more relaxed atmosphere at Le Diptyque, the choice is yours depending on your mood.

XXX ✿

La Truffe Noire

bd de la Cambre 12 ✉ *1000 – ☎ 0 2 640 44 22 – www.truffenoire.com – Closed 1 week at Easter, first 2 weeks August, Christmas-New Year, Saturday lunch and Sunday* **K3**

Rest – Menu 50 € (lunch), 175/225 € – Carte 80/209 €

Spec. Carpaccio de bœuf aux truffes. Truffe "à la croque au sel". Ravioli à la truffe.

♦ Italian ♦ Luxury ♦ Elegant ♦

As you might expect, The Black Truffle serves the famous *Tuber Melanosporum* in all manner of dishes. An elegant decor with a patio-terrace. Charismatic owner. Splendid choice of wines... some at staggering prices!

XX

Odette en ville with rm

r. Châtelain 25 ✉ *1050 – ☎ 0 2 640 26 26 – www.chez-odette.com*

8 rm – †250/425 € ††250/425 €, ☕ 25 € **J2**

Rest – Menu 18 € (lunch), 50/75 € – Carte 37/78 €

♦ Contemporary ♦ Trendy ♦

The place to be and be seen! Here, you will rub shoulders with a mixed clientele in a trendy atmosphere. Quality cuisine and conscientious, professional service. This discreetly luxurious hotel with monochrome decor has a cosy lounge with a well-stocked library and designer guestrooms.

XX

Basil & Co

av. Louise 156 ✉ *1050 – ☎ 0 2 642 22 22 – www.basil-co.be – Closed 1 week after Easter, 3 weeks in August, Saturday and Sunday*

Rest – Menu 28 € (lunch)/35 € **J1**

♦ Contemporary ♦ Fashionable ♦

A charming restaurant in a townhouse with a decor that incorporates mouldings, marble fireplaces, high ceilings and a contemporary design. Modern cuisine with an exotic feel, including a choice of tapas in summer.

XX

La Porte des Indes

av. Louise 455 ✉ *1050 – ☎ 0 2 647 86 51 – www.laportedesindes.com – Closed Sunday lunch* **K3**

Rest – Menu 12 € (lunch), 43/58 € bi – Carte 33/69 €

♦ Indian ♦ Exotic ♦

Enjoy the classic dishes of Indian and Thai cuisine amid the authentic, evocative and colourful decor of La Porte des Indes.

X

Notos

r. Livourne 154 ✉ *1000 – ☎ 0 2 513 29 59 – www.notos.be – Closed 3 weeks in August, 1 week late December, Monday lunch and Sunday* **J2**

Rest – *(open until 11 pm)* Menu 18 € (lunch), 35/65 € – Carte 44/61 €

♦ Greek ♦ Minimalist ♦

A 'new generation' Greek restaurant located in what used to be a garage. Restrained contemporary setting, authentic Greek dishes with a modern touch, and a good selection of Hellenic wines.

X

L'Atelier de la Truffe Noire

av. Louise 300 ✉ *1050 – ☎ 0 2 640 54 55 – www.atelier.truffenoire.com – Closed 1 week at Easter, first 2 weeks August, first week January, Monday dinner and Sunday* **K2**

Rest – Menu 22 € (lunch), 3735/95 € – Carte 38/84 €

♦ Italian ♦ Bistro ♦

This chic eatery serving Italian and world cuisine is a tea-room, trattoria and bistro rolled into one. Perfect for a quick coffee and pastry, a lunch or a relaxed dinner which might even include a dish flavoured by the eponymous truffle.

Marie

r. Alphonse De Witte 40 ✉ 1050 – ✆ 0 2 644 30 31
– Closed 17 July-16 August, 24 December-4 January, Saturday lunch, Sunday and Monday **K2**
Rest – Menu 19 € (lunch)/65 € – Carte 46/58 €
♦ Traditional ♦ Bistro ♦
A very pleasant bistro serving high quality traditional cuisine. Interesting decor and an extensive choice of wines (particularly by the glass) presented by the attentive sommelier.

De la Vigne... à l'Assiette

r. Longue Haie 51 ✉ 1000 – ✆ 0 2 647 68 03
– Closed Christmas-New Year, Saturday lunch, Sunday and Monday
Rest – Menu 16 € (lunch), 25/40 € – Carte 38/55 € **J2**
♦ Contemporary ♦ Bistro ♦
This 'gastro bistro' serves unusual, hearty cuisine washed down with a choice of reasonably priced world wines. Professional and knowledgeable staff.

Sérafine

av. Adolphe Buyl 104 ✉ 1050 – ✆ 0 2 646 00 14 – www.serafine.be
– Closed Saturday lunch and Sunday *Plan I* **C3**
Rest – Menu 10 € (lunch), 28/40 € – Carte 33/50 €
♦ Italian influences ♦ Bistro ♦
The name of this gourmet bistro beside the ULB pays homage to the chef's Sicilian "mamma", whose delicious recipes he has inherited. French-Italian menu. Nostalgic decor.

Kamo (Kamo Tomoyasu)

av. des Saisons 123 ✉ 1050 – ✆ 0 2 648 78 48
– closed Monday lunch and Sunday *Plan I* **C3**
Rest – *(booking essential)* Menu 10 € (lunch), 40/70 € – Carte 33/76 €
Spec. Sushi et sashimi (lunch). Bol de riz aux tempura variés. Terriyaki de buri grillé et laqué, sauce soja.
♦ Japanese ♦ Trendy ♦
A slice of Tokyo in Ixelles: the classics of Japanese cuisine and remarkable suggestions with bold flavours are served in a pared-down setting with a trendy atmosphere. Sit at the counter to admire the skills of the two chefs at work. Good lunch *bento*.

Magenta

chaussée de Waterloo 421 ✉ 1050 – ✆ 0 2 347 01 75 – www.magenta-restaurant.com
– Closed 1 week in July, carnival holidays, Monday dinner, Saturday lunch and Sunday **J3**
Rest – Menu 20 € (lunch), 28/45 € – Carte 50/64 €
♦ Contemporary ♦ Friendly ♦
The owner is all smiles as she welcomes you into this little restaurant with cream and magenta walls. The chef cooks up tasty dishes with the onus on refinement, at very reasonable prices.

Chalet Robinson

Sentier de l'Embarcadère 1 (pontoon) ✉ 1000 – ✆ 0 2 372 92 92 – www.chaletrobinson.be *Plan I* **C3**
Rest – *(open until midnight)* Menu 17 € (lunch), 25/50 € – Carte 32/52 €
♦ Brasserie ♦ Fashionable ♦
This large chalet on a little island in the Bois de la Cambre is a unique place, full of nostalgia. Classic interior design and food at accessible prices. Small boats can be rented. Venue for events.

Renaissance

r. Parnasse 19 ✉ 1050 – ✆ 0 2 505 29 29 – www.renaissancebrussels.com
256 rm – 99/249 € 99/249 €, 25 € – 6 suites **G3**
Rest – Menu 25 € (lunch), 29/40 € bi – Carte 38/53 €
♦ Chain hotel ♦ Business ♦ Modern ♦
A modern chain hotel adjoining the European institutions district. Well-appointed bedrooms, studios in the annexe, conference rooms, business facilities, and a 'health academy'. Traditional cuisine and a three-course lunch menu provided at this brasserie.

Radisson Blu EU

r. Idalie 35 ✉ 1050 – ✆ 0 2 626 81 11 – www.radissonblu.com/euhotel-brussels
145 rm – 99/227 € 109/245 € – 4 suites **G3**
Rest – Menu 42/52 € – Carte 50/70 €
♦ Chain hotel ♦ Business ♦ Modern ♦
A new, ultra-contemporary hotel offering three types of rooms: Fresh, Chic and Fashion. Popular with a business clientele and European civil servants. Classic, modern cuisine served at your table or at the large, designer bar. Trendy, contemporary decor.

Sofitel Brussels Europe

pl. Jourdan 1 ✉ 1040 – ✆ 0 2 235 51 00
– www.sofitel-brussels-europe.com **G3**
137 rm – 100/465 € 100/465 €, 30 € – 11 suites
Rest – Menu 35 € – Carte approx. 55 €
♦ Palace ♦ Business ♦ Design ♦
A modern luxury hotel overlooking a busy square at the heart of the European institutions district. Glass hall-atrium, leisure facilities, and fully equipped rooms, junior suites and suites. This smart restaurant has a relaxed feel and trendy decor.

Stanhope

r. Commerce 9 ✉ 1000 – ✆ 0 2 506 91 11 – www.stanhope.be
125 rm – 140/350 € 140/525 €, 25 € – 9 suites *Plan IV* **O3**
Rest *Brighton* – *✆ 0 2 506 90 35 (closed Saturday and Sunday) (lunch only except Easter holidays, 12 July-3 September and carnival holidays)* Menu 42 € – Carte 41/57 €
♦ Grand Luxury ♦ Traditional ♦ Stylish ♦
The splendours of the Victorian era are brought to life in this British-style townhouse. It offers varying categories of rooms, including superb suites and duplexes. Elegant and classic dining room in line with the menu. Pretty courtyard-terrace.

Eurostars Montgomery

av. de Tervuren 134 ✉ 1150 – ✆ 0 2 741 85 11
– www.eurostarsmontgomery.com *Plan I* **C2**
61 rm – 120/550 € 140/600 €, 20 € – 2 suites
Rest – *(closed Saturday and Sunday)* Carte 40/61 €
♦ Chain hotel ♦ Business ♦ Classic ♦
An elegant and intimate business hotel facing the Square Montgomery. Early-20C façade, guestrooms of varying styles, penthouses, lounge-library, English bar, fitness room and sauna. A cosy restaurant serving international cuisine adapted to a business clientele.

Crowne Plaza Europa

r. Loi 107 ✉ 1040 – ✆ 0 2 230 13 33 – www.europahotelbrussels.com
236 rm – 69/499 € 69/499 €, 27 € – 2 suites **G2**
Rest – *(closed lunch Saturday and Sunday)* Menu 16 € (lunch), 29/39 € – Carte 36/58 €
♦ Chain hotel ♦ Business ♦ Classic ♦
This 16-storey chain hotel is at the heart of the European institutions district. Comfortable guestrooms, modern lobby, fitness room, conference facilities and business centre. The Gallery is known for its fashionable decor, global menu and lunch and dinner buffets.

Silken Berlaymont

bd Charlemagne 11 ✉ 1000 – ☎ 0 2 231 09 09 – www.hotelsilkenberlaymont.com **G2**

212 rm – †79/325 € ††79/325 €, ☕ 25 € – 2 suites

Rest *L'Objectif* – *(closed lunch Saturday and Sunday)* Menu 19 € (lunch), 25/39 € – Carte 36/52 €

♦ Business ♦ Modern ♦

A hotel with functional but comfortable rooms; those to the rear are generally quieter. Interior decor based on the theme of contemporary photography. Enjoy varied cuisine in this restaurant's contemporary setting.

Park without rest

av. de l'Yser 21 ✉ 1040 – ☎ 0 2 735 74 00 – www.parkhotelbrussels.be

54 rm ☕ – †115/399 € ††135/750 € **H2**

♦ Traditional ♦ Classic ♦

This intimate hotel comprising of two impressive mansions dating from 1903 that face the Parc du Cinquantenaire. Traditional breakfast room overlooking an attractive town garden.

Martin's Central Park

rest,

bd Charlemagne 80 ✉ 1000 – ☎ 0 2 230 85 55 – www.martinshotels.com **G2**

97 rm – †130/275 € ††150/295 €, ☕ 20 € – 3 suites

Rest *Icones* – *(closed 20 July-20 August, Saturday lunch and Sunday lunch)* Menu 19 € (lunch), 25/38 € – Carte 39/56 €

♦ Chain hotel ♦ Traditional ♦ Modern ♦

A modern hotel near the Berlaymont building with three categories of guestrooms and excellent business and seminar facilities. Designer public areas adorned with snapshots of Hollywood stars. Trendy brasserie with a decor and special effects inspired by the world of film. Lounge bar.

Leopold

rest,

r. Luxembourg 35 ✉ 1050 – ☎ 0 2 511 18 28 – www.hotel-leopold.be

111 rm ☕ – †150/270 € ††170/290 € *Plan IV* **O3**

Rest *Salon Les Anges* – *(closed Saturday lunch and Sunday) (lunch only except Friday and Saturday)* Menu 35 € (lunch), 65 € bi/80 € bi – Carte approx. 49 €

♦ Business ♦ Family ♦ Functional ♦

The Leopold continues to expand and improve at the same time. Smart public areas, welcoming guestrooms, and a large winter garden used as a breakfast room. Classic cuisine served in a romantic and refined atmosphere. Relaxed brasserie serving a range of dishes.

Holiday Inn Schuman without rest

r. Breydel 20 ✉ 1040 – ☎ 0 2 280 40 00 – www.holiday-inn.com/brusselschuman **H2**

59 rm – †50/460 € ††60/470 €, ☕ 22 € – 2 suites

♦ Chain hotel ♦ Business ♦ Classic ♦

An unbeatable location in the heart of the European quarter, with facilities that are popular with members of parliament, civil servants and businessmen and women.

New Hotel Charlemagne without rest

bd Charlemagne 25 ✉ 1000 – ☎ 0 2 230 21 35 – www.new-hotel.com **H2**

68 rm – †75/425 € ††75/425 €, ☕ 22 €

♦ Business ♦ Family ♦ Functional ♦

Located between the Square Ambiorix and the Berlaymont complex, this small, comfortable hotel is popular with European politicians and civil servants. The renovated guestrooms are perhaps preferable.

XX

Stirwen

chaussée St-Pierre 15 ✉ 1040 – ✆ 0 2 640 85 41 – www.stirwen.be
– Closed August, 2 weeks in December, Saturday and Sunday **G3**
Rest – Menu 35 € (lunch) – Carte 54/75 €
♦ Classic ♦ Retro ♦
A restaurant with a plush, elegant feel enhanced by attractive Belle Époque-style wood decor. Traditional cuisine, include specialities from around France. Popular with diplomats.

XX

Le buone maniere

av. de Tervuren 59 ✉ 1040 – ✆ 0 2 762 61 05
– Closed 1-17 August, Saturday lunch and Sunday Plan I **C2**
Rest – Menu 30/70 € bi – Carte 42/52 €
♦ Italian ♦ Elegant ♦
Le buone maniere occupies a mansion along a busy road. Authentic Italian-Mediterranean cuisine served to a backdrop of contemporary decor or on the front terrace.

X

L'Ancienne Poissonnerie

r. Trône 65 ✉ 1050 – ✆ 0 2 502 75 05 – www.anciennepoissonnerie.be
– closed 1-16 August, Saturday lunch and Sunday Plan IV **G3**
Rest – *(open until 11 pm)* Carte 38/50 €
♦ Italian ♦ Minimalist ♦
A designer influenced, family-run Italian restaurant in a former Art Nouveau fishmonger's. Open kitchen, and period decor including the façade and painted wall tiles. No menu.

X

Take Sushi

bd Charlemagne 21 ✉ 1000 – ✆ 0 2 230 56 27
– Closed Saturday and Sunday **G-H2**
Rest – Menu 17 € (lunch), 32/52 € bi – Carte 43/59 €
♦ Japanese ♦ Minimalist ♦
Established in 1985, this Japanese restaurant in the heart of the European district has a sushi bar and courtyard terrace. Typical bento (box) set menus. Particularly popular weekday lunchtimes.

X

Chou

pl. de Londres 4 ✉ 1050 – ✆ 0 25 11 92 38 – www.restaurantchou.eu
– Closed late July-early August, Saturday and Sunday Plan III **K1**
Rest – Menu 20 € (lunch), 45/80 € bi – Carte 55/70 €
♦ Contemporary ♦ Trendy ♦
At the Chou restaurant (the nickname of the French owner) the elegant decor is enhanced by soft lighting. The decor includes old casting moulds which act as tables, a sloping dresser, a red plexiglass floor above the wine cellar, and a kitchen that opens out on to the dining room.

X

Foro Romano

r. Joseph II 19 ✉ 1000 – ✆ 0 2 280 15 14 – www.fororomano.be
– Closed 15-31 August, Saturday except the first of the month and Sunday Plan IV **O2**
Rest – *(lunch only except Thursday and Friday)* Carte 31/45 €
♦ Italian ♦ Neighbourhood ♦
The oenothèque offers hearty Italian cuisine, created with its international clientele firmly in mind, and gets very busy at lunchtime. Eat in the dining room or at the counter.

X

Les Caprices d'Harmony

r. Noyer 236 ✉ 1030 – ✆ 0 2 733 14 02
– Closed Monday dinner, Saturday lunch and Sunday **H2**
Rest – Menu 15/50 € bi – Carte 19/34 €
♦ Classic ♦ Brasserie ♦
The understated decor of dark brown hues is perfectly in keeping with the classic menu. The owner is also the chef; his two specialities are onglet à l'échalote and sole meunière.

Sheraton

pl. Rogier 3 ✉ 1210 – ☎ 0 2 224 31 11 – www.sheraton.com/brussels
488 rm – 85/375 € 85/375 €, ☕ 27 € – 23 suites **F1**
Rest – Menu 29 € (lunch)/35 € – Carte 29/58 €
♦ Chain hotel ♦ Business ♦ Modern ♦
Imposing tower hotel with superb facilities for a mainly international business and conference clientele. Spacious standard and club rooms, as well as numerous suites. Attractive contemporary bar. Traditional cuisine in this hotel restaurant facing Place Rogier. Lunch buffet.

Crowne Plaza "Le Palace"

r. Gineste 3 ✉ 1210 – ☎ 0 2 203 62 00 – www.crowneplazabrussels.com **F1**
346 rm – 75/350 € 75/350 €, ☕ 28 € – 8 suites
Rest – Menu 21 €, 33/38 € – Carte approx. 40 €
♦ Chain hotel ♦ Business ♦ Classic ♦
This Belle Époque palace, which celebrated its centenary in 2008, has rediscovered its former glory. Impressively elegant public areas, a brand-new bar, neo-retro-style guestrooms and new suites. Cosmopolitan cuisine to a backdrop of chic and trendy decor.

Bloom!

r. Royale 250 ✉ 1210 – ☎ 0 2 220 66 11 – www.hotelbloom.com
305 rm – 100/350 € 100/350 €, ☕ 25 € **F1**
Rest *Smoods* – *☎ 0 2 220 06 66 (open until 11 pm)* Menu 26 € (lunch) – Carte 48/75 €
♦ Business ♦ Design ♦ Personalised ♦
This fashionable business hotel has made quite an impression with its breathtaking design. Bright, art-inspired bedrooms, each embellished with a modern fresco. Meeting rooms, fitness area, sauna and hammam. Contemporary cuisine is served in a trendy ambience.

Le Dome

rm,

bd du Jardin Botanique 12 ✉ 1000 – ☎ 0 2 218 06 80 – www.hotel-le-dome.be **F1**
125 rm ☕ – 80/132 € 90/146 €
Rest – *(closed Saturday and Sunday)* Carte 25/45 €
♦ Chain hotel ♦ Business ♦ Functional ♦
A building with a façade dating from 1900 and a dome that stands proudly over Place Rogier. Art Nouveau decor in the hotel's guestrooms and public areas. A modern brasserie with a mezzanine. The menu focuses on traditional Belgian fare, in addition to a choice of salads and snacks.

322 without rest

av. Lambermont 322 ✉ 1030 – ☎ 0 2 242 55 95 – www.lambermonthotels.com Plan I **C2**
45 rm – 85/140 € 85/140 €, ☕ 18 €
♦ Business ♦ Family ♦ Modern ♦
This family-run hotel looks deceptively like a residential block. Minimalist, functional rooms. Guests are invited to leave their mark on the walls of the breakfast room.

Senza Nome (Giovanni Bruno)

r. Royale Ste-Marie 22 ✉ 1030 – ☎ 0 2 223 16 17 – www.senzanome.be
Closed last week July-15 August, Christmas, New Year, Saturday lunch and Sunday
Rest – *(pre-book)* Menu 65/85 € – Carte 60/84 € **G1**
Spec. Spaghetti à l'encre de seiche, coulis de tomates à l'arrabiata. Feuilles de pâtes au double beurre et Grana Padano. Osso buco sans l'os avec sa purée de légumes.
♦ Italian ♦ Bistro ♦ Fashionable ♦
The best of Italian cuisine and wine are on offer in this restaurant near the Halles de Schaerbeek. Welcoming decor and popular with politicians and celebrities. Bookings essential for lunch and dinner.

Les Dames Tartine

chaussée de Haecht 58 ✉ 1210 – ✆ 0 2 218 45 49
– Closed first 3 weeks August, Saturday lunch, Sunday and Monday
Rest – Menu 19 € (lunch), 35/46 € – Carte 43/51 € **G1**
◆ Traditional ◆ Rustic ◆ Family ◆
Two women run this restaurant with great panache. Excellent seasonal cuisine, an intimate atmosphere and an impressive wine list.

GARE DU MIDI *Plan I*

Be Manos

Square de l'Aviation 23 ✉ 1070 – ✆ 0 2 520 65 65 – www.bemanos.com
59 rm – 130/345 € 150/385 € – 1 suite *Plan II* **E2**
Rest *Be Lella* – *(closed Saturday lunch and Sunday)* Menu 18 € (lunch) – Carte 43/63 €
◆ Luxury ◆ Design ◆
Ultra trendy and high on design, superlatives barely do justice to this hotel opened in 2007 in a fashionable district of Anderlecht. Attractive terraces and a spa. This very trendy restaurant serves both Belgian and Brussels specialities.

De Fierlant without rest

r. De Fierlant 67 ✉ 1190 – ✆ 0 2 538 60 70 – www.hoteldefierlant.be
40 rm – 66/99 € 69/109 € **B3**
◆ Family ◆ Functional ◆
The De Fierlant is located between the Midi TGV train station and the Forest-National concert hall. Well-maintained guestrooms, modern (buffet) breakfast area, lounge and bar.

Agenda Midi without rest

bd Jamar 11 ✉ 1060 – ✆ 0 2 520 00 10 – www.hotel-agenda.com
35 rm – 85/125 € 85/140 € *Plan II* **E2**
◆ Traditional ◆ Functional ◆
The Agenda Midi occupies a building just a stone's throw from the Midi TGV station. Bright, well-maintained guestrooms with those to the rear perhaps preferable. Business corner and buffet breakfast.

Saint Guidon

av. Théo Verbeeck 2 ✉ 1070 – ✆ 0 2 520 55 36 – www.saint-guidon.be
– Closed 21 June-21 July, Christmas-New Year, Saturday, Sunday and days of club home games **A3**
Rest – *(lunch only)* Menu 35/60 € bi – Carte 50/102 €
◆ Contemporary ◆ Elegant ◆
This popular restaurant is located inside the RSC Anderlecht football stadium with views of the pitch. Refined, traditional cuisine served by an attentive and professional staff.

Bon-Bon (Christophe Hardiquest)

r. Carmélites 93 ✉ 1180 – ✆ 0 2 346 66 15 – www.bon-bon.be
– Closed 21 July-15 August, first week January, Saturday, Sunday and Monday
Rest – *(pre-book)* Menu 40 € (lunch), 67/140 € – Carte 63/104 € **B3**
Spec. La tuile d'argile de foie gras de canard aux baies de genévrier. Bar de ligne cuit en coquilles d'huîtres brisées. Turbot au fenouil et jambon d'Ardenne fumé.
◆ Contemporary ◆ Bistro ◆
Wood panelling, parquet flooring, mirrors and grey velvet make up the decor in this restaurant. It serves modern dishes created using certified, and often unusual, ingredients.

Alain Cornelis

av. Paul Janson 82 ✉ 1070 – ✆ 0 2 523 20 83 – www.alaincornelis.be
– Closed 1 week at Easter, first 2 weeks August, Christmas-New Year, Wednesday dinner, Saturday lunch, Sunday and bank holidays **A3**
Rest – Menu 22 € (lunch), 32/47 € – Carte 32/48 €
◆ Contemporary ◆ Elegant ◆
A restaurant with a somewhat grand, traditional ambience, with cuisine and service in the same vein. Garden terrace close to an ornamental pool. Set menu and à la carte choices.

La Brouette

bd Prince de Liège 61 ✉ 1070 – ✆ 0 2 522 51 69 – www.labrouette.be
– Closed 25 July-19 August, 7-9 January, carnival, Saturday lunch, Sunday dinner and Monday **A2**

Rest – Menu 35/55 € – Carte 50/62 €

◆ Contemporary ◆ Friendly ◆

Restaurant with an interior renovated in grey and claret tones, and adorned with artistic photos taken by the owner-cum-sommelier, who is a permanent presence in the dining room. The 'Brouette' menu is particularly recommended.

La Paix (David Martin)

r. Ropsy-Chaudron 49 (opposite abattoirs) ✉ 1070 – ✆ 0 2 523 09 58
– www.lapaix.eu
– Closed July, Christmas-New Year, Saturday and Sunday **B2**

Rest – *(lunch only except Friday)* Carte 50/74 €

Spec. Mousse de jambon, patta negra et gelée de consommé. Onglet de veau de lait, légumes rôtis au beurre salé. Poulet de Bresse cuit au foin en cocotte, en deux services.

◆ Bistro ◆ Brasserie ◆

In an establishment that was formerly a café frequented by butchers, the French chef explores and reinvents bistro cuisine in a typical Brussels ambience. Diners have a view over the kitchens, where the meat is cooked in a wood-fired oven.

ATOMIUM QUARTER *Plan I*

Rijckendael

Luitberg 1 ✉ 1853 Strombeek-Bever – ✆ 0 2 267 41 24
– www.rijckendael.be **B1**

49 rm – 🚹75/181 € 🚹🚹95/225 € **Rest** – Menu 23 € (lunch)/42 €

◆ Business ◆ Functional ◆

This modern-style hotel is located in a residential district with easy access to the Atomium and Heysel stadium. Functional guestrooms. Private car park. Restaurant with rustic charm in an old farmhouse dating from 1857. Classic, traditional cuisine.

La Roseraie

De Limburg Stirumlaan 213 ✉ 1780 Wemmel – ✆ 0 2 456 99 10
– www.laroseraie.be **A1**

8 rm – 🚹107/250 € 🚹🚹130/360 €

Rest – *(closed Saturday lunch, Sunday dinner and Monday)* Menu 14 € bi (lunch), 35/48 € – Carte 48/62 €

◆ Family ◆ Personalised ◆ Functional ◆

La Roseraie is a friendly, family-run hotel occupying a 1930s building. Meticulous guestrooms decorated according to different themes, such as African, Japanese, Roman, etc. A contemporary restaurant decorated in bright tones, with a unique piano lobster tank!

't Stoveke (Daniel Antuna)

Jetsestraat 52 ✉ 1853 Strombeek-Bever – ✆ 0 2 267 67 25
– www.tstoveke.be
– Closed August, late December-early January, Saturday lunch, Sunday dinner, Tuesday and Wednesday **B1**

Rest – *(number of covers limited, pre-book)* Menu 30 € (lunch), 55/67 €

Spec. Escalope de foie de canard à la mousseline de rhubarbe et estragon. Baby homard en croûte de fleurs de fenouil et asperges au lard fumé. Barbue poêlée, carottes et mouseline de pommes de terre et queue de bœuf.

◆ Contemporary ◆ Elegant ◆

Occupying a modernised house (both inside and out) in a residential district near the Heysel stadium. Enticing à la carte and set menu choices encompassing the traditional and contemporary. Kitchens visible from the dining room, plus an attractive hidden terrace.

Le gril aux herbes

Brusselsesteenweg 21 ✉ 1780 Wemmel – ✆ 0 2 460 52 39 – www.evanrestaurants.be – Closed Monday in July-August, Saturday lunch and Sunday **A1**

Rest – Menu 35 € (lunch), 50/110 € – Carte 62/92 €

Rest *La table d'Evan* – Menu 45/55 € – Carte approx. 50 €

♦ Contemporary ♦ Trendy ♦

Two dining concepts are on offer at the Gril aux Herbes, with a focus on traditional/contemporary gastronomy to a backdrop of chic, neo-Baroque decor. Views of the garden. Enjoy a choice of refined tapas on the high stools to the rear of the Table d'Evan, where the culinary philosophy is expressed on the walls.

L'Auberge de l'Isard

Romeinsesteenweg 964 ✉ 1780 Wemmel – ✆ 0 2 479 85 64 – www.isard.be – Closed 1 week Easter holidays, 21 July-early August, Sunday dinner and Monday

Rest – Menu 25 € (lunch), 35/55 € – Carte approx. 50 € **A-B1**

♦ Contemporary ♦ Formal ♦

This restaurant is located between the ring road and Heysel Stadium. It has a modern dining room with round tables and comfortable armchairs, as well as a pergola on the terrace. Contemporary à la carte menu. The affordable, flexible lunch and set menus mean you can eat well even on a budget.

French Kiss

r. Léopold Ier 470 ✉ 1090 – ✆ 0 2 425 22 93 – www.restaurantfrenchkiss.be – Closed 28 July-18 August, 24 and 31 December and Monday **B2**

Rest – Menu 23 € (lunch)/33 € – Carte 32/57 €

♦ Traditional ♦ Friendly ♦

A pleasant restaurant renowned for its excellent grilled dishes and impressive wine list. Dining area with a low ceiling and bright paintings adding colour to the brick walls.

AIRPORT & NATO *Plan I*

Sheraton Airport

rm, rm,

aéroport Bruxelles National ✉ 1930 Zaventem – ✆ 0 2 710 80 00 – www.sheraton.com/brusselsairport **D1**

294 rm – 🚹159/295 € 🚹🚹159/295 €, ☕ 25 € – 2 suites

Rest – *(open until 11 pm) (dinner only by reservation)* Carte 41/58 €

♦ Chain hotel ♦ Business ♦ Modern ♦

This comfortable chain hotel is part of the airport terminal. Redesigned lounges and public areas, and bright, contemporary bedrooms. Popular with business travellers. A full range of guest services. Restaurant offering an international menu from Belgian ingredients.

Crowne Plaza Airport

Da Vincilaan 4 ✉ 1831 Diegem – ✆ 0 2 416 33 33 – www.crowneplaza.com/cpbrusselsarpt **D1**

312 rm – 🚹95/445 € 🚹🚹95/445 €, ☕ 22 € – 3 suites

Rest – *(closed Friday dinner and Saturday) (open until 11 pm)* Menu 25 € (lunch) – Carte 41/56 €

♦ Chain hotel ♦ Business ♦ Modern ♦

This upmarket chain hotel is located in a business district close to the airport. Central atrium, well-appointed guestrooms, a full range of conference facilities, fitness room and sauna. Club floor with a private lounge. A restaurant with an adjoining lounge bar. Buffet lunch midweek. Terrace overlooking a public park.

Holiday Inn Airport

Holidaystraat 7 ✉ 1831 Diegem – ✆ 0 2 720 58 65 – www.skoj.be

310 rm – 🚹85/230 € 🚹🚹85/230 €, ☕ 23 € **D1**

Rest – *(dinner only)* Carte 33/42 €

♦ Chain hotel ♦ Business ♦ Modern ♦

A 1970s hotel near the airport that has just embarked on an extensive programme of modernisation. Extensive leisure and business facilities. Contemporary in style, with traditional à la carte choices and buffet menus.

Pullman Airport

Bessenveldstraat 15 ✉ 1831 Diegem – ☎ 0 2 713 66 66
– www.pullmanhotels.com **C1**
125 rm – ♂90/200 € ♂♂115/300 €, ☕ 23 €
Rest – *(closed Friday dinner, Saturday and Sunday)* Menu 29 € bi (lunch) – Carte 38/51 €
◆ Chain hotel ◆ Business ◆ Stylish ◆
Quiet, cosy guestrooms, seven meeting rooms and a variety of leisure facilities are on offer in this hotel along the motorway, just 4km from Zaventem airport. A friendly bar and restaurant with the feel of an upmarket brasserie.

Novotel Airport

Leonardo Da Vincilaan 25 ✉ 1831 Diegem – ☎ 0 2 725 30 50
– www.novotel.com **D1**
209 rm – ♂79/250 € ♂♂79/260 €, ☕ 18 €
Rest – *(open until 11.30 pm)* Menu 23 € – Carte 33/48 €
◆ Chain hotel ◆ Business ◆ Functional ◆
Convenient for stopover or business travellers, this Novotel is being gradually upgraded in line with the rest of the chain. Outdoor pool, fitness centre and meeting rooms. Modern brasserie with buffet menus (except weekends).

Stockmansmolen

H. Henneaulaan 164 ✉ 1930 Zaventem – ☎ 0 2 725 34 34
– www.stockmansmolen.be
– Closed first 3 weeks August, 22 December-4 January, Saturday and Sunday
Rest – Menu 80 € bi (lunch), 54/74 € – Carte 60/88 € **D1**
◆ Brasserie ◆ Elegant ◆
This 13C water mill has a brasserie downstairs and a restaurant upstairs with the decor combining old and modern. The best option is the traditionally inspired set menu.

Orange

Leuvensesteenweg 614 ✉ 1930 Nossegem – ☎ 0 2 757 05 59
– www.orangerestaurant.be
– Closed Monday dinner, Saturday lunch and Sunday **D1**
Rest – Menu 20 € (lunch), 25/34 € – Carte 37/60 €
◆ Brasserie ◆ Friendly ◆
A modern take on good old brasserie cooking, served in an inviting setting: terracotta and chocolate tones, banquettes with fake crocodile-skin upholstery, and designer lighting. Pretty terrace surrounded by greenery.

Brasserie Mariadal

Kouterweg 2 (in the communal park) ✉ 1930 Zaventem – ☎ 0 2 720 59 30
– www.brasseriemariadal.be **D1**
Rest – Menu 17 € (lunch)/34 € – Carte 28/61 €
◆ Contemporary ◆ Brasserie ◆
This modern brasserie occupies an attractive manor house in a public park with a lake. Find an uncluttered, stylish decor, an orangerie, reception rooms and play area. A good value for money menu.

piu...

Leuvensessteenweg 491 ✉ 1930 Zaventem – ☎ 0 2 720 60 96
– www.piu-zaventem.be
– Closed Saturday lunch and Sunday **D2**
Rest – Menu 15 € (lunch)/33 € – Carte 32/61 €
◆ Italian ◆ Brasserie ◆
Art Deco brasserie-style. Tasty Italian cooking placing the onus on vegetables; in season, shellfish feature on the menu. Large terrace at the back.

ANTWERP

ANVERS – ANTWERPEN

Population: 472 071 – Altitude: sea level

imbus/Fotolia.com

Antwerp calls itself the pocketsize metropolis, and with good reason. Although it's Belgium's second-largest port with a population of half a million, it still retains a compact intimacy, defined by bustling squares and narrow streets. It's a place with many facets, not least its marked link to Rubens and the diamond trade; in recent years it's become a fashion hotspot due to the success of the renowned design collective The Antwerp Six in the 1990s.

The city's centre teems with ornate gabled guildhouses. In summer, open-air cafés line the area beneath the towering cathedral, giving the place a festive, almost bohemian air. It's a fantastic place to shop; besides the clothing boutiques, there are antiques emporiums and diamond stores that can't help but entice the eye. That's to say nothing of the chocolate shops, whose window displays are a visitor attraction in themselves. Bold regeneration projects have transformed the skyline over the last decade, and the waterfront has undergone a big change with its decrepit warehouses starting a new life as ritzy storerooms of twenty-first century commerce. Nightlife here is the best in Belgium, while the beer is savoured with a cellar bar reverence, a satisfied sniff and a glorious gargle, the way others in Europe might treat a vintage wine.

LIVING THE CITY

Antwerp lies on the east bank of the **River Scheldt**. The **Old Town** is defined by **Grote Markt** and **Groenplaats,** and slightly further east, The **Meir** shopping street. These are a kind of dividing line between Antwerp's north and south. The city can be defined as an island, cut off from the suburbs by a ring road. North of the centre is **Het Eilandje**, the hip former warehouse area. To the east is the **Diamond District** and the main **railway station**. Antique and bric-a-brac shops are in abundance in the 'designer heart' **Het Zuid** south of the centre. This is also where you'll find the best museums and art galleries. The smart suburb of **Zurenborg** is to the southeast.

PRACTICAL INFORMATION

ARRIVAL-DEPARTURE

If arriving at Brussels (Zaventem) Airport take the SN Brussels Airlines shuttle bus to Central Station which runs on the hour and takes 45min. Antwerpen-Deurne Airport is 7km from the city - take bus number 16 to Pelikaanstraat. Inter-city trains stop at Antwerpen-Central and Antwerpen-Berchem stations.

TRANSPORT

Antwerp has an efficient network of trams, buses and premetro, which is a tram that runs underground at some stage of the journey. Invest in a Dagpas Stad – a city day pass – which gives unlimited travel on the whole of the city's public transport system; it's obtainable on board buses and trams and from De Lijn kiosks.

On many occasions you'll find it quicker to walk around, for this is a compact city made for pedestrians. Or if you want to get about by bike, head into the Tourism Antwerp on Grote Markt for more information.

EXPLORING ANTWERP

Antwerp is a feast for the eyes. It can give you medieval character, Gothic splendour and scintillating fashion creations in a single three- hundred-and-sixty degree visual sweep. Although steeped in modern folklore due to the exploits of its now legendary designers-with-attitude, Antwerp is essentially a fine old Flanders town, living easily with its old age. Stroll just off the central Grote Markt to get a feel for its ancient bones. Off the adjacent **Oude Koornmarkt** you'll find **Vlaeykensgang**, a baffling maze of alleys that date back to the 16C. There's a little square here that allows you to wallow in the atmosphere of bygone times. Take a deep breath and head back out into the full glare of tourist heaven – Grote Markt is the heart of the Old Centre, and the home of Antwerp's finest sixteenth century architecture, including the awesome town hall and a selection of wonderfully impressive guildhouses. Gaze at the iconic **Brabo Fountain** in the middle of the square and you gaze at the very epicentre of the city.

MAKING ITS MARKT

Grote Markt's great Gothic cathedral, **Onze Lieve Vrouwekathedraal** (Our Lady's Cathedral) holds two titles of distinction: it's the largest Gothic church in the Low Countries, and the most popular visitor attraction in Flanders. Nearly five hundred years old, its intricate spire dominates the skyline, but its greatest treasures await within. Despite the beautiful nooks, crannies, altars and aisles, all eyes inevitably fall on four paintings by Rubens, including two spectacular triptychs. There's another fine church nearby: **Carolus Borromeuskerk** took six years to build in the early 17C and the result is a fabulously ornate baroque confection: it would have been even more spectacular if thirty nine ceiling paintings by Rubens hadn't been destroyed in a fire in 1718. Confound your disappointment by heading into the church's beautiful square, it's called **Hendrik Conscienceplein**, and rivals Grote Markt for the old town's top plaudits. Stop here for a drink at one of its smart cafés.

RUBENS QUEUE

No apologies for bringing up the name of Antwerp's most famous son again. **Rubens' House** is situated just off the Meir shopping street. It's easy to find, just attach yourself to the queues of tourists waiting at the front door. This is where almost all of his great works were produced; its collections are on an intimate scale, with only ten paintings by Rubens to see, but the house gives you a vivid picture of his personality and his daily life. He would have approved of the **Royal Museum of Fine Arts** (way down south of the centre), not least because it devotes two of its large rooms to his paintings. There are over seven thousand works here, making it one of the most important collections in Europe. You'll also find Van Eyck, Magritte, Breughel the Younger and Memling in an eclectic array of highlights. Unlike Rubens' House, the light and airy rooms allow you some welcome space to manoeuvre. What if your tastes are more up-to-date? Well, for a modern hit, head west a little way to the river where you'll find the **Museum of Contemporary Art**, an old grain silo converted into a happening space of post-1970 artworks, grungy and cutting-edge pieces with a decent place to squat. This is a modernist's heaven but, for the most dynamic gallery in Antwerp, you have to retrace your steps and head back towards the centre. Only five years old, **MoMu** chronicles the history of fashion in what is now one of Europe's leading design cities. Its permanent collection is fascinating, but what really draw the crowds are the hip and happening temporary exhibits, a fitting tribute to the Antwerp 6, whose exploits took the fashion world by storm twenty years ago. To enhance the modish experience, you can dine in a seriously snazzy brasserie and flick through the coolest pages in the zeitgeist in the glossily smart bookshop.

SMART STRAAT-EGY

MoMu is flush in the heart of Het Zuid, the neighbourhood just south of the old centre. Twenty years ago, this was a rundown quarter with art nouveau buildings that had pretty much gone to seed. Largely as a result of the fashion industry waving its magic wand over the area, it's now the most glamorous address in town; smart boutiques and chic dressers meet at every turn. Two of the city's best shopping streets run parallel here. **Nationalestraat** is a wide nineteenth-century boulevard of designer stores (a more discerning address than the nearby mainstream Meir), while a short stroll to its west is **Kloosterstraat**, the antiques street of Antwerp. Rummage through the bizarre artefacts tumbling onto the pavement, and you'll sooner or later find something truly out of this world. That's the theory, and often enough it bears fruit (or something a little more exotic).

To get a feel for the city's nicely weighted schizophrenia (the old town balanced by the new 'hipdom'), take a hike to two of its suburbs. Zurenborg is a village-like quarter in the 'far' southeast of Antwerp, by the railway line leading up towards the station. The wealthy merchant classes built it up, and today it's where the city's moneyed bohemians and artists live. There are sumptuous belle-epoque buildings here; the most interesting walk is up and down the seven avenues that fan out from **Draakplaats Tramplein**, where you can take in the fine – not to say eccentic – art nouveau buildings. Right up the other end of town is Het Eilandje, a one-time collection of mangy warehouses and storage facilities that the world steered clear of. Nowadays it's alive with quirky shops, cafés and offices; notable names have moved in, including Antwerp 6 fashion guru Dries Van Noten, whose workshop and office is based in a local warehouse.

ROCK SOLID

Another aspect of the city is the area around the mighty Centraal station, a terminus that ranks as one of Europe's finest, with its sweeping staircases and vaulted dome. It's relevant that the station displays a wealth of gold gilt, because this is also the **Diamond District**, a grungy kind of area after dark, but during the day the centre of the city's historic diamond industry, where many billions of euros' worth of shiny things are handled each year. If the sight of all those sparklers proves too much, take a pew at the nearby triangular shaped **Stadspark**, Antwerp's largest green space, where you can watch the cosmopolitan mix that for many decades has defined the area. Take a deep breath, then head back to that diamond shop to double-check the price of that rock…

CALENDAR HIGHLIGHTS

Laundry Day only comes once a year in Antwerp, but the hip Het Eilandje area cleans up when it happens early every September. This is the coolest event of the year, bringing in forty thousand revellers who dance to the various DJs at outdoor stages in the area. Why Laundry Day? Well, the first one in the mid-1990s was held at a weekend, when Belgians traditionally hang their washing out to dry…Later in the month, it's the turn of architecture addicts to hit the streets for Open Monument Day, when various historic buildings, usually closed to the public, open their doors for a day. The city is well known for its antiques, and in March this reputation comes to the fore when twenty thousand visitors head to the Bouwcentrum for the Eurantica Antwerp Antiques Festival, a grand fair with paintings,

ANTWERP IN…

➜ ONE DAY

Grote Markt, Our Lady's Cathedral, MoMu, Het Zuid

➜ TWO DAYS

Rubens' House, Royal Museum of Fine Arts, a stroll across to the Left Bank via the Sint-Anna tunnel

➜ THREE DAYS

Het Eilandje, a river trip, Kloosterstraat, Nationalestraat

jewellery, furniture and objets d'art up for grabs. May brings out revellers for five weeks of ghost trains and roller-coasters at the Sinksefoor funfair, which takes over a capacious square in southern Antwerp. The free carillon concerts on Monday nights between May and September have become hugely popular. The Groenplaats is heaving in June with ale quaffers for Beer Passion Weekend, with over 150 tipples on offer. You can lie on Antwerp Beach through the summer – a long stretch of sand in the dock area south of the centre boasting terraces with comfy sun-loungers - or, in July, you might prefer classical music at the Festival of Flanders (at venues across the city), or the International Summer Festival, which has street theatre, open-air cinema and jazz concerts happening on various city squares. Antwerp wouldn't be Antwerp without Rubens, and the Rubens Market in August sees Grote Markt's traders donning their best sixteenth century garb in honour of the great man.

EATING OUT

With Antwerp being Europe's second-largest commercial port, it's no surprise that fish and seafood play a big part in the local diet. The menus of Flanders are heavily influenced by the proximity to the North Sea, lush meadows and canals swarming with eels. But the eating culture in Antwerp offers a lot more than crustacean flavours. With its centuries old connection to more exotic climes, there's no shortage of fragrant spices such as cinnamon finding their way regularly into local dishes: check out the rich stews so beloved by the locals. Having such a high ratio of trend-setting types flitting around, there's always a good chance of finding a restaurant devoted to the latest in food fads. If you want to eat with the chic, hang around the Het Eilandje dockside or the rejuvenated ancient warehouses south of Grote Markt. For early risers, grand cafés are a popular port of call here. They're open nice and early in the morning, and are ideal for a slow coffee and trawl through the papers. Overall the city boasts the same tempting Belgian gastronomic specialities as Brussels (eg, stewed eel in chervil sauce, mussels in various sauces, dishes with rabbit, beef stew and chicory), the focus in Antwerp is more on contemporary cuisine, matched with up-to-date décor. Don't miss out on the local chocolate, shaped like a hand in keeping with the local legend which tells of a Roman soldier who cut off the hand of a giant and threw it in the river, and in the process gave the city its name: Hand werpen, meaning 'to throw a hand'. And make sure you try your hand at the local beer: Antwerp's De Koninck brewery serves the popular keuninkske, served in a glass shaped like an open bowl.

→ SCHELDT SHOCKED

The best view of Antwerp's dramatic skyline is from the west bank of the Scheldt. Firstly, stroll through the listed Sint-Anna tunnel with its lovely art deco interior, and, at the other side, go 'wow' as you take in the superb panoramic view of the city from the Left Bank.

The river has always been Antwerp's lifeline, and you can make the most of it on fifty-minute river cruises, which depart from Steenplein on a regular basis in the afternoons. The trip offers up a taste of the city's maritime history; you'll also get a good look at modern riverside landmarks such as the unmistakable Palace of Justice, an iconic twenty-first century building that resembles a white-sailed ship – fittingly, in a city whose port has been its fortune.

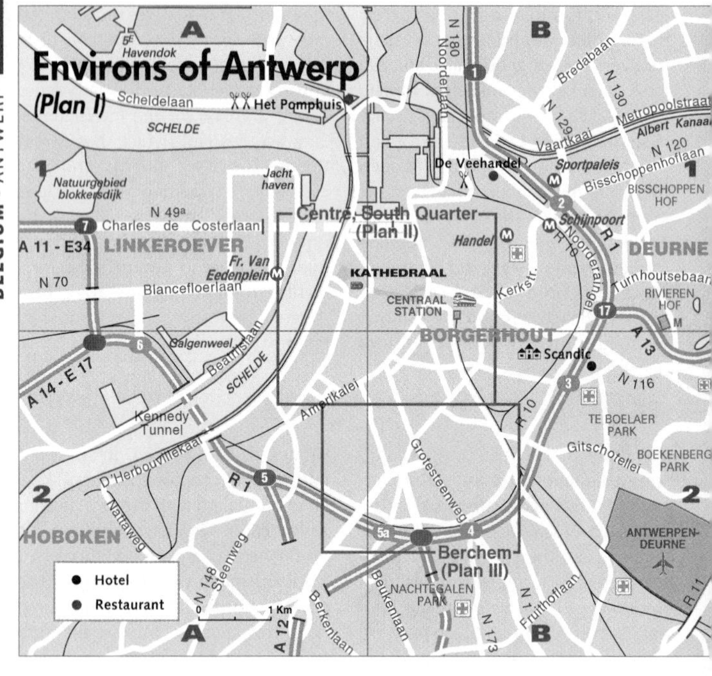

CENTRE (Old Town and Main Station) *Plan II*

Hilton

Groenplaats 32 – ✆ 0 3 204 12 12
– www.antwerp.hilton.com **D2**
193 rm – 🚹159/369 € 🚹🚹159/369 €, ☕ 25 € – 17 suites
Rest *Brasserie Terrace Café* – Menu 29 € (lunch)
– Carte 29/60 €
♦ Chain hotel ♦ Luxury ♦ Stylish ♦
A luxury hotel established in 1994 within the walls of the superb, early-20C Grand Bazar building. Sumptuous Belle Époque ballroom. Suites facing the city, standard guestrooms overlooking the courtyard. Views of the cathedral and busy Groenplaats from the Terrace Café's veranda.

Radisson Blu Astrid

rm,

Koningin Astridplein 7 ✉ 2018 – ✆ 0 3 203 12 34
– www.radissonblu.com/astridhotel-antwerp **F2**
247 rm – 🚹109/295 € 🚹🚹109/295 €, ☕ 22 € – 3 suites
Rest – Menu 20 € (lunch), 30/77 € bi – Carte 34/48 €
♦ Chain hotel ♦ Luxury ♦ Stylish ♦
This modern, elegant hotel caters admirably for guests in the city on business or for pleasure. The Aquatopia oceanarium inside the hotel is home to 10,000 fish and reptiles. This bright and trendy canteen-style brasserie has a distinctly urban atmosphere.

Radisson Blu Park Lane

Van Eycklei 34 ✉ *2018 –* ☏ *0 3 285 85 85 – www.radissonblu.com/parklanehotel-antwerp* **E3**

161 rm – †99/239 € ††99/239 €, ☕ 27 € – 13 suites

Rest – Menu 25 € (lunch), 40 € bi/75 € bi – Carte 33/53 €

♦ Chain hotel ♦ Business ♦ Stylish ♦

This luxury hotel is on a main road alongside a park. The bedrooms and suites are well appointed. It also offers a conference centre, lounge-bar, swimming pool, fitness room and sauna. The hotel's brasserie offers an international menu including pastas and pizzas. Valet parking.

De Witte Lelie without rest

Keizerstraat 16 – ☏ *0 3 226 19 66 – www.dewittelelie.be* **D1**

8 rm – †195/295 € ††245/295 €, ☕ 25 € – 3 suites

♦ Luxury ♦ Stylish ♦

This small and tranquil luxury hotel combines old-world charm and modern design. Find personalised service and bedrooms that are gradually being refurbished with great attention to detail. Breakfast is served in an elegant dining room near the open kitchen, or on the patio in summer.

't Sandt without rest

Het Zand 17 – ☏ *0 3 232 93 90 – www.hotel-sandt.be* **C2**

28 rm ☕ – †150/280 € ††170/300 € – 1 suite

♦ Luxury ♦ Stylish ♦

This establishment is in an attractive building with a fine Rococo façade near the banks of the Escaut. It offers attentive service, bedrooms full of character, meeting rooms, a patio and a roof terrace.

Theater

Arenbergstraat 30 – ☏ *0 3 203 54 10 – www.vhv-hotels.be* **E2**

122 rm – †110/220 € ††130/240 €, ☕ 20 € – 5 suites

Rest – *(closed 18 July-16 August, 23 December-2 January, Saturday, Sunday and bank holidays) (dinner only)* Menu 18/54 € – Carte 32/41 €

♦ Business ♦ Classic ♦

This modern business hotel is in a strategic location close to the theatre, museums and luxury boutiques. There are two generations of guestrooms, a cosy lounge and meeting rooms. This restaurant has a cosy dining room with wood flooring and wrought-iron furnishings. A cosmopolitan menu is on offer.

Rubens without rest

Oude Beurs 29 – ☏ *0 3 222 48 48 – www.hotelrubensantwerp.be*

35 rm ☕ – †145/230 € ††150/230 € – 1 suite **D1**

♦ Family ♦ Classic ♦

The Rubens occupies a stately building near the Grand Place, in which some of the guestrooms have a terrace overlooking the garden. Welcoming breakfast room and lounge, as well as a colonnaded courtyard filled with flowers. Peace and quiet guaranteed.

Hyllit without rest

De Keyserlei 28 (access via Appelmansstraat) ✉ *2018 –* ☏ *0 32 02 68 00 – www.hyllithotel.be* **E2**

180 rm – †110/180 € ††130/200 €, ☕ 20 € – 20 suites

♦ Business ♦ Stylish ♦

This hotel on a busy shopping street has obliging staff. There are large and well-appointed rooms, suites and junior suites, as well as an extensive breakfast buffet, meeting rooms, lounge and leisure facilities.

Plaza without rest

Charlottalei 49 ✉ *2018 –* ☏ *0 3 287 28 70 – www.plaza.be* **F3**

81 rm – †79/350 € ††79/350 €, ☕ 9 €

♦ Business ♦ Stylish ♦

A family-run hotel perfect for a good night's sleep. Spacious bedrooms and cosy suites, a lounge with Chesterfield chairs, plus a pleasant breakfast area and bar.

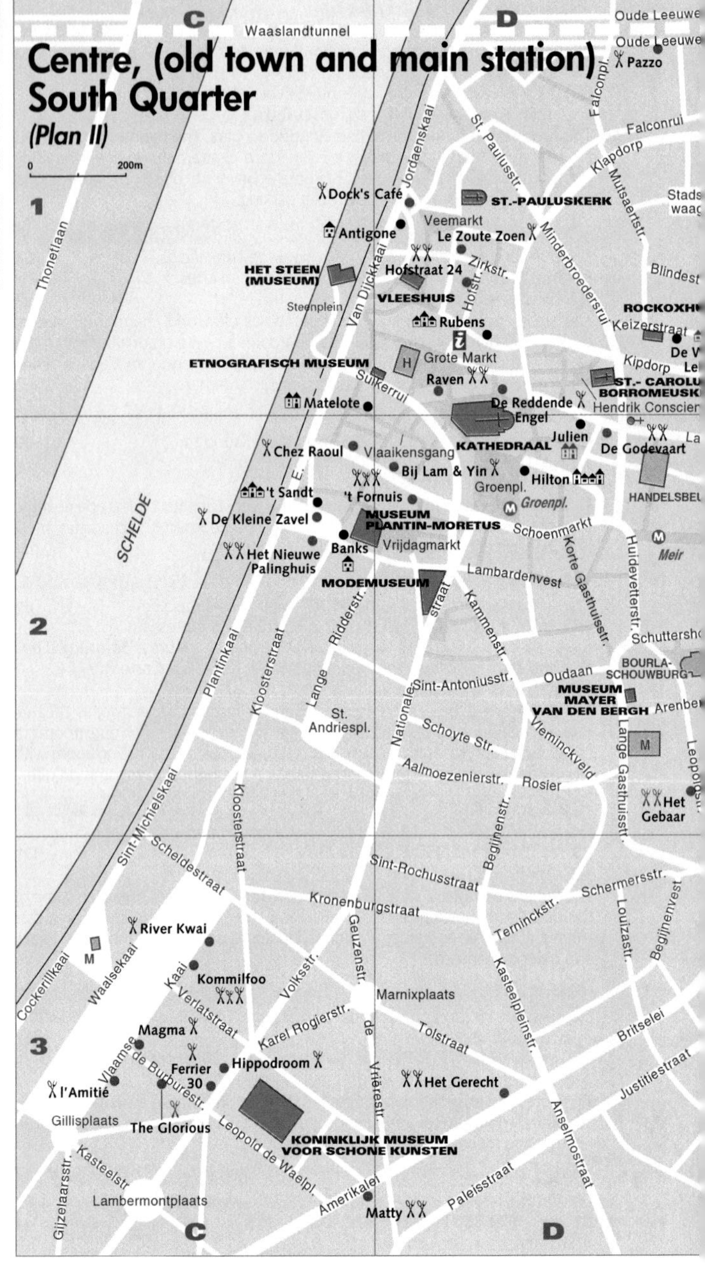
Centre, (old town and main station) South Quarter
(Plan II)
0 200m
C
D
1
2
3
Waaslandtunnel
Oude Leeuwe
Pazzo
Falconpl.
Falconrui
Klapdorp
Jordaenskaai
St. Paulusstr.
Mutsaertstr.
Dock's Café
ST.-PAULUSKERK
Antigone
Veemarkt
Le Zoute Zoen
Minderbroedersrui
Thonetlaan
HET STEEN (MUSEUM)
Hofstraat 24
Zirkstr.
Hofstr.
Blindest
Steenplein
Van Dijckkaai
VLEESHUIS
ROCKOXH
Rubens
Keizerstraat
Grote Markt
Kipdorp
ETNOGRAFISCH MUSEUM
Raven
ST.- CAROLU BORROMEUSK
Suikerrui
Matelote
De Reddende Engel
Hendrik Conscien
Julien
De Godevaart
Chez Raoul
Vlaaikensgang
KATHEDRAAL
Bij Lam & Yin
Hilton
Groenpl.
HANDELSBEU
't Sandt
't Fornuis
Groenpl.
De Kleine Zavel
MUSEUM PLANTIN-MORETUS
Schoenmarkt
SCHELDE
Het Nieuwe Palinghuis
Banks
Vrijdagmarkt
Korte Gasthuisstr.
Huidevettersstr.
Meir
Lambardenvest
MODEMUSEUM
Kammenstr.
Ridderstr.
Schuttersh
Plantinkaai
Kloosterstraat
Lange
Sint-Antoniusstr.
Oudaan
BOURLA-SCHOUWBURG
MUSEUM MAYER VAN DEN BERGH
Arenbe
St. Andriespl.
Nationalestraat
Schoyte Str.
Vleminckveld
Lange Gasthuisstr.
Leopoldstr.
Aalmoezenierstr.
Rosier
Het Gebaar
Sint-Michielskaai
Kloosterstraat
Begijnenstr.
Scheldestraat
Sint-Rochusstraat
Schermersstr.
Kronenburgstraat
Ternickstr.
Louizastr.
Begijnenvest
River Kwai
Geuzenstr.
M
Cockerillkaai
Waalsekaai
Kaai
Kommilfoo
Verlatstraat
Volksstr.
Marnixplaats
Kasteelpleinstr.
Karel Rogierstr.
de Vrièrestr.
Tolstraat
Britselei
Magma
Ferrier 30
Hippodroom
Het Gerecht
Justitiestraat
Vlaamse
de Burburestr.
l'Amitié
Gillisplaats
The Glorious
Leopold de Waelpl.
KONINKLIJK MUSEUM VOOR SCHONE KUNSTEN
Anselmostraat
Kasteelstr.
Amerikalei
Paleisstraat
Lambermontplaats
Matty
Gijzelaarsstr.

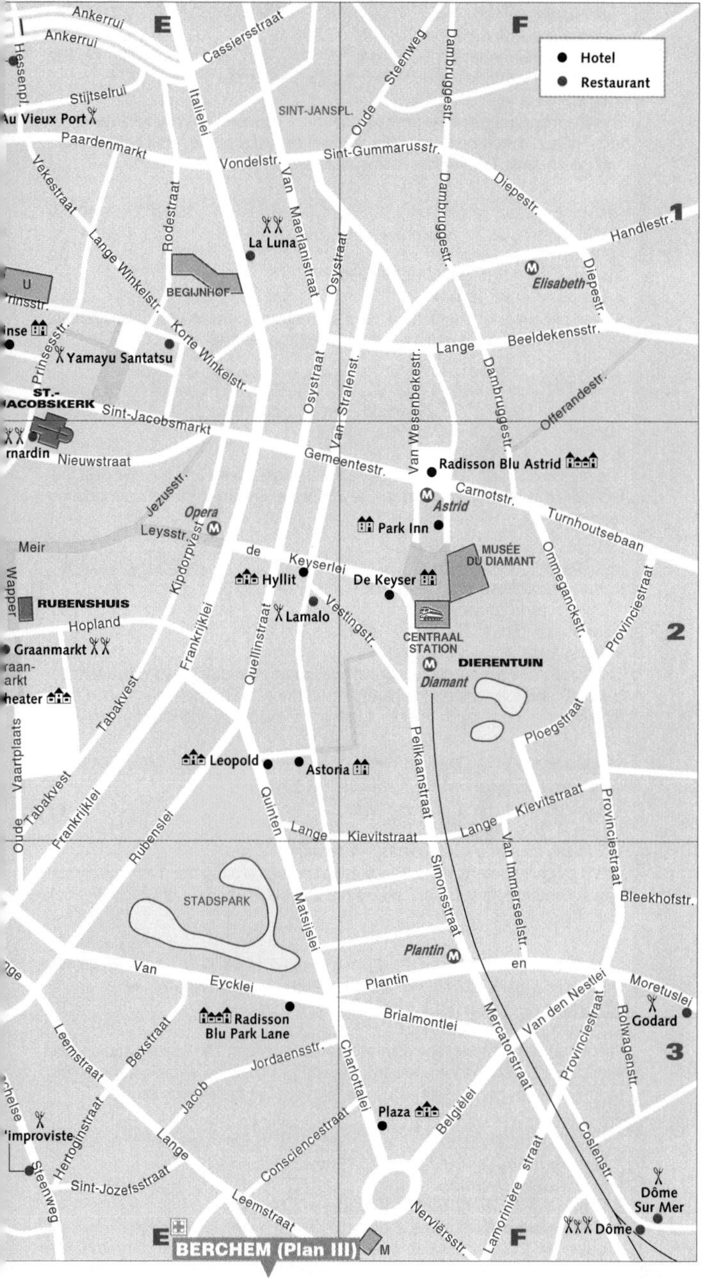

E
F
Hotel
Restaurant
1
2
3
Ankerrui
Cassiersstraat
Steenweg
Dambruggestr.
Stijtselrui
Au Vieux Port
SINT-JANSPL.
Oude
Italielei
Paardenmarkt
Vondelstr.
Sint-Gummarusstr.
Diepestr.
Vekestraat
Van Maerlanistraat
Dambruggestr.
Rodestraat
La Luna
Osystraat
Handlestr.
Lange Winkelstr.
Elisabeth
BEGIJNHOF
Diepestr.
Prinsesstr.
Korte Winkelstr.
Lange
Beeldekensstr.
Yamayu Santatsu
Osystraat
Van Stralenst.
Van Wesenbekestr.
Dambruggestr.
Offerandestr.
ST.-JACOBSKERK
Sint-Jacobsmarkt
Nieuwstraat
Gemeentestr.
Radisson Blu Astrid
Carnotstr.
Astrid
Jezusstr.
Opera
Leysstr.
Park Inn
Turnhoutsebaan
Meir
de Keyserlei
MUSÉE DU DIAMANT
Kipdorpvest
Hyllit
De Keyser
Ommeganckstr.
Wapper
RUBENSHUIS
Frankrijklei
Quellinstraat
Lamalo
Vestingstr.
Provinciestraat
Hopland
CENTRAAL STATION
Graanmarkt
DIERENTUIN
Diamant
Tabakvest
Ploegstraat
Vaartplaats
Leopold
Astoria
Pelikaanstraat
Oude Tabakvest
Frankrijklei
Quinten
Kievitstraat
Lange
Lange Kievitstraat
Van Immerseelstr.
Provinciestraat
Rubenslei
Simonsstraat
STADSPARK
Matsijslei
Bleekhofstr.
Plantin
Van Eycklei
Plantin en Moretuslei
Godard
Radisson Blu Park Lane
Brialmontlei
Van den Nestlei
Leemstraat
Bexstraat
Mercatorstraat
Provinciestraat
Rolwagenstr.
Jordaensstr.
Charlottalei
Jacob
L'improviste
Hertoginstraat
Plaza
Belgiëlei
Conscienceestraat
Lange Leemstraat
Coslenstr.
Lamorinière straat
Steenweg
Sint-Jozefsstraat
Dôme Sur Mer
Dôme
Nerviërsstr.
BERCHEM (Plan III)
M

Leopold without rest

Quinten Matsijslei 25 ✉ 2018 – ✆ 0 32 31 15 15
– www.leopoldhotels.com/antwerp **E2**

126 rm – 🚹99/139 € 🚹🚹99/139 €, ☕ 15 € – 1 suite

◆ Business ◆ Design ◆

This chain boutique hotel is located opposite a park near the city's diamond district. There is a modern decor with plenty of character in the hotel's public areas and guestrooms. Conference rooms available.

Julien without rest

– ✆ 0 3 229 06 00 – www.hotel-julien.com
– Closed last week July-first week August **D2**

22 rm ☕ – 🚹170/290 € 🚹🚹170/290 €

◆ Luxury ◆ Stylish ◆

A pearl of a hotel hidden behind a carriage entrance. Attentive staff, an intimate and cosy ambience, lounge-bar, spa and rooftop terrace.

Matelote without rest

Haarstraat 11a – ✆ 0 3 201 88 00 – www.matelote.be **C1**

10 rm – 🚹90/190 € 🚹🚹90/190 €, ☕ 13 €

◆ Luxury ◆ Modern ◆

The Matelote's main selling points are the friendly service and the chic designer feel, which is in stark contrast to the 16C walls. Breakfast in the neighbouring restaurant.

Astoria without rest

Korte Herentalsestraat 5 ✉ 2018 – ✆ 0 3 227 31 30
– www.astoria-antwerp.com **E2**

66 rm ☕ – 🚹69/129 € 🚹🚹69/149 €

◆ Business ◆ Functional ◆

The Astoria offers modern, functional guestrooms (including two with a terrace-balcony), and fully equipped apartments in the annexe. These are a good base for a short or long stay in the city. Close to the diamond district.

Park Inn without rest

Koningin Astridplein 14 ✉ 2018 – ✆ 0 3 202 31 70
– www.parkinn.com/hotel-antwerp **F2**

59 rm – 🚹89/149 € 🚹🚹89/149 €, ☕ 16 €

◆ Chain hotel ◆ Business ◆ Design ◆

This new chain hotel is handily located in the area around the main railway station. A contemporary feel extends to the bedrooms, the best of which overlook Place Reine Astrid.

De Keyser without rest

De Keyserlei 66 ✉ 2018 – ✆ 0 3 206 74 60 – www.vhv-hotels.be

120 rm ☕ – 🚹110/190 € 🚹🚹130/210 € – 3 suites **F2**

◆ Business ◆ Modern ◆

This hotel has an excellent central location between the railway station and shopping district. Modern guestrooms and public areas, a choice of meeting rooms, a trendy bar, as well as a swimming pool and relaxation centre.

Prinse without rest

Keizerstraat 63 – ✆ 0 3 226 40 50 – www.hotelprinse.be
– Closed 23-27 December **E1**

32 rm ☕ – 🚹110/120 € 🚹🚹135/150 € – 2 suites

◆ Business ◆ Classic ◆

A quiet 16C private mansion offering spacious, contemporary comfort. Courtyards embellished with box plants. Modern breakfast room, plus a designer lounge.

Antigone without rest

Jordaenskaai 11 – ✆ 03 231 66 77 – www.antigonehotel.be **D1**

21 rm – 75/100 € 85/100 € – 2 suites

◆ Traditional ◆ Functional ◆

An old corner house on the banks of the Escaut near the Steen Museum. Smart, renovated façade embellished with blue window awnings. Reasonably priced, functional and modern guestrooms.

Banks without rest

Steenhouwersvest 55 – ✆ 03 232 40 02 – www.hotelbanks.com

68 rm – 75/145 € 100/155 € **C2**

◆ Business ◆ Functional ◆ Minimalist ◆

This new hotel has a minimalist design and is ideally located in the old centre. Welcome aperitif at reception (open until 8pm), compact bedrooms, and breakfast served at your table.

't Fornuis (Johan Segers)

Reyndersstraat 24 – ✆ 03 233 62 70

– Closed 17 July-15 August, Saturday and Sunday **D2**

Rest – *(pre-book)* Carte 55/120 €

Spec. Crabe aux biscuits d'herbes. Sole pochée à la rhubarbe. Ris de veau aux lentilles.

◆ Traditional ◆ Rustic ◆

Fine classic cuisine and quality wines are served in this rustic restaurant housed in an old building. The owner/chef introduces the menu in person. He has been running the show since 1976 and was awarded his first Michelin star in 1986. Miniature stoves exhibited downstairs.

Dôme (Julien Burlat)

Grote Hondstraat 2 ✉ 2018 – ✆ 03 239 90 03 – www.domeweb.be

– Closed 2 weeks in August, 24 December-9 January, Saturday lunch, Sunday and Monday **F3**

Rest – *(booking essential at dinner)* Menu 39 € (lunch)/78 € – Carte 72/91 €

Spec. Cuisses de grenouilles, réglisse, salade de Cecina del Buey. Fera du lac Léman poché au beurre salé et à l'érable. Filet de taureau de Camargue, oignons doux et jus épicé (Easter).

◆ Contemporary ◆ Elegant ◆

Enjoy French gastronomy based around the very best products beneath the Baroque stucco cupola in this circular dining room. Astute wine list compiled by a young and talented sommelier. A true sense of hospitality and service.

La Luna (Dirk De Koninck)

(dinner)

Italiëlei 177 – ✆ 03 232 23 44 – www.laluna.be

– Closed 1 week at Easter, 1-15 August, Christmas-New Year, Saturday lunch, Sunday and Monday **E1**

Rest – Menu 38 € (lunch)/85 € – Carte 55/77 €

Spec. Sashimi au thon et au saumon, daikon et gingembre. Agneau de lait aux légumes du sud. Turbot aux moules bouchots provençale.

◆ Contemporary ◆ Design ◆

This restaurant has a refined setting with grey benches, interesting light effects, a gas fire and a high-tech kitchen. Here the father and son team produce a range of sophisticated dishes. Excellent selection of wines.

Raven

Grote Markt 14 – ✆ 03 233 28 33 – www.restaurant-raven.be

– Closed Sunday and Monday **D1**

Rest – Menu 30/60 € – Carte 56/80 €

◆ Classic ◆ Fashionable ◆

This house on the Grote Markt teems with character. It has been taken over by a talented chef who loves to cook in the pure French tradition, with the occasional touch of modernity.

XX

Het Nieuwe Palinghuis

Sint-Jansvliet 14 – ✆ 0 3 231 74 45 – www.hetnieuwepalinghuis.be – Closed June, Monday and Tuesday **C2**

Rest – Menu 39/125 €

◆ Seafood ◆ Friendly ◆

This restaurant specialises in fish and seafood. It has an old-fashioned veranda, and a dining room with a ship's wheel and photos of Antwerp from bygone days. The interesting decor extends to the toilets!

XX

Hofstraat 24

Hofstraat 24 – ✆ 0 3 225 05 45 – www.hofstraat24.be – Closed 2 weeks at Easter, last week July-first 2 weeks August, 2 weeks at Christmas, Wednesday and Sunday **D1**

Rest – *(dinner only except Friday)* Carte 46/61 €

◆ Classic ◆ Cosy ◆

À la carte dishes (no menus) that are changed monthly are served beneath the restaurant's glass roof or in two pleasant rooms, one of which is a more intimate library. The owner-chef is at the helm in the kitchen.

XX

Het Pomphuis

Siberiastraat ✉ 2030 – ✆ 0 3 770 86 25 – www.hetpomphuis.be – Closed 24 December *Plan I* **A1**

Rest – Menu 28 € (lunch)/45 € bi – Carte 46/60 €

◆ Contemporary ◆ Retro ◆

This extraordinary restaurant occupies a huge warehouse dating from 1920, where the decor includes three enormous bilge pumps. Enjoy the sophisticated, contemporary menu and views of the docks from the terrace.

XX ✿

Het Gebaar (Roger Van Damme)

Leopoldstraat 24 – ✆ 0 3 232 37 10 – www.hetgebaar.be – closed Sunday, Monday and bank holidays **D2**

Rest – *(lunch only) (booking advisable)* Carte 62/76 €

Spec. Salade d'avocat, pomme et kingcrabe avec son duo de langoustines. Noisettes et agrumes (douceur). Petit de luxe (assortiment de desserts).

◆ Innovative ◆ Cosy ◆

This restaurant is located in an elegant building on the edge of the botanical park. Luxury tea room cuisine, which the chef enriches with modern twists; mouthwatering desserts! Non-stop service until 6pm.

XX

Graanmarkt 13

Graanmarkt 13 – ✆ 0 3 337 79 91 – www.graanmarkt13.be – Closed 1-21 August, Sunday and Monday **E2**

Rest – Menu 25 € (lunch), 60/80 € – Carte 47/92 €

◆ Contemporary ◆ Minimalist ◆ Trendy ◆

This trendy, minimalist loft in the mezzanine of a bourgeois house lies in the heart of Antwerp, behind the Théâtre Bourla. Tasty and originally presented dishes.

XX

De Godevaart

Sint-Katelijnevest 23 – ✆ 0 3 231 89 94 – www.degodevaart.org – Closed 1 week Easter holidays, first 2 weeks September, first week Janaury, Saturday lunch, Sunday and Monday **D2**

Rest – *(pre-book)* Menu 37 € (lunch), 65/115 € – Carte 64/85 €

◆ Innovative ◆ Fashionable ◆

The cutting-edge gastronomy of this young, ambitious chef is well worth discovering. The restaurant is set in an old house, which has retained part of its original decor (stuccowork and fireplace). Valet parking in the evening.

XX

Bernardin

Sint-Jacobsstraat 17 – ✆ 0 3 213 07 00
– www.restaurantbernardin.be
– Closed 1 week at Easter, last 2 weeks August, 25 December-4 January, Saturday lunch, Sunday and Monday **E2**

Rest – Menu 30 € (lunch)/35 €

♦ Contemporary ♦ Fashionable ♦

This 17C house has been renovated inside and out. Depending on the season and the weather, choose between the modern, sober decor of the dining room or the delightful courtyard in the shadow of St Jacob's church.

X

Dock's Café

Jordaenskaai 7 – ✆ 0 3 226 63 30 – www.docks.be
– Closed Sunday **D1**

Rest – *(open until 11.30 pm)* Menu 15 € (lunch), 26/42 €
– Carte 35/73 €

♦ Brasserie ♦ Fashionable ♦

Set in the post-industrial landscape of the docks, this brasserie encapsulates contemporary taste: Jules Verne decor, trendy clientele and tasty "terre-mer" cuisine (oyster bar). Booking advisable.

X

Chez Raoul

Vlasmarkt 21 – ✆ 0 3 213 09 77 – www.chezraoul.be
– Closed 3 weeks in July, Tuesday and Wednesday **C2**

Rest – *(dinner only)* Menu 50 € – Carte 44/67 €

♦ Contemporary ♦ Bistro ♦

This pocket-sized dining room has a welcoming atmosphere, specials listed on slate boards on the walls, a seasonal menu and lunches that live up to expectations. Champagnes and digestifs listed on a blackboard.

X

Le Zoute Zoen

Zirkstraat 17 – ✆ 0 3 226 92 20
– Closed Saturday lunch and Monday **D1**

Rest – Menu 18 € (lunch), 29/45 € – Carte 31/50 €

♦ Classic ♦ Bistro ♦

This is an intimate and cosy bistro. The culinary emphasis of its female chef is placed as much as possible on Belgian dishes and produce, including the set 'Zoenmenu'.

X

De Reddende Engel

Torfburg 3 – ✆ 0 3 233 66 30
– www.de-reddende-engel.be
– closed mid August-mid September, 6-15 March, Saturday lunch, Tuesday and Wednesday **D1**

Rest – Menu 28/34 € – Carte 35/53 €

♦ Traditional ♦ Rustic ♦

Provence and Gascony come together in this rustic house near the cathedral. Enjoy dishes such as bouillabaisse from Marseille, brandade from Nîmes, duck liver from the Landes, cassoulet etc.

X

De Kleine Zavel

Stoofstraat 2 – ✆ 0 3 231 96 91 – www.kleinezavel.be
– Closed 22-28 December, Saturday lunch and Monday **C2**

Rest – Menu 30 € (lunch), 70/95 € bi – Carte 46/58 €

♦ Contemporary ♦ Bistro ♦

This is a typical Antwerp bistro with old wooden floorboards and a retro-style counter. Old wooden beer crates and shelves of wine partition the small, wood tables.

Bij Lam & Yin (Lap Yee Lam)

Reyndersstraat 17 – ✆ 0 3 232 88 38
– Closed Easter holidays, Monday and Tuesday **D2**
Rest – *(dinner only) (number of covers limited, pre-book)* Carte 36/53 €
Spec. Crevettes à la vermicelli et sauce chili. Bar à la vapeur, vinaigrette de soja et gingembre aux légumes croquants. Pigeon aux noix de Cashew, aux poivrons doux et bettes rouges.

♦ Chinese ♦ Minimalist ♦ Exotic ♦

This Chinese restaurant goes against the grain, challenging preconceived ideas about Asian cuisine. It has a minimalist decor and a small menu placing the onus on fresh ingredients, originality and flavour. Be sure to book a table!

Dôme Sur Mer

Arendstraat 1 ✉ 2018 – ✆ 0 3 281 74 33 – www.domeweb.be
– Closed 2 weeks early September, 24 December-10 January and Saturday lunch **F3**
Rest – *(open until 11 pm)* Carte 37/78 €

♦ Seafood ♦ Bistro ♦

This manor house has been transformed into a trendy seafood brasserie. It has a whitewashed decor punctuated by several bluish coloured aquariums full of goldfish.

Pazzo

Oude Leeuwenrui 12 – ✆ 0 3 232 86 82 – www.pazzo.be
– Closed 15 July-15 August, late December-early January, Saturday, Sunday and bank holidays **D1**
Rest – *(open until 11 pm)* Menu 20 € (lunch) – Carte 40/71 €

♦ Contemporary ♦ Friendly ♦ Fashionable ♦

This trendy brasserie with a lively atmosphere occupies a former warehouse near the docks. Enjoy Mediterranean- and Asian-inspired bistro cuisine with excellent wine recommendations from the owner-sommelier.

Lamalo

Appelmansstraat 21 ✉ 2018 – ✆ 0 3 213 22 00 – www.lamalo.com
– Closed first 2 weeks August, Jewish bank holidays, Friday and Saturday
Rest – Menu 22 € (lunch) – Carte approx. 40 € **E2**

♦ Kosher ♦ Cosy ♦

This restaurant in the city's diamond district is a popular haunt for Antwerp's Jewish community. Tasty Kosher cuisine with a Mediterranean twist. Bright and welcoming decor.

Yamayu Santatsu

Ossenmarkt 19 – ✆ 0 3 234 09 49 – www.santatsu.be
– Closed Sunday lunch and Monday **E1**
Rest – Menu 23 € (lunch), 35/60 € – Carte 34/65 €

♦ Japanese ♦ Friendly ♦

A lively and authentic Japanese restaurant that only uses the best hand picked ingredients, and prepares sushi in full view of diners. Assorted à la carte options with four different menus for two people.

De Veehandel

Lange Lobroekstraat 61 ✉ 2060 – ✆ 0 3 271 06 06
– www.de-veehandel.be
– Closed 25 December, 1st January, Saturday lunch and Sunday lunch
Rest – Menu 35 € – Carte approx. 45 € *Plan I* **B1**

♦ Meat specialities ♦ Bistro ♦ Friendly ♦

Where can you find the best steaks in the city? Look no further than this old bistro with a profusion of wood decor near the city's abattoir. Limousin beef takes pride of place.

Godard

Wolfstraat 35 ✉ 2018 – ☎ 0 3 283 68 21 – www.restaurantgodard.be
– Closed Saturday lunch, Sunday and Monday **F3**
Rest – *(booking advisable)* Menu 20 € (lunch), 36/56 € – Carte 38/57 €
♦ Contemporary ♦ Bistro ♦ Neighbourhood ♦
This new local bistro is always full – a good reason to book a table here! Charming service, a modern setting, 'spontaneous' cuisine, as well as a pavement terrace (drinks only).

À l'improviste

Mechelsesteenweg 112 ✉ 2018 – ☎ 0 3 216 33 03 – www.alimproviste.be
– Closed Saturday lunch, Sunday and bank holidays **E3**
Rest – *(number of covers limited, pre-book)* Menu 22 € (lunch), 38/53 €
♦ Contemporary ♦ Bistro ♦ Trendy ♦
Don't show up unexpectedly (à l'improviste) at this "culinary theatre" which is full every lunchtime. Interesting choices on the set daily menu, to a backdrop of modern decor, including an open kitchen.

Au Vieux Port

Napelsstraat 130 – ☎ 0 3 290 77 11
– Closed 25 July-15 August, 27 December-2 January, Saturday and Sunday
Rest – *(booking advisable)* Carte 43/73 € **E1**
♦ Brasserie ♦ Bistro ♦
This brasserie is worth keeping in mind for its simple, rustic and tasty cuisine, its gently nostalgic air, and its ritualised service (flambés and carving at guests' tables). Busy atmosphere at lunchtime.

SOUTH QUARTER AND BERCHEM *Plan III*

Crowne Plaza

Gerard Legrellelaan 10 ✉ 2020 – ☎ 0 3 259 75 00
– www.crowneplaza.com **G1**
262 rm – †85/185 € ††85/185 €, ☕ 21 € **Rest** – Carte 36/71 €
♦ Business ♦ Functional ♦
Located close to the ring road and a main road into the city. This huge chain hotel has 260 guestrooms on 16 floors, which are being renovated in stages. Numerous meeting rooms. A relaxed gastro-lounge in which to enjoy a meal or meet with friends or business colleagues.

Firean

Karel Oomsstraat 6 ✉ 2018 – ☎ 0 3 237 02 60 – www.hotelfirean.com
– Closed 24 July-18 August and 24 December-10 January **G1**
12 rm – †134/193 € ††144/211 €, ☕ 17 €
Rest *Minerva* – see below
♦ Luxury ♦ Stylish ♦
This property full of charm occupies an Art Deco-style building (1929). It features public rooms in the style of the period, a flower-filled patio, and personalised guestrooms with antique furnishings. Impeccable service.

Kommilfoo

Vlaamse Kaai 17 – ☎ 0 3 237 30 00
– Closed first 2 weeks July, Christmas, Saturday lunch, Sunday and Monday
Rest – Menu 33 € (lunch), 55/65 € – Carte 62/85 € *Plan II* **C3**
♦ Innovative ♦ Cosy ♦
A comfortable, modern dining room is the setting for the culinary creations of this innovative chef who alternates ever-evolving recipes with molecular experimentation. Pyrenean goat is an ever-present dish on the menu here!

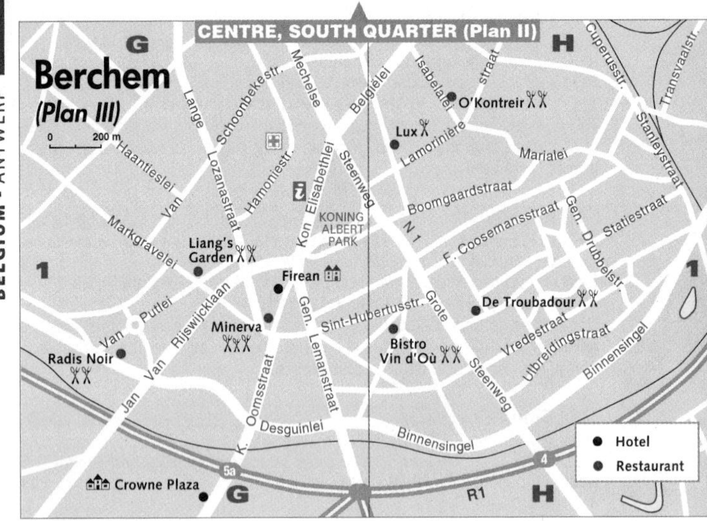

Minerva – Hôtel Firean

XXX

Karel Oomsstraat 36 ✉ 2018 – ✆ 0 3 216 00 55
– www.restaurantminerva.be
– Closed last week July-first 2 weeks August, late December-early January, Saturday and Sunday **G1**

Rest – Menu 38 € (lunch)/60 € – Carte 50/87 €

♦ Traditional ♦ Elegant ♦

Highly professional service and chic decor in the improbable setting of the ex Minerva garage, which has even retained its old car inspection pit. Modern take on classic dishes.

Liang's Garden

XX

Markgravelei 141 ✉ 2018 – ✆ 0 3 237 22 22
– www.liangsgarden.be
– Closed 11 July-8 August and Sunday **G1**

Rest – Menu 26 € (lunch), 45/70 € – Carte 32/82 €

♦ Chinese ♦ Exotic ♦ Luxury ♦

A stalwart of Chinese cuisine in the city! A spacious and elegant restaurant where the authentic menu covers specialities from Canton (dim sum), Peking (duck) and Szechuan (fondue).

Radis Noir

XX

Desguinlei 186 ✉ 2018 – ✆ 0 3 238 37 70 – www.radisnoir.be
– Closed 14-25 April, 21 July-11 August, 24 December-3 January, bank holidays, Saturday lunch, Sunday and Wednesday **G1**

Rest – Menu 30 € (lunch), 52/100 € – Carte 57/105 €

♦ Contemporary ♦ Minimalist ♦ Design ♦

This minimalist dining room is hidden behind a modernised old façade. The owner who steers clear of the latest culinary and molecular trends continually updates the concise menu.

De Troubadour

Driekoningenstraat 72 ✉ 2600 Berchem – ☎ 0 3 239 39 16 – www.detroubadour.be – Closed first 3 weeks August, Sunday and Monday **H1**

Rest – Menu 25 € (lunch), 35/39 € – Carte 35/64 €

♦ Contemporary ♦ Trendy ♦

A modern, cosy dining room where the gregarious owner fosters a warm and friendly atmosphere. Classic, creative à la carte options, as well as appetising menus and daily specials announced at your table. Parking available (prior booking required).

Bistro Vin d'Où

Terlinckstraat 2 – ☎ 0 3 230 55 99 – www.vindou.be – Closed 24 April-8 May, 16 July-16 August, 24 December-5 January, dinner Monday, Tuesday and Wednesday, Saturday lunch and Sunday **H1**

Rest – Carte 42/86 €

♦ Classic ♦ Brasserie ♦

This old house in a residential area has been transformed into a cosy bistro. Modern, artisanal-style cuisine, which only uses carefully selected high quality products. Attractive patio for summer dining.

Het Gerecht

Amerikalei 20 – ☎ 0 3 248 79 28 – www.hetgerecht.be – Closed Easter holidays, last 2 weeks July-first week August, first week January, Saturday lunch, Sunday and Monday *Plan II* **D3**

Rest – Menu 24 € (lunch) – Carte 53/72 €

♦ Contemporary ♦ Cosy ♦

Contemporary cuisine prepared by the male chef, with the female half of the partnership running the front of house. Cosy, modern and elegant decor, plus a decked courtyard terrace enclosed by brick walls.

Matty

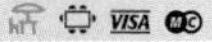

Brederodestraat 23 ✉ 2018 – ☎ 0 3 293 54 41 – www.restaurantmatty.be – Closed last 2 weeks July-first week August, Saturday lunch, Sunday and Monday *Plan II* **C3**

Rest – *(booking advisable)* Menu 28 € (lunch), 38/50 € – Carte 46/62 €

♦ Contemporary ♦ Design ♦

Contemporary cuisine prepared by a chef who can be seen at work from one of the two dining rooms. Modern, startlingly white decor and an outdoor terrace for summer dining.

Hippodroom

Leopold de Waelplaats 10 – ☎ 0 3 248 52 52 – www.hippodroom.be – closed Saturday lunch and Sunday *Plan II* **C3**

Rest – *(open until 11 pm)* Menu 23 € (lunch) – Carte 40/79 €

♦ Brasserie ♦ Trendy ♦

This brasserie mixes an arty atmosphere with trendy, imaginatively presented cuisine in a mansion opposite the city's Fine Arts Museum. Outdoor terraces on the street and to the rear.

The Glorious

– ☎ 0 3 237 06 13 – www.theglorious.be – Closed 3 weeks Whitsun holidays, Sunday and Monday *Plan II* **C3**

Rest – Menu 35 € – Carte 38/63 €

♦ Traditional ♦ Wine bar ♦ Formal ♦

This former industrial warehouse has a carefully designed, trendy interior. It features an à la carte Wining & Dining concept.

The Glorious Inn

– Closed 3 weeks Whitsun holidays

3 rm – 140/190 € 140/190 €, 15 €

♦ Luxury ♦ Personalised ♦

Second-hand furniture makes for an original, contemporary interior decoration. Delicious breakfast prepared by the owner.

l'Amitié

Vlaamse Kaai 43 – ✆ 0 3 257 50 05 – www.lamitie.net – Closed 2 weeks in June, Christmas-New Year, Saturday lunch, Sunday and Monday Plan II **C3**

Rest – Menu 25 € (lunch), 35/65 € – Carte 48/72 €

♦ Contemporary ♦ Bistro ♦

This welcoming address, located in one of the city's liveliest districts, dedicates itself to the concept of bistronomy (traditional dishes with an inventive twist). On fine sunny days take advantage of the Mediterranean-style terrace.

Ferrier 30

Leopold de Waelplaats 30 – ✆ 0 3 216 50 62 – www.ferrier-30.be – Closed Wednesday Plan II **C3**

Rest – *(open until 11 pm)* Carte 36/58 €

♦ Italian ♦ Design ♦

Italian cuisine and wine is served amid the black and white decor inside or on the terrace overlooking the Fine Arts Museum. The more intimate basement room is used for private gatherings. Efficient service.

River Kwai

Vlaamse Kaai 14 – ✆ 0 3 237 46 51 – www.riverkwai.be – Closed Wednesday Plan II **C3**

Rest – *(dinner only except Thursday and Friday)* Menu 20 € (lunch), 25/49 € bi – Carte 30/47 €

♦ Thai ♦ Exotic ♦

This reliable restaurant has been serving authentic Thai cuisine for the past 20 years. Find an attractive retro façade, dining rooms on separate floors with a typical decor, an elegant lounge and a front terrace.

Lux

(lunch)

Adriaan Brouwerstraat 13 – ✆ 0 3 233 30 30 – www.luxantwerp.com – Closed 1st January and Saturday lunch **H1**

Rest – *(open until 11 pm)* Menu 20 € (lunch), 25/34 € – Carte 39/75 €

♦ Contemporary ♦ Luxury ♦

This restaurant occupies the house of a former ship owner, and has a terrace that overlooks the port. There is a profusion of marble (columns, fireplaces), a wine and cocktail bar, à la carte options, plus an attractive lunch menu.

AT THE AIRPORT *Plan I*

Scandic

rm,

Luitenant Lippenslaan 66 ✉ 2140 Borgerhout – ✆ 0 3 235 91 91 – www.scandichotels.com/antwerpen **B2**

204 rm – †95/185 € ††95/185 €

Rest – *(closed lunch Saturday and Sunday)* Menu 35 € – Carte 31/47 €

♦ Chain hotel ♦ Functional ♦

This chain hotel has a number of advantages: easy access to the ring road and centre of the city, a full range of creature comforts in its guestrooms, as well as meeting and leisure facilities. A restaurant offering a classic international à la carte menu. Bar with a terrace.

CZECH REPUBLIC

ČESKÁ REPUBLIKA

PROFILE

→ **Area:**
78 864 km² (30 449 sq mi).

→ **Population:**
10 515 818 inhabitants (est. 2010), density = 130 per km².

→ **Capital:**
Prague (population 1 249 026 inhabitants).

→ **Currency:**
Czech crown (Kč); rate of exchange: CZK 100 = € 4.06 = US$ 5.59 (Dec 2010).

→ **Government:**
Parliamentary republic (since 1993). Member of European Union since 2004.

→ **Language:**
Czech; also German and English.

→ **Specific public holidays:**
Liberation Day (8 May); St. Cyril and St. Methodius Day (5 July); Martyrdom of Jean Hus (6 July); Czech Statehood Day (28 September); Independence Day (28 October); Freedom and Democracy Day (17 November); Boxing Day (26 December).

→ **Local Time:**
GMT + 1 hour in winter and GMT + 2 hours in summer.

→ **Climate:**
Temperate continental with cold winters and warm summers (Prague: January: 0°C, July: 20°C).

→ **International Dialling Code:**
00 420 followed by area code (Prague: 2), and then the local number.

→ **Emergency:**
Police: ✆ **158**; Ambulance: ✆ **155**; Fire Brigade: ✆ **150**.

→ **Electricity:**
220 volts AC, 50Hz; 2-pin round-shaped continental plugs.

→ **Formalities**
Travellers from the European Union (EU), Switzerland, Iceland and the main countries of North and South America need a national identity card or passport (America: passport required) to visit Czech Republic for less than three months (tourism or business purpose). For visitors from other countries a visa may be required, in addition to a passport, especially for those wishing to stay for longer than three months. We advise you to check with your embassy before travelling.

PRAGUE
PRAHA

Population: 1 223 368 – Altitude: 250m

urtyardpix/Fotolia.com

The most important thing to remember about Prague is that its history stretches back to the Dark Ages. In the ninth century a princely seat comprising a simple walled-in compound was built where today stands the castle. In the tenth century the first bridge over the Vltava arrived. By the thirteenth century the enchanting cobbled alleyways below the castle were complete. Wherever you tread here, the musty scent of the past travels with you. But Prague has come of age and in many ways it's had to. It now receives ten times as many visitors as it did 20 years ago, and that figure could jump to double again (15 million) by 2012. Europe's most perfectly preserved capital now proffers consumer choice as well as medieval marvels. Its state-of-the-art shopping malls and pulsing nightlife bear testament to its popularity with tourists, the iron glove of communism long since having given way to the silk purse of western consumerism. These days there are practically two versions of Prague - the lively, youthful version which has spawned the unfortunate, headline grabbing epithet of 'stag party central', and the sedate, enchanting version most people have succumbed to, the 'city of a hundred spires', where cathedrals, churches, chapels and monasteries – exuberant and extraordinary - prod the skyline. And this is the city, prosperous, cosmopolitan and orderly, where music of all shades seeps into your senses.

LIVING THE CITY

The four main zones of Prague were originally independent towns in their own right. The river Vltava winds its way through their heart, and they're linked by the iconic Charles Bridge, possibly the most charismatic of Europe's spans. On the west side lie Hradèany, the castle quarter, built on a rock spur commanding the river bend, and Malá Strana, Prague's most perfectly preserved district at the bottom of the castle hill. Over the river are Staré Město, the old town with its vibrant medieval square and outer boulevards, and Nové Město, the new town, which is the city's commercial heart extending south and east of the old town. It's where you find Wenceslas Square and it's where Prague's suited and booted new execs hang out and the young things go to party.

PRACTICAL INFORMATION

ARRIVAL-DEPARTURE

Ruzyně (Prague Airport) is 20km west of the city. Take a taxi displaying an 'Airport Cars' sign ; this should cost around CZK650. The shuttle bus leaves every 30min. International trains stop at Hlavni nádraží.

TRANSPORT

Trams and buses are frequent in Prague and run from early morning to past midnight. There's also a 49-station Metro comprising three lines and covering much of the city. All three are invariably cheap.

Be wary of taxis. Although regulations specify rates, it's not uncommon to be grossly overcharged. Always use a designated rank, and avoid flagging down a cab anywhere.

If you think you'll be public transport hopping on a pretty regular basis, then buy a short-term season pass that allows unlimited travel on bus, tram, metro and Petrin funicular.

EXPLORING PRAGUE

No other capital in Europe can match Prague's enviable mix of Medieval, Gothic, Baroque and art nouveau. It creates a heady fairytale patchwork set off by glinting spring sunshine or a pure blanket of winter snow.

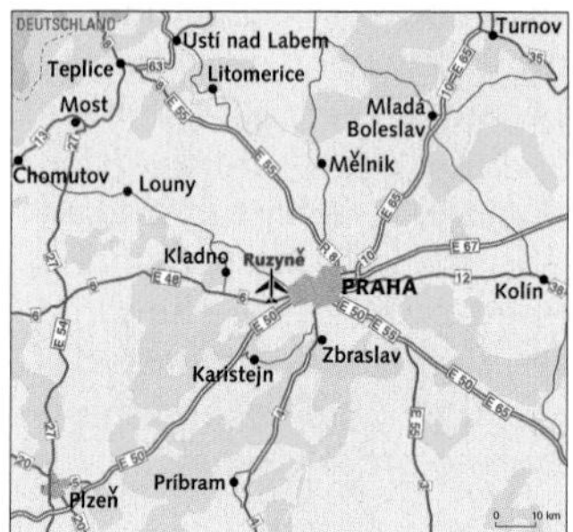

The city's laid-back citizens sit in their gloomily atmospheric pubs and relax with a beer, leaving the hard work to the tourists. Outside, many of those are trying to decide just how to fit the jigsaw pieces together...museums, art galleries, churches, synagogues, a chamber concert in an ornate chapel. Or perhaps they're trying to find their way around the labyrinthine web of lanes and passageways that may link those very tourist landmarks.

→ YOU'LL BE A-MAZED

If you're all set to 'do' Staré Město or Malá Strana, be prepared to lose yourself in a maze of crooked streets and narrow alleyways; don't be afraid to peek down passageways and slip into secret courtyards hemmed in by old-style dwellings. The real itch of Prague is feeling you haven't discovered it until it's concocted a way of getting you lost. As confused as you may be, you can take heart in the knowledge that before too long you'll end up by the Vltava or catch sight of a recognizable landmark. If it all gets a little bit too claustrophobic, you can take refuge in the Nové Město. Here the medieval town planner has taken pity on the confused visitor and the streets and squares are logically laid out, as typified by the broad boulevard of **Wenceslas Square**.

To get a real perspective on the city, everyone – and we mean everyone – takes a stroll over the **Charles Bridge** (completed in 1402) with its various bronze saints staring down implacably on the never-ending shuffle of passers-by. At each end is a tower, open to visitors, both offering superb views from their roofs. This merely whets the appetite for the climb up to **Prague Castle**, with its commanding cliff-top outlook. Its scale is breathtaking; quite simply, it's the biggest ancient castle in the world. So big that within its third courtyard stands the immense Gothic structure that is **St Vitus Cathedral,** complete with massive main tower, scintillating rose window, spectacular stained-glass windows, and a chapel to St Wenceslas that glitters with gold, silver and semi-precious stones. There are other jewels in the Castle's crown, such as the Royal Garden, the Old Royal Palace and the Summer Palace, while close by are the smart boutiques of the tiny, magical Golden Lane, where Franz Kafka, at number 22, wrote much of his work. There's so much to take in around here that it might be worth doing it in more than one visit.

→ THROUGH TICK AND TYN

If you just love the warm glow of big crowds, then cross the river for another fix. This time the masses gather every hour in Staré Město's Old Town Square beneath the Orloj, or **Astronomical Clock,** which has three hands to show the position of the sun, moon and stars. On the hour, with the crowds in tow, carved figures do a turn, death wags his hourglass, and a cockerel crows to bring the drama to its conclusion. There are other great charms to the historical square (aside from the ubiquitous restaurants and bars to rest weary feet); every hue and nuance of architectural style vies for attention in the shape of the rococo Kinsky Palace, the Gothic/Baroque House of the Stone Bell, the Renaissance façade of Storch House, and the dramatic twin spires signalling the great Gothic landmark of the Church of Our Lady Before Tyn. Here, inside the richly adorned interior, search out the tomb of Tycho Brahe, Renaissance astronomer, who lost the tip of his nose in a duel, had it replaced in gold and silver, and died when his bladder burst after an excess of beer and wine. He might have appreciated the Municipal House, an art nouveau masterpiece close to Old Town Square where you can wine and dine in luxuriously refined surroundings. It's a great place for concerts, too.

To the north of Staré Město is Josefov, the Jewish quarter, where the Old Jewish Cemetery is a fascinating place to visit. Hemmed in by buildings and high walls, there was only so much space for the 12,000 tombstones, and these topple across each other in chaotic disarray. The synagogues of the area remain, some used as museums outlining the long history of Jews in Prague, others as places of worship. The Old-New Synagogue, near the cemetery, is one of Europe's oldest functioning synagogues, and boasts an eye-catching high brick gable and an atmospheric feel. Josefov is a rather small area that does get packed, so a good time to go along is early in the day.

→ GRAND NATIONAL

At the other end of town, at the southern end of Wenceslas Square, looms the brooding bulk of another great Prague institution, **the National Museum.** With its vast natural history and archaeology collections, it's a city institution, but some may find the most intriguing aspect of the place its cavernous atrium and grand staircases (incidentally, there are many quirky museums in Prague, devoted to the likes of spiders and scorpions, medieval torture and Barbie). The National Museum is a towering experience under a big roof, and you can get a similar kind of awesome hit at **the National Theatre**, south of Charles Bridge by the river, an opulent home of opera, ballet and theatre, full of lavish decorations from the country's top nineteenth century artistic talents.

To appreciate a complete contrast, head back over the river to **Petrin Hill,** which towers gloriously over Malá Strana's dappled squares and aristocratic palaces. It offers great vistas over the city, and features lots of leafy trails that criss-cross the surface. Sitting atop of it all is Prague's mini Eiffel Tower, the Petrin Tower, gifting you more stunning views. Heading back down to river level, you might be surprised to find the John Lennon Wall, painted after his murder in 1980, covered in graffiti, slightly tatty and peeling, but preserved as a totem to free expression.

However hard-wired to the newly opened-up, globalized world Prague aspires to be, it'll surely never lose its magical medieval appeal. It's at its best in the winter with damp mists swirling off the river, and the crowds mysteriously evaporated. In November or February, you can walk unsullied across Charles Bridge and appreciate this stunning city at its best.

CALENDAR HIGHLIGHTS

There's an English language paper in the city, **The Prague Post**, which is particularly good for listing details of what's on where. And there are so many people handing out leaflets announcing recitals and concerts that your hand will soon start to feel like a mini JCB. Many of these events are worth looking into, so don't just stuff that bit of paper away in your pocket. The Prague Spring Festival, which takes place in May and offers a scintillating variety of classical concerts at many venues, is internationally lauded, but there's also an Autumn Festival in September, and a Winter

PRAGUE IN...

→ ONE DAY

Old Town Square, the astronomical clock, Charles Bridge, Prague Castle, take it all in on Petrin Hill

→ TWO DAYS

Josefov, the National Theatre, Golden Lane

→ THREE DAYS

Wenceslas Square and the National Museum, across the bridge for a detailed look round Malá Strana

Festival in January, so...if you miss one, remember there'll be another along soon. Fans of gipsy roots music have a treat every May, with the World Roma Festival, which, as well as gipsy music, features films and theatre shows in various locations. Dance Prague, every June, is another highlight of the cultural year, while, without employing a trace of the city's trademark irony, June the third is devoted to the death of Kafka, with admirers flocking to his burial place. December is a good time to be in Old Town Square, with its huge Christmas tree and surrounding markets selling all manner of things you might not really want. On New Year's Eve, the square is a manic place to be, and the fireworks over the castle are something else.

EATING OUT

Prague was and still is to an extent famous for its infinite variety of dumplings. These were the glutinous staple that saw locals through the long years of stark Communist rule. It's still as easy as bumping into another tourist on Charles Bridge to get the favoured local nosh: pork, pickled cabbage and dumplings. You can also mix the likes of schnitzel, beer and ginger cake for a ridiculously cheap outlay. But since '89's Velvet Revolution, Prague has undergone a bit of a foodie revolution, and the heavy traditional cuisine is now served, in the better establishments, with a creative flair and international approach. Global menus are now common currency here. Less palatably, the city has earned a reputation for rather straight-faced and indifferent service: lots of restaurants include a tip in your final bill, so check closely to make sure you don't tip twice. It's worth remembering that lunch is the main meal of the Czech day, and many restaurants have shut up shop well before midnight.

Czechs consume more beer than anyone else in the world, and there are some excellent microbrewery tipples to be had. In Staré Město there's a very popular establishment, with an amazing selection of beers, conveniently called Alcohol Bar. Harder to find in the city, but well worth the effort, are the brilliant flea markets, which set up their stalls depending on the time of year. A good place to check out details is the Globe English language bookstore by the Vltava near the National Theatre. Everyone knows everything there, and the coffee's good too!

→ RISING DAMP

The floods of 2002 were a wake-up call to locals that the Vltava is no respecter of the tourist trade. The costs reached some 70 billion crowns in structural damage and loss of visitors. Although buildings were smartly renovated in good time, the city has learnt its lesson and the authorities have built a new flood wall and early warning system in case the river decides to put them to the test again.

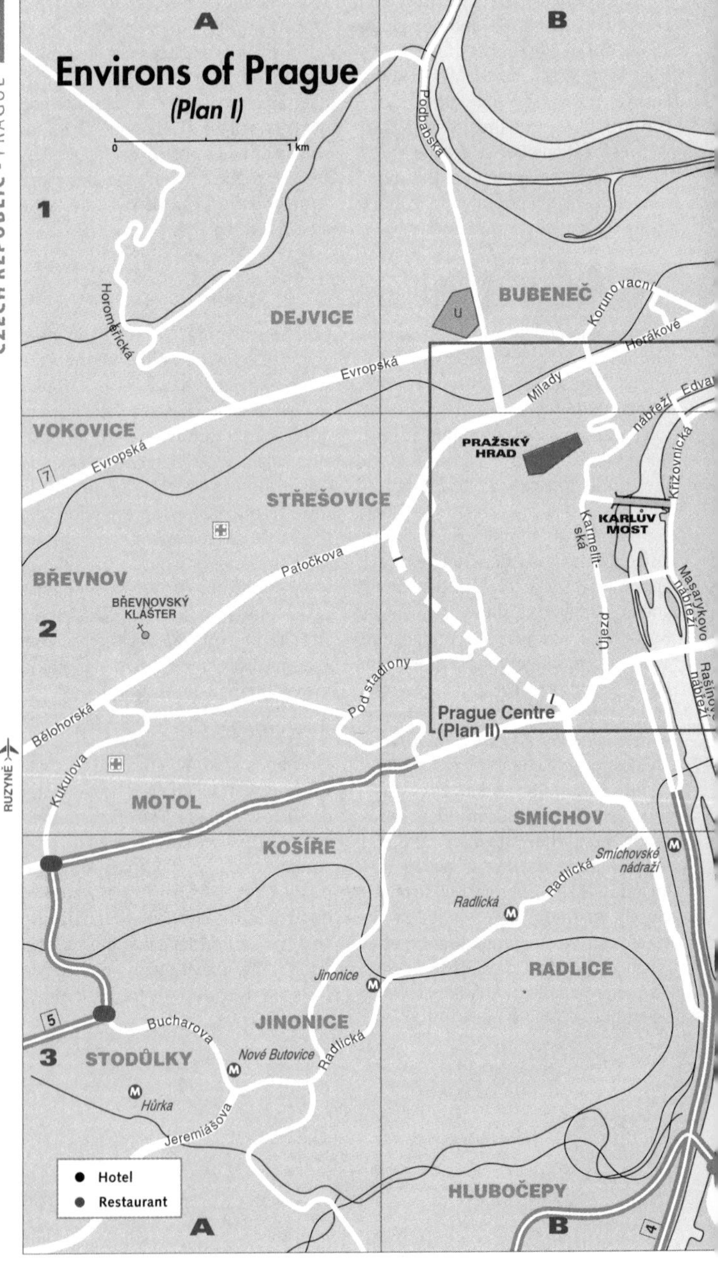
Environs of Prague
(Plan I)
0
1 km
A
B
1
2
3
DEJVICE
BUBENEČ
VOKOVICE
STŘEŠOVICE
BŘEVNOV
BŘEVNOVSKÝ KLÁŠTER
PRAŽSKÝ HRAD
KARLŮV MOST
MOTOL
KOŠÍŘE
SMÍCHOV
RADLICE
JINONICE
STODŮLKY
HLUBOČEPY
Podbabská
Horoměřická
Evropská
Milady
Horákové
Korunovační
nábřeží
Edvard
Křižovnická
Karmelitská
Újezd
Masarykovo nábřeží
Rašínovo nábřeží
Patočkova
Pod stadiony
Bělohorská
Kukulova
Bucharova
Jeremiášova
Radlická
Smíchovské nádraží
Jinonice
Nové Butovice
Hůrka
Prague Centre (Plan II)
RUZYNĚ
U
7
5
4
Hotel
Restaurant

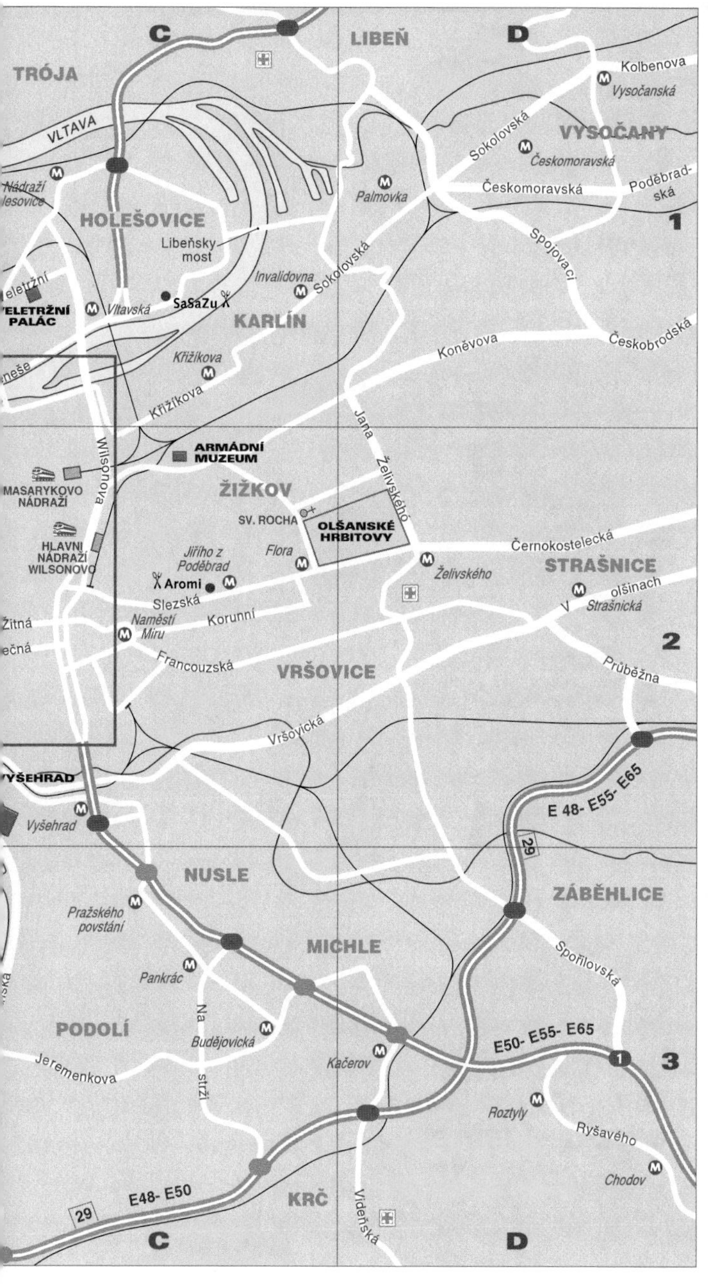
C
D
TRÓJA
LIBEŇ
VLTAVA
Kolbenova
Vysočanská
VYSOČANY
Sokolovská
Českomoravská
Českomoravská
Poděbradská
Nádraží Holešovice
Palmovka
HOLEŠOVICE
1
Libeňsky most
Spojovací
Invalidovna
Sokolovská
Veletržní
VELETRŽNÍ PALÁC
Vltavská
SaSaZu
KARLÍN
Českobrodská
Koněvova
Křižíkova
Křižíkova
Jana Želivského
ARMÁDNÍ MUZEUM
Wilsonova
MASARYKOVO NÁDRAŽÍ
ŽIŽKOV
SV. ROCHA
OLŠANSKÉ HRBITOVY
Černokostelecká
HLAVNI NÁDRAŽÍ WILSONOVO
Jiřího z Poděbrad
Flora
Želivského
STRAŠNICE
Aromi
Slezská
V olšinach
Strašnická
Žitná
Náměstí Míru
Korunní
2
Francouzská
VRŠOVICE
Průběžna
Vršovická
VYŠEHRAD
E 48- E55- E65
Vyšehrad
29
NUSLE
ZÁBĚHLICE
Pražského povstání
MICHLE
Spořilovská
Pankrác
Na strži
PODOLÍ
Budějovická
E50- E55- E65
Kačerov
1
3
Jeremenkova
Roztyly
Ryšavého
Chodov
E48- E50
29
KRČ
Vídeňská
C
D

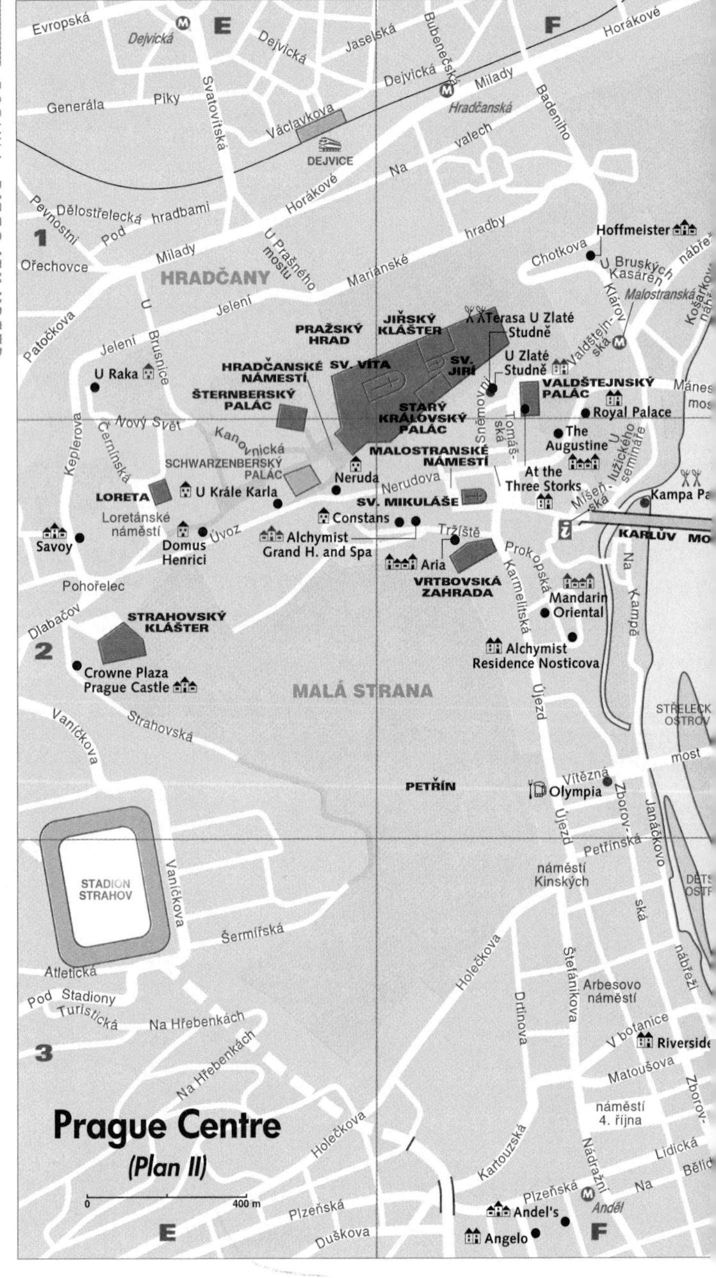
Prague Centre
(Plan II)
HRADČANY
MALÁ STRANA
PETŘÍN
PRAŽSKÝ HRAD
JIŘSKÝ KLÁŠTER
HRADČANSKÉ NÁMESTÍ
SV. VÍTA
SV. JIŘÍ
ŠTERNBERSKÝ PALÁC
STARÝ KRÁLOVSKÝ PALÁC
SCHWARZENBERSKÝ PALÁC
MALOSTRANSKÉ NÁMESTÍ
SV. MIKULÁŠE
VALDŠTEJNSKÝ PALÁC
LORETA
STRAHOVSKÝ KLÁŠTER
VRTBOVSKÁ ZAHRADA
KARLŮV MO
STADION STRAHOV
Hoffmeister
Terasa U Zlaté Studně
U Zlaté Studně
Royal Palace
The Augustine
At the Three Storks
Kampa Pa
U Raka
U Krále Karla
Neruda
Constans
Alchymist Grand H. and Spa
Aria
Mandarin Oriental
Alchymist Residence Nosticova
Savoy
Domus Henrici
Crowne Plaza Prague Castle
Olympia
Riverside
Andel's
Angelo
Dejvická
Hradčanská
Malostranská
Anděl
DEJVICE
Evropská
Generála
Piky
Svatovítská
Dejvická
Jaselská
Bubenečská
Milady
Horákové
Václavkova
Badeniho
Na valech
Pevnostní
Dělostřelecká
Pod hradbami
Ořechovce
Milady
U Prašného mostu
Mariánské hradby
Chotkova
U Bruských Kasáren
Klárov
Valdštejnská
Jelení
Patočkova
U Brusnice
Nový Svět
Černínská
Keplerova
Kanovnická
Nerudova
Sněmovní
Tomášská
U lužického semináře
Míšeňská
Loretánské náměstí
Úvoz
Tržiště
Prokopská
Karmelitská
Na Kampě
Pohořelec
Dlabačov
Újezd
STŘELECK OSTROV
most
Vítězná
Zborov-ská
Strahovská
Vaníčkova
Petřínská
náměstí Kinských
Janáčkovo nábřeží
DĚTS OSTR
Šermířská
Atletická
Pod Stadiony
Turistická
Na Hřebenkách
Holečkova
Drtinova
Štefánikova
Arbesovo náměstí
V botanice
Matoušova
náměstí 4. října
Kartouzská
Nádražní
Lidická
Plzeňská
Na Bělid
Duškova
Mánes most
Košarkovo nábř
E
F
1
2
3
0
400 m

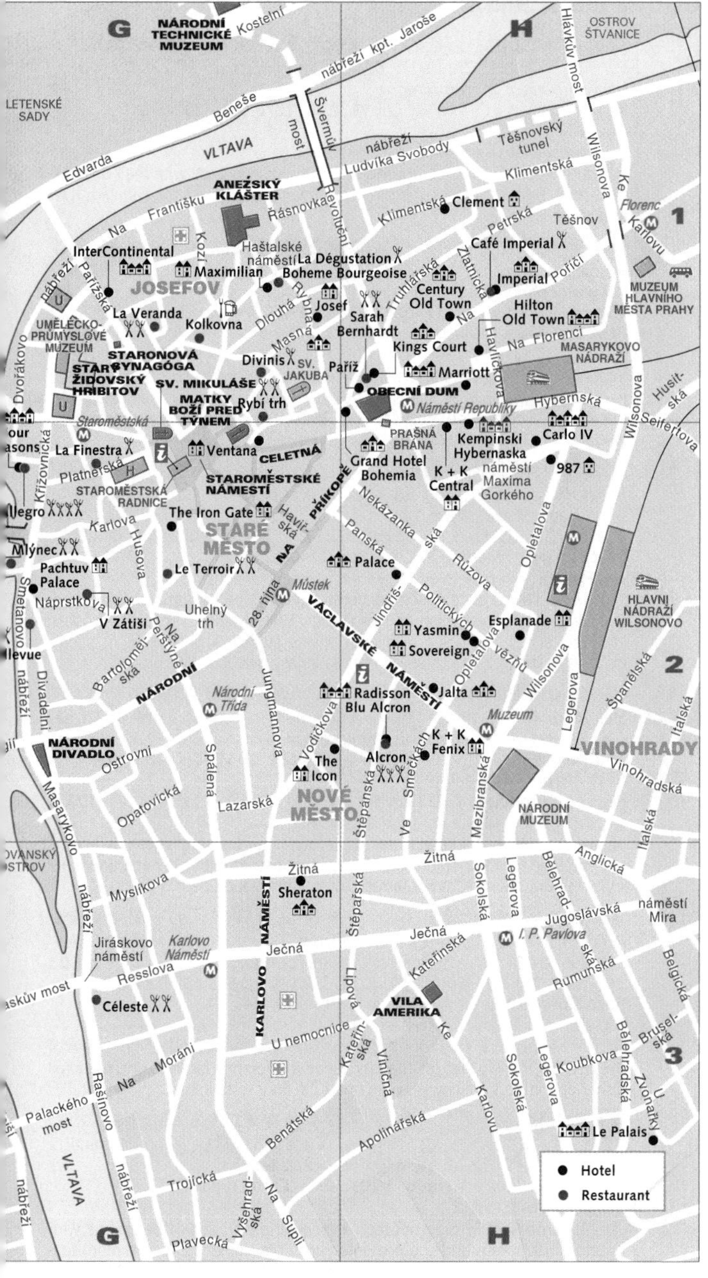
G
H
1
2
3
NÁRODNÍ TECHNICKÉ MUZEUM
Kostelní
nábřeží kpt. Jaroše
OSTROV ŠTVANICE
Hlávkův most
LETENSKÉ SADY
Edvarda Beneše
VLTAVA
most
Švermův
nábřeží Ludvíka Svobody
Těšnovský tunel
Wilsonova
Klimentská
ANEŽSKÝ KLÁŠTER
Na Františku
Řásnovka
Revoluční
Klimentská
Clement
Petrská
Těšnov
Ke Karlovu
Florenc
Kozí
Haštalské náměstí
La Dégustation
InterContinental
Maximilian
Boheme Bourgeoise
Truhlářská
Café Imperial
nábřeží
Pařížská
JOSEFOV
Dlouhá
Rybná
Century Old Town
Zlatnická
Imperial
Na Poříčí
MUZEUM HLAVNÍHO MĚSTA PRAHY
La Veranda
Kolkovna
Josef
Sarah Bernhardt
Hilton Old Town
UMĚLECKO-PRŮMYSLOVÉ MUZEUM
Masná
Kings Court
Havlíčkova
Na Florenci
Dvořákovo
STARONOVÁ SYNAGÓGA
STARÝ ŽIDOVSKÝ HŘBITOV
Divinis
SV. JAKUBA
Paříž
Marriott
MASARYKOVO NÁDRAŽÍ
SV. MIKULÁŠE
OBECNÍ DUM
MATKY BOŽÍ PRED TÝNEM
Rybí trh
Náměstí Republiky
Hybernská
Husitská
Staroměstská
Seifertova
Four Seasons
Křižovnická
La Finestra
Ventana
CELETNÁ
PRAŠNÁ BRÁNA
Kempinski Hybernaska
Carlo IV
Platnéřská
STAROMĚSTSKÉ NÁMĚSTÍ
Grand Hotel Bohemia
K + K Central
náměstí Maxima Gorkého
987
STAROMĚSTSKÁ RADNICE
Allegro
The Iron Gate
Havířská
NA PŘÍKOPĚ
Nekázanka
Karlova
Husova
STARÉ MĚSTO
Panská
Opletalova
Mlýnec
Pachtuv Palace
Le Terroir
Palace
Růžova
Smetanovo nábřeží
Náprstkova
V Zátiší
Můstek
Politických vězňů
Jindřišská
Uhelný trh
28. října
HLAVNÍ NÁDRAŽÍ WILSONOVO
Bellevue
Na Perštýně
VÁCLAVSKÉ NÁMĚSTÍ
Yasmin
Esplanade
Bartolomějská
Sovereign
Wilsonova
Divadelní
NÁRODNÍ
Jungmannova
Opletalova
Španělská
Národní Třída
Radisson Blu Alcron
Jalta
Legerova
Italská
Muzeum
Vodičkova
K + K Fenix
VINOHRADY
NÁRODNÍ DIVADLO
Ostrovní
Spálená
The Icon
Alcron
Smečkách
Vinohradská
Masarykovo
Lazarská
NOVÉ MĚSTO
Štěpánská
Ve Smečkách
Mezibranská
NÁRODNÍ MUZEUM
Opatovická
SLOVANSKÝ OSTROV
Žitná
Žitná
Anglická
Sokolská
Legerova
Bělehradská
Italská
Myslíkova
Sheraton
Štěpařská
náměstí Míra
nábřeží
KARLOVO NÁMĚSTÍ
Jugoslávská
Jiráskovo náměstí
Karlovo Náměstí
Ječná
Ječná
I. P. Pavlova
Resslova
Kateřinská
Jiráskův most
Rumunská
Belgická
Céleste
VILA AMERIKA
Lipová
U nemocnice
Ke Karlovu
Kateřinská
Na Moráni
Viničná
Sokolská
Bruselská
Bělehradská
Koubkova
Legerova
Palackého most
Rašínovo nábřeží
Apolinářská
Benátská
Karlovu
Zvonařky
Le Palais
VLTAVA
Trojická
Vyšehradská
Na Slupi
Plavecká
Hotel
Restaurant

ON THE RIGHT BANK

Four Seasons

Veleslavínova 1098/2A ✉ *110 00 – Ⓜ Staroměstská – ✆ 221 427 000 – www.fourseasons.com/prague* **G2**
141 rm – 6150/10087 CZK 7750/11070 CZK – 20 suites
Rest *Allegro* – see below
◆ Grand Luxury ◆ Modern ◆
Imposing riverside hotel composed of three buildings; each with their own distinct style. Elegant, well-kept bedrooms of varying sizes; ask for one with river and castle views.

Carlo IV

Senovážné Nám. 13 ✉ *110 00 – Ⓜ Náměsti Republiky – ✆ 224 593 111 – www.boscolohotels.com* **H2**
150 rm – 13532 CZK 46252 CZK, 492 CZK – 2 suites
Rest *Box Block* – Carte 785/1085 CZK
◆ Grand Luxury ◆ Stylish ◆
Impressive former bank with stunning marble lobby, ornate ceiling and pillars in neo-Renaissance style. Roman spa and pool. Luxurious bedrooms; those in the original building are the most spacious. Elegant, contemporary restaurant serving modern Italian dishes.

Kempinski Hybernská

Hybernská 12 ✉ *110 00 – Ⓜ Náměsti Republiky – ✆ 226 226 111 – www.kempinski-prague.com* **H2**
13 rm – 9381/18515 CZK 9381/123431 CZK – **62 suites**, 642 CZK
Rest *Le Grill* – Menu 720 CZK – Carte 740/1250 CZK
◆ Historic ◆ Stylish ◆
200 year old listed building with delightful glass-topped atrium, cosy bar, inner courtyard and formally planted rear garden. Well-equipped, stylish bedrooms; including suites that boast their own private jacuzzis and terraces. Spacious, bistro-style dining room offers an internationally influenced menu.

Radisson Blu Alcron

Štěpánská 40 ✉ *110 00 – Ⓜ Muzeum – ✆ 222 820 000 – www.radissonblu.com* **H2**
200 rm – 3674/5154 CZK 3674/5154 CZK, 641 CZK – 6 suites
Rest *Alcron* – see below
Rest *La Rotonde* – ✆ *222 820 410* – Menu 590 CZK – Carte 640/1410 CZK
◆ Luxury ◆ Business ◆ Modern ◆
Imposing 1930s building with executive lounge and warmly styled bedrooms offering high levels of comfort and good facilities. Attentive service. Brasserie-style restaurant with summer terrace; international and Czech dishes.

Inter-Continental

Pařížská 30 ✉ *110 00 – Ⓜ Staroměstská – ✆ 296 631 111 – www.intercontinental.com/prague* **G1**
349 rm – 5615/6350 CZK 5615/7332 CZK, 638 CZK – 23 suites
Rest *Zlatá Praha* – *(dinner only)* Carte 950/1440 CZK
◆ Grand Luxury ◆ Modern ◆
Elegant bedrooms in hues of soft caramel and fresh apple; most enjoy views of the river or the old part of the city. Good conference facilities. International dishes and impressive city views in smart 7th floor restaurant.

Le Palais

U Zvonařky 1 ✉ *120 00 – Ⓜ I. P. Pavlova – ✆ 234 634 111 – www.palaishotel.cz*
60 rm – 7153 CZK 7646 CZK – 12 suites **H3**
Rest *Le Papillon* – Menu 642/1036 CZK – Carte 1036/1332 CZK
◆ Luxury ◆ Classic ◆
Late 19C mansion in quiet location overlooking city. Stylish bedrooms with luxurious bathrooms and complimentary mini bar; corner rooms are more spacious. Classically styled dining room with delightful outlook from terrace. Contemporary, seasonal cooking.

Marriott

V Celnici 8 ✉ *110 00 –* Ⓜ *Náměsti Republiky –* ☎ *222 888 888 – www.marriottprague.com* **H1**

258 rm – †3800/5500 CZK ††3800/5500 CZK, ☕ 800 CZK – 35 suites

Rest – Menu 480 CZK (lunch) – Carte 785/1225 CZK

♦ Business ♦ Classic ♦

International hotel providing first class conference facilities and excellent leisure club. Spacious, comfortable bedrooms are decorated in red and gold, and boast king-size beds. Red leather furnished brasserie offers an internationally influenced menu.

Hilton Old Town

V Celnici 7 ✉ *111 21 –* Ⓜ *Náměsti Republiky –* ☎ *221 822 100 – www.hilton.com* **H1**

300 rm – †3253/5717 CZK ††4066/6530 CZK, ☕ 641 CZK – 3 suites

Rest *Zinc* – ☎ *221 822 420* – Carte 641/1356 CZK

♦ Business ♦ Modern ♦

Located in the heart of the city and boasting an art deco style lobby with white marble, mirrors and gold décor. Soft, contemporary colour schemes in well-equipped bedrooms. Zinc offers modern European cooking with Asian influences under a shimmering zinc ceiling.

Sheraton

Zitna 8 ✉ *120 00 –* Ⓜ *Karlovo Náměstí –* ☎ *225 999 999 – www.sheratonprague.com* **G3**

122 rm – †7000 CZK ††7000 CZK, ☕ 675 CZK – 38 suites

Rest *Brasserie Délice* – Menu 490/890 CZK – Carte 700/1490 CZK

♦ Townhouse ♦ Stylish ♦

Modern, boutique-style hotel composed of four 19C buildings. Comfortable bedrooms, some with balconies; ask for one of the newer rooms facing the back. Rooftop terrace with impressive views. International dishes in Brasserie Délice.

Palace

Panská 12 ✉ *111 21 –* Ⓜ *Můstek –* ☎ *224 093 111 – www.palacehotel.cz* **H2**

122 rm – †2962/4690 CZK ††2692/4690 CZK, ☕ 444 CZK – 2 suites

Rest *Gourmet Club* – *(dinner only)* Menu 1605 CZK – Carte 1230/1510 CZK

♦ Traditional ♦ Classic ♦

Original Viennese art nouveau style façade dating back to 1909. Elegant interior; bedrooms combine period furniture with modern facilities and services. Classic French dishes, intimate ambience and professional staff in Gourmet Club.

Grand Hotel Bohemia

rest,

Králodvorská 4 ✉ *110 00 –* Ⓜ *Náměsti Republiky –* ☎ *234 608 111 – www.grandhotelbohemia.cz* **H1**

78 rm ☕ – †3689/5658 CZK ††4450/6027 CZK

Rest – Menu 550/750 CZK – Carte 570/1020 CZK

♦ Traditional ♦ Modern ♦

Friendly, professional staff in this classic 1920s hotel, with its splendid neo-Baroque ballroom. Immaculately kept, contemporary bedrooms with good level of facilities; compact bathrooms boast underfloor heating. Classic dishes in Franz Josef bistro.

Imperial

Na Poříčí 15 ✉ *110 00 –* Ⓜ *Náměsti Republiky –* ☎ *246 011 600 – www.hotel-imperial.cz* **H1**

126 rm – †3750/5500 CZK ††3750/5500 CZK, ☕ 280 CZK

Rest *Café Imperial* – see below

♦ Business ♦ Retro ♦

This historic hotel's listed façade dates from 1914 and its interior features exquisite ceramic mosaics in an art deco style. Its well-kept dark wood bedrooms combine retro styling with modern comforts.

Paříž

U obecniho domu 1 ✉ 110 00 – Ⓜ Náměsti Republiky – ✆ 222 195 195 – www.hotel-pariz.cz **H1**

83 rm – †7755 CZK ††7755 CZK, ☕ 490 CZK – 1 suite

Rest *Sarah Bernhardt* – see below

♦ Traditional ♦ Classic ♦

Charming art nouveau townhouse, its bright corridors hung with art. Well-equipped bedrooms; corner rooms are the largest. Chandelier and red leather furnished café open for lunch.

Kings Court

U Obecního domu 3 ✉ 110 00 – Ⓜ Náměsti Republiky – ✆ 224 222 888 – www.hotelkingscourt.cz **H1**

131 rm ☕ – †7540 CZK ††7540 CZK – 4 suites

Rest – Carte 595/795 CZK

♦ Townhouse ♦ Stylish ♦

Former chamber of commerce located beneath the Obecni Dum; now a contemporary hotel with smart, well-equipped bedrooms and a basement spa zone. Original art nouveau windows feature. International menu and buffet breakfasts in café-restaurant with summer terrace.

Jalta

Václavské Nám. 45 ✉ 110 00 – Ⓜ Muzeum – ✆ 222 822 111 – www.hoteljalta.com **H2**

89 rm ☕ – †5421/7393 CZK ††5421/7393 CZK – 5 suites

Rest *Como* – Carte 585/815 CZK

♦ Traditional ♦ Stylish ♦

Well-kept hotel named after the historical Jalta conference, with a façade protected by UNESCO. Spacious, comfortable, well-equipped bedrooms boast art deco styling and balconies. Tapas and Mediterranean cooking in Como, complete with a pianist at weekends.

Century Old Town

Na Poříčí 7 ✉ 110 00 – Ⓜ Náměsti Republiky – ✆ 221 800 800 – www.accor.com **H1**

143 rm – †3196 CZK ††3196 CZK, ☕ 423 CZK – 1 suite

Rest *Felice* – Menu 375 CZK – Carte 520/895 CZK

♦ Business ♦ Functional ♦

Modern hotel in 19C building, ideally situated in city centre. Well-maintained, contemporary bedrooms and compact, functional bathrooms. Felice restaurant named after one of Kafka's lovers. Pleasant terrace; brasserie-style food.

Josef without rest

Rybná 20 ✉ 110 00 – Ⓜ Náměsti Republiky – ✆ 221 700 111 – www.hoteljosef.com **G1**

109 rm ☕ – †2936 CZK ††3182 CZK

♦ Townhouse ♦ Design ♦

Boutique hotel with light-filled lobby and delightful courtyard garden. Smart, design-led bedrooms feature glass bathrooms; ask for a room with a view on either the 7th or 8th floor.

Pachtuv Palace rm,

Karolíny Světlé 34 ✉ 110 00 – Ⓜ Staroměstská – ✆ 234 705 111 – www.mamaison.com **G2**

20 rm – †5500/8000 CZK ††8500/19000 CZK – **30 suites**, ☕ 520 CZK

Rest *Amade* – *✆ 230 234 316* – Carte 610/845 CZK

♦ Traditional ♦ Cosy ♦

17C residence near the river; renovated in a baroque style, with elegant lobby and charming courtyard terrace. Spacious, antique-furnished bedrooms; ask for one with a river view. Informal restaurant with modern, seasonal menu of Czech and international dishes.

Yasmin

Politických vězňu 12/913 ✉ 110 00 – Ⓜ Muzeum – ☏ 234 100 111 – www.hotel-yasmin.cz **H2**

196 rm – 5921 CZK 5921/6901 CZK **Rest** – Carte 257/567 CZK

◆ Business ◆ Modern ◆

Contemporary styling in this design-led hotel; spacious, green-hued bedrooms come with all mod cons and dark tiled bathrooms. Entrance to garden from Wenceslas Square. International/Asian dishes served in colourful restaurant.

Maximilian without rest

Haštalská 14 ✉ 110 00 – Ⓜ Náměsti Republiky – ☏ 225 303 111 – www.maximilianhotel.com **G1**

70 rm – 2195/3923 CZK 2443/4910 CZK, 350 CZK – 1 suite

◆ Business ◆ Modern ◆

Well-maintained, modern hotel in a quiet area. Comfortable, contemporary bedrooms. Basement Thai massage spa. Good choice from the breakfast buffet in the glass and steel winter garden.

K + K Central

Hybernská 10 ✉ 110 00 – Ⓜ Náměsti Republiky – ☏ 225 022 000 – www.kkhotels.com/central **H2**

126 rm – 6909 CZK 7401 CZK – 1 suite **Rest** – Carte 613/859 CZK

◆ Business ◆ Modern ◆

Beautifully restored hotel in centre of city, with wonderful art nouveau façade and well-kept, green and lilac-hued bedrooms. Glass cube conference room. Breakfast served in impressive former theatre. Light dishes in modern bar/bistro.

The Icon

V Jámě 6 ✉ 110 00 – Ⓜ Muzeum – ☏ 725 634 100 – www.iconhotel.eu

29 rm – 2250/3500 CZK 2250/3500 CZK – 2 suites **G2**

Rest – Carte 480/795 CZK

◆ Business ◆ Modern ◆

Ultra-modern, centrally located hotel, with friendly, helpful staff and a relaxed feel. Well-equipped bedrooms and all-day breakfasts. Look out for the art installation, 'The Ages of Life'. Small purple basement bar/restaurant, with large menu and a hip vibe.

Ventana without rest

Celetná 7 ✉ 110 00 – Ⓜ Náměsti Republiky – ☏ 221 776 600 – www.ventana-hotel.net **G2**

27 rm – 3455/4935 CZK 3948/5428 CZK, 246 CZK – 2 suites

◆ Traditional ◆ Classic ◆

Former residential house with art deco façade, near the Old Town market. Spacious, well-kept bedrooms in muted shades set over 4 floors; top floor loft rooms have separate lounge.

The Iron Gate

Michalská 19 ✉ 110 00 – Ⓜ Staroměstská – ☏ 225 777 777 – www.irongaterestaurant.cz **G2**

12 rm – 2500/7500 CZK 4500/15000 CZK – **31 suites**

Rest *Zelezná vrata* – *(dinner only)* Carte 790/1570 CZK

◆ Traditional ◆ Classic ◆

14C building hidden away in cobbled streets; now a luxury hotel, with wooden ceilings and original wall paintings. Functional bedrooms and pleasant courtyard garden. Modern restaurant with funky basement bar offers mix of Italian and traditional Czech dishes.

K + K Fenix

Ve Smečkách 30 ✉ 110 00 – Ⓜ Muzeum – ☏ 225 012 000 – www.kkhotels.com **H2**

128 rm – 6645 CZK 7140 CZK **Rest** – Carte 480/720 CZK

◆ Business ◆ Modern ◆

Located in area busy with nightlife; an up-to-date interior behind a classic façade. Ask for one of the refurbished bedrooms, which are contemporary in greys and greens. Light dishes in modern bar/restaurant.

Esplanade

Washingtonova 1600-19 ✉ 110 00 – Ⓜ Muzeum – ✆ 224 501 111 – www.esplanade.cz **H2**

74 rm – 2194/3821 CZK 2440/3919 CZK

Rest – Menu 247/616 CZK – Carte 606/887 CZK

♦ Traditional ♦ Classic ♦

Charming and atmospheric; this art nouveau building is something of an architectural gem. Original features abound; variously sized bedrooms enjoy style and a timeless elegance. International menu offered in friendly surroundings.

Sovereign

Politických Veznu 16 ✉ 110 00 – Ⓜ Muzeum – ✆ 242 454 545 – www.hotel-sovereign.cz **H2**

50 rm – 2954/4800 CZK 3223/4800 CZK

Rest *Epicure* – *✆ 242 454 143 (closed Saturday lunch and Sunday)*
Menu 296/443 CZK – Carte 419/837 CZK

♦ Historic ♦ Modern ♦

Steps away from Wenceslas Square, this former bank, built in 1898, is now a well-maintained, modern hotel. Spacious bedrooms have high ceilings, good facilities and soft brown colour schemes. Contemporary, bistro-style Epicure offers an international menu.

Clement without rest

Klimentská 30 ✉ 110 00 – Ⓜ Náměsti Republiky – ✆ 221 314 350 – www.hotelclement.cz **H1**

77 rm – 1234/3703 CZK 1358/3703 CZK

♦ Business ♦ Functional ♦

Former office building not far from either the river or the city centre; now a modern hotel featuring clean, functional bedrooms in a contemporary style. Friendly, helpful staff.

987 without rest

Senovážné Nám.15 ✉ 110 00 – Ⓜ Náměsti Republiky – ✆ 255 737 100 – www.987hotelsl.com **H2**

77 rm – 2698/5150 CZK 2698/5150 CZK – 3 suites

♦ Traditional ♦ Modern ♦

Small, modern hotel in central location; well-equipped, comfortable bedrooms are set over 6 floors and feature modern design and furnishings. Colourful ground floor breakfast room.

Allegro – at Four Seasons Hotel

Veleslavínova 1098/2a ✉ 11000 – Ⓜ Staroměstská – ✆ 221 426 880 – www.fourseasons.com/prague **G2**

Rest – Carte 1755/2770 CZK

Spec. Cod with wild fennel oil, olives and cauliflower. Veal baked in clay with shallots and foie gras. Poached black figs in honey with sangria ice cream.

♦ Italian ♦ Elegant ♦

High-ceilinged, wood-panelled restaurant overlooking river and featuring beautiful flower arrangements. High quality ingredients used to create Italian/Mediterranean dishes with contemporary touches. Impressive wine list, including some lovely reds.

Alcron – at Radisson Blu Alcron Hotel

Štěpánská 40 ✉ 110 00 – Ⓜ Muzeum – ✆ 222 820 038 – www.alcron.cz – Closed Saturday and Sunday **H2**

Rest – *(booking essential)* Carte 1570/1890 CZK

♦ Contemporary ♦ Design ♦

Intimate semi-circular restaurant dominated by art deco mural. Well-presented, contemporary cooking; choice of hot and cold tasting dishes from international menu. Friendly, professional staff.

XX

La Degustation Bohême Bourgeoise

Haštalská 18 ✉ 11000 – Ⓜ Náměsti Republiky
– ✆ 222 311 234 – www.ladegustation.cz
– Closed July, 24 December, Sunday and lunch Monday, Friday and Saturday
Rest – Menu 360/1000 CZK **G1**
♦ Modern ♦ Intimate ♦
Cosy L-shaped restaurant with elegant dark wood interior. European dishes make good use of quality regional produce. Open kitchen; chef's table. Professional service from well-versed team.

XX

Le Terroir

Vejvodova 1 (Entrance from Jilskà Street) ✉ 110 00 – Ⓜ Můstek
– ✆ 222 220 260 – www.leterroir.cz
– Closed 22-26 February, 2-7 August, 25 December, Sunday and Monday
Rest – Menu 1290 CZK (dinner) – Carte 1000/1480 CZK **G2**
♦ Innovative ♦ Rustic ♦
Small but charming cellar restaurant hidden away in centre of city. Good value European cooking, fantastic fromagerie and professional service. Superb wine list with some excellent Riesling/Bordeaux/Burgundy.

XX

La Veranda

Elišky Krásnohorské 2 ✉ 110 00 – Ⓜ Staroměstská – ✆ 224 814 733
– www.laveranda.cz
– Closed Sunday **G1**
Rest – Carte 525/1120 CZK
♦ Innovative ♦ Design ♦
Choose between the main restaurant, decorated in bright, sunny colours and the more intimate downstairs room with its contemporary styling. Mediterranean dishes. Friendly service.

XX

Céleste

Rasínovo Nábr. 80 (Tandící dům, Dancing House) ✉ 120 00
– Ⓜ Karlovo Náměstí – ✆ 221 984 160 – www.celesterestaurant.cz
– Closed 24-26 December and Sunday **G3**
Rest – *(booking essential at dinner)* Menu 550 CZK – Carte 1170/1565 CZK
♦ French ♦ Minimalist ♦
Located on the 7th floor of the Dancing House, with superb views of the city and castle, this busy, modern restaurant offers creative French-based cooking with contemporary twists.

XX

V Zátiši

Liliová 1, Betlémské Nám. ✉ 110 00 – Ⓜ Můstek – ✆ 222 221 155
– www.zatisigroup.cz
– Closed 24 December **G2**
Rest – *(booking essential at dinner)* Menu 990 CZK
♦ Modern ♦ Cosy ♦
Popular, modern, city centre restaurant with a name meaning 'timeless'. Traditional Czech dishes with some Asian influences. Friendly, attentive service. Wines for sale to take away.

XX

Sarah Bernhardt – at Hotel Paříž

U obecniho domu 1 ✉ 110 00 – Ⓜ Náměsti Republiky – ✆ 222 195 195
– www.hotel-paris.cz **H1**
Rest – *(dinner only)* Menu 690 CZK – Carte 720/830 CZK
♦ International ♦ Brasserie ♦ Retro ♦
High-ceilinged art deco restaurant, named after the famous actress. Keenly prepared international dishes make good use of quality ingredients. Friendly, professional service.

XX **Bellevue**

Smetanovo Nábřeží 18 ✉ 110 00 – Ⓜ Staroměstská – ✆ 222 221 443 – www.zatisigroup.cz **G2**

Rest – Menu 1090 CZK

♦ Traditional ♦ Formal ♦

Elegant 19C townhouse with pleasant summer terrace and river views; contemporary interior decorated in a pastel palette, with neo-baroque lighting. Fixed price, international menu.

XX **Mlýnec**

Novotného Lávka 9 ✉ 110 00 – Ⓜ Staroměstská – ✆ 221 000 777 – www.zatisigroup.cz – Closed 24 December **G2**

Rest – Menu 590 CZK – Carte 885/985 CZK

♦ Contemporary ♦ Retro ♦

Contemporary styling with paintings, antiques and crystal lighting. Well presented, modern European and Czech cuisine. Terrace views of Charles Bridge on fine summer evenings.

XX **Rybí trh**

Týnský dvůr 5 ✉ 110 00 – Ⓜ Náměsti Republiky – ✆ 602 295 911 – www.rybitrh.cz **G1**

Rest – Menu 790 CZK – Carte 390/1720 CZK

♦ Seafood ♦ Friendly ♦

Seafood restaurant in picturesque spot in heart of the city. Marine-themed décor with turquoise walls, aquariums, open kitchen and fish counter. Contemporary cooking and a pleasant terrace.

X **Aromi**

Mánesova 78/1442 ✉ 120 00 – Ⓜ Jiřiho z Poděbrad – ✆ 222 713 222 – www.aromi.cz *Plan I* **C2**

Rest – *(booking essential at dinner)* Menu 165 CZK – Carte 575/805 CZK

♦ Italian ♦ Rustic ♦

Charming neighbourhood restaurant with rustic interior, open kitchen and lively atmosphere. Open all day for fresh, tasty, simply prepared and great value Italian dishes; choose the daily specials. Excellent choice of Italian wines. Attentive, charming service.

X **Divinis**

Týnská 21 ✉ 110 00 – Ⓜ Staromestská – ✆ 222 325 440 – www.divinis.cz – Closed 24-25 December and Sunday **G1**

Rest – *(booking essential) (dinner only)* Carte 675/1060 CZK

♦ Italian ♦ Bistro ♦ Friendly ♦

Intimate, popular, candlelit restaurant with wooden décor, flowers and a friendly, homely atmosphere. Imaginative, passionate kitchen offers concise, sensibly priced menu of fresh, tasty, well-prepared Italian dishes. Relaxed, informed service.

X **La Finestra**

Platnérská 90/13 – Ⓜ Staroměstská – ✆ 222 325 325 – www.lafinestra.cz **G2**

Rest – *(booking essential)* Menu 195 CZK (lunch) – Carte 945/1225 CZK

♦ Italian ♦ Rustic ♦ Cosy ♦

Located in the basement of a townhouse, with a cosy, rustic, red-brick interior. Italian menu, with emphasis on fresh, good quality meat. Superb Italian wine list; friendly staff.

X **Café Imperial** – at Hotel Imperial

Na Poříčí 15 ✉ 110 00 – Ⓜ Náměsti Republiky – ✆ 246 011 440 – www.hotel-imperial.cz **H1**

Rest – *(booking essential)* Carte 362/625 CZK

♦ International ♦ Brasserie ♦ Retro ♦

Popular restaurant with the feel of a Parisian brasserie and a remarkable backdrop of colourfully tiled pillars and walls in an art deco style. Seasonal, international menu.

Kolkovna

V Kolkovně 8 ✉ 110 00 – Ⓜ Staroměstská – ✆ 224 819 701 – www.kolkovna.cz **G1**
Rest – Carte 285/625 CZK
♦ Traditional ♦ Inn ♦
Popular pub/brasserie located in the Jewish Quarter; with vaulted ceilings and beer counter. Traditional Czech cooking comes in generous portions and is good value for money.

ON THE LEFT BANK *Plan II*

Mandarin Oriental

Nebovidská 459/1 ✉ 118 00 – Ⓜ Malostranská – ✆ 233 088 888 – www.mandarinoriental.com **F2**
79 rm – †5769/11171 CZK ††5769/11171 CZK, ☕ 715 CZK – 20 suites
Rest *Essensia* – Menu 790 CZK (lunch) – Carte 1060/1470 CZK
♦ Luxury ♦ Stylish ♦
Former 14C monastery in peaceful setting in a central quarter; now a charming, modern hotel featuring warm, contemporary décor with an Asian edge. Luxurious, well-equipped bedrooms. Delightful spa in former chapel. Wine cellar. Essensia offers Asian and Czech dishes presented in a European style. Professional service.

The Augustine

Letenská 12/33 ✉ 118 000 – Ⓜ Malostranská – ✆ 266 112 233 – www.roccofortecollection.com – Closed 28 December-2 January **F1**
90 rm – †12000 CZK ††12500 CZK, ☕ 625 CZK – 11 suites
Rest *The Monastery* – Menu 614 CZK – Carte 795/1178 CZK
♦ Historic ♦ Design ♦
Set in seven buildings, including the monastery after which it is named. Spacious bedrooms in a cubist style, with all mod cons and luxury bathrooms; best is the 3-floored Tower Suite, with its impressive views. Brasserie-style restaurant offers international dishes.

Aria

Tržiště 9 ✉ 118 00 – Ⓜ Malostranská – ✆ 225 334 111 – www.aria.cz
37 rm ☕ – †5142/7108 CZK ††5142/7108 CZK – 7 suites **F2**
Rest *Coda* – *✆ 225 334 761* – Carte 1080/1760 CZK
♦ Luxury ♦ Design ♦
Stylish hotel with musical motif; its warmly decorated, variously sized bedrooms individually themed to different composers or styles of music. International influences on tasting menu in art deco Coda. Superb rooftop terrace with view to castle.

Alchymist Grand H. and Spa

Tržíště 19 ✉ 118 00 – Ⓜ Malostranská – ✆ 257 286 011 – www.alchymisthotel.com **F2**
37 rm – †7109/8580 CZK ††7109/8580 CZK, ☕ 491 CZK – 7 suites
Rest *Aquarius* – *✆ 257 286 019* – Carte 785/4290 CZK
♦ Luxury ♦ Classic ♦
Charming, cosy 16C townhouse with carefully chosen décor and sumptuous furniture. Bedrooms are in a neo-baroque or Renaissance style and feature good-sized bathrooms. Impressive oriental spa. Aquarius offers contemporary international cooking and features interesting Indian paintings, along with a pleasant terrace.

Crowne Plaza Prague Castle

Strahovská 128 ✉ 118 00 – ✆ 226 080 000 – www.cpcastle.com **E2**

135 rm – 5638 CZK 6006 CZK, 368 CZK – 3 suites

Rest – Menu 858/980 CZK – Carte 711/1152 CZK

♦ Business ♦ Historic ♦

Located in a UNESCO designated area behind the Strahov Monastery. Warmly decorated, well-kept bedrooms; those in the 16C building are more spacious. Small, Zen-style massage area. International dishes offered in Mediterranean-themed restaurant with terrace.

Andel's

Stroupeznického 21 ✉ 150 00 – Ⓜ Anděl – ✆ 296 889 688 – www.andelshotel.com **F3**

261 rm – 4800 CZK 4800 CZK, 245 CZK – 33 suites

Rest *Oscar's* – Menu 592 CZK – Carte 455/616 CZK

♦ Business ♦ Modern ♦

Stylish hotel in business area near shopping centre Nový Smíchov, and with good rail and road connections. Spacious, contemporary bedrooms and luxurious long stay apartments. Oscar's serves international cuisine in a modern setting.

Savoy

rm,

Keplerova 6 ✉ 118 00 – ✆ 224 302 430 – www.savoyhotel.cz

55 rm – 6860 CZK 6860 CZK – 2 suites **E2**

Rest *Hradčany* – *(Closed Sunday)* Menu 560 CZK (lunch) – Carte 530/1020 CZK

♦ Luxury ♦ Classic ♦

Former cinema complex rebuilt as hotel, with relaxed atmosphere. Classically styled bedrooms come with complimentary mini-bar; opt for one of the spacious suites. Elegant restaurant with open roof in summer. International dishes.

Hoffmeister

Pod Bruskou 7 ✉ 118 00 – Ⓜ Malostranská – ✆ 251 017 111 – www.hoffmeister.cz **F1**

43 rm – 4802/5294 CZK 4679/5664 CZK, 444 CZK – 5 suites

Rest *Ada* – Carte 838/1231 CZK

♦ Traditional ♦ Classic ♦

Situated in a busy corner location; its charming lobby decorated with caricatures of artists by Adolf Hoffmeister. Variously sized, individually styled bedrooms; some with underfloor heated bathrooms or jacuzzis. Classic French-influenced menu in elegant Ada.

U Zlaté Studně

U Zlaté Studně 166/4 ✉ 118 00 – Ⓜ Malostranská – ✆ 257 011 213 – www.goldenwell.cz **F1**

17 rm – 5515/6986 CZK 5515/6986 CZK, 613 CZK – 2 suites

Rest *Terasa U Zlaté Studně* – see below

♦ Historic ♦ Classic ♦

Charming, intimate hotel, situated in a quiet cobbled street close to Charles Bridge and the Royal Gardens. Cosy, antique-furnished bedrooms, most with a view over the city; some of the castle. Pleasant heated roof terrace. Professional, friendly staff.

Riverside without rest

Janáčkovo Nábřeži 15 ✉ 150 00 – Ⓜ Anděl – ✆ 225 994 611 – www.mamaison.com **F3**

77 rm – 4000/5500 CZK 6500/8000 CZK, 390 CZK – 3 suites

♦ Business ♦ Modern ♦

Well-kept riverside hotel with stylish, characterful bedrooms. The newer rooms are more modern, with spacious bathrooms; some have lake views and the quieter ones look onto the courtyard.

At The Three Storks

Tomášská 20 ✉ 118 00 – Ⓜ Malostranská – ✆ 257 210 779 – www.utricapu.cz **F1**

20 rm – 🚹1875/3657 CZK 🚹🚹2750/3800 CZK

Rest – Menu 280/380 CZK – Carte 700/1000 CZK

♦ Townhouse ♦ Modern ♦

Renovated 17C house with white 19C façade. Superior or deluxe bedrooms: the latter are more spacious; all have luxury bathrooms. Modern lobby bar and panoramic lift. Contemporary restaurant with clean, bright interior, serving mix of international and Czech dishes.

Royal Palace

Letenská 11 ✉ 118 19 – Ⓜ Malostranská – ✆ 224 811 281 – www.hotelroyalpalace.cz **F1**

34 rm – 🚹3683/5261 CZK 🚹🚹3946/5524 CZK – 2 suites

Rest – Menu 350 CZK (lunch) – Carte 700/1050 CZK

♦ Townhouse ♦ Classic ♦

Neo-Renaissance style 19C building, whose classically styled bedrooms are well-equipped and boast views to either side. Opt for the presidential suite with its sublime castle outlook. Elegant restaurant offers appealing menu of international dishes.

Alchymist Residence Nosticova

Nosticova 1, Malá Strana ✉ 118 00 – Ⓜ Malostranská – ✆ 257 312 513 – www.nosticova.com **F2**

12 rm – 🚹3224/5580 CZK 🚹🚹5580/6100 CZK, 390 CZK – 4 suites

Rest *Alchymist* – *(closed Sunday between 10 October-3 March)* Carte approx. 970 CZK

♦ Townhouse ♦ Classic ♦

17C building in quiet street; spacious, high-ceilinged, antique-furnished bedrooms; all with a kitchenette. Guests can use spa facilities at sister hotel, the Alchymist Grand. Mediterranean cooking served in flamboyantly-styled restaurant. Splendid garden terrace.

Angelo without rest

Radlicka 1g ✉ 150 00 – Ⓜ Anděl – ✆ 234 801 111 – www.angelohotel.com **F3**

168 rm – 🚹4658 CZK 🚹🚹4658 CZK, 450 CZK

♦ Business ♦ Modern ♦

Jazz is the theme of this brightly coloured hotel, with its red, yellow and black décor. Uniform bedrooms and spacious bathrooms with showers. Executive suites on top two floors.

U Raka without rest

Černínská 10 ✉ 118 00 – ✆ 220 511 100 – www.romantikhotel-uraka.cz

6 rm – 🚹2206/2942 CZK 🚹🚹2942/3799 CZK **E1**

♦ Family ♦ Cosy ♦

Cosy, rustic, family-run hotel; tucked away in a quiet neighbourhood. Warmly decorated, tidy bedrooms; ask for the luxury room with its own fireplace and garden terrace. Friendly, attentive staff. Fresh breakfast buffet served on typical Czech plates.

Domus Henrici without rest

Loretánská 11 ✉ 11 800 – ✆ 220 511 369 – www.hidden-places.com

7 rm – 🚹2084/2819 CZK 🚹🚹2451/3187 CZK – 1 suite **E2**

♦ Townhouse ♦ Minimalist ♦

Privately run townhouse in tranquil location close to the castle. Spacious, antique-furnished bedrooms; some with jacuzzi baths. South-facing terrace with unique view of city.

Neruda

Nerudova 44 ✉ 118 00 – ✆ 257 535 557 – www.hotelneruda.eu
42 rm – 1900/4280 CZK 1900/4800 CZK **E2**
Rest – Carte 500/900 CZK
♦ Townhouse ♦ Modern ♦
Named after local Czech writer, whose poems decorate the corridors. Cosy bedrooms in original 14C building; ask for one of the more spacious, more modern rooms in the newer building. Roof terrace overlooking castle. International dishes in restaurant.

Constans without rest

Břetislavova 309 ✉ 110 00 – Ⓜ Malostranská – ✆ 234 091 818 – www.hotelconstans.cz **F2**
31 rm – 1545/3383 CZK 1716/3726 CZK, 275 CZK
♦ Townhouse ♦ Classic ♦
Three converted townhouses situated in quiet street. Very spacious bedrooms boast period furniture and marble bathrooms; four also have a balcony. Traditional breakfast room.

U Krále Karla without rest

Úvoz 4 ✉ 118 00 – ✆ 257 531 211 – www.romantichotels.cz
19 rm – 2500/3000 CZK 3000/3200 CZK **E2**
♦ Historic ♦ Classic ♦
Quiet baroque townhouse; formerly a Gothic-style home to a Benedictine order. Splendid staircase leads to traditional bedrooms featuring parquet floors. Stunning stained glass ceiling.

Kampa Park

Na Kampě 8b, Malá Strana ✉ 118 00 – Ⓜ Malostranská – ✆ 296 826 102 – www.kampagroup.com **F2**
Rest – *(booking essential at dinner)* Carte 1105/1785 CZK
♦ Modern ♦ Fashionable ♦
Popular, well-run, modern restaurant, stunningly located at water's edge by Charles Bridge. In winter, dine in the winter garden; in summer enjoy the terrace. Fairly priced global menu; carefully prepared dishes use quality produce. Charming, professional service.

Terasa U Zlaté Studně – at U Zlaté Studně Hotel

U Zlaté Studně 4 ✉ 118 00 – Ⓜ Malostranská – ✆ 257 533 322 – www.terasauzlatestudne.cz **F1**
Rest – Carte 930/2260 CZK
♦ Modern ♦ Design ♦
Magnificent views over the city from this top floor restaurant and its heated terrace. Blue and gold décor, fine china, professional service. Well-presented, full-flavoured modern dishes.

SaSaZu

Bubenské nábr. 306/13 ✉ 170 04 – Ⓜ Vltavská – ✆ 284 097 455 – www.sasazu.cz *Plan I* **C1**
Rest – Carte 450/785 CZK
♦ Asian ♦ Exotic ♦ Fashionable ♦
Funky, stylish restaurant and bar located on the Prague Market and decorated with unique statues and huge red lamps. Well-balanced, innovative Asian cooking; dishes are prepared with care and offered at a reasonable price. Attentive, knowledgeable service.

Olympia

Vítězná 7 ✉ 110 00 – Ⓜ Národni Třída – ✆ 251 511 080 – www.kolkovna.cz **F2**
Rest – Carte 284/625 CZK
♦ Traditional ♦ Inn ♦
Converted bank; now an atmospheric pub-owned brasserie with beer on draught, close to tramstop 22. Traditional, international menu; try the tasty Czech dishes and the homemade sausages.

DENMARK

DANMARK

PROFILE

→ **Area:**
43 069 km² (16 629 sq mi) excluding the Faroe Islands and Greenland.

→ **Population:**
5 511 451 inhabitants (est. 2009), density = 127 per km².

→ **Capital:**
Copenhagen (conurbation 1 875 179 inhabitants).

→ **Currency:**
Danish Krone (DKK) divided into 100 øre; rate of exchange: DKK 1 = € 0.13 = US$ 0.18 (Dec. 2010).

→ **Government:**
Constitutional parliamentary (single chamber) monarchy (since 1849). Member of European Union since 1973.

→ **Languages:**
Danish; many Danes also understand and speak English.

→ **Specific public holidays:**
Maundy Thursday (the day before Good Friday); Good Friday (Friday before Easter); Prayer Day (4th Friday after Easter); Constitution Day (5 June); Boxing Day (26 December).

→ **Local Time:**
GMT + 1 hour in winter and GMT + 2 hours in summer.

→ **Climate:**
Temperate northern maritime with cold winters and mild summers (Copenhagen: January: 1°C, July: 18°C).

→ **International dialling Code:**
00 45 followed by full local number. Directory Enquiries: ✆ **118**.

→ **Emergency:**
Dial ✆ **112** for Police, Ambulance and Fire Brigade.

→ **Electricity:**
220 volts AC, 50Hz; 2-pin round-shaped continental plugs.

→ **Formalities**
Travellers from the European Union (EU), Switzerland, Norway, Iceland and the main countries of North and South

America need a national identity card or passport (America: passport required) to visit Denmark for less than three months (tourism or business purpose). For visitors from other countries a visa may be required, in addition to a passport, especially for those wishing to stay for longer than three months. If you plan to visit Greenland or Faroe Islands while in Denmark, you must purchase a visa in advance in your own country. We advise you to check with your embassy before travelling.

SA 93

COPENHAGEN
KØBENHAVN

Population: 514 000 (conurbation 1 875 179) Altitude: approx 13m above sea level

aPu99/Fotolia.com

You have to go right over to the far eastern coast of Denmark to find Copenhagen. It stares straight across the Öresund Straight at Sweden, as though anxious to leave its own shores. They've even built a bridge connecting it to Malmö on the other side. But once you've idled away some time in the Danish capital, you'll wonder why anyone might ever want to leave. This bright, sleek city has a nicely digestible, compact feel and is an easy place to discover on foot. It's a laid-back, hassle-free city generally free from threatening behaviour, and there are lots of elegant, smartly designed buildings to look at. The people fall pretty much into that category, too.

Though Denmark is one of the richest countries in the world, the citizens of Copenhagen are not given to brashness; if anything, they get embarrassed by what they call their provincialism, at being way out on the margins of Europe. But at the same time, they have an infectious enthusiasm for the arts and a world-renowned appreciation of design. Ingest this alongside a good cup of coffee, an open fire and sleek, cosy surroundings, and you'll be partaking of Danish hygge, a word much prized by locals loosely translated as 'warm conviviality'. To the list can now be added good food: fresh regional ingredients have revolutionized the menus of Copenhagen's hip restaurants.

LIVING THE CITY

Some cities overwhelm you, and give the impression that there's too much of them to take in. Not Copenhagen. Most of its key sights are neatly compressed within its central **Slotsholmen** 'island', an area that enjoyed its first golden age in the early seventeenth century in the reign of Christian IV, when it became a harbour of great consequence. It has canals on three sides and opposite the harbour is the area of **Christianshavn**, home of the legendary freewheeling 'free-town' community of Christiania. Further up from the centre are **Nyhavn**, the much-photographed canalside with brightly coloured buildings where the sightseeing cruises leave from, and the elegant **Frederiksstaden**, whose wide streets contain palaces and museums. West of centre is where Copenhageners love to hang out: the **Tivoli Gardens**, a kind of magical fairyland. Slightly more down-to-earth are the western suburbs of Vesterbro and Nørrebro, which were run-down areas given a street credible spit and polish for the 21st century, and are now two of the trendiest districts.

PRACTICAL INFORMATION

ARRIVAL-DEPARTURE

Copenhagen Airport is located in Kastrup, 9km southeast of the city. The new extension to the metro allows you to now travel to the centre in 15min. A taxi, meanwhile, will cost about Kr250-300 and take 25min.

TRANSPORT

If you wish to dart about the city by rail, the metro is a triumph of sleek, smooth, beautifully detailed efficiency which runs 24 hours a day.

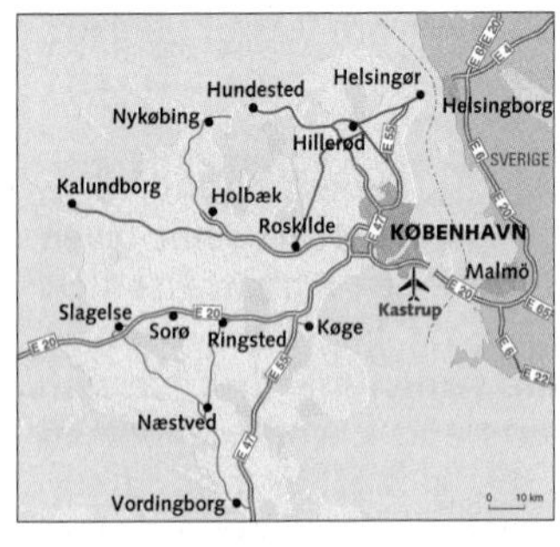

Want to see as much of Copenhagen as possible without continually digging into your pocket for cash? Get a Copenhagen Card, which gives free entry to all museums and galleries, as well as free bus, train and metro travel. Get one from the main tourist office just across the road from the central railway station.

It's not every day you're offered a free city bike ride but brightly painted bicycles, lined up in racks, are available for the deposit of a Dkr20 coin. The coin releases a cycle from a stand for an unlimited period and is retrieved when the cycle is returned to any of the 150 stands in the city. It takes about two hours to circumnavigate the major attractions.

It's possible to see the city... by kayak. Kajak Ole (that's Ole's Kayaks) can get you paddling round the central harbour area for a very different perspective. No previous experience is necessary, and it beats taking a crowded bus.

EXPLORING COPENHAGEN

The medieval centre of Copenhagen is a walker's paradise, compounded by the fact that the longest shopping street in Europe, **Strøget**, is these days pedestrianised. (It's actually a collective name for five streets running from east to west, in case you're looking for Strøget on a map). Some of the world's top retail names are squashed into its eastern end, while for half a mile further west run fountains, churches, squares and cafés (and a wealth of shops, of course). The cluster of grand brand names gives a clue to Copenhagen's love affair with design and style. Turn any corner in the central area and you'll find an elegant 17C building rubbing shoulders with a sleek example from the modern age.

The city's royal history stretches back for a millennium, and the rich architectural legacy is seen in its castles, museums and palaces. These merge so well with the new buildings around them that you might well think they were made for each other. The city presents a user-friendly modern ambience with its extensive waterfronts, quirky little shops and hundreds of cafés, but it also boasts world class art collections, museums, and impressive parks, gardens and lakes, all of which bear the mark of an earlier time. A design footprint of impeccable taste remains a pedestrian's constant companion. Even the airport has smart wooden floors and a clean, fresh charm about it.

→ DESIGNED TO PLEASE

The place to go to find out what's causing the latest aesthetic stir is the **Danish Design Centre** just south of Tivoli on the splendidly named Hans Christian Andersens Boulevard. It's a beautiful, five-storey, smoked-glass building opened in 2000 that houses temporary exhibitions and interactive installations. And it's right opposite one of Copenhagen's crown jewels, the nineteenth century **Ny Carlsberg Glyptotek**, which contains a superb art collection including world-renowned French Impressionist paintings housed in a graceful modern extension. To complete a stylish trio, all within the space of half a mile, head to the waterfront to take in the **Black Diamond**, a dramatic name for a radical building. Just over a decade old, it's the extension to the old Royal Library, and the clash of styles is breathtaking. So is the Black Diamond's reflective surface (made up of glass, silk concrete, sandstone, maple and granite) which changes colour moment by moment as it ripples against the water and sky.

The most recent of the modernist eye-catchers to turn heads is over the canal on Dock Island: the colossal **Opera House** was opened in 2005 and its knife-edge roof abuts the water, leaning across towards the rococo royal palaces on the other side (a fact that horrified some locals at the time). It's nine floors high, on a scale with the Met in New York, and is seen as a kind of gargantuan twin of The Black Diamond. Until recently, Copenhagen was an almost exclusively low-rise city, but these two big, bold intruders have certainly stirred up the cool, calm Danish waters.

→ TIVOLI OR NOT TIVOLI...

For a more traditional experience, it's hard to beat the **National Gallery** (in a lovely park setting in the northern area of Rosenborg), with its superb collection of Matisse paintings, or the National Museum in the heart of town. This imposing centerpiece is housed in a gorgeous one-time royal palace, and boasts some of the finest rooms in the city. It also lays claim to the most extensive collection of Danish artefacts in the world. Star turn must be the 3,500 year-old Sun Chariot unearthed by a Sjaelland farmer in 1902; it's exquisite to look at, still bearing some of its gold leaf. Walk a few blocks down from here and you come to that city icon so traditional that it would make even the Sun Chariot feel like a new cart on the block: the **Tivoli Gardens** seem to have been around forever (they actually opened in 1843) and, judging by admission figures, it seems the whole of Scandinavia has been taken for a ride here. There are roller-coasters, open air shows, troubadours, jugglers, orchestras, parades, ice-cream and beer stands. At night Tivoli turns into a fairyland with over 100,000 lights illuminating the sky as the Demon rollercoaster whirls through the air and fireworks crackle heavenwards. The whole smorgasbord of innocent delights might not be to everyone's taste, considering the refined air of the rest of Copenhagen, but in the end even the biggest cynic is usually won over by the relentlessly magical atmosphere. And if you really can't stand all the showground stuff, you can at least admire the lovely lake, gushing fountains and eye-catching flowerbeds.

→ THE ROYAL FAMILIARITY

It might seem strange to visitors that egalitarian Denmark stands fast behind a monarchy, but the Danes love their populist, chain-smoking Queen Margrethe II, and tourists love to visit where she lives, **Amalienborg Palace,** in the posh Frederiksstaden part of town. Its four palaces stand around a rather grand cobbled square, and when Margrethe is in, a flag flies from the roof. There's a rumour that if they sing loud enough from the new Opera House opposite, the production can be enjoyed from the royal apartments. At the diametrically opposite end of the tourist radar scan, but no less a tourist attraction, is the free state of **Christiania**, an eastern section of Christianshavn that until 1971 was a military camp. When it was abandoned, hundreds of hippies moved in and attracted hundreds more from around Denmark. Their concepts of recycling, solar and wind power have over time become mainstream, and the government has allowed the 'free state' to continue as a social experiment. With three quarters of a million tourists coming to visit a year, an odd 'human zoo' ambience can prevail.

These days, the edgier parts of town are to the west – **Vesterbro** and **Nørrebro.** They offer a couple of interesting alternatives to the city centre for those wanting a taste of how Copenhageners live. Vesterbro was a rough quarter sprawling from the Central station, but regeneration has given it a creative boost, with a younger, racially mixed population running bohemian cafés, trendy clothes emporiums and independent design shops. Nørrebro's deep, dark working-class streets were fashioned in the mid-19th century, and the 1970s and 80s saw a wave of Muslim immigrants come into the area. These days it's home to vinyl stores, junk shops, coffee dens and middle-class teenagers drawn by its ethnic appeal. Some of Copenhagen's trendier restaurants and bars can also be found in the old meat packing district.

COPENHAGEN IN...

→ ONE DAY

Walk along Strøget, visit The National Museum, Ny Carlsberg Glyptotek, Black Diamond on waterfront; sit at Nyhavn and watch the boats go by.

→ TWO DAYS

Spend most of the day in Tivoli Gardens; head on across to the trendy Vesterbro; take in the Opera House and Christiania

→ THREE DAYS

The royal palaces at Frederiksstaden; a train ride along the Danish coastline

CALENDAR HIGHLIGHTS

Spring and summer are the times to visit Copenhagen for its festivals (deepest winter is a time of hibernation in Denmark). You can get your bearings at the May Day Festival when brass bands and marchers descend on Faelled Park (in the shadow of the national stadium in Osterbro) for much food, drink and music. There's more beer to be consumed at the Copenhagen Beer Festival, also in May: you don't just have to put up with Carlsberg here but can enjoy the offerings from microbreweries too. Dance it all off at the Latin American Festival, in venues around the city centre in May, when rhythms from Cuba and Brazil typically include salsa, samba and tango. June kicks off with the Whitsun Carnival in Faelled Park, while lagers are to the fore again at the St Hans Eve Festival, in the same park and along the northern beaches near the city, as locals celebrate the longest day of the year. Northern Europe's largest music festival, a four-day rock jaunt at Roskilde, is a 25-minute train journey away from the capital in June, and jazz lovers can gorge themselves with 600 concerts as the Jazz Festival takes over the city in July. The more sophisticated Ballet Festival, featuring the Royal Danish Ballet, is in August, while pre-1971 Bentleys, Bugattis and Alfa Romeos make their own kind of music at the Copenhagen Historic Grand Prix in the same month ; which is later brought to a close by the Copenhagen Cooking Festival. Finally, if you go to see the Little Mermaid while you're in the city, try the 23 August – that was the date in 1913 she was placed in her location at the harbour, so they call it her birthday.

EATING OUT

Copenhagen's reputation for its food just keeps getting bigger and bigger. The city's dining establishments manage to marry Danish dining traditions such as herring or frikkadeller meatballs with global influences to impressive effect. So impressive that in recent times the city has earned itself more Michelin stars, for its crisp and precise cooking, than any other in Scandinavia. Top- and bottom-end restaurants and cafés – those most expensive and those most cheap - are pretty well catered for but the trick is to find one that fits the mid-range, so be warned: you could use up much energy trying to locate a smart restaurant with reasonable prices. Many good restaurants blend French methods and dishes with fresh regional ingredients and innovative touches and there is a trend towards fixed price, no choice menus involving several courses. Danes love their coffee and drink more of it per capita than anywhere else; you're guaranteed a good, strong cup all around the city. There's no need to tip, as it should be included in the cost of the meal. Danes, though, have a very good reputation as cheerful, helpful waiting staff, so you might feel like adding a bit extra. But be warned, many restaurants – and even hotels – charge between 2.5% and 5% for using a foreign credit card.

→ ROUND AND ROUND WE GO

You don't have to go to the top of Black Diamond or the Opera House to get a view over the city. The **Rundetårn** (Round Tower), just off Strøget, is Europe's oldest working observatory, and from the top of its long spiral staircase you get a fine vista of Copenhagen's low-rise symmetry.

→ FALLEN LADY

She may be a tourist attraction, but locals aren't that keen on The **Little Mermaid**. In her near century long residence along the Langelinie docks she's been painted red, had her head hacked off and arm lopped off – and then, in 2003, she was actually bombed into the water! Are residents trying to tell us something?

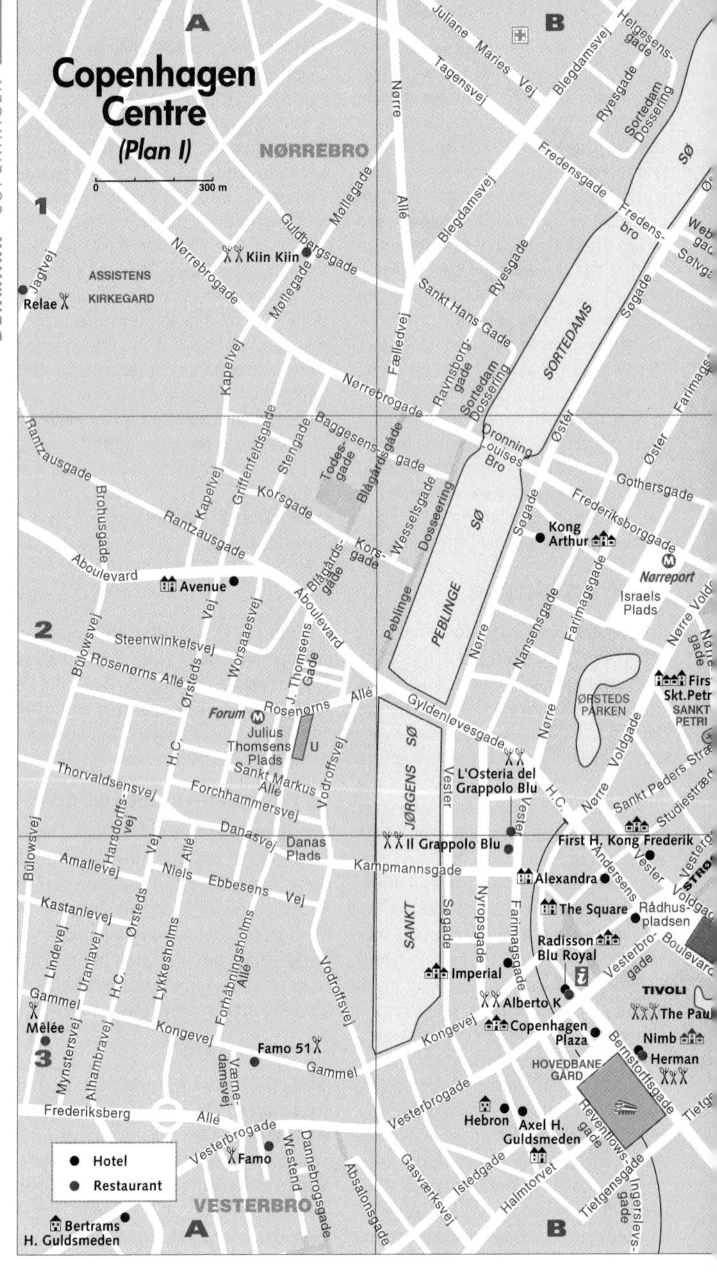
Copenhagen Centre
(Plan I)
0
300 m
A
B
1
2
3
NØRREBRO
VESTERBRO
ASSISTENS
KIRKEGARD
Relae
Kiin Kiin
Avenue
Forum
Julius Thomsens Plads
Kong Arthur
Nørreport
Israels Plads
ØRSTEDS PARKEN
L'Osteria del Grappolo Blu
Il Grappolo Blu
First H. Kong Frederik
Alexandra
The Square
Rådhus-pladsen
Radisson Blu Royal
Imperial
Alberto K
Copenhagen Plaza
TIVOLI
The Paul
Nimb
Herman
HOVEDBANE GÅRD
Hebron
Axel H. Guldsmeden
Mêlée
Famo 51
Famo
Bertrams H. Guldsmeden
Hotel
Restaurant
PEBLINGE SØ
SORTEDAMS SØ
SANKT JØRGENS SØ
Nørrebrogade
Jagtvej
Guldbergsgade
Møllegade
Nørre Allé
Tagensvej
Juliane Maries Vej
Blegdamsvej
Fredensgade
Fredens-bro
Ryesgade
Sankt Hans Gade
Fælledvej
Kapelvej
Rantzausgade
Baggesensgade
Blågårdsgade
Korsgade
Stengade
Griffenfeldsgade
Todesgade
Wesselsgade
Peblinge Dosseringen
Sortedam Dosseringen
Dronning Louises Bro
Øster Søgade
Gothersgade
Frederiksborggade
Farimagsgade
Nansensgade
Åboulevard
Brohusgade
Steenwinkelsvej
Rosenørns Allé
Bülowsvej
Ørsteds Vej
Worsaaesvej
J. Thomsens Gade
Vodroffsvej
Gyldenløvesgade
H.C. Ørsteds Vej
Thorvaldsensvej
Forchhammersvej
Sankt Markus Allé
Danasvej
Danas Plads
Kampmannsgade
Vester Søgade
Nyropsgade
Vester Farimagsgade
H.C. Andersens Boulevard
Vester Voldgade
Nørre Voldgade
Sankt Peders Stræde
Studiestræde
Amalievej
Niels Ebbesens Vej
Harsdorffsvej
Kastanievej
Lindevej
Uraniavej
Lykkesholms Allé
Forhåbningsholms Allé
Gammel Kongevej
Mynstersvej
Alhambravej
Værnedamsvej
Frederiksberg Allé
Vesterbrogade
Westend
Dannebrogsgade
Absalonsgade
Gasværksvej
Istedgade
Halmtorvet
Reventlowsgade
Bernstorffsgade
Tietgensgade
Ingerslevsgade
Helgesensgade
Sortedam Dosseringen
Webersgade
Sølvgade
Søgade

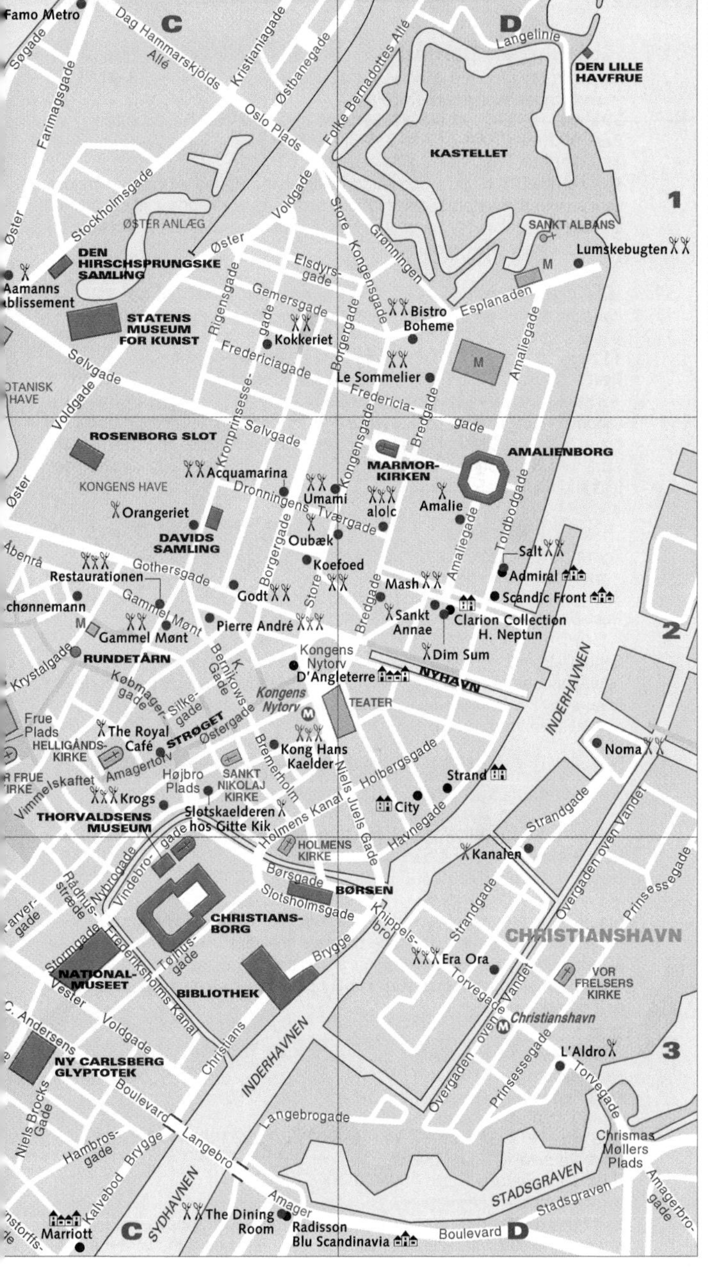
C
D
1
2
3
Famo Metro
Dag Hammarskjölds Allé
Kristianiagade
Østbanegade
Folke Bernadottes Allé
Langelinie
DEN LILLE HAVFRUE
Søgade
Farimagsgade
Oslo Plads
KASTELLET
Stockholmsgade
ØSTER ANLÆG
Voldgade
Store Kongensgade
Grønningen
SANKT ALBANS
Lumskebugten
Øster
DEN HIRSCHSPRUNGSKE SAMLING
Øster
Elsdyrsgade
M
Aamanns Etablissement
Gemersgade
Esplanaden
Bistro Boheme
STATENS MUSEUM FOR KUNST
Rigensgade
Kokkeriet
Borgergade
Amaliegade
Fredericiagade
Le Sommelier
M
Sølvgade
BOTANISK HAVE
Voldgade
Kronprinsessegade
Fredericiagade
Bredgade
ROSENBORG SLOT
Sølvgade
Kongensgade
AMALIENBORG
MARMORKIRKEN
Acquamarina
KONGENS HAVE
Dronningens Tværgade
Umami
a|o|c
Amalie
Orangeriet
Toldbodgade
Øster
DAVIDS SAMLING
Oubæk
Salt
Åbenrå
Gothersgade
Koefoed
Admiral
Restaurationen
Store
Mash
Scandic Front
Schønnemann
Godt
Bredgade
Sankt Annae
Clarion Collection H. Neptun
Gammel Mønt
M
Gammel Mønt
Pierre André
Dim Sum
Krystalgade
RUNDETÅRN
Bernikows Gade
Kongens Nytorv
D'Angleterre
NYHAVN
INDERHAVNEN
Købmagergade
Silkegade
Kongens Nytorv
TEATER
Frue Plads
Kirkegade
The Royal Café
STRØGET
Østergade
HELLIGÅNDSKIRKE
Noma
Kong Hans Kaelder
Amagertorv
Bremerholm
Holbergsgade
VOR FRUE KIRKE
Vimmelskaftet
Højbro Plads
SANKT NIKOLAJ KIRKE
Strand
Krogs
Niels Juels Gade
City
THORVALDSENS MUSEUM
Slotskaelderen hos Gitte Kik
Holmens Kanal
Strandgade
Havnegade
Overgaden oven Vandet
Vindebrogade
HOLMENS KIRKE
Kanalen
Nybrogade
Børsgade
BØRSEN
Prinsessegade
Rådhusstræde
Slotsholmsgade
Knippelsbro
Farvergade
CHRISTIANSBORG
CHRISTIANSHAVN
Strandgade
Stormgade
Frederiksholms Kanal
Tøjhusgade
Brygge
Era Ora
NATIONALMUSEET
Torvegade
VOR FRELSERS KIRKE
Vester
BIBLIOTHEK
Christianshavn
H.C. Andersens
Voldgade
Christians
INDERHAVNEN
Overgaden oven Vandet
Prinsessegade
L'Aldro
Torvegade
NY CARLSBERG GLYPTOTEK
Boulevard
Niels Brocks Gade
Langebrogade
Hambrosgade
Brygge
Langebro
Christmas Møllers Plads
Kalvebod
STADSGRAVEN
Stadsgraven
Amagerbrogade
SYDHAVNEN
Amager
The Dining Room
Radisson Blu Scandinavia
Boulevard
Marriott
Tietgensgade

Copenhagen Marriott

Kalvebod Brygge 5 ✉ 1560 V – ✆ 88 33 99 00 – www.copenhagenmarriott.com **C3**

391 rm – ♦999/2999 DKK ♦♦999/2999 DKK, ☕ 215 DKK – 10 suites

Rest *Midtown Grill* – Carte 335/580 DKK

♦ Luxury ♦ Business ♦ Modern ♦

Striking hotel with large, open-fired lounge-bar and floor-to-ceiling windows overlooking the water. Bright, spacious bedrooms are handsomely appointed and afford canal or city views. American grill offers steaks, chops and seafood, and has a lively open kitchen.

D'Angleterre

Kongens Nytorv 34 ✉ 1050 K – Ⓜ Kongens Nytorv – ✆ 33 12 00 95 – www.dangleterre.dk **C2**

117 rm ☕ – ♦1430/6030 DKK ♦♦1930/6030 DKK – 6 suites

Rest – Menu 365/385 DKK – Carte 575/945 DKK

♦ Traditional ♦ Historic ♦ Classic ♦

Landmark hotel dating back over 250 years, boasting an elegant lobby and grand ballroom. Classical bedrooms come in various shapes and sizes; pay the extra for a Royal Square view or stylish suite. Light lunches, popular afternoon teas and traditional dinners.

First H. Skt. Petri

Krystalgade 22 ✉ 1172 K – Ⓜ Nørreport – ✆ 33 45 91 00 – www.firsthotels.com **B2**

257 rm – ♦1195/3695 DKK ♦♦1195/3695 DKK, ☕ 195 DKK – 11 suites

Rest *Brasserie Petri* – Carte 280/405 DKK

♦ Business ♦ Modern ♦

Centrally located former department store, close to St Peter's Church. Spacious open-plan atrium with large, lively bar. White bedrooms boast stylish design features by Per Arnoldi. Huge brasserie dining room with courtyard terrace; concise Mediterranean menu.

Nimb

Bernstorffsgade 5 ✉ 1577 V – Ⓜ København Hovedbane Gård – ✆ 88 70 00 00 – www.nimb.dk **B3**

13 rm ☕ – ♦2000/2500 DKK ♦♦3500/6500 DKK

Rest *Herman* – see below

Rest *Brasserie* – Menu 400 DKK – Carte 375/550 DKK

♦ Luxury ♦ Design ♦

Moorish-style, former private residence built in 1909, situated beside Tivoli Gardens. Baronial lounge with stone fireplace; pleasant bar in former ballroom. Sympathetically designed bedrooms are well-equipped. Wine bar boasts over 1,700 bottles. Informal brasserie, with 3 open kitchens, offers a popular weekend brunch.

Radisson Blu Royal

Hammerichsgade 1 ✉ 1611 V – Ⓜ København Hovedbane Gård – ✆ 33 42 60 00 – www.radissonblu.com **B3**

258 rm – ♦1395/2095 DKK ♦♦1495/2095 DKK, ☕ 195 DKK – 2 suites

Rest *Alberto K* – see below

Rest *Café Royal* – Carte 400/420 DKK

♦ Business ♦ Design ♦

Vast hotel designed by Arne Jacobson. Large lobby with shops; extensive conference and fitness facilities. Scandinavian-style bedrooms: the largest are the double-aspect corner rooms; 606 has its original décor. Informal restaurant boasts floor-to-ceiling windows.

Radisson Blu Scandinavia

Amager Boulevard 70 ✉ 2300 S – Ⓜ Island Brygge
– ✆ 33 96 50 00 – www.radissonblu.com/scandinaviahotel-copenhagen
538 rm – 795/1795 DKK 895/1795 DKK, ☕ 175 DKK **C3**
– 24 suites
Rest *The Dining Room* – see below
Rest *Blue Elephant* – *✆ 33 96 59 70 (closed Christmas-New Year and Sunday) (dinner only)* Carte 310/495 DKK
Rest *Kyoto* – *✆ 33 32 16 74 (dinner only)* Menu 310/550 DKK – Carte 270/460 DKK

♦ Business ♦ Personalised ♦

Modern tower block with busy bar, shops and casino. Fitness and conference rooms on first floor. Six different themes to bedrooms, including 'Oriental' and 'High-Tech'; all have great views. Exotic décor in appealing Thai restaurant. Wide-ranging Japanese menu in Kyoto.

Tivoli

Arni Magnussons Gade 2-4 (via Kalvebod Brygge C 3) ✉ 1577 V
– ✆ 44 87 00 00 – www.tivolihotel.dk
388 rm – 1770/2070 DKK 1770/2070 DKK, ☕ 150 DKK – 8 suites
Rest *Tivoli Brasserie* – Carte 280/460 DKK
Rest *Sticks 'n' Sushi* – *✆ 88 32 95 95* – Carte 200/500 DKK

♦ Family ♦ Business ♦ Modern ♦

Contemporary tower block beside a huge congress centre. Basement leisure facilities and kids' play room; colourful bedrooms with boldly patterned fabrics. Spacious brasserie offers international menu. Trendy, top floor sushi restaurant and bar boast great views.

Copenhagen Plaza

Bernstorffsgade 4 ✉ 1577 V – Ⓜ København Hovedbane Gård
– ✆ 33 14 92 62 – www.profilhotels.dk **B3**
91 rm – 1595/2395 DKK 1795/2395 DKK, ☕ 145 DKK – 2 suites
Rest – *(dinner only)* Carte 285/375 DKK

♦ Traditional ♦ Retro ♦

Located next to the railway station and Tivoli Gardens, an early 20C hotel commissioned by King Frederik VIII. Mix of charmingly old-fashioned bedrooms and more contemporary ones; some are being refurbished. Lovely library bar and welcoming, modern restaurant.

Island

Kalvebod Brygge 53 (via Kalvebod Brygge C 3) ✉ 1560 V – ✆ 33 38 96 00
– www.copenhagenisland.dk
325 rm – 935/2055 DKK 1135/2055 DKK, ☕ 150 DKK
Rest *The Harbour* – Menu 245/295 DKK

♦ Business ♦ Modern ♦

Contemporary glass and steel hotel, set outside the city, on a man-made island in the harbour. Well-equipped bedrooms, some with balconies; choose water over a city view. Allergy friendly rooms available. Multi-level lounge bar and restaurant. Wide-ranging menu.

Admiral

Toldbodgade 24-28 ✉ 1253 K – Ⓜ Kongens Nytorv – ✆ 33 74 14 14
– www.admiralhotel.dk **D2**
314 rm – 1195/1890 DKK 1490/1890 DKK, ☕ 135 DKK – 52 suites
Rest *Salt* – see below

♦ Business ♦ Modern ♦

Impressive 1787 former grain-drying warehouse. Extensive conference facilities. Maritime theme runs throughout. Bedrooms boast vintage beams, bespoke wood furniture and harbour or city views.

Kong Arthur without rest

Nørre Søgade 11 1370 K – Nørreport – 33 11 12 12 – www.kongarthur.dk **B2**

155 rm – †980/1590 DKK ††1080/5000 DKK, 145 DKK

♦ Business ♦ Classic ♦

Four 1881 buildings set around a courtyard, in elegant residential avenue close to Peblinge Lake. Vaulted breakfast room. Well-equipped bedrooms vary in size; courtyard rooms are quietest.

First H. Kong Frederik

rm,

Vester Voldgade 25 1552 V – Vesterport – 33 12 59 02 – www.firsthotels.dk **D2**

109 rm – †995/2390 DKK ††995/2390 DKK, 135 DKK – 1 suite

Rest *Public House* – *70 26 23 20* – Carte 250/280 DKK

♦ Townhouse ♦ Personalised ♦

One hundred year old townhouse in the very centre of the city, 5min from Tivoli Park. Intimate lobby in dark hues; cosy bedrooms with colourful feature walls, set around a glass-roofed courtyard. Contemporary gastropub-style dining room offers a concise menu.

Scandic Front

rm, rm,

Sankt Annae Plads 21 1250 K – Kongens Nytorv – 33 13 34 00 – www.scandichotels.com **D2**

129 rm – †920/2390 DKK ††1120/2590 DKK – 3 suites

Rest *Scandic Front* – Menu 275 DKK – Carte 218/380 DKK

♦ Business ♦ Modern ♦

Contemporary harbourside hotel with pleasant lobby-lounge, airy function rooms and well-equipped fitness area. White-walled bedrooms boast design furniture; some are duplex or have balconies and harbour views. Modern dining room serves salads, tapas and grills.

Imperial

Vester Farimagsgade 9 1606 V – Vesterport – 33 12 80 00 – www.imperialhotel.dk **B3**

266 rm – †1865 DKK ††2195/3515 DKK, 150 DKK – 1 suite

Rest – *(closed dinner 24 December)* Carte 435/575 DKK

♦ Business ♦ Modern ♦

Spacious, mid-20C hotel set on a wide city thoroughfare. Mix of bedroom styles: older rooms are functional and well-equipped; ask for the newer rooms, which have a more appealing, contemporary style. Informal restaurant offers concise menu of international dishes.

The Square without rest

Rådhuspladsen 14 1550 V – København Hovedbane Gård – 33 38 12 00 – www.thesquarecopenhagen.com **B3**

267 rm – †900/2085 DKK ††1085/4095 DKK, 110 DKK

♦ Business ♦ Modern ♦

Set on the Town Hall Square, close to the station and Tivoli Gardens. Modern lobby. Fairly compact bedrooms with 'square' theme in décor; a few have balconies. Bright 6th floor breakfast room.

Avenue without rest

Åboulevard 29 1960 C – Forum – 35 37 31 11 – www.avenuehotel.dk – Closed 22 December-3 January **A2**

68 rm – †950/1350 DKK ††1050/1650 DKK

♦ Business ♦ Modern ♦

Set within a building dating back to 1899, not far from the metro station. Pleasant lounge, relaxing bar and nice courtyard patio. Comfortable, well-maintained bedrooms with bright, crisp style.

Axel H. Guldsmeden

Helgolandsgade 11 ✉ 1653 K – Ⓜ København Hovedbane Gård – ✆ 33 31 32 66 – www.hotelguldsmeden.com **B3**

129 rm – 1495/1995 DKK 1995 DKK, ☕ 125 DKK

Rest – Menu 295 DKK

♦ Business ♦ Oriental ♦

Stylish hotel with charming courtyard and uniquely styled inner. Exotic bedrooms boast furniture from Indonesia and other Asian knick-knacks: most have four-posters; some have small balconies. Relaxation area in basement. Restaurant offers original, organic tapas.

Alexandra without rest

H.C. Andersens Boulevard 8 ✉ 1553 V – Ⓜ København Hovedbane Gård – ✆ 33 74 44 44 – www.hotel-alexandra.dk – Closed 24-27 December **B3**

61 rm – 1445/1845 DKK 1745/2145 DKK, ☕ 99 DKK

♦ Traditional ♦ Personalised ♦

Traditional city centre hotel boasting an entire 'allergy friendly' floor. Uniquely styled bedrooms come in a range of styles; the 13 'Design' rooms are decorated by famous Danish designers.

Clarion Collection H. Neptun without rest

Sankt Annae Plads 18-20 ✉ 1250 K – Ⓜ Kongens Nytorv – ✆ 33 96 20 00 – www.choicehotels.dk **D2**

133 rm ☕ – 740/1590 DKK 990/1990 DKK – 15 suites

♦ Business ♦ Functional ♦

Adjoining 1854 houses in a residential area of bustling Nyhavn. Bedrooms vary in size from tiny singles to large doubles, and boast classical Gustavian-style furniture. Courtyard breakfasts.

City without rest

Peder Skrams Gade 24 ✉ 1054 K – Ⓜ Kongens Nytorv – ✆ 33 13 06 66 – www.hotelcity.dk **D2**

81 rm ☕ – 1050/1400 DKK 1195/1700 DKK

♦ Business ♦ Functional ♦

Modern hotel in quiet street between the city and the docks. Designer furniture, including Jacobsen armchairs, features throughout. Bedrooms boast monochrome Jan Persson jazz photos. Cosy bar.

Strand without rest

Havnegade 37 ✉ 1058 K – Ⓜ Kongens Nytorv – ✆ 33 48 99 00 – www.copenhagenstrand.dk – Closed 21-29 December **D2**

172 rm – 1620/1960 DKK 1960 DKK, ☕ 110 DKK – 2 suites

♦ Business ♦ Functional ♦

Centrally located hotel in a 19C former paper factory on the harbourside. Comfortable, functional bedrooms in light maritime colours with polished wood furnishings. Large basement lobby-lounge.

Bertrams H. Guldsmeden without rest

Vesterbrogade 107 ✉ 1620 V – ✆ 70 20 81 07 – www.bertramshotel.com **A3**

46 rm – 1015/1495 DKK 1271/1795 DKK, ☕ 130 DKK

♦ Townhouse ♦ Personalised ♦

Younger sister to Axel H. Guldsmeden, with similarly styled Indonesian interior. Largest, most peaceful bedrooms overlook the courtyard; some boast four-posters or balconies. Good breakfasts.

Hebron without rest

Helgolandsgade 4 ✉ 1653 V – Ⓜ København Hovedbane Gård – ✆ 33 31 69 06 – www.hebron.dk – Closed 23 December-2 January **B3**

93 rm – †855/1255 DKK ††1155/1355 DKK – 6 suites

◆ Traditional ◆ Functional ◆

This was one of the city's biggest hotels when it opened in 1899 and some original features still remain. Set close to the shops and gardens, it's simple, functional and ideal for short stays.

Geranium

Per Henrik Lings Allé 4 (8th Fl), Parken National Stadium (via Dag Hammaraskjölds Allé C 1) ✉ 2100 Ø – ✆ 69 96 00 20 – www.geranium.dk – Closed 3 weeks July, Christmas-New Year and Sunday-Tuesday

Rest – *(booking essential) (dinner only) (set menu only)* Menu 998 DKK

◆ Innovative ◆ Design ◆ Elegant ◆

Spacious, modern restaurant and elegant lounge-bar on the 8th floor of the Parken National Stadium. Views into the impressive-looking kitchen and over the treetops. Interesting, innovative set menus; skilled cooking relies on local, organic and biodynamic produce.

Kong Hans Kaelder

Vingårdsstraede 6 ✉ 1070 K – Ⓜ Kongens Nytorv – ✆ 33 11 68 68 – www.konghans.dk – Closed mid July-mid August, first 2 weeks January, Sunday and bank holidays

Rest – *(booking essential) (dinner only)* Menu 1100 DKK – Carte 870/1340 DKK **C2**

Spec. 'Late Summer by the Lake' with crayfish and sweet 'n' sour rose hip. Roasted turbot with braised fennel and fennel pollen sauce. Blackberries with molasses and junket ice cream.

◆ Danish ◆ Elegant ◆

Well-established and enthusiastically run restaurant, in a vaulted Gothic cellar. Cooking is classically grounded with a modern edge; choice of concise à la carte or 9 course Innovation Menu. Well-kept Danish cheeses come with their own individual accompaniments.

Mielcke & Hurtigkarl

Runddel 1 (via Frederiksberg Allé A 3) ✉ 2000 C – ✆ 38 34 84 36 – www.mhcph.com – Closed 18 December-10 January, Tuesday-Wednesday in winter, Sunday and Monday

Rest – *(booking essential) (dinner only and lunch April-September)* Menu 435/850 DKK

◆ Innovative ◆ Elegant ◆

1744 orangery with lovely summer terrace, set in Frederiksberg Gardens. Charming inner boasts walls painted with garden scenes and backing tracks of birdsong. Confident chef follows the seasons closely – ambitious, innovative dishes often display several elements.

formel B (Kristian Møller)

Vesterbrogade 182-184, Frederiksberg (via Vesterbrogade A 3) ✉ 1800 C – ✆ 33 25 10 66 – www.formel-b.dk – Closed 11-31 July, 23-26 December and Sunday

Rest – *(booking essential) (dinner only) (set menu only)* Menu 500/900 DKK

Spec. Langoustine with carrots and nage sauce. Breast of pigeon with morels and celeriac. Chocolate dessert.

◆ Innovative ◆ Elegant ◆

Modern restaurant with sleek, split-level inner of polished marble and stainless steel; sit by the window or above the glass-ceilinged wine cellar. Well-balanced set menu of skilfully prepared modern dishes. Confident young team and knowledgeable sommelier.

XXX ✿

Herman – at Nimb Hotel

Bernstorffsgade 5 ✉ 1577 V – Ⓜ København Hovedbane Gård – ✆ 88 70 00 20 – www.nimb.dk – Closed 23-26 December, 31 December-17 January, Saturday lunch and Sunday **B3**

Rest – *(booking advisable) (set menu only)* Menu 475/900 DKK

Spec. Seared foie gras with cherries and meringues. Veal with wild mushrooms and pickled gherkins. 'Sweet memories' in two servings.

♦ Modern Danish ♦ Formal ♦

Split-level hotel restaurant, affording views over Tivoli Gardens from its floor-to-ceiling windows and drinks terrace. Danish dishes rely on seasonal ingredients and feature lots of sweet and sour combinations. 4 to 6 courses served at dinner. Formal service.

XXX ✿

a|o|c

Dronningens Tvaergade 2 ✉ 1302 K – Ⓜ Kongens Nytorv – ✆ 33 11 11 45 – www.restaurantaoc.dk – Closed 23-30 December, 1-4 January, July, Sunday, Monday and bank holidays **D2**

Rest – *(dinner only) (set menu only)* Menu 595/1105 DKK

Spec. Gravadmax in hay ash with green tomatoes and dill. Tenderloin of beef with beetroot, parsley and smoked marrow. Buttermilk 'iceberg', white chocolate and hazelnuts.

♦ Modern Danish ♦

Large 17C vaulted cellar restaurant, owned and run by an experienced sommelier. 4, 5, 6 and 7 course set menus provide the full sensory experience, featuring well-presented, very innovative combinations. Dishes are flavoursome and arrive with a touch of theatre.

XXX ✿

Era Ora

Overgaden neden Vandet 33B ✉ 1414 K – Ⓜ Christianshavn – ✆ 32 54 06 93 – www.era-ora.dk – Closed Easter Monday, 23-27 December and Sunday **D3**

Rest – *(booking essential)* Menu 375/880 DKK

Spec. Scallop with pumpkin. Veal tongue with grapefruit and fennel. White chocolate with grape sorbet.

♦ Italian ♦ Elegant ♦

Old warehouse dating back to the 1600s, set in a lovely canalside location. Modern inner of glass and beaten copper. Well-stocked cellar features Tuscan and Piedmont wines. Weekly set menu offers imported Italian produce in well-executed dishes with personality.

XXX

Restaurationen

Møntergade 19 ✉ 1116 K – Ⓜ Kongens Nytorv – ✆ 33 14 94 95 – www.restaurationen.com – Closed Easter, July, August, 20 December-5 January, Sunday and Monday

Rest – *(booking essential) (dinner only and lunch 15 November-20 December) (set menu only)* Menu 785 DKK **C2**

♦ Classic ♦ Formal ♦ Romantic ♦

Long-standing restaurant run by a well-known chef, who also owns the next door wine bar. Romantically lit dining room. Accomplished, classically based cooking displays French influences.

XXX

Krogs

Gammel Strand 38 ✉ 1202 K – Ⓜ Kongens Nytorv – ✆ 33 15 89 15 – www.krogs.dk – Closed 22 December-3 January and Sunday **C2**

Rest – *(booking essential) (dinner only)* Menu 785 DKK – Carte 690/1185 DKK

♦ Seafood ♦ Formal ♦

Characterful 18C house beside the canal, with classical, high-ceilinged dining room. Traditional seafood à la carte mixes French and Danish touches; tasting menu offers more creative dishes.

XXX

Pierre André

Ny Østergade 21 ✉ 1101 K – Ⓜ Kongens Nytorv – ☎ 33 16 17 19 – www.pierreandre.dk
– Closed Easter, 3 weeks July-August, 23-26 December, 1 January, Sunday, Monday and bank holidays **C2**

Rest – *(booking essential) (dinner only)* Menu 395 DKK – Carte 365/520 DKK

♦ French ♦ Formal ♦

Smart French restaurant with formal, classical styling and intimate atmosphere, set in an attractive old building. Classical menus feature tasty Gallic cooking; lighter dishes offered at lunch.

XX
✿✿

Noma (Rene Redzepi)

Strandgade 93 ✉ 1401 K – Ⓜ Christianshavn – ☎ 32 96 32 97 – www.noma.dk
– Closed 2 weeks July, first week August, 23 December-5 January, Sunday and Monday **D2**

Rest – *(booking essential) (set menu only)* Menu 1095/1395 DKK

Spec. Tartar with wood sorrel and crushed juniper. Beef cheek with pickled apple and chickweed. Porridge of rye bread, skyr and whipped cream.

♦ Innovative ♦ Design ♦

Stylish restaurant in converted harbourside warehouse, with just 12 tables but over 65 staff. Highly skilled kitchen uses quality Nordic ingredients to create unique, innovative dishes that stimulate the senses and test culinary boundaries. Professional yet friendly service.

XX
✿

Kiin Kiin (Lertchai Treetawatchaiwong)

Guldbergsgade 21 ✉ 2200 N – ☎ 35 35 75 55 – www.kiin.dk
– Closed Christmas and Sunday **A1**

Rest – *(booking essential) (dinner only) (set menu only)* Menu 775 DKK

Spec. Frozen red coconut currry with baby lobster and lychee. Guinea fowl with green plum sauce. Earl Grey ice cream with jasmine foam and crispy white chocolate.

♦ Thai ♦ Exotic ♦

Charming restaurant whose name means 'come and eat'. Comfortable lounge for canapés. Tasteful dining room with gold masks and fresh flowers. Set menu of modern, personal interpretations of Thai dishes in some unusual flavour combinations. Excellent service.

XX
✿

Kokkeriet (Lasse Askov)

Kronprinsessegade 64 ✉ 1306 K – ☎ 33 15 27 77 – www.kokkeriet.dk
– Closed 24-26 December, Sunday and Monday **C1**

Rest – *(dinner only) (set menu only)* Menu 500/700 DKK

Spec. Salted mullet with cabbage in white sauce and crispy skin. Chicken and lobster with giblets, bacon and forest mushrooms. Elderberry soup with liquorice and chocolate.

♦ Modern ♦ Intimate ♦

Small neighbourhood restaurant in cosy, narrow room, with attentive service and lively atmosphere. Cooking displays a modern Danish base, with well-balanced, clearly defined flavours and contemporary presentation. 3 to 7 course menus come with wines to match.

XX

Umami

Store Kongensgade 59 ✉ 1264 K – Ⓜ Kongens Nytorv – ☎ 33 38 75 00 – www.restaurantumami.dk
– Closed 23 December-3 January and Sunday **C/D2**

Rest – *(dinner only)* Menu 575/850 DKK – Carte 395/720 DKK

♦ Euro-asiatic ♦ Fashionable ♦

Attractive, modern building with large cocktail bar and lounge on the ground floor. Elegant upper level boasts a stylish dining room and sushi counter. Japanese dishes have a European slant.

XX

Salt – at Admiral Hotel

Toldbodgade 24-28 ✉ 1253 K – Ⓜ Kongens Nytorv – ☎ 33 74 14 44 – www.salt.dk **D2**

Rest – Menu 375 DKK – Carte 355/540 DKK

♦ Modern ♦ Design ♦

Trendy hotel restaurant with terrace, inspired by a French brasserie. Old wood beams and colourful, contemporary furniture blend together nicely. European cooking displays Scandinavian touches.

XX

Le Sommelier

Bredgade 63-65 ✉ 1260 K – ☎ 33 11 45 15 – www.lesommelier.dk – Closed 22 December-3 January, Saturday and Sunday **D1**

Rest – Menu 270/395 DKK – Carte 365/475 DKK

♦ French ♦ Brasserie ♦

Attractive French brasserie in the heart of the Old Town. Traditional main room and 3 private rooms boast simple wooden furniture and wine posters. Carefully prepared, daily set menu uses quality ingredients and offers classic French dishes. Excellent wine list.

XX

Koefoed

Landgreven 3 (basement) ✉ 1301 K – Ⓜ Kongens Nytorv – ☎ 56 48 22 24 – www.restaurant-koefoed.dk – Closed 23 December-5 January and Sunday **C2**

Rest – *(booking essential at dinner)* Menu 375 DKK (dinner) – Carte 375/515 DKK

♦ Modern Danish ♦ Intimate ♦

Intimate restaurant where everything from the produce to the glassware celebrates the island of Bornholm. Set menu and upscale smørrebrød at lunch; concise à la carte and tasting menu at dinner.

XX

Gammel Mønt

Gammel Mønt 41 ✉ 1117 K – Ⓜ Kongens Nytorv – ☎ 33 15 10 60 – www.gammel-moent.dk – Closed 23 June-15 August, Christmas, Saturday, Sunday and bank holidays

Rest – *(lunch only)* Menu 395 DKK – Carte 385/635 DKK **C2**

♦ Traditional ♦ Cosy ♦

18C house with striking red façade. Simple basement room with communal tables; elegant, linen-laid restaurant above. Authentic, generous, seasonal cooking. Tasty herring and home-aged beef.

XX

The Dining Room – at Radisson Blu Scandinavia Hotel

Amager Boulevard 70, (25th Fl) ✉ 2300 S – Ⓜ Island Brygge – ☎ 33 96 58 58 – www.thediningroom.dk – Closed Sunday, Monday and bank holidays **C3**

Rest – *(dinner only)* Carte 325/455 DKK

♦ Modern ♦ Romantic ♦

Independently run hotel restaurant on the 25th floor of the Radisson Blu Scandinavia. Long, modern room boasts delightful city and sea views. Concise but appealing contemporary Danish menu.

XX

Lumskebugten

Esplanaden 21 ✉ 1263 K – ☎ 33 15 60 29 – www.lumskebugten.dk – Closed Easter, July, Christmas-New Year, Sunday and bank holidays

Rest – *(lunch only)* Menu 248/388 DKK – Carte 200/320 DKK **D1**

♦ Traditional ♦ Cosy ♦ Retro ♦

19C quayside pavilion, where the Royal Family occasionally dine. Several small rooms adorned with maritime memorabilia and paintings. Local menus offer wide selection of classical fish dishes.

XX **Il Grappolo Blu**

Vester Farimagsgade 35 ✉ 1606 V – Ⓜ Vesterport – ☎ 33 11 57 20 – www.ilgrappoloblu.com
– Closed Easter, July, Christmas-New Year, Sunday and Monday lunch
Rest – *(booking essential) (set menu only)* Menu 350/750 DKK **B3**

♦ Italian ♦ Rustic ♦ Elegant ♦

Cosy, personally run restaurant displaying rustic wood panelling and ornate carving. Set menu offers well-prepared, authentic Italian antipasti and tasty pastas. Booking essential for lunch.

XX **Alberto K** – at Radisson Blu Royal Hotel

Hammerichsgade 1 ✉ 1611 V – Ⓜ København Hovedbane Gård – ☎ 33 42 61 61 – www.alberto-k.dk
– Closed Sunday **B3**
Rest – *(dinner only) (set menu only)* Menu 775 DKK

♦ Modern ♦ Design ♦

Located on the 20th floor of the Radisson Blu Royal hotel and boasting stunning panoramic views over the city. 1960s inspired Danish design interior. Contemporary European set dinner menu.

XX **Godt**

Gothersgade 38 ✉ 1123 K – Ⓜ Kongens Nytorv – ☎ 33 15 21 22 – www.restaurant-godt.dk
– Closed 15-19 February, 19-23 April, 5 July-6 August, 18-22 October, Christmas-New Year, Sunday, Monday and bank holidays. **C2**
Rest – *(dinner only) (set menu only)* Menu 500/660 DKK

♦ Classic ♦ Friendly ♦

Stylish restaurant seating just 20, with old WWII shells acting as unique candle holders. Traditional French and European 4 and 5 course daily menus, formed around the latest market produce.

XX **Bistro Boheme**

Esplanaden 8 ✉ 1263 K – ☎ 33 93 98 44 – www.bistroboheme.dk
– Closed 24-26 December and Sunday **D1**
Rest – Carte 388/538 DKK

♦ Classic ♦ Bistro ♦

Former florist and gallery near the Old Town. Airy, split-level interior with buzzy atmosphere. Unfussy, classical French menus display Danish overtones. Good choice of wines by the glass.

XX **Frederiks Have**

Smallegade 41, (entrance on Virginiavej) (West : 1.5 km. via Gammel Kongevej A 3) ✉ 2000 F – Ⓜ Frederiksberg – ☎ 38 88 33 35 – www.frederikshave.dk
– Closed 17-25 April, 22 December-5 January and Sunday
Rest – Menu 250/385 DKK – Carte 410/510 DKK

♦ Danish ♦ Neighbourhood ♦

Sweet neighbourhood restaurant with large terrace, set just off the main street in a residential area. Choice of set price menu or à la carte, each consisting of well-presented, modern Danish dishes with a classical base. Tasty sweet and sour combinations feature.

XX **Mash**

Bredgade 20 ✉ 1260 K – Ⓜ Kongens Nytorv – ☎ 33 13 93 00 – www.mashsteak.dk
– Closed Saturday and Sunday lunch **D2**
Rest – *(booking essential at dinner)* Carte 330/575 DKK

♦ Steakhouse ♦ Brasserie ♦

Smart, American-style steakhouse with trendy bar, red leather booths and aged meat on display. Simple, classical steak dishes and some fish alternatives. Largely French and American wine list.

Acquamarina

Borgergade 17a ✉ 1300 K – Ⓜ Kongens Nytorv – ☎ 33 11 17 21 – www.acquamarina.dk
– Closed Easter, Christmas, Sunday and Monday **C2**
Rest – *(booking essential) (dinner only) (set menu only)* Menu 325 DKK
♦ Seafood ♦ Design ♦

Fashionable restaurant displaying modern artwork and 2 huge copper chandeliers. Now open for dinner only and serving a daily set menu of quality fish and shellfish dishes with an Italian touch.

L' Osteria del Grappolo Blu

Vester Farimagsgade 37 ✉ 1606 V – Ⓜ Vesterport – ☎ 33 12 57 20 – www.osteria.dk
– Closed Easter, July, Christmas-New Year and Sunday **B2/3**
Rest – *(dinner only)* Carte 395/595 DKK
♦ Italian ♦ Friendly ♦

More informal counterpart to Il Grappolo Blu, with smart osteria styling. Authentic homemade dishes have their roots in southern Italy; bread and ice cream are made on the premises daily.

Orangeriet

Kronprinsessegade 13, (Kongens Have) ✉ 1306 K – Ⓜ Kongens Nytorv – ☎ 33 11 13 07 – www.restaurant-orangeriet.dk
– Closed 1 week late October, Christmas, Sunday dinner and Monday
Rest – Menu 250/400 DKK – Carte 235/505 DKK **C2**
♦ Danish ♦ Romantic ♦

In a charming location, with a bright dining room and delightful terrace overlooking the King's Garden. Typical orangery style with white walls, simple design furniture and lush plants, including an orange tree. Appealing selection of unfussy Danish dishes.

Kanalen

Christianshavn-Wilders Plads 1-3 ✉ 1403 K – Ⓜ Christianshavn – ☎ 32 95 13 30 – www.restaurant-kanalen.dk
– Closed 24-30 December, Sunday and bank holidays **D3**
Rest – *(booking essential)* Menu 275/360 DKK – Carte 360/538 DKK
♦ Danish ♦ Bistro ♦ Cosy ♦

Former Harbour Police office with lovely terrace, in delightful canalside location. Red façade masks simple, informal dining room with numerous French windows facing the water. Tiny open kitchen prepares a well-balanced Danish menu with light French touches.

M/S Amerika

Dampfaergevej 8, Pakhus 12, Amerikakaj (via Folke Bernadottes Allée C 1) ✉ 2100 K – ☎ 35 26 90 30 – www.msamerika.dk
– Closed Sunday and bank holidays
Rest – Menu 295/325 DKK – Carte 355/490 DKK
♦ Danish ♦ Brasserie ♦

Characterful 19C warehouse on the quayside. Industrial/brasserie-style interior with open kitchen, friendly atmosphere and popular terrace. Daily blackboard menu of Danish brasserie dishes.

L'Altro

Torvegade 62 ✉ 1400 K – Ⓜ Christianshavn – ☎ 32 54 54 06 – www.laltro.dk
– Closed Easter, Christmas and Sunday **D3**
Rest – *(booking essential) (dinner only) (set menu only)* Menu 340/440 DKK
♦ Italian ♦ Intimate ♦

Cosy restaurant with warm, rustic style, that celebrates *la cucina de la casa* – the homely Italian spirit of 'mama's kitchen'. Regularly changing menus feature tasty family recipes from Umbria and Tuscany; appealing dishes rely on fresh, good quality ingredients.

Relæ

Jægersborggade 41 ✉ 2200 N – ✆ 36 96 66 09 – www.restaurant-relae.dk
– Closed January, July, Sunday-Tuesday and bank holidays **A1**
Rest – *(booking essential) (dinner only)* Menu 345 DKK
◆ Seasonal cuisine ◆ Minimalist ◆
Located in an interesting street full of up-and-coming shops and galleries. Simple wood-furnished interior with large benches and stools at the counter, facing the open kitchen. Two daily set menus – one featuring meat and one vegetarian. Seasonal, modern cooking.

Famo 51

Gammel Kongevej 51 ✉ 1610 V – ✆ 33 22 22 50 – www.famo.dk
– Closed Easter and 23 December-3 January **A3**
Rest – *(booking essential) (dinner only)* Menu 400 DKK
◆ Italian ◆ Minimalist ◆
Laid-back restaurant with intimate, two-tabled cellar. Extensive daily set menu offers rustic Italian dishes and relies on seasonal ingredients. On Fridays they offer only fish and shellfish.

Sorte Hest

Vesterbrogade 135 (via Vesterbrogade A 3) ✉ 1620 V – ✆ 33 25 22 23
– www.sortehestetspisested.dk
– Closed July, Christmas and Sunday-Tuesday
Rest – *(booking essential) (dinner only)* Menu 425 DKK – Carte approx. 390 DKK
◆ Modern Danish ◆ Bistro ◆
Informal bistro dating from 1906; try for one of the seats at the tiny counters facing the open kitchen. Passionate chef uses seasonal ingredients to create appealing French and Danish dishes.

Kødbyens Fiskebar

Den Hvide Kødby, Flaesketorvet 100 (via Halmtorvet and Sønder Blvd B3)
✉ 1711 V – ✆ 32 15 56 56 – www.fiskebaren.dk
– Closed Sunday and Monday
Rest – *(dinner only)* Carte 355/445 DKK
◆ Seafood ◆ Trendy ◆
Set in a former meat market, with a buzzy atmosphere and trendy, industrial feel. Sit on wall-mounted banquettes or on high stools at the central aluminium bar. Concise menu features fresh, simply prepared seafood dishes, which are based around the latest catch.

Enomania

Vesterbrogade 187 (via Vesterbrogade A 3) ✉ 1800 C – ✆ 33 23 60 80
– www.enomania.dk
– Closed Christmas-New Year, 2 weeks July, 1 week late October, Sunday and Monday
Rest – *(booking essential) (dinner only and lunch Thursday-Friday)(set menu only)* Menu 350 DKK
◆ Italian ◆ Wine bar ◆
Simple, bistro-style restaurant near Frederiksberg Park; its name meaning 'Wine Mania'. Wine cellar with a table for tasting; excellent list of over 600 bins, mostly from Piedmont and Burgundy. Straightforward, tasty Italian dishes from a daily 4 course set menu.

Mêlée

Martensens Allé 16 ✉ 1828 – Ⓜ Frederiksberg – ✆ 35 13 11 34
– www.melee.dk
– Closed 1 week autumn, 2 weeks Christmas-New Year, Saturday-Monday
Rest – *(booking essential) (dinner only)* Carte 290/355 DKK **A3**
◆ Friendly ◆ Bistro ◆
Bustling neighbourhood bistro with friendly atmosphere, run by an experienced team. Modern, country-style French cooking with Danish influences; expect bold flavours and generous portions. Concise menu and a daily blackboard special; French wines accompany.

Soren K

Søren Kierkegaard Plads 1 ✉ 1221 K – ✆ 33 47 49 49 – www.soerenk.dk – Closed Sunday and bank holidays **C3**

Rest – Menu 490 DKK (dinner) – Carte 285/485 DKK

♦ Modern Danish ♦ Minimalist ♦

Located in the contemporary 'Black Diamond' building. Modern dining room with design furniture and floor-to-ceiling windows overlooking the quayside; lovely terrace. Menu features Danish recipes, Scandinavian ingredients, French influences and a modern touch.

Famo

Saxogade 3 ✉ 1662 V – ✆ 33 23 22 50 – www.famo.dk – Closed 23 December-3 January **A3**

Rest – *(booking essential) (dinner only) (set menu only)* Menu 370 DKK

♦ Italian ♦ Bistro ♦

Simple Italian restaurant set in a small street; its red and white walls hung with contemporary art. Extensive daily menus are presented orally; with a choice of eight antipasti, followed by tasty homemade pasta, generous main courses and authentic desserts.

Aamanns Etablissement

Øster Farimagsgade 12 ✉ 2100 Ø – Ⓜ Nørreport – ✆ 35 55 33 10 – www.aamanns.dk – Closed 23 December-2 January and Sunday **C1**

Rest – *(booking advisable)* Menu 315 DKK (dinner) – Carte lunch 315/360 DKK

♦ Danish ♦ Bistro ♦

Cosy, pastel-hued restaurant with cheery team. Concise, seasonal menus blend classical techniques and traditional smørrebrød with more modern 'small plates'. Dinner menu comes with wine pairings.

Oubaek

Store Kongensgade 52 ✉ 1264 K – Ⓜ Kongens Nytorv – ✆ 33 32 32 09 – www.rasmusoubaek.dk – Closed July, 20 December-3 January and Sunday **C/D2**

Rest – *(booking essential) (dinner only)* Menu 425 DKK – Carte 310/430 DKK

♦ French ♦ Friendly ♦

Unassuming restaurant with tables beside the open kitchen and on a mezzanine. Unfussy, simply presented French dishes with a Danish touch; dinner consists of 'taster' plates. Friendly team.

Dim Sum

Sankt Annae Plads 16 ✉ 1250 K – Ⓜ Kongens Nytorv – ✆ 35 35 60 05 – www.restaurantdimsum.dk – Closed Christmas, Sunday and Monday **D2**

Rest – *(booking essential) (dinner only)* Menu 350 DKK – Carte 245/325 DKK

♦ Chinese (Dim Sum) ♦ Fashionable ♦

Narrow restaurant with large black counter overlooking an open kitchen. Contemporary Chinese cooking; fixed price menu offers good selection of dim sum. Well-paced service. Laid-back ambience.

Famo Metro

Øster Søgade 114 ✉ 2100 Ø – ✆ 35 55 66 30 – www.famo.dk – Closed 2 weeks Christmas and Sunday **C1**

Rest – Menu 375 DKK – Carte 405/460 DKK

♦ Italian ♦ Minimalist ♦

The 3rd in the Famo group. Modern dining room boasts floor-to-ceiling windows and water views. Second basement room has a rotisserie fireplace. Classical Italian dishes include homemade pastas.

IN TIVOLI

XXX ✿

The Paul (Paul Cunningham)

Vesterbrogade 3 ✉ 1630 K – Ⓜ København Hovedbane Gård – ✆ 33 75 07 75 – www.thepaul.dk
– Closed January-March and Sunday **B3**
Rest – *(set menu only)* Menu 425/745 DKK
Spec. Turbot with vanilla and caviar. Guinea fowl with almond praline, wild fungi and coffee jus. Tea infused mallows with smoked lemon ice cream.
♦ Innovative ♦ Elegant ♦
Elegant 20C glass-domed building overlooking the lake in Tivoli Gardens. Bright, airy inner with passionate British chef's cookbooks and art on display. Confident modern Danish cooking with classical base; techniques are kept simple but presentation is original.

SMØRREBRØD *The following list of simpler restaurants and cafés/bars specialise in Danish open sandwiches and are generally open from 10.00am to 4.00pm.*

X

Sankt Annae

Sankt Annae Plads 12 ✉ 1250 K – Ⓜ Kongens Nytorv – ✆ 33 12 54 97 – www.restaurantsanktannae.dk
– Closed mid July-7 August, Christmas-New Year, Sunday and bank holidays
Rest – *(booking essential) (lunch only)* Carte 185/385 DKK **D2**
♦ Smørrebrød ♦ Cosy ♦
Attractive terraced building from 1837, with charming maritime décor. Seasonal à la carte and daily blackboard menu. The lobster salad and shrimps – fresh from the local fjords – are a hit.

X

Amalie

Amaliegade 11 ✉ 1256 K – Ⓜ Kongens Nytorv – ✆ 33 12 88 10 – www.restaurantamalie.dk
– Closed Easter, July, Christmas-New Year, Sunday and bank holidays
Rest – *(booking essential) (lunch only)* Menu 218 DKK **D2**
– Carte approx. 250 DKK
♦ Smørrebrød ♦ Intimate ♦ Inn ♦
Charming 18C townhouse next to Amalienborg Palace. Two tiny, cosy rooms displaying old paintings and elegant porcelain. Authentic Danish menu, with a large choice of herring, salmon and salads.

X

Schønnemann

Hauser Plads 16 ✉ 1127 K – Ⓜ Nørreport – ✆ 33 12 07 85 – www.danskfrokost.dk
– Closed Easter, 23 December-4 January, Sunday and bank holidays
Rest – *(booking essential) (lunch only)* Menu 318/428 DKK **C2**
– Carte 180/300 DKK
♦ Smørrebrød ♦ Rustic ♦
Opened in 1877 and still putting sand on the floor of the rustic basement room in memory of its early days. Offers smørrebrød, open sandwiches and large selection of herring and tartar dishes.

X

The Royal Cafe

Amagertorv 6 ✉ 1160 K – Ⓜ Kongens Nytorv – ✆ 33 12 11 22 – www.theroyalcafe.dk **C2**
Rest – *(lunch only)* Carte 180/225 DKK
♦ Smørrebrød ♦ Fashionable ♦
Funky eatery in Royal Copenhagen china showroom. Homemade pastry counter and peaceful courtyard terrace. Breakfast, afternoon tea and original 21C 'smushies' (smørrebrød crossed with sushi).

X

Slotskælderen hos Gitte Kik

Fortunstræ 4 ✉ *1065 K* – Ⓜ *Kongens Nytorv* – ✆ *33 11 15 37*
– Closed July, Sunday, Monday and public holidays **C2**
Rest – *(booking essential) (lunch only)* Carte 159/230 DKK
♦ Smørrebrød ♦ Family ♦
Established restaurant, family-run since 1910, that sets the benchmark for this type of cuisine. Rustic inner filled with portraits and city scenes. Around 50 choices of appealing smørrebrød.

ENVIRONS OF COPENHAGEN

AT HELLERUP North : 7.5 km by Østbanegade and Road 2 - ✉ 2900 Hellerup

XX

Saison

Strandvejen 203 ✉ *2900* – ✆ *39 62 21 40* – *www.saison.dk*
– Closed 3 weeks July, 25 December, Sunday and bank holidays
Rest – Menu 350/440 DKK – Carte 425/600 DKK
♦ Seasonal cuisine ♦ Friendly ♦
Bright and airy hotel restaurant with high ceilings and oversized windows. Carefully prepared dishes change daily, depending on the latest market produce available. Cookery school in basement.

AT SKOVSHOVED North : 10 km by Østbanegade and Road 2

Skovshoved

Strandvejen 267 ✉ *2920* – ✆ *39 64 00 28* – *www.skovshovedhotel.com*
20 rm – †1025/1525 DKK ††1325/1725 DKK, ☕ 145 DKK – 2 suites
Rest – Menu 295/395 DKK – Carte 370/470 DKK
♦ Inn ♦ Cosy ♦
Set in a charming village and dating back to the 1890s, after the original 1660 hotel burnt down. Modern lounge furnished with white sofas and armchairs. Cosy, Scandinavian-style bedrooms, some looking out to sea and some boasting balconies. Appealing Danish dishes at lunch; more creative options served in the evening.

AT KLAMPENBORG North : 13 km by Østanegade and Road 2

X

Den Røde Cottage

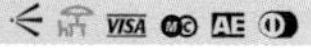

Strandvejen 550 ✉ *2930* – Ⓜ *Klampenborg* – ✆ *39 90 46 14*
– www.dengulecottage.dk
– Closed February and 22 December-3 January
Rest – *(booking essential)* Menu 400/600 DKK
♦ Seasonal cuisine ♦ Design ♦
Charming former Forestry Officer's house, built in 1881 and located on an old plantation. Small but romantic dining room laid with Royal Copenhagen porcelain; lovely terrace offers partial sea view. Monthly changing, seasonal Nordic menu relies on quality produce.

X

Den Gule Cottage

Strandvejen 506 ✉ *2930* – Ⓜ *Klampenborg* – ✆ *39 64 06 91*
– www.dengulecottage.dk
– Closed February and 22 December-3 January
Rest – *(booking advisable)* Carte 265/315 DKK
♦ Danish ♦ Inn ♦ Minimalist ♦
Lovely 1844 cottage facing the beach; from the same team as Den Røde. Two tiny, simply decorated rooms and large terrace with sea view. Unfussy menu of 5 main dishes, salads and cheese plates.

AT SØLLERØD North : 20 km by Tagensvej (take the train to Holte then taxi) - ✉ 2840 Holte

XXX ✿

Søllerød Kro

Søllerødvej 35 ✉ 2840 – ✆ 45 80 25 05 – www.soelleroed-kro.dk – Closed 14-20 February, 18-24 April, 11-31 July, Monday and Tuesday

Rest – Menu 375/875 DKK – Carte 650/930 DKK

Spec. Baerii caviar 'en surprise'. Lobster with morels and white asparagus. Danish berries with vanilla.

♦ Classic ♦ Inn ♦

Characterful 17C thatched inn with three small but stylish dining rooms and a delightful courtyard terrace. Superb wine list features plenty of Burgundy and champagne. Choose from an array of menus that offer light, refined dishes with fresh, sharp flavours.

AT KASTRUP AIRPORT Southeast : 10 km by Amager Boulevard

Hilton Copenhagen Airport

Ellehammersvej 20 ✉ 2770 – Ⓜ København Lufthavn Kastrup – ✆ 32 50 15 01 – www.hilton.com

375 rm – †1095/2595 DKK ††1095/3495 DKK, ☕ 195 DKK – 1 suite

Rest *Hamlet* – *(closed Sunday) (dinner only)* Carte 550/720 DKK

Rest *Horizon* – *(Sunday Brunch)* Carte 325/522 DKK

♦ Business ♦ Modern ♦

Smart business hotel accessed from the airport via a glass walkway. Spacious, well-maintained bedrooms with excellent sound-proofing and good views from the higher floors. Asian-inspired Ni'mat Spa. Nordic specialties served in Hamlet. Buffet meals in Horizon.

AT ØRESTAD South : 6 km by Amager Boulevard and Amagerfaelledvej

Crowne Plaza Towers

Ørestads boulevard 114-118 ✉ 2300 S – Ⓜ Ørestads – ✆ 88 77 66 55 – www.cpcopenhagen.dk

362 rm – †900/2195 DKK ††900/2195 DKK, ☕ 175 DKK – 4 suites

Rest *Storm* – Menu 320 DKK – Carte 340/500 DKK

♦ Business ♦ Modern ♦

Modern tower block between the city and the airport, next to a huge shopping mall. Airy, minimalist lobby and bar. Spacious, contemporary bedrooms with bright furniture and good views. One of the world's greenest hotels. Restaurant offers Scandinavian cuisine.

FINLAND
SUOMI

PROFILE

→ **Area:**
338 145 km^2
(130 558 sq mi).

→ **Population:**
5 351 427 inhabitants (est. 2009),
density = 15 per km^2.

→ **Capital:**
Helsinki (conurbation 1 320 220 inhabitants).

→ **Currency:**
Euro (€); rate of exchange: € 1 = US$ 1.37 (Dec. 2010).

→ **Government:**
Parliamentary republic (since 1917). Member of European Union since 1995.

→ **Languages:**
Finnish (a Finno-Ugric language related to Estonian) spoken by 92% of Finns, Swedish (6%) and Sami (some 7 000 native speakers). English is widely spoken.

→ **Specific public holidays:**
Epiphany (6 January); Good Friday (Friday before Easter); Midsummer's Eve Day (mid June); Independence Day (6 December); Boxing Day (26 December).

→ **Local time:**
GMT + 2 hours in winter and GMT + 3 hours in summer.

→ **Climate:**
Temperate continental with very cold winters and mild summers (Helsinki: January: -7°C, July: 17°C). Midnight sun: the sun never sets for several weeks around Midsummer in the north. Snow settles in early December to April in the south and centre of the country. Northern Lights *(Aurora Borealis)* visible in the north on clear, dark nights; highest frequency in Feb-Mar and Sep-Oct.

→ **International dialling Code:**
00 358 followed by area code (Helsinki: 9) and then the local number.

→ **Emergency:**
Fire Brigade, Ambulance, Police: ✆ **112.**

→ **Electricity:**
220 volts AC, 50Hz; 2-pin round-shaped continental plugs.

→ **Formalities**
Travellers from the European Union (EU), Switzerland, Iceland and the main countries of North and South America need a national identity card or passport (America: passport required) to visit Finland for less than three months (tourism or business purpose). For visitors from other countries a visa may be required, in addition to a passport, especially for those wishing to stay for longer than three months. If you plan to visit Russia while in Finland, you must purchase an appropriate visa in advance in your own country. We advise you to check with your embassy before travelling.

HELSINKI

HELSINGFORS

Population; 583 000 (conurbation 1 303 126) – Altitude: sea level

. Robic/MICHELIN

Cool, clean and chic, the 'Daughter of the Baltic' sits prettily on a peninsula, jutting out between the landmasses of its historical overlords, Sweden and Russia. Surrounded on three sides by water, Helsinki is a busy port, but that only tells a small part of the story: forests grow in abundance around here and trees reach down to the lapping shores. This is a striking city to look at: it was rebuilt in the nineteenth century after fire, and many of the buildings have a handsome neoclassical or art nouveau façade. Shoppers can browse the picturesque outdoor food and tourist markets stretching along the main harbour, where island-hopping ferries ply their trade.

Wherever you are here, you get the feeling of man and nature thinking pretty much along the same lines. In a country with over 200,000 lakes it would be pretty hard to escape a green sensibility, and the Finnish capital has made sure that concrete and stone have never taken priority over its distinctive features of trees, water and open space. There are bridges at every turn connecting the city's varied array of small islands, and a ten kilometre strip of parkland acts as a spine running vertically up from the centre. Renowned as a city of cool, it's somewhere that also revels in a hot nightlife and even hotter saunas – this is where they were invented. And if your blast of dry heat has left you wanting a refreshing dip, there's always a freezing lake close at hand.

LIVING THE CITY

The harbour is the hub of Helsinki. Arrive by boat and **Senate Square,** identified by the proud lines of its Lutheran cathedral, beckons in the background. To your east juts the headland of **Katajanokka,** while moving away from the harbour the city centre continues to the northwest, pierced by the elongated **Mannerheimintie** shopping street. To the east as you proceed along this thoroughfare is **Töölönlahti Bay**, the southern-most tip of **Central Park's** gloriously green spine. To the west is **Sibelius Park**, named after Finland's greatest composer. Helsinki sits in an archipelago and islands around it include **Suomenlinna** to the south, which houses an eighteenth century sea fortress, now a UNESCO World Heritage site.

PRACTICAL INFORMATION

ARRIVAL-DEPARTURE

Helsinki-Vantaa Airport is 19km north of the city. By taxi it'll cost around €40 and take 20-30min. There are also buses to Central Bus Station which will take 40min.

TRANSPORT

Getting across Helsinki is fast and easy: trams and buses whizz you round efficiently. A single ticket is cheap and good for any transfers you make within an hour: buy them from the driver, ticket machines, kiosks, metro stations or ferry terminal.

If you expect to use public transport often, it might be worth buying a tourist ticket, valid for one, three or five days and available from railway stations, ticket machines or the tourist office.

The Helsinki Card is another good option: it's valid for one, two or three days with a sliding scale of prices, and allows you unlimited transport plus free admission to museums and attractions.

There are regular ferries from the harbour to Suomenlinna; they sail a little less frequently to the other main islands.

EXPLORING HELSINKI

There's something about a harbour. See one and it becomes the pivotal part of a town or city. In Helsinki that feeling is accentuated by the grand hubbub of the daily market that takes place there. It's a colourful gathering of farmers and fishermen, traders and crafts people, and the buzzy atmosphere is enhanced by the aromas from impromptu cafés selling fresh and smoked fish grilled on planks of cedar. For the surrounding elegant neoclassical look, we can thank the German architect Carl Engel, who engraved on a clean slate nearly 200 years ago. This chunk of the city is an ideal place just to stroll round for an hour or two, enjoying the juxtaposition of fine architecture and waterfront life.

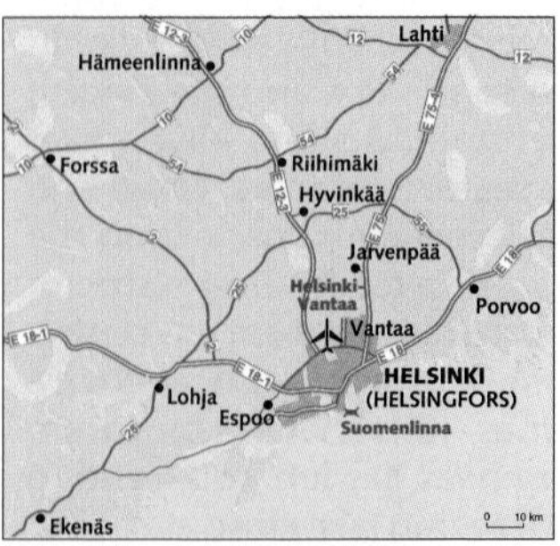

When it comes to cathedrals, you'll encounter double vision as you step off your boat onto the waterside. The vivid green dome of the **Lutheran Cathedral** has been a focal point for visitors for over 150 years, standing majestically up the hill from the harbour in **Senate Square**. The buildings that surround it create a fine symmetry; this is recognized as one of Europe's most aesthetically satisfying squares. Dominating the far side of the harbour, meanwhile, is **Uspensky Cathedral,** western Europe's largest Orthodox church, a confident testimony to Russia's past influence in Finland. It has thirteen gold cupolas, and an equally elaborate interior redolent of black marble and glinting gold. Helsinki spreads westwards along the boutique-edged avenues of **Esplanadi,** a strip of parkland that comes alive on summer evenings as everyone promenades during the long hours of light.

This is a city that takes its culture seriously. There are a host of good museums within a small area up from Senate Square and Esplanadi. The **Ateneum** (National Gallery) is a suitably grand building to house the best of Finnish art, given international enhancement by a splattering of works by Gauguin, Cézanne, Degas, Modogliani and Van Gogh. Half a mile up the road stands the eye-catching, **Kiasma,** a picture itself with its curvy zinc roof and vertical aluminium elevations. This is the home of Finnish modern art, complete with theatre for experimental drama, dance and music. Carry on a little further up Mannerheimintie and you reach the **National Museum**, another show-stopping building, chock full with Finnish artefacts from prehistoric times to the present day. The sense of classy cool so permeates these places that it's no surprise to find a museum itself dedicated to style: The **DesignMuseo** (go back south past Esplanadi) pits all the famous design styles side-by-side in a kaleidoscope of good taste, with a main emphasis on Finnish masters of the art.

➜ NOUVEAU RICH

If you get a slight feeling of déjà vu when your eyes alight on the DesignMuseo's art nouveau exhibits, there's a good chance you've already spent some time in Katajanokka, the art nouveau quarter of the city jutting out like a wiggly foot as you approach the harbour by boat. Art nouveau took off in Helsinki as the Arts and Crafts Movement of the early twentieth century happily coincided with a flowering of inspired Finnish architects, and dozens of their landmark buildings are found in eye-

HELSINKI IN...

➜ ONE DAY

Harbour market place, Uspensky Cathedral, Lutheran Cathedral, Katajanokka, a slow stroll up Mannerheimintie taking in the cultural sights

➜ TWO DAYS

A ferry to Suomenlinna and most of the day at the sea fortress, Church in the Rock, the lively nightlife of Fredrikinkatu area (west of city)

➜ THREE DAYS

A trip through Central Park, the Sibelius monument, the design area round Esplanadi

catching clusters, chief of which is Katajanokka, the first neighbourhood of this type in Europe, and still the continent's best preserved. As you walk along its streets, you'll notice fine stone ornamentation, dreamy towers and fanciful details of all kinds. Two other examples of jaw-dropping art nouveau are the **Helsinki Railway Station** with its sumptuous interior and iconic lamp-holding figures to welcome you in (if somewhat menacingly), and the **Pohjola** insurance building, near Esplanadi, which mixes stone with local wood to dramatic effect. Head to the west of the city, though, for one of Finland's top visitor attractions. **Temppeliaukio**, or the Church in the Rock, is exactly that. It was hollowed out from living bedrock in 1969, and to visit is like staring at an altar in a quarry. The copper roof offsets the deadening effect of the granite walls, and the acoustics are stunning: it's a top-notch venue for concerts.

➜ SOUR NOTE

The world of Finnish music is dominated by one man...**Jean Sibelius**. In Helsinki they think so much of him they not only gave him a monument, they gave him a park to go with it. It's in the west of the city and the monument certainly caused a stir when it was unveiled back in 1967. Made up of a collection of different sized metallic pipes that make their own kind of music when the wind blows, it was subject to a torrent of abuse at the time because people couldn't see the connection with Sibelius. So they added a statue of his head (some way from the pipes) and things quietened down. Judge for yourself. Whatever you may think, the park is a lovely, peaceful place to take a stroll, and it's very close to the water's edge. The best place to hear the music of Sibelius is the impressive **Finlandia Hall**, opposite the National Museum and overlooking Toolo Bay. It's a stunning building of white marble and black granite to remind you of a piano keyboard, and its acoustics do wonders for the likes of the Helsinki Philharmonic who regularly hold court there.

➜ GOING UNDERGROUND

This is an excellent city for shopping. Just looking in the windows is like a lesson in artistic design. Actually, just looking in the windows may be your wisest move, especially if you're on a tight budget, as prices tend to shoot in a distinctly northerly direction. The smartest shops are around Esplanadi and Mannerheimintie, where fashion, furniture, jewellery and homeware stores jostle for attention. Go to Senate Square and its surrounds for handicrafts and art shops. If the weather's bad, you can hide from it beneath the central streets in a maze of connected underground passages replete with shops, cafés, restaurants and food markets. You could spend a day browsing down there without ever emerging into daylight!

A short ferry trip to the island of Suomenlinna is a good idea in the summer. Certainly UNESCO thinks so: it made the sea fortress on the island's headland a World Heritage Site in 1991. The fortress, built by the Swedes in the mid-eighteenth century, was used as a defence against Russia, and some of the island's 900-strong population now lives in its converted naval buildings. There are several museums and exhibition halls, balanced by delightful walks, bays and coves, making it a good location for a whole day's excursion. The calm of the island is a kind of microcosm of Helsinki: a restful place that seems to run quietly, smoothly and apparently without much effort.

CALENDAR HIGHLIGHTS

Helsinki has been around since 1550, and Helsinki Day, its birthday, is celebrated on 12 June. There are plenty of festivities and events around the city – Esplanadi and Senate Square are filled with music and the performing arts, while sailing boats in the harbour let you on-board (for a fee). Also in June, Juhannus (midsummer) is celebrated with bonfires and gusto. Football fans can get a summer fix at the International Youth Tournament when hundreds of young players from around the world gather to compete for the Helsinki Cup. August's Helsinki Festival includes a Night of Arts with street shows till dawn, as well as classical music, dance, theatre and visual arts. Herring lovers should make for the Market Square in October – the Baltic Herring Festival has been held here for over 200 years. Traditional Christmas markets light up the harbour in December, when there's also the dramatic Lucia Parade to the Lutheran Cathedral.

EATING OUT

Jacques Chirac may not have been very complimentary about the Finnish diet but he had clearly never visited any of the superbly stylish restaurants in Helsinki regularly serving imaginative cuisine where local – and we mean local – ingredients are very much to the fore. Produce is sourced from the country's abundant lakes, forests and seas, so that your menu will assuredly be laden with the likes of reindeer, smoked reindeer, reindeer's tongue, elk in aspic, lampreys, Arctic char, Baltic herring, snow grouse and cloudberries. Generally speaking, complicated, fussy preparations are overlooked for those that let the natural flavours shine through. In the autumn, markets are piled high with woodland mushrooms, often from Lapland, and chefs make the most of this bounty. Local alcoholic drinks include schnapps, vodka and liqueurs made from local berries, while *lakka* (made from cloudberries) and *mesimarja* (brambleberries) are definitely worth discovering – you may not find them in any other European city. You'd find coffee anywhere in Europe, but not to the same extent as here: Finns are among the world's biggest coffee drinkers. In the gastronomic restaurants, lunch is a simpler affair with limited choice.

→ WILD CITY

If you go for a walk in Central Park, you'll be surrounded by animal life. These include weasel, raccoon dog, muskrat, elk, arctic and brown hare. Birds are everywhere in the spring; in particular keep an eye open for Eurasian jay, dunnock, red-breasted flycatcher and garden and wood warblers.

→ OLYMPIAN HEIGHTS

Although Helsinki is a pretty low-lying city, you can reach the heights at the 240ft Olympic Stadium tower, built in 1938. The view takes in the whole of the city and the outlying Gulf of Finland.

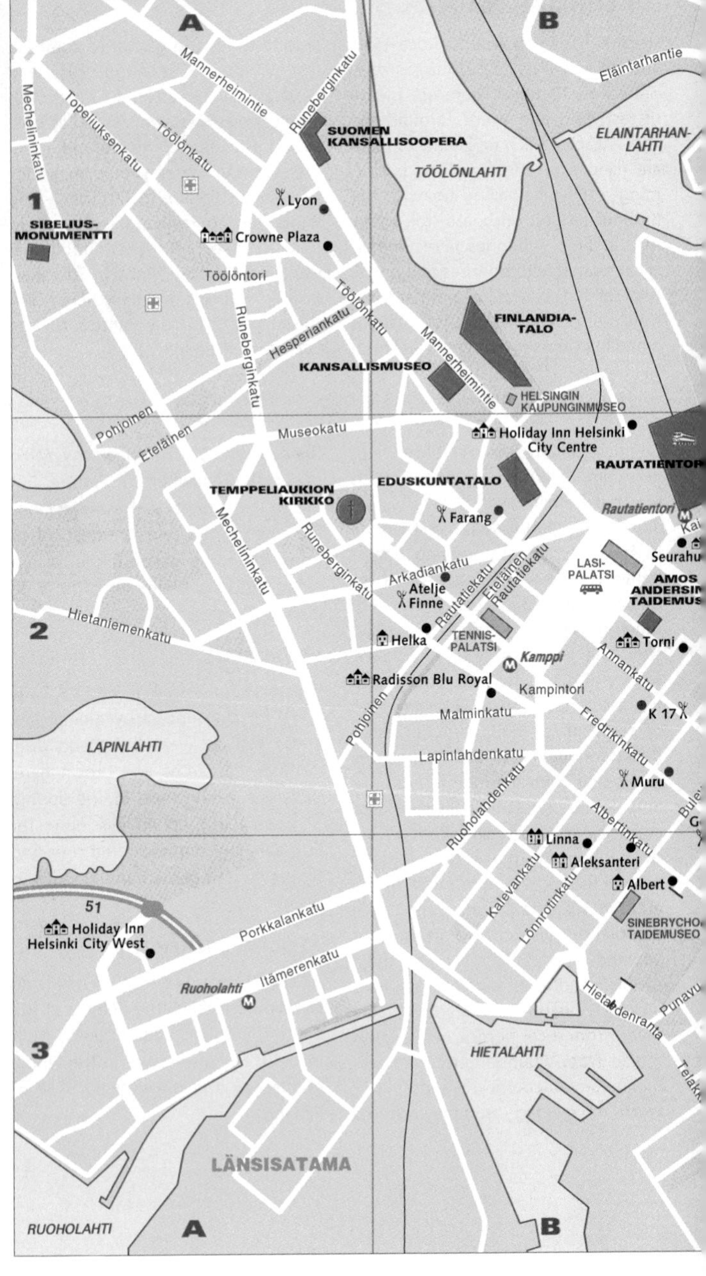
A
B
1
2
3
Mannerheimintie
Runeberginkatu
Mechelininkatu
Topeliuksenkatu
Töölönkatu
Eläintarhantie
SUOMEN KANSALLISOOPERA
ELAINTARHAN-LAHTI
TÖÖLÖNLAHTI
Lyon
SIBELIUS-MONUMENTTI
Crowne Plaza
Töölöntori
FINLANDIA-TALO
Hesperiankatu
KANSALLISMUSEO
HELSINGIN KAUPUNGINMUSEO
Pohjoinen
Eteläinen
Museokatu
Holiday Inn Helsinki City Centre
RAUTATIENTORI
EDUSKUNTATALO
TEMPPELIAUKION KIRKKO
Farang
Rautatientori
Seurahu
LASI-PALATSI
AMOS ANDERSIN TAIDEMUS
Arkadiankatu
Atelje Finne
Rautatiekatu
Eteläinen Rautatiekatu
Hietaniemenkatu
Helka
TENNIS-PALATSI
Kamppi
Torni
Annankatu
Radisson Blu Royal
Kampintori
Malminkatu
K 17
Fredrikinkatu
LAPINLAHTI
Lapinlahdenkatu
Muru
Ruoholahdenkatu
Albertinkatu
Linna
Aleksanteri
Kalevankatu
Lönnrotinkatu
Albert
51
SINEBRYCHOFF TAIDEMUSEO
Holiday Inn Helsinki City West
Porkkalankatu
Itämerenkatu
Ruoholahti
Hietalahdenranta
Punavu
HIETALAHTI
LÄNSISATAMA
RUOHOLAHTI

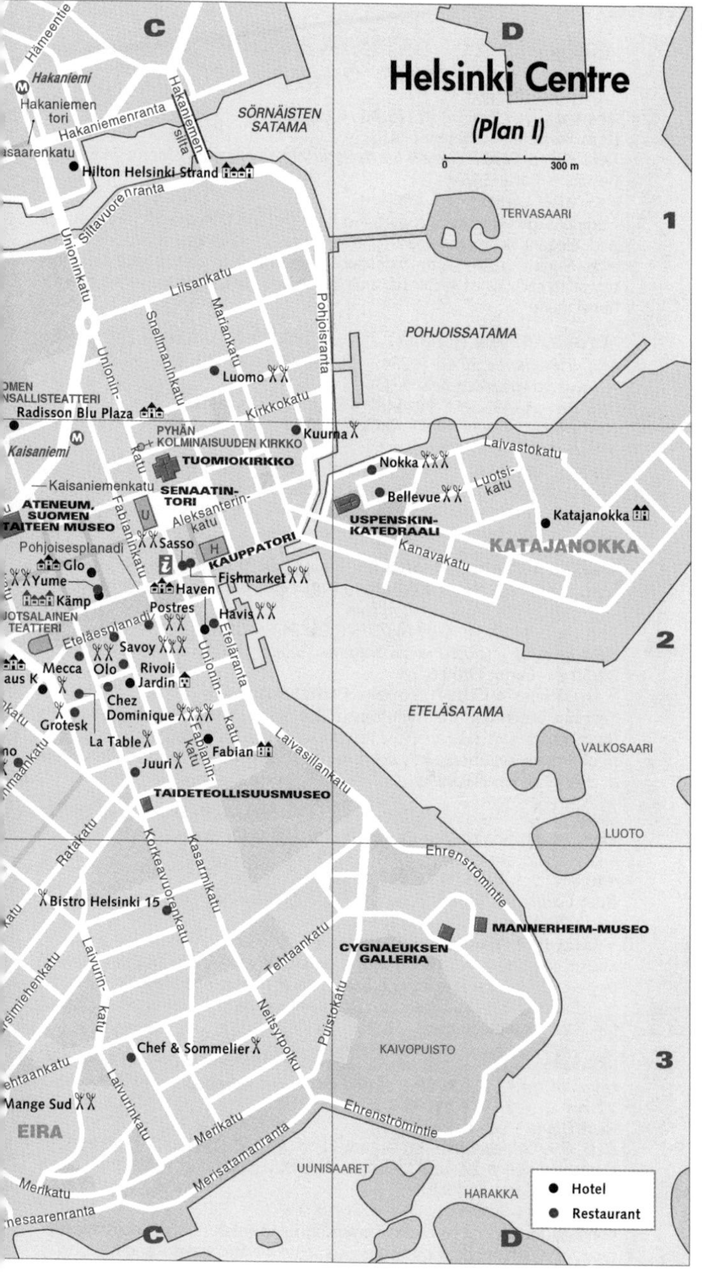
Helsinki Centre
(Plan I)
0
300 m
C
D
1
2
3
Hakaniemi
Hakaniemen tori
Hakaniemenranta
Hakaniemen silta
SÖRNÄISTEN SATAMA
Hilton Helsinki Strand
Siltavuorenranta
Unioninkatu
Liisankatu
Snellmaninkatu
Mariankatu
Pohjoisranta
POHJOISSATAMA
TERVASAARI
Luomo
Kirkkokatu
Radisson Blu Plaza
PYHÄN KOLMINAISUUDEN KIRKKO
Kuurna
Kaisaniemi
TUOMIOKIRKKO
Kaisaniemenkatu
SENAATIN-TORI
ATENEUM, SUOMEN TAITEEN MUSEO
Aleksanterinkatu
Fabianinkatu
Nokka
Bellevue
Laivastokatu
Luotsikatu
Katajanokka
USPENSKIN-KATEDRAALI
KATAJANOKKA
Kanavakatu
Pohjoisesplanadi
Sasso
KAUPPATORI
Glo
Yume
Kämp
Fishmarket
Haven
Postres
Havis
Eteläesplanadi
Savoy
Mecca
Olo
Rivoli
Jardin
Chez Dominique
Grotesk
La Table
Eteläranta
Unioninkatu
ETELÄSATAMA
VALKOSAARI
Fabian
Fabianinkatu
Juuri
Laivasillankatu
TAIDETEOLLISUUSMUSEO
LUOTO
Ratakatu
Korkeavuorenkatu
Kasarmikatu
Ehrenströmintie
Bistro Helsinki 15
MANNERHEIM-MUSEO
Laivurinkatu
Tehtaankatu
CYGNAEUKSEN GALLERIA
Neitsytpolku
Puistokatu
KAIVOPUISTO
Chef & Sommelier
Laivurinkatu
Mange Sud
EIRA
Merikatu
Merisatamanranta
Ehrenströmintie
UUNISAARET
HARAKKA
Merikatu
Hotel
Restaurant

Kämp

Pohjoisesplanadi 29 ✉ 00100 – Ⓜ Kaisaniemi – ✆ (09) 576 111 – www.hotelkamp.fi C2
174 rm – 🛉175/465 € 🛉🛉175/465 €, ☕ 26.90 € – 5 suites
Rest *Yume* – see below
Rest *Kämp Café* – *(closed lunch Saturday and Sunday)* Menu 31 € (lunch) – Carte 34/54 €
♦ Grand Luxury ♦ Classic ♦
Luxurious 19C hotel with superb top floor spa and fitness facility. Well-equipped, elegant bedrooms boast spacious marble bathrooms; suites are named after Finnish artists. Large nightclub offers excellent champagne selection; tempting cocktail list in chic bar area. Brasserie-style Kämp Café serves international menu.

Crowne Plaza Helsinki

Mannerheimintie 50 ✉ 00260 – ✆ (09) 2521 0000 – www.crowne.plaza-helsinki.fi A1
345 rm – 🛉149/299 € 🛉🛉164/314 €, ☕ 21 € – 4 suites
Rest *Macu* – Menu 49 € – Carte 26/50 €
♦ Business ♦ Modern ♦
Spacious hotel specialising in conferences. Comfortable, contemporary bedrooms boast good facilities – the higher the floor, the better the grade – and city or lake views. Large fitness room and spa. Warm, welcoming restaurant offers Mediterranean cuisine.

Hilton Helsinki Strand

John Stenbergin Ranta 4 ✉ 00530 – Ⓜ Hakaniemi – ✆ (09) 393 51 – www.hilton.com C1
184 rm – 🛉129/340 € 🛉🛉149/375 €, ☕ 24 € – 6 suites
Rest *Bridges* – *(closed lunch Saturday, Sunday and bank holidays)* Menu 32/50 € – Carte 39/60 €
♦ Business ♦ Chain hotel ♦ Functional ♦
Spacious waterfront hotel with classic '80s design, impressive atrium and 8th floor fitness and relaxation centre; take in city views from the sauna or pool. Smartly kept bedrooms boast marble bathrooms. Restaurant offers a mix of classics and local cuisine.

Glo

Kluuvikatu 4 ✉ 00100 – Ⓜ Kaisaniemi – ✆ (010) 3444 400 – www.palacekamp.fi C2
140 rm ☕ – 🛉105/325 € 🛉🛉115/335 € – 4 suites
Rest *Carlito's* – *(closed Saturday lunch, Sunday and bank holidays)* Carte 29/47 €
♦ Luxury ♦ Modern ♦ Design ♦
Stylish, centrally located hotel with good spa/fitness facilities and complimentary bicycle service. Spacious bedrooms have a contemporary look and boast hi-tech extras. Bar has a lively atmosphere at weekends. Carlito's offers a buffet lunch and gourmet pizzas.

Haven

Unioninkatu 17 ✉ 00130 – ✆ (09) 681930 – www.hotelhaven.fi C2
77 rm ☕ – 🛉470 € 🛉🛉505 €
Rest *Havis* – see below
Rest *G W Sundmans* – Eteläranta 16, ✆ *(09) 61285400 (closed 23-30 December, lunch 27 June-9 August, Saturday lunch and Sunday)* Menu 33/59 € – Carte 62/79 €
♦ Luxury ♦ Townhouse ♦ Stylish ♦
Centrally located office block conversion in townhouse style, boasting four types of stylish, modern bedroom – some with water views – and top quality beds, fabrics and furniture. Comfy bar. Formal restaurant serves traditional Finnish and French cuisine.

Klaus K

Bulevardi 2 ✉ 00120 – Ⓜ Rautatientori – ☎ (20) 770 4700 – www.klauskhotel.com – Closed 22-27 December **C2**

135 rm – 121/200 € 200/250 € – 2 suites

Rest *Toscanini* – *☎ (20) 770 4713* – Menu 25/44 € – Carte 34/51 €

♦ Traditional ♦ Design ♦

Late 19C landmark building with great façade. Striking interior is designed to reflect the epic themes of The Kalevala. The four styles of bedroom – Envy, Desire, Passion and Mystical – reflect this. Stylish bar. Modern Tuscan cuisine in lively Toscanini.

Radisson Blu Royal

Runeberginkatu 2 ✉ 00100 – Ⓜ Kamppi – ☎ (20) 1234 701 – www.radissonblu.com/royalhotel-helsinki **B2**

255 rm – 95/230 € 95/230 €, 23 € – 7 suites

Rest *Grill it!* – *(closed Sunday lunch)* Menu 37/50 € – Carte 31/63 €

♦ Business ♦ Modern ♦

Two-winged hotel with pleasant bar, close to the metro station. Spacious bedrooms boast good sized desks; the larger Business Class rooms offer even more facilities and inclusive breakfast. Grilled specialities in the restaurant.

Radisson Blu Plaza

Mikonkatu 23 ✉ 00100 – Ⓜ Kaisaniemi – ☎ (20) 1234 703 – www.radissonblu.com/plazahotel-helsinki **C1-2**

290 rm – 95/175 € 110/190 € – 1 suite

Rest *Pääkonttori* – *(closed lunch Saturday and Sunday)* Menu 30/40 € – Carte 35/49 €

♦ Chain hotel ♦ Historic ♦ Functional ♦

Early 20C building set close to the station – formerly a company HQ – and completed by a more modern wing. Choice of 'Italian', 'Nordic' or 'Classic' bedrooms. Elegant Italian restaurant boasts impressive columns and stained glass windows.

Torni

Yrjönkatu 26 ✉ 00100 – Ⓜ Rautatientori – ☎ (20) 1234 604 – www.sokoshotels.fi – Closed Christmas **B2**

146 rm – 81/247 € 101/247 € – 6 suites

Rest – *(closed Sunday)* Carte 34/61 €

♦ Business ♦ Stylish ♦

Charming early 20C city centre hotel with 11 floor tower and palpable sense of history. Warm, elegant décor with choice of 'Art Deco', 'Functionalism' or 'Art Nouveau' bedrooms. Choice of three bars. Pleasant art deco restaurant offers various types of cooking.

Seurahuone

Kaivokatu 12 ✉ 00100 – Ⓜ Rautatientori – ☎ (09) 69 141 – www.hotelliseurahuone.fi **B2**

118 rm – 135/270 € 185/270 €

Rest – *(closed Sunday and bank holidays)* Menu 35/45 € – Carte 41/67 €

♦ Historic ♦ Classic ♦

Early 20C hotel – one of the oldest in Finland – where a sympathetic renovation has retained a pleasant period feel. Bedrooms display dark wood furniture and Gustav Klimt prints. Traditional bar and an elegant, high-ceilinged restaurant hung with chandeliers.

Holiday Inn Helsinki

Messuaukio 1 (near Pasila Railway Station) (North : 5 km by Mannerheimintie, Nordenskiöldink, Savonkatu off Ratapihantie) ✉ 00520 – ☎ (09) 150 900 – www.finland.holidayinn.com

239 rm – 115/255 € 135/275 €, 15.75 € – 5 suites

Rest *Terra Nova* – Menu 38/44 € – Carte 32/53 €

♦ Business ♦ Modern ♦

Set just outside the city – but close to a station – in the Masscentrum Fair Centre, this chain hotel is popular for conferences. Bright, warm bedrooms offer varying levels of facilities. Welcoming Terra Nova serves international cuisine.

Holiday Inn Helsinki City West

Sulhasenkuja 3 ✉ 00180 – Ⓜ Ruoholahti – ✆ (09) 4152 1000 – www.restel.fi/holidayinn **A3**

256 rm – 🚹122/235 € 🚹🚹140/253 €, ☕ 18 €

Rest *Fokka* – *(Closed lunch Saturday and Sunday)* Menu 35 € (lunch) – Carte dinner 28/88 €

♦ Business ♦ Functional ♦

Sited in a business park well away from the city centre but close to a railway station. Modern bedrooms display touches of colour, pleasant furniture and excellent soundproofing; bathrooms are compact. Contemporary restaurant serves international cuisine.

Holiday Inn Helsinki City Centre

Elielinaukio 5 ✉ 00100 – Ⓜ Rautatientori – ✆ (09) 5425 5000 – www.holidayinn.com/hihelsinki.cc **B2**

174 rm ☕ – 🚹145/265 € 🚹🚹160/280 €

Rest *Verde* – *(closed Saturday lunch and Sunday) (buffet lunch)* Menu 35/45 € – Carte 25/45 €

♦ Chain hotel ♦ Functional ♦

Contemporary chain hotel located close to the post office, station and main shopping areas. Modern bedrooms boast good soundproofing, light wood furnishings and shower-only bathrooms; most have city views. Restaurant serves international and Finnish dishes.

Fabian without rest

Fabiankatu 7 – Ⓜ Kaisaniemi – ✆ (09) 6128 2000 – www.hotelfabian.fi – closed 22-27 December **C2**

58 rm – 🚹140/240 € 🚹🚹170/270 €

♦ Townhouse ♦ Stylish ♦ Modern ♦

Charming and stylish boutique hotel in the heart of the city, opened in 2010 and sister to the Haven hotel. Individually decorated bedrooms with wood floors and tiled bathrooms.

Katajanokka

Vyökatu 1 ✉ 00160 – ✆ (09) 686 450 – www.bwkatajanokka.fi **D2**

106 rm ☕ – 🚹99/207 € 🚹🚹109/227 €

Rest *Jailbird* – *(closed lunch Saturday and Sunday)* Menu 28 € – Carte 29/47 €

♦ Historic ♦ Modern ♦

Pleasantly restored late 19C former prison with high ceilinged corridors and original staircases still in situ. Old cells are now comfortable, well-equipped bedrooms. Large cellar restaurant serves international cuisine and features a preserved prison cell.

Aleksanteri

Albertinkatu 34 ✉ 00180 – Ⓜ Kamppi – ✆ (20) 1234 643 – www.sokoshotels.fi – Closed 1 week Christmas **B3**

151 rm ☕ – 🚹88/239 € 🚹🚹98/249 €

Rest *Fransmanni* – *(closed lunch Saturday and Sunday)* Carte 32/48 €

♦ Business ♦ Modern ♦

Two renovated buildings set by the Alexander Theatre. The 1920s building offers modern, comfortable well-equipped bedrooms, while the 1880s building boasts larger rooms and more characterful features. Restaurant serves French cuisine.

Linna without rest

Lönnrotinkatu 29 ✉ 00180 – Ⓜ Kamppi – ✆ (010) 344 4100 – www.palacekamp.fi – Closed 20 December-2 January **B3**

47 rm – 🚹245/265 € 🚹🚹265 €, ☕ 16.70 € – 1 suite

♦ Townhouse ♦ Modern ♦

Early 20C landmark building with striking art nouveau styling, contemporary interior and friendly staff. Soundproofed bedrooms are in a more recent extension. Breakfast in converted cellar.

Pasila

Maistraatinportti 3 (North : 5 km by Mannerheimintie, Nordenskiöldink off Vetuvitie) ✉ 00240 – ✆ (20) 1234 613 – www.sokoshotels.fi – Closed 18-31 December

178 rm – †71/165 € ††80/250 €

Rest *Sevilla* – *(lunch weekdays only)* Carte 26/53 €

◆ Business ◆ Modern ◆

Spacious hotel in a peaceful area close to the Hartwall Arena and Congress Centre; popular with business types during the week. Modern bedrooms display local decoration and furnishings. Spanish cuisine in Sevilla, with its Andalusian décor.

Rivoli Jardin without rest

Kasarmikatu 40 ✉ 00130 – Ⓜ Kaisaniemi – ✆ (09) 681 500 – www.rivoli.fi – Closed Christmas **C2**

55 rm – †110/210 € ††130/250 €

◆ Townhouse ◆ Classic ◆

Small city centre hotel with pleasant breakfast room and functional, cosy and well maintained bedrooms; top floor rooms have terraces. Sauna and meeting room in the cellar.

Albert

Albertinkatu 30 ✉ 00120 – Ⓜ Kamppi – ✆ (20) 1234 638 – www.sokoshotels.fi – Closed 1 week Christmas **B3**

95 rm – †78/234 € ††93/234 €

Rest *Papa Albert* – *(closed lunch Saturday and Sunday) (dinner only)* Menu 45 € – Carte 30/36 €

◆ Business ◆ Modern ◆

Late 19C building with welcoming lounge bar. Standard bedrooms are compact but well-equipped and are useful for business travellers; superior rooms are slightly larger. Contemporary Papa Albert offers an Italian menu.

Helka

Pohjoinen Rautatiekatu 23 ✉ 00100 – Ⓜ Kamppi – ✆ (09) 613 580 – www.helka.fi – Closed 23-27 December **B2**

146 rm – †100/189 € ††124/189 € – 3 suites

Rest *Helkan Keittiö* – *(dinner only)* Menu 35 € – Carte 30/42 €

◆ Business ◆ Functional ◆

Early 20C building redesigned around the concept of 'nature'. Well-kept, contemporary bedrooms have white walls and huge photos of flora and fauna on the ceilings. In the restaurant, Finnish cuisine can be enjoyed among real tree trunks and large forest prints.

Chez Dominique (Hans Valimaki)

Rikhardinkatu 4 ✉ 00130 – Ⓜ Rautatientori – ✆ (09) 612 7393 – www.chezdominique.fi – Closed Sunday, Monday and lunch Tuesday

Rest – *(booking essential)* Menu 29/59 € – Carte approx. 120 € **C2**

Spec. Duck foie gras with liquorice and pear. Grilled turbot with crab, peas and mint. Oats with wild honey and turnip.

◆ Inventive ◆ Elegant ◆

Elegant restaurant displaying neutral hues and retro furnishings. Skilled kitchen produces modern, well-balanced dishes, crafted from high quality produce. Complex, flavoursome combinations are presented in an innovative manner. Formal yet friendly service.

Savoy

Eteläesplanadi 14 (8th floor) ✉ 00130 – Ⓜ Kaisaniemi – ✆ (09) 6128 5300 – www.royalravintolat.com/savoy – Closed Easter, mid summer and 24 December-10 January **C2**

Rest – Menu 54/70 € – Carte 75/95 €

◆ Finnish ◆ Formal ◆

Opened in 1937, an elegant 8th floor restaurant with a pleasant '30s feel. Terrific views from the summer roof terrace. Carefully sourced ingredients used in largely classical, Finnish dishes.

XXX

Nokka

Kanavaranta 7F ✉ 00160 – ✆ (09) 6128 5600 – www.royalravintolat.com – Closed Easter, mid summer, Christmas, lunch July, 1 and 6 January, 6 December, Saturday lunch and Sunday **D2**

Rest – *(booking advisable)* Menu 39/50 € – Carte dinner 49/58 €

♦ Modern Finnish ♦ Elegant ♦

Converted harbourside warehouse with exposed brick walls, elegant bar, a wine cellar and cookery school. An open kitchen prepares modern Finnish cuisine and relies on small farm producers.

XX ✿

Postres (Vesa Parviainen/Samuli Wirgentius)

✉ 00130 – Ⓜ Kaisaniemi – ✆ (09) 663 300 – www.postres.fi – Closed 3 weeks July, 2 weeks December, Easter, Saturday lunch, Sunday and Monday **C2**

Rest – Menu 29/53 € – Carte dinner 62/78 €

Spec. Nordic sea shrimps with Baltic herring, oysters and gravadlax. Slow-roasted pork belly with ceps and rosemary jus. Tarte Tatin with vanilla ice cream and caramel sauce.

♦ Modern ♦ Design ♦

Modern glass-fronted restaurant on the main esplanade, divided into two bright and stylish rooms. Classical Scandinavian cooking uses French techniques alongside modern, innovative touches to produce dishes that are full of flavour.

XX ✿

Olo (Pekka Terävä)

Kasarmikatu 44 ✉ 00130 – Ⓜ Kaisaneimi – ✆ (09) 665 565 – www.olo-ravintola.fi – Closed 1 July-4 August, 24-27 June, 22-25 September, 23-27 December, Monday dinner and Sunday **C2**

Rest – *(booking advisable)* Menu 48/69 €

Spec. Jerusalem artichoke with vendace roe. Laveret with celery and mushrooms. Whipped porridge with yoghurt and fudge.

♦ Contemporary ♦ Elegant ♦

Attractive, comfortable and immaculately kept corner restaurant, with pleasant service from a young, efficient team. Elegant wine cellar and kitchen studio for private dining. Cooking is refined and unfussy, with some modern touches, and prepared with confidence.

XX ✿

Luomo (Jouni Toivanen)

Vironkatu 8 ✉ 00170 – Ⓜ Kaisaniemi – ✆ (09) 1357287 – www.luomo.fi – Closed midsummer, Easter, 25 December, Sunday and Monday

Rest – *(booking essential) (dinner only) (set menu only)* **C1**

Menu 55/79 €

Spec. Eel and egg. Moroccan goose. Tangerine and liquorice.

♦ Innovative ♦ Intimate ♦ Neighbourhood ♦

Intimate restaurant on residential city street, with antique candelabras and artwork for sale from a local gallery. Modern 3, 5 or 7 course menus display flavoursome ingredients in bold, imaginative combinations, prepared with a high level of skill and technique.

XX

Sasso

Pohjoisesplanadi 17 ✉ 00170 – Ⓜ Kaisaniemi – ✆ (09) 1345 6240 – www.palacekamp.fi/sasso – Closed Christmas, Easter, lunch Saturday, Sunday and bank holidays

Rest – Menu 37 € – Carte (dinner) 37/58 € **C2**

♦ Italian ♦ Fashionable ♦

Spacious harbourside restaurant decorated in contemporary brown hues, with stylish bar and lounge. Well-organised kitchen produces northern Italian dishes, crafted from Scandinavian ingredients.

XX ✿ **Demo** (Tommi Tuominen/Teemu Aura)

Uudenmaankatu 11 ✉ 00120 – Ⓜ Rautatientori – ✆ (09) 228 90 840 – www.restaurantdemo.fi
– Closed 16-31 July, 20 December-6 January, Easter, Sunday, Monday and bank holidays **C2**

Rest – *(dinner only) (booking essential)* Menu 57 € – Carte 62/76 €
Spec. Pigeon breast stuffed with foie gras and apple terrine. Pot roasted wild duck with braised red cabbage. Caramel soufflé with raspberry ice cream.
♦ Modern Finnish ♦ Intimate ♦

Atmospheric candlelit restaurant on busy street, with neutral hues and relaxed, shabby-chic style; sit on retro chairs or comfy banquettes. Classical cooking combines French and Finnish influences to produce robust and satisfying dishes. Good wine recommendations.

XX **Mange Sud**

Tehtaankatu 34 D2 ✉ 00150 – ✆ (020) 711 8350 – www.mangesud.fi
– Closed 23 December-3 January, 23-27 June, Sunday and Monday

Rest – *(dinner only and Saturday lunch)* Menu 29/42 € – Carte 41/53 € **C3**
♦ Mediterranean ♦ Neighbourhood ♦

Eye-catching red property in smart, southern residential area. Stylish dining rooms; actors appear occasionally for some impromtu theatre. Confident cooking displays Mediterranean influences.

XX **FishMarket**

Pohjoisesplanadi 17 ✉ 00170 – Ⓜ Kaisaniemi – ✆ (09) 1345 6220 – www.palacekamp.fi – Closed Sunday **C2**

Rest – *(dinner only)* Menu 52 € – Carte 47/88 €
♦ Seafood ♦ Elegant ♦

Several different dining areas set within the basement of a former pharmacy, with elegant décor and bright, contemporary Scandinavian furnishings. The daily catch is displayed at the bar.

XX **Yume** – at Kämp Hotel

Kluuvikatu 2 ✉ 00100 – Ⓜ Kaisaniemi – ✆ (09) 57611718 – www.palacekamp.fi
– Closed 8 May, 25 June, 5 and 13 November, 6 and 24-26 December and Sunday **C2**

Rest – *(dinner only)* Menu 40/50 € – Carte 34/61 €
♦ Japanese ♦ Fashionable ♦

Contemporary restaurant set in the Kämp Hotel, with pleasant, seasonal décor. Menus present a wide selection of Japanese cuisine, with some dishes adapted to suit European tastes.

XX **Alia**

Mustikkamaankuja 1 (North : 3 km by Hämeentie) ✉ 00570 – ✆ (09) 66 00 66 – www.alia.fi
– Closed Easter, 24 December-6 January, Sunday dinner and Monday

Rest – Menu 29 € – Carte 46/55 €
♦ Finnish ♦ Rustic ♦

This country sister to Postres is housed within a traditional wooden building, surrounded by trees. More modern interior is divided into four rooms. Expect classic Finnish and French dishes.

XX **Bellevue**

Rahapajankatu 3 ✉ 00160 – Ⓜ Kaisaniemi – ✆ (09) 179 560 – www.restaurantbellevue.com
– Closed July, 23-26 December, Sunday and Monday **D2**

Rest – Menu 27/58 € – Carte 39/65 €
♦ Russian ♦ Cosy ♦

Opened in 1917, this townhouse restaurant boasts several dining rooms adorned with paintings and knick-knacks. Russian cuisine proudly maintains tradition; waiters wear authentic costumes.

XX

Havis – at Haven Hotel

Eteläranta 16 ✉ 00130 – ✆ (09) 6128 5800 – www.royalravintolat.com/havis **C2**

Rest – *(Closed Easter, Sunday and Saturday lunch except summer)*
Menu 42 € – Carte 48/54 €

♦ Seafood ♦ Elegant ♦

19C harbourside restaurant serving carefully crafted seafood dishes. Two rooms – one with elegant vaulted ceiling and maritime knick-knacks, the other with contemporary open kitchen and terrace.

X

Muru

Fredrikinkatu 41 ✉ 00120 – Ⓜ Kamppi – ✆ (09) 42891213 – www.murudining.fi **B2**

Rest – *(booking advisable) (dinner only)* Menu 42/49 €

♦ Modern ♦ Neighbourhood ♦ Trendy ♦

Four young owners have created a vibrant, welcoming spot. The rustic feel comes with a contemporary edge and the cooking is refined yet also gutsy. All dishes are available as starters or main courses. The bar is made from old wine boxes.

X

Grotesk

Ludviginkatu 10 ✉ 00130 – Ⓜ Rautatientori – ✆ (10) 470 2100 – www.grotesk.fi
– Closed 23-27 December, Monday dinner, Saturday lunch and Sunday

Rest – Menu 25/42 € – Carte dinner 39/51 € **C2**

♦ Modern Finnish ♦ Fashionable ♦

Trendy city centre restaurant with stylish black and red décor, canopy-covered patio terrace and buzzy atmosphere. Modern Finnish cooking is heartwarming and flavoursome. The lounge bar is open in the evening and attracts a younger crowd. Informal service.

X

Goce

Fredrikinkatu 37 – ✆ (010) 548 63 03 – www.goce.fi
– Closed 22 December-3 January, 1-4 April, Sunday, lunch Saturday and dinner Monday-Tuesday **B2**

Rest – *(booking essential) (set menu only)* Menu 24/38 €

♦ Innovative ♦ Trendy ♦

Cosy, bustling restaurant kitted out with a knowing, retro look and featuring clear plastic chairs. Cooking comes in small plates; simply decide on the number and leave the rest to the kitchen.

X

La Table

Ludviginkatu 3-5 ✉ 00100 – Ⓜ Rautatientori – ✆ (09) 673 236 – www.latable.fi
– Closed Saturday and Sunday **C2**

Rest – *(booking essential)* Menu 27/39 €

♦ Modern ♦ Design ♦ Bistro ♦

Flavoursome and well-priced regional dishes from a simple but balanced menu are the draw at this friendly little bistro-style restaurant in the centre of town. Comic faces adorning the white and green walls add to the bonhomie. The chef also teaches cookery.

X

Solna

Solnantie 26 (Northwest : 5 km by Mannerheimintie, Tukholmankatu, Paciusgatan and Munkkiniemen puistotie, by tram N° 4 alighting at Laaja Ladhden Aukio) ✉ 00330 – ✆ (09) 530 1400 – www.solna.fi
– Closed Easter, 23 December-3 January, Saturday lunch and Sunday

Rest – Menu 37/44 €

♦ Scandinavian ♦ Bistro ♦

Keenly run neighbourhood restaurant set within a residential building and boasting contemporary bistro styling and a warm atmosphere. Concise, well-priced menus offer hearty, flavoursome dishes crafted from quality ingredients. Friendly, efficient service.

Farang

Ainonkatu 3 (inside the Kunsthalle) – Ⓜ Kamppi – ✆ (09) 454 4212 – www.farang.fi
– Closed July, Saturday lunch, Sunday, Monday and bank holidays
Rest – Menu 26/59 € – Carte 34/51 € **B2**
♦ Thai ♦ Trendy ♦
The Kunsthalle exhibition venue also plays host to this stylish, modern restaurant, decorated in hues of black, grey and red. Black wood tables and chairs separated by transparent curtains. Zesty, harmonious, vibrant dishes from South East Asia. Friendly service.

Chef & Sommelier

Huvilakatu 28A ✉ 00150 – ✆ (400) 959 440 – www.chefetsommelier.fi
– Closed Easter, July, Christmas, Sunday and Monday **C3**
Rest – *(booking advisable) (dinner only)* Menu 42 €
♦ Organic ♦ Neighbourhood ♦
Cosy and simply decorated restaurant with a friendly atmosphere. The open kitchen uses organic and Fairtrade ingredients for its Finnish cuisine. Set menus include a vegetarian option.

Lyon

Mannerheimintie 56 ✉ 00260 – ✆ (09) 408 131 – www.ravintolalyon.fi
– Closed Easter, midsummer, July, Christmas, Sunday, Monday and bank holidays **A1**
Rest – *(dinner only and lunch 3 weeks before Christmas)* Menu 44 € – Carte 44/68 €
♦ French ♦ Bistro ♦
Well-established restaurant with traditional French bistro feel, set close to the Opera. Wide-ranging menus offer seasonal French and vegetarian dishes crafted from good Finnish ingredients.

Mecca

Korkeavuorenkatu 34 ✉ 00130 – Ⓜ Kaisaniemi – ✆ (09) 1345 6200 – www.palacekamp.fi
– Closed Easter, 6 and 23-30 December and Sunday **C2**
Rest – *(dinner only)* Menu 35/65 € – Carte 29/52 €
♦ International ♦ Fashionable ♦ Musical ♦
Large, moodily lit restaurant with lively atmosphere and clubby feel; the chef's abstract art adorns the walls. The open kitchen delivers creative, wide-ranging, international cuisine.

Ateljé Finne

Arkadiankatu 14 ✉ 00100 – Ⓜ Kamppi – ✆ (09) 493 110 – www.ateljefinne.fi
– Closed July and 23 December-5 January **B2**
Rest – *(dinner only) (booking advisable)* Menu 39 € – Carte 39/45 €
♦ Modern Finnish ♦ Bistro ♦
Formerly the studio of famous Finnish sculptor Gunnar Finne, now three small bistro-style dining rooms decorated with local art. Local dishes are given contemporary and international twists.

Juuri

Korkeavuorenkatu 27 ✉ 00130 – ✆ (09) 635 732 – www.juuri.fi
– Closed 24-26 December and Sunday lunch **C2**
Rest – Carte 36/45 €
♦ Finnish ♦ Bistro ♦
Small bistro with traditional feel and friendly service, close to the Design Museum. Classic Finnish cuisine and tapas-style starters; lunch menu more concise. Organic deli next door.

Kuurna

Meritullinkatu 6 ✉ 00170 – Ⓜ Kaisaniemi – ☎ (09) 670 849 – www.kuurna.fi
– Closed July, 2 weeks Christmas, Sunday and Monday **C2**
Rest – *(booking essential) (dinner only)* Menu 37 € – Carte 37/48 €
♦ Finnish ♦ Neighbourhood ♦
Small but very popular restaurant with vaulted ceiling and seating for just twenty. Set menu offers three choices and is supplemented by blackboard specials. Seasonal Finnish cooking.

K17

Kalevankatu 17 ✉ 00100 – Ⓜ Kamppi – ☎ (040) 1711117 – www.k17.fi
– Closed Saturday lunch, Sunday and bank holidays **B2**
Rest – *(set menu only)* Menu 27/55 €
♦ Trendy ♦ Individual ♦
Fashionable spot known as much for its cocktails as its food. Minimalist in style, with all white decoration in the dining room and all black in the bar. Understated, modern menu.

Bistro Helsinki 15

Korkeavuorenkatu 4B ✉ 00150 – ☎ (09) 4242 7650 – www.bistrohelsinki.fi
– Closed Easter, 25-27 June, lunch 27 June-5 August, 23-26 December, Monday dinner, Saturday lunch and Sunday **C3**
Rest – Menu 42/49 € – Carte 41/48 €
♦ Italian ♦ Bistro ♦ Elegant ♦
Friendly neighbourhood restaurant with a narrow dining room and chrome bar. Italian cooking has a modern edge and incorporates some Finnish touches; simpler menu offered at lunch.

AT HELSINKI-VANTAA AIRPORT

Hilton Helsinki Vantaa

Lentàjànkuja 1 ✉ 01530 – ☎ (09) 732 20
– www.helsinki-vantaa-airport.hilton.com
241 rm – †125/245 € ††125/245 €, ☕ 24 € – 5 suites
Rest *Gui* – *(closed Saturday and Sunday lunch)* Menu 34 €
– Carte 42/51 €
♦ Business ♦ Modern ♦
Spacious glass hotel with relaxed ambience, 3min from the international terminal. Soundproofed bedrooms boast locally designed furniture, good facilities and large bathrooms; some have saunas. Contemporary restaurant serves Finnish and international dishes.

FRANCE

PROFILE

→ **Area:**
551 500 km^2
(212 934 sq mi).

→ **Population:**
64 667 000 inhabitants (est. 2010), density = 110 per km^2.

→ **Capital:**
Paris (conurbation 11 598 866 inhabitants).

→ **Currency:**
Euro (€); rate of exchange: € 1 = US$ 1.37 (Dec. 2010).

→ **Government:**
Parliamentary republic (since 1946). Member of European Union since 1957 (one of the 6 founding countries).

→ **Language:**
French.

→ **Specific public holidays:**
Victory Day 1945 (8 May), Bastille Day-National Day (14 July), Armistice Day 1918 (11 November).

→ **Local Time:**
GMT + 1 hour in winter and GMT + 2 hours in summer.

→ **Climate:**
Temperate with cool winters and warm summers (Paris: January: 3°C, July: 20°C). Mediterranean climate in the south (mild winters, hot and sunny summers, occasional strong wind called the mistral).

→ **International dialling Code:**
00 33 followed by regional code without the initial **0** and then the local number.

→ **Emergency:**
Police: ✆ **17**;
Ambulance: ✆ **15**;
Fire Brigade: ✆ **18**.

→ **Electricity:**
220 volts AC, 50Hz. 2-pin round-shaped continental plugs.

→ **Formalities**
Travellers from the European Union (EU), Switzerland, Iceland and the main countries of North and South America need a national identity card or passport (America: passport required) to visit France for less than three months (tourism or business purpose). For visitors from other countries a visa may be required, in addition to a passport, especially for those wishing to stay for longer than three months. We advise you to check with your embassy before travelling.

PARIS

PARIS

Population (est.2010): 2 203 817 (conurbation 11 598 866) – Altitude: 30m

'rille Lips/Fotolia.com

It may be the city of a hundred and one clichés, but Paris never fails to come up with the goods. The French capital is one of the truly great cities of the world, a metropolis that eternally satisfies the desires of its beguiled visitors. With its harmonious layout, typified by the grand geometric boulevards radiating from the Arc de Triomphe like the spokes of a wheel, Paris is designed to enrapture.

Despite its ever-widening tentacles, most of the things worth seeing are contained within the city's ring road, the Boulevard Périphérique. The very heart of Paris is an island, the Ile de la Cité, where over two thousand years ago Celtic tribes first eked out a living. Later the Romans took control, attracted by the strategic possibilities of this settlement in the middle of the Seine. In time, a series of French kings achieved the centralisation of France, with Paris its cultural, political and economic nerve centre. Romance still pervades the streets of the twenty-first century city – a stroll along the Left Bank conjures images of Doisneau's magical monochrome photographs, while the narrow, cobbled streets of Montmartre vividly call up the colourful cool of Toulouse-Lautrec. But Paris is not resting on its laurels. New buildings and new cultural sensations are never far away: most recent has been the headline-grabbing Musée du Quai Branly. Les Grands Travaux are forever in the wings, waiting to inspire.

LIVING THE CITY

Paris wouldn't be Paris *sans* its Left and Right Banks. The **Left Bank** takes in the city south of the Seine; the **Right Bank** comprises the north and west. There are twenty **arrondissements** (quarters) set within the **Boulevard Périphérique**. The **Ile de la Cité** is the nucleus around which the city grew and the oldest quarters around this site are the 1st, 2nd, 3rd, 4th arrondissements on the Right Bank and 5th and 6th on the Left Bank. The remaining arrondissements fan out in a clockwise direction from here. Landmarks are universally known: the **Eiffel Tower** and the **Arc de Triomphe** are to the west of the centre (though on different sides of the river), the **Sacré-Coeur** is to the north, **Montparnasse Tower** to the south, and, of course, **Notre-Dame Cathedral** slap bang in the middle (of the Seine).

PRACTICAL INFORMATION

ARRIVAL-DEPARTURE

Roissy-Charles-de-Gaulle Airport is 23km northeast of Paris and by taxi will cost around €55. Air France Bus to Montparnasse or Porte Maillot runs every 15min. Orly Airport is 14km south and a taxi will be approximately €35. The Air France Bus runs to Invalides or Montparnasse. The Eurostar runs from the Gare du Nord, on the Rue de Dunkerque in the 10th arrondissement.

TRANSPORT

Paris has an excellent public transport system, and it's inexpensive too. Choose between the bus or the metro. A single ticket has a flat fare however far you travel; a carnet (book of ten tickets) works out at very good value for money.

There are three different travel cards you can also buy. Paris Visite is a one-day pass for three zones, or five-day pass for five zones; Mobilis is a one-day pass giving unlimited travel in either zones 1-2, or zones 1-6; Pass Navigo is a weekly or monthly pass valid from Monday-Sunday or from the first of the month, offering an advantageous rate (you'll need a photograph for this one).

In 2007 Paris introduced the Velib. It's a self-service bicycle system – you pick up one of the fifteen thousand bikes stationed at any of 1200 points across the city, and leave it at another one. Subscription is a euro a day - the first half-hour of the journey is free, then after that you pay another euro if you require another half hour. Swiping a normal travel card will free up your bike – then it's just you versus the Parisian traffic...

EXPLORING PARIS

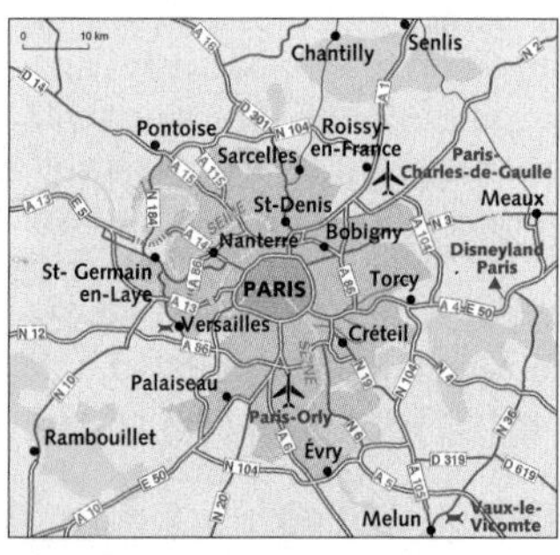

There are so many ways to enjoy the aura of Paris that even those who have never set foot in the city will recognise the familiar poetic selling points. A boat trip along the **Seine**; a café pose in **Boulevard St Germain**; the majestic glories of Notre-Dame cathedral; the utterly emblematic **Eiffel Tower**; a casual meander through the arty alleyways of **Montmartre** (enjoying the fabulous view, of course); the importance of the **Louvre's** mighty collection; getting to grips with the **Centre Pompidou** (still futuristic after more than thirty years). However often you're reminded of them, these are images that never lose their power to seduce.

More than any other European city, Paris is defined by its river. The Seine slices its way through the centre, dividing the capital into two distinct areas. The Left Bank has, for centuries, been the home of poets, writers and artists. Inspired by the proximity of **the Sorbonne**, France's first university, radicals and intellectuals have throughout the ages flourished their quills and philosophised upon the world; many of their tracts can be found languishing in *les bouquinistes*, the Seine-side bookstalls it's impossible not to stop and browse over. Latin speaking students of the Sorbonne gave this area its name; today the **Latin Quarter** is filled with art galleries, cafés and bookshops. It's still the done thing to linger in the legendary cafés and brasseries of Boulevard St-Germain and reflect on more than the price of handbags in the smart boutiques lining the street. The classic trio – **Café de Flore, Les Deux Magots** and **Brasserie Lipp** – sit within a beguiling proximity to each other: a triangle of culinary and intellectual temptation.

→ THE SEINE CHOICE

Many of the major sights of Paris are famously strung out along the river, like an imposing architectural necklace. Two, of more recent vintage, have created quite a stir on the waterfront. If you're in Paris in the summer time, go down to the river at the eastern end of the Louvre, in the shadow of the **Pont des Arts**, and there you'll find sandy beaches, palm trees, ice-cream stalls, water sprinklers and deckchairs, not to mention fitness classes, too. This is **Paris Plage**, which, over the last eight years, has become a bit of an institution. Further west, in the long shadow of the Eiffel Tower, a museum has been pulling in visitors by the thousand. The **Musée du Quai Branly** squats low like a barge and invites you in along a sensuously swooping white ramp, while inside, mud-coloured walls form the dimly lit backdrop to powerful displays of tribal and folk art from France's colonial past. This was President Chirac's pet project, and it's shaping up to become as popular as those of his predecessors Pompidou and Mitterrand.

→ CREATING AN IMPRESSION

Mind you, it'll have to go some to catch the city's other artistic institutions. Further east along the riverfront, for example, the magical **Musée d'Orsay** continues to inspire. Everything about it is striking, from its Industrial Age railway station shell to its fabulous collections of nineteenth century art, which read like the greatest hits of Impressionist painting; realists and symbolists are there too, and substantial arrays of Van Gogh, Gauguin and Cézanne. Across the Seine, The Louvre – the museum to end all museums – is where to go for a daunting array of antiquities and French neo-classical grandeur, while the Centre Pompidou brings you bang up to date with a peerless collection of works by the likes of Picasso, Kandinsky, Matisse and Miro, right up to the latest trends.

→ EAST SIDE STORY

Taking a trip on the water doesn't have to mean taking a trip on the Seine. There's a hauntingly evocative sojourn you can take to a forgotten Paris – a liquid journey that takes you right under the **Bastille**. The **Canal Saint-Martin** winds its way up the eastern side of the city from the **Porte de l'Arsenal**, just below the Bastille, to **Parc de la Villette**, some four kilometres away. Alleys of chestnut trees cloak the peaceful, still waters of the two hundred year old canal, at one point just a stone's throw from the roaring **Place de la République**. The journey includes idyllic stretches with arching iron footbridges and boatman's pathways. It has ghoulish landmarks, too: the elegant **Maison des Morts** is where they used to pay rewards for bodies fished from the canal, and immediately below the Bastille, in a deep, dark netherworld, the boat slows to reveal a crypt, wherein lie the remains of the victims of the revolutions of 1830 and 1848. Open-topped tourist boats cover the fascinating two-and-a-half hour trip a few times a day.

→ THREE CEMETERIES

A cemetery may not be on every city's visitor hit-list, but every city isn't Paris, which has three great *cimetières*, full of history's rich and famous, and **Père-Lachaise** is the greatest of them all. Visit this massive sea of sepulchres, where the only movement appears to be the flapping of crows' wings above the deadly calm, and you'll pick out a long list of the great and the good who happen to have breathed their last in the city. Then you'll understand the wisdom of the saying: "You haven't lived until you've died in Paris". The twelfth century lovers Abelard and Heloise were the first to be reburied here, and in the last two hundred years, they've been followed by a veritable A-list Who's Who. The range is phenomenal, from Chopin to Jim Morrison, Balzac to Piaf, Rossini to Oscar Wilde and Molière to Isadora Duncan. Despite the great clamour they may have made in their lives, they now rest in a stunningly tranquil oasis of peace, the largest green space in Paris.

For contrast, what better than the life-affirming paintings of the twentieth century's most acclaimed artist. The **Picasso Museum** is hidden in a fine seventeenth century mansion in R**ue de Thorigny**, a back street in the fascinating **Marais Quarter**. It holds nearly four thousand of his works, from childhood sketches to important late works.

CALENDAR HIGHLIGHTS

Whatever your fancy, Paris can satisfy it. March is a good time for book lovers to indulge a wordy fix: the Salon du Livre Paris at the Parc des Expositions Paris-Nord Villepinte is a five day orgy *des mots* with a shelf-full of performances, while Poets' Springtime has over five thousand well versed events in streets, cafés, markets, museums, schools and stations. Later in the year, October's Reading Festival boasts hundreds of written word events. The music world takes to the City of Light with an eclectic flourish. The Open-Air Classical Music Festival on weekends in August and September brings world-class performers to Parc Floral, and in the same month Jazz à

PARIS IN…

→ ONE DAY

Eiffel Tower and a boat trip on the Seine, Musée d'Orsay, people watching in a St-Germain brasserie

→ TWO DAYS

Musée du Quai Branly (or The Louvre), Montmartre, Picasso Museum and the Marais

→ THREE DAYS

Père-Lachaise, Canal Saint-Martin, Centre Pompidou

la Villette, in Parc de la Villette, grows annually in stature as a home for innovative, experimental jazz. Dramatic Spanish rhythms cut through the springtime air in March's International Flamenco Festival at Le Grand Rex. Meantime, in north-east Paris, Seine St-Denis chills to the Banlieues Bleues, also in March. If your springtime fancy turns to art, then head to Art Paris, at Grand Palais, for a high quality small collection of paintings, sculptures and photos. You can stay up late either at La Nuit des Musées (May) when museums keep their doors open until 1am, or at Nuit Blanche (October) when it seems every public space in the city lets you in for a nocturnal cultural nose around. Catch a diverse programme of movies at springtime's Paris Film Festival, at the Cinéma Gaumont Marignan on the Champs-Élysées, or indulge your taste for wine at October's Montmartre Grape Harvest Festival (la Butte has its own vineyard). Hang around for a month and you can carouse on the Carrousel du Louvre at November's Great Wines Fair. If your taste is for beer and chips, a world away from the cultural clichés of Paris, then lose yourself amongst five million others at Europe's largest funfair, the Foire du Trône, at Pelouse de Reuilly, in the spring.

EATING OUT

Three hundred years ago, the social philosopher Montesquieu famously said, "Lunch kills half of Paris, supper the other half." Food plays such an important role in Gallic life that eating well is deemed a citizen's birthright. Stroll around any part of the capital and lavish looking shops offer perfectly presented treats: the Place de la Madeleine, for instance, has a lip-smacking range of treats. Parisians are intensely knowledgeable about their food and wine to the extent that restaurant, bistro and brasserie offerings here are of a higher quality than just about any other European city. Mind you, the French capital has had a lot on its plate in recent years with the rest of Europe seemingly playing catch up, by way of strong gastronomic performances coming from the likes of Barcelona, London and Copenhagen. As though Paris would rest on its laurels! Young chefs have taken up the cudgels and are opening their own crowd-pulling bistros and inventing their own styles; they've broken away from more formulaic regimes to achieve their own goals. They can call on the strongest backup team around: specialist produce shops line every Parisian thoroughfare, and there are not far short of a hundred city-wide markets teeming with fresh produce. Remember, when eating in Paris, to enjoy your meal at a leisurely pace – this is the city, after all, that practically shuts up shop at 12.30pm for lunch. People think nothing of spending up to three hours at the table, so if you're pressed for time, go to a brasserie or café. A service charge of fifteen per cent is normally included in the price of the meal, but locals leave an additional five per cent in smaller restaurants, and five to ten per cent in the grander establishments, which pride themselves on their service. (If you think the service has been a bit brusque or haughty, just remember that a Parisian waiter walks on average between six and twelve miles a day attending to customers' whims).

HOTELS FROM A TO Z

M

N

O

P

R

S

T

V

W

RESTAURANTS FROM A TO Z

OPEN SATURDAY AND SUNDAY

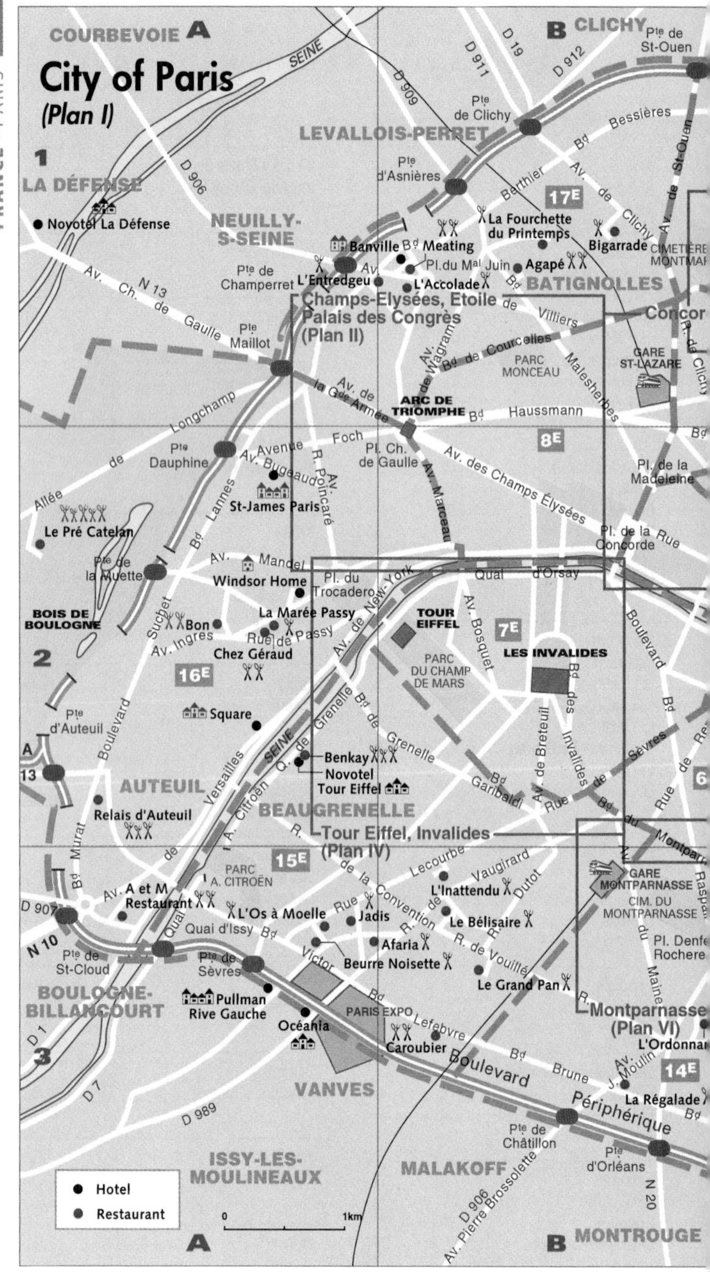
City of Paris
(Plan I)
Novotel La Défense
Banville
Meating
La Fourchette du Printemps
Bigarrade
Agapé
L'Entredgeu
L'Accolade
Champs-Elysées, Etoile Palais des Congrès (Plan II)
St-James Paris
Le Pré Catelan
Windsor Home
La Marée Passy
Bon
Chez Géraud
Square
Benkay
Novotel Tour Eiffel
Relais d'Auteuil
Tour Eiffel, Invalides (Plan IV)
A et M Restaurant
L'Os à Moelle
Jadis
L'Inattendu
Le Bélisaire
Afaria
Beurre Noisette
Le Grand Pan
Pullman Rive Gauche
Océania
Caroubier
Montparnasse (Plan VI)
L'Ordonnan
La Régalade
Hotel
Restaurant
0
1km

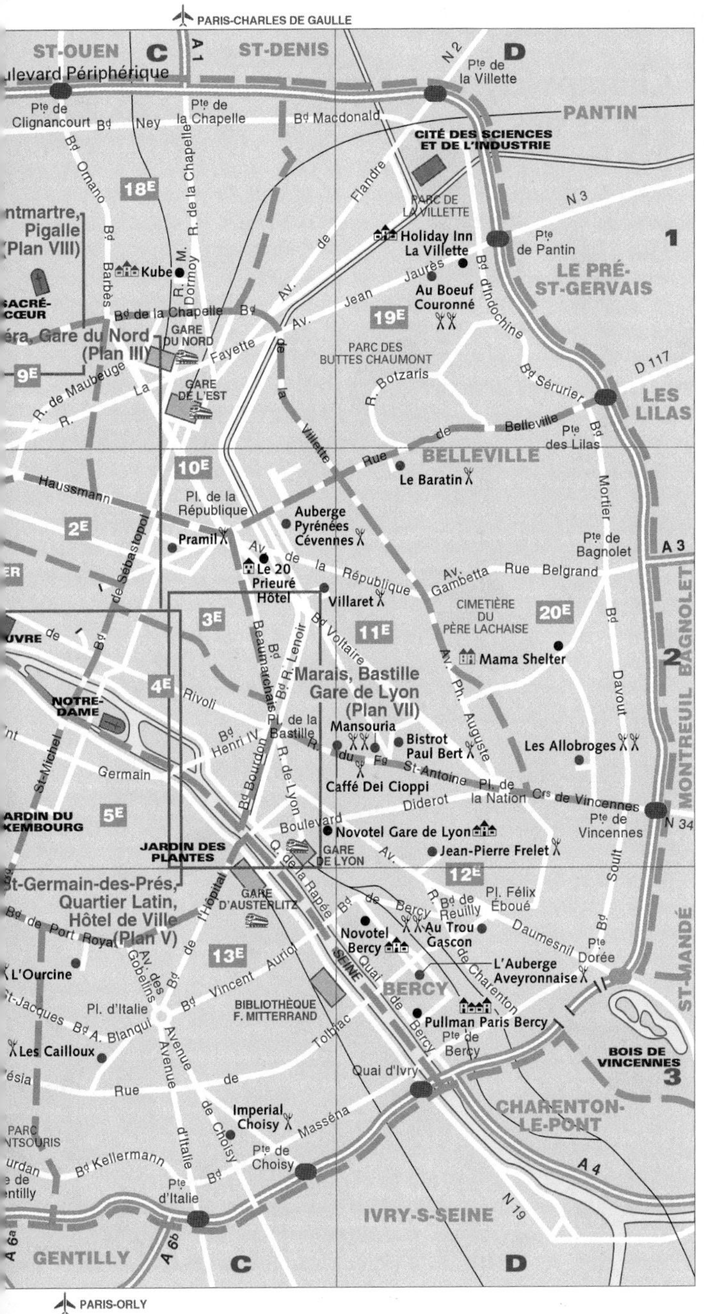
PARIS-CHARLES DE GAULLE
ST-OUEN
ST-DENIS
PANTIN
CITÉ DES SCIENCES ET DE L'INDUSTRIE
PARC DE LA VILLETTE
Holiday Inn La Villette
Kube
Au Boeuf Couronné
LE PRÉ-ST-GERVAIS
PARC DES BUTTES CHAUMONT
GARE DU NORD
GARE DE L'EST
LES LILAS
BELLEVILLE
Le Baratin
Auberge Pyrénées Cévennes
Pramil
Le 20 Prieuré Hôtel
Villaret
CIMETIÈRE DU PÈRE LACHAISE
Mama Shelter
Marais, Bastille Gare de Lyon (Plan VII)
NOTRE-DAME
Mansouria
Bistrot Paul Bert
Les Allobroges
Caffé Dei Cioppi
JARDIN DES PLANTES
Novotel Gare de Lyon
Jean-Pierre Frelet
GARE DE LYON
GARE D'AUSTERLITZ
St-Germain-des-Prés, Quartier Latin, Hôtel de Ville (Plan V)
Novotel Bercy
Au Trou Gascon
L'Auberge Aveyronnaise
L'Ourcine
BIBLIOTHÈQUE F. MITTERRAND
BERCY
Pullman Paris Bercy
Les Cailloux
BOIS DE VINCENNES
CHARENTON-LE-PONT
Imperial Choisy
IVRY-S-SEINE
GENTILLY
PARIS-ORLY

Champs-Élysées, Étoile, Palais des Congrès
(Plan II)

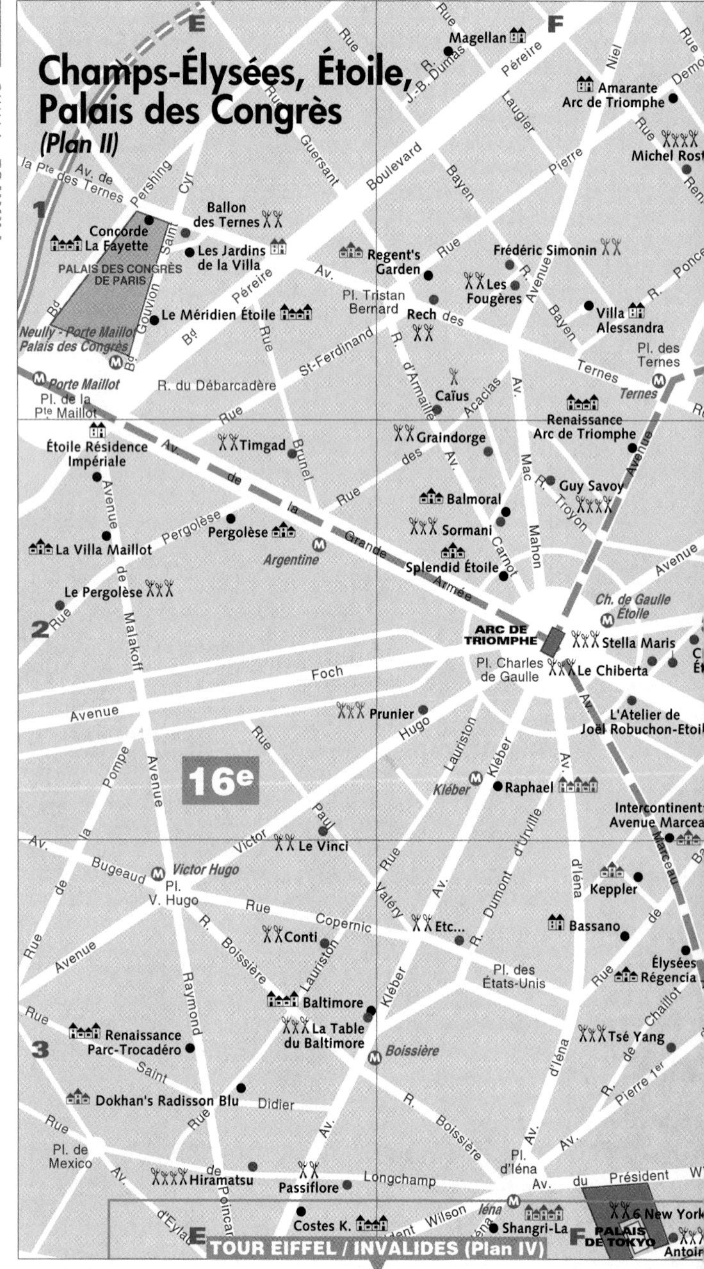

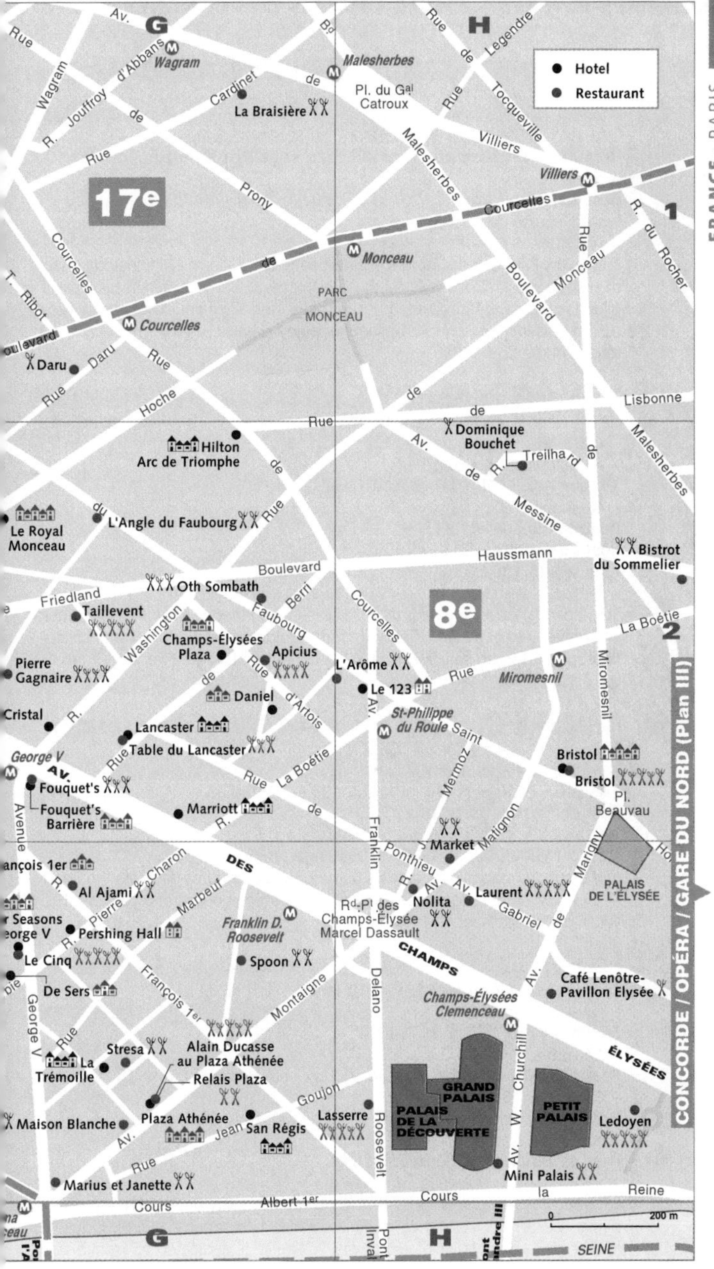
Hotel
Restaurant
17e
8e
La Braisière
Daru
Hilton Arc de Triomphe
Dominique Bouchet
Le Royal Monceau
L'Angle du Faubourg
Bistrot du Sommelier
Oth Sombath
Taillevent
Champs-Élysées Plaza
Apicius
L'Arôme
Le 123
Pierre Gagnaire
Daniel
Cristal
Lancaster
Table du Lancaster
Bristol
Fouquet's
Fouquet's Barrière
Marriott
Market
Al Ajami
Laurent
Nolita
Pershing Hall
Le Cinq
Spoon
Café Lenôtre-Pavillon Elysée
De Sers
Stresa
Alain Ducasse au Plaza Athénée
Relais Plaza
La Trémoille
Maison Blanche
Plaza Athénée
San Régis
Lasserre
Ledoyen
Mini Palais
Marius et Janette
GRAND PALAIS
PALAIS DE LA DÉCOUVERTE
PETIT PALAIS
PALAIS DE L'ÉLYSÉE
PARC MONCEAU
Pl. Beauvau
Pl. du Gal Catroux
Rd-Pt des Champs-Élysée Marcel Dassault
Wagram
Malesherbes
Villiers
Monceau
Courcelles
Miromesnil
St-Philippe du Roule
George V
Franklin D. Roosevelt
Champs-Élysées Clemenceau
SEINE
200 m
CONCORDE / OPÉRA / GARE DU NORD (Plan III)

Plaza Athénée

25 av. Montaigne (8th) – Ⓜ *Alma Marceau* – ✆ *01 53 67 66 65*
– *www.plaza-athenee-paris.com* **G3**
146 rm – †590/935 € ††700/935 €, ☕ 50 € – 45 suites
Rest *Alain Ducasse au Plaza Athénée et Le Relais Plaza*
– see below
Rest *La Cour Jardin* – ✆ *01 53 67 66 02 (open from mid May-mid September)* Carte 78/136 €
♦ Palace ♦ Grand Luxury ♦ Classic ♦
This luxury Parisian hotel par excellence opened its doors in 1911. In addition to the classic and Art Deco styles of the guestrooms, the Plaza Athénée also boasts gilded fixtures and fittings, marble furnishings, and a luxurious Dior beauty centre. The essence of comfort! In summer enjoy classic dishes on the charming terrace of the Cour Jardin.

Four Seasons George V

31 av. George-V (8th) – Ⓜ *George V*
– ✆ *01 49 52 70 00*
– *www.fourseasons.com/paris* **G3**
197 rm – †750/1095 € ††750/1095 €, ☕ 50 €
– 48 suites
Rest *Le Cinq* – see below
Rest *La Galerie* – ✆ *01 49 52 70 06*
– Carte 115/180 €
♦ Palace ♦ Grand Luxury ♦ Personalised ♦
This legendary palace dating from 1928 is embellished with all the splendour and refinement of the 18C. Spacious and luxurious guestrooms, artwork collections, plus a superb spa. In summer, the tables in this restaurant are set out in the delightful interior courtyard.

Le Bristol

112 r. Fg St-Honoré (8th) – Ⓜ *Miromesnil* – ✆ *01 53 43 43 00*
– *www.lebristolparis.com* **H2**
148 rm – †650 € ††770/1600 €, ☕ 39 € – 39 suites
Rest *Le Bristol* – see below
♦ Palace ♦ Grand Luxury ♦ Stylish ♦
This luxury hotel, built in 1925 and boasting a new wing added in 2009, is arranged around a magnificent garden. Sumptuous guestrooms decorated in Louis XV or Louis XVI style, as well as a stunning swimming pool, reminiscent of a 19C yacht, on the top floor.

Shangri-La

10 av. d'Iéna (16th) ✉ *75116* – Ⓜ *Iéna* – ✆ *01 53 67 19 98*
– *www.shangri-la.com* **F3**
54 rm – †750/1675 € ††750/1675 €, ☕ 48 €
– 27 suites
Rest *L'Abeille* – *(closed August, Sunday and Monday)* Menu 180 €
– Carte 110/150 €
Rest *Shang Palace* – *(opening scheduled in April) (closed Tuesday and Wednesday)* Carte 50/200 €
Rest *La Bauhinia* – Carte 75/120 €
♦ Palace ♦ Historic ♦ Stylish ♦
Late-19C Paris meets Asia in the most recent of the city's palatial hotels occupying the former residence of Prince Roland Bonaparte (1896). Opulent luxury and a distinct air of exclusivity. L'Abeille is dedicated to French cuisine. Cantonese specialities in the Shang Palace. Enjoy all-day dining at the Bauhinia.

Le Royal Monceau

37 av. Hoche (8th) – Ⓜ Charles de Gaulle-Etoile – ✆ 01 42 99 88 00 – www.leroyalmonceau.com **G2**

117 rm – 780/1800 € 780/1800 €, 49 € – 32 suites

Rest *La Cuisine* – Carte 62/95 €

Rest *Il Carpaccio* – *(closed Sunday and Monday)* Carte 70/92 €

Rest *Le Grand Salon* – Carte 49/85 €

♦ Palace ♦ Grand Luxury ♦ Design ♦

Le Royal received a facelift in 2010, transforming it into a luxury hotel fit for the 21C. Redesigned by Philippe Starck, the decor is in keeping with the contemporary theme, with an art gallery, bookshop and high-tech cinema. Art-filled decor in La Cuisine. Enjoy attractively prepared Italian cuisine at Le Carpaccio. This luxurious lounge area is the perfect setting for a drink or snack.

Raphael

17 av. Kléber (16th) ✉ 75116 – Ⓜ Kléber – ✆ 01 53 64 32 00 – www.raphael-hotel.com **F2**

83 rm – 375/535 € 375/535 €, 39 € – 37 suites

Rest *Les Jardins Plein Ciel* – *✆ 01 53 64 32 30 (open from May-September and closed Saturday lunch and Sunday)* Menu 55 € bi (lunch)/65 € bi – Carte 80/150 €

Rest *La Salle à Manger* – *(closed August, Saturday and Sunday)* Menu 55 € bi (lunch)/65 € bi – Carte 80/120 €

♦ Palace ♦ Stylish ♦

The Raphael, built in 1925, offers a superb wood-panelled gallery, refined rooms, a rooftop terrace with a panoramic view and a trendy English bar. A lovely view of Paris and seasonal cuisine are the hallmarks of the Jardins Plein Ciel (seventh floor). Enjoy traditional gourmet dining in the palatial surroundings of this restaurant.

Fouquet's Barrière

46 av. George-V (8th) – Ⓜ George V – ✆ 01 40 69 60 00 – www.fouquets-barriere.com **G2**

81 rm – 750/960 € 750/960 €, 46 € – 31 suites

Rest *Le Diane* – *✆ 01 40 69 60 60 (closed 31 July-22 August, 2 to 10 January, Saturday lunch, Sunday and Monday)* Menu 78/125 € bi – Carte 83/136 €

♦ Grand Luxury ♦ Modern ♦

This hotel, a member of the Barrière, bears the decorative imprint of Jacques Garcia, featuring a mix of Art Deco and Empire styles. Elegant guestrooms, a superb spa and a patio. Find a hushed ambience at Le Diane with its brightly lit niches adorned with flowers. Pleasant terrace.

Champs-Élysées Plaza without rest

35 r. de Berri (8th) – Ⓜ George V – ✆ 01 53 53 20 20 – www.champselyseesplaza.com **G2**

25 rm – 350/1100 € 350/1100 €, 30 € – 10 suites

♦ Luxury ♦ Personalised ♦

With its elegance, space, harmony of colours, fusion of styles and attentive service, this hotel is the epitome of opulent and cosy luxury. Fitness centre.

Renaissance Parc-Trocadéro

55 av. R. Poincaré (16th) ✉ 75116 – Ⓜ Victor Hugo – ✆ 01 44 05 66 66 – www.renaissanceleparctrocadero.com – Opening scheduled end of March after renovation **E3**

122 rm – 219/569 € 269/599 €, 27 € – 4 suites

Rest *Le Relais du Parc* – *✆ 01 44 05 66 10 (closed 1 to 22 August, Christmas Holidays, Saturday lunch and Sunday)* Menu 37 € (lunch), 47/95 € bi – Carte 35/55 €

♦ Grand Luxury ♦ Chain hotel ♦ Elegant ♦

From spring 2011 guests can enjoy the benefits of this hotel's meticulous renovation. Comfort in abundance in an excellent location in the north of the arrondissement. Enjoy contemporary cuisine in the chic bistro atmosphere of this restaurant.

Hilton Arc de Triomphe

51 r. de Courcelles (8th) – Ⓜ Courcelles – ✆ 01 58 36 67 00 – www.hilton.com **G2**

383 rm – †295/730 € ††295/730 €, ☕ 35 € – 80 suites

Rest *Safran* – *✆ 01 58 36 67 96* – Menu 40 € (lunch) – Carte 39/77 €

♦ Luxury ♦ Chain hotel ♦ Personalised ♦

Inspired by the cruise liners of the 1930s, this hotel has revived their luxurious and refined spirit, with its elegant Art Deco bedrooms designed by Jacques Garcia – those facing the patio are particularly quiet. Fitness centre. The brasserie-style menu at the Safran is adapted to international tastes.

Lancaster

7 r. Berri (8th) – Ⓜ George V – ✆ 01 40 76 40 76 – www.hotel-lancaster.fr

46 rm – †320/670 € ††390/670 €, ☕ 35 € – 11 suites **G2**

Rest *La Table du Lancaster* – see below

♦ Luxury ♦ Classic ♦

Marlene Dietrich loved the discreet luxury of this property built in 1889 just a stone's throw from the Champs-Élysées. Pleasant lobby and lounges filled with antique furniture.

Baltimore

88 bis av. Kléber (16th) ✉ 75116 – Ⓜ Boissière – ✆ 01 44 34 54 54 – www.hotel-baltimore-paris.com **E3**

102 rm – †195/580 € ††195/580 €, ☕ 26 € – 1 suite

Rest *La Table du Baltimore* – see below

♦ Historic ♦ Personalised ♦

Simple furniture, trendy fabrics, and old photos: the contemporary decor of the rooms contrast with the architecture of this 19C building. Warm, cosy lounge-bar.

Costes K.

81 av. Kléber (16th) ✉ 75116 – Ⓜ Trocadéro – ✆ 01 44 05 75 75 – www.costes.com **E3**

83 rm – †250/550 € ††300/550 €, ☕ 20 €

Rest *Costes K.* – Carte 50/60 €

♦ Luxury ♦ Minimalist ♦ Design ♦

Designed by Ricardo Bofill, this modern hotel has a calm, discreet atmosphere. The spacious, minimalist-style guestrooms are arranged around an attractive Japanese-style patio. Contemporary cuisine served in a bright, modern dining room.

San Régis

12 r. J. Goujon (8th) – Ⓜ Champs-Elysées Clemenceau – ✆ 01 44 95 16 16 – www.hotel-sanregis.fr **G3**

41 rm – †360/650 € ††485/650 €, ☕ 36 € – 3 suites

Rest – *(closed August and Sunday)* Menu 40 € (weekday lunch) – Carte 50/65 €

♦ Luxury ♦ Stylish ♦

This townhouse dating from 1857 has been restored with great taste. Features include a fine staircase adorned with stained glass and statues which leads to delightful guestrooms, some classic in style, others more contemporary. This restaurant occupies a delightful, luxuriously elegant dining room which pays full homage to tradition.

Renaissance Arc de Triomphe

39 av. Wagram (17th) – Ⓜ Ternes – ✆ 01 55 37 55 37 – www.renaissancearcdetriomphe.fr **F2**

118 rm – †279/649 € ††279/649 €, ☕ 28 € – 5 suites

Rest *Makassar* – Menu 39 € (lunch) – Carte 40/56 €

♦ Luxury ♦ Chain hotel ♦ Design ♦

Occupying the site of the Théâtre de l'Empire, this hotel opened in 2009 was designed by Christian de Portzamparc. High-tech gadgets and guestrooms that reinterpret the decor of the 1970s. This restaurant specialising in local cuisine and Indonesian delicacies has a lounge-style atmosphere.

Le Méridien Étoile

81 bd Gouvion St-Cyr (17th) – Ⓜ Neuilly-Porte Maillot – ✆ 01 40 68 34 34 – www.lemeridienetoile.fr **E1**

1004 rm – 169/559 € 169/559 €, 23 € – 21 suites

Rest *L'Orénoc* – *✆ 01 40 68 30 40 (closed 26 July-30 August, 1 week Christmas Holidays, Saturday lunch and Sunday dinner)* Menu 38/75 € – Carte 48/75 €

Rest *Le Jazz Club Lounge* – *✆ 01 40 68 30 42* – Carte 35/68 €

♦ Business ♦ Modern ♦

This huge hotel's new look would not be out of place in a high-tech space station. Some of the guestrooms, with their steel lights and distinct colours, have a slightly Seventies feel. The Orénoc serves contemporary cuisine to a backdrop of welcoming, colonial-style decor. Sushi-lovers and live music enthusiasts will enjoy the contemporary feel of the Jazz Club Lounge.

Concorde La Fayette

3 pl. Gén. Koenig (17th) – Ⓜ Porte Maillot – ✆ 01 40 68 50 68 – www.concorde-lafayette.com **E1**

950 rm – 165/600 € 165/600 €, 30 € – 21 suites

Rest *La Fayette* – *✆ 01 40 68 51 19* – Menu 35 € – Carte 51/72 €

♦ Business ♦ Modern ♦

This 33-floor tower block, part of the city's convention centre, offers wonderful views of Paris, in particular from its panoramic bar. The highly contemporary and newly renovated guestrooms are the pick of the bunch here. Eat as much as you like at the buffet of the La Fayette restaurant.

Marriott

70 av. des Champs-Élysées (8th) – Ⓜ Franklin D. Roosevelt – ✆ 01 53 93 55 00 – www.marriottchampselysees.com **G2**

173 rm – 359/789 € 359/789 €, 29 € – 19 suites

Rest *Le Restaurant* – *✆ 01 53 93 55 44 (closed Saturday lunch and Sunday lunch)* Menu 45 € – Carte 45/75 €

♦ Luxury ♦ Chain hotel ♦ Modern ♦

A beautiful Haussmann-style building along the Champs-Élysées. The spacious guestrooms, renovated in 2009, are the epitome of restrained contemporary elegance, with some boasting views of the city's famous avenue and others overlooking the atrium or interior courtyard. The menu in Le Restaurant is centred around traditional dishes and grilled meats.

La Trémoille

14 r. Trémoille (8th) – Ⓜ Alma Marceau – ✆ 01 56 52 14 00 – www.hotel-tremoille.com **G3**

88 rm – 305/765 € 305/765 €, 35 € – 5 suites

Rest *Louis²* – *(closed Saturday lunch, Sunday and Bank Holidays)* Menu 50 € (weekday dinner)/68 € – Carte 42/69 €

♦ Luxury ♦ Modern ♦

Moulded fittings, attractive stretched fabrics, and black and white marble in the bathrooms combine to create a neo-retro feel in the bedrooms. Contemporary cuisine in a lounge-style atmosphere.

Keppler without rest

10 r. Keppler (16th) ✉ 75116 – Ⓜ George V – ✆ 01 47 20 65 05 – www.keppler.fr **F3**

34 rm – 220/370 € 240/400 €, 22 € – 5 suites

♦ Luxury ♦ Personalised ♦ Cosy ♦

This luxurious, sophisticated establishment is the work of designer Pierre-Yves Rochon. A magical blend of styles, materials and light sets the tone in the lobby and rooms.

Dokhan's Radisson Blu without rest

117 r. Lauriston (16th) ✉ 75116 – Ⓜ Trocadéro – ✆ 01 53 65 66 99 – www.radissonblu.com/dokhanhotel-paristrocadero **E3**

41 rm – 230/720 € 230/720 €, 28 € – 4 suites

♦ Luxury ♦ Cosy ♦ Personalised ♦

Attractive town house (1910) with Palladian architecture and neo-Classical interior decor. 18C celadon wood panelling in the cosy lounges and intimate champagne bar.

De Sers rm, A/C VISA AE

41 av. Pierre 1er de Serbie (8th) – George V – 01 53 23 75 75 – www.hoteldesers.com **G3**

45 rm – 450/680 € 480/680 €, 35 € – 7 suites

Rest – *(closed August)* Menu 49/99 € – Carte 50/80 €

♦ Luxury ♦ Modern ♦ Personalised ♦

This late-19C townhouse is a successful fusion of varying styles. While the lobby has retained its original character, the guestrooms are thoroughly modern in style. Organic products and a contemporary à la carte menu are on offer in this design-inspired restaurant with a pleasant terrace.

François 1er without rest A/C VISA AE

7 r. Magellan (8th) – George V – 01 47 23 44 04 – www.hotelfrancoispremier.com **G3**

40 rm – 250/480 € 270/490 €, 22 € – 2 suites

♦ Luxury ♦ Personalised ♦

Carrara marble, moulded fittings, curios, antique furniture and a plethora of paintings set the scene in this luxuriously elegant hotel created by French architect Pierre Yves Rochon. Substantial buffet breakfast.

Intercontinental Avenue Marceau A/C VISA AE

64 av. Marceau (8th) – George V – 01 44 43 36 36 – www.ic-marceau.com **F2-3**

55 rm – 450/1600 € 550/1600 €, 30 €

Rest *M64* – *01 44 43 36 50 (closed Sunday dinner)* Menu 44/49 € – Carte 56/98 €

♦ Luxury ♦ Business ♦ Modern ♦

A luxurious designer-inspired hotel a stone's throw from Place de l'Étoile. Decor incorporating cutting-edge technology, modern furnishings and sketches and replicas of frescoes from the Italian Renaissance. A lounge ambience sets the scene for contemporary seasonal cuisine with a spontaneous touch.

Daniel rm, A/C VISA AE

8 r. Frédéric Bastiat (8th) – St-Philippe du Roule – 01 42 56 17 00 – www.hoteldanielparis.com **G2**

23 rm – 290/350 € 390/570 €, 24 € – 3 suites

Rest – *(closed 31 July-31 August, Saturday and Sunday)* Menu 40 € (weekdays) – Carte 45/76 €

♦ Luxury ♦ Personalised ♦ Oriental ♦

The theme in the Daniel hotel is the world of travel, with an elegant and welcoming decor of Liberty prints and decorative objects from around the globe. Refined cuisine with Mediterranean influences and seasonal specials.

Regent's Garden without rest A/C P VISA AE

6 r. P.-Demours (17th) – Ternes – 01 45 74 07 30 – www.hotel-regents-paris.com **F1**

40 rm – 290/490 € 290/490 €, 20 € – 1 suite

♦ Modern ♦ Cosy ♦

This historic mansion boasts a successful blend of the traditional (fireplace, period furniture) and modern (dark colour scheme, original patterns). An exquisite Japanese-style garden adds to the charm.

La Villa Maillot without rest A/C VISA AE

143 av. Malakoff (16th) ✉ 75116 – Porte Maillot – 01 53 64 52 52 – www.lavillamaillot.fr **E2**

39 rm – 150/430 € 150/430 €, 25 € – 3 suites

♦ Business ♦ Personalised ♦

Situated near Porte Maillot, this hotel has well-soundproofed guestrooms decorated in soft colours. Breakfast is served in a glass conservatory. Sauna and hammam.

Splendid Étoile

1bis av. Carnot (17th) – Ⓜ Charles de Gaulle-Etoile – ✆ 01 45 72 72 00 – www.hsplendid.com **F2**

54 rm – 330/370 € 330/370 €, 25 € – 3 suites

Rest *Le Pré Carré* – *✆ 01 46 22 57 35 (closed 7 to 22 August, Saturday lunch and Sunday)* Menu 36 € (dinner) – Carte 45/65 €

♦ Traditional ♦ Classic ♦

This hotel has a beautiful classical façade adorned with wrought-iron balconies. Spacious guestrooms full of character furnished in Louis XV style, with some overlooking the Arc de Triomphe. Two mirrors reflect the infinite elegance of this restaurant's decor. Updated cuisine.

Pergolèse without rest

3 r. Pergolèse (16th) ✉ 75116 – Ⓜ Argentine – ✆ 01 53 64 04 04 – www.parishotelpergolese.com **E2**

40 rm – 130/276 € 140/348 €, 17 €

♦ Business ♦ Modern ♦ Design ♦

The elegant façade of this hotel in the 16th arrondissement contrasts with the modern interior design of white walls and light wood furnishings. Attractive breakfast room facing a patio. Cosy bar.

Élysées Régencia without rest

41 av. Marceau (16th) ✉ 75116 – Ⓜ George V – ✆ 01 47 20 42 65 – www.regencia.com **F3**

43 rm – 175/355 € 195/375 €, 19 €

♦ Business ♦ Modern ♦

With its designer-style decor, this hotel offers modern, stylish rooms (in blue, fuchsia or aniseed), and two junior suites in Provençal colours. Elegant lounge, bar and library.

Balmoral without rest

6 r. Gén. Lanrezac (17th) – Ⓜ Charles de Gaulle-Etoile – ✆ 01 43 80 30 50 – www.hotel-balmoral.com **F2**

57 rm – 100/245 € 100/245 €, 11 €

♦ Traditional ♦ Personalised ♦

A hushed ambience and refined interior of period furniture and wood panelling are the Balmoral's defining characteristics. Snug and comfortable guestrooms which have been renovated with a modern eye.

Pershing Hall

49 r. Pierre Charron (8th) – Ⓜ George V – ✆ 01 58 36 58 00 – www.pershinghall.com **G3**

20 rm – 282/780 € 282/780 € – 6 suites

Rest – Carte 53/110 €

♦ Luxury ♦ Modern ♦ Minimalist ♦

The home of General Pershing and a club for veterans has been transformed into this trendy hotel bearing the hallmark of the designer Andrée Putman. Soothing decor, which includes the extraordinary vertical garden. The Pershing Hall's contemporary atmosphere sets the scene for trendy cuisine based around classic dishes. A fine choice of champagnes.

Les Jardins de la Villa without rest

5 r. Bélidor (17th) – Ⓜ Porte Maillot – ✆ 01 53 81 01 10 – www.jardinsdelavilla.com **E1**

33 rm – 290/480 € 290/480 €, 27 €

♦ Luxury ♦ Design ♦

Fashion addicts will be bowled over by this small hotel which is big on couture. With its black and shocking pink decor, the references to the world of fashion are numerous. Original, chic and comfortable.

Le 123 without rest

123 r. du Faubourg St-Honoré (8th) – Ⓜ St-Philippe-du-Roule – ✆ 01 53 89 01 23 – www.astotel.com **H2**

41 rm – 199/529 € 199/529 €, 22 €

◆ Luxury ◆ Personalised ◆

The 123 is a fusion of varying styles, materials and colours. Haute-couture guestrooms, which are the perfect base for a shopping trip in this highly fashionable district of the city.

Cristal without rest

9 r. Washington (8th) – Ⓜ George V – ✆ 01 45 63 27 33 – www.hotel-le-cristal.com **G2**

25 rm – 169/260 € 169/450 €, 18 € – 1 suite

◆ Business ◆ Design ◆

A hotel with an urban-chic design featuring an explosion of colours and a decor that is built around rock crystals. A mass of optical effects and designer furniture.

Bassano without rest

15 r. Bassano (16th) ✉ 75116 – Ⓜ George V – ✆ 01 47 23 78 23 – www.hotel-bassano.com – Closed August **F3**

33 rm – 175/325 € 195/345 €, 19 € – 1 suite

◆ Business ◆ Modern ◆

Fully renovated in 2008, this hotel is situated away from the busy avenues nearby. The decor is firmly 21C with elegant, functional guestrooms in shades of blue and grey.

Amarante Arc de Triomphe without rest

25 r. Th.-de-Banville (17th) – Ⓜ Pereire – ✆ 01 47 63 76 69 – www.amarantearcdetriomphe.com **F1**

50 rm – 150/250 € 180/300 €, 20 €

◆ Chain hotel ◆ Classic ◆

A well-located hotel with elegant guestrooms inspired by the Directoire style, some of which overlook the patio. Popular with business and leisure travellers alike.

Étoile Résidence Impériale without rest

155 av. de Malakoff (16th) ✉ 75116 – Ⓜ Porte Maillot – ✆ 01 45 00 23 45 – www.residenceimperiale.com **E2**

37 rm – 150/240 € 150/240 €, 14 €

◆ Business ◆ Modern ◆ Cosy ◆

A stone's throw from the Palais des Congrès, this hotel offers rooms that are either contemporary (attractive brown and beige decor) or functional (first and second floors) in style. All rooms are well-soundproofed.

Villa Alessandra without rest

9 pl. Boulnois (17th) – Ⓜ Ternes – ✆ 01 56 33 24 24 – www.villa-alessandra.com **F1**

49 rm – 129/280 € 189/380 €, 15 €

◆ Business ◆ Functional ◆

A quiet, charming hotel fronting a delightful small square in the Ternes quarter. With their wrought-iron beds and painted wood furniture, the guestrooms evoke Provence.

Magellan without rest

17 r. J.-B. Dumas (17th) – Ⓜ Porte de Champerret – ✆ 01 45 72 44 51 – www.hotelmagellan.com **F1**

72 rm – 90/149 € 131/164 €, 16 €

◆ Business ◆ Design ◆

The Magellan's charming guestrooms are gradually being refurbished in this building dating from 1900. The attractive garden, always a bonus in Paris, is used for breakfast in summer.

XXXXX ✿✿

Le Cinq – Hôtel Four Seasons George V

31 av. George V (8th) – Ⓜ George V – ✆ 01 49 52 71 54 – www.fourseasons.com/paris **G3**

Rest – Menu 78 € (lunch), 170/230 € – Carte 200/350 €

Spec. Ormeaux, Saint-Jacques et couteaux au beurre d'algues, soupe crémeuse au cresson. Dos de cabillaud nacré, soleil de courgette-fleur à la marjolaine, beurre à la prune salée (spring-summer). Fraises, croustillant au fenouil, sorbet marbré fromage blanc-fraise (spring-summer).

♦ Innovative ♦ Luxury ♦

Against a backdrop of Grand Trianon-inspired splendour, uniformed waiters perform a perfectly orchestrated ballet with a succession of dishes which intoxicate the senses. First-rate cuisine courtesy of chef Éric Briffard. Superb wine list.

XXXXX ✿✿✿

Alain Ducasse au Plaza Athénée – Hôtel Plaza Athénée

25 av. Montaigne (8th) – Ⓜ Alma Marceau – ✆ 01 53 67 65 00 – www.alain-ducasse.com – Closed 23 July-29 August, 17 to 30 December, Monday lunch, Tuesday lunch, Wednesday lunch, Saturday, Sunday and Bank Holidays **G3**

Rest – Menu 360 € – Carte 160/240 €

Spec. Langoustines rafraîchies, caviar. Volaille Albufera, tartufi di Alba (15 October-31 December). Caillé de brebis, caramel-poivre.

♦ Innovative ♦ Luxury ♦

Alain Ducasse's quintessential touch is very much to the fore in this famous luxury hotel, with a focus on the finest authentic ingredients and honest cuisine which avoids the superfluous to focus on core flavours. The beauty of the cuisine is matched by the Regency decor, which has been reworked by Patrick Jouin.

XXXXX ✿✿✿

Le Bristol – Hôtel Bristol

112 r. Fg St-Honoré (8th) – Ⓜ Miromesnil – ✆ 01 53 43 43 00 – www.lebristolparis.com **H2**

Rest – Menu 85 € (lunch)/260 € – Carte 135/280 €

Spec. Macaronis farcis, truffe noire, artichaut et foie gras de canard. Poularde de Bresse cuite en vessie au vin jaune, royale d'abats. Précieux chocolat "nyangbo", cacao liquide, fine tuile croustillante.

♦ A la mode ♦ Luxury ♦ Intimate ♦

This exceptional restaurant boasts one dining room adorned with wood panelling and tapestries, and a second which opens out on to a rare garden. The cuisine bears the classic hallmarks of chef Éric Fréchon, who employs a freedom of expression which pays homage to the great tradition and flavours of the finest French cuisine.

XXXXX ✿✿✿

Ledoyen

8 av. Dutuit (carré Champs-Élysées) (8th) – Ⓜ Champs Elysées Clemenceau – ✆ 01 53 05 10 01 – Closed 1 to 21 August, Monday lunch, Saturday and Sunday **H3**

Rest – Menu 88 € (lunch), 199/299 € bi – Carte 160/220 €

Spec. Grosses langoustines à l'émulsion d'agrumes. Blanc de turbot braisé, pommes rattes truffées. Croquant de pamplemousse cru et cuit.

♦ Innovative ♦ Luxury ♦

This neo-Classical pavilion is located within the gardens of the Champs-Élysées. Superb setting, luxurious decor and a remarkable dining experience. Christian Le Squer champions cuisine that is unpretentious yet cooked to perfection. An incomparable and intense pleasure for the senses.

Taillevent

15 r. Lamennais (8th) – Charles de Gaulle-Etoile – 01 44 95 15 01 – www.taillevent.com – Closed 30 July-29 August, Saturday, Sunday and Bank Holidays

Rest – *(number of covers limited, pre-book)* Menu 80 € (lunch)/190 € – Carte 130/225 € **G2**

Spec. Rémoulade de tourteau à l'aneth, sauce fleurette citronnée. Selle et côte d'agneau de Lozère frottées à la sarriette, saveurs orientales. Tarte renversée au chocolat et au café grillé.

♦ Classic ♦ Luxury ♦

Wainscoting and works of art adorn this former private residence dating from the 19C. It was once home to the Duke of Morny, and is now a guardian of French haute cuisine. Exquisite cuisine and magnificent wine list.

Lasserre

17 av. F.-D.-Roosevelt (8th) – Franklin D. Roosevelt – 01 43 59 53 43 – www.restaurant-lasserre.com – Closed August, Tuesday lunch, Wednesday lunch, Saturday lunch, Sunday and Monday **H3**

Rest – Menu 85 € (lunch)/185 € – Carte 150/200 €

Spec. Macaroni aux truffes noires et foie gras. Rouget crosutillant à la marjolaine et courgette-fleur (May-December). Fraises des bois à l'eau de rose, granité à la chartreuse.

♦ Classic ♦ Luxury ♦

One of the temples of Parisian gastronomy. With its columns, heavy fabrics and crystal chandeliers, Lasserre's decor steers well clear of contemporary influence. The same is true in the kitchen, where the restaurant's new team succeeds in creating classic cuisine with a fresh approach.

Laurent

41 av. Gabriel (8th) – Champs Elysées Clemenceau – 01 42 25 00 39 – www.le-laurent.com – Closed 23 December-5 January, Saturday lunch, Sunday and Bank Holidays

Rest – Menu 80/141 € – Carte 136/225 € **H3**

Spec. Araignée de mer dans ses sucs en gelée, crème de fenouil. Flanchet de veau braisé, blettes à la moelle (April-October). Glace vanille minute.

♦ Classic ♦ Luxury ♦

The Laurent's classic menu of traditional French fare has made this restaurant a long-time favourite of regulars and celebrities alike. Neo-Classical decor of pilasters, columns, pediments and antique capitals.

Apicius (Jean-Pierre Vigato)

20 r. d'Artois (8th) – St-Philippe du Roule – 01 43 80 19 66 – www.restaurant-apicius.com – Closed August, Saturday, Sunday and Bank Holidays **G2**

Rest – Menu 160/180 € – Carte 120/210 €

Spec. Variation de langoustines, à la plancha, mi-cuite et en tempura. Milieu de très gros turbot rôti, jus tranché aux épices. Soufflé à la vanille et fondue de framboises, glace vanille (season).

♦ Innovative ♦ Elegant ♦

Apicius occupies an 18C listed building. An elegant setting which is contemporary, Baroque and Rococo all at once without being over-bearing. The experienced self-taught chef Jean-Pierre Vigato serves honest cuisine using the finest ingredients as his guide. Superb wine cellar.

Guy Savoy

18 r. Troyon (17th) – Charles de Gaulle-Etoile – 01 43 80 40 61 – www.guysavoy.com – Closed 3 weeks in August, 24 December-2 January, Saturday lunch, Sunday and Monday **F2**

Rest – Menu 285/360 € – Carte 168/324 €

Spec. "Colors of caviar". Bar en écailles grillées aux épices douces. Chariot des glaces, sorbets, les bocaux et biscuits d'autrefois.

♦ Innovative ♦ Trendy ♦

Glass, leather and wenge wood combine with African sculpture and works by some of the greatest names in contemporary art to provide the setting for the refined and inventive cuisine in this resolutely 21C restaurant.

XXXX ✿✿

Michel Rostang

20 r. Rennequin (17th) – Ⓜ Ternes – ✆ 01 47 63 40 77
– www.michelrostang.com
– Closed Monday except dinner from September-June, Saturday lunch and Sunday **F1**

Rest – Menu 76 € (lunch), 169/198 € – Carte 125/182 €

Spec. Salade de homard bleu cuit au moment, servi entier. Canette au sang en deux services. Tarte moelleuse au chocolat amer.

◆ Classic ◆ Elegant ◆ Luxury ◆

Wood panelling, Robj statuettes, Lalique glass and Art Deco stained glass combine to give this restaurant a luxurious and original look. Exquisite classic cuisine and an equally outstanding wine list.

XXXX ✿✿✿

Pierre Gagnaire

6 r. Balzac (8th) – Ⓜ George V – ✆ 01 58 36 12 50
– www.pierre-gagnaire.com
– Closed 30 July-15 August, Christmas Holidays, Sunday lunch and Saturday

Rest – Menu 105 € (lunch)/265 € – Carte 300/350 € **G2**

Spec. Les langoustines. L'agneau de Lozère. Le grand dessert Pierre Gagnaire.

◆ Innovative ◆ Elegant ◆

The chic and hushed contemporary setting fades into the background in comparison with the myriad dishes bursting with creativity and inventiveness. Jazz fan and art lover Pierre Gagnaire makes the flavours, colours and textures sing! A feast for the senses.

XXXX ✿

Hiramatsu

(dinner)

52 r. Longchamp (16th) ✉ 75116 – Ⓜ Trocadéro – ✆ 01 56 81 08 80
– www.hiramatsu.co.jp
– Closed August, 24 December-3 January, Saturday and Sunday **E3**

Rest – *(number of covers limited, pre-book)* Menu 48 € (lunch), 95/130 € – Carte 164/212 €

Spec. Gourmandise de homard et pigeon fumé, œuf poché, crème de noix. Fines lamelles d'agneau, compotée d'oignons blancs, jus de truffe au thym. Gâteau au chocolat "Hiramatsu".

◆ Classic ◆ Elegant ◆ Luxury ◆

Beneath his Japanese sign, Hiramatsu honours French cuisine with inventiveness and talent. High-class gastronomy in an extremely elegant setting decorated with flowers. Magnificent wine list.

XXX

Prunier

16 av. Victor-Hugo (16th) – Ⓜ Charles de Gaulle-Etoile – ✆ 01 44 17 35 85
– www.prunier.com
– Closed August, Sunday and Bank Holidays **F2**

Rest – Menu 45 € (weekday lunch), 65/150 € – Carte 70/180 €

◆ Seafood ◆ Retro ◆ Luxury ◆

Superb listed Art Deco interior (black marble, mosaics, stained glass) at this institution, created in 1925 by the architect Boileau. Excellent fish and seafood (caviar, salmon etc).

XXX ✿

La Table du Lancaster – Hôtel Lancaster

7 r. de Berri (8th) – Ⓜ George V – ✆ 01 40 76 40 18
– www.hotel-lancaster.fr – Closed Saturday lunch **G2**

Rest – Menu 52 € bi (weekday lunch), 115/145 € – Carte 82/149 €

Spec. Poêlée de grenouilles meunière, satay de tamarin. Sole à la ciboulette selon la recette historique des frères Troisgros. Soufflé à la noix de coco et à l'ananas (summer).

◆ Contemporary ◆ Elegant ◆

An elegant setting with chinoiseries and a zen-inspired garden. It is fitting that this legendary name in Parisian cuisine called upon a chef of the renown of Michel Troisgros (of Roanne fame) to supervise its menu. Light, elegant and contemporary cuisine with a variety of themes, namely products, flavours and the senses.

XXX

Maison Blanche

15 av. Montaigne (8th) – Ⓜ Alma Marceau – ✆ 01 47 23 55 99
– www.maison-blanche.fr
– Closed 5 to 25 August, Saturday lunch and Sunday lunch **G3**

Rest – Menu 55 € (lunch), 69/110 € – Carte 80/150 €

♦ A la mode ♦ Elegant ♦

A modern, loft-style restaurant overlooking Paris from the top of the Théâtre des Champs-Élysées. Contemporary cuisine with Mediterranean and Asian influences.

XXX

Fouquet's

99 av. Champs Élysées (8th) – Ⓜ George V – ✆ 01 40 69 60 50
– www.lucienbarriere.com **G2**

Rest – Menu 78 € – Carte 60/150 €

♦ Classic ♦ Formal ♦

The favourite haunt of everyone who's anyone in Paris since 1899. You visit Fouquet's for the same reason as the Eiffel Tower, namely its listed decor and terrace overlooking the Champs-Élysées. Classic brasserie fare.

XXX ✿

La Table du Baltimore – Hôtel Baltimore

1 r. Léo Delibes (16th) ✉ 75016 – Ⓜ Boissière
– ✆ 01 44 34 54 34 – www.hotel-baltimore-paris.com
– Closed August, Saturday and Sunday **E3**

Rest – Menu 51 € bi (lunch), 59/78 € – Carte 60/98 €

Spec. Le foie gras (autumn-winter). Le bœuf. Le chocolat.

♦ A la mode ♦ Cosy ♦

Period wood-panelling, modern furnishings, warm colours and a collection of drawings characterise this restaurant. Fine contemporary-style cuisine.

XXX ✿

Le Chiberta

3 r. Arsène-Houssaye (8th) – Ⓜ Charles de Gaulle-Etoile – ✆ 01 53 53 42 00
– www.lechiberta.com
– Closed 2 weeks in August, Saturday lunch and Sunday **F2**

Rest – Menu 49/155 € bi – Carte 80/100 €

Spec. Crème de petits pois rafraichis à l'huile d'amande. Bar de petit bateau à la plancha, aubergines et jus de citron confit. Terrine de pamplemousse, thé earl grey.

♦ Innovative ♦ Design ♦

Find a serene atmosphere, soft lighting and simple decor designed by J M Wilmotte (dark colours and unusual wine bottle walls). This provides the setting for inventive cuisine supervised by Guy Savoy.

XXX

Sormani

4 r. Gén. Lanrezac (17th) – Ⓜ Charles de Gaulle-Etoile – ✆ 01 43 80 13 91
– Closed 1 to 21 August, Saturday, Sunday and Bank Holidays **F2**

Rest – Menu 60 € – Carte 64/135 €

♦ Italian ♦ Romantic ♦

Latin charm predominates in this restaurant near the Place de l'Etoile. Attractive Baroque-style decor featuring a red colour scheme and Murano glass chandeliers. A "dolce vita" atmosphere in which to enjoy Italian cuisine.

XXX ✿

Antoine

10 av. de New-York (16th) ✉ 75116 – Ⓜ Alma Marceau
– ✆ 01 40 70 19 28 – www.antoine-paris.fr
– Closed August **F3**

Rest – Menu 48 € (lunch) – Carte 76/128 €

Spec. Tartare de saint-pierre. Sole de l'Île d'Yeu meunière, purée de rattes. Déclinaison de chocolat noir grands crus en chaud-froid.

♦ Seafood ♦ Elegant ♦

With its direct links to Breton, Basque and Mediterranean ports, the Antoine serves the best fresh fish and seafood, prepared with great finesse and originality. Contemporary decor.

XXX ✿

Le Pergolèse (Stéphane Gaborieau)

40 r. Pergolèse (16th) ✉ 75116 – Ⓜ Porte Maillot – ✆ 01 45 00 21 40 – www.lepergolese.com
– Closed 3 weeks in August, Saturday lunch and Sunday **E2**

Rest – Menu 48 € bi (lunch)/95 € – Carte 80/100 €

Spec. Moelleux de sardines marinées, sorbet tomate. Volaille de Bresse en ballottine, truffe et foie gras. Baba au rhum au carpaccio de figue.

♦ A la mode ♦ Elegant ♦

Classically inspired cuisine attractively prepared with a modern twist is on offer in this restaurant run by a recipient of the Meilleur Ouvrier de France award. A pleasant, elegant setting defined by wood decor and taupe and claret tones.

XXX ✿

Stella Maris (Tateru Yoshino)

4 r. Arsène Houssaye (8th) – Ⓜ Charles de Gaulle-Etoile – ✆ 01 42 89 16 22
– Closed Saturday lunch, Sunday and Bank Holidays **F2**

Rest – Menu 49 € (lunch), 70/130 € – Carte 114/182 €

Spec. Millefeuille de thon mariné et aubergine, tapenade et caviar français. Lièvre à la royale (October-December). Kouign aman façon penthièvre, sorbet cidre.

♦ A la mode ♦ Elegant ♦

A brilliant Japanese chef who is fanatical about fine French cuisine has created a classic menu at this refined restaurant near the Arc de Triomphe. Sleek decor with Art Deco touches.

XXX

Tsé Yang

25 av. Pierre-1er-de-Serbie (16th) – Ⓜ Iéna – ✆ 01 47 20 70 22
– www.tse-yang.fr **F3**

Rest – Menu 39/49 € – Carte 34/90 €

♦ Chinese ♦ Luxury ♦ Exotic ♦

Traditional cuisine from Beijing, Shanghai and Szechuan is served in this Chinese restaurant. Elegant dining rooms in black tones with gold coffered ceilings.

XXX

Oth Sombath

184 r. du Fg-St-Honoré (8th) – Ⓜ St-Philippe-du-Roule – ✆ 01 42 56 55 55
– www.othsombath.com
– Closed August and Sunday **G2**

Rest – Menu 32 €, 40/70 € – Carte 55/75 €

♦ Thai ♦ Elegant ♦

There is nothing traditional about this Thai restaurant with its elegant, modern decor and dishes such as foie gras spring roll, sea bass with lime, yellow prawn curry, and minced beef with Thai basil.

XXX

Citrus Étoile

6 r. Arsène-Houssaye (8th) – Ⓜ Charles de Gaulle-Étoile – ✆ 01 42 89 15 51
– www.citrusetoile.com
– Closed 23 December-4 January, Saturday, Sunday and Bank Holidays

Rest – Menu 39 € (lunch), 69 € bi/85 € – Carte 66/93 € **F2**

♦ A la mode ♦ Elegant ♦

Gilles Épié creates original cuisine that is inspired by his sound classic training and rich experiences abroad (California). Elegant decor and delightful service.

XX

Mini Palais

Au Grand Palais - 3 av. Winston Churchill (8th)
– Ⓜ Champs Elysées Clemenceau – ✆ 01 42 56 42 42
– www.minipalais.com **H3**

Rest – Carte 30/62 €

♦ A la mode ♦ Elegant ♦

Concealed within the Grand Palais, the Mini Palace is dedicated to the full pleasures of the palate, with a focus on generosity, abundance and the finest ingredients. The snack menu is available from midday to midnight. Tea room and an exquisite terrace.

Frédéric Simonin

25 r. Bayen (17th) – Ternes – 01 45 74 74 74 – www.fredericsimonin.com – Closed 30 July-22 August, Sunday and Monday **F1**

Rest – Menu 38 € (lunch), 120/170 € bi – Carte 60/110 €

Spec. Tourteau dans une gelée acidulée à l'avocat. Pomme de ris de veau dorée aux girolles. Soufflé chaud au yuzu et sa glace.

♦ A la mode ♦ Cosy ♦ Elegant ♦

A white-and-black decor forms the backdrop to this chic restaurant opened in 2010 close to Place des Ternes. Fine, delicate cuisine from this chef with quite a career behind him already.

Le Relais Plaza – Hôtel Plaza Athénée

25 av. Montaigne (8th) – Alma Marceau – 01 53 67 64 00 – www.plaza-athenee-paris.com – Closed 24 July-29 August **G3**

Rest – Menu 48 € – Carte 68/138 €

♦ A la mode ♦ Brasserie ♦ Luxury ♦

The chic and intimate "local" for staff from the nearby fashion houses. Beautiful 1930s decor inspired by the Normandie cruise ship. Classic cuisine with a contemporary twist.

Passiflore (Roland Durand)

33 r. de Longchamp (16th) ✉ 75116 – Trocadéro – 01 47 04 96 81 – www.restaurantpassiflore.com – Closed 14 July-15 August, Saturday lunch, Sunday and Monday

Rest – Menu 49/75 € – Carte dinner 72/90 € **E3**

Spec. Ravioles de homard en nage aux herbes d'Orient. Caille de Vendée en forestière gourmande aux girolles. Gâteau chaud au chocolat grand cru, sorbet cacao.

♦ A la mode ♦ Trendy ♦ Fashionable ♦

This restaurant offers fine, modern cuisine that is full of flavour. It is served in a contemporary-style dining room decorated in tones of violet and grey with mushroom-shaped lamps.

Spoon

12 r. Marignan (8th) – Franklin D. Roosevelt – 01 40 76 34 44 – www.spoon-restaurants.com – Closed August, Saturday and Sunday **G3**

Rest – Menu 33 € (weekday lunch)/76 € – Carte 36/62 €

♦ A la mode ♦ Design ♦

An Alain Ducasse restaurant in the Hôtel Marignan, where the concept is "natural, simple, healthy and good". A sleek, ultra-hip and bright eatery with open kitchens.

Conti

72 r. Lauriston (16th) – Boissière – 01 47 27 74 67 – Closed 1 to 21 August, 26 December-2 January, Saturday and Sunday

Rest – Menu 34 € (lunch) – Carte 49/75 € **E3**

♦ Italian ♦ Intimate ♦ Cosy ♦

Red and black predominate in this restaurant's decor, where mirrors and crystal chandeliers glitter. Italian cuisine; wonderful wine list.

L'Angle du Faubourg

195 r. Fg St-Honoré (8th) – Ternes – 01 40 74 20 20 – www.taillevent.com – Closed August, Saturday, Sunday and Bank Holidays **G2**

Rest – Menu 40 € (lunch), 82 € bi/132 € bi – Carte 66/75 €

Spec. Rémoulade de chair de crabe et d'avocat, gelée de tomate (June-September). Risotto crémeux de bouche à oreille. Délice au chocolat manjari, glace à la fraise (June-September).

♦ A la mode ♦ Friendly ♦

Part of the Taillevent empire, L'Angle du Faubourg is located on the corner of Rue Faubourg-St-Honoré and Rue Balzac close to the Salle Pleyel concert hall. An elegant, contemporary backdrop for a concise menu of refined, harmonious cuisine.

XX

Marius et Janette

4 av. George V (8th) – Ⓜ Alma Marceau – ✆ 01 47 23 41 88 **G3**

Rest – Menu 48 € – Carte 71/117 €

♦ Seafood ♦ Formal ♦

An elegant yacht-style interior complete with fishing nets. The speciality here is obviously seafood and the menu is changed daily according to what fresh fish is available.

XX

Timgad

21 r. Brunel (17th) – Ⓜ Argentine – ✆ 01 45 74 23 70 – www.timgad.fr

Rest – Carte 65/115 € **E2**

♦ Moroccan ♦ Friendly ♦

Experience the historic splendour of the city of Timgad in this elegant Moroccan restaurant adorned with fine stuccowork. Fragrant North African cuisine, including couscous and tagines.

XX ✿

etc...

2 r. La Pérouse (16th) ✉ 75016 – Ⓜ Kléber – ✆ 01 49 52 10 10
– Closed 1 to 22 August, Saturday lunch and Sunday **F3**

Rest – Menu 45 € (lunch)/62 € – Carte 68/80 €

Spec. Fantaisie voyageuse "terre et mer". Boudin maison, jus de fruit passion. Caramel au goût de carambar glacé.

♦ A la mode ♦ Trendy ♦ Design ♦

Stylish new bistro-style restaurant in black and grey tones from chef Christian Le Squer. Restricted menu featuring high quality, modern cuisine highlighting seasonal produce.

XX

Rech

62 av. des Ternes (17th) – Ⓜ Ternes – ✆ 01 45 72 29 47
– www.alain-ducasse.com
– Closed August, 24 to 31 December, Sunday and Monday **F1**

Rest – Menu 30/54 € – Carte 52/79 €

♦ Seafood ♦ Retro ♦

A renowned Art Deco-style restaurant with an enticing list of house specialities: shellfish, whole fish served for two people, Rech's own camembert and supersized éclairs.

XX ✿

Agapé

51 r. Jouffroy-d'Abbans (17th) – Ⓜ Wagram – ✆ 01 42 27 20 18
– www.agape-paris.fr
– Closed August, Saturday and Sunday *Plan I* **B1**

Rest – Menu 35 € (lunch), 90/120 € – Carte 80/100 €

Spec. Noix de veau crue fumée au bois de hêtre, citron-vanille. Pêche de petit bateau des côtes bretonnes. Chocolat Oropucce Trinidad, vanille bourbon.

♦ A la mode ♦ Minimalist ♦

This smart restaurant, whose name means love in Greek, sports a minimalist decor. Concise, enticing menu. Extremely popular with gourmets.

XX ✿

L'Arôme

3 r. St-Philippe-du-Roule (8th) – Ⓜ St-Philippe-du-Roule – ✆ 01 42 25 55 98
– www.larome.fr
– Closed 3 weeks in August, 1 week in December, Saturday and Sunday

Rest – Menu 79/175 € bi **G-H2**

Spec. Fleur de courgette farcie au tourteau breton (May-September). Lièvre à la royale, airelles au sirop de poivre de Tasmanie (15 September-15 December). Millefeuille destructuré aux fraises des bois (15 April-30 September).

♦ A la mode ♦ Elegant ♦

Éric Martins (front of house) recommends wines that perfectly match Thomas Boullault's refined and inventive French cuisine showcasing seasonal produce. Chic, friendly and seriously good.

XX

Graindorge

VISA MC AE

15 r. Arc-de-Triomphe (17th) – Ⓜ Charles de Gaulle-Étoile – ✆ 01 47 54 00 28 – Closed 1 to 15 August, Saturday lunch and Sunday **F2**

Rest – Menu 28 € (lunch), 35/55 € – Carte 44/70 €

♦ Flemish cuisine ♦ Retro ♦

Potjevlesch (potted meat), bintje farcie (stuffed potatoes), waterzoï (a stew with Ostend grey prawns) and kippers from Boulogne are just some of the hearty Northern dishes on offer in the Graindorge's attractive Art Deco setting, washed down with some delicious traditional beers.

XX

Bistrot du Sommelier

A/C VISA MC AE

97 bd Haussmann (8th) – Ⓜ St-Augustin – ✆ 01 42 65 24 85 – www.bistrotdusommelier.com – Closed 1 to 28 August, 24 December-1 January, Saturday and Sunday

Rest – Menu 39 € (lunch), 43 € bi/110 € bi – Carte 53/75 € **H2**

♦ A la mode ♦ Bistro ♦

This bistro of free-flowing Bacchanalian pleasure belongs to Philippe Faure-Brac, elected World's Best Sommelier in 1992.

XX ✿

La Braisière (Jacques Faussat)

A/C VISA MC AE

54 r. Cardinet (17th) – Ⓜ Malesherbes – ✆ 01 47 63 40 37 – Closed August, 24 December-2 January, Saturday except dinner from October-April and Sunday **G1**

Rest – Menu 38 € (lunch) – Carte 59/83 €

Spec. Esturgeon de l'Adour mariné au citron vert et piquillos. Croustillant de pigeon fermier du Gers (February-September). Soufflé chaud aux fruits de saison.

♦ South-western France ♦ Elegant ♦

This restaurant decorated in a tasteful, restrained style is located in a quiet district of the city. The delicious cuisine, which changes according to the season and the whim of the chef, takes its inspiration from southwest France.

XX

Market

A/C VISA MC AE

15 av. Matignon (8th) – Ⓜ Franklin D. Roosevelt – ✆ 01 56 43 40 90 – www.jean-georges.com **H3**

Rest – Carte dinner 47/80 €

♦ Fusion ♦ Design ♦

Polished concrete, linen, wood and ethnic touches set the scene for this chic, trendy bistro serving wonderful fusion cuisine supervised by New Yorker Jean-Georges Vongerichten.

XX

6 New-York

A/C VISA MC AE

6 av. de New-York (16th) ✉ 75016 – Ⓜ Alma Marceau – ✆ 01 40 70 03 30 – www.6newyork.fr – Closed August, Saturday lunch and Sunday **F3**

Rest – Menu 35 € (lunch), 63/78 € bi – Carte 49/66 €

♦ A la mode ♦ Design ♦

This resolutely modern restaurant is situated on Avenue de New York (hence the name). It focuses on attractively presented contemporary cuisine, which is in perfect harmony with its surroundings.

XX

Le Vinci

A/C VISA MC AE

23 r. P. Valéry (16th) ✉ 75116 – Ⓜ Victor Hugo – ✆ 01 45 01 68 18 – Closed August, Saturday and Sunday **E2-3**

Rest – Menu 35 € (dinner) – Carte 55/65 €

♦ Italian ♦ Elegant ♦ Friendly ♦

Delicious Italian cuisine, a pleasant colourful interior and friendly service characterises this very popular restaurant a stone's throw from the chic boutiques along Avenue Victor Hugo.

XX

Le Ballon des Ternes

103 av. Ternes (17th) – Porte Maillot – 01 45 74 17 98 – www.leballondesternes.fr **E1**

Rest – Carte 38/65 €

♦ Brasserie ♦ Retro ♦

No, you have not had a glass of wine too many! The table set upside down on the ceiling is part of the 1900 decor of this brasserie next to the Palais des Congrès.

XX

Al Ajami

58 r. François 1er (8th) – George V – 01 42 25 38 44 – www.ajami.com

Rest – Menu 25 € (weekday lunch)/48 € – Carte 31/60 € **G3**

♦ Lebanese ♦ Elegant ♦

The Paris outpost of a Lebanese establishment founded in Beirut in 1920 with a loyal following of international diners. Good, reasonably priced "Beyrouthin" lunchtime menu.

XX

Nolita

1 av. Matignon (Motor Village - 2nd Floor) (8th) – Franklin D. Roosevelt – 01 53 75 78 78 – www.motorvillage.fr **H3**

Rest – Carte 45/90 €

♦ Italian ♦ Design ♦

A restaurant with a chic black-and-white decor in the MotorVillage (the showroom of a major Italian car maker) where the focus is on authentic Italian cuisine.

XX

Les Fougères

10 r. Villebois-Mareuil (17th) – Ternes – 01 40 68 78 66 – www.restaurant-les-fougeres.fr – Closed 24 April-2 May, 1 to 21 August, 25 December-2 January, Saturday and Sunday **F1**

Rest – Menu 38/60 € – Carte 65/85 €

♦ A la mode ♦ Cosy ♦

A cosy fern-themed decor and a menu inspired by the changing season : mushrooms and game in autumn, truffles in winter, tender young vegetables in spring...

XX

Le Stresa

7 r. Chambiges (8th) – Alma Marceau – 01 47 23 51 62 – www.lestresa.com – Closed August, 20 December-4 January, 1 to 8 May, Saturday and Sunday

Rest – *(pre-book)* Carte 80/130 € **G3**

♦ Italian ♦ Family ♦

A trattoria in the Golden Triangle district frequented by the in-crowd. Compression sculptures by César and works by Arman among others on display. Artists love the Italian cuisine here too.

X

Café Lenôtre - Pavillon Elysée

10 av. des Champs-Elysées (8th) – Champs Elysées Clemenceau – 01 42 65 85 10 – www.lenotre.fr – Closed 3 weeks in August, 12 to 28 February, Sunday except lunch from April-October and Monday from November-March **H3**

Rest – Carte 45/78 €

♦ A la mode ♦ Friendly ♦

This elegant, well-restored pavilion was built for the 1900 World Fair. It is home to a boutique, catering school and a distinctly modern restaurant.

X

L'Atelier de Joël Robuchon - Etoile

133 av. des Champs-Élysées (Publicis Drugstore basement) (8th) – Charles de Gaulle-Etoile – 01 47 23 75 75 – www.joel-robuchon.com – Open 11.30am to 3.30pm and 6.30pm to midnight. Reservations possible for certain times only: call for more information **H2**

Rest – Menu 150 € – Carte 60/130 €

Spec. Caviar en gelée de crustacés, crème de chou-fleur. Saint-pierre avec fondue de tomate à la coriandre et citron vert. Clafoutis tradition.

♦ Innovative ♦ Design ♦ Minimalist ♦

Next to the Arc de Triomphe, the newest "Atelier" created by the famous chef Joël Robuchon. A successful concept (long counter with high stools, red and black modern décor) serving refine and simple recipes mixing French, Spanish and Asian influences.

Dominique Bouchet

11 r. Treilhard (8th) – Miromesnil – 01 45 61 09 46 – www.dominique-bouchet.com – Closed 1 to 22 August, Saturday, Sunday and Bank Holidays **H2**

Rest – *(pre-book)* Menu 98 € (dinner) – Carte 60/85 €

Spec. Charlotte de tomate et crabe, avocat, pomme verte, mangue et basilic (May-September). Bar sur pomme ratte façon carbonara, huile d'olive à la vanille, câpres et citron (May-September). Tarte au chocolat, sorbet de saison.

♦ A la mode ♦ Bistro ♦ Trendy ♦

Tasteful contemporary decor, a friendly atmosphere and delicious, traditionally-based cuisine using market produce are the hallmarks of this small, successful and trendy bistro.

Caïus

6 r. d'Armaillé (17th) – Charles de Gaulle-Etoile – 01 42 27 19 20 – Closed 10 to 25 August, 22 December-2 January, Saturday and Sunday

Rest – Menu 39 € – Carte 39/51 € **F1**

♦ Innovative ♦ Cosy ♦

Every season the inventive chef in this chic and elegant restaurant creates playful cuisine full of interesting flavours using spices and often-forgotten ingredients.

Daru

(dinner)

19 r. Daru (8th) – Courcelles – 01 42 27 23 60 – www.daru.fr – Closed August and Sunday **G1**

Rest – Carte 60/100 €

♦ Russian ♦ Exotic ♦

Founded in 1918, Daru was the first Russian grocer's shop in Paris. It continues to uphold Slav traditions and transports you to the Russia of yesteryear with its taramas, beef Strognanov and blinis.

L'Accolade

23 r. Guillaume-Tell (17th) – Péreire – 01 42 67 12 67 – www.laccolade.com – Closed August, 1 week Christmas Holidays, Sunday and Monday

Rest – Menu 34 € *Plan I* **B1**

♦ A la mode ♦ Bistro ♦

Find a mix of old and new styles in this bistro, where traditional banquettes and a wooden floor contrasts with the modern, bright-green walls. Classic cuisine with a contemporary twist.

L'Entredgeu

83 r. Laugier (17th) – Porte de Champerret – 01 40 54 97 24 – Closed 1 week end April-early May, 3 weeks in August, 1 week Christmas Holidays, Sunday and Monday *Plan I* **AB1**

Rest – Menu 33 €

♦ Bistro ♦ Bistro ♦

Friendly service, a lively atmosphere, a decor that is reminiscent of southwest France, and delicious seasonally based cuisine are the hallmarks of this restaurant with a tongue-twisting name.

CONCORDE – OPÉRA – BOURSE – GARE DU NORD *Plan III*

Le Meurice

rm,

228 r. Rivoli (1st) – Tuileries – 01 44 58 10 55 – www.lemeurice.com

137 rm – †540/665 € ††620/810 €, 48 € – 23 suites **J-K3**

Rest ***Le Meurice*** – see below

Rest ***Le Dali*** – *01 44 58 10 44* – Carte 50/130 €

♦ Palace ♦ Grand Luxury ♦ Historic ♦

One of the first luxury hotels to open in Paris (early 19C), located opposite the Jardins des Tuileries. Sumptuous guestrooms plus a magnificent suite on the top floor with breathtaking panoramic views. Philippe Starck has added his contemporary touch, ensuring that the Le Meurice continues to sparkle. An impressive canvas by Ara Starck adorns the ceiling of the Dali.

Ritz

15 pl. Vendôme (1st) – Ⓜ Opéra – ✆ 01 43 16 30 30 – www.ritzparis.com
123 rm – 850/9600 € 850/9600 €, ☕ 67 € – 36 suites **K3**
Rest *L'Espadon* – see below
Rest *Bar Vendôme* – *✆ 01 43 16 33 63* – Carte 75/125 €
♦ Grand Luxury ♦ Palace ♦ Stylish ♦
In 1898, César Ritz opened the 'perfect hotel' of his dreams, boasting Valentino, Proust, Hemingway and Coco Chanel among its guests. Exquisitely sophisticated. Superb pool. Chic interior and lovely terrace at the Bar Vendôme, which turns into a tea-room in the afternoon.

Crillon

10 pl. de la Concorde (8th) – Ⓜ Concorde – ✆ 01 44 71 15 00 – www.crillon.com **D3**
119 rm – 770/950 € 770/950 €, ☕ 62 € – 28 suites
Rest *Les Ambassadeurs* – see below
Rest *L'Obé* – *✆ 01 44 71 15 15* – Menu 35 € (weekday lunch), 55/75 € bi – Carte 56/96 €
♦ Palace ♦ Grand Luxury ♦ Stylish ♦
This masterpiece of 18C architecture, ideally located on Place de la Concorde, has preserved its opulent ornamentation, with Sonia Rykiel and Sybille de Margerie combining to rework the decor of its guestrooms without betraying the overall ambience. An iconic Parisian luxury hotel!

Intercontinental Le Grand

2 r. Scribe (9th) – Ⓜ Opéra – ✆ 01 40 07 32 32 – www.paris.intercontinental.com **K2**
442 rm – 250/920 € 250/920 €, ☕ 39 € – 28 suites
Rest *Café de la Paix* – see below
♦ Palace ♦ Stylish ♦ Historic ♦
This famous luxury hotel, opened in 1862, was refurbished in 2003. It is a perfect mix of elegant Second Empire-style and modern creature comforts.

Park Hyatt

5 r. de la Paix (2nd) – Ⓜ Opéra – ✆ 01 58 71 12 34 – www.paris.vendome.hyatt.fr **K3**
124 rm – 560/800 € 560/800 €, ☕ 42 € – 38 suites
Rest *Pur'* – see below
Rest *Les Orchidées* – *✆ 01 58 71 10 60 (lunch only)* Carte 70/135 €
♦ Luxury ♦ Personalised ♦ Design ♦
This Haussmannian building has been converted into an ultra-modern, luxury hotel with the decor by Ed Tuttle. Collection of modern art, a spa and high-tech equipment throughout. Cuisine in keeping with current tastes, served to diners beneath a glass roof.

The Westin Paris

rm,

3 r. Castiglione (1st) – Ⓜ Tuileries – ✆ 01 44 77 11 11 – www.westin.com/paris **J3**
440 rm – 200/800 € 200/800 €, ☕ 39 € – 29 suites
Rest *Le First* – *✆ 01 44 77 10 40* – Menu 35 € (weekdays)/85 € bi – Carte approx. 53 €
Rest *La Terrasse* – *(open from April-September)* Menu 35 € (weekdays)/68 € bi – Carte approx. 53 €
♦ Luxury ♦ Stylish ♦
This hotel built in 1878 combines old-world charm (Napoleon III lounges) and elegant contemporary touches. Some guestrooms boast views across the Tuileries gardens. The designer Jacques Garcia has brought his chic and opulent modern boudoir style to the interior of Le First. The courtyard is secluded from the Paris hurly-burly.

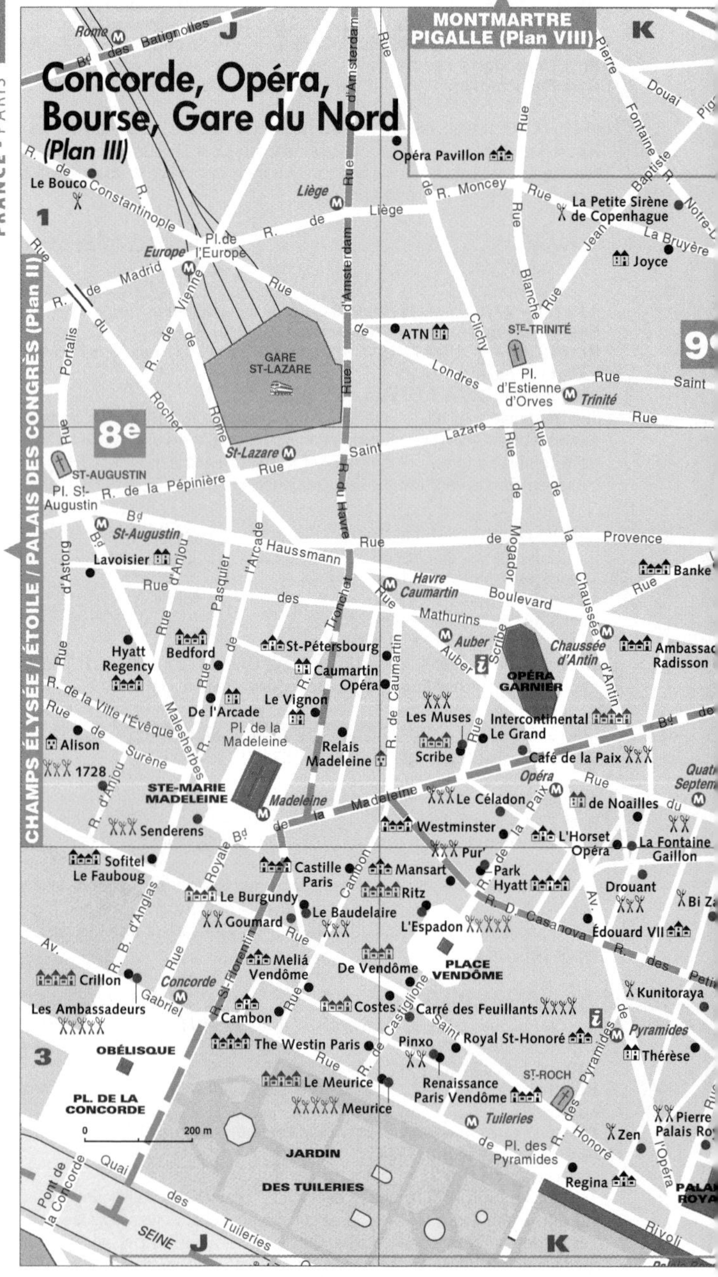
Concorde, Opéra, Bourse, Gare du Nord
(Plan III)
MONTMARTRE PIGALLE (Plan VIII)
CHAMPS ÉLYSÉE / ÉTOILE / PALAIS DES CONGRÈS (Plan II)
8e
GARE ST-LAZARE
OPÉRA GARNIER
STE-MARIE MADELEINE
PLACE VENDÔME
OBÉLISQUE
PL. DE LA CONCORDE
JARDIN DES TUILERIES
SEINE
Le Bouco
Opéra Pavillon
La Petite Sirène de Copenhague
Joyce
ATN
Lavoisier
Banke
Hyatt Regency
Bedford
St-Pétersbourg
Caumartin Opéra
Le Vignon
De l'Arcade
Relais Madeleine
Les Muses
Scribe
Intercontinental Le Grand
Ambassador Radisson
Café de la Paix
Alison
1728
Senderens
Le Céladon
de Noailles
Westminster
L'Horset Opéra
La Fontaine Gaillon
Sofitel Le Faubourg
Castille Paris
Mansart
Park Hyatt
Le Burgundy
Ritz
Drouant
Le Baudelaire
Goumard
L'Espadon
Édouard VII
Meliá Vendôme
De Vendôme
Crillon
Les Ambassadeurs
Costes
Carré des Feuillants
Kunitoraya
Cambon
Royal St-Honoré
The Westin Paris
Pinxo
Thérèse
Le Meurice
Meurice
Renaissance Paris Vendôme
Zen
Pierre Palais Royal
Regina
Liège
Europe
St-Lazare
St-Augustin
Havre Caumartin
Auber
Chaussée d'Antin
Opéra
Madeleine
Concorde
Trinité
Tuileries
Pyramides
Quatre Septembre
Rome
ST-AUGUSTIN
STE-TRINITÉ
ST-ROCH
0 200 m

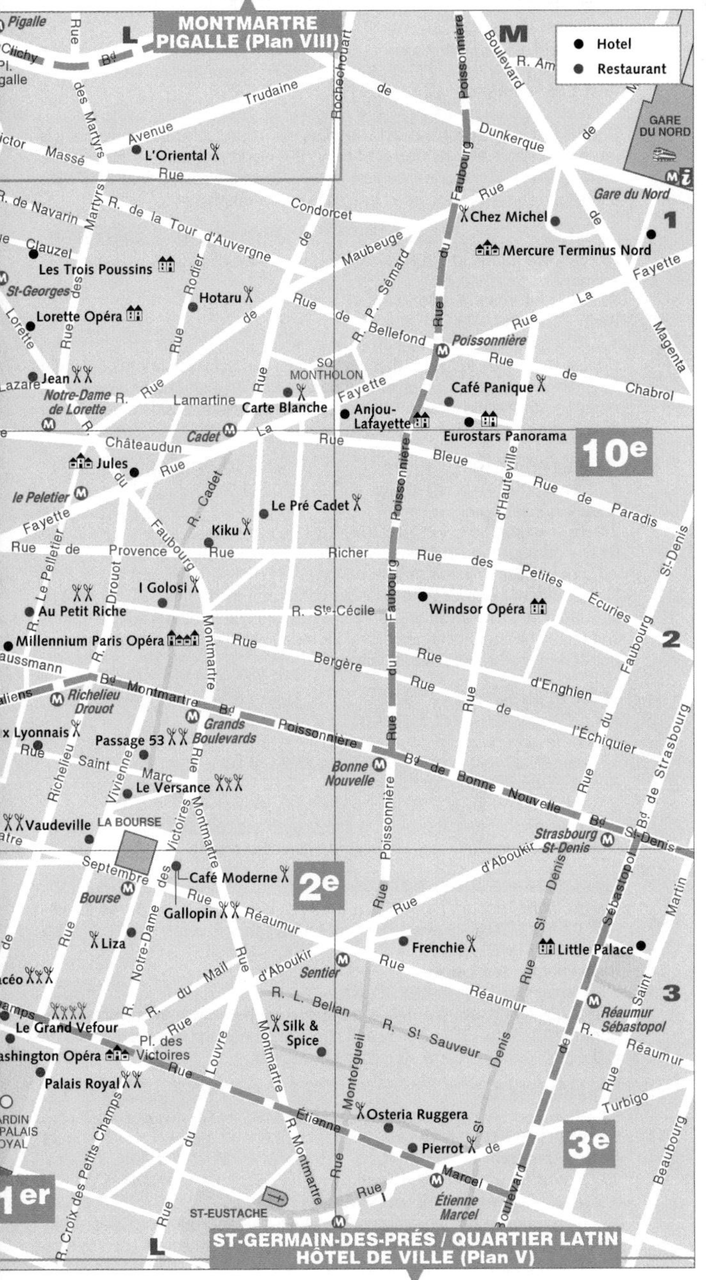
MONTMARTRE PIGALLE (Plan VIII)
Hotel
Restaurant
GARE DU NORD
Gare du Nord
L'Oriental
Chez Michel
Mercure Terminus Nord
Les Trois Poussins
Hotaru
Lorette Opéra
Jean
Carte Blanche
Anjou-Lafayette
Café Panique
Eurostars Panorama
10e
Jules
Le Pré Cadet
Kiku
I Golosi
Au Petit Riche
Windsor Opéra
Millennium Paris Opéra
Passage 53
Le Versance
Vaudeville
LA BOURSE
Café Moderne
Gallopin
2e
Liza
Frenchie
Little Palace
Le Grand Vefour
Silk & Spice
Palais Royal
Osteria Ruggera
Pierrot
3e
1er
ST-EUSTACHE
ST-GERMAIN-DES-PRÉS / QUARTIER LATIN HÔTEL DE VILLE (Plan V)

Scribe

1 r. Scribe (9th) – Ⓜ Opéra – ✆ 01 44 71 24 24
– www.hotel-scribe-paris.com **K2**
204 rm – 🛉260/780 € 🛉🛉260/780 €, ☕ 35 € – 9 suites
Rest *Café Lumière* – Carte 45/95 €
♦ Grand Luxury ♦ Palace ♦ Personalised ♦
Housed in a fine Haussmann-style building, this impeccably maintained hotel is much appreciated for its discreet luxury. The world première of the Lumière brothers' first film was screened here in 1895. There is a cosy, refined ambience at the Café Lumière, brightened by a glass roof. Modern menu.

Costes

239 r. St-Honoré (1st) – Ⓜ Concorde – ✆ 01 42 44 50 00
– www.hotelcostes.com **K3**
82 rm – 🛉400/850 € 🛉🛉550/850 €, ☕ 32 € – 3 suites
Rest – Carte 44/108 €
♦ Luxury ♦ Personalised ♦ Cosy ♦
Updated Napoleon III style in the hotel's purple and gold guestrooms. Splendid Italianate courtyard and impressive fitness centre. An extravagant luxury hotel popular with the hip crowd. The restaurant of the Hôtel Costes is a shrine to the latest trend in lounge-style decor.

De Vendôme

1 pl. Vendôme (1st) – Ⓜ Opéra – ✆ 01 55 04 55 00
– www.hoteldevendome.com **K3**
24 rm – 🛉450/550 € 🛉🛉520/620 €, ☕ 35 € – 5 suites
Rest – *(closed August)* Menu 72 € (dinner) – Carte approx. 70 €
♦ Grand Luxury ♦ Palace ♦ Stylish ♦
Place Vendôme provides the splendid backdrop for this fine 18C townhouse converted into a luxury hotel. Bedrooms with antique furniture, marble fittings and high-tech equipment. This first-floor restaurant with a contemporary, boudoir-style decor serves seasonal cuisine.

Le Burgundy

6-8 r. Duphot (1st) – Ⓜ Madeleine – ✆ 01 42 60 34 12
– www.leburgundy.com **J3**
51 rm – 🛉380/530 € 🛉🛉400/950 €, ☕ 44 € – 8 suites
Rest *Le Baudelaire* – see below
♦ Grand Luxury ♦ Design ♦ Personalised ♦
Luxurious and refined, this elegant hotel combines colourful fabrics, designer furniture and contemporary artworks in a luminous setting.

Renaissance Paris Vendôme

4 r. du Mont-Thabor (1st) – Ⓜ Tuileries
– ✆ 01 40 20 20 00 – www.renaissanceparisvendome.com **K3**
97 rm – 🛉319/659 € 🛉🛉319/659 €, ☕ 29 € – 15 suites
Rest *Pinxo* – see below
♦ Business ♦ Cosy ♦ Modern ♦
A 19C building converted into a contemporary hotel with interesting decor from the 1930s to 1950s. Honey and chocolate tones and wood predominate in the high-tech bedrooms. Attractive Chinese bar.

Castille Paris

33 r. Cambon (1st) – Ⓜ Madeleine – ✆ 01 44 58 44 58 – www.castille.com
91 rm – 🛉500/1700 € 🛉🛉500/1700 €, ☕ 28 € – 17 suites **J3**
Rest *L'Assaggio* – 37 r. Cambon, *✆ 01 44 58 45 67 (closed August, 24 to 30 December, Saturday and Sunday)* Menu 45 € – Carte 60/200 €
♦ Luxury ♦ Personalised ♦ Classic ♦
This establishment has a delightful Venetian-inspired decor in the Opéra wing, as well as black and white chic in the Rivoli wing - in homage to the nearby Chanel fashion house. L'Assaggio serves Italian cuisine in a Villa d'Este-style dining room. Patio-terrace.

Westminster

13 r. de la Paix (2nd) – Ⓜ Opéra – ✆ 01 42 61 57 46 – www.hotelwestminster.com **K2**
85 rm – 220/590 € 220/590 €, 30 € – 17 suites
Rest *Le Céladon* – see below
Rest *Le Petit Céladon* – *✆ 01 47 03 40 42 (open weekends)* Menu 55 € bi
♦ Luxury ♦ Stylish ♦
In was in 1846 that this elegant hotel took the name of its most loyal guest, the Duke of Westminster. Luxurious rooms and apartments. The Céladon becomes the Petit Céladon at the weekend, with a simplified menu and more relaxed service.

Hyatt Regency

24 bd Malhesherbes (8th) – Ⓜ Madeleine – ✆ 01 55 27 12 34 – www.paris.madeleine.hyatt.com **J2**
82 rm – 330/520 € 330/520 €, 32 € – 4 suites
Rest *Café M* – Menu 48 €
♦ Luxury ♦ Chain hotel ♦ Modern ♦
A discreetly decorated hotel exuding a welcoming ambience. Features include an Eiffel-designed glass dome, pleasant contemporary guestrooms, a sauna and hammam. Contemporary cuisine at the Café M, plus a champagne bar in the evening.

Millennium Paris Opéra

12 bd Haussmann (9th) – Ⓜ Richelieu Drouot – ✆ 01 49 49 16 00 – www.millenniumhotels.com **L2**
163 rm – 500/1000 € 500/1000 €, 25 € – 21 suites
Rest *Brasserie Haussmann* – *✆ 01 49 49 16 64* – Carte 39/70 €
♦ Luxury ♦ Personalised ♦
This hotel built in 1927 has lost none of its Roaring Twenties charm. Tastefully appointed rooms with stylish or period furniture. Modern facilities. Enjoy typical brasserie fare amid the Haussmann's sympathetically refurbished decor.

Banke

20 r. Lafayette (9th) – Ⓜ Chaussée d'Antin – ✆ 01 55 33 22 22 – www.derbyhotels.com **K2**
94 rm – 190/475 € 190/580 €, 28 €
Rest – Menu 29 € (weekday lunch)/54 € – Carte 32/68 €
♦ Luxury ♦ Design ♦
This bank building from the early 20C was transformed into a luxury hotel in 2009. The opulent lobby (gold and crimson tones and a huge glass roof) is particularly impressive. This restaurant serves contemporary cuisine with a distinct Mediterranean influence.

Ambassador Radisson Blu

16 bd Haussmann (9th) – Ⓜ Richelieu Drouot – ✆ 01 44 83 40 40 – www.radissonblu.com/ambassadorhotel-paris **K2**
297 rm – 260/2000 € 260/2000 €, 28 € – 8 suites
Rest *16 Haussmann* – *✆ 01 48 00 06 38 (closed 4 to 25 August, Saturday lunch and Sunday)* Menu 37 € (dinner), 39/44 €
♦ Business ♦ Art Deco ♦ Classic ♦
Painted wood panels, crystal chandeliers and antiques adorn this elegant Art Deco hotel dating from the 1920s. The most recently renovated guestrooms are more contemporary in style. At 16 Haussmann, sample modern cuisine that changes with the seasons, while observing the lively boulevard outside.

Bedford

17 r. de l'Arcade (8th), Ⓜ Madeleine, ✆ 01 44 94 77 77 – www.hotel-bedford.com
135 rm – 174/214 € 214/276 €, 20 € – 10 suites **J2**
Rest *Le Victoria* – *(closed August, Saturday, Sunday and Bank Holidays) (lunch only)* Menu 43/48 € – Carte 60/80 €
♦ Luxury ♦ Personalised ♦
This hotel founded in 1848 perpetuates with elegance the traditional notions of hotel hospitality. Pleasant, discreetly refined guestrooms. 1900s-style decor with an abundance of decorative, stucco motifs and a lovely cupola. The restaurant room is the Bedford's real jewel.

Sofitel le Faubourg

15 r. Boissy-d'Anglas (8th) – Ⓜ Concorde – ✆ 01 44 94 14 14 – www.sofitel.com **J3**
122 rm – †450/950 € ††450/950 €, ☕ 42 € – 25 suites
Rest *Café Faubourg* – *✆ 01 44 94 14 24 (closed Saturday lunch and Sunday lunch)* Menu 35 € – Carte 60/88 €
♦ Chain hotel ♦ Luxury ♦ Modern ♦
An elegant hotel occupying two buildings from the 18C and 19C respectively. Delightful suites renovated in 2010 in a contemporary style, in addition to plush guestrooms, a lounge crowned by a glass roof, fitness centre and hammam. The Café Faubourg boasts a trendy decor, modern cuisine and a relaxing interior garden.

Regina

2 pl. des Pyramides (1st) – Ⓜ Tuileries – ✆ 01 42 60 31 10 – www.regina-hotel.com **K3**
120 rm – †230/380 € ††230/380 €, ☕ 32 € – 10 suites
Rest – Carte 37/59 €
♦ Business ♦ Personalised ♦
This 1900s-style hotel has managed to preserve its traditional atmosphere and Art Nouveau decor. Superb lobby and antique furniture in the guestrooms. Those on the patio side are quieter, and some offer views of the Eiffel Tower. Indulge in traditional cuisine in the dining room embellished with a pretty Majorelle fireplace, or in the flower-decked courtyard.

Cambon without rest

3 r. Cambon (1st) – Ⓜ Concorde – ✆ 01 44 58 93 93 – www.hotelcambon.com **J3**
40 rm – †280/380 € ††390/490 €, ☕ 22 € – 6 suites
♦ Functional ♦ Classic ♦
This hotel between the Tuileries gardens and the Rue St-Honoré has a loyal following thanks to its friendly staff and pleasant guestrooms with their mix of contemporary furnishings and old paintings.

Royal St-Honoré without rest

221 r. St-Honoré (1st) – Ⓜ Tuileries – ✆ 01 42 60 32 79 – www.hotel-royal-st-honore.com **K3**
72 rm – †220/390 € ††270/440 €, ☕ 22 €
♦ Business ♦ Classic ♦ Functional ♦
This opulent looking 19C building is on the site of the former Hôtel de Noailles. Find elegant and refined guestrooms, with a Louis XVI decor in the breakfast room. Cosy bar.

Meliá Vendôme without rest

8 r. Cambon (1st) – Ⓜ Concorde – ✆ 01 44 77 54 00 – www.solmelia.com
83 rm – †241/389 € ††241/409 €, ☕ 28 € – 4 suites **J3**
♦ Business ♦ Functional ♦ Cosy ♦
An elegant hotel with a hushed atmosphere and decorated in tones of red and gold. Romantic feel in the guestrooms, a lounge with a Belle-Époque glass roof, plus an attractive breakfast area.

Édouard VII

39 av. de l'Opéra (2nd) – Ⓜ Opéra – ✆ 01 42 61 56 90 – www.edouard7hotel.com **K3**
62 rm – †195/570 € ††200/570 €, ☕ 25 € – 8 suites
Rest *Cuisine L'E 7* – Carte 30/40 €
♦ Luxury ♦ Modern ♦ Cosy ♦
Shimmering fabrics and refined decor in the Couture rooms, while the mood in the Edouard VII rooms is more understated. The hotel exudes elegance and the suites are superb. Cosy bar and light meals in a very pleasant contemporary setting.

Mercure Terminus Nord without rest

12 bd Denain (10th) – Ⓜ Gare du Nord – ✆ 01 42 80 20 00 – www.mercure.com **M1**

236 rm – 🚹120/340 € 🚹🚹140/360 €, ☕ 15 €

♦ Chain hotel ♦ Business ♦ Functional ♦

A sympathetic renovation has restored this 19C hotel to its former glory. Art Nouveau stained glass, "British" decor and a cosy atmosphere give it the air of an elegant Victorian mansion.

Opéra Pavillon without rest

7 r. de Parme (9th) – Ⓜ Liège – ✆ 01 55 31 60 00 – www.pavillonparis.com **K1**

30 rm ☕ – 🚹210/270 € 🚹🚹270/310 €

♦ Business ♦ Design ♦

Contemporary-style hotel in a quiet street. The rooms are on the small side, but have a sober, luxurious decor and a pleasant intimate atmosphere. Japanese garden in the mini-courtyard.

Washington Opéra without rest

50 r. Richelieu (1st) – Ⓜ Palais Royal – ✆ 01 42 96 68 06 – www.washingtonopera.com **L3**

36 rm – 🚹195/215 € 🚹🚹215/245 €, ☕ 15 €

♦ Luxury ♦ Classic ♦

Former townhouse of the Marquise de Pompadour. Directoire or 'Gustavian'-style rooms. The 6th floor terrace offers beautiful views over the gardens of the Palais-Royal.

Mansart without rest

5 r. des Capucines (1st) – Ⓜ Opéra – ✆ 01 42 61 50 28 – www.espritdefrance.com **K3**

57 rm – 🚹170/380 € 🚹🚹180/380 €, ☕ 15 €

♦ Business ♦ Functional ♦ Classic ♦

This hotel is a beautiful tribute to Mansart, architect to Louis XIV and of the adjoining Place Vendôme. Classic guestrooms furnished in Empire or Directoire style, along with a more contemporary lobby.

L'Horset Opéra without rest

18 r. d'Antin (2nd) – Ⓜ Opéra – ✆ 01 44 71 87 00 – www.hotelhorsetopera.com **K2-3**

54 rm ☕ – 🚹180/265 € 🚹🚹195/295 €

♦ Luxury ♦ Cosy ♦

The atmosphere inside this hotel a short distance from the Garnier Opera House is very hushed. The rooms are tastefully and classically decorated with matching wall hangings and fabrics, and warm wood panelling.

Jules without rest

49 r. La Fayette (9th) – Ⓜ Le Peletier – ✆ 01 42 85 05 44 – www.hoteljules.com **L2**

101 rm – 🚹170/320 € 🚹🚹190/650 €, ☕ 18 €

♦ Traditional ♦ Design ♦

This hotel has embraced contemporary design without sacrificing any of its inherent elegance. Bright and lively breakfast room (orange decor with floral motif). Gym.

St-Pétersbourg without rest

33 r. Caumartin (9th) – Ⓜ Havre Caumartin – ✆ 01 42 66 60 38 – www.hotelsaintpetersbourg.com **J2**

98 rm ☕ – 🚹153/179 € 🚹🚹190/249 €

♦ Classic ♦

A large, traditional, family-run hotel. Elegant entrance with chandeliers and a marble floor, numerous lounges and meeting rooms. Spacious guestrooms.

De Noailles without rest

9 r. de la Michodière (2nd) – Ⓜ Quatre Septembre – ✆ 01 47 42 92 90 – www.hoteldenoailles.com **K2**

52 rm – ♦200/375 € ♦♦210/535 €, ☕ 18 € – 5 suites

♦ Modern ♦ Cosy ♦

Hip, contemporary elegance behind a pretty 1900 façade. Sleek, minimalist rooms, most of which open on to the patio (with a balcony on the 5th and 6th floors).

De l'Arcade without rest

9 r. de l'Arcade (8th) – Ⓜ Madeleine – ✆ 01 53 30 60 00 – www.hotel-arcade.com **J2**

44 rm – ♦153/194 € ♦♦174/330 €, ☕ 15 € – 4 suites

♦ Family ♦ Personalised ♦

The same family has run this hotel near the Madeleine for the past four generations. Soberly decorated guestrooms with prints and paintings adorning the walls.

ATN without rest

21 r. d'Athènes (9th) – Ⓜ St-Lazare – ✆ 01 48 74 00 55 – www.atn-hotel-paris-opera.com **K1**

36 rm – ♦137/320 € ♦♦137/320 €, ☕ 12 €

♦ Business ♦ Design ♦

Situated just a stone's throw from St-Lazare station, ATN can be summed up by its trendy contemporary design, high quality materials and attention to detail.

Lorette Opéra without rest

36 r. Notre-Dame-de-Lorette (9th) – Ⓜ St-Georges – ✆ 01 42 85 18 81 – www.astotel.com **L1**

84 rm – ♦139/269 € ♦♦139/269 €, ☕ 17 €

♦ Business ♦ Modern ♦

The decor in this completely renovated hotel is a harmonious mix of bare stone and contemporary style. Pleasant, modern rooms. Breakfast is served in the vaulted cellar.

Windsor Opéra without rest

10 r. G.-Laumain (10th) – Ⓜ Bonne Nouvelle – ✆ 01 48 00 98 98 – www.hotelwindsor.com **M2**

24 rm – ♦145/296 € ♦♦150/296 €, ☕ 14 €

♦ Modern ♦ Functional ♦

Parquet flooring, white wood furniture and high-quality materials feature prominently at the Windsor Opéra. Well-maintained, reasonably spacious guestrooms in a quiet street with little traffic.

Eurostars Panorama without rest

9 r. des Messageries (10th) – Ⓜ Poissonnière – ✆ 01 47 70 44 02 – www.eurostarshotels.com **M1**

43 rm – ♦95/545 € ♦♦100/550 €, ☕ 14 €

♦ Business ♦ Design ♦

This brand new hotel stands out due to its ultra contemporary style. Designer decor with references to French culture.

Le Lavoisier without rest

21 r. Lavoisier (8th) – Ⓜ St-Augustin – ✆ 01 53 30 06 06 – www.hotellavoisier.com **J2**

27 rm – ♦164/315 € ♦♦178/315 €, ☕ 15 € – 3 suites

♦ Luxury ♦ Modern ♦

A hotel with cosy guestrooms, a small lounge-library doubling as a bar and a vaulted breakfast room close to the Saint-Augustin church.

Little Palace without rest

4 r. Salomon de Caus (3rd) – Ⓜ Réaumur Sébastopol – ✆ 01 42 72 08 15 – www.littlepalacehotel.com **M3**

49 rm – ♦178/230 € ♦♦198/265 €, ☕ 15 € – 4 suites

♦ Traditional ♦ Personalised ♦

The charming Little Palace is a successful fusion of Belle Époque and contemporary styles. Welcoming guestrooms with those on the 6th and 7th floors (with a balcony and views of Paris) preferable.

Le Vignon without rest A/C VISA AE
23 r. Vignon (8th) – Ⓜ Madeleine – ✆ 01 47 42 93 00 – www.levignon.com **J2**
28 rm – †180/330 € ††180/390 €, ☐ 20 €
◆ Business ◆ Functional ◆
A welcoming hotel just a stone's throw from Place de la Madeleine. In the guest-rooms the colourful, almost pop-style furniture contrasts sharply with the whitewashed walls. Charming attic-style rooms on the 6th floor.

Thérèse without rest A/C VISA AE
5 r. Thérèse (1st) – Ⓜ Pyramides – ✆ 01 42 96 10 01 – www.hoteltherese.com **K3**
43 rm – †160/320 € ††160/320 €, ☐ 13 €
◆ Business ◆ Personalised ◆
The charm of this hotel lies in its elegant contemporary decor of paintings, wood-panelling and pastel shades. Cosy lounge and breakfast room in the vaulted cellar.

Caumartin Opéra without rest A/C VISA AE
27 r. Caumartin (9th) – Ⓜ Havre Caumartin – ✆ 01 47 42 95 95 – www.astotel.com **J-K2**
40 rm – †165/259 € ††165/259 €, ☐ 17 €
◆ Minimalist ◆
This small hotel is near the city's major department stores. Guestrooms have a modern feel and immaculate, white bathrooms.

Anjou Lafayette without rest A/C VISA AE
4 r. Riboutté (9th) – Ⓜ Cadet – ✆ 01 42 46 83 44 – www.hotelanjoulafayette.com **M1**
39 rm – †109/170 € ††129/190 €, ☐ 12 €
◆ Modern ◆
This hotel near the leafy Square Montholon has Second Empire wrought-iron gates. It offers comfortable, soundproofed rooms decorated in warm tones.

Les Trois Poussins without rest A/C VISA AE
15 r. Clauzel (9th) – Ⓜ St-Georges – ✆ 01 53 32 81 81 – www.les3poussins.com **L1**
40 rm – †150/165 € ††150/250 €, ☐ 13 €
◆ Traditional ◆ Classic ◆
Elegant rooms offering several levels of comfort. View of Paris from the top floors. Prettily vaulted breakfast room. Small courtyard-terrace.

Joyce without rest A/C VISA AE
29 r. La Bruyère (9th) – Ⓜ St-Georges – ✆ 01 55 07 00 01 – www.astotel.com **K1**
44 rm – †149/299 € ††149/299 €, ☐ 17 €
◆ Design ◆ Personalised ◆
Architect's drawings of headboards, bookshelves and wood panelling add a unique aspect to the decor in the guestrooms of this brand-new and stylish hotel. Attractive, glass-fronted breakfast room.

Relais Madeleine without rest A/C VISA AE
11 bis r. Godot-de-Mauroy (9th) – Ⓜ Havre Caumartin – ✆ 01 47 42 22 40 – www.relaismadeleine.fr **J2**
23 rm – †180/210 € ††210/460 €, ☐ 13 €
◆ Luxury ◆ Personalised ◆ Classic ◆
Recently refurbished throughout with an elegant decor that resembles that of a family home (period furniture, portraits). Contemporary facilities and attentive service.

Alison without rest

21 r. de Surène (8th) – Ⓜ Madeleine – ☎ 01 42 65 54 00 – www.hotelalison.com **J2**

34 rm – †99/177 € ††122/197 €, ☕ 10 €

◆ Family ◆ Functional ◆

This small hotel in a quiet street near the Théâtre de la Madeleine offers good value for money. Functional guestrooms offering high levels of comfort.

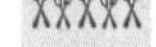

Le Meurice – Hôtel Le Meurice

228 r. de Rivoli (1st) – Ⓜ Tuileries – ☎ 01 44 58 10 55 – www.lemeurice.com – Closed 29 July-29 August, 11 to 28 February, Saturday, Sunday and Bank Holidays **J-K3**

Rest – Menu 90 € (lunch), 240/400 € bi – Carte 165/250 €

Spec. Chair de tourteau en feuilles de calamar (spring). Blanc de turbot étuvé en écailles de gros champignons de Paris (September-November). Palet fondant au chocolat, mikado de meringues au yuzu (winter).

◆ Innovative ◆ Luxury ◆ Romantic ◆

The fabulous decor calls to mind the style of the 17C, and the State Apartments at Versailles. Head chef Yannick Alleno's cuisine reveals a brilliant alliance of classicism and inventiveness, where even the simplest ingredients are transformed into the most extravagant flavours. Service fit for a king!

L'Espadon – Hôtel Ritz

15 pl. Vendôme (1st) – Ⓜ Opéra – ☎ 01 43 16 30 80 – www.ritzparis.com **K3**

Rest – Menu 70 € (weekday lunch), 105/340 € bi – Carte 170/240 €

Spec. Rafraîchi de tourteau et langoustine, légumes à la verveine citron. Ris de veau cuit au sautoir, petits pois à la française et girolles crémées. Mille-feuille "Tradition Ritz".

◆ Classic ◆ Elegant ◆

The dazzling dining room is awash with gold and drapery. In this magical setting, Michel Roth's faultlessly classic cuisine finds its true expression. Impeccable service.

Les Ambassadeurs – Hôtel Crillon

10 pl. de la Concorde (8th) – Ⓜ Concorde – ☎ 01 44 71 16 16 – www.crillon.com – Closed August, Sunday and Monday **J3**

Rest – Menu 68 € (weekday lunch)/140 € – Carte 98/160 €

Spec. Foie gras de canard des Landes, mousse parfumée à l'Irish coffee. Sole aux langues d'oursin, pommes de terre ratte et poireaux. Poire Belle Hélène, crème glacée à la vanille Bourbon, sauce aux deux chocolats.

◆ Contemporary ◆ Luxury ◆

The opulent 18C dining room of the famous Hôtel Crillon was once a ballroom. A young team took over the reins of this embassy of haute cuisine in 2010, creating a delicious, harmonious menu on a par with the decor.

Le Grand Véfour (Guy Martin)

17 r. Beaujolais (1st) – Ⓜ Palais Royal – ☎ 01 42 96 56 27 – www.grand-vefour.com – Closed 18 to 22 April, 1 to 29 August, 24 December-1 January, Friday dinner, Saturday and Sunday **L3**

Rest – Menu 88 € (lunch)/268 € – Carte 185/269 €

Spec. Ravioles de foie gras, crème foisonnée truffée. Parmentier de queue de bœuf aux truffes. Palet noisette et chocolat au lait, glace au caramel et prise de sel de Guérande.

◆ Innovative ◆ Romantic ◆ Luxury ◆

Many famous personalities have dined in the elegant Directoire-style rooms of this historic and luxurious restaurant, located in the gardens of the Palais Royal. Inventive cuisine under the baton of Guy Martine.

Carré des Feuillants (Alain Dutournier)

14 r. Castiglione (1st) – Tuileries – 01 42 86 82 82 – www.carredesfeuillants.fr – Closed August, Saturday and Sunday **K3**

Rest – Menu 58 € (lunch), 150/190 € – Carte 135/175 €

Spec. Bar de ligne émincé, amandes fraîches, copeaux de poutargue, tomate ancienne (summer). Tronçon de turbot sauvage étuvé dans son jus de cuisson, caviar ébène, semoule de brocoli (summer). Envie de vacherin, grosses framboises, chiboust au yuzu, crème fermière et mascavo (spring-summer).

♦ A la mode ♦ Luxury ♦ Elegant ♦

Elegant and minimalist contemporary restaurant on the site of the old Feuillants convent. Modern menu with strong Gascony influences. Superb wines and Armagnacs.

Senderens

9 pl. de la Madeleine (8th) – Madeleine – 01 42 65 22 90 – www.senderens.fr – Closed 2 to 22 August and Bank Holidays **J2**

Rest – Menu 90/150 € bi – Carte 100/150 €

Spec. Encornets à la plancha, brunoise de tomates confites et dés de chorizo. Cochon de lait de Burgos, rougail de poireaux et mangue. Figues en impression d'épices, glace aux spéculos (season).

♦ Innovative ♦ Design ♦

Formerly Lucas-Carton and now Senderens, this exclusive restaurant boasts a decor which fuses Art Nouveau wood with futuristic furnishings to create a relaxed ambience. The pleasures of the palate remain the priority here, as witnessed by the superbly creative and refined cuisine.

1728

8 r. d'Anjou (8th) – Madeleine – 01 40 17 04 77 – www.restaurant-1728.com – Closed 5 to 25 August, Sunday and Bank Holidays **J2**

Rest – Menu 55 € (dinner) – Carte 52/122 €

♦ Innovative ♦ Romantic ♦

The 1728 occupies an 18C mansion house with romantic period lounges and serving a fusion of Eastern and Western cuisine. A journey through time and around the world.

Le Céladon – Hôtel Westminster

15 r. Daunou (2nd) – Opéra – 01 42 61 77 42 – www.leceladon.com – Closed August, Saturday and Sunday **K2**

Rest – Menu 49/55 € – Carte 90/120 €

Spec. Saint-Jacques bretonnes mi-cuites au poivre long, bisque glacée de homard et perles du Japon. Turbot de petit bateau rôti sur l'arête, tellines en croûte de moutarde torréfiée. Pomme cuite au beurre salé, glace caramel et pain perdu.

♦ Contemporary ♦ Romantic ♦

A sophisticated decor that combines Regency-style furniture, old paintings and a collection of pale green Chinese porcelain and celadon vases. Contemporary-style cuisine with its roots in classic dishes.

Café de la Paix – Intercontinental Le Grand

12 bd des Capucines (9th) – Opéra – 01 40 07 36 36 – www.cafedelapaix.fr **K2**

Rest – Menu 46 € (lunch)/83 € – Carte 60/130 €

♦ A la mode ♦ Elegant ♦ Formal ♦

Frescoes, gilded panelling and Napoleon III-inspired furniture provide the backdrop for this luxurious and legendary brasserie. Open from 7am to midnight, it is still the place to meet in Paris.

XXX ✿ **Pur'** – Hôtel Park Hyatt

5 r. de la Paix (2nd) – Ⓜ Opéra – ✆ 01 58 71 10 61 – www.paris.vendome.hyatt.fr – Closed August **K3**

Rest – Menu 85/135 € – Carte 85/170 €

Spec. Coquillages en marinière, fine gelée de concombre, fleur de bourrache et neige de raifort. Filet de rouget, aubergines fumées et fines céréales. Biscuits gaufrette au chocolat noir grand cru et miel de romarin.

♦ Innovative ♦ Fashionable ♦ Design ♦

The kitchens open theatrically on to the chic and contemporary dining room, where diners can enjoy creative dishes prepared using top-quality ingredients. Attractive, fun and elegant at the same time!

XXX **Drouant**

16 pl. Gaillon (2nd) – Ⓜ Quatre Septembre – ✆ 01 42 65 15 16 – www.drouant.com **K3**

Rest – Menu 43 € (lunch) – Carte 68/89 €

♦ A la mode ♦ Elegant ♦

A legendary restaurant where the Prix Goncourt has been awarded since 1914. With Antoine Westermann at the helm, it serves traditional cuisine with a modern touch. Elegant, richly decorated interior.

XXX ✿ **Le Baudelaire** – Hôtel Le Burgundy

6-8 r. Duphot (1st) – Ⓜ Madeleine – ✆ 01 42 60 34 12 – www.leburgundy.com – Closed Sunday **J3**

Rest – Carte 57/109 €

Spec. Escabèche de rouget. Suprême de volaille en croûte d'amande. Mousse de datte, ananas rôti, croustillant chocolat.

♦ Contemporary ♦ Luxury ♦ Elegant ♦

A newcomer to the scene (the chic hotel that houses the restaurant opened in 2010) but already a firm favourite for the delicate and flavourful cuisine of a talented chef.

XXX **Macéo**

15 r. Petits-Champs (1st) – Ⓜ Bourse – ✆ 01 42 97 53 85 – www.maceorestaurant.com – Closed 30 July-22 August, Saturday lunch, Sunday and Bank Holidays

Rest – Menu 33/48 € – Carte 49/65 € **L3**

♦ Innovative ♦ Friendly ♦

A Second Empire interior with mouldings, parquet flooring and beautiful mirrors is the setting for modern cuisine showcasing seasonal produce. Vegetarian menu and international wine list.

XXX **Le Versance**

16 r. Feydeau (2nd) – Ⓜ Bourse – ✆ 01 45 08 00 08 – www.leversance.fr – Closed August, 24 December-5 January, Saturday lunch, Sunday and Monday

Rest – Menu 38 € bi (lunch) – Carte 57/86 € **L2**

♦ A la mode ♦ Fashionable ♦

A sleek interior with a winning combination of exposed beams, stained-glass windows and modern furniture. Equally as impressive is the globetrotting chef's cuisine: think lobster curry, calf's sweetbread and spiced pears.

XX **La Fontaine Gaillon**

pl. Gaillon (2nd) – Ⓜ Quatre Septembre – ✆ 01 47 42 63 22 – www.la-fontaine-gaillon.com – Closed 6 to 20 August, Saturday and Sunday **K2-3**

Rest – Menu 45 € (weekday lunch) – Carte 60/90 €

♦ Seafood ♦ Cosy ♦

Beautiful 17C townhouse supervised by Gérard Depardieu with a hushed setting and terrace around a fountain. Spotlight on seafood, accompanied by a pleasant selection of wines.

XX

Goumard

9 r. Duphot (1st) – Ⓜ Madeleine – ✆ 01 42 60 36 07 – www.goumard.com **J3**

Rest – Menu 39/49 € – Carte 50/75 €

♦ Seafood ♦ Cosy ♦

This restaurant dating back over a century has been given a new lease of life. Contemporary decor, a selection of meat dishes, plus a choice of seafood specialities (oysters at the bar). Open from midday to midnight.

XX

Pierre au Palais Royal

10 r. Richelieu (1st) – Ⓜ Palais Royal – ✆ 01 42 96 09 17 – www.pierreaupalaisroyal.com – Closed 3 weeks in August, Saturday lunch and Sunday **K3**

Rest – Menu 39/80 € bi – Carte 45/55 €

♦ A la mode ♦ Neighbourhood ♦ Friendly ♦

This famous Parisian restaurant has changed its style over the years with its simple, chic dining room now decorated in black and white. The cuisine is inspired by southwest France, and presented with enthusiasm by the owner.

XX

Palais Royal

110 Galerie de Valois - Jardin du Palais Royal (1st) – Ⓜ Bourse – ✆ 01 40 20 00 27 – www.restaurantdupalaisroyal.com – Closed Sunday **L3**

Rest – Carte 50/75 €

♦ Traditional ♦ Retro ♦

Beneath the windows of writer Colette's apartment, this Art Deco-style restaurant with an idyllic terrace overlooks the Palais Royal garden. Traditional cuisine.

XX ✿

Jean

8 r. St-Lazare (9th) – Ⓜ Notre-Dame de Lorette – ✆ 01 48 78 62 73 – www.restaurantjean.fr – Closed 8 to 22 Augsut, Saturday and Sunday **L1**

Rest – Menu 46/95 € – Carte 66/85 €

Spec. Escargots, crémeux de risotto, herbes hachées, beaufort, épices. Lotte, navets longs, pois gourmands, radis roses, coquillages, algues, sauce au pinot gris. Sablé cœur caramel coulant, quinoa soufflé caramélisé, framboises au citron vert.

♦ Innovative ♦ Friendly ♦ Inn ♦

Tempting modern cuisine is on offer in the welcoming atmosphere of this restaurant. It has pink and white tones, striped fabrics, floral motifs and floor mosaics. Cosy private room on the first floor.

XX

Au Petit Riche

25 r. Le Peletier (9th) – Ⓜ Richelieu Drouot – ✆ 01 47 70 68 68 – www.aupetitriche.com – Closed Saturday and Sunday from mid July-end August and Bank Holidays

Rest – Menu 28/34 € bi – Carte 32/50 € **L2**

♦ Traditional ♦ Bistro ♦

Red velvet banquettes, mirrors and elegant tables add to the charm of this bistro with a distinct 19C atmosphere. The cuisine is inspired by the Tours region and is accompanied by a fine selection of Loire Valley wines.

XX

Gallopin

40 r. N.-D.-des-Victoires (2nd) – Ⓜ Bourse – ✆ 01 42 36 45 38 – www.brasseriegallopin.com **L3**

Rest – Menu 31/36 € bi – Carte 30/63 €

♦ Brasserie ♦ Retro ♦

Located just opposite the Palais Brongniart, this brasserie with refined Victorian decor opened in 1876 and is named after its founder. Classic cuisine and bistro-style dishes.

XX

Pinxo – Hôtel Renaissance Paris Vendôme

9 r. d'Alger (1st) – Ⓜ Tuileries – ✆ 01 40 20 72 00 – www.pinxo.fr – Closed August **K3**

Rest – Menu 32 € (lunch) – Carte 42/60 €

♦ Innovative ♦ Fashionable ♦ Friendly ♦

The minimalist furniture, black-and-white colour scheme and open kitchen create an understated, stylish setting in which to share Alain Dutournier's creative dishes.

XX

Vaudeville

29 r. Vivienne (2nd), Ⓜ Bourse – ✆ 01 40 20 04 62 – www.vaudevilleparis.com

Rest – Menu 30 € – Carte 40/85 € **L2**

♦ Brasserie ♦

This large, quintessentially Parisian Art Deco brasserie is a favourite lunch haunt for journalists by day, and a popular post-theatre eatery by night.

XX ✿✿

Passage 53

53 passage des Panoramas (2nd) – Ⓜ Grand Boulevards – ✆ 01 42 33 04 35 – www.passage53.com – Closed August, February Holidays, Sunday and Monday **L2**

Rest – *(number of covers limited, pre-book)* Menu 53 € (lunch)/95 €

Spec. Menu dégustation surprise.

♦ Innovative ♦ Design ♦ Minimalist ♦

Situated in a well-preserved covered passageway, this restaurant offers an impressive choice of contemporary, market-inspired dishes to a backdrop of minimalist decor. The young Japanese chef, who trained at the Astrance, creates precise, perfectly presented dishes using top-quality ingredients.

X

Liza

14 r. de la Banque (2nd) – Ⓜ Bourse – ✆ 01 55 35 00 66 – www.restaurant-liza.com – Closed Saturday lunch and Sunday dinner **L3**

Rest – Menu 42 € (dinner)/49 € – Carte 35/50 €

♦ Lebanese ♦ Exotic ♦ Elegant ♦

There's nothing clichéd about this Lebanese restaurant styled by Middle Eastern designers (lounge-style decor), where the focus is on fine, fragrant reinterpretations of traditional dishes.

X

Café Moderne

40 r. N.-D.-des-Victoires (2nd) – Ⓜ Bourse – ✆ 01 53 40 84 10 – Closed 1 to 24 August, Saturday lunch and Sunday **L3**

Rest – Menu 35/45 €

♦ Contemporary ♦ Elegant ♦ Fashionable ♦

An elegant, modern restaurant near the Paris Stock Exchange that is packed at lunchtimes and has a more intimate atmosphere in the evening. The decor and menu showcase fine French wines. The chef here has a real penchant for seasonal produce.

X

Aux Lyonnais

32 r. St-Marc (2nd) – Ⓜ Richelieu Drouot – ✆ 01 42 96 65 04 – www.alain-ducasse.com – Closed August, Saturday lunch, Sunday and Monday **L2**

Rest – *(pre-book)* Menu 26 € (weekday lunch)/34 € – Carte 39/57 €

♦ Lyons cuisine ♦ Bistro ♦ Retro ♦

This bistro founded in 1890 serves delicious cuisine which explores the gastronomic history of the city. Deliciously retro decor, featuring a zinc counter, banquettes, bevelled mirrors and moulded fixtures and fittings.

X

Hotaru

18 r. Rodier (9th) – Ⓜ Notre-Dame de Lorette – ✆ 01 48 78 33 74 – Closed 2 weeks in August, 24 December-3 January, Sunday and Monday

Rest – Menu 37/72 € – Carte 29/65 € **L1**

♦ Japanese ♦ Rustic ♦

The restrained decor in this Japanese eatery, occupying the premises of a former local restaurant, is enlivened by a number of Far Eastern touches. Traditional cuisine with a firm focus on fish.

Café Panique

12 r. des Messageries (10th) – Ⓜ Poissonnière – ✆ 01 47 70 06 84 – www.cafepanique.com – Closed August,1 week in February, Saturday, Sunday and Bank Holidays

Rest – Menu 35 € **M1**

◆ A la mode ◆ Intimate ◆

This former textile workshop is now a contemporary loft-style restaurant. Inventive cuisine featuring foie gras ravioli, cappuccino of verbena, veal gateau etc.

La Petite Sirène de Copenhague

47 r. N.-D.-de-Lorette (9th) – Ⓜ St-Georges – ✆ 01 45 26 66 66 – Closed August, 23 December-2 January, Saturday lunch, Sunday and Monday

Rest – *(pre-book)* Menu 29 € (lunch)/34 € – Carte 42/60 € **K1**

◆ Danish ◆ Cosy ◆

Dine on typical Danish specialities in this restaurant with a sober decor of whitewashed walls and soft lighting. Attentive service.

Carte Blanche

6 r. Lamartine (9th) – Ⓜ Cadet – ✆ 01 48 78 12 20 – www.restaurantcarteblanche.com – Closed 1 to 24 August, Saturday lunch, Sunday and Bank Holidays

Rest – Menu 35/42 € **L1**

◆ A la mode ◆

The owners of this restaurant are great travellers: photos and souvenirs from their trips around the world can be seen in the dining room. Exotic tableware and cuisine that shows French and international influence.

Kunitoraya

5 r. Villedo (1st) – Ⓜ Pyramides – ✆ 01 47 03 07 74 – www.kunitoraya.com – Closed 2 weeks in August, February Holidays and Wednesday **K3**

Rest – Menu 37/90 € – Carte 38/58 €

◆ Japanese ◆ Retro ◆ Minimalist ◆

With its old zinc counter, mirrors and Métro-style tiling, Kunitoraya has the feel of a late-night Parisian restaurant from the early 1900s. Refined Japanese cuisine based around "udon", a thick homemade noodle made with wholemeal flower imported from Japan.

Zen

8 r. de L'Échelle (1st) – Ⓜ Palais Royal – ✆ 01 42 61 93 99 – www.restaurant-zen.fr.cc – Closed 10 to 20 August **K3**

Rest – Menu 20/45 € bi – Carte 20/34 €

◆ Japanese ◆

Japanese restaurant serving an extensive, traditional menu against a contemporary, all-white decor with sleek curves and flashes of acid green.

I Golosi

6 r. Grange-Batelière (9th) – Ⓜ Richelieu Drouot – ✆ 01 48 24 18 63 – Closed 6 to 22 August, Saturday dinner and Sunday **L2**

Rest – Carte 26/50 €

◆ Italian ◆ Friendly ◆

On the 1st floor, Italian designer decor with a minimalism made up for by the joviality of the service. Café, shop and little spot for tasting things on the ground floor. Italian cuisine.

Silk & Spice

6 r. Mandar (2nd) – Ⓜ Sentier – ✆ 01 44 88 21 91 – www.silkandspice.fr

Rest – Menu 25/52 € – Carte 28/55 € **L3**

◆ Thai ◆ Exotic ◆

Hushed atmosphere and delicious Thai-inspired cuisine. The signature dishes here are king prawns and shrimps in a lemon grass reduction, and green beef curry.

Le Pré Cadet

A/C VISA MC AE

10 r. Saulnier (9th) – Ⓜ Cadet – ✆ 01 48 24 99 64
– Closed 1 to 8 May, 3 to 21 August, 24 December-1 January, Saturday lunch and Sunday **L2**

Rest – *(number of covers limited, pre-book)* Menu 30 € – Carte 30/50 €

◆ Bistro ◆ Friendly ◆

The success of this small restaurant close to the Folies Bergères is based on its relaxed and friendly atmosphere and no-nonsense cuisine, including the house speciality, tête de veau. Excellent choice of coffees.

Pierrot

A/C (dinner) VISA MC AE

18 r. Étienne Marcel (2nd) – Ⓜ Etienne Marcel – ✆ 01 45 08 00 10
– Closed Sunday **M3**

Rest – Carte 37/50 €

◆ Traditional ◆ Bistro ◆

This friendly bistro run by two young people from the Aveyron serves meat from the Aubrac, house foie gras and herbed rack of lamb which is popular with regulars and visitors alike!

Chez Michel

VISA MC

10 r. Belzunce (10th) – Ⓜ Gare du Nord – ✆ 01 44 53 06 20
– Closed 2 weeks in August, Monday lunch, Saturday and Sunday

Rest – Menu 32/45 € **M1**

◆ Traditional ◆ Bistro ◆

A retro-style bistro with a slightly rustic feel offering delicious Breton dishes in homage to the chef's native region, with game on the menu in season.

Bi Zan

VISA MC AE

56 r. Ste-Anne (2nd) – Ⓜ Quatre Septembre – ✆ 01 42 96 67 76
– Closed 2 weeks in August and Sunday **K3**

Rest – Menu 45 € (lunch)/85 €

◆ Japanese ◆ Minimalist ◆

Bi Zan, also the name of a mountainous region in Japan, is a popular Japanese eatery with a zen-like minimalist decor. Upstairs bar and dining room, plus an impressive sake list.

Frenchie

A/C VISA MC AE

5 r. du Nil (2nd), Ⓜ Sentier – ✆ 01 40 39 96 19 – www.frenchie-restaurant.com
– Closed 2 weeks in August, Christmas Holidays, Monday lunch, Saturday and Sunday **M3**

Rest – *(number of covers limited, pre-book)* Menu 35 €

◆ A la mode ◆ Friendly ◆ Fashionable ◆

Near the Sentier metro station, this small, loft-style restaurant has exposed brickwork, stones and beams. It specialises in contemporary-style cuisine created by a young chef who has worked abroad.

Le Bouco

VISA MC AE

10 r. de Constantinople (8th) – Ⓜ Europe – ✆ 01 42 93 73 33
– www.lebouco.com
– Closed August, Saturday, Sunday and Bank Holidays **J1**

Rest – *(number of covers limited, pre-book)* Menu 29 € (lunch)/35 € – Carte 33/49 €

◆ South-western France ◆ Bistro ◆

This tiny modern bistro serves its own simple take on cuisine from southwest France, through dishes such as Basque ham, chicken liver terrine and Camembert with truffles. Good value for money.

Kiku

A/C VISA AE

56 r. Richer (9th) – Ⓜ Cadet – ✆ 01 44 83 02 30
– Closed Saturday lunch and Sunday **L2**

Rest – Menu 25 € (lunch)/35 €

◆ Japanese ◆

Contemporary izakaya-style restaurant (sake bar which serves a selection of small dishes). Modern authentic Japanese cuisine (no sushi).

Osteria Ruggera
35 r. Tiquetonne (2nd) – Ⓜ Étienne Marcel – ✆ 01 40 26 13 91 – www.restaurant-osteriaruggera-paris.com – Closed 14 to 28 August, Saturday lunch and Sunday lunch **M3**
Rest – *(number of covers limited, pre-book)* Menu 23 € (lunch) Carte 30/50 €
♦ Italian ♦ Rustic ♦
A small Italian eatery in the very hip Montorgueil district whose watchword is simplicity. Rustic decor and authentically flavoured Sicilian specialities.

TOUR EIFFEL – INVALIDES *Plan IV*

Sezz without rest
6 av. Frémiet (16th) ✉ 75016 – Ⓜ Passy – ✆ 01 56 75 26 26 – www.hotelsezz.com **N2**
35 rm – 🛉400/600 € 🛉🛉600/800 €, ☕ 32 € – 1 suite
♦ Luxury ♦ Design ♦
Attractive hotel dating from 1913, which has been completely renovated in a modern style (shades of grey, original furniture and high-tech equipment). Attentive staff, hammam and Jacuzzi.

Mercure Suffren Tour Eiffel
20 r. Jean-Rey (15th) – Ⓜ Bir-Hakeim – ✆ 01 45 78 50 00 – www.mercure.com **N2**
405 rm – 🛉180/315 € 🛉🛉195/315 €, ☕ 20 € **Rest** – Carte 32/45 €
♦ Chain hotel ♦ Business ♦ Functional ♦
This modern hotel is gradually renovating its guestrooms; some of which enjoy views of the Eiffel Tower. Fitness room open 24hrs a day. This lounge-style restaurant has a bar and wine cellar.

Le Marquis without rest
15 r. Dupleix (15th) – Ⓜ Dupleix – ✆ 01 43 06 31 50 – www.lemarquisparis.com **O2**
36 rm – 🛉149/350 € 🛉🛉149/350 €, ☕ 19 €
♦ Business ♦ Modern ♦ Personalised ♦
This is a handy address close to the Champ de Mars. It offers comfortable guestrooms that show attention to detail and are decorated in warm, contemporary tones (brown, cream and chocolate).

Bourgogne et Montana without rest
3 r. de Bourgogne (7th) – Ⓜ Assemblée Nationale – ✆ 01 45 51 20 22 – www.bourgogne-montana.com **Q1**
28 rm ☕ – 🛉230/305 € 🛉🛉230/305 € – 4 suites
♦ Traditional ♦ Personalised ♦
Elegance and beauty pervade this 18C hotel that mingles old with new. The top floor rooms offer superb views over the Palais Bourbon (French parliament house).

Le Walt without rest
37 av. de la Motte-Picquet (7th) – Ⓜ École Militaire – ✆ 01 45 51 55 83 – www.lewaltparis.com **P2**
25 rm – 🛉169/350 € 🛉🛉169/350 €, ☕ 19 €
♦ Personalised ♦
This hotel has comfortable and contemporary guestrooms. An original feature is the reproductions of classical art masterpieces above the headboard. Pleasant patio.

Muguet without rest
11 r. Chevert (7th) – Ⓜ École Militaire – ✆ 01 47 05 05 93 – www.hotelmuguet.com **P2**
43 rm – 🛉100/115 € 🛉🛉140/205 €, ☕ 12 €
♦ Family ♦ Classic ♦
In a quiet street a stone's throw from Les Invalides, this hotel has been refurbished in a classic style. Attractively maintained guestrooms; those overlooking the small flower-decked garden are generally quieter.

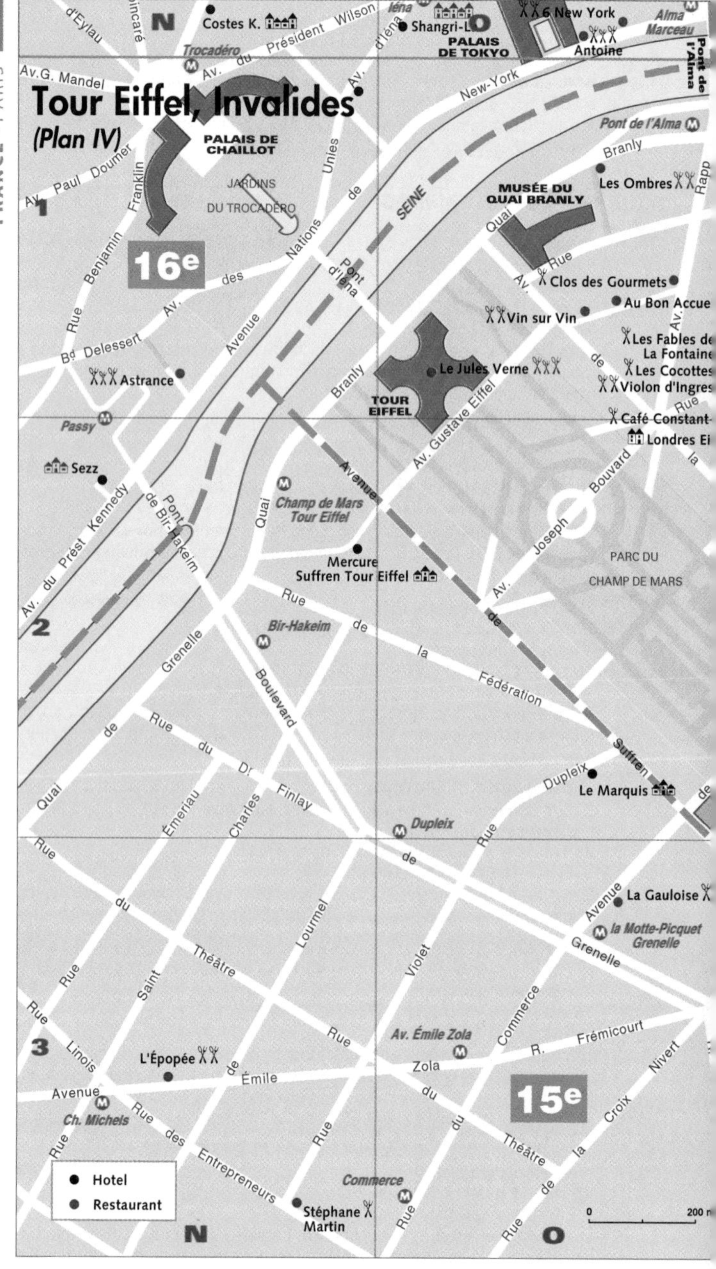
Tour Eiffel, Invalides
(Plan IV)
16e
15e
PALAIS DE CHAILLOT
JARDINS DU TROCADÉRO
PALAIS DE TOKYO
MUSÉE DU QUAI BRANLY
TOUR EIFFEL
PARC DU CHAMP DE MARS
SEINE
Costes K.
Shangri-La
6 New York
Antoine
Les Ombres
Clos des Gourmets
Au Bon Accue
Vin sur Vin
Les Fables de La Fontaine
Les Cocottes
Violon d'Ingres
Le Jules Verne
Café Constant
Londres Ei
Astrance
Sezz
Mercure Suffren Tour Eiffel
Le Marquis
La Gauloise
L'Épopée
Stéphane Martin
Trocadéro
Iéna
Alma Marceau
Pont de l'Alma
Passy
Champ de Mars Tour Eiffel
Bir-Hakeim
Dupleix
la Motte-Picquet Grenelle
Av. Émile Zola
Ch. Michels
Commerce
Hotel
Restaurant
N
O
1
2
3
0
200 m

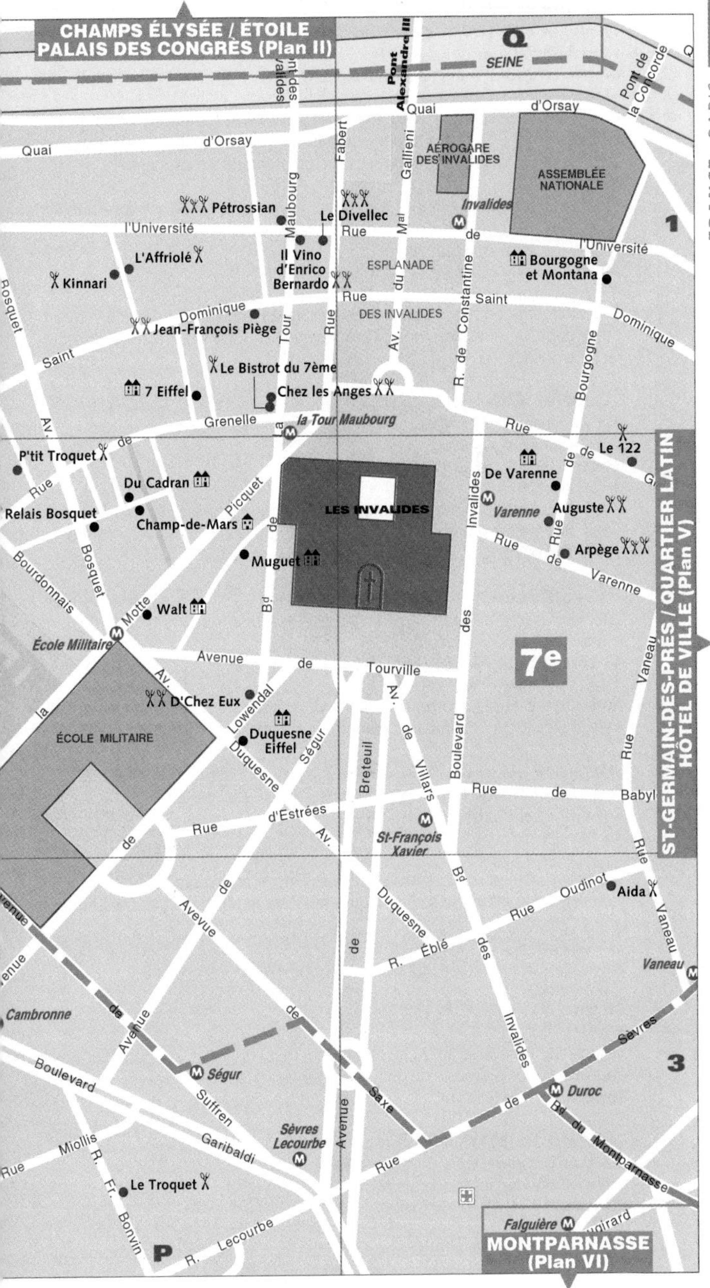
CHAMPS ÉLYSÉE / ÉTOILE
PALAIS DES CONGRÈS (Plan II)
SEINE
Pont Alexandre III
Pont de la Concorde
Quai d'Orsay
AÉROGARE DES INVALIDES
ASSEMBLÉE NATIONALE
Invalides
Pétrossian
Le Divellec
Il Vino d'Enrico Bernardo
L'Affriolé
Kinnari
Bourgogne et Montana
ESPLANADE DES INVALIDES
Jean-François Piège
Le Bistrot du 7ème
7 Eiffel
Chez les Anges
la Tour Maubourg
P'tit Troquet
Du Cadran
Relais Bosquet
Champ-de-Mars
Le 122
De Varenne
Varenne
Auguste
Arpège
LES INVALIDES
Muguet
Walt
École Militaire
ÉCOLE MILITAIRE
D'Chez Eux
Duquesne Eiffel
7e
St-François Xavier
Aida
Vaneau
Cambronne
Ségur
Duroc
Sèvres Lecourbe
Le Troquet
Falguière
MONTPARNASSE (Plan VI)
ST-GERMAIN-DES-PRÉS / QUARTIER LATIN
HÔTEL DE VILLE (Plan V)
1
3
Q
P

7 Eiffel without rest

17 bis r. Amélie (7th) – Ⓜ La Tour Maubourg – ✆ 01 45 55 10 01 – www.7eiffel.com **P1**

32 rm – 240/370 € 240/370 €, ☕ 19 €

♦ Business ♦ Design ♦

Completely renovated in 2010, the 7 Eiffel now has something of an avant-garde ambience. Designer furniture and the clever use of vibrant materials and lighting combine to create a modern and comfortable atmosphere.

Relais Bosquet without rest

19 r. du Champ-de-Mars (7th) – Ⓜ École Militaire – ✆ 01 47 05 25 45 – www.hotelrelaisbosquet.com **P2**

40 rm – 145/250 € 145/250 €, ☕ 17 €

♦ Family ♦ Classic ♦ Functional ♦

This discreet hotel has an attractively decorated interior and classically styled guestrooms in refreshing tones. Those overlooking the small courtyard to the rear are quieter.

Londres Eiffel without rest

1 r. Augereau (7th) – Ⓜ École Militaire – ✆ 01 45 51 63 02 – www.londres-eiffel.com **O1-2**

30 rm – 120/165 € 150/250 €, ☕ 14 €

♦ Family ♦ Personalised ♦

Warm tones and an intimate atmosphere are the main features of this hotel's small but well-maintained guestrooms (half of which were refurbished in 2009). The building overlooking the courtyard is particularly quiet.

Du Cadran without rest

10 r. du Champ-de-Mars (7th) – Ⓜ École Militaire – ✆ 01 40 62 67 00 – www.hotelducadran.com **P2**

41 rm – 150/270 € 165/270 €, ☕ 13 €

♦ Business ♦ Modern ♦

Access to this newly refurbished hotel is via a chocolate shop! Contemporary in style, the decor in its compact bedrooms is minimalist to the letter.

De Varenne without rest

44 r. de Bourgogne (7th) – Ⓜ Varenne – ✆ 01 45 51 45 55 – www.hoteldevarenne.com **Q2**

25 rm – 139/169 € 139/239 €, ☕ 11 €

♦ Family ♦ Classic ♦

A well-maintained hotel embellished with Empire and Louis XVI furniture in a relatively quiet setting. In summer, breakfast is served in a small, leafy courtyard.

Duquesne Eiffel without rest

23 av. Duquesne (7th) – Ⓜ École Militaire – ✆ 01 44 42 09 09 – www.hde.fr **P2**

40 rm – 133/250 € 133/250 €, ☕ 12 €

♦ Business ♦ Cosy ♦

Completely renovated in 2008, this hotel offers its guests comfortable, well-appointed rooms. Those on the fifth-floor boast superb views of the Eiffel Tower and École Militaire.

Champ de Mars without rest

7 r. du Champ-de-Mars (7th) – Ⓜ École Militaire – ✆ 01 45 51 52 30 – www.hotelduchampdemars.com **P2**

25 rm – 93 € 100 €, ☕ 8 €

♦ Cosy ♦

This small, reasonably priced family-run hotel has cosy and romantic rooms between the Champ-de-Mars and the Invalides. Attractive Liberty-style decor, which is at its best in the rooms already renovated.

Le Jules Verne

2nd floor Eiffel Tower, private lift, South pillar (7th)
– Bir-Hakeim – 01 45 55 61 44
– www.lejulesverne-paris.com **O1**

Rest – Menu 85 € (weekday lunch), 165/200 € – Carte 160/210 €

Spec. Homard de nos côtes, sabayon au fumet de crustacés et caviar gold. Tournedos poêlé, foie gras de canard, sauce Périgueux et pommes soufflées. L'écrou au chocolat et praliné croustillant, glace noisette.

♦ Contemporary ♦ Design ♦ Formal ♦

The designer decor on the second floor of the Eiffel Tower lives up to expectations, with a magical view as a bonus! French culinary heritage is the focus here, where classic dishes are accompanied by some excellent wines.

Arpège (Alain Passard)

84 r. de Varenne (7th) – Varenne – 01 45 51 47 33
– www.alain-passard.com
– Closed Saturday and Sunday **Q2**

Rest – Menu 120 € (lunch)/320 € – Carte 190/290 €

Spec. Couleur, saveur, parfum et dessin du jardin. Aiguillettes de homard de l'archipel de Chausey au savagnin. Tarte aux pommes bouquet de roses.

♦ Innovative ♦ Elegant ♦

Choose the elegant modern dining room, with rare wood and glass decorations by Lalique, rather than the basement. Savour dazzling vegetable garden-based cuisine by a master chef and poet of the land.

Astrance (Pascal Barbot)

4 r. Beethoven (16th) ✉ 75016 – Passy – 01 40 50 84 40
– Closed 28 July-30 August, 29 October-7 November, 19 February-1 March, Saturday, Sunday, Monday and Bank Holidays **N1**

Rest – (number of covers limited, pre-book) Menu 70 € (lunch), 120/190 €

Spec. Homard poché, nectarine en salade, herbes et fleurs sauvages. Ris de veau grillé, girolles cuisinées aux abricots et amandes. Tartelette aux fruits de la passion et thé vert.

♦ Innovative ♦ Minimalist ♦ Elegant ♦

No menu or à la carte choices in this restaurant, where chef Pascal Barbot produces a different 'surprise menu' at each sitting. Sample the inventive cuisine of a chef at the height of his art, who focuses on excellent ingredients and creative flair. An unforgettable culinary experience.

Le Divellec (Jacques Le Divellec)

107 r. de l'Université (7th) – Invalides – 01 45 51 91 96
– Closed 25 July-25 August, 25 December-2 January, Saturday and Sunday

Rest – Menu 50 € (lunch), 65/160 € – Carte 110/220 € **P1**

Spec. Carpaccio de turbot aux truffes. Homard à la presse avec son corail. Soufflé chaud à l'infusion de truffe.

♦ Seafood ♦ Elegant ♦

This restaurant, with its ocean-inspired decor, prides itself on outstanding fish and seafood on the doorstep of Les Invalides. Reasonably priced lunch menus, along with more expensive à la carte options.

Pétrossian

144 r. de l'Université (7th) – Invalides – 01 44 11 32 32
– www.petrossian.fr
– Closed August, Sunday and Monday **P1**

Rest – Menu 70/90 € – Carte 70/120 €

♦ Seafood ♦ Formal ♦

The Petrossians have been serving Parisians with caviar from the Caspian Sea since 1920. Enjoy fish and seafood in the elegant dining room above the boutique.

Jean-François Piège

79 r. St-Dominique (1st floor) (7th), Ⓜ *La Tour Maubourg – ✆ 01 47 05 79 79 – Closed August, Sunday and Monday* **P1**

Rest – *(number of covers limited, pre-book)* Menu 90/115 €

Spec. Sélection des meilleurs produits de saison.

♦ A la mode ♦ Design ♦ Cosy ♦

Jean-François Piège has left the Crillon to revive this brasserie. It dates from 1923 and has been treated to a modern makeover. Sample the personalised cuisine with a few tributes to its brasserie heritage.

Il Vino d'Enrico Bernardo

13 bd La Tour-Maubourg (7th) – Ⓜ *Invalides – ✆ 01 44 11 72 00 – www.ilvinobyenricobernardo.com – Closed Saturday lunch* **P1**

Rest – Menu 70 € bi (lunch), 98 € bi/165 € bi – Carte 105/150 €

Spec. Saint-pierre en carpaccio, huile de noix, pomme verte, vinaigrette à la moutarde à l'ancienne. Cabillaud rôti, concassé de tomate, olive noire, salade de fenouil. Chocolat blanc, mangue, glace noix de coco.

♦ A la mode ♦ Design ♦

Choose the wine and let the meal take care of itself! In his chic designer restaurant, the Best Sommelier 2004 reverses the trend by linking the food to the wine.

Les Ombres

27 quai Branly (Quai Branly museum - 5th Floor) (7th) – Ⓜ *Alma Marceau – ✆ 01 47 53 68 00 – www.lesombres-restaurant.com* **O1**

Rest – Menu 38 € (lunch), 95/145 € bi – Carte 62/103 €

♦ A la mode ♦ Design ♦ Trendy ♦

This restaurant on the roof terrace of the Musée du Quai Branly boasts splendid views of the Eiffel Tower. Contemporary dining amid a designer decor featuring an abundance of glass.

Le Violon d'Ingres (Christian Constant et Stéphane Schmidt)

135 r. St-Dominique (7th) – Ⓜ *École Militaire – ✆ 01 45 55 15 05 – www.leviolondingres.com* **O1**

Rest – Menu 36 € (weekday lunch), 49/80 € – Carte 57/86 €

Spec. Œufs pochés frits, jambon croustillant, piperade de poivron doux au vieux vinaigre. Suprême de bar croustillant, ravigote aux câpres. Soufflé chaud à la vanille, sauce caramel au beurre salé.

♦ Contemporary ♦ Elegant ♦

This elegant dining room in the style of a contemporary bistro is popular with food enthusiasts. They are attracted by the high quality traditional cuisine that focuses on seasonal ingredients.

Vin sur Vin

20 r. de Monttessuy (7th) – Ⓜ *Pont de l'Alma – ✆ 01 47 05 14 20 – Closed 29 May-6 June, August, 24 December-4 January, Monday except dinner from September-March, Saturday lunch and Sunday* **O1**

Rest – *(number of covers limited, pre-book)* Carte 80/120 €

Spec. Ravioles aux truffes. Ris de veau croustillant. Soufflé chaud.

♦ Classic ♦ Cosy ♦

This restaurant has friendly service, an elegant decor and the ambience of a private house. Its delicious, traditional cuisine is accompanied by an extensive 600-strong wine list.

Chez les Anges

54 bd de la Tour-Maubourg (7th) – Ⓜ *La Tour Maubourg – ✆ 01 47 05 89 86 – www.chezlesanges.com – Closed Saturday and Sunday* **P1**

Rest – Menu 31/40 € – Carte 45/85 €

♦ Traditional ♦ Design ♦

A minimalist, contemporary decor sets the scene for delicious, honest cuisine that blends the traditional and the modern, with dishes like pig's trotter pancake, fillet of whiting, and calf's liver with braised red cabbage.

Auguste (Gaël Orieux)
54 r. Bourgogne (7th) – Ⓜ Varenne – ✆ 01 45 51 61 09 – www.restaurantauguste.fr – Closed 1 to 22 August, Saturday and Sunday **Q2**
Rest – Menu 35 € (lunch) – Carte 72/115 €
Spec. Huîtres creuses "perle noire" en gelée à la diable, mousse de raifort (September-December). Noix de ris de veau croustillante et cacahuètes caramélisées, pleurotes et vin jaune. Soufflé au chocolat pur caraïbe.
♦ A la mode ♦ Design ♦
Pleasant, colourful and contemporary decor provides the setting for cuisine that is both full of flavour and inventiveness. Attractively priced lunch menu, with more expensive options for dinner.

D'Chez Eux
2 av. Lowendal (7th) – Ⓜ École Militaire – ✆ 01 47 05 52 55 – www.chezeux.com – Closed August **P2**
Rest – Menu 34 € (lunch) – Carte 50/100 €
♦ Terroir ♦ Rustic ♦
For 40 years customers have been flocking to this restaurant with the atmosphere of a provincial inn. Hearty dishes from southwest France served by waiters in traditional white aprons.

La Gauloise
59 av. La Motte-Picquet (15th) – Ⓜ La Motte Picquet Grenelle – ✆ 01 47 34 11 64 **O3**
Rest – Menu 22/28 € – Carte 31/50 €
♦ Brasserie ♦ Neighbourhood ♦
This 1900 brasserie must have seen many celebrities pass through, judging from the signed photos on the walls. A pleasant, kerbside terrace.

L'Épopée
89 av. Émile-Zola (15th) – Ⓜ Charles Michels – ✆ 01 45 77 71 37 – www.lepopee.fr – Closed 9 to 17 August, 24 December-3 January and Sunday dinner
Rest – Menu 35 € **N3**
♦ Traditional ♦ Family ♦
A concise menu of traditional cuisine with a modern twist, and a good choice of estate wines, continue to attract a loyal following here.

Au Bon Accueil
14 r. Monttessuy (7th) – Ⓜ Pont de l'Alma – ✆ 01 47 05 46 11 – www.aubonaccueilparis.com – Closed 1 to 15 August, Saturday lunch and Sunday **O1**
Rest – Menu 27 € (lunch)/31 € – Carte 45/65 €
♦ A la mode ♦ Bistro ♦ Cosy ♦
In the shadow of the Eiffel Tower, this chic and discreet restaurant serves appetising cuisine based around seasonal produce. Excellent value.

Les Fables de La Fontaine (Sébastien Gravé)
131 r. St-Dominique (7th) – Ⓜ École Militaire – ✆ 01 44 18 37 55 – www.lesfablesdelafontaine.net – Closed 23 to 28 December **O1**
Rest – *(number of covers limited, pre-book)* Menu 35 € bi (weekday lunch)/90 € – Carte 62/85 €
Spec. Tartare de bar au citron confit, mousse parmesan et sablé craquant. Saint-Jacques à la plancha, gratin de macaronis à la truffe noire et jambon Ibaïona (15 November-31 March). Gâteau basque.
♦ Seafood ♦ Fashionable ♦ Intimate ♦
This bistro specialises in seafood served in a small dining room (brown tones, banquettes, tiles) and on a summer terrace. Restricted, carefully planned menu and good wines available by the glass.

Stéphane Martin

67 r. des Entrepreneurs (15th) – Ⓜ Charles Michels – ✆ 01 45 79 03 31 – www.stephanemartin.com – Closed 17 to 25 April, 31 July-22 August, 24 December-3 January, Sunday and Monday **N3**

Rest – Menu 21 € (weekday lunch)/35 € – Carte 38/55 €

♦ A la mode ♦

This inviting restaurant with a library theme (mural of bookshelves), serves up-to-date market fresh cuisine.

Le Clos des Gourmets

16 av. Rapp (7th) – Ⓜ Alma Marceau – ✆ 01 45 51 75 61 – www.closdesgourmets.com – Closed 1 to 25 August, Sunday and Monday **O1**

Rest – Menu 30 € (lunch)/35 € – Carte lunch 35/60 €

♦ A la mode ♦ Design ♦

Wood panelling and beige and grey tones set the scene in this simply furnished yet elegant restaurant with a welcoming ambience. The creative and flavoursome cuisine includes signature dishes such as crème brûlée with asparagus, wok-fried vegetables with Pata Negra ham, and confit of fennel with mild spices.

Les Cocottes

135 r. St-Dominique (7th) – Ⓜ École Militaire – www.lesrestaurantsdeconstant.com – Closed Sunday **O1**

Rest – Carte 27/50 €

♦ A la mode ♦ Fashionable ♦

The concept in this friendly eatery is based around bistro cuisine with a modern touch cooked in cast-iron casserole pots (cocottes), including popular dishes such as country paté, roast veal etc. No advance booking.

Aida (Koji Aida)

1 r. Pierre Leroux (7th) – Ⓜ Vaneau – ✆ 01 43 06 14 18 – www.aidaparis.com – Closed 1 week in March, 3 weeks in August, Monday and lunch **Q3**

Rest – *(number of covers limited, pre-book)* Menu 140/160 €

Spec. Sashimi. Teppanyaki de chateaubriand de bœuf limousin. Sorbet au sencha.

♦ Japanese ♦ Minimalist ♦

A Zen feel to this discreet Japanese restaurant with a bar counter and private dining room. Japanese cuisine and teppanyaki menus, and a rich list of Burgundy wines chosen by the passionate chef.

Le 122

122 r. de Grenelle (7th) – Ⓜ Solférino – ✆ 01 45 56 07 42 – www.le122.fr – Closed 23 July-17 August, Saturday and Sunday **Q2**

Rest – Menu 23 € (lunch)/35 € – Carte 30/38 €

♦ A la mode ♦ Design ♦

A designer decor of luminous globes, Starck chairs, and grey and mauve tones. Inventive, good value dishes full of flavour, including a daily menu.

Kinnari

8 r. Malar (7th) – Ⓜ La Tour Maubourg – ✆ 01 47 05 18 18 – Closed Sunday **P1**

Rest – Menu 22 € (lunch)/25 € – Carte 30/45 €

♦ Thai ♦ Exotic ♦

Run by the brother of the owner of the Suan Thaï, Kinnari has successfully copied its decor and recipes, which include green papaya salad with shrimps and duck magret with a tamarind sauce.

L'Affriolé

17 r. Malar (7th) – Invalides – 01 44 18 31 33 – Closed 3 weeks in August, Sunday and Monday **P1**

Rest – Menu 29 € (lunch)/34 €

♦ A la mode ♦ Design ♦

Daily specials posted on a slate board, plus a menu and à la carte choices that change monthly according to what's in season. A 2009 facelift saw a shift to a more modern, designer look.

P'tit Troquet

28 r. de l'Exposition (7th) – École Militaire – 01 47 05 80 39 – Closed August, Saturday lunch, Monday lunch and Sunday **P2**

Rest – *(number of covers limited, pre-book)* Menu 32/40 €

♦ Bistro ♦ Retro ♦

Although its size lives up to its name, this bistro has a nostalgic charm, with its old posters, zinc counter and classic dishes such as veal casserole, beef bourguignon and chocolate caramel tart.

Le Troquet

21 r. François-Bonvin (15th) – Cambronne – 01 45 66 89 00 – Closed 1 week in May, 3 weeks in August, 1 week in December, Sunday and Monday **P3**

Rest – Menu 32 € (lunch)/41 €

♦ Terroir ♦ Neighbourhood ♦ Bistro ♦

This authentic Parisian café boasts a retro decor and impressive seasonal cuisine created by Christian Etchebest, the famous chef from southwest France. Popular with locals and visitors alike.

Le Bistrot du 7ème

56 bd de La Tour-Maubourg (7th) – La Tour Maubourg – 01 45 51 93 08 – Closed Saturday lunch and Sunday lunch **P1**

Rest – Menu 16 € (lunch)/25 € – Carte 29/44 €

♦ Bistro ♦

This authentic bistro has a traditional counter, old posters, paper napkins, and a typical brasserie-style menu. It features old favourites, such as rabbit terrine and duck confit.

Café Constant

139 r. St-Dominique (7th) – École Militaire – 01 47 53 73 34 – www.lesrestaurantsdeconstant.com – Closed Monday **O1**

Rest – Menu 23 € – Carte 34/51 €

♦ Bistro ♦ Friendly ♦

This unpretentious and friendly brasserie run by Christian Constant occupies an old café. The gourmet bistro cuisine includes classics such as eggs mimosa, oyster tartare, roast lamb, rice pudding etc. No advance booking.

SAINT-GERMAIN DES PRES – QUARTIER LATIN – HOTEL DE VILLE

Plan V

Lutetia

45 bd Raspail (6th) – Sèvres Babylone – 01 49 54 46 46 – www.lutetia-paris.com **R2**

231 rm – 600/850 € 600/850 €, 26 € – 11 suites

Rest *Paris* – see below

Rest *Brasserie Lutetia* – *01 49 54 46 76* – Menu 35 € (lunch), 42/50 € bi – Carte 54/73 €

♦ Luxury ♦ Art Deco ♦

Built in 1910, this luxury hotel on the Left Bank has lost none of its sparkle. It happily blends Art Deco fixtures with contemporary details (sculptures by César, Arman etc). One of the city's most popular culinary haunts. A traditional atmosphere, enlivened by its jazz evenings.

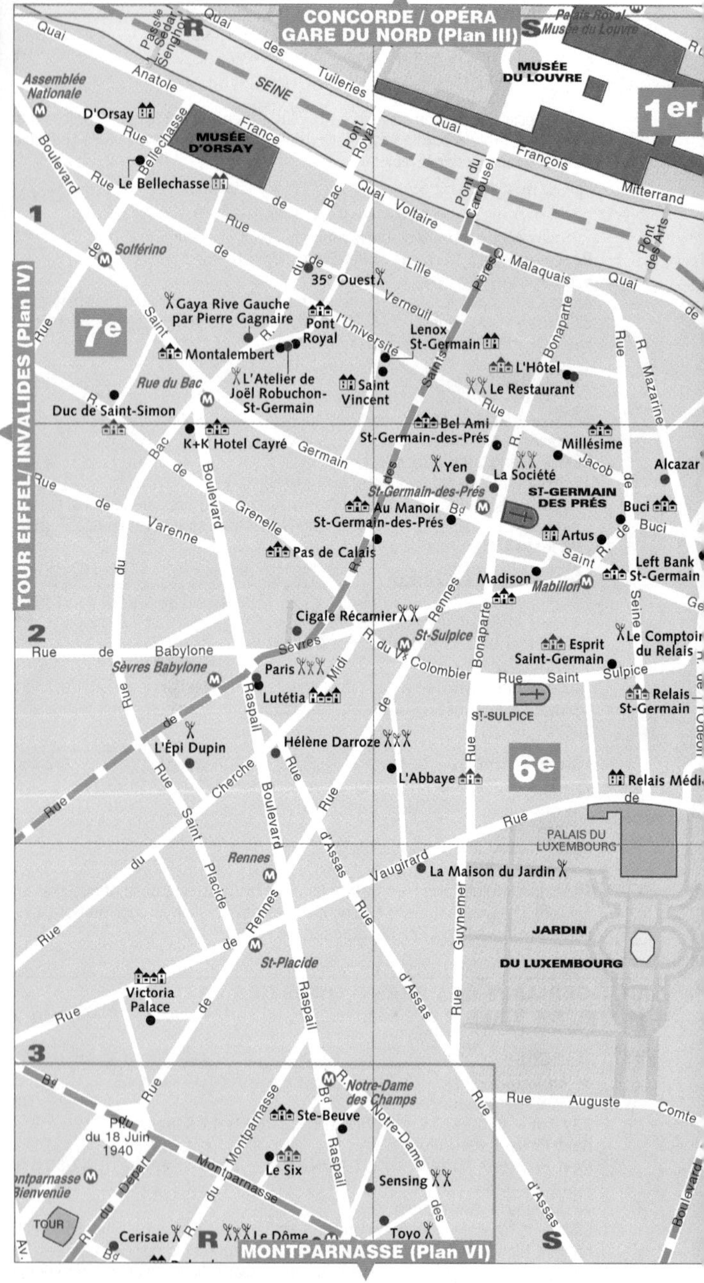
CONCORDE / OPÉRA
GARE DU NORD (Plan III)
TOUR EIFFEL/ INVALIDES (Plan IV)
MONTPARNASSE (Plan VI)
MUSÉE DU LOUVRE
MUSÉE D'ORSAY
1er
7e
6e
SEINE
Assemblée Nationale
D'Orsay
Le Bellechasse
Solférino
Gaya Rive Gauche par Pierre Gagnaire
35° Ouest
Pont Royal
Montalembert
L'Atelier de Joël Robuchon-St-Germain
Lenox St-Germain
Saint Vincent
L'Hôtel
Le Restaurant
Rue du Bac
Duc de Saint-Simon
K+K Hotel Cayré
Bel Ami
St-Germain-des-Prés
Millésime
Yen
La Société
Alcazar
St-Germain-des-Prés
ST-GERMAIN DES PRÉS
Au Manoir St-Germain-des-Prés
Buci
Artus
Pas de Calais
Madison
Mabillon
Left Bank St-Germain
Cigale Récamier
St-Sulpice
Esprit Saint-Germain
Le Comptoir du Relais
Sèvres Babylone
Paris
Lutétia
ST-SULPICE
Relais St-Germain
L'Épi Dupin
Hélène Darroze
L'Abbaye
Relais Médi
PALAIS DU LUXEMBOURG
Rennes
La Maison du Jardin
JARDIN DU LUXEMBOURG
St-Placide
Victoria Palace
Notre-Dame des Champs
Ste-Beuve
Pl. du 18 Juin 1940
Le Six
Sensing
Montparnasse Bienvenüe
TOUR
Cerisaie
Le Dôme
Toyo
Quai Anatole France
Quai des Tuileries
Quai François Mitterrand
Quai Voltaire
Q. Malaquais
Pont du Carrousel
Pont des Arts
Pont Royal
Rue de Lille
Rue de Verneuil
R. de l'Université
Rue Jacob
R. Mazarine
Rue Bonaparte
Rue de Seine
Bd Saint-Germain
Rue de Grenelle
Rue de Varenne
Rue de Babylone
Rue de Sèvres
R. du Vx Colombier
Rue Saint Sulpice
R. de Buci
Rue de Rennes
Boulevard Raspail
Rue du Cherche-Midi
Rue d'Assas
Rue de Vaugirard
Rue Guynemer
Rue Auguste Comte
Rue Saint Placide
Bd du Montparnasse
Bd Notre-Dame des Champs
R. du Départ
Rue des Saints-Pères
Boulevard Saint-Germain
Rue de Bellechasse
Rue du Bac
Passle L. Sedar Senghor

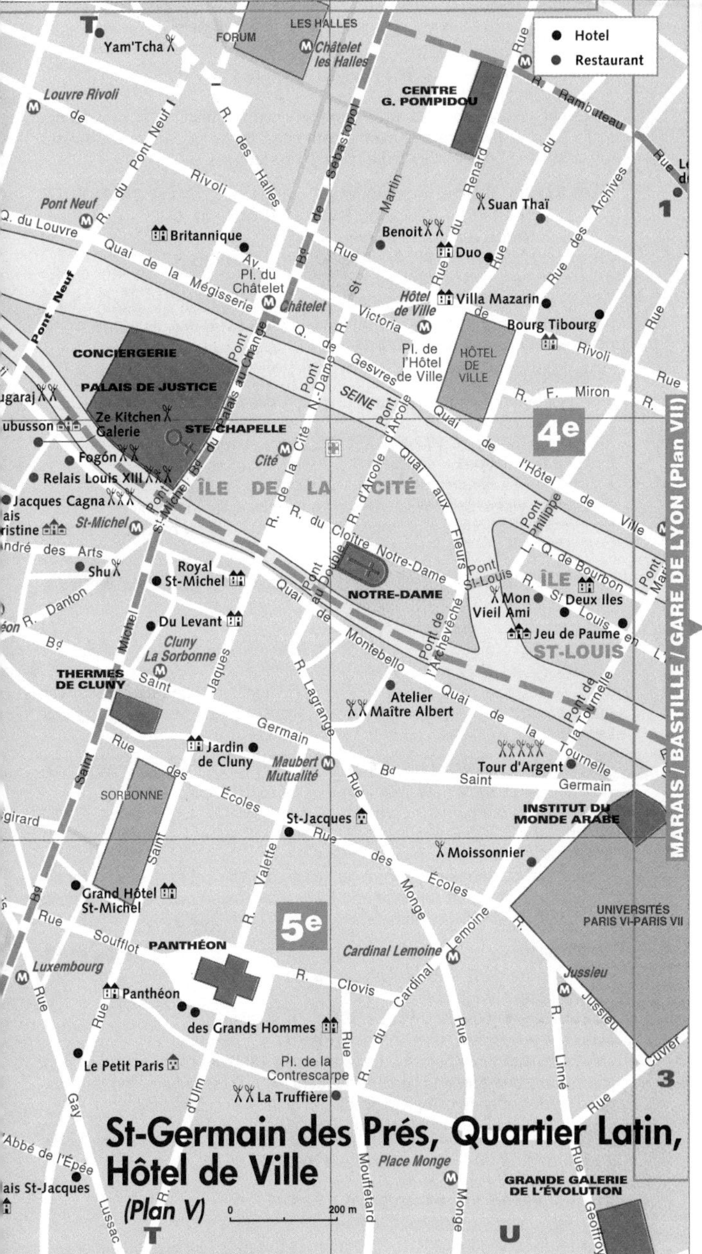

St-Germain des Prés, Quartier Latin, Hôtel de Ville (Plan V)

Victoria Palace without rest

6 r. Blaise-Desgoffe (6th) – Ⓜ St-Placide – ☎ 01 45 49 70 00
– www.victoriapalace.com **R3**
58 rm – 284/378 € 284/378 € – 4 suites
♦ Traditional ♦ Stylish ♦
This small luxury hotel has an undeniable charm. It features elegant fabrics, Louis XVI-style furniture and marble bathrooms in the guestrooms. Canvases, red velvet and porcelain are to be found in the lounges.

Duc de St-Simon without rest

14 r. St-Simon (7th) – Ⓜ Rue du Bac – ☎ 01 44 39 20 20
– www.hotelducdesaintsimon.com **R1**
29 rm – 250/290 € 250/290 €, 15 € – 5 suites
♦ Luxury ♦ Personalised ♦
With its elegant fabrics, wood-panelling, antique furniture and decorative items, the atmosphere here is of an old bourgeois house. Courteous service, as well as peace and quiet adds to its attraction.

L'Hôtel

13 r. des Beaux-Arts (6th) – Ⓜ St-Germain des Prés – ☎ 01 44 41 99 00
– www.l-hotel.com **S1**
20 rm – 280/740 € 280/740 €, 16 € – 4 suites
Rest *Le Restaurant* – see below
♦ Luxury ♦ Historic ♦ Personalised ♦
This hotel is where Oscar Wilde passed away, leaving an unpaid bill behind him. It sports a vertiginous well of light and an extravagant decor by Garcia (Baroque, French Empire and Oriental).

D'Aubusson without rest

33 r. Dauphine (6th) – Ⓜ Odéon – ☎ 01 43 29 43 43
– www.hoteldaubusson.com **T2**
49 rm – 255/625 € 275/625 €, 25 €
♦ Luxury ♦ Cosy ♦ Personalised ♦
A 17C townhouse with character, offering elegant, renovated rooms with Versailles parquet and Aubusson tapestries. There are jazz evenings at the Café Laurent at the weekend.

Esprit St-Germain without rest

22 r. St-Sulpice (6th) – Ⓜ Mabillon – ☎ 01 53 10 55 55
– www.espritsaintgermain.com **S2**
28 rm – 330/810 € 330/810 €, 28 € – 5 suites
♦ Luxury ♦ Personalised ♦
Elegant and contemporary rooms featuring soothing colours, leopard motifs, modern paintings and furniture, old beams and bathrooms with slate walls. Very modern yet with an intimate feel.

L'Abbaye without rest

10 r. Cassette (6th) – Ⓜ St-Sulpice – ☎ 01 45 44 38 11
– www.hotel-abbaye.com **S2**
40 rm – 260/270 € 380/395 € – 4 suites
♦ Luxury ♦ Historic ♦ Personalised ♦
This hotel with rare charm occupies a former 18C convent. It features bright guestrooms boasting traditional refinement, with those overlooking the courtyard garden offering complete peace and quiet. Meticulous service.

Relais Christine without rest

3 r. Christine (6th) – Ⓜ St-Michel – ☎ 01 40 51 60 80
– www.relais-christine.com **T2**
51 rm – 310/930 € 310/930 €, 30 €
♦ Traditional ♦ Historic ♦ Personalised ♦
Breakfast is served in a 13C vaulted room of this mansion, built on a medieval site. Handsome cobbled courtyard, fitness facilities, and rooms with a personal touch.

Relais St-Germain

9 carr. de l'Odéon (6th) – Ⓜ Odéon – ✆ 01 44 27 07 97 – www.hotelrsg.com
22 rm ☕ – 🚹180/220 € 🚹🚹230/440 € **S2**
Rest *Le Comptoir du Relais* – see below
◆ Luxury ◆ Personalised ◆
This elegant hotel is spread across three 17C buildings. Polished beams, shimmering fabrics and antique furniture add to the charm of its guestrooms.

Pont Royal without rest

7 r. Montalembert (7th) – Ⓜ Rue du Bac – ✆ 01 42 84 70 00 – www.hotel-pont-royal.com **R1**
65 rm – 🚹420/560 € 🚹🚹420/560 €, ☕ 27 € – 10 suites
◆ Historic ◆ Personalised ◆
A historic 'literary' hotel that embodies the true bohemian spirit of the Left Bank. Comfortable facilities amid a chic, pleasant decor without ostentation.

Bel Ami St-Germain des Prés without rest

7 r. St-Benoit (6th) – Ⓜ St-Germain des Prés – ✆ 01 42 61 53 53 – www.hotel-bel-ami.com **S2**
106 rm – 🚹260/550 € 🚹🚹260/550 €, ☕ 25 € – 4 suites
◆ Luxury ◆ Minimalist ◆ Design ◆
Although this attractive building dates from the 19C, it has nothing in common with the novel by Maupassant! It has a resolutely modern interior where minimalist luxury rubs shoulders with high-tech design. Well-being centre.

Montalembert

3 r. Montalembert (7th) – Ⓜ Rue du Bac – ✆ 01 45 49 68 68 – www.montalembert.com **R1**
52 rm – 🚹240/650 € 🚹🚹240/650 €, ☕ 24 € – 4 suites
Rest – Carte 45/75 €
◆ Historic ◆ Personalised ◆ Design ◆
With their dark wood, designer furnishings and brown, purple and beige colour scheme, the guestrooms here show all the hallmarks of contemporary design. A dozen or so rooms are in Louis Philippe-style. Modern dining room and pavement terrace.

Pas de Calais without rest

59 r. des Saints-Pères (6th) – Ⓜ St-Germain des Prés – ✆ 01 45 48 78 74 – www.hotelpasdecalais.com **R2**
38 rm – 🚹150/165 € 🚹🚹165/320 €, ☕ 15 €
◆ Traditional ◆ Personalised ◆
The hotel lobby is crowned by a glass ceiling and embellished with a plant wall made up of orchids. Attractive rooms with individual touches, and exposed beams on the top floor. Attentive service.

K+K Hotel Cayré without rest

4 bd Raspail (7th) – Ⓜ Rue du Bac – ✆ 01 45 44 38 88 – www.kkhotels.com/cayre **R1-2**
125 rm – 🚹250/435 € 🚹🚹290/465 €, ☕ 27 €
◆ Business ◆ Modern ◆
The Haussmann façade of this hotel contrasts with its elegant designer-style rooms. A fitness centre with a sauna and massage facilities is available in the basement.

Madison without rest

143 bd St-Germain (6th) – Ⓜ St-Germain des Prés – ✆ 01 40 51 60 00 – www.hotel-madison.com **S2**
50 rm ☕ – 🚹220/550 € 🚹🚹220/550 €
◆ Personalised ◆ Design ◆
Camus loved to stay at this hotel. Choose from a choice of elegant guestrooms: those on the lower floors are classic in style and enhanced with modern touches; those on the upper floors, some of which enjoy views of the church, have a more cosy feel.

Left Bank St-Germain without rest

9 r. de l'Ancienne Comédie (6th) – Ⓜ Odéon – ✆ 01 43 54 01 70 – www.paris-hotels-charm.com **S2**

31 rm – 130/280 € 140/290 €

◆ Traditional ◆ Classic ◆

With its solid Louis XIII furniture, Aubusson tapestries, damask fabrics and half-timbers, this hotel is very much for those with a penchant for old-style decor. Several rooms have the bonus of Notre Dame views.

Millésime without rest

15 r. Jacob (6th) – Ⓜ St-Germain des Prés – ✆ 01 44 07 97 97 – www.millesimehotel.com **S2**

21 rm – 195/225 € 195/225 €, 16 €

◆ Traditional ◆ Cosy ◆

Colours of the south and select furniture and fabrics create a warm atmosphere in the splendid rooms at this hotel. Superb 17C staircase, patio and fine vaulted dining room.

Au Manoir St-Germain-des-Prés without rest

153 bd St-Germain (6th) – Ⓜ St-Germain des Prés – ✆ 01 42 22 21 65 – www.paris-hotels-charm.com **S2**

28 rm – 170/330 € 170/330 €

◆ Traditional ◆ Cosy ◆

This hotel facing the Café de Flore and a 1000 year-old church has retained all of its charm following renovation work in 2008. Find wood-panelling, antique furniture and old-style creature comforts. Opt for a room with a view.

Buci without rest

22 r. Buci (6th) – Ⓜ Mabillon – ✆ 01 55 42 74 74 – www.buci-hotel.com

24 rm – 207/385 € 207/570 € **S2**

◆ Traditional ◆ Personalised ◆

This intimate hotel enjoys an ideal location at the heart of St-Germain-des-Prés. Find stylish guestrooms, some with canopies above the beds and English period furniture, while others have been renovated in a more contemporary style.

Jeu de Paume without rest

54 r. St-Louis-en-l'Ile (4th) – Ⓜ Pont Marie – ✆ 01 43 26 14 18 – www.jeudepaumehotel.com **U2**

28 rm – 145/255 € 205/350 €, 20 € – 2 suites

◆ Historic ◆ Personalised ◆

This 17C building on the Ile St-Louis, once a venue for real tennis, is now a charming boutique hotel. Entirely renovated in 2010, the rooms offer understated contemporary elegance with exposed beams and high ceilings.

Bourg Tibourg without rest

19 r. Bourg Tibourg (4th) – Ⓜ Hôtel de Ville – ✆ 01 42 78 47 39 – www.hotelbourgtibourg.com **U1**

30 rm – 180 € 230/260 €, 16 €

◆ Luxury ◆ Personalised ◆ Cosy ◆

Hotel entirely styled by Jacques Garcia. Each room has its own individual decor (neo-Gothic, Baroque, Eastern etc) and exudes luxury and refinement. A little gem in the heart of the Marais district.

Le Bellechasse without rest

8 r. de Bellechasse (7th) – Ⓜ Musée d'Orsay – ✆ 01 45 50 22 31 – www.lebellechasse.com **R1**

34 rm – 220/390 € 220/390 €, 21 €

◆ Luxury ◆ Personalised ◆ Design ◆

Top couturier Christian Lacroix designed the rooms of this hotel. He has joyfully mixed colour with antique and modern details to create an almost dreamlike but distinctly fashionable setting.

D'Orsay without rest

93 r. de Lille (7th) – Ⓜ Solférino – ✆ 01 47 05 85 54 – www.espritdefrance.com **R1**

40 rm – †145/180 € ††165/380 €, ☕ 15 € – 1 suite

♦ Traditional ♦ Classic ♦

This hotel occupies two late-18C buildings. Find attractive and spacious rooms with period furniture. There is a welcoming lounge overlooking a small, leafy patio.

St-Vincent without rest

5 r. Pré aux Clercs (7th) – Ⓜ Rue du Bac – ✆ 01 42 61 01 51 – www.hotel-st-vincent.com **S1**

22 rm – †160/260 € ††260 €, ☕ 14 €

♦ Historic ♦ Personalised ♦

A charming and quiet hotel in the heart of the Left Bank. This 18C private mansion is home to elegant and welcoming rooms decorated in the style of the Napoleon III era.

Des Grands Hommes without rest

17 pl. Panthéon (5th) – Ⓜ Luxembourg – ✆ 01 46 34 19 60 – www.hoteldesgrandshommes.com **T3**

31 rm – †150/320 € ††160/320 €, ☕ 10 €

♦ Historic ♦ Stylish ♦

This perfectly maintained hotel is decorated in Directoire-style with antique furniture. Many of the rooms enjoy views of the Pantheon; those on the fifth and six floors have a balcony or terrace.

Royal St-Michel without rest

3 bd St-Michel (5th) – Ⓜ St-Michel – ✆ 01 44 07 06 06 – www.hotelroyalsaintmichel.com **T2**

39 rm – †149/260 € ††159/320 €, ☕ 15 €

♦ Business ♦ Modern ♦

Standing opposite the famous St-Michel fountain, this welcoming hotel enjoys an excellent location in the heart of the lively Latin quarter. Contemporary, fairly plain guestrooms.

Deux Îles without rest

59 r. St-Louis-en-l'Ile (4th) – Ⓜ Pont Marie – ✆ 01 43 26 13 35 – www.hoteldesdeuxiles.com **U2**

17 rm – †159 € ††195 €, ☕ 13 €

♦ Family ♦ Cosy ♦ Modern ♦

Beige and brown tones, rattan and exposed beams set the scene in this hotel which was fully renovated in 2010. Although the rooms are on the small side they are particularly comfortable.

Relais Médicis without rest

23 r. Racine (6th) – Ⓜ Odéon – ✆ 01 43 26 00 60 – www.relaismedicis.com **S2**

16 rm ☕ – †142/172 € ††172/258 €

♦ Personalised ♦ Cosy ♦

A hint of Provence pervades the guestrooms of this hotel near the Odéon theatre; those overlooking the patio are quieter. Interesting array of antique furniture.

Panthéon without rest

19 pl. Panthéon (5th) – Ⓜ Luxembourg – ✆ 01 43 54 32 95 – www.hoteldupantheon.com **T3**

36 rm – †160/320 € ††160/320 €, ☕ 13 €

♦ Cosy ♦ Stylish ♦

Choose between cosy or Louis XVI-style rooms with views of the Pantheon's dome. Attractive lounge and vaulted breakfast room.

Villa Mazarin without rest

6 r. des Archives (4th) – Ⓜ Hôtel de Ville – ✆ 01 53 01 90 90 – www.villamazarin.com **U1**

29 rm – 190/350 € 190/350 €, 12 €

♦ Family ♦ Personalised ♦ Modern ♦

This central hotel is a stone's throw from Notre Dame, Place des Vosges and Beaubourg. It offers a contemporary look at the Second Empire. There are a few split-level rooms.

Grand Hôtel St-Michel without rest

19 r. Cujas (5th) – Ⓜ Luxembourg – ✆ 01 46 33 33 02 – www.grand-hotel-st-michel.com **T3**

45 rm – 215/350 € 215/350 €, 20 € – 2 suites

♦ Business ♦ Modern ♦

Renovated in 2008, this hotel has successfully combined modern design and a harmony of colours in its comfortable guestrooms. Fitness room, hammam, plus a vaulted breakfast room.

Relais St-Jacques without rest

3 r. Abbé-de-l'Épée (5th) – Ⓜ Luxembourg – ✆ 01 53 73 26 00 – www.relais-saint-jacques.com **T3**

22 rm – 169/349 € 169/349 €, 17 €

♦ Family ♦ Cosy ♦

Rooms of various styles (Directoire, Louis Philippe, etc.), a glass-roofed breakfast room, Louis XV lounge and 1920s bar, make this a stylish hotchpotch hotel!

Artus without rest

34 r. de Buci (6th) – Ⓜ Mabillon – ✆ 01 43 29 07 20 – www.artushotel.com **S2**

27 rm – 199/285 € 199/415 €

♦ Design ♦ Modern ♦

This contemporary yet intimate hotel has modern bedrooms ornamented with antiques. There is a design-inspired bar, and paintings from nearby galleries on display. Copious breakfast.

Lenox St-Germain without rest

9 r. de l'Université (7th) – Ⓜ St-Germain des Prés – ✆ 01 42 96 10 95 – www.lenoxsaintgermain.com **S1**

34 rm – 140/290 € 140/290 €, 15 €

♦ Business ♦ Cosy ♦

A discreetly luxurious hotel with an Art Deco feel in the lobby, and a Baroque and more classic decor in the guestrooms, all of which were renovated in 2009. Duplex on the top floor.

Jardin de Cluny without rest

9 r. du Sommerard (5th) – Ⓜ Maubert Mutualité – ✆ 01 43 54 22 66 – www.hoteljardindecluny.com **T2**

40 rm – 139/199 € 139/239 €, 15 €

♦ Personalised ♦ Modern ♦

An Ecolabel certified hotel with attractively appointed guestrooms. Breakfast buffet served in a large stone-vaulted dining room.

Du Levant without rest

18 r. de la Harpe (5th) – Ⓜ St-Michel – ✆ 01 46 34 11 00 – www.hoteldulevant.com **T2**

47 rm – 76/138 € 120/170 €

♦ Personalised ♦ Art Deco ♦

This reasonably priced hotel built in 1875 has guestrooms that are high in colour, with walls decorated in red, yellow and bright pink. Perfect location from which to explore the city.

Duo without rest

11 r. Temple (4th) – Ⓜ Hôtel de Ville – ✆ 01 42 72 72 22 – www.duoparis.com **U1**

56 rm – †160/200 € ††210/380 €, ☕ 15 € – 2 suites

◆ Modern ◆ Design ◆

Well-preserved period features (listed staircase, 16C vaulted cellar) combined with elegant and trendy contemporary interior design: a winning Duo run by the same family since 1918.

Britannique without rest

20 av. Victoria (1st) – Ⓜ Châtelet – ✆ 01 42 33 74 59 – www.hotel-britannique.fr **T1**

39 rm – †168/198 € ††215/230 €, ☕ 13 €

◆ Family ◆ Cosy ◆

Established by an English family during the reign of Queen Victoria, this hotel has retained its British Imperial elegance. Richly furnished rooms with a refined and exotic feel. Charming lounge.

Le Petit Paris without rest

214 r. St-Jacques (5th) – Ⓜ Luxembourg – ✆ 01 53 10 29 29 – www.hotelpetitparis.com **T3**

20 rm – †240/360 € ††240/360 €, ☕ 12 €

◆ Luxury ◆ Design ◆

Each guestroom has its own ambience (Louis XV, the 1970s, the Roaring Twenties etc.), and each floor its own colour. Reopened in 2009 with a highly personalised decor.

St-Jacques without rest

35 r. des Écoles (5th) – Ⓜ Maubert Mutualité – ✆ 01 44 07 45 45 – www.paris-hotel-stjacques.com **T2**

36 rm – †89/121 € ††137/184 €, ☕ 13 €

◆ Traditional ◆ Personalised ◆

A small, family-run hotel offering traditional guestrooms decorated with moulded ceilings and original frescoes. The deluxe rooms have been attractively renovated in a more opulent style.

La Tour d'Argent

15 quai de la Tournelle (5th) – Ⓜ Maubert Mutualité – ✆ 01 43 54 23 31 – www.latourdargent.com

– Closed August, 13 to 28 February, Sunday and Monday **U2**

Rest – Menu 65 € (lunch)/160 € – Carte 250/300 €

Spec. Quenelles de brochet André Terrail. Caneton "Tour d'Argent". Crêpes Belle Époque.

◆ Classic ◆ Luxury ◆

An unforgettable view of Notre-Dame cathedral and a quintessentially traditional restaurant serving classic dishes from the gastronomic hall of fame, including legendary Challans duck. Formal, elegant service, like in the old days. Superb wine list.

Paris – Hôtel Lutetia

45 bd Raspail (6th) – Ⓜ Sèvres Babylone – ✆ 01 49 54 46 90 – www.lutetia-paris.com

– Closed August, Saturday, Sunday and Bank Holidays **R2**

Rest – Menu 60 € bi (lunch), 80/130 € – Carte 60/160 €

Spec. Foie gras en cannelloni à la truffe noire, artichaut aux noisettes (December-March). Turbot de Bretagne cuit sur l'os, jeunes légumes à la dulce marine et à la laitue de mer. Le "Tout Chocolat" d'un gourmand de cacao.

◆ A la mode ◆ Cosy ◆ Elegant ◆

In keeping with the style of the hotel, the Sonia Rykiel Art Deco dining room reproduces one of the lounges from the Normandie ocean liner. Inspired updated cuisine.

XXX ✿

Jacques Cagna (dinner)

14 r. des Grands-Augustins (6th) – M St-Michel – ☎ 01 43 26 49 39 – www.jacques-cagna.com – Closed 1 to 26 August, Monday lunch, Saturday lunch and Sunday

Rest – Menu 45 € (lunch)/95 € – Carte 84/153 € **T2**

Spec. Langoustines de l'Atlantique en croustillant, salade, purée d'avocat, chips d'artichaut. Noix de ris de veau cuite en croûte de pâte à sel au romarin, pomme Anna, épinards. Paris-brest au praliné à l'ancienne.

♦ Traditional ♦ Intimate ♦ Rustic ♦

This restaurant occupies one of the oldest houses in Paris. Attractive dining room embellished with solid beams, 16C wood-panelling and Flemish paintings. Refined, traditional cuisine.

XXX ✿✿

Relais Louis XIII (Manuel Martinez)

8 r. des Grands-Augustins (6th) – M Odéon – ☎ 01 43 26 75 96 – www.relaislouis13.com – Closed August, Sunday and Monday **T2**

Rest – Menu 50 € (lunch), 80/125 € – Carte 100/130 €

Spec. Ravioli de homard breton, foie gras et crème de cèpes. Caneton challandais arrosé d'un jus d'orange au vieux vinaigre, cuisse en salade. Millefeuille, crème légère à la vanille Bourbon.

♦ Classic ♦ Intimate ♦

This 16C house has three Louis XIII-style dining rooms adorned with balustrades, striped fabrics and open stonework. Classic cuisine with a subtle touch.

XXX ✿

Hélène Darroze

4 r. d'Assas (6th) – M Sèvres Babylone – ☎ 01 42 22 00 11 – www.helenedarroze.com **R2**

Rest – *(1st floor) (closed lunch from 20 July-30 August, Sunday and Monday)* Menu 52 € (lunch), 125/175 € bi

Rest *Le Salon* – *(closed 20 July-30 August, Sunday and Monday)* Menu 85/105 € bi

Spec. Chipiron sauté au chorizo, riz carnaroli acquarello, noir et crémeux. Pigeonneau de Racan cuit au feu de bois, foie gras de canard des Landes grillé. Chocolat Caraïbes, tarte parfumée à la framboise (summer).

♦ A la mode ♦ Cosy ♦

This restaurant offers delicious cuisine and wines from southwest France. The modern, discreet and soft decor is in tones of aubergine and orange. On the ground floor, Hélène Darroze presides over the Salon, serving tapas and snacks with a rustic Landes accent.

XX ✿

Le Restaurant – Hôtel L'Hôtel

13 r. des Beaux-Arts (6th) – M St-Germain des Prés – ☎ 01 44 41 99 01 – www.l-hotel.com – Closed August, 21 to 28 December, Sunday and Monday **S1**

Rest – Menu 95/155 € bi – Carte 77/111 €

Spec. Ravioles de cèpes (autumn). Ris de veau. Le chocolat.

♦ Innovative ♦ Elegant ♦

Occupying the equally economically named L'Hôtel, Le Restaurant has a decor designed by Jacques Garcia and a small internal courtyard. Superbly prepared contemporary cuisine.

XX

La Société

4 pl. St-Germain-des-Prés (6th) – M St-Germain des Prés – ☎ 01 53 63 60 60 **S2**

Rest – Carte 50/100 €

♦ A la mode ♦ Design ♦ Luxury ♦

The Costes family opened this glamorous restaurant in the heart of St-Germain-des-Prés in 2009. A temple to architectural design and stylish living. Contemporary cuisine.

XX

Cigale Récamier

4 r. Récamier (7th) – Ⓜ Sèvres Babylone – ✆ 01 45 48 86 58 – Closed Sunday
Rest – Carte 40/55 € **R2**

♦ Traditional ♦ Friendly ♦

This discreet restaurant is popular with politicians, lawyers and publishers. Classic cuisine and sweet and savoury soufflé specialities. The quiet terrace here is always popular.

XX ✿

Benoit

20 r. St-Martin (4th) – Ⓜ Châtelet-Les Halles – ✆ 01 42 72 25 76
– www.alain-ducasse.com – Closed August **U1**
Rest – Menu 34 € (lunch) – Carte 55/84 €

Spec. Escargots en coquille, beurre d'ail, fines herbes. Tête de veau sauce ravigote. Profiteroles sauce chocolat chaud.

♦ Classic ♦ Bistro ♦

Alain Ducasse runs this chic and lively bistro, one of the oldest in Paris. Classic cuisine, respecting the soul of this fine, authentic establishment.

XX

Yugaraj

14 r. Dauphine (6th) – Ⓜ Odéon – ✆ 01 43 26 44 91
– Closed August, Monday lunch and Thursday lunch **T1**
Rest – Menu 28/66 € – Carte 40/60 €

♦ Indian ♦ Exotic ♦

Step right into India in this acclaimed restaurant with its typical decor of wood, silk, antiques etc. Extensive à la carte choices.

XX

La Truffière

4 r. Blainville (5th), Ⓜ Place Monge – ✆ 01 46 33 29 82 – www.latruffiere.com
– Closed 18 to 26 December, Sunday and Monday **T3**
Rest – Menu 28 € (weekday lunch), 38/115 € – Carte 60/140 €

♦ A la mode ♦ Intimate ♦

In addition to his mainstay traditional cuisine, the chef also creates more contemporary dishes, including a few Japanese-inspired creations. Rustic yet intimate ambience and a superb wine list.

XX

Atelier Maître Albert

1 r. Maître Albert (5th) – Ⓜ Maubert Mutualité – ✆ 01 56 81 30 01
– www.ateliermaitrealbert.com
– Closed 1 to 15 August, Christmas Holidays, Saturday lunch and Sunday lunch
Rest – Menu 32 € (dinner) – Carte dinner 40/59 € **U2**

♦ Traditional ♦ Cosy ♦

An attractive medieval fireplace and roasting spits take pride of place in this handsome interior designed by Jean-Michel Wilmotte. Guy Savoy is responsible for the mouthwatering menu.

XX

Alcazar

62 r. Mazarine (6th) – Ⓜ Odéon – ✆ 01 53 10 19 99 – www.alcazar.fr
- www.blogalcazar.fr **S2**
Rest – Menu 40 € (dinner) – Carte 40/60 €

♦ Trendy ♦ Brasserie ♦

Sir Conrad's establishment attracts fans of electro-chic atmospheres and modern tastes. The glass wall, mezzanine and view of the kitchens give the location its individuality.

XX ✿

Fogón (Juan Alberto Herráiz)

(dinner)

45 quai des Grands Augustins (6th) – Ⓜ St-Michel – ✆ 01 43 54 31 33
– www.fogon.fr
– Closed 15 August-7 September, 23 December-7 January, Monday and lunch except Saturday and Sunday **T2**
Rest – Menu 48/55 € – Carte 40/55 €

Spec. Tapas selon le marché. Riz en paella. Tapas sucrées.

♦ Spanish ♦ Design ♦

Spanish cuisine (tapas, paellas) reworked with flair and ingenuity, using top quality produce. The setting here is chic, and contemporary, with a distinct designer feel.

L'Atelier de Joël Robuchon - St-Germain

5 r. de Montalembert (7th) – Ⓜ Rue du Bac
– ✆ 01 42 22 56 56 – www.joel-robuchon.com
– Open from 11.30am to 3.30pm and 6.30pm to midnight. Reservations possible for certain times only : please enquire **R1**
Rest – Menu 150 € – Carte 59/128 €
Spec. Tomates anciennes, relevées de sumac à l'huile vierge (15 June-30 September). Agneau de lait en côtelettes à la fleur de thym. "Chocolat tendance", ganache onctueuse au chocolat araguani, glace au grué de cacao.
♦ Innovative ♦ Design ♦ Minimalist ♦
An original concept in a chic décor designed by Rochon: no tables, just high stools in a row facing the counter, where you can sample fine, modern cuisine, served tapas style.

Gaya Rive Gauche par Pierre Gagnaire

44 r. du Bac (7th) – Ⓜ Rue du Bac – ✆ 01 45 44 73 73
– www.pierre-gagnaire.com
– Closed 23 December-3 January and Sunday **R1**
Rest – Carte 60/100 €
Spec. Pressé de tourteau. Escalope de bar sauvage. Biscuit chocolat gayas.
♦ Seafood ♦ Design ♦ Elegant ♦
In this delightful contemporary and relaxed bistro with a grey-blue décor designed by Christian Ghion, you are served a succession of creative seafood dishes.

Ze Kitchen Galerie (William Ledeuil)

4 r. des Grands-Augustins (6th) – Ⓜ St-Michel – ✆ 01 44 32 00 32
– www.zekitchengalerie.fr
– Closed Saturday lunch and Sunday **T2**
Rest – Menu 39 € bi (lunch)/76 € – Carte dinner approx. 68 €
Spec. Crabe d'Alaska aux herbes thaïes, gaspacho de tomate cœur de bœuf (summer). Plats à la plancha. Glace chocolat blanc, wasabi, condiment pistache et fraise.
♦ Fusion ♦ Design ♦ Trendy ♦
Tempting fusion menu influenced by Asia, refined interior with a loft atmosphere, contemporary paintings and visible kitchens: Ze Kitchen is 'ze' hip place to be on the Left Bank.

Yam'Tcha (Adeline Grattard)

4 r. Sauval (1st) – Ⓜ Louvre Rivoli – ✆ 01 40 26 08 07
– www.yamtcha.com
– Closed August, Christmas Holidays, Sunday dinner, Monday and Tuesday
Rest – *(number of covers limited, pre-book)* Menu 50 € (weekday lunch)/85 € **T1**
Spec. Homard, jaune d'œuf, maïs. Cochon de lait noir de Bigorre, aubergines à la séchuanaise. Cheese cake, gingembre confit, shiso.
♦ Fusion ♦ Cosy ♦
Enjoy remarkable cuisine produced by a young chef who trained in Hong Kong and at the Astrance. Simple, yet memorable dishes with both French and Asian influences, as well as an excellent selection of teas. Space for just twenty diners!

Mon Vieil Ami

69 r. St-Louis-en-l'Île (4th) – Ⓜ Pont Marie – ✆ 01 40 46 01 35
– www.mon-vieil-ami.com
– Closed 1 to 20 August, 1 to 20 January, Monday and Tuesday **U2**
Rest – Menu 43 €
♦ Traditional ♦ Inn ♦ Elegant ♦
Old wooden beams and contemporary decor characterise this trendy, auberge-style restaurant. Delicious traditional recipes with a lovely modern touch and Alsace influences.

Yen

22 r. St-Benoît (6th) – Ⓜ St-Germain-des-Prés – ✆ 01 45 44 11 18 – Closed 2 weeks in August and Sunday **S2**

Rest – Menu 68 € (dinner) – Carte 35/70 €

♦ Japanese ♦ Minimalist ♦

Two dining rooms with highly refined Japanese decor, the one on the first floor is slightly warmer in style. Pride of place on the menu for the chef's speciality: soba (buckwheat noodles).

L'Épi Dupin

11 r. Dupin (6th), Ⓜ Sèvres Babylone – ✆ 01 42 22 64 56 – www.epidupin.com – Closed 1 to 24 August, Monday lunch, Saturday and Sunday **R2**

Rest – *(number of covers limited, pre-book)* Menu 33 €

♦ A la mode ♦ Friendly ♦

Exposed stone, half-timbering and wooden beams create a convivial backdrop for delicious traditional cuisine with a modern touch. This pocket-sized eatery a stone's throw from Le Bon Marché department store has a loyal local following.

35° Ouest

35 r. de Verneuil (7th) – Ⓜ Rue du Bac – ✆ 01 42 86 98 88 – Closed 1 to 29 August, 24 December-2 January, Sunday and Monday

Rest – *(number of covers limited, pre-book)* Carte 45/107 € **R1**

Spec. Rémoulade de tourteau et granny-smith. Turbot rôti en tronçon, champignons du moment. Tarte chocolat-cannelle.

♦ Seafood ♦ Minimalist ♦

The simple, modern decor in the small dining room provides a backdrop for fish and seafood, with an emphasis on the freshest products and superb flavours.

La Maison du Jardin

27 r. Vaugirard (6th) – Ⓜ Rennes – ✆ 01 45 48 22 31 – Closed 1 to 24 August, Saturday lunch, Sunday and Bank Holidays

Rest – *(pre-book)* Menu 31 € **S3**

♦ Traditional ♦ Bistro ♦

This bistro close to the Luxembourg gardens serves cuisine which blends simplicity and tradition through classic dishes such as homemade pâté, seasonal soups, mousse au chocolat etc, accompanied by affordably priced wines.

Le Comptoir du Relais – Hôtel Relais St-Germain

5 carr. de l'Odéon (6th) – Ⓜ Odéon – ✆ 01 44 27 07 97 – www.hotelrsg.com **S2**

Rest – *(number of covers limited, pre-book)* Menu 50 € (weekday dinner) – Carte 40/70 €

♦ Bistro ♦

In this pleasant little bistro, Yves Camdeborde offers tasty, generous, traditional cuisine, including specialities from southwest France. Authentic 1930s decor.

Shu

8 r. Suger (6th) – Ⓜ St-Michel – ✆ 0146 34 25 88 – www.restaurant-shu.com – Closed 2 weeks in August, Easter Holidays and Sunday **T2**

Rest – *(dinner only) (number of covers limited, pre-book)* Menu 38/56 €

♦ Japanese ♦ Minimalist ♦

A Japanese restaurant housed in an old cellar in the St-Michel quarter. Quality products and technical expertise are the hallmarks of the native chef, who is a master in the art of kushiage (small, deep-fried kebabs).

Moissonnier

28 r. des Fossés-St-Bernard (5th) – Ⓜ Jussieu – ✆ 01 43 29 87 65 – Closed August, Sunday and Monday **U3**

Rest – Carte 29/57 €

♦ Lyons cuisine ♦ Bistro ♦

The typical decor of this bistro, with its gleaming bar, old walls and cosy banquettes, has not changed in years. Cuisine from Lyon with the occasional foray into the Franche-Comté.

Suan Thaï

41 r. Ste-Croix-de-la-Bretonnerie (4th) – Ⓜ Rambuteau – ✆ 01 42 77 10 20 **U1**

Rest – Menu 17 € (weekday lunch), 28/38 € – Carte 35/60 €

♦ Thai ♦ Exotic ♦

Chefs from Thailand create authentic, delicate flavours amid a discreetly exotic decor. Reasonably priced and increasingly popular, so make sure you book.

MONTPARNASSE – DENFERT *Plan VI*

Pullman Montparnasse

19 r. du Cdt Mouchotte (14th) – Ⓜ Montparnasse Bienvenüe – ✆ 01 44 36 44 36 – www.pullmanhotels.com **V1**

918 rm – †179/449 € ††179/449 €, ☕ 27 € – 35 suites

Rest – Menu 35 € – Carte 45/70 €

♦ Business ♦ Art Deco ♦

The spacious rooms in this glass and concrete building have been revamped in a contemporary style with an Art Deco flourish. Beautiful view of the capital from the upper floors.

Concorde Montparnasse

40 r. du Cdt Mouchotte (14th) – Ⓜ Gaîté – ✆ 01 56 54 84 00 – www.concorde-montparnasse.com **V1**

354 rm – †150/450 € ††150/450 €, ☕ 23 €

Rest – Menu 31 € (weekdays) – Carte 31/52 €

♦ Business ♦ Modern ♦

This hotel on Place de Catalogne offers guests quiet, well-sized rooms with a contemporary feel. Interior garden and trendy bar. This modern, soberly designed restaurant features exotic wood and colourful fabrics. It serves international cuisine.

Le Six without rest

14 r. Stanislas (6th) – Ⓜ Notre-Dame des Champs – ✆ 01 42 22 00 75 – www.hotel-le-six.com **W1**

37 rm – †199/450 € ††209/450 €, ☕ 22 € – 4 suites

♦ Luxury ♦ Design ♦

This modern hotel is between the Luxembourg gardens, St-Germain des Prés and Montparnasse. Find spacious rooms, warm colours and photos of famous visitors to the area. Small, well-equipped spa.

Aiglon without rest

232 bd Raspail (14th) – Ⓜ Raspail – ✆ 01 43 20 82 42 – www.aiglon.com

36 rm – †140/175 € ††140/212 €, ☕ 12 € – 10 suites **W1**

♦ Classic ♦ Modern ♦

This one time home to Giacometti and Bunuel is gradually being modernised. Bright colours and stylish details (mosaics in the bathrooms, photos etc.) set the scene here.

Ste-Beuve without rest

9 r. Ste-Beuve (6th) – Ⓜ Notre-Dame des Champs – ✆ 01 45 48 20 07 – www.parishotelcharme.com **W1**

22 rm – †159/255 € ††159/365 €, ☕ 15 €

♦ Cosy ♦ Personalised ♦

The intimate atmosphere of this establishment makes it feel like a private home. The guestrooms have been renovated in a tasteful modern style; bathrooms in black and white.

Lenox Montparnasse without rest

15 r. Delambre (14th) – Ⓜ Vavin – ✆ 01 43 35 34 50 – www.hotellenox.com

52 rm – †200/350 € ††200/350 €, ☕ 16 € **W1**

♦ Business ♦ Classic ♦

A stylish, elegant hotel with an intimate bar and lounges, bedrooms in a variety of colour schemes (with period furniture and decorative objects), and pleasant suites on the sixth floor.

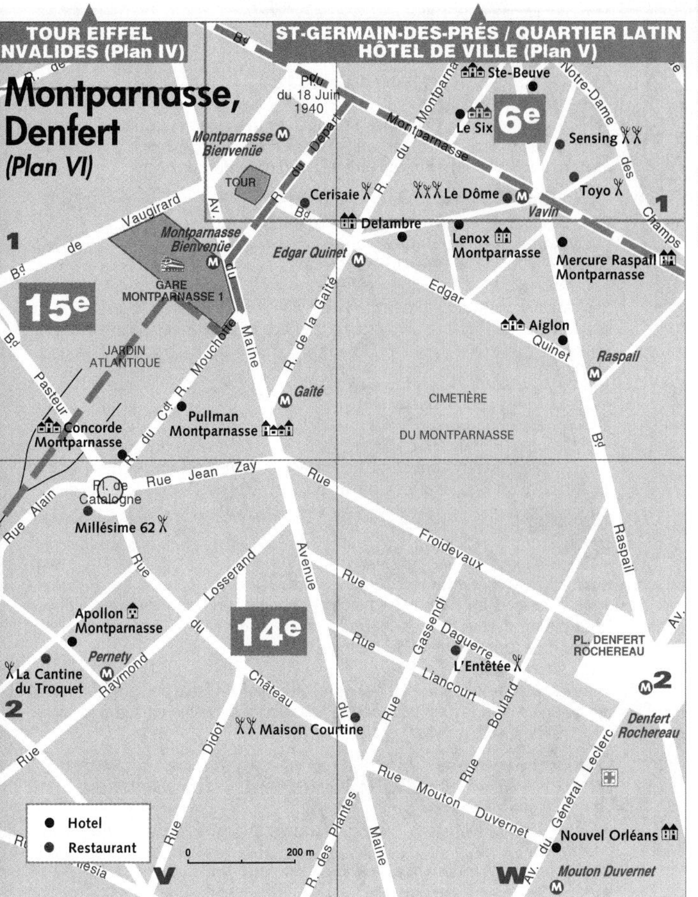

Nouvel Orléans without rest

25 av. du Gén.-Leclerc (14th) – Ⓜ Mouton Duvernet – ✆ 01 43 27 80 20 – www.hotelnouvelorleans.com **W2**

46 rm – 90/145 € 145 €, 12 €

♦ Business ♦ Functional ♦

A well-maintained hotel close to the Porte d'Orléans. The guestrooms have contemporary-style furniture and warm, colourful fabrics; the quieter rooms are to the rear of the hotel.

Delambre without rest

35 r. Delambre (14th) – Ⓜ Edgar Quinet – ✆ 01 43 20 66 31 – www.hoteldelambreparis.com **W1**

30 rm – 85/160 € 99/160 €, 11 €

♦ Business ♦ Functional ♦

André Breton stayed in this hotel located in a quiet street close to Montparnasse railway station. The decor is modern, the rooms simple but bright, and many are spacious.

Mercure Raspail Montparnasse without rest

207 bd Raspail (14th) – Ⓜ Vavin – ✆ 01 43 20 62 94
– www.mercure.com **W1**

63 rm – 130/220 € 140/230 €, ☕ 15 €

◆ Business ◆ Modern ◆

This building from the Haussmann era is close to the famous brasseries in the Montparnasse district. It offers well-maintained guestrooms with a restrained modern decor (varnished wood furniture and colourful curtains).

Apollon Montparnasse without rest

91 r. Ouest (14th) – Ⓜ Pernety – ✆ 01 43 95 62 00
– www.apollon-montparnasse.com **V2**

33 rm – 90/115 € 99/139 €, ☕ 12 €

◆ Traditional ◆ Functional ◆

A pleasantly renovated family-run hotel with well-maintained guestrooms in which stripes and floral curtains provide the decorative backdrop. Courteous staff.

Le Dôme

108 bd Montparnasse (14th) – Ⓜ Vavin – ✆ 01 43 35 25 81
– Closed Sunday and Monday in August **W1**

Rest – Carte 75/160 €

◆ Seafood ◆ Elegant ◆

This temple of literary and artistic bohemian life in the Roaring Twenties is now an attractive Art Deco brasserie offering old-style service. Fish and seafood.

Sensing

19 r. Bréa (6th) – Ⓜ Vavin – ✆ 01 43 27 08 80 – www.restaurant-sensing.com
– Closed August, Monday lunch and Sunday **W1**

Rest – Menu 55 € bi (lunch)/95 € – Carte 60/93 €

Spec. Tourteau en carapace et écume, brioche noire au beurre d'algues. Saint-pierre snacké, jeunes légumes et cœur de salade. Fruits de saison poêlés, financier et sorbet du moment.

◆ A la mode ◆ Trendy ◆

With Guy Martin at the helm, the Sensing offers light, refined and elegantly crafted cuisine with a strong focus on the finest ingredients. An uncluttered, ultra-design setting with a stylish contemporary feel.

Maison Courtine

157 av. du Maine (14th) – Ⓜ Mouton Duvernet – ✆ 01 45 43 08 04
– www.lamaisoncourtine.com
– Closed 3 weeks in August, 1 week in February, Monday lunch, Saturday lunch and Sunday **W2**

Rest – Menu 24 € (lunch), 30/35 € – Carte approx. 33 €

◆ A la mode ◆ Friendly ◆

This former bastion of cuisine from southwest France was transformed in 2009 into a contemporary restaurant with pink and grey-green tones. The emphasis is now on seasonal Mediterranean cuisine.

La Cerisaie

70 bd E.-Quinet (14th) – Ⓜ Edgar Quinet – ✆ 01 43 20 98 98
– www.restaurantlacerisaie.com
– Closed 14 July-15 August, 19 December-4 January, Saturday and Sunday

Rest – *(pre-book)* Menu 32/39 € – Carte 32/46 € **V1**

◆ South-western France ◆ Bistro ◆

A tiny restaurant in the heart of the Breton quarter. Every day, the owner chalks up on a blackboard the carefully prepared south-western dishes.

Millésimes 62

13 pl. de Catalogne (14th) – Ⓜ Gaîté – ✆ 01 43 35 34 35
– www.millesimes62.com – Closed Saturday lunch and Sunday

Rest – Menu 23 € (lunch), 26/29 € – Carte 28/38 € **V2**

◆ Friendly ◆ Fashionable ◆

Enjoy affordably priced seasonal cuisine on Place de Catalogne, where the culinary highlights include beef with Szechuan pepper and crème brûlée with bergamot.

La Cantine du Troquet

101 r. de l'Ouest (14th) – Ⓜ Pernety **V2**
Rest – Menu 30 € – Carte 29/39 €
♦ Bistro ♦ Friendly ♦
A simplified version of its sister restaurant, Le Troquet in the 15th arrondissement. Conviviality is the theme here, with its red banquettes, wooden tables and daily specials posted on a blackboard. No reservations – and not even a telephone!

L'Entêtée

4 r. Danville (14th) – Ⓜ Denfert Rochereau – ✆ 01 40 47 56 81 – www.wix.com/lentetee – Closed August, Sunday, Monday and Bank Holidays **W2**
Rest – *(dinner only) (number of covers limited, pre-book)* Menu 32/30 € – Carte approx. 39 €
♦ A la mode ♦ Bistro ♦
This discreet bistro is a short distance from rue Dagerre. The female chef takes her inspiration from seasonal cuisine flavoured with herbs and spices.

L'Ordonnance

51 r. Hallé (14th) – Ⓜ Mouton Duvernet – ✆ 01 43 27 55 85 – Closed 1 to 15 August, Saturday except dinner in winter and Sunday *Plan I* **B3**
Rest – Menu 32 €
♦ Traditional ♦ Bistro ♦
This new-wave bistro near Place Michel-Audiard is run by its friendly and welcoming owner. The honest and precise cuisine here includes favourites such as roast loin of lamb with thyme, poached eggs, pan-fried foie gras.

Toyo

17 r. Jules Chaplain (6th) – Ⓜ Vavin – ✆ 01 43 54 28 03 – Closed August, Sunday and Monday **W1**
Rest – Menu 35 € (lunch), 55/75 €
♦ A la mode ♦ Design ♦ Minimalist ♦
In a former life Toyo worked for a leading Japanese fashion designer. Nowadays, he excels in the art of combining flavours and textures from France and Asia. Refined cuisine with a fresh touch.

MARAIS – BASTILLE – GARE DE LYON *Plan VII*

Pavillon de la Reine without rest

28 pl. des Vosges (3rd) – Ⓜ Bastille – ✆ 01 40 29 19 19 – www.pavillon-de-la-reine.com **Y2**
38 rm – †330/900 € ††330/900 €, ☕ 34 € – 16 suites
♦ Luxury ♦ Historic ♦ Personalised ♦
This elegant and luxurious hotel showcases the discreet noble ambience of the Paris of yesteryear. Once through the vaulted arcades of Place des Vosges, the first feast for the eyes is the beautiful verdant courtyard. Inside, the guestrooms are both plush and elegant, with a small spa providing the icing on the cake.

Les Jardins du Marais

rm,

74 r. Amelot (11th) – Ⓜ St-Sébastien Froissart – ✆ 01 40 21 22 23 – www.lesjardinsdumarais.com **Y1**
263 rm – †350/750 € ††350/750 €, ☕ 20 € – 8 suites
Rest – *(closed Sunday)* Menu 22/30 €
♦ Luxury ♦ Art Deco ♦
Partly listed buildings overlooking an old cul-de-sac with small, private terraces. Designer entrance hall and bar, and Art Deco touches in the bedrooms.

Mercure Gare de Lyon without rest

2 pl. Louis-Armand (12th) – Ⓜ Gare de Lyon – ✆ 01 43 44 84 84 – www.mercure.com **Y3**

315 rm – 140/300 € 155/315 €, 17 €

♦ Chain hotel ♦ Modern ♦

The modern architecture of this hotel contrasts with the belfry of the Gare de Lyon next door. The bedrooms, refurbished in 2009, are soundproofed and air-conditioned. Wine bar.

Du Petit Moulin without rest

29 r. du Poitou (3rd) – Ⓜ St-Sébastien Froissart – ✆ 01 42 74 10 10 – www.hoteldupetitmoulin.com **X1**

17 rm – 190/350 € 190/350 €, 15 €

♦ Luxury ♦ Personalised ♦

Christian Lacroix is behind the unique and refined decor in this hotel in the Marais, which plays on the contrasts between the traditional and the modern. Every bedroom is a delight, with vibrant tones and free-standing bathtubs.

Le Standard Design without rest

29 r. des Taillandiers (11th) – Ⓜ Bastille – ✆ 01 48 05 30 97 – www.standard-design-hotel-paris.com **Y2**

36 rm – 115/250 € 115/280 €, 15 €

♦ Cosy ♦ Design ♦

A contemporary interior in black and white with touches of colour in the bedrooms. Bright breakfast room under sloping ceilings.

Paris Bastille without rest

67 r. de Lyon (12th) – Ⓜ Bastille – ✆ 01 40 01 07 17 – www.hotelparisbastille.com **Y2**

37 rm – 181/278 € 195/278 €, 13 €

♦ Business ♦ Functional ♦ Modern ♦

Up-to-date comfort, modern hardwood furnishings and carefully chosen colour schemes characterise the rooms in this hotel facing the Opéra. Bar area.

L'Ambroisie (Bernard Pacaud)

9 pl. des Vosges (4th) – Ⓜ St-Paul – ✆ 01 42 78 51 45 – Closed August, February Holidays, Sunday and Monday **X2**

Rest – Carte 200/310 €

Spec. Foie gras de canard landais en croûte de poivre gris, chutney de cerises noires. Noix de ris de veau braisée à la financière, timbale de macaronis. Boule nacrée à la pêche blanche et cassis, glace verveine.

♦ Classic ♦ Luxury ♦

Regal decor and subtle cuisine that is close to perfection beneath the arcades of the Place des Vosges. In classical mythology, ambrosia (the restaurant's name) was the food of the gods.

Bofinger (dinner)

5 r. Bastille (4th) – Ⓜ Bastille – ✆ 01 42 72 87 82 – www.bofingerparis.com **Y2**

Rest – Menu 31 € – Carte 40/70 €

♦ Brasserie ♦ Retro ♦

This is a real Paris institution with a striking, Alsace-style decor, including a dome, inlaid wood, mirrors, and paintings by Hansi. Opened in 1864, this brasserie is as charming as ever.

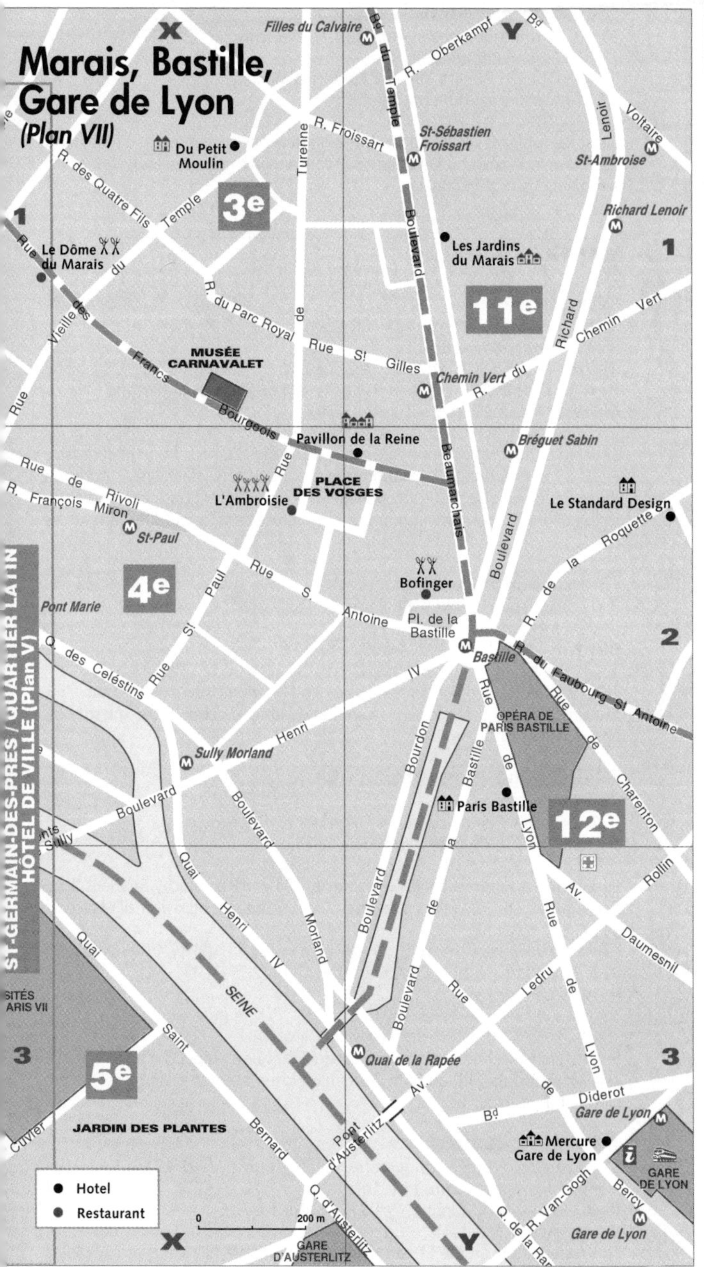

Marais, Bastille, Gare de Lyon
(Plan VII)
Du Petit Moulin
Le Dôme du Marais
MUSÉE CARNAVALET
Pavillon de la Reine
PLACE DES VOSGES
L'Ambroisie
Les Jardins du Marais
Le Standard Design
Bofinger
Pl. de la Bastille
OPÉRA DE PARIS BASTILLE
Paris Bastille
Mercure Gare de Lyon
GARE DE LYON
GARE D'AUSTERLITZ
JARDIN DES PLANTES
SEINE
3e
4e
5e
11e
12e
Filles du Calvaire
St-Sébastien Froissart
St-Ambroise
Richard Lenoir
Chemin Vert
Bréguet Sabin
St-Paul
Pont Marie
Bastille
Sully Morland
Quai de la Rapée
Gare de Lyon
R. Oberkampf
R. Froissart
R. des Quatre Fils
R. du Parc Royal
Rue St Gilles
Rue Vieille du Temple
Rue des Francs Bourgeois
Rue de Rivoli
R. François Miron
Rue St Antoine
Rue St Paul
Q. des Célestins
Boulevard Henri IV
Quai Henri IV
Boulevard Morland
Boulevard Bourdon
Boulevard Beaumarchais
Boulevard du Temple
Boulevard Richard Lenoir
R. du Chemin Vert
R. de la Roquette
R. du Faubourg St Antoine
Rue de Charenton
Rue de Lyon
Rue de la Bastille
Boulevard de la Bastille
Av. Daumesnil
Av. Ledru Rollin
Bd Diderot
R. Van-Gogh
Rue de Bercy
Q. de la Rapée
Av. Pont d'Austerlitz
Q. d'Austerlitz
Quai Saint Bernard
Cuvier
Voltaire
Lenoir
Turenne
ST-GERMAIN-DES-PRES / QUARTIER LATIN HÔTEL DE VILLE (Plan V)
Hotel
Restaurant
0
200 m
X
Y
1
2
3

Le Dôme du Marais

53 bis r. Francs-Bourgeois (4th) – Ⓜ Rambuteau – ✆ 01 42 74 54 17 – www.ledomedumarais.fr – Closed 7 to 31 August, Tuesday lunch and Monday **X1**

Rest – Menu 25 € (lunch), 32/48 €

◆ Romantic ◆ Elegant ◆

Seasonal cuisine is served under the pretty dome of the former Crédit Municipal (stated-owned pawnbroker's) auction room and in the conservatory. Perfect for a romantic, candlelit dinners.

MONTMARTRE – PIGALLE *Plan VIII*

Terrass' Hôtel

12 r. J.-de-Maistre (18th) – Ⓜ Place de Clichy – ✆ 01 46 06 72 85 – www.terrass-hotel.com **Z1**

98 rm – †285/550 € ††285/550 €, ☐ 17 €

Rest *Le Diapason* – *✆ 01 44 92 34 00 (closed Sunday dinner and Monday)* Menu 29/38 € – Carte 45/70 €

◆ Grand Luxury ◆ Classic ◆ Personalised ◆

Situated at the foot of Montmartre, this discreetly luxurious hotel features spacious, simply furnished guestrooms that are perfectly maintained. Attractive lounge and piano-bar, plus an open fire in winter. Modern cuisine served either in the contemporary dining room or on the roof terrace, with its views of the city.

Mercure Montmartre without rest

3 r. Caulaincourt (18th) – Ⓜ Place de Clichy – ✆ 01 44 69 70 70 – www.mercure.com **Z2**

305 rm – †89/320 € ††104/335 €, ☐ 17 €

◆ Chain hotel ◆ Business ◆ Functional ◆

This fully refurbished Mercure enjoys a good location close to Place Clichy, the Moulin Rouge and Montmartre cemetery. Modern, comfortable guestrooms and obliging staff.

Holiday Inn Paris Montmartre without rest

23 r. Damrémont (18th) – Ⓜ Lamarck Caulaincourt – ✆ 01 44 92 33 40 **Z1**

54 rm – †145/300 € ††145/300 €, ☐ 13 €

◆ Chain hotel ◆ Business ◆ Functional ◆

Located in a quiet street between Montmartre hill and Place Clichy. Spacious, functional guestrooms, as well as a breakfast room that opens onto a small terrace.

Timhotel without rest

11 r. Ravignan (18th) – Ⓜ Abbesses – ✆ 01 42 55 74 79 – www.timhotel.com **AA2**

59 rm – †75/170 € ††85/180 €, ☐ 10 €

◆ Chain hotel ◆ Modern ◆ Functional ◆

Smart, functional hotel on one of the neighbourhood's most charming squares. The rooms on the 4th and 5th floors have been renovated and offer superb views of the capital.

Chamarré Montmartre

52 r. Lamarck (18th) – Ⓜ Lamarck Caulaincourt – ✆ 01 42 55 05 42 – www.chamarre-montmartre.com **AA1**

Rest – Menu 37 € (lunch), 49/95 € – Carte 62/73 €

◆ Franco-Mauritian ◆ Design ◆

This restaurant is on the Lamarck side of Montmartre hill. It has a cosy dining room with a restricted view of the kitchens, a bar with chairs for diners, and a pleasant terrace. French-Mauritian cuisine.

L'Oriental

47 av. Trudaine (9th) – Ⓜ Pigalle
– ✆ 01 42 64 39 80
– www.loriental-restaurant.com **AA2**

Rest – Menu 34 € – Carte 31/50 €

♦ Moroccan ♦ Exotic ♦

Choose from the pleasant outdoor terrace or the welcoming and comfortable dining room with its oriental decor. Evocatively flavoured Moroccan cuisine, including signature couscous dishes.

Miroir

94 r. des Martyrs (18th) – Ⓜ Abbesses
– ✆ 01 46 06 50 73
– Closed 3 weeks in August, 23 to 31 December, Sunday, Monday and Bank Holidays **AA2**

Rest – Menu 25/32 € – Carte 32/45 €

♦ Bistro ♦ Friendly ♦

A young and professional team runs this typical Parisian bistro, where one dining room is illuminated by natural light through its glass roof. Seasonally inspired menus and an attractive choice of wines.

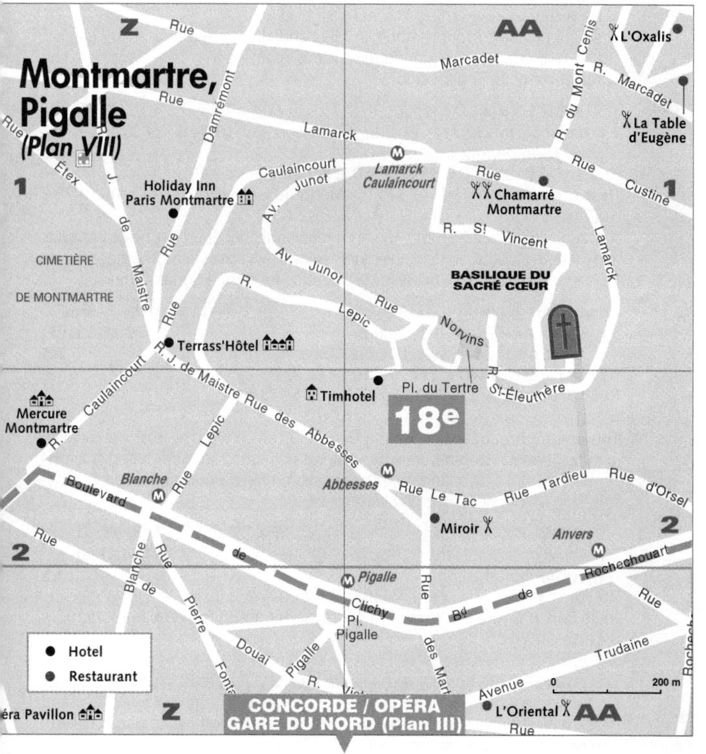

La Table d'Eugène

18 r. Eugène-Sue (18th) – Ⓜ *Jules Joffrin* – ✆ *01 42 55 61 64*
– *Closed 1 to 25 August, 24 December-3 January, Sunday and Monday*
Rest – *(number of covers limited, pre-book)* Menu 35 € **AA1**

♦ A la mode ♦ Minimalist ♦

Dishes include seven-hour lamb with ras el hanout, and apricot crumble. A winning formula close to the city hall in the 18th arrondissement. Nostalgic decor (bistro tables, ceiling mouldings) and lots of flavour.

L'Oxalis

14 r. Ferdinand-Flocon (18th) – Ⓜ *Jules Joffrin* – ✆ *01 42 51 11 98*
– *www.restaurantoxalis.com*
– *Closed 8 to 23 August, Sunday and Monday* **AA1**
Rest – Menu 18 € (weekday lunch)/28 € – Carte approx. 38 €

♦ Traditional ♦ Neighbourhood ♦

Oxalis is the Latin name for wild wood sorrel. This small restaurant close to the Mairie, run by a charming couple, serves an attractive selection of traditional dishes.

OUTSIDE CENTRAL AREA *Plan I*

St-James Paris

43 av. Bugeaud (16th) ✉ *75116* – Ⓜ *Porte Dauphine* – ✆ *01 44 05 81 81*
– *www.saint-james-paris.com* **A2**
18 rm – †320/590 € ††320/590 € – **30 suites** – ††500/920 €, ☐ 32 €
Rest – *(closed Saturday, Sunday and Bank Holidays) (resident only)*
Menu 60 € – Carte 64/220 €

♦ Historic ♦ Luxury ♦ Personalised ♦

Beautiful private townhouse built in 1892 and surrounded by a shady garden. Find a majestic staircase, modern, spacious rooms, and a bar-library with the atmosphere of an English club.

Pullman Paris Bercy

1 r. de Libourne (12th) – Ⓜ *Cour St-Émilion* – ✆ *01 44 67 34 00*
– *www.pullmanhotels.com* **D3**
385 rm – †180/350 € ††180/350 €, ☐ 22 € – 11 suites
Rest *Café Ké* – ✆ *01 44 67 34 71* – Menu 33 € (weekdays) – Carte 52/73 €

♦ Chain hotel ♦ Functional ♦ Design ♦

A beautiful glass façade, contemporary interior in shades of brown, beige and blue, and modern facilities. Some of the rooms enjoy views across Paris. The elegant Café Ké is a pleasant option in the Bercy village. Modern cuisine; Sunday brunch.

Pullman Rive Gauche

8 r. L.-Armand (15th) – Ⓜ *Balard*
– ✆ *01 40 60 30 30* – *www.pullmanhotels.com* **A3**
612 rm – †129/440 € ††129/440 €, ☐ 22 € – 15 suites
Rest *Brasserie* – ✆ *01 40 60 33 77* – Carte 38/80 €

♦ Chain hotel ♦ Business ♦ Modern ♦

This hotel opposite the heliport has been refurbished with the business traveller in mind. It offers contemporary guestrooms with good soundproofing, a fitness centre, internet access and meeting rooms. Unpretentious cuisine, an English-style bar, and a panoramic breakfast room.

Square

3 r. Boulainvilliers (16th) ✉ *75016* – Ⓜ *Mirabeau* – ✆ *01 44 14 91 90*
– *www.hotelsquare.com* **A2**
20 rm – †300/650 € ††300/650 €, ☐ 25 € – 4 suites
Rest *Zébra Square* – ✆ *01 44 14 91 91* – Menu 38 € (weekday lunch)
– Carte 50/60 €

♦ Luxury ♦ Design ♦

This jewel of contemporary architecture is across from the Maison de la Radio. Find modern guestrooms in grey or red tones with high-tech facilities and modern art. This restaurant has a trendy decor with soothing colours. Contemporary-style cuisine is on the menu.

Kube without rest

1-5 passage Ruelle (18th) – Ⓜ *La Chapelle* – ✆ *01 42 05 20 00*
– *www.kubehotel.com* **C1**

41 rm – †250 € ††300/900 €, ☕ 25 €

◆ Luxury ◆ Design ◆ Modern ◆

The 19C façade belies this hotel's high-tech 21C designer interior. Loft-style bedrooms with an emphasis on raw materials. Two bars, including the Ice Kube (minus 10°C – warm clothing provided!) on the first floor.

Holiday Inn La Villette

216 av. J. Jaurès (19th) – Ⓜ *Porte de Pantin*
– ✆ *01 44 84 18 18* – *www.holidayinn-parisvillette.com* **D1**

182 rm – †120/250 € ††120/250 €, ☕ 18 €

Rest – *(closed Saturday and Sunday)* Menu 18 € – Carte 29/51 €

◆ Chain hotel ◆ Business ◆ Modern ◆

This modern building is opposite the Cité de la Musique. It offers spacious and well-soundproofed rooms with a restful decor and modern comforts. Meeting rooms, auditorium and gym. Traditional cuisine served with the backdrop of a modern brasserie decor.

Novotel Tour Eiffel

61 quai de Grenelle (15th) – Ⓜ *Charles Michels*
– ✆ *01 40 58 20 00* – *www.novotel-paris-convention.com* **A2**

758 rm – †179/400 € ††179/400 €, ☕ 22 € – 6 suites

Rest *Benkay* – see below

Rest *L'Envie* – ✆ *01 40 58 20 75* – Carte 31/45 €

◆ Chain hotel ◆ Business ◆ Modern ◆

This hotel overlooking the Seine has comfortable, modern rooms (wood, light colours); most of which enjoy views of the river. High-tech conference centre. The menu at L'Envie is firmly focused on Mediterranean cuisine.

Océania without rest

52 r. Oradour-sur-Glane (15th) – Ⓜ *Porte de Versailles* – ✆ *01 56 09 09 09*
– *www.oceaniahotels.com* **A3**

232 rm – †270 € ††287 €, ☕ 17 € – 18 suites

◆ Business ◆ Modern ◆

This modern hotel built in 2005 offers modern comforts in an elegant, contemporary setting. Well-appointed guestrooms, fully equipped well-being centre, and an exotic terrace-garden.

Novotel Bercy

85 r. de Bercy (12th) – Ⓜ *Bercy* – ✆ *01 43 42 30 00* **D3**

151 rm – †115/260 € ††115/260 €, ☕ 15 €

Rest – Carte 18/49 €

◆ Chain hotel ◆ Business ◆ Functional ◆

The bright rooms in this Novotel are decorated in an attractive contemporary style. The nearby Parc de Bercy occupies the site of an old wine depot. Good value for money. Dining room/veranda and popular terrace in summertime. Traditional menu.

Novotel Gare de Lyon

2 r. Hector-Malot (12th) – Ⓜ *Gare de Lyon*
– ✆ *01 44 67 60 00* – *www.accorhotels.com* **D2**

253 rm – †119/299 € ††119/299 €, ☕ 16 €

Rest – Carte approx. 25 €

◆ Chain hotel ◆ Functional ◆

This modern hotel overlooking a tranquil square offers comfortable guestrooms typical of the Novotel chain - those on the sixth floor have a terrace. Swimming pool, fitness club and well-equipped children's area. A 'Novotel Café' modern menu is served at the Côté Jardin restaurant. Contemporary decor.

Mama Shelter

109 r. de Bagnolet (20th) – Ⓜ Gambetta – ✆ 01 43 48 48 48
– www.mamashelter.com **D2**

169 rm – 🛉79/299 € 🛉🛉89/309 €, ☕ 15 € – 1 suite
Rest – Menu 29 € (dinner) – Carte 29/79 €

♦ Design ♦

Starck's imagination breaths originality into the sleek and fanciful designer decor of this new and vast hotel at the leading edge of modernity. Large lounge bar. Restaurant lit by wide bay windows, and a long terrace runs along one side.

Banville without rest

166 bd Berthier (17th) – Ⓜ Porte de Champerret – ✆ 01 42 67 70 16
– www.hotelbanville.fr **B1**

38 rm – 🛉250/320 € 🛉🛉250/500 €, ☕ 20 €

♦ Luxury ♦ Personalised ♦

This charming boutique hotel is decorated with great taste, with guestrooms embellished with shiny wood and opulent detail. Jazz evenings in the piano-bar every Tuesday.

Windsor Home without rest

3 r. Vital (16th) ✉ 75016 – Ⓜ La Muette – ✆ 01 45 04 49 49
– www.windsorhomeparis.com **A2**

8 rm – 🛉90/170 € 🛉🛉105/195 €, ☕ 15 €

♦ Historic ♦ Family ♦ Personalised ♦

This charming, 100 year-old residence looks more like a guesthouse than a hotel. It features old furniture, mouldings, bright colours and contemporary touches.

Le 20 Prieuré Hôtel without rest

20 r. Grand Prieuré (11th) – Ⓜ Oberkampf – ✆ 01 47 00 74 14
– www.20ph-paris.com **C2**

32 rm – 🛉105/150 € 🛉🛉115/170 €, ☕ 12 €

♦ Design ♦

Refurbished in 2007 in a contemporary, urban style. Compact yet pleasant guestrooms in white tones, with designer furniture and huge photos of Paris behind each bed.

Le Pré Catelan

✿✿✿

rte de Suresnes (16th) ✉ 75016 – ✆ 01 44 14 41 14
– www.precatelanparis.com – Closed 31 July-22 August, 23 to 31 October, 19 February-5 March, Sunday and Monday **A2**

Rest – Menu 85 € (weekday lunch), 180/230 € – Carte 180/250 €

Spec. Crabe préparé en coque, fine gelée de corail et caviar de France, soupe de fenouil. Cabillaud cuit meunière, fondue d'aubergine, crème légère d'avocat. Pomme soufflée croustillante, crème glacée caramel, cidre et sucre pétillant.

♦ Innovative ♦ Luxury ♦ Elegant ♦

Based on classic recipes that pay homage to the local produce, Frédéric Anton's inventive cuisine is perfectly accomplished. Each dish is a masterpiece, to be enjoyed to the full amid a magnificent decor of white and silver in the heart of the Bois de Boulogne.

La Grande Cascade

✿

allée de Longchamp (16th) ✉ 75016 – ✆ 01 45 27 33 51
– www.grandecascade.com

Rest – Menu 65/185 € – Carte 140/190 €

Spec. Macaronis farcis au céleri rave, foie gras et truffe noire. Pomme de ris de veau, olives, câpres et croûtons. Dégustation d'un chocolat pure origine "Baïano" du Brésil.

♦ A la mode ♦ Luxury ♦

This charming pavilion dating from 1850 is just a few metres from the Grande Cascade in the Bois de Boulogne. Refined cuisine served in the rotunda or on the delightful terrace.

XXX ✿

Relais d'Auteuil (Patrick Pignol)

31 bd Murat (16th) ✉ 75016 – Ⓜ Michel Ange Molitor – ✆ 01 46 51 09 54 – www.relaisdauteuil-pignol.com
– Closed August, Christmas Holidays, Saturday lunch, Sunday and Monday
Rest – Menu 75 € (lunch), 125/145 € – Carte 105/170 € **A2**
Spec. Crevettes "Cristal Bay" à l'huile de crustacés. Pigeon rôti, béatilles farcies au parfum de bergamote. Beignets de chocolat bitter.
♦ Contemporary ♦ Elegant ♦ Luxury ♦
Intimate atmosphere, in which the neutral decor highlights the modern paintings and sculptures. Fine modern cuisine with game in season. Excellent wine list and a good selection of champagnes.

XXX

Benkay – Novotel Tour Eiffel

61 quai de Grenelle (15th) – Ⓜ Bir-Hakeim – ✆ 01 40 58 21 26 – www.restaurant-benkay.com – Closed August **A2**
Rest – Menu 32 € (lunch), 38/150 € – Carte 55/150 €
♦ Japanese ♦ Exotic ♦ Elegant ♦
Elegant Japanese setting on the top floor of a hotel overlooking the Seine. Teppanyaki cuisine (prepared on hot plates in front of guests) and washoku (table service).

XX

Bon

25 r. de la Pompe (16th) ✉ 75116 – Ⓜ La Muette – ✆ 01 40 72 70 00 – www.restaurantbon.fr **A2**
Rest – Menu 30 € bi (lunch) – Carte 40/59 €
♦ Fusion ♦ Design ♦ Trendy ♦
Three original dining rooms with very different atmospheres (vinothéque, fireplace room and library), all designed by Philippe Starck. Fusion cuisine with a strong Asian influence.

XX ✿

Au Trou Gascon

40 r. Taine (12th) – Ⓜ Daumesnil – ✆ 01 43 44 34 26 – www.autrougascon.fr
– Closed August, 25 December-3 January, Saturday and Sunday **D3**
Rest – Menu 38 € (lunch)/49 € – Carte 53/73 €
Spec. Crabe royal, fraîcheurs du jardin et tomate de "plein champ" en gaspacho (summer). Filet de colvert, épices et coing confit (winter). Crumble rhubarbe, fraises mara des bois en gelée, sorbet au caillé de brebis (summer).
♦ South-West of France ♦ Elegant ♦
The decor of this old bistro dating from 1900 combines period mouldings, designer furniture and grey tones. The menu features generous portions of delicious dishes from the Landes and Chalosse, as well as seafood.

XX

Meating

122 av. de Villiers (17th) – Ⓜ Péreire – ✆ 01 43 80 10 10 – www.restaurantmeating.com
– Closed Saturday lunch and Sunday **B1**
Rest – Menu 35 € bi – Carte 40/75 €
♦ Meat specialities ♦ Elegant ♦
A young, energetic chef is at the helm of this chic and trendy restaurant serving highly refined cuisine with an obvious emphasis on meat. High-quality cuts prepared to your exact specifications.

XX

Chez Géraud

31 r. Vital (16th) ✉ 75016 – Ⓜ La Muette – ✆ 01 45 20 33 00
– Closed 29 July-29 August, Saturday and Sunday **A2**
Rest – Menu 30 € – Carte 50/70 €
♦ Traditional ♦ Bistro ♦
Discreet, traditional cuisine is to the fore in this restaurant, which offers classic dishes and game in season. The daily menu (not available on Friday evenings) is particularly interesting.

Mansouria

11 r. Faidherbe (11th) – Faidherbe Chaligny – 01 43 71 00 16 – www.mansouria.fr – Closed Monday lunch and Sunday **D2**

Rest – *(pre-book)* Menu 28/36 € – Carte 32/50 €

♦ Moroccan ♦ Exotic ♦

Tajines, couscous, and crème à la fleur d'oranger are among the aromatic dishes prepared by the talented female chefs here under the baton of Fatema Hal, an ethnologist, writer and leading figure in North Africa gastronomy.

Le Caroubier

82 bd Lefèbvre (15th) – Porte de Vanves – 01 40 43 16 12 – www.restaurant-lecaroubier.com – Closed 24 July-25 August and Monday **B3**

Rest – Menu 18 € (weekday lunch)/28 € – Carte 30/45 €

♦ Moroccan ♦ Exotic ♦

Delicate couscous dishes, subtly flavoured and unfussy tajines, and pastillas blessed with the sun from the Atlas mountains are on offer in this oasis of calm close to the Porte de Versailles.

A et M Restaurant

136 bd Murat (16th) ✉ 75016 – Porte de St-Cloud – 01 45 27 39 60 – www.am-restaurant.com – Closed August, Saturday lunch and Sunday **A3**

Rest – Menu 30 € – Carte 37/45 €

♦ A la mode ♦ Elegant ♦ Friendly ♦

Beef parmentier and iced mousse with confit of fennel are just two of the dishes on the menu of this fashionable bistro with a chic and welcoming decor. In terms of value for money, the menu here is one of the best in Paris.

Au Bœuf Couronné

188 av. Jean-Jaurès (19th) – Porte de Pantin – 01 42 39 44 44 – www.rest-gj.com **D1**

Rest – Menu 32 € bi – Carte 27/75 €

♦ Meat specialities ♦ Brasserie ♦

This restaurant opposite the former Villette market is as successful as ever. Hearty portions, friendly service and a retro-style decor.

Les Allobroges

71 r. des Grands-Champs (20th) – Maraîchers – 01 43 73 40 00 – Closed 2 weeks in August, Sunday dinner and Monday **D2**

Rest – Menu 19 € (weekdays), 33/44 €

♦ Traditional ♦ Neighbourhood ♦ Formal ♦

Step off the beaten track to discover this friendly restaurant close to Porte de Montreuil. Fine traditional cuisine offering excellent value for money. Attentive service.

La Marée Passy

71 av. P. Doumer (16th) ✉ 75016 – La Muette – 01 45 04 12 81 – www.lamareepassy.com **A2**

Rest – Carte 39/50 €

♦ Seafood ♦ Friendly ♦

The nautical decor of this red toned, wood-panelled dining room is the perfect backdrop for its seafood based menu. Friendly atmosphere.

Bigarrade (Christophe Pelé)

106 r. Nollet (17th) – Brochant – 01 42 26 01 02 – www.bigarrade.fr – Closed August, Christmas Holidays, Saturday, Sunday and Monday **B1**

Rest – *(number of covers limited, pre-book)* Menu 35 € (lunch), 45/85 €

Spec. Menu du marché.

♦ Innovative ♦ Design ♦ Elegant ♦

A small, stylish restaurant decorated in white and green apple tones, where Christophe Pelé and his team run the open kitchen. Impeccable presentation of dishes combining simplicity and invention. No à la carte or set menu choices – guests here trust the chef's inspiration.

La Régalade

49 av. Jean-Moulin (14th) – Porte d'Orléans – 01 45 45 68 58 – Closed 25 July-20 August, 1 to 10 January, Monday lunch, Saturday and Sunday **B3**

Rest – *(pre-book)* Menu 32 €

♦ Bistro ♦ Friendly ♦

An informal setting for copious and well-prepared cuisine which is seasonally inspired and accompanied by a judicious wine list. A popular address so booking ahead is recommended.

Jean-Pierre Frelet

25 r. Montgallet (12th) – Montgallet – 01 43 43 76 65 – Closed 16 to 24 May, 30 July-30 August, Saturday lunch and Sunday

Rest – Menu 29 € (dinner) – Carte 44/55 € **D2**

♦ Traditional ♦ Friendly ♦

The minimalist decor and tightly packed tables create a friendly atmosphere here. Generous portions, with the emphasis firmly on seasonal produce.

Villaret

(dinner)

13 r. Ternaux (11th) – Parmentier – 01 43 57 75 56 – Closed August, 24 December-4 January, Saturday lunch and Sunday

Rest – Menu 25 € (lunch)/32 € – Carte 40/50 € **C2**

♦ Bistro ♦ Friendly ♦

This simple but characterful bistro has hit on a winning formula: a friendly atmosphere, good, seasonal cuisine and a fine selection of wines.

Auberge Pyrénées Cévennes

106 r. Folie-Méricourt (11th) – République – 01 43 57 33 78 – Closed 30 July-20 August, Saturday lunch, Sunday and Bank Holidays

Rest – Menu 30 € – Carte 30/82 € **C2**

♦ Terroir ♦ Inn ♦

A fun atmosphere reigns in this restaurant popular with serious gourmets. The female owner's welcome is second to none, while the cuisine – a veritable gastronomic Tour de France – is both delicious and abundant.

Afaria

15 r. Desnouettes (15th) – Convention – 01 48 56 15 36 – Closed 31 July-22 August, Sunday and Monday **A-B3**

Rest – Menu 24 € (weekday lunch)/45 € – Carte 33/61 €

♦ Innovative ♦

This successful restaurant pays homage to Basque cuisine, with a few culinary contributions from other parts of the world. Bookings essential.

Beurre Noisette

68 r. Vasco-de-Gama (15th) – Lourmel – 01 48 56 82 49 – Closed 1 to 24 August, Sunday and Monday **A3**

Rest – Menu 30 € (weekday lunch), 32/48 € – Carte 32/45 €

♦ A la mode ♦

A welcoming address run by a chef who has worked in the kitchens of some of the city's finest restaurants . A mix of unpretentious and more ambitious cuisine, prepared using seasonal produce, accompanied by a impressive choice of wines.

Le Bélisaire

2 r. Marmontel (15th) – Vaugirard – 01 48 28 62 24 – Closed 30 July-21 August, 24 December-1 January, Saturday lunch and Sunday

Rest – Menu 24 € (lunch), 33/35 € – Carte 22/32 € **B3**

♦ Bistro ♦

This elegant bistro has built up a solid reputation in the Convention district thanks to its excellent contemporary cuisine and friendly service.

Bistrot Paul Bert

18 r. Paul-Bert (11th) – Ⓜ Faidherbe Chaligny – ✆ 01 43 72 24 01 – Closed August, Sunday and Monday **D2**

Rest – *(pre-book)* Menu 17 € (weekday lunch), 34/49 €

♦ Bistro ♦ Retro ♦

Home cooking is very much to the fore in this friendly bistro, with dishes such as beef parmentier and steak on the menu. Make sure you save space for the rum baba!

L'Auberge Aveyronnaise

40 r. Gabriel-Lamé (12th) – Ⓜ Cour St-Émilion – ✆ 01 43 40 12 24 – Closed 1 to 15 August **D3**

Rest – Menu 25 € (lunch)/31 €

♦ Terroir ♦ Rustic ♦ Brasserie ♦

Checked tablecloths and rather rustic decoration help create this corner of the Aveyron a stone's throw from Bercy Village, with specialities such as "tripoux" (mutton tripe) and "aligot" (creamed potato with cheese).

Le Grand Pan

20 r. Rosenwald (15th) – Ⓜ Plaisance – ✆ 01 42 50 02 50 – Closed 1 week in May, 10 to 30 August, Christmas Holidays, Saturday and Sunday

Rest – Menu 28 € (lunch) – Carte 30/50 € **B3**

♦ Meat specialities ♦ Bistro ♦ Neighbourhood ♦

A local bistro once frequented by Georges Brassens, who lived nearby. Soup starters, superb meat main courses, and traditional desserts.

Pramil

9 r. Vertbois (3rd) – Ⓜ Temple – ✆ 01 42 72 03 60 – Closed 3 to 9 May, 15 to 29 August, Sunday lunch and Monday

Rest – Menu 30/38 € – Carte 30/47 € **C2**

♦ Bistro ♦

The Pramil's restrained yet stylish decor (paintings and white orchids) accentuates the generous seasonal cuisine with a contemporary touch created by Alain Pramil.

La Fourchette du Printemps (Nicolas Mouton)

30 r. du Printemps (17th) – Ⓜ Wagram – ✆ 01 42 27 26 97 – Closed August, Christmas Holidays, Saturday lunch and Sunday **B1**

Rest – *(number of covers limited, pre-book)* Menu 26 € (lunch)/42 €

Spec. Crème d'artichaut aux langoustines. Lotte et Saint-pierre en bouillabaisse. Paris-brest.

♦ Contemporary ♦ Bistro ♦

Enjoy springtime throughout the year in this contemporary bistro which stands out from the crowd, where the two young chefs, both trained in a number of top restaurants, accentuate the full flavour of their cuisine. Even simplicity is done with finesse here.

Les Cailloux

58 r. des Cinq-Diamants (13th) – Ⓜ Corvisart – ✆ 01 45 80 15 08 – www.lescailloux.fr – Closed 1 week in August and Christmas Holidays

Rest – Menu 17 € bi (lunch) – Carte 22/60 € **C3**

♦ Italian ♦ Bistro ♦

The Butte-aux-Cailles district is home to many restaurants, including this informal Italian bistro that serves delicious sun-blessed food at reasonable prices.

L'Ourcine

92 r. Broca (13th) – Ⓜ Les Gobelins – ✆ 01 47 07 13 65 – Closed 3 weeks in August, Sunday and Monday **C3**

Rest – Menu 34/54 €

♦ Bistro ♦

This small bistro, recognisable by its dark red façade, keeps things simple with inspired, seasonal cuisine. Menu of the day plus specials on the blackboard.

Jadis

208 r. de la Croix-Nivert (15th) – Ⓜ Convention – ☎ 01 45 57 73 20
– Closed 3 weeks in August, Saturday and Sunday **A3**

Rest – Menu 34/65 € – Carte 42/60 €

♦ A la mode ♦ Bistro ♦

This charming restaurant with a bistro feel is a mirror image of its young and promising owner-chef. Modern menu that changes with the seasons.

L'Os à Moelle

3 r. Vasco-de-Gama (15th) – Ⓜ Lourmel – ☎ 01 45 57 27 27
– Closed 2-25 August, Saturday lunch, Sunday and Monday **A3**

Rest – Menu 28 € (lunch)/35 €

♦ Bistro ♦ Friendly ♦

A paradise for lovers of good food. Enjoy delicious, seasonally inspired bistro dishes marked up on a slate board amid a decor of brightly coloured walls.

Impérial Choisy

32 av. de Choisy (13th) – Ⓜ Porte de Choisy – ☎ 01 45 86 42 40

Rest – Carte 25/50 € **C3**

♦ Chinese ♦ Minimalist ♦

An authentic Chinese restaurant very popular with Asian diners who flock here to enjoy the delicious Cantonese specialities on offer.

Le Baratin

3 r. Jouye-Rouve (20th) – Ⓜ Pyrénées – ☎ 01 43 49 39 70
– Closed 1 to 8 May, August, 10 to 16 January, Saturday lunch, Sunday and Monday

Rest – *(pre-book)* Menu 30/42 € – Carte 31/40 € **D2**

♦ Bistro ♦ Wine bar ♦

Enticing dishes chalked up on the blackboard, reasonable prices, choice of fine wines... it's easy to understand the appeal of this neighbourhood bistro.

Caffé dei Cioppi

159 r. du Faubourg-St-Antoine (11th) – Ⓜ Ledru Rollin – ☎ 01 43 46 10 14
– Closed August, 24 December-2 January, Monday dinner, Tuesday dinner, Saturday and Sunday **CD2**

Rest – *(number of covers limited, pre-book)* Carte 22/34 €

♦ Italian ♦ Neighbourhood ♦

This mini-trattoria with seating for just 16 diners is run by a chef from Sicily (and formerly the Relais Plaza) and his female partner from Milan. Delicious Italian cuisine.

L'Inattendu

99 r. Blomet (15th) – Ⓜ Vaugirard – ☎ 01 55 76 93 12
– www.restaurant-inattendu.fr – Closed August, Saturday lunch and Sunday

Rest – Menu 30/37 € **B3**

♦ Contemporary ♦

L'Inattendu has been created by two experienced restaurant professionals, with Loïc front of house and Patrick in the kitchen. Reasonably priced cuisine with flavours galore, including some unexpected combinations.

LA DÉFENSE *Plan I*

Pullman La Défense

rm,

11 av. Arche (exit La Défense 6) ✉ 92081 – ☎ 01 47 17 50 00
– www.pullmanhotels.com

368 rm – †175/470 € ††175/470 €, ☐ 22 € – 16 suites

Rest *Avant Seine* – ☎ *01 47 17 50 99 (closed 29 July-21 August, 17 December-2 January, Friday dinner, Saturday, Sunday and Bank Holidays)* Carte approx. 54 €

♦ Luxury ♦ Modern ♦

Beautiful architecture, resembling a ship's hull, a combination of glass and ochre stonework. Spacious, elegant rooms, lounges and very well-equipped auditorium (with simultaneous translation booths). The Avant Seine offers you quality designer décor and spit-roast dishes.

Renaissance

60 Jardin de Valmy (on the ring road, exit La Défense 7)
✉ 92918 – ☎ 01 41 97 50 50
– www.renaissanceladefense.fr
324 rm – †169/450 € ††169/450 €, ☕ 25 € – 3 suites
Rest – *(closed Bank Holiday lunch, Sunday lunch and Saturday)*
Menu 34 € (lunch)/45 € bi – Carte 51/68 €
♦ Luxury ♦ Personalised ♦
Luxurious sophistication defines this contemporary hotel at the foot of the Grande Arche: quality materials, flawless comfort and inviting, perfectly equipped guestrooms. This brasserie serves traditional dishes and seasonal suggestions overlooking the Valmy gardens.

Hilton La Défense

2 pl. de la Défense ✉ 92053 – ☎ 01 46 92 10 10
– www.hilton.com
148 rm – †195/550 € ††195/550 €, ☕ 26 € – 9 suites
Rest *Côté Parvis* – *(closed Friday dinner, Sunday lunch and Saturday)*
Menu 55 € bi (weekday lunch) – Carte 39/72 €
♦ Luxury ♦ Modern ♦
Hotel situated within the CNIT complex. Some of the rooms have been particularly designed with the business traveller in mind: work, rest, relaxation and Jacuzzi tubs in the bathrooms. At Côté Parvis, modern cuisine and a fine view of the Arch of La Défense.

Sofitel Paris La Défense

34 cours Michelet (on the ring road, exit La Défense 4)
✉ 92060 Puteaux – ☎ 01 47 76 44 43
– www.sofitel-paris-ladefense.com
150 rm – †150/535 € ††150/535 €, ☕ 26 € – 1 suite
Rest *L'Italian Lounge* – *☎ 01 47 76 72 40* – Menu 37 € (weekdays), 60/115 € – Carte 55/85 €
♦ Luxury ♦ Design ♦
The scalloped façade of this hotel blends in among the skyscrapers of La Défense. Spacious, well-equipped rooms, which sport a fashionable look. A contemporary setting for Mediterranean cuisine and a fine wine list.

Novotel La Défense

2 bd Neuilly (exit La Défense 1) – ☎ 01 41 45 23 23
– www.novotel.com **A1**
280 rm – †79/390 € ††79/490 €, ☕ 16 €
Rest – Carte 25/40 €
♦ Business ♦ Modern ♦
This hotel is at the foot of La Défense, a genuine open-air museum. Some of the renovated rooms overlook Paris. Trendy new Novotel Café-style bar. Contemporary decor in the restaurant, whose cuisine evolves with the seasons.

PARIS AIRPORT ORLY

Hilton Orly

(near Orly Sud airport) ✉ 94544 – ☎ 01 45 12 45 12
– www.hilton.fr
340 rm – †99/295 € ††99/295 €, ☕ 25 €
Rest – Menu 30/39 € – Carte 32/61 €
♦ Chain hotel ♦ Functional ♦ Personalised ♦
A popular choice for corporate clients, this 1960s hotel has a designer interior, discreet yet elegant bedrooms and state of the art business facilities. The Hilton's contemporary-style restaurant focuses on traditional cuisine.

Mercure

allée Cdt Mouchotte (exit Orlytech) ✉ *94547 – ✆ 01 49 75 15 50 – www.mercure.com*
192 rm – 80/215 € 90/225 €, ☕ 15 €
Rest – *(closed Saturday and Sunday)* Carte 27/40 €
♦ Chain hotel ♦ Functional ♦
This Mercure is a convenient option for stopover passengers. Friendly service, a pleasant verdant setting, and bedrooms which have been revamped in contemporary tones. Bar snacks and traditional dishes adapted to the timetables of travellers in transit.

PARIS AIRPORT ROISSY

Z. I. Paris Nord II

Hyatt Regency

351 av. Bois de la Pie – ✆ 01 48 17 12 34 – www.paris.charlesdegaulle.hyatt.com
376 rm ☕ – 105/420 € 105/420 € – 12 suites
Rest – Carte 42/55 €
♦ Business ♦ Modern ♦
Spectacular, contemporary architecture in a good location close to the airport. Large, stylish bedrooms equipped with ultra-modern facilities for its predominantly corporate guests. Enjoy buffet cuisine or classic à la carte choices in the Hyatt Regency's glass-ceilinged restaurant.

À l'aérogare n° 2

Sheraton

– ✆ 01 49 19 70 70 – www.sheraton.com/parisairport
252 rm – 199/599 € 199/599 €, ☕ 30 €
Rest *Les Étoiles* – *✆ 01 41 84 64 54 (closed 22 July-26 August and 21 December-3 January)* Menu 49 € (weekdays) – Carte 70/105 €
Rest *Les Saisons* – Menu 31 € (weekday lunch) – Carte approx. 35 €
♦ Chain hotel ♦ Modern ♦
Leave your plane or train and take a trip on this "luxury liner" with its futuristic architecture. Decor by Andrée Putman, a view of the runways, absolute quiet and refined rooms. Les Étoiles offers modern cuisine and beautiful contemporary setting. Brasserie dishes at Les Saisons.

À Roissypole

Hilton

– ✆ 01 49 19 77 77 – www.hilton.com
385 rm – 159/600 € 159/600 €, ☕ 25 €
Rest *Les Aviateurs* – *✆ 01 49 19 77 95* – Carte 36/65 €
♦ Business ♦ Modern ♦
Daring architecture, space and light are the main features of this hotel. Its ultra-modern facilities make it an ideal place in which to work and relax. Brasserie fare at Les Aviateurs.

Pullman

Zone centrale Ouest – ✆ 01 49 19 29 29 – www.pullmanhotels.com
339 rm – 145/525 € 145/525 €, ☕ 22 € – 5 suites
Rest *L'Escale* – Menu 40 € (weekdays) – Carte 31/54 €
♦ Business ♦ Classic ♦
A personal welcome, comfortable atmosphere, conference rooms, an elegant bar and well-looked-after rooms are the advantages of this hotel between two airport terminals. A pleasant port of call dedicated to travel, this restaurant offers a menu of world flavours.

À Roissy-Ville

Marriott

allée du Verger – ✆ 01 34 38 53 53 – www.parismarriottcharlesdegaulle.fr
298 rm – 139/459 € 139/459 €, 22 € – 2 suites
Rest – Menu 35 € – Carte 31/67 €
♦ Business ♦ Classic ♦
Behind its colonnaded white façade, this establishment has modern facilities perfectly in tune with the requirements of businessmen transiting through Paris. Themed brasserie menu served in a large and carefully decorated dining room.

Millennium

allée du Verger – ✆ 01 34 29 33 33 – www.milleniumhotels.com
239 rm – 350/380 € 350/380 €, 20 € **Rest** – Carte 25/50 €
♦ Business ♦ Modern ♦ Art Deco ♦
Bar, Irish pub, fitness centre, attractive swimming pool, conference rooms, and spacious bedrooms with one floor specially equipped for businessmen: a hotel with good facilities. International cuisine and brasserie buffet or fast food served at the bar.

Novotel Convention et Wellness

allée du Verger – ✆ 01 30 18 20 00 – www.novotel.com
289 rm – 99/350 € 99/350 €, 18 € – 7 suites
Rest – Menu 12 € – Carte 18/41 €
♦ Chain hotel ♦ Modern ♦
This modern hotel offers a range of impressive services, ranging from a huge conference area with an integrated network, a kids' corner and a fully equipped business centre. In the contemporary setting of the spacious Novotel Café, guests can enjoy traditional brasserie fare and a menu focused on healthy eating.

Mercure

allée du Verger – ✆ 01 34 29 40 00 – www.mercure.com
203 rm – 89/320 € 99/330 €, 19 €
Rest – Menu 24 € (weekday lunch) – Carte 30/50 €
♦ Business ♦ Classic ♦
This hotel has a meticulous decor comprising Provençal style in the hall, old-fashioned zinc in the bar and spacious rooms in light wood. A contemporary menu that changes with the seasons served in the pleasant dining room or on the terrace overlooking the garden.

LYONS

LYON

Population (2010): 472 305 (conurbation 1 348 832) Altitude: 175m

lzada/Fotolia.com

Lyons is a city that needs a second look. The first may be to its disadvantage: from the outlying autoroute, passers speeding by get a vision of the petrochemical industry. But strip away that industrial façade and look what lies within: the gastronomic epicentre of France; a wonderfully characterful old town with medieval and Renaissance buildings plus a World Heritage Site stamp of approval; and the peaceful flow of not one but two great rivers, the Rhône and the Saône.

Lyons has been a wealthy place since the Roman Empire, but it really came of age in the sixteenth century thanks to its silk industry; many of the city's finest buildings were erected by Italian silk merchants who flocked here at the time. What they left behind was the largest Renaissance quarter in France, with glorious architecture and an imposing cathedral. Much of this character could have been lost when demolition of the old town was threatened, but an enlightened twentieth century mayor instead made it safe, sanitary and a living embodiment of the past. Nowadays it's an energised city whose modern industries give it a twenty first century buzz – on the outside. But that feeling hasn't pervaded the three-hour lunch ethos of the older quarters: there are more restaurants per square metre of the old town than anywhere else on earth. Step inside a Lyonnais bouchon for a real encounter with the city…

LIVING THE CITY

Two great waterways, the rivers **Saône** (west) and **Rhône** (east) have their confluence in Lyons, and provide the liquid heart of the city. Modern Lyons in the shape of the shiny new Villeurbanne and La Part Dieu districts are to the east of the Rhône. The medieval sector, the old town, is west of the Saône.

Between the two rivers is a peninsula, the **Presqu'ile**, which is indeed almost an island, and appears on maps like an extended tongue. This area is renowned for its red-roofed sixteenth and seventeenth century houses. Just north of here on a hill is the old silk-weavers' district, La Croix-Rousse.

PRACTICAL INFORMATION

ARRIVAL-DEPARTURE

Lyon-Saint-Exupéry Airport is 27km east of the city centre. The Express Bus takes 45min and runs every 20min. A taxi will cost around €48.

TRANSPORT

The transport system in the city even includes the funicular, as well as bus, tram and metro. The 'Liberty' ticket is valid for one day for travel on the network. You can also buy single tickets and a carnet of ten tickets.

The Lyons City Card is available for one, two or three days, and grants unlimited access to the transport network, plus nineteen museums (including the Roman ruins in St-Romain-en-Gal), short river trips and guided city tours. The card is available from the tourist office and major public transport offices.

Lyons boasts one of Europe's biggest 'swipe a bike' schemes: with a smart card, you help yourself to a cycle at two hundred places around town, at a flat rate for every hour in which you're pedalling.

EXPLORING LYONS

So you've worked your way into the heart of Lyons past the not-so-endearing outskirts. Standing in the Presqu'ile, you can see why France's second biggest city made its name in history. The two rivers holding you in their grip ensured this old Roman town evolved into an essential stopover for Renaissance merchants arriving from Italy and northern Europe. Lyons became the French land and river trade capital, and four annual fairs took place here, ensnaring merchants from all over the continent. But you'll need to take one of the city's twenty-eight bridges, and cross the Saône into the old town, to discover where Lyons' ancient heart really began to beat.

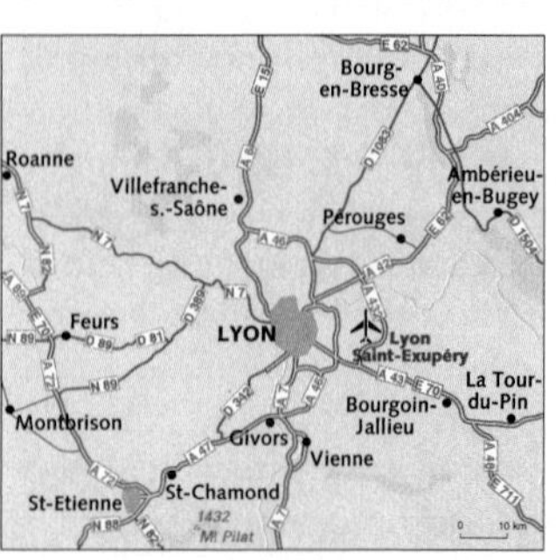

→ TRIPS ALONG THE TRABOULES

Old town is made up of three villages: **St-Georges, St-Jean**, and **St-Paul**. The characterful streets are pressed close together displaying a winning picture of medieval and Renaissance facades, interspersed with narrow alleys, paved courtyards, Italian built towers, and dozens of restaurants to settle into and absorb the atmosphere. Many diners will be enjoying the rest after taking on another element of the old town that's unique to Lyons: the traboules, or tunnelled passageways leading to courtyards open to the sky. There are more than three hundred of these shortcuts through ancient buildings, built in the 15C to make the transport of silk easier in rainy weather. Many traboules wind their way around the Croix-Rousse district as well as the old town, but you'll get lost trying to locate these fascinating medieval tunnels unless you've got a special traboule guide from the tourist office in your hand. The longest, by the way, is at number 27 in the old town's enchanting Rue du Boeuf.

→ OLD TREASURES

If you like your landmarks to be a little bit more familiar than the traboules, then you can't do much better than the old town's two massive churches. St Jean Cathedral is an imposing Gothic structure built from the 12C to the 15C, and boasts eight hundred year old stained glass above the altar and in the rose windows. Its main glory, though, is an astronomical clock built by 14C monks to calculate thousands of moveable feast days, such as Easter. Amazingly, it'll stop its workings in 2019 when its seven-hundred-year programme runs out! Up on Fourvière hill (reached by funicular) behind the Cathedral is an even more conspicuous pile: the **Notre-Dame Basilica** of Fourvière, built in the 19C. It's a monumental church with an outlandish interior that throws together marble and mosaics in an anarchic free for all, and the outside is a bit of a wedding cake, too. Best thing about your journey up here is the superb view you get of the city ranged below, showing the sweep of the rivers and the distinguishing marks of the different quartiers. Other highlights of the old town include the remains of two ruined Roman theatres, close to the basilica, and, from the other end of the cultural compass, an entertaining Marionnette Museum, whose biggest draw is the 18C Lyonnais creations Guignol and Madelon, the famous puppets who embody the spirit of the local people.

→ ALMOST PERFECT!

The Presqu'ile is dominated by its great red-sanded square Place Bellecour: it's a vast space, with good views across the Saône to the basilica. It has some interesting streets running off it: to the south the rue Auguste Comte is an antiquarian's heaven. This is the place to come if you're looking for a French Regency sideboard, Louis XVI armchair, tapestry or early edition of Voltaire. More than one hundred antiques shops are nestled around here. Meanwhile, running parallel is Rue Victor Hugo, renowned for its stylish, contemporary boutiques. North of the Place Bellecour, a leisurely stroll takes you to possibly Lyons' most beautiful square, **Place des Terreaux**, an arresting space with magnificent fountains and a mighty hôtel de ville. It also lays claim to the **Musée des Beaux-Arts**, which just happens to be rated the best art collection in France outside the Louvre. You name it: they've got it, from Tintoretto, El Greco and Rubens, to Picasso, Matisse, Canova and Rodin. The museum also includes an eye-catching collection of medieval woodcarvings, plus an eclectic range of objets d'art and antiquities.

→ A TISSUS

A more unexpected highlight of the Presqu'ile is to be found back south of Place Bellecour: the **Musée des Tissus** is considered by many - despite the competition - to be the best in Lyons. It tells the story of silk, with luxurious 17C to 19C hangings produced in Lyons, including those from a rather impressive client list that includes Marie-Antoinette, Empress Josephine, and Catherine the Great of Russia. It's not just local silks that are on display; there are also superb examples from Baghdad, as well as carpets from Iran, Turkey and India, and beautifully artistic decorative work from almost two thousand years ago. Afterwards, you'll probably be tempted to venture up to La Croix-Rousse, the old silk-weavers' district north of Place des Terreaux. Only a few looms still operate in the neighbourhood, but if you attempt the long ascent of Montée de la Grande Côte, you'll get a fair impression of what the area was like five hundred years ago. This is a quartier of many traboules and giant street murals depicting local life. At the top of **Croix-Rousse** (you can get there by metro) is a pleasant square of cafés and swaying trees, and, maybe best of all, grand city views.

→ FOOD AND WATER

Although Lyons is rightly renowned for its restaurants and bouchons, you can also grab your food on the hoof with confidence. A great bet is the bustling open-air market which runs along Quai des Célestins and St Antoine, two quays by the Saône in the heart of the Presqu'île. Saunter along here and you can pick up any amount of French delicacies, including sausages, cakes, breads, hams, chocolates, fruits and jams. After lunch à pied, a good idea is to unwind on a river jaunt. Boats set off regularly along the Saône, travel around the southern end of the peninsula, and return by the Rhône. A night cruise is the top tip, when this beautifully illuminated city bathes its best bits in sumptuous light. If it's not too late, the ideal way to end the evening is a concert at Lyons' swanky Opera House, behind the hotel de ville. Its silver stairways are set off by a totally black interior, and its concerts range all the way from opera to jazz.

CALENDAR HIGHLIGHTS

As Lyons is famous for its gastronomy, what better than being here in October to celebrate Tasting Week? Chefs and cooks demonstrate their art, while markets and festivals bring the joys of Lyonnais' produce and recipes to one and all. The city's most time-honoured event occurs in December: it's the Festival of Lights, when a lantern lit procession, inaugurated in 1852, brings even more aura to the famously lauded illuminations of Lyons. Concerts and activities all add weight to this now four-day extravaganza. Also in December is the Vieux-Lyon Ancient Music Festival (at the Chapelle de la Trinité), which is one of the major events of its kind in

LYONS IN...

→ ONE DAY

Old town including funicular up Fourvière hill, Musée des Beaux-Arts, dining in a bouchon

→ TWO DAYS

Musée des Tissus, La Croix-Rousse, evening river trip, Opera House

→ THREE DAYS

Traboule hunting (map in hand), antique shops in rue Auguste Comte, meal in one of Lyons' famously starred restaurants

France, and features inspiring music by the likes of Mozart, Handel and Bach. On the same theme, Les Musicades (March) is an international chamber music festival which takes place in a number of venues around Lyons, while May's Nuits Sonores Panorama of Electronic Music is pretty much self-explanatory: electronic dance music through the night in various streets and squares. Les Estivales in May continues the musical thread, with a host of free events in outdoor spaces and parks; particularly noteworthy are the shows in the courtyard of the Hotel de Ville. Theatre and music dominates the Nuits de Fourvière Festival in June, when the two Roman amphitheatres on the hill provide an atmospheric setting. Day long street parties and fireworks (also on Fourvière Hill) provide the blistering backdrop to Bastille Day festivities in July. The action's fast and furious at September's Lyons Dance Biennial, with the dance traditions of twenty world cities being celebrated at twenty-three different venues, not to mention three hundred thousand parade-goers thronging the city streets. Things slow down to a more sedate air at the Red Carpet Antiques Festival (October) when a huge red carpet is thrown down on Rue Auguste Comte and all sorts of wonderful antiques are put on display for buyers and browsers.

EATING OUT

Lyons is a great place for eating. If your budget won't run to one of the smarter breed of restaurants, then pop into a local bouchon. These are the true gastronomic heart and soul of the city, atmospheric little establishments where the cuisine revolves round the sort of thing the silkworkers ate all those years ago: tripe, pigs' trotters, calf's head. Fish lovers will instead go for quenelles (fish dumplings); typical are quenelles de brochet of blended pike in a crayfish sauce. For the most atmospheric example of the bouchon, try and get to one in the tunnel-like recess inside a medieval building in the old town. Lyons also offers restaurants serving dishes from every region in France, as well as most places you can think of overseas. It's a city that loves its wine: it's said that Lyons is kept afloat on three rivers: the Saône, the Rhône, and the Beaujolais…Hours of repast in the city begin at 12.30 for lunch (and can continue for many an hour afterwards) and 7.30 in the evenings. With the reputation the city has for its restaurants, it's advisable to book ahead. The bill will include a service charge, but if you've been particularly happy with the service, then a tip of five to ten per cent is normal.

→ SPYING AS YOU'RE FRYING

On sunny summer days, the Lyonnais find their green relaxation in the Parc de la Tête d'Or, on the modern side of town east of the Rhône. Here there are ponds, botanical gardens, rose gardens and a small zoo. One curious interloper you can't miss: the spindly antennae overlooking the park that happens to be part of the international HQ of Interpol…

→ CORKING GOOD LUNCH

'Bouchon' is translated as 'cork'. The theory is that the buzzy local food hotspots acquired their name in the old days when corks from empty bottles were lined up along the bar and the waiter counted them to work out the bill. Earthy locals pour scorn on Parisians, who they believe have abandoned the concept of lunch. In Lyons, regulars at the bouchon embrace the three-hour midday meal with passion and flair.

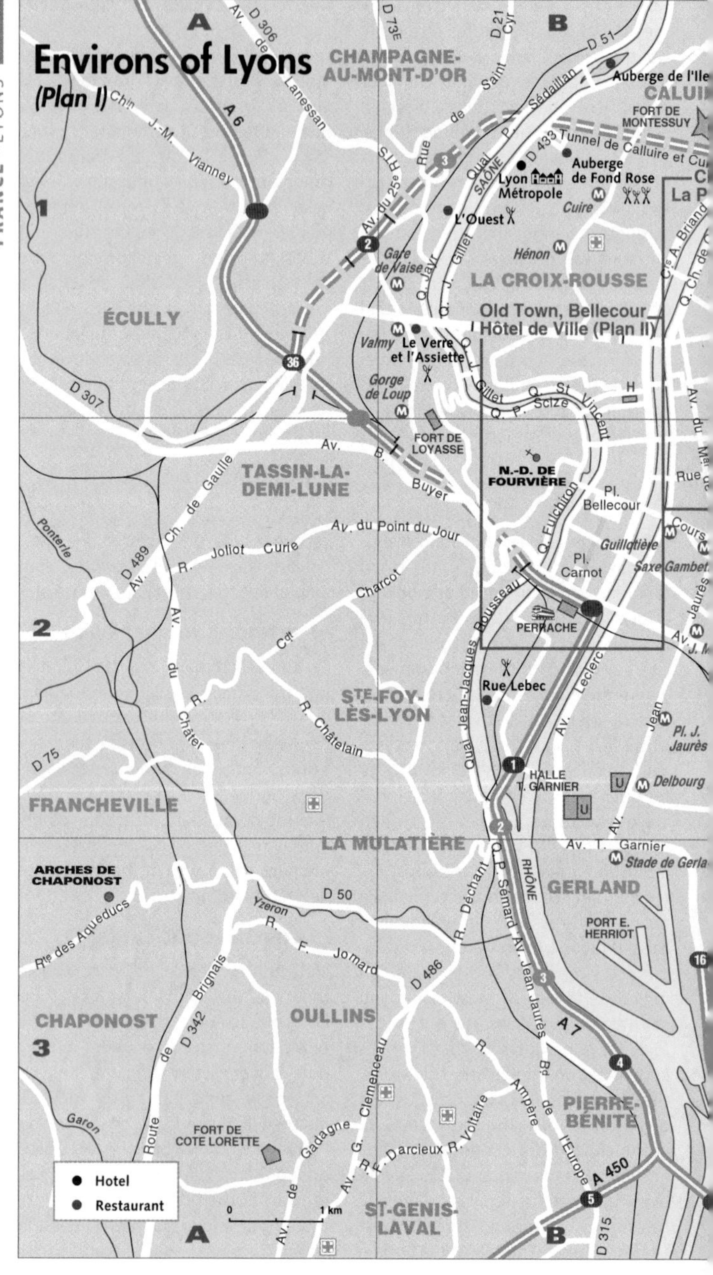

Environs of Lyons
(Plan I)
A
B
1
2
3
CHAMPAGNE-AU-MONT-D'OR
CALUIRE
ÉCULLY
LA CROIX-ROUSSE
Old Town, Bellecour
Hôtel de Ville (Plan II)
TASSIN-LA-DEMI-LUNE
ST-FOY-LÈS-LYON
FRANCHEVILLE
LA MULATIÈRE
GERLAND
ARCHES DE CHAPONOST
CHAPONOST
OULLINS
PIERRE-BÉNITE
ST-GENIS-LAVAL
Auberge de l'Ile
FORT DE MONTESSUY
Tunnel de Caluire et Cuire
Auberge de Fond Rose
Lyon Métropole
Cuire
L'Ouest
Hénon
Gare de Vaise
Valmy
Le Verre et l'Assiette
Gorge de Loup
FORT DE LOYASSE
N.-D. DE FOURVIÈRE
Pl. Bellecour
Guillotière
Pl. Carnot
Saxe Gambetta
PERRACHE
Rue Lebec
Pl. J. Jaurès
HALLE T. GARNIER
Delbourg
Stade de Gerland
PORT E. HERRIOT
FORT DE COTE LORETTE
Hotel
Restaurant
0
1 km
A6
A7
A 450
D 306
D 73E
D 21
D 51
D 433
D 307
D 489
D 75
D 50
D 486
D 342
D 315
Av. de Lanessan
Ch. J.-M. Vianney
Rue de Saint Cyr
P. Sédaillan
Quai Saône
Q. J. Gillet
Q. Jayr
Av. du 25e RTS
Q. P. Scize
Q. St Vincent
Av. B. Buyer
Ch. de Gaulle
Av. du Point du Jour
R. Joliot Curie
Cdt Charcot
Av. du R. Châter
R. Châtelain
Q. Fulchiron
Quai Jean-Jacques Rousseau
Av. Leclerc
Av. T. Garnier
Q. P. Sémard
Av. Jean Jaurès
R. Déchant
RHÔNE
Rte des Aqueducs
Yzeron
R. F. Jomard
Route de Brignais
Garon
Av. G. Clemenceau
Av. de Gadagne
R. F. Darcieux
R. Voltaire
R. Ampère
Bd de l'Europe
Pontet

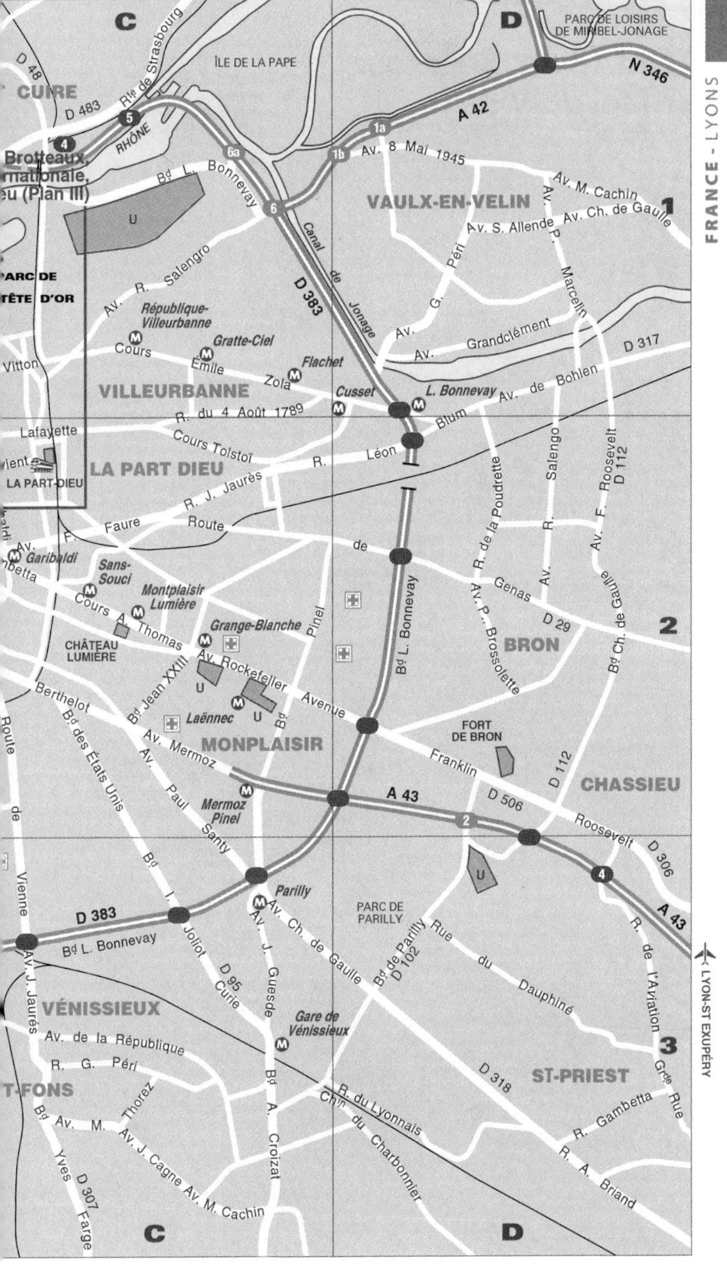
C
D
ÎLE DE LA PAPE
PARC DE LOISIRS DE MIRIBEL-JONAGE
N 346
A 42
CUIRE
D 483
Rte de Strasbourg
RHÔNE
Av. 8 Mai 1945
Bd L. Bonnevay
VAULX-EN-VELIN
Av. M. Cachin
Av. Ch. de Gaulle
Av. S. Allende
Av. P. Marcelin
Av. G. Péri
Canal de Jonage
D 383
Av. R. Salengro
République-Villeurbanne
Gratte-Ciel
Cours Émile Zola
Flachet
Cusset
L. Bonnevay
Av. Grandclément
D 317
Av. de Bohlen
VILLEURBANNE
R. du 4 Août 1789
Cours Tolstoï
R. Léon Blum
LA PART DIEU
R. J. Jaurès
Route de Genas
R. de la Poudrette
Av. R. Salengo
Av. F. Roosevelt
D 112
Garibaldi
Sans-Souci
Montplaisir Lumière
Cours A. Thomas
Grange-Blanche
Pinel
Bd L. Bonnevay
D 29
BRON
Av. P. Brossolette
Bd Ch. de Gaulle
CHÂTEAU LUMIÈRE
Bd Jean XXIII
Av. Rockefeller
Laënnec
Avenue Franklin Roosevelt
Berthelot
Bd des États Unis
Av. Mermoz
MONPLAISIR
FORT DE BRON
CHASSIEU
D 506
A 43
Mermoz Pinel
Av. Paul Santy
D 306
Route de Vienne
Bd I. Joliot Curie
D 95
Parilly
PARC DE PARILLY
Av. Ch. de Gaulle
Bd de Parilly
D 102
Rue du Dauphiné
R. de l'Aviation
LYON-ST EXUPÉRY
D 383
Bd L. Bonnevay
Av. J. Jaurès
VÉNISSIEUX
Av. J. Guesde
Gare de Vénissieux
Av. de la République
R. G. Péri
D 318
ST-PRIEST
Bd A. Croizat
R. du Lyonnais
Ch. du Charbonnier
R. Gambetta
Gde Rue
Av. M. Thorez
Av. J. Cagne
Av. M. Cachin
Bd Yves Farge
D 307
R. A. Briand
1
2
3

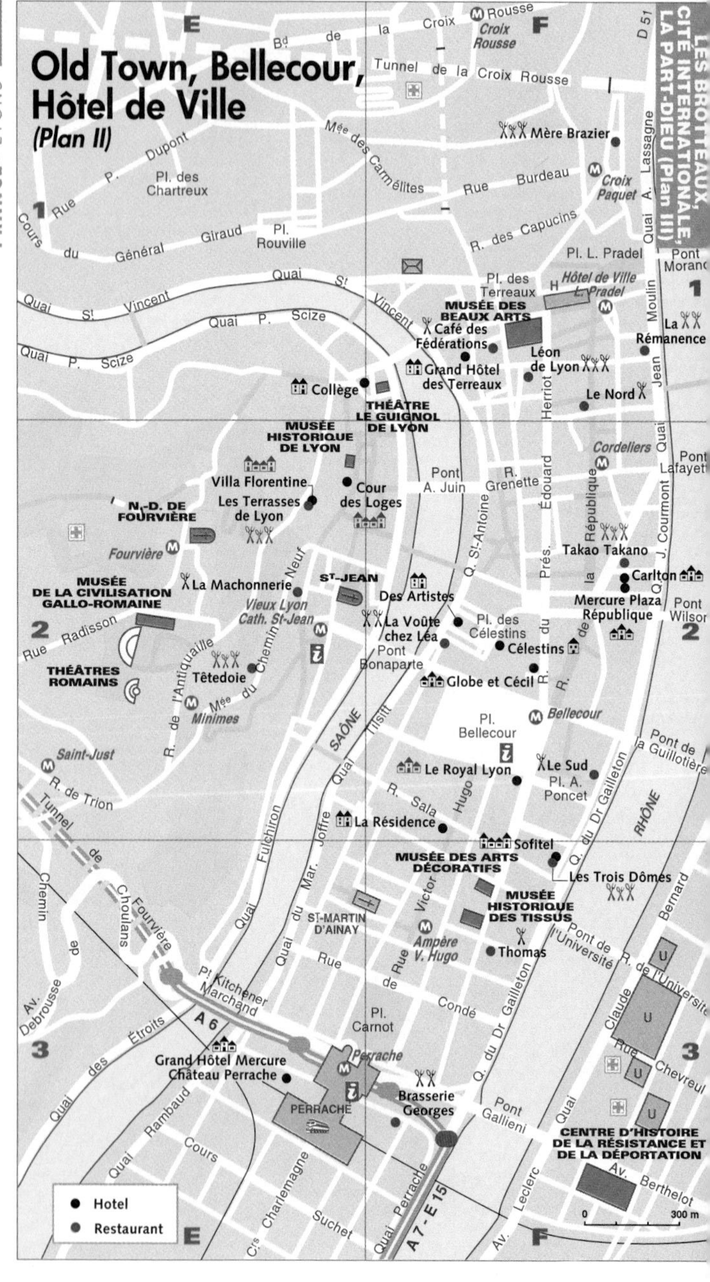
Old Town, Bellecour, Hôtel de Ville
(Plan II)
LES BROTTEAUX, CITÉ INTERNATIONALE, LA PART-DIEU (Plan III)
Mère Brazier
Musée des Beaux Arts
Café des Fédérations
Grand Hôtel des Terreaux
Léon de Lyon
La Rémanence
Le Nord
Collège
Théâtre Le Guignol de Lyon
Musée Historique de Lyon
Villa Florentine
Les Terrasses de Lyon
Cour des Loges
N.-D. de Fourvière
Fourvière
Musée de la Civilisation Gallo-Romaine
La Machonnerie
St-Jean
Des Artistes
La Voûte chez Léa
Théâtres Romains
Têtedoie
Célestins
Globe et Cécil
Takao Takano
Carlton
Mercure Plaza République
Le Royal Lyon
Le Sud
La Résidence
Sofitel
Musée des Arts Décoratifs
Les Trois Dômes
Musée Historique des Tissus
Thomas
Grand Hôtel Mercure Château Perrache
Brasserie Georges
Perrache
Centre d'Histoire de la Résistance et de la Déportation
Hotel
Restaurant
0 300 m

Sofitel

20 quai Gailleton ✉ *69002 – Ⓜ Bellecour – ✆ 04 72 41 20 20 – www.sofitel.com* **F3**
164 rm – 🯅230/380 € 🯅🯅230/380 €, ☕ 26 € – 26 suites
Rest *Les Trois Dômes* – see below
Rest *Silk Brasserie* – *✆ 04 72 41 20 80* – Menu 23 € – Carte 35/55 €
♦ Luxury ♦ Modern ♦
The cubic architecture of this hotel contrasts with its luxurious interior. It features a new-look, contemporary-style lobby, tastefully furnished modern guestrooms, smart shops and a hairdressing salon. Find a new trendy atmosphere at the Silk Brasserie where the menu offers international dishes and specialities from Lyon.

Le Royal Lyon

20 pl. Bellecour ✉ *69002 – Ⓜ Bellecour – ✆ 04 78 37 57 31 – www.lyonhotel-leroyal.com* **F2**
69 rm – 🯅260/390 € 🯅🯅340/390 €, ☕ 20 € – 5 suites
Rest – *(closed 1 to 21 August)* Menu 27 € – Carte 39/48 €
♦ Traditional ♦ Personalised ♦
Recently renovated, this 19C hotel run by the Paul Bocuse Institute has regained its former splendour. Magnificent guestrooms. Kitchen-style breakfast room. Updated menu at the restaurant.

Carlton without rest

4 r. Jussieu ✉ *69002 – Ⓜ Cordeliers – ✆ 04 78 42 56 51 – www.mercure.com*
83 rm – 🯅99/219 € 🯅🯅109/229 €, ☕ 17 € **F2**
♦ Traditional ♦ Classic ♦
Purple and gold prevail in this traditional hotel, decorated in the manner of an old-fashioned luxury hotel. The period lift cage has a charm all of its own. Comfortable rooms.

Globe et Cécil without rest

21 r. Gasparin ✉ *69002 – Ⓜ Bellecour – ✆ 04 78 42 58 95 – www.globeetcecilhotel.com* **F2**
60 rm ☕ – 🯅140/145 € 🯅🯅175/180 €
♦ Traditional ♦ Personalised ♦
One of the last silk-merchants of the town decorated the conference room of this hotel. Antique and modern furniture adorns the tastefully decorated rooms. Irresistible welcome.

Mercure Plaza République without rest

5 r. Stella ✉ *69002 – Ⓜ Cordeliers – ✆ 04 78 37 50 50 – www.mercure.com* **F2**
78 rm – 🯅99/209 € 🯅🯅109/219 €, ☕ 17 €
♦ Business ♦ Modern ♦
This hotel with 19C architecture is particularly popular with business travellers. It has a central location, a renovated modern interior, full range of comforts and conference facilities.

Grand Hôtel des Terreaux without rest

16 r. Lanterne ✉ *69001 – Ⓜ Hôtel de ville – ✆ 04 78 27 04 10 – www.hotel-lyon.fr* **F1**
53 rm – 🯅85/90 € 🯅🯅115/160 €, ☕ 12 €
♦ Traditional ♦ Personalised ♦
Personalised, tastefully decorated rooms, a small indoor pool and attentive service ensure that guests can relax to the full in this former 19C posthouse.

Des Artistes without rest

8 r. Gaspard André ✉ *69002 – Ⓜ Cordeliers – ✆ 04 78 42 04 88 – www.hoteldesartistes.fr* **F2**
45 rm – 🯅90/140 € 🯅🯅100/160 €, ☕ 12 €
♦ Traditional ♦ Personalised ♦
The hotel is named after the "artistes" of the neighbouring Célestins theatre. Stylish rooms; a Cocteau style fresco adorns the breakfast room.

La Résidence without rest

18 r. V. Hugo ✉ 69002 – Ⓜ Bellecour – ✆ 04 78 42 63 28
– www.hotel-la-residence.com **F2**
67 rm – 88 € 88 €, 8 €
♦ Business ♦ Functional ♦
In a pedestrian street near Bellecour square, this hotel provides rooms and a lounge in a 1970s style. A few rooms are more elegant and graced with wainscoting.

Célestins without rest

4 r. des Archers ✉ 69002 – Ⓜ Guillotière – ✆ 04 72 56 08 98
– www.hotelcelestins.com **F2**
25 rm – 73/123 € 79/129 €, 9 €
♦ Traditional ♦ Cosy ♦
This hotel occupies several floors of a residential building. It offers bright rooms that are gradually being refurbished; those at the front enjoy views of the Fourvière hill.

Takao Takano

14 r. Grolée ✉ 69002 – Ⓜ Cordeliers – ✆ 04 78 42 15 35
– Closed August, Sunday and Monday **F2**
Rest – Menu 45 € (weekday lunch)/85 €
– Carte 60/100 €
Spec. Foie gras de canard grillé. Aiguillette de rumsteack cuite au barbecue, jus de paleron. Fine tartelette au caramel mou et beurre salé.
♦ A la mode ♦ Design ♦
This restaurant, which first made its name thanks to the cuisine of Nicolas Le Bec, was taken over in 2010 by Japanese chef Takao Takano who is making his mark with inventive and delicious creations showing influences from around the world. Hushed, pearl-grey decor.

Les Trois Dômes – Hôtel Sofitel

20 quai Gailleton (8th Floor) ✉ 69002 – Ⓜ Bellecour – ✆ 04 72 41 20 97
– www.les-3-domes.com
– Closed 24 July-23 August, 27 February-7 March, Sunday and Monday
Rest – Menu 79 € (weekday lunch), 125/135 € **F3**
– Carte 105/160 €
Spec. Millefeuille de crabe et avocat. Bœuf Angus d'Écosse en miroir de porto, parmentier de joue de bœuf français. Trois "grands crus" de chocolat.
♦ A la mode ♦ Formal ♦
Admire the superb view from the top floor restaurant of the Sofitel hotel, which serves delicious inventive cuisine accompanied by a good selection of wines. The silver and white decor is contemporary in style, with silk-like motifs on the walls.

Mère Brazier (Mathieu Viannay)

12 r. Royale ✉ 69001 – Ⓜ Hôtel de Ville – ✆ 04 78 23 17 20
– www.lamerebrazier.fr
– Closed 30 July-29 August, 18 to 26 February, Saturday and Sunday
Rest – Menu 37 €, 58/118 € – Carte 82/139 € **F1**
Spec. Araignée de mer aux condiments, fine gelée acidulée, émulsion de crustacés (May-October). Volaille de Bresse demi-deuil, petits légumes et cerises au vinaigre. Paris-brest, glace aux noisettes caramélisées, pralin.
♦ A la mode ♦ Elegant ♦
This iconic restaurant has been taken over by an award-winning chef. Despite the modern decor, the sense of history has been preserved. It has an enticing menu that combines the classic and the contemporary.

XXX

Léon de Lyon

1 r. Pleney (corner of r. du Plâtre) ✉ 69001 – Ⓜ Hôtel de ville – ✆ 04 72 10 11 12 – www.leondelyon.com **F1**

Rest – Menu 23 € (weekdays), 30/34 € – Carte 38/48 €

◆ Brasserie ◆ Formal ◆

This institution in Lyons, treated to a lavish brasserie decor, has lost nothing of its friendly, plush appeal. Excellent choice of produce that does full justice to local gourmet specialities and delicacies.

XX

La Rémanence

31 r. du Bât-d'Argent ✉ 69001 – Ⓜ Hôtel de Ville – ✆ 04 72 00 08 08 – www.laremanence.fr – Closed 2 to 24 August, Sunday and Monday **F1**

Rest – Menu 37/71 € – Carte 50/60 €

◆ Innovative ◆

Occupying an 18C Jesuit refectory with vaulted dining rooms and golden stone walls, La Rémanence is run by a friendly young couple whose culinary focus is on inventive cuisine.

XX

Brasserie Georges

30 cours Verdun ✉ 69002 – Ⓜ Perrache – ✆ 04 72 56 54 54 – www.brasseriegeorges.com **F3**

Rest – Menu 19/24 € – Carte 25/40 €

◆ Brasserie ◆

"Great Beer and Great Food since 1836", this listed brasserie is one of the landmarks of Lyon. It has a carefully preserved Art Deco-style dining room and a relaxed atmosphere.

XX

La Voûte - Chez Léa

11 pl. A. Gourju ✉ 69002 – Ⓜ Bellecour – ✆ 04 78 42 01 33 – Closed Sunday and Bank Holidays **F2**

Rest – Menu 18 € (weekday lunch), 28/39 € – Carte 35/55 €

◆ Traditional ◆ Friendly ◆

One of the oldest restaurants in Lyons, it continues to brilliantly uphold the region's gastronomic traditions. Welcoming ambiance and decor. Game menu in autumn.

X

Le Nord

18 r. Neuve ✉ 69002 – Ⓜ Hôtel de ville – ✆ 04 72 10 69 69 – www.nordsudbrasseries.com **F1**

Rest – Menu 23 € (weekdays)/29 € – Carte 30/56 €

◆ Brasserie ◆

The authentic 1900s decor in this restaurant – the first brasserie opened by Paul Bocuse – includes red banquettes, a colourful tiled floor, wood-panelling and spherical lamps. Traditional cuisine.

X

Le Sud

11 pl. Antonin-Poncet ✉ 69002 – Ⓜ Bellecour – ✆ 04 72 77 80 00 – www.nordsudbrasseries.com **F2**

Rest – Menu 23 € (weekdays)/29 € – Carte 33/52 €

◆ Brasserie ◆

Another of chef Paul Bocuse's creations, Le Sud evokes the Mediterranean both in its cuisine and its colourful decor. Delightful summer terrace.

X

Thomas

6 r. Laurencin ✉ 69002 – Ⓜ Bellecour – ✆ 04 72 56 04 76 – www.restaurant-thomas.com – Closed 22 April-2 May, 7 to 30 August, 24 December-2 January, Saturday and Sunday **F3**

Rest – Menu 18 € (lunch), 41/55 €

Rest *Comptoir Thomas* – *✆ 04 72 41 92 99* – Carte 31/57 €

◆ Elegant ◆

This restaurant's enthusiastic young chef serves appetising cuisine in a cosy, modern dining room. A new menu is created monthly. Three annexes in the same street serve cuisine of an equally high standard, including dishes at the trendy Comptoir.

BOUCHONS *Regional wine tasting and local cuisine in a typical lyonnaise atmosphere*

Daniel et Denise

156 r. Créqui ✉ 69003 – Ⓜ Place Guichard – ✆ 04 78 60 66 53 – www.daniel-et-denise.fr – Closed 23 July-23 August, 23 December-4 January, Saturday, Sunday and Bank Holidays Plan III **G3**

Rest – Menu 26 € (lunch) – Carte 29/45 €

◆ Lyons cuisine ◆ Bistro ◆

This attractive bistro has a traditional feel, relaxed informal atmosphere, and tasty cuisine based around high quality produce. It is a typical 'bouchon Lyonnais' run by an award-winning chef.

Café des Fédérations

8 r. Major Martin ✉ 69001 – Ⓜ Hôtel de ville – ✆ 04 78 28 26 00 – www.lesfedeslyon.com – Closed 24 December-3 January and Sunday

Rest – *(pre-book)* Menu 19 € (lunch)/24 € **F1**

◆ Lyons cuisine ◆ Bistro ◆

Checked tablecloths, tightly packed tables, giant sausages hanging from the ceiling and a relaxed informal atmosphere: a genuine "bouchon" for sure!

OLD TOWN *Plan II*

Villa Florentine

25 montée St-Barthélémy ✉ 69005 – Ⓜ Fourvière – ✆ 04 72 56 56 56 – www.villaflorentine.com **E2**

21 rm – †255/465 € ††255/465 €, ☕ 25 € – 7 suites

Rest *Les Terrasses de Lyon* – see below

◆ Luxury ◆ Personalised ◆

On the Fourvière hill, this Renaissance-inspired abode commands a matchless view of the town. The interior sports an elegant blend of old and new.

Cour des Loges

6 r. Boeuf ✉ 69005 – Ⓜ Vieux Lyon Cathédrale Saint-Jean – ✆ 04 72 77 44 44 – www.courdesloges.com **E2**

57 rm – †204/240 € ††255/505 €, ☕ 25 € – 4 suites

Rest *Les Loges* – *(closed July, August, Sunday, Monday and lunch)* Menu 60/85 € – Carte 75/89 €

◆ Luxury ◆ Personalised ◆

An exceptional group of 14C-18C houses set around a splendid galleried courtyard has been decorated by contemporary designers and artists. Creative cuisine and decor with a personal touch.

Collège without rest

5 pl. St Paul ✉ 69005 – Ⓜ Vieux Lyon Cathédrale Saint-Jean – ✆ 04 72 10 05 05 – www.college-hotel.com **E-F1**

39 rm – †125/155 € ††125/155 €, ☕ 12 €

◆ Business ◆ Minimalist ◆

Take a trip down memory lane: old-fashioned school desks, a pommel horse and geography maps. The rooms are white, resolutely modern, with a balcony or terrace.

Les Terrasses de Lyon – Hôtel Villa Florentine

25 montée St-Barthélémy ✉ 69005 – Ⓜ Fourvière – ✆ 04 72 56 56 02 – www.villaflorentine.com – Closed Sunday and Monday **E2**

Rest – Menu 38 € (lunch), 48/95 € – Carte 72/120 €

Spec. Foie gras de canard frais, chutney de mangue (summer). Dos de bar poêlé sur peau, pointes d'asperges rôties et girolles. Soufflé au citron, madeleines et tuiles craquantes.

◆ Contemporary ◆ Elegant ◆

Breathtaking view of Lyons from the terrace. The interior and conservatory are stylish and the modern cuisine subtly enhances excellent produce.

XXX ✿

Têtedoie (Christian Têtedoie)

(dinner)

montée du Chemin-Neuf ✉ 69005 – Ⓜ Minimes
– ✆ 04 78 29 40 10 – www.tetedoie.com
– Closed 2 weeks in August **E2**

Rest – Menu 40 € bi (weekday lunch), 65/96 €
– Carte approx. 80 €

Spec. Salade de homard rôti au beurre d'orange. Quenelles de brochet aux trois saveurs. Chaud-froid de poire.

♦ Innovative ♦ Elegant ♦ Design ♦

An elegant, contemporary restaurant overlooking the city from the Fourvière hill. The chef serves traditional French cuisine with a sublime modern twist. The wine cellar is home to over 700 appellations.

X

La Machonnerie

36 r. Tramassac ✉ 69005 – Ⓜ Vieux Lyon – ✆ 04 78 42 24 62
– www.lamachonnerie.com
– Closed 15 to 30 July, 2 weeks in January, Sunday and lunch except Saturday **E2**

Rest – *(pre-book)* Menu 28/45 € bi – Carte 35/45 €

♦ Lyons cuisine ♦ Rustic ♦

The traditions of informal service, a friendly atmosphere and authentic regional cuisine are kept alive in this typical neighbourhood bistro. Attractive lounge dedicated to jazz music.

PERRACHE

Plan II

Grand Hôtel Mercure Château Perrache

12 cours Verdun ✉ 69002 – Ⓜ Perrache
– ✆ 04 72 77 15 00
– www.mercure.com **E3**

111 rm – †90/250 € ††110/270 €, ☕ 17 € – 2 suites

Rest *Les Belles Saisons* – *(closed 25 July-25 August, weekends and Bank Holidays)* Carte 22/35 €

♦ Traditional ♦ Art Deco ♦

This hotel built in 1900 has partially conserved its Art Nouveau setting: intricate wood carving in the lobby and period furniture in some of the rooms and suites. Les Belles Saisons boasts a Majorelle style decor, a contemporary atmosphere, and traditional cuisine.

LES BROTTEAUX – CITÉ INTERNATIONALE – LA PART-DIEU

Plan III

Hilton

rm,

70 quai Ch.-de-Gaulle ✉ 69006 – ✆ 04 78 17 50 50 – www.hilton.com

199 rm – †150/365 € ††150/365 €, ☕ 24 € – 5 suites **H1**

Rest *Blue Elephant* – *✆ 04 78 17 50 00 (closed 15 July-15 August, Saturday lunch and Sunday)* Menu 28/55 € – Carte 35/55 €

Rest *Brasserie* – *✆ 04 78 17 51 00* – Menu 24 € (weekday lunch) – Carte 38/55 €

♦ Chain hotel ♦ Modern ♦

This impressive modern hotel built in brick and glass is equipped with a comprehensive business centre. Fully equipped bedrooms and apartments facing the Tête d'Or park or the Rhône. Thai specialities and decor at the Blue Elephant. Traditional food is served at the Brasserie, which boasts a retro-style decor and a pleasant terrace.

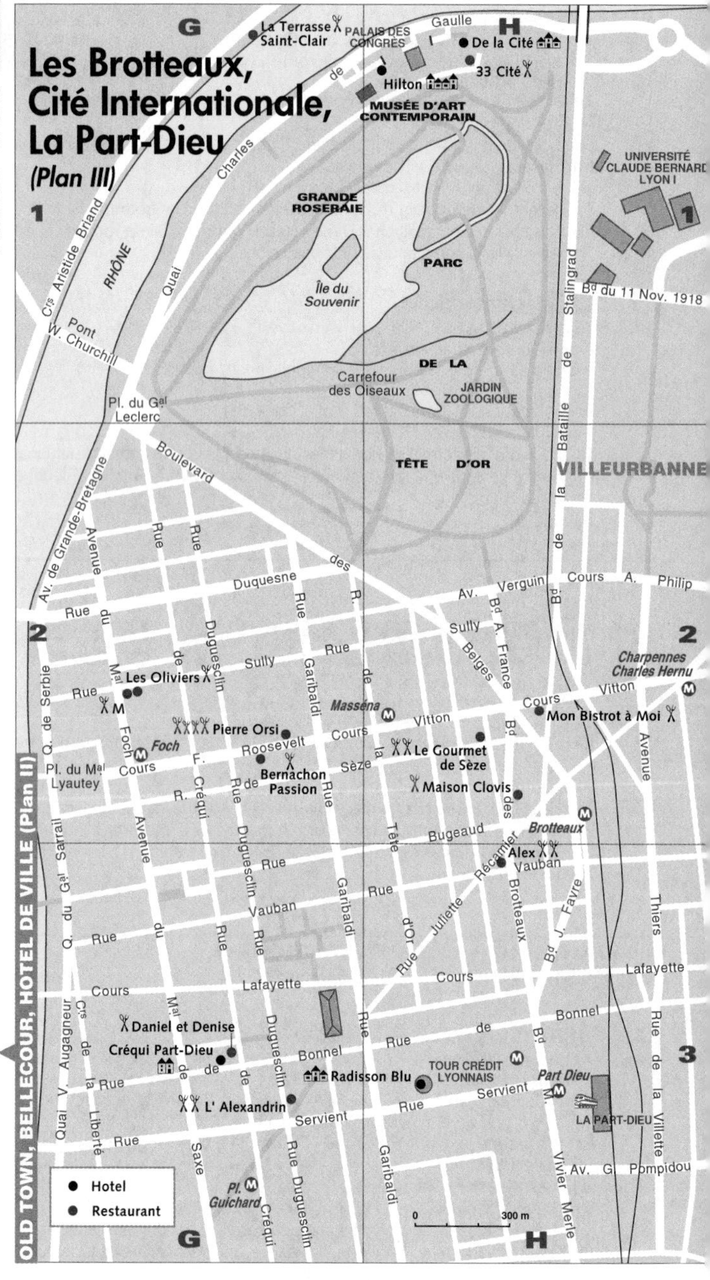
Les Brotteaux,
Cité Internationale,
La Part-Dieu
(Plan III)
G
H
1
2
3
La Terrasse Saint-Clair
PALAIS DES CONGRÈS
De la Cité
33 Cité
Hilton
MUSÉE D'ART CONTEMPORAIN
UNIVERSITÉ CLAUDE BERNARD LYON I
GRANDE ROSERAIE
Île du Souvenir
PARC
DE LA
TÊTE D'OR
Carrefour des Oiseaux
JARDIN ZOOLOGIQUE
RHÔNE
Quai Charles de Gaulle
Crs Aristide Briand
Pont W. Churchill
Pl. du Gal Leclerc
Boulevard des Belges
Bd du 11 Nov. 1918
Bd de la Bataille de Stalingrad
VILLEURBANNE
Av. de Grande-Bretagne
Avenue du Mal Foch
Rue Duquesne
Rue Duguesclin
Rue Garibaldi
Rue de Créqui
Av. Verguin
Cours A. Philip
Bd A. France
Rue Sully
Charpennes Charles Hernu
Les Oliviers
Pierre Orsi
Masséna
Cours Vitton
Mon Bistrot à Moi
Q. de Serbie
Foch
Pl. du Mal Lyautey
Cours F. Roosevelt
Bernachon Passion
Rue de Sèze
Le Gourmet de Sèze
Maison Clovis
Rue Tête d'Or
Bd des Brotteaux
Brotteaux
Rue Bugeaud
Alex
Rue Vauban
Rue Juliette Récamier
Bd J. Favre
Avenue Thiers
Q. du Gal Sarrail
Cours Lafayette
Crs de la Liberté
Quai V. Augagneur
Daniel et Denise
Créqui Part-Dieu
Rue de Bonnel
Radisson Blu
TOUR CRÉDIT LYONNAIS
Part Dieu
Bd M. Vivier Merle
Rue Servient
L' Alexandrin
LA PART-DIEU
Rue de la Villette
Av. G. Pompidou
Rue Saxe
Pl. Guichard
Hotel
Restaurant
0
300 m
OLD TOWN, BELLECOUR, HOTEL DE VILLE (Plan II)

Radisson Blu

129 r. Servient (32th Floor) ✉ 69003 – Ⓜ Part Dieu – ✆ 04 78 63 55 00 – www.radissonblu.com/hotel-lyon **H3**

245 rm – 135/165 € 135/320 €, ☕ 20 €

Rest *L'Arc-en-Ciel* – *(closed from mid July-end August, Saturday lunch and Sunday)* Menu 46/146 € bi – Carte 64/103 €

Rest *Bistrot de la Tour* – *(closed 25 July-16 August, Saturday and Sunday) (lunch only)* Menu 18 € – Carte 20/40 €

◆ Business ◆ Functional ◆

At the top of a building known as the "pencil", this hotel is inspired by the style of the houses of old Lyon, with an inner courtyard and galleries. Superb view from some of the guestrooms. On the 32nd floor of a tower block, the Arc-en-Ciel specialises in seasonal, contemporary cuisine. Packed at lunchtime.

De la Cité

22 quai Ch.-de-Gaulle ✉ 69006 – ✆ 04 78 17 86 86 – www.lyon.concorde-hotels.com **H1**

164 rm – 99/355 € 99/355 €, ☕ 22 € – 5 suites

Rest – Menu 22 € – Carte 28/44 €

◆ Chain hotel ◆ Modern ◆

This modern building designed by Renzo Piano stands between the Tête d'Or park and the Rhône. Bright rooms decorated in a contemporary style. Traditional cuisine is to the fore in this restaurant with a terrace opening on to the patio of the Cité Internationale. Impressive cocktail list in the bar.

Créqui Part-Dieu

rm,

37 r. Bonnel ✉ 69003 – Ⓜ Place Guichard – ✆ 04 78 60 20 47 – www.bestwestern-lyonpartdieu.com **G3**

46 rm – 77/175 € 77/185 €, ☕ 15 € – 3 suites

Rest *La Cantine du Palais* – *✆ 04 78 60 83 96 (Closed August, Saturday and Sunday)* Menu 18 € (lunch)/23 €

◆ Business ◆ Functional ◆

This hotel is located opposite the Cité Judiciaire. Split between two buildings, the guestrooms are decorated in warm tones, with those in the new wing resolutely contemporary in style. Family cooking and a 'school yard' ambience in the well-renovated restaurant.

XXXX

Pierre Orsi

3 pl. Kléber ✉ 69006 – Ⓜ Masséna – ✆ 04 78 89 57 68 – www.pierreorsi.com – Closed Sunday and Monday except Bank Holidays **G2**

Rest – Menu 45 € (weekday lunch), 60/115 € – Carte 61/153 €

Spec. Ravioles de foie gras de canard au jus de porto et truffes. Pigeonneau en cocotte aux gousses d'ail confites en chemise. Crêpes suzette au beurre d'orange.

◆ Contemporary ◆ Elegant ◆ Cosy ◆

This old house is home to elegant dining rooms and a rose garden terrace. Fine up-to-date cuisine and good wine list.

XX

L'Alexandrin (Laurent Rigal)

83 r. Moncey ✉ 69003 – Ⓜ Place Guichard – ✆ 04 72 61 15 69 – www.lalexandrin.com – Closed 1 to 23 August, 24 to 29 December, Sunday and Monday

Rest – Menu 38 € (weekday lunch), 60/150 € **G3**

Spec. Cappuccino de cèpes à la fève tonka et châtaignes éclatées (October-January). Véritable mousseline de brochet et son crémeux d'écrevisse. Madeleines au chocolat guanaja et marmelade d'orange confite au Grand Marnier.

◆ A la mode ◆ Cosy ◆

This welcoming, colourful restaurant is very popular with locals. Pleasant terrace, good choice of Côtes du Rhône, and regional dishes prepared with an original flair.

Le Gourmet de Sèze (Bernard Mariller)

129 r. Sèze ✉ 69006 – Ⓜ Masséna – ☎ 04 78 24 23 42 – www.le-gourmet-de-seze.com – Closed 2 to 6 June, 23 July-23 August, 27 February-3 March, Sunday, Monday and Bank Holidays **H2**

Rest – *(number of covers limited, pre-book)* Menu 35 € (weekday lunch), 47/95 €

Spec. Croustillants de pieds de cochon compotés à la moutarde en grains. Saint-Jacques de la baie de Saint-Brieuc (October-March). Grand dessert du gourmet en quatre assiettes.

♦ A la mode ♦ Cosy ♦

This restaurant has an attractive dining room with tones of pale yellow and chocolate, mirrors, paintings, and well-spaced round tables. This complements the carefully prepared, traditional cuisine with a modern twist.

Alex

44 bd des Brotteaux ✉ 69006 – Ⓜ Brotteaux – ☎ 04 78 52 30 11 – Closed August, Sunday and Monday **H3**

Rest – Menu 22 € (weekday lunch), 28/59 € – Carte 52/60 €

♦ A la mode ♦ Design ♦

Bold colours, designer furniture and contemporary art come together to create the simple yet chic decor in this restaurant. The owner-chef's menu highlights seasonal produce.

Maison Clovis (Clovis Khoury)

19 bd Brotteaux ✉ 69006 – Ⓜ Brotteaux – ☎ 04 72 74 44 61 – www.maisonclovis.com – Closed 1 to 22 August, 2 to 10 January, Sunday and Monday **H2**

Rest – Menu 26 € (weekday lunch), 42/70 € – Carte 50/80 €

Spec. Oursin dans sa coque, risotto aux supions, cuisses de grenouille et raviolis aux champignons (September-April). Homard cuit à l'étouffée, champignons, artichauts, légumes fanes, jus de carapace. Harmonie gourmande au chocolat grand cru.

♦ A la mode ♦ Design ♦

This welcoming contemporary bistro has a designer feel. Unfussy yet delicious modern cooking based around the best products. The art of simplicity.

33 Cité

33 quai Charles-de-Gaulle ✉ 69006 – ☎ 04 37 45 45 45 – www.33cite.com – Closed 8 to 21 August **H1**

Rest – Menu 23/27 € – Carte 33/55 €

♦ Traditional ♦ Design ♦

Contemporary designer setting opposite the Salle 3000 at the Cité Internationale. View of the Parc de la Tête d'Or through the large windows. Choice of modern and classic dishes.

La Terrasse St-Clair

2 Grande Rue St-Clair ✉ 69300 Caluire-et-Cuire – ☎ 04 72 27 37 37 – www.terrasse-saint-clair.com – Closed 5 to 22 August, 23 December-15 January, Sunday and Monday

Rest – Menu 25 € **G1**

♦ Traditional ♦ Bistro ♦

This restaurant has the atmosphere of an open-air dance hall. Good traditional cuisine. Terrace shaded by plane trees, plus a pétanque area.

Les Oliviers

20 r. Sully ✉ 69006 – Ⓜ Foch – ☎ 04 78 89 07 09 – www.lesolivierslyon.fr – Closed 1 to 8 May, August, Saturday, Sunday and Bank Holidays

Rest – Menu 24/45 € – Carte 24/45 € **G2**

♦ A la mode ♦ Friendly ♦

This restaurant is a tiny corner of Provence hidden away in Paris' 6th arrondissement. It has an intimate, simply furnished, contemporary-style dining room, and delicious Mediterranean cuisine.

M

47 av. Foch ✉ 69006 – Ⓜ Foch – ☎ 04 78 89 55 19
– www.mrestaurant.fr
– Closed 30 July-22 August, 26 February-7 March, Saturday and Sunday
Rest – Menu 24/38 € **G2**
◆ A la mode ◆ Trendy ◆
This establishment is very appealing with its open plan, minimalist, faintly psychedelic interior dotted with orange arabesques. Updated cuisine steeped in flavour.

Bernachon Passion

42 cours Franklin-Roosevelt ✉ 69006 – Ⓜ Foch – ☎ 04 78 52 23 65
– www.bernachon.com
– Closed 24 July-25 August, Sunday, Monday and Bank Holidays
Rest – *(lunch only) (number of covers limited, pre-book)* **G2**
Menu 25 € – Carte approx. 35 €
◆ Traditional ◆ Design ◆
This restaurant is run by Paul Bocuse's daughter and her children, owner of the renowned chocolate shop next door. Classic menu; dish of the day at lunchtime. Tea room.

Mon Bistrot à Moi

84 cours Vitton ✉ 69006 – Ⓜ Brotteaux
– ☎ 04 78 52 47 28
– Closed 1 week in February, 1 to 22 August, Saturday and Sunday
Rest – *(number of covers limited, pre-book)* Menu 21 € **H2**
◆ Bistro ◆
A new address in the Les Brotteaux district. It offers copper pans hanging from the walls, honest bistro cuisine, wines listed on a blackboard, and excellent value.

AROUND LYONS

Lyon Métropole

85 quai J. Gillet ✉ 69004 – ☎ 04 72 10 44 44
– www.lyonmetropole.com **B1**
118 rm – †149/220 € ††149/220 €, ☕ 18 €
Rest *Le Lyon Plage* – *☎ 04 72 10 44 30* – Menu 23 € – Carte 25/42 €
◆ Business ◆ Modern ◆
This hotel is popular for its excellent sports facilities, which include an Olympic swimming pool, superb spa, gym, tennis and squash courts, as well as a golf practice area. The renovated modern guestrooms are preferable here. Seafood takes pride of place on the menu of the Brasserie Lyon Plage.

Auberge de Fond Rose (Gérard Vignat)

23 quai G. Clemenceau ✉ 69300 Caluire-et-Cuire
– ☎ 04 78 29 34 61 – www.aubergedefondrose.com
– Closed February Holidays, Sunday dinner, Monday and Tuesday
Rest – Menu 38 € bi (weekday lunch), 55/85 € **B1**
– Carte 66/95 €
Spec. Carpaccio de pétoncles, royale de jus de coquillages (September-April). Veau cuit en cocotte aux morilles et Côtes du Jura. Fondant au chocolat manjari, crème glacée à la vanille.
◆ A la mode ◆ Formal ◆
This handsome 1920s house features an idyllic terrace leading into the garden planted with ancient trees. Fine up-to-date menu and interesting wine list.

XX ✿✿

Auberge de l'Ile (Jean-Christophe Ansanay-Alex)
(on Barbe Island) ✉ *69009* (dinner) P VISA MC AE
– ✆ 04 78 83 99 49 – www.aubergedelile.com
– Closed Sunday and Monday **B1**
Rest – Menu 110 € – Carte 95/136 €
Spec. Foie gras de canard cuit au torchon servi froid, brioche mousseline tiède. Agneau de pré salé en croûte de sel et thym, tomate cœur de pigeon (July-September). Soufflé pêche blanche (July-September).
♦ Innovative ♦ Friendly ♦
With its location on the lush Ile Barbe on the Saône, this inn seems as if it is almost in the country. Dating from 1601, it boasts a warm, intimate interior (wood and baked clay decor) and fine cuisine offering striking taste combinations and creative flights of fancy.

X

L'Ouest A/C VISA MC AE
1 quai du Commerce (North via the banks of the Saône, D 51)
✉ *69009 – ✆ 04 37 64 64 64*
– www.nordsudbrasseries.com **B1**
Rest – Menu 23 € (weekdays)/29 € – Carte 35/50 €
♦ Brasserie ♦ Fashionable ♦
A distinctive modern building of wood, concrete and metal. Bar, giant screens, open kitchen, river facing terrace and exotic dishes. Bocuse is on a western course!

X

Rue Le Bec 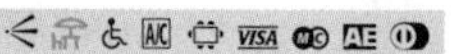
43 quai Rambaud (new Confluence district) ✉ *69002 – Ⓜ Perrache*
– ✆ 04 78 92 87 87 – www.nicolaslebec.com **B2**
Rest – Carte 31/69 €
♦ A la mode ♦ Design ♦
This unique gourmet hall covers 2000mE>2 in the new Confluence district of the city. It brings together a number of different food ventures under the same roof as part of a project led by Nicolas Le Bec. A cross between a market and a restaurant.

X

Le Verre et l'Assiette A/C VISA MC
20 Grande-Rue-de-Vaise ✉ *69009 – Ⓜ Valmy – ✆ 04 78 83 32 25*
– www.leverreetlassiette.com
– Closed 22 July-16 August, 25 February-6 March, Monday dinner, Tuesday dinner, Wednesday dinner, Saturday and Sunday **B1**
Rest – Menu 24 € (weekday lunch), 28/44 €
♦ A la mode ♦
The talented chef here reworks traditional Lyon dishes and a number of classics of French cuisine with great originality. Friendly service to a backdrop of pleasant modern decor featuring wood and stone.

Collonges-au-Mont-d'Or

XXXXX ✿✿✿

Paul Bocuse A/C P VISA MC AE
40 r. de la Plage, au pont de Collonges
(12 km North via the banks of the Saône, D 433 and D 51) ✉ *69660*
– ✆ 04 72 42 90 90
– www.bocuse.fr
Rest – Menu 130/215 € – Carte 115/205 €
Spec. Rouget barbet en écailles de pommes de terre. Volaille de Bresse en vessie "Mère Fillioux". Gâteau Président " Maurice Bernachon".
♦ Classic ♦ Formal ♦
A high temple of tradition and old-style service, which is oblivious to passing culinary trends. Paul Bocuse is still offering the same "presidential" truffle soup first served in 1975, and has had three Michelin since 1965!

CHARBONNIÈRES-LES-BAINS

Le Pavillon de la Rotonde

3 av. du Casino – ✆ 04 78 87 79 79
– www.pavillon-rotonde.com
– Closed August
16 rm – 325 € 355 €, 33 €
Rest *Philippe Gauvreau* – see below
♦ Luxury ♦ Design ♦ Personalised ♦
A stone's throw from the casino, a luxurious hotel with contemporary decor and discreet Art Deco touches. Spacious rooms with terrace giving onto the gardens. Heated indoor swimming pool and spa.

Philippe Gauvreau – Hôtel Le Pavillon de la Rotonde

3 av. du Casino – ✆ 04 78 87 79 79
– www.pavillon-rotonde.com
– Closed August, 2 to 11 January, Saturday lunch, Sunday and Monday
Rest – Menu 58 € bi (weekday lunch), 115/148 € – Carte 115/180 €
Spec. Il était une fois... quatre foies pressés. Homard breton entier cuit en tajine, petits farcis. Cannellonis de chocolat amer à la glace de crème brûlée, sauce chocolat guanaja.
♦ Innovative ♦ Formal ♦
This modern, elegant and welcoming restaurant opens out onto the gardens and park. The cuisine here is a perfect fusion of top quality products and flavours.

Maison des Tanneurs
Gerwerstub 1572
SON RESTAURANT SES 1ers CRUS DU PAYS
La Maison de la Choucroute

Strasbourg

STRASBOURG

Population (est. 2010): 272 123 (conurbation 427 245) – Altitude: 143m

X/Fotolia.com

Would it be stretching things to call Strasbourg the ultimate European city? It can make an impressive claim: although in France, it sits just across the Rhine from Germany; it's home to the Court of Human Rights and the Council of Europe; its stunning Cathedral is the highest medieval building on the continent; and it's a major communications hub as it connects the Mediterranean with the Rhineland, Central Europe, the North Sea and the Baltic. Oh, and the Old Town is a UNESCO World Heritage Site.

What's more, there's a real cosmopolitan buzz here. A large student population, courtesy of the city's ancient university, helps generate a year-round feeling of liveliness. The name 'Strasbourg' translates as 'crossroads' and the city bounced back and forth between France and Germany for over three hundred years before its final acceptance as French over half a century ago. Its unique geographical position also lends the city a great gastronomic tradition, with two cuisine cultures colliding head on, and hungry visitors reaping the culinary benefits. Meantime, street signs in both French and Alsatian add to a gently teasing schizophrenia, enhanced by distinct areas of medieval French and German architecture. The final brushwork of this striking picture is the handsome waterway that completely encircles the Old Town, the ideal setting for a lingering boat journey on a summer's afternoon.

LIVING THE CITY

The **River Rhine** flows a short distance to the east of Strasbourg; the waterway that encircles the historical centre is the **River Ill** and the **Fossé des Remparts** canal. This effectively means that the heart of the city, the tourist epicentre, is an island: The Grande Ile. The **Petite France** neighbourhood is on the island's southwest tip, while the '**German district**' is northeast. The smart **European Parliament** zone is a couple of miles beyond this. Strasbourg's 'happening' district, **Krutenau**, lies near the university campus to the east of town. Right across from here, on the western fringes, is the main arrival point to the city, the central railway station.

PRACTICAL INFORMATION

ARRIVAL-DEPARTURE

Strasbourg-Entzheim International Airport is found 12km southwest of the city. The train to Central Station runs from Entzheim Station (a 5min walk from the terminal) and takes 15min. A taxi to the city centre will be about €30.

TRANSPORT

Strasbourg is covered by a bus and tram service. Tickets are valid for the whole transport network. You can buy a single ticket or carnets (multipass). There's also a Tour-Pass which gives unlimited travel for 24hr.

The city has impressive green credentials. Buses run on natural gas, trams are slick and efficient, and there are 130,000 cyclists and 270 miles of cycle paths – hiring a bike is a great way of getting about here.

If you're staying longer, invest in a Strasbourg-Pass. This is a three-day pass which offers free travel, plus free admission (and numerous discounts) to city-wide monuments and visitor attractions.

EXPLORING STRASBOURG

Set on its island between the tree-lined embrace of the River Ill, Strasbourg's old town is a classic medieval gem, but the capital of Alsace is a lot more than one-dimensional. The strikingly modern European Parliament building

ensures the presence of smart shops; the large population of university students guarantees a youthful buzz; and what look like German wine taverns turn out to be cosy French bistros.

Visitors who arrive expecting a rather straight-laced city full of politicians are knocked out by its time-honed beauty and elegance. The World Heritage Site status is richly deserved: there are rows of half-timbered medieval buildings, glorious mansions and narrow pedestrianised streets dotted with leafy squares and lined with pavement cafés. The German quarter is the more northerly stretch of the old town, marked by sturdy public buildings and graceful gardens. Much of the architecture in these parts is of the grand nineteenth century neoclassical sort: witness a group of imposing structures such as the **Palace of the Rhine** and the **Strasbourg National Theatre** in the rather un-Germanic sounding Place de la Republique. Then a bit further down, on **Place Broglie**, nip inside the much-frequented **Rhine Opera** building to book tickets: performances here have earned Strasbourg a worldwide reputation for classical music.

→ TRULY IN-SPIRED

The centre of the old town is also its busiest point. Many people here are making tracks to the magnificent **Notre-Dame Cathedral**. It's not hard to find, as its unmistakable single spire towers over crouching medieval roofs lying humbly in its wake. The cathedral's stark silhouette is visible from miles round, but on closer inspection, lace-like stonework softens its lines, though it won't do much to lessen the leering stares of countless gargoyles. This is a tremendous 11C sandstone confection that changes colour with the light, from dawn pink to afternoon ochre. Inside there's an elaborate astronomical clock that brings forth a parade of apostles when it chimes at 12.30pm. Crowning glory is the kaleidoscope of the rose window: on sunny days, the stained glass is a joy to behold. Two other medieval churches in the old town are worth visiting: **St-Pierre-le-Jeune** (in Place St-Pierre-Le-Jeune) is a superb Gothic pile from 1053, and you can still see the base of the bell tower and a number of walls from the original building, though what you might appreciate most are the church's wonderful 14C frescoes. Meantime, a similar reverie can be felt at the **Church of Saint Thomas** on the Quai Saint-Thomas. It dates back to the 13C, and pride of place within goes to the organ that was played by Mozart and Albert Schweitzer.

→ PETITE PLEASURES

The southern district of the old town (which contains St Thomas) is the predominantly Gallic part of Strasbourg – Petite France. This is the prettiest area of all, like a fairytale scene peopled by 21C tourists. It's made up of 15C black-and-white half-timbered houses, once the homes of tanners and dyers, with geranium-filled balconies. All around is a jumble of cobbled streets punctuated by canals and camel-back stone bridges. Stop at the characterful **Pont des Moulins** and listen to the gushing water as it's channelled through a narrow passageway. All around here you can take in memorable views. Climb to the top of the nearby **Vauban Dam**, which crosses the Ill at its widest point, and look across to the **Ponts Couverts**, covered bridges linked by grand medieval watchtowers that in turn provide an observation point for the four Ill canals.

→ ART OF THE MATTER

Looking the other way from the dam you see the modish façade of the **Museum of Modern and Contemporary Art**. This is the crème de la crème of Strasbourg's museums, perhaps because of the striking steel-and-plate-glass structure in which it's housed as much as for the artworks themselves. Step inside and admire delightful floor-to-ceiling windows that enhance the powerful paintings on the walls...then finish your coffee in the Art Café and head on through to the actual permanent collection. This features Picasso, Braque, Ernst, Gauguin, Kandinsky and Magritte. The museum's upper gallery is a different concept altogether: an off-the-wall contemporary art ragbag that might have had even Picasso stroking his chin. If your taste in museums is a bit more conservative, check out the elegant **Rohan Palace**, in the shadow of the cathedral. Not only is this a fine eighteenth century building, it also boasts three museums, which delve into the worlds of archaeology, fine and applied arts. Across the water, on **quai Saint-Nicolas**, three adjoining sixteenth century houses make up the **Alsatian Museum**, dedicated to the history and traditions of the city and area you're visiting. If local history (or local signposts) have left you confused, this is the place to sort yourself out.

→ MEET THE KRU

Strasbourg's 'playground' is Krutenau, a bohemian quarter that used to be occupied by 'water folk' such as fishermen and boatmen. It always had an alternative air, and it's kept that bohemian feel to this day, enhanced by the big student population that descends on its bars and clubs. This funky district has an eclectic mix of hole-in-the-wall restaurants serving everything from spicy Lebanese meals to rich Thai curries. If, however, your idea of playing is a gentle cruise on a boat, then it's simplicity itself to jump on one at the landing stage behind the Rohan Palace, and relax on a one-hour trip that does the classic circular trip taking in the grandiose European Parliament building to the north and the Ponts-Couverts to the south. Then again, a stroll along the banks of the Ill gives you a first-hand chance to appreciate the tastefully landscaped river-banks that typify a superior kind of European city.

CALENDAR HIGHLIGHTS

Alsatians look forward to September in the city, not for any particularly autumnal reasons, but because this is the month when Festival Musica comes to town, and wonderfully diverse works from the modern classical music genre are performed at venues throughout Strasbourg. This lights the blue touch paper for two more influential events in the city. November's St'Art at the Strasbourg Centre de Congrès is lauded as the second-biggest contemporary art fair in France (after the FIAC in Paris) and draws art-lovers from around Europe to the 'crossroads' of the continent. That same month sees Jazz d'Or, a highly popular jazz festival over two weeks with forty concerts spread across venues in the city. The main summer event here is the Route Romane Festival (August and September), when Strasbourg's shared Franco-German cultural heritage is celebrated with a feast of medieval and traditional music. Christmas markets in the city are worth a particular mention. They're amongst the oldest and the best in Europe, and have been held here since 1570. The market in Place Broglie, in the old town, is recognised as the one at the top of the tree.

STRASBOURG IN...

→ ONE DAY

Old Town, Notre-Dame Cathedral, Petite France

→ TWO DAYS

Boat trip on the Ill, Museum of Modern and Contemporary Art, meal in a winstub

→ THREE DAYS

Alsatian Museum (or Rohan Palace museums), European Parliament, Orangerie

EATING OUT

Strasbourg is generally considered one of the best cities in France for delicious cuisine and places in which to eat it. There's the attention to quality and detail that's the epitome of the French gourmet philosophy allied to bold and hearty Alsatian fare with its roots firmly set across the Rhine. A favourite of the region is choucroute (or sauerkraut if you're leaning towards Germany), which is a rumbustious mixture of cabbage, potatoes, pork, sausage and ham; then there's baeckoffe, a tasty Alsace stew, which translates as 'ovenbake' and blends pieces of stewing lamb, beef and pork with liberal dollops of Riesling. Talking of which, the fragrant wines of the area have a distinct character of their own: they're white, spicy and floral. The local fruit liquor, eau de vie, has a definite Alsatian kick, too – it's sweetened entirely by fruit without a hint of sugar. A good place in which to sample the local produce is a typical Strasbourg winstub. The smarter restaurants – highly prized and requiring advance reservation – are around the cathedral, in the Petite France quarter, and along the canal and river banks. As this is a eurocrat zone, expect a smart set to be at a table close to you. As in other parts of France, a fifteen per cent service charge is already added to your bill, but round it up for good service.

➔ FOLLY IN THE PARK

The Orangerie is Strasbourg's most popular park, just across from the European Council offices. Not only is it full of people in serious suits – it also boasts a zoo and a bowling alley.

➔ ARTY ANTHEM

Strasbourg can lay claim to three famous sons. Two of them, Gustave Dore and Jean Arp, became world renowned for their abilities with a paintbrush. The third, Frederic de Dietrich, was the mayor who commissioned the French national anthem, La Marseillaise.

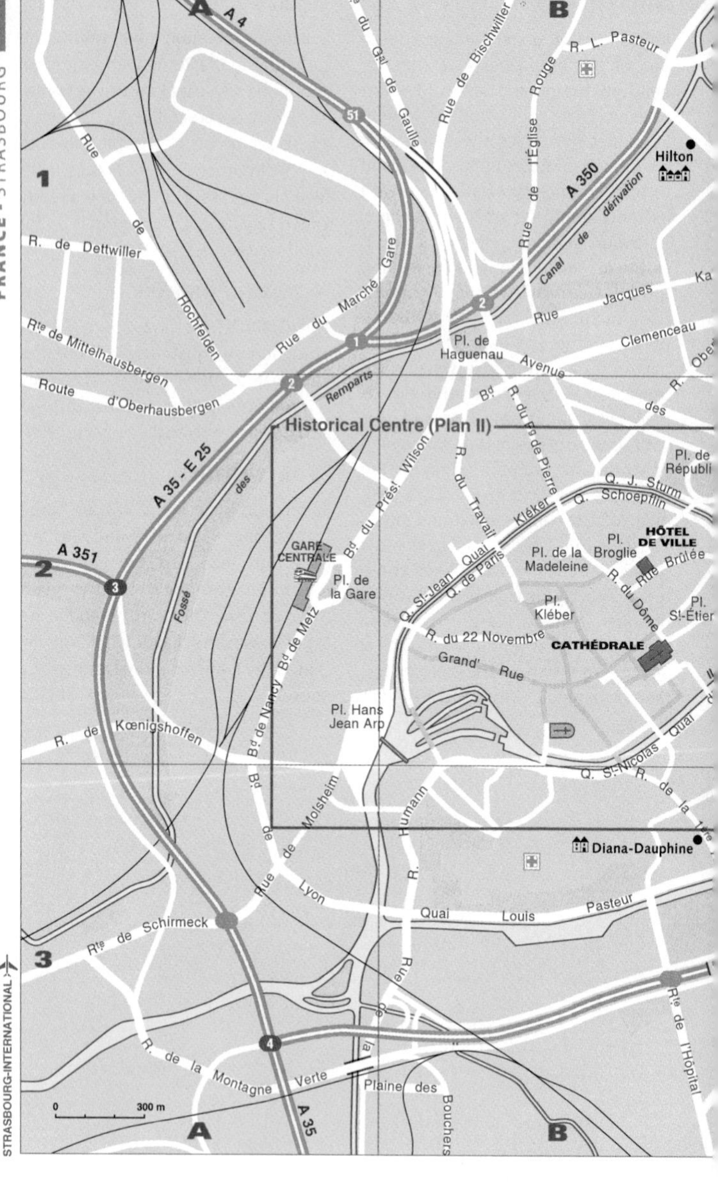

STRASBOURG-INTERNATIONAL

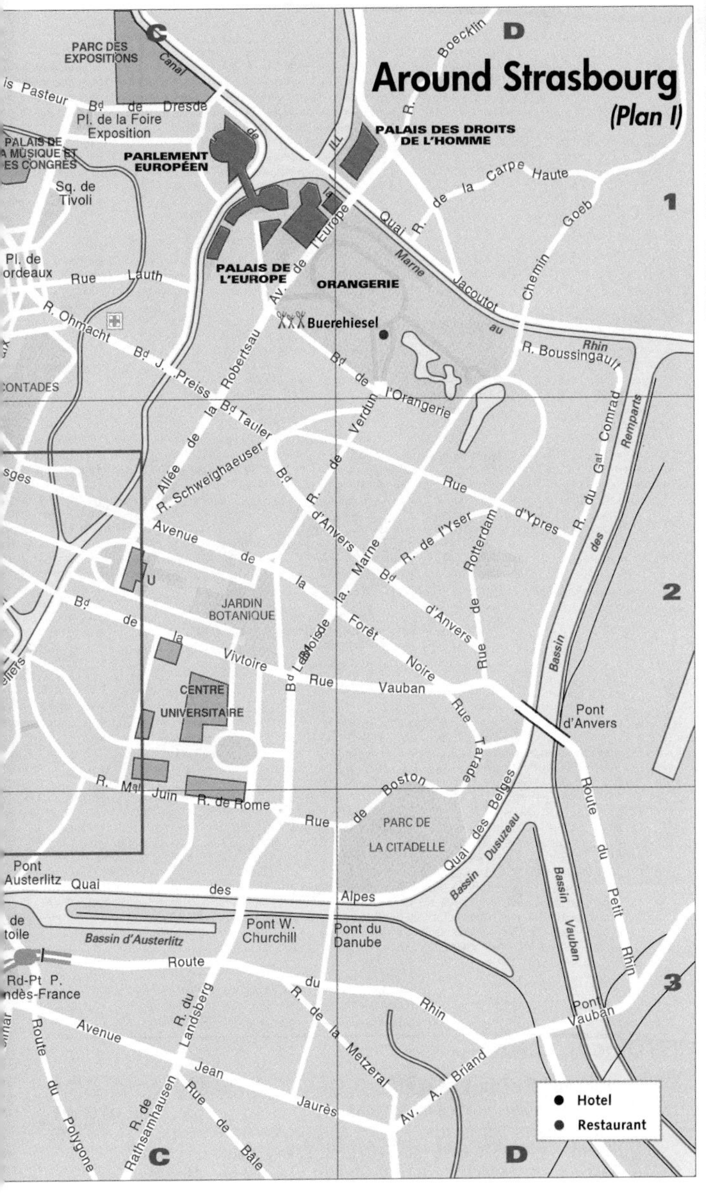
Around Strasbourg
(Plan I)
PARC DES EXPOSITIONS
PALAIS DES DROITS DE L'HOMME
PARLEMENT EUROPÉEN
PALAIS DE L'EUROPE
ORANGERIE
Buerehiesel
JARDIN BOTANIQUE
CENTRE UNIVERSITAIRE
PARC DE LA CITADELLE
Pont d'Anvers
Pont W. Churchill
Pont du Danube
Bassin d'Austerlitz
Pont Vauban
Hotel
Restaurant

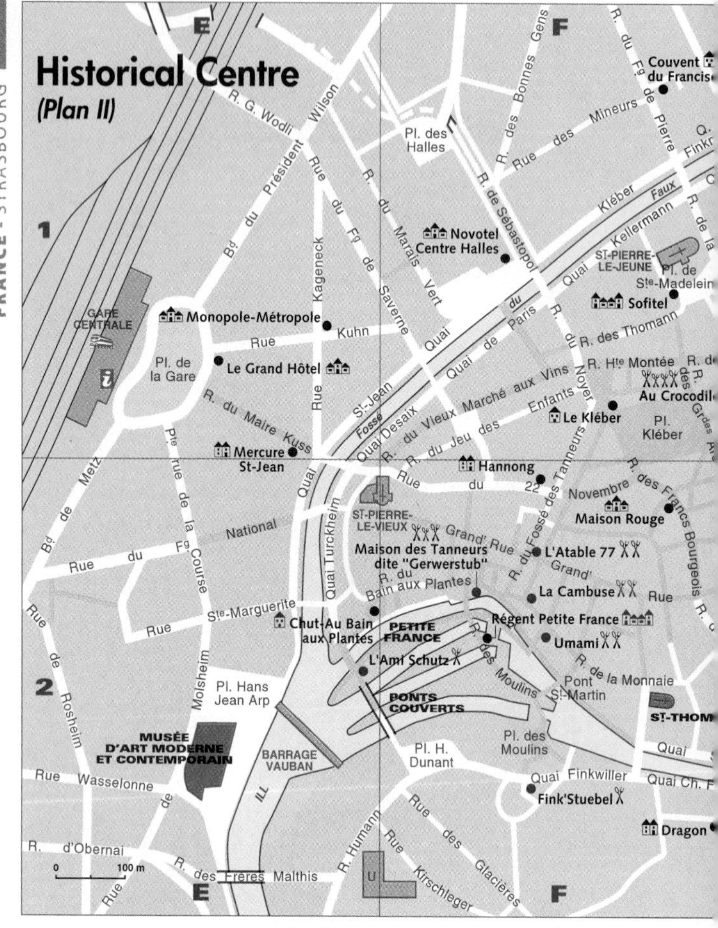

HISTORICAL CENTRE

Plan II

Régent Petite France

5 r. des Moulins – *03 88 76 43 43*
– *www.regent-hotels.com*

F2

63 rm – 155/575 € 155/575 €, 22 € – 9 suites
Rest – *(closed lunch except July-August, Sunday and Monday)*
Carte 42/50 €

♦ Grand Luxury ♦ Business ♦ Design ♦

A beautiful, large hotel occupying a former ice-making factory on the banks of the river Ill in the historic Petite France district. Comfortable, modern, stylish and unostentatious interior with pleasantly hushed rooms. A restaurant with a modern menu, lounge bar and terrace over the river.

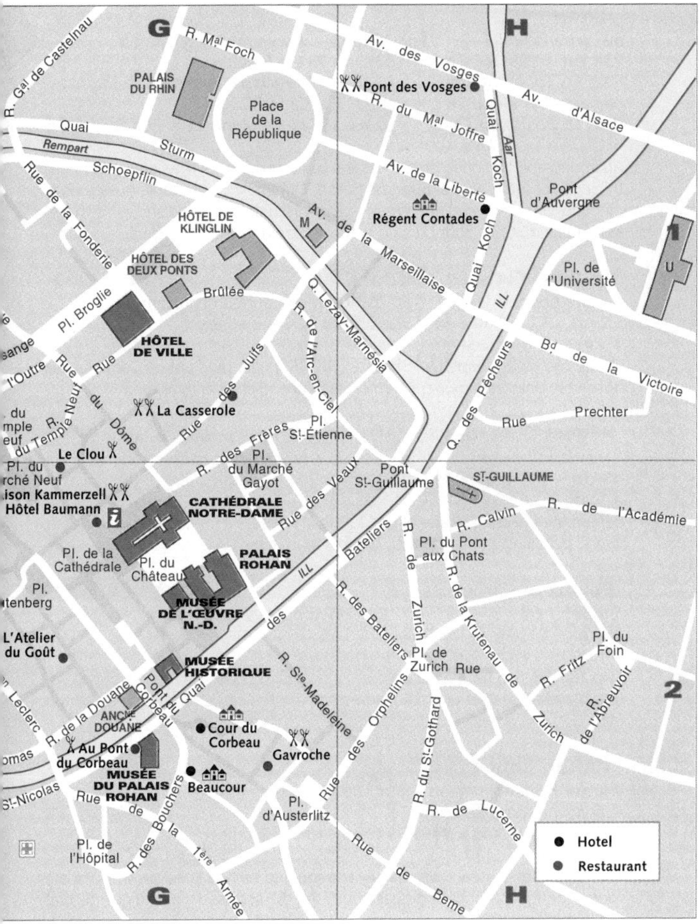

Sofitel

4 pl. St-Pierre-le-Jeune
– ✆ 03 88 15 49 00
– www.sofitel-strasbourg.com **F1**

151 rm – 🚹105/345 € 🚹🚹105/345 €, ☕ 23 € – 2 suites
Rest *Goh* – *✆ 03 88 15 49 10 (closed 3 weeks in August, 1 week in January, Saturday lunch, Sunday and Bank Holidays)* Menu 31 € bi/65 € – Carte 46/78 €

♦ Chain hotel ♦ Luxury ♦ Functional ♦

This hotel situated in a quiet area north of the cathedral combines space, contemporary decor and faultless upkeep. The rooms and bar are oases of calm. The Goh has an elegant decor and a "stammtisch" (regulars' table), where guests can enjoy local specialities with a modern twist.

Hilton

av. Herrenschmidt – ☎ 03 88 37 10 10 – www.strasbourg.hilton.fr
238 rm – †99/360 € ††99/360 €, ☐ 23 € – 5 suites *Plan I* **B1**
Rest *La Table du Chef* – ☎ *03 88 37 41 42 (closed July-August, Saturday and Sunday)* Menu 28 € (lunch)/34 € – Carte 33/58 €
Rest *Le Jardin du Tivoli* – ☎ *03 88 35 72 61* – Menu 31 € – Carte 30/48 €
♦ Chain hotel ♦ Business ♦
An impeccably designed glass and steel building opposite the Convention Centre, ideal for international business guests. Extremely comfortable guestrooms, meeting rooms, bar and numerous facilities. Traditional cuisine and a British feel at La Table du Chef. Buffet dining at the Le Jardin du Tivoli brasserie.

Cour du Corbeau without rest

6 r. des Couples – ☎ 03 90 00 26 26 – www.cour-corbeau.com
55 rm – †155/550 € ††155/550 €, ☐ 22 € – 2 suites **G2**
♦ Historic ♦ Design ♦ Personalised ♦
Occupying several superb old houses (16C-19C) near the Pont du Corbeau, this hotel combines very modern comfort with period architectural charm.

Régent Contades without rest

8 av. de la Liberté – ☎ 03 88 15 05 05 – www.regent-contades.com
45 rm – †110/525 € ††110/525 €, ☐ 20 € – 2 suites **H1**
♦ Luxury ♦ Historic ♦ Classic ♦
Behind the beautiful façade of this 19C townhouse is a refined, classical interior (wood panelling, paintings) with services to match.

Beaucour without rest

5 r. Bouchers – ☎ 03 88 76 72 00 – www.hotel-beaucour.com
49 rm – †110 € ††135/169 €, ☐ 14 € **G2**
♦ Family ♦ Classic ♦ Personalised ♦
Two 18C Alsatian houses built around a charming flower-filled patio. Very comfortable Alsatian-style or classic rooms, some with wooden beams, spa bathtub etc.

Maison Rouge without rest

4 r. des Francs-Bourgeois – ☎ 03 88 32 08 60
– www.maison-rouge.com **F2**
140 rm – †79/158 € ††95/174 €, ☐ 15 € – 2 suites
♦ Luxury ♦ Business ♦ Stylish ♦
Traditional hotel offering top-quality comfort and service. Spacious, immaculate rooms (designer fabrics, top-quality furnishings), accessed via landings decorated with objets d'art.

Le Grand Hôtel without rest

12 pl. de la Gare – ☎ 03 88 52 84 84 – www.le-grand-hotel.com
83 rm ☐ – †177/287 € ††177/287 € **E1**
♦ Business ♦ Design ♦
This hotel opposite the TGV station is definitely on a modern track with its minimalist contemporary decor, understated yet plush furnishings, and meticulously maintained amenities. Five minutes from the city centre.

Monopole-Métropole without rest

16 r. Kuhn – ☎ 03 88 14 39 14
– www.bw-monopole.com **E1**
86 rm ☐ – †85/200 € ††90/220 €
♦ Family ♦ Rustic ♦ Design ♦
A smart 19C building located between the train station and the historic Petite France district. Charming features include Alsatian antiques and paintings by great local artists. Traditional or more contemporary rooms.

Novotel Centre Halles

4 quai Kléber – ✆ 03 88 21 50 50 – www.novotel.com **F1**
96 rm – 107/222 € 107/222 €, 14 € **Rest** – Carte 20/40 €
♦ Chain hotel ♦ Modern ♦ Functional ♦
A hotel with bright, spacious rooms located in the Les Halles shopping centre. Gym on the top floor with a view of the cathedral. A simple, practical menu is on offer in this bar and restaurant which open on to the shopping centre.

Diana-Dauphine without rest

30 r. de la 1ère Armée – ✆ 03 88 36 26 61
– www.hotel-diana-dauphine.com
– Closed 22 December-2 January Plan I **B3**
45 rm – 90/150 € 90/170 €, 11 €
♦ Luxury ♦ Business ♦ Design ♦
Located on the tram line leading to the old quarter, this hotel has a modern lobby-cum-lounge and understated contemporary rooms, most of which are spacious. Locked garage accessible 24 hours a day.

Hannong without rest

15 r. du 22 Novembre – ✆ 03 88 32 16 22 – www.hotel-hannong.com
– Closed 2 to 9 January **F2**
72 rm – 65/184 € 75/222 €, 14 €
♦ Family ♦ Business ♦ Classic ♦
This hotel full of character is built on the site of the Hannong earthenware factory (18C). Objets d'art, contemporary facilities, quality materials and meticulous upkeep. Pleasant terrace area.

Du Dragon without rest

12 r. du Dragon – ✆ 03 88 35 79 80 – www.dragon.fr **F2**
32 rm – 79/116 € 89/129 €, 12 €
♦ Family ♦ Modern ♦ Design ♦
Two 17C houses built around a flower-filled patio garden (where breakfast is served in summer) in a quiet area of the city. Comfortable, modern rooms, built into the eaves on the top floor.

Mercure St-Jean without rest

3 r. Maire Kuss – ✆ 03 88 32 80 80 – www.mercure.com **E1**
61 rm – 79/165 € 79/175 €, 16 €
♦ Chain hotel ♦ Business ♦ Design ♦
Modern hotel with pleasant rooms offering contemporary comforts between the train station and old quarter. Try the "2030 room" for its imaginative and futuristic amenities.

Chut - Au Bain aux Plantes

4 r. Bain-aux-Plantes – ✆ 03 88 32 05 06 – www.hote-strasbourg.fr
8 rm – 75/95 € 95/160 €, 12 € – 1 suite **E2**
Rest – *(closed 1 to 10 May, 6 to 16 August, 30 October-8 November, 23 to 27 December, 2 to 6 January, 20 February-1 March, Sunday and Monday)* Menu 18 € (weekday lunch), 35/49 € bi – Carte 32/50 €
♦ Inn ♦ Luxury ♦ Personalised ♦
Hotel with all the charm of a guesthouse, located in a picturesque street near the historic Petite France district. Contemporary and antique decorative objects and furniture in a tranquil, minimalist atmosphere. The spice-infused cuisine changes daily. Intimate dining room with a courtyard terrace.

Le Kléber without rest

29 pl. Kléber – ✆ 03 88 32 09 53 – www.hotel-kleber.com **F1**
30 rm – 60/88 € 67/95 €, 8.50 €
♦ Family ♦ Personalised ♦ Cosy ♦
All the rooms here have a colourful, sweet and savoury theme (names include Meringue, Fraise and Cannelle). Unbeatable location on the famous Place Kléber.

Couvent du Franciscain without rest

18 r. du Fg de Pierre – ✆ 03 88 32 93 93 – www.hotel-franciscain.com – Closed 24 July-7 August **F1**

43 rm – †43/74 € ††78/84 €, ☕ 10 €

♦ Family ♦ Functional ♦ Retro ♦

This hotel on the site of an old convent at the end of a cul-de-sac offers simple, neat rooms at competitive rates. Breakfast is served in a winstub-style cellar with an amusing mural.

Au Crocodile

10 r. de l'Outre – ✆ 03 88 32 13 02 – www.au-crocodile.com – Closed 24 July-8 August, Sunday and Monday **F1**

Rest – Menu 35 € (weekday lunch), 69/138 € – Carte 101/196 €

Spec. Foie de canard poêlé, choucroute imaginaire. Cabillaud en viennoise, purée légère à la livèche. Forêt noire revisitée à notre façon.

♦ Classic ♦ Romantic ♦ Formal ♦

Although this restaurant changed hands in 2009, it has retained the famous crocodile brought back from the Egypt campaign by a military captain from Alsace. Elegant, refined decor and fine, classic cuisine.

Buerehiesel (Éric Westermann)

dans le parc de l'Orangerie – ✆ 03 88 45 56 65 – www.buerehiesel.com – Closed 1 to 22 August, 1 to 23 January, Sunday and Monday *Plan I* **D1**

Rest – Menu 33 € (weekday lunch), 65/88 € – Carte 52/85 €

Spec. Schniederspaetle et cuisses de grenouille poêlées au cerfeuil. Poulette pattes noires cuite entière comme un baeckeofe. Brioche caramélisée à la bière, glace à la bière et poire rôtie.

♦ Regional ♦ Formal ♦ Friendly ♦

An exquisite restaurant housed in a beautiful half-timbered 17C farmhouse that was dismantled from its original location and rebuilt in the Parc de l'Orangerie (bucolic views from the conservatory dining room and terrace). Refined and reliable regional cuisine, accompanied by a wonderful choice of Alsace wines. Pleasant service.

Maison des Tanneurs dite "Gerwerstub"

42 r. Bain aux Plantes – ✆ 03 88 32 79 70 – www.maison-des-tanneurs.com – Closed 26 July-8 August, 30 December-24 January, Sunday and Monday

Rest – Menu 20 € (weekday lunch)/26 € – Carte 30/50 € **F2**

♦ Terroir ♦ Elegant ♦ Friendly ♦

This typical Alsace house with lots of character (1572) overlooking the river Ill in the historic Petite France district is an institution for sauerkraut and other famous regional specialities.

La Cambuse (Babette Lefebvre)

1 r. des Dentelles – ✆ 03 88 22 10 22 – Closed 1 to 10 May, 1 to 23 August, 24 December-12 January, Sunday and Monday **F2**

Rest – *(number of covers limited, pre-book)* Carte 40/55 €

Spec. Œuf fermier au crabe et écrevisses. Lotte aux shiitakés et coriandre. Tarte au chocolat amer, crème à la noix de coco.

♦ Fish ♦ Cosy ♦ Intimate ♦

La Cambuse's intimate dining room is decorated in the style of a boat cabin. Simple yet refined fish and seafood are the specialities here, prepared in a fusion of French and Asian styles based around spices and a minimum of cooking time.

XX

L'Atable 77

77 Grand'Rue – ✆ 03 88 32 23 37 – www.latable77.com – Closed 22 April-2 May, 31 July-21 August, 1 to 10 January, Sunday, Monday and Bank Holiday lunch **F2**

Rest – Menu 33/85 € bi

♦ Contemporary ♦ Cosy ♦ Design ♦

An attractive, trendy restaurant with a resolutely contemporary feel throughout. Sleek decor dotted with bright paintings, designer tableware and very appetising modern cuisine.

XX

Le Violon d'Ingres

1 r. Chevalier Robert (at La Robertsau) – ✆ 03 88 31 39 50 – www.violondingres.com – Closed 25 April-5 mai, 15 to 29 August, 2 to 10 January, Saturday lunch, Sunday dinner and Monday

Rest – Menu 29/65 € – Carte 52/62 €

♦ A la mode ♦ Elegant ♦

This historic Alsace house in the Robertsau district near the European Parliament serves impeccably prepared modern cuisine in an elegant dining room or on the shady terrace.

XX

Maison Kammerzell et Hôtel Baumann with rm

16 pl. de la Cathédrale – ✆ 03 88 32 42 14 – www.maison-kammerzell.com **G2**

9 rm – †110 € ††135 €, ☕ 10 € **Rest** – Menu 27/46 € – Carte 28/64 €

♦ Terroir ♦ Inn ♦

A typical 16C Strasbourg house near the cathedral with an authentic medieval feel, featuring stained-glass windows, paintings, wood carvings and Gothic vaulting. Local cuisine (sauerkraut is a speciality) and brasserie-style dishes. Plainly decorated rooms.

XX ✿

La Casserole (Éric Girardin)

24 r. des Juifs – ✆ 03 88 36 49 68 – www.restaurantlacasserole.fr – Closed 22 April-2 Mai, 31 July-17 August, 24 December-2 January, Saturday lunch, Sunday, Monday and Bank Holiday lunch **G1**

Rest – *(number of covers limited, pre-book)* Menu 39 € (lunch), 60/80 € – Carte 66/83 €

Spec. Langoustines juste saisies, carpaccio de fenouil, agrume (autumn-winter). Carré d'agneau cuit au four, polenta moelleuse aux olives noires. Vanille de Madagascar en crème légère et onctueuse.

♦ Innovative ♦ Neighbourhood ♦ Formal ♦

A magical restaurant behind the cathedral where Éric Girardin creates refined, harmonious dishes with striking skill. A hushed, contemporary setting and charming service.

XX

Gavroche

4 r. Klein – ✆ 03 88 36 82 89 – www.restaurant-gavroche.com – Closed 25 July-16 August, 24 December-3 January, Saturday and Sunday

Rest – Menu 38/56 € – Carte 59/81 € **G2**

♦ A la mode ♦ Elegant ♦

There's little fanfare in this restaurant offering a pleasant welcome and elegant, contemporary decor. Beautifully presented modern and creative cuisine influenced by seasonal produce.

XX ✿

Umami (René Fieger)

8 r. des Dentelles – ✆ 03 88 32 80 53 – www.restaurant-umami.com – Closed 24 April-1 May, 28 August-18 September, 31 December-12 January, Sunday and lunch except Saturday **F2**

Rest – *(number of covers limited, pre-book)* Menu 45/60 €

Spec. Menu du marché.

♦ Innovative ♦ Cosy ♦

Sweet, salty, sour, bitter and... "umami" (savoury), the fifth taste in Japanese cuisine and the hallmark of the cuisine here, which showcases flavours from around the world. Attractive modern decor.

Pont des Vosges

15 quai Koch – ✆ 03 88 36 47 75
– Closed Sunday **H1**
Rest – Carte 30/55 €
◆ Brasserie ◆ Retro ◆ Friendly ◆
Located on the corner of an old building, this brasserie is renowned for its copious, traditional cuisine. Advertising posters and mirrors decorate the dining room.

L'Atelier du Goût

17 r. des Tonneliers – ✆ 03 88 21 01 01 – www.atelier-du-gout.fr
– Closed 1 week February Holidays, 2 weeks in August, Sunday and Bank Holidays **G2**
Rest – Menu 29 € (weekday lunch)/36 € – Carte 40/48 €
◆ Contemporary ◆ Trendy ◆ Design ◆
A colourful designer decor sets the scene in this former winstub, turned into a laid-back restaurant devoted to good food. Appetising dishes made with organic and seasonal produce.

WINSTUBS *Regional specialities and wine tasting in a typical Alsatian atmosphere*

L'Ami Schutz

1 Ponts Couverts – ✆ 03 88 32 76 98 – www.ami-schutz.com
– Closed 23 December-12 January **E2**
Rest – Menu 27/42 € – Carte 28/55 €
◆ Alsatian cuisine ◆ Rustic ◆ Friendly ◆
L'Ami Schutz enjoys a timeless setting on the river Ill in the historic Petite France district. Delightful shady terrace and two typical dining rooms (one rustic, the other more refined) with a menu to match.

Le Clou

3 r. Chaudron – ✆ 03 88 32 11 67 – www.le-clou.com
– Closed Wednesday lunch, Sunday and Bank Holidays **G1-2**
Rest – *(pre-book)* Menu 19 € (weekday lunch) – Carte 26/55 €
◆ Alsatian cuisine ◆ Rustic ◆ Friendly ◆
Located a short distance from the cathedral, this authentic winstub (typical Alsace bistro) is packed with olde worlde objects and scenes from yesteryear (beautiful marquetry). Typical cuisine which pays homage to the region.

Fink'Stuebel with rm

26 r. Finkwiller – ✆ 03 88 25 07 57 – http://finkstuebel.free.fr
– Closed 9 to 30 August, Sunday and Monday **F2**
5 rm – †68 € ††68 €, ☐ 9 €
Rest – Menu 10 € – Carte 30/55 €
◆ Alsatian cuisine ◆ Family ◆ Inn ◆
Half-timbering, wooden floorboards, painted woodwork, regional furniture and floral tablecloths provide the decor in the Fink'Stuebel, the epitome of a traditional winstub. Local cuisine predominates here, of course, with foie gras to the fore. This establishment offers recently refurbished and well-appointed guestrooms decorated in Alsatian-style.

Au Pont du Corbeau

21 quai St-Nicolas – ✆ 03 88 35 60 68
– Closed 3 weeks in August, 1 week February Holidays, Sunday lunch and Saturday except in December **G2**
Rest – Carte 24/38 €
◆ Alsatian cuisine ◆ Rustic ◆ Inn ◆
Experience local gastronomic specialities and traditional decor (Renaissance features, posters) in this restaurant next door to the Musée Alsacien, with its displays of popular art.

TOULOUSE

TOULOUSE

Population (est. 2010): 439 453 (conurbation 761 090) – Altitude: 146m

udiuk/Fotolia.com

The first thing you notice about Toulouse is its pink buildings, leaving you in little doubt as to why France's fourth biggest city has the enchanting epithet 'La Ville Rose'. The rouge shade of brickwork lends the place a distinctly sunny charm, enhanced by a lovely old town infused with sixteenth century merchant houses and grand Romanesque churches.

It's here that the Toulousains throng, particularly at dusk when the town's bars and cafes are bathed in a sumptuous rosy glow. This is a confident, easy-going city whose rich architectural heritage is matched by an intellectual verve: its 115,000 students make it second only to Paris as a French university centre. You wouldn't think it to be sitting at a sunny bar with an Armagnac, but Toulouse is also at the heart of the European aerospace industry, and it's on the outskirts here that the space shuttle programme is based. Pre-eminence has come the way of this city before. From the tenth to the thirteenth centuries, the Counts of Toulouse ran a resplendent court populated by troubadours and poets whose works inspired the likes of Dante and Chaucer. Then in the sixteenth century, it flourished again through the cultivation of woad, and newly enriched merchants built the most magnificent town houses - ***hotels particuliers*** -which make up one of the best reasons to wander the streets on a sunny day.

LIVING THE CITY

Toulouse sits handsomely midway between the Mediterranean and the Atlantic. The visitor-friendly old town is bounded to the east by the Canal du Midi and to the west by the gently curving River Garonne. This charming area is even more tightly hemmed in by a ring of nineteenth-century boulevards (d'Arcole, Strasbourg, Lazare Carnot, Verdier and Jules Guesde). A sharply defined 'cross' of streets cuts the centre into four quarters (Rue d'Alsace Lorraine/Rue du Languedoc running north/south; Rue de Metz east/west). Over the river three kilometres to the northwest is Toulouse Blagnac airport, while the same distance southeast is the huge Cité de l'Espace centre.

PRACTICAL INFORMATION

ARRIVAL-DEPARTURE

Toulouse-Blagnac Airport is located 7km west of the city centre. The Express bus takes 20min while a taxi will cost about €27. High speed trains to Paris go from Gare Matabiau.

TRANSPORT

Toulouse offers a bus and metro system to get you around town. A one-trip red ticket allows you to travel anywhere on the network for an hour. There's a slightly more expensive round trip ticket, plus a Day ticket and 10-12 trip tickets.

The main railway station is situated in a picturesque setting by the Canal du Midi. It's a short five minute hop on the metro to the old town centre, but if you're not weighed down by luggage it's a pleasant twenty minute stroll over the canal on foot. On your walk into town, just before the central Place du Capitole, you'll find the main tourist office on the square Charles-de-Gaulle.

EXPLORING TOULOUSE

"Pink at dawn, red at noon and purple at dusk." How many cities can you say that about? At around the time of the colour purple, particularly in the summertime, you'll hear the sound of screeching chairs as everyone grabs a table at the bars around the capacious **Place du Capitole**, and waits for the daily free light show. As the sun sets, the long, neoclassical facade of the city hall begins to glow. At first it's a soft blush, then a warm fiery light, as the sun works on the golden balconies of its eighteenth century, rose-coloured frontage. All this, and dinner too.

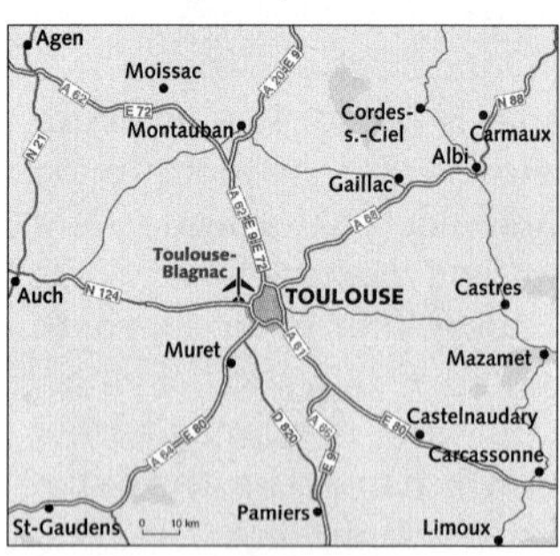

You don't have to go far to find another great treasure of old Toulouse. Just to the north of Capitole is **St-Sernin**, the largest Romanesque basilica in Europe and considered the finest in France. It was begun in 1080 as a stopping point for pilgrims on their way to Santiago de Compostela, and took another three centuries to complete. Nearly a thousand years after the first brick was laid it still has the power to knock you back in your stride. Its octagonal belfry is a masterpiece of its kind, while its cavernous, pale pink interior is full of soaring arches, and there's an array of ancient relics in the crypt. If St-Sernin is the towering landmark here, it's not the only church to impress. As the medieval streets spill out in a rich patchwork southwest of the basilica, you come across **Les Jacobins** on Rue Lakanal. A great Gothic pile built in the thirteenth century, it boasts elegant vaulting ribs like sprouting palm fronds, and lovingly maintained cloisters full of quiet, atmospheric splendour; beneath the altar lie the remains of the philosopher St Thomas Aquinas. Down Rue Gambetta from here is the baroque **Notre-Dame-de-la-Daurade**, whose dark and brooding interior is watched over by a black Madonna.

→ PARTICULIER-LY FINE

When the visitor's eye hasn't been taken by one of the churches, there's a good chance it's seized on the delights of a ***hôtel particulier***. These are the superb Renaissance town houses and mansions which were built by the city's merchants from the wealth of the woad trade. Nearly all are built of red Toulousain brick, decorated with costly stone (brought over from the Pyrenees) in the form of ornate doorways, vaulted cloisters, statues, turrets and pillars. Most are closed, but you can peek at many by strolling casually into courtyards; particularly good is the elaborate **Hôtel de Bernuy** with its fine stone-galleried courtyard on Rue Gambetta. But the pick of les *particuliers* is **Hôtel d'Assezat**, on Rue de Metz, not least because it's open to the public. It's a superb twenty eight metre high building of brick and stone, enhanced by classic columns and a tower with octagonal lantern. Thanks to its Bemberg collection, there's a great assortment of artwork on view, including a roomful of Bonnards, and works by Monet, Canaletto, Dufy and Cranach the Elder. Eclectic is the word!

→ SCULPTURE, SPACE – AND A SLAUGHTERHOUSE

In keeping with its venerable surroundings, Toulouse's old town offers up a museum dedicated to the distant past. Musée des Augustins is itself a nineteenth-century building based round the cloisters of an Augustinian priory. Inside, the wonderful collections of Romanesque and medieval sculpture bring alive the fashions of the day; these are 'fleshed out' by sixteenth to nineteenth century European paintings. For the shock of the new, you have to head over the Garonne to the left bank and a mighty brick-built former nineteenth-century slaughterhouse – Les Abattoirs, opened in 2000 – which dives head first into the world of modern art from the 1950s onwards. It includes the head-turning La Depouille du Minotaure by Picasso – a stage curtain from 1936 (okay, not everything here is post-50s). Toulouse's up-to-the-minute face, however, is found in the southeastern suburbs at Cité de l'Espace, the science park that leaves earth to deal with all things galactic. This is the place to come if you want to dock your virtual capsule on a space station, or find out about weightlessness, satellite communications and planetary movements. You can also walk inside a mock-up of the Mir space station (but the bus back to Place du Capitole may seem a bit mundane afterwards).

→ KEEPING WATCH

Back on the old town's reassuring 'terra firma', fine detail appears in every nook and cranny; for somewhere apparently timeless, there's a fascination with the hours of the day, whether it's via the charming twenty-four hour clock on the face of an eighteenth-century townhouse, or in the absorbing **Musee Paul-Dupuy** (south of Capitole), which has an elegantly displayed collection of clocks and watches. All round this part of town are narrow lanes and pretty streets; the prettiest **is Rue Croix-Baragnon**, with its galleries and designer boutiques renowned for their chic interiors. Stroll about here to pick up interesting art and antiques or funky, bohemian one-offs. And when you've had your fill of street life, you'll be pleased to know that this is also the area where the city's best green spots are to be found. You can take your pick from either the enchanting formal gardens of the **Grand-Rond**, or the slightly larger and equally beguiling **Jardin des Plantes.**

→ MARKET FRESH

This is a city that makes the most of the outdoor life, and that includes its markets. The Place du Capitole is the place to be on a Wednesday, when a huge market sells food, clothes and bric-à-brac. And twice a week, they bring out the organic food, too: hang around and you'll be able to try all manner of breads, cheeses and cakes before you delve in your pocket for cash. Up at the Basilica St-Sernin on a Sunday, the antiques and bric-à-brac market is way too good to just call a flea-market – this is the place for gilded mirrors and chandeliers, so better keep some extra space in your rucksack. Market or not, the little squares dotted all over town are always humming with life, be it unicyclists or accordionists, roller-bladers or skateboarders. Or maybe just students. There are 115,000 of them here, not just adding to the weight of grey matter within the city walls, but, even more crucially if you're visiting, helping keep the prices down in the cafés and bars.

CALENDAR HIGHLIGHTS

La Ville Rose views its festivals and events through violet-tinted spectacles, even in the gloom of February, when it hosts the International Violet Meeting. Toulouse is the world capital of violets, and this celebration of the city's favourite flower includes exhibitions, markets, and various flower-based attractions. A month later, the Parc des Expositions de Toulouse is the venue for the Toulouse International Fair, when 150,000 visitors congregate for exhibitions and activities based around an international theme. In June, the action moves down to the river. The Garonne Festival livens up the banksides with art happenings, music and parades, while also that month the Electronic Siestas Festival brings free afternoon concerts to the Garonne: it's innovative music to snooze-in-the-sun by. Toulouse is a cultural hothouse, and

TOULOUSE IN...

→ ONE DAY

Place du Capitole, St-Sernin, Les Jacobins, Hôtel d'Assezat, dusk back at Capitole

→ TWO DAYS

Musée des Augustins, Les Abattoirs (or Cité de l'Espace), the streets around rue Croix-Baragnon, a stroll along the banks of the Canal du Midi (or the Garonne)

→ THREE DAYS

Jardin des Plantes, Musée Paul-Dupuy, a boisterous market (if Sunday, at St-Sernin)

the Marathon des Mots, also in June, celebrates the written word, with more than three hundred writers and artists taking part in a series of readings and performances at more than forty venues. There's an eclectic air about the Toulouse d'Éte Music Festival in July and August. International names rub shoulders with local musicians in a wide range of concerts at venues across the city, and the music ranges from flamenco to jazz to piano recital. Fans of the latter will be in seventh heaven, because September sees the Piano Aux Jacobins Festival, at the Church of the Jacobins, an atmospheric occasion with recitals by some of the world's best pianists in the cloisters of the ancient church. A huge contemporary art showpiece dominates the end of September and October: Printemps de Septembre is a free exhibition covering many artistic genres that takes place all over the city with special street lighting to enhance the effect. Alongside runs the Festival Occitania (also September) with more than fifty cultural events covering film, music, poetry, theatre, painting and more besides. To top it all off, November's Toulouse Antiques Fair, at the Parc des Expositions, has been voted France's premier event in its category by the trade press, so expect three impressive displays: Prestige, Antiques and Arts and Crafts.

EATING OUT

The food of the Toulousain is not for the faint-hearted. A lot of the city's favoured dishes concentrate on the parts of animals many prefer to forget. Neck, brain, ears and liver find their way onto the menu stuffed, slow-cooked or in eye-popping combinations. At the smart restaurants, it's possible to order the likes of pigeon stuffed with langoustines or foie gras with spiced fruits. Traditionally, the mainstay of the southwest is the cassoulet, a hearty stew with basic ingredients such as pork, duck fat, beans and garlic. You need to be hungry to take it on, so you'll be pleased to know that proper evening dining in Toulouse doesn't really start till at least 8.30 or 9 in the evening when your appetite should be well and truly whetted. Get there earlier and you'll be dining alone. This is a city that lives the late life: it's only sixty miles from the Spanish border, and its dining style is cheerily overseen as 'la mode espagnole'. There's a third element to the food scene here: wander down some of the narrower streets in the evening and you'll realise how close you are to North Africa. Exotic scents waft from darkened doorways and Moroccan restaurants – lots of them – tempt you inside. Wherever you decide to eat, the bill includes a service charge, but if you're happy with the service, it's usual to leave a tip of between five and ten per cent. And remember, if you've been excited by a particular ingredient then stock up at the farmers' markets that are popular in the city: these are the places for foie gras, sausages, creamy wads of goats' cheese, and bread the size of local rugby balls.

→ TOULOUSE L'EAU-TREK

If you get the chance, come into the city by the Canal du Midi. It's lined with plane trees and fine nineteenth-century houses, and winds its calm way up from the Mediterranean. The most atmospheric way to see it is by cycling, walking or just floating along its seductive course on a slow boat.

→ BIG ON OPERA

The city hall in the Place du Capitole is so big because it also contains Toulouse's main musical venue, the Opera House. This is a refurbished eighteenth century gem, with opulent gilt mouldings and painted cartouches. It's one of France's most prestigious homes of opera, but get along to see ballet, chamber music and recitals as well.

Environs of Toulouse *(Plan I)*

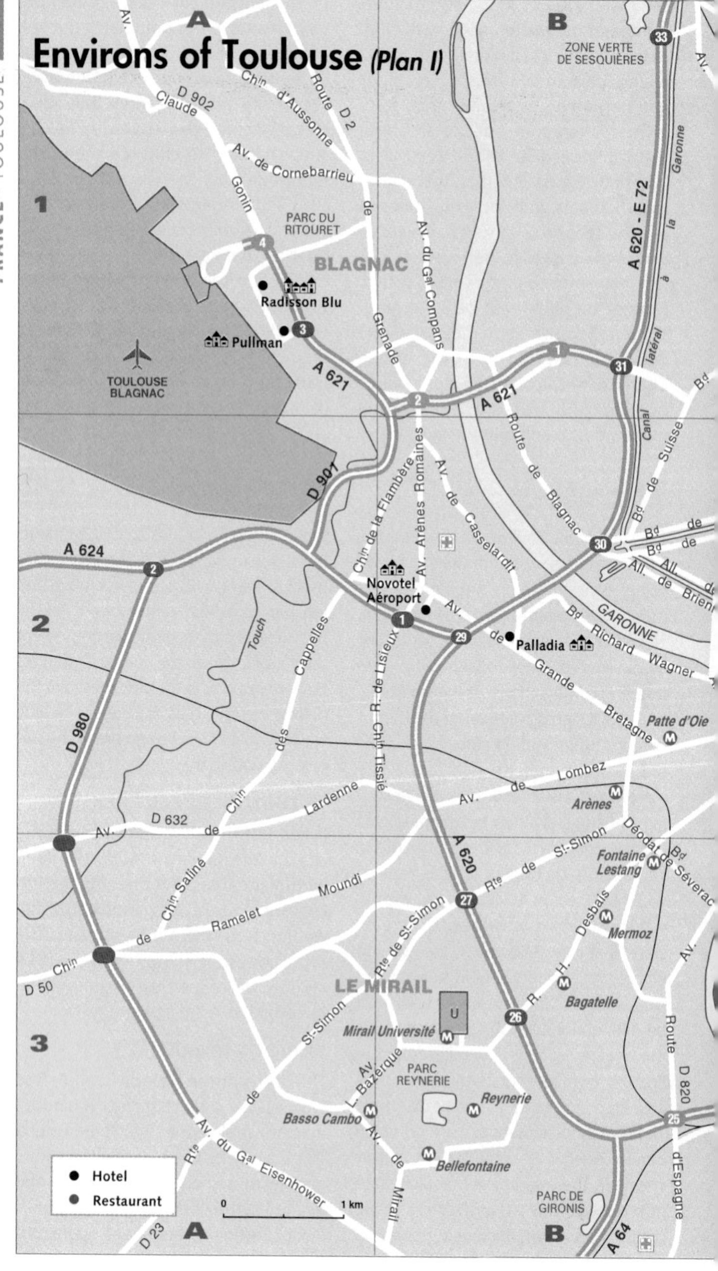

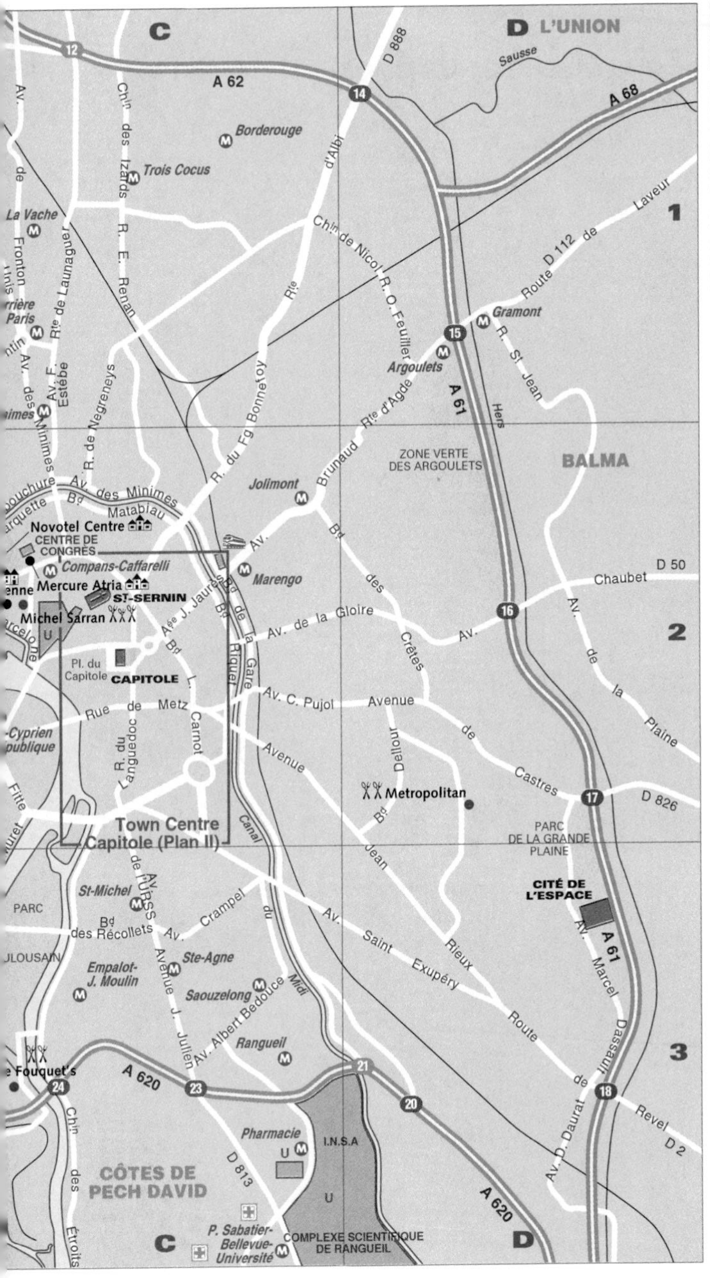
C
D
L'UNION
A 62
A 68
A 61
A 620
D 888
Sausse
Borderouge
Trois Cocus
La Vache
Gramont
Argoulets
Jolimont
Marengo
Compans-Caffarelli
Novotel Centre
CENTRE DE CONGRÈS
Mercure Atria
ST-SERNIN
Michel Sarran
Pl. du Capitole
CAPITOLE
ZONE VERTE DES ARGOULETS
BALMA
D 50
Chaubet
Av. de la Gloire
Av. C. Pujol
Avenue de Castres
Rue de Metz
Metropolitan
D 826
PARC DE LA GRANDE PLAINE
CITÉ DE L'ESPACE
Town Centre Capitole (Plan II)
St-Michel
Bd des Récollets
Ste-Agne
Empalot-J. Moulin
Saouzelong
Rangueil
Av. Saint Exupéry
Route de Revel
D 2
Fouquet's
Pharmacie
I.N.S.A
CÔTES DE PECH DAVID
D 813
P. Sabatier-Bellevue-Université
COMPLEXE SCIENTIFIQUE DE RANGUEIL
1
2
3

Town Centre, Capitole
(Plan II)

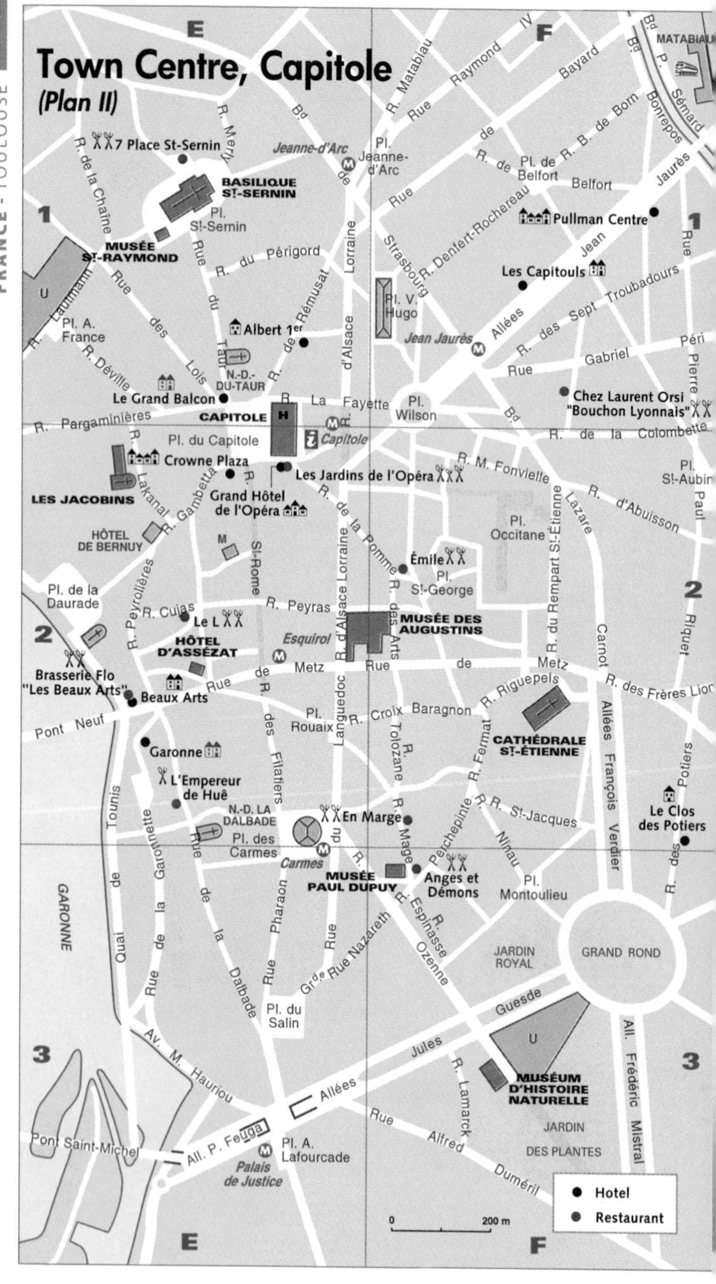

Pullman Centre

84 allées Jean Jaurès – ✆ 05 61 10 23 10 – www.pullmanhotels.com
119 rm – †185/240 € ††185/240 €, ☕ 22 € – 6 suites **F1**
Rest *S W Café* – *✆ 05 61 10 23 40 (closed Saturday lunch and Sunday lunch)* Menu 23 € (weekday dinner) – Carte 28/48 €
♦ Luxury ♦ Chain hotel ♦ Design ♦
The Pullman Centre was completely renovated in 2009 in a more contemporary style. It features refined guestrooms and high-tech equipment (business centre and fitness room). S W Café has a minimalist decor and a menu that favours regional produce and spices from around the world.

Crowne Plaza

7 pl. du Capitole – ✆ 05 61 61 19 19 – www.crowne-plaza-toulouse.com
162 rm – †120/295 € ††135/310 €, ☕ 23 € – 3 suites **E2**
Rest – *(closed August)* Menu 21 € (lunch), 26/45 € – Carte 37/63 €
♦ Business ♦ Chain hotel ♦ Classic ♦
This hotel plus business centre enjoys a prestigious location on the Place du Capitole. Spacious, well-equipped rooms, some of which overlook the town hall. The restaurant opens onto a delightful Florentine-inspired patio.

Grand Hôtel de l'Opéra without rest

1 pl. du Capitole – ✆ 05 61 21 82 66
– www.grand-hotel-opera.com **E2**
49 rm – †120/490 € ††150/490 €, ☕ 20 €
♦ Luxury ♦ Cosy ♦ Stylish ♦
This hotel in a 17C convent has an air of serenity and charm. It features beautiful rooms with wood panels and velvet furnishings. Pleasant lounge-bar and attractive lobby.

Mercure Atria

8 espl. Compans Caffarelli – ✆ 05 61 11 09 09 – www.mercure.com
136 rm – †80/190 € ††90/205 €, ☕ 16 € – 2 suites *Plan I* **C2**
Rest – *(closed 1 to 21 August)* Carte 25/40 €
♦ Chain hotel ♦ Modern ♦
This modern building with a striking glass façade is situated near the Palais des Congrès. It boasts comfortable guestrooms decorated according to an operatic theme. Modern cuisine served in a contemporary, bistro-style restaurant.

Novotel Centre

5 pl. A. Jourdain – ✆ 05 61 21 74 74 – www.novotel.com *Plan I* **C2**
135 rm – †80/195 € ††80/195 €, ☕ 14 € – 2 suites **Rest** – Carte 25/47 €
♦ Chain hotel ♦ Modern ♦ Functional ♦
This hotel situated in a residential part of the city centre has spacious rooms furnished in the typical style of the chain. Japanese garden and park nearby. The restaurant overlooking the hotel swimming pool specialises in traditional cuisine.

Le Grand Balcon without rest

10 r. Romiguière – ✆ 05 34 25 44 09 – www.grandbalconhotel.com
47 rm – †160/190 € ††160/390 €, ☕ 20 € **E1**
♦ Luxury ♦ Design ♦
The hotel once used by the Aéropostale pilots has just reopened, celebrating its former guests in its imaginative contemporary design. Room n° 32 is a reproduction of Saint Exupéry's old room.

Garonne without rest

22 descente de la Halle-aux-Poissons – ✆ 05 34 31 94 80
– www.hotelgaronne.com **E2**
14 rm – †95/230 € ††95/230 €, ☕ 19 €
♦ Luxury ♦ Personalised ♦
An old building in one of the Old Town's narrow streets. A fine contemporary interior: stained-oak parquet flooring, design furniture, silk draperies and the odd Japanese touch.

Des Beaux Arts without rest

1 pl. du Pont-Neuf – ✆ 05 34 45 42 42 – www.hoteldesbeauxarts.com
19 rm – †110/250 € ††110/250 €, ☕ 14 € **E2**

◆ Business ◆ Modern ◆ Cosy ◆

This tastefully furnished 18C house has cosy, elegant rooms, most with a view of the Garonne. N° 42 enjoys the additional benefit of a mini-terrace.

De Brienne without rest

20 bd du Mar.-Leclerc – ✆ 05 61 23 60 60 – www.hoteldebrienne.com
70 rm – †75/100 € ††85/110 €, ☕ 11 € – 1 suite *Plan I* **C2**

◆ Chain hotel ◆ Classic ◆ Functional ◆

This hotel near the city centre offers simply decorated, functional guestrooms; the quieter rooms are to the rear. Free parking and pleasant lounge area.

Les Capitouls without rest

29 allées Jean-Jaurès – ✆ 05 34 41 31 21
– www.bestwestern-capitouls.com **F1**
55 rm – †110/181 € ††110/181 €, ☕ 15 € – 2 suites

◆ Chain hotel ◆ Classic ◆

This attractive old townhouse in the city centre has a distinctive foyer with pink brick vaulting. Comfortable, functional guestrooms.

Le Clos des Potiers without rest

12 r. des Potiers – ✆ 05 61 47 15 15 – www.le-clos-des-potiers.com
9 rm – †100/220 € ††100/220 €, ☕ 13 € **F2**

◆ Family ◆ Personalised ◆

This townhouse in a quiet street near the city centre is full of charm. The guestrooms are decorated in a classic style. It is a cosy address, halfway between a hotel and a bed and breakfast.

Albert 1er without rest

8 r. Rivals – ✆ 05 61 21 17 91 – www.hotel-albert1.com **E1**
47 rm – †55/109 € ††65/119 €, ☕ 10 €

◆ Family ◆ Functional ◆

This family-run hotel is an ideal base for discovering the 'ville rose' on foot. The well-appointed, functional guestrooms are gradually being refurbished; the quieter rooms are to the rear.

Michel Sarran

21 bd A. Duportal – ✆ 05 61 12 32 32 – www.michel-sarran.com
– Closed August, 20 to 28 December, Wednesday lunch, Saturday and Sunday *Plan I* **C2**

Rest – *(pre-book)* Menu 44 € bi (lunch), 98/165 € bi – Carte 95/135 €

Spec. Foie gras en éclair pâtissier à la feuille d'or et éclats de noisette. Pigeon du Mont Royal, suprêmes frits en kadaïf et jus à l'encre, abattis en croquette. Pommes granny en compote et mousseux, glace blanche à la cannelle, soufflé "pomme d'Amour".

◆ Innovative ◆ Intimate ◆ Fashionable ◆

This delightful 19C residence, with its friendly atmosphere and plain modern decor, offers delicious inventive cuisine. Attractive Italian-style terrace for summer dining.

Les Jardins de l'Opéra

1 pl. du Capitole – ✆ 05 61 23 07 76 – www.lesjardinsdelopera.com
– Closed Bank Holiday lunch, Sunday and Monday **E2**

Rest – Menu 29/99 € – Carte 54/88 €

◆ Inventive ◆ Luxury ◆ Formal ◆

Elegant dining room under a glass roof that provides a pool of light. The inventive, contemporary cuisine focuses on quality ingredients. Flower-decked inner courtyard.

XX ✿

En Marge (Frank Renimel)

8 r. Mage – ✆ 05 61 53 07 24 – www.restaurantenmarge.com
– Closed 4 to 10 May, 13 July-10 August, Sunday, Monday and Tuesday
Rest – *(number of covers limited, pre-book)* Menu 60/120 € **F2**
Spec. Tartare de Saint-Jacques, crème de potimarron, émulsion à la truffe (November-March). Suprême de pigeon rôti, tatin de céleri, jus de viande au caviar citron (March-April). Cigare au rhum et à la feuille de tabac.
♦ Innovative ♦ Friendly ♦ Family ♦
Friendly atmosphere, attentive service and delicious, innovative cuisine. There is a limited number of tables to a backdrop of modern decor with a hint of Baroque.

XX ✿

Metropolitan

2 pl. Auguste-Albert – ✆ 05 61 34 63 11 – www.metropolitan-restaurant.fr
– Closed 1 to 15 August, Saturday lunch, Sunday and Monday *Plan I* **D2**
Rest – Menu 39 € (weekdays), 64/92 € – Carte 76/100 €
Spec. Canneloni de tourteau et ananas à la coriandre. Volaille fermière et homard au vin jaune, fricassée de légumes d'été (June-July.). Barre glacée au chocolat ivoire et violette, cristalline et sirop de violette.
♦ A la mode ♦ Design ♦
This fashionable restaurant is near the Cité de l'Espace. It gets full marks for its delicious, contemporary cuisine, designer-style dining room and friendly service.

XX

Le L

24 pl. de la Bourse – ✆ 05 61 21 69 05 – www.restaurantlel.com
– Closed 5 to 25 August, Sunday and Monday **E2**
Rest – Menu 48 € (dinner)/89 € – Carte 25/40 €
♦ Innovative ♦ Fashionable ♦
This contemporary restaurant is in the heart of the old town. It features a regularly renewed creative menu of Asian inspiration, more elaborate in the evenings. Summer terrace.

XX

Anges et Démons

1 r. Perchepinte – ✆ 05 61 52 66 69 – www.restaurant-angesetdemons.com
– Closed Sunday dinner, Monday and lunch except Sunday **F3**
Rest – Menu 40/55 €
♦ A la mode ♦ Cosy ♦
This engaging restaurant in the old town has an original concept – the price of the main dish chosen determines the price of the full menu. Cosy dining rooms with 16C vaults in the cellar.

XX

Le Fouquet's

18 chemin de la Loge – ✆ 05 61 33 37 77 – www.lucienbarriere.com
Rest – Menu 32 € bi (lunch)/34 € – Carte 33/68 € **C3**
♦ A la mode ♦ Brasserie ♦
Fouquet's most recent restaurant is situated on an island on the Garonne river. It serves contemporary cuisine amid a decor of gold leaf, discreet lighting and old photos.

XX

7 Place St-Sernin

7 pl. St-Sernin – ✆ 05 62 30 05 30 – www.7placesaintsernin.com
– Closed 1 to 15 August, 1 week in December, Saturday lunch and Sunday
Rest – Menu 22 € bi (lunch), 28/55 € bi – Carte 53/82 € **E1**
♦ A la mode ♦ Fashionable ♦
This elegant restaurant occupies a typical Toulouse-style house with contemporary paintings on the walls. The cuisine, traditional with a modern twist, matches the setting. Terrace facing the St Sernin basilica.

XX

Brasserie Flo "Les Beaux Arts"

1 quai Daurade – ✆ 05 61 21 12 12 – www.brasserielesbeauxarts.com
Rest – Menu 23/38 € – Carte 27/56 € **E2**
♦ Brasserie ♦ Retro ♦ Brasserie ♦
Popular with locals, this brasserie on the banks of the Garonne was once frequented by Ingres, Matisse and Bourdelle. Retro decor and a varied menu.

Chez Laurent Orsi "Bouchon Lyonnais"

13 r. de l'Industrie – ☎ 05 61 62 97 43 – www.le-bouchon-lyonnais.com **F1**

Rest – Menu 22/37 € – Carte approx. 38 €

♦ Bistro ♦ Retro ♦ Brasserie ♦

A large bistro whose leather banquettes, closely packed tables and mirrors create an attractive, old-fashioned atmosphere. Dishes from southwest France and Lyon, as well as fish and seafood.

Émile

13 pl. St-Georges – ☎ 05 61 21 05 56 – www.restaurant-emile.com – Closed 21 December-10 January, Monday except dinner May-September and Sunday **F2**

Rest – Menu 20 € (lunch), 30/55 € – Carte 39/61 €

♦ Terroir ♦ Friendly ♦

A restaurant with a popular terrace and a menu focused on local dishes and fish (cassoulet is the house speciality). Fine wine list.

L'Empereur de Huê

17 r. des Couteliers – ☎ 05 61 53 55 72 – www.empereurdehue.com – Closed lunch, Sunday and Monday **E2**

Rest – *(pre-book)* Menu 37 € (weekdays) – Carte 47/54 €

♦ Vietnamese ♦ Design ♦ Minimalist ♦

The talented chef combines carefully selected products and aromatic herbs to create fine cuisine in this Vietnamese culinary outpost with a resolutely contemporary feel.

AROUND TOULOUSE

Blagnac

Radisson Blu

2 r. Dieudonné-Costes – ☎ 05 61 16 18 00 – www.toulouse.radissonblu.com

200 rm – †120/300 € ††120/300 € **A1**

Rest – Menu 20 € (weekday lunch)/27 € – Carte 30/45 €

♦ Chain hotel ♦ Business ♦ Design ♦

A stone's throw from the airport, this contemporary hotel has a striking façade adorned with multicoloured transparent shutters. The modern theme continues in the guestrooms. This restaurant with large picture windows serves contemporary-style cuisine. Covered terrace and patio.

Pullman

2 av. Didier Daurat (direction airport, exit 3) – ☎ 05 34 56 11 11 – www.pullmanhotels.com **A1**

100 rm – †95/335 € ††95/335 €, 22 €

Rest *Le Corridor* – *(closed 24 July-21 August, Friday dinner, Saturday, Sunday and Bank Holidays)* Menu 30 € – Carte 42/74 €

♦ Chain hotel ♦ Business ♦ Modern ♦

Don't be fooled by the 1970s architecture of this hotel. Inside it boasts trendy public areas and contemporary-style guestrooms in tones of red and aubergine. Tapas-type snacks served at the bar and more traditional menu in the dining room.

Purpan

Palladia

271 av. de Grande Bretagne – ☎ 05 62 12 01 20 – www.hotelpalladia.com

90 rm – †99/260 € ††99/260 €, 18 € – 1 suite **B2**

Rest – *(closed Sunday and Bank Holidays)* Menu 28/59 € bi – Carte 39/74 €

♦ Business ♦ Modern ♦

An imposing building with a glass and concrete façade, whose location between the airport and city centre makes it ideal for business. The spacious rooms are gradually being renovated. Comfortable restaurant with a terrace for fine weather.

Novotel Aéroport

23 impasse Maubec – ✆ 05 61 15 00 00 – www.novotel.com **B2**

123 rm – 77/175 € 79/175 €, 14 €

Rest – *(closed Saturday lunch and Sunday lunch except July-August)* Carte 33/50 €

♦ Chain hotel ♦ Functional ♦

With a full range of leisure facilities (children's play area, tennis court and swimming pool), this hotel is ideal for both business and leisure. The decor is typical of the latest Novotel style. The contemporary restaurant and terrace offer a view of the pool. Traditional cuisine.

Colomiers

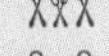

L'Amphitryon (Yannick Delpech)

chemin de Gramont – ✆ 05 61 15 55 55 – www.lamphitryon.com

Rest – Menu 30 € (weekday lunch), 69/120 € – Carte 98/168 €

Spec. Caviar des Pyrénées et sardine taillée au couteau, crème de morue et condiments. Pigeonneau du Mont-Royal rôti et fumé au bois de hêtre, les cuisses en "vrai faux" sushi. Tajine de clémentines et olives taggiasche, grog au rhum et glace à l'huile d'olive (winter).

♦ Innovative ♦ Fashionable ♦ Design ♦

A glass roof, fireplace and table d'hôte dining are the new innovations at this restaurant. It serves superb, creative and highly original cuisine based around local produce.

GERMANY
DEUTSCHLAND

PROFILE

→ **Area:**
357 111 km^2
(137 735 sq mi).

→ **Population:**
81 757 600 inhabitants (est. 2010), density = 231 per km^2.

→ **Capital:**
Berlin (conurbation 3 761 000 inhabitants).

→ **Currency:**
Euro (€); rate of exchange: € 1 = US$ 1.37 (Dec. 2010).

→ **Government:**
Parliamentary federal republic, comprising 16 states (Länder) since 1990. Member of European Union since 1957 (one of the 6 founding countries).

→ **Language:**
German.

→ **Specific public holidays:**
Epiphany (6 January in Baden-Württemberg, Bayern and Sachsen-Anhalt only); Good Friday (Friday before Easter); Corpus Christi (in Baden-Württemberg, Bayern, Hessen, Nordrhein-Westfalen, Rheinland-Pfalz, Saarland, Sachsen, Thüringen and those communities with a predominantly Roman Catholic population only); Day of German Unity (3 October); Reformation Day (31 October – in new Federal States only); 26 December.

→ **Local Time:**
GMT + 1 hour in winter and GMT + 2 hours in summer.

→ **Climate:**
Temperate continental, with cold winters and warm summers (Berlin: January: 0°C, July: 20°C).

→ **International dialling Code:**
00 49 followed by area code and then the local number. International directory enquiries ✆ **11 834.**

→ **Emergency:**
Police: ✆ **110**; Fire Brigade: ✆ **112.**

→ **Electricity:**
220 volts AC, 50HZ; 2-pin round-shaped continental plugs.

→ **Formalities**
Travellers from the European Union (EU), Switzerland, Iceland and the main countries of North and South America need a national identity card or passport (America: passport required) to visit Germany for less than three months (tourism or business purpose). For visitors from other countries a visa may be required, in addition to a passport, especially for those wishing to stay for longer than three months. We advise you to check with your embassy before travelling.

Population: 3 416 000 (conurbation 3 761 000) – Altitude: 34m

ıillot/MICHELIN

It's not every city parliament that has to scratch its head and decide where to put its centre, but that's the intriguing dilemma facing Berlin. Although homogeneous in many other ways, the east and the west of the city still lay claim to centres after their forty years of partition, and it may be that in time the exciting new – and central - Potsdamer Platz comes to be accepted as the city's hub. That's the thing about Germany's biggest metropolis – it's an invigorating mix of old and new, and constantly redefining itself.

After 1990, there were a tempestuous few years as Berlin sought to resolve its new identity, but it now stands proud as one of the most dynamic and forward thinking cities in the world. Alongside its idea of tomorrow, it's never lost sight of its bohemian past, and many parts of the city retain the arty sense of adventure that characterised downtown Berlin during the 1920s. Turn any corner and you might find a modernist art gallery, a tiny cinema or a cutting-edge club. Culture seeps through the very pores of life here.

LIVING THE CITY

The eastern side of the river Spree, around Nikolaiviertel, is the historic heart of the city, dating back to the 13C. Meanwhile, way over to the west of the centre lie Kurfürstendamm and Charlottenburg, smart districts which came to the fore after World War II as the heart of West Berlin. Between the two lie imposing areas which swarm with visitors: **Tiergarten** is the green lung of the city, and just to its east is the great boulevard of Unter den Linden. Continuing eastward, the self-explanatory Museum Island sits snugly and securely in the tributaries of the Spree. The most southerly of Berlin's sprawling districts is **Kreuzberg**, renowned for its bohemian, alternative character.

PRACTICAL INFORMATION

ARRIVAL-DEPARTURE

Berlin is served by two airports : Berlin-Tegel Airport lies 12km northwest of the city centre and Berlin-Schönefeld is 21km to the southeast. U-Bahn and S-Bahn trains operate from all two.

TRANSPORT

Invest in a Berlin-Potsdam Welcome Card. It gives you unlimited travel on the S-Bahn (trains), and discounts for selected theatres, museums, attractions and city tours. Available at public transport ticket desks, many hotels, and tourist information offices.

To get from one side of Berlin to the other, you'll need to travel by public transport. The U- and S-Bahn are quick and efficient, but the bus is another good alternative. Routes 100 and 200 are special double-decker services ideal for the visitor, as they incorporate most of the top attractions. Trams operate mainly within East Berlin. A tram ticket can be used on buses, U- and S-Bahn trains. There are various ticketing options which prevail in the city: check with tourist information offices.

Cyclists are well looked after here, so a good idea might be to hire a bike. There are many cycling routes around the city: most of the main roads have separate cycling lanes and even special traffic lights at intersections.

EXPLORING BERLIN

Sooner or later, the visitor to Berlin will take a stroll down Unter den Linden. To all intents and purposes, this is the city's central avenue, and you'll find none more attractive. It's an imposing boulevard, and it begins at its western end with the symbol of German reunification, The Brandenburg Gate. This magnificent neo-classical structure was completed in 1795, and has borne witness to many of the city's momentous episodes, most recently the celebrations of 1989 when the detested Wall it overlooked was triumphantly torn down. Earlier this decade the Gate was painstakingly renovated to its original Acropolis-like glory.

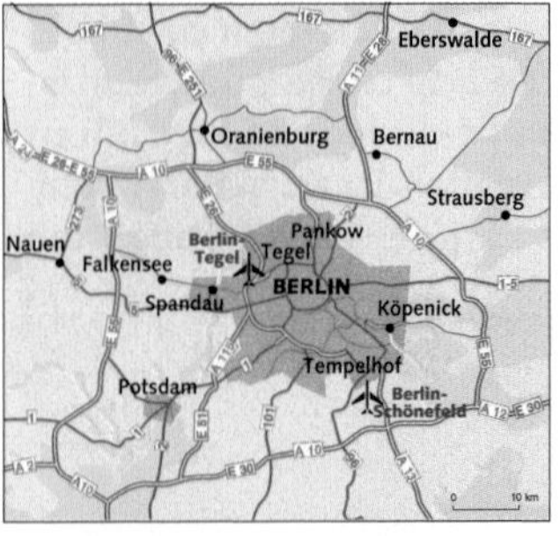

The wide, tree-lined Unter den Linden contains many of the city's historic landmarks, with a high concentration of 18C buildings sporting a prestigious pedigree. There's a line of fine stop-off points a little way up, the highlight being the **German History Museum**, which is housed in a magnificent former arsenal of pink baroque built just over three hundred years ago. Its fascinating exhibits range from a stern looking Martin Luther to the jacket of a concentration camp prisoner. Close to here is the neo-classical façade of the **State Opera House**, home to some of Berlin's finest performances, and the **State Library**, which boasts a tranquil inner courtyard with fountain and snug café providing a welcome break from the bustling grandeur of the boulevard.

→ ON A SPREE

Crossing **Schlossbrücke**, the eye-catching bridge over the Spree, you're on Berlin's very own island, named after what's made it famous. There are five museums here, and they're all in a grand huddle to your left. Pick of the bunch is the **Pergamon Museum**, which has one of the best collections of antiquities in the world, impressive enough to draw thousands of art lovers from across the globe. The other museums are hardly put in the shade: the **Alte Nationalgalerie** has a fine collection of German Romantics and French Impressionists; the **Altes** and **Neues Museums** highlight intriguing collections of Greek and Roman antiquities, and Egyptian art respectively; and the **Bodemuseum** has an eclectic mix of sculpture and coins. Give yourself an hour in each to do them justice. Most visually arresting of the island's buildings is the huge **Berliner Dom**, the city's cathedral, which has been painstakingly rebuilt since the War. Its impressive neo-Baroque exterior is modelled on St Peter's in Rome.

→ MEDIEVAL RECREATION

Just east from the island, across another bridge, lies the historic centre of Berlin, the Nikolaiviertel. By the time the city celebrated its seven hundred and fiftieth anniversary in 1987, the East German authorities of the time had rebuilt the area's pristine buildings: many of them having been lost in the War. What you see now is their attempt to recreate a medieval village. Centrepiece is the (originally) 13C **Nikolai Church**, which now includes a fascinating Berlin history exhibition. For true authenticity, make for the nearby **Knoblauchhaus**. This is the only house in Nikolaiviertel to escape War damage, and it's the oldest building still standing in Berlin. It's a beautiful mid-eighteenth century merchant's home, and its interior is now a household museum. For a radically different experience, head a little further east to the **TV Tower** – you're bound to have spotted it from practically any vantage point in the city. It's Berlin's tallest structure, like a giant toothpick that's bored its way up from the ground, and the view from its revolving café is spectacular: you'll see the whole of the city from up here, and you can enjoy a *Kaffee und Kuchen* while you're at it.

→ TOP OF THE POTS

Will **Potsdamer Platz** be recognised one day as the centrepoint of Berlin? It's ticking all the right boxes. Located just off the luxuriant Tiergarten, it was a mass of rubble not too many years ago. Now it's been developed as Germany's architectural showpiece, a shimmering zone of shiny new arcades and office buildings, where corporate domes merge with bright-as-a-button cafés and splashy fountains. This reborn area also does a nice line in irony: step out from one of its swish 21C entertainment complexes and spot the line of metal plaques thrusting from the street paving to denote where the Berlin Wall once stood.

Potsdamer Platz also draws in a lot of visitors who've been to the nearby **Gemäldegalerie**, generally considered to be the best in Berlin. It contains nearly three thousand paintings covering five hundred years from the thirteenth to the eighteenth centuries, painstakingly acquired by experts whose task was to select high quality examples from all major European schools. Thus one can admire great works by Botticelli, Caravaggio, Rubens, Rembrandt, Bruegel, Vermeer and others. In keeping with the zeitgeist feel of Potsdamer Platz is the nearby **Reichstag** parliament building. Its wondrous late twentieth century glass beehive dome is visible for miles around, and adds another powerful visual statement to Berlin's modernist account. One more architectural wonder near the Gemäldegalerie is the 'circus tent' **Philharmonie** building, home to one of Europe's most renowned orchestras, the Berlin Philharmonic.

→ ALTERNATIVE CHECKPOINT

South of the centre is the 'alternative' highlight, Kreuzberg, the city's most bohemian quarter. Bizarrely enough, the 'entry point' to Kreuzberg could hardly be less bohemian (though it could possibly be termed 'alternative'): **Checkpoint Charlie** was the notorious crossing point between East and West Berlin during the Cold War. It's now marked by a single hut, but nearby is a fascinating Checkpoint Charlie museum full of weird ephemera relating to it. These days, this buzzing quarter is more renowned for its Turkish bazaars, arty boutiques, galleries and nightclubs: the latter often open in the early hours, not closing until long after the rising of the sun.

→ WEST SIDE STORY

Many tourists concentrate on the district that was East Berlin, where the origins of the city lie, but the western side also has much to commend it. Kurfürstendamm is a snazzy boulevard that runs through the heart of the area. It's not hard to realise that this was the 'free market' side of Berlin during the days of the Wall, as Ku'damm (the locals' name) runs the gamut of exclusive designer stores. The fashionable side-streets off it are also lined with boutiques and cafés tailor made to ensnare the *beau monde*. The area also boasts Europe's largest department store, **Kaufhaus des Westens** ('KaDeWe'), now over a hundred years old. The main attraction here is the gourmet's paradise, which has the largest collection of foodstuffs in the whole of Europe, including live fish and nearly two thousand five hundred different wines. Further west, Charlottenburg is possibly the most enchanting part of the city. It only became part of Berlin in 1920, and its heart is the seventeenth century former royal summer palace of Queen Sophie Charlotte. Its collection of richly decorated interiors is unequalled in Berlin, and the beautifully picturesque park that surrounds it is a magnet for weekending locals.

BERLIN IN...

→ ONE DAY

Unter den Linden, Museum Island, Nikolaiviertel, coffee at TV Tower

→ TWO DAYS

Potsdamer Platz, Reichstag, Gemäldegalerie, concert at Philharmonie

→ THREE DAYS

KaDeWe, Kurfürstendamm, Charlottenburg Palace

CALENDAR HIGHLIGHTS

The importance of Berlin as a cultural centre begins early in the year with the world renowned Berlin Film Festival, which attracts top international movies and stars. Throughout the summer the city holds the Museumsinsel Festival, during which special music, theatre and film productions are held for the public: Potsdamer Platz's open-air cinema is a popular venue. At the beginning of summer, in May, Kreuzberg's hip streets play host to the Karneval der Kulturen, which is three days of singing and dancing in celebration of multicultural Berlin. The massive Global City celebration in August attracts up to three million visitors to Ku'damm. Now twenty years old, it hosts ten stages, featuring music of every description. A month later Musikfest Berlin offers two weeks of top classical performances in the Opera House and Philharmonie. The International Literary Festival (September) packs out Bebelplatz, as writers and poets from all over the world read to thousands. In October the focus is on a glittering metropolis when its top attractions are seductively illuminated in the Berlin Festival of Lights.

EATING OUT

Although by tradition Berlin hasn't been a gourmet stronghold, it does have a reputation for simple, hearty dishes, inspired by the long, hard winters. It's amazing how when the temperatures plummet, the city's comfort food can have an irresistible allure. Come the winter, who's for pork knuckle, Schnitzel, Bratwurst in mustard, chunky dumplings…or the real Berlin favourite Currywurst, which enjoins curry sauce and sausage. Be sure to try the local beer – Berliner Weisse mit Schuss – which is a light beer with a dash of raspberry or woodruff. Of course, that's not the whole story. Over the last fifteen years or so, Berlin has become so cosmopolitan that it can now claim a wider range of restaurants than any other German city. Many of the best restaurants are found within grand hotels and you only have to get to Savignyplatz near Ku'damm to realise how smart dining has taken off in a big way: the square is bursting with popular cafés and restaurants serving good food. There are lots too in Gendarmenmarkt. In the city as a whole there are almost unlimited options for the visitor: Asian restaurants of all kinds have sprung up in recent years. On the local front, bread and potatoes are ubiquitous – indeed Berlin has its own unique breads and rolls – but since reunification, the signature dishes have incorporated a global influence, so produce from the local forests, rivers and lakes may well have an Asian or Mediterranean twist. You can invariably eat late in Berlin: lots of places stay open until late, which can mean 2 or 3 in the morning. As dinner is the popular meal so there are plenty of inexpensive lunch menus available. Service is included in the price of your meal, but it's customary to round up the bill.

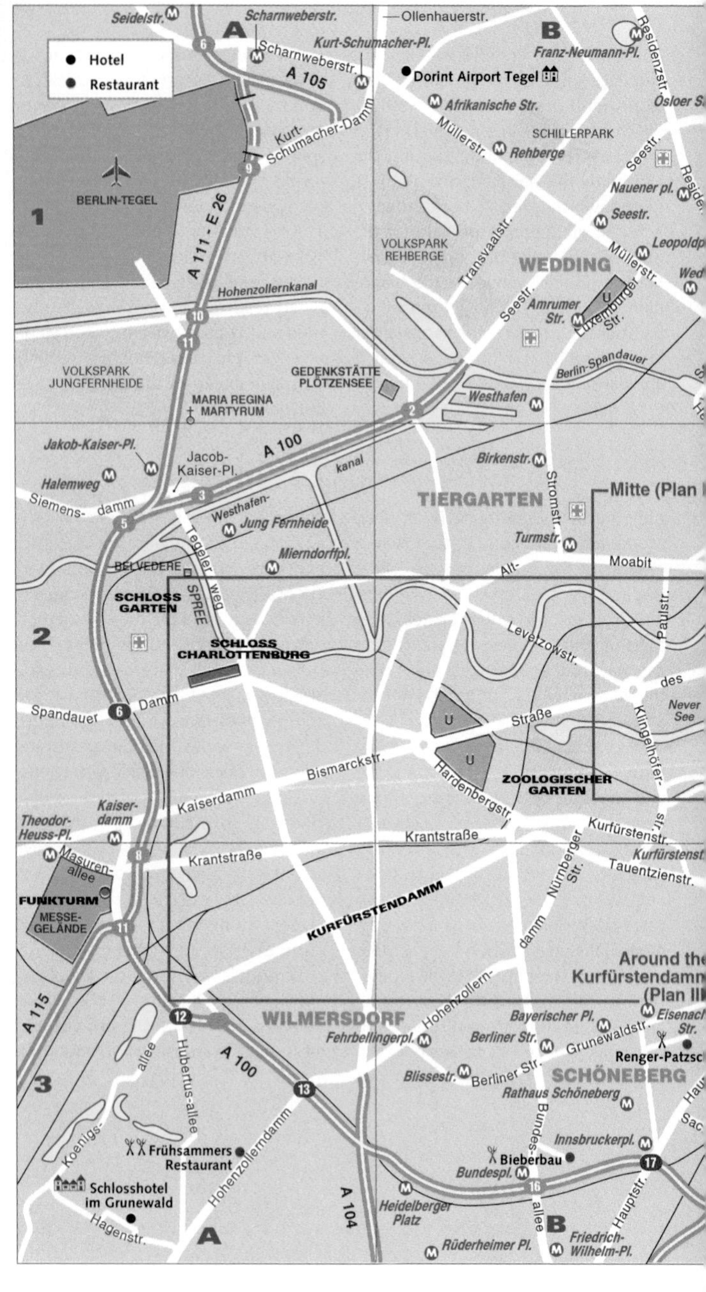
Hotel
Restaurant
A
B
1
2
3
BERLIN-TEGEL
Dorint Airport Tegel
Frühsammers Restaurant
Schlosshotel im Grunewald
Bieberbau
Renger-Patzsc
WEDDING
TIERGARTEN
WILMERSDORF
SCHÖNEBERG
SCHLOSS CHARLOTTENBURG
ZOOLOGISCHER GARTEN
FUNKTURM
MESSE-GELÄNDE
KURFÜRSTENDAMM
Mitte (Plan
Around the Kurfürstendamm (Plan II

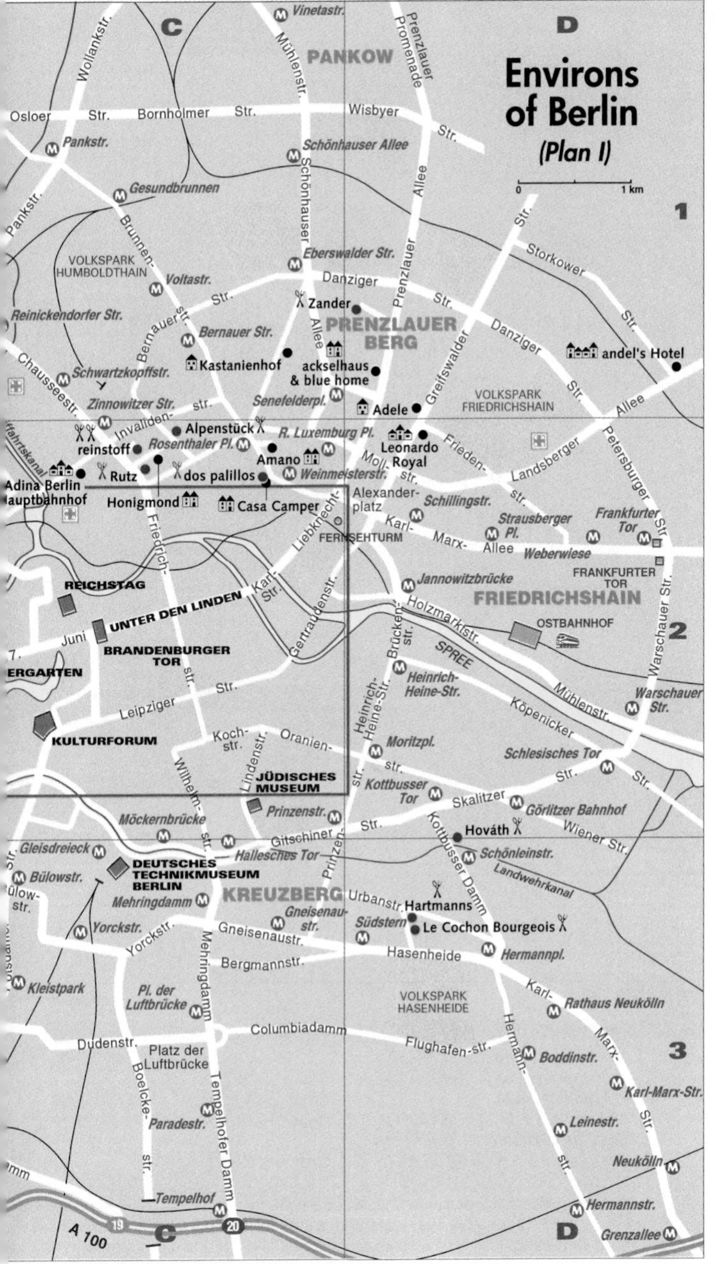
Environs of Berlin
(Plan I)
0
1 km
C
D
1
2
3
PANKOW
PRENZLAUER BERG
FRIEDRICHSHAIN
KREUZBERG
VOLKSPARK HUMBOLDTHAIN
VOLKSPARK FRIEDRICHSHAIN
VOLKSPARK HASENHEIDE
REICHSTAG
UNTER DEN LINDEN
BRANDENBURGER TOR
KULTURFORUM
JÜDISCHES MUSEUM
DEUTSCHES TECHNIKMUSEUM BERLIN
FERNSEHTURM
OSTBAHNHOF
FRANKFURTER TOR
SPREE
Zander
Kastanienhof
ackselhaus & blue home
Adele
Leonardo Royal
andel's Hotel
Alpenstück
reinstoff
Rutz
dos palillos
Amano
Adina Berlin Hauptbahnhof
Honigmond
Casa Camper
Hováth
Hartmanns
Le Cochon Bourgeois
Vinetastr.
Pankstr.
Gesundbrunnen
Schönhauser Allee
Eberswalder Str.
Voltastr.
Bernauer Str.
Reinickendorfer Str.
Schwartzkopffstr.
Zinnowitzer Str.
Senefelderpl.
Rosenthaler Pl.
R. Luxemburg Pl.
Weinmeisterstr.
Schillingstr.
Strausberger Pl.
Frankfurter Tor
Weberwiese
Jannowitzbrücke
Heinrich-Heine-Str.
Warschauer Str.
Moritzpl.
Schlesisches Tor
Kottbusser Tor
Görlitzer Bahnhof
Prinzenstr.
Möckernbrücke
Hallesches Tor
Gleisdreieck
Bülowstr.
Mehringdamm
Yorckstr.
Kleistpark
Pl. der Luftbrücke
Schönleinstr.
Südstern
Hermannpl.
Rathaus Neukölln
Boddinstr.
Karl-Marx-Str.
Leinestr.
Neukölln
Hermannstr.
Grenzallee
Paradestr.
Tempelhof
Wollankstr.
Osloer Str.
Bornholmer Str.
Wisbyer Str.
Prenzlauer Promenade
Mühlenstr.
Schönhauser Allee
Prenzlauer Allee
Pankstr.
Brunnenstr.
Bernauer str.
Danziger Str.
Storkower Str.
Greifswalder Str.
Chausseestr.
Invalidenstr.
Alexanderplatz
Liebknecht-
Karl-Str.
Moll-str.
Friedenstr.
Landsberger Allee
Petersburger Str.
Karl-Marx-Allee
Holzmarktstr.
Brückenstr.
Mühlenstr.
Köpenicker Str.
Warschauer Str.
Friedrichstr.
Gertraudenstr.
Juni
Leipziger Str.
Kochstr.
Oranienstr.
Lindenstr.
Wilhelmstr.
Skalitzer Str.
Wiener Str.
Kottbusser Damm
Landwehrkanal
Gitschiner Str.
Prinzenstr.
Urbanstr.
Gneisenaustr.
Yorckstr.
Bergmannstr.
Hasenheide
Karl-Marx-Str.
Mehringdamm
Columbiadamm
Flughafen-str.
Hermannstr.
Dudenstr.
Platz der Luftbrücke
Boelckestr.
Tempelhofer Damm
A 100
19
20

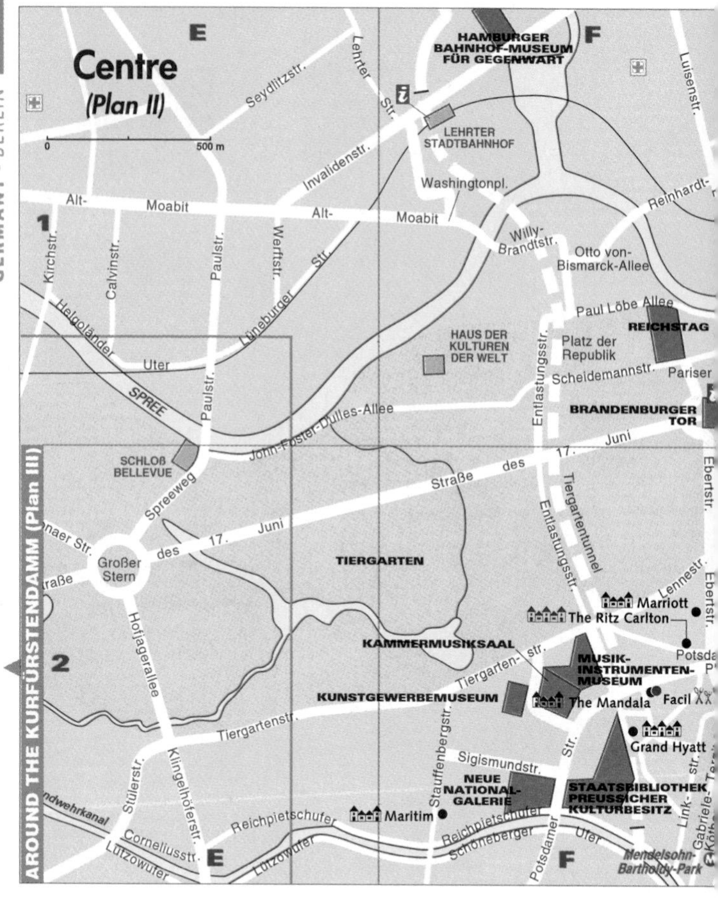

CENTRE

Plan II

Adlon Kempinski

Unter den Linden 77 ✉ *10117*
– Ⓜ Brandenburger Tor – ✆ (030) 2 26 10
– www.hotel-adlon.de

G1

304 rm – 🕴220/600 € 🕴🕴220/600 €, ☕ 39 € – 29 suites
Rest *Lorenz Adlon* – see below
Rest *Quarré* – *✆ (030) 22 61 15 55* – Carte 58/75 €

◆ Grand Luxury ◆ Historic ◆ Classic ◆

This magnificent five-star hotel has an international reputation. It has successfully copied the original 1907-style and stands for traditional living and luxurious furnishings. There is a spacious spa area and presidential suites with a limousine and butler service. The Quarré is classical in style and has views over the Brandenburg Gate from the terrace.

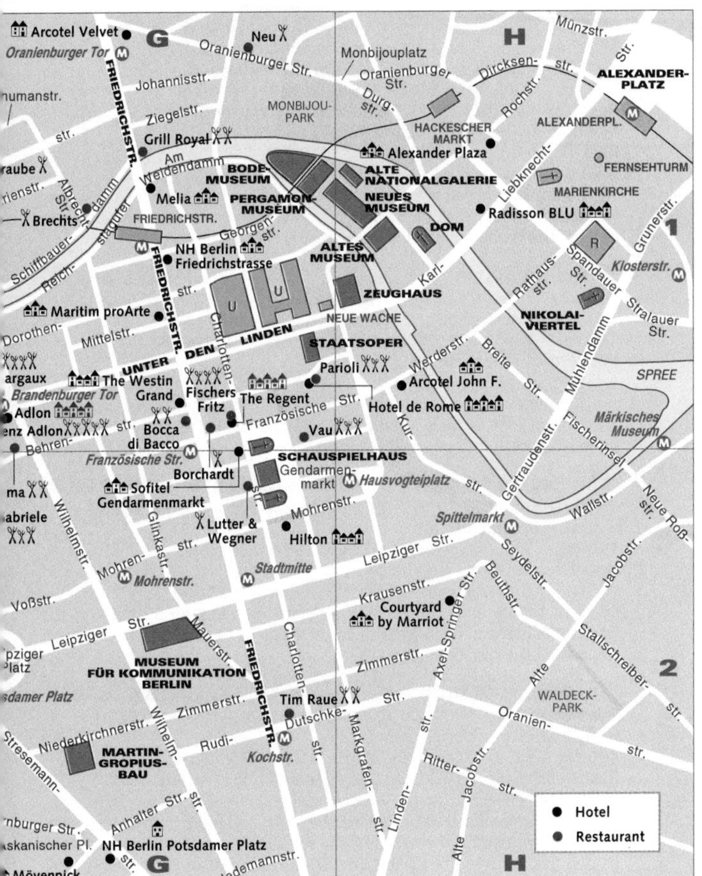

The Ritz-Carlton

Potsdamer Platz 3 ✉ 10785
– Ⓜ Potsdamer Platz
– ✆ (030) 33 77 77
– www.ritzcarlton.de **F2**

303 rm – 235/295 € 265/325 €
– 40 suites

Rest *Brasserie Desbrosses* – *✆ (030) 3 37 77 63 40*
– Carte 38/87 €

♦ Grand Luxury ♦ Chain hotel ♦ Classic ♦

An exclusive, elegant address. The splendid, lobby with its suspended marble staircase also houses a stylish lounge where guests can meet for an afternoon tea. This original French brasserie, which was founded in 1875 and serves typical meals, has an informal atmosphere.

Grand Hyatt

Marlene-Dietrich-Platz 2 (entrance Eichhornstraße) ✉ 10785 – Ⓜ Potsdamer Platz – ✆ (030) 25 53 12 34 – www.berlin.grand.hyatt.com
342 rm – 🚹205/395 € 🚹🚹205/425 €, ☕ 32 € – 16 suites **F2**
Rest *Vox* – *✆ (030) 25 53 17 72 (closed Saturday lunch and Sunday lunch)*
Menu 46/66 € (dinner) – Carte 43/64 €
Rest *Tizian* – Carte 42/55 €

◆ Grand Luxury ◆ Chain hotel ◆ Design ◆

This trapezoidal-shaped hotel on the Potsdamer Platz stands out for its modern, well-equipped rooms of purist design. Contemporary design with open-plan kitchen. This restaurant has a lounge opening onto a hall.

Hotel de Rome

Behrenstr. 37 ✉ 10117 – Ⓜ Französische Str. – ✆ (030) 4 60 60 90 – www.hotelderome.de **G1**
146 rm – 🚹395/495 € 🚹🚹395/495 €, ☕ 30 € – 9 suites
Rest *Parioli* – see below

◆ Grand Luxury ◆ Classic ◆

A luxury hotel on the Bebelplatz in the impressive framework of a building dating from 1889, formerly used by the Dresdner Bank. Today, the old strong-room is a pool.

The Regent

Charlottenstr. 49 ✉ 10117 – Ⓜ Französische Str. – ✆ (030) 2 03 38 – www.theregentberlin.de **G1**
196 rm – 🚹235/425 € 🚹🚹235/425 €, ☕ 35 € – 39 suites
Rest *Fischers Fritz* – see below

◆ Grand Luxury ◆ Classic ◆

Excellent service and sophisticated elegance give this luxury hotel in the Gendarmenmarkt an exclusive feel. One of the many treats on offer is afternoon tea in English, Indian or Russian-style.

The Westin Grand

Friedrichstr. 158 ✉ 10117 – Ⓜ Französische Str. – ✆ (030) 2 02 70 – www.westingrandberlin.com **G1**
400 rm – 🚹139/490 € 🚹🚹159/510 €, ☕ 29 € – 16 suites
Rest *Relish* – *✆ (030) 20 27 31 77* – Menu 44/66 € – Carte 38/68 €

◆ Chain hotel ◆ Luxury ◆ Modern ◆

This classic grand hotel has an impressive lobby and modern rooms. Some of the suites are stylishly themed, as is the spa suite. A highlight is the 3,000m2 garden in the middle of Berlin! The Relish restaurant serves contemporary, modern cuisine.

Radisson BLU

Karl-Liebknecht-Str. 3 ✉ 10178 – Ⓜ Alexanderplatz – ✆ (030) 23 82 80 – www.radissonblu.de/hotel-berlin **H1**
427 rm – 🚹155/380 € 🚹🚹155/380 €, ☕ 26 € – 1 suite
Rest *HEat* – *✆ (030) 2 38 28 34 72* – Carte 23/49 €

◆ Business ◆ Chain hotel ◆ Modern ◆

What catches your eye when you look into the contemporary, atrium lobby of this hotel is the cylindrical aquarium 25m high. Some of the simply designed, modern, functional rooms have a view of the Spree or the AquaDom. The HEat restaurant serves international cuisine.

Marriott

Inge-Beisheim-Platz 1 ✉ 10785 – Ⓜ Potsdamer Platz – ✆ (030) 22 00 00 – www.berlinmarriott.de **F2**
379 rm ☕ – 🚹159/259 € 🚹🚹179/279 € – 9 suites **Rest** – Carte 34/94 €

◆ Chain hotel ◆ Luxury ◆ Contemporary ◆

The lobby of this typical American chain hotel is a 40m high atrium. The comfortable and luxurious rooms are ideally designed for the business guest. This bistro-style restaurant has an open kitchen and a large window façade.

Maritim

Stauffenbergstr. 26 ✉ 10785 – Ⓜ Mendelssohn-Bartholdy-Park – ✆ (030) 2 06 50 – www.maritim.de **F2**

505 rm – 155/295 € 170/310 €, 24 € – 27 suites

Rest *Grand Restaurant M* – *✆ (030) 20 65 10 90 (closed Sunday)* Carte 35/50 €

♦ Conference hotel ♦ Elegant ♦ Contemporary ♦

This hotel has a sophisticated, elegant lobby, and spacious premises for conferences and events. It offers guestrooms with well-equipped technical facilities and large suites, including the 350m2 Presidential Suite! The Grand Restaurant M is a 1920s style restaurant.

Hilton

Mohrenstr. 30 ✉ 10117 – Ⓜ Stadtmitte – ✆ (030) 2 02 30 – www.hilton.de/berlin **G2**

601 rm – 145/345 € 145/345 €, 26 € – 15 suites

Rest *Mark Brandenburg* – *✆ (030) 20 23 46 55* – Carte 28/49 €

♦ Chain hotel ♦ Luxury ♦ Functional ♦

This city hotel stands out for its impressive lobby, its wide range of wellness and fitness facilities, and its rooms, some of which look onto the Gendarmenmarkt. Mark Brandenburg offers regional dishes.

The Mandala

Potsdamer Str. 3 ✉ 10785 – Ⓜ Potsdamer Platz – ✆ (030) 5 90 05 00 00 – www.themandala.de **F2**

157 rm – 190/270 € 190/350 €, 27 € – 13 suites

Rest *Facil* – see below

♦ Business ♦ Design ♦

This hotel in the Potsdamer Platz opposite the Sony Center with its range of spacious and simple yet luxurious rooms and suites boasts an unusual spa. The trendy Bar Qiu serves business lunches.

Soho House

Torstr. 1 ✉ 10119 – Ⓜ Senefelderpl. – ✆ (030) 4 05 04 40 – www.sohohouseberlin.com *Plan I* **D1**

40 rm – 120/210 € 120/210 €, 15 €

Rest – *(resident only)* Carte 21/43 €

♦ Townhouse ♦ Design ♦ Personalised ♦

As the first Soho House in Germany, the concept and design of this very unconventional hotel (no name on the building!) appeals to creative and artistic minds. Club floor and outdoor roof pool with view of the city.

andel's Hotel

Landsberger Allee 106 ✉ 10369 – ✆ (030) 4 53 05 30 – www.andelsberlin.com

557 rm – 99/199 € 119/219 € – 23 suites *Plan I* **D1**

Rest *a.choice* – *✆ (030) 45 30 53 26 21 (dinner only)* Menu 34/64 € – Carte 40/51 €

♦ Conference hotel ♦ Modern ♦

This remarkable building is an events and conference hotel. It has a modern design, very large lobby, and an excellent events area. Executive floors with free W-LAN. The restaurant decor is elegant with clean lines.

Arcotel John F.

Werderscher Markt 11 ✉ 10117 – Ⓜ Französische Str. – ✆ (030) 4 05 04 60 – www.arcotelhotels.com **H1**

190 rm – 95/325 € 95/325 €, 18 € – 3 suites

Rest *Foreign Affairs* – *✆ (030) 40 50 46 18 00* – Carte 31/48 €

♦ Business ♦ Modern ♦

This designer hotel located next to the German Foreign Office is dedicated to John F. Kennedy and offers attractive, modern rooms with rocking chairs, including themed 'Kennedy' and 'International Style' rooms. This restaurant serves international dishes.

Leonardo Royal

Otto-Braun-Str. 90 ✉ 10249 Berlin – Ⓜ Alexander Platz – ✆ (030) 7 55 43 00 – www.leonardo-hotels.com *Plan I* **D2**

346 rm – 89/199 € 99/229 € **Rest** – Carte 27/52 €

♦ Business ♦ Modern ♦

This modern business hotel near Friedrichshain Park offers good transport links and smart rooms including special "Ladies Rooms". It also has conference facilities for up to 700 participants. This spacious restaurant serves international cuisine.

Maritim proArte

Friedrichstr. 151 (access via Dorotheenstr. 55) ✉ 10117 – Ⓜ Friedrichstr. – ✆ (030) 2 03 35 – www.maritim.de **G1**

403 rm – 159/299 € 174/314 €, 22 €

Rest *Atelier* – *✆ (030) 20 33 45 20 (closed mid July - end August and Sunday) (dinner only)* Menu 44/55 € – Carte 32/43 €

Rest *Bistro media* – *✆ (030) 20 33 45 30* – Carte 24/30 €

♦ Chain hotel ♦ Business ♦ Modern ♦

This modern and functionally equipped hotel has good meeting facilities and the pleasant Checkpoint Charlie bar. Throughout the hotel there are pictures by Jungen Wilden. The Atelier is a modern, designer-style restaurant.

NH Berlin Friedrichstrasse

Friedrichstr. 96 ✉ 10117 – Ⓜ Friedrichstr. – ✆ (030) 2 06 26 60 – www.nh-hotels.com **G1**

268 rm – 99/320 € 99/320 €, 21 €

Rest – *(closed July - August and Sunday - Monday)* Carte 28/60 €

♦ Business ♦ Modern ♦

The spacious lobby and cosy rooms in this hotel are furnished in a modern style. Breakfast is offered in the bright, glass annexe. Light, open plan restaurant with modern cuisine.

Sofitel Gendarmenmarkt

Charlottenstr. 50 ✉ 10117 – Ⓜ Französische Str. – ✆ (030) 20 37 50 – www.sofitel.com **G1-2**

92 rm – 134/320 € 159/345 €, 28 €

Rest *Aigner* – *✆ (030) 2 03 75 18 50* – Menu 27 € (lunch)/85 € Carte 37/58 €

♦ Chain hotel ♦ Business ♦ Modern ♦

This hotel is directly opposite the Gendarmenmarkt. It offers modern, designer-style rooms and a small leisure area on the top floor. This restaurant has been decorated with the original fixtures and fittings from an old Viennese coffee house.

Courtyard by Marriott

Axel-Springer-Str. 55 ✉ 10117 – Ⓜ Spittelmarkt – ✆ (030) 8 00 92 80 – www.courtyard.com/bermt **H2**

267 rm – 99/139 € 99/139 €, 21 € – 4 suites

Rest – Carte 23/37 €

♦ Chain hotel ♦ Business ♦ Functional ♦

The various conference areas, the functional rooms with good working spaces, and the large lobby area all contribute to making this hotel an ideal business address. Oléo Pazzo is a Mediterranean bistro-style restaurant with a bar.

Melia

Friedrichstr. 103 ✉ 10117 – Ⓜ Friedrichstr. – ✆ (030) 20 60 79 00 – www.meliaberlin.com **G1**

364 rm – 97/167 € 97/167 €, 22 € – 4 suites

Rest – Carte 34/48 €

♦ Business ♦ Modern ♦

The first Berlin hotel of the Spanish Sol-Melia Group is in a central location. It offers modern, technically up-to-date rooms, some with a view of the Spree. There are executive facilities on the seventh and eighth floors. The Café Madrid restaurant on the first floor serves international cuisine. There is also a comfortable tapas bar.

Mövenpick

Schönebergerstr. 3 ✉ 10963 – Ⓜ Potsdamer Platz – ✆ (030) 23 00 60 – www.moevenpick-berlin.com **G2**

243 rm – ♦109/259 € ♦♦109/259 €, ☕ 22 € – 1 suite

Rest – Carte 29/48 €

♦ Historic ♦ Design ♦

This former Siemens building combines external heritage architecture with a modern interior. The lovely studio rooms on the top floor are particularly attractive; some have free-standing baths. This interior courtyard restaurant has a glass roof that can be left open in summer.

Adina Berlin Hauptbahnhof

Platz vor dem Neuen Tor 6 (access via Hannoversche Straße) ✉ 10178 – Ⓜ Zinnowitzer Str. – ✆ (030) 2 00 03 20 – www.adina.eu *Plan I* **C2**

139 rm – ♦99/209 € ♦♦119/459 €, ☕ 18 €

Rest *Alto* – *(dinner only)* Carte 18/25 €

♦ Business ♦ Design ♦ Contemporary ♦

A non-smoking hotel opposite the Charité hospital, not far from the main railway station. It offers good quality rooms and modern, comfortably appointed apartments with a kitchenette. "Berlin-Style Tapas" at Alto.

Alexander Plaza

Rosenstr. 1 ✉ 10178 – Ⓜ Alexanderplatz – ✆ (030) 24 00 10 – www.hotel-alexander-plaza.de **H1**

94 rm – ♦105/165 € ♦♦115/175 €, ☕ 12 € – 4 suites

Rest – Carte 19/32 €

♦ Business ♦ Functional ♦

Between the Marienkirche and the market, this restored old building provides modern rooms and apartments with small kitchen facilities. International dishes are served in the restaurant with conservatory.

Casa Camper

Weinmeisterstr. 1 ✉ 10178 – Ⓜ Weinmeisterstr. – ✆ (030) 20 00 34 10 – www.casacamper.com *Plan I* **C2**

51 rm ☕ – ♦145/265 € ♦♦185/305 € – 3 suites

Rest *dos palillos* – see below

♦ Business ♦ Design ♦ Functional ♦

Fernando Amat and Jordi Tio are behind the design of this high quality interior. The room are decorated in striking red and warm wood. Free snacks in "Tentempié" on the seventh floor.

Arcotel Velvet

Oranienburger Str. 52 ✉ 10117 – Ⓜ Oranienburger Tor – ✆ (030) 2 78 75 30 – www.arcotel.com/velvet **G1**

85 rm – ♦89/325 € ♦♦89/325 €, ☕ 16 €

Rest *Lutter & Wegener* – *✆ (030) 24 78 10 78* – Carte 27/37 €

♦ Business ♦ Modern ♦ Functional ♦

The glass façade and an appealing combination of dark furniture and strong reds characterise the rooms. The portraits of famous personalities are a nice detail. A delicatessen bar and decorative wine racks are features of the Lutter & Wegener.

Amano without rest

Auguststr. 43 (access via Kleine Rosenthalerstraße) ✉ 10119 – Ⓜ Rosenthaler Platz – ✆ (030) 8 09 41 50 – www.hotel-amano.com

163 rm – ♦75/220 € ♦♦85/230 €, ☕ 11 € – 20 suites *Plan I* **C2**

♦ Business ♦ Modern ♦

Tailored perfectly for the business traveller, this smart, contemporary-style hotel located close to the Hackesche Höfe boasts a panoramic roof terrace and bar.

Honigmond

Tieckstr. 11 ✉ *10115* – Ⓜ *Zinnowitzer Str.* – ☎ *(030) 2 84 45 50*
– *www.honigmond.de* *Plan I* **C2**
35 rm ☕ – †95/135 € ††145/165 € – 2 suites
Rest – Carte 20/32 €
◆ Historic ◆ Classic ◆ Personalised ◆
Built in 1895 this house in a quiet side street has individually-styled rooms. The Garden Hotel 350m away has a lovely inner courtyard garden. Pleasant coffee shop-cum-restaurant in a classic setting.

ackselhaus & blue home without rest

Belforter Str. 21 ✉ *10405* – Ⓜ *Senefelderplatz* – ☎ *(030) 44 33 76 33*
– *www.ackselhaus.de* *Plan I* **D1**
35 rm ☕ – †110/170 € ††140/170 € – 4 suites
◆ Townhouse ◆ Historic ◆ Personalised ◆
This establishment has a really special historical charm. It is Venetian in style with blue tones. The green inner courtyards with their lounge feel are very pretty.

Adele without rest

Greifswalder Str. 227 ✉ *10405* – Ⓜ *Alexanderplatz* – ☎ *(030) 44 32 43 10*
– *www.adele-berlin.de* *Plan I* **D1**
15 rm ☕ – †85/145 € ††105/165 € – 3 suites
◆ Townhouse ◆ Design ◆
This small and very exclusive boutique hotel is furnished in Art Deco-style. It has comfortable, pretty guestrooms and a very modern breakfast room.

NH Berlin Potsdamer Platz without rest

Stresemannstr. 47 ✉ *10963* – Ⓜ *Potsdamer Platz*
– ☎ *(030) 2 25 07 10* – *www.nh-hotels.com* **G2**
89 rm ☕ – †99/149 € ††99/149 €
◆ Business ◆ Contemporary ◆
This business hotel is close to Potsdamer Platz. It offers modern and freshly designed rooms with parquet flooring and the latest technology. Good underground and local railway connections.

Kastanienhof without rest

Kastanienallee 65 ✉ *10119* – Ⓜ *Senefelderpl.* – ☎ *(030) 44 30 50*
– *www.kastanienhof.biz* *Plan I* **C1**
35 rm – †68/85 € ††87/122 €, ☕ 9 € – 3 suites
◆ Townhouse ◆ Functional ◆
This well-managed hotel offering functional rooms is run by a real Berliner who has decorated it with a vast array of mementos of "his" city.

Lorenz Adlon – Hotel Adlon Kempinski

Unter den Linden 77 ✉ *10117* – Ⓜ *Brandenburger Tor*
– ☎ *(030) 22 61 19 60* – *www.hotel-adlon.de*
– *Closed August and Sunday - Monday* **G1**
Rest – *(dinner only)* Menu 105/160 €
– Carte 95/140 €
Spec. Dorade und Sardine mit Bisque. Geschmorter Kalbsschwanz mit Rettich, Petersilie und Aubergine. Erdbeeren, Himbeeren und Joghurt mit Schokoladenmousse.
◆ Classic ◆ Luxury ◆ Elegant ◆
The classic cuisine at this luxurious restaurant bears the signature of Hendrik Otto. The very best products are painstakingly combined to create dishes bursting with flavour. Very good service and expert wine recommendations. Some of the tables have a view of the Brandenburg Gate.

XXXX
✿✿

Fischers Fritz – Hotel The Regent

Charlottenstr. 49 ✉ 10117 – Ⓜ Französische Str. – ✆ (030) 20 33 63 63 – www.fischersfritzberlin.com **G1**

Rest – *(booking advisable)* Menu 47 € (lunch)/160 € – Carte 115/149 €

Spec. Doppeltes Filet von der Rotbarbe, Mairübe gefüllt mit weißen Zwiebeln und Coulis von Sauerampfer. Mittelstück vom Steinbutt mit Stangenspargel und Sauce Choron. Pochiertes Onsen-Ei mit Pfifferlingen, marinierter Gänsestopfleber und Erbsen-Bärlauch-Infusion.

◆ Inventive ◆ Elegant ◆

With his creative dishes Christian Lohse displays skill and precision in the kitchen of this elegant gourmet address. Flavours are harmoniously combined and the classics are given new interpretations. Good value lunch menu.

XXXX
✿

Margaux (Michael Hoffmann)

Unter den Linden 78 (entrance Wilhelmstraße) ✉ 10117 – Ⓜ Brandenburger Tor – ✆ (030) 22 65 26 11 – www.margaux-berlin.de – Closed Sunday, Juli - mid August: Sunday and Monday **G1**

Rest – *(dinner only)* Menu 95/180 €

Spec. "Bar de Ligne" und Bouillabaisse. Sellerie und Schnittlauch. Taube mit Gewürzen.

◆ Inventive ◆ Minimalist ◆ Fashionable ◆

At his modern restaurant close to the Brandenburg Gate Michael Hoffmann will send you off on the multifarious "Voyage de Cuisine" – the vegetarian version of which is also worth the journey. Attentive and well-trained service.

XXX
✿

FACIL – Hotel The Mandala

Potsdamer Str. 3 (5th floor) ✉ 10785 – Ⓜ Potsdamer Platz – ✆ (030) 5 90 05 12 34 – www.facil.de – Closed 2 - 18 January, 23 July - 7 August and Saturday - Sunday

Rest – *(booking advisable)* Menu 39 € (lunch)/140 € – Carte 79/118 € **F2**

Spec. Makrele-Escabèche mit Gänseleber und Wasserkresse. Wildlachs mit Dashi-Emulsion und Algen. Lammherz mit Rübstiel und Zitruspüree.

◆ Inventive ◆ Minimalist ◆

Find a small oasis on the fifth floor of the inner courtyard of this high-rise building. Michael Kempf's creative dishes are served in a completely glassed-in restaurant overlooking the countryside. Cheaper lunchtime menu.

XXX

Gabriele

Behrenstr. 72 ✉ 10117 – Ⓜ Brandenburger Tor – ✆ (030) 20 62 86 10 – www.gabriele-restaurant.de – Closed 2 weeks January, 2 weeks July - mid August and Monday

Rest – *(dinner only)* Menu 96/138 € – Carte 72/106 € **G2**

◆ Italian ◆ Elegant ◆ Luxury ◆

A high-class restaurant decorated with paintings and beautiful lights serving traditional and modern Italian cuisine. The wine list contains some little-known gems from Italy.

XXX
✿

VAU (Kolja Kleeberg)

Jägerstr. 54 ✉ 10117 – Ⓜ Französische Str. – ✆ (030) 2 02 97 30 – www.vau-berlin.de – Closed Sunday **G1**

Rest – Menu 65 € (lunch)/120 € – Carte 79/94 €

Spec. Pochierte Forelle mit Kräuterrührei und "Pumpernickel-Öl". Gesottenes Kalbsscherzel mit Galuschki, Sud und Sprosse von der Erbse. Eisschokolade mit Cannelle und weißem Granitée.

◆ Inventive ◆ Fashionable ◆

The renowned architect Meinrad von Gerkan designed this restaurant. Enjoy fresh, creative food and good wine recommendations in a select, modern interior. More inexpensive lunchtime menu.

XXX

Parioli – Hotel de Rome

Behrenstr. 37 ✉ 10117 – Ⓜ Französische Str. – ✆ (030) 4 60 60 90 – www.pariolirestaurant.de **G1**

Rest – Menu 76/89 € – Carte 52/77 €

♦ Mediterranean ♦ Elegant ♦

This elegant restaurant is decorated in dark wood and gold tones. It offers international cuisine with a Mediterranean influence. There is a terrace in the beautiful interior courtyard.

XX ✿

Tim Raue

Rudi-Dutschke-Str. 26 ✉ 10969 – Ⓜ Kochstr. – ✆ (030) 37 59 12 04 – www.tim-raue.com – Closed 2 weeks January, 2 weeks July - August, Sunday - Monday and Bank Holidays lunch **G2**

Rest – Menu 38 € (lunch)/148 € – Carte 110/134 €

Spec. Rote Garnele, Rosenschnaps und Shiso. Peking Ente Interpretation. Macaron von Grüntee, Meerrettich, Vanillecreme und Erbeeren mit Eis von weißem Balsamico.

♦ Asian ♦ Friendly ♦

Tim Raue has relocated and now welcomes his guests in a former gallery near Checkpoint Charlie. Yet the concept remains the same: interesting and well thought out Euro-Asian food.

XX ✿

reinstoff (Daniel Achilles)

Schlegelstr. 26c (Edison Höfe) ✉ 10115 – Ⓜ Zinnowitzerstr. – ✆ (030) 30 88 12 14 – www.reinstoff.eu – Closed 2 weeks January, 2 weeks August and Sunday - Monday

Rest – *(dinner only)* Menu 59/119 € *Plan I* **C2**

Spec. Leipziger Allerlei. Gänseleber, Fichtenknospen, Ziegenquark und Wildkräuter. Rücken vom Schwein mit gelben Rüben, Algen, Ingwer und Bier.

♦ Inventive ♦ Fashionable ♦ Intimate ♦

This historic factory building in the Edison Höfe is home to a minimalist restaurant in a room-in-a-room concept. Three cubes create an interesting atmosphere in which creative dishes and wines from Germany and Spain are served.

XX

Grill Royal

Friedrichstr. 105 b ✉ 10117 – Ⓜ Oranienburger Tor – ✆ (030) 28 87 92 88 – www.grillroyal.com **G1**

Rest – *(dinner only) (booking essential)* Carte 30/133 €

♦ International ♦ Trendy ♦ Fashionable ♦

The place to eat on the River Spree, known for its grilled meats. Diners select the cuts themselves from a glass chiller cabinet! Great selection of Bordeaux and Italian wines.

XX

uma

Behrenstr. 72 ✉ 10117 – Ⓜ Brandenburger Tor – ✆ (030) 3 01 11 73 24 – www.uma-restaurant.de – Closed 2 weeks July - August and Sunday **G1**

Rest – *(dinner only)* Menu 48/98 € – Carte 37/52 €

♦ Japanese ♦ Intimate ♦ Exotic ♦

In this restaurant and shochu bar located to the south of the Adlon Hotel chef Stephan Zuber serves traditional Japanese food with a European spin.

XX

Bocca di Bacco

Friedrichstr. 167 ✉ 10117 – Ⓜ Französische Str. – ✆ (030) 20 67 28 28 – www.boccadibacco.de – Closed Sunday lunch and Bank Holidays lunch **G1**

Rest – Menu 20 € (lunch) – Carte 36/50 €

♦ Italian ♦ Fashionable ♦

This restaurant with a modern design has a bar and lounge area where good Italian cuisine is served. Very friendly atmosphere. Beautiful function room on the first-floor.

Rutz

Chausseestr. 8 ✉ 10115 – Ⓜ Oranienburger Tor – ✆ (030) 24 62 87 60 – www.rutz-weinbar.de
– Closed January - mid February and Sunday - Monday Plan I **C2**

Rest – *(dinner only)* Menu 62/137 € – Carte 76/93 €
Rest *Weinbar* – *(open from 4 pm)* Menu 62/90 € – Carte 43/67 €
Spec. Zweimal Thunfisch und Ingwer, Cashewkerne, Mango, Rettich-Wasabisalat und Wiesenkräuter. Gegrilltes Entrecote und geschmorte Brust vom Rind mit Rosmarinpüree. Schokolade und Passionsfrucht mit Vanille-Mispeln, Krokant und Guaveneis.

♦ Inventive ♦ Trendy ♦

Guests are cordially looked after on two floors. The restaurant upstairs is simple and modern in style, and there is a vine-covered terrace facing the inner courtyard. Marco Müller's cooking is creative and Mediterranean inspired. The Weinbar on the ground floor serves regional specialities.

Hartmanns

Fichtestr. 31 ✉ 10967 – Ⓜ Südstern – ✆ (030) 61 20 10 03 – www.hartmanns-restaurant.de
– Closed Sunday Plan I **D3**

Rest – *(dinner only) (booking advisable)* Menu 21 € (lunch)/74 € – Carte 52/58 €
Spec. Marinierte Kalbshaxenscheiben mit sautierten Pfifferlingen. Pochierter Saibling mit geröstetem und püriertem Blumenklohl. Zitronentarte mit Joghurtsorbet.

♦ Modern ♦ Cosy ♦ Neighbourhood ♦

In the evening the attentive team serves sophisticated contemporary dishes by Stefan Hartmann in intimate surroundings. Nice terrace at the front of the house.

dos palillos – Hotel Casa Camper

Weinmeisterstr. 1 (entrance Rosenthalerstr. 53) ✉ 10178 – Ⓜ Weinmeisterstr. – ✆ (030) 20 00 34 13 – www.dospalillos.com
– Closed Sunday - Tuesday lunch and Wednesday Plan I **C2**

Rest – Menu 45/60 € – Carte 24/32 €

♦ Asian ♦ Design ♦ Fashionable ♦

This restaurant is an extraordinary concept and has a minimalist design in white. The Asian dishes are served in tapas form – the chefs are in direct contact with the guests and are pleased to advise them. Eat at the long bar looking into the open kitchen.

Traube

Reinhardtstr. 33 ✉ 10117 – Ⓜ Oranienburger Tor – ✆ (030) 27 87 93 93 – www.traube-berlin.de
– Closed Saturday lunch and Sunday **G1**

Rest – Menu 59 € – Carte 34/52 €

♦ International ♦ Friendly ♦

This very attractive, classically modern restaurant has a bistro area. It also serves international dishes on the terrace in the inner courtyard. There is also a small midday menu.

Brechts

Schiffbauerdamm 6 ✉ 10117 – Ⓜ Oranienburger Tor – ✆ (030) 28 59 85 85 – www.brechts.de **G1**

Rest – Menu 33/49 € – Carte 34/51 €

♦ Austrian ♦ Fashionable ♦

Named after Bertolt Brecht, this appealing restaurant is centrally located by the river Spree. Red walls, pictures and clean-lined design create a very pleasant atmosphere. Good Austrian and international cuisine is served here.

Borchardt

Französische Str. 47 ✉ 10117 – Ⓜ Französische Str. – ✆ (030) 81 88 62 62
Rest – Carte 28/64 € **G1**

◆ International ◆ Brasserie ◆

A traditional townhouse in the Gendarmenmarkt is home to this trendy restaurant serving international cuisine with a charming interior courtyard terrace.

Lutter & Wegner

Charlottenstr. 56 ✉ 10117 – Ⓜ Französische Str. – ✆ (030) 2 02 95 40 – www.l-w-berlin.de **G2**
Rest – Carte 31/52 €

◆ Austrian ◆ Wine bar ◆

This restaurant with its cosy wine bar is a lively venue serving Austrian-influenced cuisine. More concise lunchtime menu. Selection of over 700 wines with something to suit every pocket.

Neu

Oranienburgerstr. 32 (at Heckmannhöfen) ✉ 10117 – Ⓜ Oranienburger Tor – ✆ (030) 66 40 84 27 – www.restaurant-neu.de – Closed Sunday dinner - Monday except Bank Holidays **G1**
Rest – Menu 19 € (lunch)/39 € – Carte 31/44 €

◆ Seasonal cuisine ◆ Trendy ◆

Find tasty, seasonal and value for money cuisine in this trendy restaurant in the artistic quarter. Smaller lunchtime menu. Pretty conservatory and inner courtyard terrace.

Alpenstück

Gartenstr. 9 ✉ 10178 – Ⓜ Rosenthaler Platz – ✆ (030) 21 75 16 46 – www.alpenstueck.de *Plan I* **C1**
Rest – *(dinner only) (booking advisable)* Carte 32/37 €

◆ Regional ◆ Fashionable ◆

This pleasant, lively restaurant is in a quiet side street. Indulge in tasty, Alpine, seasonal food served by friendly staff. Many organic and regional products are used. Rustic terrace at the front.

Le Cochon Bourgeois

Fichtestr. 24 ✉ 10967 – Ⓜ Südstern – ✆ (030) 6 93 01 01 – www.lecochon.de – Closed 1 - 17 January, 2 - 16 August and Sunday - Monday *Plan I* **D3**
Rest – *(dinner only)* Menu 35/53 € – Carte 32/55 €

◆ French ◆ Cosy ◆

French bistro-style cuisine is served in this fine historical setting with stucco-like woodwork and parquet floors. The wine selection includes some little-known gems.

Horváth

Paul-Lincke-Ufer 44a ✉ 10999 – Ⓜ Schönleinstr. – ✆ (030) 61 28 99 92 – www.restaurant-horvath.de – Closed Monday *Plan I* **D2**
Rest – *(dinner only) (booking advisable)* Menu 38/76 € – Carte 36/59 €

◆ International ◆ Minimalist ◆

This restaurant has period parquet flooring and minimalist decor in warm brown tones. Contemporary and Austrian cuisine served with goods wines and friendly service.

Zander

Kollwitzstr. 50 ✉ 10405 – Ⓜ Senefelder Platz – ✆ (030) 44 05 76 79 – www.zander-restaurant.de – Closed 1 - 17 January and Monday *Plan I* **D1**
Rest – *(dinner only) (booking advisable)* Menu 33/49 € – Carte 35/54 €

◆ International ◆ Bistro ◆

This friendly restaurant located in a trendy residential area serves fresh, international cuisine on two floors. Changing art exhibitions. Close to the underground.

Concorde

Augsburger Str. 41 ✉ *10789* – Ⓜ *Kurfürstendamm* – ✆ *(030) 8 00 99 90* – *www.concorde-hotels.com/concordeberlin* **K2**

311 rm – †140/450 € ††140/450 €, ☕ 28 € – 22 suites

Rest *Brasserie Le Faubourg* – ✆ *(030) 80 09 99 77 00* – Carte 40/72 €

◆ Business ◆ Grand Luxury ◆ Modern ◆

This modern luxury hotel stands in the middle of the lively city centre. It has spacious public areas and generously sized rooms. It also offers individual suites, some of which have beautiful views. There is art throughout the hotel. The Brasserie Le Faubourg is elegant and modern.

Palace

Budapester Str. 45 ✉ *10787* – Ⓜ *Zoologischer Garten* – ✆ *(030) 2 50 20* – *www.palace.de* **K2**

282 rm – †175/630 € ††175/630 €, ☕ 26 € – 19 suites

Rest *First Floor* – see below

◆ Grand Luxury ◆ Classic ◆

This luxurious hotel is at the Europa Center. It offers a large lobby, attentive service and rooms in a classical or modern style, as well as elegant suites. It also provides an 800m2 Mediterranean spa area.

InterContinental

Budapester Str. 2 ✉ *10787* – Ⓜ *Zoologischer Garten* – ✆ *(030) 2 60 20* – *www.berlin.intercontinental.com* **L2**

577 rm – †135/350 € ††135/350 €, ☕ 30 € – 13 suites

Rest *Hugos* – see below

Rest *L.A. Cafe* – Carte 28/54 €

◆ Chain hotel ◆ Luxury ◆ Classic ◆

The modern, elegant and very well-equipped guestrooms are large and good value. There is also a tasteful vitality club, as well as the conference and meeting areas. The L.A. Cafe serves Chinese and international cuisine.

Grand Hotel Esplanade

Lützowufer 15 ✉ *10785* – Ⓜ *Wittenbergplatz* – ✆ *(030) 25 47 80* – *www.esplanade.de* **L2**

394 rm – †89/399 € ††89/399 €, ☕ 18 € – 24 suites

Rest – Carte 30/53 €

Rest *Eckrestaurant* – *(closed Sunday) (dinner only)* Carte 28/47 €

◆ Luxury ◆ Modern ◆

In this hotel on the Landwehr canal find a modern and lively lobby, very cosy and friendly rooms and individual suites. Outside the building is the MS Esplanade yacht, home to events of all kinds. The Ellipse Lounge offers international cuisine. Sample local specialities in the Eckrestaurant.

Swissôtel

Augsburger Str. 44 ✉ *10789* – Ⓜ *Kurfürstendamm* – ✆ *(030) 22 01 00* – *www.swissotel.com/berlin* **K2**

316 rm – †140/260 € ††140/260 €, ☕ 21 €

Rest *44* – see below

◆ Business ◆ Modern ◆

This modern town hotel with its glass façade welcomes its guests with a spacious atrium hall. It has comfortable guestrooms, including business and executive rooms.

Pullman Schweizerhof

Budapester Str. 25 ✉ *10787* – Ⓜ *Zoologischer Garten* – ✆ *(030) 2 69 60* – *www.pullmanhotels.com*

383 rm – †125/385 € ††125/385 €, ☕ 24 € – 10 suites **L2**

Rest – Carte 31/50 €

◆ Chain hotel ◆ Business ◆ Design ◆

A modern hotel designed for business travel and meetings. It features technically well-equipped and comfortable guestrooms, and a fashionable wellness area. Bistro-style restaurant

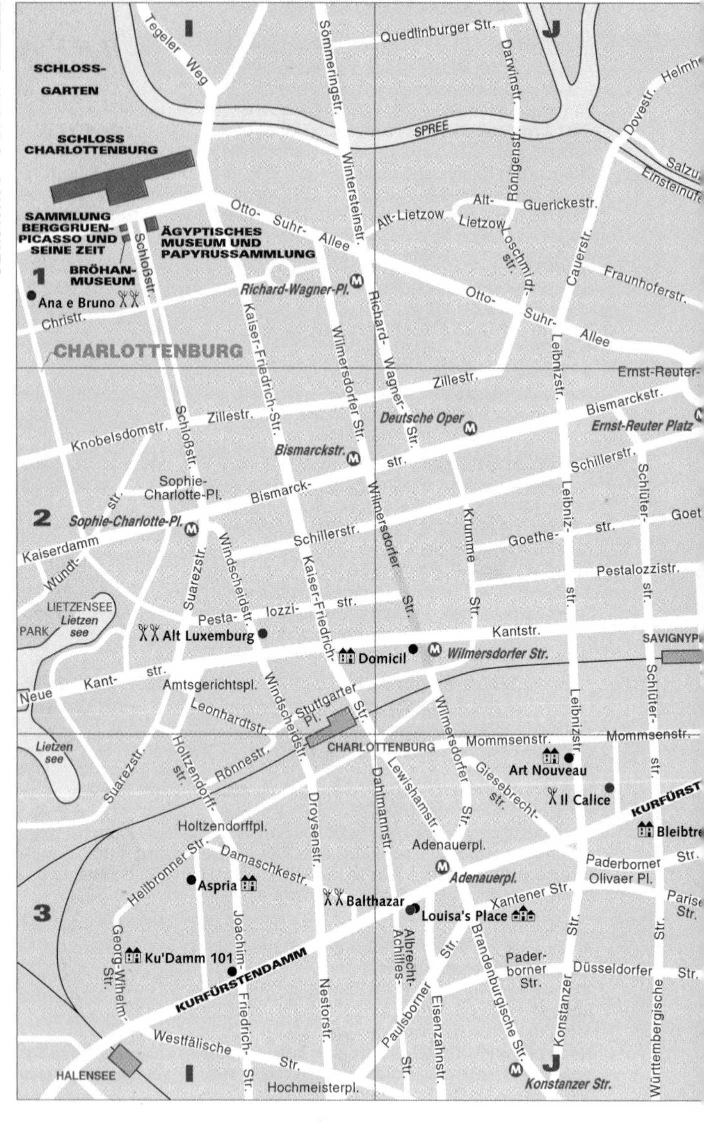

SCHLOSS-GARTEN
SCHLOSS CHARLOTTENBURG
SAMMLUNG BERGGRUEN-PICASSO UND SEINE ZEIT
BRÖHAN-MUSEUM
ÄGYPTISCHES MUSEUM UND PAPYRUSSAMMLUNG
Ana e Bruno
CHARLOTTENBURG
Richard-Wagner-Pl.
Deutsche Oper
Bismarckstr.
Ernst-Reuter Platz
Sophie-Charlotte-Pl.
LIETZENSEE PARK
Lietzen see
Alt Luxemburg
Domicil
Wilmersdorfer Str.
SAVIGNYPL
CHARLOTTENBURG
Art Nouveau
Il Calice
KURFÜRST
Bleibtr
Adenauerpl.
Aspria
Balthazar
Louisa's Place
Ku'Damm 101
KURFÜRSTENDAMM
HALENSEE
Konstanzer Str.
Tegeler Weg
Quedlinburger Str.
Darwinstr.
Sömmeringstr.
SPREE
Dovestr.
Helmholtz
Salzufer
Einsteinufer
Wintersteinstr.
Rönigenstr.
Alt-Lietzow
Guerickestr.
Otto-Suhr-Allee
Loschmidtstr.
Cauerstr.
Fraunhoferstr.
Schloßstr.
Kaiser-Friedrich-Str.
Wilmersdorfer Str.
Richard-Wagner-Str.
Leibnizstr.
Christstr.
Zillestr.
Ernst-Reuter-
Bismarckstr.
Knobelsdomstr.
Schillerstr.
Schlüterstr.
Sophie-Charlotte-Pl.
Krumme Str.
Goethestr.
Kaiserdamm
Wundtstr.
Windscheidstr.
Suarezstr.
Pestalozzistr.
Kantstr.
Neue Kantstr.
Amtsgerichtspl.
Leonhardtstr.
Stuttgarter Pl.
Mommsenstr.
Lietzen see
Holtzendorffstr.
Rönnestr.
Dahlmannstr.
Lewishamstr.
Giesebrechtstr.
Holtzendorffpl.
Droysenstr.
Adenauerpl.
Paderborner Str.
Olivaer Pl.
Heilbronner Str.
Damaschkestr.
Pariser Str.
Xantener Str.
Georg-Wilhelm-Str.
Joachim-Friedrich-Str.
Albrecht-Achilles-Str.
Brandenburgische Str.
Düsseldorfer Str.
Westfälische Str.
Nestorstr.
Paulsborner Str.
Eisenzahnstr.
Konstanzer Str.
Württembergische Str.
Hochmeisterpl.
I
J
1
2
3

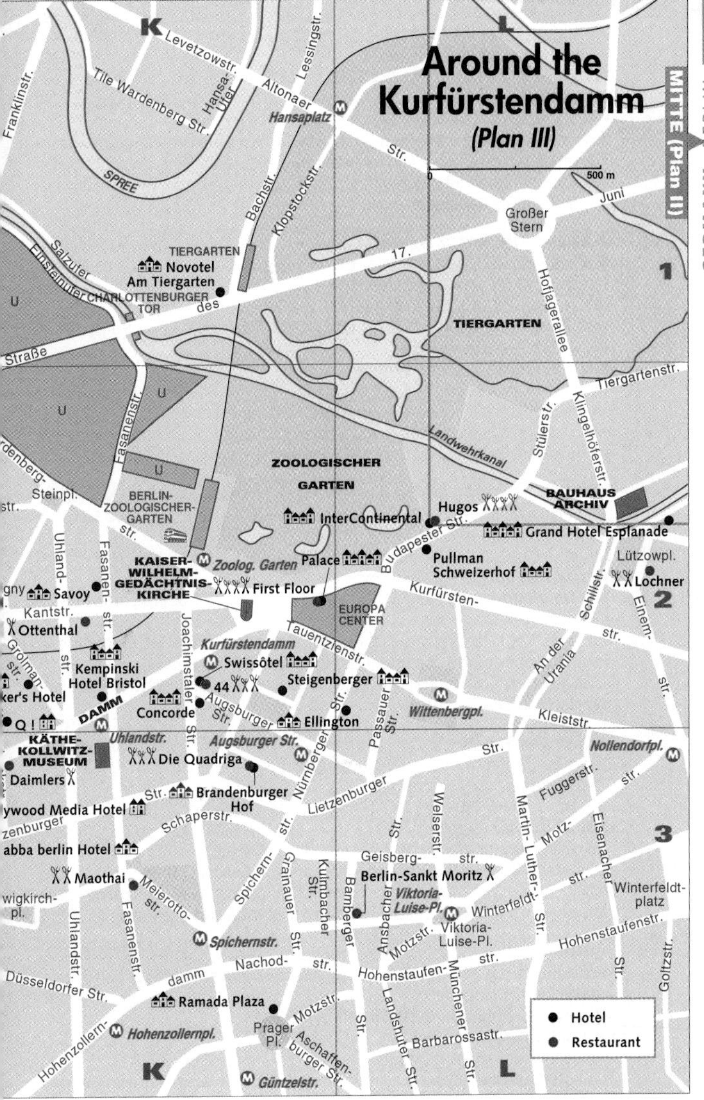
Around the Kurfürstendamm
(Plan III)
MITTE (Plan II)
500 m
Hotel
Restaurant
Novotel Am Tiergarten
InterContinental
Hugos
Grand Hotel Esplanade
Palace
Pullman Schweizerhof
Lochner
Savoy
First Floor
Ottenthal
Kempinski Hotel Bristol
Swissôtel
44
Steigenberger
Concorde
Ellington
Die Quadriga
Daimlers
Brandenburger Hof
Maothai
Berlin-Sankt Moritz
Ramada Plaza
TIERGARTEN
ZOOLOGISCHER GARTEN
BAUHAUS ARCHIV
KAISER-WILHELM-GEDÄCHTNIS-KIRCHE
KÄTHE-KOLLWITZ-MUSEUM
EUROPA CENTER
Großer Stern
Kurfürstendamm
Zoolog. Garten
Wittenbergpl.
Nollendorfpl.
Augsburger Str.
Uhlandstr.
Viktoria-Luise-Pl.
Spichernstr.
Hohenzollernpl.
Güntzelstr.
Hansaplatz

Steigenberger

Los-Angeles-Platz 1 ✉ 10789 – Ⓜ Augsburger Str. – ✆ (030) 2 12 70 – www.berlin.steigenberger.de **K2**

397 rm – 🚹125/655 € 🚹🚹125/655 €, ☕ 23 € – 11 suites

Rest *Berliner Stube* – *✆ (030) 2 12 77 50* – Carte 25/48 €

♦ Conference hotel ♦ Business ♦ Modern ♦

This hotel has an attractive lobby area with bar and smokers' lounge and beautiful, modern rooms decorated in earth tones with clean lines. Executive suites are located on the sixth floor with access to a private lounge. This friendly Berliner Stube has a traditional touch.

Kempinski Hotel Bristol

Kurfürstendamm 27 ✉ 10719 – Ⓜ Uhlandstr. – ✆ (030) 88 43 40 – www.kempinski-berlin.com **K2**

301 rm ☕ – 🚹140/350 € 🚹🚹140/350 € – 22 suites

Rest *Kempinski Grill* – *✆ (030) 88 43 47 67 (closed 12 July - 8 August)* Menu 73 € – Carte 47/75 €

Rest *Reinhard's* – Carte 24/42 €

♦ Luxury ♦ Classic ♦

The impressive building on the renowned Ku'damm is an elegant luxury hotel, which has already welcomed many a distinguished guest. The Kempinski Grill has been a Berlin institution since 1952. Reinhard's has a pleasant brasserie style.

Brandenburger Hof

Eislebener Str. 14 ✉ 10789 – Ⓜ Augsburger Str. – ✆ (030) 21 40 50 – www.brandenburger-hof.com **K3**

72 rm – 🚹180/280 € 🚹🚹265/315 €, ☕ 34 € – 8 suites

Rest *Die Quadriga* – see below

Rest *Quadriga-Lounge* – *✆ (030) 21 40 56 51* – Menu 51/63 € – Carte 48/65 €

♦ Historic ♦ Design ♦ Elegant ♦

The Berlin City Palace retains all the classical elegance of the 19C in the simple, clean lines of its rooms. It also boasts an exclusive Thaleia massage suite and a lavish à-la-carte breakfast menu. There is a conservatory atmosphere in the light and airy Quadriga Lounge.

abba Berlin Hotel

Lietzenburger Str. 89 ✉ 10719 – Ⓜ Uhlandstr. – ✆ (030) 8 87 18 60 – www.abbaberlinhotel.com/de **K3**

216 rm – 🚹110/190 € 🚹🚹110/190 €, ☕ 18 € – 4 suites

Rest *abba mía* – Carte 22/43 €

♦ Business ♦ Contemporary ♦ Functional ♦

This hotel is ideal for business travellers and conferences. There is a spacious smart lobby, as well as modern, comfortable, pleasantly simple rooms, each with a lovely crystal chandelier. The menu is Spanish and international.

Louisa's Place

Kurfürstendamm 160 ✉ 10709 – Ⓜ Adenauerplatz – ✆ (030) 63 10 30 – www.louisas-place.de **J3**

47 suites – 🚹155/595 € 🚹🚹155/595 €, ☕ 20 €

Rest *Balthazar* – see below

♦ Business ♦ Personalised ♦ Cosy ♦

This hotel has a friendly service and offers tasteful, spacious suites with kitchens. There is also a stylish breakfast room and library.

Ramada Plaza

Pragerstr. 12 ✉ 10779 – Ⓜ Güntzelstr. – ✆ (030) 2 36 25 00 – www.ramada-plaza-berlin.de **K3**

184 rm – 🚹89/259 € 🚹🚹89/259 €, ☕ 20 €, 67 suites **Rest** – Carte 30/46 €

♦ Chain hotel ♦ Modern ♦

A business hotel providing elegant rooms and suites with American cherry wood furnishings and the latest technical facilities. With executive suites on the sixth floor. A classic style restaurant.

Ellington

Nürnberger Str. 50 ✉ *10789* – Ⓜ *Wittenbergplatz* – ✆ *(030) 68 31 50* – *www.ellington-hotel.com* **L2**

285 rm – 118/258 € 128/268 €, 19 € – 3 suites **Rest** – Carte 30/58 €

◆ Business ◆ Modern ◆ Minimalist ◆

Numerous photographs of the Duke Ellington, after whom the hotel is named, adorn this simply furnished hotel. It has a beautiful lobby area and a lounge-style interior courtyard. Many details preserve its historic charm. A restaurant with a straightforward style

Novotel am Tiergarten

Straße des 17. Juni 106 ✉ *10623* – Ⓜ *Hansaplatz* – ✆ *(030) 60 03 50* – *www.novotel-berlin.com* **K1**

274 rm – 89/299 € 104/314 €, 19 € – 6 suites **Rest** – Carte 25/55 €

◆ Chain hotel ◆ Modern ◆

Located near the Tiergarten overland station, this business hotel provides modern rooms equipped with the latest technology and extensive fitness facilities as well as a lounge-style roof terrace.

Savoy

rm,

Fasanenstr. 9 ✉ *10623* – Ⓜ *Zoologischer Garten* – ✆ *(030) 31 10 30* – *www.hotel-savoy.com* **K2**

125 rm – 119/248 € 146/277 €, 22 € – 7 suites

Rest – *(closed Sunday)* Menu 33/48 € (dinner) – Carte 23/56 €

◆ Business ◆ Modern ◆

The elegant lobby area of this traditional hotel has a personal feel and is dominated by red tones. The Casa del Habano has a good selection of cigars. Modern interior with a rugged, red wine colour scheme.

Q!

Knesebeckstr. 67 ✉ *10623* – Ⓜ *Uhlandstr.* – ✆ *(030) 8 10 06 60* – *www.loock-hotels.com* **K2**

77 rm – 105/255 € 105/265 € **Rest** – *(resident only)* Carte 30/44 €

◆ Business ◆ Design ◆

Design reigns supreme. The modern, technically well laid out rooms are minimalist with their dark tones. Stylish restaurant with Euro-Asian fare.

Hollywood Media Hotel without rest

Kurfürstendamm 202 ✉ *10719* – Ⓜ *Uhlandstr.* – ✆ *(030) 88 91 00* – *www.filmhotel.de* **K3**

182 rm – 95/139 € 115/159 € – 5 suites

◆ Business ◆ Modern ◆

This residence is devoted to Hollywood and the world of film. The tasteful, contemporary rooms are decorated with numerous film posters and photos of stars. The hotel has its own small cinema.

Aspria

Karlsruher Str. 20 ✉ *10711* – Ⓜ *Adenauerpl.* – ✆ *(030) 8 90 68 88 68* – *www.aspria-hotel.de* **I3**

42 rm – 89/189 € 89/199 €, 10 € **Rest** – Carte 19/22 €

◆ Business ◆ Contemporary ◆ Design ◆

This hotel features tasteful modern rooms with very good technical equipment. Directly adjoining is the "Sporting Club"'; which is open to the public and has outstanding amenities. This timeless restaurant also has a bistro and a terrace.

Domicil

Kantstr. 111a ✉ *10627* – Ⓜ *Wilmersdorfer Str.* – ✆ *(030) 32 90 30* – *www.hotel-domicil-berlin.de* **J2**

70 rm – 90/120 € 110/140 € – 10 suites **Rest** – Carte 18/37 €

◆ Business ◆ Modern ◆

This privately run hotel is furnished with warm shades and pretty materials providing a homely Italian style. Rooms to the rear are particularly quiet. This restaurant has lobby, breakfast and dining areas on the seventh-floor with a beautiful roof terrace. International cuisine.

Hecker's Hotel

Grolmanstr. 35 ✉ 10623 – Ⓤ Uhlandstr. – ☎ (030) 8 89 00 – www.heckers-hotel.de **K2**

69 rm – †110/250 € ††120/280 €, ☕ 16 € – 3 suites

Rest *Cassambalis* – *☎ (030) 8 85 47 47 (closed Sunday lunch)*

Carte 33/47 €

◆ Business ◆ Design ◆

This establishment offers contemporary living just a few steps from the Kurfürstendamm. The Bauhaus, Toskana and Colonial themed rooms are tastefully done out. There is a quiet sun terrace on the fourth-floor, and a modern breakfast room. The Cassambalis offers Mediterranean cuisine in a warm and charming atmosphere.

Bleibtreu

Bleibtreustr. 31 ✉ 10707 – Ⓤ Uhlandstr. – ☎ (030) 88 47 40 – www.bleibtreu.com **J3**

60 rm – †112/198 € ††118/198 €, ☕ 17 €

Rest – Carte 21/43 €

◆ Business ◆ Design ◆

This refurbished patrician house from around 1900 provides friendly and good value guestrooms furnished in a modern style. Rooms have a free mini bar and some have W-LAN. The restaurant offers sandwiches, steaks and burgers. There are terraces on the street and in the interior courtyard.

Ku' Damm 101 without rest

Kurfürstendamm 101 ✉ 10711 – Ⓤ Adenauerplatz – ☎ (030) 5 20 05 50 – www.kudamm101.com **I3**

170 rm – †101/205 € ††118/222 €, ☕ 15 €

◆ Business ◆ Design ◆

Deliberately understated designs and natural rubber flooring set the atmosphere. Rooms are bright and technically well-equipped. The breakfast room offers a view over the town, and there is a modern bar.

Art Nouveau without rest

Leibnizstr. 59 ✉ 10629 – Ⓤ Adenauerplatz – ☎ (030) 3 27 74 40 – www.hotelartnouveau.de **J3**

17 rm ☕ – †96/146 € ††126/186 € – 3 suites

◆ Townhouse ◆ Personalised ◆ Cosy ◆

The lift of this very special and charming hotel on the fourth-floor dates back to 1906. Find individually decorated rooms, partly with antique furniture and wooden floorboards.

Hugos – Hotel InterContinental

Budapester Str. 2 (14th floor) ✉ 10787 – Ⓤ Zoologischer Garten – ☎ (030) 26 02 12 63 – www.hugos-restaurant.de – Closed 2 weeks early January, 1 week end April, 4 weeks July - August, Sunday and Bank Holidays **L2**

Rest – *(dinner only)* Menu 90/112 € – Carte 89/109 €

Spec. Makrele mit Paprika, Bohnen und Safran-Craker. Rücken von Lamm mit Artischocken, gepfefferten Karotten und Djah Oftadeh. Kaymak und Erdbeere karamellisiert, Mousse und Erdbeer-Goa-Curryeis.

◆ Modern ◆ Fashionable ◆ Elegant ◆

Take the lift to this smart restaurant on the 14th floor, where in addition to Thomas Kammeier's contemporary cuisine, the amazing view of the city makes any visit worthwhile. There is choice of three menus, accompanied by the appropriate wines.

XXXX ✿

First Floor – Hotel Palace

Budapester Str. 45 ✉ 10787 – Ⓜ Zoologischer Garten – ✆ (030) 25 02 10 20 – www.firstfloor.palace.de – Closed 1 - 13 January, 11 July - 8 August, Saturday lunch and Sunday lunch

Rest – Menu 39 € (lunch)/112 € – Carte 77/94 € **K2**

Spec. Gebratene Langustinen auf Duo vom grünen und weißen Spargel. Rinderfilet "Rossini Art" neu interpretiert. Rhabarber mit Essigkaramell und Vanille.

♦ Classic ♦ Elegant ♦

Chef Matthias Diether cooks very good classic food with contemporary elements at this restaurant on the first floor of the hotel. The adept service team competently recommends the right wines from a selection of around 1 500 vineyards.

XXX ✿

Die Quadriga – Hotel Brandenburger Hof

Eislebener Str. 14 ✉ 10789 – Ⓜ Augsburger Str. – ✆ (030) 21 40 56 51 – www.brandenburger-hof.com – Closed 1 - 17 January, 17 July - 15 August and Sunday - Monday

Rest – *(dinner only)* Menu 110/145 € – Carte 77/92 € **K3**

Spec. Rentier und Tanne mit Rosmarin. Lachs und Jakobsmuscheln mit Estragon. Schokolade und Fenchel, Holzkohle.

♦ Seasonal cuisine ♦ Elegant ♦ Classic ♦

Chef Sauli Kemppainen who spoils guests at this classic, stylish restaurant with his seasonal dishes, hails from Finland. His cooking is creative and very precise.

XXX

44 – Hotel Swissôtel

Augsburger Str. 44 ✉ 10789 – Ⓜ Kurfürstendamm – ✆ (030) 2 20 10 22 88 – www.restaurant44.de – Closed 1 - 9 January, 24 July - 14 August and Sunday **K2**

Rest – Menu 33/82 € – Carte 61/80 €

♦ Innovative ♦ Fashionable ♦

This simple, modern and elegant restaurant serves imaginative food in the form of a tasting menu. Glass frontage and terrace overlooking the Kurfurstendamm.

XX

Ana e Bruno

Sophie-Charlotten-Str. 101 ✉ 14059 – Ⓜ Sophie-Charlotte-Pl. – ✆ (030) 3 25 71 10 – www.ana-e-bruno.de **I1**

Rest – *(dinner only)* Menu 59/95 € – Carte 45/74 €

♦ Mediterranean ♦ Elegant ♦

Find attentive and dedicated service, as well as an ambitious and tasty Mediterranean cuisine in this elegant and pleasant, brightly decorated restaurant. There is an excellent Italian wine list.

XX

Alt Luxemburg

Windscheidstr. 31 ✉ 10627 – Ⓜ Wilmersdorfer Str. – ✆ (030) 3 23 87 30 – www.altluxemburg.de – Closed Sunday **I2**

Rest – *(dinner only) (booking advisable)* Menu 48/70 € – Carte 51/70 €

♦ Classic ♦ Family ♦

Attractive, friendly colours contribute to the atmosphere of this restaurant. It offers classic cuisine, and has been traditionally run by the Wannemacher family since 1982.

XX

Balthazar – Hotel Louisa's Place

Kurfürstendamm 160 ✉ 10709 – Ⓜ Adenauerplatz – ✆ (030) 89 40 84 77 – www.balthazar-restaurant.de **J3**

Rest – *(dinner only)* Menu 42/44 € – Carte 35/55 €

♦ International ♦ Fashionable ♦ Trendy ♦

This restaurant is on the Kurfürstendamm. It features timeless furnishings in warm shades, and carefully laid out tables. Enjoy the good service and the modern, international menu.

Lochner

Lützowplatz 5 ✉ 10785 – Ⓜ Nollendorfplatz – ✆ (030) 23 00 52 20 – www.lochner-restaurant.de – Closed 2 weeks end July - early August and Monday **L2**

Rest – *(dinner only)* Menu 45/70 € – Carte 38/59 €

◆ International ◆ Friendly ◆

This is a pleasant, family-run restaurant with many regular customers. Your host cooks ambitiously, and friendly service is encouraged from the top down.

Maothai

Meierottostr. 1 ✉ 10719 – Ⓜ Spichernstr. – ✆ (030) 8 83 28 23 – www.maothai-am-fasanenplatz.de **K3**

Rest – *(dinner only)* Carte 21/49 €

◆ Asian ◆ Exotic ◆

Enjoy the intimate, candle lit atmosphere in this restaurant near the Fasanen square. It serves authentic Thai cuisine, and there is a charming terrace dining area.

Bieberbau

Durlacher Str. 15 ✉ 10715 – Ⓜ Bundesplatz – ✆ (030) 8 53 23 90 – www.bieberbau-berlin.de – Closed Sunday - Monday *Plan I* **B3**

Rest – *(dinner only) (booking advisable)* Menu 35/53 €

◆ International ◆ Cosy ◆

Enjoy excellent wining and dining in the former studio of the master stuccoer Richard Bieber. It is adorned with listed 19C craftsmanship, has friendly and professional waitresses, as well as a lovely terrace at the front.

Berlin-Sankt Moritz

Regensburger Str. 7 ✉ 10777 – Ⓜ Viktoria-Luise-Pl. – ✆ (030) 23 62 44 70 – www.restaurant-sankt-moritz.de – Closed Sunday **L3**

Rest – *(dinner only)* Menu 41/88 € – Carte 41/58 €

◆ International ◆ Cosy ◆

This cosy restaurant located in a residential area serves ambitious contemporary cuisine and has a good choice of wines – just follow the recommendations of the knowledgeable staff.

Ottenthal

Kantstr. 153 ✉ 10623 – Ⓜ Uhlandstr. – ✆ (030) 3 13 31 62 – www.ottenthal.com **K2**

Rest – *(dinner only) (booking advisable)* Carte 29/46 €

◆ Austrian ◆ Bistro ◆

There is a bistro-like feel at this pleasant restaurant named after chef Arthur Schneller's home village in Lower Austria. Tasty Austrian influenced dishes and a good wine selection are on offer. Friendly service.

Daimlers

Kurfürstendamm 203 ✉ 10719 – Ⓜ Uhlandstr. – ✆ (030) 39 01 16 98 – www.daimlers.de – Closed Sunday dinner **K3**

Rest – Carte 26/53 €

◆ International ◆ Bistro ◆

A bistro-style restaurant hides behind the glass frontage of this car dealership. The classic international cuisine is complemented by the "Berlin Menu". Good German wines sold to drink on the premises or take away.

Il Calice

Walter-Benjamin-Platz 4 ✉ 10629 – Ⓜ Adenauerpl. – ✆ (030) 3 24 23 08 – www.ilcalice.de – Closed Sunday lunch **J3**

Rest – Carte 39/67 €

◆ International ◆ Friendly ◆ Brasserie ◆

By the Leibniz Kolonnaden, this friendly restaurant has a brasserie-like atmosphere. It features good Italian and international cuisine and more refined dining in the evening. The food is accompanied by very good Italian wines.

Renger-Patzsch

Wartburgstr. 54 ✉ *10823 –* Ⓤ *Eisenacher Str. –* ✆ *(030) 7 84 20 59*
– www.renger-patzsch.com *Plan I* **B3**
Rest – *(dinner only) (booking essential)* Carte 24/34 €
♦ Home cooking ♦ Inn ♦ Cosy ♦
This cosy restaurant is named after the pioneer of landscape photography – black and white pictures adorn the walls. Good traditional cooking and tarte flambée are on the menu.

ENVIRONS OF BERLIN *Plan I*

AT BERLIN-GRUNEWALD

Schlosshotel im Grunewald

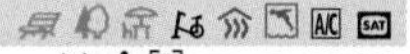

Brahmsstr. 10 ✉ *14193 –* ✆ *(030) 89 58 40*
– www.schlosshotelberlin.com **A3**
53 rm – †219/259 € ††219/259 €, ☕ 26 € – 10 suites
Rest *Alter Wintergarten* – *(Tuesday - Saturday lunch only)* Carte 48/61 €
Rest *Vivaldi* – ✆ *(030) 89 58 47 34 (closed 2 weeks January and Sunday - Monday) (dinner only)* Menu 65/115 € – Carte 53/77 €
♦ Rural ♦ Luxury ♦ Design ♦
This 19C palace located in the upmarket Grunewald district offers a perfect combination of wonderful historical detail and refined, modern style. Remarkable library. Set in small grounds. A friendly welcome awaits in this lovely restaurant. A stylishly elegant restaurant with a pleasant terrace.

Frühsammers Restaurant

Flinsberger Platz 8 ✉ *14193 –* ✆ *(030) 89 73 86 28*
– www.fruehsammers-restaurant.de
– Closed 1 - 11 January, 21 - 25 March and Saturday lunch, Sunday - Monday
Rest – *(booking advisable)* Menu 26 € (lunch)/98 € (dinner) **A3**
♦ International ♦ Friendly ♦
The Frühsammer family serve excellent international food along with the chef's wine recommendations in this elegant villa belonging to the Grunewalder Tennis Club. Good-value lunch menu.

AT BERLIN-TEGEL (AIRPORT)

Dorint Airport Tegel

Gotthardstr. 96 ✉ *13403 –* Ⓤ *Kurt-Schuhmacher-Platz –* ✆ *(030) 49 88 40*
– www.dorint.com/berlin-tegel **B1**
303 rm – †62/143 € ††72/153 €, ☕ 14 € **Rest** – Carte 20/32 €
♦ Chain hotel ♦ Functional ♦
A functional business hotel with good transport links. The luxury rooms on the upper floors offer extras including air conditioning and a late check-out facility, as well as an hour's free wireless LAN. Restaurant serving international cuisine.

Cologne
KÖLN

Population (est 2010) 998 105 - Altitude: 53m.

:rgen/Fotolia.com

Based in the very centre of Europe on the banks of the Rhine, Cologne is Germany's oldest city (its name was instigated by the Romans, a 'colony' set up to fend off Barbarians). It became a Free City, and later fell under the rule of Napoleon and then the Prussians; all of which has given the locals a cosmopolitan, laid-back and sociable outlook. To illustrate the point, they have their own beer named after them, *Kölsch*, which enjoys the same regional status as Champagne, meaning it can't be brewed anywhere else in the country.

Although it may never be described as Europe's prettiest city, it has an eye-catching old town (largely rebuilt after World War II) and some world-class museums, with subjects ranging from modern art via sport and the Olympics to chocolate. It also boasts one of the finest collections of medieval churches in Europe (lovingly restored in the last half-century), and ploughs its own furrow by celebrating Carnival like it's Rio (no-one seems to care that there's no beach and not much sunshine). Most famously, Cologne has its Cathedral, a massive structure that stood tall during the War, and remains the biggest tourist attraction in Germany. Many of the people craning their necks to take in the exterior are also marvelling at the fact that the whole great edifice took over half a millennium to build…

LIVING THE CITY

The **River Rhine** cuts a swathe right through the heart of Cologne, with four central bridges allowing you plentiful passage from east to west. The main hub of the city is on the west bank, with the **Altstadt** (old town), dominated by its **Cathedral**, practically on the river bank itself. Out to the west, the old medieval walls are now a ring road, which neatly encircles the city centre. Just northwest of the ring road is **Mediapark,** a brash modern development, while to the east of the Rhine is the massive **Trade Fair Centre**, with its 80m-high tower. To its north is Cologne's biggest and most popular park, **Rheinpark.**

PRACTICAL INFORMATION

ARRIVAL-DEPARTURE

Cologne-Bonn Airport lies 17km southeast of the city centre. A taxi will cost approximately €30 or take the S13 train.

TRANSPORT

You can get around Cologne by bus, tram or metro. Validate (stamp) each ticket whenever you board. You can buy a single trip ticket for Cologne, which is valid for anywhere in the city. This is also valid for a journey to nearby Bonn. There are also day tickets covering the same area.

If you're in the city for a while, invest in a Köln Welcome Card. This offers almost ninety offers of reduced admission, ranging from art and culture, leisure facilities, shopping and eating establishments, to free travel on the public transport network. It's available from tourist information offices and many hotels.

EXPLORING COLOGNE

A lot of people come to Cologne for its trade fairs; this is a city renowned across Germany for people in suits making a beeline for the great redbrick Kölnmesse building on the Rhine's right bank. Any visitor not heading for this imposing Trade Fair Centre is invariably headed towards the city's other mighty landmark, rearing like a huge blackened monster over on the left bank. When Cologne **Cathedral** was completed in 1880, it was the tallest building in the world, a record it held for nine years until the rise of the Eiffel Tower. The massive Dom on the Rhine took an astonishing 632 years to complete, because its high Gothic style fell out of fashion in the mid-sixteenth century and tools were downed for another three hundred years, when it became popular again.

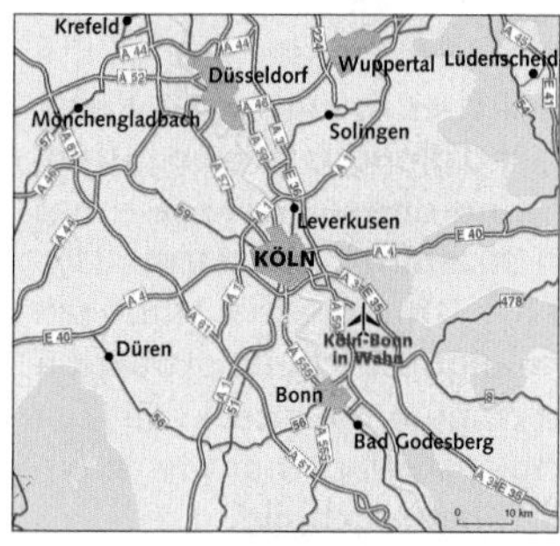

Two million visitors pass through its huge main door each year; the pluckier ones ascend the 509 steps that lead to an observation platform in one of the towers. Halfway up, many take a breather to look at the largest free-swinging bell in the world. At ground level, the massive oak stalls, now seven hundred years old, are the largest ever made in Germany; there's a beautiful fifteenth century altar painting of the patrons of Cologne, and a huge Romanesque reliquary, the Shrine of the Three Kings. After all this, the rest of the city might appear to suffer from an inferiority complex. Look closer, though, and you'll see the city's been fighting back.

➜ ALL ROADS LEAD TO ROMANESQUE

Cologne was a powerful centre for the Church in medieval times and the result is the impressive circle of **Romanesque churches** huddled together in a circle in the old town. They were all badly damaged in the War, but the loving reparations carried out since have returned most to their former glory. Amongst the most startling are **St Ursula**, with a Baroque golden chamber full of ornate, gilded carving, wild-eyed busts and hundreds of skulls wearing sequinned caps, and **St Gereon**, with its massive, ten-sided dome making it one of the most distinctive and unusual buildings in Germany. The Romanesque church most identified with the city is **Great St Martin's**, mainly because its wonderful tower and steeple dominate the **Fischmarkt**, a popular tourist spot by the river. The houses and street lay-out around here have been rebuilt to historic designs, making it a romantically picturesque neighbourhood in which to wander.

➜ DOM-MINIONS

Over the last few years, Cologne has rightly built itself a reputation as a cultural metropolis. Its museums are a by-word for excellence, and two of them are within the shadow of the Dom. The **Romano-Germanic Museum** is essential viewing for anyone keen on 'what the Romans did for us'. Its centrepiece is a fabulous Dionysius mosaic discovered in 1941 during excavations for an air-raid shelter. The mosaic features maids in flowing blue capes being attended by muscular satyrs, and it's made from over a million pieces of ceramic. On display elsewhere is a superb array of artefacts, including beautiful oil lamps, jewellery, sandals, snake thread glassware, dice and even bridge foundations. Almost next door, perfectly placed to provide a nice contrast, is the **Museum Ludwig**, which propels you forward two thousand years with a mind-blowing collection of twentieth century art. It's in a magically light, airy building that seems just right for the biggest collection of Pop Art outside the US. Over four floors, you cross continents and all sorts of borders and boundaries to take in Russian avant-garde, German Expressionism, surrealism, and contemporary installations. Expect the ubiquitous Picasso, Dali, Magritte and Chagall, and a whole lot more besides.

➜ TASTY SELECTION

If your taste is for art from earlier, more classical, times, Cologne has that covered, too. A few minutes' walk south leads you to the **Wallraf-Richartz Museum**, a shiny edifice opened in 2001. This should cater to most tastes, as the range of Western art from the thirteenth to the nineteenth centuries is pretty comprehensive. On the second floor is the very earliest depiction of Cologne – six hundred years old – in *The Martyrdom of St Ursula at the City of Cologne*. Go up a floor and you're face to face with a fantastic collection of works by the masters of Dutch and Flemish painting; up again and you'll find the Impressionists, plus the likes of Cezanne, Munch and Van Gogh. Nearby, on the banks of the Rhine, you'll find two more museum big hitters, rather incongruously plonked down next to each other. The **German Sport and Olympic Museum** gives you the chance to burn off energy by racing a cycle through a wind tunnel or playing football up on the roof, while at the **Chocolate**

Museum you can put the pounds back on via a very tasty trip through three millennia's worth of the brown stuff.

→ OUT OF STEP?

Underground music takes on a very literal meaning in Cologne. Go down the steps of the Ludwig Museum and immediately underneath is the **Philharmonic Hall**, home to a wide range of concerts from classical to folk and pop. In the past, the Hall has also played host to the unwelcome sound of intrusive footsteps from pedestrians in the street above, so perhaps you should avoid performances with too many quiet passages. No such considerations at the city's classy **Opera House**, in the heart of the city centre, south west of the Dom. It's situated in Germany's largest theatre complex, and holds 1300, so you've a pretty good chance of getting a seat; as well as classic and modern opera, ballet is featured heavily, too. One of the city's coolest musical venues is in the peaceful confines of the **Stadtgarten** (City Park) just beyond the ring road. **Stadtgarten** is set on the **Venloer Strasse** side of the park and has been the top jazz venue in the city for over thirty years. These days, it's widened its remit and features other strands of contemporary music. This is in general the 'cool' side of town, frequented by students and the media denizens who work in the nearby Mediapark. There are lots of fashionable restaurants and clubs, and, just to the west of the ring road, the **Belgian Quarter**, easily identified by its street names. This boasts handsome old buildings and chic apartments which make it one of the classiest places to live – and to stroll – in the city.

CALENDAR HIGHLIGHTS

As Cologne is a city of museums, it's fitting that one of its most acclaimed events is the Long Night of Cologne Museums (October). Around forty of them are open through most of the hours of darkness at a very low price. There's no real question, though, about what's the main festival in the city: Carnival. Unlike Rio or Venice, it begins on 11 November at 11.11am with a day of fancy dress and drinking in the old town and goes on until it reaches its climax about three months later with five days of hard partying, culminating in a street parade on Rose Monday (just before Lent) watched by a million spectators. As a complete contrast, the city takes on a bookish air in March when it hosts Europe's largest international literature festival, lit.cologne, featuring a whole array of renowned authors. In June, half a million pairs of eyes look upwards as Cologne Lights illuminates the skies over the

COLOGNE IN…

→ ONE DAY

Altstadt, Dom, Romanesque churches

→ TWO DAYS

Museum Ludwig, Wallraf-Richartz Museum (or Chocolate Museum, depending on your taste), Stadtgarten (or Opera House, again depending on your taste)

→ THREE DAYS

Romano-Germanic Museum, Rheinpark

Rhine with the world's largest musically synchronised fireworks display; a convoy of boats adds to the spectacle. A month later, the Christopher Street Day gay pride gathering descends on an open-air stage in the old town for its off-the-wall parade; these days the event actually takes up a whole weekend. Also in July, the Summerjam (around the fields of Lake Fuhlinger) brings a Caribbean flair to Cologne in the shape of a reggae and world music jamboree. Not many cities can lay claim to concerts on their ring road, but Ringfest (August) sees a line of stages set up for two miles along the Ringstrassen (don't worry, it's closed to traffic) and two million rock fans descend on the area for a batch of free concerts.

EATING OUT

Cologne has a good variety of international restaurants, but before you consider eating, you should consider the local beer. The city is renowned throughout Germany for its Kölsch. It's the name of the local people and it's the name of their brew, a light beer with the yeast risen to the top rather than sunk to the bottom of the glass. There are twenty local breweries producing their own versions, and you can try them out in an old town brauhaus, atmospheric places with dark wood-panelled interiors and buzzy waiters always at hand to fill your empty stangen (small 0.2 litre glasses) whether you want them to or not. You haven't experienced Cologne properly till you've downed your Kölsch. That accomplished, you can make the most of the city's ethnic diversity by selecting a restaurant from an impressive global range; pick of the bunch are the fine Italian, Japanese and Turkish establishments. Seek out an Italian ice-cream parlour in the summertime, sit under a parasol and tuck into their renowned, full-on sundaes. If your preference is for something local, your best bet is not to be an animal lover. Favoured dishes include Himmer un Äad (bloodsausage and mash), Sauerbraten vom Pferd (braised horse) or Töttchen (ragout of brains and calf's head, cooked with herbs). As well as restaurants, cafés and bars stay open through the afternoon until late, maybe 11.00pm or midnight. Service charge is generally included but a tip of up to ten per cent is the norm.

ON THE RHEIN LINES

Pop over to the east bank for the city's biggest green space, Rheinpark. It's a whopping 125 acres and if you want to get from one end to the other you can climb aboard the park's very own miniature railway, or, if you fancy reaching it in dramatic fashion from the west bank, take a trip on the cable car that leaves from the zoo and crosses the river at head-spinning height.

Environs of Cologne
(Plan I)
0
2 km
A
B
1
2
3
PESCH
LONGERICH
WEIDENPESCH
MAUENHEIM
OSSENDORF
BICKENDORF
VOGELSANG
EHRENFELD
MÜNGERSDORF
WEIDEN
JUNKERSDORF
LINDENTHAL
SÜLZ
KLETTENBERG
HÜRTH
A 57-E 31
A 1-E 37
A 57
A 1-E 31
A 4-E 40
Neusser Landstr.
Industriestr.
Militärringstr.
Neusser
Venloer
Str.
Parkgürtel
Äußere Kanalstr.
Ehrenfeld-gürtel
Centre (Plan II)
Innere Kanalstr.
Melatengürtel
Aachener
Str.
Maître im Landhaus Kuckuck
MUSEUM FÜR OSTASIATISCHE KUNST
Universitätsstr.
STADTWALD
Brenner'scher Hof
Dürener
Fellini
Sülzgürtel
Horbeller
Bonn-
Holzstr.
Kölner
Frechener
Luxemburger
Klettenberg-gürtel
Zollstock-gürtel
Brühler
27
28
29
30
102
103
104
11

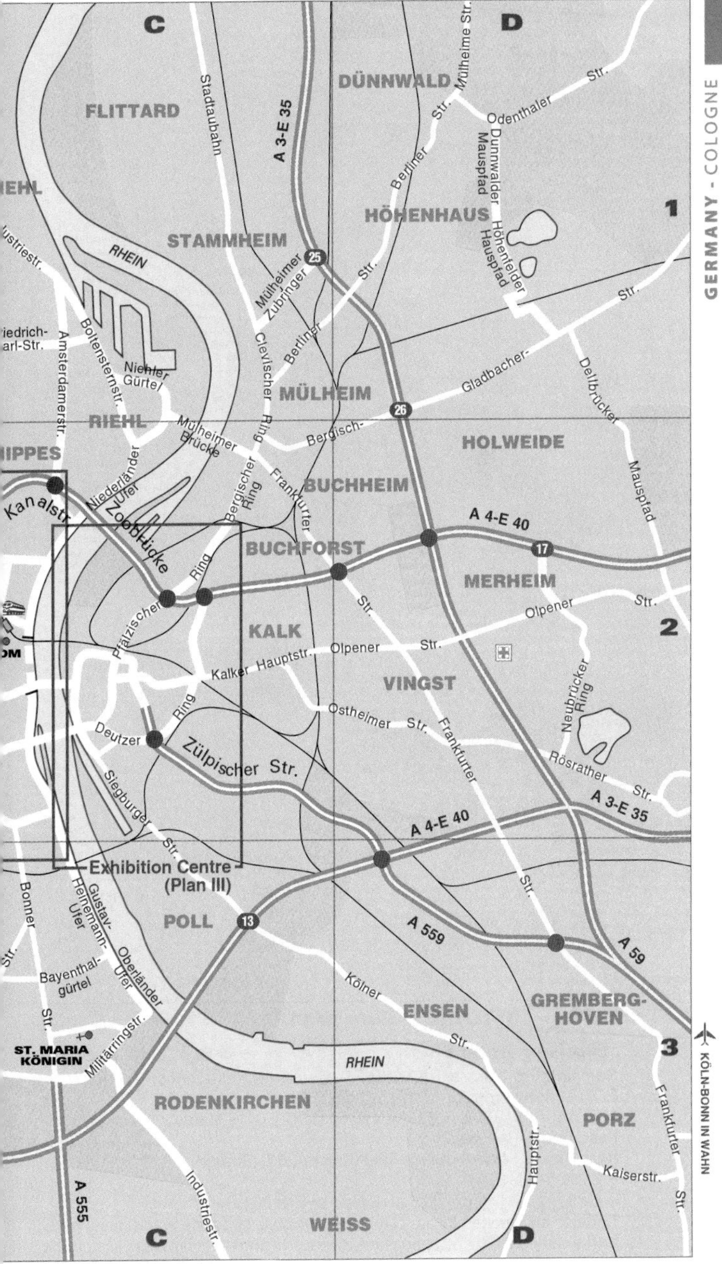
C
D
FLITTARD
DÜNNWALD
STAMMHEIM
HÖHENHAUS
MÜLHEIM
RIEHL
HOLWEIDE
BUCHHEIM
BUCHFORST
MERHEIM
KALK
VINGST
POLL
ENSEN
GREMBERG-HOVEN
RODENKIRCHEN
PORZ
WEISS
ST. MARIA KÖNIGIN
RHEIN
A 3-E 35
A 4-E 40
A 559
A 59
A 555
Stadtaubahn
Mülheimer Str.
Odenthaler Str.
Berliner Str.
Dünnwalder Mauspfad
Höhenfelder Hauspfad
Mülheimer Zubringer
Clevischer Ring
Gladbacher- Str.
Dellbrücker Mauspfad
Bergisch-
Niehler Gürtel
Boltensternstr.
Amsterdamerstr.
Mülheimer Brücke
Niederländer Ufer
Bergischer Ring
Frankfurter Str.
Kanalstr.
Zoobrücke
Olpener Str.
Kalker Hauptstr.
Pfälzischer Ring
Ostheimer Str.
Neubrücker Ring
Rösrather Str.
Deutzer Ring
Zülpischer Str.
Siegburger Str.
Exhibition Centre (Plan III)
Bonner Str.
Gustav-Heinemann-Ufer
Oberländer Ufer
Bayenthal-gürtel
Militärringstr.
Kölner Str.
Hauptstr.
Kaiserstr.
Industriestr.
KÖLN-BONN IN WAHN
1
2
3

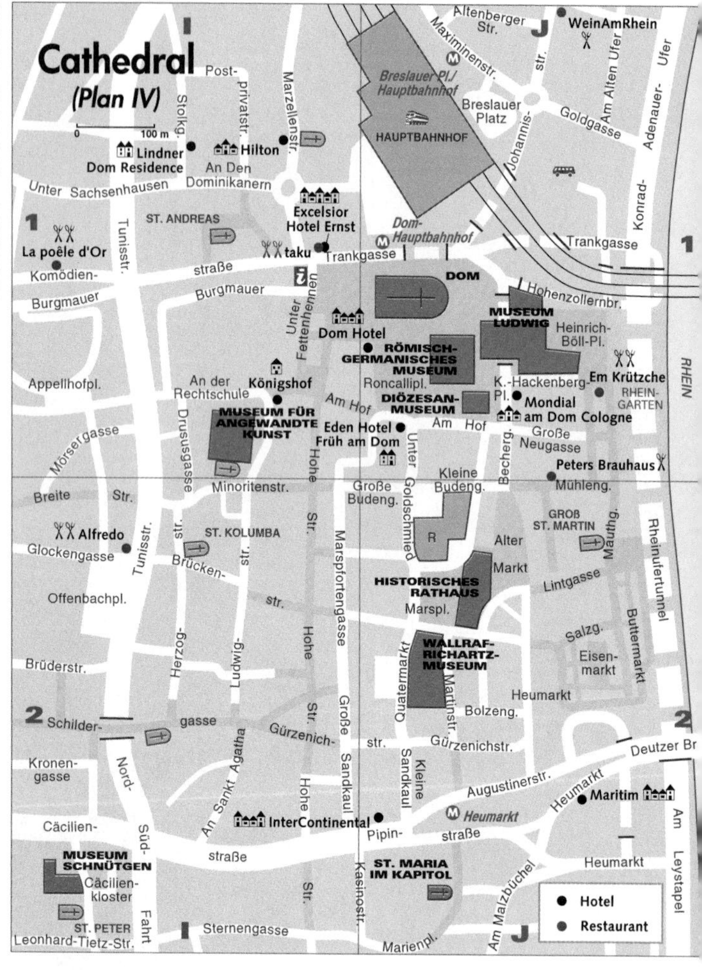

CATHEDRAL – HISTORIC TOWN HALL *Plan IV*

Excelsior Hotel Ernst

Domplatz/Trankgasse 1 ✉ 50667 – Ⓜ Dom-Hauptbahnhof – ✆ (0221) 27 01 – www.excelsior-hotel-ernst.de **I1**

142 rm – 🚹210/380 € 🚹🚹230/490 €, ☕ 27 € – 19 suites
Rest *Taku* – see below
Rest *Hanse Stube* – Menu 59 € (lunch)/86 € (dinner) – Carte 54/78 €

♦ Grand Luxury ♦ Traditional ♦ Classic ♦

Tradition and modernity are combined with style and taste in this grand hotel by the cathedral. The reception area is exclusive and the rooms are elegant. The rooms in the Hanse wing are particularly stately. A stylish classical atmosphere prevails in the Hanse Stube.

InterContinental

Pipinstr. 1 ⊠ 50667 – Ⓜ Heumarkt – ✆ (0221) 2 80 60 – www.koeln.intercontinental.com **J2**
262 rm – †149/425 € ††179/455 €, ☕ 29 € – 9 suites
Rest *Maulbeers* – *✆ (0221) 28 06 12 70 (closed Sunday and Monday) (dinner only)* Menu 39/55 € – Carte 40/63 €

♦ Business ♦ Luxury ♦ Retro ♦

In all categories, this hotel offers fashionable rooms in muted colours with the most up-to-date technology and views of the cathedral. The special extras include executive rooms and the Club floor. The Maulbeers restaurant on the first-floor offers international cuisine.

Dom Hotel

Domkloster 2a ⊠ 50667 – Ⓜ Dom-Hauptbahnhof – ✆ (0221) 2 02 40 – www.domhotel.de **J1**
124 rm – †150/300 € ††175/325 €, ☕ 28 € – 4 suites
Rest – Menu 32 € (lunch) – Carte 32/57 €

♦ Traditional ♦ Luxury ♦ Classic ♦

Built in 1857, this traditional hotel is situated right next to the cathedral. It has a classically elegant, yet modern style. The bar and one of the junior suites are dedicated to Peter Ustinov. At Restaurant Le Merou, enjoy sitting at the large window front. There is a terrace onto Roncalliplatz.

Maritim

Heumarkt 20 ⊠ 50667 – Ⓜ Heumarkt – ✆ (0221) 2 02 70 – www.maritim.de
454 rm – †128/350 € ††148/370 €, ☕ 19 € – 12 suites **J2**
Rest *Bellevue* – *✆ (0221) 2 02 78 75* – Menu 68/86 € (dinner) – Carte 50/67 €

♦ Chain hotel ♦ Functional ♦

This hotel by the Deutz bridge on the edge of the old town offers comfortable, functional rooms. The impressive, airy glass-roofed lobby, with its boulevard flair, invites you to stroll around. The Bellevue has a roof terrace and views over the Rhine. Interesting water list.

Hilton

Marzellenstr. 13 ⊠ 50668 – Ⓜ Dom-Hauptbahnhof – ✆ (0221) 13 07 10 – www.hilton.de/koeln **I1**
296 rm – †99/450 € ††109/480 €, ☕ 24 €, 2 suites **Rest** – Carte 29/65 €

♦ Business ♦ Modern ♦

This business travellers' hotel is just a stone's throw from the cathedral. From its lobby to the Ice Bar and guestrooms, it is laid out in a clean-lined, modern design. The Konrad restaurant with show kitchen has a simple, modern ambience.

Mondial Am Dom Cologne

Kurt-Hackenberg-Platz 1 ⊠ 50667 – Ⓜ Dom-Hauptbahnhof – ✆ (0221) 2 06 30 – www.hotel-mondial-am-dom-cologne.com **J1**
207 rm – †119/455 € ††139/475 €, ☕ 24 € **Rest** – Carte 36/65 €

♦ Business ♦ Modern ♦

This hotel lies in the town centre near the cathedral. It provides modern, well-furnished and technically equipped rooms, including spacious deluxe rooms. Havana cigar lounge. This contemporary restaurant offers a tapas bar, brasserie and fine dining.

Lindner Dom Residence

An den Dominikanern 4a (entrance Stolkgasse) ⊠ 50668 – Ⓜ Dom-Hauptbahnhof – ✆ (0221) 1 64 40 – www.lindner.de
125 rm – †89/169 € ††109/189 €, ☕ 20 € **I1**
Rest *La Gazetta* – Carte 26/53 €

♦ Townhouse ♦ Functional ♦

This modern, glazed, atrium building is a functional business hotel close to the cathedral. There are first-class rooms with balconies on the seventh-floor, and a good fitness area (charged extra). Taste predominantly Italian cuisine in La Gazetta, which has a view of the interior courtyard.

Eden Hotel Früh am Dom without rest

Sporergasse 1 ✉ 50667 – Ⓜ Dom-Hauptbahnhof – ✆ (0221) 27 29 20 – www.hotel-eden.de **J1**

38 rm – 95/253 € 120/293 €

◆ Townhouse ◆ Modern ◆

Close to the Domplatz is this hotel with modern rooms, some with views of the Dom. The breakfast room provides lovely views of the Heinzelmännchenbrunnen.

Königshof without rest

Richartzstr. 14 ✉ 50667 – Ⓜ Dom-Hauptbahnhof – ✆ (0221) 2 57 87 71 – www.hotelkoenigshof.com **I1**

82 rm – 68/139 € 98/215 € – 1 suite

◆ Townhouse ◆ Functional ◆

Just a few paces from Cologne cathedral, this hotel offers functional rooms and a good breakfast buffet.

taku – Excelsior Hotel Ernst

Domplatz (Trankgasse 1) ✉ 50667 – Ⓜ Dom-Hauptbahnhof – ✆ (0221) 2 70 39 10 – www.taku.de – Closed 4 weeks July - August **I1**

Rest – Menu 29 € (lunch) – Carte 43/69 €

◆ Asian ◆ Minimalist ◆ Fashionable ◆

This restaurant offers authentically prepared Asian dishes from Chinese to Indonesian, in a clear-cut, contemporary setting. Highly attentive service.

Alfredo (Roberto Carturan)

Tunisstr. 3 ✉ 50667 – ✆ (0221) 2 57 73 80 – www.ristorante-alfredo.com – Closed 3 weeks August - early September, Saturday - Sunday and Bank Holidays

Rest – *(booking advisable)* Carte 40/63 € **I2**

Spec. Langzeit gegarter Schweinebauch. Gnocchi mit Scampi. Seezunge mit Kapern und Kräutern.

◆ Italian ◆ Friendly ◆

Together with his wife Susanne, Roberto Carturan runs this restaurant – which was founded by and named after his father. She cordially attends to the guests while he cooks tasty, authentic Italian dishes, and also advises you in person.

La Poêle d'Or

Komödienstr. 50 ✉ 50667 – Ⓜ Dom-Hauptbahnhof – ✆ (0221) 13 98 67 77 – www.lapoeledor.de – Closed 23 December - 14 January, Sunday - Monday and Bank Holidays **I1**

Rest – Menu 49/77 € – Carte 51/57 €

Rest *Bistrot B* – Carte 27/35 €

◆ Classic ◆ Trendy ◆

After a break of several years, Jean-Claude Bado has returned to his old workplace. His head waiter at the time now attentively manages the service. Modern ambience, classic cuisine and fine wines. Casual bistro with a down-to-earth menu.

Em Krützche

Am Frankenturm 1 ✉ 50667 – Ⓜ Dom-Hauptbahnhof – ✆ (0221) 2 58 08 39 – www.em-kruetzche.de – Closed 23 - 25 December, 30 March - 13 April and Monday **J1**

Rest – Carte 31/40 €

◆ Regional ◆ Traditional ◆ Family ◆

This historical guesthouse has been run by the Fehn family for over 30 years. The lovely rooms are spread over two floors and range from rustically charming to elegant. The winter speciality is goose.

WeinAmRhein

Johannisstr. 64 ✉ 50668 – Ⓜ Breslauer Pl./Hauptbahnhof – ✆ (0221) 91 24 88 85 – www.weinamrhein.eu – Closed Saturday lunch, Sunday - Monday **J1**

Rest – *(Bank Holidays dinner only)* Menu 43 € (dinner) – Carte 31/58 €

◆ International ◆ Fashionable ◆

This restaurant offers good, international cuisine and an extensive European wine list in a very modern setting. The decor, including floor tiles, chairs and the striking wall hangings, are based around the theme of wine.

Peters Brauhaus

Mühlengasse 1 ✉ 50667 – Ⓜ Dom-Hauptbahnhof – ✆ (0221) 2 57 39 50 – www.peters-brauhaus.de – Closed over Christmas **J1**

Rest – Carte 19/36 €

♦ Regional ♦ Cosy ♦

A rustic inn with a beautiful decorated façade. Worth a look around: each room has a character of its own. Serves good, solid food with fresh Kölsch beer on draught.

CENTRE

Plan II

Marriott

Johannisstr. 76 ✉ 50668 – Ⓜ Breslauer Pl. / Hauptbahnhof – ✆ (0221) 94 22 20 – www.koelnmarriott.de **F1-2**

365 rm – †129/480 € ††129/480 €, ☕ 25 € – 10 suites

Rest *Fou* – *✆ (0221) 9 42 22 61 01 (closed Sunday dinner)* Carte 20/42 €

♦ Business ♦ Modern ♦

A spacious lobby and "Plusch-Bar" greet you at this comfortable business hotel near the cathedral. The rooms are comfortable and very modern. This restaurant has the casual, French brasserie-style.

Pullman

Helenenstr. 14 ✉ 50667 – Ⓜ Friesenplatz – ✆ (0221) 27 50 – www.pullmanhotels.com **E2**

275 rm – †108/408 € ††108/408 €, ☕ 22 € – 10 suites

Rest – *(closed Sunday and Monday)* Carte 25/57 €

♦ Chain hotel ♦ Conference hotel ♦ Modern ♦

Its central location and modern design distinguish this conference hotel. All suites are on the eleventh floor and have a fabulous view of the cathedral. On the twelfth floor is the 'George M' wine bar with its international menu.

Im Wasserturm

rest,

Kaygasse 2 ✉ 50676 – Ⓜ Poststr. – ✆ (0221) 2 00 80 – www.hotel-im-wasserturm.de **F2**

78 rm – †225 € ††255 €, ☕ 28 € – 7 suites

Rest *La Vision* – see below

Rest *d/\blju "W"* – Menu 33/44 € – Carte 36/68 €

♦ Historic ♦ Business ♦ Design ♦

The impressive architecture of this 130-year-old former water tower provides a unique setting for this elegant, modern hotel. Beauty and massage treatments are available at "Atelier Beauté". With its clean, contemporary design d/\blju "W" serves regional and international cuisine.

Renaissance

Magnusstr. 20 ✉ 50672 – Ⓜ Friesenplatz – ✆ (0221) 2 03 40 – www.renaissancekoeln.de **E2**

236 rm – †125/495 € ††125/550 €, ☕ 24 €

Rest *Raffael* – Carte 27/43 €

♦ Chain hotel ♦ Classic ♦

This city centre hotel is timelessly elegant. The club floor offers particular comfort with its own lounge and special facilities. The Raffael restaurant serves international cuisine.

Savoy

Turiner Str. 9 ✉ 50668 – Ⓜ Breslauer Pl. / Hauptbahnhof – ✆ (0221) 1 62 30 – www.savoy.de **F1**

98 rm ☕ – †140/325 € ††185/385 € – 13 suites **Rest** – Carte 37/56 €

♦ Business ♦ Personalised ♦

This building has been laid out in a high class, sophisticated and individual style. No two of the tasteful and elegant rooms are the same. The James Bond Suite for example is particularly interesting. Dinner is served in the Mythos restaurant; lunch is served in the bar. Beautiful roof terrace.

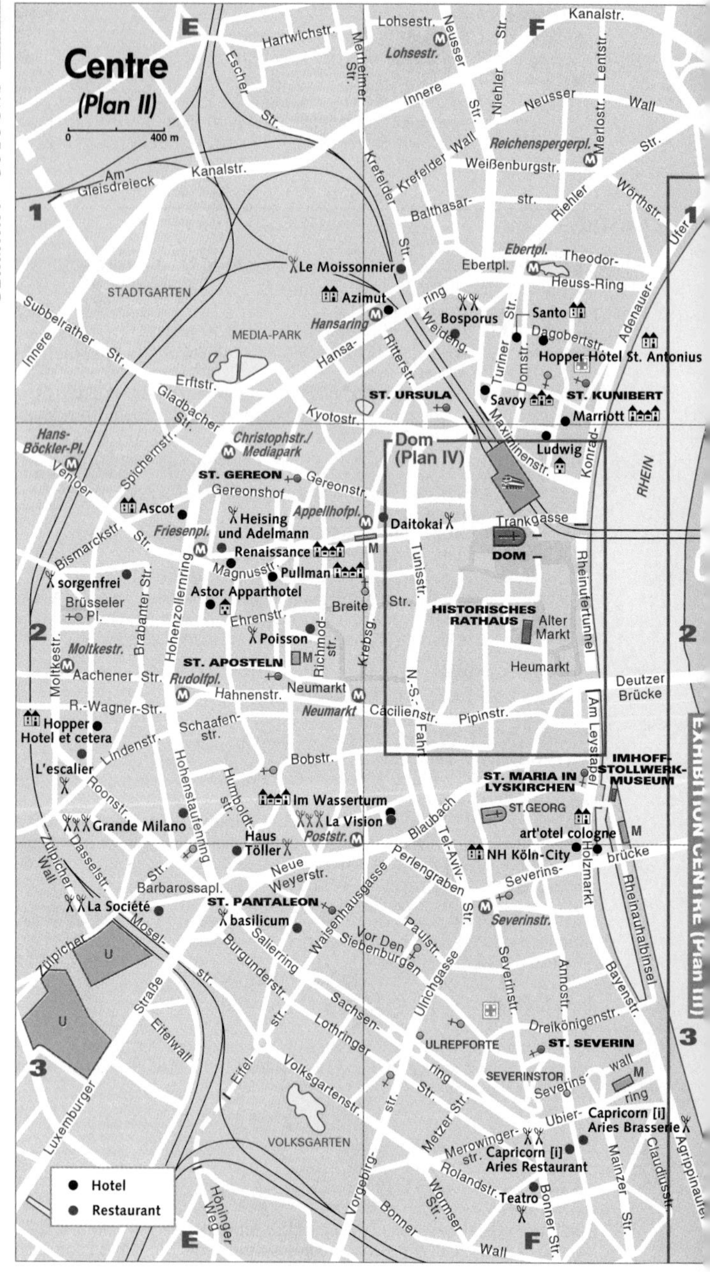
Centre
(Plan II)
0
400 m
E
F
1
2
3
Hotel
Restaurant
Le Moissonnier
Azimut
Bosporus
Santo
Hopper Hotel St. Antonius
Savoy
Marriott
Ludwig
Ascot
Heising und Adelmann
Daitokai
Renaissance
Pullman
sorgenfrei
Astor Apparthotel
Poisson
Hopper Hotel et cetera
L'escalier
Im Wasserturm
La Vision
Grande Milano
Haus Töller
art'otel cologne
NH Köln-City
La Société
basilicum
Capricorn [i] Aries Brasserie
Capricorn [i] Aries Restaurant
Teatro
STADTGARTEN
MEDIA-PARK
ST. URSULA
ST. KUNIBERT
ST. GEREON
Dom (Plan IV)
DOM
HISTORISCHES RATHAUS
ST. APOSTELN
ST. MARIA IN LYSKIRCHEN
IMHOFF-STOLLWERK-MUSEUM
ST.GEORG
ST. PANTALEON
ULREPFORTE
ST. SEVERIN
SEVERINSTOR
VOLKSGARTEN
RHEIN
EXHIBITION CENTRE (Plan III)
Lohsestr.
Reichenspergerpl.
Ebertpl.
Hansaring
Christophstr./ Mediapark
Hans-Böckler-Pl.
Appellhofpl.
Friesenpl.
Moltkestr.
Rudolfpl.
Neumarkt
Poststr.
Severinstr.
Kanalstr.
Hartwichstr.
Escher Str.
Merheimer Str.
Neusser Str.
Niehler Str.
Lentstr.
Merlostr.
Innere Kanalstr.
Neusser Wall
Krefelder Wall
Krefelder Str.
Weißenburgstr.
Balthasar-str.
Riehler Str.
Wörthstr.
Theodor-Heuss-Ring
Am Gleisdreieck
Subbelrather Str.
Innere
Hansa-ring
Ritterstr.
Weideng.
Turiner Str.
Domstr.
Dagobertstr.
Adenauer-
Uferstr.
Erftstr.
Gladbacher Str.
Kyotostr.
Maximinenstr.
Konrad-
Venloer
Spichernstr.
Gereonstr.
Gereonshof
Trankgasse
Bismarckstr.
Magnusstr.
Tunisstr.
Rheinufertunnel
Brüsseler Pl.
Brabanter Str.
Hohenzollernring
Ehrenstr.
Breite Str.
Richmodstr.
Krebsg.
Alter Markt
Heumarkt
Aachener Str.
Hahnenstr.
N.-S.-Fahrt
Cäcilienstr.
Pipinstr.
Deutzer Brücke
Am Leystapel
R.-Wagner-Str.
Schaafenstr.
Lindenstr.
Bobstr.
Roonstr.
Hohenstaufenring
Humboldtstr.
Blaubach
Tel-Aviv-Str.
Holzmarkt
brücke
Zülpicher Wall
Dasselstr.
Barbarossapl.
Neue Weyerstr.
Perlengraben
Severins-
Waisenhausgasse
Rheinauhafeninsel
Zülpicher Straße
Moselstr.
Salierring
Burgunderstr.
Vor Den Siebenburgen
Paulstr.
Ulrichgasse
Severinstr.
Annostr.
Bayenstr.
Luxemburger
Eifelwall
Eifelstr.
Sachsen-ring
Lothringer Str.
Volksgartenstr.
Dreikönigenstr.
Severinswall
Vorgebirgstr.
Metzer Str.
Ubierring
Merowingerstr.
Claudiusstr.
Agrippinaufer
Rolandstr.
Bonner Str.
Wormser Str.
Mainzer Str.
Bonner Wall
Höninger Weg

art'otel cologne

Am Holzmarkt 4 ✉ 50676 – Ⓜ Severinstr. – ✆ (0221) 80 10 30 – www.artotels.com **F3**

218 rm – 🚹92/142 € 🚹🚹92/142 €, ☕ 18 €

Rest – *(dinner only)* Carte 32/36 €

◆ Business ◆ Design ◆

Modern designer hotel at the Rhine port. Simple styling as well as numerous works by the Korean artist SEO can be found throughout The Chino Latino restaurant serves Asian food and has a terrace with views of the chocolate museum.

Azimut without rest

Hansaring 97 ✉ 50670 – Ⓜ Hansaring – ✆ (0221) 88 87 60 – www.azimuthotels.de **F1**

190 rm – 🚹105/145 € 🚹🚹105/145 €, ☕ 15 €

◆ Business ◆ Modern ◆

This modern business hotel in a historic brick building is equipped with good technical facilities.

Ascot without rest

Hohenzollernring 95 ✉ 50672 – Ⓜ Friesenplatz – ✆ (0221) 9 52 96 50 – www.hotel-ascot.de – Closed Christmas - 2 January **E2**

44 rm ☕ – 🚹99/300 € 🚹🚹109/300 €

◆ Townhouse ◆ Cosy ◆ Classic ◆

The English style of this hotel can be seen from its bedrooms to its pretty lobby with a small library and bar. There is a friendly breakfast room with an interior courtyard terrace.

Santo without rest

Dagobertstr. 22 ✉ 50668 – Ⓜ Ebertplatz – ✆ (0221) 9 13 97 70 – www.hotelsanto.de **F1**

69 rm ☕ – 🚹89/128 € 🚹🚹114/148 €

◆ Business ◆ Modern ◆

This hotel is distinguished by its contemporary design and the pleasing, specially designed lighting concept from Christian Türmer. Attentive service.

Hopper Hotel St. Antonius

Dagobertstr. 32 ✉ 50668 – Ⓜ Ebertpl. – ✆ (0221) 1 66 00 – www.hopper.de **F1**

54 rm ☕ – 🚹105/125 € 🚹🚹150 € – 5 suites

Rest *L. Fritz im Hopper* – *(closed Saturday lunch and Sunday lunch)* Carte 26/42 €

◆ Business ◆ Personalised ◆

A historic building fabric and a clear, modern style are combined in this former Kolping guesthouse. Large and small suites are available. The Tiefrot theatre is also housed here. Restaurant with a bistro atmosphere and a beautiful round ceiling arch. It has a pleasant terrace in the interior courtyard.

Hopper Hotel et cetera

Brüsseler Str. 26 ✉ 50674 – Ⓜ Moltkestr. – ✆ (0221) 92 44 00 – www.hopper.de – Closed 1 - 9 January **E2**

49 rm ☕ – 🚹95/120 € 🚹🚹135/145 €

Rest – *(closed Sunday - Monday)* Carte 31/44 €

◆ Townhouse ◆ Personalised ◆

In this former monastery, simple, modern furnishing and historic elements have been combined beautifully. The hotel is in the Belgian quarter near the old town. This interior, courtyard, terrace restaurant is set under the trees. There is an impressive altar painting that will catch your eye.

NH Köln-City rest, VISA AE

Holzmarkt 47 ✉ 50676 – Ⓜ Severinstr. – ✆ (0221) 2 72 28 80 – www.nh-hotels.de **F3**

204 rm – †69/199 € ††69/199 €, ☕ 18 €

Rest – *(closed 23 - 31 December)* Carte 24/41 €

♦ Chain hotel ♦ Modern ♦

This modern hotel is close to the Severin bridge and not far from the Stollwerck chocolate museum. Some of the modern, functional rooms are superior in that they face the peaceful interior courtyard. This modern restaurant has a small conservatory.

Astor Apparthotel without rest VISA AE

Friesenwall 68 ✉ 50672 – Ⓜ Friesenplatz – ✆ (0221) 20 71 20 – www.hotelastor.de – Closed Christmas - 3 January **E2**

50 rm ☕ – †85/125 € ††95/145 € – 1 suite

♦ Townhouse ♦ Functional ♦

This highly personally managed hotel consists of two houses that have been joined together. Some of the rooms are particularly comfortable and modern. Art is displayed in the form of pictures.

Ludwig without rest VISA AE

Brandenburger Str. 24 ✉ 50668 – Ⓜ Breslauer Pl. / Hauptbahnhof – ✆ (0221) 16 05 40 – www.hotelludwig.de – Closed Christmas - 1 January

55 rm ☕ – †88/98 € ††114/129 € – 1 suite **F2**

♦ Townhouse ♦ Functional ♦

This hotel is close to the centre and the station. Other advantages are its very friendly service and its well-maintained, modern rooms. Some of the rooms on the fourth-floor have air-conditioning and a balcony.

La Vision – Hotel Im Wasserturm VISA AE

Kaygasse 2 (11th floor) ✉ 50676 – Ⓜ Poststr. – ✆ (0221) 2 00 80 – www.hotel-im-wasserturm.de – Closed 2 weeks January, 4 weeks end July - August and Sunday - Monday

Rest – *(dinner only)* Menu 73/118 € – Carte 60/83 € **F2**

Spec. Marinierte Jakobsmuschelscheiben mit zweierlei Broccoli, Nelkenpfeffer und leichter Ingwercreme. Tranchen vom Rindsonglet im Röstkartoffelsud mit feinem Spitzkohl. Knusprige Tarte von der Schokolade mit geeistem Fenchel.

♦ Inventive ♦ Elegant ♦

At this restaurant a captivating, restrained elegance is combined with a magnificent view over Cologne. Yet the environment is surpassed by the creative culinary skills of Hans Horbeth. The attentive team serves the excellent "1872" and "John Moore" menus.

Grande Milano VISA AE

Hohenstaufenring 29 ✉ 50674 – Ⓜ Rudolfpl. – ✆ (0221) 24 21 21 – www.grandemilano.com – Closed Saturday lunch and Sunday

Rest – Menu 59/89 € – Carte 42/75 € **E2**

Rest *Pinot di Pinot* – Menu 14 € (lunch)/20 € (dinner) – Carte 22/40 €

♦ Italian ♦ Elegant ♦ Friendly ♦

This family-run restaurant has an elegant atmosphere, attentive service and exceptional Italian cuisine. The speciality in autumn is white Alba truffle. Pinot di Pinot provides a light alternative with a bistro atmosphere.

Capricorn [i] Aries Restaurant (Klaus Jaquemod)

Alteburger Str. 34 ✉ 50678 – Ⓜ Severinstr. – ✆ (0221) 32 31 82 – www.capricorniaries.com – Closed 3 - 9 March, 22 - 25 April, July and Monday - Tuesday **F3**

Rest – *(dinner only) (booking essential)* Menu 75/95 €

Spec. Laubfrosch vom Lachs in Kaviarvinaigrette. Seezungen-Hummerroulade mit Topinamburmousse. Vol-au-vent von Meeresfrüchten mit Spargel.

♦ Inventive ♦ Intimate ♦ Individual ♦

Klaus Jaquemod and Judith Kräeber have jointly run this restaurant for many years. In its unostentatious elegant white room excellent dishes in the form of two menus are served at only four tables. Professional wine recommendations.

XX ✿

La Société

Kyffhäuser Str. 53 ✉ 50674 – ✆ (0221) 23 24 64 – www.lasociete.info
– Closed 3 weeks July - August **E3**
Rest – *(dinner only) (booking advisable)* Menu 67/95 €
– Carte 53/82 €

Spec. Fünf verschiedene Suppen mit kleiner Beilage im Reagenzglasständer. Seeteufel für zwei Personen im Ganzen gebraten mit Kalbscroûtons. Karamellisierte Taubenbrust mit Gänseleber, Lauch und Speck-Datteln.

◆ Inventive ◆ Individual ◆ Intimate ◆

Mario Kotaska and Dominic Jeske are in charge of the kitchen at this restaurant close to the university district. The food is creative, the atmosphere intimate, and the well-trained service team are appealingly natural and provide good wine recommendations.

XX

Bosporus

Weidengasse 36 ✉ 50668 – Ⓜ Hansaring – ✆ (0221) 12 52 65
– www.bosporus.de
– Closed Sunday lunch **F1**
Rest – Carte 26/36 €

◆ Turkish ◆ Classic ◆ Friendly ◆

This classically furnished restaurant has a pleasant terrace and a beautiful function room on the first-floor. Authentic Turkish cuisine is prepared in the open kitchen.

X ✿✿

Le Moissonnier

Krefelder Str. 25 ✉ 50670 – Ⓜ Hansaring – ✆ (0221) 72 94 79
– www.lemoissonnier.de
– Closed 2 weeks Christmas - early January, 1 week over Easter, 3 weeks July - August and Sunday - Monday, except Bank Holidays **F1**
Rest – *(booking essential)* Menu 65/103 € – Carte 58/103 €

Spec. Foie Gras Maison. Coquilles Saint-Jacques. Pigeonneau rôti.

◆ Innovative ◆ Bistro ◆

Mr and Mrs Moissonnier and chef Eric Mechon are a well-matched trio and bring a touch of Paris to Cologne in this delightful bistro. Unusual combinations define the food. Ask for the rarities wine list.

X ✿

L'escalier (Jens Dannenfeld)

Brüsseler Str. 11 ✉ 50674 – Ⓜ Moltkestr. – ✆ (0221) 2 05 39 98
– www.lescalier-restaurant.de
– Closed 3 - 10 March, 18 - 28 April, 24 October - 3 November and Saturday lunch, Sunday - Monday lunch **E2**
Rest – Menu 38/60 € – Carte 50/61 €

Spec. Gefüllte Topinambur mit Datteln und Löffelerbsen, Minze. Gebackener Krautwickel vom Hecht mit Majoran. Rinderrücken auf Meerrettichkohlrabi und Roten Zwiebeln.

◆ Classic ◆ Fashionable ◆ Bistro ◆

Enter this lovely old building in the Belgian quarter via the eponymous three steps and enjoy the modern classic cuisine of Jens Dannenfeld. You will be well looked after by the attentive service team led by Melanie Dannenfeld.

X

Poisson

Wolfsstr. 6 ✉ 50667 – Ⓜ Neumarkt – ✆ (0221) 27 73 68 83
– www.poisson-restaurant.de
– Closed over Carnival, Sunday - Monday and Bank Holidays **E3**
Rest – *(booking advisable)* Menu 35 € (lunch) – Carte 48/84 €

◆ Fish ◆ Bistro ◆ Trendy ◆

The highlight of this modern bistro, in the middle of the old town, is its fish dishes. The chef cooks modern, product specific dishes with classical, Asian and Mediterranean elements.

Capricorn [i] Aries Brasserie

Alteburgerstr. 31 ✉ 50678 – Ⓜ Severinstr. – ✆ (0221) 3 97 57 10 – www.capricorniaries.com – Closed Saturday lunch and Sunday

Rest – Menu 35/55 € – Carte 27/52 € **F3**

♦ French ♦ Bistro ♦ Cosy ♦

This cosy brasserie, with a terrace on the street, is a lighter alternative to the restaurant opposite with the same name. Pleasant atmosphere, friendly service and international cuisine.

Heising und Adelmann

Friesenstr. 58 ✉ 50670 – Ⓜ Friesenplatz – ✆ (0221) 1 30 94 24 – www.heising-und-adelmann.de – Closed 1 week over Easter, Sunday - Monday and Bank Holidays

Rest – Menu 36 € – Carte 32/48 € **E2**

♦ International ♦ Bistro ♦ Trendy ♦

Guests are served modern international cuisine in the relaxed atmosphere of this lively bistro restaurant with its delightful terrace. Pleasant Lounge and large bar area.

basilicum

Am Weidenbach 33 ✉ 50676 – Ⓜ Poststr. – ✆ (0221) 32 35 55 – www.basilicum.org – Closed 8 - 16 February, 6 - 19 September and Sunday

Rest – *(dinner only) (booking advisable)* Carte 39/49 € **E3**

♦ International ♦ Friendly ♦

Find good contemporary, international cuisine in this small bistro-style restaurant, which is run in a friendly and dedicated manner. Attractive covered inner courtyard terrace.

Teatro

Zugweg 1 ✉ 50667 – Ⓜ Severinstr. – ✆ (0221) 80 15 80 20 – Closed Tuesday, Saturday lunch, Sunday lunch **F3**

Rest – *(booking advisable)* Carte 35/46 €

♦ Italian ♦ Fashionable ♦ Family ♦

Italian dishes can be selected from a board at the Spatola family's vibrant restaurant. The decor features black and white photographs of film stars. Good value lunchtime menu.

Sorgenfrei

Antwerpenerstr. 15 ✉ 50672 – Ⓜ Moltkestr. – ✆ (0221) 3 55 73 27 – www.sorgenfrei-koeln.com – Closed Saturday lunch - Sunday

Rest – Menu 34/41 € (dinner) – Carte 32/45 € **E2**

♦ International ♦ Friendly ♦ Cosy ♦

Pleasant cosy restaurant in the Belgian quarter featuring friendly service, international cuisine and good wine recommendations. Smaller lunchtime menu. Wine shop next door.

Daitokai

Kattenbug 2 ✉ 50667 – Ⓜ Appellhofpl. – ✆ (0221) 12 00 48 – www.daitokai.de – Closed Monday except exhibitions **F2**

Rest – *(Tuesday - Thursday dinner only)* Menu 36 € (lunch)/61 € – Carte 38/63 €

♦ Japanese ♦ Friendly ♦

In this authentic Japanese restaurant in the town centre, the cooks demonstrate their finger skills at Teppanyaki tables. The waitresses are appropriately dressed in Kimonos.

Haus Töller

Weyerstr. 96 ✉ 50676 – Ⓜ Poststr. – ✆ (0221) 2 58 93 16 – www.haus-toeller.de – Closed end July - early September, Sunday and Bank Holidays **E3**

Rest – *(dinner only) (booking advisable)* Carte 19/26 €

♦ Regional ♦ Traditional ♦ Cosy ♦

Find the Wirtshaus tradition in its genuine form: wooden tables and floors, conferred ceilings and even a 'confessional', all the same as they were 100 years ago. It is also worth seeing the scroll on display from 1942. Friday evening is potato pancakes.

AT THE EXHIBITION CENTRE *Plan III*

Hyatt Regency

Kennedy-Ufer 2a ✉ 50679 – Ⓜ Deutzer Freiheit
– ✆ (0221) 8 28 12 34 – www.cologne.regency.hyatt.de **G2**
306 rm – ♦190/450 € ♦♦220/480 €, ☕ 29 € – 18 suites
Rest *Glashaus* – *✆ (0221) 82 81 17 73* – Carte 45/66 €

♦ Chain hotel ♦ Luxury ♦ Classic ♦

This luxury hotel offering elegant rooms in the clean, modern style is located on the banks of the River Rhine. Some rooms have river views. This restaurant with its atrium-style glass lobby serves international cuisine.

Dorint An der Messe

Deutz-Mülheimer-Str. 22 ✉ 50679 – Ⓜ Bf. Deutz
– ✆ (0221) 80 19 00 – www.dorint.com/koeln **G1**
313 rm ☕ – ♦129/424 € ♦♦167/449 € – 47 suites
Rest *L'Adresse* – *(closed Sunday - Monday) (dinner only)* Carte 24/52 €
Rest *Düx* – Carte 23/42 €

♦ Chain hotel ♦ Business ♦ Modern ♦

This elegant, modern hotel located opposite the Exhibition Centre has a 650m² spa and a bright and friendly breakfast room which also lays on a buffet lunch during trade fairs and exhibitions. For the ultimate in luxury try the exclusive Konrad Adenauer Suite. L'Adresse offers an upmarket menu. The Düx is a typical Cologne restaurant.

Radisson BLU

Messe Kreisel 3 ✉ 50679 – Ⓜ Bf. Deutz – ✆ (0221) 27 72 00
– www.cologne.radissonblu.com **G1**
393 rm – ♦145/195 € ♦♦145/195 €, ☕ 23 € – 1 suite
Rest – *(closed Satuday lunch, Sunday lunch and Bank Holidays lunch)* Carte 36/52 €

♦ Chain hotel ♦ Stylish ♦ Modern ♦

This ultra-modern business hotel next to the Exhibition Centre boasts an impressive glass lobby which houses the bar, and the luxury Capitolium Suite complete with cathedral view. Paparazzi serves Italian cuisine including pizzas fresh from its authentic pizza oven.

Günnewig Hotel Stadtpalais

Deutz-Kalker-Str. 52 ✉ 50667 – Ⓜ Deutz-Kalker Bad
– ✆ (0221) 88 04 20 – www.guennewig.de **G2**
115 rm – ♦135/302 € ♦♦145/322 €, ☕ 18 € – 2 suites
Rest – *(dinner only)* Menu 20/50 € – Carte 24/61 €

♦ Business ♦ Modern ♦

This attractive group of building directly opposite the LANXXES Arena combines historical and modern architecture. Technically well equipped rooms in purist style. Small range of dishes available in menu form.

Burns Art Hotel without rest

Adam-Stegerwald-Str. 9 ✉ 51063 – Ⓜ Bf. Deutz – ✆ (0221) 6 71 16 90
– www.hotel-burns.de – closed 22 - 30 December **H1**
83 rm ☕ – ♦85/194 € ♦♦105/220 €

♦ Business ♦ Functional ♦

This hotel boasts a relatively calm location in a residential area. Guests can choose between contemporary "Fair & More" rooms and the pure lines of its designer "Burns Art" rooms.

Inselhotel without rest

Constantinstr. 96 ✉ 50679 – Ⓜ Bf. Deutz – ✆ (0221) 8 80 34 50
– www.inselhotel-koeln.de **G2**
42 rm ☕ – ♦79/185 € ♦♦109/265 €

♦ Townhouse ♦ Functional ♦

This corner townhouse opposite Deutz railway station offers its guests friendly service and well-maintained, functional rooms. Close to the Exhibition Centre and LANXXES Arena.

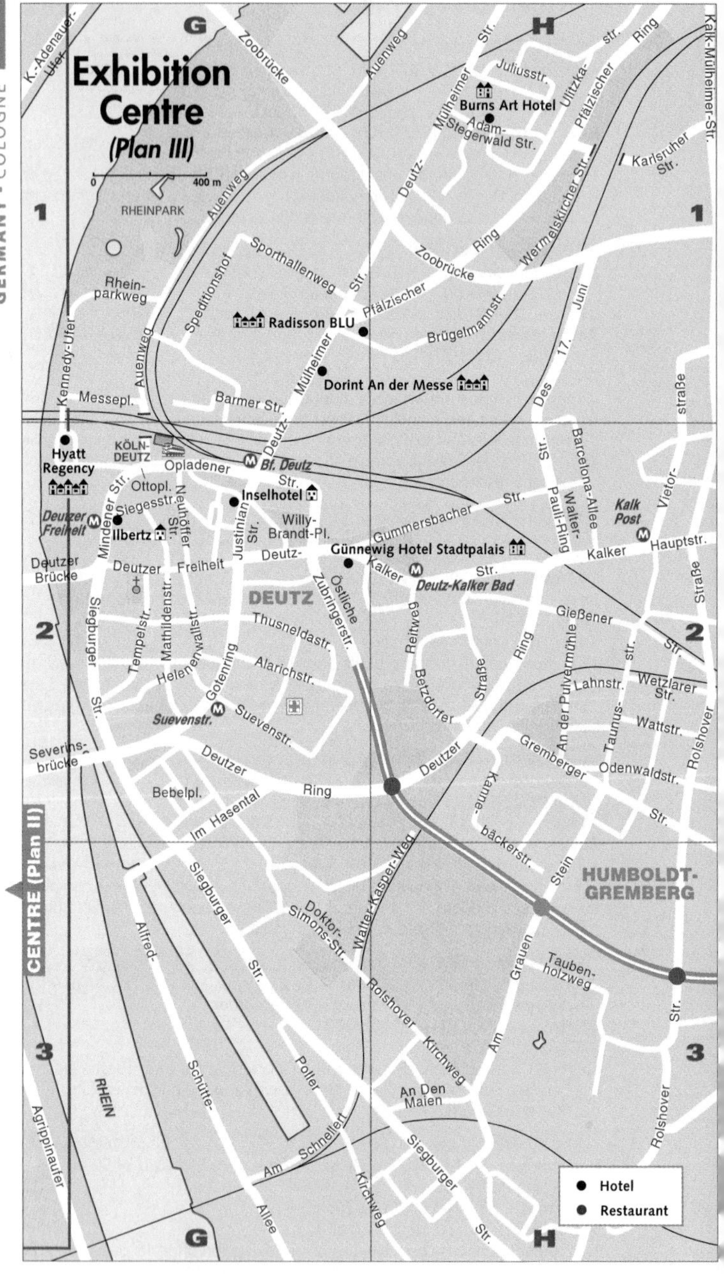
Exhibition Centre
(Plan III)
0
400 m
RHEINPARK
Rhein-parkweg
Kennedy-Ufer
K.-Adenauer-Ufer
Messepl.
Auenweg
Zoobrücke
Speditionshof
Sporthallenweg
Radisson BLU
Dorint An der Messe
Burns Art Hotel
Juliusstr.
Adam-Stegerwald Str.
Mülheimer Str.
Deutz-Mülheimer Str.
Pfälzischer Ring
Ulitzka-str.
Wermelskircher Str.
Karlsruher Str.
Kalk-Mülheimer-Str.
Brügelmannstr.
Des 17. Juni Str.
Barmer Str.
Hyatt Regency
KÖLN-DEUTZ
Opladener Str.
Bf. Deutz
Ottopl.
Siegesstr.
Neuhöffer Str.
Inselhotel
Justinianstr.
Willy-Brandt-Pl.
Gummersbacher Str.
Barcelona-Allee
Walter-Pauli-Ring
Kalk Post
Vietor-straße
Deutzer Freiheit
Mindener Str.
Ilbertz
Deutzer Brücke
Deutzer Freiheit
Deutz-Kalker Str.
Günnewig Hotel Stadtpalais
Deutz-Kalker Bad
Kalker Hauptstr.
DEUTZ
Östliche Zubringerstr.
Thusneldastr.
Alarichstr.
Reitweg
Betzdorfer Straße
Gießener Str.
Siegburger Str.
Tempelstr.
Mathildenstr.
Helenenwallstr.
Gotenring
Suevenstr.
Lahnstr.
Wetzlarer Str.
An der Pulvermühle
Taunus-str.
Wattstr.
Rolshover Straße
Severinsbrücke
Deutzer Ring
Gremberger Str.
Odenwaldstr.
Bebelpl.
Im Hasental
Kannebäckerstr.
Stein
HUMBOLDT-GREMBERG
Walter-Kasper-Weg
Doktor-Simons-Str.
Alfred-Schütte-Allee
Siegburger Str.
Am Grauen Stein
Taubenholzweg
Rolshover Str.
Rolshover Kirchweg
Poller Kirchweg
An Den Maien
Am Schnellert
Siegburger Str.
RHEIN
Agrippinaufer
CENTRE (Plan II)
Hotel
Restaurant
G
H
1
2
3

Ilbertz without rest

Mindener Str. 6 (access via Siegesstr. 5) ✉ 50679 – Ⓜ Deutzer Freiheit – ✆ (0221) 8 29 59 20 – www.hotel-ilbertz.de
– Closed Christmas - 6 January **G2**

26 rm ☕ – 🚹92/170 € 🚹🚹115/190 €

♦ Family ♦ Functional ♦

This immaculate, family-run hotel with its characteristic yellow façade offers functional rooms equipped with the latest technology and a traditional breakfast room.

ENVIRONS OF COLOGNE

Brenner'scher Hof

Wilhelm-von-Capitaine-Str. 15 ✉ 50858 – ✆ (0221) 9 48 60 00 – www.brennerscher-hof.de **A2**

41 rm ☕ – 🚹99/119 € 🚹🚹109/129 € – 2 suites

Rest *Anno Pomm* – ✆ *(0221) 4 84 98 82* – Carte 16/31 €

♦ Country house ♦ Historic ♦ Cosy ♦

This beautify country house dating back to 1754 has been decorated in Mediterranean style. The guest accommodation is in a series of charming and comfortable individually designed rooms, suites and maisonettes. Anno Pomm offers a range of dishes based around the humble potato.

Maître im Landhaus Kuckuck (Erhard Schäfer)

Olympiaweg 2 (by Friedrich-Schmitt-Straße) ✉ 50933 – ✆ (0221) 48 53 60 – www.landhaus-kuckuck.de
– Closed 2 weeks end April, 4 weeks August - early September and Sunday - Monday **A2**

Rest – *(dinner only) (booking essential)* Menu 99/119 € – Carte 70/77 €

Rest *Landhaus Kuckuck* – *(closed Sunday dinner - Monday)* Menu 38 € – Carte 35/55 €

Spec. Gebratene Felsenrotbarbe mit Zuckerschotenmousseline und Verjus du Périgord. Tournedo vom Rinderfilet mit geschmortem Ochsenschwanz und römischen Nocken. Karamell-Schockoladen-Savarin mit Mispeln und Eiskaffee.

♦ Classic ♦ Elegant ♦

"Maître" is the name of the small gourmet restaurant in this pretty country house where Erhard Schäfer carefully prepares seasonal, classic dishes. Friendly and competent service. There is a terrace under chestnut trees and a Davidoff smoking lounge. Landhaus Kuckuck offers international and regional cuisine.

Fellini

Zülpicher Str. 327 ✉ 50937 – ✆ (0221) 44 19 00 – www.felliniristorante.de

Rest – Carte 34/55 € **B2**

♦ Italian ♦ Friendly ♦

This pleasant restaurant is decorated with posters and photographs honouring the eponymous film maker. The traditional menu is replaced by a board announcing seasonal Italian dishes. Good selection of grappas.

AT THE AIRPORT South-East: 17 km by A59 D3

Holiday Inn Airport

Waldstr. 255 (at airport Köln/Bonn) ✉ 51147 – ✆ (02203) 56 10 – www.koeln-bonn-airport-hi-hotel.de

177 rm – 🚹139/169 € 🚹🚹159/179 €, ☕ 18 € **Rest** – Carte 28/40 €

♦ Chain hotel ♦ Functional ♦

Ideal for the business traveller, this hotel with its modern reception area and well-appointed contemporary rooms offers a free airport shuttle service. An elegant restaurant serving predominantly international cuisine with a great bar.

FRANKFURT

FRANKFURT AM MAIN

Population (est.2005) 649 000 (conurbation 1 489 000) – Altitude:112m

m Bayer/Fotolia.com

European travellers might feel there's no need to go all the way to New York when they've got Frankfurt. After all, it's earned itself the nickname 'Mainhattan' what with all those slinky, shiny skyscrapers reaching up from the banks of the river Main. This may be a city of brash towers housing big corporations (hence its other nickname 'Bankfurt') but you'll also find half-timbered medieval houses (admittedly rebuilt), and a blistering array of museums along the south bank of the river.

Located at the crossing point of Germany's north-south and east-west roads, Frankfurt is the financial powerhouse of the country, but a city that takes its cultural scene very seriously. It's said that it spends more money on the arts per year than any other European city, and from being something of a gastronomic back water, it's become a gourmet hotspot with its cuisine range becoming more eclectic by the month. The city has also joined the recent trend in turning local venues into summer beach clubs, complete with palm trees and sand. One man who wouldn't believe his eyes if he saw Frankfurt today is Germany's great poet, novelist and dramatist Johann Wolfgang von Goethe…he was born and bred here.

LIVING THE CITY

The centre of Frankfurt is **Cathedral Hill**, where the cathedral has stood for eight hundred years. It towers over **Römerberg**, the medieval square, rebuilt following the War. To the west, amongst the mighty skyscrapers of international banks and corporations, lies the main railway station and **Exhibition Centre**, while south of the **river Main**, which cuts east-west through the city, is the famous **'museum embankment'** and Frankfurt's oldest area, **Sachsenhausen**, full of bars, cafés and restaurants.

PRACTICAL INFORMATION

ARRIVAL-DEPARTURE

Frankfurt Airport is only 9km southeast from the city centre. A taxi will cost around €25. S-Bahn trains S8 and S9 leave every 15min for Frankfurt station and the journey takes just over 10min.

TRANSPORT

Frankfurt runs an efficient bus, metro and tram system. You can buy a day ticket for one person or a group (maximum five), which is valid until the last ride of the day. Tickets are available at vending machines and from bus drivers, but not on trams, the U-Bahn or S-Bahn.

Be a smart Frankfurter and invest in a Frankfurt Card. This entitles you to free public transport and discounts at a variety of museums and attractions. There are also reductions of up to thirty per cent on selected boat trips. You can buy the Card at many travel agencies, at tourist information offices and in both terminals at the airport. It's valid for 24 or 48 hours.

EXPLORING FRANKFURT

During Germany's post-war economic miracle, Frankfurt soon re-established itself as the economic hub of the country. As part of a big drive to show that there was more to the city than Deutschmarks, the authorities poured millions into invigorating its cultural life, using old plans to faithfully rebuild key parts of the war-torn old town and at the same time launch a succession of exciting opera companies, museums and theatres. The city was reborn, and is now the closest thing western Germany has to a high-rise metropolis. To view its skyline from the south bank at night is to see a twinkling fairyland of light, its resemblance to Manhattan evident to all.

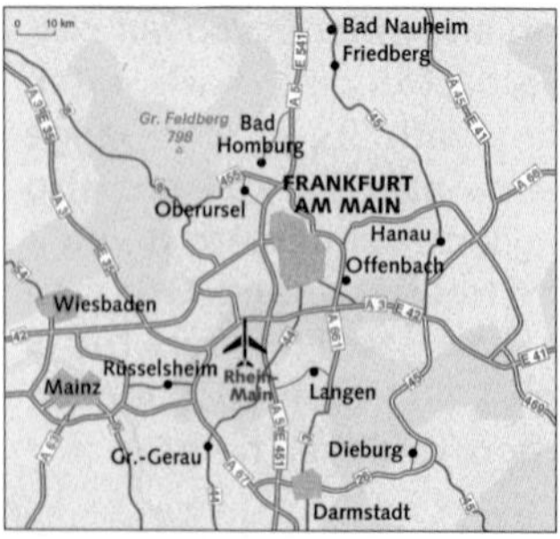

Just to the north of the curving River Main is a compact area that speaks of a far older Frankfurt, where once Holy Roman Emperors were crowned, and where market fairs rang to the cries of traders over a thousand years ago. The dominant feature of the district is the Römerberg, the old centre with its eye-catching half-timbered buildings lovingly rebuilt in 1986 with the aid of historical plans. Römerberg is a cobbled, octagonal square known locally as the 'Great Parlour', and its most striking landmark is the **town hall**, originally three 14C town houses linked by a Gothic triple-gabled frontage. It's not just pretty façades around here, there's a great gallery on the square – the **Kunsthalle Schirn**, opened little more than twenty years ago. It hosts a range of high-powered art, archaeology and cultural exhibitions, and in a short period has become one of Europe's most prestigious spaces. As a contrast, the twin-naved church of **St Nicholas**, just west of the Schirn, dates back to 1290, and twice a day reverberates to the sound of German folk songs. On the eastern side of the old town is the Kaiserdom, the city's thirteenth century cathedral, which remained standing throughout Allied bombing, and boasts stunning views from its Gothic tower: you'll have to climb 324 steps first, though.

→ BANKING ON CULTURE

Visitors don't have to travel far to find out more about the centuries long, incident-filled history of Frankfurt. Close by St Nicholas is the **History Museum**, finished in 1972, which includes a fascinating model of the medieval town, and colourful fragments of buildings that were lost in World War II. By now, you're just about at the water's edge. Cross the river and you'll be face to face with one of the best cultural neighbourhoods in Europe: the Museum Embankment. Along here, strung out like pearls, are nine exhibition buildings, enough to keep an art lover engrossed for many hours, if not days. Some of the museums are quite new (such as those looking at **German Film**, or **World Cultures**), but the **Stadel Art Institute** – perhaps the jewel in the crown – is nearly two hundred years old. The imposing neo-renaissance building boasts work by the likes of Vermeer, Rembrandt, Botticelli, Bosch and van Eyck. If Old Masters are not to your taste, then you can try your luck at other exhibitions around here, which deal with architecture, icons, sculpture, communications, applied art, or – the newest baby on the block – local artists from the Rhine-Main area. In terms of sheer novelty, head back over the Main for the **Modern Art Museum**: the collections from the 1960s onwards are innovative enough, but just gazing at the building itself is an absorbing experience – it looks like a rather tasty slice of cake.

→ MAIN PLAYERS

You can't avoid looking at buildings in this city. In the centre, the now emblematic skyscrapers tower endlessly up to the clouds; if you're of a mind, you could even call them gigantic works of art themselves. One of them, the **Commerzbank Tower**, just happens to be the tallest office building in Europe. Slightly dwarfed, but still very large indeed, is the **Main Tower**, and this is the one that's of interest to visitors. It's the only one in Frankfurt with a public viewing platform, which can be located up on the roof. It hardly needs saying that the vista from here is astounding.

The contrast between the new and the old is thrown up again back in the old town where, a short way up from the north bank of the Main, stands the **Goethe house**. The great man was born here in 1749, and it's where he lived for the next twenty-six years. It's a fascinating example of a mid-eighteenth century home of the upper middle classes, lovingly restored with an interior that includes his writing desk and an astronomical clock. Next door is the decade-old **Goethemuseum**, which includes a collection of items related to Goethe, and an absorbing library with his writings. Another cultural highlight of the area is the **Opera House**, completely rebuilt in a compelling Italian Renaissance style. What happens inside, too, is of a high order:

this is Frankfurt's top venue for a wide range of concerts, which take place in either the Great Hall or the Mozart Hall – expect anything from chamber and symphony concerts to jazz, pop and comedy.

Frankfurt is home to some of the country's best shopping streets. Number one on the list is the pedestrianised **Zeil Promenade**, which is lined with department stores. There are more specialised streets dotted around: the nearby **Goethestrasse** (for exclusive designer boutiques); **Berger Strasse** (for trendy fashion); **Schillerstrasse** (for shoes). Seek out the **Kleinmarkthalle,** the city's huge indoor grocery market, for some superbly fresh German foodstuffs. A slightly more out of the way quarter to hit is Sachsenhausen, which is over the river and to the southeast of Museum Embankment. It's a leafy, laidback area, very popular for chilling out, so, after checking its quirky little specialist shops (and Saturday flea market), locals like to sip beer or coffee in one of the neighbourhood's many bars and restaurants.

Of course, if relaxing by a beach is more your thing, then even somewhere seriously landlocked like Frankfurt can come up with a solution. In the summer, many of the city's venues set up outdoor beach clubs, complete with sand and palm trees. The rooftops of some city centre buildings are fair game to double as the faux-seaside; for instance, the roof of the car park of the **Frankfurt Stock Exchange** boasts two pools and a five-hundred strong capacity, while **City Beach Frankfurt**, on the roof of the car park of (this time) a department store, goes that extra mile, with a pool and sand, open air cinema, beach volley ball, and salsa evenings.

CALENDAR HIGHLIGHTS

Practically everyone in Europe's heard of Frankfurt's main event, and with good reason. The Book Fair (in October) is a major jamboree for publishers and book lovers, and reflects the latest trends in global literature. Not by any means is every celebration in the city so cerebral. Frankfurt's Carnival in February is a riot of colour, music and festivities, and it kick-starts an impressive array of spring and summer events. The Forest Folk Festival (May) in Niederrad Forest, a stone's throw from the city, boasts a fairground, bustling market and traditional festivities. A month later, the Opernplatz Festival (in the square with the Opera House) has a stage with music, a motley collective of cabaret artists and a fine range of international gourmet treats (enough to bring local bankers down from their towers). The Rose and Light Festival (also June) transforms the city's Palm Garden into a wonderland of lanterns and candles, which complement the

FRANKFURT IN...

→ ONE DAY

Old Town, Römerberg, the view from Main Tower

→ TWO DAYS

Goethe House, Museum Embankment (take your pick of one or two museums), a restaurant in Sachsenhausen

→ THREE DAYS

Boat trip on the Main, window shopping (Zeil), concert at Opera House

music going on all around. Zeil's inner-city pavements are shaken in July by the Sound of Frankfurt, when the likes of techno, rock and pop throb round the pedestrian zones. The river hosts two big entertainments in August: the River Main Festival, and the Museum Quay Festival. Both rejoice in Frankfurt's waterway, with music, fireworks, a regatta, the museums, and local concert halls all playing a big part. The end of summer is announced with Autumn Dippe Fair, at Festplatz am Ratsweg in September. The last big open-air fair before winter is a riot of old-fashioned fun, with carousels, rollercoasters, and fireworks to set it all off and close it down.

EATING OUT

Not so long ago, Frankfurt's gastronomic fame came courtesy of its Apfelwein (a sweet or dry variant of cider) and Handkäs mit Musik (small yellow cheese with vinegar, oil and onions). Not forgetting Grüne Sauce (a mixture of various herbs and sour cream served with boiled eggs). That's not the case now. Head along to the Fressgass (near Opernplatz) and you've got a pedestrian mile of fine eateries – food on the hoof or to graze over at good prices. Fressgass, by the way, translates as 'Eatery Alley' or 'Glutton's Lane', so you get the picture. Nearly thirty per cent of Frankfurt's citizens have come to live here from overseas, so a wealth of eating possibilities has been opened up and it's now no problem to 'eat globally' all round the city. Foreign communities have added a real touch of spice to the culinary landscape, which is full of the likes of Turkish, Italian and Chinese establishments. Nevertheless, a visit to this city wouldn't be complete without a trip to the äppelwoilokale in Sachsenhausen, the casual but lively cafés where tradition is the key, and Apfelwein served up in ceramic mugs is the drink. Any down sides to eating here? In a city full of bankers, it can prove a bit difficult locating good but inexpensive food, but if in doubt (or potential penury) - hit the Fressgass!

→ EXPRESS DELIVERY

For a leisurely trip round Frankfurt, try the Ebbelwei Express. This colourful tram takes visitors all over the city from Römer to the zoo, across the river to Sachsenhausen and back – and you get a free bottle of cider. But it only runs at weekends and on public holidays.

→ A RIVER RUNS

Taking to the water makes a great day out here. Only a few steps away from the Römerberg is the Main quay at the Eiserner Steg, from where you can catch boats up and down the river. You can choose between day trips up to the Rhine or shorter journeys taking in the amazing skyline of the city.

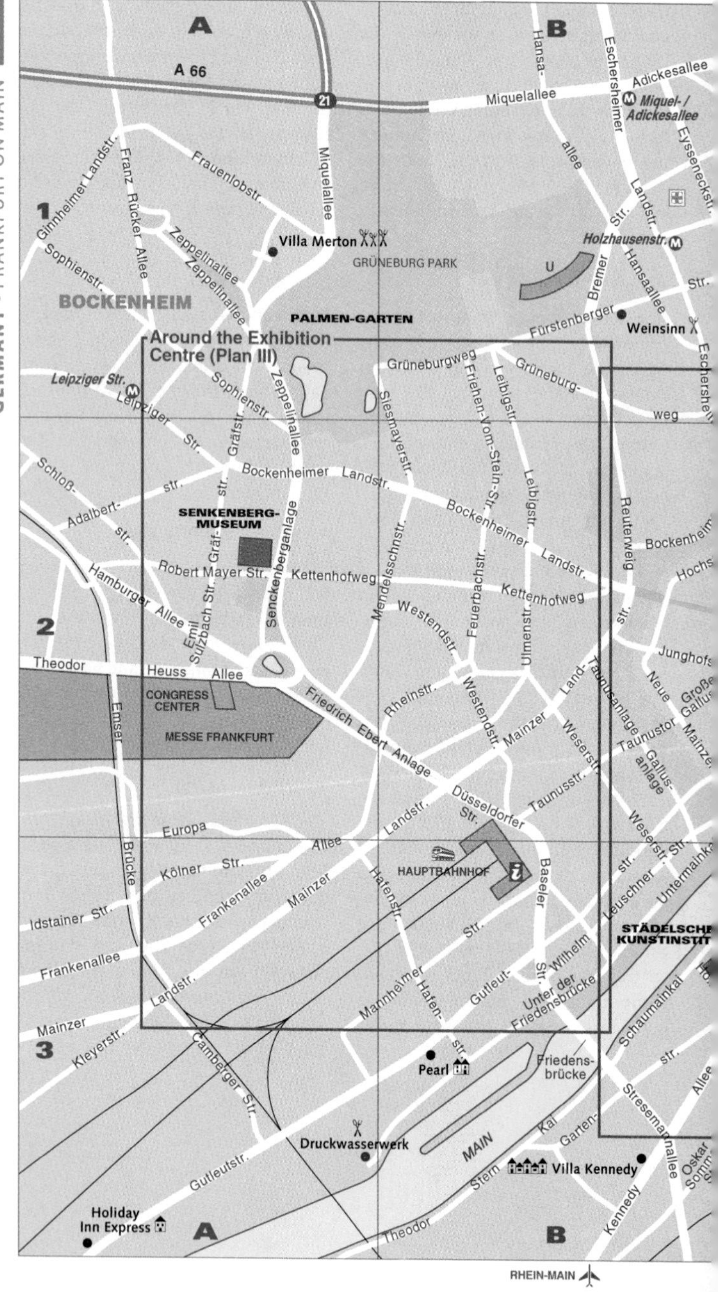
A
B
A 66
21
Miquelallee
Adickesallee
Miquel- / Adickesallee
Eschersheimer Landstr.
Hansa-allee
Eysseneckstr.
Frauenlobstr.
Ginnheimer Landstr.
Franz Rücker Allee
Sophienstr.
Zeppelinallee
Villa Merton
GRÜNEBURG PARK
Holzhausenstr.
U
Bremer Str.
Hansaallee
BOCKENHEIM
PALMEN-GARTEN
Fürstenberger Str.
Weinsinn
Around the Exhibition Centre (Plan III)
Grüneburgweg
Leipziger Str.
Leipziger Str.
Gräfstr.
Siesmayerstr.
Frihen-Vom-Stein-Str.
Leibigstr.
Bockenheimer Landstr.
Schloß-str.
Adalbert-str.
SENKENBERG-MUSEUM
Senckenberganlage
Mendelsschnstr.
Reuterweg
Robert Mayer Str.
Kettenhofweg
Hamburger Allee
Emil Sulzbach Str.
Westendstr.
Feuerbachstr.
Ulmenstr.
Theodor Heuss Allee
CONGRESS CENTER
MESSE FRANKFURT
Friedrich Ebert Anlage
Rheinstr.
Mainzer Landstr.
Taunusanlage
Weserstr.
Junghofstr.
Neue Mainzer
Taunustor
Gallusanlage
Emser Brücke
Europa Allee
Düsseldorfer Str.
Taunusstr.
Kölner Str.
Hafenstr.
HAUPTBAHNHOF
Baseler Str.
Leuschner str.
Idstainer Str.
Frankenallee
Mainzer Landstr.
STÄDELSCHE KUNSTINSTITUT
Gutleut-str.
Wilhelm
Unter der Friedensbrücke
Mannheimer Str.
Schaumainkai
Kleyerstr.
Camberger Str.
Pearl
Friedens-brücke
Druckwasserwerk
MAIN
Kai
Garten-str.
Stresemannallee
Villa Kennedy
Kennedy
Gutleutstr.
Holiday Inn Express
Stern
Theodor
RHEIN-MAIN
1
2
3

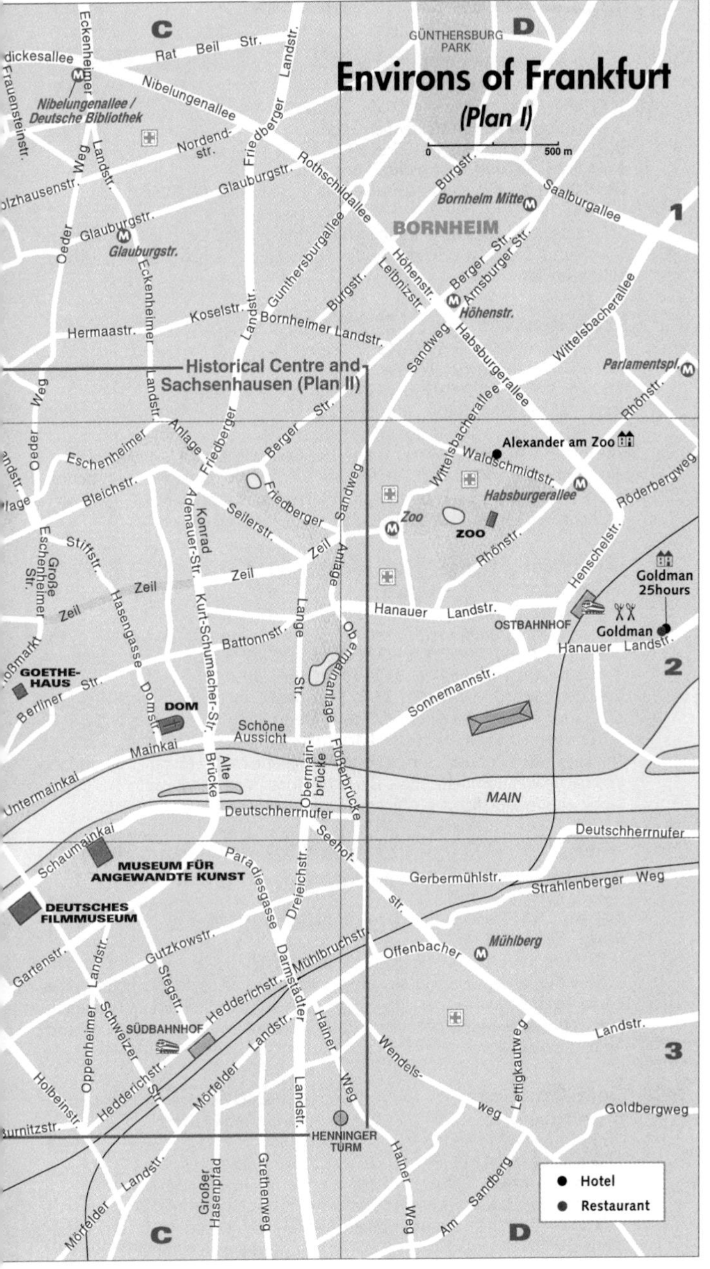

Environs of Frankfurt
(Plan I)
0
500 m
C
D
1
2
3
GÜNTHERSBURG PARK
BORNHEIM
Bornheim Mitte
Höhenstr.
Parlamentspl.
Nibelungenallee / Deutsche Bibliothek
Glauburgstr.
Historical Centre and Sachsenhausen (Plan II)
Alexander am Zoo
Habsburgerallee
Zoo
ZOO
Goldman 25hours
Goldman
OSTBAHNHOF
GOETHE-HAUS
DOM
MAIN
MUSEUM FÜR ANGEWANDTE KUNST
DEUTSCHES FILMMUSEUM
SÜDBAHNHOF
Mühlberg
HENNINGER TURM
Hotel
Restaurant

Steigenberger Frankfurter Hof

Am Kaiserplatz ✉ 60311
– Ⓜ Willy-Brandt-Platz – ✆ (069) 2 15 02
– www.frankfurter-hof.steigenberger.de **E1**
321 rm – †175/229 € ††175/229 €, ☐ 32 € – 20 suites
Rest *Français and Rest Iroha* – see below
Rest *Oscar's* – *(booking advisable)* Menu 30 € – Carte 41/66 €
♦ Luxury ♦ Traditional ♦ Classic ♦

This traditional luxury hotel has been welcoming guests since 1876. It boasts a magnificent façade which sets the classical tone of the hotel. Oscar's, with its light bistro atmosphere

Villa Kennedy

Kennedyallee 70 ✉ 60596 – Ⓜ Schweizer Platz – ✆ (069) 71 71 20
– www.villakennedyhotel.de *Plan I* **B3**
163 rm – †220/495 € ††295/550 €, ☐ 32 € – 25 suites
Rest – Menu 60/110 € – Carte 58/82 €
♦ Grand Luxury ♦ Villa ♦ Classic ♦

The former Villa Speyer (1904) has now been extended into a luxury hotel complex in the museum district. The interior successfully combines the historical and the contemporary. Excellent spa. This restaurant facing onto a pretty interior courtyard serves international cuisine with an Italian influence.

The Westin Grand

Konrad-Adenauer-Str. 7 ✉ 60313
– Ⓜ Konstablerwache – ✆ (069) 2 98 10
– www.westingrandfrankfurt.com **F1**
369 rm – †189/729 € ††189/729 €, ☐ 31 € – 17 suites
Rest *san san* – *✆ (069) 91 39 90 50* – Carte 29/54 €
Rest *Sushimoto* – *✆ (069) 1 31 00 57 (closed Sunday lunch and Monday, except trade fairs) (booking advisable)* Menu 35/105 € – Carte 27/56 €
♦ Luxury ♦ Chain hotel ♦ Modern ♦

This cosy, modern, business hotel in the city centre has an elegant tone and an international atmosphere. There is a 24hr fitness room, and exhibitions in the lobby. This restaurant offers Chinese cuisine. Japanese in the Sushimoto.

Hilton

Hochstr. 4 ✉ 60313 – Ⓜ Eschenheimer Tor – ✆ (069) 13 38 00
– www.hilton.de/frankfurt **E1**
342 rm – †175/349 € ††175/349 €, ☐ 33 € – 3 suites
Rest – Carte 43/81 €
♦ Business ♦ Chain hotel ♦ Contemporary ♦

A generous, impressive and airy atrium welcomes you into this hotel at the Bockenheimer centre. The 25m indoor pool, a former municipal swimming pool, is the largest hotel pool in Frankfurt. Restaurant with an international and American menu.

InterContinental

Wilhelm-Leuschner-Str. 43 ✉ 60329 – Ⓜ Willy-Brandt-Platz – ✆ (069) 2 60 50 – www.frankfurt.intercontinental.com **E2**
770 rm – †149/426 € ††149/426 €, ☐ 31 € – 35 suites
Rest *Signatures* – Carte 40/57 €
♦ Business ♦ Conference hotel ♦ Functional ♦

This hotel, situated on the Main, offers classical-style guestrooms in its two buildings, the City Wing and River Wing. The best views are seen from the Club area on the 21st-floor. This restaurant has a modern conservatory. It serves international cuisine, mostly in buffet form.

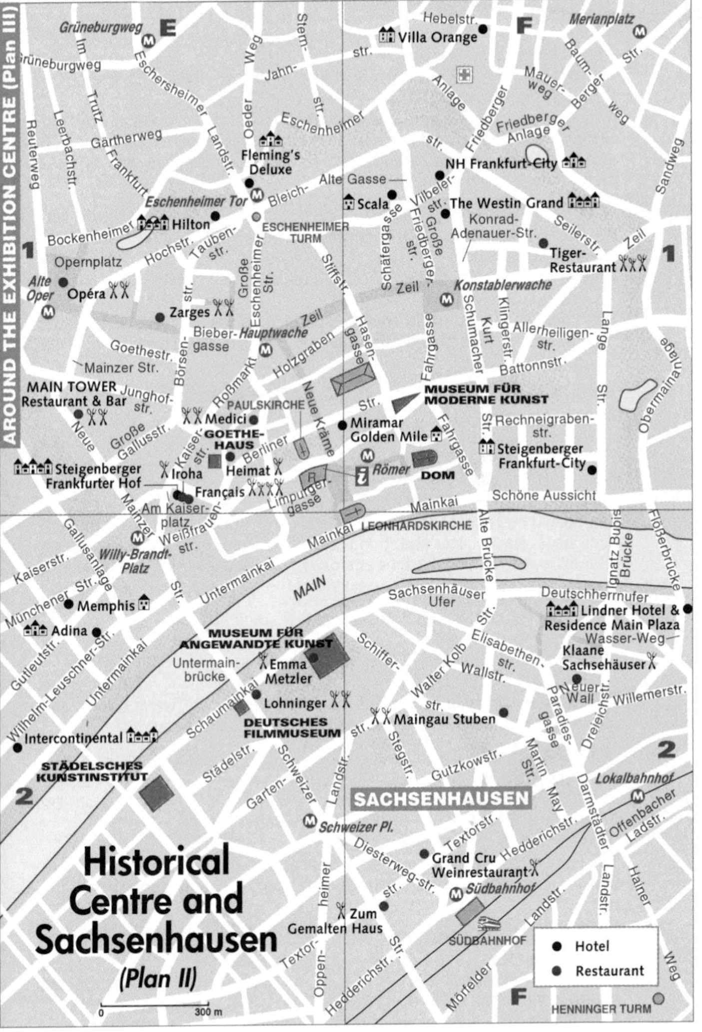

Lindner Hotel & Residence Main Plaza

Walther-von-Cronberg Platz 1
✉ 60594 – Ⓜ *Lokalbahnhof* – ✆ *(069) 66 40 10* – *www.lindner.de*
118 rm – †149/299 € ††169/429 €, ☕ 23 € – 7 suites **F2**
Rest *New Brick* – ✆ *(069) 6 64 01 44 03* – Carte 36/55 €
♦ Business ♦ Luxury ♦ Modern ♦

Behind its red brick façade, this striking high rise tower on the banks of the Main houses a luxury hotel with spacious, elegant rooms, many with views over the city, and a 450m² beauty and spa centre. New Brick serves Californian cuisine prepared before your eyes in the open kitchen.

Fleming's Deluxe

Eschenheimer Tor 2 ✉ 60318 – Ⓜ Eschenheimer Tor – ☎ (069) 4 27 23 20 – www.flemings-hotels.com **E1**

106 rm – 🛉148/289 € 🛉🛉168/314 € – 6 suites **Rest** – Carte 32/70 €

◆ Business ◆ Modern ◆

At the Eschenheimer centre find this listed, former office building from the 1950s with a still operating original Paternoster. It has modern furnishings with a bar and lounge on the seventh-floor. This roof top restaurant with its show kitchen offers a view of the Skyline.

NH Frankfurt-City

Vilbelerstr. 2 ✉ 60313 – Ⓜ Konstablerwache – ☎ (069) 9 28 85 90 – www.nh-hotels.com **F1**

256 rm – 🛉159/179 € 🛉🛉159/179 €, 24 €, 8 suites **Rest** – Carte 35/54 €

◆ Chain hotel ◆ Contemporary ◆

This modern and functionally equipped business address is located in the inner city, just a few steps from the pedestrian zone. Restaurant on the first floor with a large buffet.

Adina

Wilhelm-Leuschner-Str. 6 ✉ 60329 – Ⓜ Willy-Brandt-Platz – ☎ (069) 2 47 47 40 – www.adina.eu **E2**

134 rm – 🛉119/159 € 🛉🛉119/159 €, 19 € – 84 suites

Rest – *(dinner only)* Carte 31/49 €

◆ Business ◆ Modern ◆

Apartment hotel close to the river Main and the city centre, with classic modern furnishings clear cut lines and strong colours. All rooms have a kitchenette. Suites also have a washing machine and dryer. International dishes and tapas.

Villa Orange without rest

Hebelstr. 1 ✉ 60318 – Ⓜ Merianplatz – ☎ (069) 40 58 40 – www.villa-orange.de **F1**

38 rm – 🛉80/215 € 🛉🛉90/255 €, 10 €

◆ Family ◆ Modern ◆ Cosy ◆

This well run, villa-style hotel offers a modern atmosphere, warm colours and organic breakfasts. Some of the rooms have free-standing baths.

Alexander am Zoo without rest

Waldschmidtstr. 59 ✉ 60316 – Ⓜ Habsburgerallee – ☎ (069) 94 96 00 – www.alexanderamzoo.de *Plan I* **D2**

66 rm – 🛉108/240 € 🛉🛉128/240 € – 9 suites

◆ Business ◆ Contemporary ◆

This hotel is located on a small side street at the corner of the zoo. It houses timeless, cosy rooms. The conference rooms on the sixth-floor open onto the roof terrace.

Goldman 25hours

Hanauer Landstr. 127 ✉ 60314 – ☎ (069) 40 58 68 90 – www.25hours-hotels.com *Plan I* **D2**

49 rm – 🛉105/185 € 🛉🛉105/185 €, 14 €

Rest *Goldman* – see below

◆ Business ◆ Design ◆ Personalised ◆

An unusual hotel of modern design in which many small details, including fashionable objets and fresh, friendly colours, combine to create a fascinating and unique whole.

Steigenberger Frankfurt-City

Lange Str. 5 ✉ 60311 – Ⓜ Römer – ☎ (069) 21 93 00 – www.frankfurt-city.steigenberger.de **F1**

149 rm – 🛉115/195 € 🛉🛉130/215 € – 1 suite **Rest** – Carte 26/45 €

◆ Business ◆ Functional ◆

This modern and functional hotel is well suited to business guests. Some of the rooms offer a view over the Frankfurt skyline. Restaurant with a visible kitchen and an international menu.

Miramar Golden Mile without rest

Berliner Str. 31 ✉ 60311 – Ⓜ Römer – ✆ (069) 9 20 39 70
– www.miramar-frankfurt.de
– Closed 23 - 31 December **E-F1**

39 rm – 100/260 € 130/280 €

◆ Townhouse ◆ Functional ◆

Between the Zeil and the Römer, with well-tended, functional rooms and a friendly breakfast room.

Memphis without rest

Münchener Str. 15 ✉ 60329 – Ⓜ Willy-Brandt-Platz – ✆ (069) 2 42 60 90
– www.memphis-hotel.de **E2**

42 rm – 50/250 € 60/299 €

◆ Business ◆ Functional ◆

This hotel is located in the centre of the city just five minutes' walk from the railway station. The rooms are small but modern and well-equipped. Those facing the interior courtyard are quieter.

Scala without rest

Schäfergasse 31 ✉ 60313 – Ⓜ Konstablerwache – ✆ (069) 1 38 11 10
– www.scala.bestwestern.de **F1**

40 rm – 60/110 € 80/130 €, 14 €

◆ Business ◆ Townhouse ◆ Functional ◆

This hotel has a central location in the centre of the city. It offers functional, though not overly large rooms. The reception and drinks service is staffed 24hrs a day.

Français – Hotel Steigenberger Frankfurter Hof

Am Kaiserplatz ✉ 60311 – Ⓜ Willy-Brandt-Platz
– ✆ (069) 21 51 38 – www.frankfurter-hof.steigenberger.de
– Closed 2 weeks April, 5 weeks July - August, Saturday - Sunday and Bank Holidays **E1**

Rest – *(booking advisable)* Menu 59 € (lunch)/129 € (dinner)
– Carte 66/116 €

Spec. Lasagne von Pfifferlingen mit Jakobsmuschel, Perlhuhneigelb und Rote Bete. Steinbutt mit Lardo und Mimolette. Himbeertörtchen und Crème brûlée mit Balsamicoeis.

◆ French ◆ Elegant ◆ Classic ◆

Patrick Bittner's cooking stands for classic dishes prepared from top quality produce. The fireplace room and the conservatory provide an elegant setting. In summer it is pleasant to dine in the Ehrenhof.

Tiger-Restaurant

Heiligkreuzgasse 20 ✉ 60313 – Ⓜ Konstablerwache – ✆ (069) 92 00 22 25
– www.tigerpalast.de
– Closed 13 - 15 February, 19 June - 23 August and Sunday - Monday

Rest – *(dinner only) (booking essential)* Menu 96/120 € **F1**

Rest *Palast-Bistrot* – *✆ (069) 92 00 22 92 (closed Monday) (dinner only)*
Menu 49/54 € – Carte 42/52 €

Spec. Schnitte von der Gänseleber mit Haselnuss-Nougat und Zitrusgelee. Filet vom Seeteufel mit Auberginen, Kichererbsen, Merguez und Kreuzkümmel. Rücken und Rippe vom Rind mit Flammkuchen von weißen Zwiebeln und Pastrami.

◆ Classic ◆ Elegant ◆ Fashionable ◆

A very pleasant modern restaurant in the basement of the Tiger Palace – under the same roof as the Varieté Theatre. Predominantly French wines accompany Alfred Friedrich's classic cooking. The Palast-Bistro restaurant features a historic vaulted brick ceiling.

XX **Opéra**

Opernplatz 1 ✉ 60313 – Ⓜ Alte Oper – ✆ (069) 1 34 02 15 – www.opera-restauration.de **E1**

Rest – Carte 39/59 €

♦ International ♦ Classic ♦

Restaurant in the former foyer of the Old Opera House with elaborate wall decorations and original Art Nouveau candlesticks. Terrace with lovely views. Saturday snacks and Sunday brunch.

XX **MAIN TOWER Restaurant & Bar**

Neue Mainzer Str. 52 (53th floor, charge) ✉ 60311 – Ⓜ Alte Oper – ✆ (069) 36 50 47 77 – www.maintower-restaurant.de – Closed Monday

Rest – *(dinner only) (booking essential)* Menu 59/99 € **E1**

♦ International ♦ Fashionable ♦

This modern restaurant is 187m up and provides fantastic views over the city. An impressive international cuisine is served here.

XX **Goldman** – Hotel Goldman 25hours

Hanauer Landstr. 127 ✉ 60314 – ✆ (069) 40 58 68 90 – www.25hours-hotels.com – Closed Sunday and Bank Holidays *Plan I* **D2**

Rest – *(dinner only)* Menu 72 € – Carte 42/58 €

♦ Mediterranean ♦ Trendy ♦

This comfortable modern restaurant with open kitchen and huge shop-window-style frontage serves Mediterranean cuisine with a modern twist.

XX **Lohninger**

Schweizer Str. 1 ✉ 60594 – Ⓜ Schweizer Pl. – ✆ (069) 2 47 55 78 60 – www.hoeren-sehen-schmecken.net **E2**

Rest – Menu 88 € – Carte 37/87 €

♦ Austrian ♦ Friendly ♦ Fashionable ♦

This modern, minimalist-style restaurant is set in the attractive, high ceilinged rooms of a classic townhouse. Austrian food with international influences is served.

XX **Maingau Stuben**

Schifferstr. 38 ✉ 60594 – Ⓜ Lokalbahnhof – ✆ (069) 61 07 52 – www.maingau.de – Closed Saturday lunch, Sunday dinner - Monday **F2**

Rest – Menu 36 € (veg.)/60 € – Carte 31/55 €

♦ International ♦ Friendly ♦

This family-run restaurant located close to the River Main offers a pleasant contemporary atmosphere and serves international and some classic cuisine. Good value lunchtime menu.

XX **Medici**

Weißadlergasse 2 ✉ 60311 – Ⓜ Hauptwache – ✆ (069) 21 99 07 94 – www.restaurantmedici.de – Closed Sunday and Bank Holidays **E1**

Rest – Menu 16 € (lunch)/62 € (dinner) – Carte 41/59 €

♦ International ♦ Formal ♦

The centrally located restaurant run by two brothers is modern in style and serves international cuisine.

XX **Zarges**

Kalbächer Gasse 10 ✉ 60311 – Ⓜ Hauptwache – ✆ (069) 29 90 30 – www.zarges-frankfurt.com – Closed Sunday, except trade fairs **E1**

Rest – Menu 35 € – Carte 30/59 €

♦ Seasonal cuisine ♦ Cosy ♦

Enjoy the French and international dishes, as well as the good, fairly priced selection of German wines in this stylish restaurant in Frankfurt's Fressgass'. There is also a bakery shop with homemade tarts and fine patisseries.

XX

Emma Metzler

Schaumainkai 17 ✉ 60594 – Ⓜ Schweizer Platz – ☎ (069) 61 99 59 06 – www.emma-metzler.com
– Closed Sunday dinner - Monday, except trade fairs **E2**

Rest – Menu 27 € (lunch) – Carte 48/59 €

♦ Seasonal cuisine ♦ Fashionable ♦

With its bright, modern interior the restaurant in the Frankfurt Museum of Applied Art offers good seasonal cuisine with attentive service. Attractive terrace looking onto the park.

X

Heimat

Berliner Str. 70 ✉ 60311 – Ⓜ Hauptwache – ☎ (069) 29 72 59 94 – www.restaurant-heimat.de
– Closed 22 December - 3 January and Bank Holidays **E1**

Rest – *(dinner only) (booking advisable)* Carte 38/53 €

♦ Seasonal cuisine ♦ Trendy ♦

A simple, friendly restaurant serving tasty seasonal cuisine with a good wine selection. This glass-fronted building is centrally located near the Römer, the Paulskirche and the Goethe House.

X

Iroha – Hotel Steigenberger Frankfurter Hof

Bethmannstr. 35 ✉ 60311 – Ⓜ Willy-Brandt-Platz – ☎ (069) 21 99 49 30 – www.iroha-frankfurt.de
– Closed Sunday and Bank Holidays **E1**

Rest – Menu 50/120 €

♦ Japanese ♦ Friendly ♦

There is a Japanese restaurant in the hotel cellar. In the Teppanyaki area food is prepared before your eyes on the traditional iron griddle. There is also a sushi bar.

X

Grand Cru Weinrestaurant

Textorstr. 56 ✉ 60594 – Ⓜ Südbahnhof – ☎ (069) 62 62 60 – www.grand-cru-weinrestaurant.de **F2**

Rest – *(dinner only)* Menu 28/60 € – Carte 30/50 €

♦ Seasonal cuisine ♦ Cosy ♦

You can be certain to dine well in this very fine restaurant. The fresh seasonal cuisine offers "Tradition" and "Innovation". The cordial and competent service team make excellent wine recommendations.

X

Klaane Sachsehäuser

Neuer Wall 11 (Sachsenhausen) ✉ 60594 – Ⓜ Lokalbahnhof – ☎ (069) 61 59 83 – www.klaanesachsehaeuser.de
– Closed 22 December - 10 January and Sunday **F2**

Rest – *(open from 4 pm)* Carte 14/30 €

♦ Regional ♦ Rustic ♦

This popular pub-style restaurant reached through an interior courtyard has been serving traditional "Stöffche" brewed on the premises and good Frankfurt fare since 1876. And you'll always find someone to share your evening with!

X

Zum gemalten Haus

Schweizer Str. 67 (Sachsenhausen) ✉ 60594 – Ⓜ Schweizer Platz – ☎ (069) 61 45 59 – www.zumgemaltenhaus.de
– Closed Monday **F2**

Rest – Carte 13/24 €

♦ Regional ♦ Rustic ♦

Huddle up, talk shop and chat in the midst of these wall murals and mementoes from bygone days. The main thing is the "Bembel" is always full!

Hessischer Hof

Friedrich-Ebert-Anlage 40 ✉ *60325 –* Ⓜ *Hauptbahnhof –* ✆ *(069) 7 54 00 – www.hessischer-hof.de* **G2**

117 rm – ♦170/465 € ♦♦200/525 €, ☕ 26 € – 7 suites

Rest – Menu 51/65 € – Carte 49/66 €

♦ Luxury ♦ Classic ♦ Personalised ♦

The service provided for guests in this classical hotel opposite the exhibition ground is first-class. A display of exquisite Sèvres porcelain decorates this elegant restaurant.

Marriott

Hamburger Allee 2 ✉ *60486 –* Ⓜ *Bockenheimer Warte –* ✆ *(069) 7 95 50 – www.frankfurt-marriott.de* **G1**

588 rm – ♦159/385 € ♦♦159/385 €, ☕ 27 € – 11 suites

Rest – *(closed Saturday - Sunday)* Carte 36/54 €

♦ Chain hotel ♦ Business ♦ Modern ♦

Opposite the exhibition centre, this hotel stands out for its well-equipped rooms in an elegant, classical style with views over the city. Increased privacy is offered on the executive floor. Restaurant with a pleasant brasserie ambience and French cuisine.

Radisson BLU

Franklinstr. 65 (by Theodor Heuss Allee **A2***)* ✉ *60486 –* ✆ *(069) 7 70 15 50 – www.radissonblu.com/hotel-frankfurt*

428 rm – ♦119/199 € ♦♦119/199 €, ☕ 26 € – 5 suites

Rest *Gaia* – ✆ *(069) 77 01 55 22 00* – Carte 30/53 €

♦ Business ♦ Conference hotel ♦ Design ♦

Various designers contributed to the layout of this fashionable, lifestyle hotel whose unusual architecture immediately catches the eye. Designer rooms include the 'At home', 'Chic', 'Fashion' and 'Fresh' rooms. Gaia with Mediterranean cuisine.

Maritim

Theodor-Heuss-Allee 3 ✉ *60486 –* Ⓜ *Bockenheimer Warte –* ✆ *(069) 7 57 80 – www.maritim.de* **G2**

543 rm – ♦119/385 € ♦♦149/415 €, ☕ 27 € – 24 suites

Rest – *(dinner only)* Menu 36/46 € – Carte 42/66 €

♦ Chain hotel ♦ Conference hotel ♦ Functional ♦

This hotel, which is directly linked with the Exhibition and Congress Park, is an ideal conference venue with timeless rooms. The rooms on the upper floors have a particularly beautiful view. The Classico and SushiSho restaurants offer international cuisine.

Le Méridien Parkhotel

Wiesenhüttenplatz 28 ✉ *60329 –* Ⓜ *Hauptbahnhof – ✆ (069) 2 69 70 – www.lemeridienparkhotelfrankfurt.com* **H2**

297 rm – ♦145/499 € ♦♦145/519 €, ☕ 26 € – 2 suites

Rest – Carte 27/62 €

♦ Luxury ♦ Chain hotel ♦ Design ♦

This city hotel comprises of a historic palace with stylish, elegant rooms and a stately atmosphere, as well as a modern businesslike extension. Le Parc bistro-style restaurant.

Roomers

Gutleutstr. 85 ✉ *60329 –* Ⓜ *Hauptbahnhof –* ✆ *(069) 2 71 34 20 – www.roomers.eu* **H2**

117 rm – ♦220/370 € ♦♦220/370 €, ☕ 29 € – 1 suite

Rest – *(closed Saturday - Sunday and Bank Holidays lunch)* Carte 37/142 €

♦ Business ♦ Design ♦ Modern ♦

This hotel boasts a beautifully crafted interior featuring high-quality materials and tasteful design. Attentive service. Excellent spa and fitness suite. Like everything else in this establishment, the restaurant is high class and modern.

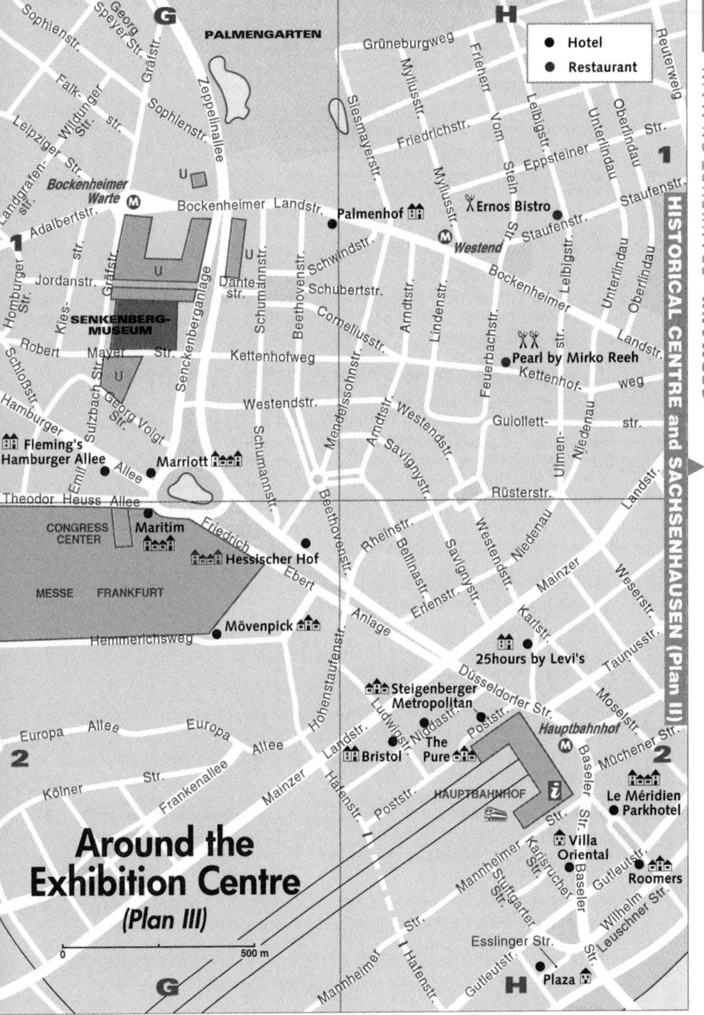

Steigenberger Metropolitan

Poststr. 6 ✉ 60329 – Ⓜ Hauptbahnhof
– ✆ (069) 5 06 07 00 – www.steigenberger.com
H2

131 rm – 🚹139/196 € 🚹🚹139/236 € – 2 suites
Rest – Carte 28/57 €

♦ Business ♦ Contemporary ♦

This beautiful city palace by the main station dates from the 19C. It is fitted out in a modern style that is both functional and elegant. Art Deco components adorn the façade and interior. The Brasserie restaurant enjoys a contemporary atmosphere.

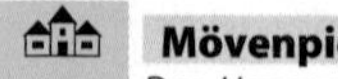

Mövenpick

Den Haager Str. 5 (access via Platz der Einheit) ✉ 60327 – ✆ (069) 7 88 07 50 – www.moevenpick-frankfurt-city.com **G2**

288 rm – 135/255 € 155/275 €, 23 € **Rest** – Carte 24/52 €

♦ Chain hotel ♦ Modern ♦

This business hotel is directly on the exhibition ground and has a conspicuous red-green façade. The rooms feature clean, modern and functional design. There is a fitness area with roof terrace. Bistro-style restaurant with international menu.

The Pure without rest

Niddastr. 86 ✉ 60329 – Ⓜ Hauptbahnhof – ✆ (069) 7 10 45 70 – www.the-pure.de **H2**

50 rm – 120/350 € 140/420 €

♦ Business ♦ Design ♦

Find minimalist, modern elegance at this hotel, which is exclusively in white. Close to the railway station, the tasteful, modern and elegant rooms are not always generously sized.

Fleming's Hamburger Allee

Hamburger Allee 47 ✉ 60486 – Ⓜ Bockenheimer Warte – ✆ (069) 2 01 74 10 – www.flemings-hotels.com **G1**

45 rm – 116/175 € 116/225 € – 2 suites

Rest – *(closed Christmas - 2 January)* Carte 21/43 €

♦ Business ♦ Townhouse ♦ Modern ♦

Just a few minutes from the exhibition centre, this townhouse in a quiet side street is a modern business hotel. Typical of this group of hotels are the open bathrooms. Trams stop right at the door. Bistro-style restaurant

25hours by Levi's

Niddastr. 58 ✉ 60329 – Ⓜ Hauptbahnhof – ✆ (069) 2 56 67 70 – www.25hours-hotels.com **H2**

76 rm – 110/230 € 110/230 €, 14 €

Rest – *(closed Sunday)* Carte 24/38 €

♦ Townhouse ♦ Design ♦ Modern ♦

This trendy hotel centrally located near the railway station pays homage to the famous Levi's jeans. Each floor is dedicated to a different decade of the 20th century from the 1930s to the 1980s. This American-style restaurant recalls the original "workers" jeans.

Pearl without rest

Gutleutstr. 173 ✉ 60327 – ✆ (069) 27 13 66 90 – www.pearlhotel.de

55 rm – 119/299 € 139/349 € *Plan I* **B3**

♦ Business ♦ Modern ♦

The hotel is of a contemporary design throughout and adapted to the needs of business travellers. The main station is about five minutes walk away.

Bristol without rest

Ludwigstr. 15 ✉ 60327 – Ⓜ Hauptbahnhof – ✆ (069) 24 23 90 – www.bristol-hotel.de **H2**

145 rm – 95/270 € 115/320 €

♦ Business ♦ Contemporary ♦

This hotel is distinguished by its proximity to the main railway station and the inner city, as well as its modern furnishing in fashionable brown shades. Snacks can be ordered in the bar until 5am.

Palmenhof without rest

Bockenheimer Landstr. 89 ✉ 60325 – Ⓜ Westend – ✆ (069) 7 53 00 60 – www.palmenhof.com – Closed Christmas - 2 January **G1**

45 rm – 122/152 € 162/182 €, 16 €

♦ Business ♦ Townhouse ♦ Classic ♦

This privately run hotel in the banking quarter was built in 1890. Behind its Gründerzeit façade it houses pretty rooms furnished with antiques from various periods.

Plaza without rest

Esslinger Str. 8 ✉ 60329 – ✆ (069) 2 71 37 80 – www.plaza-frankfurt.bestwestern.de **H2**

45 rm – 89/108 € 127/135 €, ☕ 14 €

◆ Business ◆ Contemporary ◆

The guestrooms of this hotel are bright, modern and practically furnished. It is located in a relatively quiet side street near the station.

Holiday Inn Express without rest

Gutleutstr. 296 ✉ 60327 – ✆ (069) 50 69 60 – www.hiexpress.com/exfrankfurtmes *Plan I* **A3**

175 rm ☕ – 85/155 € 85/155 €

◆ Chain hotel ◆ Functional ◆

Ideal for business travellers, this modern, well-equipped hotel is conveniently located near the exhibition centre and the local station.

Villa Oriental

A/C rm,

Baseler Str. 21 ✉ 60329 – Ⓜ Hauptbahnhof – ✆ (069) 27 10 89 50 – www.villa-oriental.com **H2**

24 rm ☕ – 99/139 € 139/159 €

Rest *Hafez* – *✆ (069) 23 23 01* – Carte 20/35 €

◆ Business ◆ Personalised ◆

A piece of the orient has been brought to Frankfurt in the form of this hotel in an ornate town house, featuring tasteful and authentic furniture, colours and accessories. The ambience and food at the Hafez are Persian inspired.

Villa Merton

Am Leonhardsbrunn 12 (corner Ditmarstraße) ✉ 60487 – ✆ (069) 70 30 33 – www.koflerkompanie.com – Closed 23 December - 10 January, Saturday - Sunday and Bank Holidays

Rest – *(booking advisable)* Menu 105/117 € – Carte 68/84 € *Plan I* **A1**

Spec. Bachsaibling und grüner Spargel. Lamm mit Karotte und konfiertem Knoblauch. Erdbeere und Frischkäse mit Lakritztagetes.

◆ Inventive ◆ Classic ◆ Elegant ◆

This beautiful villa with its tasteful interior is in an exclusive location in the elegant diplomatic quarter. Matthias Schmidt creatively prepares and harmoniously puts together the dishes. Simpler business lunch.

Pearl by Mirko Reeh

Kettenhofweg 64 ✉ 60325 – Ⓜ Westend – ✆ (069) 71 40 20 46 – www.pearl-frankfurt.de – Closed Saturday lunch, Sunday and Bank Holidays **H1**

Rest – Menu 39/58 € – Carte 37/47 €

◆ Seasonal cuisine ◆ Fashionable ◆ Intimate ◆

Good contemporary cuisine is available in this modern restaurant decorated in warm colours. Situated in a residential district, it also has a small, pretty terrace.

Ernos Bistro

Liebigstr. 15 ✉ 60323 – Ⓜ Westend – ✆ (069) 72 19 97 – www.ernosbistro.de – Closed 2 weeks end December - early January, 3 weeks end June - early August, Saturday - Sunday and Bank Holidays **H1**

Rest – *(booking advisable)* Menu 36 € (lunch)/125 € – Carte 67/101 €

Spec. Hausgemachte Gänsestopfleber. Pochiertes Kalbsfilet mit Mangold und Ragoût von Cocobohnen. Nougat-Millefeuille mit leichter Schokolade und Vanilleeis.

◆ French ◆ Bistro ◆ Cosy ◆

Charming Westend bistro, which from the decor, via the cuisine to the wine is French-orientated. In addition to the food, the informal atmosphere is popular with the guests.

X **Druckwasserwerk**

Am Druckwasserwerk 1 ✉ 60237 – ☎ (069) 2 56 28 77 00
– www.restaurant-druckwasserwerk.de *Plan I* **A3**
Rest – Carte 29/40 €
♦ Seasonal cuisine ♦ Friendly ♦
This brick building of the historic waterworks in the west port is an industrial monument. The loft atmosphere is very appealing. Enjoy the good international food in a casual, modern atmosphere.

X **Weinsinn**

Fürstenbergerstr. 179 ✉ 60322
– Ⓜ Holzhausenstr. – ☎ (069) 56 99 80 80
– www.weinsinn-frankfurt.de
– Closed 19 April - 1 May, 12 - 24 July, Sunday - Monday and Bank Holidays
Rest – *(dinner only)* Menu 44/54 € *Plan I* **B1**
– Carte 32/55 €
♦ International ♦ Minimalist ♦ Retro ♦
Clean lines with a retro touch define this restaurant and wine bar. Enjoy carefully prepared contemporary food in a pleasantly informal and cosy atmosphere. Good wine recommendations.

ENVIRONS OF FRANKFURT

AT FRANKFURT-FECHENHEIM by Hanauer Landstraße D2

XX ✿ **Silk** (Mario Lohninger)

Carl-Benz-Str. 21 ✉ 60386 – ☎ (069) 90 02 00
– www.hoeren-sehen-schmecken.net
– Closed 2 weeks early January, mid July - mid August and Sunday - Monday
Rest – *(dinner only)* Menu 119 €
Rest *Micro Fine Dining* – *(closed 2 weeks early January and Sunday - Wednesday) (dinner only)* Menu 88 €
– Carte 43/85 €
Spec. Lauwarmer Skrei mit Petersilie und Miso-Vinaigrette. Carabinero mit Schwarzwurzel und Blutorange. Mozartdessert.
♦ Innovative ♦ Minimalist ♦ Trendy ♦
Delicious, creative cuisine with its own style meets an extraordinary dining experience. Enjoy the numerous bite-sized dishes on comfortable upholstered couches. There is a harmonious lounge atmosphere characterised by a minimalist design in white. Micro features an open cuisine where you can watch the fusion food being prepared before your eyes. The Cocoon Club is just next door.

AT THE RHEIN-MAIN AIRPORT by Kennedy Allee B3

Kempinski Hotel Gravenbruch

Graf zu Ysenburg und Büdingen-Platz 1 ✉ 63263 – ☎ (069) 38 98 80
– www.kempinski-frankfurt.com
284 rm – †119/299 € ††119/299 €, ☕ 26 € – 23 suites
Rest *Forsthaus* – Menu 69 € – Carte 43/60 €
Rest *L'olivo* – Carte 33/61 €
♦ Chain hotel ♦ Classic ♦
This hotel stands in attractive gardens with its own lake. The rooms are decorated in either a classic country or a more contemporary style. Beauty and massage treatments available. An elegant forester's lodge with garden views. This restaurant serves Italian/international cuisine.

Steigenberger Airport

Unterschweinstiege 16 ✉ 60549 – ✆ (069) 6 97 50
– www.airporthotel.steigenberger.de
570 rm – 🚹159/229 € 🚹🚹169/249 €, ☕ 28 € – 10 suites
Rest *Faces* – see below
Rest *Unterschweinstiege* – *✆ (069) 69 75 25 00* – Carte 33/59 €
♦ Chain hotel ♦ Modern ♦
This hotel is characterised by its elegant hall, comfortable rooms (in particular the modern Tower room) and the 'Open Sky' leisure area with fantastic views. A cosy atmosphere in the Unterschweinstiege.

Faces – Hotel Steigenberger Airport

Unterschweinstiege 16 ✉ 60549 – ✆ (069) 69 75 24 00
– www.airporthotel.steigenberger.de
– Closed 6 weeks July - August, 3 weeks December - early January and Saturday - Sunday
Rest – *(dinner only)* Menu 56 € – Carte 47/83 €
♦ International ♦ Design ♦
Behind the glass frontage lies a smart, modern restaurant with original lighting. It serves contemporary international cuisine focusing on high quality ingredients. Separate bar.

EMMA
LIBELLE

HAMBURG

HAMBURG

Population (est.2005): 1 770 000 (conurbation 2 290 000) – Altitude: at sea level

tthias Krüttgen/Fotolia.com

With a maritime role stretching back centuries, Germany's second largest city has a lively and liberal ambience. Hamburg's motto is 'The Gateway to the World', and there's certainly a visceral feel here, particularly around the big, buzzy and bustling port area. Locals enjoy a long-held reputation for their tolerance and outward looking stance, cosmopolitan to the core. This tolerance extends famously to the city's nightlife, which in the St Pauli area is renowned for its racy characteristics.

But there's another side to Hamburg. Despite its northerly position, it sits easily with a Mediterranean style café culture, and boasts waterside areas that have seen a significant amount of renovation and restyling in recent years. This is a big city for culture; it's where you come for the Long Theatre Night and the Art Mile Day. And, of course, it's where the Beatles paid their dues: the Reeperbahn is a classic first stop for many visitors. Eight hundred years' worth of trading with the world has left another favourable legacy: Hamburg's cuisine scene touches on all four corners of the globe. And space to breathe is seen as very important here: the city authorities have paid much attention to green spaces, and Hamburg can proudly claim an enviable amount of parks, lakes and tree-lined canals.

LIVING THE CITY

There's no cathedral in Hamburg (at least not a standing one, as war-destroyed St Nikolai remains a ruin) so the **Town Hall** acts as the central landmark. Just north of here is the Binnenalster (inner) and Aussenalster (outer) lake. The old walls of the city, dating back over eight hundred years, are delineated by a distinct semicircle of boulevards that curve attractively in a wide arc south of the lakes. Further south from here is the port and harbour area, defined by Landungsbrücken to the west, and Speicherstadt to the east. The district to the west of the centre is **St Pauli**, famed for its clubs and bars, particularly along the notorious Reeperbahn, which pierces the district from east to west. The contrastingly smart **Altona** suburb and delightful **Blankenese** village are west of St Pauli.

PRACTICAL INFORMATION

ARRIVAL-DEPARTURE

Hamburg Airport is 15km from the city centre. A taxi costs approximately €20. Airport buses leave for Hamburg Hauptbahnhof every 15-20min and Altona Station every 30min, with a journey time for both of 20min.

TRANSPORT

Hamburg Transport Authority controls all bus routes, S-Bahn and U-Bahn underground lines, and several river and ferry services. Tickets are available for single journeys, or for one day or three day duration. Buy from vending machines or bus drivers. Information available from many underground stations and the main railway station (Hauptbahnhof).

The Hamburg Card is valid for the transport network, and offers free entrance to eleven state-run museums, discounts on other activities, and on tours on water and land. Buy it from Tourist Information offices, vending machines, hotels and travel agents.

EXPLORING HAMBURG

If it weren't for the **Elbe**, there would be no Hamburg, so why not get the feel of the place by heading down to the water and sniffing the salty harbour air? An endless stream of ships calls at the twenty-seven miles of quayside to transport goods to and from ports far and wide. Take a boat yourself from the Landungsbrücken pier for an invigorating harbour tour. The views of the Elbe are wonderful, and you can pick and choose how you want to travel, either by basic boat or slinky cruiser. These will carry you upriver towards the huge modern container docks or eastwards through a network of canals, leading to the fascinating **Speicherstadt**. This is a wondrous place to be, the biggest warehouse complex in the world – the 'City of Warehouses'. It's a hauntingly Hanseatic dark-red brick complex from the mid-nineteenth century, and it's no ghost building:

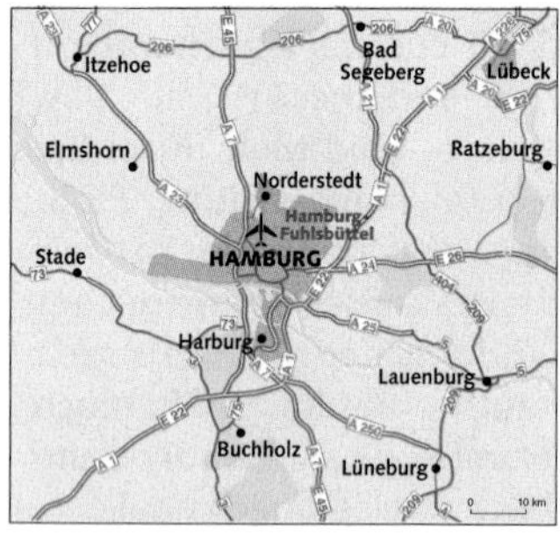

wholesalers still keep a range of goods here. It's also alive with museums (four in total) relating to the Speicherstadt's history. Close to here, in Deichstrasse, and the nearby old Cremon road, stand charmingly romantic merchants' houses, dating back to the seventeenth and eighteenth centuries. As much of the city was rebuilt after the War, this nugget of old Hamburg offers a tantalising flavour of what the port quarter must once have been like.

→ WATER, WATER EVERYWHERE

Water dominates this city. Go up through the old town, and the liquid quality takes on a different feel altogether, as you arrive at the shimmering **Alster**. Locals proudly ask a rhetorical question: what other bustling metropolis can boast such a wondrous lake in its centre? Surrounded by cafés, promenades and invigorating lungfuls of greenery, you can actually walk around the entire 160-hectare lake without having to cross a single road. For the energetically challenged, steamboats leave from the Jungfernstieg pier, pass under two bridges connecting the outer lake from the inner, and take in a view which incorporates elaborate nineteenth century merchants' villas and delightful parks full of poplars, chestnuts and oaks. If the chance arises, hop off your boat and down a coffee at one of the tempting lakeside cafés: memorable views of the Hamburg skyline, with its dominant spires and steeples, are guaranteed. The third watery option is a cruise along inner-city canals, where weeping willows bow down gracefully and grand-looking villas offer a haughty eye as you make your stately procession between Alster and Elbe.

→ PICTURE PERFECT

Not only can Hamburgers crow about the glory of their lake, they can also lay claim to the most important art gallery in northern Germany. The **Kunsthalle** is made up of three interconnected buildings and the paintings and artworks contained within make an entrance in the fifteenth century and an exit at the present day, taking in the likes of Master Bertram of Minden, Friedrichs, Runge, Monet, Manet, Renoir, Warhol and Beuys. A refuelling point well worth a look round itself is the Café Liebermann, where you can enjoy cake and coffee in the rarefied splendour of marble-columned surroundings. If your appreciation of art isn't quite yet sated, then continue south along the boulevard arc, past the railway station, and very soon you'll reach the Arts and Crafts Museum. This is an eclectic wonderland, with exhibits ranging from the Orient, ancient Greece and Rome right through to musical instruments down the ages and handsome examples of Art Nouveau.

You have to go right across to the inner city's west side to locate the third in Hamburg's winning triumvirate of galleries and museums, and many think this is the most satisfying of the three. The **Hamburg History Museum** covers just about every aspect of the city; particularly impressive are the models of Hamburg showing the stark differences over a five hundred year period. It's interesting, too, to enter into the elegant seventeenth century merchant's home, or see just what the medieval authorities did with huge nails and the skulls of pirates who dared terrorise the port.

→ CONVERSION OF ST PAULI

Of course, lots of tourists come to Hamburg and make a beeline for the St Pauli district, just up from the western docks, and it's safe to say that visiting churches and opera houses is probably not top of their tour agenda. St Pauli is the district where the Beatles cut their teeth in the early 60s, and its pulsating nightlife is still a big draw. The Reeperbahn has kept its reputation as the street where you wouldn't bring your great aunt: the sex shows and strip clubs are as lurid as ever, but times are a–changing. Tourists are making for the area because in recent years it's become a lively theatre and restaurant quarter in its own right. Hip young Hamburgers come here too because the bars and clubs have taken on a trendy, rather than garish, aspect. It's now a well-regulated area, and the nightlife is multi-layered, rather than notoriously one-dimensional as of old. In fact, your great aunt may demand to be taken there.

→ FOR FISH

If early starts are your thing, then St Pauli's world-famous **fishmarket**, down by the Elbe, is the ideal destination. A Sunday stalwart for three hundred years, it kicks off at five in the morning, and is often frequented by revellers unwilling to draw a line under their Saturday night. It's a cross between a rock concert and a flea-market with an impressive sideline in exotic fruit and smoked fish. There are great bargains to be had in plants and vegetables, too, and the salty-sounding vendors are an integral part of the experience. A cavernous steel and glass hall, on two floors, is given over for the morning to eating, drinking and live bands belting out a fine collection of old favourites to sing along with. For anyone still in the mood to savour the delights of St Pauli, just up the road is the Erotic Art Museum, which has nearly two thousand exhibits spanning five hundred years.

→ TOP PERFORMERS

Performance venues of another shade are high on Hamburg's cultural hit-list. In fact, they're the best of their kind in northern Germany. Just west of the inner Alster lake is the **Hamburg State Opera** and Ballet, where the best international names regularly perform. Meanwhile, The Musikhalle, which is by the Wallanlagen Gardens on aptly named Johannes-Brahms-Platz, celebrated its hundredth birthday in 2008. It's one of the most beautiful concert venues in Germany, an ornate building with three fine halls offering a wide range of orchestral and vocal performances. Hamburg can even boast two local orchestras of high renown, and the Musikhalle is their home.

CALENDAR HIGHLIGHTS

The event that really puts Hamburg on the map is the **Dom Festival**: 'Dommarkt' (in summer 'Sommer-Dom', in winter 'Winter-Dom'), which happens three times a year (usually April, August and November). It goes back to the fourteenth century, and translates as the Cathedral Festival. Basically, it's a huge funfair, with thrill rides, live music and beer tents

HAMBURG IN...

→ ONE DAY

Boat trip from Landungsbrücken, Speicherstadt, Kunsthalle, Fishmarket (if it's a Sunday morning!)

→ TWO DAYS

Steamboat on the Alster, Hamburg History Museum, St Pauli by night

→ THREE DAYS

Arts and Crafts Museum, canal trip between lake and harbour, concert at Musikhalle

– it attracts a phenomenal nine million visitors a year. The city's other major annual event is the harbour's birthday celebration every May – Hafengeburtstag - fun and games (and tug boats dancing) happen all along the harbour. There's a month-long market to celebrate the arrival of Spring, every March and April, in St Pauli's Heiligengeistfeld. In September movie fans wallow in a glut of celluloid at the Film Festival Hamburg. May's Long Night of Hamburg Museums and November's Art Mile Day cement the city's reputation as a cultural behemoth: on both occasions arty hothouses are kept open deep into the night.

EATING OUT

Being a city immersed in water, it's no surprise to find Hamburg is pretty hot on fish. Though its fishing industry isn't the powerhouse of old, the city still boasts a giant trawler's worth of seafood places to eat. Eel dishes are mainstays of the traditional restaurant's menu, as is the herring stew with vegetables called Labskaus. Also unsurprisingly, considering it's the country's gateway to the world, this is somewhere that offers a vast range of international dishes. As good restaurants tend to open where the media gathers, and Hamburg is Germany's media capital, you're assured of a range of smart and swanky places to dine. Wherever you eat here, the portions are likely to be generous. There's no problem with finding somewhere early: cafes are often open at seven, with the belief that it's never too early for coffee and cake. Bakeries, too, believe in an early start, and the calorie content here, too, can be pretty high. Bistros and restaurants, usually open by midday, are proud of their local ingredients, so keep your eyes open for Hamburgisch on the menu. Service charges are always included in the bill, so tipping is not compulsory, although most people will round it up to the next euro, and possibly add five to ten per cent.

➜ TIME FOR THE TOWN HALL

Hamburg's nineteenth-century town hall, in **Rathausplatz**, is an eye-catching place with nearly six hundred and fifty rooms. It does battle as the city's main landmark with 'Michel' – St Michael's Church – which stands proudly over the port as a centuries-old guide to sailors. Its massive clock face is the biggest in Germany, and at midday every day its three organs put on an awesome, ear-piercing show.

➜ VIEW FROM A BRIDGE

Hamburg's a great place to look at the world from a bridge. You won't have trouble finding one. There are a whopping 2,247 of them around the city. Bear in mind that Venice has a measly 450, and you might begin to get the picture.

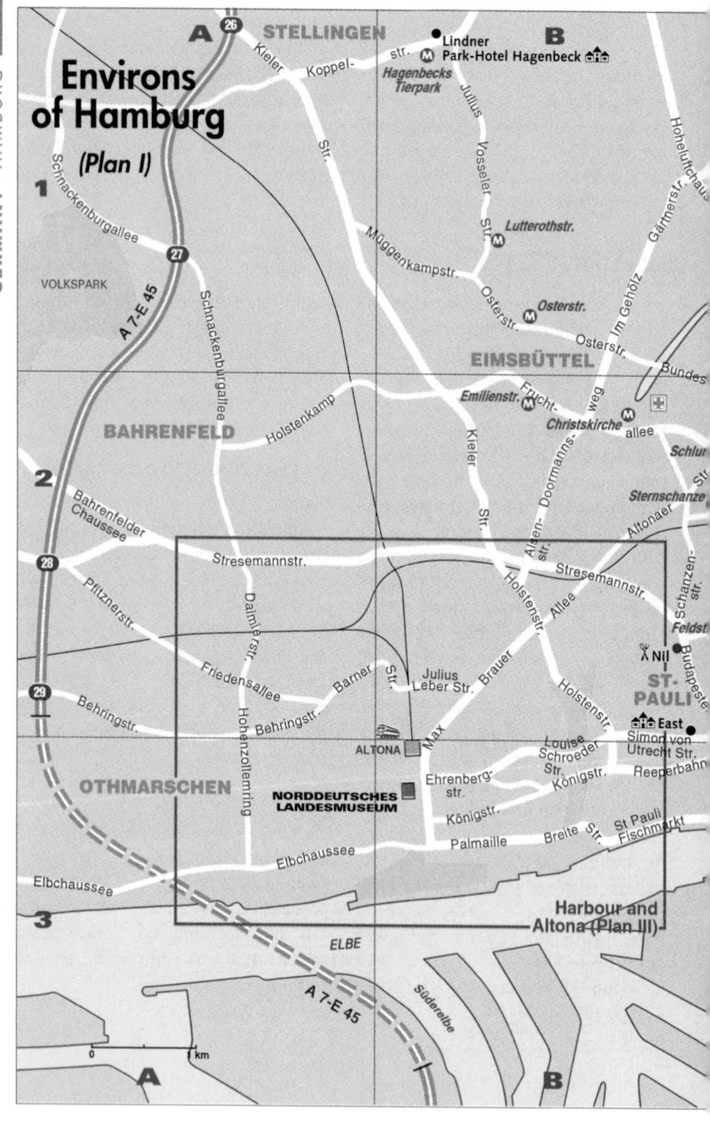
Environs of Hamburg
(Plan I)
A
B
1
2
3
STELLINGEN
Lindner Park-Hotel Hagenbeck
Hagenbecks Tierpark
Kieler Str.
Koppel-str.
Julius Vosseler Str.
Lutterothstr.
Müggenkampstr.
Osterstr.
Hoheluftchaus
Gärtnerstr.
Im Gehölz
Bundes
EIMSBÜTTEL
Emilienstr.
Fruchtallee
Christkirche
Doormannsweg
Alsen-str.
Schlu
Sternschanze
Altonaer
Schanzen-str.
Feldst
Nil
Budapester
ST.-PAULI
East
Simon von Utrecht Str.
Reeperbahn
Schnackenburgallee
VOLKSPARK
A 7-E 45
BAHRENFELD
Holstenkamp
Kieler Str.
Bahrenfelder Chaussee
Stresemannstr.
Pfitznerstr.
Daimlerstr.
Friedensallee
Barner Str.
Julius Leber Str.
Max Brauer Allee
Holstenstr.
Behringstr.
Hohenzollernring
ALTONA
Louise Schroeder Str.
Königstr.
Ehrenberg-str.
OTHMARSCHEN
NORDDEUTSCHES LANDESMUSEUM
Palmaille
Breite Str.
St Pauli Fischmarkt
Elbchaussee
Harbour and Altona (Plan III)
ELBE
Süderelbe
0
1 km

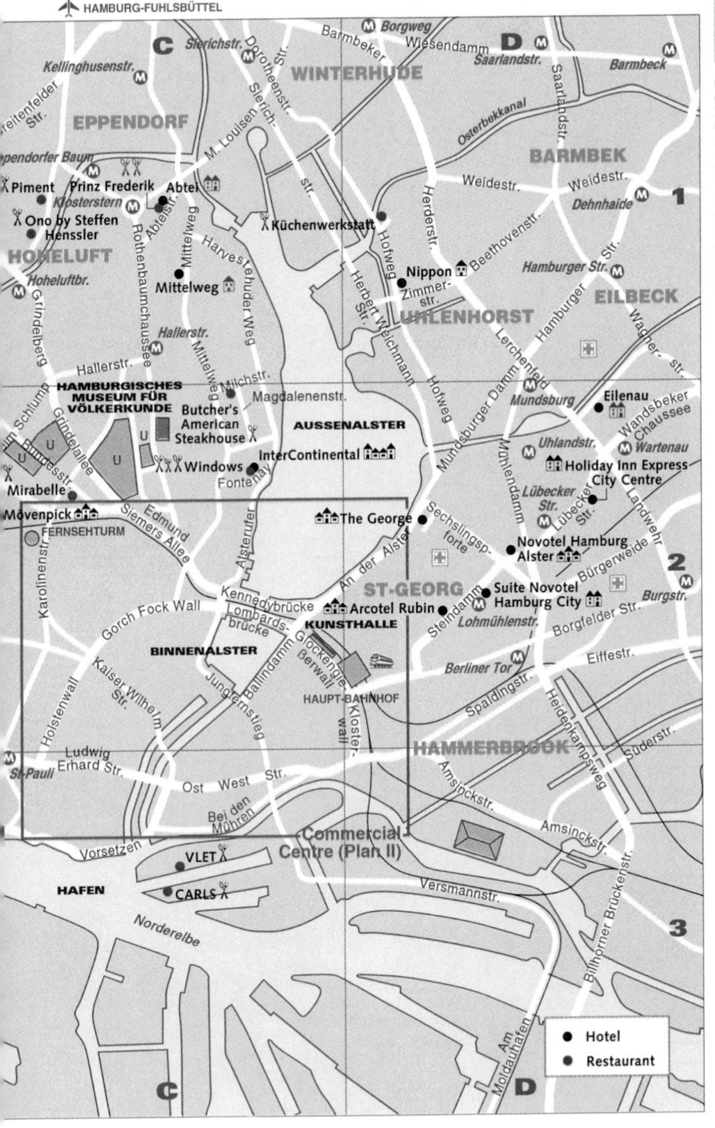
WINTERHUDE
EPPENDORF
BARMBEK
HOHELUFT
UHLENHORST
EILBECK
HAMBURGISCHES MUSEUM FÜR VÖLKERKUNDE
AUSSENALSTER
BINNENALSTER
ST-GEORG
KUNSTHALLE
HAUPT-BAHNHOF
HAMMERBROOK
HAFEN
FERNSEHTURM
Piment
Prinz Frederik
Abtei
Ono by Steffen Henssler
Küchenwerkstatt
Nippon
Mittelweg
Butcher's American Steakhouse
Windows
InterContinental
Mirabelle
Mövenpick
The George
Eilenau
Holiday Inn Express City Centre
Novotel Hamburg Alster
Suite Novotel Hamburg City
Arcotel Rubin
VLET
CARLS
Commercial Centre (Plan II)
Norderelbe
Hotel
Restaurant

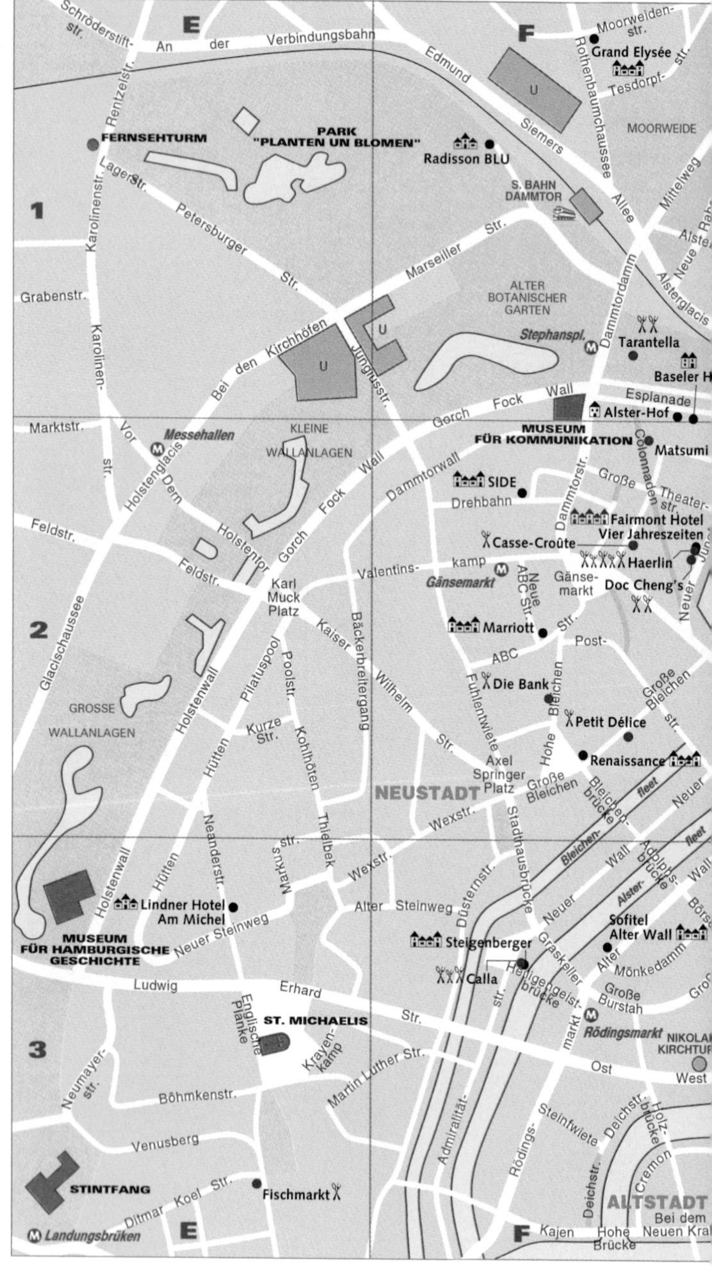
E
F
1
2
3
Schröderstift-str.
An der Verbindungsbahn
Edmund Siemers Allee
Moorweiden-str.
Grand Elysée
Tesdorpf-str.
Rothenbaumchaussee
MOORWEIDE
Rentzelstr.
FERNSEHTURM
PARK "PLANTEN UN BLOMEN"
Radisson BLU
Lagerstr.
S. BAHN DAMMTOR
Mittelweg
Karolinenstr.
Petersburger Str.
Marseiller Str.
Alster
Neue Rabenstr.
Alsterglacis
Dammtordamm
Grabenstr.
ALTER BOTANISCHER GARTEN
Karolinen-
Bei den Kirchhöfen
Jungiusstr.
Stephanspl.
Tarantella
Baseler H
Gorch Fock Wall
Esplanade
Alster-Hof
Marktstr.
Vor
Messehallen
KLEINE WALLANLAGEN
MUSEUM FÜR KOMMUNIKATION
Matsumi
Colonnaden
str.
Holstenglacis
Dem
Dammtorwall
SIDE
Große Theater-str.
Dammtorstr.
Drehbahn
Fairmont Hotel Vier Jahreszeiten
Feldstr.
Holstentor
Gorch Fock Wall
Casse-Croûte
Haerlin
Valentins-kamp
Gänsemarkt
Neue ABC Str.
Gänse-markt
Doc Cheng's
Neuer Jungfernstieg
Karl Muck Platz
Kaiser Wilhelm Str.
Bäckerbreitergang
Marriott
ABC Str.
Post-
Glacischaussee
Pilatuspool
Poolstr.
Die Bank
Fühlentwiete
Große Bleichen
GROSSE WALLANLAGEN
Holstenwall
Kurze Str.
Hohe Bleichen
Petit Délice
Hütten
Kohlhöfen
Renaissance
Axel Springer Platz
Große Bleichen
Bleichen-brücke
NEUSTADT
fleet
Neuer Wall
Neanderstr.
Thielbek
Wexstr.
Stadthausbrücke
Bleichen-
Adolphs-brücke
Alster-
Wexstr.
Markusstr.
Hütten
Holstenwall
Lindner Hotel Am Michel
Alter Steinweg
Düsternstr.
Neuer Wall
Börse
Sofitel Alter Wall
MUSEUM FÜR HAMBURGISCHE GESCHICHTE
Neuer Steinweg
Steigenberger
Graskeller
Alter Wall
Mönkedamm
Calla
Heiligengeist-brücke
Ludwig Erhard Str.
Große Burstah
Englische Planke
ST. MICHAELIS
markt
Rödingsmarkt
NIKOLAI KIRCHTURM
Krayenkamp
Martin Luther Str.
Ost West
Neumayer-str.
Böhmkenstr.
Admiralitätstr.
Rödings-
Steinfwiete
Deichstr.
Holzbrücke
Venusberg
Cremon
STINTFANG
Ditmar Koel Str.
Fischmarkt
ALTSTADT
Landungsbrüken
Kajen
Hohe Brücke
Bei dem Neuen Kran

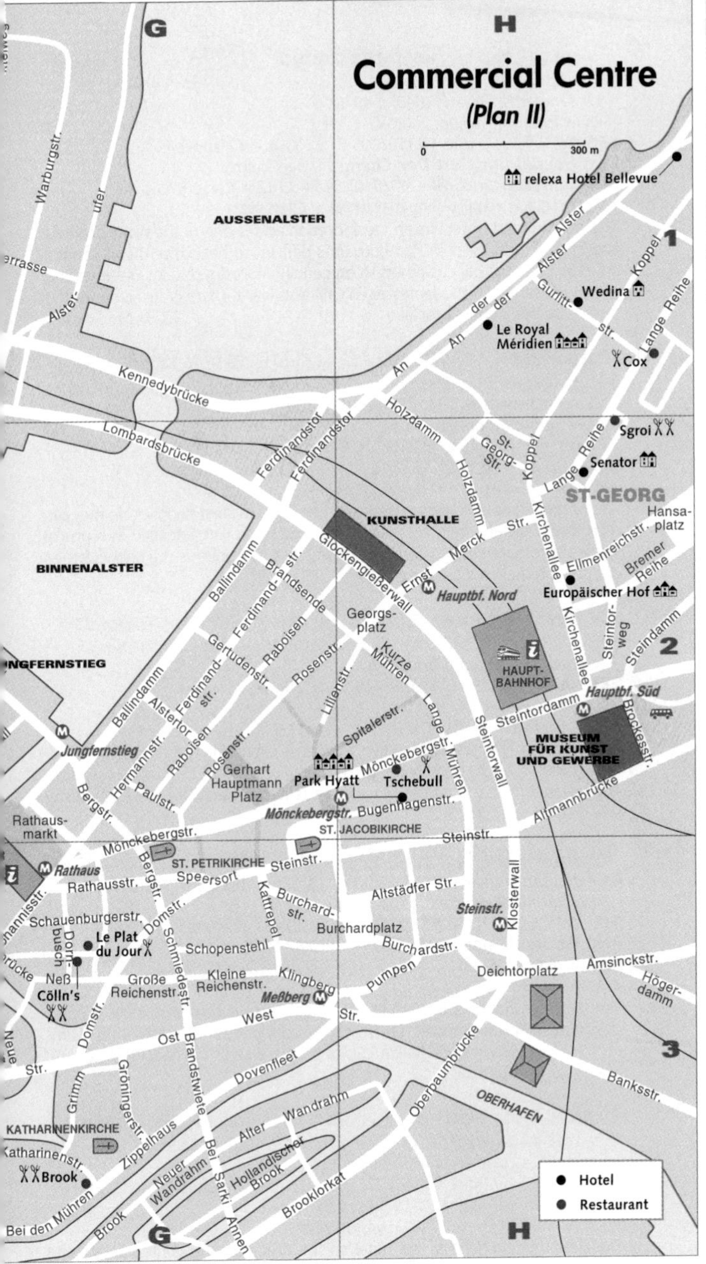

Commercial Centre
(Plan II)
0
300 m
relexa Hotel Bellevue
AUSSENALSTER
BINNENALSTER
KUNSTHALLE
ST-GEORG
Wedina
Le Royal Méridien
Cox
Sgroi
Senator
Europäischer Hof
Hauptbf. Nord
HAUPT-BAHNHOF
Hauptbf. Süd
MUSEUM FÜR KUNST UND GEWERBE
Park Hyatt
Tschebull
Gerhart Hauptmann Platz
Mönckebergstr.
ST. JACOBIKIRCHE
ST. PETRIKIRCHE
Rathaus
Rathausmarkt
Jungfernstieg
Le Plat du Jour
Cölln's
Meßberg
Steinstr.
Deichtorplatz
OBERHAFEN
KATHARINENKIRCHE
Brook
Kennedybrücke
Lombardsbrücke
Ballindamm
Glockengießerwall
Steintordamm
Steintorwall
Klosterwall
Amsinckstr.
Banksstr.
Oberbaumbrücke
Brooktorkai
Hotel
Restaurant
G
H
1
2
3

Fairmont Hotel Vier Jahreszeiten

Neuer Jungfernstieg 9 ✉ *20354*
– Ⓜ *Jungfernstieg* – ✆ *(040) 3 49 40*
– *www.fairmont-hvj.de* **F2**
156 rm – 🚹260/315 € 🚹🚹310/395 €, ☕ 32 € – 17 suites
Rest *Haerlin and Rest Doc Cheng's* – see below
Rest *Jahreszeiten Grill* – ✆ *(040) 34 94 33 12* – Carte 37/66 €
♦ Grand Luxury ♦ Traditional ♦ Classic ♦

This noble grand hotel has an ideal location and is one of the most beautiful and elegant addresses in Hamburg. It is difficult to beat in terms of comfort and service. In the bar customers sit on genuine Rolls Royce seats. International dishes are served in the Jahreszeiten Grill restaurant. There is also an attractive terrace on the Binnenalster lake.

Park Hyatt

Bugenhagenstr. 8 (at Levantehaus) ✉ *20095*
– Ⓜ *Mönckebergstr.* – ✆ *(040) 33 32 12 34*
– *www.hamburg.park.hyatt.de* **H2**
252 rm – 🚹180/340 € 🚹🚹210/370 €, ☕ 31 € – 21 suites
Rest *Apples* – ✆ *(040) 33 32 15 11* – Menu 59 € – Carte 35/61 €
♦ Grand Luxury ♦ Chain hotel ♦ Modern ♦

This former office building welcomes its guests on the first-floor, where they can relax in the tasteful lounge. It is a luxury hotel that is unequalled in terms of value and modern elegance. The eye-catcher at Apples is the show kitchen offering international cuisine.

Le Royal Méridien

An der Alster 52 ✉ *20099* – Ⓜ *Hauptbf. Nord* – ✆ *(040) 2 10 00*
– *www.lemeridien.com/hamburg* **H1**
284 rm – 🚹169/399 € 🚹🚹189/419 €, ☕ 28 € – 12 suites
Rest – Carte 45/67 €
♦ Chain hotel ♦ Luxury ♦ Modern ♦

This modern hotel has an attractive, clear style extending from the brightly furnished rooms (with specially designed therapeutic beds) to the wellness area. The restaurant on the ninth floor offers a fantastic view over the Außenalster lake.

Grand Elysée

Rothenbaumchaussee 10 ✉ *20148* – Ⓜ *Stephanspl.* – ✆ *(040) 41 41 20*
– *www.grand-elysee.com* **F1**
511 rm – 🚹140/200 € 🚹🚹160/220 €, ☕ 20 € – 17 suites
Rest *Piazza Romana* – ✆ *(040) 41 41 27 34* – Carte 34/58 €
Rest *Brasserie Flum* – ✆ *(040) 41 41 27 23* – Carte 25/45 €
♦ Luxury ♦ Classic ♦

The generous hotel lobby with its café greets you in boulevard style. It offers classic, elegant rooms, quiet garden courtyard rooms, and south-facing rooms on the Moorweiden park. Italian cuisine in the Piazza Romana. Brasserie and oyster bar with seafood.

Sofitel Alter Wall

Alter Wall 40 ✉ *20457* – Ⓜ *Rödingsmarkt* – ✆ *(040) 36 95 00*
– *www.sofitel.com* **F3**
241 rm – 🚹145/255 € 🚹🚹165/275 €, ☕ 26 € – 10 suites
Rest – Carte 32/47 €
♦ Chain hotel ♦ Luxury ♦ Design ♦

The clear modern style of this hotel on the Alster canal is contemporary and luxurious - it even has its own landing stage. Chic little spa in the basement. Restaurant with a straightforward layout.

Steigenberger

Heiligengeistbrücke 4 ✉ 20459 – Ⓜ Rödingsmarkt – ✆ (040) 36 80 60 – www.hamburg.steigenberger.de **F3**

233 rm – 139/249 € 159/269 €, ☕ 23 € – 6 suites

Rest *Calla* – see below

Rest *Bistro am Fleet* – Carte 24/54 €

♦ Luxury ♦ Classic ♦

Right beside the Alster canal stands this well-run and elegant hotel in the shape of a ship. From the fitness area roof terrace there is a wonderful view over the city. International cuisine in the bistro.

SIDE

Drehbahn 49 ✉ 20354 – Ⓜ Stephansplatz – ✆ (040) 30 99 90 – www.side-hamburg.de **F2**

178 rm – 150/300 € 150/300 €, ☕ 23 € – 10 suites

Rest – *(Saturday, Sunday and Bank Holidays dinner only)* Carte 38/99 €

♦ Luxury ♦ Design ♦

Behind the natural stone and glass façade lays the impressive 30m high lobby, with a lighting design by Robert Wilson. The hotel has tasteful rooms designed in white and brown by Matteo Thun. The "(m)eatery" is a "high-end steakhouse" and bar.

Renaissance

Große Bleichen ✉ 20354 – Ⓜ Jungfernstieg – ✆ (040) 34 91 80 – www.renaissance-hamburg.com **F2**

205 rm – 149/200 € 159/245 €, ☕ 24 € – 1 suite **Rest** – Carte 29/40 €

♦ Luxury ♦ Classic ♦

This classic and sophisticated hotel is equipped with functional, liveable and comfortable guestrooms. On the sixth-floor relax in the sauna and enjoy the view. This restaurant is the former residence of the Broschek printing family, who have provided its name and atmosphere.

Marriott

ABC-Str. 52 ✉ 20354 – Ⓜ Gänsemarkt – ✆ (040) 3 50 50 – www.hamburgmarriott.de **F2**

278 rm – 179/239 € 189/239 €, ☕ 26 € – 3 suites **Rest** – Carte 30/41 €

♦ Chain hotel ♦ Modern ♦

This classic hotel is close to the Gänsemarkt. It has a sophisticated atmosphere in its lobby and guestrooms, and an attractive swimming, sauna and beauty area. Restaurant Speicher 52 has a friendly and modern presentation.

Radisson BLU

Marseiller Str. 2 ✉ 20355 – Ⓜ Stephanspl. – ✆ (040) 3 50 20 – www.radissonblu.com/hotel-hamburg **F1**

556 rm – 130/185 € 130/185 €, ☕ 20 € – 9 suites

Rest *Fillini* – Carte 23/39 €

Rest *Trader Vic's* – *(dinner only)* Carte 38/52 €

♦ Chain hotel ♦ Functional ♦

This high-rise business hotel with great city views is connected to the Congress Centre. It offers spacious common areas and comfortable "Natural", "Urban" and "New York Mansion" rooms. Fillini serves international cuisine. Trader Vic's serves Polynesian cuisine.

Arcotel Rubin

Steindamm 63 (access via Danzingerstraße) ✉ 20099 – Ⓜ Lohmühlenstr. – ✆ (040) 2 41 92 90 – www.arcotelhotels.com/rubin *Plan I* **D2**

217 rm – 89/250 € 89/250 €, ☕ 12 €

Rest – Menu 19 € – Carte 23/36 €

♦ Chain hotel ♦ Business ♦ Design ♦

This elegantly designed hotel close to the main railway station is decorated in beautiful tones of ruby red. There is even a themed "Red Room". The sauna and fitness facilities offer views over Hamburg. The "Wiener Kaffee" café-restaurant serves international cuisine with an Austrian influence.

The Goerge

Barcastr. 3 ✉ 22087 – Ⓜ Lohmühlenstr. – ✆ (040) 2 80 03 00 – www.thegeorge-hotel.de Plan I **D2**

125 rm – 🚹135/185 € 🚹🚹135/185 €, ☕ 12 € – 2 suites

Rest – *(closed Sunday dinner)* Carte 39/69 €

◆ Townhouse ◆ Design ◆ Elegant ◆

The elegant British style has been successfully brought up-to-date in this design hotel. Pleasant roof terrace with a view over Hamburg, and a garden at the back. This restaurant with a large bar area serves international cuisine.

Mövenpick

Sternschanze 6 ✉ 20357 – Ⓜ Sternschanze – ✆ (040) 3 34 41 10 – www.moevenpick-hamburg.com Plan I **C2**

226 rm – 🚹120/240 € 🚹🚹140/260 €, ☕ 21 € – 2 suites

Rest – Carte 29/43 €

◆ Chain hotel ◆ Historic ◆ Modern ◆

The guestrooms, in this former water tower from around 1900, have a modern style and technology. There is a very chic roof suite with a particularly impressive view over the city. International cuisine is served in this restaurant with a terrace facing the Schanzen park.

Novotel Hamburg Alster

Lübecker Str. 3 ✉ 22087 – Ⓜ Lübecker Str. – ✆ (040) 39 19 00 – www.novotel.com Plan I **D2**

210 rm – 🚹99/179 € 🚹🚹99/179 €, ☕ 18 € – 2 suites

Rest – Carte 17/47 €

◆ Chain hotel ◆ Modern ◆

This contemporary hotel provides modern, well-equipped rooms and good conference facilities. Children under 16 years old can sleep free in their parents' room. Restaurant accessed from the hotel lobby.

Europäischer Hof

rest,

Kirchenallee 45 ✉ 20099 – Ⓜ Hauptbahnhof Süd – ✆ (040) 24 82 48 – www.europaeischer-hof.de **H2**

275 rm ☕ – 🚹115/195 € 🚹🚹145/232 €

Rest ***Paulaner's*** – Carte 21/37 €

◆ Business ◆ Classic ◆

A large, dignified hall welcomes you to this hotel, which is located opposite the main station. Find the seven-storey 'Euro-therme' with a 150m waterslide over six floors. The atmosphere in Paulaner's is rustic and relaxed.

Lindner Hotel Am Michel

Neanderstr. 20 ✉ 20459 – ✆ (040) 3 07 06 70 – www.lindner.de/hotel-hamburg **E3**

259 rm – 🚹129/509 € 🚹🚹149/529 €, ☕ 20 € – 8 suites

Rest – Menu 29/43 € – Carte 29/46 €

◆ Business ◆ Chain hotel ◆ Contemporary ◆

This brick building is in a relatively quiet and central location, close to the 'Michel'. It offers modern, well-appointed rooms in warm colours. There is a view over the city from the sauna area. The restaurant Sonnin serves international cuisine.

Eilenau without rest

Eilenau 36 ✉ 22089 – Ⓜ Wartenau – ✆ (040) 2 36 01 30 – www.eilenau.de Plan I **D2**

17 rm ☕ – 🚹126/220 € 🚹🚹165/320 € – 5 suites

◆ Townhouse ◆ Personalised ◆ Elegant ◆

Two over 100-year old town houses have been converted into a dapper and stylish hotel, combining the modern and antique, stucco and old parquet. Free W-LAN and telephone, as well as fresh fruit and water. Small breakfast garden.

relexa Hotel Bellevue

An der Alster 14 (access via Koppel) ✉ 20099 – ✆ (040) 28 44 40 – www.relexa-hotels.de **H1**

85 rm – 59/115 € 109/159 € – 2 suites **Rest** – Carte 21/35 €

◆ Villa ◆ Personalised ◆

This classic townhouse on the Alster, and two further buildings, accommodate cosy guestrooms and small, but modern, single rooms. There is also a pleasant cellar bar. During the day diners are served in the restaurant with a view of the Alster lake; and in the evening, in the cosy basement maritime restaurant.

Senator without rest

Lange Reihe 18 ✉ 20099 – Ⓜ Hauptbf. Nord – ✆ (040) 24 19 30 – www.hotel-senator-hamburg.de **H2**

56 rm – 109/159 € 129/189 €

◆ Townhouse ◆ Functional ◆

Expect bright and practically furnished guestrooms in this hotel behind the station. There are also some 'wellness rooms' with steam massage showers available.

Baseler Hof

Esplanade 11 ✉ 20354 – Ⓜ Stephansplatz – ✆ (040) 35 90 60 – www.baselerhof.de **F1**

168 rm – 89/125 € 145/155 € – 4 suites

Rest *Kleinhuis* – *✆ (040) 35 33 99* – Menu 26 € – Carte 28/40 €

◆ Traditional ◆ Functional ◆

This hotel is located between the Außenalster lake and the Botanical Gardens, and is a member of the Association of Christian Hotels. A well maintained and run hotel. The Kleinhuis is a friendly, bistro-style restaurant.

Suite Novotel Hamburg City without rest

Lübeckertordamm 2 ✉ 20099 – Ⓜ Lohmühlenstr. – ✆ (040) 27 14 00 – www.suitenovotel.com *Plan I* **D2**

186 rm – 89/119 € 89/119 €, 13 €

◆ Business ◆ Functional ◆

The no-nonsense guestrooms in this hotel are quite spacious and functional. The internet and telephone can be used at no extra charge. Snacks are available to take away in the lobby.

Holiday Inn Express City Centre without rest

Lübecker Str. 109 ✉ 22087 – Ⓜ Lübecker Str. – ✆ (040) 7 34 45 10 – www.fmhos.com *Plan I* **D2**

179 rm – 89/129 € 89/129 €

◆ Business ◆ Modern ◆

An ideal centrally-located business hotel with technically well equipped rooms in fresh warm colours (pillows available in two hardnesses).

Wedina without rest (with guesthouses)

Gurlittstr. 23 ✉ 20099 – ✆ (040) 2 80 89 00 – www.wedina.de – Closed 24 - 28 December **H1**

59 rm – 98/148 € 118/168 €

◆ Family ◆ Cosy ◆

There are four buildings with façades in red, yellow, blue and green, which house modern rooms from colourful to literary. An idyllic garden draws you to breakfast. Bicycle rental.

Alster-Hof without rest

Esplanade 12 ✉ 20354 – Ⓜ Stephansplatz – ✆ (040) 35 00 70 – www.alster-hof.de – Closed 23 December - 2 January **F1**

111 rm – 85/110 € 130/165 € – 3 suites

◆ Traditional ◆ Functional ◆

This well cared for hotel is in the city centre, near to the Alster. It has functional guestrooms decorated in homely colours. These include sometimes rather small single rooms.

XXXXX ✿

Haerlin – Fairmont Hotel Vier Jahreszeiten

Neuer Jungfernstieg 9 ✉ 20354 – Ⓜ Jungfernstieg – ✆ (040) 34 94 33 10 – www.fairmont-hvj.de
– Closed 22 - 30 April, 11 July - 8 August and Sunday - Monday **F2**
Rest – *(dinner only)* Menu 105/117 € – Carte 76/107 €
Spec. Gänseleberparfait mit Holunderblütengelée und Kaisergranat mit karamellisierter Grapefruit. Wolfsbarsch in Meersalz gegart mit Artischocken à la barigoule und Bohnencassoulet. Knusprige Ente in zwei Gängen serviert.
♦ Classic ♦ Luxury ♦
Christoph Rüffer has developed an interesting contemporary style of cooking. It is classically based and makes this elegant restaurant into an outstanding gourmet establishment. Fantastic view of the Binnenalster Lake.

XXX

Calla – Hotel Steigenberger

Heiligengeistbrücke 4 ✉ 20459 – Ⓜ Rödingsmarkt – ✆ (040) 36 80 60 – www.calla.steigenberger.de
– Closed Christmas - 3 January, 30 June - 10 August, Sunday - Monday and Bank Holidays **F3**
Rest – *(dinner only)* Menu 42/79 € – Carte 41/72 €
♦ International ♦ Elegant ♦ Fashionable ♦
With a view over the River Alster, this bright and tastefully modern restaurant offers refined dining and friendly service. Creative international cuisine with more than a hint of the Far East.

XX

Cölln's

Brodschrangen 1 ✉ 20457 – Ⓜ Rathaus – ✆ (040) 36 41 53 – www.coellns-restaurant.de
– Closed Saturday lunch, Sunday and Bank Holidays **G3**
Rest – *(booking advisable)* Carte 40/75 €
♦ Classic ♦ Cosy ♦
This tastefully restored historic building has many charming small rooms. There are mostly fish dishes on the menu. Specialities are oysters, lobster and caviar.

XX ✿

Sgroi

Lange Reihe 40 ✉ 20099 – Ⓜ Hauptbf. Nord – ✆ (040) 28 00 39 30 – www.sgroi.de
– Closed Saturday lunch, Sunday - Monday and Bank Holidays lunch
Rest – Menu 35 € (lunch)/82 € – Carte 66/80 € **H1-2**
Spec. Calamaretti gefüllt mit Tatar von Garnelen, Salat von Rucola, Radieschensprossen und grünen Äpfeln. Rosa gebratener Thunfisch in Noriblatt auf jungem Spinat mit geschmorter Gurke. Bricolage von Kalbsbries und Mark mit Kalbskopfgalantina, jungen Artischocken, Frisée und Balsamico Tradizionale.
♦ Italian ♦ Minimalist ♦
For Anna Sgroi the produce is at the centre of her modern, Italian inspired food. The clean-lined style is reflected in the bright, unfussy decor where guests are cordially and attentively looked after. Cheaper and simpler midday menu.

XX

Tarantella

Stephansplatz 10 (at Casino Esplanade) ✉ 20354 – Ⓜ Stephanspl. – ✆ (040) 65 06 77 90 – www.tarantella.cc **F1**
Rest – Carte 29/69 €
♦ International ♦ Fashionable ♦
This restaurant with its noble and yet simple, modern design is housed in the historic casino building. It offers international dishes from its show kitchen. There is a bistro area and a beautiful terrace with plants.

Brook

Bei den Mühren 91 ✉ 20457 – Ⓜ Meßberg – ✆ (040) 37 50 31 28 – www.restaurant-brook.de – Closed Sunday **G3**

Rest – Carte 34/47 €

♦ International ♦ Fashionable ♦

A modern restaurant with friendly service and high quality international cuisine. In the evening there is a pretty view of the illuminated Speicherstadt (warehouses) opposite.

Doc Cheng's – Fairmont Hotel Vier Jahreszeiten

Neuer Jungfernstieg 9 ✉ 20354 – Ⓜ Jungfernstieg – ✆ (040) 3 49 43 33 – www.fairmont-hvj.de – Closed Sunday **F2**

Rest – *(dinner only)* Carte 35/49 €

♦ Asian ♦ Individual ♦

The Far East inspires both the design and cuisine of this restaurant. Euro-Asian cuisine is served here.

Die Bank

Hohe Bleichen 17 ✉ 20354 – Ⓜ Gänsemarkt – ✆ (040) 2 38 00 30 – www.diebank-brasserie.de – Closed Sunday and Bank Holidays

Rest – Menu 53/69 € – Carte 38/69 € **F2**

♦ International ♦ Brasserie ♦ Trendy ♦

This brasserie and bar are one of the city's hotspots. The banking hall on the first-floor of this former bank, built in 1897, is an impressive feature of this fashionable venue.

CARLS

Am Kaiserkai 69 ✉ 20457 – ✆ (040) 3 00 32 24 00 – www.carls-brasserie.de *Plan I* **C3**

Rest – Menu 36 € – Carte 32/77 €

♦ French ♦ Brasserie ♦

This elegant brasserie located next to the new Elbphilharmonie concert hall has a fantastic view over the port and serves French cuisine with a North-German flavour. Snacks and pastries are available in the bistro.

La Mirabelle

Bundesstr. 15 ✉ 20146 – Ⓜ Hallerstr. – ✆ (040) 4 10 75 85 – www.la-mirabelle-hamburg.de – Closed Sunday *Plan I* **C2**

Rest – *(dinner only)* Menu 39/49 € – Carte 46/57 €

♦ French ♦ Cosy ♦

In this charming little restaurant, the pleasant and informal atmosphere, together with the modern dishes on offer, reflect the French roots of the chef.

Tschebull

Mönckebergstr. 7 (at Levantehaus) ✉ 20095 – Ⓜ Mönchebergstr. – ✆ (040) 32 96 47 96 – www.tschebull.de – Closed Sunday and Bank Holidays **H2**

Rest – Menu 26 € (lunch)/85 € (dinner) – Carte 32/63 €

♦ Austrian ♦ Cosy ♦

Find a modern, uncomplicated ambience with an Alpine touch on the first floor of this smart shopping arcade. Sample the Austrian cuisine of the Carinthian-born chef.

VLET

Sandtorkai 23 (at Markthalle, 1st floor) ✉ 20457 – ✆ (040) 3 34 75 37 50 – www.vlet.de – Closed Saturday lunch and Sunday *Plan I* **C3**

Rest – Menu 65 € (dinner) – Carte 39/63 €

♦ Modern ♦ Trendy ♦

Contemporary regional cuisine is served in this characteristic Speicherstadt brick building. This young, modern restaurant is reached via the Kibbelsteg bridge.

Fischmarkt

Ditmar-Koel-Str. 1 ✉ 20459 – Ⓜ Landungsbrücken – ✆ (040) 36 38 09 – www.restaurant-fischmarkt.de
– Closed Sunday **E3**
Rest – *(booking advisable)* Menu 33/49 € – Carte 30/71 €
♦ Fish ♦ Bistro ♦
At the Schaarmarkt close to the harbour, this bistro on two levels has a Mediterranean decor. It serves many fish specials and the fish display is very appetising.

Le Plat du Jour

Dornbusch 4 ✉ 20095 – Ⓜ Rathaus – ✆ (040) 32 14 14 – www.leplatdujour.de **G3**
Rest – *(booking advisable)* Menu 29 € (dinner) – Carte 27/41 €
♦ French ♦ Bistro ♦
A pleasant and lively establishment – just as a typical French bistro should be. Black and white photographs emphasise the authentic ambience. The no-nonsense dishes are all freshly prepared.

Casse-Croûte

Büschstr. 2 ✉ 20354 – Ⓜ Gänsemarkt – ✆ (040) 34 33 73 – www.cassecroute.de
– Closed over Christmas, Sunday lunch and Bank Holidays lunch **F2**
Rest – *(booking advisable)* Menu 30 € – Carte 25/52 €
♦ French ♦ Bistro ♦
Tasty, French influenced food is prepared at this appealing bistro near the Gänsemarkt and Jungfernstieg. The atmosphere is pleasant and relaxed. Modern pictures adorn the restaurant.

Petit Délice

Große Bleichen 21 ✉ 20354 – Ⓜ Jungfernstieg – ✆ (040) 34 34 70
– Closed Sunday and Bank Holidays **F2**
Rest – *(booking advisable)* Menu 39 € – Carte 32/73 €
Rest *Traiteur* – *✆ (040) 33 44 19 80* – Carte 17/44 €
♦ French ♦ Friendly ♦
This small, bright restaurant is located in a passage in a shopping centre. It specialises in fresh, French dishes. Traiteur offers a bistro ambiance and good traditional and international food as well coffee and cakes

Cox

Lange Reihe 68 ✉ 20099 – Ⓜ Hauptbf. Nord – ✆ (040) 24 94 22 – www.restaurant-cox.de
– Closed Saturday lunch, Sunday lunch and Bank Holidays lunch
Rest – Carte 27/45 € **H1**
♦ International ♦ Bistro ♦
A very pleasant team serves the guests delicious and carefully prepared international dishes in a cosy bistro ambience. Smaller lunch menu.

Matsumi

Colonnaden 96 (1st floor) ✉ 20354 – Ⓜ Stephansplatz – ✆ (040) 34 31 25 – www.matsumi.de
– Closed Christmas - early January, Sunday - Monday and Bank Holidays lunch **F2**
Rest – Menu 59 € – Carte 17/59 €
♦ Japanese ♦ Minimalist ♦
You will find this classic Japanese restaurant in the pedestrian zone. The authentic fare is served at the table, at the sushi bar or in the tatami rooms (for groups).

InterContinental

Fontenay 10 ✉ 20354 – ✆ (040) 4 14 20
– www.hamburg.intercontinental.com **C2**
281 rm – †145/290 € ††145/390 €, ☕ 26 € – 21 suites
Rest *Windows* – see below
Rest *Signatures* – *✆ (040) 41 42 25 20* – Carte 32/46 €
♦ Chain hotel ♦ Luxury ♦ Functional ♦
This hotel is located on the Alster. It will charm guests with its extravagant appearance and the technically perfect design of the rooms. The Signatures conservatory restaurant has an international menu and is bright and pleasant.

Lindner Park-Hotel Hagenbeck

Hagenbecksstr. 150 ✉ 22527
– Ⓜ Hagenbecks Tierpark – ✆ (040) 8 00 80 81 00
– www.lindner.de/hotel-hagenbeck **B1**
158 rm – †109/359 € ††129/379 €, ☕ 17 € – 3 suites
Rest – Carte 34/46 €
♦ Business ♦ Holiday hotel ♦ Retro ♦
Tasteful colonial-style is the main theme of this establishment. With selected authentic details, the themed floors reflect the exoticness of African and Asia. The colonial atmosphere of the hotel continues in the restaurant. Pretty terrace.

Abtei

Abteistr. 14 ✉ 20149 – Ⓜ Klosterstern – ✆ (040) 44 29 05
– www.abtei-hotel.de – Closed over Christmas **C1**
11 rm ☕ – †145/200 € ††190/260 €
Rest *Prinz Frederik* – see below
Rest *Bistro* – *(closed Sunday - Monday)* Carte 39/43 €
♦ Villa ♦ Personalised ♦
This noble villa from 1897 is a real gem. Enjoy the calm, beautiful living area, the exquisite and individual furnishings, as well as the atmosphere of privacy. Bistro dishes are served in the restaurant 'Le jardin de la maison Pommery'.

Mittelweg without rest

Mittelweg 59 ✉ 20149 – Ⓜ Klosterstern – ✆ (040) 4 14 10 10
– www.hotel-mittelweg-hamburg.de **C1**
30 rm ☕ – †95/125 € ††135/158 €
♦ Villa ♦ Cosy ♦
This former businessman's villa of 1890 is an atmospheric hotel in a secluded little garden. The historic ambience is retained in its tasteful, classic rooms, the beautiful staircase, and the cosy breakfast room with its high stucco ceiling.

Nippon

Hofweg 75 ✉ 22085 – ✆ (040) 2 27 11 40 – www.nipponhotel.de
– Closed Christmas - 1 January **D1**
42 rm – †104/127 € ††122/158 €, ☕ 15 €
Rest – *(closed Monday) (dinner only)* Carte 22/37 €
♦ Townhouse ♦ Minimalist ♦
With a truly Far Eastern appearance, the rooms are furnished in a simple style with tatami floors, shoji walls and futons. The Wa-Yo restaurant with sushi bar offers classic Japanese cuisine and premium sake.

Windows – Hotel InterContinental

Fontenay 10 ✉ 20354 – ✆ (040) 4 14 20
– www.hamburg.intercontinental.com
– Closed 3 weeks January, end July - end August and Sunday - Monday
Rest – *(dinner only)* Carte 50/92 € **C2**
♦ Classic ♦ Elegant ♦
This restaurant high above the city offers an elegant atmosphere and fabulous views over Hamburg and the Alster. International cuisine.

XX ✿

Prinz Frederik – Hotel Abtei

Abteistr. 14 ✉ 20149 – Ⓜ Klosterstern – ✆ (040) 44 29 05
– www.abtei-hotel.de
– Closed over Christmas and Sunday - Monday **C1**

Rest – *(dinner only) (booking essential)* Menu 69/100 €

Spec. Gâteau von der Gänseleber mit Apfelkraut und Gewürz-Franzbrötchen. Taubenbrust mit Mon-Chéri-Jus und Rote Bete im Salzteig gegart. Schokoladenschnitte mit Kirschsorbet und gebackenem Schokoladencroustillant.

♦ Classic ♦ Elegant ♦

The extremely stylish ambience, the friendly service, and the classic cooking of Jochen Kempf assure that guests enjoy many a pleasant hour in this small restaurant. In the anteroom there is a cosy, elegant lounge with an open fireplace.

XX ✿

Piment (Wahabi Nouri)

Lehmweg 29 ✉ 20251 – Ⓜ Eppendorfer Baum – ✆ (040) 42 93 77 88
– www.restaurant-piment.de
– Closed Sunday **C1**

Rest – *(dinner only) (booking advisable)* Menu 75/95 € – Carte 73/81 €

Spec. Gebeiztes und Tatar vom Loup de Mer mit Charmoula. Geschmorte Ochsenschulter mit Schalloten und Kalbsmaske gratiniert. Zweierlei von der Schokolade mit geschmorter Ananas und Ingwer-Vanille-Aufguss.

♦ Inventive ♦ Friendly ♦

Enjoy the flavour-rich, classic French food, which with its spices reflects the Moroccan origins of the patron. Warm red and cream colours create a cosy atmosphere in the restaurant.

X ✿

Küchenwerkstatt (Gerald Zogbaum)

Hans-Henny-Jahnn-Weg 1 (entrance Hofweg) ✉ 22085 – ✆ (040) 22 92 75 88 – www.kuechenwerkstatt-hamburg.de
– Closed 1 - 14 January and Sunday - Monday **D1**

Rest – Menu 26 € (lunch)/126 € (dinner) – Carte 67/76 €

Spec. Sorbet von grünen Tomaten mit aromatischen kleinen Frühlingsgemüsen, Spargelgewürz, Gemüsekrokant, Wachtelei und Blütenblätter. Langostino gebraten, roh und als Essenz. Dessertvariation von Rhabarber und Himbeere.

♦ Inventive ♦ Trendy ♦

A former ferry house dating from 1880 offers modern-style in a historic setting. The contemporary, creative cuisine of Gerald Zogbaum can also be ordered at midday from the evening menu – in addition to good lunch dishes. Competent service and wine recommendations.

X

Ono by Steffen Henssler

Lehmweg 17 ✉ 20251 – Ⓜ Hoheluftbr. – ✆ (040) 88 17 18 42
– www.onobysh.de
– Closed Christmas - 5 January and Sunday **C1**

Rest – Carte 23/43 €

♦ Asian ♦ Minimalist ♦

Tasty Asian and sushi dishes from the show kitchen are served at small tables in this bright, modern and lively bistro.

X

Speisewirtschaft Wattkorn with rm 

Tangstedter Landstr. 230 (by Hamburger Str. **D1***) ✉ 22417 – ✆ (040) 5 20 37 97 – www.wattkorn.de*

13 rm – †45/80 € ††80/120 €

Rest – *(booking advisable)* Menu 20 € (lunch)/26 € – Carte 18/58 €

♦ Regional ♦ Rustic ♦

Host Michael Wollenberg serves very tasty regional and seasonal dishes with game specialities, but sushi is also on the menu. There is a cosy, rustic ambience and friendly service. Very pleasant terrace and garden area. Country house style guestrooms.

Butcher's American Steakhouse

Milchstr. 19 ✉ 20148 – ✆ (040) 44 60 82 – www.butchers-steakhouse.de – Closed Saturday lunch, Sunday and Bank Holidays **C2**

Rest – Carte 52/87 €

♦ International ♦ Trendy ♦

Here you can taste fine Nebraska beef that the chef presents to the table. A cosy restaurant with a decor dominated by dark wood and warm colours.

HARBOUR – ALTONA *Plan III*

Empire Riverside Hotel

Bernhardt-Nocht-Str. 97 (by Davidstraße) ✉ 20359 – Ⓜ Reeperbahn – ✆ (040) 31 11 90 – www.empire-riverside.de **J1**

327 rm – †130/349 € ††130/349 €, ☕ 18 €

Rest *Waterkant* – *✆ (040) 31 11 97 04 80 (dinner only)* Carte 35/67 €

♦ Business ♦ Conference hotel ♦ Design ♦

Famous architect David Chipperfield designed this contemporary hotel close to the St Pauli pontoon bridges. Rooms have a view of either the river or the city as does "20 up", the panoramic bar on the 20th floor. This wharf-side restaurant offers international cuisine in a simple, contemporary setting.

East

Simon-von-Utrecht-Str. 31 ✉ 20359 – Ⓜ St. Pauli – ✆ (040) 30 99 30 – www.east-hamburg.de *Plan I* **B2**

127 rm – †155/195 € ††175/220 €, ☕ 19 € – 3 suites

Rest – *(closed Saturday lunch and Sunday lunch)* Carte 26/63 €

♦ Business ♦ Design ♦

This trendy hotel built in an old foundry offers the very latest in design across the board, from its rooms to its bar/lounge, and its leisure and beauty centre with a professionally staffed fitness club. Unusual restaurant serving Euro-Asian cuisine in a converted factory.

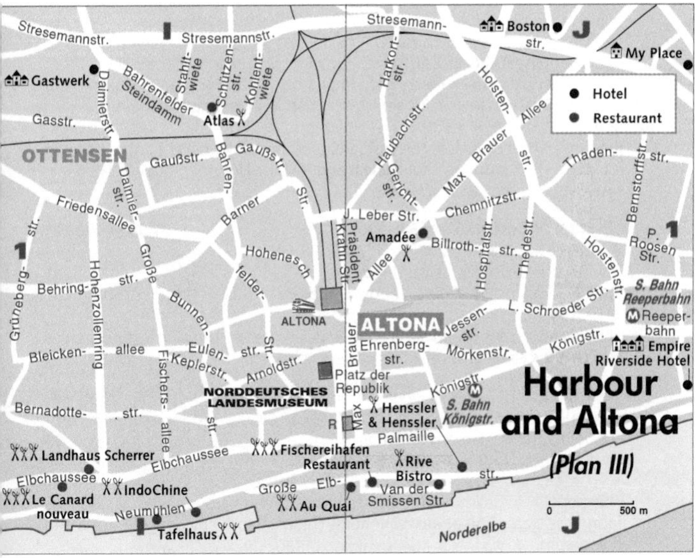

Harbour and Altona
(Plan III)

● Hotel
● Restaurant

Boston

Missundestr. 2 ✉ 22769 – Ⓜ Feldstr. – ☎ (040) 5 89 66 67 00 – www.boston-hamburg.de J1

46 rm – 🚹140/260 € 🚹🚹160/280 €, ☕ 16 €

Rest – *(closed Sunday) (dinner only)* Carte 30/47 €

♦ Business ♦ Design ♦ Modern ♦

A modern business hotel with tasteful and straightforward fittings. Rooms are available in the categories Design and Business – the latter with a kitchenette. This trendy restaurant has an adjoining lounge and bar.

My Place without rest

Lippmannstr. 5 ✉ 22769 – Ⓜ Feldstr. – ☎ (040) 28 57 18 74 – www.myplace-hamburg.de J1

18 rm – 🚹60/70 € 🚹🚹80/90 €, ☕ 4 € – 4 suites

♦ Townhouse ♦ Design ♦ Cosy ♦

Close to the trendy Schanze district the dedicated hostess runs a small hotel with individually styled, charming modern rooms named after districts of Hamburg.

Landhaus Scherrer (Heinz O. Wehmann)

Elbchaussee 130 ✉ 22763 – ☎ (040) 8 80 10 11 – www.landhausscherrer.de – Closed Sunday I1

Rest – Menu 89/119 € – Carte 56/98 €

Rest *Wehmann's Bistro* – Menu 33 € – Carte 33/49 €

Spec. Fischsuppe à la Bouillabaisse mit Crostini und Sauce Rouille. Steinbuttrücken am Stück gekocht mit Wasabi-Meerrettich, Meerretichwurzel und zerlassener Butter. Krosse Ente auf Spitzkohl, Selleriepüree und Kubeben-Pfeffersauce.

♦ Classic ♦ Elegant ♦

Emmi Scherrer and Heinz O. Wehmann focus on the product related classic cuisine, which has distinguished this elegant restaurant for many years. Among the around 12 000 bottles in the well-established wine cellar are a number of top vintages. This beautifully panelled bistro offers a less formal alternative.

Le Canard nouveau (Ali Güngörmüs)

Elbchaussee 139 ✉ 22763 – ☎ (040) 88 12 95 31 – www.lecanard-hamburg.de – Closed 1 week early January, 1 week mid March, 1 week early - mid Oktober and Sunday - Monday I1

Rest – Menu 39 € (lunch)/95 € – Carte 60/75 €

Spec. Morcheln mit Erbsen und Spargel in Sherry à la crème. Lauwarmer Lachs mit Zitronen-Pfefferkruste, Rhabarber und Macadamianüssen. Ali's Schokoladenkuchen mit Johannisbroteis und eingelegten Mispeln.

♦ International ♦ Fashionable ♦

In terms of its architecture this restaurant resembles the bow of a ship heading into port. The rooms are bright, linear and elegant. Unfussy product related cuisine. Simpler menu at lunchtime.

Fischereihafen Restaurant

Große Elbstr. 143 ✉ 22767 – ☎ (040) 38 18 16 – www.fischereihafenrestaurant.de J1

Rest – *(booking advisable)* Menu 30 € (lunch)/60 € – Carte 34/58 €

♦ Fish ♦ Classic ♦

This fish restaurant overlooking the port is a veritable Hamburg institution. The service is excellent as is the great value lunchtime menu.

Au Quai

Grosse Elbstr. 145 b ✉ 22767 – ☎ (040) 38 03 77 30 – www.au-quai.com – Closed Saturday lunch and Sunday J1

Rest – Menu 35 € (lunch)/59 € – Carte 32/77 €

♦ Fusion ♦ Trendy ♦

This popular establishment is situated close to the harbour and has a terrace facing the water. The modern interior is complemented by designer items and holographs.

XX

IndoChine

Neumühlen 11 ✉ 22763 – ✆ (040) 39 80 78 80 – www.indochine.de
– Closed Saturday lunch **I1**

Rest – Menu 40 € – Carte 34/67 €

♦ Asian ♦ Trendy ♦

This elegant modern restaurant with views over the Elbe serves wonderfully authentic Cambodian-, Laotian- and Vietnamese-inspired cuisine. The IceBar (pay on entry) is worth seeing and feeling!

XX ✿

Tafelhaus (Christian Rach)

Neumühlen 17 ✉ 22763 – ✆ (040) 89 27 60 – www.tafelhaus.de
– Closed Saturday lunch and Sunday - Monday, Restaurant closes down October 2011 **I1**

Rest – *(booking advisable)* Menu 46 € (lunch)/85 €

Spec. Hummer mit grünen Pistazien, Tomatenmarmelade und Ingwer-Chiboust. Zweierlei vom Milchkalb mit Schwarzen Oliven, Sellerie und Kartoffel-Kefirschaum. Weißer Pfirsich als Mousse und Sorbet mit Rosmarin und Nougat.

♦ Inventive ♦ Minimalist ♦ Fashionable ♦

Clean lines determine the interior. The cuisine style is creative and contemporary. From the restaurant and terrace guests can watch the busy shipping traffic on the Elbe.

X

Henssler Henssler

Große Elbstr. 160 ✉ 22767 – Ⓜ Königstr. – ✆ (040) 38 69 90 00
– www.hensslerhenssler.de
– Closed Sunday **J1**

Rest – *(booking advisable)* Menu 19 € (lunch)/50 € – Carte 29/46 €

♦ Japanese ♦ Minimalist ♦

This minimalist restaurant is in a former fish auction hall. Fresh fish products from neighbouring suppliers are used for the Californian influenced Japanese dishes. Guests have an interesting insight into the open kitchen from the sushi bar.

X

Rive Bistro

Van-der-Smissen-Str. 1 (at Kreuzfahrt-Center) ✉ 22767 – Ⓜ Königstr.
– ✆ (040) 3 80 59 19 – www.rive.de **J1**

Rest – *(booking advisable)* Menu 50 € – Carte 30/49 €

♦ Fish ♦ Trendy ♦ Bistro ♦

This bistro with its superb view of the Elbe is right by the harbour, close to the fish market. Tasty international food is served, including oysters from the bar, as well as sushi and sashimi.

X

Nil

Neuer Pferdemarkt 5 ✉ 20359 – Ⓜ Feldstr. – ✆ (040) 4 39 78 23
– www.restaurant-nil.de
– Closed Tuesday except December *Plan I* **B2**

Rest – *(dinner only)* Menu 37 € – Carte 32/42 €

♦ International ♦ Neighbourhood ♦

It is a little cramped but cosy on the three floors of this establishment. It serves tasty, international food – on the pleasant garden terrace at the back too.

X

Amadée

Max-Brauer-Allee 80 ✉ 22765 – Ⓜ S. Bahn Königstr. – ✆ (040) 98 23 93 30 – www.restaurant-amadee.de
– Closed Monday **J1**

Rest – *(dinner only)* Menu 33 € – Carte 27/34 €

♦ Austrian ♦ Classic ♦ Individual ♦

Tasty Austrian food is served in the former set designer's workshop of the Allee Theatre. Find decorative Venetian ceiling paintings and elaborate frescos in the Engelzimmer.

Louis C. Jacob

Elbchaussee 401 (by Elbchaussee **A3**) ✉ *22609 – ✆ (040) 82 25 50 – www.hotel-jacob.de*

85 rm – 198/258 € 258/485 €, ☕ 28 € – 10 suites

Rest ***Jacobs Restaurant and Rest Weinwirtschaft Kleines Jacob*** – see below

♦ Luxury ♦ Traditional ♦ Classic ♦

The successful management and services in this elegant hotel on the Elbe are exemplary. Equally pleasant is the classical furnishing of the rooms, some of which are as spacious as junior suites.

Gastwerk

Beim Alten Gaswerk 3 (corner of Daimlerstraße) ✉ *22761 – ✆ (040) 89 06 20 – www.gastwerk-hotel.de* **I1**

141 rm – 130/200 € 130/200 €, ☕ 18 € – 3 suites

Rest – *(closed Saturday lunch and Sunday lunch)* Carte 35/56 €

♦ Business ♦ Design ♦

A successful combination of imposing industrial architecture and modern design. Pleasant rooms, lofts and suites – two of the suites have room terraces. A modern restaurant serving Italian cuisine.

Landhaus Flottbek

Baron-Voght-Str. 179 (by Stresemannstraße **A2**) ✉ *22607 – ✆ (040) 8 22 74 10 – www.landhaus-flottbek.de*

25 rm – 90/120 € 120/150 €, ☕ 16 €

Rest – *(closed Saturday lunch and Sunday lunch)* Carte 24/57 €

♦ Family ♦ Cosy ♦

A group of 18C farmhouses set in a lovely garden with tasteful, individually furnished rooms. Two of the rooms have a terrace or winter garden. This comfortable restaurant serves seasonal cuisine and has a lovely terrace facing the garden.

Jacobs Restaurant – Hotel Louis C. Jacob

Elbchaussee 401 (by Elbchaussee **A3**) ✉ *22609 – ✆ (040) 82 25 50 – www.hotel-jacob.de*

– Closed Monday - Tuesday

Rest – *(booking advisable)* Menu 62 € (lunch)/129 € – Carte 86/106 €

Spec. Hummersalat mit Argan-Krustentieröl, Radieschen und Staudensellerie. Steinbutt mit Curry gebraten und Macadamia-Pok-Choi. Geschmorte Ochsenschulter mit Rotweinreduktion und Kartoffelschaum.

♦ Classic ♦ Elegant ♦

This stylish, bright restaurant exudes Hanseatic elegance. Under the direction of Thomas Martin, the kitchen team prepares classic based contemporary cuisine. In summer a highlight is the Linden Terrace with its views of the Elbe.

Süllberg - Seven Seas (Karlheinz Hauser) with rm

Süllbergsterrasse 12 (by Elbchaussee **A3**) ✉ *22587 – ✆ (040) 8 66 25 20 – www.suellberg-hamburg.de*

– Closed 3 January - 2 February and Monday - Tuesday

10 rm – 170/190 € 190/230 €, ☕ 17 € – 1 suite

Rest – *(Wednesday - Saturday dinner only)* Menu 89/128 € – Carte 72/98 €

Rest ***Bistro*** – *✆ (040) 86 62 52 77* – Menu 36/42 € – Carte 30/62 €

Spec. Thunfisch, Lachs und Königskrabbe mit Avocado, Emulsion von Zitrusfrüchten und Wasabi-Sorbet. Geangelter Loup de Mer mit Lardo, Tomatenconfit, Parmesansauce und gebackenen Ginos. Rehrücken im Kräuter-Bergpfeffermantel mit Essigkirschen, zweierlei Wacholdersaucen und Sellerietaschen.

♦ Mediterranean ♦ Luxury ♦

In a splendid location overlooking Blankenese and the Elbe stands this historic building that forms the appropriate setting for this luxurious restaurant. Classic cuisine based on exquisite products. The service is competent and friendly. Tasteful rooms and beauty treatments await guests in this hotel.

XX

Witthüs

Elbchaussee 499a (by Elbchaussee **A3***) ✉ 22587 – ✆ (040) 86 01 73*
– www.witthues.com
– Closed Monday
Rest – *(dinner only)* Menu 30/33 € – Carte 32/44 €
♦ International ♦ Classic ♦
This historic farmhouse is idyllically located near the Elbe. Enjoy international cuisine and professional service in a classic, elegant setting with Nordic flair. Outdoor terrace.

X

Weinwirtschaft Kleines Jacob – Hotel Louis C. Jacob

Elbchaussee 404 (by Elbchaussee **A3***) ✉ 22609*
– ✆ (040) 82 25 55 10 – www.hotel-jacob.de
Rest – *(Monday - Saturday dinner only)* Menu 32 € – Carte 32/48 €
♦ Mediterranean ♦ Wine bar ♦ Cosy ♦
Make yourself comfortable at this little establishment opposite the hotel. A wine themed decor and open kitchen, accompanied by tasty Mediterranean food and good wine, defines the atmosphere here.

X

Atlas

Schützenstr. 9a (entrance Phoenixhof) ✉ 22761 – ✆ (040) 8 51 78 10
– www.atlas.at
– Closed Saturday lunch and Sunday dinner **I1**
Rest – Menu 25 € (lunch)/28 € (dinner) – Carte 26/40 €
♦ International ♦ Bistro ♦
This former fish smokery is now a restaurant in the modern bistro style. Shorter menu available at lunchtimes. Pleasant ivy-covered terrace.

AT THE AIRPORT

Radisson BLU Airport

Flughafenstr. 1 ✉ 22355 – ✆ (040) 3 00 30 00
– www.radissonblu.com/hotel-hamburgairport
266 rm – †128/178 € ††128/178 €, ☕ 20 € – 1 suite
Rest – Carte 28/37 €
♦ Business ♦ Modern ♦
Modern circular hotel complex with access to terminals 1 and 2. Purist design throughout, rooms in "Ocean" and "Urban" style, including large business rooms. This bright, stylish restaurant has an integrated bar.

MUNICH
MÜNCHEN

Population: 1 311 000 (conurbation 1 656 000) – Altitude: 520m

chtblick/Fotolia.com

Situated in a stunning position not far north of the Alps, Munich is a cultural titan, rather unfairly overshadowed in publicity terms by its world-famous Oktoberfest bier extravaganza. Famously described as the 'village with a million inhabitants', its mix of German organisation and Italian lifestyle makes for a magical merge, with an enviable amount of Italian restaurants to seek out and enjoy.

This capital of Southern Germany boasts over forty theatres and dozens of museums, temples of culture that blend charmingly with the Bavarian love of folklore and lederhosen – the cliché actually does ring true, and locals will proudly don their traditional garb at the drop of a green hat (with jauntily set feather). Perhaps in no other world location – certainly not in Western Europe – is there such an enjoyable abundance of folk festivals and groups dedicated to playing the local music. And there's an abundance of places to see them, too: Munich is awash with Bierhallen, Bierkeller, and Biergarten. Surrounded by green fields and rolling hills (on good days, you can see across to the Alps) it's not difficult to see why Munich is currently seen as one of – if not the most – liveable city in the world.

LIVING THE CITY

The heart of Munich is the Old Town, and its epicentre the **Marienplatz** in the south and **Residenz** to the north: there are many fine historic buildings around here. Running to the east is the **River Isar**, with fine urban thoroughfares and green areas for walks. Head north for the area dissected by the **Ludwigstrasse** and **Leopoldstrasse** – **Schwabing** – which is full of students as it's the University district. To the east is the **English Garden**, a denizen of peace. West of here, the Museums district, dominated by the **Pinakothek**, is characterised by bookshops, antique stores and galleries.

PRACTICAL INFORMATION

ARRIVAL-DEPARTURE

A taxi from Airport Frank-Josef Strauss, which is 28km northeast of the city, will cost around €55. Alternatively, take the Munich S-Bahn Lines S1 or S8 to the centre, which will take 45 minutes.

TRANSPORT

On buses and trams, Munich's not the most straightforward city to travel around. It's divided into four ring-shaped price zones; zone 1 (the white zone) is the most important for visitors, as it covers the city centre. Prices rise in accordance with the amount of zones you intend to travel. If you plan to make several journeys, invest in a strip card, which costs ten euros. You can also buy a one- or three-day Tageskarte, which are good value for tourists. Available from tourist information offices, hotel receptions, travel agents and newsagents.

The underground network (U-Bahn) opened in 1971, and some stretches of the network are still not finished. It operates the same fare system as on Munich's buses and trams.

The München Welcome Card is valid for use on public transport in the city centre and for discounts of up to fifty per cent for more than thirty sights, museums, castles and palaces, city tours and bicycle hire. The card is available for one or three days.

EXPLORING MUNICH

There's really only one building you can identify as your marker for a tour of Munich, and that's the **Frauenkirche**, the largest Gothic church in Southern Germany. Its distinctive onion domes, standing high and mighty on twin towers, have been an impressive sight since the mid-fifteenth century. Around them sits snugly the old town, a tourist mecca with an intimacy and warmth enhanced by fine historic architecture and an absence of modern buildings zooming to the sky. Aesthetically, this looks great, but the reason for it is more prosaic: if the top rung of the city's fire engines can't reach, then it won't get built...

Marienplatz is the focal point for visitors. It's the central square, just a stone's throw from Frauenkirche, and Munich life emanates from this busy, bustling hub. In its immediate vicinity stand three other distinctive churches: **Peterskirche**, built in the twelfth century, is the oldest in Munich; **Michaelskirche** is famous for its magnificent barrel vaulting; and **Asamkirche** is a riot of colourful frescoes and gold leaf. Marienplatz's town hall – the **Rathaus** – took over fifty years to build at the end of the 19C, and is a testimony to Gothic splendour, with Glockenspiel marionettes performing a daily dance high up the façade. Just up the road (or, more precisely, medieval street) from here is the majestic Residenz, the grand palatial home of the Wittelsbach dynasty who ruled over Bavaria for seven hundred years, right up until the end of the First World War. It boasts the jaw-dropping **Antiquarium** – a great hall built in the 17C – and a Rococo theatre (the **Cuvillies**) just bursting with grand operatic pomp.

→ DRINK, ANYONE?

You might feel the need to balance all this civic glory with something a little more down-to-earth: a drink maybe. Well, just a hop, skip and jump away from Residenz, across the luxurious boulevard **Maximilianstrasse,** is what locals modestly call the most famous pub in the world. **Hofbräuhaus** was opened in 1828, and, perhaps unsurprisingly, it's the city's greatest tourist attraction. It can seat around 2,500 drinkers. There's a hall with long tables for a thousand on the ground floor, and a vaulted hall for thirteen hundred on the first. Side rooms make up the number. Every day, nearly eighteen thousand pints of beer are drunk, but Muncheners rather turn their noses up at it as a tourist honeypot. They have their more cherished and authentic bierhallen to keep them in liquid company.

If induced to claustrophobia at the thought of all that humanity reaching for a frothing litre of ale, then head to the **Viktualienmarkt**. It's another great landmark of the old town, and it celebrated its two hundredth birthday in 2007. Here you can get your beer and wine on the hoof, along with fruit and vegetables, meat and fish, cheese and flowers, sausages and salamis. This is Munich's oldest and most picturesque market, where you'll find fellow shoppers knocking back mugs of beer and tots of schnapps under canvas awnings.

→ PICTURE THIS

Head north and you hit the newer part of Munich, much of it built in the 19C. This part of town is famous for its stylish art galleries, and they don't come much more stylish than the Pinakothek, which boasts no less than three completely individual galleries each with its own distinctive allure. The oldest is the **Alte Pinakothek**, now considered one of the world's most important art galleries, with an outstanding collection of work from the 14C and 18C. Cross the road to the **Neue Pinakothek**, opened in 1853 and home to an impressive range of European art from the 19C. Most recent addition to this revered grouping is the **Pinakothek der Moderne**, opened only in 2002. As you might have guessed from the name, this is a temple to the world of modern art, architecture and design, housed in a spacious, three-floor structure of glass and concrete just demanding to be noticed by the passing public. Museums abound in this district; jostling for your attention in one compact and classy area are grand buildings with collections that include ancient classical antiquities, dazzling mineral formations, Greek and Roman sculpture, fossilised palm trees (and a mastodon), and artworks by Kandinsky, Klee, Beuys and Warhol. A respite from cultural overload can be taken at the **Old Botanical Gardens**, a short walk south from the museums. It has a delightful café garden, shaded by exotic trees.

➜ IN AN ENGLISH CITY GARDEN

Mind you, when it comes to green spaces, there's nothing in the city to compare with the **English Garden**, so called because of its naturalistic landscaped style. It's one of Europe's largest city parks, and, looked at on a map, resembles a great green lung breathing life into the surrounding *strassen*. It's in a favourable position on the east side of Munich, close to the river Isar, and is a huge attraction in the summer months. You can, if you so wish, sunbathe naked here, or go for a swim in the winding streams that weave their way amongst the trees and shrubs. Many head for the 18C **Chinese Tower**, not for the view it offers (though that's good) but because it proffers a famous biergarten in its shadow. This is the university quarter: there are sixty thousand students, and the streets in the vicinity are full of life and noise. A grand boulevard runs right through, south to north. Ludwigstrasse, at the southern end, is elegantly neo-Classical in style, but as you walk northwards along Leopoldstrasse, the ambience becomes much less formal. The students come into their own, and there are pubs and swish boutiques lining the way. This is the famous Schwabing area, renowned since the late nineteenth century as a bohemian hang out, populated in its pre-World War I heyday by the likes of Thomas Mann, Kandinsky and Klee.

➜ BEER IN BAVARIA

One of the main attractions of Munich lies in wait in a most fortuitous spot between the English Garden and the Isar. It's the **Bavarian National Museum** and it covers all aspects of life in this part of Germany from classical antiquity until the nineteenth century. It's laid out over three fascinating floors, and leaves barely a stone unturned if that stone may reveal an interesting nugget of Bavarian life. What it doesn't feature, ironically, is the one subject great hordes come exclusively to Munich for…the Oktoberfest. The largest beer orgy in the world takes up two weeks of September (and a little bit of October) and welcomes six million (yes, six million) visitors, who quaff around six million litres of golden stuff in fourteen giant tents. Sausages, ox meat and roast chickens are devoured in frightening proportions, and the songs hammered out with much gusto are invariably of the Bavarian kind. The Oktoberfest began life in 1810 to celebrate royal nuptials, so in two years' time it'll be putting on its two hundredth anniversary party. Imagine what *that's* going to be like…

CALENDAR HIGHLIGHTS

Festivals, many of them free, come thick and fast in Munich. The beer festivals (unfortunately, not free) kick off in March with Starkbierfest (The Festival

MUNICH IN…

➜ ONE DAY

The old town, Frauenkirche, English Garden, Wagner (if possible!) at the National Theatre

➜ TWO DAYS

Schwabing, Pinakothek, Hofbräuhaus

➜ THREE DAYS

Olympic Park, Schloss Nymphenburg, last night 'hurrah' at a traditional Bavarian inn

of Strong Beer), carry on with the Maibockausschank at the Hofbräuhaus in May, and end with a quiet little affair in September and October...A few measures will probably be raised at the Biennale in April; this is Germany's largest contemporary music festival, heralding a host of musical events in the city. The Tollwood Festival in July, in the Olympic Park, features jazz and rock, while in June the Münchner Opernfestspiele is for opera and ballet lovers. Jazz Summer, also in July, lights up the swish Hotel Bayerischer Hof; meanwhile, rock and jazz fans are catered for in August's Theatron Music Summer in the Olympic Park's open-air theatre. The dramatic sounding Long Night of Museums is a dream for culture vultures, with over seventy museums and galleries staying open till 2am (October). Runners can get their hit also in October with the Munich Media Marathon, not a long-distance run for journos, but a twenty-six miler for one and all – over ten thousand 'ordinary' runners took part in 2009.

EATING OUT

Munich is a city in which you can eat well (especially if you're not vegetarian), and in large quantities. The local specialities are meat and potatoes, with large dollops of cabbage on the side ; you won't have trouble finding roast pork and dumplings or meatloaf and don't forget the local white veal sausage or weisswurst. The meat is invariably succulent, and cabbage is often adorned with the likes of juniper berries. Potatoes, meanwhile, have a tendency to evolve into soft and buttery dumplings. And sausage? Take your pick from over 1,500 recognised species. Other specialities include Schweinshaxe (knuckle of pork) or Leberkäs (meat and offal pâté). Eating out in Munich, or anywhere in Bavaria, is an experience in itself, with the distinctive background din of laughter, singing and the clinking of mugs of Bavarian Weissbier. It's famous for the Brauereigaststätten or brewery inns. When you've found your inn, be prepared for much noise, and don't be afraid to 'muck in' on a long bench, i.e. fall into conversation of a kind with fellow diners and drinkers. If that's not your idea of a good night out, then the many Italian restaurants in the city provide an excellent alternative. Most restaurants stay open until midnight or 1am. Service is included in the bill, but it's customary to leave an extra 10 per cent tip.

→ BAROQUE

Head west from the city for the baroque palace to beat all baroque palaces. The Schloss Nymphenburg – the Nymphs' Castle - was once the home of Bavaria's monarchs, and it boasts wondrous landscaping with canals, a gallery of thirty-six beautiful women, and a museum that includes 'mad' King Ludwig's coronation coach.

→ RING FIRST

If you want a night at the opera, then head to the National Theatre, right next to the Residenz. Modelled on a Greek temple, it specialises in the work of Wagner; in fact, it's where the great man actually made his name. He would have loved the latest version of the auditorium: its décor is sky blue, ivory, purple and gold.

→ PARK LIFE

Munich's most arguably famous sight is actually a few miles to the northwest of the city itself. The Olympic Park, and its iconic Olympic Tower, were built for the 1972 Games. The hills around the park aren't natural...they were made from rubble taken away from the city at the end of World War II.

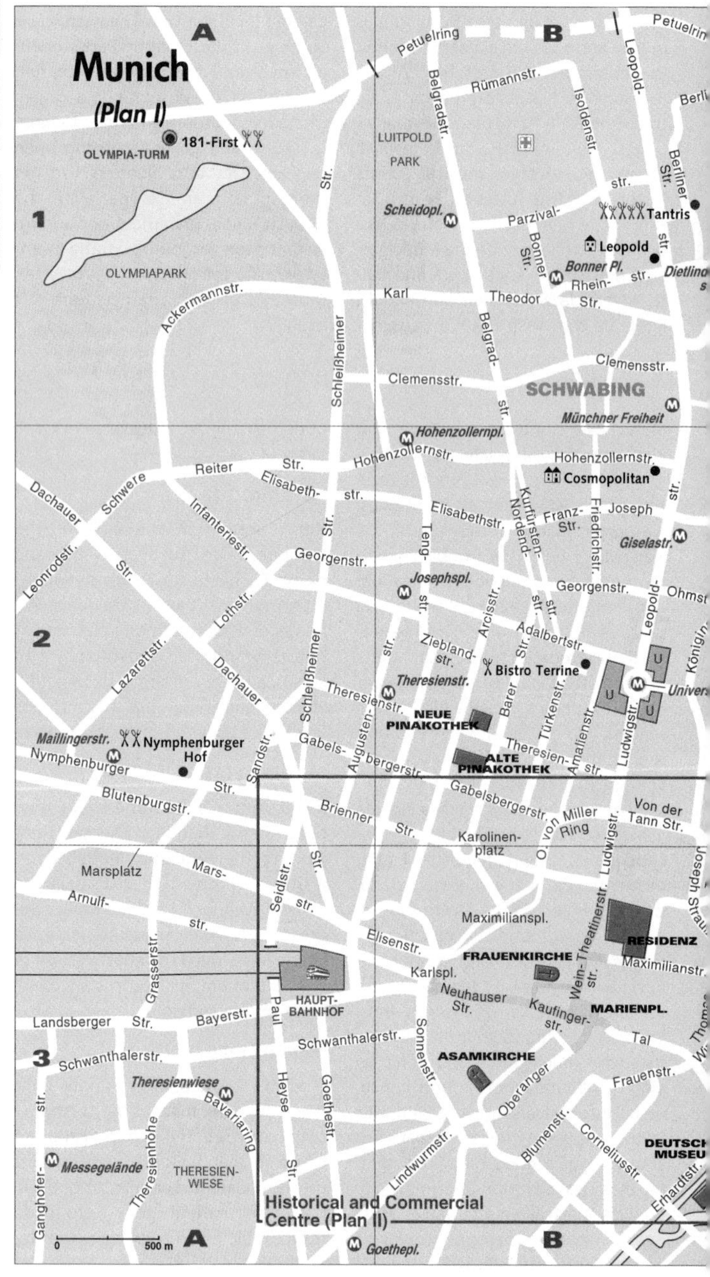
Munich
(Plan I)
181-First
OLYMPIA-TURM
OLYMPIAPARK
LUITPOLD PARK
Scheidopl.
Tantris
Leopold
Bonner Pl.
SCHWABING
Münchner Freiheit
Hohenzollernpl.
Cosmopolitan
Giselastr.
Josephspl.
Bistro Terrine
Theresienstr.
NEUE PINAKOTHEK
ALTE PINAKOTHEK
Universität
Maillingerstr.
Nymphenburger Hof
Karolinenplatz
Maximiliansplatz
RESIDENZ
FRAUENKIRCHE
MARIENPL.
Karlspl.
HAUPT-BAHNHOF
ASAMKIRCHE
Theresienwiese
THERESIEN-WIESE
Messegelände
DEUTSCHES MUSEUM
Goethepl.
Historical and Commercial Centre (Plan II)
0
500 m

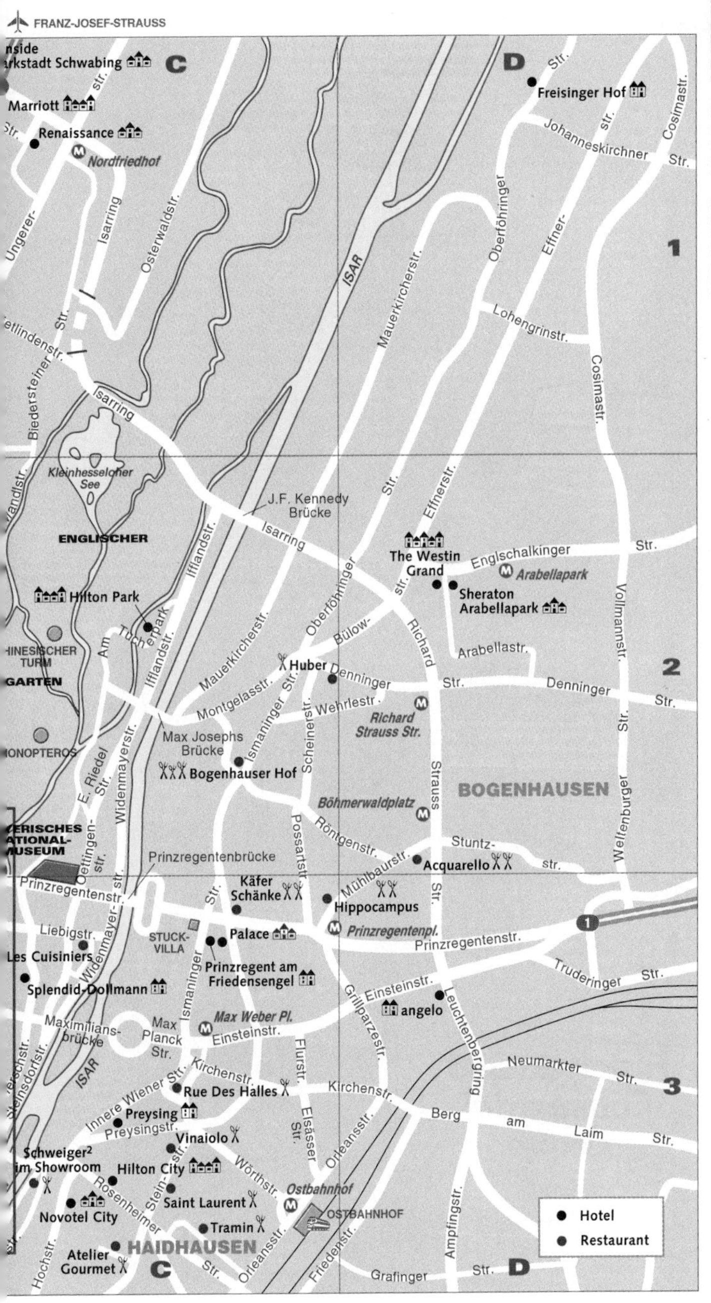
FRANZ-JOSEF-STRAUSS
Freisinger Hof
Marriott
Renaissance
Nordfriedhof
Isarring
Osterwaldstr.
ISAR
Mauerkircherstr.
Oberföhringer
Effner-
Johanneskirchner Str.
Cosimastr.
Lohengrinstr.
Biedersteiner Str.
Kleinhesseloher See
ENGLISCHER
J.F. Kennedy Brücke
Ifflandstr.
The Westin Grand
Englschalkinger Str.
Arabellapark
Sheraton Arabellapark
Arabellastr.
Vollmannstr.
Hilton Park
Tucherpark
Bülow-
Richard Strauss Str.
Huber
Denninger Str.
Montgelasstr.
Ismaninger Str.
Wehrlestr.
Richard Strauss Str.
Max Josephs Brücke
Bogenhauser Hof
Scheinerstr.
BOGENHAUSEN
Böhmerwaldplatz
Weltenburger Str.
E. Riedel Str.
Widenmayerstr.
Oettingen-str.
Prinzregentenbrücke
Röntgenstr.
Stuntz-str.
Possartstr.
Acquarello
Mühlbaurstr.
Käfer Schänke
Hippocampus
Prinzregentenstr.
Prinzregentenpl.
Liebigstr.
Stuck-Villa
Palace
Les Cuisiniers
Prinzregent am Friedensengel
Splendid-Dollmann
Truderinger Str.
Einsteinstr.
angelo
Grillparzerstr.
Maximiliansbrücke
Max Planck Str.
Max Weber Pl.
Leuchtenbergring
Neumarkter Str.
Kirchenstr.
Rue Des Halles
Flurstr.
Innere Wiener Str.
Preysing
Preysingstr.
Elsässer Str.
Berg am Laim Str.
Vinaiolo
Schweiger[2] im Showroom
Hilton City
Wörthstr.
Orleansstr.
Ostbahnhof
OSTBAHNHOF
Rosenheimer Str.
Steinstr.
Saint Laurent
Novotel City
Tramin
Ampfingstr.
Friedenstr.
Atelier Gourmet
HAIDHAUSEN
Hochstr.
Grafinger Str.
Hotel
Restaurant
C
D
1
2
3

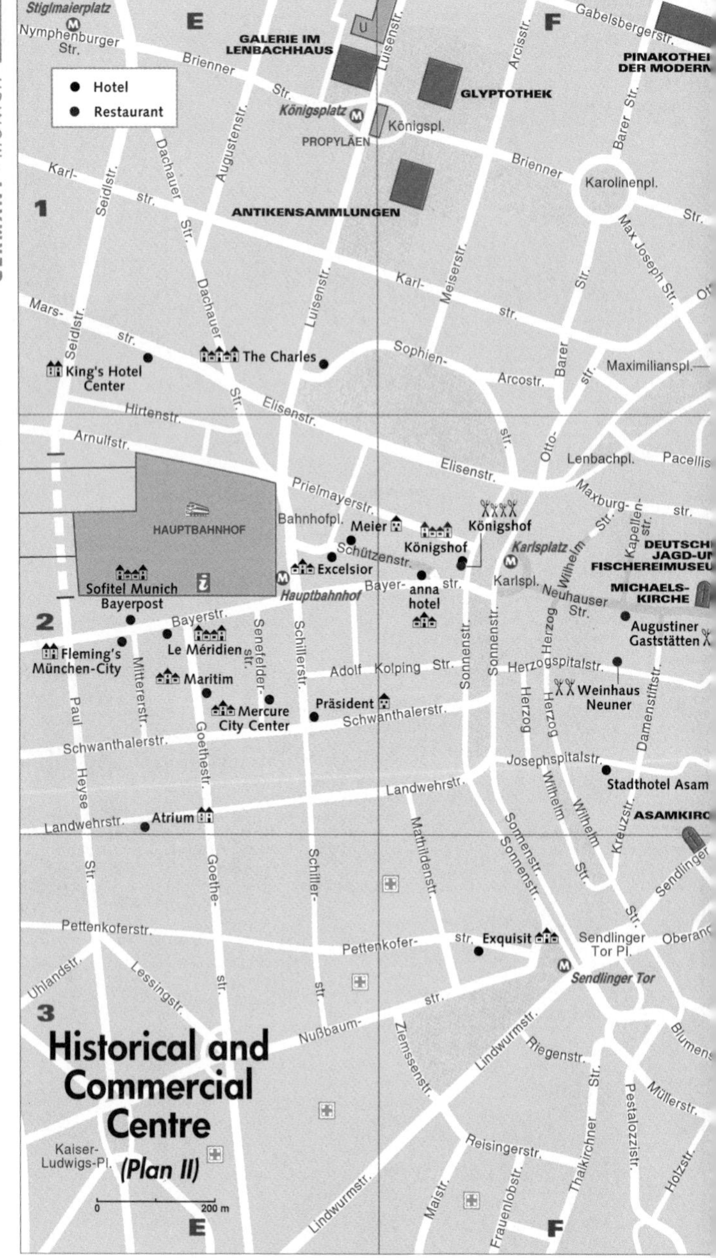
Historical and Commercial Centre (Plan II)
Hotel
Restaurant
E
F
1
2
3
Stiglmaierplatz
Nymphenburger Str.
Brienner Str.
GALERIE IM LENBACHHAUS
Luisenstr.
Arcisstr.
Gabelsbergerstr.
GLYPTOTHEK
Königsplatz
Königspl.
PROPYLÄEN
Augustenstr.
Dachauer Str.
Seidlstr.
Karl-str.
ANTIKENSAMMLUNGEN
Karolinenpl.
Barer Str.
Max Joseph Str.
Meiserstr.
Mars-str.
The Charles
King's Hotel Center
Sophien-str.
Arcostr.
Maximilianspl.
Hirtenstr.
Elisenstr.
Arnulfstr.
Lenbachpl.
Maxburg-str.
Prielmayerstr.
HAUPTBAHNHOF
Bahnhofpl.
Meier
Königshof
Karlsplatz
Karlspl.
Schützenstr.
Excelsior
Hauptbahnhof
Bayer-str.
anna hotel
Neuhauser Str.
Sofitel Munich Bayerpost
MICHAELS-KIRCHE
Augustiner Gaststätten
Bayerstr.
Le Méridien
Senefelder-str.
Schillerstr.
Sonnenstr.
Fleming's München-City
Mittererstr.
Maritim
Adolf Kolping Str.
Herzogspitalstr.
Weinhaus Neuner
Mercure City Center
Präsident
Schwanthalerstr.
Paul Heyse Str.
Goethestr.
Josephspitalstr.
Stadthotel Asam
Landwehrstr.
Atrium
Mathildenstr.
Herzog Wilhelm Str.
Damenstiftstr.
Kreuzstr.
Pettenkoferstr.
Exquisit
Sendlinger Tor Pl.
Sendlinger Tor
Uhlandstr.
Lessingstr.
Nußbaum-str.
Ziemssenstr.
Lindwurmstr.
Riegenstr.
Thalkirchner Str.
Pestalozzistr.
Müllerstr.
Reisingerstr.
Kaiser-Ludwigs-Pl.
Maistr.
Frauenlobstr.
Holzstr.
0
200 m

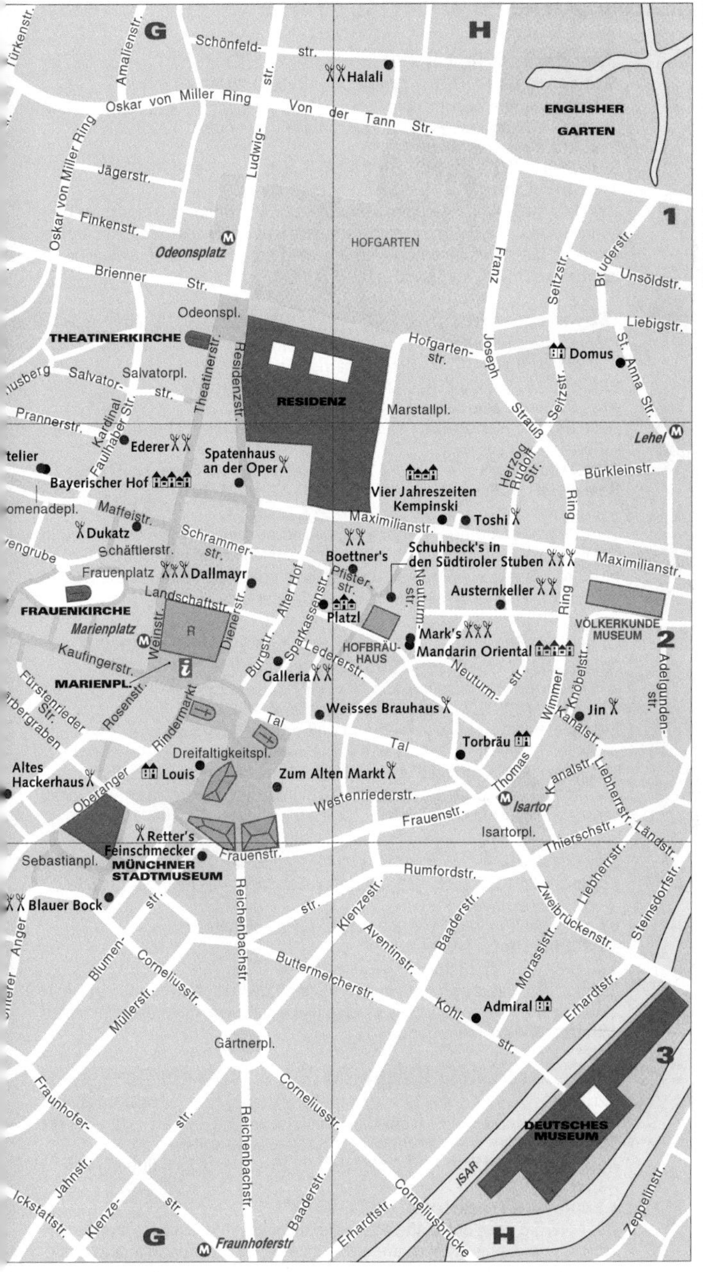

ENGLISHER GARTEN
HOFGARTEN
RESIDENZ
THEATINERKIRCHE
FRAUENKIRCHE
Marienplatz
MARIENPL.
HOFBRÄU-HAUS
VÖLKERKUNDE MUSEUM
MÜNCHNER STADTMUSEUM
DEUTSCHES MUSEUM
Odeonsplatz
Lehel
Isartor
Fraunhoferstr
Halali
Domus
Ederer
Spatenhaus an der Oper
Bayerischer Hof
Vier Jahreszeiten Kempinski
Toshi
Dukatz
Boettner's
Schuhbeck's in den Südtiroler Stuben
Dallmayr
Austernkeller
Platzl
Mark's
Mandarin Oriental
Galleria
Jin
Weisses Brauhaus
Torbräu
Altes Hackerhaus
Louis
Zum Alten Markt
Retter's Feinschmecker
Blauer Bock
Admiral
Schönfeld-str.
Oskar von Miller Ring
Von der Tann Str.
Ludwig-str.
Jägerstr.
Finkenstr.
Brienner Str.
Odeonspl.
Salvatorpl.
Salvator-str.
Prannerstr.
Kardinal Faulhaber Str.
Theatinerstr.
Residenzstr.
Hofgarten-str.
Marstallpl.
Franz Joseph Strauß Ring
Seitzstr.
Bruderstr.
Unsöldstr.
Liebigstr.
St. Anna Str.
Herzog Rudolf Str.
Bürkleinstr.
Maximilianstr.
Maffeistr.
Schrammer-str.
Schäftlerstr.
Frauenplatz
Landschaftstr.
Pfister-str.
Neuturm-str.
Alter Hof
Sparkassenstr.
Burgstr.
Ledererstr.
Dienerstr.
Weinstr.
Kaufingerstr.
Fürstenrieder Str.
Rosenstr.
Rindermarkt
Tal
Dreifaltigkeitspl.
Oberanger
Westenriederstr.
Frauenstr.
Isartorpl.
Thomas Wimmer Ring
Knöbelstr.
Kanalstr.
Liebherrstr.
Adelgunden-str.
Thierschstr.
Lândstr.
Sebastianpl.
Rumfordstr.
Reichenbachstr.
Klenzestr.
Aventinstr.
Baaderstr.
Zweibrückenstr.
Morassistr.
Steinsdorfstr.
Buttermelcherstr.
Kohl-str.
Erhardtstr.
Blumen-str.
Corneliusstr.
Müllerstr.
Gärtnerpl.
Fraunhofer-str.
Jahnstr.
Klenze-str.
Ickstattstr.
Corneliusbrücke
ISAR
Zeppelinstr.
Anger

Mandarin Oriental

Neuturmstr. 1 ✉ *80331 –* Ⓜ *Isartor –* ☎ *(089) 29 09 80 – www.mandarinoriental.com* **H2**

73 rm – †325/555 € ††325/555 €, ☕ 36 € – 8 suites

Rest *Mark's* – see below

Rest *Bistro MO* – ☎ *(089) 29 09 88 75 (lunch only)* Carte 45/73 €

◆ Grand Luxury ◆ Historic ◆ Classic ◆

This classy hotel which occupies a beautiful period townhouse is one of the best addresses in Germany. The exemplary service is perfectly complemented by the luxurious but tasteful interior. With a heated pool on the roof. At lunchtime international dishes are served in the Bistro MO.

Bayerischer Hof

Promenadeplatz 2 ✉ *80333 –* Ⓜ *Marienplatz – ☎ (089) 2 12 00 – www.bayerischerhof.de* **G2**

350 rm – †280/520 € ††420/520 €, ☕ 30 € – 17 suites

Rest *Atelier* – see below

Rest *Garden-Restaurant* – *(booking advisable)* Menu 33 € (lunch)/58 € – Carte 38/75 €

Rest *Trader Vic's* – ☎ *(089) 2 12 09 95 (dinner only)* Carte 32/77 €

Rest *Palais Keller* – ☎ *(089) 2 12 09 90* – Carte 21/40 €

◆ Grand Luxury ◆ Traditional ◆ Classic ◆

This five-star grand hotel, built in a magnificent palatial style, was opened in 1841. The rooms have been decorated in six different but exclusive styles. The blue spa has a view of Munich. International dishes are served at the Garden Restaurant. Polynesian cuisine is served at Trader Vic's.

The Charles

Sophienstr. 28 ✉ *80333 –* Ⓜ *Hauptbahnhof –* ☎ *(089) 5 44 55 50 – www.roccofortecollection.com* **E1**

132 rm – †495/550 € ††495/550 €, ☕ 29 € – 28 suites

Rest *Davvero* – ☎ *(089) 54 45 55 12 00* – Carte 50/65 €

◆ Grand Luxury ◆ Elegant ◆ Modern ◆

This luxury hotel is situated in the old botanic garden. Its fine decor has a simple, modern and elegant style. There is a high quality spa area, as well as every service you could possibly wish for. Italian food is served at Davvero.

Königshof

Karlsplatz 25 ✉ *80335 –* Ⓜ *Karlsplatz (Stachus) –* ☎ *(089) 55 13 60 – www.geisel-privathotels.de* **F2**

87 rm – †270/450 € ††310/490 €, ☕ 27 € – 8 suites

Rest *Königshof* – see below

◆ Luxury ◆ Traditional ◆ Elegant ◆

Built in 1900, this stylish restaurant is run with dedication by the Geisel family and their attentive team. Ideally situated in the Karlsplatz, it has been decorated with taste and sophistication.

Vier Jahreszeiten Kempinski

Maximilianstr. 17 ✉ *80539 –* Ⓜ *Lehel –* ☎ *(089) 2 12 50 – www.kempinski.com/munich* **H2**

303 rm – †220/379 € ††260/827 €, ☕ 35 € – 30 suites

Rest *Vue Maximilian* – ☎ *(089) 21 25 21 25* – Menu 23 € (lunch)/52 € – Carte 48/92 €

◆ Luxury ◆ Traditional ◆ Classic ◆

This hotel has been one of the classic grand hotels in Munich since it opened in 1858. Combines historical charm with contemporary comfort in a most attractive way. Diners in the Vue Maximilian restaurant have a view over the Maximilianstraße.

Sofitel Munich Bayerpost

Bayerstr. 12 ✉ 80335 – Ⓜ Hauptbahnhof
– ✆ (089) 59 94 80 – www.sofitel.com **E2**
396 rm – 🚹219/499 € 🚹🚹219/499 €, ☕ 28 € – 8 suites
Rest *Schwarz & Weiz* – *(closed Saturday - Sunday and Bank Holidays) (dinner only)* Carte 49/64 €
Rest *Sophie's Bistro* – Carte 39/55 €
♦ Chain hotel ♦ Luxury ♦ Design ♦
Modern architecture and contemporary design has been very successfully integrated into this listed building from the Gründerzeit. The restaurant offers a classic, international menu. The specialities at Sophie's Bistro are dishes from the grill.

Hilton Park

Am Tucherpark 7 ✉ 80538 – ✆ (089) 3 84 50
– www.hilton.de/muenchenpark *Plan I* **C2**
484 rm – 🚹109/429 € 🚹🚹109/429 €, ☕ 28 € – 3 suites
Rest *Tivoli & Club* – *✆ (089) 38 45 27 69* – Carte 31/49 €
♦ Chain hotel ♦ Luxury ♦ Modern ♦
Besides being located on the Englischer Garten, the benefits of this hotel include contemporary, well-equipped rooms, as well as business and executive rooms. This restaurant serves international cuisine and boasts a beer garden by the River Eisbach.

Le Méridien

Bayerstr. 41 ✉ 80335 – Ⓜ Hauptbahnhof – ✆ (089) 2 42 20
– www.lemeridienmunich.com **E2**
381 rm – 🚹139/445 € 🚹🚹139/445 €, ☕ 28 € – 8 suites **Rest** – Carte 32/60 €
♦ Chain hotel ♦ Luxury ♦ Design ♦
Opposite the main station, this hotel offers a contemporary, understated elegance. The fashionable rooms have good technical facilities. The restaurant looks onto the pleasant courtyard garden.

Excelsior

rest,

Schützenstr. 11 ✉ 80335 – Ⓜ Hauptbahnhof – ✆ (089) 55 13 70
– www.geisel-privathotels.de **E2**
112 rm – 🚹165/215 € 🚹🚹185/310 €, ☕ 19 € – 3 suites
Rest *Geisel's Vinothek* – *✆ (089) 55 13 71 40 (closed Sunday lunch)*
Menu 19 € (lunch)/38 € (dinner) – Carte 29/47 €
♦ Business ♦ Classic ♦
This hotel, with its individual and cosy rooms, is the sister enterprise of the Königshof. Here you will also find the leisure area. There is a good breakfast buffet in a stylish atmosphere. This pleasant, rustic-style winery shop offers a wide range of wines.

Maritim

Goethestr. 7 ✉ 80336 – Ⓜ Hauptbahnhof – ✆ (089) 55 23 50
– www.maritim.de **E2**
347 rm – 🚹120/231 € 🚹🚹167/278 €, ☕ 22 € – 6 suites
Rest – Carte 29/47 €
♦ Business ♦ Functional ♦
This hotel is close to the main station, the Stachus and the Theresienwiese. Find relatively quiet, classical-style rooms, and a pool on the seventh-floor with view over the Frauenkirche. The grill-room and bistro restaurants serve international cuisine.

Mercure City Center

rm,

Senefelder Str. 9 ✉ 80336 – Ⓜ Hauptbahnhof – ✆ (089) 55 13 20
– www.mercure.com **E2**
167 rm – 🚹89/269 € 🚹🚹89/269 €, ☕ 19 € **Rest** – Carte 28/45 €
♦ Chain hotel ♦ Modern ♦
The theatre theme runs throughout the whole hotel with red shades dominating. The rather spacious guestrooms are cosy and have a modern design. Opening off the lobby, the restaurant features international fare.

Platzl

Sparkassenstr. 10 ✉ 80331 – Ⓜ Marienplatz – ✆ (089) 23 70 30 – www.platzl.de **G2**

167 rm – 131/226 € 193/246 € – 1 suite

Rest *Pfistermühle* – *✆ (089) 23 70 38 65 (closed Sunday)* Menu 51 € – Carte 38/59 €

Rest *Ayingers* – *✆ (089) 23 70 36 66* – Carte 18/38 €

♦ Traditional ♦ Cosy ♦

This hotel in the centre of the old town has rooms that very successfully combine classic and modern styles. There is a recreation area in the style of Ludwig II's Moorish Kiosk. Find an old Munich atmosphere in the vaults of the Pfistermühle. Ayingers offers tavern tradition

Exquisit

Pettenkoferstr. 3 ✉ 80336 – Ⓜ Sendlinger Tor – ✆ (089) 5 51 99 00 – www.hotel-exquisit.com **F3**

50 rm – 152/245 € 189/305 € – 5 suites

Rest – *(Closed August, Saturday - Sunday and Bank Holidays) (lunch only)* Carte 20/30 €

♦ Business ♦ Classic ♦

This well-managed hotel not for from the Sendlinger Tor is characterised by a classical style and high quality facilities. Modern bistro with a small menu.

anna hotel

Schützenstr. 1 ✉ 80335 – Ⓜ Karlsplatz (Stachus) – ✆ (089) 59 99 40 – www.geisel-privathotels.de **F2**

73 rm – 200/255 € 220/275 € – 1 suite **Rest** – Carte 41/51 €

♦ Business ♦ Modern ♦

Modern design is what marks the atmosphere of this comfortable hotel, right on the Stachus. The rooms have state of the art technology, with panoramic views on the top floor. This bistro-style restaurant has an international menu and sushi bar.

Splendid-Dollmann without rest

Thierschstr. 49 ✉ 80538 – Ⓜ Lehel – ✆ (089) 23 80 80 – www.hotel-splendid-dollmann.de *Plan I* **C3**

36 rm – 130/170 € 160/200 €, 13 € – 2 suites

♦ Historic ♦ Personalised ♦

This 19C middle class house has a stylish lobby, presented as a library. Find individually decorated rooms, some with antiques, and a pretty breakfast room with an arched ceiling.

Stadthotel Asam without rest

Josephspitalstr. 3 ✉ 80331 – Ⓜ Sendlinger Tor – ✆ (089) 2 30 97 00 – www.hotel-asam.de – Closed Christmas - 3 January **F2**

25 rm – 124/161 € 149/211 €, 19 € – 8 suites

♦ Business ♦ Classic ♦

Bright, cosy rooms with high quality baths can be found in this hotel in the city centre - some face peacefully onto the interior court. There is a pleasant breakfast area with a small terrace.

Louis

Viktualienmarkt 6 ✉ 80331 – Ⓜ Marienplatz – ✆ (089) 41 11 90 80 – www.louis-hotel.com **G2**

72 rm – 195/395 € 195/395 €, 20 € – 1 suite

Rest *EMIKO* – *(dinner only)* Carte 38/76 €

♦ Townhouse ♦ Elegant ♦

The outstanding features here are the very central location on the Viktualienmarkt as well as the high-quality rooms in a timeless elegant style offering wonderful views. Asian menu in the restaurant.

Torbräu

Tal 41 ✉ 80331 – Ⓜ Isartor – ✆ (089) 24 23 40 – www.torbraeu.de
90 rm – 154/204 € 194/252 € – 3 suites **H2**
Rest *La Famiglia* – *✆ (089) 22 80 75 23* – Carte 35/48 €
♦ Traditional ♦ Classic ♦
Built in 1490, this hotel is the oldest in the city. It is a well-attended family business, which is being constantly modernised. There is a bright, pleasant breakfast room on the first-floor. The La Famiglia restaurant serves Italian cuisine in a Tuscan atmosphere.

Fleming's München-City

Bayerstr. 47 ✉ 80335 – Ⓜ Hauptbahnhof – ✆ (089) 4 44 46 60 – www.flemings-hotels.com **E2**
112 rm – 115/216 € 148/249 € **Rest** – Carte 24/42 €
♦ Business ♦ Modern ♦
Centrally located near the main railway station, this hotel offers functional, modern rooms. Bistro-style restaurant with bar and delicatessen.

Admiral without rest

Kohlstr. 9 ✉ 80469 – Ⓜ Isartor – ✆ (089) 21 63 50 – www.hotel-admiral.de **H3**
32 rm – 120/280 € 120/310 € – 1 suite
♦ Family ♦ Classic ♦
This family-run hotel comes across as classic, stylish and comfortable. Some rooms face peacefully onto the garden where, in summer, it is possible to enjoy the good breakfast on offer.

King's Hotel Center without rest

Marsstr. 15 ✉ 80335 – Ⓜ Hauptbahnhof – ✆ (089) 51 55 30 – www.kingshotels.de – Closed over Christmas **E1**
90 rm – 99/270 € 140/400 €, 12 €
♦ Business ♦ Cosy ♦
This hotel, close to the town centre, has comfortable rooms with four-poster beds. The single rooms are rather small. The wood-panelled breakfast room offers a good selection from the buffet.

Atrium without rest

Landwehrstr. 59 ✉ 80336 – Ⓜ Theresienwiese – ✆ (089) 51 41 90 – www.atrium-hotel.de **E2**
162 rm – 89/299 € 109/399 €
♦ Business ♦ Functional ♦
This hotel is located between the main station and Theresienwiese. It offers practical rooms, a modern breakfast room with a generous buffet, and a beautifully planted interior courtyard with a lounge.

Domus

St.-Anna-Str. 31 ✉ 80538 – Ⓜ Lehel – ✆ (089) 2 17 77 30 – www.domus-hotel.de **H1**
45 rm – 115/165 € 150/210 €
Rest *facile* – *✆ (089) 21 77 73 67 (closed Saturday lunch and Sunday)* Carte 27/41 €
♦ Business ♦ Functional ♦
This personally run hotel lies peacefully between Maximilianstrasse and Prinzregentenstrasse. The rooms are modern and practical, and most have balconies. The 'facile' restaurant has an easy atmosphere and Italian cuisine.

Präsident without rest

Schwanthalerstr. 20 ✉ 80336 – Ⓜ Hauptbahnhof – ✆ (089) 5 49 00 60 – www.hotel-praesident.de **E2**
42 rm – 69/209 € 79/249 €
♦ Business ♦ Functional ♦
This convenient hotel is diagonally opposite the Deutsche Theatre. It has practical, modern rooms and a breakfast buffet offering good food.

Meier without rest

Schützenstr. 12 ✉ 80335 – Ⓜ Hauptbahnhof – ☎ (089) 5 49 03 40 – www.hotel-meier.de **E2**

50 rm – †98/145 € ††130/180 €

♦ Business ♦ Functional ♦

This multi-floored hotel is on a shopping street between the main station and Stachus. It offers visitors uniform, functional rooms.

XXXX ✿

Königshof – Hotel Königshof

Karlsplatz 25 (1st floor) ✉ 80335 – Ⓜ Karlsplatz (Stachus) – ☎ (089) 55 13 61 42 – www.geisel-privathotels.de – Closed 1 - 12 January, August, Sunday - Monday and Bank Holidays

Rest – *(booking advisable)* Menu 42 € (lunch)/132 € – Carte 74/97 € **F2**

Spec. Hummer mit Erbsen, Passionsfrucht und Pata Negra Schinken. Rehmedaillon mit knusprigen Ravioli und Pfifferlingen. Erdnüsse und Salz-Mürbteig, Milchkaramell, Parfait und Schokolade.

♦ Classic ♦ Elegant ♦

This very elegant restaurant has lavishly set tables, where Martin Fauster's kitchen team prepares excellent classic dishes. From the windows watch the hustle and bustle on the Stachus.

XXX ✿

Mark's – Hotel Mandarin Oriental

Neuturmstr. 1 (1st floor) ✉ 80331 – Ⓜ Isartor – ☎ (089) 29 09 88 75 – www.mandarinoriental.com – Closed Sunday - Monday **H2**

Rest – *(dinner only)* Menu 49/95 € – Carte 60/111 €

Spec. Gänseleber mit Maisbisquit und Kaninchen. St. Pierre auf Calamaretti-Risotto mit Bärenkrebsen und Kerbelnage. Gebratenes und Geschmortes vom Milchzicklein mit Saubohnen.

♦ Classic ♦ Elegant ♦

A lovely staircase leads from the lobby of this exclusive hotel up to the elegant restaurant on the gallery. It features the contemporary, classic cuisine and good service.

XXX ✿

Atelier – Hotel Bayerischer Hof

Promenadeplatz 2 ✉ 80333 – Ⓜ Marienplatz – ☎ (089) 22 07 43 – www.bayerischerhof.de – Closed August and Sunday - Monday **G2**

Rest – *(dinner only)* Menu 74/115 €

Spec. Steinbutt mit Demeter-Eigelb und Wiesenkräutern. Rinderrücken mit Morcheln, Mark und Bärlauch. Bananensplit.

♦ Seasonal cuisine ♦ Fashionable ♦

Steffen Mezger's uses top quality products to prepare contemporary-style classic dishes. The ambience is created by the tasteful design in warm earthy tones and the attentive service.

XXX ✿✿

Dallmayr

Dienerstr. 14 (1st floor) ✉ 80331 – Ⓜ Marienplatz – ☎ (089) 2 13 51 00 – www.dallmayr.de – Closed Christmas - 11 January, 18 April - 3 May, 1 - 23 August, Sunday - Monday and Bank Holidays **G2**

Rest – *(booking advisable)* Menu 80/140 € – Carte 88/114 €

Spec. Cannelloni von Kalb in Sojagelee mit Thunfisch-Carpaccio und Avocado. Steinbutt mit zweierlei Langostino, Quinoa, grüner Spargel und Krustentierjus. Taube in der Meersalzkruste gebacken mit Trüffeljus und Gänseleberflan.

♦ Classic ♦ Elegant ♦

The name Dallmayr is inextricably associated with tradition and quality. For this reason only the best products in the form of classic dishes are served at the splendidly laid tables at the fine restaurant of this delicatessen. Diethard Urbansky is the chef.

XXX ✿

Schuhbecks in den Südtiroler Stuben

Platzl 6 ✉ 80331 – Ⓜ Isartor – ☎ (089) 2 16 69 00 – www.schuhbeck.de
– Closed 1 week early January and Sunday - Monday lunch **H2**

Rest – *(booking essential)* Menu 78/118 €

Spec. Salat vom gebackenen Bauernhendl mit Buttermilch, Sellerie, Zitrone, Piment und Lorbeer. Getrüffeltes Nudelgangerl aus dem Parmesanlaib mit a bisserl Gemüse. Böfflamott von der Ochsenschulter mit viererlei Pfeffer, geschmortem Frühlingslauch und Ofentomaten.

♦ Regional ♦ Rustic ♦ Elegant ♦

Schuhbeck's gourmet emporium is on the square in the centre of the old town. It comprises of an elegant Alpine restaurant serving Patrick Raaß regional cuisine, various shops selling ice cream, chocolate, spices and wine, as well as a café-bistro and a cookery school.

XX

Blauer Bock

Sebastiansplatz 9 ✉ 80331 – Ⓜ Marienplatz – ☎ (089) 45 22 23 33
– www.restaurant-blauerbock.de
– Closed Sunday and Bank Holidays **G3**

Rest – Menu 37 € (lunch)/82 € – Carte 56/59 €

♦ French ♦ Minimalist ♦ Fashionable ♦

This fashionable, modern restaurant is just a few steps from the Viktualienmarkt. Ambitious cuisine with French roots.

XX

Ederer

Kardinal-Faulhaber-Str. 10 (1st floor) ✉ 80333 – Ⓜ Odeonsplatz
– ☎ (089) 24 23 13 10 – www.restaurant-ederer.de
– Closed Sunday and Bank Holidays **G2**

Rest – *(booking advisable)* Menu 33 € (lunch)/37 € (dinner)
– Carte 42/72 €

♦ International ♦ Fashionable ♦

This comfortable, chic and modern restaurant belongs to the 'Fünf Höfe' quarter of the city. Here, Karl Ederer offers international cuisine made from fresh products. There is a lovely interior courtyard.

XX

Boettner's

Pfisterstr. 9 ✉ 80331 – Ⓜ Marienplatz – ☎ (089) 22 12 10
– www.boettners.de
– Closed Sunday and Bank Holidays **H2**

Rest – *(booking advisable)* Menu 32 € (lunch)/86 € – Carte 43/105 €

♦ Classic ♦ Cosy ♦

This tradition rich establishment not far from the Platzl was founded in 1901. Classic ambience and cuisine. In the summer tables are set out on the terrace in front.

XX

Halali

Schönfeldstr. 22 ✉ 80539 – Ⓜ Odeonsplatz – ☎ (089) 28 59 09
– www.restaurant-halali.de
– Closed Saturday lunch, Sunday and Bank Holidays **H1**

Rest – *(booking advisable)* Menu 24 € (lunch)/58 € – Carte 41/63 €

♦ International ♦ Cosy ♦

The sophisticated restaurant in this 19C guesthouse has almost become an institution already. The dark wood panelling and lovely decoration has created a cosy atmosphere.

XX

Nymphenburger Hof

Nymphenburger Str. 24 ✉ 80335 – Ⓜ Maillingerstr. – ☎ (089) 1 23 38 30
– www.nymphenburgerhof.de
– Closed 24 December - 8 January, Saturday lunch, Sunday and Bank Holidays

Rest – *(booking advisable)* Menu 22 € (lunch)/78 € (dinner) *Plan I* **A2**
– Carte 36/58 €

♦ International ♦ Friendly ♦

This bright, informal restaurant is inviting with its lovely terrace. The cuisine has an Austrian influence.

XX

Galleria

Sparkassenstr. 11 (corner Ledererstraße) ✉ *80331* – Ⓜ *Marienplatz*
– ✆ *(089) 29 79 95* **G2**
Rest – *(booking advisable)* Menu 25 € (lunch)/64 € (dinner)
– Carte 43/49 €
◆ Italian ◆ Cosy ◆
A small, cosy restaurant in the inner city with Italian cuisine. Temporary art displays in the dining area.

XX

Weinhaus Neuner

Herzogspitalstr. 8 ✉ *80331* – Ⓜ *Karlsplatz (Stachus)* – ✆ *(089) 2 60 39 54*
– *www.weinhaus-neuner.de*
– *Closed Sunday and Bank Holidays* **F2**
Rest – Menu 23 € (lunch)/58 € – Carte 34/51 €
◆ International ◆ Traditional ◆
It is worth visiting this 1641 wine house to see the crossed vault 'Tirolian arches'. There is also a beautiful wall painting, old panelling, and the preserved, original carvings.

XX

Austernkeller

Stollbergstr. 11 ✉ *80539* – Ⓜ *Isartor* – ✆ *(089) 29 87 87*
– *www.austernkeller.de* **H2**
Rest – *(dinner only) (booking advisable)* Carte 33/59 €
◆ Fish ◆ Cosy ◆
Guests particularly enjoy fish and seafood in this listed cellar vault decorated with porcelain plates.

XX

Les Cuisiniers

Reitmorstr. 21 ✉ *80538* – Ⓜ *Lehel* – ✆ *(089) 23 70 98 90*
– *www.lescuisiniers.de*
– *Closed Saturday lunch and Sunday* *Plan I* **C3**
Rest – *(booking advisable)* Menu 42 € – Carte 31/48 €
◆ French ◆ Bistro ◆
This lovely bright restaurant has the air of a bistro with its lively atmosphere and friendly, informal service. The French menu is displayed on a board.

X ✿

Schweiger² im Showroom

Lilienstr. 6 ✉ *81669* – ✆ *(089) 44 42 90 82* – *www.schweiger2.de*
– *Closed Christmas - 9 January, 1 - 14 August, Saturday - Sunday and Bank Holidays* *Plan I* **C3**
Rest – *(dinner only) (booking advisable)* Menu 63/120 €
Spec. Variation vom Langostino mit Zitronenconfitroulade, Gurkenspaghetti und Avocadomousseline. Konfierter Rochenflügel auf Pok Choi und das Gelbe vom 40 Minuten Bauernei. Dreierlei vom Lamm mit Selleriepüree und Portweinschalotten.
◆ Inventive ◆ Friendly ◆ Trendy ◆
Andreas Schweiger is pursuing a very young and very modern concept in this small restaurant. He values personal contact with his guests, deliberately dispenses with a menu, and personally announces the creatively put together dishes at the table.

X

Dukatz

Maffeistr. 3a (1st floor) ✉ *80333* – Ⓜ *Marienplatz* – ✆ *(089) 7 10 40 73 73*
– *www.dukatz.de*
– *Closed Sunday and Bank Holidays* **G2**
Rest – *(booking advisable)* Carte 30/49 €
◆ French ◆ Bistro ◆ Friendly ◆
Find this lovely bistro-style restaurant on the first floor of the Schäfflerhof, right in the middle of town. Delicious uncomplicated French food is served.

Retter's Feinschmecker

Frauenstr. 10 ✉ 80469 – Ⓜ Isartor – ✆ (089) 23 23 79 23
– www.retters.de
– Closed 1 - 11 January, 25 May - 7 June, Sunday - Monday and Bank Holidays
Rest – Menu 27 € (lunch)/70 € (dinner) – Carte 22/55 € **G3**

◆ Seasonal cuisine ◆ Cosy ◆

Next to the market, this is a cosy, down-to-earth, modern restaurant with antique, Swiss pine panelling. Seasonal dishes are served from a daily changing menu, and wines from their own business next door.

Toshi

Wurzerstr. 18 ✉ 80539 – Ⓜ Lehel – ✆ (089) 25 54 69 42
– www.toshi.de.com
– Closed Saturday lunch, Saturday and Bank Holidays lunch **H2**
Rest – Menu 65/120 € – Carte 34/84 €

◆ Japanese ◆ Minimalist ◆

This Japanese restaurant is close to the elegant Maximilianstrasse. Dine on fresh cuisine from the Far East in an authentic ambience. Sushi bar and teppanyaki.

Zum Alten Markt

Dreifaltigkeitsplatz 3 ✉ 80331 – Ⓜ Marienplatz – ✆ (089) 29 99 95
– www.zumaltenmarkt.de
– closed Sunday and Bank Holidays **G2**
Rest – Carte 23/39 €

◆ International ◆ Cosy ◆

This personally run, quaint bar is next to the Viktualienmarkt. It is furnished with original 400 year-old wood from a south Tirolian, councilman's room.

Jin

Kanalstr. 14 ✉ 80538 – Ⓜ Isartor – ✆ (089) 21 94 99 70
– www.restaurant-jin.de
– Closed Monday **H2**
Rest – Menu 28/68 € – Carte 33/57 €

◆ Asian ◆ Friendly ◆

Simply designed in dark wood, this restaurant offers outstanding Asian cuisine and friendly service. Sushi is also on the menu.

Altes Hackerhaus

Sendlinger Str. 14 ✉ 80331 – Ⓜ Marienplatz – ✆ (089) 2 60 50 26
– www.hackerhaus.de **G2**
Rest – Carte 16/48 €

◆ Bavarian specialities ◆ Cosy ◆

A very cared-for and well-run rustic restaurant where Bavarian delicacies are served in warm and homely rooms. There is a beautiful covered interior courtyard.

Weisses Bräuhaus

Tal 7 ✉ 80331 – Ⓜ Isartor – ✆ (089) 2 90 13 80
– www.weisses-brauhaus.de **G2**
Rest – Carte 14/31 €

◆ Bavarian specialities ◆ Cosy ◆

Its long tradition and Bavarian cuisine have made this smart old townhouse restaurant with its numerous dining rooms something of a Munich institution. Steak specialities.

Spatenhaus an der Oper

Residenzstr. 12 ✉ 80333 – Ⓜ Marienplatz – ✆ (089) 2 90 70 60
– www.kuffler.de **G2**
Rest – Carte 27/54 €

◆ Bavarian specialities ◆ Traditional ◆

The attractive rooms in this townhouse, opposite the Bavarian State Opera, exude rural charm. On the ground floor the food is local; on the first-floor the menu is international.

Augustiner Gaststätten

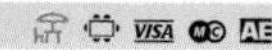

Neuhauser Str. 27 ✉ 80331 – Ⓜ Karlsplatz (Stachus)
– ✆ (089) 23 18 32 57 – www.augustiner-restaurant.com **F2**
Rest – Carte 12/35 €
◆ Bavarian specialities ◆ Traditional ◆
For as long as can be recalled this striking brewery guesthouse in the pedestrian zone has been known for its good beer, which has been brewed here since 1885. The interior courtyard is one of the city's loveliest beer gardens.

ENVIRONS *Plan I*

The Westin Grand

Arabellastr. 6 ✉ 81925 – Ⓜ Arabellapark
– ✆ (089) 9 26 40 – www.westin.com/munich **D2**
627 rm – 🚹130/399 € 🚹🚹130/399 €, ☕ 27 € – 28 suites
Rest *ZEN* – *✆ (089) 92 64 81 10 (closed Sunday dinner)* Carte 31/60 €
Rest *Paulaner's* – *✆ (089) 92 64 81 15 (closed Saturday lunch, Sunday lunch and Bank Holidays lunch)* Carte 24/39 €
◆ Business ◆ Luxury ◆ Contemporary ◆
This luxury business hotel and conference venue boasts a wonderful 1500m² spa with adjoining fitness facilities. Great roof lounge for the executive rooms. ZEN offers Asian cuisine cooked in its open kitchen.

Marriott

Berliner Str. 93 ✉ 80805 – Ⓜ Nordfriedhof – ✆ (089) 36 00 20
– www.marriott-muenchen.de **C1**
348 rm – 🚹189/239 € 🚹🚹189/239 €, ☕ 26 € – 14 suites
Rest – Carte 30/42 €
◆ Chain hotel ◆ Contemporary ◆
A comfortable business hotel in the contemporary style with pleasant, spacious lobby. Massage and beauty treatments available. Modern restaurant serving international cuisine.

Hilton City

Rosenheimer Str. 15 ✉ 81667 – Ⓜ Ostbahnhof – ✆ (089) 4 80 40
– www.hilton.de **C3**
480 rm – 🚹109/429 € 🚹🚹109/429 €, ☕ 28 € – 3 suites **Rest** – Carte 28/51 €
◆ Chain hotel ◆ Contemporary ◆
This business hotel with its contemporary, functional rooms is conveniently located for the conference centres and has a direct overland railway link to the airport. Regional and international cuisine is served in this rustic restaurant.

Palace

rm,

Trogerstr. 21 ✉ 81675 – Ⓜ Prinzregentenplatz – ✆ (089) 41 97 10
– www.muenchenpalace.de **C3**
74 rm – 🚹165/310 € 🚹🚹225/380 €, ☕ 25 € – 2 suites **Rest** – Carte 35/47 €
◆ Business ◆ Classic ◆ Elegant ◆
This tasteful, impeccably run hotel includes many musicians amongst its regulars. The natural tones and parquet floors combine to create a warm and friendly atmosphere. Pleasant garden and roof terrace. This restaurant serves classic international cuisine.

Innside Parkstadt Schwabing

rest,

Mies-van-der-Rohe-Str. 10 ✉ 80807
– Ⓜ Nordfriedhof – ✆ (089) 35 40 80 – www.innside.de **C1**
160 rm ☕ – 🚹99/429 € 🚹🚹109/459 €
Rest – *(closed Saturday lunch, Sunday lunch and Bank Holidays)* Carte 35/46 €
◆ Business ◆ Functional ◆
Designed by famous architect Helmut Jahn, this hotel enjoys a convenient location close to the striking HighLight Towers. The whole building is beautifully light, with clean modern lines. This bistro-style restaurant decorated with its modern white interior serves international cuisine.

Renaissance

Theodor-Dombart-Str. 4 (corner Berliner Straße) ✉ 80805 – Ⓜ Nordfriedhof – ✆ (089) 36 09 90 – www.renaissance-munich.de **C1**

261 rm – 128/188 € 128/188 €, 26 € – 40 suites

Rest – Carte 32/42 €

♦ Chain hotel ♦ Contemporary ♦

This business hotel close to the English Gardens offers cosy yet spacious rooms and roomy, elegant suites and junior suites. This restaurant, known as 46°-47°, is in a modern bistro-style and has an internal courtyard terrace.

Novotel City

Hochstr. 11 ✉ 81669 – Ⓜ Ostbahnhof – ✆ (089) 66 10 70 – www.novotel.com **C3**

307 rm – 95/295 € 115/315 €, 19 € – 2 suites

Rest – Carte 25/65 €

♦ Business ♦ Modern ♦

This business hotel with its modern, well-equipped rooms is located close to the River Isar and the German Museum. The restaurant reflects the light and airy, contemporary design of the hotel.

Sheraton Arabellapark

Arabellastr. 5 ✉ 81925 – Ⓜ Arabellapark – ✆ (089) 9 23 20 – www.sheratonarabellapark.com **D2**

rm,

446 rm – 125/370 € 125/370 €, 24 € – 35 suites

Rest – Carte 28/48 €

♦ Business ♦ Modern ♦

This hotel with its simple, modern rooms complete with balconies is situated close to the English Garden. Views over the city from the indoor pool on the 22nd floor. "Audrey's" and "66" offer international cuisine together with grilled meats and organic dishes.

Cosmopolitan without rest

Hohenzollernstr. 5 ✉ 80801 – Ⓜ Münchner Freiheit – ✆ (089) 38 38 10 – www.geisel-privathotels.de **B2**

71 rm – 125/185 € 135/195 €

♦ Business ♦ Functional ♦

Located close to the Leopoldstraße with good underground connections this privately run hotel offers functional, modern rooms equipped with the latest technology.

Suitehotel without rest

*Lyonel-Feininger-Str. 22 (by Isarring **C1**) ✉ 80807 – ✆ (089) 35 81 90 – www.suitehotel.com*

149 rm – 94/109 € 119/225 €, 13 €

♦ Chain hotel ♦ Contemporary ♦

Contemporary hotel with modern design. The comfortable rooms are spacious and functional, with the state-of-the-art technology.

Prinzregent am Friedensengel without rest

Ismaninger Str. 42 ✉ 81675 – Ⓜ Prinzregentenplatz – ✆ (089) 41 60 50 – www.prinzregent.de **C3**

65 rm – 125/185 € 155/215 € – 2 suites

♦ Business ♦ Cosy ♦

This lovely old hotel with its beautiful woodwork is full of Bavarian charm. The cosy, wood-panelled bar offers bar snacks.

Freisinger Hof

Oberföhringer Str. 189 ✉ 81925 – ✆ (089) 95 23 02 – www.freisinger-hof.de – Closed end December - 10 January (hotel only) **D1**

51 rm – 115/125 € 145/160 € **Rest** – Carte 30/52 €

◆ Country house ◆ Cosy ◆

The hotel annexe which has been added to this historical inn offers comfortable country-style rooms. The small lobby is bright and welcoming. Enjoy tasty regional food in this cosy inn dating from 1875. Boiled beef and other classic Austrian dishes served.

angelo

rm, rm,

Leuchtenbergring 20 ✉ 81677 – Ⓜ Prinzregentenpl. – ✆ (089) 1 89 08 60 – www.angelo-munich.com **D3**

146 rm – 99/249 € 124/274 € – 2 suites **Rest** – Carte 18/36 €

◆ Business ◆ Contemporary ◆

This modern business hotel with direct access to the overland railway is located close to a large fitness and wellness studio for which it provides a daily menu. Bistro-style restaurant.

Preysing without rest

Preysingstr. 1 / Stubenvollstr. 2 ✉ 81667 – Ⓜ Max Weber Pl. – ✆ (089) 45 84 50 – www.hotel-preysing.de – Closed Christmas - 4 January **C3**

62 rm – 138/220 € 198/280 € – 5 suites

◆ Townhouse ◆ Cosy ◆

This tip-top furnished hotel has up-to-date guestrooms with granite floors. It is very suited to business travellers.

Leopold

Leopoldstr. 119 ✉ 80804 – Ⓜ Dietlindenstr. – ✆ (089) 36 04 30 – www.hotel-leopold.de – Closed 23 - 30 December **B1**

63 rm – 98/175 € 132/245 € **Rest** – *(dinner only)* Carte 18/38 €

◆ Family ◆ Contemporary ◆

This impeccably run, family hotel offers a range of well-appointed rooms furnished in different styles some of which have lovely garden views. Rustic restaurant with international menu.

Tantris

Johann-Fichte-Str. 7 ✉ 80805 – Ⓜ Dietlindenstr. – ✆ (089) 3 61 95 90 – www.tantris.de – Closed 1 - 11 January, Sunday - Monday and Bank Holidays **B1**

Rest – *(booking advisable)* Menu 65 € (lunch)/160 € – Carte 80/118 €

Spec. Lauwarmer Lachs mit Lauchpüree und brauner Butter. Hummer mit Saubohnen, Ravioli und Zitronengras-Krustentiersud. Gratiniertes Carré vom Lammrücken mit Artischocken, Ofentomaten und geschmorten Kartoffeln.

◆ Classic ◆ Retro ◆

For over 20 years the native-born Austrian Hans Haas has been delighting guests with product related, contemporary-classic dishes in his very own style. With its orange-red and black interior this 1970's building has retained its original character.

Bogenhauser Hof

Ismaninger Str. 85 ✉ 81675 – Ⓜ Böhmerwaldplatz – ✆ (089) 98 55 86 – www.bogenhauser-hof.de – Closed Christmas - 6 January, Sunday and Bank Holidays **C2**

Rest – *(booking advisable)* Menu 49/107 € – Carte 47/68 €

◆ Classic ◆ Traditional ◆ Cosy ◆

This elegant yet comfortable restaurant housed in a building dating back to 1825 and serving classic cuisine prepared using the finest ingredients has many regulars. Leafy garden complete with mature chestnut trees.

XX ✿

181 - First (Otto Koch)

Spiridon-Louis-Ring 7 ✉ 80809 – ✆ (089) 30 66 85 85
– www.restaurant181.com
– Closed 2 weeks early January, 1 week end August, 1 week early September and Sunday - Monday **A1**

Rest – *(dinner only) (booking essential)* Menu 95/145 €
Rest *181 - Business* – *✆ (089) 3 50 94 81 81* – Menu 25 € (lunch)/65 € – Carte 45/63 €

Spec. Steinpilzsuppe mit frischem Moosschaum. Milchlammvariation. Arganöl-Mango-Gelee mit gefrorenem "Steinklotz" und Pina Colada-Soufflé.

♦ Modern ♦ Elegant ♦

At a height of 181m this modern restaurant rotates about its own axis and offers impressive views. The friendly and attentive Fritz family welcomes guests. Otto Koch prepares both classic and contemporary dishes. This restaurant serves international cuisine.

XX ✿

Acquarello (Mario Gamba)

Mühlbaurstr. 36 ✉ 81677 – Ⓜ Böhmerwaldplatz – ✆ (089) 4 70 48 48
– www.acquarello.com
– Closed 1 - 3 January, Saturday lunch, Sunday lunch and Bank Holiday lunch

Rest – Menu 39 € (lunch)/98 € – Carte 46/82 € **D2**

Spec. Neun Geschmacksrichtungen für ein Roastbeef. Feigentortelli mit Gänseleber und Cassissauce. Rinderschmorbraten mit Barolosauce und Selleriepüree.

♦ Italian ♦ Friendly ♦

Mario Gamba is a native-born Italian whose classic dishes are inspired by his Mediterranean homeland. The ambience also has a certain southern easiness about it. Friendly service.

XX

Käfer Schänke

Prinzregentenstr. 73 (1st floor) ✉ 81675 – Ⓜ Prinzregentenplatz
– ✆ (089) 4 16 82 47 – www.feinkost-kaefer.de
– Closed Sunday and Bank Holidays **C3**

Rest – *(booking essential)* Carte 48/97 €

♦ International ♦ Cosy ♦ Individual ♦

In this popular restaurant with its 12 highly individual dining rooms the international menu is determined by the availability of the best quality produce. The delicatessen sells a range of fine foods.

XX

Hippocampus

Mühlbaurstr. 5 ✉ 81677 – Ⓜ Prinzregentenplatz – ✆ (089) 47 58 55
– www.hippocampus-restaurant.de
– Closed Saturday lunch **C3**

Rest – Menu 53 € – Carte 40/55 €

♦ Italian ♦ Elegant ♦

Hippocampus offers friendly service, an informal atmosphere and ambitious Italian cuisine. Beautiful fixtures and fittings help create the elegant yet warm and welcoming interior.

X

Acetaia

Nymphenburger Str. 215 (by **A2***) ✉ 80639 – ✆ (089) 13 92 90 77*
– www.restaurant-acetaia.de
– Closed Saturday lunch

Rest – Menu 27 € (lunch)/65 € – Carte 45/57 €

♦ Italian ♦ Cosy ♦

This friendly restaurant with its Art Nouveau decor offers Italian cuisine and the best espresso in the city. The olive oil and balsamic vinegar which gave the place its name are also very good. Attractive terrace.

Terrine

Amalienstr. 89 (Amalien-Passage) ✉ 80799 – Ⓜ Universität – ☎ (089) 28 17 80 – www.terrine.de
– Closed 2 weeks early January, 2 weeks June and Saturday lunch, Sunday - Monday **B2**
Rest – Menu 39 € (lunch)/120 € (dinner) – Carte 63/84 €
Spec. Wildkräuter-Ravioli mit Gänseleber, Aubergine, Erbsen und Nussbutter. Rehkeule mit Rote Bete, Ingwer-Joghurt, Pfifferlingen und Malzjus. Maracuja-Parfait mit Kaktusfeigencreme, Marzipan, Aloe Vera und Weißbier.
♦ Seasonal cuisine ♦ Bistro ♦
This light, charming bistro has friendly service and features the creative cooking of Jakob Stüttgen. Wine, vinegar, spices, chocolates etc. can be purchased in the little shop next door.

Tramin

Lothringer Str. 7 ✉ 81667 – Ⓜ Ostbahnhof – ☎ (089) 44 45 40 90 – www.tramin-restaurant.de
– Closed Sunday - Monday **C3**
Rest – *(dinner only)* Menu 52/78 € – Carte 45/55 €
♦ Inventive ♦ Fashionable ♦
This interesting establishment has a casual atmosphere, friendly service and ambitious, creative cuisine in a deliberately unpretentious atmosphere. A very good selection of wines is also available.

Huber

Newtonstr. 13 ✉ 81679 – Ⓜ Richard Strauss Str. – ☎ (089) 98 51 52 – www.huber-restaurant.de
– Closed Saturday lunch and Sunday - Monday **C2**
Rest – Menu 25 € (lunch)/69 € (dinner) – Carte 35/60 €
♦ Classic ♦ Fashionable ♦
This appealing, modern restaurant offers friendly service and quality contemporary cuisine created by a young chef. The selection of Austrian wines is particularly good. The interior is by a Munich designer.

Saint Laurent

Steinstr. 63 ✉ 81667 – Ⓜ Ostbahnhof – ☎ (089) 47 08 40 00
– Closed Monday **C3**
Rest – *(dinner only)* Menu 25 € – Carte 34/53 €
♦ French ♦ Cosy ♦
A comfortable restaurant where the French-inspired atmosphere and French music provide the ideal backdrop to the chef's cooking style. There is a terrace some 50m from the restaurant.

Atelier Gourmet

Rablstr. 37 ✉ 81669 – Ⓜ Ostbahnhof – ☎ (089) 48 72 20 – www.ateliergourmet.de
– Closed Sunday **C3**
Rest – *(dinner only) (booking advisable)* Menu 34/41 € – Carte 34/43 €
♦ French ♦ Friendly ♦
An informal small evening restaurant with a modern ambience and friendly service. Guests order carefully prepared and reasonably priced French bistro dishes from a blackboard. Good range of wines available.

Vinaiolo

Steinstr. 42 ✉ 81667 – Ⓜ Ostbahnhof – ☎ (089) 48 95 03 56 – www.vinaiolo.de
– Closed Saturday lunch **C3**
Rest – Menu 59 € – Carte 42/47 €
♦ Italian ♦ Cosy ♦
Part of the decor in this friendly Italian restaurant, including the beautiful old cabinets in which the wines are displayed, originally came from the interior of a 1904 grocer's shop.

Rue Des Halles

Steinstr. 18 ✉ *81667* – Ⓜ *Max Weber Platz* – ✆ *(089) 48 56 75*
– *www.rue-des-halles.de* **C3**

Rest – *(dinner only) (booking advisable)* Menu 23/52 € – Carte 28/45 €

◆ French ◆ Bistro ◆

Experience the typical French atmosphere of this bistro-style restaurant. It has both classic and regional French dishes on the menu.

AT THE EXHIBITION CENTRE

Schreiberhof

Erdinger Str. 2 ✉ *85609 Aschheim* – ✆ *(089) 90 00 60*
– *www.schreiberhof.de*

87 rm – †95/115 € ††115 € **Rest** – Menu 50 € – Carte 31/45 €

◆ Inn ◆ Conference hotel ◆ Functional ◆

Once a traditional inn, Schreiberhof has been developed into a modern city centre hotel with functional rooms. The light-flooded winter garden makes an unusual conference setting. This restaurant offers a number of dining rooms in different styles ranging from the stylish to the cosy and informal and a beer garden set under mature trees.

Prinzregent an der Messe

Riemer Str. 350 ✉ *81829* – ✆ *(089) 94 53 90*
– *www.prinzregent.de*

91 rm – †145/175 € ††185/225 € – 4 suites **Rest** – Carte 22/49 €

◆ Business ◆ Inn ◆ Cosy ◆

This lovely hotel, converted from a period inn, offers comfortable rooms in the Bavarian style and a great sauna. Located conveniently close to the exhibition centre. A cosy restaurant with a touch of elegance.

Innside München Neue Messe

rest,

Humboldtstr. 12 (Industrialpark-West)
✉ *85609 Aschheim* – ✆ *(089) 94 00 50* – *www.innside.de*

134 rm – †169/189 € ††199/219 € **Rest** – Carte 29/40 €

◆ Business ◆ Modern ◆

A modern design characterises this hotel, from the light hall area in atrium style, through to the cosy guestrooms. Unusual features include the freestanding glass showers. Bistro-style restaurant with international cuisine.

Novotel Messe

Willy-Brandt-Platz 1 ✉ *81829* – ✆ *(089) 99 40 00*
– *www.novotel.com/5563*

278 rm – †89/299 € ††89/299 €, 19 € **Rest** – Carte 28/48 €

◆ Chain hotel ◆ Business ◆ Modern ◆

Located in the former airport grounds next to the convention centre, this hotel is modem and functional. Good transport connections with the motorway and underground. Bright, friendly restaurant with a glass frontage.

AT THE AIRPORT

Kempinski Airport München

Terminalstraße Mitte 20 ✉ *85356 München*
– ✆ *(089) 9 78 20* – *www.kempinski-airport.de*

389 rm – †149/385 € ††149/385 €, 31 € – 46 suites

Rest ***charles lindbergh*** – ✆ *(089) 97 82 45 00* – Menu 89 €
– Carte 31/55 €

◆ Business ◆ Contemporary ◆

This business hotel has an imposing glass atrium complete with 18m-high palm trees. The rooms are contemporary but tasteful and the leisure facilities excellent. International cuisine features at the timeless charles lindbergh restaurant.

STUTTGART

STUTTGART

Population: 601 646 – Altitude: 245m

uriy Davats/Fotolia.com

Baden-Württemberg, in Germany's south west, is one of the country's most popular tourist destinations, defined by superb castles, delectable resorts, and renowned wine-growing areas. The capital of the region, Stuttgart, sits easily within this framework. Its valley location, surrounded by steeply rising slopes, has allowed vineyards to approach the city centre from all around: the twisting branches of grapes are as much a part of the inner city picture as the sleek museums for Mercedes or Porsche.

There's an enviable amount of open space in Stuttgart. Parks, forests and orchards cover more than half of its area. It seems appropriate that the city started life as a horse stud farm in the tenth century, growing to become Germany's most prosperous metropolis by way – incongruously or not - of its association with the world's sleekest cars. This is also a city of fine squares, majestic palaces, architecturally diverse buildings and cultural vigour. Three years ago a spectacular glass cube announced itself as the city's new museum of art, while theatre, ballet and opera are housed together in the largest 'three function' building in Europe. Meanwhile, many visitors keep an eye open for Stuttgart's Beer Festival, which gives Munich's Oktoberfest a run for its money.

LIVING THE CITY

Stuttgart is enviably situated amongst picturesque hills. It's surrounded on three sides by wooded elevations, while to the east it's open to the river **Neckar.** The old town is bounded to the east by the district of **Obertürkheim**, a popular destination as it's the home of the Mercedes-Benz Museum. The city is in the heart of Germany's most scenic state (with the possible exception of Bavaria), and to its northwest lies Heidelberg, and to its west is Baden-Baden.

PRACTICAL INFORMATION

ARRIVAL-DEPARTURE

The Airport is 13km south of the city centre. S-Bahn commuter trains S2 and S3 run to Central Station in 30min, while a taxi will cost around € 20.

TRANSPORT

There's an impressively integrated public transport system in Stuttgart, which covers nearby towns as well as the city itself. Once you've bought a ticket, you can switch between buses, trams, U-Bahns, and mainline and S-Bahn trains.

There are three types of ticket you might need. If you're only in town for a short time, buy a day ticket. If you're around for longer, invest in either a city explorer Stuttcard or Stuttcard plus; these give free admission to most museums, reduced entry to theatres, and free travel on public transport for three days, including transport to the airport (the Stuttcard plus is more expensive, but offers a few more benefits).

EXPLORING STUTTGART

Stuttgart breathes well-being and good living. Even its neighbours are of the very top drawer, in the shape of nearby Heidelberg and Baden-Baden. It's a city that was always favoured by the local bigwigs, becoming first ducal, then royal, capital of Württemberg. Its beautiful position, cosseted by rolling hills, may have had something to do with this, but the local hierarchy of the past would have been bamboozled at the source of Stuttgart's current success: fast cars. Both Mercedes-Benz and Porsche have made their names in this city, and both manufacturers boast slinky museums devoted to their pride and joy.

→ SQUARE DEAL

Visitors here invariably make for **Schlossplatz,** the imposing square at the centre of the city. Its huge dimensions are breathtaking, especially when you take in the proportions of the vast **Neues Schloss**, the palace that eats up the whole of the square's east side. It was the last Baroque castle-residence to be built in Germany, and its construction lasted throughout much of the eighteenth century's latter half. The idea was to make it a second Versailles, and a pretty good job they made of it. The only part you can visit are the cellars, but it's worth it to see the **Römisches Lapidarium**, a collection of Roman stone fragments dating back to 200AD. The grandeur of the square extends still further: opposite the Neues Schloss is **Königsbau**, a fine Neo-Classical structure from the mid-nineteenth century, which has been turned to modern day use by lining it with glitzy shops.

➔ STATE OF PERFECTION

You get a clue to Stuttgart's cultural import a short stroll from Schlossplatz, by arriving at the nineteenth century **Staatsgalerie**, or Old State Gallery. Reckoned to be one of the top art museums in the country, it boasts a fantastic collection of old masters and a fascinating inventory of graphics, which includes illustrated books, posters and photographs. Its stature was enhanced in 1984 when a dazzling new extension was added – the New State Gallery – which contains works from the twentieth century by the likes of Modigliani, Picasso and Beuys. This is now one of Germany's most visited museums, but its status has been challenged in the past couple of years by the new kid on the block, The **Kunstmuseum,** just off Schlossplatz. Maybe that should read the new *block* on the block, because this twenty first century upstart is in the shape of a cube made of glass, and even if you don't intend going in, you'll want to stop and look at it. It features the work of German artists, including Otto Dix and Swabian Impressionists, and its hidden tunnels of art are an unexpected delight for the first-time visitor.

➔ SCHILL-OUT ZONE

You only have to cross the smart shopping street, **Königstrasse,** to indulge in a bit more of Stuttgart's cultural scene. On the beautiful **Schillerplatz**, the remains of a fourteenth century castle were given a sixteenth century makeover, and the **Altes Schloss** got its Renaissance look with atmospheric arcaded cloisters encircling a spooky inner courtyard. You might not expect to find a museum here, but this is the home of the **Württembergisches Landesmuseum**, which has an eclectic mix of Italian sculptures, Renaissance curios, and – on the top floor – the nineteenth century crown jewels.

Hang around a bit on Schillerplatz. It's the city's one example of a truly historic square, as it was here that the stud farm that gave Stuttgart its name is said to have stood. It's surrounded by historic buildings: apart from the Altes Schloss, there's the sixteenth century **Old Chancellery**, which is now a restaurant; a **gabled granary**, also from the sixteenth century, where you can find a museum of musical instruments and the elegant seventeenth century **Prinzenbau**.

➔ GET YOUR MOTOR RUNNING

You often read about somewhere being a 'city of contrasts', but in Stuttgart they really mean it. To the east of the centre, away from the charms of the past, lies the roaring glory of the **Mercedes-Benz Museum**, a must for petrol-heads. Here you can see the first cars in the world, Carl Benz's three-wheeled automobile from 1886, and Gottlieb Daimler's horseless carriage. There are over seventy vehicles on display, all in mint condition, from the earliest models to today's state-of-the-art cars. One of the most impressive exhibits is the Blitzen Benz, which was driven at 228mph to set the world record at Daytona Beach nearly one hundred years ago. Of course, where there's Merc, there's **Porsche,** and Stuttgart's other legendary car manufacturer has its own museum, too, ranging from the 356 Roadster of 1948 to the latest models. A spectacular new Porsche Museum opened in the city, and is even more comprehensive than its predecessor.

If you like to see a play, or you're a bit partial to the opera or the ballet, it's possible to combine all three at Stuttgart's **State Theatre**. It's big enough and it's bold enough to house all three within the same premises, either in the **Playhouse** or the **Opera house.** The foyer, with its busts of writers and composers, is an imposing place to gather.

→ GREEN U-TURN

Stuttgart cherishes its verdant surroundings. Not only swathed in hills and vineyards, it also boasts an enviable amount of parks and green space. In fact, this has a collective name, The Green U, named after the rough shape this 'natural trail' takes. It's eight kilometres in length, starting at the Schlossplatz, and heading away via magnificent gardens (the Schlossgarten) north of Neues Schloss, before taking in the glorious Rosenstein Park, with its lake, rose garden, grand old trees, and showy Schloss Rosenstein, the former country house of the Württemberg kings. If it sounds rather idyllic from ground level, get bird's eye confirmation by heading nearly 220m up the city's famous TV Tower. Now over fifty years old, it stands on top of a wooded hill, and from either its observation platform or crows nest café you can indulge uninterrupted, jaw-dropping views of Stuttgart, the vineyards of the Neckar Valley, the Black Forest and the Alps.

CALENDAR HIGHLIGHTS

As the home to two of the world's most famous marques, it's not surprising that Stuttgart should honour the motor car. It does this in March with Retroclassics (at the Messe Stuttgart), which is a show full of vintage favourites, such as Aston Martins, Rolls Royces and Porsches, alongside a 'history of classic cars' exhibit. A month earlier, the year gets a stately opening with the Stuttgart Bach Week, at the Liederhalle, during which international artists celebrate the great man's music over a ten-day festival. The art world comes to the fore in March with Long Art Night at the Staatsgalerie: the idea is to enjoy an evening meal, then head to the museum and get into the unique experience of taking on Picasso and Munch till the midnight hour. The coming of summer is a good time to be a beer drinker in this city. The Stuttgart Spring Beer Festival (April/May), at Cannstatter Wasen, is a three-week ale celebration, with the distraction of hot-air balloon flights and fireworks. July sees two big events. Schlossplatz hosts the Jazz Open wich features many international artists giving it their all for a week at the Liederhalle or on the adjacent open-air stage.

STUTTGART IN…

→ ONE DAY

Schlossplatz, Staatsgalerie, Mercedes-Benz Museum

→ TWO DAYS

Kunstmuseum, Altes Schloss, amble through Schlossgarten, Porsche Museum, State Theatre Stuttgart

→ THREE DAYS

Stroll in Rosenstein park, outing to Heidelberg or Baden-Baden

Meanwhile, the Stuttgart Christopher Street Day parade is a gay pride event lasting a week, with special events running alongside stage and cabaret shows. The elegant Summer Festival (August) shimmers across three days of white pavilions, fairy lights and lanterns, with music, food and entertainment keeping thousands happy outside Neues Schloss and the Opera House. The grape and the grain hit the forefront again with the city's final two big festivals of the year. The Stuttgarter Weindorf (Aug/Sep) attracts a million wine lovers to the Marktplatz and Schlossplatz for twelve days of serious imbibing. Fifty local wineries create the famous "wine village", with over one hundred lovingly-decorated arbours. A month later, the Stuttgart Beer Festival at Cannstatter Wasen has almost two hundred years of history behind it. 'Fleshed out' with a giant Ferris wheel and numerous fairground attractions, it's the world's second biggest beer extravaganza, behind Munich's Oktoberfest.

EATING OUT

Württemberg's viniculture has a tradition of more than a thousand years and the most popular variety amongst the locals is the ruby red Trollinger. You might be surprised how it's served to you: in quarter litre glasses with handles. You won't be surprised that the 'Schwäbische Weinstuben' (local wine taverns) are rollicking good places to go. Beer is a flourishing trade too, with large Stuttgart breweries vying for your palate. That's not to say that food takes a back seat. On the contrary, this south western city isn't far from the French border, and prides itself on accomplished French inspired menus. Italian restaurants, and lots of them, jostle for position as well. There's a renowned 'local kitchen', with *Gaisburger Marsch* the pick of the dishes: it's a tasty stew made of *Spätzle* (the staple Stuttgart noodle), potatoes, beef pieces, vegetables, broth and roasted onions. *Spätzles* turn up everywhere, and are very popular *'mit Linsen'* (lentils), especially when they're teamed up and served with warm sausages, or accompanying a Swabian roast, another hearty dish featuring roasted slices of beef with lots of roasted onions, served with Sauerkraut and *Maultaschen* (square dumplings with a savoury filling). There's an impressive range of international restaurants in the city, so if you want to eat good cuisine from beyond European borders, you won't have a problem. Prices include service, but it's usual to leave a tip of around ten per cent of the bill.

→ NATURAL MAGNETISM

Plant and animal lovers in Stuttgart will want to head for the Wilhelma, Europe's largest zoological/botanical gardens. Not only can you gaze at more than ten thousand animals, you can also take in the glory of rare orchids, a large magnolia grove, and all kinds of exotic plants. It can get rather crowded: nearly two million visitors turn up each year, so be prepared to have your space invaded.

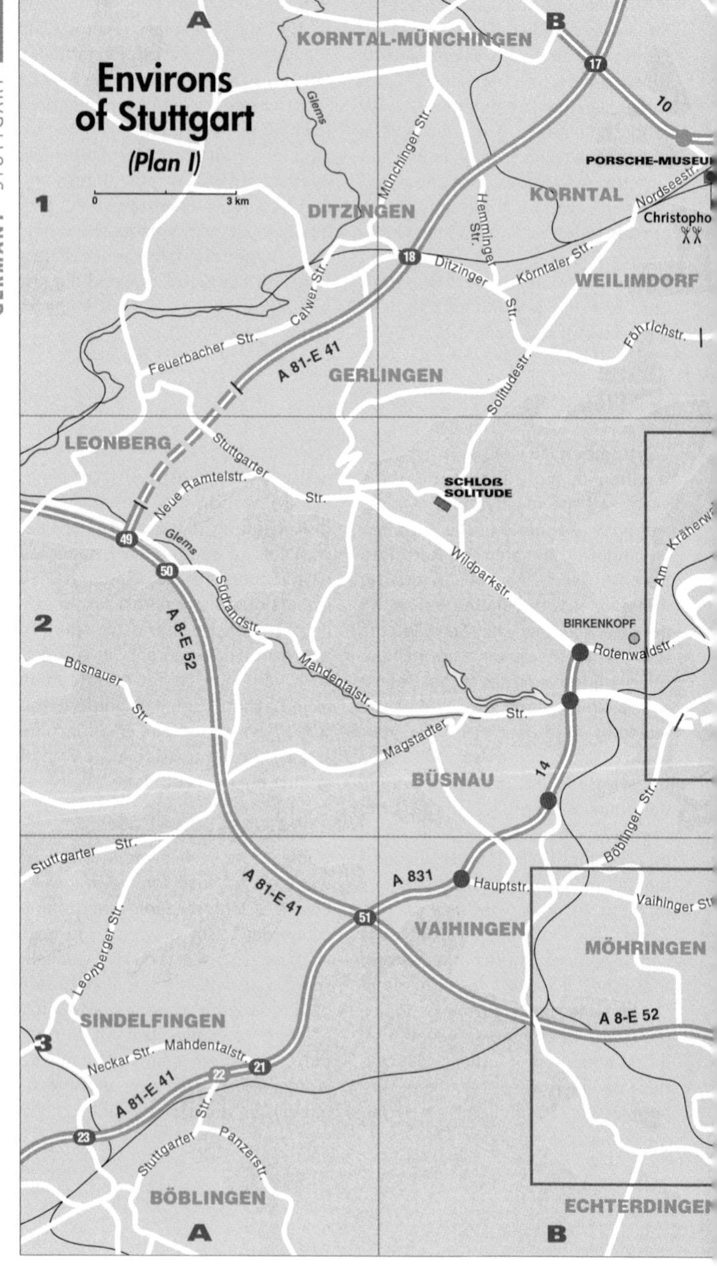
Environs of Stuttgart
(Plan I)
0
3 km
A
B
1
2
3
KORNTAL-MÜNCHINGEN
DITZINGEN
KORNTAL
WEILIMDORF
GERLINGEN
LEONBERG
SCHLOß SOLITUDE
BIRKENKOPF
BÜSNAU
VAIHINGEN
MÖHRINGEN
SINDELFINGEN
BÖBLINGEN
ECHTERDINGEN
PORSCHE-MUSEU
Christopho
Glems
Münchinger Str.
Hemminger Str.
Ditzinger Str.
Körntaler Str.
Nordseestr.
Föhrichstr.
Calwer Str.
Feuerbacher Str.
A 81-E 41
Solitudestr.
Stuttgarter Str.
Neue Ramtelstr.
Wildparkstr.
Am Kräherwa
Südrandstr.
Mahdentalstr.
Rotenwaldstr.
Büsnauer Str.
A 8-E 52
Magstadter Str.
14
Böblinger Str.
A 831
Hauptstr.
Vaihinger Str
Stuttgarter Str.
Leonberger Str.
Neckar Str.
Mahdentalstr.
Stuttgarter Str.
Panzerstr.
10
17
18
49
50
51
21
22
23

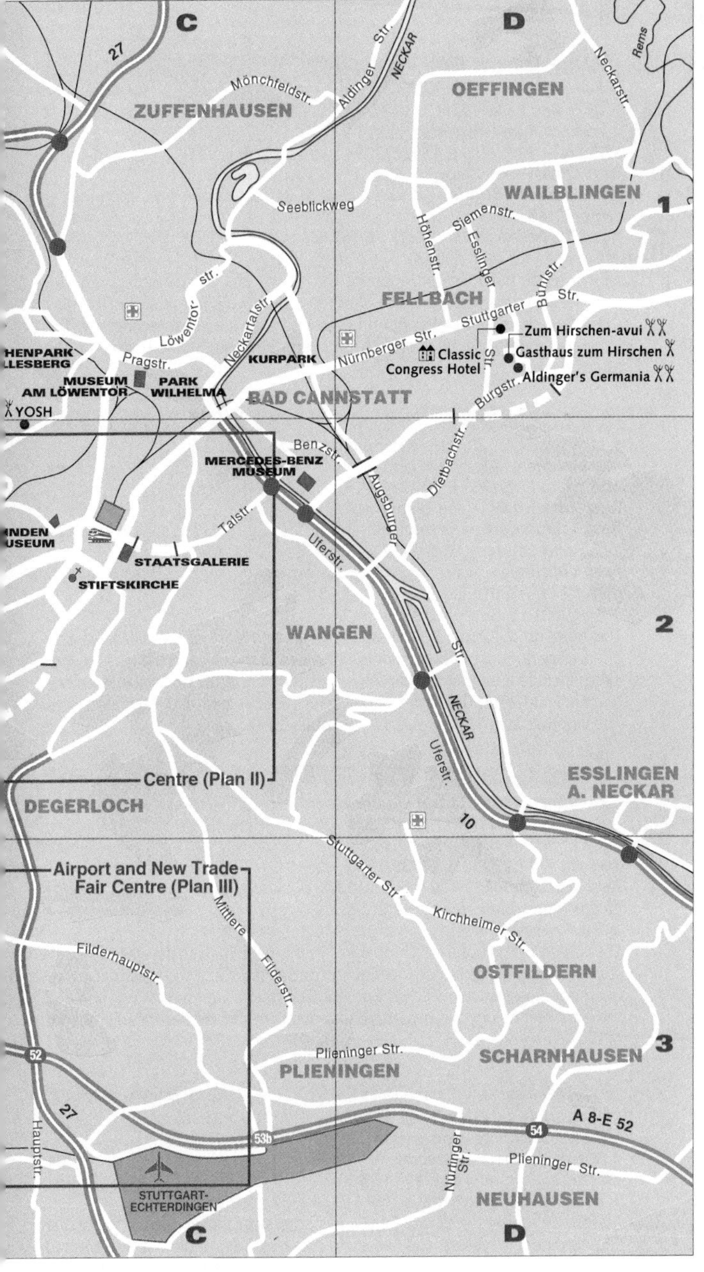

C
D
ZUFFENHAUSEN
OEFFINGEN
WAILBLINGEN
FELLBACH
KURPARK
BAD CANNSTATT
MUSEUM AM LÖWENTOR
PARK WILHELMA
YOSH
MERCEDES-BENZ MUSEUM
STAATSGALERIE
STIFTSKIRCHE
WANGEN
Zum Hirschen-avui
Gasthaus zum Hirschen
Aldinger's Germania
Classic Congress Hotel
Mönchfeldstr.
Aldinger Str.
NECKAR
Neckarstr.
Rems
Seeblickweg
Höhenstr.
Siemenstr.
Esslinger Str.
Bühlstr.
Stuttgarter Str.
Nürnberger Str.
Burgstr.
Löwentor-str.
Pragstr.
Neckartalstr.
Benzstr.
Augsburger Str.
Dietbachstr.
Talstr.
Uferstr.
ESSLINGEN A. NECKAR
Centre (Plan II)
DEGERLOCH
Airport and New Trade Fair Centre (Plan III)
Mittlere Filderstr.
Filderhauptstr.
Stuttgarter Str.
Kirchheimer Str.
OSTFILDERN
Plieninger Str.
PLIENINGEN
SCHARNHAUSEN
A 8-E 52
Hauptstr.
Nürtinger Str.
NEUHAUSEN
STUTTGART-ECHTERDINGEN
1
2
3

Steigenberger Graf Zeppelin

Arnulf-Klett-Platz 7 ✉ 70173
– Ⓜ S. Bahn – ✆ (0711) 2 04 80
– www.stuttgart.steigenberger.de **N1**
155 rm – 115/235 € 125/295 €, 22 € – 1 suite
Rest *Olivo* – see below
Rest *Zeppelin Stüble* – *✆ (0711) 2 04 81 84 (closed Sunday - Monday)*
Carte 22/46 €
Rest *Zeppelino's* – *✆ (0711) 2 04 83 63* – Carte 33/61 €
♦ Chain hotel ♦ Classic ♦
This business hotel located opposite the railway station will offer a reduced number of rooms when it opens after renovation work in mid-2011. The new rooms will be modern, elegant and equipped with the latest technology. The elegant Davidoff Lounge is open to smokers. Zeppelin Stüble boasts a rustic atmosphere.

Am Schlossgarten

Schillerstr. 23 ✉ 70173 – Ⓜ S. Bahn – ✆ (0711) 2 02 60
– www.hotelschlossgarten.com **N1**
106 rm – 222/251 € 279/311 €, 22 € – 4 suites
Rest *Zirbelstube* – see below
Rest *Schlossgarten-Restaurant* – *✆ (0711) 2 02 68 30 (closed Friday lunch and Saturday lunch)* Menu 35/75 € – Carte 40/53 €
Rest *Vinothek* – *✆ (0711) 2 02 68 36 (closed Sunday and Bank Holidays)*
Menu 27 € – Carte 22/29 €
♦ Townhouse ♦ Classic ♦
This hotel on the edge of Schlossgarten Park and close to the railway station offers elegant, contemporary rooms with views of the city and the park. Service extras include a morning paper for every guest. Currently undergoing renovation until mid-2011. The Schlossgarten serves international and regional cuisine. The Vinothek is a Mediterranean-style restaurant and café.

Arcotel Camino

Heilbronner Str. 21 (access via Im Kaisemer 1) ✉ 70191
– Ⓜ S. Bahn – ✆ (0711) 25 85 80
– www.arcotelhotels.com/camino **M1**
168 rm – 135/250 € 135/250 €, 18 € – 3 suites
Rest *Weissenhof* – *✆ (0711) 2 58 58 42 00 (closed Saturday lunch, Sunday lunch)* Menu 25/65 € – Carte 26/46 €
♦ Business ♦ Design ♦
The design of the hotel which operates in this beautifully restored 1890 sandstone building is inspired by the "Camino de Santiago" and the style of the Weißenhofsiedlung residential development. The rooms offer modern design and the latest technology. An elegant, contemporary restaurant decorated in shades of brown and ochre.

Kronen-Hotel without rest

Kronenstr. 48 ✉ 70174 – Ⓜ S. Bahn – ✆ (0711) 2 25 10
– www.kronenhotel-stuttgart.de
– Closed Christmas - 3 January **M1**
80 rm – 108/120 € 149/180 €
♦ Business ♦ Functional ♦
Attentively run by the Berger family, this hotel near the city centre is popular with business travellers and weekend-breakers alike. Individually furnished rooms and the excellent breakfast (served on the terrace in the summer months) add to its charms.

Wörtz zur Weinsteige

Hohenheimer Str. 30 ✉ 70184 – Ⓜ Dobelstr. – ✆ (0711) 2 36 70 00 – www.zur-weinsteige.de **N2**

32 rm – 99/124 € 124/144 €

Rest – *(closed 2 weeks early January, 2 weeks end August, Sunday - Monday and Bank Holidays)* Menu 32/80 € – Carte 36/72 €

♦ Townhouse ♦ Rustic ♦

In the main building the Scherle family hotel offers simple, homely rooms, while those in the annexe, including the stylish Louis XVI junior suite, are more comfortable and elegant. The fish pond contains coy carp for display and sale. Tasty, regional and international food is served at this cosy restaurant.

Der Zauberlehrling

Rosenstr. 38 ✉ 70182 – Ⓜ Olgaeck – ✆ (0711) 2 37 77 70 – www.zauberlehrling.de **N2**

17 rm – 120/195 € 180/270 €, 19 € – 4 suites

Rest *Der Zauberlehrling* – see below

♦ Townhouse ♦ Personalised ♦

This small hotel which occupies two townhouses is run by the Heldmann family. The themed rooms are individually designed and furnished with particular attention to detail. Some have roof terraces.

Unger without rest

Kronenstr. 17 ✉ 70173 – Ⓜ S. Bahn – ✆ (0711) 2 09 90 – www.hotel-unger.de **N1**

114 rm – 104/153 € 143/219 €

♦ Townhouse ♦ Functional ♦

This hotel with its functional rooms is situated just off the pedestrian zone. Some of the rooms on the top floor have balconies. The hotel's art exhibition is particularly interesting.

City-Hotel without rest

Uhlandstr. 18 ✉ 70182 – Ⓜ Olgaeck – ✆ (0711) 21 08 10 – www.cityhotel-stuttgart.de **N2**

31 rm – 79/89 € 95/119 €

♦ Townhouse ♦ Functional ♦

This contemporary hotel close to the pedestrian zone offers individually designed rooms in the contemporary style and a light and airy breakfast room with winter garden and terrace.

Abalon without rest

Zimmermannstr. 7 (access via Olgastr. 79) ✉ 70182 – Ⓜ Olgaeck – ✆ (0711) 2 17 10 – www.abalon.de **N2**

42 rm – 79/89 € 98/129 €

♦ Business ♦ Functional ♦

Located just north of the city centre, this hotel offers functional rooms (with fruit juice and mineral water provided free of charge), a modern breakfast area and leafy roof terrace.

Zirbelstube – Hotel Am Schlossgarten

Schillerstr. 23 ✉ 70173 – Ⓜ S. Bahn – ✆ (0711) 2 02 68 28 – www.hotelschlossgarten.com – Closed 1 - 8 January, 25 - 30 April, 15 August - 6 September and Sunday - Monday **N1**

Rest – *(booking advisable)* Menu 65 € (lunch)/120 € – Carte 99/137 €

Spec. Marinierte Gänsestopfleber auf Erdbeerganache mit Erdbeerschmarrn und Waldmeistergelee. Medaillon von Seeteufel auf Erbsencreme mit Erbsensprossen und Frischkäsenocken. Rinderfilet auf Café de Paris-Creme mit Potpourri von Frühlingsgemüsen und Markknödel.

♦ Classic ♦ Elegant ♦

The gourmet restaurant on the first floor has beautiful pine panelling and a friendly, elegant atmosphere. This is a harmonious setting for Bernhard Diers' modern, classic cuisine, which is presented in the form of three menus. The terrace overlooks the château park.

XXX ✿

Olivo – Hotel Steigenberger Graf Zeppelin

Arnulf-Klett-Platz 7 ✉ 70173 – Ⓜ S. Bahn – ✆ (0711) 2 04 82 77
– www.stuttgart.steigenberger.de
– Closed August - early September and Sunday - Monday **N1**

Rest – Menu 48 € (lunch)/119 € – Carte 69/94 €

Spec. Thunfisch mit Avocado, Ananas und Tomaten-Chili Nage. Lammrücken und confierte Lammkeule mit Tomaten und Oliven. Crema Catalana "légère" mit Erdbeeren und weißem Schokoladenmousse.

♦ Modern ♦ Elegant ♦

Modern, yet classic describes the ambience in this restaurant. Chef Marc Rennhack cooks with contemporary and Mediterranean influences. Lunch menu at midday.

XX ✿

Délice

Hauptstätter Str. 61 ✉ 70178 – Ⓜ Österreichischer Pl.
– ✆ (0711) 6 40 32 22 – www.restaurant-delice.de
– Closed Christmas - 9 January, 1 week over Easter, 2 weeks over Whitsun,
2 weeks end August, Saturday - Sunday and Bank Holidays **M2**

Rest – *(dinner only) (booking essential)* Menu 70/98 € – Carte 60/70 €

Spec. Gebeizte Makrele mit Couscous, Ingwergurke und gebratener Garnele. Kalbsrücken und geschmorte Kalbsschulter mit Senfkohl. Grießnocken mit Lorbeer-Calvadosapfel und Zartbitterschokoladeneis.

♦ Seasonal cuisine ♦ Friendly ♦

In this vaulted restaurant host and sommelier Evangelos Pattas ensures personal and committed service, while chef Benjamin Schuster recommends a menu at the table. Also there is a small à la carte selection. Wine cellar with rarities.

XX

Kern's Pastetchen

Hohenheimer Str. 64 ✉ 70184 – Ⓜ Bopser – ✆ (0711) 48 48 55
– www.kerns-pastetchen.de – Closed Sunday **N2**

Rest – *(dinner only) (booking essential)* Menu 54/68 € – Carte 45/66 €

♦ Classic ♦ Friendly ♦ Rustic ♦

Marieluise and Josef Kern given their own personal welcome to guests to this friendly restaurant with its informal atmosphere and combination of Austrian- and French-inspired cuisine. Wide range of Austrian wines.

XX

San Pietro

Heusteigstr. 45 ✉ 70180 – Ⓜ Österreichischer Pl. – ✆ (0711) 6 07 18 80
– www.santedesantis.de
– Closed August, Sunday and Bank Holidays **M2**

Rest – *(dinner only)* Menu 45/110 € – Carte 36/59 €

♦ Traditional ♦ Elegant ♦ Mediterranean ♦

This Italian restaurant serves good home cooking in the old state parliament building with Piero Cuna managing front-of-house and his partner Sante de Santis looking after the kitchens and running a cookery school. There is also a relaxed wine bar-cum-lounge.

XX

La Fenice

Rotebühlplatz 29 ✉ 70178 – Ⓜ Rotebühlpl. – ✆ (0711) 6 15 11 44
– www.ristorante-la-fenice.de
– Closed Saturday lunch, Sunday and Bank Holidays **M2**

Rest – Menu 19 € (lunch)/55 € – Carte 37/57 €

♦ Italian ♦ Cosy ♦

This light, friendly restaurant with an elegant touch is where the Gorgoglione sisters offer Italian cuisine.

XX

Di Gennaro

Kronprinzstr. 11 ✉ 70173 – Ⓜ Rotebühlpl. – ✆ (0711) 22 29 60 51
– www.digennaro.de – Closed Sunday and Bank Holidays **M2**

Rest – Menu 80 € (dinner) – Carte 43/57 €

♦ Italian ♦ Bistro ♦ Cosy ♦

This modern townhouse in the city centre houses a delicatessen store, a restaurant with bar, and a winery in the cellar. Italian cuisine is on offer.

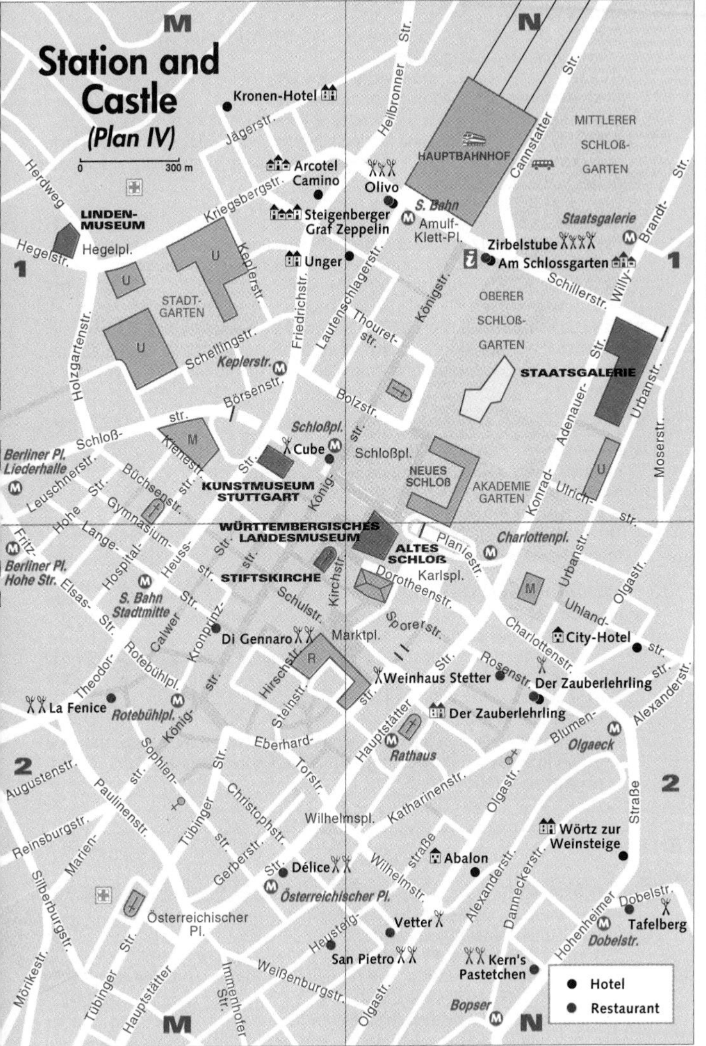

Der Zauberlehrling – Hotel Der Zauberlehrling

Rosenstr. 38 ✉ 70182 – Ⓜ Olgaeck – ✆ (0711) 2 37 77 70
– www.zauberlehrling.de
– Closed Sunday - Monday lunch, Friday lunch, Saturday lunch **N2**
Rest – *(booking advisable)* Menu 49/98 €
– Carte 55/67 €
◆ Inventive ◆ Trendy ◆ Fashionable ◆
This attractive modern hotel is decorated in bright colours with clean, modern lines and serves contemporary, creative cuisine with a regional accent.

Talfelberg

Dobelstr. 2 ✉ 70184 – Ⓜ Dobelstr. – ☎ (0711) 51 89 02 68 – www.tafelberg-stuttgart.de – Closed 15 - 29 August and Sunday - Monday **N2**

Rest – *(dinner only) (booking advisable)* Menu 26/41 € – Carte 25/41 €

♦ Seasonal cuisine ♦ Friendly ♦ Fashionable ♦

A friendly welcome from Nina Ruisinger awaits you in this contemporary style restaurant where her husband prepares ambitious contemporary seasonal dishes in the kitchen.

Cube

Kleiner Schlossplatz 1 (at Kunstmuseum, 4th floor) ✉ 70173 – Ⓜ Schloßpl. – ☎ (0711) 2 80 44 41 – www.cube-restaurant.de

Rest – Menu 30 € (lunch) – Carte 44/56 € **M1**

♦ Mediterranean ♦ Fashionable ♦

This cube-shaped, all-glass building designed by Heinz Witthöft with fantastic views of the Schlosspark and city serves Mediterranean/Asian fusion cuisine. There is also a good value lunchtime menu and snacks are served in the basement bar.

Vetter

Bopserstr. 18 ✉ 70180 – Ⓜ Österreichischer Pl. – ☎ (0711) 24 19 16 – Closed 2 weeks August, Christmas - New Year and Sunday **N2**

Rest – *(dinner only) (booking advisable)* Carte 25/48 €

♦ Regional ♦ Neighbourhood ♦

This comfortable establishment is down a side street in the town centre. Find a modern interior and a selection of regional and international dishes.

Weinhaus Stetter

Rosenstr. 32 ✉ 70182 – Ⓜ Rathaus – ☎ (0711) 24 01 63 – www.weinhaus-stetter.de – Closed 2 weeks early January, 2 weeks end August - early September, Sunday and Bank Holidays **N2**

Rest – *(Monday - Friday open from 3 pm)* Carte 15/32 €

♦ Regional ♦ Simple ♦

This rural style restaurant features regional cooking and a wine shop. The wine selection includes around 600 offerings, with a good representation of Württemberger and French wines.

CENTRE *Plan II*

Le Méridien

Willy-Brandt-Str. 30 ✉ 70173 – Ⓜ Neckartor – ☎ (0711) 2 22 10 – www.lemeridienstuttgart.com **G1**

291 rm – †138/375 € ††138/375 €, ☕ 25 € – 2 suites

Rest *Le Cassoulet* – Menu 35 € (lunch)/65 € (dinner) – Carte 38/62 €

♦ Luxury ♦ Business ♦ Classic ♦

This luxurious hotel is by the Schlossgarten. It has a spacious lobby and modern, elegantly furnished rooms with good technical facilities. Pleasant spa area. Le Cassoulet provides a range of international dishes.

Maritim

Seidenstr. 34 ✉ 70174 – Ⓜ Rosenberg-/Seidenstr. – ☎ (0711) 94 20 – www.maritim.de **F1**

555 rm – †99/229 € ††119/249 €, ☕ 18 € – 12 suites

Rest – *(dinner only)* Carte 31/53 €

♦ Chain hotel ♦ Functional ♦

This spacious hotel connected to the Liederhalle cultural and congress centre is ideal for conference visitors. Both suites and junior suites offer the height of luxury with some rooms boasting "in-room saunas". As well as the Reuchlin restaurant, there is the rotisserie and buffet.

Mercure City-Center

Heilbronner Str. 88 ✉ 70191 – Ⓜ Türlenstr. – ✆ (0711) 25 55 80 – www.mercure.com **G1**

174 rm – †69/179 € ††79/189 €, ☕ 17 € **Rest** – Carte 18/37 €

♦ Chain hotel ♦ Functional ♦

This hotel with its modern functional rooms and convenient location close to the station and motorway is popular with business travellers.

Bellevue

Schurwaldstr. 45 ✉ 70186 – Ⓜ Gaisburg – ✆ (0711) 48 07 60 – www.bellevue-stuttgart.de – Closed August **H1**

12 rm ☕ – †46/61 € ††79 €

Rest – *(closed Tuesday-Wednesday)* Menu 9/27 € – Carte 17/37 €

♦ Family ♦ Functional ♦

Some of the rooms in this small hotel, which has been in family ownership since 1913, offer fine views. A daily newspaper is delivered to guests every morning. The hotel restaurant offers good, plain mainly regional food.

Wielandshöhe (Vincent Klink)

Alte Weinsteige 71 ✉ 70597 – Ⓜ Weinsteige – ✆ (0711) 6 40 88 48 – www.wielandshoehe.de – Closed Sunday and Monday **F3**

Rest – *(booking advisable)* Menu 78/110 € – Carte 53/85 €

Spec. Ganze Seezunge mit Champagnersauce, Blattspinat und Kartoffeln (am Tisch filetiert). Confit vom Perlhuhn mit Sauce Cumberland und Pommes Carrées. Schokoladenpudding mit Vanillesauce und Vanilleglace.

♦ Classic ♦ Fashionable ♦

Enjoy Vincent Klink's cuisine at this restaurant above the city, as well as the fantastic view of Stuttgart – particularly from the window tables and the terrace. The menu is classic with a regional influence.

YOSH

Feuerbacher Weg 101 ✉ 70192 – ✆ (0711) 6 99 69 60 – www.yosh-stuttgart.de – Closed 3 weeks early January, 3 weeks early August and Monday - Tuesday

Rest – *(dinner only) (booking advisable)* Menu 79/139 € – Carte 56/105 € *Plan I* **C2**

♦ Classic ♦ Elegant ♦

Excellent, contemporary, classic based cuisine is served in the comfortable, elegant setting of this restaurant. Dishes are accompanied by a particularly good selection of French and Italian red wines.

Breitenbach

Gebelsbergstr. 97 ✉ 70199 – Ⓜ Bihlpl. – ✆ (0711) 6 40 64 67 – www.restaurant-breitenbach.de – Closed 1 week January, 1 week over Whitsun, 2 weeks August and Sunday - Monday **E3**

Rest – *(dinner only) (booking advisable)* Menu 80 € – Carte 65/89 €

Spec. Halber Hummer mit Erdnussdip, Wasabi-Kaviarrolle, Shisosprossen-Salat und Süßkartoffel-Vinaigrette. Dreierlei vom Milchkalb mit Limonen-Knoblauchsauce und gegrilltem Gemüse. Wassermelonensalat mit Mango-sorbet und Grüntee-Crème brûlée.

♦ Inventive ♦ Friendly ♦ Family ♦

Benjamin Breitenbach cooks international dishes with seasonal and partly Asian touches. Congenially attending to the guests, his wife Sun-Young guarantees a pleasant atmosphere in an elegant setting. Cosy, modern smoking lounge.

Fässle

Löwenstr. 51 ✉ 70597 – Ⓜ Degerloch – ✆ (0711) 76 01 00 – www.faessle.de – Closed Sunday - Monday lunch **F3**

Rest – *(booking advisable)* Menu 34/52 € – Carte 28/46 €

♦ International ♦ Traditional ♦ Fashionable ♦

Dine in the cosy rooms of the lovely old sandstone building, or sit out on the terrace in summer. The food is international and regional and is prepared with care and flavour.

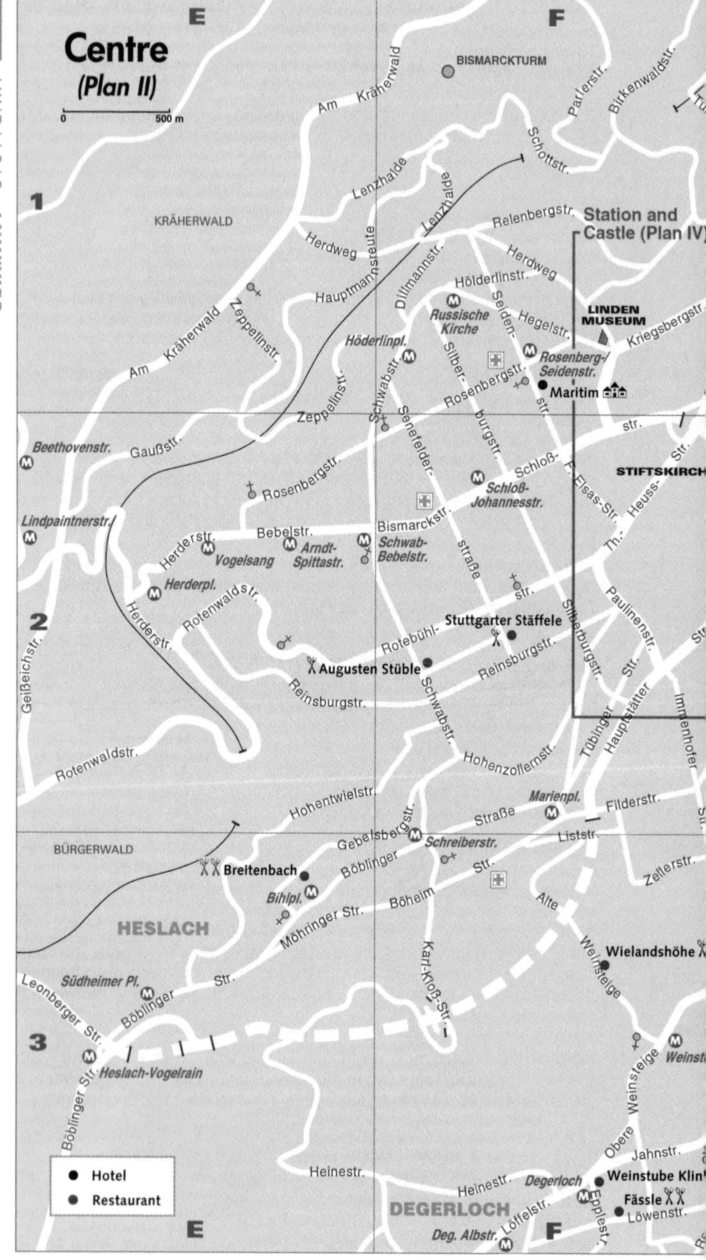
Centre
(Plan II)
0
500 m
E
F
1
2
3
KRÄHERWALD
BISMARCKTURM
Station and Castle (Plan IV)
LINDEN MUSEUM
Maritim
Stuttgarter Stäffele
Augusten Stüble
Breitenbach
Wielandshöhe
Weinstube Klin
Fässle
STIFTSKIRCH
BÜRGERWALD
HESLACH
DEGERLOCH
Russische Kirche
Höderlinpl.
Rosenberg-/ Seidenstr.
Beethovenstr.
Lindpaintnerstr.
Schloß-Johannesstr.
Vogelsang
Arndt-Spittastr.
Schwab-Bebelstr.
Herderpl.
Marienpl.
Schreiberstr.
Bihlpl.
Südheimer Pl.
Heslach-Vogelrain
Degerloch
Deg. Albstr.
Hotel
Restaurant

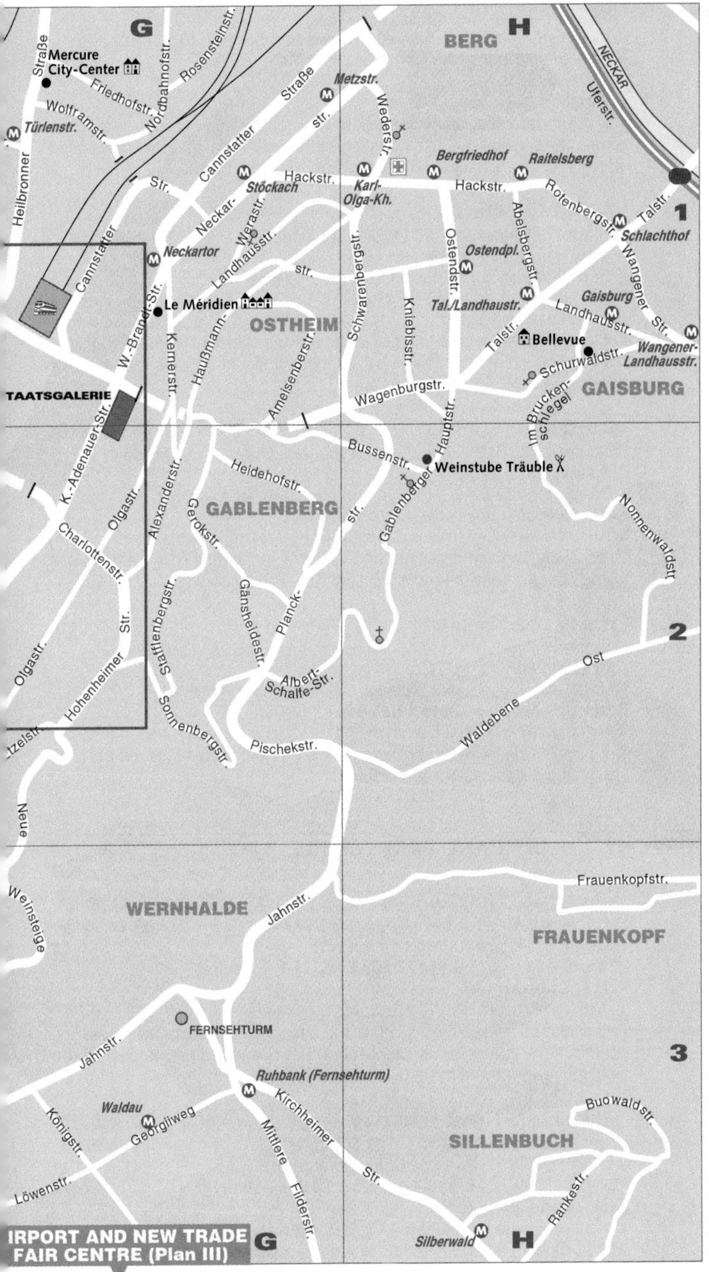
G
H
BERG
NECKAR
Uferstr.
Mercure City-Center
Straße
Friedhofstr.
Rosensteinstr.
Nordbahnhofstr.
Wolframstr.
Türlenstr.
Heilbronner
Metzstr.
Wederstr.
Straße
Str.
Cannstatter
Hackstr.
Stöckach
Karl-Olga-Kh.
Bergfriedhof
Raitelsberg
Hackstr.
Rotenbergstr.
Talstr.
Schlachthof
1
Neckar-
Werastr.
Landhausstr.
Neckartor
Str.
Schwarenbergstr.
Ostendstr.
Ostendpl.
Abelsbergstr.
Wangener
Cannstatter
Le Méridien
OSTHEIM
Kniebisstr.
Tal./Landhausstr.
Gaisburg
Landhausstr.
Str.
W.-Brandt-Str.
Kernerstr.
Haußmann-
Amelsenberstr.
Talstr.
Bellevue
Wangener-Landhausstr.
Schurwaldstr.
TAATSGALERIE
Wagenburgstr.
Im Bruckenschlegel
GAISBURG
K.-Adenauer-Str.
Bussenstr.
Hauptstr.
Weinstube Träuble
Heidehofstr.
Gablenberger
Alexanderstr.
Gerokstr.
GABLENBERG
Str.
Nonnenwaldstr.
Olgastr.
Charlottenstr.
Gänsheidestr.
Planck-
Str.
Stafflenbergstr.
2
Olgastr.
Hohenheimer
Albert-Schäffle-Str.
Ost
Sonnenbergstr.
Waldebene
Pischekstr.
Neue
Weinsteige
Frauenkopfstr.
WERNHALDE
Jahnstr.
FRAUENKOPF
FERNSEHTURM
3
Jahnstr.
Ruhbank (Fernsehturm)
Kirchheimer
Buowaldstr.
Waldau
Georgiiweg
Königstr.
Mittlere
SILLENBUCH
Löwenstr.
Str.
Filderstr.
Rankestr.
IRPORT AND NEW TRADE FAIR CENTRE (Plan III)
G
Silberwald
H

Augusten Stüble

Augustenstr. 104 ✉ 70197 – Ⓜ Schwab-Bebelstr. – ✆ (0711) 62 12 48
Rest – *(dinner only) (booking advisable)* Menu 25/42 € **F2**
– Carte 29/38 €

◆ Regional ◆ Cosy ◆

This comfortable restaurant is located in a corner block on the edge of the town centre. The seasonal menu features regional as well as classic dishes and a good selection of wines. Daily specials are displayed on the board.

Weinstube Klink

Epplestr. 1b (Degerloch) ✉ 70597 – Ⓜ Degerloch – ✆ (0711) 7 65 32 05
– www.weinstube-klink.de
– Closed Saturday lunch, Sunday and Bank Holidays **F3**
Rest – *(booking advisable)* Carte 22/39 €

◆ Regional ◆ Rustic ◆

Regular guests appreciate this restaurant, which is somewhat hidden in an interior courtyard. It offers a small Swabian menu and a good wine selection. The daily specials are displayed on a slate.

Stuttgarter Stäffele

Buschlestr. 2a ✉ 70178 – Ⓜ Schloß-Johannesstr. – ✆ (0711) 66 41 90
– www.staeffele.de
– Closed Saturday lunch, Sunday lunch and Bank Holidays lunch
Rest – *(booking advisable)* Carte 23/39 € **F2**

◆ Schwaben cuisine ◆ Cosy ◆

This friendly Swabian restaurant and wine bar has several cosy dining rooms lovingly decorated with various local artefacts. Parking service.

Weinstube Träuble

Gablenberger Hauptstraße 66 (entrance Bussenstraße) ✉ 70186
– Ⓜ Ostendpl. – ✆ (0711) 46 54 28
– Closed end August - mid September, Sunday and Bank Holidays
Rest – *(dinner only)* Carte 19/51 € **H2**

◆ Regional ◆ Wine bar ◆

The panelled dining room of this tiny 200-year-old house is extremely cosy. Snacks and daily specials are available.

AIRPORT – NEW TRADE FAIR CENTRE *Plan III*

Mövenpick Hotel Airport

Flughafenstr. 50 ✉ 70629 – ✆ (0711) 55 34 40
– www.moevenpick-stuttgart-airport.com **L2**
326 rm – †110/275 € ††125/300 €, ☕ 21 € – 2 suites
Rest – Carte 31/47 €

◆ Conference hotel ◆ Business ◆ Design ◆

This ultra-modern business hotel at the airport offers great views from the upper storeys. Luxury corner junior suites. This clean-lined grey and white restaurant offers a view of the airport terminals.

Millennium Hotel & Resort

Plieninger Str. 100 ✉ 70567 – Ⓜ Salzacker
– ✆ (0711) 72 10 – www.milleniumhotels.com **J1**
454 rm – †99/184 € ††99/184 €, ☕ 20 € – 1 suite
Rest – Carte 19/54 €

◆ Conference hotel ◆ Business ◆ Functional ◆

A large, modern hotel with rooms of various categories. The SI experience centre and its Musical Theatre are right on the doorstep. Access to the Swabian springs. Choose between 19 different restaurants, bars and cafés.

Pullman Fontana

Vollmoellerstr. 5 ✉ 70563 – Ⓜ Vaihingen – ✆ (0711) 73 00
– www.pullmanhotels.com **I1**

252 rm – 129/159 € 149/179 €, 20 € – 2 suites
Rest – Menu 31 € – Carte 29/54 €

♦ Chain hotel ♦ Business ♦ Classic ♦

This luxury hotel offers comfortable rooms in the traditional style with fine views from the upper storeys. It also has offers bright and airy modern leisure facilities. An informal yet elegant restaurant with winter garden.

Recknagels Traube

Brabandtgasse 2 ✉ 70599 – Ⓜ Plieningen – ✆ (0711) 45 89 20
– www.hotel-traube-stuttgart.de
– Closed 23 December - 3 January **L2**

19 rm – 99/149 € 129/199 €
Rest – *(closed Sunday and Bank Holidays) (dinner only)*
Carte 25/34 €

♦ Country house ♦ Rustic ♦

This small hotel run by the Recknagel family occupies an old half-timbered townhouse and two guest houses and offers comfortable, individually furnished rooms. Recki's Wirtshaus is a bar/restaurant in an old smithy serving good plain food. Attractive terrace.

Am Park

Lessingstr. 4 (Leinfelden) ✉ 70771 – Ⓜ Unteraichen – ✆ (0711) 90 31 00
– www.hotelampark-leinfelden.de
– Closed 23 December - 11 January **J2**

42 rm – 85/110 € 95/140 €
Rest – *(closed Saturday - Sunday)* Carte 30/56 €

♦ Business ♦ Functional ♦

Run by the Schienle family, this hotel with its blue and white façade is situated in a quiet location in a cul-de-sac near the park. Its rooms are meticulously maintained and well-equipped. Flavoursome regional food is served attentively in the cosy dining rooms. A pretty beer garden also belongs to the restaurant.

Gloria

Sigmaringer Str. 59 ✉ 70567 – Ⓜ Sigmaringer Str. – ✆ (0711) 7 18 50
– www.hotelgloria.de **J1**

85 rm – 78/115 € 115/150 €
Rest *Möhringer Hexle* – *✆ (0711) 7 18 51 17 (closed Sunday dinner, Bank Holidays dinner)* Carte 24/44 €

♦ Business ♦ Functional ♦

This excellent hotel with its convenient location has been run by Evelin Kraft for more than 20 years. It offers high-quality contemporary rooms, the most spacious of which are located on the top floor. This informal restaurant serves Mediterranean cuisine and has a winter garden and terrace.

top air

in the airport (Terminal 1, Level 4) ✉ 70629 – ✆ (0711) 9 48 21 37
– www.restaurant-top-air.de
– Closed end December - mid January, August, Saturday - Sunday and Bank Holidays **L2**

Rest – Menu 42 € (lunch)/108 € – Carte 61/100 €
Spec. Parfait von der Gänsestopfleber mit Feigen, Gewürzganache und Schokoladen-Haselnussgelee. Confierter Kalbsbauch und gebratene Jakobsmuscheln mit Erbsencrème, schwarze Oliven, Pfifferlingen und Röstzwiebeljus. Schokoladen-Speckkaramell mit Dreierlei von der Birne.

♦ Inventive ♦ Friendly ♦ Fashionable ♦

The large glass frontage on the top floor of the airport terminal offers a great view of the tarmac. Claudio Urru's interesting creations are French-Mediterranean inspired and display ambition and creativity.

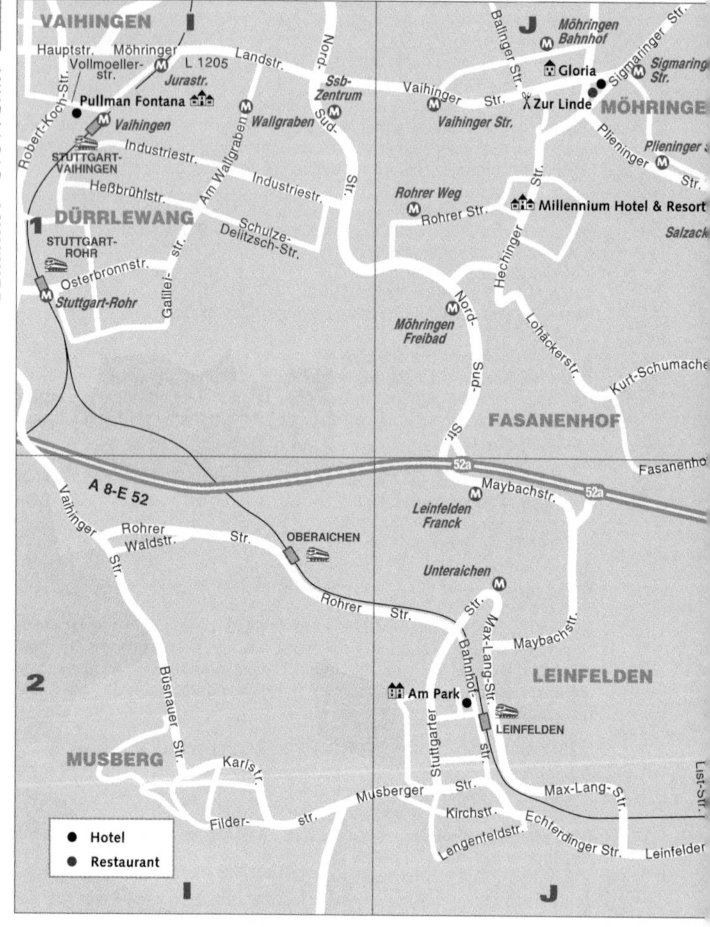

Speisemeisterei (Frank Oehler)

Schloss Hohenheim ✉ 70599 – Ⓜ Plieningen – ☎ (0711) 34 21 79 79
– *www.speisemeisterei.de*
– *Closed Tuesday* **L1**

Rest – *(booking advisable)* Menu 70/90 € – Carte 70/88 €

Spec. Gänseleberterrine mit Rhabarber, Pistazien und Vanillebrioche. Hausgemachte Pasta mit frischen Morcheln, Erbsen und Haselnüssen. Involtini vom Schwein mit Tomatenbutter, gebratenem Spargel und Florentiner Nocken.

♦ Seasonal cuisine ♦ Fashionable ♦ Classic ♦

In the stylish cavalry quarters of the château, stucco, chandeliers and antique parquet meet clean-lined, modern design. The cuisine is distinguished by the individual style of Frank Oehler, the flavour of the food and its creative presentation.

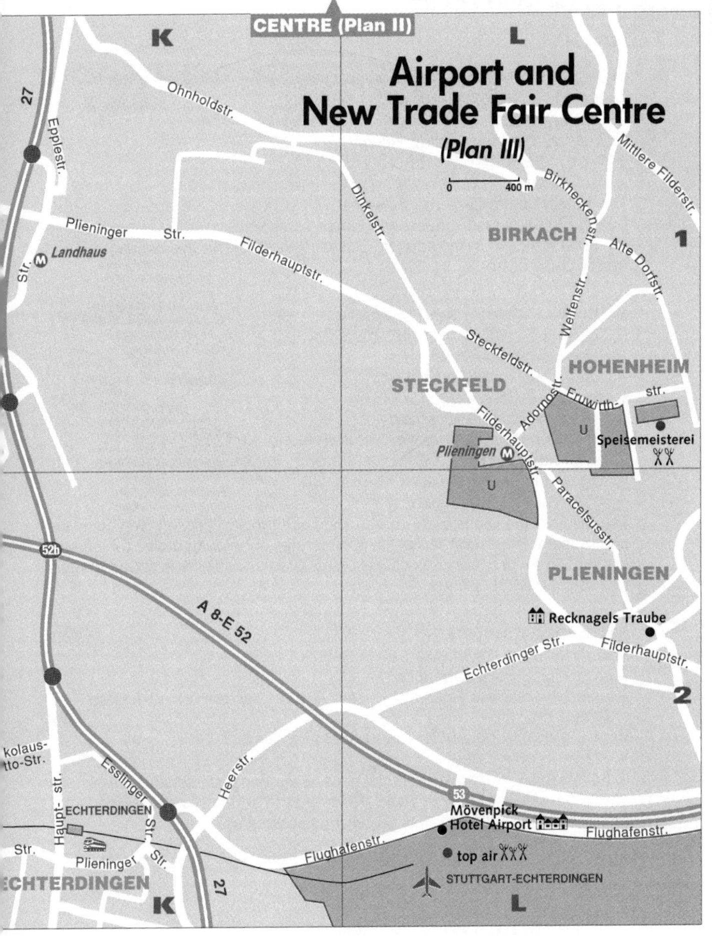

Zur Linde

Sigmaringer Str. 49 ✉ 70567
– Ⓜ Sigmaringer Str.
– ✆ (0711) 7 19 95 90
– www.joergmink.com J1

Rest – *(booking advisable)*
Carte 28/49 €

◆ Regional ◆ Inn ◆

The cosy dining rooms in this listed restaurant offer typical Swabian fare including home-made Maultaschen, a local speciality. Traditional vaulted basement room for functions.

ENVIRONS OF STUTTGART — *Plan I*

AT FELLBACH

Classic Congress Hotel without rest

Tainer Str. 7 ✉ 70734 – ✆ (0711) 5 85 90
– www.cch-bw.de
– Closed 23 December - early January **D1**
149 rm – 99/159 € 123/183 €
◆ Business ◆ Conference hotel ◆ Functional ◆

This hotel's comfortable rooms, some with park views, are accessed via the bright, high-ceilinged atrium-style lobby. Conference rooms are available in the hotel itself and in the adjacent Schwabenlandhalle. In the evenings try the trendy Chilys bistro.

Zum Hirschen - avui (Armin Karrer) with rm

Hirschstr. 1 ✉ 70734 – ✆ (0711) 9 57 93 70
– www.zumhirschen-fellbach.de
– Closed 1 week over Carnival, end July - August and Saturday - Monday
9 rm – 85/95 € 115/135 € **D1**
Rest *Gasthaus zum Hirschen* – see below
Rest – *(dinner only) (booking essential)* Menu 98/128 €
Spec. Langostinos mit Grapefuit und Ingwer. Kalbsbries mit Ahornsenf, Pfifferlingen und Rettich. Dessert-Degustation.
◆ Innovative ◆ Elegant ◆

The "avui" in the vaults of this pretty 16C half-timbered house is very intimate and modern. The patron serves flavour intensive dishes with molecular influences in the form of a four or six-course menu. These include lavish appetisers and interesting dessert tastings.

Aldinger's Germania

Schmerstr. 6 ✉ 70734 – ✆ (0711) 58 20 37
– www.aldingers-germania.de
– Closed 2 weeks mid February, 3 weeks August - September and Sunday - Monday **D1**
Rest – *(booking advisable)* Menu 35/45 € – Carte 30/48 €
◆ Regional ◆ Cosy ◆

In this Swabian family restaurant the third generation is still serving guests in its cosy rooms. Volker Adlinger cooks down-to-earth and tasty regional food with an international influence. Vaulted cellar for celebrations.

Gasthaus zum Hirschen – Restaurant Zum Hirschen - avui

Hirschstr. 1 ✉ 70734 – ✆ (0711) 9 57 93 70
– www.zumhirschen-fellbach.de
– Closed 1 week over Carnival, end July - August **D1**
Rest – *(booking advisable)* Menu 34/50 € – Carte 29/55 €
◆ Traditional ◆ Rurally ◆ Fashionable ◆

This somewhat more down-to-earth alternative to the gourmet restaurant offers good traditional food with contemporary elements. Dishes can also be enjoyed on the attractive terrace in summer.

AT ZUFFENHAUSEN

Christophorus

Porscheplatz 5 (at Porsche Museum) ✉ 70435 – ✆ (0711) 91 12 59 80
– www.porsche.com – Closed Sunday dinner and Monday **B1**
Rest – Menu 36/95 € – Carte 51/85 €
◆ Mediterranean ◆ Design ◆ Retro ◆

Seasonally influenced cuisine is served on the top floor of this modern, futuristic building. The speciality is US prime beef from the grill. There is a bistro and coffee bar on the ground floor. Smoking lounge.

GREECE

ELLÁDA

PROFILE

→ **Area:**
131 944 km²
(50 944 sq mi).

→ **Population:**
10 749 943 inhabitants (est. 2010), density = 81 per km².

→ **Capital:**
Athens (conurbation 3 761 810 inhabitants).

→ **Currency:**
Euro (€); rate of exchange: € 1 = US$ 1.37 (Dec. 2010).

→ **Government:**
Parliamentary republic (since 1974). Member of European Union since 1981.

→ **Language:**
Greek.

→ **Specific public holidays:**
Epiphany (6 January); Orthodox Shrove Monday (late February-March); Independence Day (25 March); Orthodox Good Friday (Friday before Easter); Orthodox Easter Monday; Day of the Holy Spirit (late May-June); Ochi Day (28 October); Boxing Day (26 December).

→ **Local Time:**
GMT + 2 hours in winter and GMT + 3 hours in summer.

→ **Climate:**
Temperate Mediterranean, with mild winters and hot, sunny summers (Athens: January: 10°C, July: 27°C).

→ **International dialling code:**
00 30 followed by local number.

→ **Emergency:**
General Police: ✆ **100**, Tourist Police: ✆ **171**, Ambulance: ✆ **166.**

→ **Electricity:**
220 volts AC, 50Hz; 2-pin round-shaped continental plugs.

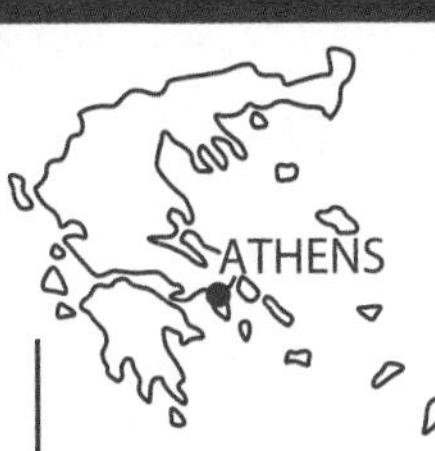

→ **Formalities**
Travellers from the European Union (EU), Switzerland, Iceland and the main countries of North and South America need a national identity card or passport (America: passport required) to visit Greece for less than three months (tourism or business purpose). For visitors from other countries a visa may be required, in addition to a passport, especially for those wishing to stay for longer than three months. We advise you to check with your embassy before travelling.

ATHENS

ATHÍNA

Population: 750 000 (conurbation 3 750 000) – Altitude: 156m

ɛfanos Kyriazis/Fotolia.com

So what did the Greeks ever do for us? Apart from inventing democracy, the theatre and the Olympic Games, that is... and planting the seeds of philosophy and Western Civilisation, of course... Athens was central to all of these, a city that became a byword for glory and learning, a place whose golden reputation could inspire such awe in later centuries that just the mention of its name was enough to turn people misty-eyed and reverential: the poets Lamartine and Byron are just two who waxed lyrical over its splendours.

It's a truly magical place, built upon eight hills and plains, with a recorded history stretching back at least 3,000 years. Its short but highly productive golden age (roughly 470BC to 430BC) resulted in the architectural glory of The Acropolis, while the likes of Plato, Aristotle and Socrates were in the business of changing the mindset of society. In more recent times, Athens suffered at the hands of the motor car, the heat and the mountains, a notorious cocktail producing a fog that would hang over the city like a heavy hand, reaching such gruesome levels that even tourists stayed away. But since the 1980s and up to and beyond the 2004 Olympics, the city has made great efforts to regenerate itself with imaginative planning and a much-needed metro. Hip clubs and restaurants have sprung up. Quaint inner city areas have been restored. Could the glory days of Athens be returning?

LIVING THE CITY

No one could possibly argue with the fact that **The Acropolis** dominates Athens. It can be seen peeking through alleyways and turnings all over the city. Beneath it lies a teeming metropolis, part urban melting pot, part uber-buzzy neighbourhood. **Plaka**, below the Acropolis, is the old quarter, and the most visited, a mixture of great charm and cheap gift shops. North and west, **Monastiraki** and **Psiri** has become a trendy zone after decades of decay; to the east, Syntagma and Kolonaki are notably modern and smart, home to the Greek parliament and the rich and famous; you can look down on them – literally and metaphorically, if you wish – from the glorious green heights of Lykkavittos Hill. The most northerly districts of central Athens are **Omonia** and **Exarcheia**, distinguished by their rugged appearance, and steeped in history; much of the life in these parts is centred round the polytechnic and the central marketplace.

PRACTICAL INFORMATION

ARRIVAL-DEPARTURE

If you're coming to the city by sea, or intending to visit the islands, then your port of call is Piraeus, a few miles from Athens. Piraeus is now the third largest port in the Mediterranean.

Athens International Airport is 33km east of the city. A taxi can take a while so your best bet is to hop on the metro and take Line 3 to Monastiraki.

TRANSPORT

Because of that traffic, the sensible way of getting around town is by the metro. Two new lines were opened in 2001 and accessibility round Athens is now markedly better than a decade ago.

Buses and trolley-buses run an excellent service (though hampered by traffic). Carnets of 10 tickets are available from newsstands, OASA booths and kiosks and at metro or subway stations.

EXPLORING ATHENS

Where can you start exploring Athens other than at the **Acropolis**? The world's most famous hill shows evidence of settlements as far back as Neolithic times, but the reign of Pericles in the fifth century BC produced buildings so stylistical-

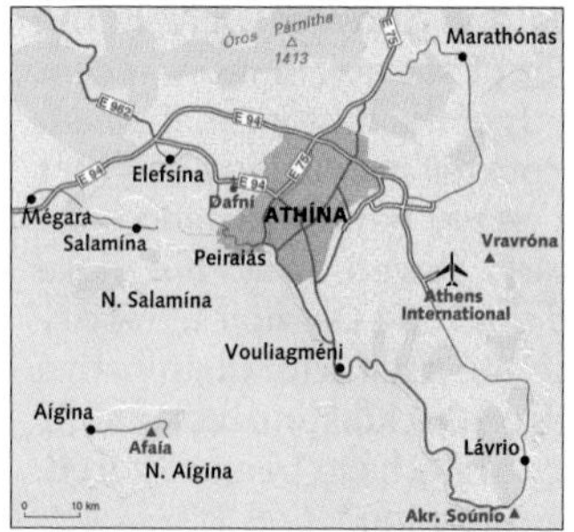

ly perfect that they're considered, 2,500 years later, the most important monuments in the Western world and the greatest-ever influence on our architecture. These great marble masterpieces were mostly temples built to honour **Athena**, the city's patron goddess. Their scale and breathtaking proportion manage to triumph on both a majestic and a human level, a testament to the ancient architects Iktinos and Kallikrates and the unerring eye of their supervising sculptor Phidias. The **Parthenon**, much of which still stands before us today, was completed in just 10 years, an amazing achievement. When you're up at the summit of the sacred rock of Athens, take your pick of the temples around you: The Parthenon (a must), Propyleia (the grand entrance temple), the small Temple of Athena Nike, or the exceptional Ionic structure of the Erechtheion. There are two ancient theatres also on the Acropolis, including one still used for the Athens Festival (Herodes Atticus Theatre). The other is the Dionysus Theatre, the world's oldest, where plays by Sophocles and Euripedes were staged. When visiting the Acropolis, try to get there in the early morning or evening, because crowds and midday heat can sap even the most enthusiastic classicist.

If it's just too damn hot up there at the summit, you don't have to walk far to find shady relief…and buildings dating back even further than the Parthenon. The ancient **Agora** is a grassy haven at the base of the hill, the one-time marketplace founded in the sixth century BC where the likes of Socrates would make impassioned speeches to interested passers-by. Its rambling and varied remains can confuse the unwary visitor, but it doesn't take much to fall into a reverie about the lively events that once happened here (it was the centre for civic activities such as commerce, politics, arts and athletics) and it's also where you come face-to-face with the best-preserved Classical temple in Greece, the **Temple of Hephaestus**. Stroll across to the area east of this at the bottom of the Acropolis and you're in **Plaka**, the old town section that's become the gathering place for tourists and travellers, especially in the warm Athenian evenings. Its charming ambience is captured in winding alleyways haunted by a medieval air (and touts in midsummer). Seek out nuggets of sheer delight, such as the irresistible Byzantine courtyards, and the delightful hidden neighbourhood of **Anafiotika**, which clings to the foot of the Acropolis, and contains idyllic blue-and-white houses built in the 19 C by Cycladic workmen. Just up from here stands The Tower of the Winds, built in 50 BC by a Syrian astronomer, with personifications of the winds on each of its eight sides – there's no other building like it in the ancient world.

➜ THE PAST AND THE PRESENTS

You can go from one end of the retail extreme to the other in central Athens; if you favour the cheaper option, then get up early on a Sunday and head for the **Monastiraki flea market**. Fabled throughout the Hellenic world, it takes place right next to the Agora, with traders and buyers filling the surrounding streets. Everything's for sale, from tat to things like antique furnishings and rare books. Just remember to haggle. At the other end of the shopping scale are the designer boutiques of **Kolonaki**, where haggling is most definitely not an option. This is the area where you can find the Parliament building, adjacent to which, along the avenue of Vassilissis Sofias, is the renowned **Museum Row**, home to four of Athens' finest. Nearest the Parliament building, The **Benaki Museum** is one of the best in Greece. It contains a fabulously all-encompassing range of prehistoric to 20 C Greek art, and its lovely rooftop garden restaurant is worth the visit in itself. Next along is the Museum of Cycladic Art, featuring elegant female figures carved 2,000 years before the Parthenon; the Byzantine Museum chronicles the rise and fall of the great Byzantine Empire from the third to the nineteenth century; and finally, the War Museum, on two huge floors, tells the history of conflict in Greece from prehistoric to modern times. Trumping all these fine collections, though, is the **National Archaeological Museum**, up in Exarcheia. Not only is this the number one museum in Greece, it's also one of the best in the world, containing a week's worth of ancient wonders to discover. Chief of these are arguably the treasures of the Mycenaean civilization, including hoards of gold and fantastical golden swords.

→ TECHNO ART

So, where does an Athenian go for the edgy, the arty and the gallery-strewn? Answer: a one-time toxin-spewing foundry in the Gaslands ('Gazi' in Greek), a former dingy neck of the woods just northwest of the Agora. This old foundry has been converted into a huge arts centre called **Technopolis**, where concerts, exhibits and arts spaces, generally of the first order, come together under one gargantuan roof with coloured lights illuminating the old chimneys. Some of the city's sleekest restaurants now nestle in the surrounding streets, while the neighbouring quarters of Thissio and Psiri have benefitted too, with grungy Greek music dives and squares dotted with bars and cafés sidling in alongside the industrial behemoths of yesteryear.

Athens is a hot and steamy place in the summer, so areas of green refuge are not just welcome but essential. South of the Acropolis is **Filopappou Hill**, the highest point in southern Athens, boasting superb views out to sea and, on its pathway up to the peak, a small cave that's said to be where Socrates was held after being sentenced to death for corrupting the youth of the city. The hill is full of shade and interesting paths. Back down to earth, you can escape the traffic in the rather wonderful National Gardens, next to the Parliament Building in Syntagma. These are full of exotic plants and winding paths, statuary and fountains. You may feel so intoxicated by this abundantly verdant oasis that you get lost (it has been known). Lykkavittos Hill, to the east of town, is accessible by foot, but most people take the funicular. It boasts stupendous views over the city from its Chapel of St George at the peak. There are a few little cafés dotted around the hill, great places to sip a drink or two as the sun goes down.

CALENDAR HIGHLIGHTS

Summer time is party time for Athenians. The Hellenic Festival runs from June to September and performances take place in a wonderful setting - the awe-inspiring Odeon of Herodes Atticus, which is backed by the floodlit Acropolis: other events featuring music, theatre and dance take place at venues around town. During the same months, The International Petra Festival at Petra Theatre gives it a good run for its money with an eclectic variety of music and theatre. The European Jazz Festival blasted off in Athens in 2001 and is now a renowned event for international names - it takes place in June at Gazi's Technopolis. Rock fans, meanwhile, should make for Terravibe in June for Rockwave Festival, the

ATHENS IN...

→ ONE DAY
Acropolis, Parthenon, Agora and Temple of Hephaestus, Plaka

→ TWO DAYS
Kolonaki, National Archaeological Museum, Filopappou Hill

→ THREE DAYS
Monastiraki flea-market (on Sunday), Benaki Museum, Technopolis, National Gardens, Lykkavittos Hill

best in Greece. It's a full-on rock celebration and includes bungee jumping and a skate park. The Dora Stratou Theatre is home to a renowned program of Greek folk dances from May to September, while The Greek Orthodox calendar highlight occurs at Easter, when a most impressive looking candlelit procession climbs Lykavittos Hill to the chapel of Agios Georgos. Talking of atmosphere: every August all Athens' monuments and archaeological sights are open to the public for free for moonlit classical performances under the title 'Nights Under The Full Moon'.

EATING OUT

In recent times, Michelin has been busy in Athens awarding stars for the smart new wave of restaurants that has hit the city. With many chefs now going abroad to train and returning home to put their nifty skills to good use, this is a fine time to eat out in the shadow of the Acropolis. If you want to get the full experience and dine with the locals (rather than the tourists), make your reservation for late evening, as Greeks rarely go out for dinner before 10pm. There's a good range of flavours in vogue, as ethnic menus have come to the fore, highlighted by Asian and Moroccan dishes. Sushi is now a big fish in Athens, too. And the trend towards a more eclectic restaurant scene now means that classic French and Italian cuisine is easily found. New modern tavernas offer good attention to detail, but this doesn't mean they're replacing the wonderfully traditional old favourites. These tavernas, along with mezedopoleia, are the backbone of Greek dining, and most visitors wouldn't think their trip was complete without eating in at least one or two. Often the waiter will just tell you what's cooking today, and you're often very welcome to go into the kitchen and make your selection. Greece is a country where it is customary to tip good service; ten per cent is the normal rate.

→ UNIFORM APPEAL

A time-honoured tourist ritual is having a gander at the changing of the guard outside the Parliament Building, on the hour every hour. Individual soldiers perform an eye-catching high kicking march, wearing mini skirts, white stockings, and red clogs with pom-poms. Selected from the ranks of Greek military conscripts, they're chosen these days not because of any warlike efficiency, but because of crowd-pleasing height and good looks.

→ MARBLES RE-FOUND

The exciting Acropolis Museum in Makrigianni, at the foot of Acropolis hill, is more than just a stunning, all-glass showpiece for its fabulous treasures. It's a sharp reminder that Greece now has a safe and adequate home for its **Marbles**, purloined by the Earl of Elgin in 1799 and sold to the British Museum where they remain to this day. After gazing at them for hours, Keats summed up the beauty of the Marbles when he famously wrote: 'Beauty is truth, truth beauty – that is all ye know on earth, and all ye need to know.'

→ A LONG WAIT FOR THE METRO

If you fancy a trip to a museum, you could do worse than nip down into the metro. During construction, many of the stations unearthed ancient remains, and these have been put on display for travellers or curious tourists; expect to find the likes of pottery and gravestones, even a skeleton still entombed. Two of the best stations are Syntagma and Akropoli. Catching a train afterwards is optional.

A
B
1
2
3
ΠΛΑΤ. ΑΙΓΥΠΤΟΥ
Pl. Egiptou
Alexandras
Ioulianou
ΑΧΑΡΝΩΝ
Γ' ΣΕΠΤΕΜΒΡΙΟΥ
Septemvriou
28
ΜΕΤΣΟΒΟΥ
ΜΠΟΥΜΠΟΥΛΙΝΑΣ
ΣΠΥΡ. ΤΡΙΚΟΥΠΗ
Larissis
ΗΠΕΙΡΟΥ
ETHNIKÓ ARHEOLOGIKÓ MOUSSÍO
ΤΟΣΙΤΣΑ
Museum
ΝΕΟΦ ΜΕΤΑΞΑ
Neof. Metaxa
ΛΙΟΣΙΩΝ
Liossion
ΙΩΑΝΝΙΝΩΝ
Deligiani
H
ΜΑΡΝΗ
Marni
Art
ΟΚΤΩΒΡΙΟΥ
Oktovriou
(Patission)
ΣΤΟΥΡΝ ΑΡΑ
POLITEHNÍOU
ΕΜΙΣΤΟΚΛΕΟΥΣ
PELOPONISSOS
ΧΙΟΥ
ΨΑΡΩΝ
ΠΛΑΤ. ΒΑΘΗΣ
Pl. Vathis
ΠΛΑΤ. ΚΑΝ ΙΓΓΟΣ
Pl. Kaningos
ΛΕΝΟΡΜΑΝ
ΦΑΒΙΕΡΟΥ
ΑΚΑΔΗΜΙΑΣ
Akadimias
Metaxourghio
Karolou
Omonia
Pl. Karaïskaki
ΑΓ. ΚΩΝΣΤΑΝΤΙΝΟΥ
Ag. Konstandinou
ΜΕΝΑΝΔΡΟΥ
ΟΜΟΝΟΙΑ
ΠΑΝ ΕΠΙΣΤΗΜΙΟΥ
Panepistimiou
ΔΕΛΗΓΙΩΡΓΗ
ΕΘΝ VIVLIOTH
ΑΧΙΛΛΕΩΣ
Ahileos
ΑΛΕΞΑΝΔΡΟΥ
ΚΟΛΟΚΥΝΘΟΥΣ
ΣΤΑΔΙΟΥ
Stadiou
METAXOURGÍO
ΠΛΑΤ. ΚΟΤΖΙΑ
Pl. Kodzia
ΘΕΡΜΟΠΥΛΩΝ
ΜΥΛΛΕΡΟΥ
Panepistimio
ΤΣΑΛΔΑΡΗ
Tsaldari
Sofokleous
KENDRIKÍ AGORÁ
ΠΛΑΤ. ΚΛΑΥΘΜΩΝΟΣ
Pl. Klafthmonos
ΜΕΓ.
ΚΕΡΑΜΕΙΚΟΥ
ΠΑΝΑΓΗ
Panagi
ΕΥΡΙΠΙΔΟΥ
Arion
ΑΙΟΛΟΥ
Eolou
M
ΠΛΑΤ. ΕΛΕΥΘΕΡΙΑΣ
Pl. Eleftherias
ΣΑΡΡΗ
ΑΡΙΣΤΟΦΑΝΟΥΣ
ETHNIK ISTORIK MOUSS
Athiri
Eridanus
Varoulko
ΚΡΙΕΖΗ
ΑΘΗΝΑΣ
Athinas
ΚΟΛΟΚΟΤΡΩΝΗ
(ΠΕΙΡΑΙΩΣ)
(Pireos)
KERAMIKÓS
O & B
Hytra
KAPNIKARÉA
Ermo
Keramikós
Mitropoleos
ΜΗΤΡΟΠΟΛΕΩ
ΕΡΜΟΥ
PL. MONASTIRÁKI
Thissio
Kuzina
MIKRÍ MITRÓPOLI
Monastiraki
Herr
ΑΔΡΙΑΝΟ
THISSÍO
MONASTIRAKI
ROMAÏKÍ AGORÁ
PLÁKA
ARHÉA AGORÁ
ΑΠΟΣΤΟΛΟΥ
Apostolou
Nileos
Psarra's
ÁRIOS PÁGOS
ASTEROSKOPÍO
AKRÓPOLI
KÉNDR MELETÓ AKROPOL
LÓFOS NIMFÓN
ΠΑΥΛΟΥ
Pavlou
ODIOU IRÓDOU ATIKOÚ
THÉATRO DIONÍSSOU
Aeropogitou
PNÍKA
Dionissiou
Akro
ΡΟΒ. ΓΚΑΛΛΙ
ΠΑΡΘΕΝΩΝΟΣ
Parthenonos
ΧΑΤΖΗΧΡ ΤΟΥ
LÓFOS FILOPÁPOU
Divani Palace Acropolis

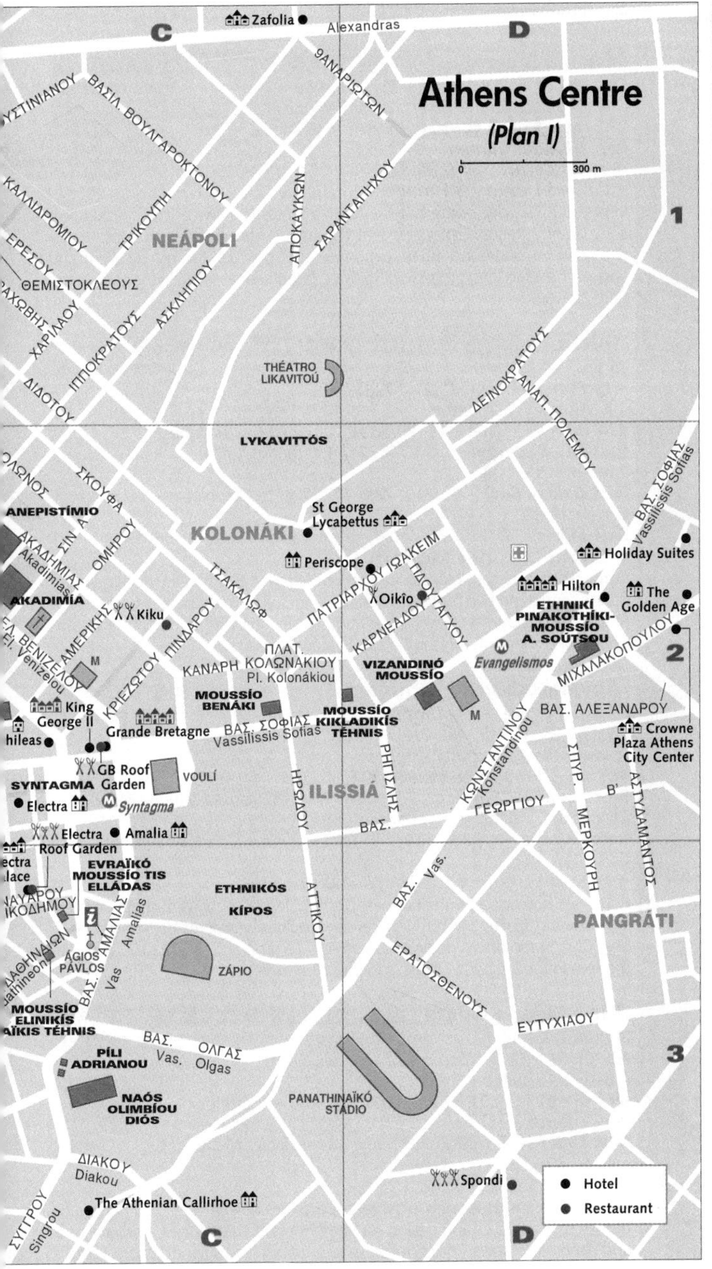

Athens Centre
(Plan I)
0
300 m
Zafolia
Alexandras
C
D
1
2
3
NEÁPOLI
LYKAVITTÓS
KOLONÁKI
ILISSIÁ
PANGRÁTI
THÉATRO LIKAVITOÚ
St George Lycabettus
Periscope
Oikîo
Holiday Suites
Hilton
The Golden Age
ETHNIKÍ PINAKOTHÍKI-MOUSSÍO A. SOÚTSOU
Evangelismos
Crowne Plaza Athens City Center
VIZANDINÓ MOUSSÍO
MOUSSÍO BENÁKI
MOUSSÍO KIKLADIKÍS TÉHNIS
ANEPISTÍMIO
AKADIMÍA
Kiku
King George II
Grande Bretagne
GB Roof Garden
VOULÍ
SYNTAGMA
Electra
Syntagma
Electra Roof Garden
Amalia
EVRAÏKÓ MOUSSÍO TIS ELLÁDAS
ETHNIKÓS KÍPOS
ÁGIOS PÁVLOS
ZÁPIO
MOUSSÍO ELINIKÍS
PÍLI ADRIANOU
NAÓS OLIMBÍOU DIÓS
PANATHINAÏKÓ STÁDIO
Spondi
The Athenian Callirhoe
Diakou
Singrou
Vassilissis Sofias
Pl. Kolonákiou
Vas. Olgas
Vas. Amalias
Konstandinou
Akadimias
El. Venizelou
Hotel
Restaurant

CENTRE

Grande Bretagne

Constitution Sq ✉ *105 64* – Ⓜ *Syntagma* – ✆ *(210) 3330 000* – *www.grandebretagne.gr* **C2**

272 rm – †540 € ††630 €, ☕ 28 € – 48 suites

Rest *GB Roof Garden* – see below

Rest *GB Corner* – ✆ *(210) 3330 750* – Carte 43/61 €

♦ Grand Luxury ♦ Palace ♦ Stylish ♦

Impressive 19C city centre hotel, affording fantastic views of the surrounding area. Grand interior displays elegant handmade furnishings. Luxurious, individually styled bedrooms boast extremely spacious bathrooms. Excellent spa and wellness facilities; professional service. International menu in formal GB Corner.

Hilton

46 Vas. Sofias Ave ✉ *115 28* – Ⓜ *Evangelismos* – ✆ *(210) 7281 000* – *www.athens.hilton.com* **D2**

474 rm – †199/369 € ††199/369 €, ☕ 32.50 € – 34 suites

Rest *The Byzantine* – ✆ *(210) 7281 400 (Buffet lunch)* Carte 40/65 €

Rest *Galaxy Roof* – ✆ *(210) 7281 402 (May to October) (dinner only)* Carte 62/86 €

Rest *Milo's* – ✆ *(210) 7244 400* – Menu 20 € – Carte 85/150 €

♦ Grand Luxury ♦ Modern ♦

Corporate hotel near Kolonaki Square, with elegant guest areas, well-equipped fitness centre and two business floors. Modern, uniform bedrooms boast balconies and sea/mountain views. Local and international dishes in informal Byzantine. Similar theme in rooftop Galaxy. Seafood in Milo's.

Athenaeum Inter-Continental

89-93 Syngrou Ave (Southwest : 2.5 km.) ✉ *117 45* – ✆ *(210) 9206 000* – *www.athens.intercontinental.com*

483 rm – †250/320 € ††250/320 €, ☕ 32 € – 60 suites

Rest *Première (9th floor)* – ✆ *(210) 9206 981 (closed Sunday-Monday) (dinner only)* Menu 48 € – Carte 60/86 €

Rest *Cafezoe* – ✆ *(210) 9206 655 (closed dinner Monday-Tuesday)* Carte 46/67 €

♦ Grand Luxury ♦ Business ♦ Modern ♦

Corporate hotel close to the business district. Elegant lobby with shops. Impressive meeting spaces and business centre. Spacious bedrooms boast latest facilities; Club floor offers dedicated services. Terrace and panoramic views in modern Première. Local dishes in informal Cafezoe.

King George Palace

3 Vasileos Georgiou A, Syntagma (Constitution) Sq ✉ *105 64* – Ⓜ *Syntagma* – ✆ *(210) 3222 210* – *www.classicalhotels.com* **C2**

89 rm – †230/260 € ††260/290 €, ☕ 35 € – 13 suites

Rest – Carte 35/57 €

Rest *Tudor Hall* – *(Closed Sunday) (dinner only)* Menu 29 € – Carte 70/91 €

♦ Luxury ♦ Classic ♦

Converted mansion located in Syntagma Square. Individually styled bedrooms display modern lines and design furniture; rooftop suite boasts a private pool and panoramic views. Stylish, informal lounge-bar serves light dinners. Elegant Tudor Hall offers more occasion with its smart terrace and modern Mediterranean menu .

Electra Palace

18-20 Nikodimou St ✉ *105 57 – Ⓜ Syntagma – ✆ (210) 3370 000 – www.electrahotels.com*
C3

135 rm – 🛉230/255 € 🛉🛉255/270 € – 20 suites
Rest *Electra Roof Garden* – see below
Rest – Carte 25/38 €

◆ Business ◆ Classic ◆

Attractive hotel set on a peaceful city street; its classical façade concealing a more recently updated interior. Smart, well-kept bedrooms; some with Acropolis views. Fantastic panoramas from the rooftop pool. Motivo restaurant serves classical Greek fare.

Ledra Marriott

115 Syngrou Ave (Southwest : 3 km) ✉ *117 45 – ✆ (210) 9300 000 – www.athensmarriott.com*

296 rm – 🛉149/209 € 🛉🛉159/219 €, 26 € – 18 suites
Rest *Kona Kai* – *(dinner only)* Menu 48 € – Carte 53/80 €
Rest *Zephyros* – *✆ (210) 9300 060 (buffet lunch)* Carte 30/62 €

◆ Business ◆ Modern ◆

On the road from the city to the sea, with panoramic views from the rooftop terrace. Traditional guest areas and classically styled bedrooms; superior furnishings in executive rooms. Authentic Polynesian dishes and teppan-yaki in Kona Kai. Local and global fare in Zephyros.

St George Lycabettus

2 Kleomenous St ✉ *106 75 – ✆ (210) 7290 711 – www.sglycabettus.gr*
C2

147 rm – 🛉155/455 € 🛉🛉200/522 €, 29 € – 6 suites
Rest *Le Grand Balcon* – Menu 38 € – Carte 44/63 €
Rest *Frame Garden* – *(closed in winter)* Menu 40/50 € – Carte 40/60 €

◆ Business ◆ Modern ◆

Elegant design hotel in exclusive district. Contemporary gold and black interior with Greek artefacts and modern art. Bedrooms boast different themes on each floor; some have balconies and views. Modern Mediterranean menu in Le Grand Balcon. Greek cuisine in Frame Garden.

Divani Palace Acropolis

19-25 Parthenonos ✉ *117 42 – Ⓜ Akropolis – ✆ (210) 9280 100 – www.divaniacropolis.gr*
B3

242 rm – 🛉235/285 € 🛉🛉235/285 €, 20 € – 8 suites
Rest *Aspassia* – Menu 30 € – Carte 36/68 €
Rest *Roof Garden* – *(closed mid October-mid May and Tuesday) (dinner only)* Carte 60/90 €

◆ Traditional ◆ Classic ◆

Classical hotel by The Acropolis, in fairly quiet street; displaying the remains of Thermistocles' wall in the basement. Well-kept, traditionally furnished bedrooms; comfy suites. Greek and Mediterranean menus in Aspassia. Modern cooking and impressive Acropolis views in Roof Garden.

Crowne Plaza Athens City Center

50 Michalakopoulou ✉ *115 28 – Ⓜ Megaro Moussikis – ✆ (210) 7278 000 – www.cpathens.com*

191 rm – 🛉150/220 € 🛉🛉150/220 €, 23 € – 2 suites
D2

Rest *Ambrosia* – Carte 35/50 €

◆ Chain hotel ◆ Business ◆ Modern ◆

Centrally located business hotel with smart, modern interior and good conference facilities. Modern bedrooms – stylish executive level display seating areas, large desks and good mod cons. Casual dining in Ambrosia, which moves to poolside roof garden in summer.

Holiday Suites without rest

4 Arnis St (by Mihalakopoulou) ✉ 115 28 – Ⓜ Megaro Moussikis – ☎ (210) 7278 500 – www.holiday-suites.com **D2**

34 rm – ††120/180 €, ☕ 19 €

◆ Business ◆ Modern ◆ Functional ◆

Converted apartments in a quiet residential street. All rooms are spacious, contemporary suites, displaying work and kitchen areas and comfy seating. Facilities shared with the Crowne Plaza.

Zafolia

87-89 Alexandras Ave ✉ 114 74 – Ⓜ Ambelokipi – ☎ (210) 6449 002 – www.zafoliahotel.gr **C1**

185 rm ☕ – †138/220 € ††145/220 € – 7 suites **Rest** – Carte 25/42 €

◆ Business ◆ Modern ◆

Privately owned business hotel to the north of the city. Contemporary guest areas; excellent views from rooftop pool and bar. Well-equipped, modern bedrooms, some with balconies. Organised service. Mezzanine dining room serves Greek and international cuisine.

Eridanus

78 Pireaus Ave, Keramikos ✉ 104 35 – Ⓜ Thissio – ☎ (210) 5205 360 – www.eridanus.gr **A2**

35 rm ☕ – †155/210 € ††175/240 € – 3 suites **Rest** – Carte 28/44 €

◆ Business ◆ Stylish ◆ Classic ◆

Contemporary design hotel set on a busy main street, boasting charming guest areas and elegant bedrooms which feature refined, modern-classical designs and plenty of extras – some have Acropolis views. Hydro-massage showers. Mediterranean cuisine served in the restaurant, which moves to the top floor terrace in summer.

The Athenian Callirhoe

32 Kallirois Ave and Petmeza ✉ 117 43 – Ⓜ Singrou-Fix – ☎ (210) 9215 353 – www.tac.gr **C3**

84 rm ☕ – †97/226 € ††108/226 €

Rest *Café Degli Artisti* – Menu 28 € – Carte 44/87 €

◆ Business ◆ Stylish ◆

Contemporary hotel near the city centre, with elegant lobby displaying design furniture and white, silver and grey hues. Comfortable, wood-furnished bedrooms; spacious executive rooms. Restaurant serves Mediterranean cuisine and moves to the roof garden in summer.

Amalia

10 Amalias Ave ✉ 105 57 – Ⓜ Syntagma – ☎ (210) 3237 300 – www.amaliahotels.com **C3**

97 rm ☕ – †100/150 € ††130/380 € – 1 suite **Rest** – Carte 29/45 €

◆ Chain hotel ◆ Modern ◆

Well-kept, minimalist hotel close to the plazas and Parliament buildings. Well-equipped, contemporary bedrooms emit a relaxing ambience; those to the front have balconies overlooking the National Gardens. Classically styled restaurant serves local cuisine.

Alexandros

8 Timoleontos Vassou St (via Vas. Sofias off Soutsou D.) ✉ 115 21 – Ⓜ Megaro Moussikis – ☎ (210) 6430 464 – www.airotel.gr

92 rm ☕ – †88/120 € ††98/164 € – 3 suites

Rest *Don Giovanni* – Carte 16/30 €

◆ Business ◆ Modern ◆

Laid-back, contemporary business hotel, set in a residential area off of a busy avenue. Well-equipped, comfy modern bedrooms in earthy hues; all are spacious 'executive' or 'suite' grades. Small restaurant offers Greek cuisine with strong Italian influences.

Electra

5 Ermou ✉ 105 63 – Ⓜ Syntagma – ☎ (210) 3378 000 – www.electrahotels.gr
106 rm – 160/185 € 185/200 € – 3 suites **C2**
Rest – Menu 25 € – Carte 25/35 €
♦ Business ♦ Modern ♦ Functional ♦
Comfortable, well-kept hotel in lively pedestrianised shopping area near Syntagma Square; ideal for short stays or business trips. Functional, soundproofed bedrooms with work desks; compact marble bathrooms. Mezzanine restaurant offers international fare.

Art without rest

27 Marni St ✉ 104 32 – Ⓜ Omonia – ☎ (210) 5240 501 – www.arthotelathens.gr
30 rm – 70/110 € 80/120 € **B1**
♦ Family ♦ Personalised ♦
Family-run hotel on busy central street, hiding behind a 19C residential façade. Modern lobby with design furniture; walls adorned with artwork. Individually styled, simply furnished bedrooms.

Periscope

22 Haritos St, Kolonaki ✉ 106 75 – Ⓜ Evangelismos – ☎ (210) 7297 200 – www.yeshotels.gr **D2**
21 rm – 135/175 € 160/280 € **Rest** – Carte 31/46 €
♦ Business ♦ Modern ♦
Modern, minimalist hotel on a quiet residential street. Individually designed bedrooms with balconies. Executive rooms display enlarged aerial photos of Athens on the ceiling. Stylish bar with Mini Cooper seating. Simple restaurant offering Mediterranean dishes.

The Golden Age

57 Michalakopoulou ✉ 115 28 – Ⓜ Megaro Moussikis – ☎ (210) 7240861 – www.goldenage.gr **D2**
115 rm – 135/160 € 145/170 € – 7 suites **Rest** – Carte 30/50 €
♦ Business ♦ Functional ♦
Modern city centre hotel with contemporary steel façade and minimalist interior. Best suited to business clientele, good-sized bedrooms are comfy and functional with up-to-date facilities; some have balconies. Small restaurant serves Greek/Mediterranean dishes.

O & B

7 Leokoriou St ✉ 105 54 – Ⓜ Thissio – ☎ (210) 331 2940 – www.oandbhotel.com **A2**
21 rm – 170/210 € 170/210 € – 1 suite **Rest** – Carte 24/43 €
♦ Townhouse ♦ Design ♦
Stylish boutique hotel in downtown Athens, with an 'O'chre & 'B'rown colour scheme running throughout. Spacious bedrooms boast quality furnishings, high attention to detail and smart marble bathrooms. Restaurant offers Mediterranean and Greek cuisine.

Hermes without rest

19 Apollonos St ✉ 105 57 – Ⓜ Syntagma – ☎ (210) 3235 514 – www.hermeshotel.gr **B3**
45 rm – 90/145 € 95/145 €
♦ Family ♦ Functional ♦
Compact, modern hotel between Monastiraki and Syntagma Square. Contemporary interior with comfy lobby and discreet breakfast room. Functional, wood-furnished bedrooms; some with balconies.

Arion without rest

18 Aglou Dimitriou St ✉ 105 54 – Ⓜ Monastiraki – ☎ (210) 3240 415 – www.arionhotel.gr **B2**
51 rm – 60/105 € 95/130 €
♦ Family ♦ Modern ♦
Small, well-priced hotel close to the subway, with modern, minimalist interior and rooftop terrace offering superb views. Smart, well-furnished bedrooms with up-to-date bathrooms – ask for one overlooking The Acropolis.

Achilleas without rest

21 Lekka St ✉ 105 62 – Ⓜ Syntagma – ✆ (210) 3233197 – www.achilleashotel.gr
36 rm ☕ – 🚹69/105 € 🚹🚹80/130 € **C2**

♦ Family ♦ Functional ♦

Friendly hotel in small street known for its silversmiths, near Constitution Square. Spacious, comfy bedrooms with up-to-date bathrooms; ideal for families. Self-service breakfast on mezzanine.

Museum without rest

16 Bouboulinas St ✉ 106 82 – Ⓜ Victoria – ✆ (210) 3805 611 – www.hotelsofathens.com **B1**
93 rm ☕ – 🚹55/70 € 🚹🚹70/145 €

♦ Family ♦ Functional ♦

Small hotel made up of two buildings and overlooking the National Archaeological Museum. Simple, minimalist style. Half of the bedrooms are in a contemporary vein; the rest, more classical.

Spondi

5 Pyronos, off Varnava Sq, Pangrati ✉ 116 36 – ✆ (210) 7564 021 – www.spondi.gr – Closed Easter and 10 days mid-August **D3**
Rest – *(dinner only)* Menu 68/118 € – Carte 78/111 €
Spec. Crab in fine herb jelly with cauliflower mousse. Fregola sarda risotto with calamari and cockles. Guanaja chocolate with thyme froth and milk sorbet.

♦ French ♦ Romantic ♦ Elegant ♦

Elegantly designed from reclaimed bricks in the style of a vaulted cellar, with a wine cave and courtyard garden to one side. Skilled chef uses top quality produce to create imaginative, deftly executed and stunningly presented modern dishes. Excellent wine list.

Electra Roof Garden – at Electra Palace Hotel

18-20 Nikodimou St ✉ 105 57 – Ⓜ Syntagma – ✆ (210) 3370 000 – www.electrahotels.gr **C3**
Rest – *(closed Sunday) (dinner only)* Carte 45/60 €

♦ Modern ♦ Romantic ♦ Elegant ♦

Stunningly located 5th floor restaurant, offering unrivalled views of The Acropolis and Athens. Original menu features traditional Greek flavours in modern, innovative interpretations. Attentive, efficient service, with many dishes delivered by the chef himself.

Varoulko (Lazarou Lefteris)

80 Pireaus Ave, Keramikos ✉ 104 35 – Ⓜ Keramikós – ✆ (210) 5228 400 – www.varoulko.gr – Closed 1 January, Easter, 25-26 December and Sunday **A2**
Rest – *(booking essential) (dinner only)* Carte 48/54 €
Spec. Crispy fish with leavened bread and aubergine mousse. John Dory with sour apple and smoked mashed potato. Chocolate cigar with crispy cuttlefish sepia ash and sparkling passion fruit.

♦ Seafood ♦ Fashionable ♦

Sleek, minimalist, split-level restaurant with part-glass roof and flooring, and remarkable roof terrace views. Well-balanced, appealingly presented seafood dishes showcase quality produce. Knowledgeable team personalise the modern 'Degustation' menu for each guest.

GB Roof Garden – at Grande Bretagne Hotel

Constitution Sq ✉ 105 64 – Ⓜ Syntagma – ✆ (210) 3330 876 – www.grandbretagne.gr **C2**
Rest – *(booking essential)* Carte 57/77 €

♦ Mediterranean ♦ Friendly ♦

Smart, comfortable and smoothly run restaurant on the rooftop of the elegant Grand Bretagne hotel. Lovely terrace boasts spectacular views over Syntagma Square and towards The Acropolis. Sunny, Mediterranean-style cooking, with an emphasis on Italian flavours.

Hytra

Navarhou Apostoli 7, Psirri ✉ 105 54 – Ⓜ Monastiraki – ✆ (210) 3316 767 – www.hytra.gr – Closed 10 April-12 October and Monday **B2**

Rest – *(booking essential) (dinner only)* Menu 40 € – Carte 53/70 €

Spec. 'Greek salad': tomato marshmallow, feta cheese mousse, olive ball and cucumber caviar. Red mullet with cauliflower and cucumber sauce. Chocolate mi-cuit with vanilla ice cream.

♦ Inventive ♦ Trendy ♦

Stylish, comfortable yet understated restaurant set in Psiri. Innovative, contemporary dishes are confidently and expertly prepared using inventive techniques; order the well-paced 'Degustation' menu to fully experience the kitchen's skill. Warm, welcoming service.

Luna Rossa

213 Sokratous, Kallithea (Southwest : 4 km) ✉ 176 74 – ✆ (210) 9423 777 – www.lunarossa.gr – Closed 1 July-31 August and Sunday

Rest – *(booking essential) (dinner only)* Menu 38/55 € – Carte 40/70 €

♦ Italian ♦ Family ♦ Elegant ♦

Unusually set in a residential property. Elegant handmade furnishings and personal service. Three romantic rooms – two with just two tables – and a pleasant terrace. Authentic Italian cooking.

Kiku

12 Dimokritou St, Kolonaki ✉ 106 73 – Ⓜ Syntagma – ✆ (210) 3647 033 – www.athenskiku.com – Closed Easter, Christmas, New Year and Sunday **C2**

Rest – *(dinner only)* Carte 70/100 €

♦ Japanese ♦ Minimalist ♦

One of the city's first Japanese restaurants, hidden away down a side street. Modern, dark, minimalist interior with large sushi counter and colour-changing mood lighting. Authentic cuisine.

Oikeîo

15 Ploutarhou St ✉ 106 76 – Ⓜ Evangelismos – ✆ (210) 7259216 – Closed 31 December-3 January, Easter, 3 weeks summer and Sunday

Rest – Carte 20/25 € **D2**

♦ Greek ♦ Rustic ♦

Small restaurant with loft room and outside tables, set in a smart quarter of Athens. Exposed red-brick walls in rustic dining room, with wicker baskets and countryside objects hanging from the ceiling. Simple Greek cooking and tasty, good value dishes.

Athiri

15 Plateon St ✉ 104 35 – Ⓜ Keramikós – ✆ (210) 3462983 – www.athirirestaurant.gr – Closed Christmas, New Year and 1 week August **A2**

Rest – *(dinner only and lunch Saturday-Sunday)* Carte 35/46 €

♦ Modern ♦ Neighbourhood ♦

Discreet address to the west of the city. Dine in minimalist inner or outdoors among the greenery. Fine, fresh, seasonal ingredients, simply prepared to reveal natural flavours. Generous portions.

Kuzina

9 Adrianou St ✉ 105 55 – Ⓜ Thissio – ✆ (210) 3240 133 – www.kuzina.gr

Rest – Carte 29/45 € **B3**

♦ Modern ♦ Bistro ♦

Lively, split-level taverna with modern open kitchen and panoramic views from the front terrace. Contemporary Greek cooking displays some Asian influences and makes good use of local produce.

Psarra's

16 Erehtheos and Erotokritou St, Plaka ✉ 105 56 – Ⓜ Monastiraki – ✆ (210) 3218 733 – www.psaras-taverna.gr **B3**

Rest – Menu 20/50 € – Carte 20/55 €

♦ Traditional ♦ Rustic ♦

Set in a small side street in a characterful district, not far from The Acropolis; a rustic Greek taverna with three wood and stone-filled dining rooms and large terrace. Simple local cuisine.

ENVIRONS OF ATHENS

AT KIFISSIA Northeast : 15 km by Vas. Sofias

Pentelikon

66 Diligianni St, Kefalari (off Harilaou Trikoupi, follow signs to Politia) ✉ 145 62 – Ⓜ Kifissia – ✆ (210) 6281 400 – www.pentelikon.gr

101 rm – 270 € 285 € – 12 suites

Rest *Vardis* – see below

Rest *La Terrasse* – Carte 26/54 €

♦ Grand Luxury ♦ Traditional ♦ Classic ♦

Elegant 1920s hotel with pleasant gardens, in affluent residential area close to the main shopping streets. Classical throughout, boasting marble, handmade furniture, antiques and oil paintings. Extensive menu in La Terrasse; dine to the accompaniment of piano music.

The Kefalari Suites without rest

1 Pentelis and Kolokotroni St, Kefalari ✉ 145 62 – Ⓜ Kifissia – ✆ (210) 6233 333 – www.yeshotels.gr

12 rm – 150/230 € 165/245 € – 1 suite

♦ Townhouse ♦ Stylish ♦

Early 20C villa in smart residential area, a stone's throw from the main square. Classical, minimalist lobby. Individually designed, elegantly furnished bedrooms with marble bathrooms.

Semiramis

48 Charilaou Trikoupi St, Kefalari ✉ 145 62 – Ⓜ Kifissia – ✆ (210) 6284 400 – www.yeshotels.gr

50 rm – 180/210 € 205/235 € – 1 suite

Rest – Carte 33/51 €

♦ Business ♦ Design ♦

Contemporary design hotel on the main plaza. Flamboyant colour schemes both inside and out, complemented by vibrant modern furnishings. Bedrooms boast hi-tech facilities and balconies. Minimalist Mediterranean restaurant overlooks the pool and decked terrace.

Twenty One

21 Kolokotroni and Mykonou St, Kefalari ✉ 145 62 – Ⓜ Kifissia – ✆ (210) 6233 521 – www.yeshotels.gr

16 rm – 145/175 € 170/200 € – 5 suites

Rest – *(dinner only)* Carte 38/50 €

♦ Business ♦ Modern ♦

Small, former 19C water mill in slate grey, located in a pleasant residential area by the main square. Choice of modern, minimalist bedrooms with feature walls or stylish loft suites. Greek and Mediterranean cuisine served in large restaurant and on terrace.

Vardis – at Pentelikon Hotel

66 Diligianni St, Kefalari (Kifissa) (off Harilaou Trikoupi, follow signs to Politia) ✉ 145 62 – Ⓜ Kifissia – ✆ (210) 6281 400 – www.pentelikon.gr
Rest – *(Closed Sunday) (booking essential) (dinner only)* Menu 65 €
– Carte 38/86 €
Spec. Squid with bulgur wheat and air-dried salami. Lamb pot roast with aubergine, artichoke and sweet peppers. Sponge cake and lemon cream with brandy and coconut sorbet.
♦ Traditional ♦ Formal ♦
Traditionally styled hotel restaurant displaying heavy drapes, elegant chandeliers, well-dressed tables and a pleasant summer terrace. Skilled chef uses modern techniques to create elegant, classically based Greek dishes. Detailed, knowledgeable service.

P Box

11 Levidou ✉ 145 62 – Ⓜ Kifissia – ✆ (210) 808 8818
– Closed New Year, Christmas and Sunday
Rest – *(Bookings not accepted)* Carte 32/49 €
♦ Modern ♦ Fashionable ♦
Set on the main shopping street of a wealthy suburb and frequented by the 'designer' set. Easy-going atmosphere and popular terrace. Modern cooking with Asian overtones. Efficient service.

AT EKALI Northeast : 20 km by Vas. Sofias

Life Gallery

103 Thisseos Ave ✉ 145 78 – ✆ (210) 6260 400
– www.bluegr.com
29 rm – 🛉165/170 € 🛉🛉175/415 € **Rest** – Carte 53/59 €
♦ Luxury ♦ Design ♦ Minimalist ♦
Modern, hi-tech hotel outside the city, with striking 'glass cube' design and pleasant gardens. Sleek, modern, minimalist interior. Stylish, well-equipped bedrooms with balconies. Spacious restaurant and terrace offer well-presented, Mediterranean-based dishes.

AT ATHENS INTERNATIONAL AIRPORT East : 35 km by Vas. Sofias

Sofitel Athens Airport

✉ 190 19 – Ⓜ Airport – ✆ (210) 3544 000
– www.sofitel.com
332 rm – 🛉200/212 € 🛉🛉200/212 €, ☕ 25 € – 13 suites
Rest *Karavi* – *(closed Sunday and Monday) (dinner only)* Carte 57/78 €
Rest *Mesoghaia* – *(closed Sunday lunch)* Carte 34/51 €
♦ Business ♦ Modern ♦
Modern hotel with small wellness centre, located just 30m from the airport terminal. Spacious, well-equipped bedrooms boast good soundproofing and pleasant bathrooms. Modern French cooking in 9th floor Karavi. Greek and Italian cuisine offered in 24hr Mesoghaia.

AT VOULIAGMENI South : 18 km by Singrou

The Westin Athens

40 Apollonos St (Vouliafmeni) ✉ 166 71
– ✆ (210) 8902 000 – www.westin.com/athens
152 rm – 🛉260/650 € 🛉🛉290/680 €, ☕ 30 € – 7 suites
Rest *Kymata* – Carte 48/63 €
Rest *Al Fresco* – *✆ (210) 8902 137* – Carte 49/63 €
♦ Luxury ♦ Palace ♦ Modern ♦
Professionally run hotel in 75 acre complex on a private peninsula. Extensive facilities include private beaches and water sports. Spacious bedrooms boast balconies/gardens and sea views. Mediterranean dishes by the pool in Kymata. Innovative Greek cuisine in Al Fresco.

Arion Resort & Spa

40 Apollonos St, Vouliagmeni ✉ *166 71*
– ✆ (210) 8902 000
– www.luxurycollection.com/arion
163 rm – ♦320/635 € ♦♦350/665 €, ☕ 30 € – 16 suites
Rest *Alia* – *(dinner only)* Carte 59/92 €
Rest *Grill Room* – *✆ (210) 8901 794 (dinner only)* Carte 59/92 €
♦ Luxury ♦ Modern ♦

In same complex as The Westin and sharing many of the facilities. Choose between large bedrooms with balconies and sea/park views or contemporary bungalows with marble bathrooms; some with private pools. Mediterranean fare in Alia. Modern French cuisine in Grill Room.

Divani Apollon Palace & Spa

10 Ag. Nikolaou and Iliou St
(Kavouri) off Athinas ✉ *166 71 – ✆ (210) 8911 100*
– www.divanis.com
279 rm – ♦420/560 € ♦♦460/600 €, ☕ 31 € – 7 suites
Rest *Mythos* – Carte 41/57 €
Rest *Anemos* – Carte 35/50 €
♦ Luxury ♦ Classic ♦

Fashionable resort hotel, with its own private beach just over the road. Bedrooms boast balconies and gulf views. Impressive spa and thalassotherapy centre with 2 inside and 2 outside pools. Fresh seafood in dockside Mythos. International dishes in modern Anemos.

Apollon Suites without rest

11 Nikolaou St ✉ *166 71 – ✆ (210) 8911 100*
– www.divanis.gr
– Restricted opening in winter
56 rm – ♦200/490 € ♦♦200/490 €
♦ Luxury ♦ Modern ♦

Peaceful annexe to the Divani Apollon. Large, well-equipped bedrooms and suites boast contemporary décor, hand-picked fabrics and furnished terraces; most have sea views. Shared facilities.

The Margi

11 Litous St, off Athinas by Apollonos ✉ *166 71 – ✆ (210) 8929 000*
– www.themargi.gr
88 rm ☕ – ♦170/210 € ♦♦180/230 € – 7 suites
Rest – Menu 32 € – Carte 33/66 €
♦ Business ♦ Stylish ♦

Stylish, contemporary hotel set close to the beach. Elegant lobby. Antique-furnished, modern colonial-style bedrooms boasting smart marble bathrooms. Breakfast and dinner can be taken on the poolside terrace. Greek cuisine displays some Mediterranean influences.

Matsuhisa

40 Apollonos St (Vouliagmeni) ✉ *16671 – ✆ (210) 8960 510*
– www.matsuhisaathens.com
– Closed 1 January, Easter, 25 December and Sunday lunch in summer.
Rest – *(booking essential) (dinner only and Sunday lunch)*
Carte 50/90 €
♦ Japanese ♦ Fashionable ♦

Stylish, sophisticated restaurant with bustling atmosphere, polished, helpful service and stunning terrace boasting sea views. Original, contemporary Japanese cooking in typical Nobu style: choose dishes from the sushi counter, stone wood oven or robata grill.

PIREAS Southwest: 8 km by Singrou

Piraeus Theoxenia

23 Karaoli and Dimitriou St ✉ 185 31 – Ⓜ Pireaus – ✆ (210) 4112 550 – www.theoxeniapalace.com

75 rm – 120 € 135 € – 1 suite

Rest *Incognito* – Menu 29 €

♦ Business ♦ Functional ♦ Modern ♦

Corporate hotel in the heart of town, close to the harbour and bustling local markets. Well-equipped gym and business centre. Spacious modern bedrooms – some with work desks and comfy seating areas. Classical restaurant offers local and Mediterranean cuisine.

AT KALAMAKI Southwest : 14 km by Singrou

Akrotiri

Vas. Georgiou B5, Agios Kosmas, Helliniko ✉ 167 77 – ✆ (210) 9859 147 – www.akrotirilounge.gr

– Closed November-April

Rest – *(dinner only)* Carte 43/74 €

♦ French ♦ Fashionable ♦ Musical ♦

Fashionable, open air seafront restaurant with pool and bridge leading to large nightclub – both get busy at midnight. Classical French menu with Greek edge; generous, well-presented dishes.

HUNGARY
MAGYARORSZÁG

PROFILE

➔ **Area:**
93 032 km^2
(35 920 sq mi).

➔ **Population:**
10 031 000 inhabitants (est. 2009), density = 108 per km^2.

➔ **Capital:**
Budapest (conurbation 2 503 205 inhabitants).

➔ **Currency:**
Forint (Ft or HUF); rate of exchange: HUF 100 = € 0.36 = US$ 0.50 (Dec 2010).

➔ **Government:**
Parliamentary republic (since 1989). Member of European Union since 2004.

➔ **Language:**
Hungarian; many Hungarians also speak English and German.

➔ **Specific public holidays:**
1848 Revolution Day (15 March); National Day-St. Stephen Day (20 August); Republic Day-1956 Uprising Remembrance Day (23 October); All Saints' Day (1 November); Boxing Day (25-26 December).

➔ **Local time:**
GMT + 1 hour in winter and GMT + 2 hours in summer.

➔ **Climate:**
Temperate continental with cold winters and warm summers (Budapest: January: -1°C, July: 22°C).

➔ **International dialling Code:**
00 36 followed by area code (1 for Budapest) and local number. International enquiries: ✆ **199**.

➔ **Emergency:**
Central emergency line: ✆ **112**; Ambulance: ✆ **104**, Fire Brigade: ✆ **105**, Police: ✆ **107**, Roadside breakdown service: ✆ **188**.

➔ **Electricity:**
220 volts, 50 Hz; 2-pin round-shaped continental plugs.

➔ **Formalities**
Travellers from the European Union (EU), Switzerland, Iceland and the main countries of North and South America need a national identity card or passport (America: passport required) to visit Hungary for less than three months (tourism or business purpose).
For visitors from other countries a visa may be required, in addition to a passport, especially for those wishing to stay for longer than three months. We advise you to check with your embassy before travelling.

BUDAPEST

BUDAPEST

Population: 1 712 210 (conurbation 2 503 205) – Altitude: 102m

›nathan/Fotolia.com

No one knows quite where the Hungarian language came from. It's not quite Slavic, not quite Turkic, and its closest relatives appear to be in Finland and Siberia. In much the same way, Hungary's capital is a bit of an enigma. A lot of what you see is not as old as it appears. Classical and Gothic buildings are mostly Neoclassical and neo-Gothic, and the fabled Baroque of the city is of a more recent vintage than in other European capitals. That's because Budapest's frequent invaders and conquerors, from all compass points of the map, left little but rubble behind them when they left; the grand look of today took shape for the most part no earlier than the mid 19C.

It's still a beautiful place to look at, with hilly Buda keeping watch via eight great bridges over sprawling Pest on the other side of the lilting, bending Danube. These were formerly two separate towns, united in 1873 to form a capital city. It reached its heyday around that time, a magnificent city that was the hub of the Austro-Hungarian Empire. Defeats in two world wars and fifty years behind the Iron Curtain put paid to the glory, but battered Budapest is used to rising from the ashes, and now it's Europe's most earthily beautiful capital, particularly when winter mists rise from the river to shroud it in a thick white cloak. The spas are good, too.

LIVING THE CITY

It's not easy to get lost in Budapest. Despite its size, it's split asunder by the great **Danube**, whose ubiquitous liquid pathway helps you keep your bearings. **Buda**, on the west bank, is very hilly and provides constant views of the river. Its southern quarter, Gellert and Taban, is smartly residential, while northern Buda is dominated by visitor hotspot The Royal Palace. This stares across to the imposing Parliament Building in **Pest**, around which large squares and wide avenues offer reminders of the Austro-Hungarian Empire. South of here is the commercial hub of Belvaros, or inner city, full of shops, cafés and summer tourists. The northeast quarter of the city, furthest from the river, is Varosliget, which translates as City Park, and it's the place the locals come to play and lounge around in the sun; this is also an area renowned for its grand buildings and monuments. In the middle of the Danube, as the city reaches its northern boundary, stands the green oasis of Margaret Island.

PRACTICAL INFORMATION

ARRIVAL-DEPARTURE

Ferihegy Budapest National Airport is 24km southeast of the city. A taxi will take about 45min and cost around 4000 HUF; there are Shuttle Mini-buses doing the rounds of the hotels or, from Terminal 1, a train will take you to the Western train station for 300 HUF.

TRANSPORT

Budapest has an extensive public transport system: its metro, with three lines, is second oldest in the world after the London Underground. Above ground, you can take your pick of buses, trolley buses or trams. Tickets must be bought in advance and validated in the ticket stampers at the start of the journey. Buy your tickets at metro stations, ticket machines, newsagents or tobacconists.

If you're in town for more than a day, then the Budapest Card is a sound investment. It includes unlimited travel on public transport, free or reduced price admission to many museums and sights, cultural and folklore programmes, as well as discounts in some shops, restaurants and thermal baths. The Card is valid for two or three days, and can be bought at the airport, main metro stations, tourist offices and some hotels.

If you're going shopping on the weekend, make sure you do it on Saturday morning. Most high street shops are shut on Saturday afternoons, and there is almost no Sunday opening, apart from the shopping malls.

EXPLORING BUDAPEST

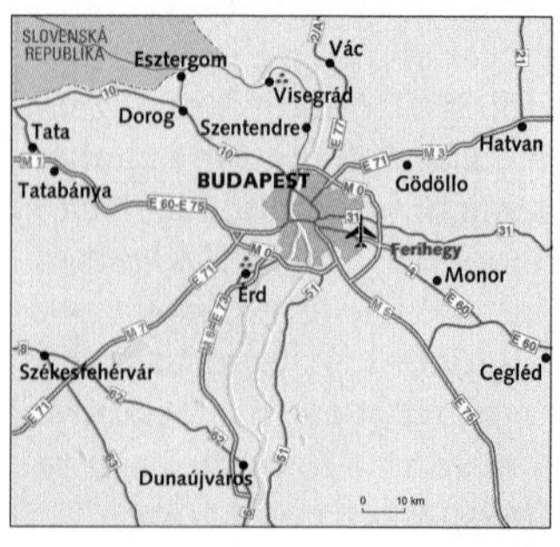

Budapest offers a thick slice of East European charm that hasn't been ruined by monotonously grey communist architecture. It's grander in scale than Vienna and Prague, the other two members of the 'Habsburg triumvirate', and you can't help but get the feeling that its art nouveau delights are modelled on nineteenth century Paris (which indeed they are, at least in Pest). Ask two locals to tell you the city's defining tourist location – its unmissable sight - and one will probably say "The Royal Palace", the other "The Parliament Building". The **Royal Palace** can certainly stake a strong claim. There's been a dominant castle or palace overlooking Buda since 1255. The latest incarnation was built in the eighteenth century after the Habsburg Empire claimed it from the Ottomans in a bloody siege. They developed not one palace but an amalgamation of buildings, spreading out along the hill. These took a big hit during World War II, and what we see today has been healthily patched up over the past sixty years: the dome, for instance, was entirely rebuilt. The **Hungarian National Gallery** was inaugurated at the Palace just over fifty years ago, in 1957, and nowhere in the city is there more treasure than here; it displays art from medieval times to the present day in six permanent exhibitions which lavish upon the visitor the very best of Hungarian creativity. Fans of the Secession (the nineteenth century arts movement devoted to bright colours and fantastical designs) will be in their element. There are actually more than 10,000 exhibits spread over much of the Royal Palace, making it one of the greatest collections in the world.

→ PARLIAMENTARY PRIVILEGE

So how does the **Parliament building** compare with all that? It's certainly nowhere near as old, as it was only completed in 1902 after two decades of construction. A symbol of Hungarian self-confidence at the beginning of the twentieth century, it certainly looks the part. It's one of Europe's finest neo-Gothic buildings and when you gaze at it from across the water its dazzling symmetry imbues it with a real sense of magnificence. Inside, its two biggest 'vote catchers' are its sweeping Grand Staircase and its Domed Hall, which houses the Crown Jewels. To see them, you'll have to join a guided tour, but as our imaginary second local would tell you, that's something well worth doing.

→ GET YOUR THERMALS ON

If you're in Budapest in the summer, you'll very likely be hot; this is a place that swelters. The good news is you won't have any trouble finding somewhere to cool down. The city is renowned for its therapeutic **thermal baths**, and when the weather's hot it can seem like the whole of Budapest is immersed. The Ottomans loved the natural springs and built some wonderful domed baths with steam rooms, hot and cold pools and peaceful chambers in which to relax. Enough original Turkish baths remain to give you (something like) the full Oriental experience. It was when spa bathing became a craze across central Europe in the nineteenth and early twentieth century that Budapest's two most famous bathing complexes opened, and they remain top visitor attractions: the Gellert Baths, in Buda, are part of the Secessionist Gellert Hotel and the stunning neo-classical main pool is surrounded by high galleries and marble columns, and studded with colourful mosaics. Meanwhile, to say Central Park's Szechenyi baths are big is like saying that Paris does some nice food and Athens has one or two interesting relics. Szechenyi is vast, the biggest in Europe, its neo-Baroque façade more like a Grand Central rail station than a bathing complex. There are splendid Belle Epoque foyers, an all-weather mixed swimming area, which includes Hungary's deepest thermal baths, single sex steam baths, and chess-players who congregate around stone chessboards in one of the expansive open-air pools.

→ PEST CONTROL

You'll know you're in the heart of Pest when you get to **Váci utca**. A teeming street in two parts (one for eating and drinking, one for hitting the shops) this is the city's buzziest thoroughfare, running parallel to the Danube. At the top end is Gerbeaud, the smartest and most famous coffee house in Budapest, at the bottom end the bustling Central Market Hall, where the locals go for their fruit and veg from local allotments on one side, and more exotic global fare on the other. Váci utca is the true hub of the city, lined with many types of store, though perhaps lacking the 'designer' glamour of more fashion-conscious cities.

Staying in Pest, go for a wonderful cultural hit at two of its most stunning buildings. The **State Opera House**, inland from the Parliament building, is a neo-Renaissance masterpiece, its interior so full of opulent splendour, you'll feel you're back at the height of the Austro-Hungarian Empire. Best of all, though: take in a concert there. Further south, beyond Váci utca, is the outstanding **Museum of Applied Arts**, its appearance a fitting tribute to the Secessionist movement and its stunning green domes worth the trip alone. Inside, dazzling Oriental artefacts complement the graceful white architecture. The creative genius behind the building was Odon Lechner, who, in the late nineteenth century, was to Budapest what Gaudi was to Barcelona. Lechner's designs adorn many structures in the city.

➔ THE GREAT ESCAPE

If you need a break from the crowds, there's one very visible, and another not so visible, refuge. **Margaret Island** (the visible one) is a tranquil oasis plonked down in the middle of the Danube. Locals sprawl around during high summer, but there's enough room for anyone to find a cool spot and relax under a tree. In the winter, with the wind gushing through the swirling branches and not a soul to be seen, it takes on a distinctly romantic feel. 2008 marked its one hundredth anniversary as a public park. And as for the hidden escape? Well, you won't discover it anywhere above ground. North of the Royal Palace, walk up Úri utca (Lords' Street) till you get to number nine, which is the entrance to the bizarre but wonderful Buda Castle Labyrinth, an underground maze of tunnels and chambers formed by hot springs half a million years ago. In the seventeenth century, a part of these catacombs was used to store wine, and there's a room today where fruity red wine gushes from a fountain – but you'll have to find it! (Your best bet is to join a guided tour). Incidentally, Úri utca itself is something to see with its Gothic and Baroque façades lining the way, but spare a thought that much of this fine street was rebuilt in the 1950s after that great shadow over Budapest – war – had once more taken its heavy toll.

BUDAPEST IN...

➔ ONE DAY

Royal Palace, the Parliament Building, a trip on the Danube

➔ TWO DAYS

Gellert Baths, a stroll down Váci utca, a concert at the State Opera House

➔ THREE DAYS

Museum of Applied Arts, Margaret Island, coffee and cake at Gerbeaud

CALENDAR HIGHLIGHTS

Music is high on the list of Hungarian passions: this is the country that gave us Liszt and Bartok. Winter is the time for high calibre concerts at great prices in venues like the Opera House and the National Concert Hall. The Spring Festival, in March, is the city's largest cultural jamboree, with a heady mixture of ballet, opera and chamber music fusing with the likes of jazz and folk dance. The Summer Festival sees theatres take their productions outside to Margaret Island. An entire Danube island is taken over by rock fans in August for the huge Sziget Festival, which goes on for a week and features roots music as well as ubiquitous four/four rhythms. From mid November to late December Vörösmarty tér plays host to the famed Christmas fair. The Autumn Festival, in October, is a kind of counterbalance to the Spring Festival: this one acts as a showcase for cutting edge theatre, dance and media arts, as well as music and film.

EATING OUT

The city is most famous for its coffee houses so before you dive into a restaurant tuck into a cream cake with a double espresso in, say, the Ruszwurm on Castle Hill, the city's oldest, and possibly cosiest, café. In tourist areas, it's not difficult to locate goulash on your menu, and you never have to travel far to find beans, dumplings and cabbage in profusion. Having said that, Budapest's culinary scene has moved on apace since the fall of communism, and Hungarian chefs have become inventive with their use of local seasonal produce. Pest is where you'll find most choice but even in Buda there are plenty of worthy restaurants in among the tourist traps. Lots of locals like to eat sausage on the run and if you fancy the idea, buy a pocket knife. Sunday brunch is popular in Budapest, especially at the best hotels. If you're in a restaurant, it might well include a service charge. Don't feel obliged to pay it, as tipping is entirely at your own discretion but you may find that the persistence of the little folk groups that pop up in many of the restaurants hard to resist.

→ WAITING FOR THE DAY

There are two outstanding places of worship in the city. The **Matthias Church**, towering over Buda, dates from 1255, but its most recent addition, the multi-coloured tiled roof, was built as recently as 1970. The magnificent **St Stephen's Basilica,** in the heart of Pest and seen from all over the city, was only completed in 1905, fifty-five years after it was begun. The great length of time in construction led to the local equivalent of 'pigs might fly' – 'when the basilica is finished'.

→ CHAIN REACTION

Budapest's most magnificent bridge is **The Chain Bridge**, linking the towns since 1848. It was designed by an Englishman, built by a Scotsman, and loved by the world: its huge towers are superbly lit at night, making it one of the city's most photographed sights.

→ TERROR TRIP

Fancy a trip to the House of Terror? You might not when you get there. Based in **Andrassy Avenue**, it's the former HQ of the fascist, then communist, secret police who ran the city for much of the twentieth century. Now a museum, it's dedicated to those who perished under both dictatorships. This is the place where confessions were extracted and victims sentenced to death. A sobering experience.

Four Seasons Gresham Palace

Roosevelt tér 5-6 ✉ *1051* – Ⓜ *Vörösmarty tér* – ✆ *(01) 268 6000* – *www.fourseasons.com/budapest* **E2**
169 rm – †57203/78976 HUF ††138882/160673 HUF, ☕ 8715 HUF – 10 suites
Rest *Gresham Kávénáz* – Carte 10076/14433 HUF
♦ Grand Luxury ♦ Palace ♦ Art Deco ♦
Beautifully renovated art nouveau building, ideally located opposite Chain Bridge, with superb views across river. Luxurious bedrooms and high quality service. Stunning lobby with mosaic floor and cupola roof. Impressive rooftop spa. Hungarian specialities at lunch; more refined international à la carte in the evening.

Corinthia Budapest

Erzsébet krt. 43-49 ✉ *1073* – Ⓜ *Oktogon* – ✆ *(01) 479 4000* – *www.corinthia.com* **F1**
390 rm – †36262/102069 HUF ††36262/118185 HUF, ☕ 7790 HUF – 24 suites
Rest *Brasserie Royale* – ✆ *(01) 479 7850 (closed Tuesday-Thursday dinner)* Carte 6900/11500 HUF
Rest *Rickshaw* – ✆ *(01) 479 7855 (closed 31 December-18 January, 4-26 July, Sunday and Monday) (dinner only)* Menu 10400 HUF – Carte 8500/11700 HUF
♦ Grand Luxury ♦ Classic ♦
Comprehensively equipped hotel with splendid façade, classic interior and two spectacular atria. Large, up-to-date bedrooms; executive grade offer more sophisticated styling. International dishes in art deco Brasserie. Asian décor and Cantonese classics in Rickshaw.

Kempinski H. Corvinus

Erzsébet tér 7-8 ✉ *1051* – Ⓜ *Deák Ferenc tér* – ✆ *(01) 429 3777* – *www.kempinski.com/budapest* **E2**
348 rm – †35096/86786 HUF ††35096/86786 HUF, ☕ 6803 HUF – 18 suites
Rest *Bistro Jardin* – *(buffet lunch)* Carte 5826/8323 HUF
Rest *Nobu* – ✆ *(01) 429 4242* – Menu 10000/20000 HUF – Carte 8300/13100 HUF
Rest *Ristorante Giardino* – ✆ *(01) 429 3990* – Carte 10067/14148 HUF
♦ Business ♦ Luxury ♦ Modern ♦
Well-equipped corporate hotel overlooking a central square. Spacious bedrooms feature Empire-style furniture and boast a good range of luxury facilities. Buffet meals in Bistro Jardin. Contemporary Japanese cooking in Nobu. Italian and Hungarian dishes in Ristorante Giardino.

Le Meridien

Erzsébet tér 9-10 ✉ *1051* – Ⓜ *Deák Ferenc tér* – ✆ *(01) 429 5500* – *www.lemeridien.com/budapest* **E2**
203 rm – †118000 HUF ††118000 HUF, ☕ 6870 HUF – 15 suites
Rest *Le Bourbon* – *(closed Saturday lunch)* Carte 7900/13200 HUF
♦ Business ♦ Luxury ♦ Classic ♦
Imposing façade and classical Hungarian interior, with cornicing and rug-covered wooden floors. Very spacious bedrooms boast high ceilings, traditional furniture and chandeliers. Atrium-styled Le Bourbon, with art deco glass dome, serves French-influenced menu.

Sofitel

Roosevelt tér 2 ✉ *1051* – Ⓜ *Vörösmarty tér* – ✆ *(01) 235 56 00* – *www.sofitel-budapest.com* **E2**
318 rm – †127611 HUF ††138705 HUF, ☕ 7400 HUF – 32 suites
Rest *Paris Budapest* – Menu 4500 HUF (lunch) – Carte 5743/27145 HUF
♦ Business ♦ Modern ♦ Stylish ♦
Modern hotel, with vast atrium and stylish lobby/lounge. Compact bedrooms boast all mod cons; those on northwest corners have Buda views. Fashionable Paris Budapest blends French and Hungarian cuisine. Unusual open kitchen; stunning castle and Danube view.

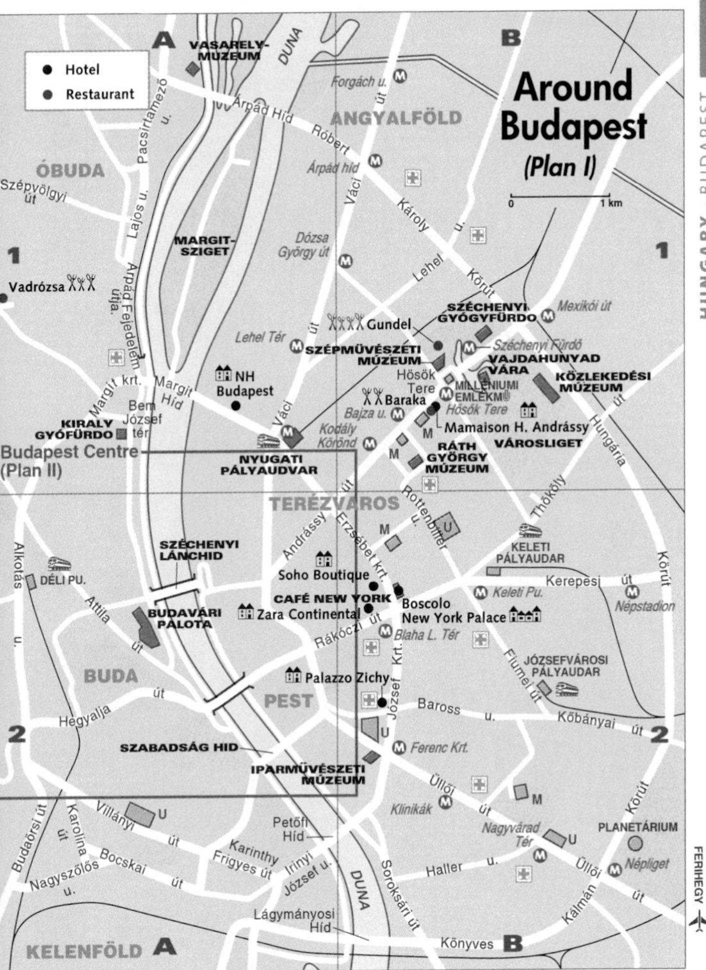

InterContinental

Apáczai Csere János utca 12-14 ✉ *1052* VISA MC AE JCB
– Ⓜ *Vörösmarty tér* – ✆ *(01) 327 6333*
– *www.budapest.intercontinental.com* **E2**

384 rm – †82100/95800 HUF ††82100/95800 HUF, ☕ 7680 HUF
– 18 suites

Rest *Corso* – ✆ *(01) 327 6392* – Carte 7800/15400 HUF

♦ Business ♦ Luxury ♦ Modern ♦

Superbly situated on banks of the Danube, with fine views to castle and palace. Well-sized, stylish bedrooms; an executive room is well worth the extra cost. International and Hungarian classics in Corso. Splendid summer terrace.

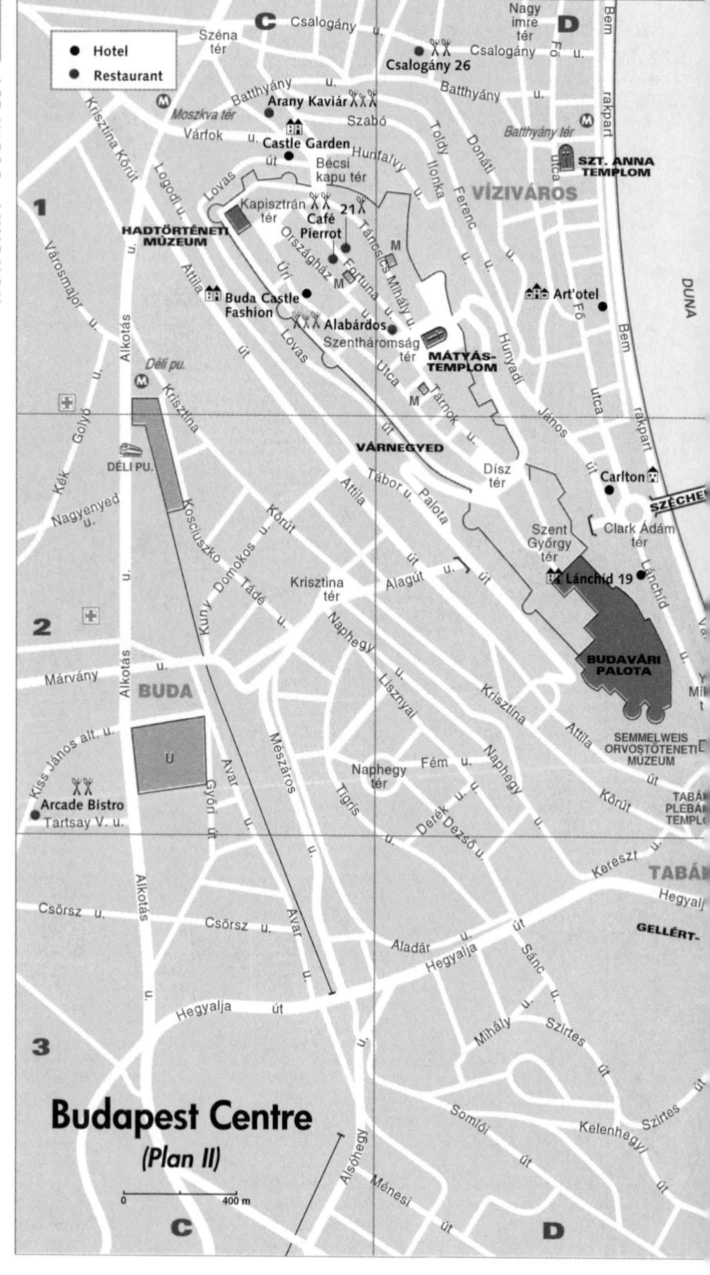
Hotel
Restaurant
Budapest Centre
(Plan II)
0
400 m
Csalogány 26
Arany Kaviár
Castle Garden
Café Pierrot
21
Buda Castle Fashion
Alabárdos
Art'otel
Carlton
Lánchíd 19
Arcade Bistro
HADTÖRTÉNETI MÚZEUM
MÁTYÁS-TEMPLOM
SZT. ANNA TEMPLOM
BUDAVÁRI PALOTA
SEMMELWEIS ORVOSTÖRTÉNETI MÚZEUM
VÍZIVÁROS
VÁRNEGYED
BUDA
DÉLI PU.
Déli pu.
Moszkva tér
Batthyány tér
DUNA
Széna tér
Nagy imre tér
Kapisztrán tér
Bécsi kapu tér
Szentháromság tér
Dísz tér
Clark Ádám tér
Szent György tér
Krisztina tér
Naphegy tér
TABÁN
GELLÉRT-

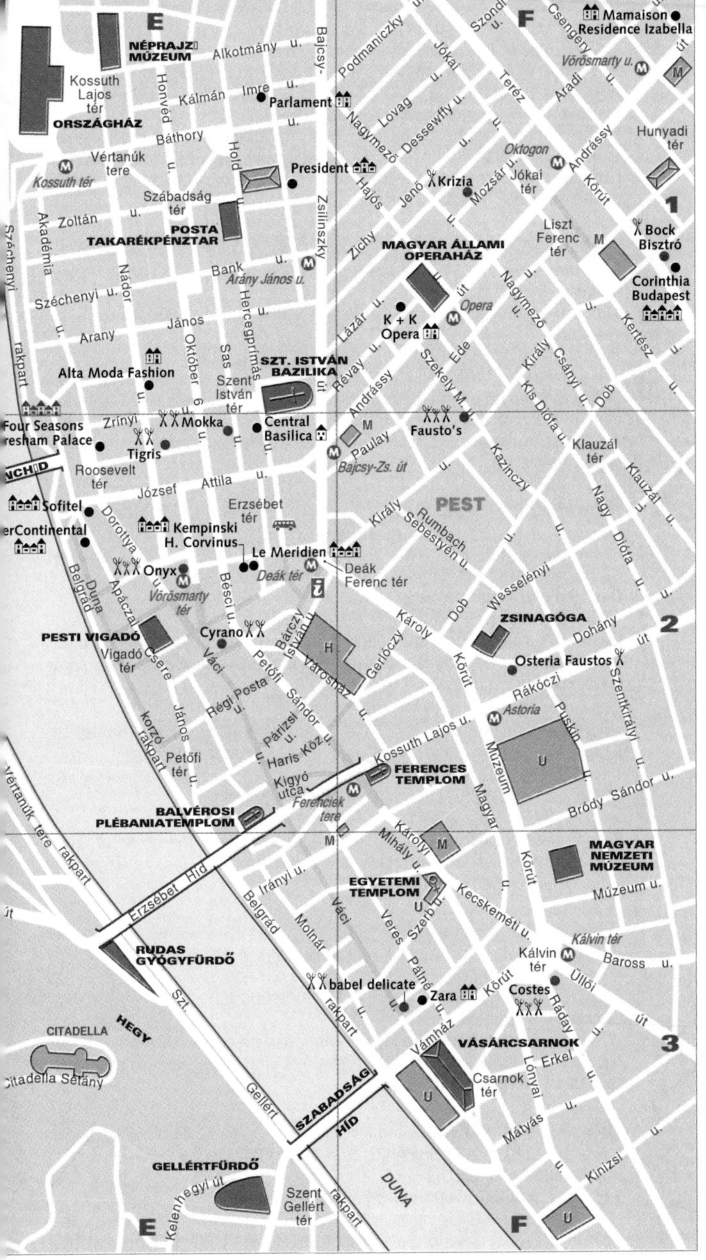
NÉPRAJZI MÚZEUM
Kossuth Lajos tér
ORSZÁGHÁZ
Parlament
President
Mamaison Residence Izabella
Hunyadi tér
Oktogon
Krizia
Jókai tér
Liszt Ferenc tér
Bock Bisztró
Corinthia Budapest
MAGYAR ÁLLAMI OPERAHÁZ
K + K Opera
Vértanúk tere
Kossuth tér
Szábadság tér
POSTA TAKARÉKPÉNZTAR
Arany János u.
Alta Moda Fashion
SZT. ISTVÁN BAZILIKA
Szent István tér
Four Seasons Gresham Palace
Mokka
Tigris
Central Basilica
Fausto's
Bajcsy-Zs. út
Roosevelt tér
Erzsébet tér
PEST
Klauzál tér
Sofitel
InterContinental
Kempinski H. Corvinus
Le Meridien
Onyx
Deák tér
Deák Ferenc tér
Vörösmarty tér
PESTI VIGADÓ
Vigadó tér
Cyrano
ZSINAGÓGA
Osteria Faustos
Astoria
Petőfi tér
FERENCES TEMPLOM
Ferenciek tere
BELVÁROSI PLÉBANIATEMPLOM
MAGYAR NEMZETI MÚZEUM
EGYETEMI TEMPLOM
Erzsébet Híd
RUDAS GYÓGYFÜRDŐ
Kálvin tér
babel delicate
Zara
Costes
CITADELLA
HEGY
Citadella Sétány
VÁSÁRCSARNOK
Csarnok tér
SZABADSÁG HÍD
GELLÉRTFÜRDŐ
Szent Gellért tér
DUNA
E
F
1
2
3

Boscolo New York Palace
Erzsébet krt. 9-11 ✉ 1073 – Ⓜ Blaha Lujza tér – ☎ (01) 886 6111 – www.boscolohotels.com VISA MC AE
Plan I **B2**
179 rm – †41449 HUF ††49742 HUF, ☕ 5527 HUF – 6 suites
Rest ***New York Salon*** – *☎ (01) 886 6167* – Carte 9990/12590 HUF
◆ Grand Luxury ◆ Stylish ◆ Design ◆
Former insurance company building with impressive atrium in Italian Renaissance style. Vast bedrooms feature silk wallpaper, chandeliers and luxurious bathrooms. Stunning baroque Salon; light café-style menu or more formal list of international/Hungarian classics.

President
rm, VISA MC AE
Hold utca 3-5 ✉ 1054 – Ⓜ Arány Janos utca – ☎ (01) 373 8200 – www.hotelpresident.hu
E1
106 rm – †23400/45700 HUF ††29500/51000 HUF, ☕ 4950 HUF – 4 suites
Rest – Menu 1650 HUF (lunch) – Carte 4740/14500 HUF
◆ Business ◆ Design ◆
Stylish, modern hotel with rooftop helipad and luxurious presidential suite. Garden City bedrooms have mirrored ceilings and murals of the city skyline, while Avenue bedrooms boast balconies. Informal, Mediterranean-themed restaurant serves international menu.

Mamaison H. Andrássy
VISA MC AE
Andrássy út 111 ✉ 1063 – Ⓜ Bajza utca – ☎ (01) 462 2100 – www.mamaison.com
Plan I **B1**
63 rm – †53130 HUF ††59455 HUF, ☕ 5060 HUF – 5 suites
Rest ***Baraka*** – see below
◆ Business ◆ Stylish ◆
Classical Bauhaus building in Embassy district. Lounge/lobby with feature pillars of stainless filigree. Spacious, modern-style bedrooms have good facilities; some feature balconies and baths.

Palazzo Zichy without rest
VISA MC AE
Lőrinc pap tér 2 ✉ 1088 – Ⓜ Ferenc körűt – ☎ (01) 235 4000 – www.hotel-palazzo-zichy.hu
Plan I **B2**
80 rm ☕ – †21500/51500 HUF ††24300/54300 HUF
◆ Business ◆ Design ◆
Rococo building with impressive 1899 façade: formerly the home of writer Count Zichy. Stylish atrium lobby with striking modern design. Generously sized, well-equipped bedrooms.

Parlament without rest
VISA MC AE
Kálmán Imre utca 19 ✉ 1054 – Ⓜ Arany János utca – ☎ (01) 374 6000 – www.parlament-hotel.hu
E1
65 rm ☕ – †20000/36000 HUF ††25000/39000 HUF
◆ Business ◆ Design ◆
Well-run hotel; stylish, modern interior contrasts with classic 19C exterior. Splendid open-plan atrium with unusual display featuring famous Hungarians. Identical bedrooms; clean, crisp design.

Alta Moda Fashion without rest
VISA MC AE
Nador U ✉ 1051 – Ⓜ Bajcsy-Zs. út – ☎ (01) 799 0080 – www.altamodahotel.hu
E1
114 rm – †32400/51000 HUF ††35900/54500 HUF
◆ Business ◆ Modern ◆
Fashionable hotel close to the shopping streets and Basilica. Dramatic lobby-lounge in contemporary style; bold designs and feature wallpapers in bedrooms – the best boast espresso machines.

Zara Continental

Dohány utca 42-44 ✉ 1074 – Ⓜ Blaha Lujza tér – ✆ (01) 8151000 – www.zarahotels.com Plan I **B2**

272 rm – †51000 HUF ††57000 HUF

Rest – Menu 1400 HUF (lunch) – Carte 3900/7350 HUF

♦ Business ♦ Modern ♦

Modern, with contemporary interior and art nouveau styling; built to resemble its former use as a public baths. Impressive copper entrance and 7th floor roof garden with loungers. Both indoor and outdoor pools. Restaurant offers Hungarian and international dishes.

NH Budapest

Vigszinház utca 3 ✉ 1137 – Ⓜ Nyugati pályaudvar – ✆ (01) 814 0000 – www.nh-hotels.com Plan I **A1**

160 rm – †24700/35960 HUF ††24700/35960 HUF, ☕ 4703 HUF

Rest – *(closed Saturday and Sunday)* Carte 4870/8354 HUF

♦ Business ♦ Chain hotel ♦ Modern ♦

Modern, purpose-built hotel located in the city suburbs. Bright, comfortable, well-equipped bedrooms; some with balconies. Impressive atrium complete with café-bar. Informal restaurant offers a mix of Hungarian and more international dishes.

Mamaison Residence Izabella without rest

Izabella utca 61 ✉ 1064 – Ⓜ Vörösmarty utca – ✆ (01) 475 5900 – www.mamaison.com **F1**

38 suites – †43400/48900 HUF ††68000/73500 HUF, ☕ 3280 HUF

♦ Townhouse ♦ Modern ♦

Well-run aparthotel; formerly a police station, with warm, open-plan reception, basement gym and sauna. Bedrooms – all suites – boast a high level of facilities; those in rear garden wing are quietest.

K + K Opera without rest

Révay utca 24 ✉ 1065 – Ⓜ Opera – ✆ (01) 269 0222 – www.kkhotels.com **F1**

203 rm ☕ – †58960 HUF ††73354 HUF – 2 suites

♦ Business ♦ Modern ♦

Handily situated next door to the Opera House and near the smart shops of Andrassy utca. Uniform bedrooms are comfortable and up-to-date. Comprehensive breakfast buffet. Friendly staff.

Soho Boutique without rest

Dohány utca 64 ✉ 1074 – Ⓜ Blaha Lujza tér – ✆ (01) 872 8292 – www.sohohotel.com Plan I **B2**

74 rm – †16600/27390 HUF ††19368/30158 HUF

♦ Business ♦ Stylish ♦ Design ♦

Well-located for tourists, with a vibrantly coloured lobby. Bedrooms boast modern art murals, red wood floors and stylish furniture; Polanski's 'Dance of the Vampires' theme runs throughout.

Zara without rest

Só utca 6 ✉ 1056 – Ⓜ Kálvin tér – ✆ (01) 577 0700 – www.zarahotels.com **F3**

74 rm ☕ – †46400 HUF ††51900 HUF

♦ Business ♦ Modern ♦

Purpose-built hotel adjacent to the river and the main shopping street. Mirrored glass façade; compact, stylish, up-to-date bedrooms with modern fabrics and good levels of comfort.

Central Basilica without rest

Hercegprímás utca 8 ✉ 1051 – Ⓜ Bajcsy-Zs. út – ☎ (01) 328 5010 – www.hotelcentral-basilica.hu **E2**

43 rm – †28500/31000 HUF ††31000/34000 HUF – 3 suites

◆ Traditional ◆ Functional ◆

Good value hotel, superbly located, close to the Basilica. Simple bedrooms, perfect for the short-stay tourist; choose one overlooking central courtyard. Cellar room for buffet breakfast.

Gundel

Állatkerti utca 2 ✉ 1146 – Ⓜ Hősök tere – ☎ (01) 468 4040 – www.gundel.hu – Closed 25 December Plan I **B1**

Rest – *(booking essential)* Menu 3800 HUF (lunch) – Carte approx. 15000 HUF

◆ Traditional Hungarian ◆ Elegant ◆ Luxury ◆

Impressive floodlit villa overlooking the city park: the country's best known restaurant. Spacious columned salon with mahogany panelling, ornate ceiling and paintings by Hungarian masters. Huge choice of traditional cuisine. Live gypsy band at dinner.

Costes

Ráday utca 4 ✉ 1092 – Ⓜ Kálvin tér – ☎ (01) 219 0696 – www.costes.hu – Closed 2 weeks January, 2 weeks August, Monday and Tuesday

Rest – *(booking essential)* Menu 6400/18000 HUF – Carte 13200/16200 HUF **F3**

Spec. Roasted quail stuffed with duck liver, baby spinach and cauliflower purée. Fillet of John Dory with zucchini, Taggiasca olives and lemon panisses. Dessert plate.

◆ Modern ◆ Design ◆ Elegant ◆

Sophisticated, tastefully furnished restaurant epitomised by clothed tables, quality glassware and formal service. Accomplished cooking of excellent ingredients: classic combinations are interpreted in an innovative style, with precise technique and clear flavours.

Onyx

Vörösmarty tér 7-8 ✉ 1051 – Ⓜ Vörösmarty tér – ☎ (01) 429 9023 – www.onyxrestaurant.hu – Closed 2 weeks January, Sunday and Monday **E2**

Rest – *(booking essential)* Menu 3590 HUF (lunch) – Carte 9600/13500 HUF

Spec. Goat's cheese ravioli, baked tomato and basil oil. Fillet, knuckle and leg of veal with celery purée. Somló sponge cake.

◆ Modern ◆ Design ◆ Elegant ◆

Stylish restaurant with black tiled floor, silver ceiling, chandeliers and onyx adorning some of the furniture. Precise, highly skilled cooking. Traditional Hungarian and European flavours to fore but with interesting modern twists and some unusual combinations.

Fausto's

Székely Mihály utca 2 ✉ 1061 – Ⓜ Opera – ☎ (01) 877 6210 – www.fausto.hu – Closed 24-26 December, 1 January, 1 May and Sunday **F1/2**

Rest – Carte 7800/11800 HUF

◆ Italian ◆ Design ◆ Elegant ◆

Smart, well-run restaurant hidden behind a discreet façade. Sophisticated, comfortable, deep red interior, divided into two. Refined, flavoursome Italian cooking. Detailed service.

Baraka – at Mamaison H. Andrássy

Andrássy út 111 ✉ 1062 – Ⓜ Bajza utca – ☎ (01) 483 1355 – www.barakarestaurant.hu Plan I **B1**

Rest – Carte 7100/11300 HUF

◆ Innovative ◆ Intimate ◆ Design ◆

Seductive, stylish restaurant with slick, professional service. Cooking is original and uses interesting combinations of high quality ingredients; dishes are modern, or classical with an innovative twist.

XX

babel delicate

Szarku utca 1 ✉ 1055 – Ⓜ Kálvin tér – ✆ (01) 338 2143
– www.babeldelicate.hu
– Closed 2 weeks January, 24-26 December, Sunday and Monday
Rest – *(booking essential)* Menu 3950/11500 HUF **F3**
– Carte 9800/12000 HUF
♦ Modern ♦ Design ♦
Tastefully decorated in black, with open kitchen and friendly service. International, Hungarian and Vegetarian menus: modern, beautifully presented dishes; stimulating flavour combinations.

XX

Tigris

Mérleg utca 10 ✉ 1051 – Ⓜ Bajcsy-Zs. út – ✆ (01) 317 3715
– www.tigrisrestaurant.hu
– Closed 1 week August, 25 December and Sunday **E2**
Rest – Menu 3500 HUF (lunch) – Carte 6700/10900 HUF
♦ Hungarian ♦ Brasserie ♦
Well-run, busy bistro serving carefully prepared, classic Hungarian dishes. Informal, efficient service and relaxed atmosphere. Excellent choice of wine from the country's top producers.

XX

Mokka

Sas utca 4 ✉ 1051 – Ⓜ Bajcsy-Zs. út – ✆ (01) 328 0081
– www.mokkarestaurant.hu **E2**
Rest – *(booking essential)* Menu 2000/7000 HUF – Carte 5860/9970 HUF
♦ Fusion ♦ Trendy ♦
Modern, stylish restaurant with vaulted ceiling and African décor. Eclectic menus offer dishes with influences ranging from Asia to Hungary; South America to the Mediterranean.

XX

Cyrano

Kristóf tér 7-8 ✉ 1052 – Ⓜ Vörösmarty tér – ✆ (01) 266 4747
– www.cyranorestaurant.info
– Closed 24 December **E2**
Rest – Menu 3000 HUF (lunch) – Carte 4995/10900 HUF
♦ International ♦ Trendy ♦ Fashionable ♦
Fashionable, modern restaurant with ornate plaster ceiling and dimly lit, intimate interior. Selection of Hungarian and international dishes. Choose a table on the mezzanine floor.

X

Bock Bisztró

Erzsébet krt. 43-49 ✉ 1073 – Ⓜ Oktogon – ✆ (01) 321 0340
– www.bockbistro.hu
– Closed 24-26 and 31 December, Sunday and bank holidays **F1**
Rest – *(booking essential)* Carte 4550/9900 HUF
♦ Hungarian ♦ Bistro ♦
Smart, vibrant, well-run little bistro with informal, stylish feel. Modern take on Hungarian classics: careful, flavoursome, satisfying cooking. Blackboard specials include bacon, ham and sausages by artisan butcher. Great wine list and an accordion player.

X

Krizia

Mozsár utca 12 ✉ 1066 – Ⓜ Oktogon – ✆ (01) 331 8711
– www.ristorantekrizia.hu
– Closed 1 week January, Easter, Christmas and Sunday **F1**
Rest – Menu 1500 HUF (lunch) – Carte 3600/8900 HUF
♦ Italian ♦ Cosy ♦ Bistro ♦
Personally run, cosy cellar restaurant on residential street. Carefully prepared seasonal Italian cooking, with regularly changing specials. Traditional feel; friendly service.

Osteria Fausto's

Dohàny utca 5 ✉ 1072 – Ⓜ Astoria – ✆ (01) 269 6806 – www.osteria.hu – Closed 24-26 December and Sunday **F2**

Rest – Menu 2500 HUF (lunch) – Carte 5500/10200 HUF

♦ Italian ♦ Bistro ♦

Informal, personally run restaurant and wine bar serving simple, rustic Italian classics supplemented by blackboard specials. Hungarian and Italian wines. Expect a friendly welcome.

BUDA

Plan II

Art'otel

Bem rkp. 16-19 ✉ 1011 – Ⓜ Batthyány tér – ✆ (01) 487 9487 – www.artotels.com **D1**

156 rm – †27000/81700 HUF ††27000/81700 HUF, ☐ 3280 HUF – 9 suites

Rest *Chelsea* – *✆ (01) 487 9439* – Menu 1990 HUF (lunch) – Carte 5390/8730 HUF

♦ Business ♦ Design ♦

Modern, purpose-built hotel on banks of Danube. Stylish interior in cool shades; over 700 pieces of art by Donald Sultan. Rooms in converted baroque houses are more spacious; those overlooking courtyard are quieter. Butterfly-themed restaurant in sunny atrium; international menu.

Lánchíd 19

Lánchíd utca 19 ✉ 1013 – ✆ (01) 419 1900 – www.lanchid19hotel.hu

48 rm – †33100/41900 HUF ††33100/41900 HUF, ☐ 3280 HUF **D2**

Rest *L19* – Menu 1915 HUF (lunch) – Carte 5500/10100 HUF

♦ Business ♦ Design ♦

Stylish hotel overlooking the Danube and castle. Designer chairs, feature walls, modern facilities and colourful bathrooms. Glass-floored lounge looks down onto 14C ruins of a water tower. Mezzanine restaurant with good river views, serving international menu.

Buda Castle Fashion without rest

Úri utca 39 ✉ 1014 – Ⓜ Moszkva tér – ✆ (01) 224 7900 – www.budacastlehotel.eu **C1**

19 rm ☐ – †19000/35000 HUF ††24000/40000 HUF – 6 suites

♦ Townhouse ♦ Stylish ♦

15C merchant's house and former HQ for the Hungarian Hunting Association, set on a quiet street in the heart of Old Buda. Spacious, comfortable bedrooms boast pleasant, modern décor.

Castle Garden

Lovas út 41 ✉ 1012 – Ⓜ Moszkva tér – ✆ (01) 224 7420 – www.castlegarden.hu **C1**

39 rm ☐ – †20500/27300 HUF ††21900/43700 HUF

Rest *Bonfini Kert* – Menu 3280 HUF (lunch) – Carte 3690/8600 HUF

♦ Business ♦ Modern ♦

Contemporary hotel just outside the castle walls. Comfortable bedrooms in natural hues boast a good level of facilities; superior rooms have enclosed terrace and views. Bonfini Kert serves menu of Italian classics with a modern touch. Pleasant terrace.

Uhu Villa without rest

Kesely utca I/a (Northwest : 8 km by Szilágyi Erzsébet fasor) ✉ 1025 – ✆ (01) 275 1002 – www.uhuvilla.hu

9 rm – †20521/40774 HUF ††32830/46513 HUF, ☐ 4105 HUF – 1 suite

♦ Traditional ♦ Cosy ♦

Friendly, discreet, personally styled early 20C villa. Surrounded by pleasant gardens and located in the peaceful Buda Hills, it is only accessible by car. Smart, contemporary bedrooms with neat décor; some boasting their own balconies. 'Uhu' means 'owl'.

Carlton without rest

Apor Péter utca 3 ✉ 1011 – ☎ (01) 224 0999 – www.carltonhotel.hu
95 rm – †23200/34100 HUF ††27300/34100 HUF **D2**
♦ Traditional ♦ Classic ♦
Friendly hotel in quiet location between Danube and castle. Neat, well-equipped, traditionally styled bedrooms; half with bath, half with shower. Extensive buffet breakfast overlooking garden.

Alabárdos

Országház utca 2 ✉ 1014 – Ⓜ Moszkva tér – ☎ (01) 356 0851
– www.alabardos.hu
– Closed Sunday **D1**
Rest – *(booking essential) (dinner only and Saturday lunch)*
Menu 10500 HUF – Carte 7400/10500 HUF
♦ Hungarian ♦ Formal ♦ Elegant ♦
Long-standing, professionally run restaurant with vaulted ceilings, antique furniture, clothed tables and detailed service. The seasonally changing menu uses locally sourced ingredients to produce traditional Hungarian dishes with a modern edge.

Arany Kaviár

Ostrom utca 19 ✉ 1015 – Ⓜ Moszkva tér – ☎ (01) 201 6737
– www.aranykaviar.hu
– Closed 24-25 December **C1**
Rest – Menu 4900/10000 HUF – Carte 6500/12900 HUF
♦ Russian ♦ Intimate ♦ Elegant ♦
Lavishly furnished restaurant serving menu of Russian/Hungarian dishes, with caviar a speciality. Well-executed, accomplished cooking uses fine ingredients. Candlelit and intimate in the evening.

Vadrózsa

Pentelei Molnár utca 15 ✉ 1025 – ☎ (01) 345 0426 – www.vadrozsa.hu
– Closed 24-26 December *Plan I* **A1**
Rest – Menu 5000 HUF (lunch) – Carte 7630/10840 HUF
♦ International ♦ Elegant ♦
Passionately run restaurant; its beautiful wood panelling, chandeliers and pianist reminiscent of a bygone era. Menu of Hungarian and international classics, with seasonal specialities.

Csalogány 26

Csalogány utca 26 ✉ 1015 – Ⓜ Batthyány tér – ☎ (01) 201 7892
– www.csalogany26.hu
– Closed 2 weeks spring, 2 weeks winter, Sunday, Monday and bank holidays
Rest – *(booking advisable)* Menu 2500 HUF (lunch) **D1**
– Carte 5500/9000 HUF
♦ Modern ♦ Bistro ♦ Friendly ♦
This modest restaurant's stark interior hides a passionate kitchen, where excellent ingredients are used to produce flavourful, rustic Hungarian dishes with a dash of modernity. Feature menu of 3, 4 or 8 courses and small à la carte offer great value. Knowledgeable service.

Café Pierrot

Fortuna utca 14 ✉ 1014 – Ⓜ Moszkva tér – ☎ (01) 375 6971
– www.pierrot.hu **C1**
Rest – Menu 7300 HUF – Carte 6140/9070 HUF
♦ Hungarian ♦ Elegant ♦
Vaulted, narrow, two-roomed restaurant in historic property within the castle walls. Hungarian classics prepared with a contemporary touch; efficient service. Pierrot theme and live piano.

Arcade Bistro

Kiss Janos Alt utca 38 ✉ 1126 – Ⓜ Déli pu. – ✆ (01) 225 1969
– www.arcadebistro.hu
– Closed 25, 31 December and Sunday dinner **C2**

Rest – Carte 6000/8400 HUF

◆ Hungarian ◆ Bistro ◆ Neighbourhood ◆

Friendly, well-run restaurant, hidden away beneath apartment blocks in a residential area. Warm Mediterranean décor, black leather banquettes and central water feature. Hungarian classics delivered in a delicate, modern manner; sizeable list of daily specials.

21

Fortuna utca 21 ✉ 1014 – Ⓜ Moszkva tér – ✆ (01) 202 2113
– www.21restaurant.hu **C1**

Rest – Menu 6300 HUF – Carte 4970/7520 HUF

◆ Hungarian ◆ Fashionable ◆ Bistro ◆

Situated within the castle walls; a contemporary take on a traditional bistro, with wood floors, rustic touches and a relaxed style. Classic Hungarian dishes, subtly reinvented with an appealing contemporary touch; blackboard specials. Efficient, friendly service.

Republic of IRELAND

ÉIRE

PROFILE

→ **Area:**
70 284 km²
(27 137 sq mi).

→ **Population:**
4 460 000 inhabitants (est. 2009), density = 63 per km².

→ **Capital:**
Dublin (population 2 688 248).

→ **Currency:**
Euro (€); rate of exchange: € 1 = US$ 1.37 (Dec. 2010).

→ **Government:**
Parliamentary republic (since 1921). Member of European Union since 1973.

→ **Languages:**
Irish and English.

→ **Specific public holidays:**
St. Patrick's Day (17 March) Good Friday (Friday before Easter); May Bank Holiday (first Monday in May); June Bank Holiday (first Monday in June); August Bank Holiday (first Monday in August); October Bank Holiday (last Monday in October); St. Stephen's Day (26 December).

→ **Local Time:**
GMT in winter and GMT + 1 hour in summer.

→ **Climate:**
Temperate maritime, with cool winters and mild summers, fairly high rainfall (Dublin : January: 5°C, July: 15°C).

→ **International dialling Code:**
00 353 followed by area code and then the local number.

→ **Emergency:**
✆ **999** for all emergency services – Fire Brigade, Police, Ambulance, Mountain, Cave, Coastguard and Sea rescue.

→ **Electricity:**
230 volts AC, 50Hz; 3 pin flat or 2-pin round-shaped wall sockets are standard.

→ **Formalities**
Travellers from the European Union

(EU), Switzerland, Iceland and the main countries of North and South America need a national identity card or passport (except for British nationals travelling from the UK; America: passport required) to visit Ireland for less than three months (tourism or business purpose). For visitors from other countries a visa may be required, in addition to a passport, especially for those wishing to stay for longer than three months. We advise you to check with your embassy before travelling.

DUBLIN

BAILE ÁTHA CLIATH

Population: 505 739 (conurbation 2 688 248) – Altitude: sea level

ırek Slusarczyk/Fotolia.com

For somewhere touted as the finest Georgian city in the British Isles, Dublin enjoys a very young image. As the 'Celtic Tiger' roared to prominence in the 1990s, Ireland's old capital took on a youthful expression, and for the first time revelled in the epithets 'chic' and 'trendy'. Nowadays it's not just the bastion of Guinness drinkers and those here for the 'craic', but a twenty-first century city with smart restaurants, grand new hotels, modern architecture, impressive galleries and ethnic diversity (and yes, the Guinness still tastes perfect).

Until the recent worldwide recession, Dublin hadn't known a period of such economic prosperity and growth for 250 years, when its handsome squares and façades took shape, designed by the finest architects of the time. In the intervening years, it's gone through uprising, civil war and independence from Britain. Now the city holds a strong fascination for foreign visitors – people are going to Dublin rather than leaving it, as was traditionally the case. Mind you, the locals don't always take too kindly to their guests: invading hordes of stag and hen parties crossing the Irish Sea for intense liquid refreshment, mostly in the Temple Bar area alongside the Liffey, put a strain on even a Dubliner's amiability. At least it leaves all those other fascinating parts of the city ripe for the rest of us to explore.

LIVING THE CITY

Dublin can be pretty well divided into three parts. The area southeast of the river is the classiest, defined by the glorious **Trinity College, St Stephen's Green**, and **Grafton Street's** smart shops. Just west of here is the second area, dominated by **Dublin Castle** and **Christ Church Cathedral** – ancient buildings abound, but it doesn't quite match the sleek aura of the city's Georgian quarter. Cross the **Liffey** to reach the third area. This northern section was the last part of Dublin to be developed during the eighteenth century. Although it lacks the glamour and affluence of its southern neighbours, it does boast the city's grandest avenue, **O'Connell Street,** as well as its most celebrated theatres, a fact that counts in a city which has been home to four Nobel Prize winning writers.

PRACTICAL INFORMATION

ARRIVAL-DEPARTURE

Dublin Airport is just over 7 miles north of the city and a taxi will cost around €20. There is no rail link to the airport but a number of coaches and buses, including Airlink and Aircoach, will take you to the city centre in approximately 30mins.

TRANSPORT

The bus network covers the whole city from the Central Bus Station in Store Street. The price of a single ticket varies depending on the number of stages you've travelled, but it's a cheap and efficient service.

The exciting LUAS (meaning 'speed') light rail network rushes you to areas of the city and suburbs previously only connected to the centre by bus. LUAS was introduced in 2004; like the buses, you pay more as you travel further by zones.

If you want to get out to the coast, then jump on a Dublin Area Rapid Transport (DART) train. They operate at regular intervals, are awesomely efficient, and leave central Dublin from Connolly, Tara Street and Pearse stations. They're as quick as they sound. Buy tickets at any station.

Get along to a Tourist Information Office for the Dublin Pass, which gains you access to just about anywhere in the city. Well, to over thirty attractions, anyway. Passes range from one to six days.

EXPLORING DUBLIN

Despite its twenty-first century gloss, Dublin still enjoys a meandering pace of life with an emphasis on the slow and relaxed. Locals will advise you to take your time over a visit; this is not the biggest metropolis on the planet, so why hurry to get around it? With almost a thousand pubs inside the city limits (never mind the new bars and cafés which have sprung up) there's certainly no problem in interrupting your sightseeing schedule. Most of the tourist hotspots are in the area to the south of the Liffey, but there's a lot of fun to be had in turning into inconspicuous alleyways and seeing

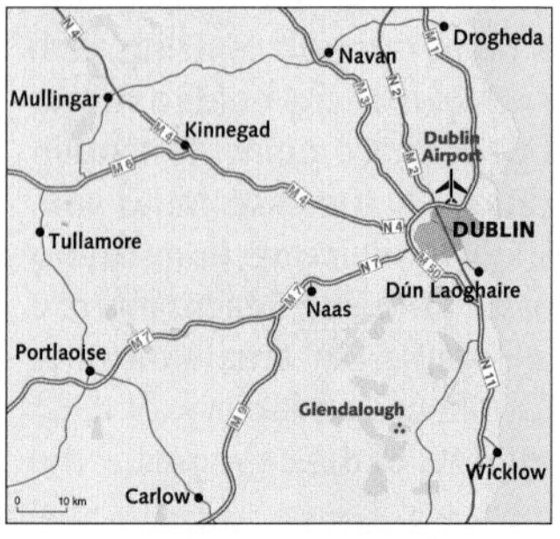

what shadowy hidden gem might be giving you the nod.

➔ BROUGHT TO BOOK

If you did happen to be in a rush, you could walk from the top of O'Connell Street over the river to the smart southern suburb of **Ballsbridge** in an hour. But then what would be the point of coming to Dublin? The best place to linger is the area around Trinity College, leading down Grafton Street. This section of the city was pretty much undeveloped until the college was founded in 1592, but it was another hundred years before St Stephen's Green, just to the south, was created. As we say, around here no-one's in a particular hurry. It's not difficult to see why people flock to the college. The alma mater of Samuel Beckett, Oliver Goldsmith and Edmund Burke, it's populated with attractive squares, an Old Library with a spectacular Long Room, and a dominant thirty metre high Campanile. Its main attraction, though, is in the Treasury, where the magnificent **Book of Kells** is housed. Dated from around AD 800, it's one of the oldest books in the world, a lavishly illustrated manuscript produced by monks on the remote Scottish island of Iona. It features superbly decorated opening letters of each chapter and dyes supposedly imported from the Middle East.

By way of a complete contrast to the intense intellectualism of Trinity College, step outside and there you'll find the fancy shops lining Grafton Street, the city's most fashionable thoroughfare. Its most exclusive store, Brown Thomas, is also one of its oldest, and locals look upon it as a Londoner might look upon Harvey Nichols. Grafton Street certainly pulls in the crowds, and for those heading south, there's the reward of a verdant sanctuary: St Stephen's Green. Landscaped with flowerbeds, trees, a lake and a fountain, it likes to remind you exactly where you are by displaying numerous memorials to eminent Dubliners: Joyce, Yeats and Wolfe Tone are all here.

➔ MAKING MERRION

This is where Georgian architecture really makes its impact felt; head north along **Merrion Street Upper** and you'll find **Merrion Square,** twelve swanky acres of mid-eighteenth century splendour, bordered on three sides by attractive town-houses featuring wrought-iron balconies and brightly painted doors. The area's sophisticated appeal is enhanced by a rash of museums and galleries, chief of these being the **National Museum** on Kildare Street, which announces itself with an eye-catching domed rotunda and beautiful jewellery from the Bronze Age. In the **National Gallery** on Clare Street, the major schools of European art are represented alongside Irish painting. One of the benefactors here was George Bernard Shaw (his own birthplace, a twenty minute walk south from here, is itself now a museum). Truly worth a visit when you're in the Georgian quarter is the **National Library**, fascinating because it contains first editions of every major Irish writer, and you don't have to think too hard to come up with an awesome list. But museum lovers need not yet feel sated, as also in the area are the **Heraldic Museum** and the **Natural History Museum**, or 'the Dead Zoo' as it's known to the locals.

➔ TEMPLE WORSHIP

You don't really feel you're strolling into a radically different area when you venture south-west of the Liffey: after all, it's just a hop, skip and jump across from Trinity College and Grafton Street. But this is an even older part of town, with **Temple Bar** boasting a wealth of attractive cobbled streets. The area is alive during the daytime as well, particularly around Temple Bar Square, which buzzes with little gallery shops, designer boutiques and a thriving book market at weekends. With its now legendary number of bars, pubs and restaurants jostling for your attention, you might feel the only way to find sanctuary is in a big church or even a castle. Wouldn't you know it, there are two on the doorstep. Christ Church Cathedral, in Christchurch Place, was established nearly a thousand years ago, making it Ireland's oldest. Its history continues right up to 2000, when the vast and fascinating twelfth century crypt was restored. Just across the way is Dublin Castle, first built in the thirteenth century, but with the **Record Tower** the only survivor from that time; luxurious state apartments and a throne presented by William of Orange can be found here, but the star turn is the **Chester Beatty Library**, in the Castle's Clock Tower Building. This outstanding collection of ancient works of art from around the world includes hundreds of illuminated manuscripts with exquisite calligraphy, and almost 300 copies of the Koran spread over a thousand years (considered to be the best example of illuminated Islamic texts in the world). There are striking Buddhist paintings, clay tablets and detailed miniatures. Not surprisingly, it was named European Museum of the Year in 2002. Oh, and the rooftop garden's a great place to eat your lunch if it's a sunny day.

→ NOT WRITTEN OFF

North of the Liffey has for many years been considered a bit of an Achilles Heel, an area 'down on its uppers' and in need of a facelift, an urban botox. That said, there are good reasons to cross the river in a northwards direction, not least a stroll along Dublin's grandest thoroughfare, O'Connell Street. This imposing avenue's mid-eighteenth century glory days may be long gone, but meandering along its central mall you can still get a feel for its heyday as you sample its mix of monuments, fine department stores and historic public buildings. At either end of O'Connell Street stand Dublin's two most famous theatres: **The Abbey** to the south is Ireland's national theatre where Irish playwrights are proudly to the fore; while **The Gate** in Parnell Square to the north has a great reputation for contemporary drama. Slipping very conveniently into this creative mix is the absorbing **Dublin Writers' Museum**, also in Parnell Square, which pays tribute to the city's long history as a literary giant, and includes letters, photos and other memorabilia. Fans of Joyce can then pop along a few streets east to the **James Joyce Cultural Centre**, housed neatly in a Georgian townhouse.

DUBLIN IN...

→ ONE DAY

Trinity College, Grafton Street, St Stephen's Green, Merrion Square, a drink and a meal in Temple Bar

→ TWO DAYS

Christ Church Cathedral, Dublin Castle, Chester Beatty Library, the quayside, a play at one of Dublin's theatres

→ THREE DAYS

A further amble round the alleyways of Temple Bar, O'Connell Street, Parnell Square, Dublin Writers' Museum, a DART train to the coast

CALENDAR HIGHLIGHTS

Some people think Dubliners celebrate a special event every day of the year – the moment the first pint of Guinness goes down. Well, that apart, there are many events and calendar highlights of an official kind in the city. St Patrick's Day in March is, surprise surprise, taken rather seriously here. It's a national holiday given over to music and carnival-style merriment. Around the same time, Celtic Flame lets rip, a citywide festival of traditional and modern music. Don't get this mixed up with the Temple Bar Fleadh, another mid-March mash-up, which resounds to traditional rhythms all around the Temple Bar area. On a more refined scale, April hosts the Colours Boat Race along the Liffey between Trinity College and University College teams, while a little later in the month Feis Ceoil is one of Europe's most well-established and prestigious classical music festivals. Temple Bar again plays host to Diversions right through the summer, an umbrella title for loads of free concerts and open-air theatre shows. The sixteenth of June is a sacred day for fans of Joyce's Ulysses, because it's Bloomsday, when walks, pub talks and lectures take place all over the city. Dublin's premier social event, the Horse Show, trots along in August and gives people a chance to dress in funny hats. Drama's back centre-stage in September with the Fringe Theatre Festival, and then in October with the Dublin Theatre Festival, where new plays are put under the spotlight. A different kind of traditional music sees Opera Ireland make its mark for a week in November at the Gaiety Theatre.

EATING OUT

It's still possible to indulge in Irish stew, but nowadays in Dublin you can also dine out on everything from Thai to tacos and Malaysian to Middle-Eastern. The last decade has seen a boom in global cuisine, often in the Temple Bar area. The city makes the most of its bay proximity, and seafood and fish are used abundantly ; in particular, smoked salmon and oysters. The latter is a staple diet of Dubliners, who love nothing better than to wash them down with Guinness. Portions here are generous, especially in pubs: a plate of roast meat and vegetables is invariably good value for money. For decades vegetables were seen as a bit of a curse in Ireland: a mere decoration, over-boiled to death. Now they're treated with the respect they deserve, and local chefs insist on the best seasonal produce, cooked for just the right amount of time to savour all the taste and goodness. There's never been a better time to be a vegetarian in Dublin, as every type of veg from asparagus to spinach and seaweed is used liberally in dishes. Meat is particularly tasty in Ireland, due to healthy livestock and a wet climate: Irish beef is world famous for its fulsome flavour. Dinner here is usually served till about 10pm, though many ethnic and city-centre restaurants stay open later. If you make your main meal at lunchtime, you'll pay considerably less than in the evening: the menus are often similar, but the bill in the middle of the day will probably be about half the price. Good restaurants nowadays include a fifteen per cent service charge, so there's no need to add a tip.

Shelbourne

27 St Stephen's Green ✉ D2 – ✆ (01) 663 4500 – www.theshelbourne.ie
243 rm – 450 € 450 €, ☕ 29 € – 19 suites **E3**
Rest *Saddle Room* – see below
◆ Grand Luxury ◆ Classic ◆
Landmark Georgian hotel with elegant guest areas, contemporary furnishings and state-of-the-art facilities. Bedrooms in original house are most characterful. High level of services and extras.

Merrion

Upper Merrion St ✉ D2 – ✆ (01) 603 0600 – www.merrionhotel.com
133 rm – 460 € 480 €, ☕ 29 € – 10 suites **F3**
Rest *Cellar* – see below
Rest *Cellar Bar* – *(closed Sunday)* Carte 26/34 €
◆ Luxury ◆ Classic ◆
Elegant hotel boasting opulent lounges and stylish cocktail bar. Spacious bedrooms – some with original features, some more corporate in style – boast smart marble bathrooms and good facilities. Characterful barrel-ceilinged bar offers concise carvery menu.

Westin

Westmoreland St ✉ D2 – ✆ (01) 645 1000 – www.thewestindublin.com
153 rm – 474 € 474 €, ☕ 19.95 € – 10 suites **E2**
Rest *Exchange* – *(closed Sunday and Monday) (dinner only and Sunday lunch)* Menu 25 € – Carte 32/43 €
Rest *Mint* – *(dinner only)* Carte 30/40 €
◆ Luxury ◆ Classic ◆
Once a bank; now a smart hotel set over 6 period buildings, with comfy lounges, impressive conference rooms and good facilities. Georgian-style bedrooms boast heavy fabrics and marble bathrooms. Modern European cooking in semi-formal Exchange. Classic pub dishes in The Mint (formerly the bank's vaults).

Dylan

Eastmoreland Pl ✉ D2 – ✆ (01) 660 3000 – www.dylan.ie
– Closed 24-26 December *Plan III* **H1**
44 rm – 175/395 € 175/395 €, ☕ 27 €
Rest *Dylan* – Menu 22/40 € – Carte 36/54 €
◆ Townhouse ◆ Stylish ◆
Modern boutique hotel with vibrant use of colour. Supremely comfortable, individually decorated bedrooms boast an opulent feel and a host of unexpected extras. French-influenced menus served in warm, stylish dining room.

Brooks

Drury St ✉ D2 – ✆ (01) 670 4000 – www.brookshotel.ie **E2**
98 rm – 350 € 430 €, ☕ 19.95 € – 1 suite
Rest *Francesca's* – *(dinner only)* Menu 26 € – Carte 29/45 €
◆ Business ◆ Stylish ◆
Commercial hotel in modish, boutique, Irish town house style. Smart lounges and stylish rooms exude contemporary panache. Extras in top range rooms, at a supplement. Fine dining with open kitchen for chef-watching.

The Clarence

6-8 Wellington Quay ✉ D2 – ✆ (01) 407 0800 – www.theclarence.ie
– Closed 24-27 December **D2**
44 rm – 139/390 € 349/390 €, ☕ 19.50 € – 5 suites
Rest *The Tea Room* – see below
◆ Luxury ◆ Design ◆
Attractive riverside hotel, formerly a warehouse. Stylish and well-run, with art deco reception, comfy lounge and famous domed bar. Plainly decorated, understated bedrooms; good facilities.

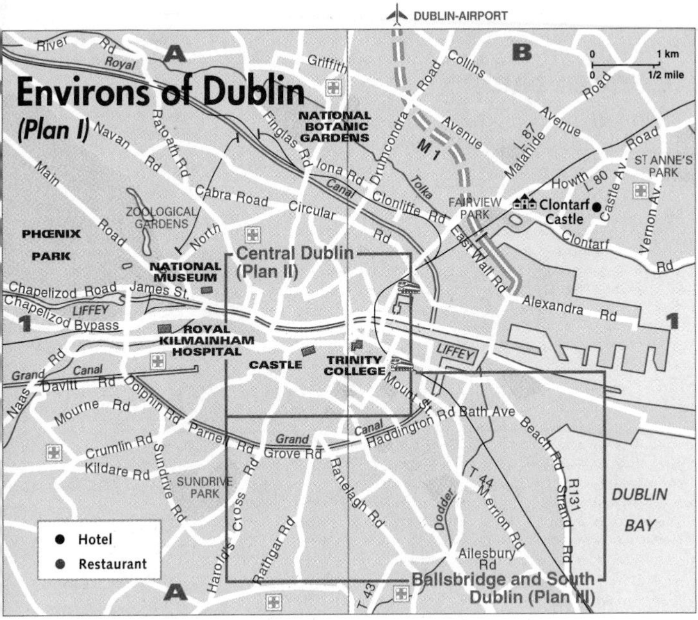

Environs of Dublin (Plan I)

Fitzwilliam

St Stephen's Grn ✉ *D2 –* ✆ *(01) 478 7000*
– www.fitzwilliamhoteldublin.com **E3**

135 rm – 🚹169/380 € 🚹🚹380 €, ☕ 24 € – 3 suites
Rest *Thornton's* – see below
Rest *Citron* – Menu 19/24 € – Carte dinner approx. 32 €

♦ Business ♦ Modern ♦

Stylish U-shaped hotel set around huge roof garden – the largest in Europe. Contemporary bedrooms display striking bold colours and good facilities; half overlook garden; half, the green. Modern first floor brasserie with international menu.

Morrison

Lower Ormond Quay ✉ *D1 –* ✆ *(01) 887 2400 – www.morrisonhotel.ie*
– Closed 24-27 December **D2**

135 rm – 🚹115/355 € 🚹🚹115/355 €, ☕ 15 € – 3 suites
Rest *Halo* – *(bar lunch)* Menu 35 €

♦ Business ♦ Design ♦

Modern riverside hotel displaying minimalist style. Contemporary lounges boast leather furniture: one has a cocktail bar. Stylish bedrooms have tranquil feel, sharp colours and good facilities. Split-level restaurant offers modern menu.

La Stampa

35-36 Dawson St ✉ *D2 –* ✆ *(01) 677 4444 – www.lastampa.ie*
– Closed 25-26 December **E3**

36 rm – 🚹260 € 🚹🚹260 €, ☕ 15 € – 1 suite
Rest *Balzac* – see below

♦ Business ♦ Personalised ♦

Deceptively large Georgian townhouse in city centre, its spacious rooms featuring bespoke furniture and a high level of facilities. Stylish guest areas and small spa with Far Eastern feel.

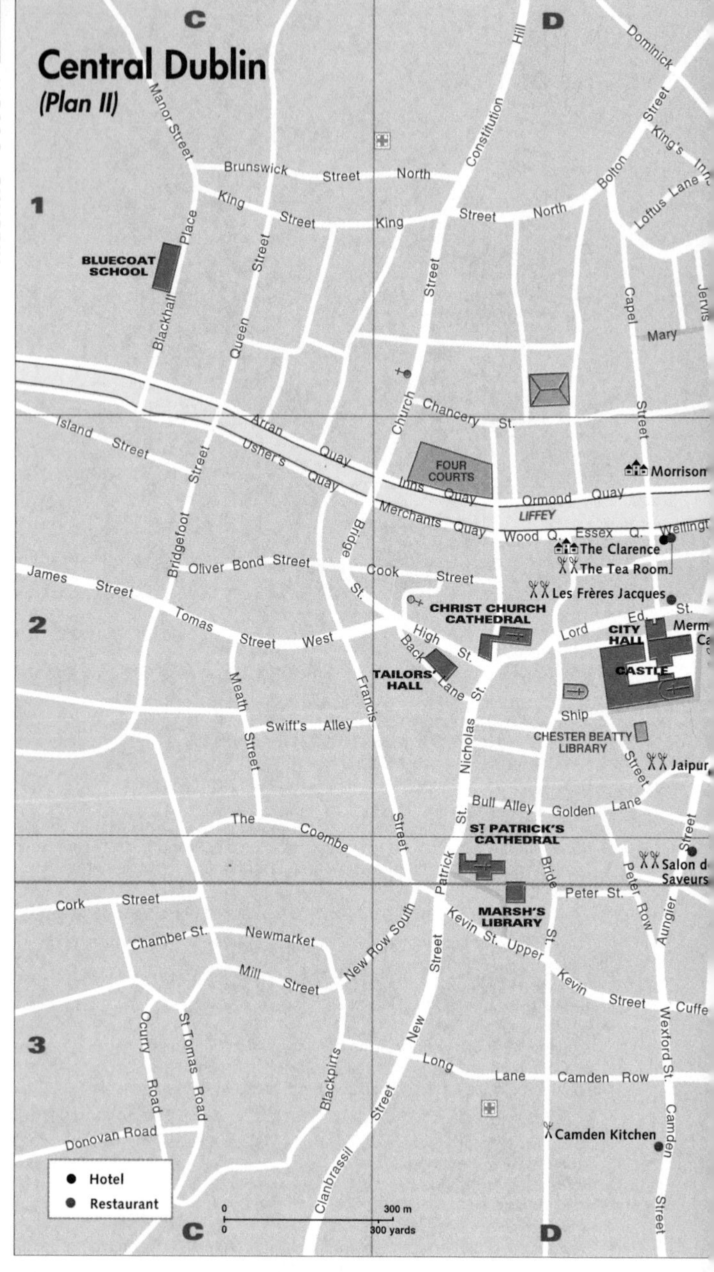

Central Dublin
(Plan II)
C
D
1
2
3
BLUECOAT SCHOOL
FOUR COURTS
LIFFEY
CHRIST CHURCH CATHEDRAL
TAILORS' HALL
CITY HALL
CASTLE
CHESTER BEATTY LIBRARY
ST PATRICK'S CATHEDRAL
MARSH'S LIBRARY
Morrison
The Clarence
The Tea Room
Les Frères Jacques
Jaipur
Salon des Saveurs
Camden Kitchen
Manor Street
Brunswick Street North
King Street North
Constitution Hill
Dominick Street
King's Inns
Bolton
Loftus Lane
Blackhall Place
Queen Street
Church Street
Capel Street
Mary
Jervis
Chancery St.
Arran Quay
Usher's Quay
Island Street
Inns Quay
Ormond Quay
Merchants Quay
Wood Q.
Essex Q.
Bridgefoot Street
Bridge St.
Oliver Bond Street
Cook Street
James Street
Tomas Street West
High St.
Back Lane
Lord Ed. St.
Meath Street
Francis Street
Swift's Alley
Nicholas St.
Ship Street
Bull Alley
Golden Lane
The Coombe
Patrick St.
Bride St.
Peter St.
Peter Row
Aungier Street
Cork Street
Chamber St.
Newmarket
Mill Street
New Row South
Kevin St. Upper
Kevin Street
Cuffe
New Street
Wexford St.
Ocurry Road
St Tomas Road
Blackpirts
Long Lane
Camden Row
Camden Street
Donovan Road
Clanbrassil Street
Hotel
Restaurant
0
300 m
300 yards

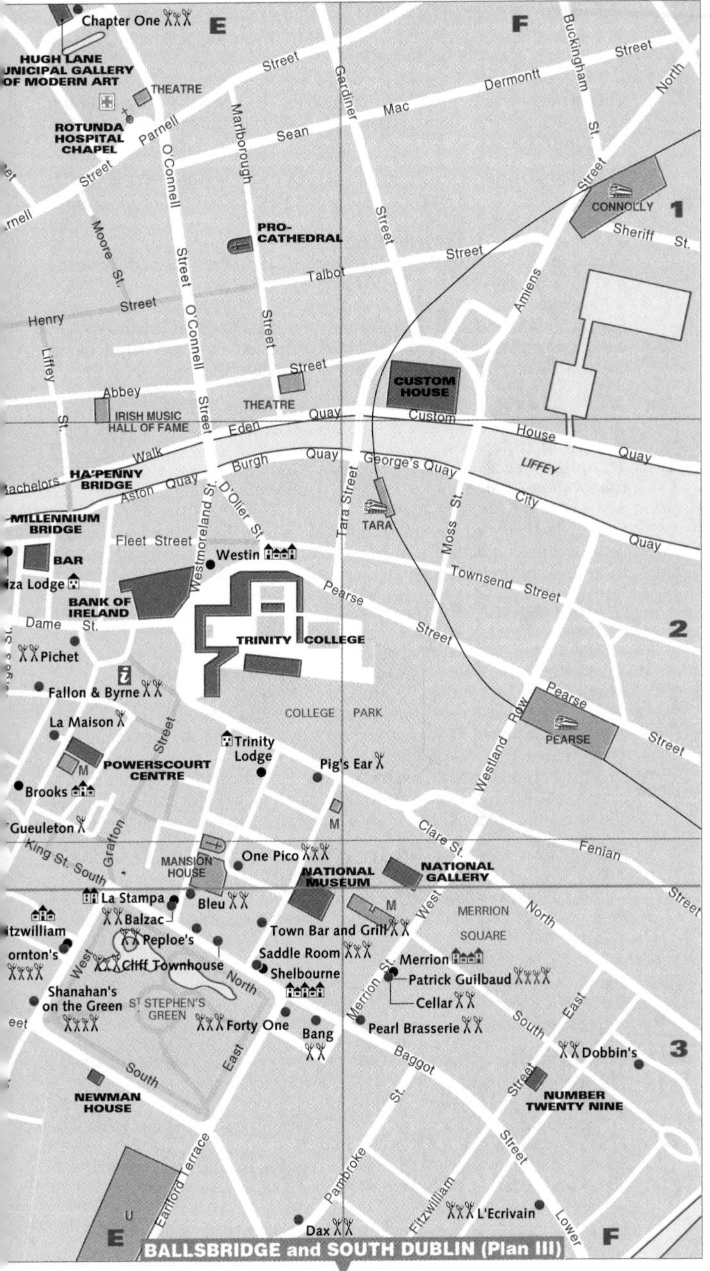
E
F
Chapter One
HUGH LANE MUNICIPAL GALLERY OF MODERN ART
THEATRE
ROTUNDA HOSPITAL CHAPEL
Parnell Street
Sean Mac Dermontt Street
Buckingham St.
North Strand
Gardiner Street
Marlborough Street
O'Connell Street
Moore St.
PRO-CATHEDRAL
CONNOLLY
Sheriff St.
Amiens Street
Talbot Street
Henry Street
Liffey St.
Abbey Street
THEATRE
CUSTOM HOUSE
IRISH MUSIC HALL OF FAME
Eden Quay
Custom House Quay
Bachelors Walk
Burgh Quay
George's Quay
LIFFEY
HA'PENNY BRIDGE
Aston Quay
D'Olier St.
Tara Street
TARA
Moss St.
City Quay
MILLENNIUM BRIDGE
Fleet Street
Westmoreland St.
Westin
BAR
Eliza Lodge
BANK OF IRELAND
Townsend Street
Pearse Street
Dame St.
TRINITY COLLEGE
Pichet
Fallon & Byrne
La Maison
COLLEGE PARK
Trinity Lodge
POWERSCOURT CENTRE
Pig's Ear
Westland Row
PEARSE
Brooks
L'Gueuleton
Grafton Street
Clare St.
Fenian Street
King St. South
MANSION HOUSE
One Pico
NATIONAL MUSEUM
NATIONAL GALLERY
La Stampa
Bleu
Balzac
Fitzwilliam
Thornton's
Peploe's
Town Bar and Grill
MERRION SQUARE
Merrion Square North
Saddle Room
Merrion
Cliff Townhouse
Shelbourne
Merrion St.
Patrick Guilbaud
Cellar
Shanahan's on the Green
ST STEPHEN'S GREEN
Forty One
Bang
Pearl Brasserie
South East
Dobbin's
Baggot St.
NUMBER TWENTY NINE
NEWMAN HOUSE
Earlsfort Terrace
Pembroke St.
Fitzwilliam
L'Ecrivain
Lower
Dax
BALLSBRIDGE and SOUTH DUBLIN (Plan III)
1
2
3

Number 31 without rest

31 Leeson Close ✉ *D2 –* ✆ *(01) 676 5011 – www.number31.ie*
21 rm ☕ – ♦90/135 € ♦♦140/175 € *Plan III* **H1**
♦ Townhouse ♦ Retro ♦
Unique house with retro styling, personally run by hospitable couple. Sunken lounge with open fire; quirky, comfortable bedrooms. Communal breakfast includes The Full Irish.

Trinity Lodge

12 South Frederick St ✉ *D2 –* ✆ *(01) 617 0900 – www.trinitylodge.com – Closed Christmas* **E2**
23 rm – ♦69/180 € ♦♦79/195 €, ☕ 7.50 €
Rest *Georges* – ✆ *(01) 679 7000 (closed 25 December-31 January, Sunday and Monday dinner)* Carte 18/30 €
♦ Townhouse ♦ Classic ♦
Elegant, centrally located Georgian town houses near local landmarks. Airy, well-furnished bedrooms with good level of comfort: the larger deluxe rooms are worth asking for. Modern restaurant and popular wine bar.

Eliza Lodge

23-24 Wellington Quay ✉ *D2 –* ✆ *(01) 671 8044 – www.elizalodge.com – Closed 20-29 December* **E2**
18 rm ☕ – ♦50/90 € ♦♦69/130 €
Rest *Italian Corner* – ✆ *(01) 671 9114* – Carte 30/40 €
♦ Family ♦ Functional ♦
Friendly, family-owned hotel ideally situated for lively Temple Bar area. Uniform bedrooms; those at the top have the best outlook over the city and river; two have balconies. Bright restaurant serves popular Italian menus overlooking the Liffey.

Patrick Guilbaud (Guillaume Lebrun)

21 Upper Merrion St ✉ *D2 –* ✆ *(01) 676 4192 – www.restaurantpatrickguilbaud.ie – Closed 25-26 December, 17 March, 22 April, Sunday and Monday*
Rest – Menu 50 € (lunch) – Carte 93/149 € **F3**
Spec. Lobster ravioli, pasta and toasted almonds. Caramelised veal sweetbreads with Cevenne onions. Warm Criollo chocolate biscuit with stout ice cream
♦ French ♦ Formal ♦
Smart, stylish and personally run restaurant within a restored and sympathetically extended Georgian house; decorated with contemporary Irish art. Accomplished and harmonious cooking, with cleverly complementing flavours and textures.

Shanahan's on the Green

119 St Stephen's Grn ✉ *D2 –* ✆ *(01) 407 0939 – www.shanahans.ie – Closed 25-26 December and Sunday* **E3**
Rest – *(dinner only and lunch Friday) (booking essential)* Menu 45 € – Carte 59/81 €
♦ Beef specialities ♦ Formal ♦
Sumptuous Georgian town house; upper floor window tables survey the Green. Supreme comfort enhances your enjoyment of strong seafood dishes and choice cuts of Irish beef.

Thornton's – at The Fitzwilliam Hotel

128 St Stephen's Grn. ✉ *D2 –* ✆ *(01) 478 7008 – www.thorntonsrestaurant.com – Closed 25 December-5 January, Sunday, Monday, lunch Tuesday and Wednesday*
Rest – Menu 49/79 € – Carte 79/125 € **E3**
Spec. Dublin bay prawns with prawn bisque. Mallard duck glazed with honey and pistachio. Prune and Armagnac soufflé, pear sorbet.
♦ Modern ♦ Formal ♦
Elegant hotel restaurant where smart glass panels divide the room; eye-catching food photos adorn the walls. Choice of classical à la carte, or modern tasting menu displaying innovative texture and flavour combinations. Knowledgeable service.

XXX ✿

L'Ecrivain (Derry Clarke)

109A Lower Baggot St ✉ D2 – ☎ (01) 661 1919 – www.lecrivain.com – Closed 24-27 December, lunch 28-30 December, 31 December-9 January, lunch 10 January, Sunday, lunch Tuesday and Wednesday, and bank holidays

Rest – *(booking essential)* Menu 25/65 € – Carte 72/81 € **F3**

Spec. Duck liver with pain d'épices, hazelnuts and pea purée. Halibut with herb gnocchi, baby leek, braised shin and parsley purée. Marshmallow and pineapple Chiboust with caramel spiced pineapple and coconut sorbet.

♦ Contemporary ♦ Formal ♦

Three-floored, former warehouse with piano bar, whiskey-themed private dining room, mezzanine and attractive terrace. Refined cooking arrives with modern touches and contemporary presentation. Service is formal but comes with personality.

XXX ✿

Chapter One (Ross Lewis)

The Dublin Writers Museum, 18-19 Parnell Sq ✉ D1 – ☎ (01) 873 2266 – www.chapteronerestaurant.com – Closed 2 weeks August, 2 weeks Christmas, Sunday and Monday **E1**

Rest – *(booking essential)* Menu 38 € (lunch) – Carte dinner 60/68 €

Spec. Terrine of foie gras with cherries and fig vinegar gel. Halibut with Dublin Bay brown shrimp and black sesame oil. Chocolate macaroon with raspberries and chocolate ganache.

♦ Modern ♦ Formal ♦

Long-established, popular restaurant in basement of historic building; contemporary lounge/bar and two smart dining rooms. Seasonal, classically-based cooking demonstrates skill and understanding. Attentive, formal service.

XXX

Forty One

41 St. Stephen's Green ✉ D2 – ☎ (01) 6620000 – www.fortyone.ie – Closed dinner 24-dinner 31 December, Sunday and Monday **E3**

Rest – *(booking advisable)* Menu 25 € (lunch) – Carte 54/71 €

♦ Modern European ♦ Elegant ♦ Intimate ♦

Richly furnished, intimate restaurant set in an attractive, creeper-clad 18C townhouse, tucked away in a corner of St Stephen's Green. Accomplished, classical cooking uses luxurious ingredients.

XXX

Cliff Townhouse with rm

A/C rest,

22 St. Stephen's Green ✉ D2 – ☎ (01) 6383939 – www.thecliftownhouse.com – Closed 25-27 December **E3**

9 rm – †125/145 € ††145/185 €

Rest – *(booking advisable)* Menu 25/45 €

♦ Modern European ♦ Brasserie ♦

Impressive Georgian townhouse overlooking the green. Large dining room with marble-topped bar and blue leather seating. Good value fixed price menus offer straightforward, classical combinations. Bedrooms display contemporary colour schemes and good comforts.

XXX

Saddle Room – at Shelbourne Hotel

27 St Stephen's Green ✉ D2 – ☎ (01) 663 4500 – www.theshelbourne.ie

Rest – Menu 24/40 € – Carte dinner 45/62 € **E3**

♦ Grills ♦ Formal ♦

Smart restaurant with well-spaced, linen-laid tables: some are set by the window; some are in booths; and some, in glass-walled private rooms. Open kitchen specialises in seafood and steaks.

XXX

One Pico

5-6 Molesworth Pl ✉ D2 – ☎ (01) 676 0300 – www.onepico.com – Closed 24-25 December and Bank Holidays **E3**

Rest – Menu 25/39 € – Carte 49/69 €

♦ Modern ♦ Fashionable ♦

Wide-ranging cuisine, classic and traditional by turns, always with an original, eclectic edge. Décor and service share a pleasant formality, crisp, modern and stylish.

XX

Salon des Saveurs

16 Aungier St ✉ D2 – ✆ (01) 4758840 – www.salondessaveurs.com
– Closed Sunday, and Monday (except December) **D2**
Rest – Menu 22 € (lunch)/56 € – Carte 26/76 €
♦ Modern European ♦ Intimate ♦
Dark, smoky, retro-chic style restaurant with mirrors and high-backed leather chairs. Set tasting menus showcase elaborate cooking, with wine pairings available. Attentive service.

XX

Pearl Brasserie

20 Merrion St Upper ✉ D2 – ✆ (01) 661 3572 – www.pearl-brasserie.com
– Closed 25 December-5 January and Sunday **F3**
Rest – Carte 31/59 €
♦ French ♦ Brasserie ♦
A metal staircase leads down to this intimate, newly refurbished, vaulted brasserie where Franco-Irish dishes are served at smart, linen-laid tables. Amiable, helpful service.

XX

Locks Brasserie

1 Windsor Terr. ✉ D8 – ✆ (01) 4200555 – www.locksbrasserie.com
– Closed 25 December-7 January and bank holidays *Plan III* **G1**
Rest – *(dinner only and lunch Thursday-Sunday)* Menu 27 € (lunch and early dinner) – Carte 29/50 €
♦ Modern European ♦ Fashionable ♦ Neighbourhood ♦
Attractive, well-lit restaurant with a relaxed atmosphere and professional, engaging staff. Dining is split over two floors, with comfy banquette seating and a cocktail bar. Menu of modern European classics; well-presented dishes make use of fine ingredients.

XX

Pichet

14-15 Trinity St ✉ D2 – ✆ (01) 6771060 – www.pichetrestaurant.com
– Closed 1-10 January **E2**
Rest – *(booking advisable)* Menu 25 € (lunch and early dinner lunch and early dinner) – Carte 31/47 €
♦ Modern European ♦ Fashionable ♦ Bistro ♦
Popular brasserie with buzzy atmosphere; its long, narrow room dominated by an open-plan kitchen counter. Front café-cum-bar for light snacks; alfresco dining on the heated terrace. Neat, flavoursome modern European cooking, with good value, daily changing menus.

XX

Dax

23 Pembroke Street Upper ✉ D2 – ✆ (01) 676 1494 – www.dax.ie
– Closed Christmas and New Year, Sunday and Monday **E3**
Rest – *(booking essential)* Menu 29/39 € (dinner Tuesday-Thursday) – Carte 44/58 €
♦ French ♦ Rustic ♦
Hidden away in basement of Georgian terrace, with rustic inner, immaculately laid tables, wine cellar and bar serving tapas. Knowledgable staff serve French influenced menus.

XX

Dobbin's

15 Stephen's Lane, (off Stephen's Place) off Lower Mount St ✉ D2 – ✆ (01) 661 9536 – www.dobbins.ie
– Closed 24 December-2 January, Saturday lunch, Sunday dinner and bank holidays **F3**
Rest – *(booking essential)* Menu 24 € (lunch)/38 € – Carte 46/54 €
♦ Traditional ♦ Neighbourhood ♦
Smart, well-established restaurant in residential area. Small bar with booths leads to spacious, neatly laid dining room with warm, modern décor. Large menu displays international influences.

XX **Cellar** - at Merrion Hotel

Upper Merrion St ✉ D2 – ✆ (01) 603 0630 – www.merrionhotel.com
Rest – *(Closed Saturday lunch)* Menu 20/30 € – Carte 36/67 € **F3**
♦ Modern ♦ Formal ♦
Set in hotel cellars, a formal restaurant with linen-laid tables, high-backed chairs and characterful curved ceiling. Good-sized menus of modern Irish cooking feature local, regional produce.

XX **The Tea Room** - at The Clarence Hotel

6-8 Wellington Quay ✉ D2 – ✆ (01) 407 0813
– Closed 24-27 December **D2**
Rest – *(booking essential)* Menu 24 € (dinner) – Carte 36/54 €
♦ Modern ♦ Fashionable ♦
Spacious hotel restaurant, where small mezzanine level overlooks larger main room with central banquette island. Ambitious cooking displays Gallic influences. Polite, formal service.

XX **Les Frères Jacques**

74 Dame St ✉ D2 – ✆ (01) 679 4555 – www.lesfreresjacques.com – Closed 25 December-2 January, Saturday lunch, Sunday and bank holiday Mondays
Rest – Menu 23 € (lunch)/38 € – Carte 48/65 € **D2**
♦ French ♦ Bistro ♦
Long-standing restaurant on narrow cobbled alley, with typical French styling and team. Classical Gallic cooking with seafood a speciality: daily fresh fish and lobster tank on display.

XX **Peploe's**

16 St Stephen's Green ✉ D2 – ✆ (01) 676 3144 – www.peploes.com
– Closed 25-29 December and 22 April **E3**
Rest – *(booking essential)* Menu 25 € (lunch and early dinner lunch and early dinner) – Carte 36/47 €
♦ Mediterranean ♦ Fashionable ♦ Brasserie ♦
Well-run, atmospheric brasserie named after Scottish artist and set in former bank vault. Small bar; main room with smart mural and linen-laid tables. Extensive menu with influences from the Med.

XX **Bleu**

Joshua House, Dawson St. ✉ D2 – ✆ (01) 676 7015 – www.bleu.ie
– Closed 25-26 December **E3**
Rest – Menu 22 € (lunch)/26 € – Carte 25/40 €
♦ Modern European ♦ Fashionable ♦
Stylish, modern eatery on a bustling street. Smart and contemporary interior, with framed mirrors a feature. The appealing, varied menu keeps its influences within Europe.

XX **Town Bar and Grill**

21 Kildare St ✉ D2 – ✆ (01) 662 4800 – www.townbarandgrill.com
– Closed 25-27 December and bank holidays **E3**
Rest – *(booking essential)* Menu 25 € (lunch) – Carte dinner 38/62 €
♦ Italian influences ♦ Rustic ♦
Located in wine merchant's old cellars: brick pillars divide a large space; fresh flowers and candles add a personal touch. Italian flair in bold cooking with innovative edge.

XX **Fallon & Byrne**

First Floor, 11-17 Exchequer St ✉ D2 – ✆ (01) 472 1000
– www.fallonandbyrne.com
– Closed 25 December, 1 January and Sunday dinner **E2**
Rest – Menu 30 € – Carte 24/39 €
♦ Bistro ♦ Rustic ♦
Food emporium boasting vast basement wine cellar, ground floor full of fresh quality produce, and first floor French style bistro with banquettes, mirrors and tasty bistro food.

XX

Balzac – at La Stampa Hotel

VISA MO AE

35-36 Dawson St ✉ D2 – ✆ (01) 677 8611 – www.lastampa.ie
– Closed Sunday **E3**

Rest – *(dinner only)* Menu 25 € – Carte 22/50 €

♦ French ♦ Fashionable ♦

Spacious restaurant in former dance hall, with high glass ceiling, linen-laid tables and banquette seating. Comfy lounge bar and appealing French themed menus.

XX

Bang

A/C VISA MO AE

11 Merrion Row ✉ D2 – ✆ (01) 400 4229 – www.bang-restaurant.com
– Closed 25 December-1 January, first week January, and Saturday-Sunday lunch **E3**

Rest – *(booking essential)* Menu 25 € (lunch lunch and early dinner)/27 € – Carte dinner 34/46 €

♦ Modern ♦ Fashionable ♦

Stylish three floor restaurant displaying impressive modern art by leading Irish/international artists. Good value lunch/early evening menus; more luxurious, modern dishes on the à la carte.

XX

Jaipur

VISA MO AE

41 South Great George's St ✉ D2 – ✆ (01) 677 0999 – www.jaipur.ie
– Closed 25-26 December **D2**

Rest – *(dinner only and lunch Thursday-Sunday)* Menu 20 € (weekday dinner) – Carte 30/46 €

♦ Indian ♦ Minimalist ♦

Long-standing restaurant set over two floors, with orange and red hues, stainless steel staircase and full length windows. Extensive menu displays interesting flavours from all over India.

X

Camden Kitchen

MO

3a Camden Mkt, Grantham St ✉ D8 – ✆ (01) 4760125
– www.camdenkitchen.ie
– Closed 25 December-7 January **D3**

Rest – *(closed Sunday dinner and Monday)* Carte 28/41 €

♦ Modern ♦ Bistro ♦

Appealing bistro with canopied façade and rustic inner, set over two floors. Open kitchen serving gutsy menu of robust, modern dishes. Relaxed, friendly service from a young team.

X

Pig's Ear

VISA MO AE

4 Nassau St ✉ D2 – ✆ (01) 6703865 – www.thepigsear.ie
– Closed 3-13 January, Sunday and bank holiday Mondays **E2**

Rest – Menu 20/22 € – Carte 32/42 €

♦ Modern European ♦ Bistro ♦

Split-level, bistro-style restaurant, in a Georgian city centre house with a striking pink door. Porcine-themed memorabilia features throughout. Well-priced, refined bistro cooking has French influences and relies on Irish produce. Attentive, personable service.

X

La Maison

A/C VISA MO

15 Castlemarket ✉ D2 – ✆ (01) 672 7258 – www.lamaisonrestaurant.ie
– Closed 25-26 and 31 December and 1 January **E2**

Rest – *(bookings not accepted)* Menu 23 € (lunch and early dinner) – Carte 32/48 €

♦ French ♦ Bistro ♦

Appealing French bistro with light blue façade, tables on the pavement and original posters decorating the walls inside. Breton-born chef offers carefully prepared, seasonal Gallic classics at a good price, which are brought to the table by a personable team.

Mermaid Café

69-70 Dame St ✉ D2 – ✆ (01) 670 8236 – www.mermaid.ie
– Closed 1 January, Good Friday, 25 and 26 December **D2**
Rest – *(Sunday brunch) (booking essential)* Menu 21 € – Carte 28/36 €
◆ Modern ◆ Minimalist ◆
This informal restaurant with unfussy décor and bustling atmosphere offers an interesting and well cooked selection of robust modern dishes. Efficient service.

L'Gueuleton

1 Fade St ✉ D2 – ✆ (01) 675 3708 – www.lgueuleton.com
– Closed dinner 24 -28 and 31 December-2 January **E2**
Rest – *(bookings not accepted)* Carte 24/45 €
◆ French ◆ Bistro ◆
Rustic restaurant with beamed ceilings, Gallic furnishings and rear terrace. Interesting French menus use local, seasonal produce. Flavoursome country cooking; friendly, efficient service.

BALLSBRIDGE *Plan III*

Four Seasons

Simmonscourt Rd ✉ D4 – ✆ (01) 665 4000 – www.fourseasons.com/dublin
157 rm – 🚹245/305 € 🚹🚹245/305 €, ☕ 29 € – 40 suites **J2**
Rest *Seasons* – Menu 35 € – Carte 35/74 €
◆ Grand Luxury ◆ Classic ◆
Set in grounds of the RDS arena. Elegant guest areas, state-of-the-art meeting rooms and impressive ballrooms boast ornate décor, antiques and Irish art. Spacious bedrooms; plenty of extras. Fine dining with fountain/garden views in Seasons.

Herbert Park

✉ D4 – ✆ (01) 667 2200 – www.herbertparkhotel.ie **J2**
151 rm – 🚹250/360 € 🚹🚹385 €, ☕ 19.50 € – 2 suites
Rest *The Pavilion* – Carte 30/45 €
◆ Business ◆ Modern ◆
Contemporary hotel overlooking suburban park, with smart marble-floored reception, stylish seating areas and chic bar. Modern bedrooms display quality furnishings and marble bathrooms. Sizeable, formal restaurant offers interesting menu.

Merrion Hall without rest

54-56 Merrion Rd ✉ D4 – ✆ (01) 668 1426 – www.halpinsprivatehotels.com
34 rm ☕ – 🚹169/189 € 🚹🚹199/229 € **J2**
◆ Business ◆ Classic ◆
Red-brick Victorian house boasts spacious, antique-furnished guest areas with a Georgian feel. Comfortable, stylish bedrooms have a traditional edge; those to rear are quieter.

Ariel House without rest

50-54 Lansdowne Rd ✉ D4 – ✆ (01) 668 5512 – www.ariel-house.net
– Closed 22-28 December **J1**
37 rm ☕ – 🚹110/150 € 🚹🚹160/250 €
◆ Townhouse ◆ Classic ◆
Personally run Victorian townhouse with comfy, traditionally styled guest areas and antique furnishings. Warmly decorated bedrooms have modern facilities and smart bathrooms; some four-posters.

Aberdeen Lodge without rest

53-55 Park Ave ✉ D4 – ✆ (01) 283 8155 – www.halpinsprivatehotels.com
17 rm ☕ – 🚹169/189 € 🚹🚹199/229 € **J2**
◆ Townhouse ◆ Classic ◆
Two Victorian townhouses in smart suburban setting, knocked through into one impressive hotel. Comfy lounge, warm homely atmosphere and well-equipped bedrooms – some with garden views.

Ballsbridge and South Dublin (Plan III)

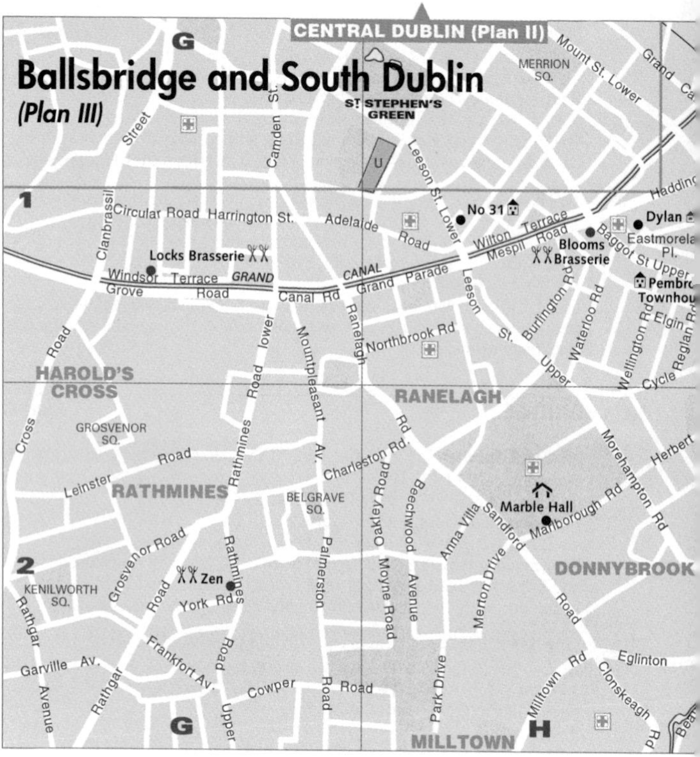

Pembroke Townhouse without rest

90 Pembroke Rd ✉ D4 – ☎ (01) 660 0277
– www.pembroketownhouse.ie
– Closed 18 December-5 January **H1**

48 rm – 🚹199 € 🚹🚹310 €, ☕ 15 €

◆ Townhouse ◆ Classic ◆

Formerly three Georgian houses, now a friendly hotel with traditional styling, comfy lounge and sunny breakfast room. Bedrooms vary in shape and size: duplex rooms are the cosiest.

Glenogra House without rest

64 Merrion Rd ✉ D4 – ☎ (01) 668 3661
– www.glenogra.com
– Closed 23-27 December **J2**

13 rm ☕ – 🚹59/119 € 🚹🚹79/139 €

◆ Family ◆ Cosy ◆

Personally run red-brick Victorian house with informal reception, comfy lounge and homely furnishings. Simply decorated bedrooms vary in shape and size; all boast modern facilities.

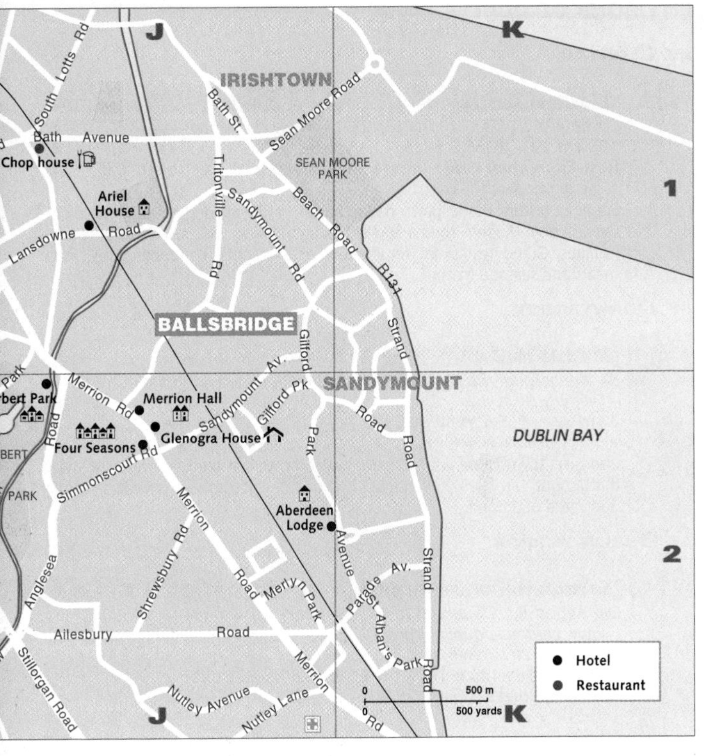

Bloom Brasserie

11 Upper Baggot St ✉ D4 – ✆ (01) 668 7170
– www.bloombrasserie.ie
– Closed 25 December **H1**
Rest – Carte 29/48 €
◆ Modern European ◆ Brasserie ◆
Sizeable basement brasserie with cool, contemporary styling, vibrant art and garden terrace. Menus offer a mix of traditional and more modern dishes; excellent value set 2 course lunch.

Chop House

2 Shelbourne Rd ✉ D4 – ✆ (1) 6602390
– www.thechophouse.ie
– Closed lunch Saturday and Sunday **J1**
Rest – Carte 23/47 €
◆ Modern European ◆ Pub ◆
Whitewashed pub in prominent position; sit in the brighter, conservatory-style area rather than the bar. Informal lunches and more elaborate dinner menu of carefully prepared, tasty dishes.

ENVIRONS OF DUBLIN

AT CLONTARF

Clontarf Castle

Castle Ave ✉ D3 – ✆ (01) 833 2321 – www.clontarfcastle.ie
108 rm – †365 € ††365 € – 3 suites *Plan I* **B1**
Rest *Fahrenheit Grill* – *(dinner only)* Menu 25 € – Carte 40/46 €
♦ Business ♦ Historic ♦

Set in an historic castle, partly dating back to 1172. Striking medieval style entrance lobby. Modern rooms and characterful luxury suites with cutting edge facilities. Grand restaurant reminiscent of a knights' banqueting hall; local meats and seafood feature.

AT DONNYBROOK

Marble Hall without rest

81 Marlborough Rd ✉ D4 – ✆ (01) 497 7350 – www.marblehall.net
– February-November *Plan III* **H2**
3 rm – †55 € ††80/90 €
♦ Townhouse ♦ Classic ♦

Georgian townhouse with effusive welcome guaranteed. Individually styled throughout, with plenty of antiques and quality soft furnishings. Stylish, warmly decorated bedrooms.

AT DUBLIN AIRPORT

Carlton H. Dublin Airport

Old Airport Rd, Cloughran (on R 132 Santry rd) – ✆ (01) 866 7500
– www.carlton.ie/dublinairport
– Closed 24-26 December
117 rm – †89/129 € ††89/129 €, 13.50 € – 1 suite
Rest *Kittyhawks* – Carte 29/46 €
♦ Business ♦ Modern ♦

Modern commercial hotel with spacious marbled reception and comfy guest areas. Uniform bedrooms display good facilities and smart bathrooms. Some rooms overlook airfield; some have balconies. Informal all-day brasserie offers popular menu.

Bewleys

Baskin Lane (East : 1½ km on A 32) – ✆ (01) 871 1000
– www.bewleyshotels.com
– Closed 25 December
466 rm – †89/199 € ††89/199 €, 12 €
Rest *The Brasserie* – Menu 20 € (lunch)/25 € – Carte dinner 25/60 €
♦ Business ♦ Functional ♦

Immense eight floor hotel, ten minutes from the airport, with selection of small meeting rooms. Immaculately kept bedrooms; good value for money. Wide-ranging menu served in The Brasserie.

AT RATHMINES

XX **Zen**

89 Upper Rathmines Rd ✉ D6 – ✆ (01) 4979428 – ww.zenrestaurant.ie
– Closed 25-27 December *Plan III* **G2**
Rest – *(dinner only and Friday lunch)* Menu 20 € – Carte 18/31 €
♦ Chinese ♦

Renowned family run Chinese restaurant in the unusual setting of an old church hall. Imaginative, authentic oriental cuisine with particular emphasis on spicy Sichuan dishes.

ITALY

ITALIA

PROFILE

→ **Area:**
301 262 km^2 (116 317 sq mi).

→ **Population:**
60 340 328 inhabitants (est. 2010), density = 200 per km^2.

→ **Capital:**
Rome (conurbation 2 743 796 inhabitants).

→ **Currency:**
Euro (**€**); rate of exchange: € 1 = 1.37 US$ (Dec 2010).

→ **Government:**
Parliamentary republic with two chambers (since 1946). Member of European Union since 1957 (one of the 6 founding countries).

→ **Language:**
Italian.

→ **Specific public holidays:**
Epiphany (6 January); Liberation Day (25 April); Anniversary of the Republic (2 June); Immaculate Conception (8 December); St. Stephen's Day (26 December). Each town also celebrates the feast day of its patron saint (Rome: 29 June St. Peter, Milan: 7 December St. Ambrose, etc details from the local tourist offices).

→ **Local Time:**
GMT + 1 hour in winter and GMT + 2 hours in summer.

→ **Climate:**
Temperate Mediterranean, with mild winters and hot, sunny summers (Rome: January: 8°C, July: 25°C).

→ **International dialling Code:**
00 39 followed by area or city code and then the local number.

→ **Emergency:**
Police: ✆ **112**; Fire Brigade: ✆ **115**; Health services: ✆ **118**.

→ **Electricity:**
220 volts AC, 50Hz; 2-pin round-shaped continental plugs.

→ **Formalities**
Travellers from the European Union (EU), Switzerland, Iceland and the main countries of North and South America need a national identity card or passport (America: passport required) to visit Italy for less than three months (tourism or business purpose). For visitors from other countries a visa may be required, in addition to a passport, especially for those wishing to stay for longer than three months.
We advise you to check with your embassy before travelling.

ROME

ROMA

Population (est. 2010): 2 743 796 – Altitude: about 100m above sea level

Marie-Louise Detoux/Fotolia.com

Rome wasn't built in a day, and it's pretty hard to do it justice in less than three. The Italian capital is so richly layered in Imperial, Renaissance, Baroque and modern architecture that it takes on the appearance of a sprawling stew, its ingredients stirred together into a spicy and multi-ingredient feast. Its broad piazzas, hooting traffic and cobbled thoroughfares all lend their part to the heady fare: a theatrical stage cradled within seven famous hills.

Being Eternal, Rome never ceases to feel like a lively, living city, while at the same time a scintillating monument to Renaissance power and an epic centre of antiquity. Nowhere else offers such a wealth of classical remains, strung together alongside palaces and churches, and bathed in the soft, golden light for which it is famous. Even when taking time off from exploring the famous sights, you can hardly fail to come across ochre-coloured façades hiding a little square with a bustling market, or stairways that lead you down to a gushing fountain. You're always aware of the steady drip of history here: over 2,700 years of it. When Augustus became the first Emperor of Rome, he could hardly have imagined the impact his city's language, laws and calendar would have upon the world.

LIVING THE CITY

The **River Tiber** snakes its way north to south through the heart of Rome. On its west bank lies the characterful and 'independent' neighbourhood of **Trastevere**, while north of here is Vatican City. Over the river the **Piazza di Spagna** area to the north has Rome's smartest shopping streets, while the southern boundary is marked by the **Aventine** and **Celian** hills, the latter overlooking the **Colosseum**. **Esquiline**'s teeming quarter is just to the east of the city's heart; that honour goes to the **Capitol,** which gave its name to the concept of a 'capital' city. Rome is surrounded by the **Lazio** countryside, beautiful in the spring and autumn months.

PRACTICAL INFORMATION

ARRIVAL-DEPARTURE

Leonardo da Vinci Airport at Fiumicino is 32km southwest of Rome ; a taxi will be around €40. The Fiumicino Leonardo Express train to Stazione Termini runs every 30min and takes 32min. Every 30min the Cotral bus travels to the Anagnina Station of Metro Line A.

TRANSPORT

Rome is served by a metro, bus and tram system. Tickets are available from metro stations, bus terminals, ticket machines, tobacconists, newsagents, cafés and tourist information centres. Choose your ticket type: a single ticket, which must be time stamped on board, or travelcards for one, three or seven days.

By the very nature of its hills and piazzas, Rome is best seen on foot, so make sure you have a good pair of walking shoes. A pair of binoculars is useful to have slung round your neck, too, as lots of sights are on ceilings or the top of columns.

Remember not to overdo the dressing down if you're visiting the religious sights around the city. You won't be allowed in if you think walking into a Roman church is akin to stepping onto an Italian beach – so avoid the likes of sleeveless tops, shorts and mini skirts.

EXPLORING ROME

To get to the very heart of Rome, you need to climb stairs. But these stairs are by Michelangelo, and once you've reached the top of the **Cordonata**,

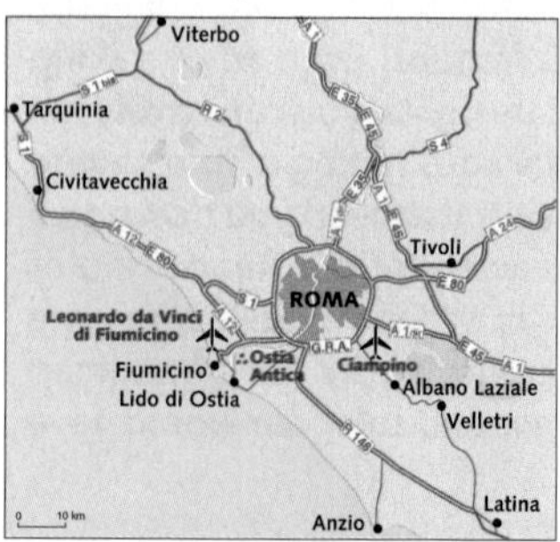

you arrive at the great man's **Piazza dei Campidoglio**, a spectacular setting for Rome's city hall, whose bell tower offers incomparable views far and wide. You are now at the Capitol, which, for Romans, has been the centre of their world and the seat of municipal government for centuries. Around the piazza are two of the city's best museums, the **Capitoline Museums**, home to a fantastic collection of Classical statues and artworks by the likes of Tintoretto, Titian and Rubens. The grandeur of these two late Middle Age temples to culture sets the tone for an even more awe-inspiring art show: the one featuring the old city's remarkable buildings themselves.

➜ FORUM...HERE TO ETERNITY

Just south of the Capitol is quite simply one of the world's great sights. It doesn't matter from which angle you come at it, there's little to compare with the drama afforded by the **Forum**'s weary old bones backed up by the brooding presence of the Colosseum. What remains of the Forum gives only a hint of its former imperial pomp, but even this relative handful of columns, temples and basilicas, scattered in a great drunken maze around you, offers a moving impression of what was once the centre of Rome's political and commercial life. Imagine it... over two thousand years ago, on this spot, Julius Caesar was building his very own temple to vanity, setting the template for future emperors from Augustus onwards. Even in its ruined state, the Colosseum, arching up in the background, is a sight to take the breath away. Rome's greatest amphitheatre was built in AD80 for over fifty thousand spectators to gawp at gladiatorial contests, but was plundered in Renaissance times for its stone. Nevertheless, it still remains an awesome presence; venture inside to the top row seats for head-spinning views.

➜ PLEASURE DOME

If you turn north from the Capitol, rather than south, you'll find not only the best-preserved ancient temple in Rome, but also one of the finest buildings in European architectural history – **The Pantheon**. This beautifully proportioned 'Temple of all the Gods' boasts a portico with granite columns, but these offer no clue as to the beauty and elegance of the building's main highlight, its vast dome. Go inside and marvel at it. The hole at the top provides the only light, and is a constant talking point for architects, who never cease to wonder just why the unreinforced dome has never come crashing to the ground!

➜ THREE COINS

A little way northeast of here is another of Rome's star turns: The **Trevi Fountain**, on the Quirinal Hill. It was only built in 1762, which makes it almost modern by the city's standards, and its theatrical figures of Neptune and two tritons take up most of the tiny **Piazza di Trevi**. The fountain resembles a stage set, and was suitably employed as the shimmering, splashy backdrop to Anita Ekberg's cavortings during Fellini's ground-breaking movie *La Dolce Vita* in 1960. Nowadays, visitors chuck coins in the Trevi, just like the secretaries in another famous 'Rome' movie, *Three Coins In the Fountain*. In the back streets around here are lots of hidden churches – neat, mysterious and charming - while further down Quirinal Hill, fine palaces built for the ancient and powerful families of the city are a splendid sight.

➜ SPANISH STROLL

Carry on northwards and you reach one of Rome's smartest areas, around Piazza di Spagna. This neighbourhood offers superb Renaissance and Baroque art in its churches, as well as one of the city's most prized ancient monuments (the **Ara Pacis**) repackaged in a 21C glass hangar. There's also fine art in the **Villa Medici**, and wonderful views of the city from the **Pincio Gardens**. But most people come up here to loll around awhile on the **Spanish Steps**. Built in 1726, the steps curve around terraces, richly flowered at Easter, to create one of the city's most famously distinctive landmarks. At their base, rather incongruously, is the **Keats-Shelley Memorial House**, a small museum dedicated to the two poets who are both buried in Rome. Latin sophistication is very much restored when you cross the Piazza di Spagna to take in the shadowy chic of **Via Condotti**. This is the home of Rome's smartest shops where early evening strollers come to gaze at the windows of the coolest designer names in the city. Another favourite is the nearby **Via del Babuino**, along which hushed art galleries and fascinating antique shops combine to create a smart feel.

Along the curving Tiber a little way south west is Rome's most handsome, most theatrical piazza – **Piazza Navona**. It's shaped like a huge oval lozenge because it was once a great athletics stadium, originally built in AD86. Today the entertainment comes from its three grandiose fountains, and the little human dramas being enacted in the pedestrian areas day and night. The eye-catching Baroque churches here provide a spectacle of their own. Close by is the fascinating **Via del Governo Vecchio**, full of 15C and 16C Renaissance houses interspersed with charming antique shops.

The east bank, just across from Trastevere, boasts a down-to-earth shrine of its own in the bustling market place of **Campo de' Fiori**, which has been in existence since medieval times when it was surrounded by inns for pilgrims; these days the lively ambience lives on and the teeming stalls of fruit and vegetables are used to supply many of the nearby restaurants. Of course, in this city you're never far from a majestic building or two to set alight the flame of inspiration. Close by is the grandiose baroque church of **Sant'Andrea della Valle**, renowned for its beautiful dome. Praying in here one day, with the cries of the market stall vendors in the distance, Puccini came up with the idea for the first act of *Tosca*.

→ THE TRASTEVERE

To get the feel for a different Rome, one that gives the impression of proletarian life in bygone times, cross the Tiber by any of the five bridges in the area, and soak up the atmosphere of **Trastevere**. It's one of the most picturesque old neighbourhoods of the city, with a distinctly laidback feel in contrast to the frenetic world over the river. The narrow cobbled alleyways here have a charm all their own and are a great place to escape to for a quiet lunch or early evening drink. The only threat to Trastevere's earthy character is the steady growth of fashionable bars, clubs and boutiques which have arrived in recent years, but in high summer the proximity of its densely packed buildings offers a welcomingly cool experience when the rest of Rome feels like a spit roast.

CALENDAR HIGHLIGHTS

You could say that Rome is an event in itself, but the city still likes to down tools for a bit of a celebration. February, for example, sees the historical thoroughfares of the city come alive for the annual Carnival. When

ROME IN...

→ ONE DAY

Capitol, Forum, Colosseum, Pantheon, Trevi Fountain, Spanish Steps

→ TWO DAYS

Via Condotti, Piazza Navona and churches in surrounding area, Capitoline museums

→ THREE DAYS

A day on the west bank of the Tiber at Trastevere and Vatican City

the azaleas appear in March, three thousand vases of them are arranged dramatically on the Spanish Steps for the Spring Festival. That same month, film fans celebrate the first of Rome's two big festivals with the Independent Film Festival, featuring more than sixty innovative movies from around the globe at a variety of cinemas. Also at that time, the city boasts its Cultural Heritage Week, with museums and monuments opening up to the public without charge. April is a big month here: Rome celebrates its birthday on the twenty-first (it was 'born' in 753BC) and the Campidoglio is the centre of activity with illuminated hillside palazzi and monster fireworks. There's also the Parklife festival at Fiera di Roma, which celebrates environmental culture with exhibits, films and installations promoting protected areas and natural parks in Italy. The Roman Summer is renowned for its oppressive heat, but the festival bearing that name (June-September) is hot in another way: the city's piazzas, palaces, parks and courtyards host a wide array of pop and jazz concerts (the outdoor film screenings late into the night may be a cooler choice). Tiberina Island is lit up like a film set for Cinema Isle (June-August) with retrospectives and blockbusters high on its agenda, while July's Festa de Noantri has two weeks' worth of art and street performances in honour of Trastevere's earthy proletarian beginnings. Also in July get cool on both banks of the Tiber at the Tevere Expo, when stalls full of arts and crafts, food and wine tempt you to buy. Two other summer highlights for music lovers: Secret Passages (July-August) boasts classical concerts and theatre performances at various locations in the city, while New Operafestival (July-September) at Basilica di San Clemente, just behind the Colosseum, is an operatic feast, featuring the likes of Mozart, Verdi and Donizetti. Autumn's Roma Europa Festival is a big one, with music, dance and theatre at stunning locations across Rome. Museums, galleries and theatres stay open till the early hours during White Night (September), while film from every angle is highlighted at the Rome Film Festival, at important movie venues, in October.

EATING OUT

Despite being Italy's capital, Rome largely favours a local, traditional cuisine to be found in typically unpretentious trattorie or osterie. Although not far from the sea, the city doesn't go in much for fish, and food is often connected to the rural, pastoral life with products coming from the surrounding Lazio hills, which also produce good wines. Pasta, of course, is not to be missed – mainly spaghetti, bucatini or rigatoni – combined with sauces such as amatriciana (prepared with tomatoes and unsmoked bacon), carbonara (eggs and unsmoked bacon) or arrabbiata (chilli). Lamb is favoured among meats for the main course; so too, the 'quinto quarto', which is another example of Roman cuisine's links to popular traditions based on rural tastes. The quinto quarto is a long-established way of indicating those parts of the beef (tail, tripe, liver, spleen, lungs, heart, kidney) left over after the best bits had gone to the richest families. Trastevere and the historical centre are full of restaurants featuring quinto quarto. For international, or more classic, cuisine combined with a more refined setting, head for the elegant hotels: very few other areas of Italy have such an increasing number of good quality restaurants within a hotel setting. Locals like to dine later in Rome than, say, Milan, with 1pm, or 8pm the very earliest you'd dream of appearing for lunch or dinner. In the famous tourist hotspots, of course, owners are only too pleased to open that bit earlier.

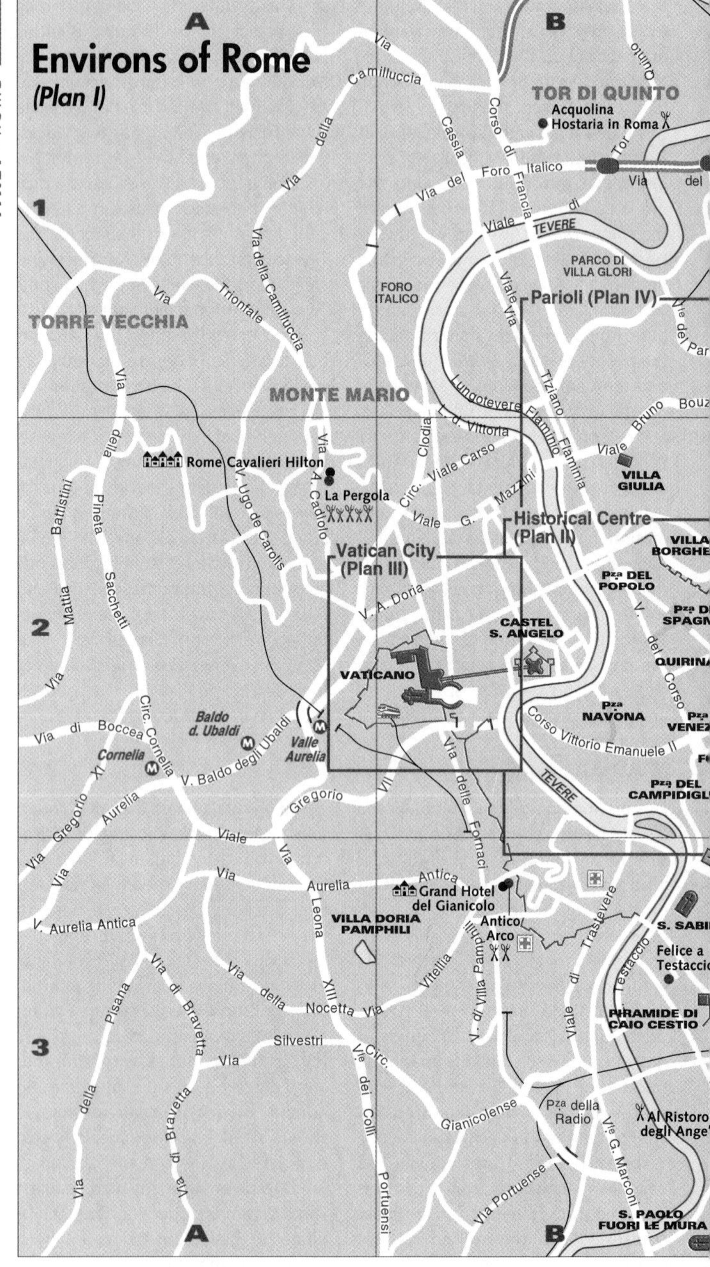
Environs of Rome
(Plan I)
TOR DI QUINTO
Acquolina Hostaria in Roma
TORRE VECCHIA
MONTE MARIO
FORO ITALICO
PARCO DI VILLA GLORI
Parioli (Plan IV)
Rome Cavalieri Hilton
La Pergola
VILLA GIULIA
Historical Centre (Plan II)
Vatican City (Plan III)
VILLA BORGHE
Pza DEL POPOLO
CASTEL S. ANGELO
VATICANO
Pza NAVONA
Baldo d. Ubaldi
Valle Aurelia
Cornelia
Pza DEL CAMPIDIGL
Grand Hotel del Gianicolo
VILLA DORIA PAMPHILI
Antico Arco
S. SABI
Felice a Testacci
PIRAMIDE DI CAIO CESTIO
Pza della Radio
Al Ristoro degli Ange
S. PAOLO FUORI LE MURA
TEVERE
Via Aurelia Antica
Via Gregorio VII
Corso Vittorio Emanuele II
Via di Boccea
Via Portuense
Via Gianicolense

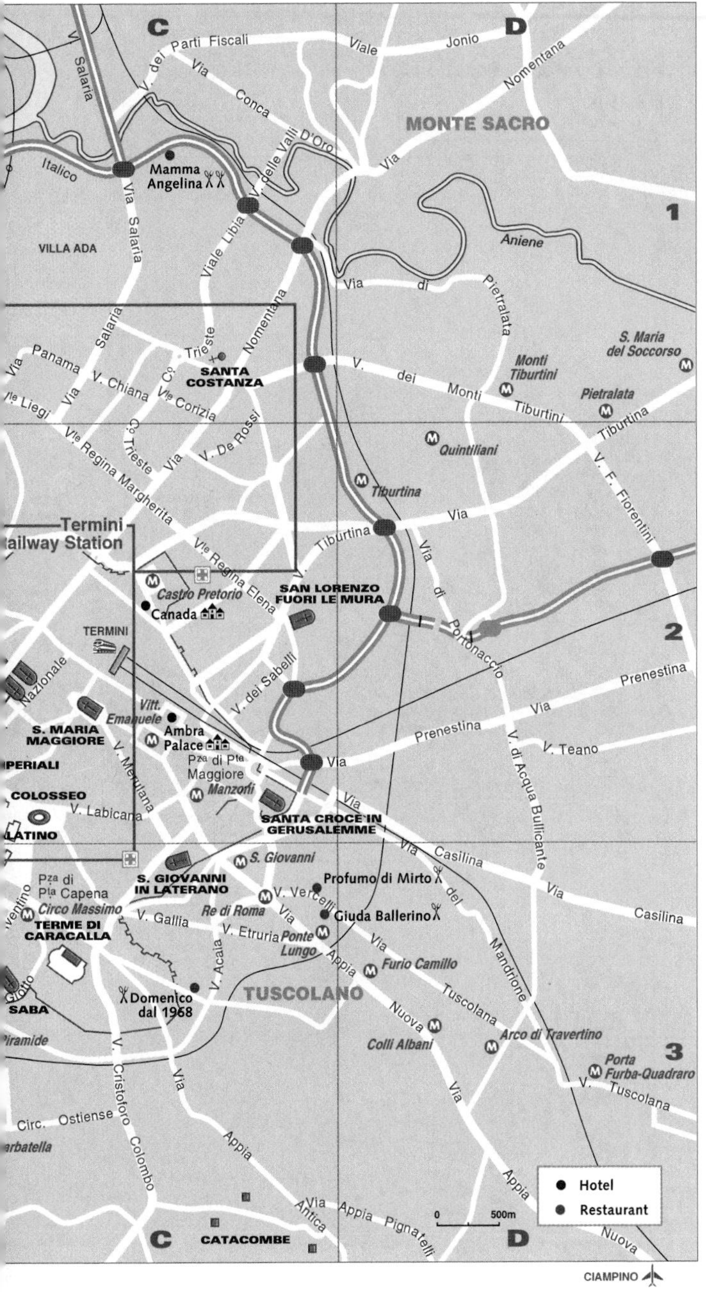

C
D
1
2
3
MONTE SACRO
VILLA ADA
Mamma Angelina
SANTA COSTANZA
Termini Railway Station
TERMINI
Castro Pretorio
Canada
SAN LORENZO FUORI LE MURA
S. MARIA MAGGIORE
COLOSSEO
Ambra Palace
Pza di Pta Maggiore
Manzoni
SANTA CROCE IN GERUSALEMME
S. GIOVANNI IN LATERANO
S. Giovanni
Profumo di Mirto
Giuda Ballerino
Re di Roma
Ponte Lungo
Furio Camillo
Circo Massimo
TERME DI CARACALLA
Pza di Pta Capena
Domenico dal 1968
TUSCOLANO
Colli Albani
Arco di Travertino
Porta Furba-Quadraro
Monti Tiburtini
Pietralata
S. Maria del Soccorso
Quintiliani
Tiburtina
Aniene
CATACOMBE
Hotel
Restaurant
0
500m
CIAMPINO

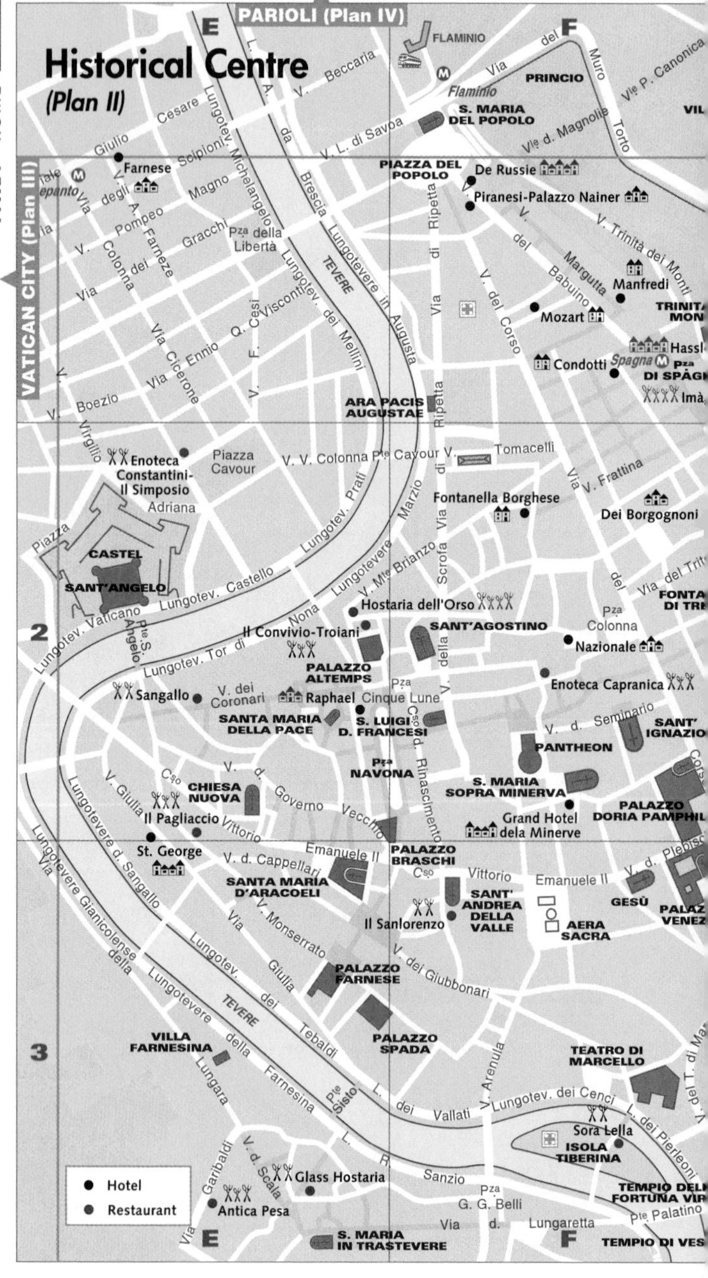

Historical Centre
(Plan II)
PARIOLI (Plan IV)
VATICAN CITY (Plan III)
FLAMINIO
PRINCIO
S. MARIA DEL POPOLO
PIAZZA DEL POPOLO
De Russie
Piranesi-Palazzo Nainer
Farnese
Manfredi
Mozart
Condotti
TRINITÀ MON
DI SPAGNA
Imà
ARA PACIS AUGUSTAE
Enoteca Constantini-Il Simposio
Piazza Cavour
Fontanella Borghese
Dei Borgognoni
CASTEL SANT'ANGELO
Hostaria dell'Orso
SANT'AGOSTINO
Il Convivio-Troiani
Nazionale
PALAZZO ALTEMPS
Enoteca Capranica
Sangallo
Raphael
SANTA MARIA DELLA PACE
S. LUIGI D. FRANCESI
PANTHEON
SANT' IGNAZIO
CHIESA NUOVA
P.za NAVONA
S. MARIA SOPRA MINERVA
PALAZZO DORIA PAMPHILI
Il Pagliaccio
Grand Hotel dela Minerve
St. George
PALAZZO BRASCHI
SANTA MARIA D'ARACOELI
SANT' ANDREA DELLA VALLE
GESÙ
Il Sanlorenzo
AERA SACRA
PALAZZO FARNESE
PALAZZO SPADA
VILLA FARNESINA
TEATRO DI MARCELLO
Sora Lella
ISOLA TIBERINA
Glass Hostaria
Antica Pesa
TEMPIO DELLA FORTUNA VIRILE
S. MARIA IN TRASTEVERE
TEMPIO DI VESTA
TEVERE
Hotel
Restaurant

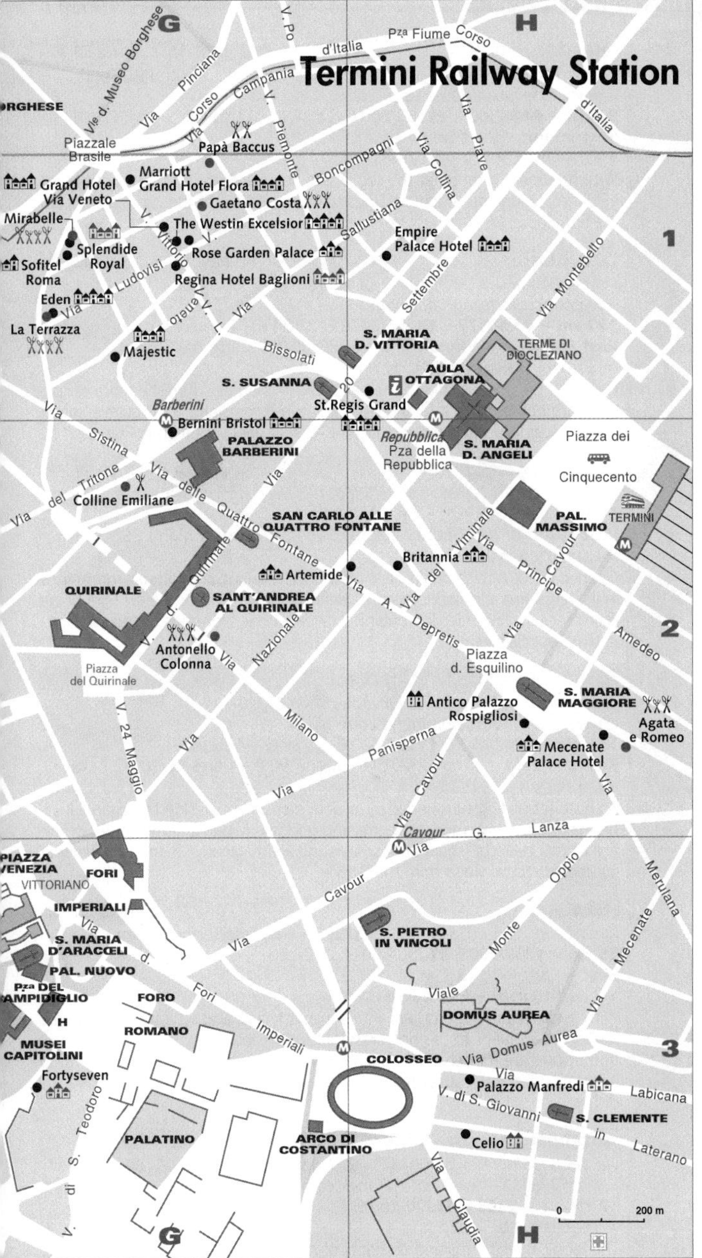

Termini Railway Station
G
H
1
2
3
Papà Baccus
Marriott Grand Hotel Flora
Grand Hotel Via Veneto
Gaetano Costa
The Westin Excelsior
Mirabelle
Splendide Royal
Sofitel Roma
Rose Garden Palace
Regina Hotel Baglioni
Empire Palace Hotel
Eden
La Terrazza
Majestic
S. MARIA D. VITTORIA
TERME DI DIOCLEZIANO
AULA OTTAGONA
S. SUSANNA
St.Regis Grand
Barberini
Bernini Bristol
Repubblica
Pza della Repubblica
S. MARIA D. ANGELI
Piazza dei Cinquecento
PALAZZO BARBERINI
Colline Emiliane
SAN CARLO ALLE QUATTRO FONTANE
PAL. MASSIMO
TERMINI
Britannia
Artemide
QUIRINALE
SANT'ANDREA AL QUIRINALE
Antonello Colonna
Piazza del Quirinale
Piazza d. Esquilino
S. MARIA MAGGIORE
Antico Palazzo Rospigliosi
Agata e Romeo
Mecenate Palace Hotel
Cavour
PIAZZA VENEZIA
VITTORIANO
FORI IMPERIALI
S. MARIA D'ARACŒLI
PAL. NUOVO
Pza DEL CAMPIDOGLIO
MUSEI CAPITOLINI
FORO ROMANO
S. PIETRO IN VINCOLI
DOMUS AUREA
COLOSSEO
Palazzo Manfredi
S. CLEMENTE
Celio
Fortyseven
PALATINO
ARCO DI COSTANTINO
0
200 m

Hassler

piazza Trinità dei Monti 6 ✉ 00187 – Ⓜ Spagna – ✆ 06 699340 – www.hotelhasslerroma.com **F1**

82 rm – †440/500 € ††550/860 €, ☕ 38 € – 13 suites

Rest *Imago* – see below

◆ Grand Luxury ◆ Stylish ◆

With its superb location at the top of the Spanish Steps, this hotel combines elegance, luxury and tradition. Unusual interpretation of the classical style on the fifth floor.

De Russie

via del Babuino 9 ✉ 00187 – Ⓜ Flaminio – ✆ 06 328881 – www.roccofortecollection.com **F1**

122 rm – †330/572 € ††486/1078 €, ☕ 34 € – 25 suites

Rest *Le Jardin de Russie* – *✆ 06 32888870* – Carte 66/131 €

◆ Grand Luxury ◆ Modern ◆

Designed by Valadier during the early 19C, this hotel is furnished in a simple and harmonious style. It features elegant guestrooms and an attractive 'secret garden' scented with roses and jasmine. One of the best hotels in Rome.

St. George

via Giulia 62 ✉ 00186 – ✆ 06 686611 – www.stgeorgehotel.it

64 rm ☕ – †260/420 € ††290/450 € **E2**

Rest *I Sofà di Via Giulia* – *(closed Sunday, Monday)* Menu 35/85 €

◆ Luxury ◆ Modern ◆

Opened in 2007, this hotel is decorated with luxurious, comfortable furnishings in its bedrooms and public lounges. Refined, elegant atmosphere. I Sofà di Via Giulia serves a fine selection of typical Italian dishes, alongside a range of international specialities.

Grand Hotel de la Minerve

piazza della Minerva 69 ✉ 00186 – ✆ 06 695201 – www.grandhoteldelaminerve.com **F2**

131 rm – †242/627 € ††297/682 €, ☕ 39 € – 4 suites

Rest *La Cesta* – *✆ 06 69520704* – Menu 90 € – Carte 56/100 €

◆ Luxury ◆ Stylish ◆

An historic building surrounded by ancient monuments. Inside: fine chandeliers, neoclassical statues, modern rooms and goddess Minerva at the center of the hall Liberty ceiling. Elegant atmosphere and an imaginative menu of traditional cuisine. Attractive views from the terrace.

Raphaël

largo Febo 2 ✉ 00186 – ✆ 06 682831 – www.raphaelhotel.com

55 rm – †230/600 € ††250/800 €, ☕ 28 € – 1 suite **E2**

Rest – Carte 60/112 €

◆ Traditional ◆ Personalised ◆

With its collection of porcelain, antiquarian artefacts and sculptures by famous artists, the entrance to this hotel resembles a museum. The recently renovated guestrooms are modern in style. The menu in this attractive restaurant with a panoramic terrace focuses mainly on Italian cuisine, along with some French dishes.

Piranesi-Palazzo Nainer without rest

via del Babuino 196 ✉ 00187 – Ⓜ Flaminio – ✆ 06 328041 – www.hotelpiranesi.com **F1**

32 rm ☕ – †168 € ††220/268 €

◆ Traditional ◆ Classic ◆

The lobby, guestrooms and corridors of this hotel are decorated with marble, elegant furnishings and an unusual exhibition of old fabrics. The hotel also boasts a roof garden and sun terrace.

Dei Borgognoni without rest

via del Bufalo 126 ✉ 00187 – Ⓜ Spagna – ✆ 06 69941505 – www.hotelborgognoni.it **F2**

51 rm ☕ – 🚹210/240 € 🚹🚹240/340 €

♦ Traditional ♦ Classic ♦

Occupying a 19C palazzo, this elegant hotel's spacious, modern public rooms and comfortable guestrooms combine both traditional and modern features.

Nazionale

piazza Montecitorio 131 ✉ 00186 – ✆ 06 695001 – www.hotelnazionale.it

100 rm ☕ – 🚹200/290 € 🚹🚹350/380 € – 1 suite **F2**

Rest – *(closed August, Sunday and Monday lunch)* Carte 40/72 €

♦ Traditional ♦ Classic ♦

This hotel is housed in an 18C building on Piazza di Montecitorio. It offers elegant public areas and guestrooms furnished with individual touches. Guests will enjoy traditional Italian cuisine in this elegant, comfortable restaurant.

Grand Hotel del Gianicolo

viale Mura Gianicolensi 107 ✉ 00152 – Ⓜ Cipro Musei Vaticani – ✆ 06 58333405 – www.grandhotelgianicolo.it

48 rm ☕ – 🚹130/380 € 🚹🚹160/410 € *Plan I* **B3**

Rest *Corte degli Angeli* – Carte 42/56 €

♦ Traditional ♦ Classic ♦

Located in an elegant villa with a well-maintained garden and swimming pool, this hotel has comfortable guestrooms and stylish public areas.

Manfredi without rest

via Margutta 61 ✉ 00187 – Ⓜ Spagna – ✆ 06 3207676 – www.hotelmanfredi.it **F1**

27 rm ☕ – 🚹🚹130/320 € – 4 suites

♦ Traditional ♦ Classic ♦

Housed on the third floor of a palazzo on the famous Via Margutta. Elegant, individually furnished guestrooms, all of which boast the latest in modern facilities. Excellent international breakfast of natural products, including yoghurt and homemade pastries.

Fontanella Borghese without rest

largo Fontanella Borghese 84 ✉ 00186 – Ⓜ Spagna – ✆ 06 68809504 – www.fontanellaborghese.com **F2**

24 rm ☕ – 🚹125/175 € 🚹🚹150/255 €

♦ Traditional ♦ Classic ♦

In a central yet peaceful location, on the 2nd and 3rd floors of a historical building looking out over Palazzo Borghese now houses a distinguished and refined hotel with classy finishings.

Mozart without rest

via dei Greci 23/b ✉ 00187 – Ⓜ Spagna – ✆ 06 36001915 – www.hotelmozart.com **F1**

72 rm ☕ – 🚹99/167 € 🚹🚹126/239 €

♦ Traditional ♦ Classic ♦

Housed in a 19C palazzo, this hotel boasts elegant public areas and stylish guestrooms. Those in the annexe are more modern and spacious.

Condotti without rest

via Mario dè Fiori 37 ✉ 00187 – Ⓜ Spagna – ✆ 06 6794661 – www.hotelcondotti.com **F1**

16 rm ☕ – 🚹139/215 € 🚹🚹179/265 €

♦ Traditional ♦ Classic ♦

The lobby of this hotel is decorated in marble and adorned with elegant chandeliers. Find small, comfortable guestrooms, some of which are in a separate building nearby.

XXXX ✿

Imàgo – Hotel Hassler

piazza Trinità dei Monti 6 ✉ 00187 – Ⓜ Spagna – ✆ 06 69934726 – www.imagorestaurant.com – closed 2 weeks in January **F1**

Rest – *(dinner only)* Menu 100/130 € – Carte 88/119 €

Spec. Crudo di mare del giorno. Capesante impanate ripiene di mozzarella di bufala, foglie di sedano e tartufo nero. Fusilloni alla carbonara con ragù di quaglia.

♦ Modern ♦ Luxury ♦

This restaurant continues to be a perennial favourite, thanks to its large windows and unforgettable views of Rome. Modern cuisine made with high quality ingredients.

XXXX

Hostaria dell'Orso

via dei Soldati 25/c ✉ 00186 – ✆ 06 68301192 – www.hdo.it – closed from 10 to 25 August and Sunday **E-F2**

Rest – *(dinner only) (booking advisable)* Menu 56/95 € – Carte 66/96 €

♦ Modern ♦ Luxury ♦

Housed in an historic building, this restaurant has intimate, romantic dining rooms decorated in a simple, elegant style. The elegant cuisine is based around the highest quality ingredients.

XXX ✿

Il Convivio-Troiani (Angelo Troiani)

vicolo dei Soldati 31 ✉ 00186 – ✆ 06 6869432 – www.ilconviviotroiani.com – closed 1 week in August and Sunday **E2**

Rest – *(dinner only)* Carte 81/109 €

Spec. Mezze penne con cozze, peperoni, latte di cocco, zafferano e basilico. Stinco d'agnello da latte con salsa alla cacciatora. Millefoglie con crema alla salvia, pepe verde e frutti di bosco.

♦ Inventive ♦ Formal ♦

This elegant restaurant is in the heart of the historic centre. Amid a decor of frescoes, paintings and modern minimalism, enjoy quintessential Italian cuisine. Choose from risottos and pasta, as well as a selection of specialities from the Lazio region.

XXX ✿✿

Il Pagliaccio (Anthony Genovese)

via dei Banchi Vecchi 129 ✉ 00186 – ✆ 06 68809595 – www.ristoranteilpagliaccio.it – closed from 8 to 31 August, from 9 to 17 January, Sunday, Monday, Tuesday midday **E2**

Rest – *(booking advisable in the evening)* Carte 100/138 €

Spec. Gnocchi di patate ripieni di ricotta di capra, zuppa di pesce e ricci di mare. Rombo al vapore di alghe, cozze e salsa al nero di seppia. Faraona laccata al tamarillo (fruit), emulsione di pompelmo e tè Earl Grey.

♦ Inventive ♦ Friendly ♦

The chef at this restaurant offers a varied menu of elaborate and ambitious dishes from around the world.

XXX

Enoteca Capranica

piazza Capranica 99/100 ✉ 00186 – ✆ 06 69940992 – www.enotecacapranica.it – closed Saturday lunchtime and Sunday **F2**

Rest – Menu 50/75 € – Carte 54/74 €

♦ Mediterranean ♦ Formal ♦

This 15C palazzo near Montecitorio has been transformed into an elegant restaurant serving Mediterranean cuisine. Colourful vaulted ceiling plus an impressive wine list.

XXX

Antica Pesa

via Garibaldi 18 ✉ *00153 – ✆ 06 5809236 – www.anticapesa.it*
– closed Sunday **E3**
Rest – *(dinner only)* Carte 48/64 €
♦ Regional ♦ Formal ♦ Luxury ♦
Typical Roman dishes made from carefully selected ingredients grace the menu of this restaurant, which is housed in a grain storehouse that once belonged to the neighbouring Papal State. Large paintings by contemporary artists hang on the walls and there is a small lounge with a fireplace near the entrance.

XX

Il Sanlorenzo

via dei Chiavari 4/5 ✉ *00186 – ✆ 06 6865097 – www.ilsanlorenzo.it*
– closed from 12 to 20 August **F3**
Rest – *(dinner only Saturday, Sunday, Monday)* Menu 75 €
– Carte 50/111 €
♦ Modern ♦ Fashionable ♦
Built over the foundations of the Teatro Pompeo, this palazzo now houses an atmospheric restaurant, which combines a sense of history with contemporary style. Modern cuisine and fish specialities.

XX

Sangallo

via dei Coronari 180 ✉ *00186 – ✆ 06 68134055*
– www.ristorantesangallo.com
– closed 15 August and Christmas **E2**
Rest – Carte 51/76 €
♦ Modern ♦ Formal ♦
This 16C palazzo, near San Salvatore church in Lauro, has an interesting contrast of old and new. It houses an elegant restaurant serving modern, innovative cuisine.

XX

Glass Hostaria (Cristina Bowerman)

vicolo del Cinque 58 ✉ *00153 – ✆ 06 58335903 – www.glasshostaria.it*
– closed 11 July-3 August , 24-25-26 December, from 10 to 19 January and Monday **E3**
Rest – *(dinner only)* Carte 53/70 €
Spec. Spaghetti affumicati, caglio di latte di capra, friggitelli e bottarga. Fichi arrostiti al pepe verde, mousse di ricotta di bufala, pancia di maiale cotta a bassa temperatura e saba. Torcione di caprino e pistacchi con ciliegie e rosmarino.
♦ Modern ♦ Design ♦
Situated in the heart of Trastevere, this restaurant boasts an ultra-modern design with an interesting play of light and slightly unsettling atmosphere. The excellent cuisine also features highly modern touches.

XX

Sora Lella

via di Ponte Quattro Capi 16 (Tiber Island) ✉ *00186 – ✆ 06 6861601*
– www.soralella.com
– closed 3 weeks in August and Sunday **F3**
Rest – Carte 38/54 €
♦ Roman ♦ Family ♦
Son and grandchildren of the famous late ""Sora Lella"", perpetuate in a dignified way the tradition both in the warmth of the welcome and in the typical Roman elements of the offer.

XX

Antico Arco

piazzale Aurelio 7 ✉ *00152 – ✆ 06 5815274 – www.anticoarco.it*
– closed 10 days in August and 1 week in December *Plan I* **B3**
Rest – *(dinner only)* Carte 52/74 €
♦ Inventive ♦ Fashionable ♦
The chef at this modern, bright and fashionable restaurant selects the best Italian ingredients to create innovative dishes based on traditional specialities.

Felice a Testaccio

via Mastrogiorgio 29 ✉ 00153 – ✆ 06 5746800
– www.feliceatestaccio.com
– closed August and Sunday evening *Plan I* **B3**
Rest – *(booking advisable)* Carte 30/45 €
♦ Roman ♦ Family ♦ Neighbourhood ♦
This restaurant is typical of an early 19C inn with its thick glass windows, exposed brick walls and wooden tables. The cuisine follows the same pattern, serving generous portions of traditional dishes from Rome and the Lazio region.

TERMINI RAILWAY STATION *Plan II*

St. Regis Grand

via Vittorio Emanuele Orlando 3 ✉ 00185 – Ⓜ Repubblica – ✆ 06 47091
– www.stregis.com/grandrome **H1**
153 rm – ††890 €, ☕ 43 € – 8 suites
Rest *Vivendo* – *✆ 06 47092736 (dinner only)* Carte 62/96 €
♦ Grand Luxury ♦ Classic ♦
Frescoes, valuable furnishings and Empire-style antiques in the luxurious bedrooms and the magnificent lounges of this hotel restored to its original splendour (1894) all add to its elegant atmosphere. A bright, eclectic decor provides the backdrop for this restaurant which serves Mediterranean cuisine with a modern twist.

The Westin Excelsior

via Vittorio Veneto 125 ✉ 00187 – Ⓜ Barberini – ✆ 0647081
– www.westin.com/excelsiorrome **G1**
285 rm – †565 € ††910 €, ☕ 25 € – 31 suites
Rest *Doney* – Carte 60/130 €
♦ Luxury ♦ Classic ♦
Spoil yourself with a stay in the royal suite (the largest in Europe) or choose one of the luxurious guestrooms, where elegant and comfortable furnishings are complemented by the very latest technology. The "dolce vita" at its best!

Eden

via Ludovisi 49 ✉ 00187 – Ⓜ Barberini – ✆ 06 478121
– www.edenroma.com **G1**
121 rm – †288/824 € ††381/999 €, ☕ 49 € – 13 suites
Rest *La Terrazza* – see below
♦ Luxury ♦ Business ♦ Stylish ♦
This large, top-end hotel has a formal atmosphere but the service is warm and friendly. Some of the rooms on the upper floors have what is perhaps the best view of Rome.

Grand Hotel Via Veneto

✉ 00187 – Ⓜ Barberini – ✆ 06 487881 – www.ghvv.it **G1**
122 rm – ††400/650 €, ☕ 40 € – 20 suites
Rest *Magnolia* – *(closed Sunday) (dinner only)* Carte 55/115 €
Rest *Time* – Carte 38/58 €
♦ Luxury ♦ Classic ♦
Situated on one of Rome's most famous streets, this hotel offers luxury in the true sense of the word, with superb, retro-style guestrooms and a collection of more than 500 original paintings on display. A love of Italian flavours and traditions is clearly evident in the cuisine served in this restaurant. This restaurant serves Italian and international cuisine, as well as a good choice of cocktails.

Regina Hotel Baglioni

via Vittorio Veneto 72 ✉ 00187 – Ⓜ Barberini – ☏ 06 421111 – www.baglionihotels.com **G1**

96 rm – 606 € 700 €, ☕ 33 € – 9 suites

Rest *Brunello Lounge & Restaurant* – *☏ 06 48902867 (closed Sunday)* Carte 105/141 €

♦ Luxury ♦ Stylish ♦

A historic hotel in an Art Nouveau building which has been recently renovated in exquisite style. Fitness enthusiasts will enjoy the small wellness centre and gym. This elegant restaurant serves international cuisine, with a lighter menu available at lunchtime.

Majestic

via Vittorio Veneto 50 ✉ 00187 – Ⓜ Barberini – ☏ 06 421441 – www.hotelmajestic.com **G1**

94 rm ☕ – 465 € 720 € – 4 suites

Rest *Filippo La Mantia* – *(closed 8 August-2 September, Saturday lunch, Sunday dinner)* Menu 35 € (lunch) – Carte dinner only 50/70 €

♦ Traditional ♦ Classic ♦

Founded in the late 19C, this hotel remains a standard-bearer for the luxury hotels along Via Veneto, with its antique furnishings and contemporary comfort. White is the dominant colour in the guestrooms. The famous chef La Mantia proposes a menu for lunch, and à la carte in the evening. The Sicilian dishes are a great success at the Sunday brunch.

Sofitel Rome Villa Borghese

via Lombardia 47 ✉ 00187 – Ⓜ Barberini – ☏ 06 478021 – www.sofitel.com **G1**

111 rm – 210/381 € 230/627 €, ☕ 25 € – 3 suites

Rest *La Terrasse* – Menu 40/110 €

♦ Luxury ♦ Classic ♦

The neo-Classical style dominates in this hotel just a stone's throw from the cosmopolitan Via Veneto. Superb guestrooms and elegant public areas. Situated on the top floor, the panoramic restaurant with its Lounge Bar boasts romantic views of the Villa Medici.

Splendide Royal

via di porta Pinciana 14 ✉ 00187 – Ⓜ Barberini – ☏ 06 421689 – www.splendideroyal.com **G1**

60 rm – 280/520 € 310/850 €, ☕ 35 € – 9 suites

Rest *Mirabelle* – see below

♦ Luxury ♦ Classic ♦

Gilded stucco, damask fabrics and sumptuous antique furnishings contribute to the Roman Baroque style of this hotel, which is in sharp contrast to the contemporary trend for minimalist design. Shades of periwinkle blue, golden yellow and cardinal red dominate in the guestrooms, creating an ambience of traditional luxury.

Bernini Bristol

piazza Barberini 23 ✉ 00187 – Ⓜ Barberini – ☏ 06 488931 – www.berninibristol.com **G2**

117 rm – 352/506 € 561/638 €, ☕ 37 € – 10 suites

Rest *L'Olimpo* – *☏ 06 488933288* – Carte 68/141 €

♦ Traditional ♦ Classic ♦

A key feature of the famous square on which it stands, this elegant hotel offers traditionally furnished and contemporary-style guestrooms. Ask for a room with a view on one of the upper floors. Roof-garden restaurant, with outdoor dining in the summer and a superb view of the Eternal City.

Marriott Grand Hotel Flora

via Vittorio Veneto 191 ✉ 00187 – Ⓜ Spagna – ✆ 06 489929 – www.grandhotelflora.net **G1**
153 rm – 289/299 € 379/419 €, ☕ 30 € – 3 suites
Rest – Carte 42/77 €
◆ Traditional ◆ Modern ◆
One of the emblematic hotels of the Italian capital. Standing at the end of Via Vittorio Veneto, the Marriott Grand Hotel Flora has an elegant, neo-Classical atmosphere brightened by contemporary touches. The food served in the restaurant here is not the usual hotel fare, but focuses on traditional Italian cuisine with a flavour of the Campania region.

Empire Palace Hotel

via Aureliana 39 ✉ 00187 – ✆ 06 421281 – www.empirepalacehotel.com
110 rm ☕ – 280/405 € **H1**
Rest *Aureliano* – (closed Sunday) Carte 47/59 €
◆ Traditional ◆ Personalised ◆
Sophisticated combination of elements of the 19C building and contemporary design, with a collection of modern art in the public areas; simple, classic bedrooms. This restaurant features cherry wood decor, tables set close together and red and blue chandeliers. Mediterranean specialities take pride of place on the menu.

Rose Garden Palace

via Boncompagni 19 ✉ 00187 – Ⓜ Barberini – ✆ 06 421741 – www.rosegardenpalace.com **G1**
65 rm ☕ – 240/380 € 260/440 €
Rest – (closed Sunday) Carte 37/76 €
◆ Traditional ◆ Modern ◆
A modern, minimalist design is the inspiration behind the furnishing of this hotel housed in an early-20C palazzo. The building has nonetheless retained some of its original architectural features, such as its high ceilings and marble decor.

Mecenate Palace Hotel

via Carlo Alberto 3 ✉ 00185 – Ⓜ Vittorio Emanuele – ✆ 06 44702024 – www.mecenatepalace.com **H2**
69 rm ☕ – 100/320 € 180/390 € – 3 suites **Rest** – Menu 28 €
◆ Traditional ◆ Stylish ◆
The warm and elegant period-style interiors are in perfect keeping with the spirit of the 19C building, which houses this hotel. Fine views of Santa Maria Maggiore from the terrace and some of the guestrooms. The restaurant on the top floor serves typical Italian cuisine.

Artemide

via Nazionale 22 ✉ 00184 – Ⓜ Repubblica – ✆ 06 489911 – www.hotelartemide.it **G-H2**
85 rm ☕ – 150/450 € **Rest** – (residents only) Carte 39/51 €
◆ Business ◆ Classic ◆
Housed in a delightful 19C Art Nouveau building, the Artemide offers all the usual comforts of a modern hotel, as well as excellent conference facilities.

Fortyseven

via Petroselli 47 ✉ 00186 – ✆ 06 6787816 – www.fortysevenhotel.com
59 rm ☕ – 200/290 € 210/300 € – 2 suites **G3**
Rest *Circus* – (dinner only except from September to June) Carte 48/70 €
◆ Luxury ◆ Art Deco ◆
The name of this hotel housed in an austere 1930s palazzo refers to the number of the street which leads down to the Teatro di Marcello. Each of the five floors here is dedicated to a 20C Italian artist (Greco, Quagliata, Mastroianni, Modigliani and Guccione) and the hotel is adorned with a collection of paintings, sculptures and lithographs.

Canada without rest

via Vicenza 58 ✉ 00185
– Ⓜ Castro Pretorio – ✆ 06 4457770
– www.hotelcanadaroma.com — *Plan I* **C2**

73 rm – 128/164 € 146/198 €

♦ Traditional ♦ Classic ♦

Housed in a period-style building near Termini railway station, this simple but elegant hotel boasts traditional furnishings and 19C frescoes, some of which adorn the guestrooms.

Ambra Palace without rest

via Principe Amedeo 257 ✉ 00185
– Ⓜ Vittorio Emanuele – ✆ 06 492330
– www.ambrapalacehotel.com — *Plan I* **C2**

78 rm – 109/230 € 129/430 €

♦ Traditional ♦ Classic ♦

Occupying a mid-19C palazzo in a lively, multi-ethnic district behind the station, this hotel has been furnished and equipped to meet the requirements of a mainly business clientele.

Britannia without rest

via Napoli 64 ✉ 00184 – Ⓜ Repubblica – ✆ 06 4883153
– www.hotelbritannia.it — **H2**

33 rm – 130/200 € 150/240 €

♦ Traditional ♦ Classic ♦

Attentive service and stylish personalised decor are some of the features of this small hotel, which offers comfortable guestrooms, most of which are brightened by a small aquarium.

Palazzo Manfredi

via Labicana 125 ✉ 00184 – Ⓜ Colosseo – ✆ 06 77591380
– www.hotelpalazzomanfredi.it — **H3**

12 rm – 260/450 € 290/680 € – 4 suites

Rest – Carte 74/113 €

♦ Luxury ♦ Classic ♦

The elegant rooms and superb suites of this hotel overlook the Colosseum and the Domus Aurea. Without a doubt the hotel's most striking feature is its delightful roof-garden terrace, which is perfect for a relaxing breakfast or romantic dinner.

Celio without rest

via dei Santi Quattro 35/c ✉ 00184
– Ⓜ Colosseo – ✆ 06 70495333
– www.hotelcelio.com — **H3**

19 rm – 130/220 € 150/250 €

♦ Traditional ♦ Classic ♦

Delightful artistic touches create an elegant atmosphere in this hotel situated opposite the Colosseum. Stylish guestrooms with individual touches, as well as a hammam and relaxation zone.

Antico Palazzo Rospigliosi without rest

via Liberiana 22 ✉ 00185 – Ⓜ Cavour
– ✆ 06 48930495 – www.hotelrospigliosi.com — **G2**

39 rm – 95/160 € 120/290 €

♦ Historic ♦ Classic ♦

This 16C mansion has retained much of its period elegance in its large lounges, as well as in the fine detail of its beautiful bedrooms. The cloister-garden, with its bubbling fountain and splendid 17C chapel, is particularly delightful.

Mirabelle – Hotel Splendide Royal

via di porta Pinciana 14 ✉ 00187 – Ⓜ Barberini – ✆ 06 42168838 – www.mirabelle.it G1

Rest – Carte 104/156 €

Spec. Terrina di foie gras tartufato con gelatina al Sauternes. Riso al salto con pistilli di zafferano, punte d'asparagi e fonduta di parmigiano. Pezzogna in guazzetto con capperi di Salina ed olive taggiasche.

♦ Modern ♦ Formal ♦ Romantic ♦

With one of the most spectacular roof gardens in Rome and views of the Vatican Gardens, this restaurant serves an interesting blend of regional and international cuisine.

La Terrazza – Hotel Eden

via Ludovisi 49 ✉ 00187 – Ⓜ Barberini – ✆ 06 47812752 G1

Rest – Carte 97/136 €

♦ Classic ♦ Formal ♦

A lift takes guests to the top floor of this building, where the dining room enjoys stunning views of the historic centre of the city. Panoramic windows allow guests to enjoy the views to the full. A unique setting for a memorable evening.

Agata e Romeo (Agata Parisella)

via Carlo Alberto 45 ✉ 00185 – Ⓜ Vittorio Emanuele – ✆ 06 4466115 – www.agataeromeo.it – closed 6 to 21 August, from 1 to 16 January, Saturday and Sunday

Rest – Menu 110/130 € – Carte 90/125 € H2

Spec. Cinque modi di cucinare il baccalà. Ravioli al basilico farciti con pappa al pomodoro (summer). Il millefoglie di Agata.

♦ Roman ♦ Friendly ♦ Formal ♦

Situated in a district that is becoming more and more multicultural, this restaurant continues to showcase Roman and Italian produce and cuisine. One of the capital's culinary institutions!

Antonello Colonna

via Milano 9/a ((Exhibition Palace)) ✉ 00184 – Ⓜ Termini – ✆ 0647822641 – www.antonellocolonna.it – closed August, Sunday, Monday G2

Rest – *(dinner only) (booking advisable)* Carte 93/121 €

Spec. Negativo di carbonara. Cubi di coda alla vaccinara. Maialino croccante.

♦ Inventive ♦ Design ♦

This open-plan, glass-walled restaurant is within the imposing Palazzo delle Esposizioni. It serves inventive cuisine inspired by traditional dishes, which will please the most discerning guests.

Gaetano Costa

via Sicilia 45 ✉ 00186 – ✆ 06 42016822 – www.gaetanocostarestaurante.com G1

Rest – Menu 50/100 € – Carte 54/70 €

♦ Modern ♦ Design ♦

A new, modern restaurant, both in terms of its decor and menu, which includes fish and meat dishes. Fixed menus are available at lunchtime, in addition to the gourmet à la carte menu. The elegant dining room becomes a popular tea room in the afternoon.

Giuda Ballerino (Andrea Fusco)

via Marco Valerio Corvo 135 (change of location to viale Appio Antico 344 scheduled for December 2007) ✉ 00174 – Ⓜ Giulio Agricola – ☎ 06 71584807 – www.giudaballelrino.it – closed August and Wednesday Plan I **C3**

Rest – *(dinner only except Sunday) (booking advisable)* Carte 57/73 €

Rest *L'Osteria* – *(closed 10 days in January)* Carte 28/34 €

Spec. Variazione di baccalà. Mezzi paccheri alla gricia con calamari croccanti e zucchine. Manzo al carbone con patata soffiata, cipollotti caramellati e asparagi al burro di vaniglia e lime.

♦ Inventive ♦ Friendly ♦

This restaurant has an unusual dual function – on one side the Osteria has a rustic feel and serves regional fare, while on the other a small, modern dining room focuses on creative, gourmet cuisine. The walls of the latter are covered with cartoons, especially of Dylan Dog, a huge favourite of the owners.

Papà Baccus

via Toscana 32/36 ✉ 00187 – Ⓜ Barberini – ☎ 06 42742808 – www.papabaccus.com – closed Saturday lunch, Sunday **G1**

Rest – Carte 51/78 €

♦ Classic ♦ Formal ♦

Although the decor of this restaurant in the Via Veneto district is traditional, the management is young and enthusiastic. The menu features delicious seafood dishes, as well as specialities from Tuscany (including Chianina beef and Cinta Senese pork), Lazio and other regions of Italy.

Domenico dal 1968

via Satrico23/25 ✉ 00183 – ☎ 06 70494602 – www.domenicodal1968.it – closed 20 days in August, Sunday and Monday midday from May to September, Sunday evening and Monday the rest of the year Plan I **C3**

Rest – *(booking advisable)* Carte 30/42 €

♦ Roman ♦ Family ♦

Roman cuisine and hearty dishes full of flavour are the specialities of this friendly, family-run trattoria. The wood furnishings in the two small dining rooms add to the warm atmosphere.

Colline Emiliane

via degli Avignonesi 22 ✉ 00187 – Ⓜ Barberini – ☎ 06 4817538 – closed August, Sunday dinner, Monday **G2**

Rest – *(booking advisable)* Carte 36/46 €

♦ Emilian specialities ♦ Family ♦

Just a stone's throw from Piazza Barberini, this simple, friendly, family-run restaurant has just a few tables arranged close together. It serves typical dishes from the Emilia region, including fresh pasta stretched by hand in the traditional way.

Profumo di Mirto

viale Amelia 8/a ✉ 00181 – ☎ 06 786206 – www.profumodimirto.it – closed August and Monday Plan I **C3**

Rest – Carte 25/52 €

♦ Fish ♦ Cosy ♦

The name Profumo di Mirto pays tribute to Sardinia, the native region of the owners of this restaurant. It specialises in fish from the Mediterranean and offers delicious, home-style cooking.

Al Ristoro degli Angeli

via Luigi Orlando ✉ 00154 – ☎ 06 51436020 – www.ristorodegliangeli.it – closed August-15 September, from 1 to 10 January and Sunday

Rest – Carte 32/46 € Plan I **B3**

♦ Roman ♦ Bistro ♦

Home to the Ente Comunale di Consumo immediately after the war, and then to a haberdashery, this building now houses a restaurant with a unique, bistro-style atmosphere. The menu focuses on dishes from Rome, but also includes a few gourmet specialities.

Vatican City
(Plan III)

● Hotel
● Restaurant

HISTORICAL CENTRE / TERMINI RAILWAY STATION (Plan II)

ST-PETER'S BASILICA
Plan II

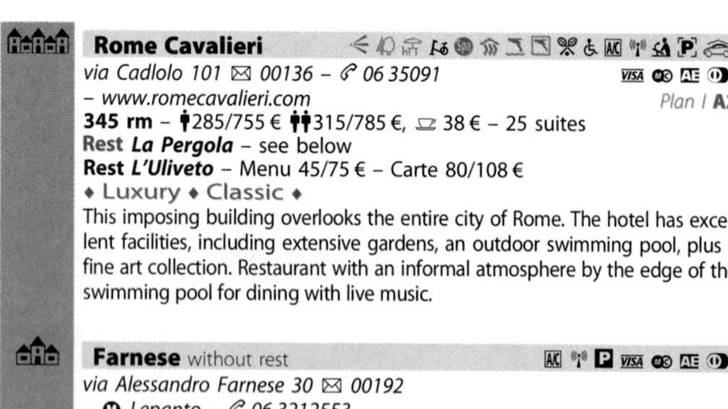

Rome Cavalieri
via Cadlolo 101 ✉ 00136 – ✆ 06 35091
– www.romecavalieri.com
Plan I **A2**
345 rm – †285/755 € ††315/785 €, ☕ 38 € – 25 suites
Rest *La Pergola* – see below
Rest *L'Uliveto* – Menu 45/75 € – Carte 80/108 €
♦ Luxury ♦ Classic ♦

This imposing building overlooks the entire city of Rome. The hotel has excellent facilities, including extensive gardens, an outdoor swimming pool, plus a fine art collection. Restaurant with an informal atmosphere by the edge of the swimming pool for dining with live music.

Farnese without rest
via Alessandro Farnese 30 ✉ 00192
– Ⓜ Lepanto – ✆ 06 3212553
– www.hotelfarnese.com
E1
23 rm ☕ – †140/220 € ††180/300 €
♦ Traditional ♦ Classic ♦

Decorated in period style, this hotel has elegant rooms and an attractive lobby housing a 17C polychrome marble frontal. Fine views of St Peter's from the terrace.

Alimandi Vaticano without rest

viale Vaticano 99 ✉ 00165
– Ⓜ Ottaviano-San Pietro
– ✆ 06 39745562
– www.alimandi.it Plan III **J1**

24 rm – 120/180 € 130/200 €

♦ Family ♦ Classic ♦

This pleasant hotel enjoys an excellent location directly opposite the Vatican Museums. The marble and wood decor in the well-appointed guestrooms adds to their elegant atmosphere.

Sant'Anna without rest

borgo Pio 133 ✉ 00193
– Ⓜ Ottaviano-San Pietro
– ✆ 06 68801602
– www.hotelsantanna.com Plan III **K1-2**

20 rm – 90/160 € 130/220 €

♦ Traditional ♦ Classic ♦

An original coffered ceiling and pleasant interior courtyard add a decorative touch to this small, welcoming hotel occupying a 16C building a short distance from St Peter's.

Bramante without rest

vicolo delle Palline 24 ✉ 00193
– Ⓜ Ottaviano-San Pietro
– ✆ 06 68806426
– www.hotelbramante.com Plan III **K2**

16 rm – 100/170 € 150/240 €

♦ Traditional ♦ Classic ♦

This historic hotel is situated in the heart of the typical, pedestrianised Borgo district. The oldest sections date back to the 15C.

La Pergola – Hotel Rome Cavalieri

via Cadlolo 101 ✉ 00136
– ✆ 06 35092152
– www.romecavalieri.com
– closed from 14 to 29 August, from 1 to 24 January, Sunday, Monday Plan I **A2**

Rest – *(dinner only) (booking essential)* Carte 125/184 €

Spec. Carpaccio tiepido di tonno su pappa al pomodoro. Spaghetti cacio e pepe con gamberi bianchi marinati al lime. Guancetta di maialino con scarola, burrata e riso soffiato al peperoncino.

♦ Inventive ♦ Luxury ♦

German chef Heinz Beck is more Italian than many of his colleagues! Served in the panoramic roof garden, the cuisine here is Roman and Mediterranean, and the service both attentive and professional.

Enoteca Costantini-Il Simposio

piazza Cavour 16 ✉ 00193
– Ⓜ Lepanto
– ✆ 06 32111131
– closed August, Saturday lunch, Sunday **E2**

Rest – Carte 40/69 €

♦ Classic ♦ Formal ♦

An evocative wrought-iron vine marks the entrance to this restaurant-cum-wine bar, which serves specialities such as foie gras, as well as a selection of different cheeses, accompanied by a glass of wine.

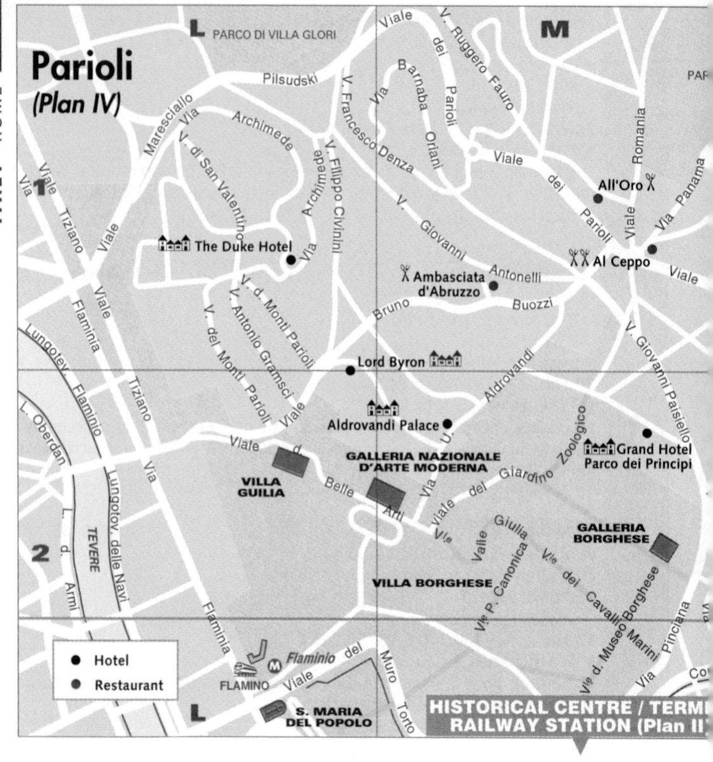

PARIOLI

Plan IV

Grand Hotel Parco dei Principi

via Gerolamo Frescobaldi 5 ✉ 00198 – ☎ 06 854421 – www.parcodeiprincipi.com

M2

166 rm – 🛉154/374 € 🛉🛉220/649 €, ☕ 28 € – 13 suites

Rest *Pauline Borghese* – Carte 55/90 €

♦ Grand Luxury ♦ Classic ♦

This hotel is situated in a quiet residential district overlooking the Villa Borghese gardens. It has views of the dome of St Peter's from the upper floors. The interior features wood-panelling, plush carpets and reproductions of famous paintings. Exclusive restaurant serving well-prepared, varied cuisine.

Aldrovandi Villa Borghese

via Ulisse Aldrovandi 15 ✉ 00197 – ☎ 06 3223993 – www.aldrovandi.com

M2

96 rm – 🛉600/800 € 🛉🛉650/850 €, ☕ 33 € – 11 suites

Rest *Baby* – *☎ 06 3216126* – Carte 75/95 €

♦ Luxury ♦ Classic ♦

In an elegant palazzo dating from the late 19C, this hotel has luxurious period-style interiors, stylish bedrooms and a delightful internal garden to the rear of the building. The restaurant is the jewel in the crown of this hotel, offering Mediterranean cuisine and fish specialities in a bright, minimalist-style dining room.

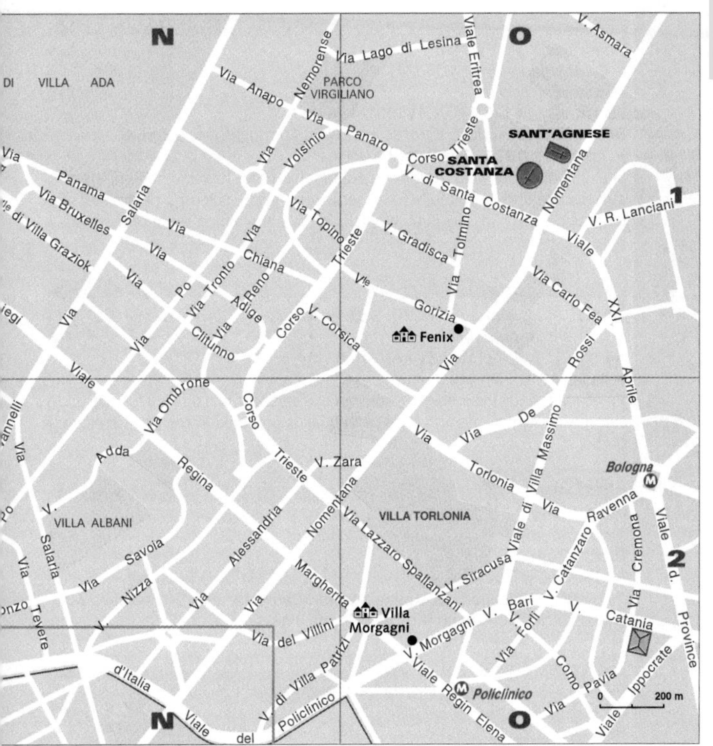

Lord Byron

via G. De Notaris 5 ✉ *00197*
– Ⓜ *Flaminio* – ✆ *06 3220404*
– *www.lordbyronhotel.com* **L-M1**

26 rm – 220/405 € 230/531 € – 6 suites

Rest *Sapori del Lord Byron* – *(closed Sunday)* Carte 53/71 €

♦ Luxury ♦ Art Deco ♦

Elegant Art Deco furnishings, luxurious guestrooms and modern facilities make this hotel near the Villa Borghese gardens an excellent base. Impeccable service. This stylish restaurant adorned with mirrors, marble and fine paintings has its own entrance. Ideal for quiet, intimate dinners.

The Duke Hotel

via Archimede 69 ✉ *00197* – ✆ *06 367221*
– *www.thedukehotel.com* **L1**

78 rm – 365/490 € 490/615 €

Rest – Carte 44/65 €

♦ Traditional ♦ Classic ♦

Situated in a quiet residential area, this hotel has the discreet, muted atmosphere of an elegant English club. Decorated in typical period style, but with all the latest modern comforts. Afternoon tea is served in front of the fireplace. Italian and international dishes are reinterpreted with a creative flair at this restaurant.

Fenix

viale Gorizia 5 ✉ 00198 – Ⓜ Bologna – ☎ 06 8540741 – www.fenixhotel.it **O1**

73 rm – 175/220 € 190/240 €

Rest – *(closed August, Saturday evening, Sunday)* Carte 25/56 €

◆ Traditional ◆ Personalised ◆

Situated near the Villa Torlonia gardens, this hotel has an modern, elegant atmosphere and is tastefully furnished with original, colourful decor. Pleasant internal garden. Soft, elegant colours dominate the dining room of the restaurant.

Villa Morgagni without rest

via G.B. Morgagni 2 ✉ 00161 – Ⓜ Policlinico – ☎ 06 44202190 – www.villamorgagni.it **O2**

34 rm – 90/150 € 120/250 €

◆ Luxury ◆ Classic ◆

Private and quiet in an elegant Art Nouveau setting with comfortable rooms. In summer or winter, the first meal of the day is prepared in the panoramic roof garden.

Al Ceppo

via Panama 2 ✉ 00198 – ☎ 06 8551379 – www.ristorantealceppo.it – closed from 12 to 24 August and Monday **M1**

Rest – Carte 52/69 €

◆ Classic ◆ Formal ◆

Innovative Mediterranean cuisine served in an elegantly rustic setting. Main courses include meat and fish grilled in the dining room.

Mamma Angelina

viale Arrigo Boito 65 ✉ 00199 – ☎ 06 8608928 – closed August and Wednesday *Plan I* **C1**

Rest – Carte 22/31 €

◆ Fish ◆ Formal ◆

Traditional Italian cuisine is the hallmark of this friendly restaurant. Specialities include an excellent buffet of antipasti, fish and seafood dishes and typical Roman delicacies.

Acquolina Hostaria in Roma (Giulio Terrinoni)

via Antonio Serra 60 ✉ 00191 – ☎ 06 3337192 – www.acquolinahostaria.com – closed 10 days in August, Christmas and Sunday *Plan I* **B1**

Rest – *(dinner only)* Carte 71/94 €

Spec. Gran crudo acquolina. Coppa di testa di rana pescatrice. Torta di baccalà e patate con bagna cauda moderna.

◆ Fish ◆ Cosy ◆

This recently restored restaurant on the outskirts of Rome offers an impressive choice of raw fish antipasti, as well as more elaborate dishes. Unequalled for its fish and seafood!

Ambasciata d'Abruzzo

via Pietro Tacchini 26 ✉ 00197 – Ⓜ Euclide – ☎ 06 8078256 – www.ambasciatadiabruzzo.com – closed from 13 to 31 August, 28 December-8 January **M1**

Rest – *(pre-book)* Carte 28/46 €

◆ Abruzzian specialities ◆ Rustic ◆

The location of this family-run trattoria in the middle of a residential district comes as something of a surprise. Good selection of antipasti, fish dishes and specialities from the Lazio and Abruzzi regions.

All'Oro (Riccardo Di Giacinto)

via Eleonora Duse 1/e ✉ 00197
– ✆ 06 97996907
– www.ristorantealloro.it
– closed 3 weeks in August, 1 week in January, Saturday lunch, Sunday, Monday lunch **M1**

Rest – Carte 59/77 €

Spec. "Tiramisù" di patate e baccalà con lardo di cinta senese. Raviolini di mascarpone con ragù d'anatra e riduzione di vino rosso. Spigola in porchetta con zuppa di carbonara e tartufo.

♦ Inventive ♦ Design ♦

This restaurant has a simple, modern decor. The inventive, personalised cuisine highlights authentic Roman traditions and flavours.

FLORENCE

FIRENZE

Population (est. 2010): 368 901 – Altitude: 50m

iovanni Simeone/Sime/Photononstop

Never one to sully itself with a political or economic role, Florence has instead always stood for beauty, and represents Italy's greatest contribution to the world of arts: the Renaissance. The city itself is much like an open air museum, with churches and squares alongside the most precious of marbles. You may have read about Florence in Forster's books or see it in Ivory's film, yet nothing prepares you for the real thing, with its works of art of unparalleled beauty. The Duomo, Michelangelo's David, Botticelli's Venere and Ponte Vecchio: the postcard becomes reality. It is said that Cupid lives in Florence and it's hard to imagine a city more romantic than this; lovers visit from around the world while those not yet in love are thought to find their match here.

Tuscany is home to one of Italy's most celebrated cuisines, as well as gorgeous olive oil and those famous Super Tuscan red wines. They form part of the fiorentini's taste for life and pursuit of excellence. It's not by chance that the Italian language originated here and that the country's national poet, Dante, was born here too. Many suggest that this brilliance must be connected to the local diet, most notably the local white cannellini beans; try them for yourself and see…

LIVING THE CITY

Florence is surrounded by a ring of hills, the **'colli'**, and winding streets flanked with cypress and olive trees lead you to the heart of Dante's beloved hometown. The city centre and many of its monuments lie on the northern side of the **Arno**, a river closely connected with Florence's history and celebrated by poets throughout the years. The river is crossed by many beautiful bridges, **Ponte Vecchio** being the most famous, but, despite its beauty, the Arno has in the past wreaked havoc in the form of regular flooding which has caused huge amounts of damage to parts of the city.

In each area of Florence, civic and religious powers each occupy their own distinct site. **Piazza della Signoria** is home to the town hall, while the **Duomo** sits in the piazza of the same name at the end of **Via Calzaiuoli**, the city's most famous shopping street and home to some of Italy's well-known brands. This area also boasts many magnificent churches. Cross one of the bridges to the south side of the city for a more relaxed, village-like atmosphere. Here you will find the **Palazzo Pitti** and the **Gardino di Boboli**. Walking eastwards will bring you to the **Piazzale Michelangelo**, which boasts probably the best views in Florence.

PRACTICAL INFORMATION

ARRIVAL-DEPARTURE

Amerigo Vespucci, Florence's airport, lies 5km outside of the city and a taxi to the centre will cost approximately €15-20. Alternatively, you can opt for a bus, which takes you to the Santa Maria Novella railway station, for €3-4.

TRANSPORT

If you are staying in the city centre the best and most interesting way to see Florence is by foot: most of the sights are within easy walking distance. Alternatively, one of the municipal orange buses will take you everywhere you need; €1,50 will buy you a 60 minute ride.

There are two main tourist offices in Florence; one is in Piazza Stazione (Santa Maria Novella), 4/a (tel. 055 212245), the other is close to Ponte alle Grazie in Borgo Santa Croce, 29r (tel. 055 2340444). More information can be obtained on the web at www.comune.fi.it or www.firenzeturismo.it.

EXPLORING FLORENCE

With so many things to see and do in Florence, it's hard to even scratch the surface in just a couple of days

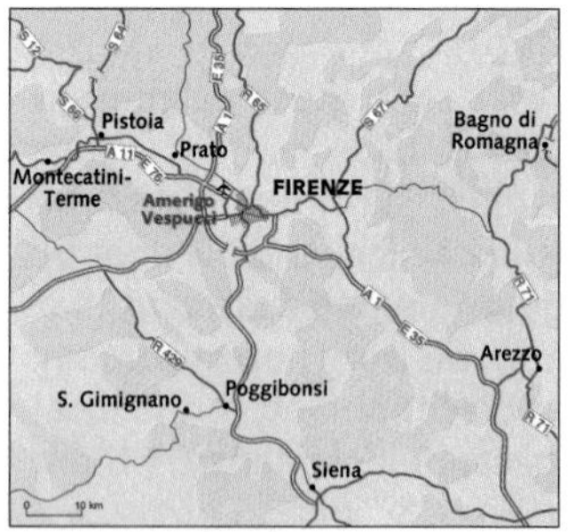

and a complete list of what's relevant would run into several pages. If you have the time, then just walk around and explore by yourself – you'll find yourself surrounded by art and beauty everywhere you go.

➜ DIVINE BEAUTY & POWER

Piazza del Duomo, the city's religious heart, is a masterpiece of marble, technical audacity and unadulterated beauty. It's composed of three parts: the Duomo, the Baptistery and the bell-tower. The Duomo itself is a magnificent example of the interpretation of Gothic style that was popular in Florence at one time and its masterpiece, Brunelleschi's Dome, is a feat that defied the rules and limits of architecture of the age. The Baptistery epitomises Florence's taste for harmony and balance and the bas-relief on its doors are one of the city's greatest treasures. Last but by no means least is Giotto's bell tower which, aside from its impressive construction, will reward you for climbing those 414 steps with breathtaking views.

In Piazza della Signoria, a 13C square, sits the stone-built Palazzo Vecchio, from where the secular powers of Florence make decisions that govern the city. Via Calzaiuoli connects Piazza della Signoria to Piazza del Duomo and it is here where you'll find all those glamorous designer shops.

Italy's most famous museum, the Uffizi, is located within a 16C Vasari Palazzo – a masterpiece of beauty with its two parallel wings – and started life as offices (uffizi) for the Medicean administration. The beauty of the construction along with the family's love for art, later convinced Francesco I to open it to the public in 1591. Today, a unique collection of artwork is on display to the public, distributed throughout 45 halls. Don't miss the three 'Madonne in Maestà' by Cimabue, Giotti and Duccio (room 2); the 'Nascita di Venere' and the 'Primavera' in Botticelli's Rooms (10-14); Leonardo da Vinci's 'L'Annunciazione' and 'L'Adorazione dei Magi' (room 15); or Tiziano's 'Venere d'Urbino' (room 28). If Florence is the heart of the Renaissance, then the Uffizi museum is the heart of Florence.

The city's most famous bridge – Ponte Vecchio – is also its oldest, dating back to 1345 and the only bridge to survive the German bombings of World War II. It stands unique, with shops and sellers flanking both sides. Butchers once occupied these shops but now they've been replaced mostly by goldsmiths. Even if the jewellery is a little too rich for your taste, then at least it's free to enjoy the romantic atmosphere that has seduced lovers over the years.

"Another Renaissance Palazzo" you may say…but this one is special; across the Ponte Vecchio towards the southern bank of the Arno, it's one of the most imposing in Florence. Its story starts with the Pitti family, ranked in the 15C among the city's most influential families together with the Medici. In an endless struggle to prove their wealth, the Pitti's ambition to build a bigger house than their rivals' brought them to financial ruin. Ironically, the Palazzo they built was then bought by the Medici themselves, who amassed an astonishing collection of works of art. Housed in the Galleria Palatina inside the Palazzo, the collection comprises paintings from the 16C to the 18C, including pieces by Raffaello and Tiziano.

→ MAGNIFICENT LORENZO

If there is one person who truly represents the city it is Lorenzo il Magnifico. Part of the Medici family who ruled Florence for more than three centuries, Lorenzo was only 20 years old when he took on the role of governing the city. Refusing every sort of official power he became a true principe and his ability as a diplomat became famous throughout Europe. The people loved him and he was hailed as a saviour after he saved Florence from invasion during the Guerra de' Pazzi. Two years after his death in 1492, Italy was invaded by Carlo VIII and one of the most magnificent periods in Florence came to an end.

No one ever matched his love for the arts and during his reign Florence became one of Europe's most influential intellectual and artistic centres. Lorenzo himself was a writer and poet, and throughout his reign he was surrounded by the best painters and sculptors of the time. He famously invited people to 'perché di doman non c'è certezza' – enjoy the best of life – because no one knows what the future holds. He also opened a school for artists that saw the young Michelangelo amongst its scholars.The legacy of this golden age has made Florence world famous: Santa Maria Novella and San Lorenzo's 'Cappelle' and 'Biblioteca Medicea Laurenziana' are only a few examples of this magnificent era.

CALENDAR HIGHLIGHTS

Florence's calendar revolves mainly around events connected with the city's rich past, many of which will be particularly appreciated by those looking to gain a deeper insight into its history. For example, The Piazza del Duomo plays host to a spectacular Easter celebration, which includes a procession of Renaissance costumes. Still going strong every April after 70 years is the handicraft exposition; while May sees the Trofeo Marzocco, a flag-waving competition. Those interested in more sporting activities should come in mid June to witness the passions engendered by a vital football match. Firework displays in Piazzale Michelangelo happen on the 24th June; while October is usually dedicated to various theatrical events. Towards the end of the year, Pitti Immagine attracts thousands of fashion lovers, so make sure you book your hotel well in advance.

EATING OUT

Tuscan food is one of the most famous and highly regarded of Italy's regional cuisines and it will come as no surprise to learn that some of the best examples are to be found here in Florence. Soups are particularly renowned and often combine popular ingredients; don't miss pappa col pomodoro – made with bread and tomatoes – or ribollita – made from cannellini, a local variety of beans, black cabbage, bread and other vegetables. You will no doubt have noticed that bread is an important feature of the Tuscan cuisine but don't be surprised if it comes with no salt, as they still follow age old traditions dating back to a time when salt was too expensive to be used lavishly.

Pasta can certainly not be ignored; pappardelle con la lepre (with hare) and pici (a sort of spaghetti) are two of the most popular. Meat is a favourite for second courses : the fiorentina, a grilled T-bone steak which takes its name from the city, has now become a favourite nationwide. Beware, restaurants in tourist areas can be very pricey – for a quick, inexpensive meal you're better off opting for a pizza.

Wines are equally important in Florence as the cooking. Buying a Super Tuscan will obviously mean digging deep into the wallet ; however, you can find good value for money with a Chianti, a Morellino di Scansano or a Nobile di Montepulciano – the Brunello di Montalcino is usually more expensive and ranked amongst the best red wines. If price is not an issue, then opt for the Super Tuscans : Ornellaia, Sassicaia, Solaia or Tignanello.

FLORENCE IN...

→ ONE DAY

Piazza della Signoria, Via Calzaiuoli, the Duomo, Santa Croce, Ponte Vecchio, the Galleria dell'Accademia

→ TWO DAYS

The Uffizi, Santa Maria Novella, San Lorenzo

→ THREE DAYS

Palazzo Pitti and the Galleria Palatina, Giardino di Boboli, Santa Maria del Carmine, Piazzale Michelangelo

Don't worry too much about the time that you go to the restaurant. Although locals may lunch around 1pm and dine around 8pm, the great number of tourists and visitors to the city has encouraged restaurants to be very flexible about timings.

Tipping has become less and less customary amongst Italians, so don't feel obliged to leave anything extra. Prices have to be displayed outside the restaurant so you'll know what to expect ; a cover charge may occasionally be added.

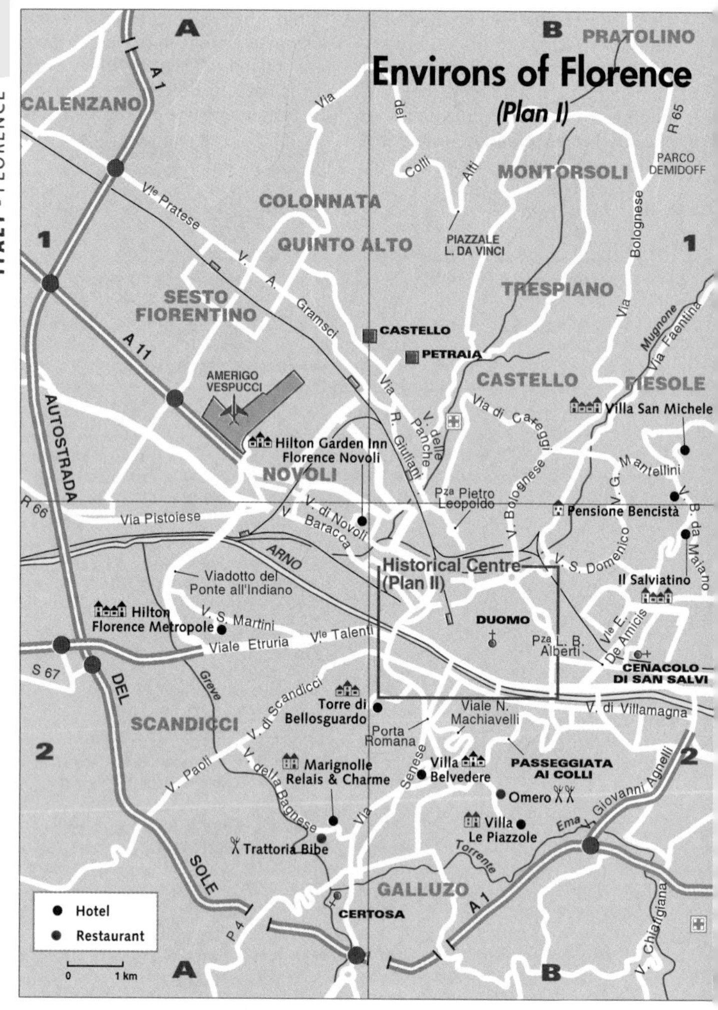

HISTORICAL CENTRE *Plan II*

The Westin Excelsior

piazza Ognissanti 3 ✉ 50123 – ☎ 055 27151 – www.westin.com/excelsiorflorence **C2**

166 rm – †670/785 € ††890/995 €, ☕ 39 € – 5 suites

Rest – Carte 41/65 €

♦ Grand Luxury ♦ Palace ♦ Historic ♦

Sumptuous interiors of an old nobleman's dwelling on the Arno, where history and tradition combine with more modern accessories for an exclusive aristocratic stay. The dining hall of this restaurant is princely. Among its features are the boxed ceilings and decor in Carrara marble.

Four Seasons Hotel Firenze

borgo Pinti 99 ✉ *50121 – ☎ 055 26261 – www.fourseasons.com/florence* **F2**
94 rm – ††330/935 €, ☕ 34 € – 24 suites
Rest *Il Palagio* – *(closed Sunday from November to March) (dinner only)* Carte 70/121 €
Rest *Al Fresco* – *(May-September) (lunch only)* Carte 40/60 €
◆ Chain hotel ◆ Grand Luxury ◆ Historic ◆
Set in delightful botanical gardens, this hotel comprises of two buildings: the Palazzo della Gherardesca and Il Conventino. The elegant decor includes frescoes and sculpted bas-reliefs, as well as oriental-style silk wallpaper. Perfect for a luxury break. The Palagio is renowned for its excellent cuisine. There is more "light" at Al Fresco.

Savoy

piazza della Repubblica 7 ✉ *50123 – ☎ 055 27351 – www.hotelsavoy.it*
102 rm – †468 € ††880 €, ☕ 32 € – 14 suites **D2**
Rest *L'Incontro* – *☎ 055 2735891* – Carte 67/86 €
◆ Luxury ◆ Palace ◆ Historic ◆
Conveniently situated near the Duomo, museums and large fashion stores, this elegant, historic hotel boasts spacious, comfortable guestrooms with mosaic-work in the bathrooms. Traditional Tuscan and Italian cuisine with an innovative twist is served in the attractive restaurant, which includes tables overlooking the piazza in summer.

Montebello Splendid

via Garibaldi 14 ✉ *50123 – ☎ 055 27471 – www.montebellosplendid.com*
60 rm ☕ – †150/350 € ††230/780 € – 2 suites **C2**
Rest – Carte 67/78 €
◆ Traditional ◆ Functional ◆
This stylishly modern hotel is the much frequented haunt of tourists and business persons; common areas are spacious and attractively furnished and give onto a delightful internal garden.

Relais Santa Croce

via Ghibellina 87 ✉ *50122 – ☎ 055 2342230 – www.baglionihotels.com*
24 rm ☕ – †200/500 € ††300/600 € – 6 suites **E3**
Rest – Carte 60/82 €
◆ Palace ◆ Personalised ◆
This hotel forms part of an 18th century mansion that also houses the famous Pinchiorri Wine library; it is characterised by a fascinating atmosphere, frescoed halls and elegantly furnished rooms. The passion for old recipes and Tuscan herbs and flavours are evident in this restaurant.

Helvetia e Bristol

via dei Pescioni 2 ✉ *50123 – ☎ 055 26651 – www.royaldemeure.com*
52 rm – †215/355 € ††280/640 €, ☕ 26 € – 15 suites **D2**
Rest *Hostaria Bibendum* – *☎ 0552665620* – Carte 62/73 €
◆ Palace ◆ Luxury ◆ Personalised ◆
Situated near the Duomo and Palazzo Strozzi, this stylish 19C residence recalls the elegance of the past with its personalised rooms furnished with period paintings and antiques. Tuscan specialities and other imaginative dishes take pride of place in this small, elegant restaurant, which also hosts cookery courses.

Regency

piazza Massimo D'Azeglio 3 ✉ *50121 – ☎ 055 245247 – www.regency-hotel.com* **F2**
31 rm ☕ – †220/405 € ††230/531 € – 3 suites
Rest *Relais le Jardin* – Carte 48/65 €
◆ Luxury ◆ Personalised ◆
This hotel, which once provided hospitality to Florence's leading political figures, has retained much of its historical charm. Tranquil atmosphere and elegant, comfortable rooms. Exquisite Italian cuisine is served in the elegant restaurant overlooking the garden.

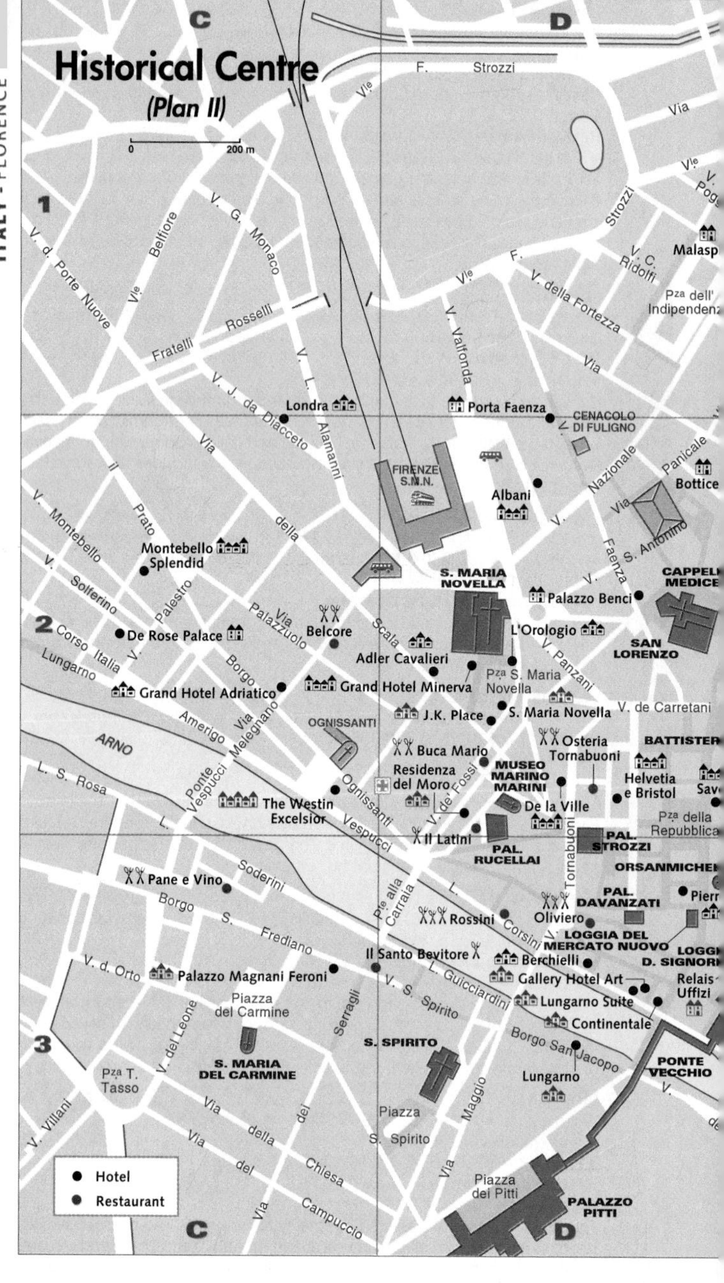
Historical Centre
(Plan II)
0
200 m
C
D
1
2
3
Hotel
Restaurant
Londra
Porta Faenza
CENACOLO DI FULIGNO
FIRENZE S.M.N.
Albani
Bottice
Malasp
Montebello Splendid
S. MARIA NOVELLA
Palazzo Benci
CAPPELLE MEDICE
SAN LORENZO
Belcore
Adler Cavalieri
L'Orologio
De Rose Palace
Grand Hotel Adriatico
Grand Hotel Minerva
Pza S. Maria Novella
S. Maria Novella
J.K. Place
OGNISSANTI
Buca Mario
Osteria Tornabuoni
BATTISTER
Residenza del Moro
MUSEO MARINO MARINI
Helvetia e Bristol
The Westin Excelsior
De la Ville
Pza della Repubblica
Il Latini
PAL. RUCELLAI
PAL. STROZZI
ORSANMICHE
Pane e Vino
PAL. DAVANZATI
Oliviero
Rossini
LOGGIA DEL MERCATO NUOVO
Il Santo Bevitore
Berchielli
Gallery Hotel Art
Relais Uffizi
Palazzo Magnani Feroni
Lungarno Suite
Continentale
Piazza del Carmine
S. SPIRITO
S. MARIA DEL CARMINE
Lungarno
PONTE VECCHIO
Pza T. Tasso
Piazza S. Spirito
Piazza dei Pitti
PALAZZO PITTI
ARNO
F. Strozzi
V. della Fortezza
V. Valfonda
Pza dell' Indipendenza
V. Nazionale
V. Faenza
V. Panzani
V. de Carretani
Via della Scala
Via Palazzuolo
V. L. Alamanni
V. J. da Diacceto
V. G. Monaco
Vle Belfiore
Vle Fratelli Rosselli
V. d. Porte Nuove
V. Montebello
V. Solferino
Corso Italia
Lungarno Amerigo Vespucci
Borgo Ognissanti
Via Melegnano
Ponte Vespucci
L. S. Rosa
L. Soderini
Borgo S. Frediano
Ple alla Carraia
L. Corsini
L. Guicciardini
V. S. Spirito
Borgo San Jacopo
V. d. Orto
V. del Leone
Serragli
Via Maggio
V. Villani
Via della Chiesa
Via del Campuccio
V. de' Fossi
Tornabuoni
V. S. Antonino
Via Panicale

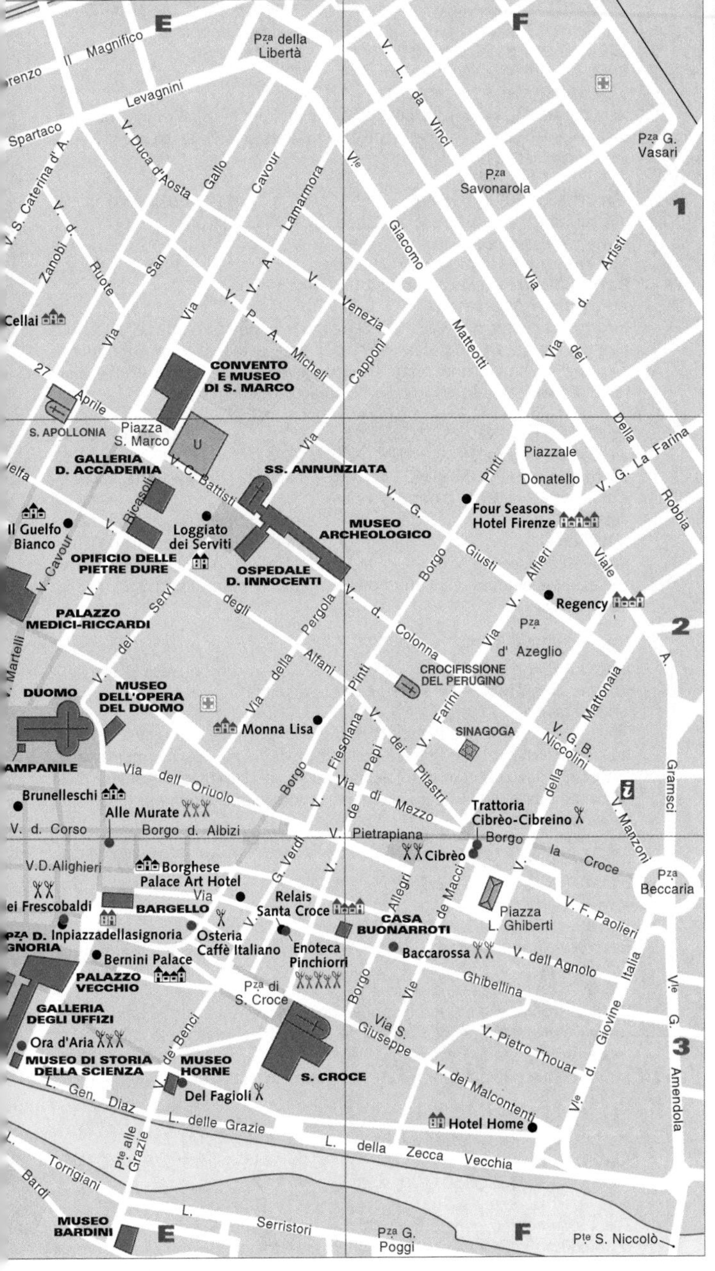
E
F
1
2
3
Pza della Libertà
Pza G. Vasari
Pza Savonarola
CONVENTO E MUSEO DI S. MARCO
S. APOLLONIA
Piazza S. Marco
GALLERIA D. ACCADEMIA
SS. ANNUNZIATA
Piazzale Donatello
Four Seasons Hotel Firenze
Il Guelfo Bianco
Loggiato dei Serviti
MUSEO ARCHEOLOGICO
OPIFICIO DELLE PIETRE DURE
OSPEDALE D. INNOCENTI
Regency
PALAZZO MEDICI-RICCARDI
Pza d' Azeglio
CROCIFISSIONE DEL PERUGINO
DUOMO
MUSEO DELL'OPERA DEL DUOMO
Monna Lisa
SINAGOGA
AMPANILE
Brunelleschi
Alle Murate
Trattoria Cibrèo-Cibreino
Cibrèo
V.D.Alighieri
Borghese Palace Art Hotel
Relais Santa Croce
Pza Beccaria
dei Frescobaldi
BARGELLO
CASA BUONARROTI
Piazza L. Ghiberti
Pza D. Inpiazzadellasignoria
GNORIA
Osteria Caffè Italiano
Enoteca Pinchiorri
Baccarossa
Bernini Palace
PALAZZO VECCHIO
Pza di S. Croce
GALLERIA DEGLI UFFIZI
Ora d'Aria
MUSEO DI STORIA DELLA SCIENZA
MUSEO HORNE
S. CROCE
Del Fagioli
Hotel Home
MUSEO BARDINI
Pza G. Poggi
Pte S. Niccolò
Pte alle Grazie
L. Gen. Diaz
L. delle Grazie
L. della Zecca Vecchia
L. Serristori
Torrigiani
Bardi

Albani

via Fiume 12 ✉ *50123 – ✆ 055 26030 – www.albanihotels.icom*

100 rm – 130/360 € 170/430 € – 2 suites **D2**

Rest – *(residents only)* Carte 28/72 €

♦ Traditional ♦ Functional ♦

Near the station, in a prestigious palace dating from the start of the 20th Century, strict neo-classical refined features in the Imperial style ambience of an extremely fascinating hotel.

Grand Hotel Minerva

piazza Santa Maria Novella 16 ✉ *50123 – ✆ 055 27230 – www.concertohotels.com* **D2**

102 rm – 129/300 € 129/500 €

Rest *I Chiostri* – *(closed Sunday)* Carte 40/65 €

♦ Palace ♦ Modern ♦

Next to the church of S.Maria Novella, a modern, very comfortable hotel, with pleasant spacious public areas; worthy of note is the view from the terrace with the swimming pool. Huge windows overlook the garden in the main room of the restaurant furnished in an attractive modern style.

Bernini Palace

piazza San Firenze 29 ✉ *50122 – ✆ 055 288621* **E3**

74 rm – 150/350 € 200/500 € – 5 suites **Rest** – Carte 47/62 €

♦ Historic ♦ Personalised ♦

When Florence was the capital of Italy, members of parliament and senators would meet in the Sala Parlamento of this hotel. With its spacious corridors, magnificent guestrooms (those on the Tuscan Floor are particularly impressive), and an excellent restaurant, this hotel now attracts visitors looking for the highest quality.

De la Ville without rest

piazza Antinori 1 ✉ *50123 – ✆ 055 2381805 – www.hoteldelaville.it*

68 rm – 110/290 € 190/420 € – 6 suites **D2**

♦ Historic ♦ Classic ♦

Situated in an elegant shopping street, this luxury hotel occupies a historical building which has been restored in classic modern style. Spacious guestrooms, as well as a new collection of suites and junior suites which will delight the most demanding of guests. Superb 180m^2 penthouse with a large terrace and 360° views of the city.

Lungarno

borgo San Jacopo 14 ✉ *50125 – ✆ 055 27261 – www.lungarnohotels.com* **D3**

69 rm – 230/630 € 330/920 €, 25 € – 4 suites

Rest *Borgo San Jacopo* – *✆ 055 281661 (closed August and Tuesday) (dinner only)* Carte 56/72 €

♦ Business ♦ Personalised ♦

Priceless "room with a view" in a hotel right on the Arno, where everything is geared towards the refined care of all of your needs; valuable collection of modern paintings. Enjoy splendid views of the river and Ponte Vecchio from the modern restaurant, which serves a range of inventive dishes.

J.K. Place without rest

piazza Santa Maria Novella 7 ✉ *50123 – ✆ 055 2645181 – www.jkplace.com* **D2**

19 rm – 350/650 € – 1 suite

♦ Grand Luxury ♦ Historic ♦

This stylish hotel overlooks the historical Piazza Santa Maria Novella. Recently restored by the architect Michele Bönan, the building now offers a surprising mix of luxury and individual details which combine to create an elegant, yet welcoming atmosphere.

Continentale without rest
vicolo dell'Oro 6 r ✉ *50123 – ☎ 055 27262 – www.lungarnohotels.com*
42 rm – 275/605 € 363/671 € – 1 suite **D3**
◆ Traditional ◆ Modern ◆
This hotel has been built up around a mediaeval tower. There is a fine view of the Ponte Vecchio from the flower-filled terrace and from some of the attractively furnished rooms.

Santa Maria Novella without rest
piazza Santa Maria Novella 1 ✉ *50123*
– ☎ 055 271840 – www.hotelsantamarianovella.it **D2**
71 rm – 150/320 € 170/450 €
◆ Traditional ◆ Modern ◆
Overlooking Piazza Santa Maria Novella, this welcoming hotel offers small lounge areas and elegant guestrooms, all of which have different decor and furnishings. Enjoy superb views of this magical city from the hotel's delightful panoramic terrace.

Gallery Hotel Art
vicolo dell'Oro 5 ✉ *50123 – ☎ 055 27263 – www.lungarnohotels.com*
69 rm – 330/528 € 352/814 € – 5 suites **D3**
Rest *The Fusion Bar & Restaurant* – *☎ 055 27266987 (closed August)*
Carte 43/67 €
◆ Business ◆ Modern ◆
Contemporary design by a well known architect and cosmopolitan art exhibited as if in a museum, are the ingredients of the uniqueness and fascination of a really "modern" hotel. Decorated in the same contemporary style as the hotel, the restaurant serves "fusion cuisine". Fixed-price buffet at lunchtime with brunch served at the weekend.

Brunelleschi
piazza Santa Elisabetta 3 ✉ *50122 – ☎ 055 27370 – www.hotelbrunelleschi.it*
95 rm – 144/365 € 169/389 € **E2**
Rest – *(closed Sunday)* Carte 57/110 €
◆ Historic ◆ Functional ◆
This hotel is housed in the Torre della Pagliazza, a Byzantine tower which is one of the oldest buildings in the city. It is also home to a small museum with exhibits dating from the Roman period.

Monna Lisa without rest
via Borgo Pinti 27 ✉ *50121 – ☎ 055 2479751 – www.monnalisa.it*
45 rm – 152/250 € 226/380 € – 4 suites **E2**
◆ Luxury ◆ Historic ◆
Situated in the historic centre, this hotel occupies an original medieval palazzo with an imposing staircase, brick flooring and coffered ceilings. Room's and communal areas have Renaissance-style furnishings. The newer rooms, which are just as elegant as the rest of the hotel, can be found in the two annexes in the splendid garden.

Palazzo Magnani Feroni without rest
borgo San Frediano 5 ✉ *50124 – ☎ 055 2399544*
– www.palazzomagnaniferoni.it **C3**
12 suites – 200/850 €
◆ Luxury ◆ Historic ◆
Located in the Oltrarno, inside a 16C building, centring on a small internal courtyard. Offering terraces with an all-round panoramic view of the city.

Borghese Palace Art Hotel without rest
via Ghibellina 174/r ✉ *50122 – ☎ 055 284363*
– www.borghesepalace.com **E3**
25 rm – 100/200 € 140/300 €
◆ Historic ◆ Functional ◆
Housed in the 19C mansion that was once the residence of Carolina Bonaparte, this attractive hotel blends classical elegance and modern furnishings, with contemporary art exhibitions often held in the public areas. The relaxation area is pretty and full of character.

Londra

via Jacopo da Diacceto 18 ✉ *50123 –* ✆ *055 27390*
– www.concertohotels.com **C1-2**
166 rm – 170/280 € 210/395 € **Rest** – Carte 40/59 €
♦ Palace ♦ Modern ♦

Near the station - a recently constructed building which is both practical and comfortable, endowed with vast public areas, business centre and conference facilities; rooms with modern furnishings. Contemporary style dining room adjoining a patio with a more romantic atmosphere.

Adler Cavalieri without rest

via della Scala 40 ✉ *50123 –* ✆ *055 277810*
– www.hoteladlercavalieri.com **D2**
60 rm – 115/275 € 120/360 €
♦ Traditional ♦ Functional ♦

This pleasant hotel is located in the immediate vicinity of the station. The soundproofing is excellent and wood has been used to very good effect. The management is youthful and competent.

Grand Hotel Adriatico

rm,

via Maso Finiguerra 9 ✉ *50123 –* ✆ *055 27931 – www.hoteladriatico.it*
126 rm – 120/230 € 130/350 € **C2**
Rest – *(closed Sunday) (dinner only)* Carte 32/72 €
♦ Traditional ♦ Functional ♦

Conveniently situated in the city centre, this hotel has a large lobby and modern guestrooms decorated in simple, yet elegant style. Tuscan and Italian cuisine is served in the quiet, recently renovated dining room, as well as in the attractive garden.

Pierre without rest

via Dè Lamberti 5 ✉ *50123 –* ✆ *055 216218 – www.remarhotels.com*
50 rm – 180/265 € 220/410 € **D3**
♦ Traditional ♦ Classic ♦

Ancient façade and interiors, recently restored, of a comfortable hotel right in the historical centre; rooms have been recently refurbished but in a Florentine or Venetian style

Lungarno Suites without rest

lungarno Acciaiuoli 4 ✉ *50123 –* ✆ *055 27268000*
– www.lungarnohotels.com **D3**
44 suites – 290/360 € 310/380 €, 15 €
♦ Luxury ♦ Functional ♦

As the name suggests, the rooms in this hotel are actually apartment suites with their own kitchen area. An ideal place for families and long-stay guests, as well as for visitors looking for spacious accommodation with hotel standard service.

Berchielli without rest

lungarno Acciaiuoli 14 ✉ *50123 –* ✆ *055 264061 – www.berchielli.it*
76 rm – 145/290 € 200/400 € **D3**
♦ Traditional ♦ Classic ♦

Stay in the heart of Florence, but along the banks of the Arno and, what is more, with a view of the Ponte Vecchio! That is the enviable opportunity that this comfortable luxury hotel offers you.

Il Guelfo Bianco without rest

via Cavour 29 ✉ *50129 –* ✆ *055 288330 – www.ilguelfobianco.it*
40 rm – 80/155 € 100/250 € **E2**
♦ Traditional ♦ Family ♦ Personalised ♦

Situated in the heart of Medici Florence, this hotel offers contemporary-style public areas and spacious guestrooms, some of which have frescoes on the ceilings. Small bistro selling hot food from 12-3pm.

L'Orologio without rest

piazza Santa Maria Novella 24 ✉ 50123 – ✆ 055 277380 – www.hotelorologioflorence.com **D2**

54 rm – 160/320 € 260/520 €

◆ Luxury ◆ Personalised ◆

The owner of this elegant hotel is one of the most important collectors of wrist watches in Europe, hence the name of the hotel ("orologio" is the Italian for watch or clock). Much of the decor relates to timepieces with a profusion of leather, parchment and wood in tobacco shades. This creates a distinctly masculine atmosphere, which is nonetheless appealing to guests of both sexes.

Cellai without rest

via 27 Aprile 14 ✉ 50129 – ✆ 055 489291 – www.hotelcellai.it

68 rm – 110/165 € 129/249 € **E1**

◆ Traditional ◆ Classic ◆

This luxurious hotel in Florence offers a welcoming atmosphere, period furnishings and antique prints of plants and animals. The top floor is home to an attractive terrace decked with jasmine, which acts as an open-air lounge in which to relax and enjoy views of the city.

Residenza del Moro without rest

via del Moro 15 ✉ 50123 – ✆ 055 290884 – www.residenzadelmoro.com

6 rm – 240 € 280 € – 5 suites **D2**

◆ Grand Luxury ◆ Personalised ◆

Returned to its original splendour after careful restoration, this 16C palazzo was built for the Marchesi Niccolini-Bourbon. Antique frescoes and magnificent works of contemporary art combine to create a luxury hotel right in the heart of Florence.

Hotel Home without rest

piazza Piave 3 ✉ 50122 – ✆ 055 243668 – www.hhflorence.it

38 rm – 180/290 € 210/350 € **F3**

◆ Townhouse ◆ Design ◆

This charming small palazzo with a predominantly white decor has a young, fashionable feel while at the same time – as the name suggests – manages to retain a homely atmosphere. Breakfast is served on three shared tables.

Porta Faenza without rest

via Faenza 77 ✉ 50123 – ✆ 055 284119 – www.hotelportafaenza.it

25 rm – 90/210 € 110/230 € **D1-2**

◆ Business ◆ Classic ◆

This small, elegant hotel housed in an 18C building not far from the Palazzo dei Congressi offers attractive, well-maintained guestrooms. Extremely attentive service.

Inpiazzadellasignoria – Hystorical building without rest

via de' Magazzini 2 ✉ 50122 – ✆ 055 2399546 – www.inpiazzadellasignoria.com **E3**

10 rm – 160/220 € 220/290 € – 2 suites

◆ Luxury ◆ Historic ◆

As the name implies, this establishment faces the Piazza della Signoria, the political centre of old Florence. It is welcoming and pleasantly elegant.

Palazzo Benci without rest

piazza Madonna degli Aldobrandini 3 ✉ 50123 – ✆ 055 213848 – www.palazzobenci.com – closed from 5 to 21 August and from 24 to 26 December **D2**

35 rm – 60/140 € 90/195 €

◆ Traditional ◆ Classic ◆

This restored historic 16C palazzo, once the residence of the Benci family, now houses an elegant hotel with coffered ceilings and original bas-reliefs adorning the communal areas. The guestrooms are comfortable and furnished with modern elegance. Delightful inner courtyard.

Botticelli without rest

via Taddea 8 ✉ 50123 – ☎ 055 290905 – www.hotelbotticelli.it

34 rm – 70/150 € 120/240 € **D2**

♦ Traditional ♦ Classic ♦

Near to the S.Lorenzo market, in a 16th Century building, is a charming hotel with frescoes in the public areas and a small covered balcony; bedrooms recently refurbished.

Relais Uffizi without rest

chiasso de' Baroncelli-chiasso del Buco 16 ✉ 50122 – ☎ 055 2676239 – www.relaisuffizi.it **D3**

12 rm – 80/120 € 140/220 €

♦ Historic ♦ Personalised ♦

This medieval palazzo is situated in a narrow alley a stone's throw from the Uffizi. It has a warm atmosphere and light, spacious rooms with period furnishings. The attractive lounge boasts large windows with views of the Piazza della Signoria.

Loggiato dei Serviti without rest

piazza strada statale Annunziata 3 ✉ 50122 – ☎ 055 289592 – www.loggiadeiservitihotel.it **E2**

35 rm – 90/150 € 130/240 € – 3 suites

♦ Historic ♦ Personalised ♦

In a 16th Century building -a twin to Brunellesci's Loggia degli Innocenti, is a hotel which has also retained in its interiors its original fascinating features.

De Rose Palace without rest

via Solferino 5 ✉ 50123 – ☎ 055 2396818 – www.florencehotelderose.com

18 rm – 90/160 € 150/230 € **C2**

♦ Traditional ♦ Classic ♦

In a renovated 19th Century building a hotel with a simple, elegant interior, with period style furnishings and beautiful Venetian lamps; pleasant family atmosphere.

Malaspina without rest

piazza dell'Indipendenza 24 ✉ 50129 – ☎ 055 489869 – www.malaspinahotel.it **D1**

31 rm – 70/163 € 90/245 €

♦ Traditional ♦ Classic ♦

In the 13C the Malaspina family received Dante as their guest at the Castello di Fosdinovo. This tradition of hospitality is upheld by the descendants of the Malaspina, who run this 20C hotel decorated in period style. Spacious, well-equipped guestrooms.

Enoteca Pinchiorri (Annie Féolde)

via Ghibellina 87 ✉ 50122 – ☎ 055 242777 – www.enotecapinchiorri.com – closed 3 weeks in August, from 15 to 27 December, Sunday, Monday and Tuesday-Wednesday lunch **E3**

Rest – *(booking essential at lunch)* Menu 200/250 € – Carte 210/335 €

Spec. Insalata di granchio reale e maionese alle patate con pompelmo rosa e petali di aglio novello. Ravioli di coniglio con olive taggiasche e tocchetti di burrata. Piccione arrostito con miele e spezie, melanzane in carrozza.

♦ Modern ♦ Luxury ♦

Spectacular from the entrance, it is Florence's gastronomic treasure. Art blends in the cuisine into a combination of Tuscan and creative twists. Legendary wine cellar.

Rossini

lungarno Corsini 4 ✉ 50123 – ☎ 055 2399224 – www.ristoranterossini.it – closed Wednesday **D3**

Rest – Menu 75 € – Carte 45/96 €

♦ Modern ♦ Formal ♦

The short distance from Ponte Vecchio and the historic literary background are the cornerstones of this refined restaurant where the traditional cuisine meets new approaches.

XXX

Alle Murate

via del Proconsolo 16 r ✉ 50122 – ✆ 055 240618 – www.allemurate.it – closed Monday **E2-3**

Rest – *(dinner only)* Carte 60/95 €

♦ Regional ♦ Intimate ♦

This restaurant is open to visitors during the day and in the evening (upon request); an audio-guide provides information on the frescoes and archaeological ruins visible here. The menu is also influenced by the past, with its emphasis on traditional, regional cuisine. A unique experience!

XXX

Ora D'Aria

via de' Georgofili 11/13 r ✉ 50122 – ✆ 055 2001699 – www.oradariaristorante.com – closed August, Sunday and Monday lunch **F3**

Rest – *(booking advisable)* Menu 50/70 € – Carte 60/78 €

♦ Inventive ♦ Formal ♦

Hidden among the narrow streets of the historic centre (behind the Uffizi museum), this attractive restaurant is traditionally furnished with wood panelling. Tuscan cuisine takes pride of place on the menu, which also features a selection of inventive dishes from elsewhere.

XXX

Oliviero

via delle Terme 51 r ✉ 50123 – ✆ 055 287643 – www.ristorante-oliviero.it – closed 3 weeks in August and Sunday **D3**

Rest – *(dinner only)* Carte 50/61 €

♦ Innovative ♦ Formal ♦

Situated in the heart of the old town, this renowned local restaurant is now under new management. Two distinct types of cuisine are on offer here – one traditional, the other a little more imaginative in style.

XX

Belcore

via dell'Albero 30r ✉ 50123 – ✆ 055 211198 – www.ristorantebelcore.it – closed from 16 to 25 August, Tuesday, Wednesday lunch **C2**

Rest – Carte 38/50 €

♦ Classic ♦ Neighbourhood ♦

An excellent selection of wines complement the different types of cuisine served in this restaurant. Taste the fish specialities, traditional favourites from Italy and Tuscany, and more modern dishes.

XX

Baccarossa

via Ghibellina 46/r ✉ 50122 – ✆ 055240620 – www.baccarossa.it

Rest – *(booking advisable)* Carte 37/46 € **F3**

♦ Mediterranean ♦ Family ♦

This elegant, bistro-style, wine bar is decorated in bright colours and furnished with wooden tables. It serves delicious Mediterranean cuisine including fish specialities, homemade pasta and some meat dishes. All the wines available can be be ordered by the glass.

XX

Buca Mario

piazza Degli Ottaviani 16 r ✉ 50123 – ✆ 055 214179 – www.bucamario.it – closed from 11 to 22 December **D2**

Rest – *(dinner only except Saturday and Sunday)* Carte 45/68 €

♦ Regional ♦ Family ♦

This typical Florentine restaurant opened in 1886. Housed in the cellars of the Palazzo Niccolini in the heart of Florence, it is popular for its excellent, traditional Tuscan cuisine.

XX

Osteria Tornabuoni

via dei Corsi 5r ✉ 50123 – ✆ 055 2773520 – www.osteriatornabuoni.it – closed 15 days in August and Sunday **D2**

Rest – Carte 35/56 €

♦ Tuscany ♦ Fashionable ♦

This fashionable, modern restaurant is housed on the ground floor of the famous palazzo of the same name. It serves high quality, regional produce including meat, cheeses and charcuterie, accompanied by an excellent selection of wines.

XX

Cibrèo

via A. Del Verrocchio 8/r ✉ 50122 – ✆ 055 2341100
– www.edizioniteatrodelsalecibreofirenze.it
– closed August, 31 December-6 January, Sunday, Monday **F3**

Rest – Carte 71/81 €

◆ Tuscany ◆ Formal ◆

This restaurant has an informal, fashionable atmosphere, with young, confident staff and fine, inventive cuisine inspired by traditional dishes.

XX

Pane e Vino

piazza di Cestello 3 rosso ✉ 50124 – ✆ 055 2476956
– www.ristorantepaneevino.it
– closed 10 days in August and Sunday **C3**

Rest – *(dinner only)* Carte 34/55 €

◆ Tuscany ◆ Family ◆

Friendly, well maintained and furnished with an unusual wooden mezzanine, this pleasant restaurant offers traditional regional cuisine with a creative twist.

XX

dei Frescobaldi

via dè Magazzini 2/4 r ✉ 50122 – ✆ 055 284724
– www.deifrescobaldi.it
– closed from 10 to 31 August, from 1 to 7 January, Sunday, Monday lunchtime **E3**

Rest – Carte 36/53 €

◆ Tuscany ◆ Friendly ◆

Owned by a wine producer, this restaurant boasts two welcoming rooms adorned with stone and frescoes. The menu here focuses on regional cuisine, as well as dishes from elsewhere. Simpler fare is served in the adjacent wine bar.

X

Il Santo Bevitore

via Santo Spirito 64/66 r ✉ 50125 – ✆ 055 211264
– www.ilsantobevitore.com
– closed from 10 to 20 August and Sunday at midday **C3**

Rest – Carte 23/38 €

◆ Tuscany ◆ Fashionable ◆ Wine bar ◆

Young and welcoming establishment, in a prominent position in the Sanfrediano quarter. The cuisine is in the Tuscan tradition with some interesting touches of creativity. Good quality-price ratio.

X

Osteria Caffè Italiano

via Isola delle Stinche 11 ✉ 50122
– ✆ 055 289368 – www.caffeitaliano.it
– closed Monday **E3**

Rest – Carte 34/45 €

◆ Italian ◆ Friendly ◆

These fine premises are part of a historic building. Wood furnishings predominate in the three small dining halls where the cuisine is largely based on Tuscan recipes. There is a fine wine list.

X

Trattoria Cibrèo-Cibreino

via dei Macci 122/r ✉ 50122 – ✆ 055 2341100
– www.edizioniteatrodelsalecibreofirenze.it
– closed August, 31 December-6 January, Sunday, Monday **F3**

Rest – Carte 28/35 €

◆ Modern ◆ Friendly ◆

Once past the queue at the entrance, you will find a charming dining room. It is very simple and informal and furnished with small tables. Extravagant traditional cuisine at competitive prices is served.

Il Latini

via dei Palchetti 6 r ✉ 50123 – ✆ 055 210916 – www.illatini.com
– closed 20 December-2 January and Monday **D2**
Rest – Carte 40/45 €
◆ Tuscany ◆ Family ◆
Tourists and locals queue at midday in order to eat in this trattoria, which is appreciated as much for the cuisine as for the exuberant and informal atmosphere.

Del Fagioli

corso Tintori 47 r ✉ 50122 – ✆ 055 244285 – www.localistorici.it
– closed August, Saturday, Sunday **E3**
Rest – Carte 22/27 €
◆ Tuscany ◆ Family ◆
Typical Tuscan trattoria in the city centre. The whole family - some of them cooking, some serving - offer a healthy Florentine cuisine and a warm welcome.

ON THE HILLS *Plan I*

Torre di Bellosguardo without rest

via Roti Michelozzi 2 ✉ 50124 – ✆ 055 2298145
– www.torrebellosguardo.com **A2**
9 rm – 110/160 € 250/290 €, 20 € – 7 suites
◆ Historic ◆ Personalised ◆
There's a hint of the past in the lounge areas and guestrooms of this simple yet elegant hotel, which has breathtaking views of Florence. It has a magical, fairy tale atmosphere. There is a park with a botanical garden, an aviary and a swimming pool.

Villa Belvedere without rest

via Benedetto Castelli 3 ✉ 50124 – ✆ 055 222501
– www.villabelvederefirenze.it
– March-20 November **B2**
26 rm – 80/100 € 100/180 €
◆ Historic ◆ Personalised ◆
Villa dating from the 1950s, with a swimming pool in the gardens and a splendid view over the town and the hills, for a quiet stay in a luxury but family orientated environment.

Villa Le Piazzole

via Suor Maria Celeste 28 – ✆ 055 223520 – www.lepiazzole.com
– closed 20 December-8 January **B2**
14 rm – 200/230 € 230/270 €
Rest – *(booking essential) (residents only)* Menu 40/90 €
◆ Traditional ◆ Personalised ◆
Enjoying a panoramic location overlooking the Ema valley with its old churches and farms, this extensive olive oil and wine estate offers individually decorated rooms with elegant period furnishings. The hotel is surrounded by a delightful Italian-style garden.

Marignolle Relais & Charme without rest

via di San Quirichino 16, Marignolle
– ✆ 055 2286910 – www.marignolle.com **A2**
7 rm – 115/225 € 130/275 €
◆ Family ◆ Personalised ◆
The pleasant rooms in this rustic dwelling in a holding in the hills are all different from one another and are characterized by refined blends of lively materials; panoramic swimming pool in the greenery.

Omero

via Pian de' Giullari 49 – ✆ 055 220053 – www.ristoranteomero.it
– closed Tuesday **B2**
Rest – Carte 44/55 €
◆ Tuscany ◆ Friendly ◆
Passing under the hams hung in a pork butcher's shop you enter a country trattoria with a view over the hills and service in summer on the terrace; typical cuisine.

Trattoria Bibe with rm

via delle Bagnese 15 – ✆ 055 2049085 – www.trattoriabibe.com
– closed 21 January-8 February, from 10 to 25 November **AS**
3 rm – 50/80 € 100/120 €
Rest – *(dinner only except Saturday and Bank Holidays)* Carte 26/33 €
◆ Tuscany ◆ Family ◆
The Italian writer Montale immortalised this trattoria in his poetry. Run by the same family for nearly two centuries, the restaurant serves typical Tuscan cuisine. It also boasts a delightful garden for summer dining. Montale immortalised in his verses this really rustic trattoria, managed by the same family since the mid 19th Century; typical dishes and service in the summer outside.

AT BAGNO A RIPOLI

Villa La Massa

via della Massa 24 – ✆ 055 62611 – www.villalamassa.it
– 25 March-6 November
24 rm – 285/510 € 445/560 €, 27 € – 13 suites
Rest *Il Verrocchio* – Carte 72/122 €
◆ Palace ◆ Luxury ◆ Historic ◆
Nestling amid tranquil green hills, this 17C Medici villa offers spectacular views of the Arno and an attractive interior with period-style furnishings. Shuttle bus to the centre of Florence. An elegant restaurant with vaulted ceilings, columns and a large fireplace. Traditional cuisine on the menu, as well as special dishes for children.

Villa Olmi Resort

via degli Olmi 4/8 – ✆ 055 637710 – www.villaolmiresort.com
59 rm – 254/330 € 269/510 € – 3 suites
Rest – Carte 64/86 €
◆ Business ◆ Modern ◆
An 18C villa with a recent addition, connected via an underground passage. Offers elegant and personalised rooms, furnished with antique pieces. In the dining room find antique chandeliers on the ceiling, a natural finish on the walls and fanciful Italian cuisine.

AT FIESOLE *Plan I*

Villa San Michele

via Doccia 4 – ✆ 055 5678200 – www.villasanmichele.com
– April-14 November **B1**
40 rm – 605 € 946/1177 € – 6 suites **Rest** – Carte 82/149 €
◆ Grand Luxury ◆ Historic ◆
Enjoy the peaceful setting and magnificent views of this hotel which occupies an elegant 15C building surrounded by greenery. If you find that you miss the hustle and bustle of Florence, a shuttle bus takes just 10 minutes to get to the city centre. Enjoy Tuscan specialities and modern cuisine in the cloisters and dining room of this restaurant. Summer dining on the terrace with fine views of Florence.

Il Salviatino

via del Salviatino 21 – ✆ 055 9041111
– www.salviatino.com **B2**
36 rm – 410/480 € 510/780 € – 9 suites
Rest *Grappolo* – *(dinner only)* Carte 70/103 €
♦ Luxury ♦ Historic ♦
Luxury is evident not only in the rooms of this 16C villa – which is surrounded by gardens and boasts fine views of the city – but also in its "service ambassadors", who are on hand to deal with guests' requests 24 hours a day. A truly idyllic place to stay!

Pensione Bencistà

via Benedetto da Maiano 4 – ✆ 055 59163 – www.bencista.com
– 15 March-15 November **B1**
38 rm – 80/130 € 143/180 € – 2 suites
Rest – Carte 19/35 €
♦ Family ♦ Historic ♦
Surrounded by extensive grounds and olive trees, this 14C villa boasts elegant public rooms decorated with period furnishings, where afternoon tea is served daily. Attractive guestrooms. The hotel's simple, spotless dining room is the setting for typical Tuscan cuisine at breakfast, lunch and dinner.

Tullio a Montebeni

via Ontignano 48 – ✆ 055 697354 – www.ristorantetullio.it
– closed August, Monday, Tuesday lunch
Rest – Carte 23/44 €
♦ Tuscany ♦ Family ♦
Everything started in a village shop, as some warm dish to restore farmers and hunters in the area. Today, the cuisine reproposes the same flavours and home produced wines.

AT SAN CASCIANO IN VAL DI PESA

Villa il Poggiale

via Empolese 69 (North-West: 1 km) – ✆ 055 828311
– www.villailpoggiale.it – closed February
20 rm – 130/180 € 150/240 € – 4 suites
Rest – *(April-October) (resident only)* Menu 30 €
♦ Family ♦ Historic ♦
This delightful villa is reminiscent of the Tuscany of E.M. Forster and Merchant Ivory, with its hundred-year-old cypress trees, Italian-style garden and Renaissance loggia. Superb guestrooms, as well as massages and beauty treatments available by prior appointment.

La Tenda Rossa (Salcuni e Santandrea)

piazza del Monumento 9/14 – ✆ 055 826132
– www.latendarossa.it
– closed from 8 to 18 August, from 3 to 13 January, Sunday, Monday midday
Rest – Carte 65/95 €
Spec. Ravioli di ribollita con emulsione di fagioli neri e cozze pelose tarantine. Agnello dell'Appennino: il magro in salsiccia con pecorino, la costoletta a scottadito con sedano rapa e salsa di frattaglie. Soufflé freddo al Vin Santo con passata di lamponi.
♦ Inventive ♦ Luxury ♦
Italian restaurants are traditionally family-run, and three families run this one! Its quality of service and the food is three times as good.

AT THE AIRPORT *Plan I*

Hilton Florence Metropole

VISA AE

via del Cavallaccio 36 ✉ 50142 – ✆ 055 78711
– www.florencemetropole.hilton.com **A2**
208 rm – ††120/195 €, ☕ 15 € – 4 suites **Rest** – *(residents only)*
♦ Chain hotel ♦ Business ♦ Modern ♦
Easily accessible from the airport, this modern hotel offers minimalist-style guestrooms and public areas, as well as a spacious conference centre. This spacious restaurant is on the first floor.

Hilton Garden Inn Florence Novoli

via Sandro Pertini 2/9, Novoli ✉ 50127 VISA AE
– ✆ 055 42401 – www.florencenovoli.hgi.com **A1**
121 rm – †110/210 € ††130/210 €, ☕ 12 €
Rest *City* – Carte 45/57 €
♦ Chain hotel ♦ Business ♦ Modern ♦
This modern hotel near the motorway offers bright and airy public areas, as well as comfortable guestrooms furnished in tasteful modern style and equipped with all the latest facilities.

MILAN

MILANO

Population (est. 2010): 1 307 495 – Altitude: 122m

runo Bermier/Fotolia.com

If it's the romantic charm of places like Venice, Florence or Rome you're looking for, then best avoid Milan. If you're hankering for a permanent panorama of Renaissance chapels, palazzi, shimmering canals and bastions of fine art, then you're in the wrong place. What Milan does is relentless fashion, churned out with oodles of attitude and style. Italy's second largest city is constantly reinventing itself, and when Milan does a makeover, it invariably does it with flair and panache.

That's not to say that Italy's capital of fast money and fast fashion doesn't have an eye for its past. The centrepiece of the whole city is the magnificent gleaming white Duomo, which took five hundred years to complete, while up *la via* a little way, La Scala is quite simply the world's most famous opera house. But this city is known primarily for its sleek and modern towers, many housing the very latest threads from the very latest fashion gurus. There are cutting-edge art galleries here, rubbing shoulders with space-age spas and bars, some of them opened by exclusive high-street designers. You know you've arrived in Milan not so much when you stare at a Renaissance piece of art as when you take an *aperitivo* at cocktail hour in a snazzy bar.

LIVING THE CITY

When you see the great bulk of the **Duomo**, you know you're in the centre of landlocked Milan. Just north lies **Brera,** with its much prized old-world charm, and **Quadrilatero d'Oro**, with no little new-world glitz. The popular **Giardini Pubblici** are a little way further north east from here. South of the centre is the **Navigli** quarter, home to rejuvenated Middle Age canals, while to the west are the green lungs of the **Parco Sempione.** The artily trendy neighbourhood of **Lambrate** is way up to the north east of Milan.

PRACTICAL INFORMATION

ARRIVAL-DEPARTURE

Malpensa Airport is 48km northwest of the city and Linate Airport 7km east. A train connects Malpensa with Stazione Cadorna every 30min which takes 40min, while a taxi will cost around €85. From Linate take the Airport bus no. 73 to Piazza San Babila metro station (every 10min, time 25min).

TRANSPORT

The best way to get about Milan is by bus, tram or metro. Tickets are valid for one metro ride, or seventy five minutes of travel on buses or trams. You can also purchase books of ten tickets, or unlimited one-day or two-day passes. Buy them at metro stations, kiosks, bars or tobacconists.

The metro provides a fast and efficient service, with frequent trains running on three different coloured lines. If you don't fancy waiting around for public transport, then walking is also advised: although Milan may seem too big to conquer on foot, most of its attractions are based in the small and compact centre.

EXPLORING MILAN

Milan's fashion designers pride themselves on peering into the future and dreaming up the garments of tomorrow. But high up in the city centre you get the chance to project your own vision even further than them. Just climb to the roof of the mighty Duomo and take in the spectacular views, which, on a clear day, will let you gaze on the Alps sixty miles away. Come back down to comprehend the wonders of a building which took half a millennium to complete. This immense Gothic cathedral, begun in 1387, reflects the whims of fashion over the centuries and is a surreal amalgam of architectural styles. The spires are capped by thousands of sculptures in an awesome embrace of High Gothic. Much of the building is marble, but the interior highlight, La Madonnina, is pure gold. It doesn't take very long to realise that this is the shade of choice for much of Milan: you'll see it in the glitter of handbags and the flash of credit cards. Cross the piazza and the sight of gold will be much in evidence at the **Galleria Vittorio Emanuele II**. Built in 1878, this fabulous salotto (drawing room) lays claim to being the first shopping arcade in Europe. For much more than a century, stylish Milanese have browsed in this elegant neoclassical structure with its landmark glass roof.

➜ FADING GLORY

Head west for the city's most lauded artistic experience (but make sure you've booked first). Invariably most visitors will find their way to see Leonardo da Vinci's **The Last Supper**. It's not in a cathedral or church, but is painted on the wall of a convent dining hall at the **Santa Maria delle Grazie**, half a mile west of the Duomo. The effect of the years (over six hundred of them) and damp Milan winters has resulted in the masterpiece literally fading in front of the onlookers' eyes. But you can still read the apostles' reactions in their movements and positions; you can still admire the brilliant colours used in the original. Your appetite for high culture whetted, head a short distance north east to the city's very own castle stronghold, **Castello Sforzesco**. Built in the fourteenth century to protect Milan's assets, over the centuries its use was adapted to showcase what the city does best: creativity. Now it's the home to no less than ten museums, and some are well worth a visit. Particularly impressive is the **Museo d'Arte Antica**, which includes a fresco believed to be by Leonardo -Sala delle Asse - and Michelangelo's extraordinary, unfinished final work, Rondanini Pieta, which he toiled over for years until his death in 1564. There's also the **Photographic Archive**, full of fascinating pictures of Italian life dating back to 1840, and the **Achille Bertarelli Prints Collection**, which seems to show that before Milan was obsessed with fashion it was rather partial to postcards, maps and all kinds of printed ephemera.

➜ PARK ART

Step out of Castello Sforzesco, and you're in one of the city's top green spaces - the Parco Sempione. It's a rambling quadrangle of grassy hillocks and leafy avenues named after philosophers and writers. Because this is Milan, there's also a temple to design here, **The Triennale,** where the way the temporary exhibitions are presented is often as impressive as the subject matter. More evidence that they like to mix relaxation and up-to-the-minute art can be found in the city's other main park, Giardini Publicci, northeast of the centre, where a double dose of culture lies in wait amongst the rose bushes and pebble paths. The **Galleria d'Arte Moderna** is chock full of Futurists and twentieth century Realists; next door the **Padiglione d'Arte Contemporanea** puts on the gutsiest and most daring exhibitions in town. Afterwards step back outside and enjoy an ice cream in the park.

The city's best art collection is in the Brera quarter, the one neighbourhood of Milan that breathes old-style Italian charm, with its low stucco buildings and cobblestone streets. This is the ideal setting for **Pinacoteca Brera**, which celebrated its two hundredth birthday in 2009. It contains over seven hundred years' worth of Italian art, including Raphael's Marriage of the Virgin, Piero della Francesca's Brera Altarpiece and Veronese's Last Supper (a very different take to Leonardo's!). Throw in the likes of Caravaggio, Canaletto, Titian, Tintoretto, Botticelli and Mantegna, and you may well convince yourself that, despite its best efforts, Milan does appreciate things other than shopping and fashion.

➜ FOOLS' GOLD?

Mind you, if that really is the reason you're here, then you'll certainly have no trouble striking gold – quite literally, in the quarter north east of the Duomo, which the locals call Quadrilatero d'Oro, or 'Golden Quad'. This is the part of town where plastic is the only currency, and if you're here on a tight budget, then a visit will be for anecdotal or research purposes only. The 'Quad' lies along and between four lengthy streets, and has earned its gold status because of the outlandishly expensive boutiques all around here. The big design names are gathered in clusters; many are so exclusive they don't bother with price tags. The good news for those financially challenged is that it isn't really necessary to shop here: the primary pastime is to perfect your strutting.

For a complete contrast, go to the south of the city centre where, in Navigli, you'll find canals from the Middle Ages. This is a rather shabby but fascinating district; artists and designers are taking over the old warehouses, particularly in **Zona Tortona**, where you can pick up well-priced trinkets from the refashioned artisans' studios. A leisurely stroll along the main drag of Ripa di Porta Ticinese brings you into contact with antiques shops during the day and trendy bars by night.

→ DIVA

To 'do' Milan properly, there's only one way to finish the evening, and that's to take in a performance at **La Scala**. The legendary venue was completely refurbished in 2004, but the history lives on: in the eighteenth and nineteenth centuries it was normal practice for the audience to chat, gamble and walk in and out during shows, while up to the middle of the last century even Italy's top divas would shy away from performing here because of the cat calls and whistles that could come their way courtesy of the nation's harshest critics located in the upper tiers. Nowadays, the diva is safe: aficionados reserve their thoughts until the bar at intermission.

CALENDAR HIGHLIGHTS

Some locals would say that the Milan calendar means nothing until early December, when the opera season at La Scala gets underway. But if you can't grab a seat for a performance for love or money, you can instead get all at sea at the Milan Aquarium's The Sea In Milan (also in December), a series of aquatic activities with marine related exhibitions and art-based events. The Fiera Milano plays host to MiArt in March, an international modern art fair that gives you the chance to check out four fascinatingly different sections: Preview, Modern, Contemporary, and Art&Co. April is the time to head down to the canals for the Naviglio Grande Flower Market, when two hundred 'flower pros' from all over Italy set up a beautiful carnival of flowers and fragrance along the wharf complex. Something completely different in June: the Gods of Metal Festival at Idropark Fila, when heavy metal music reigns for two days. In the same month, the rhythms are of a very different nature at the Festival Latino Americano, in the grounds of Datchforum: a South American village is set up to host not

MILAN IN...

→ ONE DAY

Duomo, The Last Supper (remember to book first), Brera, Navigli

→ TWO DAYS

Pinacoteca Brera, Castello Sforzesco, Parco Sempione, a night at La Scala

→ THREE DAYS

Giardini Publicci and its museums, trendy Lambrate district

only top musicians from that continent, but also literature, art and films. June's a busy month in Milan: there's the Festa del Naviglio, with music, food and special events around the canals, and also Notte Bianca (on the third Saturday of the month) when a variety of concerts and performances go on right through the night. During September Music, they continue right through a whole month, and feature the work of famous composers, as well as the world's regional music. Panoramica (also in September) is a top film festival featuring a selection of the best movies from the Venice and Locarno Festivals: get along to the Anteo or Multisala Plinius cinemas for the reel deal. More than twenty thousand visitors jog along to the Fiera Milano in October for a fitness fiesta at the Wellness World Exhibition, while the ambience is more on the decadent side the same month for the Celtic New Year celebrations, when the Castello Sforzesco is turned into a medieval north European site for traditional music and revelry.

EATING OUT

For a taste of Italy's regional cuisines, Milan is a great place to be. The city is often the goal of those leaving their home regions in the south or centre of the country; many open trattoria or restaurants with the result that Milan offers a wide range of provincial menus. Excellent fish restaurants, inspired by recipes from the south, are a big draw despite the fact that the city is a long way from the sea. Going beyond the local borders, that emphasis on really good food continues and the quality (if not always the number) of ethnically diverse places to eat is better in Milan than just about anywhere else in Italy, including Rome. Japanese restaurants are all the rage now and they're having a growing influence on menus here: raw fish is very popular. You'd expect avant-garde eating destinations to be the thing in this city of fashion and style, and you'd be right: there are some top-notch cutting-edge restaurants, thanks to Milan's famous tendency to reshape and experiment as it goes. For those who want to try out the local gastronomic traditions, *risotto allo zafferano* is not to be missed, nor either the *cotoletta alla Milanese* (veal cutlet), or the *casoeula* (a winter special made with pork and cabbage). Then, of course, there's the ubiquitous *panettone*, to be enjoyed at Christmas. Milanesi tend to eat earlier than diners in Rome, starting the evening meal at roughly eight o'clock. If you want to stay up that much later lingering with the beautiful people, your best bet is the bohemian Navigli quarter, with its unique atmosphere created by old fashioned houses and laidback canal side eateries. The bill will always include service charge.

→ HAVING A BALL AT THE GALLERIA

A couple of things you should know about the oh-so-stylish Galleria Vittorio Emanuele II. Architect Giuseppe Mengoni spent fourteen years working on this, his pet project, but died falling from the roof the day before it opened in 1878. Bring yourself good luck by rubbing your feet on the genitals of the bull in the central mosaic. Decades of grinding stilettos meant the bull required a recent touch up.

If you can't get enough of this century's art scene, then head out of town (fifteen minutes on the metro) to the suburb of Lambrate. The provocative and highly singular gallerias beckon you inside for audacious artworks and flights of fancy with a technological twist. What would Leonardo have made of it all?

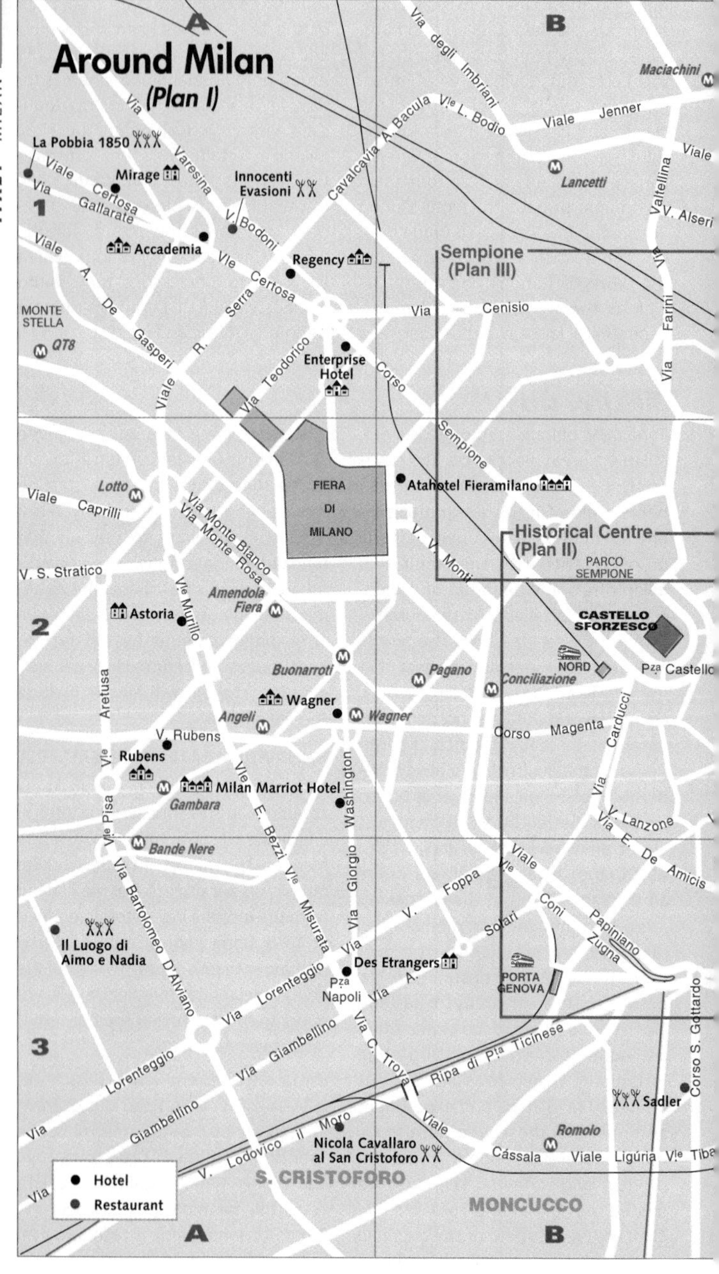

Around Milan
(Plan I)
La Pobbia 1850
Mirage
Innocenti Evasioni
Accademia
Regency
Enterprise Hotel
Atahotel Fieramilano
FIERA DI MILANO
Sempione (Plan III)
Historical Centre (Plan II)
PARCO SEMPIONE
CASTELLO SFORZESCO
NORD
Astoria
Wagner
Rubens
Milan Marriot Hotel
Des Etrangers
Il Luogo di Aimo e Nadia
Sadler
Nicola Cavallaro al San Cristoforo
PORTA GENOVA
S. CRISTOFORO
MONCUCCO
MONTE STELLA
QT8
Lotto
Amendola Fiera
Buonarroti
Pagano
Conciliazione
Angeli
Wagner
Gambara
Bande Nere
Romolo
Lancetti
Maciachini
Hotel
Restaurant

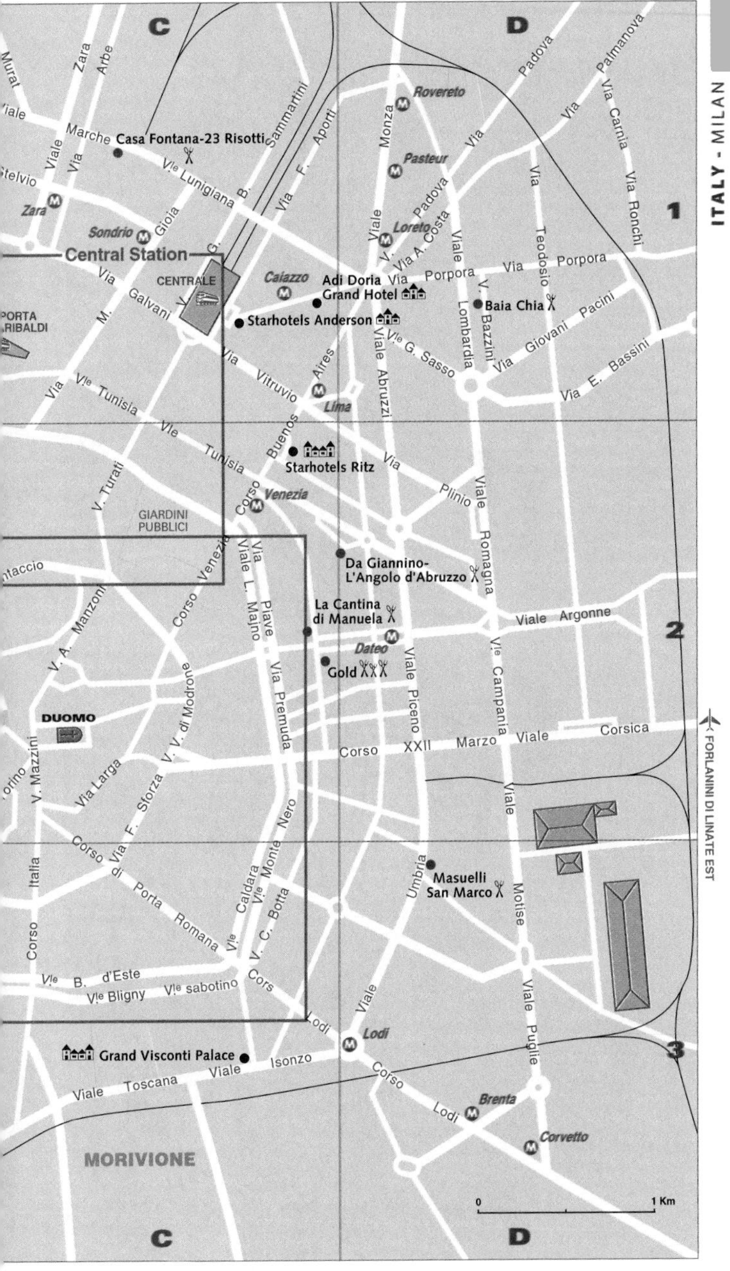
C
D
Central Station
CENTRALE
Casa Fontana-23 Risotti
Adi Doria Grand Hotel
Starhotels Anderson
Baia Chia
Starhotels Ritz
Da Giannino-L'Angolo d'Abruzzo
La Cantina di Manuela
Gold
Masuelli San Marco
Grand Visconti Palace
GIARDINI PUBBLICI
DUOMO
MORIVIONE
Roverleto
Pasteur
Loreto
Zara
Sondrio
Caiazzo
Lima
Venezia
Dateo
Lodi
Brenta
Corvetto
Viale Monza
Via Padova
Viale Abruzzi
Viale Romagna
Viale Argonne
Viale Piceno
Corso XXII Marzo
Viale Corsica
Viale Campania
Viale Molise
Viale Puglie
Corso Lodi
Viale Isonzo
Viale Toscana
Via Vitruvio
Via Plinio
Vle Tunisia
Corso Venezia
Viale L. Majno
Via Piave
Via Premuda
V. V. di Modrone
Corso di Porta Romana
Corso Italia
V. Mazzini
Via Larga
V. A. Manzoni
V. Turati
Viale Umbria
Via Porpora
Via Teodosio
Via Giovani Pacini
Via E. Bassini
V. Bazzini
Viale Lombardia
Via Ronchi
Via Carnia
Via Palmanova
Vle G. Sasso
Via A. Costa
Via Buenos Aires
Via F. Aporti
Vle Lunigiana
Viale Marche
Via Galvani
Via Zara
Arbe
Stelvio
Murat
Gioia
Sammartini
Vle B. d'Este
Vle Bligny
Vle sabotino
Vle Caldara
Vle Monte Nero
V. C. Botta
Via F. Sforza
PORTA GARIBALDI
FORLANINI DI LINATE EST
0
1 Km
1
2
3

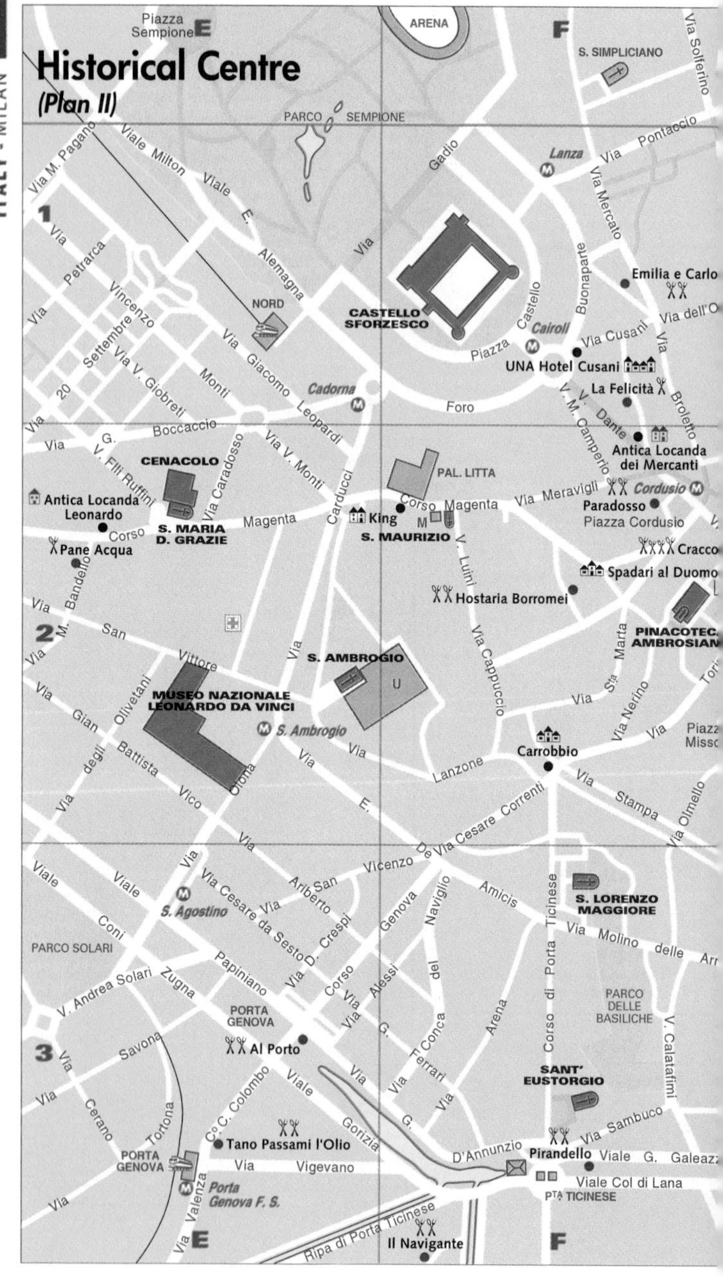

Historical Centre
(Plan II)
Piazza Sempione
ARENA
S. SIMPLICIANO
PARCO SEMPIONE
Via Solferino
Lanza
Via Pontaccio
Via Mercato
Viale Milton
Viale E. Alemagna
Via M. Pagano
Via Gadio
Via Petrarca
Via Vincenzo
NORD
CASTELLO SFORZESCO
Piazza Castello
Cairoli
Via Buonaparte
Emilia e Carlo
Via dell'O
Via Cusani
UNA Hotel Cusani
La Felicità
Via 20 Settembre
Via V. Giobreti
Monti
Via Giacomo Leopardi
Cadorna
Foro
V. M. Camperio
V. Dante
Broletto
Antica Locanda dei Mercanti
Via G. Boccaccio
V. F.lli Ruffini
CENACOLO
Via Caradosso
Via V. Monti
PAL. LITTA
Via Meravigli
Cordusio
Antica Locanda Leonardo
S. MARIA D. GRAZIE
Corso Magenta
Carducci
King
S. MAURIZIO
Paradosso
Piazza Cordusio
Pane Acqua
Cracco
Spadari al Duomo
V. Luini
Hostaria Borromei
Via M. Bandello
Via San Vittore
Via Cappuccio
PINACOTEC. AMBROSIAN
S. AMBROGIO
Via Sta Marta
MUSEO NAZIONALE LEONARDO DA VINCI
Via Olivetani
S. Ambrogio
Via Nerino
Piazz Missc
Via Gian Battista Vico
Via degli Olona
Via Lanzone
Carrobbio
Via E. De Amicis
Via Stampa
Via Olmello
Via Cesare Correnti
Via San Vicenzo
Viale Coni Zugna
S. Agostino
Via Cesare da Sesto
Via Ariberto
Via D. Crespi
Corso Genova
S. LORENZO MAGGIORE
Via Molino delle Arm
PARCO SOLARI
Via Papiniano
V. Andrea Solari
PORTA GENOVA
Via Alessi
Via del Naviglio
Via Conca
Corso di Porta Ticinese
PARCO DELLE BASILICHE
V. Calatafimi
Via Savona
Al Porto
Via G. Ferrari
Arena
SANT' EUSTORGIO
Via Cerano
Via Tortona
C.so C. Colombo
Viale Gorizia
Via Sambuco
Tano Passami l'Olio
PORTA GENOVA
Via Vigevano
D'Annunzio
Pirandello
Viale G. Galeazz
Viale Col di Lana
Pta TICINESE
Via Valenza
Porta Genova F. S.
Ripa di Porta Ticinese
Il Navigante

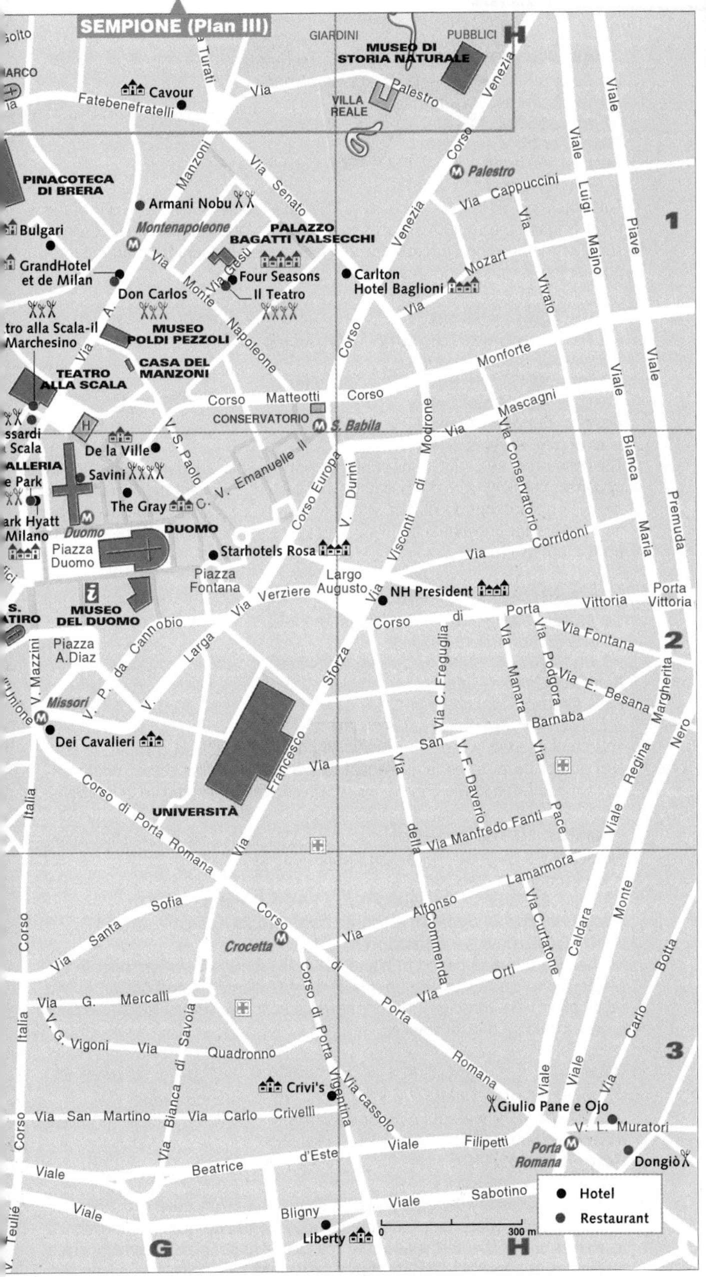
SEMPIONE (Plan III)
GIARDINI PUBBLICI
MUSEO DI STORIA NATURALE
VILLA REALE
PINACOTECA DI BRERA
Cavour
Armani Nobu
Bulgari
GrandHotel et de Milan
Don Carlos
Four Seasons
Il Teatro
PALAZZO BAGATTI VALSECCHI
Carlton Hotel Baglioni
MUSEO POLDI PEZZOLI
CASA DEL MANZONI
TEATRO ALLA SCALA
CONSERVATORIO
S. Babila
Palestro
Montenapoleone
De la Ville
Savini
The Gray
Park Hyatt Milano
DUOMO
Piazza Duomo
Starhotels Rosa
Piazza Fontana
Largo Augusto
NH President
MUSEO DEL DUOMO
Piazza A.Diaz
Missori
Dei Cavalieri
UNIVERSITÀ
Crocetta
Crivi's
Giulio Pane e Ojo
Porta Romana
Dongiò
Liberty
Porta Vittoria
Hotel
Restaurant
0
300 m
1
2
3
G
H

Four Seasons
via Gesù 6/8 ✉ *20121* – Ⓜ *Montenapoleone* – ✆ *02 770888* – *www.fourseasons.com/milan* **G1**
67 rm – †600 € ††820 €, ☕ 35 € – 51 suites
Rest*Il Teatro* – see below
Rest *La Veranda* – ✆ *02 77881478* – Carte 64/110 €
♦ Grand Luxury ♦ Stylish ♦
This hotel, housed in a 15C monastery in Milan's "Golden Triangle", is one of the most elegant and exclusive places to stay in the city. The hotel has retained some of the building's original decorative features. Restaurant facing the interior garden. Refined atmosphere.

Park Hyatt Milano
via Tommaso Grossi 1 ✉ *20121* – Ⓜ *Duomo* – ✆ *02 88211234* – *www.milan.park.hyatt.it* **G2**
78 rm – ††450/510 €, ☕ 35 € – 30 suites
Rest*The Park* – see below
Rest *La Cupola* – Menu 50 €
♦ Luxury ♦ Modern ♦
The contemporary design of this hotel occupying a palazzo dating from 1870 is in perfect harmony with the building's architecture. Excellent modern facilities, spacious guestrooms decorated with Venetian stucco and Murano glass lamps, and an elegant Imperial Suite. Find traditional or buffet cuisine at La Cupola from 11am to 11pm.

Grand Hotel et de Milan
via Manzoni 29 ✉ *20121* – Ⓜ *Montenapoleone* – ✆ *02 723141* – *www.grandhoteletdemilan.it* **G1**
95 rm – †625 € ††689 €, ☕ 35 € – 8 suites
Rest*Don Carlos* – see below
Rest *Caruso* – *(lunch only)* Carte 51/68 €
♦ Luxury ♦ Traditional ♦ Stylish ♦
This hotel opened over 150 years ago. Big names in the field of music, theatre and politics have stayed in its elegant rooms that are full of charm. Bright restaurant dedicated to the great tenor, who recorded his first record in this hotel.

Carlton Hotel Baglioni
via Senato 5 ✉ *20121* – Ⓜ *San Babila* – ✆ *02 77077* – *www.baglionihotels.com* **H1**
83 rm – †530/805 € ††585/860 €, ☕ 36 € – 9 suites
Rest *Il Baretto al Baglioni* – *(closed from 6 to 29 August)* Carte 64/132 €
♦ Grand Luxury ♦ Classic ♦
Refined features and period furniture, valuable fabrics with warm tones in the public rooms and in the bedrooms of a most elegant "bomboniera" in the heart of fashion conscious Milan. The restaurant has several elegant dining rooms, including one for smokers.

Bulgari
via privata Fratelli Gabba 7/b ✉ *20121* – Ⓜ *Montenapoleone* – ✆ *02 805805* – *www.bulgarihotels.com* **G1**
49 rm – †550 € ††650 €, ☕ 30 € – 11 suites
Rest – Carte 66/110 €
♦ Luxury ♦ Stylish ♦
The famous jewellery designer Bulgari is behind this luxury hotel in the heart of Milan. The hotel offers warmly decorated guestrooms adorned with fine fabrics, as well as one of the best spas in the city, with a green glass hammam which resembles an emerald. This excusive restaurant overlooks an unexpected, attractive garden.

Starhotels Rosa Grand

piazza Fontana 3 ✉ 20122 – Ⓜ Duomo – ✆ 02 88311 – www.starhotels.com **G2**

320 rm – 👥180/1300 € – 7 suites **Rest** – Menu 45/58 €

◆ Chain hotel ◆ Classic ◆

Situated in the heart of Milan, this hotel has recently undergone a major refurbishment. The interior is arranged around a courtyard, with simple, square shapes creating a naturally elegant look. The guestrooms here are comfortable and stylish, although only a few offer views of the Duomo.

Grand Visconti Palace

viale Isonzo 14 ✉ 20135 – Ⓜ Lodi TIBB – ✆ 02 540341 – www.grandviscontipalace.com *Plan I* **C3**

162 rm – 👤130/610 € 👥180/700 € – 10 suites

Rest *Al Quinto Piano* – Carte 50/70 €

◆ Palace ◆ Classic ◆

This elegant hotel occupies the extensive buildings of an old industrial mill. Facilities include conference rooms, a delightful garden, and a welcoming well-being centre. As its name suggests, this restaurant is situated on the fifth floor. Creative, imaginative cuisine.

NH President

largo Augusto 10 ✉ 20122 – Ⓜ San Babila – ✆ 02 77461 – www.nh-hotels.it **H2**

251 rm – 👤250/470 € 👥350/710 € – 10 suites

Rest *Il Verziere* – Carte 44/76 €

◆ Chain hotel ◆ Modern ◆

An international standard hotel for business travellers or tourists. It has attractive, spacious lounge areas as well as facilities for fashion shows, business lunches and conferences. The restaurant serves specialities from Lombardy, as well as Mediterranean-style dishes.

UNA Hotel Cusani

via Cusani 13 ✉ 20121 – Ⓜ Cairoli – ✆ 02 85601 – www.unahotels.it

87 rm – 👥199/695 € – 5 suites **Rest** – Carte 45/65 € **F1**

◆ Business ◆ Classic ◆

Located in the heart of the historic town centre, this hotel is in an ideal location for business and sightseeing. It has simple and modern, very large attractive rooms. Choose from classic Italian or international dishes at this cosy restaurant.

De la Ville

via Hoepli 6 ✉ 20121 – Ⓜ Duomo – ✆ 02 8791311 – www.sinahotels.com **G2**

109 rm – 👤396/418 € 👥429/440 € – 1 suite

Rest *L'Opera* – *✆ 02 8051231* – Carte 39/59 €

◆ Luxury ◆ Classic ◆

Located near the Duomo, this chic hotel with warm surroundings is decorated with marble and colourful silk. It has a relaxing swimming pool on the top floor covered with a transparent dome. Ideal for after theatre dinner, this restaurant serves Mediterranean cuisine reinterpreted with a creative flair.

The Gray

via San Raffaele 6 ✉ 20121 – Ⓜ Duomo – ✆ 02 7208951 – www.sinahotels.com – closed August **G2**

21 rm – 👤473 € 👥638 €, ☕ 37 € – 5 suites **Rest** – Carte 68/94 €

◆ Luxury ◆ Design ◆

Near the Galleria, this elegant hotel's modern design has rooms with stylish touches. There is also a fitness centre. This cosy restaurant with a creative décor offers a gourmet menu.

Spadari al Duomo without rest

via Spadari 11 ✉ 20123 – Ⓜ Duomo – ✆ 02 72002371
– www.spadarihotel.com
– closed from 23 to 27 December **F2**

40 rm – 198/368 €

◆ Business ◆ Design ◆

With its extensive collection of contemporary art, this small hotel combines comfort with a penchant for new and exciting forms of artistic expression.

Cavour

via Fatebenefratelli 21 ✉ 20121 – Ⓜ Turati – ✆ 02 620001
– www.hotelcavour.it
– closed August **G1**

113 rm – 105/273 € 116/313 €

Rest *Conte Camillo* – *✆ 02 6570516 (dinner only Saturday-Sunday)*
Carte 46/67 €

◆ Business ◆ Functional ◆

This traditional, family-run hotel, situated near the city's main cultural sights, cafés and restaurants, offers its guests well-furnished, sound-proofed rooms and excellent service. This discreetly stylish restaurant in the centre of Milan offers traditional dishes with a modern touch.

Dei Cavalieri without rest

piazza Missori 1 ✉ 20123 – Ⓜ Missori – ✆ 02 88571
– www.hoteldeicavalieri.com **G2**

177 rm – 129/509 €

◆ Traditional ◆ Business ◆

You are sure to find a relaxing atmosphere in this hotel that has stylish, comfortably furnished rooms with contemporary décor and facilities for conferences, business lunches and banquets.

Carrobbio without rest

via Medici 3 ✉ 20123 – Ⓜ Duomo – ✆ 02 89010740
– www.hotelcarrobbiomilano.com
– closed August **F2**

56 rm – 117/198 € 147/356 €

◆ Business ◆ Classic ◆

This recently renovated hotel is in a quiet area and near the historic town centre. It has a small and relaxing winter garden.

Liberty without rest

viale Bligny 56 ✉ 20136 – ✆ 02 58318562 – www.hotelliberty-milano.com
– closed August and from 23 to 27 December **G3**

58 rm – 100/250 € 200/360 €

◆ Traditional ◆ Stylish ◆

This elegant hotel close to the Bocconi University has public areas decorated in Art Nouveau (also known as Liberty) style, with coloured glass and antique furniture. The attractive guestrooms are warm and welcoming; those overlooking the garden are particularly quiet.

Crivi's without rest

corso Porta Vigentina 46 ✉ 20122 – Ⓜ Crocetta – ✆ 02 582891
– www.crivis.com
– closed August and Christmas **G3**

86 rm – 120/250 € 140/350 €

◆ Business ◆ Modern ◆

In a convenient location near the metro, this comfortable hotel has pleasant public areas and traditionally furnished, reasonably comfortable and spacious guestrooms.

King without rest

corso Magenta 19 ✉ 20123 – Ⓜ Cadorna F.N.M. – ☎ 02 874432 – www.mokinba.it **F2**

50 rm – 115/300 € 246/410 €

◆ Business ◆ Classic ◆

Housed in a six-storey building not far from the Duomo, this hotel has been renovated with opulent and elegant furnishings. The guestrooms, although not that spacious, are very comfortable.

Antica Locanda dei Mercanti without rest

via San Tomaso 6 ✉ 20121 – Ⓜ Cordusio – ☎ 02 8054080 – www.locanda.it **F2**

10 rm – 175/205 € 225/275 €, 15 € – 5 suites

◆ Townhouse ◆ Family ◆ Personalised ◆

A small, cosy hotel, simple and elegant in style, and furnished with antique furniture. Many of the light and spacious guestrooms have a small terrace.

XXXX **The Park** – Hotel Park Hyatt Milano

via Tommaso Grossi 1 ✉ 20121 – Ⓜ Duomo – ☎ 02 88211234 – www.milan.park.hyatt.com – closed from 8 to 29 August, Saturday lunch and Sunday **G2**

Rest – Carte 50/90 €

◆ Modern ◆ Design ◆

This restaurant serves innovative, seasonal Mediterranean cuisine to a sophisticated backdrop of simple elegance. Works of art by the American painter Kim Rebholz adorn the walls.

XXXX ✿✿ **Cracco**

via Victor Hugo 4 ✉ 20123 – Ⓜ Duomo – ☎ 02 876774 – www.ristorantecracco.it – closed 3 weeks in August, 24 December-11 January, Saturday at midday, Sunday, Monday at midday **F2**

Rest – Menu 130/160 € – Carte 105/152 €

Spec. Musetto di maiale fondente con scampi e pomodori verdi. Risotto con ricci di mare, midollo e nero di seppia. Rombo chiodato al forno in crosta al cacao, patata bianca e pomodoro.

◆ Inventive ◆ Fashionable ◆

Decorated in a simple, modern style, this restaurant serves excellent contemporary cuisine with a focus on innovative and inventive dishes.

XXXX **Il Teatro** – Hotel Four Seasons

via Gesù 6/8 ✉ 20121 – Ⓜ Montenapoleone – ☎ 02 77081435 – www.fourseasons.com/milan/dining – closed 17 July-5 September and Sunday **G1**

Rest – *(dinner only) (booking advisable)* Menu 85 € – Carte 80/96 €

◆ Modern ◆ Formal ◆

The restaurant, contained in the splendid premises of the Four Seasons hotel, is characterised by exclusiveness and class. The cuisine highlights interpretive creativity.

XXXX **Savini**

galleria Vittorio Emanuele II ✉ 20121 – Ⓜ Duomo – ☎ 02 72003433 – www.savinimilano.it – closed 10 days in January and 20 days in August **G2**

Rest – *(closed Saturday midday, Sunday) (booking advisable)* Carte 88/114 €

Rest *Caffetteria* – Carte 58/84 €

◆ Classic ◆ Luxury ◆ Formal ◆

This perennial Milanese favourite has benefited from a recent facelift. The new menu focuses on a fusion of innovative flavours and traditional, regional specialities. Enjoy the informal atmosphere by the bar in the Caffetteria, which serves pizza, salads and a range of specialities from Lombardy.

XXX **Don Carlos** – Grand Hotel et de Milan

via Manzoni 29 ✉ 20121 – Ⓜ Montenapoleone – ☎ 02 72314640 – www.ristorantedoncarlos.it – closed August **G1**

Rest – *(dinner only)* Menu 85 € – Carte 70/98 €

♦ Lombard-piedmontese ♦ Formal ♦

Named after one of Verdi's operas, this charming restaurant has a quiet atmosphere and elegant decor, including wood panelling, red appliqué and old photos. The menu focuses on traditional cuisine from Lombardy and Piedmont with a creative touch.

XXX ✿✿ **Trussardi alla Scala**

piazza della Scala 5 (palazzo Trussardi) ✉ 20121 – Ⓜ Duomo – ☎ 02 80688201 – www.trussardi.it – closed 3 weeks in August, from 1 to 13 January, Saturday at lunchtime, Sunday, also Saturday dinner in July **G1**

Rest – Carte 116/168 €

Spec. Insalata liquida con gnocchi di seppia e olio alle olive nere. Spalla d'agnello con patate fritte, crema di ricotta e cipolla. Biscotto di parmigiano al limone e basilico, sfoglia di pomodoro e gelato ai capperi.

♦ Modern ♦ Trendy ♦

Until recently one of Italy's emerging chefs, Andrea Berton is now one of the country's best-known names. His imaginative and inventive dishes focus on clean lines and excellent ingredients, making him a guru of avant-garde, contemporary Italian cuisine.

XXX ✿✿ **Sadler**

via Ascanio Sforza 77 ✉ 20141 – Ⓜ Romolo – ☎ 02 58104451 – www.sadler.it – closed from 8 to 23 August, from 1 to 6 January and Sunday

Rest – *(dinner only)* Menu 130/175 € – Carte 84/120 € *Plan I* **B3**

Spec. Ravioli farciti di cacio e pepe con calamari all'amatriciana. Filetto di branzino di lenza cotto al sale, germogli di finocchio, crema di fiori di zucchina. Piccione al forno, puré di sedano bianco, mandorle tostate e riduzione di aceto balsamico.

♦ Inventive ♦ Formal ♦

Harmony is the hallmark of this restaurant, with its clean lines, carefully chosen fabrics, large windows and effective lighting. Balance is also evident in the cuisine, which is a fine blend of the traditional and the innovative.

XXX **Teatro alla Scala - il Marchesino**

piazza della Scala ✉ 20121 – Ⓜ Duomo – ☎ 02 72 09 43 38 – www.ilmarchesino.it – closed from 8 to 29 August and Sunday **G1**

Rest – *(booking advisable)* Carte 72/124 €

♦ Modern ♦ Elegant ♦

Housed in the La Scala opera house, this attractive restaurant also doubles as a cafeteria and tea room. Elegant and informal at the same time, it serves fine traditional cuisine.

XX **Armani/Nobu**

via Pisoni 1 ✉ 20121 – Ⓜ Montenapoleone – ☎ 02 62312645 – www.armaninobu.it – closed from 8 to 22 August and Sunday midday **G1**

Rest – Carte 40/80 €

♦ Japanese ♦ Trendy ♦

This restaurant offers an exotic combination of fashion and gastronomy. Find Japanese 'fusion' cuisine with South American influences in a simple, elegant atmosphere inspired by Japanese design. Spacious area reserved for smokers.

XX **Emilia e Carlo** AC VISA MC AE ①

via Sacchi 8 ✉ 20121 – Ⓜ Cairoli – ✆ 02 875948 – www.emiliaecarlo.it – closed Saturday midday, Sunday **F1**

Rest – Carte 50/65 €

♦ Modern ♦ Formal ♦

Housed in an early 19C palazzo, this trattoria has a rustic feel with arches and wooden beams. Creative contemporary cuisine, and a fine choice of wines.

XX **Paradosso** AC VISA MC AE ①

via Santa Maria Segreta 7/9 ✉ 20123 – Ⓜ Cordusio – ✆ 02 89011536 – www.paradossoristorante.com – closed August, 24 December-6 January, Saturday, Sunday **F1**

Rest – *(lunch only)* Carte 41/70 €

♦ Modern ♦ Formal ♦

A flight of steps leads down to this surprisingly airy restaurant – a type of 'winter garden' crowned with a large glass dome. Delicious cuisine with an emphasis on contemporary-style dishes.

XX **Al Porto** AC VISA MC AE ①

piazzale Generale Cantore ✉ 20123 – Ⓜ Porta Genova FS – ✆ 02 89407425 – closed August, 24 December-3 January, Sunday, Monday midday

Rest – Carte 52/70 € **E3**

♦ Fish ♦ Formal ♦

There is a definite maritime flavour to this restaurant, which occupies the old 19C Porta Genova toll house. Always busy, Al Porto specialises exclusively in fresh fish dishes, including raw fish.

XX ✿ **Tano Passami l'Olio** (Gaetano Simonato) AC VISA MC AE ①

via Villoresi, 16 ✉ 20143 – ✆ 02 8394139 – www.tanopassamilolio.com – closed August, 24 December-6 January and Sunday **E3**

Rest – *(dinner only) (booking advisable)* Carte 76/100 €

Spec. Uovo di quaglia caramellato su mousse di tonno, bottarga e crudo di tonno, olio alla menta. Uovo di patata alla coque ripieno di fonduta leggera con porcini croccanti e tartufo bianco (autumn). Portafoglio di pescatrice con fegato grasso e tartufo in crema di mela con riso nero venere.

♦ Inventive ♦ Intimate ♦

The key features here are the soft lighting, romantic atmosphere and creative fish and meat dishes, flavoured with a choice of extra-virgin olive oils on display in the dining room. Smoking lounge with a sofa.

XX **Il Navigante** AC P VISA MC AE ①

via Magolfa 14 ✉ 20143 – ✆ 02 89406320 – www.navigante.it – closed August and Sunday **F3**

Rest – Carte 38/57 €

♦ Fish ♦ Intimate ♦

On a road at the back of the waterway, live music every evening in an establishment, managed by an ex-ship's cook, with an unusual aquarium on the floor; seafood cuisine.

XX **Pirandello** AC VISA MC AE

viale Gian Galeazzo 6 ✉ 20136 – ✆ 02 89402901 – closed from 7 to 30 August, Saturday at midday, Sunday **F3**

Rest – Carte 43/55 €

♦ Sicilian ♦ Formal ♦

This restaurant has a decidedly Sicilian atmosphere, management and cuisine. Sample the tasty fish dishes and traditional Sicilian cuisine in both dining rooms.

XX

Hostaria Borromei

via Borromei 4 ✉ 20123 – Ⓜ Cordusio – ✆ 02 86453760
– closed from 8 to 31 August, 24 December-7 January and Saturday-Sunday lunchtime **F2**

Rest – Carte 36/59 €

♦ Mantuan ♦ Family ♦

Housed in an 18C palazzo in the heart of the historic centre, this small restaurant serves traditional, regional cuisine, with the accent on dishes from Mantua. Outdoor dining in the courtyard in summer.

X

La Felicità

via Rovello 3 ✉ 20121 – Ⓜ Cordusio – ✆ 02 865235 **F1**

Rest – Carte 17/25 €

♦ Chinese ♦ Family ♦

This simple, well-run Chinese restaurant also serves Vietnamese, Thai and Korean cuisine. Elegant furnishings which are broadly Oriental in style.

X

Masuelli San Marco

viale Umbria 80 ✉ 20135 – Ⓜ Lodi TIBB – ✆ 02 55184138
– www.masuellitrattoria.it
– closed 3 weeks in August, 25 December - 6 January, Sunday, Monday midday

Rest – Carte 35/50 € *Plan I* **D3**

♦ Regional ♦ Friendly ♦

A rustic atmosphere with a luxurious feel in a typical trattoria, with the same management since 1921; cuisine strongly linked to traditional Lombardy and Piedmont recipes.

X

Giulio Pane e Ojo

via Muratori 10 ✉ 20135 – Ⓜ Porta Romana – ✆ 02 5456189
– www.giuliopaneojo.com
– closed 24-26 December and Sunday except December **H3**

Rest – Carte 28/34 €

♦ Roman ♦ Friendly ♦

This rustic, informal restaurant run by a young team is very popular with locals. The cuisine here is typically Roman with simpler, cheaper meals available at lunchtime. Reservations are advised for the evening.

X

Dongiò

via Corio 3 ✉ 20135 – Ⓜ Porta Romana – ✆ 02 5511372
– closed Easter, 2 weeks in August, 2 weeks in Christmas, Saturday at midday, Sunday **H3**

Rest – *(booking advisable)* Carte 24/37 €

♦ Calabrian specialities ♦ Family ♦

This family-run restaurant introduces a flavour of traditional Calabria to Milan with a simple, lively atmosphere that is quite rare nowadays. Home cooking based on fresh pasta, 'nduja (spicy sausage) and the ubiquitous peperoncino (chilli pepper).

X

Pane Acqua

via Bandello 14 ✉ 20123 – ✆ 02 48198622 – www.paneacqua.com
– closed 3 weeks in August, 25 December-6 January, Saturday and Sunday in July, Sunday and Monday lunch the rest of the year **E2**

Rest – Menu 18 € bi (lunch)/55 € – Carte 57/75 €

♦ Modern ♦ Fashionable ♦

If you're looking for an unusual address, look no further! Thanks to an agreement with a modern art gallery, the furnishings and decor in this small bistro-style restaurant change on a regular basis. Not so the cuisine, however, which is always full of flavour and imaginative flair.

Principe di Savoia

piazza della Repubblica 17 ✉ *20124* – Ⓜ *Repubblica* – ✆ *02 62301* – *www.hotelprincipedisavoia.com* **M2**

337 rm – ♦610/1250 € ♦♦760/1250 €, ☕ 45 € – 64 suites

Rest *Acanto* – ✆ *02 62302026* – Carte 77/132 €

♦ Grand Luxury ♦ Palace ♦ Stylish ♦

Period furniture, luxury, and sophistication predominate in this19th-century building with an international appeal. There are also sports facilities and a health centre. The restaurant is elegant and modern, with large windows overlooking a well-tended garden. Classic, contemporary cuisine.

The Westin Palace

piazza della Repubblica 20 ✉ *20124* – Ⓜ *Repubblica* – ✆ *02 63361* – *www.westin.com/palacemilan* **M2**

228 rm – ♦150/1000 € ♦♦200/1300 €, ☕ 37 € – 12 suites

Rest – Carte 60/75 €

♦ Grand Luxury ♦ Stylish ♦

Housed in a modern tower block, this luxury hotel offers comfort and elegance, with superb guestrooms, "Heavenly Beds" and stylish decor. The recently renovated restaurant has lost none of its elegance and now offers a private dining area. The menu focuses on Mediterranean cuisine.

Atahotel Executive without rest

viale Luigi Sturzo 45 ✉ *20154* – Ⓜ *Porta Garibaldi FS* – ✆ *02 62941* – *www.atahotels.it* **L1**

414 rm ☕ – ♦♦90/470 € – 6 suites

♦ Chain hotel ♦ Business ♦ Classic ♦

This modern hotel is situated opposite the Garibaldi railway station. Its well-equipped conference centre is ideal for business clients and meetings. Attractive and comfortable guestrooms.

Starhotels Ritz

via Spallanzani 40 ✉ *20129* – Ⓜ *Lima* – ✆ *02 2055* – *www.starhotels.com* *Plan I* **C2**

191 rm ☕ – ♦♦105/260 € – 6 suites **Rest** – Menu 35/65 €

♦ Chain hotel ♦ Classic ♦

Centrally located in a quiet area, this simple and elegant hotel is now equipped with a health centre with gym and spa facilities. A large dining room for banquets, and wall paintings are the features of this restaurant.

Four Points Sheraton Milan Center

via Cardano 1 ✉ *20124* – Ⓜ *Gioia* – ✆ *02 667461* – *www.fourpoints.com/milan* **M1**

254 rm ☕ – ♦110/400 € ♦♦125/500 €

Rest *Nectare* – Carte 39/68 €

♦ Business ♦ Palace ♦ Classic ♦

Housed in a modern building in the centre of Milan, this hotel offers relaxing public areas furnished in a simple, elegant style, as well as pleasant and comfortable guestrooms. A bright dining room with tasteful decor.

UNA Hotel Tocq

via A. de Tocqueville 7/D ✉ *20154* – Ⓜ *Porta Garibaldi FS* – ✆ *02 62071* – *www.unahotels.it* **L1**

109 rm ☕ – ♦♦119/603 € – 13 suites **Rest** – Carte 36/49 €

♦ Business ♦ Chain hotel ♦ Design ♦

Modern design is the key feature of this hotel, with its subtle, minimalist furnishings. Fully equipped with all the facilities expected of a contemporary hotel. This restaurant is decorated with summer colours and natural, Danish oak parquet flooring. There is a pleasant lounge bar for a pre-dinner aperitif.

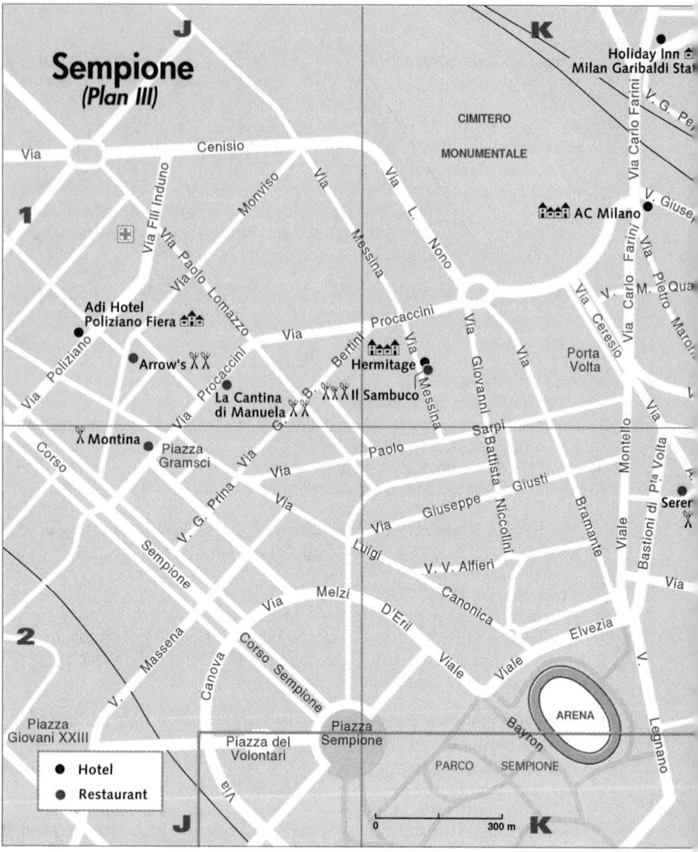

Sempione
(Plan III)

● Hotel
● Restaurant

Holiday Inn Milan Garibaldi Station

via Farini angolo via Ugo Bassi ✉ *20159 –* Ⓜ *Porta Garibaldi FS –* ✆ *02 6076801 – www.himilangaribaldi.com*

129 rm – ††99/499 €, ☕ 20 € **Rest** – Carte 39/59 € **K1**

◆ Chain hotel ◆ Business ◆ Modern ◆

This light, welcoming hotel decorated in a minimalist style continues to be a good choice for accommodation in Milan. The pleasant breakfast room has a glass cupola. Modern decor and traditional cuisine.

Maison Moschino

viale Monte Grappa 6 ✉ *20124 –* Ⓜ *Porta Garibaldi FS –* ✆ *02 29009858 – www.maisonmoschino.com* **L1-2**

65 rm – †248/539 € ††281/627 €, ☕ 24 € **Rest *Il Clandestino*** – Carte 72/97 €

◆ Business ◆ Personalised ◆

This hotel is housed in an elegant neo-Classical palazzo, which was once a railway station. It boasts bright, modern interiors furnished by the famous fashion house after which it is named. The guestrooms are designed according to 16 different styles, all on the theme of fairytales. Regional Milanese cuisine gives way to exquisite fish and seafood dishes at Il Clandestino restaurant.

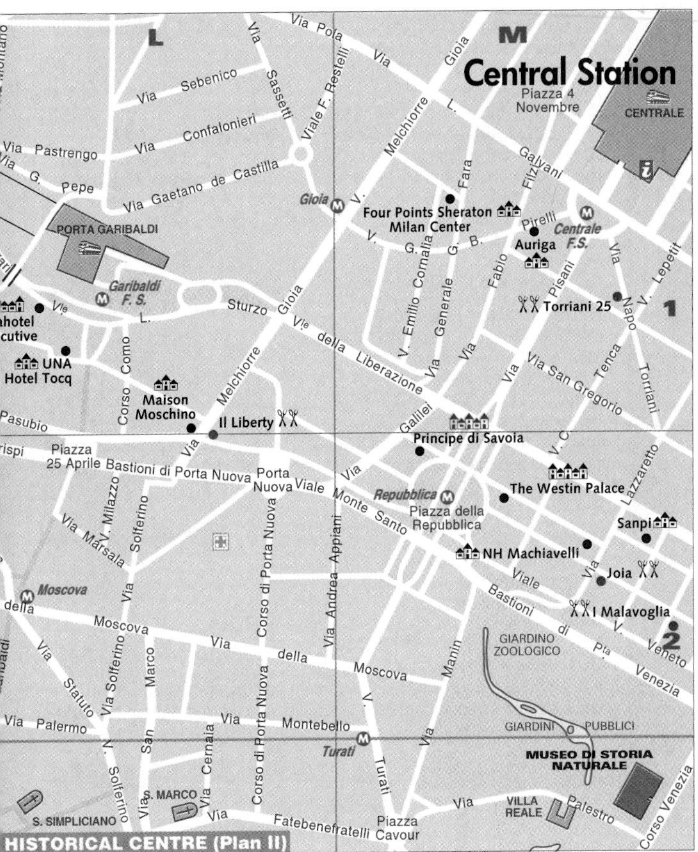

Starhotels Anderson

piazza Luigi di Savoia 20 ✉ *20124* – Ⓜ *Centrale FS* – ✆ *02 6690141*
– www.starhotels.com *Plan I* **C1**

106 rm ☕ – 👥99/750 € **Rest** – Menu 42/46 €

◆ Chain hotel ◆ Classic ◆

This hotel has a warm, designer-style atmosphere, with fashionable and intimate public rooms and welcoming guestrooms offering all the usual comforts of a hotel of this standard. The elegant lounge is home to a small restaurant (open only in the evenings) which serves contemporary-style cuisine.

NH Machiavelli

via Lazzaretto 5 ✉ *20124* – Ⓜ *Repubblica* – ✆ *02 631141*
– www.nh-hotels.it – closed 30 July-21 August **M2**

103 rm ☕ – 👤95/450 € 👥115/520 €

Rest *Caffè Niccolò* – Carte 60/74 €

◆ Chain hotel ◆ Business ◆ Modern ◆

This recently built hotel has simple, bright rooms and a large open lounge area. A small restaurant serving à la carte and buffet meals.

Adi Doria Grand Hotel

viale Andrea Doria 22 ✉ 20124
– Ⓜ Caiazzo – ✆ 02 67411411
– www.adihotels.com Plan I **C1**
122 rm – 99/385 € 99/485 € – 2 suites
Rest – *(closed August and 24 December-6 January)* Carte 38/59 €
♦ Chain hotel ♦ Classic ♦

This classical building has an elegant lobby furnished in early 20C-style and large, comfortable guestrooms. Cultural and musical events are occasionally held in the spacious public areas. This elegant restaurant serves fine regional and international cuisine.

Sanpi without rest

via Lazzaro Palazzi 18 ✉ 20124
– Ⓜ Porta Venezia – ✆ 02 29513341
– www.hotelsanpimilano.it
– closed 24 December-2 January **M2**
79 rm – 95/350 € 119/450 €
♦ Business ♦ Design ♦

Comprising three buildings in the heart of the city, this quiet hotel has well-lit public areas and guestrooms decorated in pastel shades. There is a small garden in the internal courtyard.

Auriga without rest

via Giovanni Battista Pirelli 7 ✉ 20124
– Ⓜ Centrale FS – ✆ 02 66985851
– www.auriga-milano.com
– closed 30 July- 22 August and 23 December-9 January **M1**
52 rm – 105/270 € 120/320 €
♦ Business ♦ Modern ♦

The mix of styles, unusual façade and bright colours of this hotel combine to create a striking exterior. Comfortable facilities and efficient service for tourists and business travellers alike.

Gold

via Poerio 2/A ✉ 20129 – ✆ 02 7577771
– www.dolcegabbanagold.it
– closed August and Sunday Plan I **C2**
Rest – *(dinner only)* Carte 63/81 €
Rest *Bistrot* – Carte 35/77 €
♦ Italian ♦ Fashionable ♦

This modern, contemporary-style restaurant furnished with large round tables is the creation of two leading names in the fashion world. Smoking room. Informal and yet elegant, the bistro serves food throughout the day.

Joia (Pietro Leemann)

via Panfilo Castaldi 18 ✉ 20124 – Ⓜ Repubblica – ✆ 02 29522124
– www.joia.it
– closed from 7 to 30 August, 25 December-8 January, Saturday lunchtime, Sunday **M2**
Rest – Menu 65/100 € – Carte 67/91 €
Spec. Crema di patate con pesto di nocciole, schiuma di tartufo, fave, chips di patate novelle ed erbe. Ravioli di sedano affumicato con salsa di zucca allo zafferano. Biscotto genovese di malto e mirtilli con gelato di mandorle, salsa di miele e vaniglia.
♦ Inventive ♦ Formal ♦

This restaurant is reputed to be the best vegetarian restaurant in Europe. Fish is no longer included on the menu, but despite this the restaurant continues to produce some of the most unusual and distinctive cuisine in the city.

XX

Torriani 25

via Napo Torriani 25 ✉ 20124 – Ⓜ Centrale FS – ✆ 02 67078183 – www.torriani25.it – closed from 6 to 28 August, 24 December-1 January, Saturday at midday, Sunday **M1**

Rest – Carte 37/65 €

♦ Fish ♦ Formal ♦ Friendly ♦

This modern restaurant is decorated in warm colours, with plenty of natural light. Choose from a wide selection of fish - the house speciality - on display on the buffet in the dining room.

XX

I Malavoglia

via Lecco 4 ✉ 20124 – Ⓜ Porta Venezia – ✆ 02 29531387 – www.ristoranteimalavoglia.com – closed August, 24 December-7 January, Sunday, Monday at midday

Rest – Carte 47/63 € **M2**

♦ Sicilian ♦ Formal ♦

This classic restaurant has been run by the same team for over thirty years. They serve typical Sicilian dishes in Lombardy's capital.

XX

Il Liberty

viale Monte Grappa 6 ✉ 20124 – ✆ 02 29011439 – www.il-liberty.it – closed 2 weeks in August, Saturday midday, Sunday **L2**

Rest – Menu 52 € – Carte 47/67 €

♦ Modern ♦ Retro ♦ Neighbourhood ♦

This small, friendly restaurant is housed in an Art Nouveau-style palazzo. It has two dining rooms and a mezzanine. The cuisine focuses on meat and seafood dishes. The former is sourced from the surrounding Lombardy countryside.

X

Casa Fontana-23 Risotti

piazza Carbonari 5 ✉ 20125 – Ⓜ Sondrio – ✆ 02 6704710 – www.23risotti.it – closed 26-28 April, 23 July-22 August, 1-10 January, Saturday midday, Monday *Plan I* **C1**

Rest – Menu 25/40 € – Carte 41/49 €

♦ Lombard specialities ♦ Family ♦

Despite the obligatory 25min wait for your food, this restaurant is well worth a visit for its excellent risottos. Attractive pictures of rice fields on the walls.

X

Serendib

via Pontida 2 ✉ 20121 – Ⓜ Moscova – ✆ 02 6592139 – www.serendib.it – closed from 10 to 20 August **K2**

Rest – *(dinner only)* Carte 24/29 €

♦ Indian ♦ Friendly ♦

Serendib, which means "make happy", is the old name for Sri Lanka – a tough challenge, but one that this restaurant manages to pull off! The cuisine combines Indian and Sri Lankan specialities.

X

La Cantina di Manuela

via Carlo Poerio 3 ✉ 20129 – Ⓜ Porta Venezia – ✆ 02 76318892 – www.lacantinadimanuela.it – closed from 7 to 21 August and Sunday *Plan I* **C2**

Rest – Carte 36/42 €

♦ Classic ♦ Wine bar ♦

This restaurant has an especially interesting wine list that accompanies its excellent cooking. A few tables are put on the path outside during summer.

X

Da Giannino-L'Angolo d'Abruzzo

via Pilo 20 ✉ 20129 – Ⓜ Porta Venezia – ✆ 02 29406526 – closed August and Monday *Plan I* **D2**

Rest – Carte 20/24 €

♦ Abruzzian specialities ♦ Neighbourhood ♦ Family ♦

Visitors can expect a warm welcome in this simple, cheerful and popular restaurant. Generous portions of typical Abruzzi cuisine.

Baia Chia

via Bazzini 37 ✉ 20131 – Ⓜ Piola – ☎ 02 2361131
– closed Easter, 3 weeks in August, 24 December-2 January, Sunday, Monday lunch *Plan I* **D1**
Rest – Carte 27/39 €
♦ Sardinian specialities ♦ Rustic ♦
This pleasant restaurant with a family atmosphere is divided into two small dining rooms, plus a veranda which can also be used in winter. Excellent fish dishes and Sardinian specialities on the menu. Many of the wines also come from Sardinia.

FIERA-SEMPIONE *Plan I*

Hermitage

via Messina 10 ✉ 20154 – Ⓜ Porta Garibaldi FS – ☎ 02 318170
– www.monrifhotels.it
– closed August *Plan III* **K1**
122 rm ☕ – 🛉80/290 € 🛉🛉120/320 € – 9 suites
Rest***Il Sambuco*** – see below
♦ Business ♦ Classic ♦
Style and comfort are the trademarks of this hotel, which combines the atmosphere of elegant period-style interiors with modern facilities. Situated in a quarter bustling with activity and shops.

Milan Marriott Hotel

via Washington 66 ✉ 20146 – Ⓜ Wagner – ☎ 02 48521
– www.milanmarriott.com **A2**
321 rm – 🛉🛉130/840 €, ☕ 20 €
Rest *La Brasserie de Milan* – ☎ *02 48522834* – Carte 38/76 €
♦ Business ♦ Classic ♦
Original contrast between the modern building and the imposing classic interiors of a hotel clearly geared towards Conference and Trade Fair business clientele; functional period style bedrooms. Restaurant dining room with the kitchen in full view; classical style.

Atahotel Fieramilano

viale Boezio 20 ✉ 20145 – ☎ 02 336221 – www.atahotels.it
– closed August **B2**
236 rm ☕ – 🛉84/405 € 🛉🛉94/610 € – 2 suites **Rest** – Menu 35/60 €
♦ Chain hotel ♦ Classic ♦
This tastefully furnished hotel opposite the Fiera Milano offers modern and comfortable rooms. In summer, breakfast is served in a gazebo in the garden. Quiet, elegant dining room.

AC Milano

via Tazzoli 2 ✉ 20154 – ☎ 02 20424211 – www.ac-hotels.com
156 rm ☕ – 🛉🛉100/440 € – 2 suites *Plan III* **K1**
Rest – *(residents only)* Carte 41/62 €
♦ Business ♦ Design ♦
A stone's throw from Corso Como and Milan's nightlife, this modern, designer-style hotel is popular with an upmarket business clientele. Spacious, well-appointed bedrooms in keeping with the high standards of this hotel chain.

Wagner without rest

via Buonarroti 13 – Ⓜ Buonarroti – ☎ 02 463151
– www.roma-wagner.com
– closed from 12 to 19 August **A2**
48 rm ☕ – 🛉119/398 € 🛉🛉169/519 € – 1 suite
♦ Business ♦ Personalised ♦
This hotel, next to the eponymous metro station, has attractive rooms with marble and modern furnishings.

Enterprise Hotel

corso Sempione 91 ✉ *20149* – ✆ *02 318181* – *www.enterprisehotel.com*
121 rm – †123/608 € ††133/648 € – 2 suites **A1**
Rest *Sophia's* – ✆ *02 31818855* – Carte 41/59 €
◆ Business ◆ Design ◆
Attention to detail and design is evident in every aspect of this elegant modern hotel, from the marble and granite exterior to its bespoke furnishings and pleasing geometrical lines. A pleasant and original restaurant for lunch and dinner. Outdoor dining in summer.

Regency without rest

via Arimondi 12 ✉ *20155* – ✆ *02 39216021* – *www.regency-milano.com*
– closed from 5 to 28 August and 22 December-6 January **A1**
71 rm – †100/270 € ††140/380 €
◆ Business ◆ Classic ◆
This charming and unusual mansion dating from the late-19C is built in the style of a small castle. Delightful courtyard and stylish interior furnishings.

Rubens

via Rubens 21 ✉ *20148* – Ⓜ *Gambara* – ✆ *02 40302*
– *www.hotelrubensmilano.com* **A2**
87 rm – †90/299 € ††110/390 € **Rest** – *(residents only)* Carte 35/45 €
◆ Business ◆ Personalised ◆
The spacious, comfortable guestrooms in this elegant hotel are adorned with frescoes by contemporary artists and furnished in stylish beige, golden and pastel-coloured tones. To get the day off to a good start, enjoy a copious breakfast in the evocatively named Sala delle Nuvole (Room in the Clouds) on the top floor.

Accademia

viale Certosa 68 ✉ *20155* – ✆ *02 39211122* – *www.antareshotels.com*
– closed from 6 to 22 August **A1**
66 rm – †350 € ††400 €, 10 € – 1 suite
Rest – *(residents only)* Menu 25 €
◆ Business ◆ Classic ◆
Following major renovation work, this hotel features new guestrooms in warm tones with designer-style furnishings and excellent levels of comfort thanks to the careful use of the space available. Note the typical mosaic which frames the lift doors.

ADI Hotel Poliziano Fiera

via Poliziano 11 ✉ *20154* – ✆ *02 3191911* – *www.adihotels.com*
– closed 29 July-28 August and 23 December-9 January *Plan III* **J1**
98 rm – †84/310 € ††98/410 € – 2 suites
Rest – *(residents only)* Carte 29/44 €
◆ Business ◆ Classic ◆
This modern hotel offers friendly, attentive service and spacious guestrooms furnished in light green and sand-coloured tones, as well as attractive public rooms.

Astoria without rest

viale Murillo 9 ✉ *20149* – Ⓜ *Lotto* – ✆ *02 40090095*
– *www.astoriahotelmilano.com* **A2**
69 rm – †100/300 € ††130/420 €
◆ Chain hotel ◆ Modern ◆
This hotel that caters mostly to business travellers is located along a ring road. The rooms are modern and soundproof.

Mirage

viale Certosa 104/106 ✉ *20156* – ✆ *02 39210471* – *www.hotelmirage.mi.it*
– closed 23 July-21 August and 23 December-2 January **A1**
86 rm – †90/299 € ††99/324 €
Rest – *(closed Friday, Saturday) (dinner only) (residents only)* Carte 28/36 €
◆ Business ◆ Classic ◆
Thanks to its strategic location near major motorways and not far from the Rho-Pero exhibition complex, this hotel is ideal for business travellers. The guestrooms, some of which have parquet floors, have been renovated in traditional style.

Des Etrangers without rest

via Sirte 9 ✉ 20146 – ☎ 02 48955325 – www.hoteldesetrangers.it
– closed from 7 to 23 August **A3**
94 rm – 60/150 € 80/230 €
◆ Business ◆ Classic ◆
This well-maintained hotel in a quiet street offers its guests functional and comfortable public areas and guestrooms, as well as convenient underground parking.

Antica Locanda Leonardo without rest

corso Magenta 78 ✉ 20123 – Ⓜ Conciliazione
– ☎ 02 48014197 – www.anticalocandaleonardo.com
– closed from 5 to 25 August and 31 December-6 January Plan II **E2**
16 rm – 95/120 € 165/245 €
◆ Townhouse ◆ Personalised ◆
The luxury atmosphere combines with the family-style welcome in a hotel which overlooks a small inner courtyard, in an ideal location near the place where Leonardo da Vinci's painting of the "Last Supper" is housed.

Il Luogo di Aimo e Nadia (Aimo Moroni)

via Montecuccoli 6 ✉ 20147 – Ⓜ Primaticcio
– ☎ 02 416886 – www.aimoenadia.com – closed Easter, 3 weeks in August, from 1 to 7 January, Saturday lunch, Sunday **A3**
Rest – Carte 90/130 €
Spec. Tagliatelle di farina di semi antichi con anatra muta novella, funghi porcini e caciocavallo podolico (summer-autumn). Rombo con salsa e succo di cipolle di Tropea. Dolci ortaggi: crostata di farina di castagne, arance e cioccolato, crema al bergamotto.
◆ Contemporary ◆ Formal ◆
Tuscan cuisine was brought to Milan, and later to other regions. Faithful to this, the selection of Italian products that the restaurant offers today is difficult to equal.

La Pobbia 1850

via Gallarate 92 ✉ 20151 – ☎ 02 38006641 – www.lapobbia.com
– closed August and Sunday **A1**
Rest – Carte 45/75 €
◆ Lombard specialities ◆ Formal ◆
This 19C tavern is now an elegant restaurant with an interior garden. It serves traditional Lombard and international cuisine. There is also an area set aside for smokers.

Il Sambuco – Hotel Hermitage

via Messina 10 ✉ 20154 – Ⓜ Porta Garibaldi FS – ☎ 02 33610333
– www.ilsambuco.it
– closed Easter, August, 24 December-4 January, Saturday lunch, Sunday
Rest – Menu 50 € – Carte 62/72 € Plan III **K1**
◆ Fish ◆ Formal ◆
Like the hotel of which it is a part, this restaurant is characterised by elegant decor and attentive service. The cuisine is renowned for its seafood specialities and, on Mondays, for its dishes of boiled meat.

Innocenti Evasioni (Arrigoni e Picco)

via privata della Bindellina ✉ 20155
– ☎ 02 33001882 – www.innocentievasioni.com
– closed August, from 1 to 10 January and Sunday **A1**
Rest – *(dinner only) (booking advisable)* Menu 47/68 € – Carte 47/60 €
Spec. Terrina di foie gras d'anatra, composta al rabarbaro e pan brioche tostato (June-September). Bigoli al torchio con sugo d'anatra e friabile al pecorino (winter). Filetto di maialino arrostito, pesche all'aceto balsamico e patate schiacciate all'extravergine.
◆ Innovative ◆ Formal ◆ Intimate ◆
This pleasant establishment, with large windows facing the garden, offers classic cuisine reinterpreted with imagination. Enjoyable outdoor summer dining.

XX

Nicola Cavallaro al San Cristoforo

via Lodovico il Moro 11 ✉ 20143 – ✆ 02 89126060 – www.nicolacavallaro.it – closed from 7 to 31 August, 24-25-26 December, Saturday midday, Monday

Rest – Carte 35/70 € **A3**

♦ Inventive ♦ Formal ♦

The brilliant young chef at this restaurant on the Naviglio creates original dishes with a flavour of the Orient. Fish takes pride of place, and is served either raw, or as part of more classical or elaborate dishes.

XX

Arrow's

via Mantegna 17/19 ✉ 20154 – ✆ 02 341533 – www.ristorantearrows.it – closed 3 weeks in August, Sunday, Monday at midday *Plan III* **J1**

Rest – Carte 39/54 €

♦ Fish ♦ Formal ♦

Packed, even at midday, the atmosphere becomes cosier in the evening but the seafood cuisine, prepared according to tradition, remains the same.

XX

La Cantina di Manuela

via Procaccini 41 ✉ 20154 – ✆ 02 3452034 – www.lacantinadimanuela.it – closed from 8 to 28 August and Sunday *Plan III* **J1**

Rest – Carte 33/41 €

♦ Classic ♦ Fashionable ♦

Not far from FieraMilanoCity, this restaurant-wine bar comprises of two intercommunicating dining rooms with an original display of bottles. Enjoy traditional dishes, which have been reinterpreted with a touch of lightness and a great deal of attention to the original flavours of the ingredients.

X

Trattoria Montina

via Procaccini 54 ✉ 20154 – Ⓜ Porta Garibaldi FS – ✆ 02 3490498 – closed from 8 to 30 August, 25 December - 5 January, Sunday, Monday midday *Plan III* **J2**

Rest – Carte 21/38 €

♦ Regional ♦ Intimate ♦

Nice bistro atmosphere, tables close together, defused lighting in the evening in an establishment managed by twin brothers; seasonal national and Milanese dishes.

TURIN

TORINO

Population (est. 2010): 909 538 – Altitude: 239m

mbus/Fotolia.com

If there's ever been a time to visit Turin, that time is now. In the past, the city was associated with the car industry and its somewhat sombre atmosphere never really attracted many tourists. All this changed dramatically in 2006 when the Winter Olympic Games took place and Turin underwent a complete renewal. Once the skiing and ice-skating were over an even greater transformation took place. The result was complex and fascinating, and Turin's name as a destination now ranks alongside Italy's more famous cities.

Turin has also had a glorious past. The city played a big part in the country's history, while at the same time opening many new doors to the future. Few know that the *Regno delle due Sicilie*, the little state Turin was head of, paved the way to Italy's unification in 1861 and that the city itself became Italy's first capital. Turin's royal family, the Savoia (later to be Italy's monarchs), moulded the city with their monuments and taste for grandeur, creating the squares and avenues that are now celebrated in this rediscovered capital.

LIVING THE CITY

Piazza Castello, the square from which some of the city's most celebrated avenues start, may well be considered the heart of Turin; while the city's landmark building has to be the **Mole Antonelliana** – originally designed as a Jewish synagogue – the city's tallest building and Turin's answer to the 'Tour Eiffel'. Named after an ancient Roman settlement, the **Quadrilatero Romano** is now the most fashionable quarter of Turin and boasts some of its most elegant shops ; its narrow medieval streets are a fascinating interlude to the city's orthogonal plan. Less fashionable but equally interesting is **Borgo Dora**, the quarter north of the **Piazza della Repubblica**; it's a popular area that has recently been given a facelift but still retains its old, bohemian atmosphere. Don't miss the **Cortile del Maglio**, inside the arsenal in Piazza Borgo Dora, with its markets and art. At the other end of the scale, **la Collina** provides some of Turin's poshest addresses, while crossing the River Po – the longest in Italy – at Piazza Vittorio Veneto will lead you to Turin's luxurious period houses. Those interested in residential architecture can also find some of Turin's most beautiful houses – dating back to the 19C – in the Via Galileo Ferraris area of the Crocetta quarter. For a more vibrant atmosphere, head for the embankment between Piazza Vittorio Veneto and Corso Vittorio Emanuele and you will find the 'murazzi', where you will get the best of Turin's nightlife with its bars and clubs.

PRACTICAL INFORMATION

ARRIVAL-DEPARTURE

Better known as Caselle – after the town near which you land – Turin's airport, Sandro Pertini, is located 11km north of the city. It will cost you between €25 and €40 to reach the city centre by taxi, or €5 by bus. The best bet, however, is to use the train, which runs every 30mins and brings you into Torino Dora railway station in just 19mins. The price of €3,40 also includes a 70 minute bus ride of your choice once in Turin.

TRANSPORT

Bus tickets range from a good value €1 for 70mins travel and up to €3,50 for unlimited daily use. In recent years the underground has been progressively extending its reach throughout Turin and provides a quick and easy way of getting around.

EXPLORING TURIN

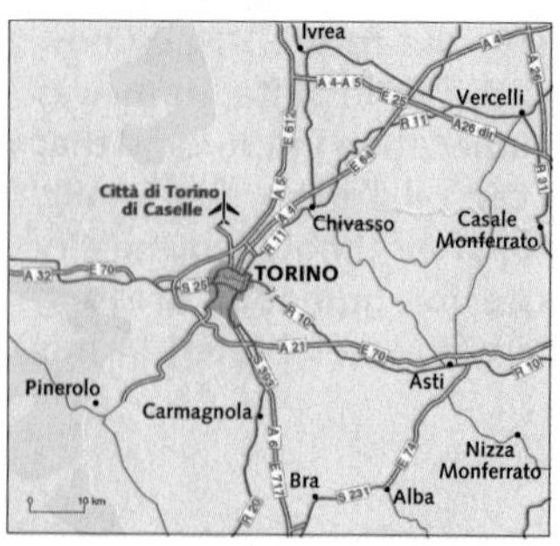

The best way to discover the city is to walk along its arcades - 18 pleasurable kilometres of shops and cafés - and all without having to worry about the weather. Famous for its long, wide avenues which interconnect at imposing squares, it's hard to get lost here. Mirroring the torinesi themselves, the city combines an air of thoroughness and order with a sense of discretion and understatement. Even baroque style churches and monuments have been reinterpreted with the native desire for measured composure; a long way from the opulence of Rome.

→ INDUSTRY & ART

Turin's love for cinema dates back to the beginning of the 20C, when the city was used as the backdrop for some of Italy's first shoots. This love affair continues today, with the Torino Film Festival having grown into one of the most interesting film events. The Mole Antonelliana plays host to the Museo del Cinema which recounts the history of cinema and displays thousands of objects relating to its birth and concluding with some spectacular recreations of famous films.

Turin has always been closely associated with Italy's car industry and in particular FIAT, a move which contributed largely to the 'miracolo economio' – the rapid economic growth that Italy experienced during the '50s and '60s. The car factories have moved on but the historical 1920s **Lingotto** plant still remains and has been ingeniously converted into a business and shopping centre, with cinemas, a picture gallery, concert hall and even two hotels. Cleverly transformed by architect Renzo Piano, it retains most of its original architectural features which lead Le Corbusier to define it as "one of the most remarkable sights industry has given us". It can be found in Via Nizza 280. Car enthusiasts should also head for the **Museo dell'Automobile Biscaretti di Ruffia**, in Corso Unità d'Italia 40, which tells the story of the car and boasts an impressive display of motor vehicles.

Turin wouldn't be the city we know today without its newspapers, bookshops and publishing houses. Those who are at ease with the Italian language will find all they need to know about what's hot in town in 'La Stampa', the daily newspaper; while book lovers will queue at the 'Fiera Internazionale del Libro' in the Lingotto, a yearly exhibition and one of Italy's most important publishing seminars. Even more unique and definitely more intriguing, is the 'Portici di Carta', which takes place in via Roma sometime in the autumn. Around 120 companies participate in the event, creating possibly the biggest ever bookshop, spread over 2 kilometres of Turin's most beautiful avenues.

→ WALK LIKE AN EGYPTIAN

As the city has never had any links with the Egyptian civilization, it may surprise you to find that Turin is home to one of the world's most important Egyptian museums. It has recently been revamped and is definitely worth a visit to view the vast range of archaeological finds. The main attraction is the collection of statues dating back to the New Reign Period, the golden age of ancient Egypt. You'll find the museum in Via Accademia delle Scienze 6, close the central Via Roma.

If you feel like a stroll in the park then **Valentino** is the most popular choice for visitors and locals alike. Relatively close to the city centre, it offers over a kilometre of pleasant walks along the Po embankment. More than just green space, it is also home to a theatre, the 17C Valentino Castle and the Borgo Medioevale – a 19C reproduction of a historic local village.

If you have the time and fancy going a little further afield, the **'corona di delizie'** deserves your attention. This refers to a series of royal palaces around Turin – hence the name 'corona' or 'crown' – built from as early as the 17C by the Savoia Royal Family. The best architects of the time contributed to these palaces and at least three deserve particular mention. Firstly, the recently restored Reggia di Venaria, once dedicated to royal hunting and now home to the richly decorated Grande Galleria; secondly, the Palazzina di Caccia di Stupingi, Juvarra's imposing 19C masterpiece;

and finally, the Castello e Museo d'Arte Contemporanea, perched on a hill 15km outside of Turin in Rivoli and host to a famous modern art museum. This last collection contributes to Turin's growing name as the capital of modern design. If you're passionate about art, don't miss the Galleria Civica di Arte Moderne e Contemporanea (GAM).

CALENDAR HIGHLIGHTS

Turin is busy throughout the year, courtesy of a multitude of business and tourist events. The Lingotto building with its post-industrial architecture, is the centre of many of these, such as Italy's most important book exhibition, the Fiera Internazionale del Libro, which usually takes place in May. Later in the year, September sees music fans flock to Turin for the annual Mito, a collection of over 200 music events lasting almost a month. Every two years in late October, food lovers can queue at the Salone del Gusto, an immense event organised by the Slow Food Movement, which gathers the best Italian producers and their products, as well as running conferences and debates. Autumn, usually November, has been attracting cinema-goers since 1982 with the Torino Film Festival (TFF) and, thanks to the quality of its selected films, it has really made a name for itself.

EATING OUT

Turin can rightly boast of being one of Italy's gastronomic centres. Faithful to its ancient role as capital, the city displays the best food the Piemonte region has to offer. Not to be missed are the fresh egg pastas (usually in the form of the very fine tajarin or as ravioli del Plin), the local braised beef (fassone), lamb and pigeons. The locals definitely have a taste for meat and most recipes use it in one form or another. Indeed, meat may keep you company throughout your meal: as an entrée such as vitello tonnato, as a filling for ravioli in your second course, as well as for the main course itself. White truffles deserve a special mention, although they've become so rare and world famous that prices are often incredibly high. Picked on the Langhe Hills between October and December, they are usually served with pasta (most commonly grated over tajarin with butter) or fonduta (cheese cream with yolks).

With some of the best Italian chocolate being produced in Turin, desserts are a real treat. You might find bonèt (chocolate pudding with almond biscuits), torta di nocciole (hazelnut

TURIN IN...

→ ONE DAY

Piazza Castello, Via Roma, Piazza San Carlo, the Mole Antonelliana, Piazza Vittorio Veneto, the Duomo and the Sacra Sindone Chapel

→ TWO DAYS

The Egyptian Museum, the Sabaudia Gallery, Palazzo Carignano, Palazzo Madama and its Museum of Ancient Arts

→ THREE DAYS

The Valentino Park, the Reggia di Venaria and the Museum of the Cinema

cake) or panna cotta (cooked cream). Alongside Tuscany, Piemontes's red wines are indisputably the best in Italy; to accompany your meal try a local Barbera, a reliable Nebbiolo or a world famous Barbaresco or Barolo – the 'king of wines'.

Cafés have a long tradition in Turin and stopping at one can be a good way of getting a little closer to local life. Dating back to 1763, *Al Bicerin* is one of the best known, and prime minister Cavour – one of the founders of Italian unity – used to be a frequent visitor here at piazza della Consolata 5. Café *San Carlo* in the elegant San Carlo Square is equally famous, as it was as the meeting point for patriots fighting for Italian independence; those more into art nouveau usually meet at Baratti & Milano, 29 Piazza Castello. Wherever you go, make sure you try a *bicerin* – a drink made from coffee, cream and chocolate – and a *gianduiotto* – added chocolate and 'tonda gentile', a famous variety of hazelnut from the Piemonte region.

The region's love for food recently paved the way to the opening of the world's biggest food market, 'Eataly': 2,500 square metres of Italy's most famous delicacies brought to you by local producers, who pride themselves of the quality of their excellent, and often rare, ingredients. The choice ranges from pasta and wine through to special varieties of rice, olive oil, cheese and all that Italy is known for. Set in via Nizza 230, close to the Lingotto, it offers a good number of restaurants too.

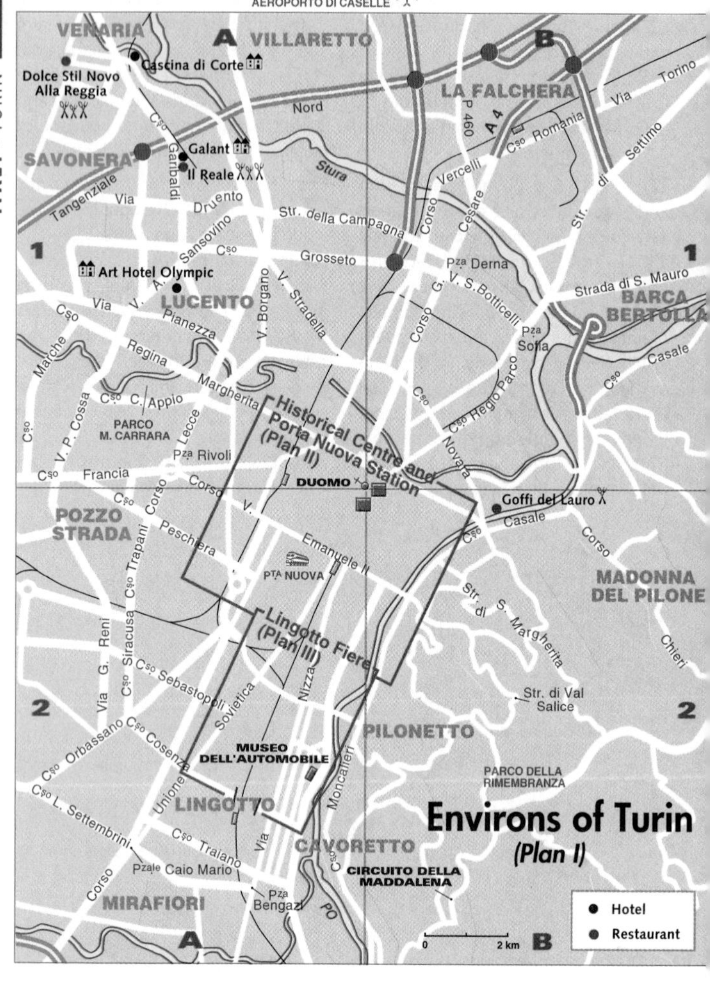

HISTORICAL CENTRE

Plan II

Golden Palace

via dell'Arcivescovado 18 ✉ *10121*
– ✆ 011 5512111 – www.goldenpalace.thi.it **D2**
183 rm – 195/398 € 220/498 € – 12 suites
Rest *Winner* – Carte 45/66 €

♦ Grand Luxury ♦ Design ♦

In the heart of the city, this new luxury hotel has been decorated in gold, silver and bronze after the colours of the Olympic medals. A whole floor is dedicated to the business clientele. A smart restaurant with designer furnishings and an innovative cuisine.

Principi di Piemonte

via Gobetti 15 ✉ *10123 – ✆ 011 55151 – www.atahotels.it* **E2**
81 rm – 150/470 € – 18 suites
Rest – Carte 46/74 €
◆ Luxury ◆ Business ◆ Modern ◆
A stone's throw from the town centre, this historic building from the 30s boasts spacious rooms that are rich in marble. They have been renovated in homage to luxury and comfort in order to create an elegant modern atmosphere. The magnificence is also taken up in the dining room, where no detail has been left to chance, so that this gastronomic stop stays in the memory.

Grand Hotel Sitea

via Carlo Alberto 35 ✉ *10123 – ✆ 011 5170171 – www.sitea.thi.it*
119 rm – 139/250 € 178/330 € – 1 suite **E2**
Rest *Carignano* – *(closed 2 weeks in August)* Carte 55/73 €
◆ Traditional ◆ Palace ◆ Classic ◆
Hospitality, atmosphere, period style furnishings: all this under the sign of a well-considered refined atmosphere in a traditional grand hotel (dating from 1925), renovated recently. This restaurant boasts large windows with views of the surrounding greenery. Mediterranean cuisine and Piedmontese specialities take pride of place here.

Starhotels Majestic

corso Vittorio Emanuele II 54 ✉ *10123 – ✆ 011 539153*
– www.starhotels.com **E2**
159 rm – 109/258 € – 2 suites
Rest *Le Regine* – *(closed Sunday)* Carte 22/45 €
◆ Traditional ◆ Chain hotel ◆ Classic ◆
Room, excellent comfort, elegance, adequate service whether in the welcoming public areas or in the bedrooms of a totally renovated hotel, in a convenient central position. A large dome of coloured glass dominates the beautiful dining room; international cuisine.

Victoria without rest

via Nino Costa 4 ✉ *10123 – ✆ 011 5611909*
– www.hotelvictoria-torino.com **E2**
106 rm – 155/200 € 245/280 €
◆ Traditional ◆ Personalised ◆
Antique furniture, symphonies of colours, four poster beds, an exacting attention to details in the personalised environment of an elegant residence with few rivals for fascination and atmosphere. Egyptian style wellness center.

Atahotel Concord without rest

via Lagrange 47 ✉ *10123 – ✆ 011 5176756 – www.atahotels.it*
139 rm – 125/300 € 150/350 € **E2**
◆ Chain hotel ◆ Traditional ◆ Classic ◆
Very centrally situated, a short distance from Porta Nuova, a comfortable building whose large equipped spaces are ideal for meetings; Well arranged public areas.

Art Hotel Boston

via Massena 70 ✉ *10128 – ✆ 011 500359 – www.arthotelboston.it*
86 rm – 80/250 € 110/350 € **D3**
Rest – Carte 32/55 €
◆ Business ◆ Design ◆
The renovation of this hotel has fully satisfied not only the requirements of comfort but also those of good taste. There is an art collection in the hall and oriental-style ornaments in the newly furnished rooms.

C
D
Piazza della Repubblica
SAN DOMENICO
PZA SAVOIA
Piazza Statuto
Principi d'Acaja
XVIII Dicembre
Porta Susa
Vinzaglio
Re Umberto
Piazza Solferino
Piazzale Duca d'Aosta
City
Galante
Solferino
Vintage 1997
NH Ambasciatori
Taverna delle Ro...
Art Hotel Boston
U
1
2
3
Hotel
Restaurant
0
300 m

Historical Centre and Porta Nuova Station

(Plan II)

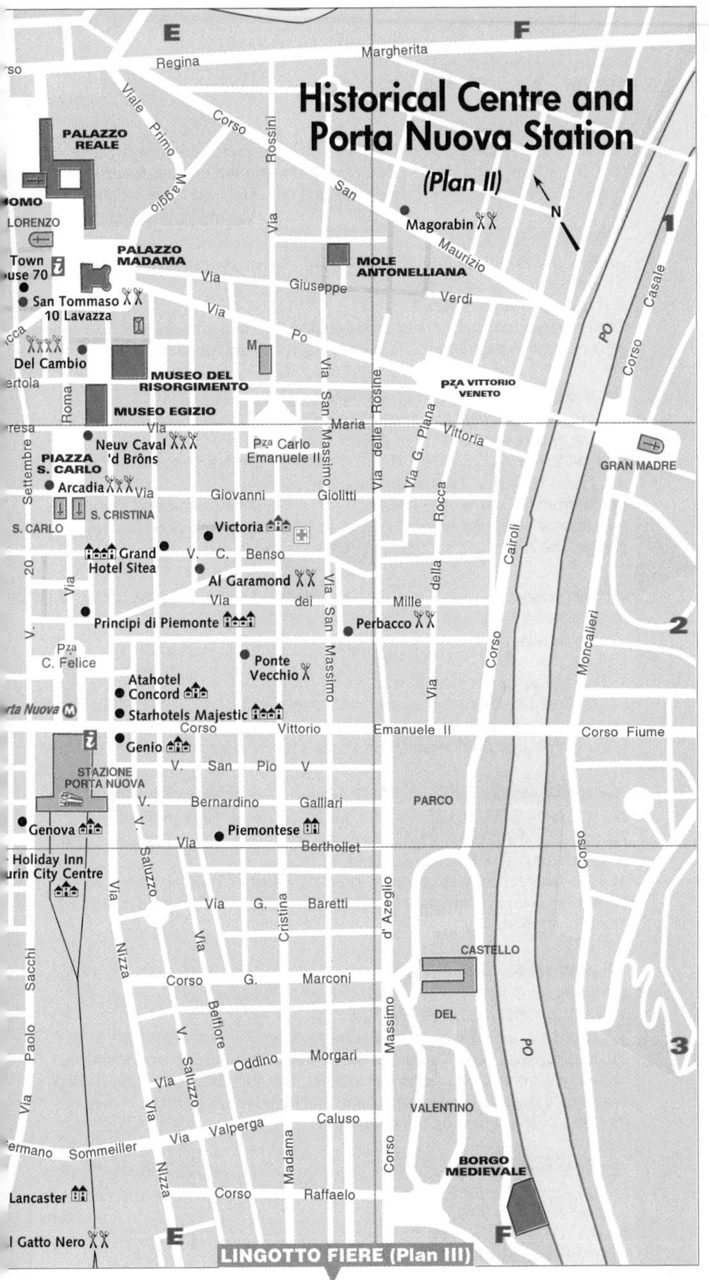

NH Ambasciatori

corso Vittorio Emanuele II 104 ✉ 10121 – ☎ 011 57521 – www.nh-hotels.it **C2**

195 rm – †75/240 € ††95/270 €, ☕ 22 € – 4 suites

Rest *Il Diplomatico* – Carte 42/56 €

♦ Chain hotel ♦ Business ♦ Classic ♦

This hotel is in a recent, square building, in continual renovation, highly suitable for Conferences; comfortable bedrooms in keeping with the standards of the chain. Large windows bathe the elegant and refined dining room in light.

City without rest

via Juvarra 25 ✉ 10122 – ☎ 011 540546 – www.bwhotelcity-to.it

61 rm ☕ – †65/200 € ††89/260 € **C1**

♦ Business ♦ Design ♦

Contemporary, original and highly individual furnishings and in a hotel in a convenient location near Porta Susa station; quiet, well-equipped bedrooms.

Holiday Inn Turin City Centre

via Assietta 3 ✉ 10128 – ☎ 011 5167111 – www.holiday-inn.com/turin-cityctr **E2**

57 rm ☕ – †92/175 € ††118/230 € **Rest** – *(dinner only)* Menu 18/25 €

♦ Chain hotel ♦ Traditional ♦ Modern ♦

Not far from the station, this hotel occupies a 19C palazzo which offers modern guestrooms equipped with all the latest technology. The hotel has its own garage. This restaurant is modern in both tone and layout.

Genio without rest

corso Vittorio Emanuele II 47 ✉ 10125 – ☎ 011 6505771 – www.hotelgenio.it **E2**

128 rm ☕ – †80/140 € ††140/220 €

♦ Traditional ♦ Classic ♦

Housed in a late-19C palazzo which was extended for the Olympics, this hotel features well-maintained guestrooms decorated with individual touches. Artistic flooring in the corridors and rooms adds a touch of elegance to the building.

Genova without rest

via Sacchi 14/b ✉ 10128 – ☎ 011 5629400 – www.albergogenova.it

78 rm ☕ – †70/180 € ††98/260 € **E2**

♦ Traditional ♦ Personalised ♦

At Porta Nuova, luxury atmosphere in an 19th century building where restorations have skilfuuly combined a classical interior with all the modern requirements of comfort.

Piemontese without rest

via Berthollet 21 ✉ 10125 – ☎ 011 6698101 – www.hotelpiemontese.it

39 rm ☕ – †69/160 € ††79/180 € **E2**

♦ Traditional ♦ Personalised ♦

Situated between Porta Nuova and the Po river, this hotel offers colourfully furnished guestrooms with individual touches; the attic-style rooms are particularly attractive with their exposed beams and hydro-massage baths. In fine weather, breakfast is served on the veranda.

Lancaster without rest

corso Filippo Turati 8 ✉ 10128 – ☎ 011 5681982 – www.lancaster.it – closed from 5 to 20 August **E3**

83 rm ☕ – †73/95 € ††100/137 €

♦ Traditional ♦ Personalised ♦

In a fairly central residential district, a luxury hotel with modern comforts and with stylish furnishing in both the public areas and upper floor bedrooms.

Art Hotel Olympic
via Verolengo 19 ✉ 10149 – ✆ 011 39997 – www.arthotelolympic.it
147 rm – 70/250 € 90/350 € **Rest** – Carte 30/51 € *Plan I* **A1**
♦ Business ♦ Design ♦
As the name suggests, the hotel brings together art and sport. Established during the recent winter games, it boasts designer rooms and communal areas adorned with artwork.

Town House 70 without rest
via XX Settembre 70 ✉ 10122 – ✆ 011 19700003 – www.townhouse.it
47 rm – 95/410 € 106/459 € – 1 suite **E1**
♦ Business ♦ Minimalist ♦
This centrally located hotel offers attractive, spacious guestrooms decorated in modern style. Breakfast is served on one large table in the small breakfast room.

Del Cambio
piazza Carignano 2 ✉ 10123 – ✆ 011 543760 – www.thi.it
– closed 3 weeks in August, 1 week in January and Sunday **E1**
Rest – *(booking advisable)* Menu 80 € – Carte 70/104 €
♦ Regional ♦ Luxury ♦ Retro ♦
The regal history of Turin and the spirit of Cavour is still ever present in the rich interiors with 19th Century decorations of this historic building; great traditional cuisine also.

Vintage 1997 (Pierluigi Consonni)
piazza Solferino 16/h ✉ 10121 – ✆ 011 535948 – www.vintage1997.com
– closed from 6 to 31 August, from 1 to 7 January, Saturday lunchtime, Sunday
Rest – Carte 48/72 € **D2**
Spec. Acciughe al verde su patata di Entraque. Tortelli di mozzarella di bufala e melanzane con pomodorini. Costata di scottona al sale grosso e rosmarino.
♦ Italian ♦ Formal ♦
Scarlet fabric, lampshades, and elegant wood-panelling soften the interior of this elegant restaurant. The creative and innovative dishes are inspired by traditional cuisine and made from carefully selected ingredients. The champagne is imported directly from France.

Neuv Caval 'd Brôns
piazza San Carlo 155 ✉ 10123 – ✆ 011 539030
– www.neuvcavaldbrons.it **E2**
Rest – Carte 45/104 €
♦ Fish ♦ Formal ♦
Innovative cuisine from the Piedmont takes pride of place in this elegant restaurant situated under the portico of a 19C palazzo, with an attractive outdoor area overlooking the square. Fish dishes also available.

Arcadia
galleria Subalpina ✉ 10123 – ✆ 011 5613898
– www.ristorantearcadia.com – closed Sunday **E2**
Rest – Carte 36/47 €
♦ Classic ♦ Luxury ♦ Elegant ♦
This impressive restaurant with high vaulted ceilings is housed in the 19C Galleria Subalpina. The menu features meat and fish with an emphasis on regional cuisine. More exotic options are available at the elegant sushi bar.

Al Garamond
via Pomba 14 ✉ 10123 – ✆ 011 8122781 – www.algaramond.it
– closed August, Saturday lunchtime, Sunday **E2**
Rest – Carte 47/75 €
♦ Modern ♦ Formal ♦ Intimate ♦
Bearing the name of a lieutenant in Napoleon's Dragoons, this restaurant offers creative modern cuisine run by young, skilled and enthusiastic management.

XX **San Tommaso 10 Lavazza** A/C VISA MC AE

via San Tommaso 10 ✉ 10122 – ✆ 011 534201 – www.lavazza.it
– closed August and Sunday **E1**

Rest – Carte 38/81 €

♦ Mediterranean ♦ Trendy ♦

Right behind the bar, beauty is the element that characterises every creation. The pleasure of looking out at the view and tempting the palate with Italian cuisine that reinterprets fantasy into delicate and intriguing recipes.

XX **Magorabin** A/C VISA MC AE

corso San Maurizio 61/b ✉ 10124 – ✆ 011 8126808 – www.magorabin.it
– closed Sunday, Monday lunchtime **F1**

Rest – Carte 48/66 €

♦ Modern ♦ Formal ♦

Full of character, the friendly owner-chef at this small restaurant moves from table to table taking orders. Creative, imaginative cuisine and a smart, modern decor – not to be missed!

XX **Al Gatto Nero** A/C VISA MC AE

corso Filippo Turati 14 ✉ 10128 – ✆ 011 590414 – www.gattonero.it
– closed 5 August-3 September and Sunday **E3**

Rest – Carte 48/64 €

♦ Fish ♦ Retro ♦

This restaurant has built up a reputation for fine dining, with a focus on Piedmontese and Tuscan dishes, as well as Mediterranean cuisine. Excellent wine list offering a selection of around 1 000 different wines.

XX **Galante** A/C VISA MC AE

corso Palestro 15 ✉ 10122 – ✆ 011532163 – www.ristorantegalante.it
– closed 23 August-7 September, Saturday lunch, Sunday **E1**

Rest – Carte 34/50 €

♦ Fish ♦ Formal ♦

Soft shades and padded seating in the small, well-cared for elegant hotel with neo classical setting; on the menu with its wide selection there are both meat and fish dishes.

XX **Perbacco** A/C VISA MC AE

via Mazzini 31 ✉ 10123 – ✆ 011 882110 – www.ristoranteperbacco.torino.it
– closed August and Sunday **E2**

Rest – *(dinner only)* Menu 32 €

♦ Regional ♦ Formal ♦

A pleasant, centrally located restaurant only open in the evenings, with a modern fairly elegant overtones; eacg guest " creates " his own menu from 4 courses chosen from the menu ; Seasonal cuisine from Piedmont.

XX **Solferino** A/C VISA MC AE

piazza Solferino 3 ✉ 10121 – ✆ 011 535851 – www.ristorantesolferino.com
– closed Saturday lunch, Sunday **D2**

Rest – Carte 33/49 €

♦ Regional ♦ Family ♦ Formal ♦

In a beautiful Turin square, competently managed for almost 30 years you will find a classic restaurant, renowned and popular - even at lunchtime; traditional cuisine.

X **Ponte Vecchio** A/C VISA MC AE

via San Francesco da Paola 41 ✉ 10123 – ✆ 011 835100
– www.ristorantino.net
– closed August, Monday, Tuesday lunchtime **E2**

Rest – Carte 30/53 €

♦ Regional ♦ Family ♦

Strong family management, unchanged since 1954, for a classic centrally located establishment furnished in early 20th century style; cuisine offers both regional and national dishes.

Taverna delle Rose

via Massena 24 ✉ 10128 – ☎ 011 538345
– closed August, Saturday lunchtime, Sunday **D3**
Rest – Carte 26/44 €
◆ Regional ◆ Friendly ◆
Typical regional cuisine served in a charming, informal atmosphere. The dining room is particularly romantic in the evening, with its exposed brickwork and soft lighting.

Goffi del Lauro

corso Casale 117 ✉ 10132 – ☎ 011 8190619 – www.ristorantegoffi.it
– closed 15 September-5 October **B2**
Rest – *(dinner only from Monday to Thursday)* Carte 28/51 €
◆ Piedmontese specialities ◆ Friendly ◆ Family ◆
This typical restaurant is situated in the city of the famous and mysterious Turin Shroud. It is traditional in both decor and cuisine. The menu features regional specialities and good value for money.

LINGOTTO FIERE *Plan III*

Le Meridien Turin Art+Tech

via Nizza 230 ✉ 10126 – ☎ 011 6642000
– www.lemeridien.com – closed August and December **H2**
139 rm – 139/410 € – 1 suite **Rest** – Carte 37/66 €
◆ Palace ◆ Design ◆
A panoramic lift takes guests from the small lobby to the top floor leading to the balcony that gives access to the rooms. The effect of this innovative layout is surprising. This restaurant combines elegance with a pleasantly informal atmosphere; the decor is in cherry wood.

Le Meridien Lingotto

via Nizza 262 ✉ 10126 – ☎ 011 6642000 – www.lemeridien.com
226 rm – 110/270 € 125/270 € – 14 suites **H2**
Rest *Torpedo* – *☎ 011 6642714* – Carte 37/66 €
◆ Palace ◆ Design ◆
This modern hotel, inside the Lingotto, one of the most successful examples of industrial architecture has a tropical garden; luxurious bedrooms with design pieces. Comfortable armchairs at the tables of the bright and elegant restaurant; high quality cuisine.

AC Torino

via Bisalta 11 ✉ 10126 – ☎ 011 6395091 – www.ac-hotels.com
89 rm – 100/345 € – 6 suites **H2**
Rest – *(residents only)* Carte 39/70 €
◆ Chain hotel ◆ Luxury ◆ Minimalist ◆
Once a pasta factory, this early 20th century building in the Lingotto area is now an up-to-date hotel that offers ideal comfort and completely modern facilities.

Giotto without rest

via Giotto 27 ✉ 10126 – ☎ 011 6637172 – www.hotelgiottotorino.it
50 rm – 60/134 € 78/162 € **H1**
◆ Traditional ◆ Modern ◆
Situated on the outskirts, not far from Lingotto and Valentino, a modern hotel with refurbished interior; bedrooms with all comforts including bath or hydro-massage baths or shower.

Cairo without rest

via La Loggia 6 ✉ 10134 – ☎ 011 3171555 – www.hotelcairo.it
59 rm – 60/150 € 80/180 € **G2**
◆ Business ◆ Classic ◆
On the outskirts of town, with parking possibilities, a family-run hotel, with welcoming interiors; the new bedrooms in the annex offer superior comfort.

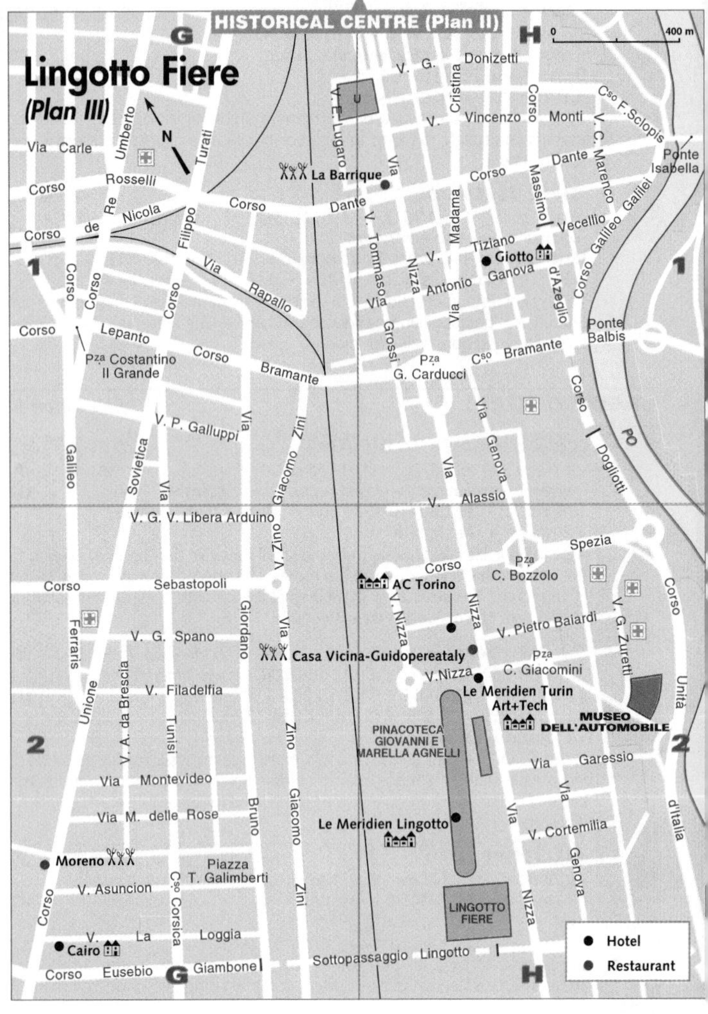

Casa Vicina-Guidopereataly (Claudio Vicina Mazzaretto)

via Nizza 224 ✉ 10126 – ✆ 011 19506840
– www.casavicina.it
– closed 10 August - 8 September, during Christmas period, Sunday evening, Monday
Rest – Menu 45 (lunch)/85 € – Carte 57/83 € **H2**
Spec. Tonno di coniglio grigio di Carmagnola con giardiniera di verdure in agrodolce. Agnolotti pizzicati a mano al sugo d'arrosto. Rognone à la coque con vellutata di senape e aglio in camicia.
♦ Regional ♦ Minimalist ♦
This restaurant in Eattaly, the first Italian supermarket to sell specialist food products, is minimalist in style and serves a wide range of creative cuisine.

XXX ✿

La Barrique (Stefano Gallo)

corso Dante 53 ✉ 10126 – ✆ 011 657900 – www.labarriqueristorante.it
– closed Sunday, Monday midday **H1**
Rest – Menu 65/85 € – Carte 59/81 €
Spec. Ravioli di patate affumicate con caviale di salmone e limone. Anatra muta nostrana ai profumi di bosco. Variazione al cioccolato.
♦ Modern ♦ Formal ♦
Friendly, family management in this restaurant that blends classical regional dishes, fresh pastas, fish, meat and the inevitable triumph of chocolate, for more creative fare.

XXX

Moreno

corso Unione Sovietica 244 ✉ 10134 – ✆ 011 3179191
– www.morenogroup.net
– closed August and Monday midday **G2**
Rest – Carte 60/70 €
♦ Modern ♦ Formal ♦
From the suburban road an unexpected lane leads into the greenery to an elegant and well-maintained establishment; pleasantly situated tables near to the glass doors looking out over the garden; traditional cuisine.

AT CASELLE TORINESE

Jet Hotel

via Della Zecca 9 – ✆ 0119913733 – www.jet-hotel.com
79 rm – †86/100 € ††95/104 €
Rest *Antica Zecca* – *✆ 0119961403 (closed Monday)* Carte 33/46 €
♦ Business ♦ Traditional ♦ Classic ♦
A beautiful 16C renovated building houses a hotel conveniently located near the airport; an elegant atmosphere, good standard of service, well-equipped bedrooms. The restaurant serves inventive dishes inspired by regional cuisine, as well as meats cooked over a grill in the dining room.

AT RIVOLI

XXXX ✿✿

Combal.zero (Davide Scabin)

piazza Mafalda di Savoia – ✆ 011 9565225 – www.combal.org
– closed from 3 to 26 August, 24 December-7 January, Sunday, Monday
Rest – *(dinner only)* Carte 115/145 €
Spec. Insalata di baccalà e pomodori. Risotto mantecato al foie gras d'oca e carciofi. Maialino caramellato al caffè con melanzana al pecorino romano.
♦ Innovative ♦ Design ♦
The modern design of this restaurant echoes that of the nearby contemporary art museum. The cuisine is eclectic in style, featuring traditional dishes from the Piedmont, alongside more original fare.

AT VENARIA REALE *Plan I*

Galant without rest

corso Garibaldi 155 – ✆ 011 4551021 – www.hotelgalant.it **A1**
39 rm – †98/146 € ††127/200 €
♦ Family ♦ Classic ♦
A modern-style structure, ideal for business clientele. Pleasant and rational common areas, comfortable bedrooms with large writing desks. There is also a meeting room.

Cascina di Corte

via Amedeo di Castellamonte 2 – ✆ 011 4593278 – www.cascinadicorte.it – closed August **A1**

10 rm – †90/110 € ††130/190 € – 2 suites **Rest** – Carte 38/60 €

◆ Historic ◆ Rustic ◆

Not far from the famous palace, this 19C farmhouse with adjoining ice-cream parlour has a simple architectural style that is typical of the region. A rustic interior with exposed brickwork in the bedrooms goes hand-in-hand with modern, comfortable furnishings and facilities.

Dolce Stil Novo alla Reggia (Alfredo Russo)

piazza della Repubblica 4 – ✆ 011 4992343 – www.dolcestilnovo.com – closed 2 weeks in August, 2 weeks in January, Sunday dinner, Monday, Tuesday midday **A1**

Rest – *(number of covers limited, pre-book)* Carte 77/114 €

Spec. Coniglio marinato in carpione di moscato. Spaghetti con bottarga di cozze ed emulsione di rucola. Crema morbida di menta di Pancalieri con menta, menta e menta.

◆ Innovative ◆ Formal ◆

Located inside the Torrione del Garove, this restaurant boasts a pretty terrace overlooking the Reggia di Venaria garden. There are two ample dining rooms with spacious tables, which are contrasted by minimalist furnishings. Sample the welcoming local cuisine with several seafood specialities.

Il Reale

corso Garibaldi 153 – ✆ 011 4530413 – www.ilreale.it – closed from 10 to 25 August **A1**

Rest – Menu 24/40 € – Carte 30/44 €

◆ Regional ◆ Formal ◆

This new restaurant opened in 2000 after in-depth renovation, offering modern luxurious elegance, enthusiastic management and cuisine with creative twists.

LUXEMBOURG
LËTZEBUERG

PROFILE

→ **Area:**
2 586 km² (998 sq mi).

→ **Population:**
502 066 inhabitants (est. 2009) nearly 62% nationals, 38% resident foreigners (mostly Belgian, French, German, Italian and Portuguese). Density = 181 per km².

→ **Capital:**
Luxembourg (conurbation 147 017 inhabitants).

→ **Currency:**
Euro (€); rate of exchange: € 1 = US$ 1.37 (Dec. 2010).

→ **Government:**
Constitutional parliamentary monarchy (since 1868). Member of European Union since 1957 (one of the 6 founding countries).

→ **Languages:**
The official language is Lëtzebuergesch, a variant of German, similar to the Frankish dialect of the Moselle valley; High German is used for general purposes and is the first language for teaching; French is the literary and administrative language.

→ **Specific public holidays:**
Carnival (Late February-March); National Day (23 June); Luxembourg City Kermesse (early September, applies to Luxembourg City only); St. Stephen's Day (26 December).

→ **Local Time:**
GMT + 1 hour in winter and GMT + 2 hours in summer.

→ **Climate:**
Temperate continental with cold winters and mild summers (Luxembourg: January: 1°C, July: 17°C).

→ **International dialling Code:**
00 352 followed by the local number of 5 or 6 or (exceptionally) 8 figures. Online telephone directory: www.editus.lu

→ **Emergency numbers:**
Police : ✆ **113** ; Medical Assistance : ✆ **112**.

→ **Electricity:**
220 volts AC, 50Hz; 2-pin round-shaped continental plugs.

→ **Formalities**
Travellers from the European Union (EU), Switzerland, Iceland and the main countries of North and South America need a national identity card or passport (America: passport required) to visit the Grand Duchy of Luxembourg for less than three months (tourism or business purpose). For visitors from other countries a visa may be required, in addition to a passport, especially for those wishing to stay for longer than three months. We advise you to check with your embassy before travelling.

LUXEMBOURG

LËTZEBUERG

Population: 507 066 – Altitude: 300m

ymond Thill/Fotolia.com

Luxembourg may be small but it's perfectly formed. And perfectly situated. It stands high above two rivers on a sandstone bluff, looking composedly back on a one thousand year history that's been anything but composed. Its commanding position over sheer gorges may be a boon to modern day visitors, but down the centuries that very setting of enviable altitude has rendered it the subject of conquest on many occasions.

Its eye-catching geography makes it a city of distinctive districts, linked by spectacular bridges spanning lush green valleys. The city squares boast elegant façades painted in pastel colours, ideally suited as the backdrop to café culture on a warm afternoon. UNESCO liked what they saw, and in 1994 conferred World Heritage Status on the old town. It may not be instantly apparent, but Luxembourg is also a hub of activity for the European Union, with new buildings and offices mushrooming in recent years – thankfully, some way from the old centre. Most visitors head in the opposite direction for wonderful walks in the valleys and across the fine bridges, finding this the best way to appreciate the capital's uniquely charming aura.

LIVING THE CITY

The absolute heart of the city is the **old town**, unmistakable at the top of its surrounding valleys, its most prominent landmark the **cathedral** spires. Winding its way deep below to the south west is the river **Pétrusse,** which has its confluence with the river **Alzette** in the south east. Directly to the south of the old town is the rather sleazy **railway station** quarter, while down at river level to the east is the altogether more attractive **Grund** district, whose northerly neighbours are **Clausen** and **Pfaffenthal**. Up in the north east, connected by the grand sounding **Pont Grand-Duchesse Charlotte**, is the EU institution quarter of **Kirchberg Plateau**.

PRACTICAL INFORMATION

ARRIVAL-DEPARTURE

Luxembourg-Findel Airport is 6km from the city centre ; a taxi should cost about €25. Alternatively, take city bus Number 16 which runs every 20min and takes 25min.

TRANSPORT

There's a good bus service in Luxembourg City, but no metro or tram. Buses run from 5am to 10pm each day, and there's an additional late night service on Fridays and Saturdays only. The most convenient bus stations for visitors are at the exit of Gare Centrale and on Place Hamilius in the old town. The fare system (valid for trains too) is simple enough: for trips of 10km or less you buy a 'short' ticket; for an unlimited day ticket (valid till 8am the next day) you buy a Billet Reseau.

You can also opt for the Luxembourg Card. This is valid for one, two or three days and, apart from giving you unlimited use of public transport, also offers free admission to lots of attractions, not just in the city but in other parts of the country too. Available from tourist offices, it's valid throughout the summer. In winter, the Stater Museeskaart offers three days of free admission to important sights in Luxembourg City.

EXPLORING LUXEMBOURG CITY

It's not every city that can boast 'Europe's Most Beautiful Balcony' in its blurb. But Luxembourg can. Along the stunning pedestrian promenade called **Chemin de la Corniche** there are scintillating views over the sheer-sided gorges that give this elegantly compact city a natural aesthetic advantage over so many others. Luxembourg City has taken a battering over the centuries. It's been taken by the Burgundians, Spanish, French, Austrians and Prussians; the stately old defensive walls that remain around the edges of the centre add an extra layer of historic charm to the place.

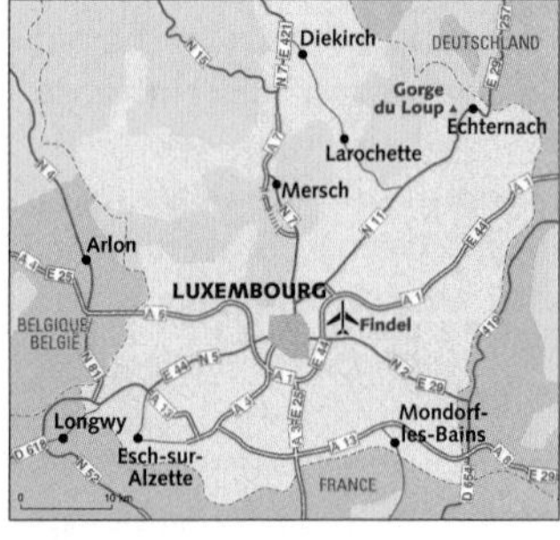

→ TAKING UP D'ARMES

The old town, nestled above the gorges, is a true delight. Its narrow streets are home to arty residents, while quirky shops, traditional cafés and fine restaurants enhance the general feel of a city contented in its skin. At the centre is the slightly formal Place Guillaume II, where you'll find the town hall. Most people, though, make a beeline for the **Place d'Armes**, the 'Parlour of the City', lined with sunny pavement terraces in the summer. The feeling of informality is enhanced when you stroll a little way east and come across the **Ducal Grand Palace**. No pomp or circumstance here, despite the fact that Louis XIV and Napoleon called in. Nowadays, with the royals having left some time ago, the Moorish-style palace, built by the Spanish in 1570, is used for functions on the inside, and as a tourist spot for photos on the outside. You're not bothered by traffic or blaring horns, and there's just a single guard on duty. All very peaceful. If you *are* searching out more life, the area right behind the Ducal Palace has several restaurants.

➜ HISTORY LESSON

There's a great museum here too, just round the corner from the palace. It's the **National Museum of History and Art**, and its show-stopping white contours come as quite a surprise after the Ducal Grand Palace. It's a state-of-the-art affair, with a glass atrium and exhibits housed over several levels. They range from the 13C to the present day and highlights include a superb Roman mosaic, absorbing works by Luxembourg's Expressionist artist Joseph Kutter, paintings by Cézanne, Picasso and Magritte, and a watercolour of the city by Turner. South from here, you can indulge a comprehensive primer on the life and times of this underestimated city at the impressive **Luxembourg City History Museum**, which, over six floors, does pretty much what it says on the label.

Luxembourg City has raised itself above the museum parapet and shone a light into the 21C with its **Museum of Modern Art,** opened in 2006. Located in the Kirchberg district, it's a stunning white concrete-and-glass palace and home to an eclectic mix of work, including photography, painting, multimedia, fashion, design and graphic arts. Close by, another new building has seen the light of day: the **Luxembourg Philharmonic Hall** is now *the* place to catch a concert in the city. It's not just home to the Philharmonic Orchestra, but also caters to a wide range of styles including jazz and world music. There are three separate concert halls, and you can squeeze in any number from 120 to 1,500.

➜ ON THE CASE

From the modern to the extremely ancient – at the end of the wonderful Chemin de la Corniche you arrive at the cliff on which the very first castle was built in 963. It's called **The Bock**, and though its mighty fort and fortifications are now no more than ruins, that's not the case with the **Casemates**. This is a labyrinth of 17C-18C underground defences carved out beneath the Bock by the Spaniards. These rock thoroughfares have known a number of uses down the years. They've seen action as slaughterhouses and bakeries and housed garrisons of soldiers. Many of the locals used them as bomb shelters during the two world wars. Further west, there are more casemates at Pétrusse, but these are slightly less accessible than those at Bock.

➜ A GRUND LIFE

Another little world exists below the Bock, and it's called the Grund, or the lower town. It's an attractive area, where the cluster of cafés, bars and restaurants sits easily alongside the meandering Alzette. Its characterful charm is enhanced by clumps of ruins offset by groups of terrace houses, once home to artisans who needed the river waters to assist them in their crafts. There's an easy way to get down here: just take the elevator from the **Plateau du St Esprit**, a hilltop bluff that itself offers stunning views over the valleys and the Grund. Although it pretty much exists in its very own green heaven, Luxembourg has fashioned itself a lovely **park,** and very moreish it is too. It's down in the valley on the same level as the Grund, but west of it in the vicinity of the Pétrusse. Get down to it from the Old Bridge, or Viaduc and, if you're here in the spring, take in the stunning display of magnolias.

CALENDAR HIGHLIGHTS

For a small place, Luxembourg packs a big festive punch. From the end of November until early January, the Winter Lights Festival uses Christmas as the excuse to let rip with street art, theatre, concerts and fireworks. Spring is celebrated with the Printemps Festival, which lasts from March until June. At concert venues throughout the city, internationally acclaimed world music and jazz musicians hold centre stage. The spotlight moves to the city's great outdoors in May with the running of the Luxembourg Marathon. This is a marathon with a difference, held in the evening and to the accompaniment of revellers soaking up the atmosphere at mini festivals in the narrow streets of the old town. Locals keep the evening of 22 June clear in their diaries: this is the eve before National Day, when fireworks are set off from the bridge over the Pétrusse Valley, and there's much partying with music and dancing on Place d'Armes and Place Guillaume II. One of Europe's biggest funfairs has evolved over the centuries from an ancient shepherd's market – it's called Schueberfouer, and it lasts two weeks from the end of August, when seemingly most of the city comes along to watch the lavish fireworks that finish it all off.

EATING OUT

The taste buds of Luxembourg have been very much influenced by French classical cuisine and the results are there for all to savour, particularly around and about the old town, an area that in the summer becomes one smart open-air terrace. The centre of town is in fact an eclectic place to eat. It runs the gauntlet from fast-style pizzeria (there are lots of Italians in the city), taverns, cafés and brasseries up to expense account restaurants favou-

LUXEMBOURG CITY IN...

→ ONE DAY

Place d'Armes, Ducal Grand Palace, National Museum of History and Art, Chemin de la Corniche

→ TWO DAYS

Leisurely coffee back on Place d'Armes, Luxembourg City History Museum, Bock Casemates, afternoon and evening in the Grund, including a meal in one of its restaurants

→ THREE DAYS

Kirchberg Plateau, Museum of Modern Art, concert at Luxembourg Philharmonic Hall

red by bankers and businessmen. On winter evenings, though, this part of town can be a bit quiet. A good bet for atmosphere, certainly in the darker months, is the Grund, which offers a variety of restaurants with a wide range of prices. It's certainly the area that boasts the most popular cafés and pubs. A few trendy places have sprouted over recent times near the Casemates, and these too are proving to be pretty hot with the younger crowd. On the menus here look out for the local speciality *Judd mat Gaardebounen*, which is a very hearty smoked neck of pork with broad beans. The Grand Duchy produces its own white and sparkling wines on the borders of the Moselle. These didn't have much of a reputation at first, but over the last decade a number of young winemakers have produced some interesting wines. You'll rarely find these abroad, as they're bought locally by business people and smart restaurants. At the end of your meal, a service charge is included in your bill, but if you want to tip, ten per cent is a reasonable amount.

→ NOTRE DAMNED

The city's Notre Dame Cathedral is unmissable, what with its black spires reaching up above the rooftops. And inside it has Luxembourg's most revered icon, The Lady Comforter of the Afflicted. But you won't see the city's greatest church in many 'must-see' lists. That's because the rest of the interior is full of renovations and mismatching styles, creating a none too inspiring mishmash. You're better off heading by on your way to the grand views of the Viaduc.

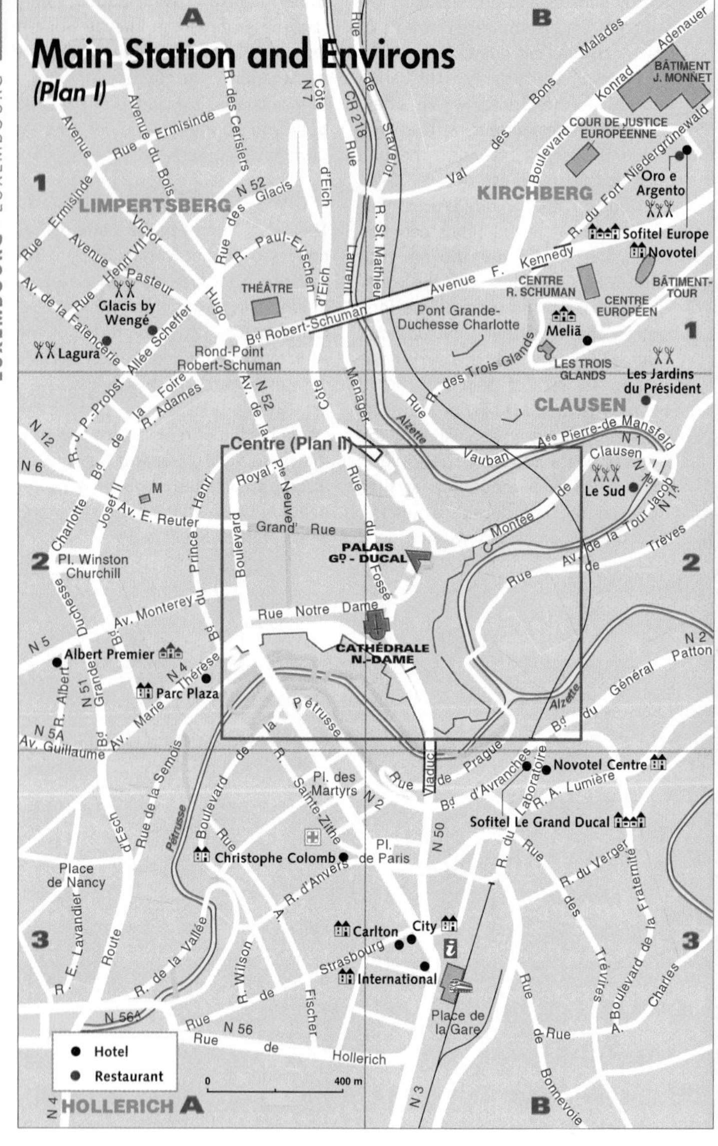
Main Station and Environs
(Plan I)
LIMPERTSBERG
KIRCHBERG
CLAUSEN
HOLLERICH
BÂTIMENT J. MONNET
COUR DE JUSTICE EUROPÉENNE
CENTRE R. SCHUMAN
CENTRE EUROPÉEN
BÂTIMENT-TOUR
THÉÂTRE
Pont Grande-Duchesse Charlotte
Rond-Point Robert-Schuman
LES TROIS GLANDS
Centre (Plan II)
PALAIS Gd - DUCAL
CATHÉDRALE N.-DAME
Pl. Winston Churchill
Pl. des Martyrs
Pl. de Paris
Place de Nancy
Place de la Gare
Viaduc
Oro e Argento
Sofitel Europe
Novotel
Meliã
Les Jardins du Président
Le Sud
Glacis by Wengé
Lagura
Albert Premier
Parc Plaza
Novotel Centre
Sofitel Le Grand Ducal
Christophe Colomb
Carlton
City
International
Hotel
Restaurant
0
400 m

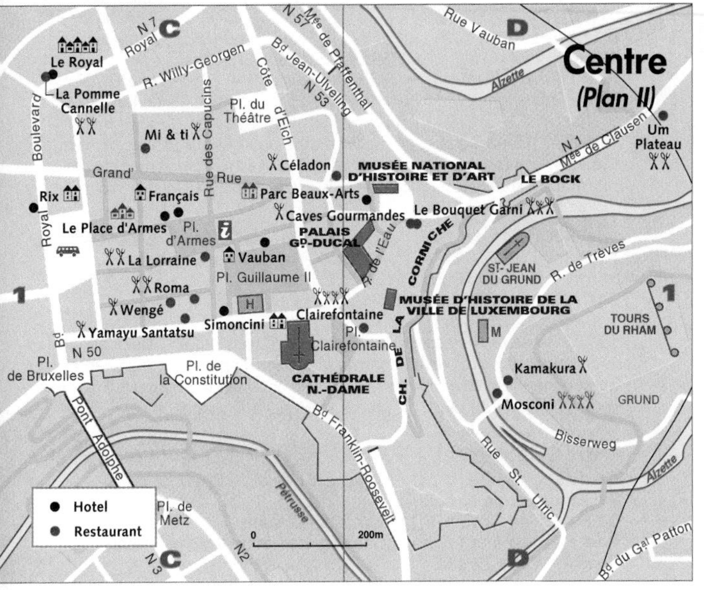

CENTRE

Plan II

Le Royal

bd Royal 12 ✉ 2449 – ✆ 241 61 61
– www.leroyalluxembourg.com **C1**
190 rm – 🚹390/530 € 🚹🚹390/530 €, ☕ 29 € – 20 suites
Rest *La Pomme Cannelle* – see below
Rest *Le Jardin* – *✆ 241 61 67 37* – Menu 35 € (lunch), 40/58 € bi – Carte 46/85 €
♦ Palace ♦ Grand Luxury ♦ Personalised ♦
A modern, luxury hotel with extremely comfortable bedrooms in the main building. The Royal Club wing is home to several types of suites. Spa, piano bar and a high level of service. The Le Jardin restaurant serves classic brasserie-style dishes. Lunch buffet every Sunday.

Sofitel Le Grand Ducal

bd d'Avranches 40 ✉ 1160 – ✆ 24 87 71
– www.sofitel.com *Plan I* **B3**
115 rm – 🚹115/315 € 🚹🚹115/315 €, ☕ 27 € – 2 suites
Rest *Top Floor* – *✆ 24 87 73 10 (closed Saturday lunch and Sunday) (open until 11 pm)* Menu 45 € (lunch) – Carte 59/79 €
♦ Chain hotel ♦ Business ♦ Modern ♦
Luxury, comfort and a designer decor are the hallmarks of this new hotel. Half of the guestrooms enjoy views of the city. Good hotel cuisine is on offer in this fashionable restaurant perched on the top floor, with picture windows overlooking the valley and the old town. Lounge-bar next door.

Le Place d'Armes

pl. d'Armes 18 ✉ 1136 – ✆ 27 47 37 – www.hotel-leplacedarmes.com
17 rm – †350/595 € ††350/595 €, ☕ 26 € – 11 suites **C1**
Rest *La Cristallerie* – Menu 45 € (lunch), 55/110 € bi – Carte 63/97 €
Rest *Plëss* – *(open until 11 pm)* Menu 26 € (lunch) – Carte 40/60 €
♦ Historic ♦ Grand Luxury ♦ Personalised ♦
This quiet 18C town house is a haven on the busiest square in the city centre. Extremely comfortable, elegant rooms. Art Nouveau refinement and classic cuisine at the first-floor restaurant. The brasserie is simpler but very pleasant.

Albert Premier

r. Albert Ier 2a ✉ 1117 – ✆ 442 44 21 – www.albertpremier.lu
38 rm – †195/390 € ††195/390 €, ☕ 18 € *Plan I* **A2**
Rest – Menu 38 € bi (lunch), 35/75 € – Carte 46/85 €
♦ Luxury ♦ Modern ♦
This old house on the edge of town is endowed with English-style public areas and lounges, as well as cosy, traditional bedrooms. Impressive designer-inspired guestrooms in the new wing. The new restaurant offers marine treats. Enjoy in a contemporary decor or on the pleasant terrace if the weather is fine.

Parc Belair

av. du X Septembre 111 (by N5) ✉ 2551 Belair – ✆ 442 32 31 – www.goeres-group.com
52 rm ☕ – †129/390 € ††153/415 € – 1 suite
Rest – *(closed lunch Saturday, Sunday and bank holidays)* Menu 13 € (lunch) – Carte 22/48 €
♦ Luxury ♦ Personalised ♦
A modern building offering comfortable guestrooms and junior suites, some with a themed decor. Quieter rooms with more attractive park views to the rear. Pleasant lounge bar. This bistro has a menu that focuses on traditional cuisine.

Parc Beaux-Arts without rest

r. Sigefroi 1 ✉ 2536 – ✆ 26 86 76 – www.goeres-group.com
10 rm ☕ – †155/445 € ††170/470 € **D1**
♦ Luxury ♦ Stylish ♦
A well-restored series of old houses adjoining the Musée d'Histoire et d'Art. Charming, neo-retro style public areas and suites. Good breakfast.

Novotel Centre

r. Laboratoire 35 ✉ 1911 – ✆ 24 87 81 *Plan I* **B3**
150 rm – †85/270 € ††85/270 €, ☕ 20 €
Rest – *(closed lunch Saturday and Sunday) (open until midnight)* Menu 28 € bi (lunch) – Carte 35/51 €
♦ Chain hotel ♦ Business ♦ Functional ♦
Opened in May 2007, this chain hotel stands midway between the railway station and the old town. Modern façade, designer-styled public areas, functional and contemporary guestrooms, as well as a choice of meeting rooms. Contemporary dining in this restaurant with its fashionable decor of claret, black and white.

Rix without rest

bd Royal 20 ✉ 2449 – ✆ 47 16 66 – www.hotelrix.lu – Closed 6-20 August and 1-8 January **C1**
21 rm ☕ – †110/160 € ††140/180 €
♦ Family ♦ Functional ♦
A family-run hotel set back from a busy road. Somewhat sober guestrooms furnished in a variety of styles. Attractive, traditionally decorated breakfast room. Free private parking for guests.

Parc Plaza

av. Marie-Thérèse 5 ✉ 2132 – ✆ 456 14 11
– www.goeres-group.com *Plan I* **A2**
89 rm – 105/250 € 125/270 €
Rest – Menu 13 € (lunch)/20 €
◆ Business ◆ Classical ◆
A modern complex divided into three sections: the Parc Plaza, with a reception area and close to 90 bedrooms, the Parc Belle-Vue, with some 60 bedroom, and the wing set aside for dining and meetings. Traditional cuisine served in the tavern-style interior or on the outdoor terrace.

Parc Belle-Vue

58 rm – 155/185 € 173/203 €
◆ Business ◆ Functional ◆
Rooms offering simpler comfort than next door.

Simoncini without rest

r. Notre-Dame 6 ✉ 2240 – ✆ 22 28 44 – www.hotelsimoncini.lu
33 rm – 110/150 € 120/180 € – 2 suites **C1**
◆ Business ◆ Minimalist ◆
This new hotel combines comfort, minimalist modernism and an arty atmosphere. Compact guestrooms, with those on the upper floors generally quieter. Underground public car park nearby.

Français

pl. d'Armes 14 ✉ 1136 – ✆ 47 45 34 – www.hotelfrancais.lu
22 rm – 99/120 € 125/140 € **C1**
Rest – *(open until 11 pm)* Menu 12 € (lunch), 22/35 €
– Carte 32/62 €
◆ Family ◆ Functional ◆
Run by the same family since 1970, this hotel overlooks the city's liveliest square. Works of art on display throughout. Superbly maintained guestrooms. A tavern-style restaurant serving classic traditional cuisine.

Vauban

pl. Guillaume II 10 ✉ 1648 – ✆ 22 04 93
– www.hotelvauban.lu **C1**
17 rm – 95/160 € 120/160 €
Rest – *(closed Sunday and Monday) (open until 11 pm)* Menu 24/45 €
– Carte 30/39 €
◆ Inn ◆ Functional ◆
This small hotel opposite the town hall overlooks a huge, lively square. It offers immaculate guestrooms, decked out in matching fabrics and parquet flooring. A restaurant offering specialities from Lebanon and Azerbaijan. Summer terrace.

Clairefontaine (Arnaud Magnier)

pl. de Clairefontaine 9 ✉ 1341 – ✆ 46 22 11
– www.restaurantclairefontaine.lu
– Closed 1 week at Easter, last 2 weeks August-first week September, 1 week Christmas-New Year, first week January, bank holidays, Saturday and Sunday
Rest – Menu 67 €, 67/115 € bi – Carte 62/109 € **D1**
Spec. Carpaccio et tartare de Saint-Jacques, céleri à la truffe (October-April). Poularde de Bresse à la truffe cuite en vessie, sauce Albufera. Variations autour du chocolat.
◆ Innovative ◆ Elegant ◆
This attractive restaurant with a terrace stands on an elegant square. It has a traditional decor with old wooden panelling and contemporary furnishings. Creative, modern cuisine and astute wine pairings.

XXXX ✿✿

Mosconi (Ilario Mosconi)

r. Münster 13 ✉ 2160 – ✆ 54 69 94 – www.mosconi.lu
– Closed 1 week at Easter, last 3 weeks August, 24 December-early January, bank holidays, Saturday lunch, Sunday and Monday **D1**
Rest – Menu 44 € (lunch), 72/120 € – Carte 78/122 €
Spec. Pâté de foies de poulet, crème de truffes blanches, polenta et câpres caramélisées. Risotto aux truffes blanches (October-December). Porcelet de lait, tortino de navet pasticciato et rettich.
♦ Italian ♦ Cosy ♦
This old manor house is on the banks of the Alzette. Romantic, discreetly luxurious lounge and dining rooms where fine Italian cuisine is served, accompanied by an excellent wine list. Attractive terrace by the water.

XXX ✿

Le Bouquet Garni (Thierry Duhr)

r. Eau 32 ✉ 1449 – ✆ 26 20 06 20 – www.lebouquetgarni.lu
– closed 15-31 August, late December-early January, Sunday and Monday
Rest – Menu 40 € (lunch)/85 € – Carte 75/97 € **D1**
Spec. Homard bleu rôti dans ses sucs, vinaigrette tiède de pomme de terre. Turbot de ligne aux girolles et asperges. Le tout chocolat.
♦ Traditional ♦ Rustic ♦
This restaurant housed in an 18C building is next to the Grand Duke's Palace. It serves refined cuisine in a chic but welcoming setting. Small, wood-decked summer terrace.

XXX

Yves Radelet

av. du X Septembre 44 (by N5) ✉ 2550 Belair – ✆ 22 26 18
– www.yvesradelet.eu
– closed last 2 weeks August, Sunday and Monday
Rest – Menu 28 € (lunch), 48/80 € – Carte 64/76 €
♦ Innovative ♦ Cosy ♦
This restaurant moved to a completely refurbished mansion in 2008. A fusion of traditional and contemporary cuisine by the inventive owner-chef who is an aficionado of molecular cuisine.

XX

La Pomme Cannelle – Hôtel Le Royal

bd Royal 12 ✉ 2449 – ✆ 241 61 67 36
– www.leroyalluxembourg.com
– Closed 1-28 August, 1-9 January, Saturday, Sunday and bank holidays
Rest – Menu 53 € (lunch), 62/87 € – Carte 73/85 € **C1**
♦ Contemporary ♦ Formal ♦ Exotic ♦
In this restaurant's elegant and warm interior, reminiscent of the Indian Empire, noble dishes such as lobster and sweetbreads feature on the menu, flavoured with the occasional hint of spice.

XX

La Lorraine

pl. d'Armes 7 ✉ 1136 – ✆ 47 14 36 – www.lalorraine-restaurant.lu
Rest – Menu 26 € (lunch)/34 € – Carte 40/68 € **C1**
♦ Seafood ♦ Trendy ♦
A gastronomic institution on Place d'Armes. Fish and seafood take pride of place, although local cuisine does feature on the menu. Gastro-chic ambience, with subtle lighting and a smart lounge atmosphere in the evening. Excellent wine cellar.

XX

Roma

r. Louvigny 5 ✉ 1946 – ✆ 22 36 92 – www.roma.lu
– Closed Sunday dinner and Monday **C1**
Rest – Carte 45/62 €
♦ Italian ♦ Friendly ♦
One of the doyens of Luxembourg's 'ristoranti'. Relaxed atmosphere and attractive furnishings. Traditional and contemporary à la carte choices, as well as an excellent selection of Italian wines.

Wengé

r. Louvigny 15 (1st floor) ✉ 1946 – ☏ 26 20 10 58
– www.wenge.lu
– Closed Sunday **C1**
Rest – Menu 30 €
♦ Contemporary ♦ Fashionable ♦
This restaurant above a delicatessen has a zen-and designer-inspired mezzanine with wenge wood panelling on the walls. A pleasant setting in which to enjoy contemporary cuisine.

Céladon

r. Nord 1 ✉ 2229 – ☏ 47 49 34 – www.thai.lu
– Closed Saturday lunch and Sunday **C1**
Rest – Menu 24 € (lunch), 40/57 € bi – Carte approx. 45 €
♦ Thai ♦ Elegant ♦
This exotic city centre restaurant is named after a precious varnish used by Thai potters. Restrained contemporary decor in the Céladon's dining rooms. Thai cuisine with vegetarian options.

Kamakura

r. Münster 4 ✉ 2160 – ☏ 47 06 04 – www.kamakura.lu
– Closed 2 weeks at Easter, 3 weeks late August, 1-4 January, Saturday lunch and Sunday **D1**
Rest – Menu 13 € (lunch), 29/68 € – Carte 36/65 €
♦ Japanese ♦ Minimalist ♦
This authentic Japanese restaurant with a minimalist, "Zen" atmosphere has been a success in Luxemburg for the last 20 years. Its wagyu-beef and sake have quite a reputation.

Mi & Ti

av. de la Porte-Neuve 8 ✉ 2227 – ☏ 26 26 22 50
– Closed last 3 weeks August, Monday dinner, Tuesday dinner and Sunday
Rest – Menu 17 € (lunch)/36 € – Carte 40/57 € **C1**
♦ Italian ♦ Fashionable ♦
A trendily decorated Italian restaurant occupying the first floor of a modern building. Authentic produce imported directly from Italy. Simplified menu at the downstairs Bottega. Busy street terrace.

Yamayu Santatsu

r. Notre-Dame 26 ✉ 2240 – ☏ 46 12 49
– Closed last week July-first 2 weeks August, late December-early January, Sunday and Monday **C1**
Rest – Menu 15 € (lunch), 30/35 € – Carte approx. 45 €
♦ Japanese ♦ Neighbourhood ♦
A minimalist-style Japanese restaurant with small dining areas upstairs for more intimate dinners. Varied choice of typical dishes, including a set menu. Sushi is freshly prepared behind the counter in the restaurant.

Caves Gourmandes

r. Eau 32 ✉ 1449 – ☏ 46 11 24
– www.caves-gourmandes.lu
– Closed 2 weeks in September, late December-early January and Sunday October-April **D1**
Rest – Menu 20 € (lunch), 35/55 € bi – Carte 40/57 €
♦ Traditional ♦ Neighbourhood ♦ Rustic ♦
The city's former salt cellars are home to this pleasant restaurant. The focus is on unpretentious, traditional local dishes, often served in cast iron dishes to add to the ambience! Summer terrace at the front of the building.

MAIN STATION *Plan I*

International

pl. de la Gare 20 ✉ *1616 – ✆ 48 59 11 – www.hotelinter.lu* **B3**
69 rm – 95/180 € 108/180 € – 1 suite
Rest – *(closed 20 December-2 January, Saturday and Sunday)* Menu 10 € (lunch), 25/38 € – Carte 26/60 €

◆ Family ◆ Classical ◆

This hotel located opposite the railway station is part of a large chain. Guestrooms in both the standard and higher categories are all well maintained. A bright and airy corner restaurant with large bay windows. An extensive menu of substantial traditional dishes with lighter fare available in the Inter-lounge.

City without rest

r. Strasbourg 1 ✉ *2561 – ✆ 29 11 22 – www.cityhotel.lu* **B3**
35 rm – 90/140 € 120/185 €

◆ Business ◆ Family ◆ Functional ◆

This building dating from the inter-war period offers a choice of reasonably spacious guestrooms in varying decor from the 1980s. A limited menu is available in the bar.

Carlton without rest

r. Strasbourg 9 ✉ *2561 – ✆ 29 96 60 – www.carlton.lu* **B3**
48 rm – 110/125 € 120/135 €

◆ Business ◆ Family ◆ Functional ◆

A delightful Art Deco building dating from 1930. Comfortable guestrooms, public areas that recall the Roaring Twenties, plus a retro-style lounge. Friendly staff and excellent service throughout.

Christophe Colomb without rest

r. Anvers 10 ✉ *1130 – ✆ 408 41 41 – www.christophe-colomb.lu*
24 rm – 75/170 € 85/185 € **A3**

◆ Family ◆ Functional ◆

Located just 500m from the station, this small hotel is ideal for rail travellers. Standard, reasonably spacious guestrooms with modern furnishings.

ENVIRONS OF LUXEMBOURG *Plan I*

Sofitel Europe rm,

r. Fort Niedergrünewald 6 (European Centre) ✉ *2015 Kirchberg – ✆ 43 77 61 – www.sofitel.com* **B1**
105 rm – 135/450 € 135/450 €, 25 € – 4 suites
Rest *Oro e Argento* – see below
Rest *Le Stübli* – *(closed July-15 August, Saturday lunch and Sunday) (open until 11 pm)* Menu 25 € (lunch)/31 €

◆ Chain hotel ◆ Business ◆ Stylish ◆

A bold, oval shaped hotel at the heart of the European Institutions district. Central atrium and spacious, extremely comfortable guestrooms. The attentive, friendly service you would expect from this upmarket chain. A typical restaurant serving regional cuisine. A warm atmosphere enhanced by the staff in traditional costume.

Meliã

Park Dräi Eechelen 1 ✉ *1499 Kirchberg – ✆ 27 33 31 – www.melia.com*
161 rm – 85/350 € 85/350 €, 20 € – 1 suite **B1**
Rest *Aqua* – *(closed lunch Saturday and Sunday)* Menu 19 € (lunch)/65 € – Carte approx. 40 €

◆ Business ◆ Design ◆

The first hotel of this Spanish chain in Benelux, located next to the conference centre. Rooms are sober, comfortable and functional. Lovely view over the city. This brasserie has Italian-style cuisine and a bar and terrace giving onto Place de l'Europe. A restrained decor, embellished with splashes of red.

NH

rte de Trèves 1 (Airport) ✉ *1019 – ✆ 34 05 71 – www.nh-hotels.com*
148 rm – 60/275 € 60/275 €, ☕ 21 € – 1 suite
Rest – *(closed lunch Saturday and Sunday) (open until 11 pm)* Menu 15 € bi (lunch)/23 € – Carte 27/50 €
◆ Chain hotel ◆ Business ◆ Modern ◆
A 1970s-style building with comfortable, functional guestrooms which are mainly popular with a business clientele. Shuttle service to Kirchberg. This bright and soberly decorated brasserie serves international cuisine. Summer dining on the terrace.

Novotel

r. Fort Niedergrünewald 6 (European Centre) ✉ *2226 Kirchberg – ✆ 429 84 81 – www.novotel.com* **B1**
260 rm – 105/250 € 105/250 €, ☕ 18 €
Rest – *(open until midnight)* Menu 16 € (lunch), 21/26 € – Carte 28/59 €
◆ Business ◆ Chain hotel ◆ Functional ◆
A neighbour to its larger sister hotel, this hotel run by the same group offers excellent facilities for business meetings and seminars. Recently refurbished guestrooms. Spacious bar and restaurant serving contemporary food.

Le Sud (Christophe Petra)

r. Emile Mousel 2 (in the ancient brasserie Mousel and Clausen, 4th floor) ✉ *2165 Clausen – ✆ 26 47 87 50 – www.le-sud.lu*
– Closed 7-29 August, Saturday lunch, Sunday and Monday **B2**
Rest – *(set menu only)* Menu 69 €
Spec. Cappuccino de pétoncles, cèpes et truffes. Risotto de Saint-pierre, pignons, olives et dentelle de parmesan (March-August). Demi pigeon en croûte, foie gras, chou et truffes.
◆ Mediterranean ◆ Elegant ◆
With dishes like cappuccino of scallops, barigoule d'artichauts du Var and croustillant of cod served with bouillabaisse jus, you may well think you are in the South of France!

Oro e Argento – Hôtel Sofitel Europe

r. Fort Niedergrünewald 6 (European Centre) ✉ *2015 Kirchberg – ✆ 43 77 61 – www.sofitel.com*
– Closed August and Saturday **B1**
Rest – Carte 39/70 €
◆ Italian ◆ Elegant ◆
An attractive Italian restaurant in a luxury hotel. Contemporary cuisine served to a backdrop of plush interior decor with a Venetian touch. Intimate atmosphere and stylish service.

The Last Supper

av. J.F. Kennedy 33 (Ellipse Kirchberg 2) ✉ *1855 Kirchberg – ✆ 27 04 54 – www.thelastsupper.lu*
– Closed Saturday lunch and Sunday
Rest – Menu 23 € (lunch), 49/59 €
◆ Contemporary ◆ Trendy ◆ Brasserie ◆
This fashionable brasserie and lounge-bar serves sushi and other contemporary delicacies. Unusual jigsaw-piece table to the rear. Pleasant terrace.

Les Jardins du President with rm

pl. Ste-Cunégonde 2 ✉ *1367 Clausen – ✆ 260 90 71 – www.jardinspresident.lu*
– Closed 10-17 April, 21 August-4 September and 25 December-10 January
7 rm ☕ – 185/250 € 185/250 € **B2**
Rest – *(closed Saturday lunch and Sunday)* Menu 29 € (lunch) – Carte 44/65 €
◆ Contemporary ◆ Cosy ◆
This restaurant stands in the middle of a verdant garden with water features, ponds, vines, ducks and rabbits. Classic cuisine with a modern twist. A cosy interior and individually furnished guestrooms.

XX

Glacis by Wengé

Allée Scheffer 21 ✉ 2520 Limpertsberg – ✆ 027 47 59 30 – www.wenge.lu
– Closed 15 August-14 September **A1**

Rest – Menu 15 € (lunch), 30/50 € – Carte 41/69 €

♦ Contemporary ♦ Brasserie ♦ Formal ♦

Earthy tones, anglepoise lamps, candles and designer seats lend the place a cosy atmosphere. Unpretentious contemporary food, prepared using quality ingredients.

XX

Lagura

av. de la Faïencerie 18 ✉ 1510 Limpertsberg – ✆ 26 27 67
– www.lagura.lu
– Closed 25-26 December and Saturday lunch **A1**

Rest – Menu 15 € (lunch)/38 € – Carte 41/57 €

♦ Italian ♦ Fashionable ♦

Brown and chocolate tones, comfortable armchairs and a cosy atmosphere provide the backdrop for this attractive Italian restaurant, whose specialities include home-made pastas, a savoury tomato tart and basil sorbet.

X

Um Plateau

Plateau Altmunster 6 ✉ 1123 Clausen – ✆ 26 47 84 26
– www.umplateau.lu
– Closed Sunday *Plan II* **D1**

Rest – Menu 25 € (lunch) – Carte 39/59 €

♦ Contemporary ♦ Trendy ♦

An elegant neo-bistro with designer chairs, pop lighting, warm colours and, for a retro touch, stained-glass windows. Contemporary cuisine: black rice risotto, salmon tartare with fennel…

NETHERLANDS
NEDERLAND

PROFILE

→ **Area:**
41 543 km²
(16 163 sq mi).

→ **Population:**
16 485 787 inhabitants (est. 2009), density = 392 per km².

→ **Capital:**
Amsterdam (755 605 inhabitants); The Hague is the seat of government and Parliament.

→ **Currency:**
Euro (€); rate of exchange: € 1 = US$1.37 (Dec. 2010).

→ **Government:**
Constitutional parliamentary monarchy (since 1815). Member of European Union since 1957 (one of the 6 founding countries).

→ **Language:**
Dutch; many Dutch people also speak English.

→ **Specific public holidays:**
Good Friday (Friday before Easter); Queen's Day Liberation Day (5 May); Boxing Day (26 December).

→ **Local Time:**
GMT + 1hour in winter and GMT + 2 hours in summer.

→ **Climate:**
Temperate maritime with cool winters and mild summers (Amsterdam: January: 2°C, July: 17°C), rainfall evenly distributed throughout the year.

→ **International dialling Code:**
00 31 followed by area code without the initial **0** and then the local number. International Directory enquiries: ✆ **06 0418**.

→ **Emergency:**
Fire Brigade: ✆ **112**; Police, Ambulance, Roadside assistance: ✆ **0900 8418**.

→ **Electricity:**
220 volts AC, 50Hz; 2-pin round-shaped continental plugs.

Formalities
Travellers from the

European Union (EU), Switzerland, Iceland and the main countries of North and South America need a national identity card or passport (America: passport required) to visit the Netherlands for less than three months (tourism or business purpose). For visitors from other countries a visa may be required, in addition to a passport, especially for those wishing to stay for longer than three months. We advise you to check with your embassy before travelling.

AMSTERDAM

AMSTERDAM

Population: 755 605 – Altitude: sea level

ackshot/Fotolia.com

Once visited, never forgotten. That's Amsterdam's great claim to fame. Its endearing horseshoe shape - defined by 17C canals cut to drain land for a growing population – allied to finely detailed gabled houses, has produced a compact city centre of aesthetically splendid symmetry and matchless consistency. Exploring the city on foot or by bike is the real joy here; visitors rarely need to jump on a tram or bus.

Amsterdam, 'the world's biggest small city', displays a host of distinctive characteristics ranging from the red light district to the brown cafés, from the wonderful art galleries to the tree-lined waterways. There's the feel of a northern Venice, but without the hallowed and revered atmosphere. It exists on a human scale, small enough to walk from one end to the other. Those who might moan that it's just *too* small should stroll along to the former derelict docklands on the east side and contemplate the shiny new apartments giving the waterfront a sleek twenty-first century feel. Most people who come here, though, are just happy to cosy up to old Amsterdam's sleepy, relaxed vibe. No European city does snug bars better: this is the place to go for cats kipping on beat-up chairs and candles flickering on wax-encrusted tables…

LIVING THE CITY

Arrive at the **Central station**, at the top end of Amsterdam's centre, and you really do have the city laid out in front of you. How many other famous European destinations can you say that about? You're in the **New Side**, although 'new' in this case refers to the medieval period. Just to your east is the **Old Side,** which began to develop in the 12C as a thriving village of fisher-folk on the River **Amstel**. Keeping these two ancient areas in a vice-like grip and fanning out beneath them in a kind of watery spider web is the **Grachtengordel**, the superb semicircle of three canals lined by elegant gabled houses and connected by pretty bridges: the Western Canal ring includes the lively, bohemian **Jordaan** district. Just beyond the Grachtengordel lies the museum quarter, a tourist must-see, as it features two of the world's most prestigious museums. The lovely **Vondelpark** is here aswell. The most easterly quarter of the city is Plantage, or 'Plantation', a name mirroring its historically green qualities. This area was once parkland, and seventeenth century Amsterdammers would come here to spend leisure time. Nowadays it's elegant and tree lined, but seems strangely undiscovered by many visitors.

PRACTICAL INFORMATION

ARRIVAL-DEPARTURE

Schipol International Airport is 18km southwest of the city and trains run regularly to Amsterdam Central Station, a journey that takes about 20 minutes. A taxi costs around €38 and there are also Airport Shuttles available.

TRANSPORT

To get around Amsterdam – take a hike. Of all Europe's main cities, this is the one most geared to walking, what with its narrow streets and canals. Avoid any thoughts of driving a car here. Word of warning: trams can be pretty silent and can move pretty fast, so look both ways when crossing tram routes. If you venture inadvertently onto a cycle path (there are many), you'll soon hear the frantic ringing of bicycle bells.

The Amsterdam Card entitles the holder to free public transport, free admission to major museums, a canal cruise and discounts in some restaurants. It's valid for 24hr, 48hr, or 72hr, and available from the Tourist Information Office opposite the central station.

Trams and buses run mostly from the central station; the metro has four short lines, mostly used by commuters. Modern white and blue trams are the most popular form of public transport; they operate from 6am on weekdays, finish just after midnight and tickets are available from the Tourist Information office or vending machines. Bus routes mainly complement the tram network.

EXPLORING AMSTERDAM

It's safe to say you won't experience the like of Amsterdam anywhere else in Europe. The city appears so well planned that it's possible to look at it on a map and sense in your head that you've got the measure of it. Most visitors arrive at the Central Railway station and get their bearings from here. Just down the road they will find two veritable old churches steeped in medieval history, a red light district famous throughout the world and a museum devoted to the history of marijuana. Such is the city they've arrived in. Central to all the action is **Dam Square** – simply 'The Dam' to locals – built on the very spot where the city's roots lie. Now somewhat faded, it nevertheless boasts the glorious Nieuwe Kerk and the Classical seventeenth century Koninklijk Paleis, once the city's town hall. The Dam's size makes it a great place for markets and all shade of al fresco events. As a complete contrast to the area's seedier elements, and not far west of the Red Light district, is the beguiling Begijnhof, an enchanting sanctuary of gabled houses (including Amsterdam's oldest) overlooking a tranquil green. Its hushed atmosphere allows for no large tour groups.

→ CANAL PLUS

Amsterdam's first canal, the **Singel**, is the tight boundary for the Old and New sides, and it is just beyond here that the Grachtengordel's concentric arrangement of canals begins. They're called Herengracht, Keizersgracht and Prinsengracht, and were cut in two stages through the seventeenth century. There's no better way of getting a feel for Amsterdam's charms than taking a slow boat along one of them, taking in the timeless appeal of the narrow houses and the steady progress of bike riders on the little waterside streets, making the most of this, the flattest country on the planet. A jaunt along the canals is best in the spring or summer, when the city blooms into a café society. Chairs and tables spill outdoors to welcome the sun, and taking in the tree-lined banks here is one of Europe's greatest pleasures. A super vantage point is from the bridge at the crossing of the Herengracht with Reguliersgracht (another pretty canal in the eastern canal ring, dug after those in the Grachtengordel): this is called the 'golden curve' and gives a view of fifteen bridges all at one time.

→ THE COLOUR BROWN

If any part of the city can claim the title of the 'real' Amsterdam, that accolade belongs to the **Jordaan**. This delightful maze of canals and backstreets on the western canal ring is a short stroll from the main visitor hotspots, yet it doesn't quite draw the same crowds. Losing yourself here is all part of the fun, idling amongst the seventeenth century workers' houses and quirky shops. This is where to stop and enjoy Amsterdam's best brown cafés, so called not just because their interiors are characterised by dark wooden panelling, but also because they've turned that rather inviting nutty colour with age and cigarette smoke. They're cosy and convivial, and often form the social hub of the neighbourhood.

At the heart of the Jordaan are two of the city's most famous sights, standing within a stone's throw of each other. The **Westerkerk** is the tallest church in Amsterdam, its spire rewarding climbers with stunning views. Rembrandt, who lived close by, is buried here, though his grave has never been found. Just along Prinsengracht is a humble abode that attracts nine hundred thousand visitors a year – **Anne Frank House**. For two years during World War II, this was where the now-famous young diarist lived with her family in a little upstairs apartment hidden behind a revolving bookcase. You can visit her room, empty except for pin-ups of wartime film stars. It's advisable, for obvious reasons, to get here either early or late in the day.

➔ SEMINAL MUSEUMS

If the weather's inclement, you can easily spend a day in the museums and galleries of this city. In fact, whatever the elements are doing, be sure to head just beyond the limits of the Grachtengordel and pay homage to the district around **Museumplein**. Here you will find the **Rijksmuseum** and the **Van Gogh Museum**, two of Europe's cultural landmarks. The Rijksmuseum has been undergoing extensive renovation and the reopened in 2008. This neo-Gothic titan is a powerhouse of art, possessing nearly seven million works, with only a fraction on display at any one time. Over two hundred years, it's built an unrivalled collection of Dutch art; try not to miss the paintings of the 17C, the Golden Age, adorned by the likes of Rembrandt, Vermeer and Hals. There are also tremendously impressive sections on Asiatic art and sculpture/applied art. It can be quite overpowering to take in this museum in a single day; best do some planning beforehand. The Van Gogh museum, on the other hand, is on a more human scale, and includes two hundred of the great man's paintings and five hundred of his drawings. There are hundreds of letters to his brother Theo, too. As if all this wasn't enough, practically opposite the homage to Van Gogh is the Stedelijk Museum, the national Museum of Modern Art, now seventy years old. Inside are works by the likes of Chagall, Cézanne and Picasso, plus, naturally enough, a fascinating insight into the Dutch De Stijl movement, iconic in the world of twentieth century abstract art.

HIPPY TRAIL

There's only one place to head after a gallery trawl, and that's the nearby **Vondelpark**. This former hippie haven boasts about eight million visitors a year. They come for the landscaped delights, the meandering footpaths, rose gardens and waterways, the parakeets which home in on the pavilion every morning, and the sheep, goats and cows which graze lazily in the pastures. They come for the free summer musical concerts and plays which the park is famous for, aswell as the film museum, where classic movies are shown each day, either in the lovingly restored interior or out on the terrace during summer. These are free to watch.

In recent decades Amsterdam has been famous for its enjoyment of plant life (mainly the sort you inhale in a brown café), but the city has been cultivating medicinal herbs for about three hundred and twenty

AMSTERDAM IN…

➔ ONE DAY

A trip on a canal boat; evening atmosphere of a brown café ; a stroll around the red light district

➔ TWO DAYS

Begijnhof, Rijksmuseum, Vondelpark

➔ THREE DAYS

The Jordaan, Van Gogh museum, Plantage and Entrepotdok

five years in the **Botanical Gardens** in the Plantage district to the east of town. These are amongst the oldest in the world, and include a three-climate greenhouse with tropical, sub-tropical and desert sections. There's an Orangery, too, with museum and terrace, which is a great place to take afternoon tea, while art shows with a botanical theme are a common sight. Plantage as a whole boasts attractively wide, tree-lined streets, and offers a vivid new take on the past: at Entrepotdok, the grand old warehouses have been redeveloped, and this dockland quarter buzzes with colour, café tables and shiny houseboats. Twenty-first century Amsterdam's evolution on water continues apace.

CALENDAR HIGHLIGHTS

Summertime is a cultural big-hit in Amsterdam. The highlight comes in the middle of August with Uitmarkt, a weekend of theatrical and musical shows on Leidseplein and Museumplein, which launches a season of dance, opera, music and drama in the city. This is also the month of the Grachtenfestival, which sees classical concerts along all sections of the Grachtengordel. September's third weekend is the time to be in Jordaan to check out its annual festival, when musical shows and fairs light up Westerkerk and its surrounding quarter. Earlier in the summer in June, look out for the Holland Festival, a three-week long jamboree, featuring theatrical drama in Amsterdamse Bos, southwest of the city, and a host of other plays, concerts and ballets around town: Vondelpark puts on some renowned shows al fresco. This is also the month for the Amsterdam Roots Festival, a celebration of global music and dance, and Open Garden Days, when picturesque private gardens are free for public perusal. Modern art is up for inspection in May at the Kunst RAI, a huge exhibition held in Amsterdam RAI, just southeast of the city. Every July, classical music fans make for the Concertgebouw for summer concerts, which continue throughout August. Brave Amsterdammers leave the comfort of cosy brown cafés on the first Saturday of November for Museumnacht, when many museums stay open during the night, with musical events and guided tours to keep eyelids from drooping.

EATING OUT

Amsterdam is a vibrant and multicultural city and, as such, offers a wide proliferation of restaurants offering a varied choice of cuisines where you can eat well without paying too much. Head for an eetcafe, and you'll get satisfying three-course menus at a reasonable price. The Dutch consider the evening to be the time to eat your main meal, so some restaurants shut at lunchtime. Aside from the eetcafe, you can top up your middle-of-day fuel levels at a bruin (brown) café, or one specialising in coffee and cake. If you wish to try local specialities, number one on the hit list could be rijsttafel or rice table, as the Dutch have imported much from their former colonies of Indonesia. Fresh raw herring from local waters is another nutritious local favourite, as are apple pies and pancakes of the sweet persuasion. Restaurants are never too big but are certainly atmospheric and busy so it's worth making reservations.

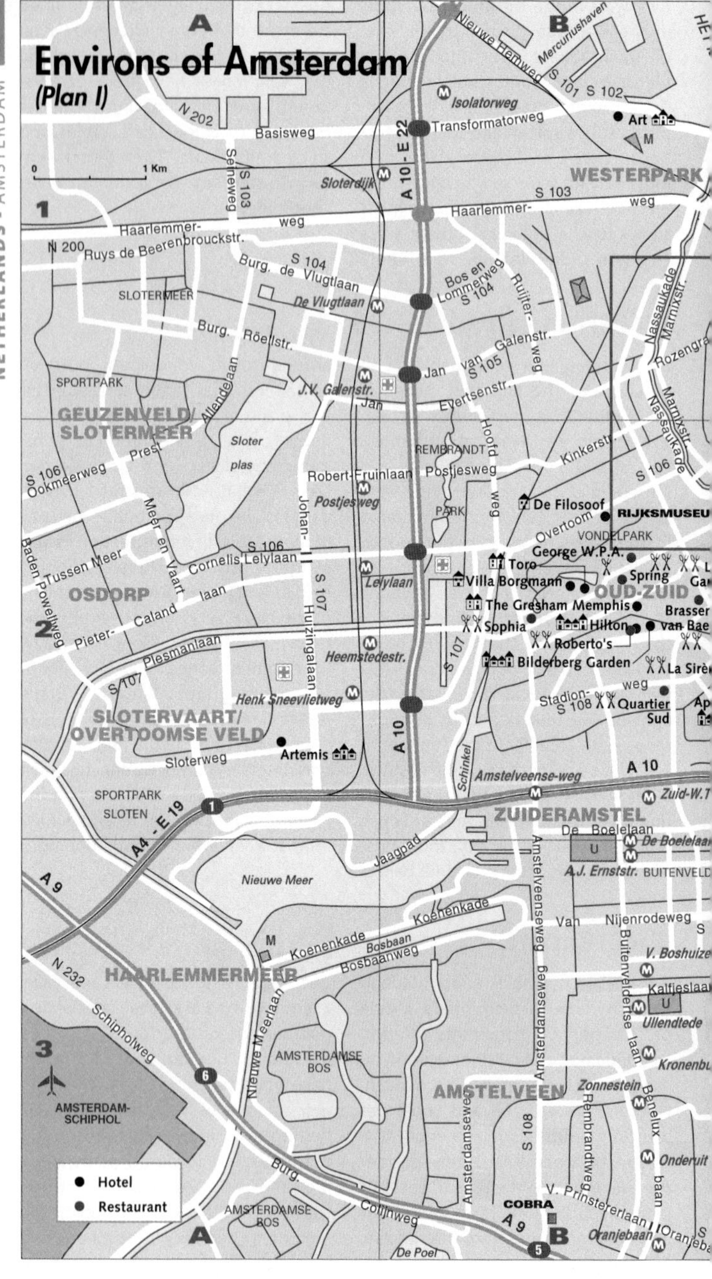

Environs of Amsterdam
(Plan I)
A
B
1
2
3
0
1 Km
Hotel
Restaurant
N 202
Basisweg
Seineweg
S 103
Isolatorweg
Transformatorweg
A 10 - E 22
Sloterdijk
Nieuwe Hemweg
Mercuriushaven
S 101
S 102
Art
M
WESTERPARK
S 103
Haarlemmer-
weg
Haarlemmer-
weg
N 200
Ruys de Beerenbrouckstr.
S 104
Burg. de Vlugtlaan
De Vlugtlaan
Bos en Lommerweg
S 104
Ruijter-
weg
SLOTERMEER
Burg. Röellstr.
Nassaukade
Marnixstr.
Rozengracht
Jan van Galenstr.
S 105
Jan Evertsensstr.
J.V. Galenstr.
SPORTPARK
GEUZENVELD/
SLOTERMEER
Allendelaan
Sloter
plas
Prest
REMBRANDT
PARK
Hoofd
weg
Kinkerstr.
S 106
Marnixstr.
Nassaukade
S 106
Ookmeerweg
Robert-Fruinlaan
Postjesweg
Postjesweg
De Filosoof
RIJKSMUSEUM
Overtoom
VONDELPARK
Johan-
Meer en Vaart
Baden Powellweg
Tussen Meer
S 106
Cornelis Lelylaan
George W.P.A.
Toro
S 107
Lelylaan
Villa Borgmann
Spring
OSDORP
laan
OUD-ZUID
The Gresham Memphis
Brasser
Huizingalaan
Sophia
Hilton
van Bae
Pieter-
Caland
Roberto's
Plesmanlaan
S 107
Heemstedestr.
Bilderberg Garden
La Sirè
S 107
Henk Sneevlietweg
Stadion-
weg
S 108
Quartier
Sud
SLOTERVAART/
OVERTOOMSE VELD
A 10
Artemis
Sloterweg
Schinkel
Amstelveense-weg
A 10
SPORTPARK
SLOTEN
A4 - E 19
1
Zuid-W.T
ZUIDERAMSTEL
De Boelelaan
U
De Boelelaan
Jaagpad
A.J. Ernststr.
BUITENVELD
A 9
Nieuwe Meer
Amstelveenseweg
Koenenkade
Van Nijenrodeweg
M
Koenenkade
Bosbaan
Bosbaanweg
Buitenveldertse laan
V. Boshuize
N 232
HAARLEMMERMEER
Kalfjeslaa
U
Ullendtede
Schipholweg
Nieuwe Meerlaan
AMSTERDAMSE
BOS
Amsterdamseweg
Kronenbu
AMSTERDAM-
SCHIPHOL
6
AMSTELVEEN
Zonnestein
Rembrandtweg
Benelux
baan
S 108
Amsterdamseweg
Onderuit
Burg.
Colijnweg
AMSTERDAMSE
BOS
COBRA
A 9
V. Prinstererlaan
Oranjebaan
5
De Poel

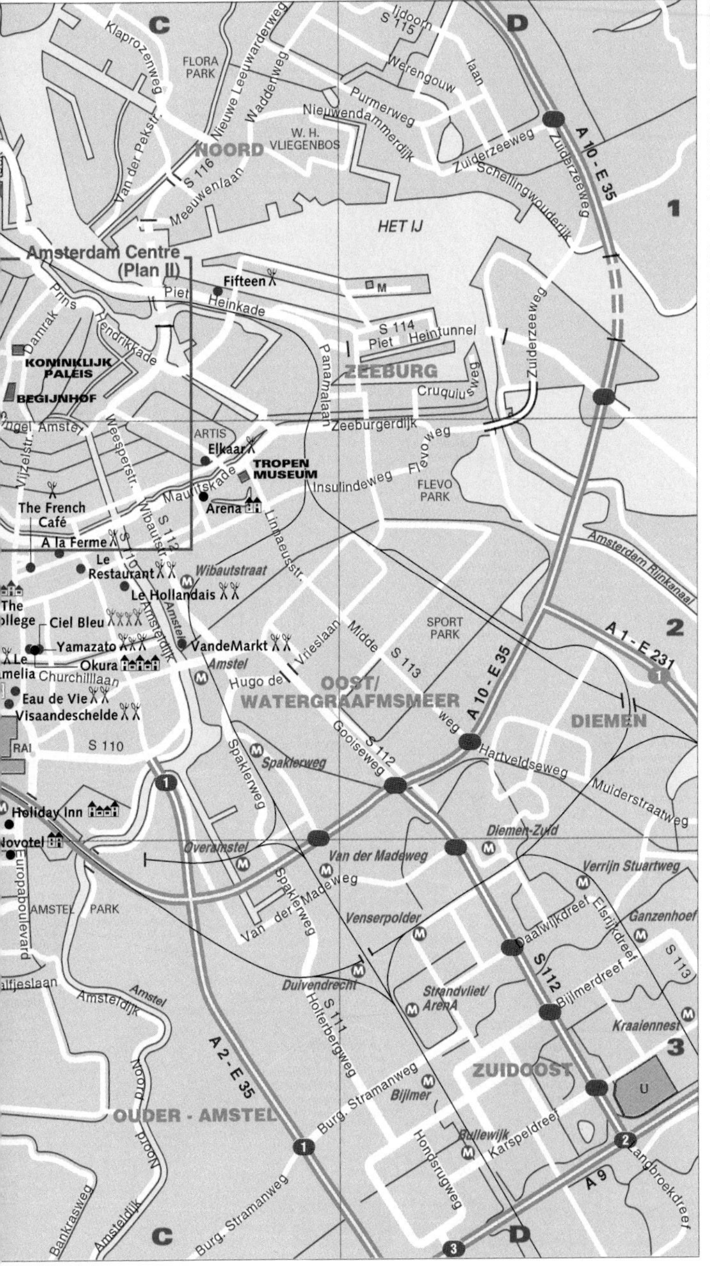
C
D
1
2
3
NOORD
HET IJ
ZEEBURG
OOST/
WATERGRAAFSMEER
DIEMEN
ZUIDOOST
OUDER - AMSTEL
Amsterdam Centre
(Plan II)
FLORA
PARK
W. H.
VLIEGENBOS
ARTIS
FLEVO
PARK
SPORT
PARK
AMSTEL PARK
KONINKLIJK
PALEIS
BEGIJNHOF
TROPEN
MUSEUM
Fifteen
Elkaar
Arena
The French
Café
A la Ferme
Le
Restaurant
Le Hollandais
The
College
Ciel Bleu
Yamazato
Okura
VandeMarkt
Le
Amelia
Eau de Vie
Visaandeschelde
Holiday Inn
Novotel
RAI
A 10 - E 35
A 1 - E 231
A 2 - E 35
A 9
S 110
S 111
S 112
S 113
S 114
S 115
S 116
Klaprozenweg
Van der Pekstr.
Nieuwe Leeuwarderweg
Wadderweg
Meeuwenlaan
Nieuwendammerdijk
Purmerweg
Werengouw
Zuiderzeeweg
Schellingwouderdijk
Piet Heinkade
Piet Heintunnel
Prins Hendrikkade
Damrak
Panamalaan
Cruquiusweg
Zeeburgerdijk
Flevoweg
Insulindeweg
Mauritskade
Weesperstr.
Wibautstr.
Vijzelstr.
Singel
Amstel
Linnaeusstr.
Middenweg
Hugo de Vrieslaan
Gooiseweg
Hartveldseweg
Muiderstraatweg
Amsterdam Rijnkanaal
Spaklerweg
Van der Madeweg
Amsteldijk
Churchilllaan
Europaboulevard
Holterbergweg
Burg. Stramanweg
Hondsrugweg
Karspeldreef
Bijlmerdreef
Daalwijkdreef
Elsrijkdreef
Langbroekdreef
Bankrasweg
Wibautstraat
Amstel
Spaklerweg
Overamstel
Van der Madeweg
Diemen-Zuid
Verrijn Stuartweg
Venserpolder
Ganzenhoef
Duivendrecht
Strandvliet/
ArenA
Kraaiennest
Bijlmer
Bullewijk
M
U

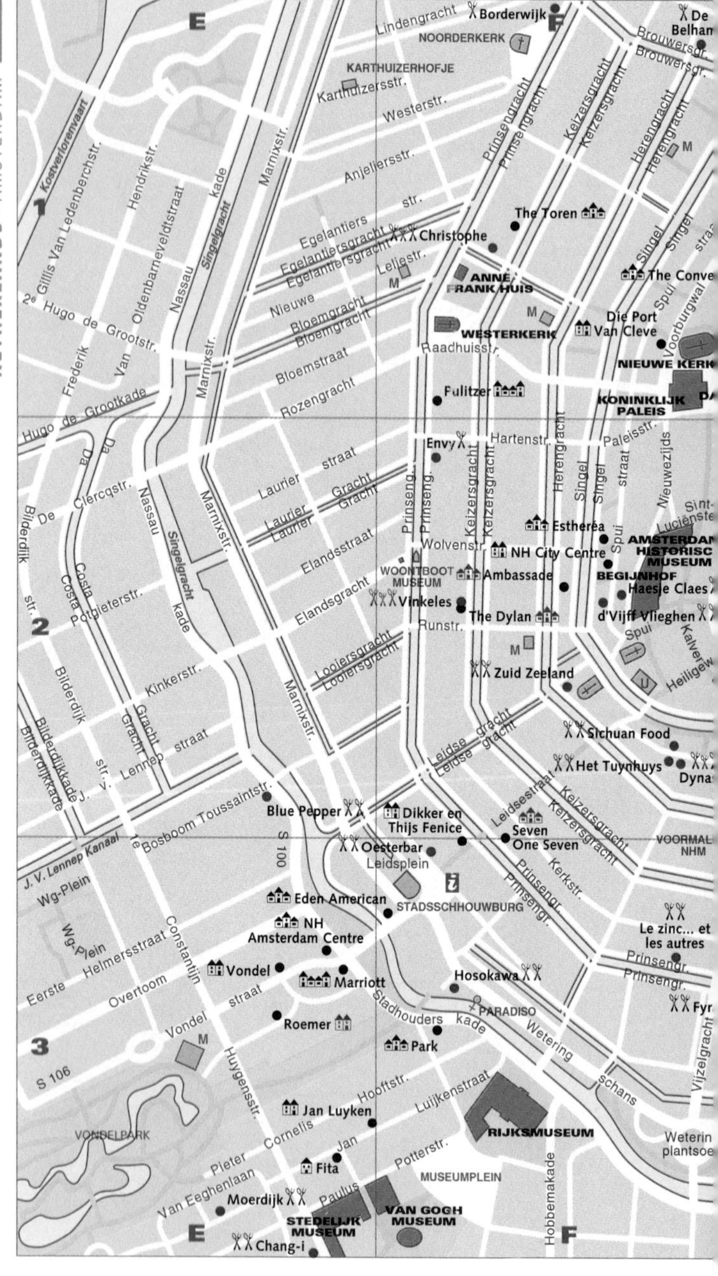

E
F
1
2
3
Lindengracht
Borderwijk
NOORDERKERK
De Belham
Brouwersgr.
KARTHUIZERHOFJE
Karthuizersstr.
Westerstr.
Anjeliersstr.
Marnixstr.
Kostverlorenvaart
Prinsengracht
Keizersgracht
Herengracht
M
The Toren
Egelantiers
Egelantiersgracht
Christophe
Leliestr.
ANNE FRANK HUIS
Singel
The Conve
Spui
Voorburgwal
Nieuwe
Bloemgracht
WESTERKERK
Die Port Van Cleve
NIEUWE KERK
Raadhuisstr.
Bloemstraat
Rozengracht
Pulitzer
KONINKLIJK PALEIS
Gillis Van Ledenberchstr.
Hendrikstr.
Oldenbarneveldtstraat
Nassau
Singelgracht
kade
2e Hugo de Grootstr.
Frederik
Van
Hugo de Grootkade
Da Clercqstr.
De
Envy
Hartenstr.
Paleisstr.
Nieuwezijds
Laurier straat
Laurier Gracht
Prinseng.
Sint-Luciënste
Estherea
AMSTERDAM HISTORISCH MUSEUM
Bilderdijk str.
Costa
Elandsstraat
Wolvenstr.
NH City Centre
WOONTBOOT MUSEUM
Ambassade
BEGIJNHOF
Haesje Claes
Potgieterstr.
Elandsgracht
Vinkeles
The Dylan
d'Vijff Vlieghen
Runstr.
Looiersgracht
Kalverstr.
Kinkerstr.
Zuid Zeeland
Heiligeweg
Bilderdijkkade
Lennep straat
J. v. Lennep
Leidse gracht
Sichuan Food
Het Tuynhuys
Dyna
Bosboom Toussaintstr.
Blue Pepper
Dikker en Thijs Fenice
Leidsestraat
Seven One Seven
VOORMALIG NHM
J. V. Lennep Kanaal
1e
S 100
Oesterbar
Leidsplein
Kerkstr.
Wg-Plein
Eden American
STADSSCHOUWBURG
NH Amsterdam Centre
Le zinc... et les autres
Eerste Helmersstraat
Constantijn
Vondel
Marriott
Overtoom
Vondelstraat
Hosokawa
Prinsengr.
Stadhouderskade
PARADISO
Fyr
Roemer
Park
Wetering schans
S 106
Vijzelgracht
Huygensstr.
Hooftstr.
Luijkenstraat
Jan Luyken
VONDELPARK
RIJKSMUSEUM
Weterin plantsoe
Pieter Cornelis
Jan
Fita
Potterstr.
MUSEUMPLEIN
Van Eeghenlaan
Moerdijk
Paulus
VAN GOGH MUSEUM
STEDELIJK MUSEUM
Hobbemakade
Chang-i

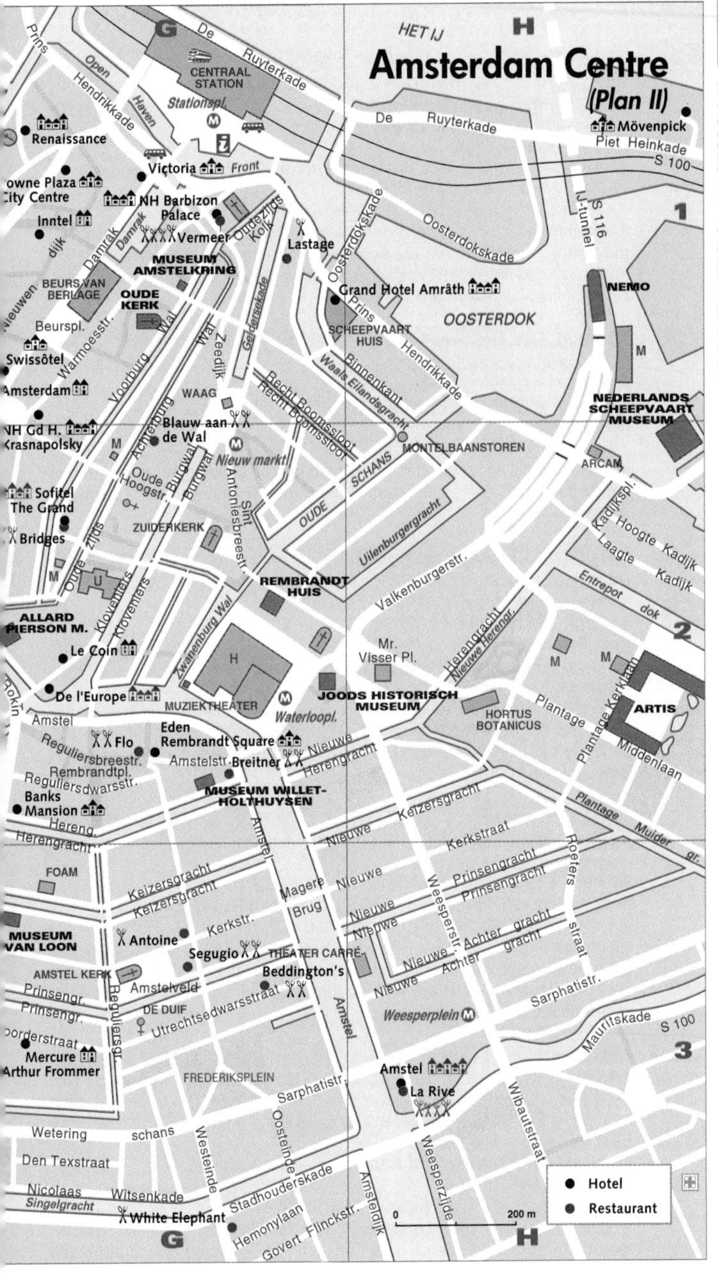
Amsterdam Centre
(Plan II)
HET IJ
CENTRAAL STATION
Stationspl.
De Ruyterkade
Prins Hendrikkade
Open Haven
Renaissance
Victoria
Crowne Plaza City Centre
NH Barbizon Palace
Inntel
Vermeer
Lastage
Damrak
MUSEUM AMSTELKRING
BEURS VAN BERLAGE
OUDE KERK
Beurspl.
Swissôtel
Amsterdam
NH Gd H. Krasnapolsky
Warmoesstr.
Voorburg
Achterburg
Wal
Zeedijk
Geldersekade
WAAG
Blauw aan de Wal
Nieuw markt
Oudezijds Kolk
Oosterdokskade
Grand Hotel Amrâth
SCHEEPVAART HUIS
Prins Hendrikkade
Binnenkant
Waals Eilandsgracht
Recht Boomssloot
OOSTERDOK
NEMO
NEDERLANDS SCHEEPVAART MUSEUM
MONTELBAANSTOREN
ARCAM
Mövenpick
Piet Heinkade
S 100
S 116
IJ-tunnel
OUDE SCHANS
Uilenburgergracht
Sofitel The Grand
Bridges
Oude Hoogstr.
Burgwal
ZUIDERKERK
Sint Antoniesbreestr.
REMBRANDT HUIS
Valkenburgerstr.
Kadijkspl.
Hoogte Kadijk
Laagte Kadijk
Entrepot dok
ALLARD PIERSON M.
Kloveniers
Zwanenburg Wal
Le Coin
De l'Europe
MUZIEKTHEATER
Waterloopl.
JOODS HISTORISCH MUSEUM
Mr. Visser Pl.
Herengracht
Nieuwe Herengr.
HORTUS BOTANICUS
Plantage Kerklaan
ARTIS
Plantage Middenlaan
Rokin
Amstel
Flo
Eden Rembrandt Square
Reguliersbreestr.
Rembrandtpl.
Reguliersdwarsstr.
Amstelstr.
Breitner
Nieuwe Herengracht
MUSEUM WILLET-HOLTHUYSEN
Banks Mansion
Hereng.
Herengracht
Nieuwe Keizersgracht
Kerkstraat
Plantage Muider gr.
Roeters straat
FOAM
Keizersgracht
Magere Brug
Nieuwe Prinsengracht
Weesperstr.
MUSEUM VAN LOON
Antoine
Kerkstr.
Segugio
THEATER CARRÉ
Nieuwe Achter gracht
AMSTEL KERK
Beddington's
Amstelveld
Prinsengr.
DE DUIF
Utrechtsedwarsstraat
Reguliersgr.
Weesperplein
Sarphatistr.
Mauritskade
Voorderstraat
Mercure Arthur Frommer
FREDERIKSPLEIN
Amstel
La Rive
Wibautstraat
Wetering schans
Den Texstraat
Westeinde
Oosteinde
Weesperzijde
Nicolaas Witsenkade
Singelgracht
White Elephant
Stadhouderskade
Hemonylaan
Govert Flinckstr.
Amsteldijk
0
200 m
Hotel
Restaurant
G
H
1
2
3

Amstel

Prof. Tulpplein 1 ✉ *1018 GX – ✆ (0 20) 622 60 60 – www.amsterdam.intercontinental.com* **H3**

62 rm – 525/625 € 525/625 €, ☕ 33 € – 17 suites

Rest *La Rive* – see below

Rest *The Amstel Bar and Brasserie* – *✆ (0 20) 520 32 69 (open until 11 pm)* Menu 50 € – Carte 58/102 €

◆ Grand Luxury ◆ Palace ◆ Personalised ◆

A veritable haven of luxury and good taste in this grand hotel on the banks of the Amstel. The vast rooms are decorated with attention to detail and stylish furnishings. Complete, efficient service. A cosy library-bar, with an appetising cosmopolitan-influenced menu.

Sofitel The Grand

O.Z. Voorburgwal 197 ✉ *1012 EX – ✆ (0 20) 555 31 11 – www.sofitel.com* **G2**

148 rm – 220/550 € 320/650 €, ☕ 32 € – 29 suites

Rest *Bridges* – see below

◆ Luxury ◆ Palace ◆ Historic ◆

Maria de Medici once stayed in this superb historic building, formerly Amsterdam's town hall. Stylish, refurbished guestrooms, lounges and a beautiful courtyard.

NH Grand Hotel Krasnapolsky

Dam 9 ✉ *1012 JS – ✆ (0 20) 554 91 11 – www.nh-hotels.com* **G1**

467 rm – 119/399 € 119/399 €, ☕ 29 € – 1 suite

Rest *Reflet* – *✆ (0 20) 554 61 14 (closed 18 July-14 August, Sunday and Monday) (dinner only)* Menu 36/63 € – Carte 39/73 €

◆ Luxury ◆ Traditional ◆ Classic ◆

Historic grand hotel on the Dam with various categories of rooms, apartments for rent by the week and buffet breakfast served under a magnificent glass roof dating from 1879. Classic menu, chic décor and well-heeled ambiance at the Reflet, founded in 1883.

De l'Europe

Nieuwe Doelenstraat 2 ✉ *1012 CP – ✆ (0 20) 531 17 77 – www.leurope.nl* **G2**

88 rm – 350/650 € 450/750 €, ☕ 30 € – 23 suites

Rest – Menu 55 € (lunch), 85/140 € bi – Carte 110/145 €

◆ Luxury ◆ Palace ◆ Personalised ◆

Luxury hotel dating from late 19C with charm and tradition. Tastefully decorated rooms. A collection of Dutch landscape paintings displayed. Beautiful water views. Up-to-date cuisine served in a sumptuous interior or on the pleasant waterside terrace. Fixed lunch menu.

NH Barbizon Palace

Prins Hendrikkade 59 ✉ *1012 AD – ✆ (0 20) 556 45 64 – www.nh-hotels.com* **G1**

271 rm – 149/209 € 149/209 €, ☕ 25 € – 3 suites

Rest *Vermeer* – see below

Rest *Hudson's Terrace and Restaurant* – *✆ (0 20) 556 48 75* – Menu 43/80 € – Carte 42/57 €

◆ Chain hotel ◆ Business ◆ Modern ◆

Modern luxury hotel near the station. A vast, luminous foyer, various types of rooms, fitness facilities, sauna, reception area in a converted church and valet parking. At Hudson's, a relaxed atmosphere, an international menu and an interior terrace set the scene.

Marriott

rm,

Stadhouderskade 12 ✉ 1054 ES – ✆ (0 20) 607 55 55 – www.amsterdammarriott.com **E3**

390 rm – ♀169/395 € ♀♀169/395 €, ☕ 25 € – 5 suites

Rest – *(closed Sunday and Monday) (dinner only)* Carte 33/60 €

♦ Chain hotel ♦ Business ♦ Cosy ♦

A high-class, American-style hotel on a major thoroughfare. The rooms are vast and well-equipped. A good seminar infrastructure and business centre. Modern steak house specialising in grilled Black Angus Beef.

Pulitzer

Prinsengracht 323 ✉ 1016 GZ – ✆ (0 20) 523 52 35 – www.luxurycollection.com/pulitzer **F1**

227 rm – ♀229/419 € ♀♀239/429 €, ☕ 29 € – 3 suites

Rest *Keizersgracht 238* – *(closed Sunday dinner)* Menu 44/56 € – Carte 35/60 €

♦ Chain hotel ♦ Luxury ♦ Historic ♦

A group of 25 admirably-restored houses, dating from the 17 and 18C set around a well-tended garden. Public areas filled with works of art; refined, individualized bedrooms. The modern grill restaurant has a unique decor (including an amusing reference to the painter, Frans Hals) and a cosy bar.

Grand Hotel Amrâth

rm,

Prins Hendrikkade 108 ✉ 1011 AK – ✆ (0 20) 552 00 00 – www.amrathamsterdam.com **G1**

158 rm – ♀250/450 € ♀♀250/450 €, ☕ 25 € – 7 suites

Rest – Menu 29 € (lunch), 36/67 € bi – Carte 40/56 €

♦ Chain hotel ♦ Business ♦ Stylish ♦

The hotel opened in 2007, in the monumental Shipping House (1916), characteristic of the Amsterdam School. Stunning Art Deco interior. Contemporary cuisine served in a large, delightfully old-fashioned dining room.

Renaissance

Kattengat 1 ✉ 1012 SZ – ✆ (0 20) 621 22 23 – www.renaissanceamsterdamhotel.com **G1**

396 rm – ♀149/395 € ♀♀149/395 €, ☕ 25 € – 6 suites

Rest – *(closed Sunday) (dinner only)* Menu 30 € bi – Carte 27/49 €

♦ Chain hotel ♦ Business ♦ Modern ♦

Rooms, suites and junior suites with modern comfort and numerous services on offer. Excellent conference facilities underneath the dome of an old Lutheran church dating from 1671. Restaurant with an international menu; simplified dining in the "brown café".

Crowne Plaza City Centre

N.Z. Voorburgwal 5 ✉ 1012 RC – ✆ (0 20) 620 05 00 – www.amsterdam-citycentre.crowneplaza.com **G1**

268 rm – ♀140/280 € ♀♀150/280 €, ☕ 25 € – 2 suites

Rest *New Dorrius* – *✆ (0 20) 420 22 24 (open until 11 pm)* Menu 24 € (lunch), 33/55 € – Carte 34/54 €

♦ Chain hotel ♦ Business ♦ Modern ♦

Fully renovated chain hotel offering modern, functional guestrooms, sauna, fitness facilities, meeting rooms and valet parking. Pleasant rooftop terrace. Brand new restaurant serving updated cuisine and Dutch delicacies.

Eden American

rm,

Leidsekade 97 ✉ 1017 PN – ✆ (0 20) 556 30 00 – www.edenamsterdamamerican.com **F3**

174 rm – ♀120/280 € ♀♀120/280 €, ☕ 20 € – 1 suite

Rest *Café Americain* – *✆ (0 20) 556 30 10* – Menu 34 € – Carte 39/75 €

♦ Palace ♦ Business ♦ Art Deco ♦

Near a lively square, this hotel with its imposing historic façade is a bit of a local institution. Bedrooms are gradually being updated. Bar popular with artists and people watchers. Elegant vaulted Art Deco café. International menu; high tea on request.

Ambassade without rest

Herengracht 341 ✉ 1016 AZ – ✆ (0 20) 555 02 22 – www.ambassade-hotel.nl **F2**

52 rm – †185/195 € ††185/245 €, ☕ 17 € – 6 suites

♦ Luxury ♦ Family ♦ Stylish ♦

Beautiful rooms and suites with a personal touch, spread over ten 17C houses overlooking the canal. Modern art and interesting library. Float and massage centre. Breakfast served in an elegant dining room.

The Dylan

Keizersgracht 384 ✉ 1016 GB – ✆ (0 20) 530 20 10 – www.dylanamsterdam.com **F2**

38 rm – †295/350 € ††395/995 €, ☕ 28 € – 3 suites

Rest *Vinkeles* – see below

♦ Grand Luxury ♦ Design ♦

"Order and beauty; luxury, peace and delight." Discover the secret harmony of the exceptional interior design of this unique hotel. Exquisite rooms by Anouska Hempel.

The Convent without rest

N.Z. Voorburgwal 67 ✉ 1012 RE – ✆ (0 20) 627 59 00 – www.theconventamsterdam.com **F1**

148 rm – †109/299 € ††109/299 €, ☕ 22 €

♦ Chain hotel ♦ Traditional ♦ Classic ♦

Three historic houses, formerly part of a convent (13C-14C) and a 20C printing works. Enjoy the lounge-cum-library, personalised guestrooms and junior suites, and a bar inspired by the Orient Express.

Seven One Seven without rest

Prinsengracht 717 ✉ 1017 JW – ✆ (0 20) 427 07 17 – www.717hotel.nl

8 rm ☕ – †425/655 € ††425/680 € **F2-3**

♦ Grand Luxury ♦ Traditional ♦ Classic ♦

Small, attractive 18C house converted into an intimate and select place to stay. The guestrooms are veritable gems. Romantic lounges; leafy courtyard where breakfast is served in summer.

Victoria

Damrak 1 ✉ 1012 LG – ✆ (0 20) 623 42 55 – www.parkplaza.com

306 rm – †105/360 € ††105/360 €, ☕ 23 € – 10 suites **G1**

Rest – *(open until 11 pm)* Menu 33 € – Carte 38/50 €

♦ Chain hotel ♦ Traditional ♦ Classic ♦

Near the station, a neoclassical 19C luxury hotel and extension dating from the 1980s. Domed lobby with modern stained glass. Refurbished rooms. Tavern-restaurant with traditional menu.

Eden Rembrandt Square

Amstelstraat 17 ✉ 1017 DA – ✆ (0 20) 890 47 47 – www.edenrembrandtsquarehotel.com **G2**

166 rm – †100/220 € ††100/220 €, ☕ 20 €

Rest *Flo* – see below

♦ Chain hotel ♦ Modern ♦

Set on a lively square, the vintage façade hides a modernised interior. Contemporary, well-equipped guestrooms. Seminar facilities and bicycles available.

Eden

Amstel 144 ✉ 1017 AE – ✆ (0 20) 530 78 70 – www.edenhotelamsterdam.com

218 rm – †75/195 € ††90/210 €, ☕ 20 €

♦ Chain hotel ♦ Functional ♦

The guestrooms in the adjoining outbuilding are pleasantly comfortable.

Banks Mansion without rest

Herengracht 519 ✉ 1017 BV – ✆ (0 20) 420 00 55 – www.banksmansion.nl **G2**

49 rm – 179/329 € 209/359 €

◆ Chain hotel ◆ Business ◆ Modern ◆

Building dating from 1923 whose interior combines the styles of Dutch architect Hendrik Petrus Berlage and American architect Frank Lloyd Wright. Modern rooms with retro touches. Alluring, intimate lounge.

Mövenpick rm,

Piet Heinkade 11 ✉ 1019 BR – ✆ (0 20) 519 12 00 – www.moevenpick-amsterdam.com **H1**

408 rm – 119/600 € 119/600 €, 23 € – 1 suite

Rest – Menu 28 € – Carte 37/46 €

◆ Chain hotel ◆ Business ◆ Modern ◆

Modern chain hotel inaugurated in 2006 in a modern district. The rooms have panoramic views. Concert hall, jazz club and congress centre next door. Restaurant serving Asian cuisine: Chinese, Thai and Indonesian.

Estheréa without rest

Singel 305 ✉ 1012 WJ – ✆ (0 20) 624 51 46 – www.estherea.nl

91 rm – 125/280 € 145/365 €, 16 € **F2**

◆ Family ◆ Traditional ◆ Personalised ◆

Since 1942, the same family have run this hotel, set in a row of old merchants' houses, with refined, neoclassical communal areas, personalised rooms and charming breakfast restaurant.

The Toren without rest

Keizersgracht 164 ✉ 1015 CZ – ✆ (0 20) 622 63 52 – www.thetoren.nl

38 rm – 115/250 € 150/480 €, 12 € **F1**

◆ Traditional ◆ Classic ◆

A charming hotel composed of several old houses, near the Anne Frank House. Neo-baroque bedrooms, elegant breakfast room with an attractive bar.

Swissôtel without rest

Damrak 96 ✉ 1012 LP – ✆ (0 20) 522 30 00 – www.swissotel.com/amsterdam **G1**

104 rm – 99/290 € 99/290 €, 20 € – 5 suites

◆ Chain hotel ◆ Business ◆ Functional ◆

Renovated chain hotel in a centrally-located traditional-looking building. Modern public areas, functional bedrooms and good reception.

NH Amsterdam Centre

Stadhouderskade 7 ✉ 1054 ES – ✆ (0 20) 685 13 51 – www.nh-hotels.com **E3**

232 rm – 100/209 € 109/209 €, 19 € – 2 suites

Rest *Sogno* – *✆ (0 20) 589 88 70 (closed Sunday and Monday) (dinner only)* Carte 47/54 €

◆ Chain hotel ◆ Business ◆ Modern ◆

Renovated chain hotel built to host athletes attending the Amsterdam Olympic Games in 1928. Designer public areas. Large modern bedrooms. Italian menu, contemporary décor and view of the Leidseplein at Sogno.

Park rm,

Stadhouderskade 25 ✉ 1071 ZD – ✆ (0 20) 671 12 22 – www.parkhotel.nl

189 rm – 120/375 € 120/375 €, 24 € **F3**

Rest *MOMO* – *✆ (0 20) 671 74 74 (open until 11 pm)* Menu 39 € – Carte 32/103 €

◆ Luxury ◆ Modern ◆

Fully renovated hi-tech hotel set between Vondelpark and the busy centre. Five types of spacious and pleasant trendy rooms. Meeting and fitness facilities. Stylish service. Fusion cuisine in a fashionable setting. Bento (Japanese lunch box) at lunchtime and tapas in the evening.

Amsterdam

Damrak 93 ✉ 1012 LP – ☎ (0 20) 555 06 66 – www.hotelamsterdam.nl
79 rm – †90/350 € ††100/360 €, ☕ 15 € **G1**
Rest *De Roode Leeuw* – Menu 30/55 € – Carte 35/50 €
♦ Traditional ♦ Classic ♦
This traditional Amsterdam hotel is located on a central section of the busy Damrak. Very comfortable rooms. Public car parks nearby. The brasserie offers traditional Dutch dishes in a modernised setting with red décor.

Die Port van Cleve

rest,

N.Z. Voorburgwal 178 ✉ 1012 SJ – ☎ (0 20) 714 20 00 – www.dieportvancleve.com **F1**
119 rm – †89/285 € ††89/295 €, ☕ 19 € – 2 suites
Rest – Menu 27 € (lunch)/35 € – Carte 38/56 €
♦ Traditional ♦ Functional ♦
The first Dutch brewers started work in the 19C behind the flamboyant façade of this building (1864). Tidy rooms. Dutch gin bar decorated with Delft china and panelling. Grill restaurant keeping a tally of the number of steaks served since 1870.

Dikker en Thijs Fenice without rest

Prinsengracht 444 ✉ 1017 KE – ☎ (0 20) 620 12 12 – www.dtfh.nl
42 rm – †125/245 € ††150/345 €, ☕ 13 € **F2-3**
♦ Business ♦ Traditional ♦ Classic ♦
Facing the canal, this complex features a 17C house and a huge 1921 building, where a pupil of famous French chef Escoffier once owned a food shop. Large guestrooms, studio and penthouse.

Inntel without rest

Nieuwezijdskolk 19 ✉ 1012 PV – ☎ (0 20) 530 18 18 – www.inntelhotels.nl
239 rm – †99/370 € ††99/370 €, ☕ 15 € **G1**
♦ Chain hotel ♦ Modern ♦
A modern glass-fronted establishment in the heart of the busy Nieuwe Zijde, the shopping area next to the station. Well sound-proofed rooms. Breakfast area entirely surrounded by glass.

NH City Centre without rest

Spuistraat 288 ✉ 1012 VX – ☎ (0 20) 420 45 45 – www.nh-hotels.com
209 rm – †99/299 € ††99/299 €, ☕ 19 € **F2**
♦ Chain hotel ♦ Business ♦ Functional ♦
Slotted between the Singel canal and the Béguine convent, this hotel has neutral, contemporary-style bedrooms typical of the NH chain. Spacious and comfortable lounge.

Mercure Arthur Frommer without rest

Noorderstraat 46 ✉ 1017 TV – ☎ (0 20) 622 03 28 – www.accorhotels.com **G3**
93 rm – †79/239 € ††99/239 €, ☕ 17 €
♦ Chain hotel ♦ Modern ♦
This renovated chain hotel, formerly a weaving factory, stands in a quiet neighbourhood, close to the Rijksmuseum. Refurbished modern bedrooms, some with designer furnishings.

Le Coin without rest

Nieuwe Doelenstraat 5 ✉ 1012 CP – ☎ (0 20) 524 68 00 – www.lecoin.nl
42 rm – †119/130 € ††139/160 €, ☕ 13 € **G2**
♦ Traditional ♦ Functional ♦
Seven houses next to the University of Amsterdam make up this hotel. Rooms of various shapes and sizes, but all decorated in a contemporary style and equipped with a kitchenette.

Roemer without rest
Roemer Visscherstraat 10 ✉ 1054 EX – ✆ (0 20) 589 08 00 – www.vondelhotels.com **E3**
23 rm – 169/549 € 299/579 €
◆ Business ◆ Design ◆
A pleasant designer-decorated hotel in an early-20C house not far from the Vondelpark. Warm welcome, well-equipped rooms, and summer breakfasts in the garden.

Vondel
Vondelstraat 26 ✉ 1054 GD – ✆ (0 20) 612 01 20 – www.vondelhotels.com
86 rm – 139/439 € 139/439 €, 20 € **E3**
Rest – Menu 15 € (lunch), 30/50 € – Carte approx. 39 €
◆ Business ◆ Luxury ◆ Design ◆
This boutique hotel was created out of seven 1900s houses. Communal areas, bedrooms and conference room in a decidedly contemporary style. Breakfasts on the stylish patio when the weather is good. Hip, stylish bistro serving local and international cuisine.

Jan Luyken without rest
Jan Luykenstraat 58 ✉ 1071 CS – ✆ (0 20) 573 07 30 – www.janluyken.nl
62 rm – 89/159 € 99/179 €, 20 € **E3**
◆ Chain hotel ◆ Traditional ◆ Cosy ◆
Three 1900s houses make up this hotel with contemporary interior décor. Modern bedrooms, designer bar with a few period touches and small courtyard terrace.

Fita without rest
Jan Luykenstraat 37 ✉ 1071 CL – ✆ (0 20) 679 09 76 – www.hotelfita.com
15 rm – 70/105 € 100/165 € **E3**
◆ Family ◆ Classic ◆
This typical family-run hotel has functional rooms in three different sizes with the added advantage of being near Amsterdam's most prestigious museums. Friendly welcome.

La Rive – Hotel Amstel
Prof. Tulpplein 1 ✉ 1018 GX – ✆ (0 20) 520 32 64 – www.restaurantlarive.com – Closed 31 July-23 August, 1-11 January, Saturday lunch, Sunday and Monday
Rest – Menu 49 € (lunch), 85/112 € – Carte 108/160 € **H3**
Spec. Langoustines in kataifi deeg gebakken, mango, komkommer en kerrie. Tarbot met hazelnoot, pompoen en couscous. Gebraden Wagyu rund met kaviaar, waterkers en selderij.
◆ Contemporary ◆ Formal ◆
A fine atmosphere with refined décor, a prestigious wine collection and high level of comfort characterize this gastronomic restaurant on the Amstel. Views of the river from the dining area at the front.

Vermeer – Hotel NH Barbizon Palace
Prins Hendrikkade 59 ✉ 1012 AD – ✆ (0 20) 556 48 85 – www.restaurantvermeer.nl – Closed 24 July-28 August, 23 December-9 January, Saturday lunch, Sunday and bank holidays **G1**
Rest – Menu 40 €, 75/100 € – Carte approx. 80 €
Spec. Zonnevis met gevulde ravioli en komkommerbloemetjes. Melklam uit de Pyreneeën met watermeloen, selderij en venkel. Taartje met krokante chocolade, hazelnootroom en peer.
◆ Contemporary ◆ Elegant ◆ Formal ◆
Classy restaurant of a luxury hotel where the chef creates inventive dishes with a bold personal touch. Fine à la carte menu with a wine list and expert sommelier to match.

XXX ✿ **Vinkeles** – Hotel The Dylan

Keizersgracht 384 ✉ 1016 GB – ☎ (0 20) 530 20 10 – www.vinkeles.com – Closed 26 December-9 January, Sunday and bank holidays **F2**

Rest – *(dinner only)* Menu 55/95 € – Carte 63/87 €

Spec. Oosterschelde kreeft met asperges, morieljes en daslookolie (April-July). Geroosterde langoustines met kalfsschenkel, gemarineerde tomaatjes en gelei van groene appel. Anjou duif, gekonfijte bospeen en jus met abrikoos.

♦ Contemporary ♦ Elegant ♦

Smart restaurant set in a characterful hotel. Creative, tasty cuisine, served stylishly in the former bakery (view of the old ovens) or facing the courtyard.

XXX **Christophe**

Leliegracht 46 ✉ 1015 DH – ☎ (0 20) 625 08 07 – www.restaurantchristophe.nl – Closed Sunday and Monday

Rest – *(dinner only)* Menu 36/66 € – Carte 64/81 € **F1**

♦ Contemporary ♦ Elegant ♦ Cosy ♦

This low-key, refined restaurant in a traditional building on the banks of the canal Lys serves good classic to modern cuisine.

XXX **Dynasty**

Reguliersdwarsstraat 30 ✉ 1017 BM – ☎ (0 20) 626 84 00 – www.fer.nl – Closed 27 December-3 February and Tuesday **F2**

Rest – *(dinner only)* Menu 43/66 € – Carte 35/69 €

♦ Asian ♦ Exotic ♦

A pleasant, longstanding restaurant featuring cuisine from around Asia. The trendy exotic décor is warm and colourful. Lovely terrace in the back and attentive service.

XX **Bridges** – Hotel Sofitel The Grand

O.Z. Voorburgwal 197 ✉ 1012 EX – ☎ (0 20) 555 35 60 – www.bridgesrestaurant.nl – Closed Saturday lunch **G2**

Rest – *(open until 11 pm)* Menu 35/59 € – Carte 51/135 €

♦ Seafood ♦ Design ♦ Fashionable ♦

Smart restaurant specialised in fish and seafood. The chef's philosophy is to keep the taste as pure as possible by adding only a few ingredients to the dishes.

XX **d'Vijff Vlieghen**

Spuistraat 294 (by Vlieghendesteeg 1) ✉ 1012 VX – ☎ (0 20) 530 40 60 – www.vijffvlieghen.nl – Closed 30 April, 25 July-7 August and 24, 25, 26 and 31 December-2 January

Rest – *(dinner only)* Menu 36/108 € bi – Carte 51/62 € **F2**

♦ Contemporary ♦ Rustic ♦

Modern cuisine prepared using typically Dutch produce and served in a restaurant taking up five 17C townhouses. Maze of fully-renovated rustic dining rooms.

XX **Breitner**

Amstel 212 ✉ 1017 AH – ☎ (0 20) 627 78 79 – www.restaurant-breitner.nl – Closed 25 July-9 August, 25 December-3 January and Sunday **G2**

Rest – *(dinner only)* Menu 35/58 € – Carte 48/76 €

♦ Contemporary ♦ Formal ♦

Creative and elaborate meals served in a classical modern setting. There are views over the Amstel with sightseeing boats and monuments (drawbridges, Amstelhof) in the background.

XX **Het Tuynhuys**

Reguliersdwarsstraat 28 ✉ 1017 BM – ☎ (0 20) 627 66 03 – www.tuynhuys.nl – Closed 28 December-3 January and lunch Saturday and Sunday

Rest – Menu 32 € (lunch), 36/60 € – Carte 42/66 € **F2**

♦ Contemporary ♦ Fashionable ♦

Mediterranean-inspired menu, attractive modern décor (white walls, wrought iron chairs, azulejo tiles) and courtyard-garden with a fine view of the baroque façade.

XX

Beddington's

Utrechtsedwarsstraat 141 ✉ 1017 WE – ✆ (0 20) 620 73 93
– Closed 17 July-8 August, 24 December-3 January, Sunday and Monday
Rest – *(dinner only)* Menu 48/55 € **G3**
♦ Contemporary ♦ Fashionable ♦
A British chef runs the open kitchen of this modern restaurant serving contemporary cuisine in her adopted home of Amsterdam. Black and white décor.

XX

Blauw aan de Wal

O.Z. Achterburgwal 99 ✉ 1012 DD – ✆ (0 20) 330 22 57
– Closed Sunday and Monday **G2**
Rest – *(dinner only until 11.30 pm) (booking advisable)* Menu 55 €
♦ Contemporary ♦ Friendly ♦
A popular restaurant at the end of a cul-de-sac in the lively red light district. Discreet décor, simple and tasty modern cuisine, good wine selection and a shady terrace.

XX

Le zinc... et les autres

Prinsengracht 999 ✉ 1017 KM – ✆ (0 20) 622 90 44 – www.lezinc.nl
– Closed 30 April, 26 July-8 August, 1 January and Sunday **F3**
Rest – *(dinner only until 11 pm)* Menu 35/55 € – Carte 48/61 €
♦ Contemporary ♦ Rustic ♦
Former 17C warehouse located off the tourist trail opposite the Prinsengracht. Superb zinc bar with refurbished rustic dining room upstairs. Extensive blackboard menu.

XX

Fyra

Noorderstraat 19 ✉ 1017 TR – ✆ (0 20) 428 36 32
– www.restaurantfyra.nl
– Closed 2 weeks in August, 22 December-2 January and Tuesday
Rest – *(dinner only)* Menu 31/63 € bi – Carte 41/56 € **F3**
♦ Contemporary ♦ Friendly ♦ Cosy ♦
Fyra means four and refers to the two couples that run this establishment. The interior is cosy and pleasant in a living room style. Current dishes with a mediteranean streak decorate the plates.

XX

Zuid Zeeland

Herengracht 413 ✉ 1017 BP – ✆ (0 20) 624 31 54 – www.zuidzeeland.nl
– Closed 4-17 January and lunch Saturday and Sunday **F2**
Rest – *(open until 11 pm)* Menu 36/62 € – Carte 56/64 €
♦ Contemporary ♦ Friendly ♦
This old establishment overlooks an attractive section of the Herengracht canal on one side and a patio on the other. Good, reasonably priced menu (simpler at lunchtimes). Pavement terrace on the canal.

XX

Hosokawa

Max Euweplein 22 ✉ 1017 MB – ✆ (0 20) 638 80 86 – www.hosokawa.nl
– Closed Sunday lunch **F3**
Rest – Menu 21 € (lunch), 38/108 € – Carte 37/78 €
♦ Japanese ♦ Minimalist ♦
A sober, modern Japanese restaurant with cooking tables, worth a detour to watch the entertaining show of food rotating past your eyes! At lunchtimes, only sushi is available.

XX

Segugio

Utrechtsestraat 96 ✉ 1017 VS – ✆ (0 20) 330 15 03 – www.segugio.nl
– Closed 30 April, 24, 25 and 31 December and Sunday **G3**
Rest – *(dinner only)* Menu 49 € – Carte 49/62 €
♦ Italian ♦ Design ♦
This establishment with three modern dining rooms on several levels features sunny Italian cuisine made right before your eyes. Good selection of regional wines.

XX **Oesterbar** A/C VISA MC AE D

Leidseplein 10 ✉ 1017 PT – ✆ (020) 623 29 88 – www.oesterbar.nl

Rest – *(open until 11 pm)* Menu 32/65 € – Carte 44/146 € **F3**

◆ Fish ◆ Retro ◆

A seafood restaurant with a new twist, featuring classic (Oude school) and evolving (Nieuwe school) cuisine served on three levels. Aquariums and lobster tanks.

XX **Flo** – Hotel Eden Rembrandt Square VISA MC AE D

Amstelstraat 9 ✉ 1017 DA – ✆ (0 20) 890 47 57
– www.floamsterdam.com
– Closed lunch Saturday and Sunday **G2**

Rest – *(open until midnight)* Menu 33 € – Carte 34/65 €

◆ Fish ◆ Brasserie ◆

Brasserie/oyster bar with a chic Parisian look featuring red velvet banquettes, sparkling brass, retro lighting and white apron service. Typical brasserie fare and good set menus.

XX **Sichuan Food** A/C VISA MC AE

Reguliersdwarsstraat 35 ✉ 1017 BK – ✆ (0 20) 626 93 27 **F2**

Rest – *(dinner only)* Menu 31/100 € bi – Carte 35/63 €

◆ Chinese ◆ Exotic ◆

Small oriental restaurant with good local reputation situated in a lively area. Typical Chinese décor. Beijing Duck prepared and served in the dining room.

XX **Blue Pepper** A/C VISA MC AE

Nassaukade 366h ✉ 1054 AB – ✆ (0 20) 489 70 39
– www.restaurantbluepepper.com
– Closed Tuesday **E2**

Rest – *(dinner only)* Menu 53/70 € – Carte 50/63 €

◆ Indonesian ◆ Fashionable ◆

An intimate modern setting and up-to-date Indonesian cuisine are featured at this establishment popular with romantic diners. Three menus. Attentive service.

X **Bordewijk** A/C VISA MC AE D

Noordermarkt 7 ✉ 1015 MV – ✆ (0 20) 624 38 99
– www.restaurantbordewijk.nl
– closed mid July-mid August, 24 December-early January, Sunday and Monday

Rest – *(dinner only)* Menu 39 € – Carte 49/76 € **F1**

◆ Contemporary ◆ Minimalist ◆

Popular restaurant due to its modern menu with inventive touches and minimalist décor: bare floorboards, Formica tables and designer chairs. Noisy atmosphere when busy.

X **Antoine** A/C VISA MC AE

Kerkstraat 377 ✉ 1017 HW – ✆ (0 20) 422 27 66
– www.restaurantantoine.nl
– Closed Sunday **G3**

Rest – *(dinner only)* Menu 35/55 € – Carte approx. 52 €

◆ Contemporary ◆ Fashionable ◆

Up-to-date cuisine served in two modern rooms, one a mezzanine, the other with a view outside. Neat tables, banquettes and comfortable seats.

X **Lastage** A/C VISA MC AE

Geldersekade 29 ✉ 1011 EJ – ✆ (0 20) 737 08 11
– www.restaurantlastage.nl
– Closed 13 July-3 August, 26 December-4 January, Monday and Tuesday

Rest – *(dinner only) (booking essential) (set menu only)* **G1**
Menu 36/56 €

◆ Contemporary ◆ Cosy ◆

A new start for this modern restaurant in a narrow 17th C house. Intimate dining rooms on two floors; the upper has a mantelpiece with "Delft" blue tiles.

Envy

Prinsengracht 381 ✉ 1016 HL – ✆ (0 20) 344 64 07 – www.envy.nl – Closed 1 January **F2**

Rest – *(dinner only except weekends until 11 pm)* Carte approx. 36 €

♦ Bistro ♦ Design ♦

Contemporary-style brasserie where guests eat on both sides of a long wengé wooden bar lit by modern globe-shaped lights or at one of the more comfortable booths.

De Belhamel

Brouwersgracht 60 ✉ 1013 GX – ✆ (0 20) 622 10 95 – www.belhamel.nl **F1**

Rest – Menu 35/45 € – Carte approx. 45 €

♦ Classic ♦ Bistro ♦

This local brasserie is at the confluence of delightful canals. Small traditional choice plus a blackboard menu (simpler at lunchtimes). Belle Epoque-style dining room with a mezzanine. Terrace near the bridge.

Haesje Claes

Spuistraat 275 ✉ 1012 VR – ✆ (0 20) 624 99 98 – www.haesjeclaes.nl – Closed 30 April and 25, 26 and 31 December **F2**

Rest – Menu 23/30 € – Carte 28/49 €

♦ Dutch regional ♦ Rustic ♦

A popular restaurant reflecting the town's atmosphere. Simple and copious Dutch cuisine served in a cheerful setting. Historical museum nearby.

Fifteen

Jollemanhof 9 ✉ 1019 GW – ✆ (0 20) 509 50 15 – www.fifteen.nl – Closed 31 December-1 January and Sunday lunch *Plan I* **C1**

Rest – *(dinner only mid July-mid August)* Carte approx. 40 €

♦ Contemporary ♦ Brasserie ♦

Jamie Oliver is behind the concept of this popular restaurant with a mission to give disadvantaged youngsters opportunities. Parking at the Passengers Terminal.

SOUTH and WEST QUARTERS *Plan I*

Okura

Ferdinand Bolstraat 333 ✉ 1072 LH – ✆ (0 20) 678 71 11 – www.okura.nl **C2**

293 rm – †160/425 € ††160/450 €, ☕ 30 € – 8 suites

Rest *Ciel bleu* and ***Yamazato*** and ***Le Camelia*** – see below

Rest *Sazanka* – *✆ (0 20) 678 74 50 (dinner only)* Menu 75/95 € – Carte 49/113 €

♦ Grand Luxury ♦ Business ♦ Modern ♦

A luxurious Japanese-style hotel set in a modern tower building. Various types of rooms and suites, superb wellness centre, extensive conference facilities and a full range of services. Japanese culinary expertise displayed at the teppanyaki dinner.

Hilton

Apollolaan 138 ✉ 1077 BG – ✆ (0 20) 710 60 00 – www.amsterdam.hilton.com **B2**

268 rm – †199/460 € ††199/460 €, ☕ 27 € – 3 suites

Rest *Roberto's* – see below

♦ Chain hotel ♦ Business ♦ Modern ♦

This classic hotel belonging to a chain has a terrace and garden with a water feature. Rooms and suites with superb views, one of which has a "John Lennon and Yoko Ono in 1969" theme.

Apollo

Apollolaan 2 ✉ 1077 BA – ✆ (0 20) 673 59 22 – www.wyndhamapolloamsterdam.com **B2**

223 rm – 109/335 € 109/335 €, 23 €

Rest ***La Sirène*** – see below

◆ Chain hotel ◆ Business ◆ Stylish ◆

An international chain hotel located at the intersection of five canals. Guestrooms designed with the business traveller in mind. Waterside bar, terrace and landing stage.

Bilderberg Garden

Dijsselhofplantsoen 7 ✉ 1077 BJ – ✆ (0 20) 570 56 00 – www.bilderberg.nl

120 rm – 129/359 € 129/359 €, 22 € – 2 suites **B2**

Rest ***De Kersentuin*** – *(closed Saturday lunch and Sunday)* Menu 28 € (lunch), 43/60 € – Carte 47/67 €

◆ Business ◆ Luxury ◆ Stylish ◆

Chain hotel catering mainly to corporate customers in the business district. Inviting interior, spacious and comfortable guestrooms, meeting facilities and valet parking. Meals in line with current tastes, modern brasserie ambience, pavement terrace.

Holiday Inn

De Boelelaan 2 ✉ 1083 HJ – ✆ (0 20) 646 23 00 – www.holidayinn.com/amsterdam **C2**

256 rm – 259/369 € 315/450 € – 8 suites

Rest – *(closed after 20.30 pm)* Carte 35/49 €

◆ Chain hotel ◆ Business ◆ Functional ◆

Chain hotel close to the RAI. Enjoy the discreet luxury and spaciousness of the communal areas and the comfortable guestrooms. Lounge-bar and restaurant in a modern setting evocative of New England. International and American cuisine.

Art

Spaarndammerdijk 302 (Westerpark) ✉ 1013 ZX – ✆ (0 20) 410 96 70 – www.westcordhotels.nl **B1**

187 rm – 99/225 € 99/225 €, 17 € – 3 suites

Rest – *(closed 23 December-16 January, Saturday lunch and Sunday)* Menu 23 € (lunch), 30/45 € – Carte 39/50 €

◆ Chain hotel ◆ Business ◆ Stylish ◆

Near a slip road off the ring, a modern hotel with very contemporary guestrooms, available in two sizes. Exhibition of paintings in the public areas. A la carte meals served in a trendy atmosphere; simpler set menu in the "eetcafé".

The College – (Hotel school training facility) rest,

Roelof Hartstraat 1 ✉ 1071 VE – ✆ (0 20) 571 15 11 – www.thecollegehotel.com **C2**

40 rm – 185/390 € 185/390 €

Rest – Menu 42/60 €

◆ Grand Luxury ◆ Design ◆

This hotel is located in a former 19C "college", redecorated with refinement. Chic and fashionable lounge bar and rooms in the same style. The modern restaurant installed in a former gym serves modern cuisine.

Toro without rest

Koningslaan 64 ✉ 1075 AG – ✆ (0 20) 673 72 23 – www.hoteltoro.nl

22 rm – 75/240 € 85/280 €, 18 € **B2**

◆ Luxury ◆ Stylish ◆

Villa set in a diplomatic and residential neighbourhood; half of the rooms overlook the Vondelpark, as does the elegant breakfast room. Convenient street parking area.

Novotel

Europaboulevard 10 ✉ 1083 AD – ✆ (0 20) 541 11 23 – www.novotelamsterdamcity.com **C3**

609 rm – 229 € 229 €, 22 €

Rest – *(open until midnight)* Menu 18/24 € – Carte 27/50 €

♦ Chain hotel ♦ Business ♦ Functional ♦

Imposing hotel block, with one of the largest guest capacities in Benelux. Fully-renovated interior. Bright, modern and functional bedrooms. Functional tavern-restaurant serving traditional classic cuisine.

Memphis without rest

De Lairessestraat 87 ✉ 1071 NX – ✆ (0 20) 673 31 41 – www.embhotels.com **B2**

78 rm – 99/200 € 119/225 €, 13 €

♦ Chain hotel ♦ Business ♦ Modern ♦

The tram line to the city centre runs in front of this ivy-covered hotel. Modern and intimate lounge bar with hushed atmosphere. Fresh bedrooms and pleasant breakfast area.

Arena

's-Gravesandestraat 51 ✉ 1092 AA – ✆ (0 20) 850 24 00 – www.hotelarena.nl **C2**

116 rm – 109/399 € 109/399 €, 19 €

Rest – *(closed Sunday) (dinner only)* Menu 35 € – Carte 36/50 €

♦ Business ♦ Design ♦ Minimalist ♦

Formerly an orphanage (1890), now an ultra-trendy hotel. Fantastic old staircase, designer bar and guestrooms of various styles and levels of comfort. Weekend nightclub (separate access). Designer setting and modern cuisine in the restaurant.

De Filosoof without rest

Anna van den Vondelstraat 6 ✉ 1054 GZ – ✆ (0 20) 683 30 13 – www.hotelfilosoof.nl **B2**

38 rm – 80/125 € 90/155 €, 15 €

♦ Family ♦ Personalised ♦

The originality of this hotel in a one-way street alongside the Vondelpark is in the décor of its rooms, based on cultural or philosophical themes. Garden.

Villa Borgmann without rest

Koningslaan 48 ✉ 1075 AE – ✆ (0 20) 673 52 52 – www.hotel-borgmann.nl **B2**

15 rm – 69/109 € 79/159 €, 12 €

♦ Family ♦ Functional ♦

A Russian couple welcome you in this large red-brick 1900s villa near the Vondelpark. Uncluttered rooms, simple breakfasts, quiet neighbourhood and convenient car park (paying).

Ciel Bleu – Hotel Okura, 23e etage

Ferdinand Bolstraat 333 ✉ 1072 LH – ✆ (0 20) 678 74 50 – www.cielbleu.nl – Closed 18 July-5 August, late December and Sunday **C2**

Rest – *(dinner only)* Menu 80/135 € – Carte 114/135 €

Spec. Drie keer langoustines. Gebakken heilbot met kreeft, ganzenlever en zwarte truffel. Warme en koude structuren van chocolade.

♦ Innovative ♦ Formal ♦

A chic restaurant at the top of the Okura Hotel with a superb contemporary décor and a fascinating urban panorama. Experience stylish service, delicious creative cuisine with exotic touches, a fine wine list and sunset views from the lounge.

XXX ✿

Yamazato – Hotel Okura

Ferdinand Bolstraat 333 ✉ 1072 LH – ✆ (0 20) 678 74 50 – www.yamazato.nl **C2**

Rest – Menu 48 € (lunch), 63/108 € – Carte 42/105 €

Spec. Kreeft Onigara-yaki. Gegrilde paling Kabayaki. Wagyu Sukiyaki.

◆ Japanese ◆ Minimalist ◆

Excellent Japanese restaurant featuring authentic Kaiseki cuisine in a Sukiya décor. Sushi bar. Meticulous and friendly service. Simplified lunch menu (lunch-box).

XX ✿

Le Restaurant (Jan de Wit)

2e Jan Steenstraat 3 ✉ 1073 VK – ✆ (0 20) 379 22 07 – www.lerestaurant.nl – Closed 3 weeks in July, late December-early January, Sunday and Monday

Rest – *(dinner only) (number of covers limited, pre-book) (set menu only)* Menu 65 € **C2**

Spec. Schelvis uit de oven met oesters, krab en groene paprika. Schouderstuk van Iberisch varken met geconfijte inktvis en zeewierchutney. Trio van fruit, groenten en chocolade.

◆ Innovative ◆ Elegant ◆

A deliciously small grand restaurant! Appetising market-fresh set menu, poised between tradition and modernity. Made with sumptuous produce, the dishes are served in an intimate and distinguished setting. Bookings essential.

XX

Visaandeschelde

(dinner)

Scheldeplein 4 ✉ 1078 GR – ✆ (0 20) 675 15 83 – www.visaandeschelde.nl – Closed 30 April, 24, 25, 26 and 31 December, 1 January and lunch Saturday and Sunday **C2**

Rest – *(open until 11 pm)* Menu 33/55 € – Carte 58/99 €

◆ Fish ◆ Fashionable ◆

Opposite the RAI congress centre, this restaurant is popular with Amsterdammers for its dishes full of the flavours of the sea, contemporary brasserie décor and lively atmosphere.

XX

Roberto's – Hotel Hilton

Apollolaan 138 ✉ 1077 BG – ✆ (0 20) 710 60 25 – www.robertosrestaurant.nl **B2**

Rest – Menu 32 € – Carte 50/113 €

◆ Italian ◆ Formal ◆

Located in the Hilton, Roberto's is one of the best Italian restaurants in the city. No fancy decor, just an understated modern dining room with smart service, top class and authentic Italian cuisine, and a menu that upholds the Bib philosophy.

XX

Le Camelia – Hotel Okura

Ferdinand Bolstraat 333 ✉ 1072 LH – ✆ (0 20) 678 74 50 – www.okura.nl **C2**

Rest – Menu 30 € (lunch)/35 € – Carte 50/62 €

◆ Contemporary ◆ Brasserie ◆

A deluxe French brasserie atmosphere and an enthusiastic young staff welcome you to this popular hotel restaurant. A move to the veranda is planned with a new name to match: La Serre.

XX

Sophia

Sophialaan 55 ✉ 1075 BP – ✆ (0 20) 305 27 60 – www.restaurantsophia.nl **B2**

Rest – Menu 22 € (lunch)/33 € – Carte 33/43 €

◆ Contemporary ◆ Design ◆ Fashionable ◆

Very trendy establishment where the well-dressed clientele samples the cuisine in a stylish setting. Small portions of several dishes served on one plate. Cocktail bar. Professional service.

XX

Le Garage
(dinner)

Ruysdaelstraat 54 ✉ 1071 XE – ✆ (0 20) 679 71 76 – www.restaurantlegarage.nl – Closed Easter, Whitsun, 25, 26, 31 December -1 January and lunch Saturday and Sunday **B2**

Rest – *(open until 11 pm)* Menu 30 € (lunch), 35/50 € – Carte 50/68 €

♦ Contemporary ♦ Trendy ♦

Excellent up-to-date establishment with an original décor. The entertainment and business clientele come to see and be seen as well as to enjoy the great food.

XX

Brasserie van Baerle

Van Baerlestraat 158 ✉ 1071 BG – ✆ (0 20) 679 15 32 – www.brasserievanbaerle.nl – Closed 30 April, 25, 26, 31 December-1 January and Saturday lunch

Rest – *(open until 11 pm)* Menu 36 € – Carte 48/63 € **B2**

♦ Brasserie ♦ Retro ♦

This retro brasserie attracts regular customers, mainly from the local area because of its attractive menu, tasty steak tartare and well-matched wines. Courtyard terrace.

XX

Spring

Willemsparkweg 177 ✉ 1071 GZ – ✆ (0 20) 675 44 21 – www.restaurantspring.nl – Closed 25, 26 and 31 December-1 January, Saturday lunch and Sunday

Rest – *(booking advisable)* Menu 32/60 € – Carte 49/59 € **B2**

♦ Contemporary ♦ Cosy ♦ Fashionable ♦

Enjoy Mediterranean cuisine in this elegant setting. It is adorned with large photos of truffle slices, rows of narrow tables, an open kitchen, and a small terrace that adds a touch of the Riviera.

XX

Quartier Sud

Olympiaplein 176 ✉ 1076 AM – ✆ (0 20) 675 39 90 – www.quartiersud.nl – Closed 25 December-2 January, Saturday lunch and Sunday **B2**

Rest – Menu 30 € (lunch), 38/44 € – Carte 36/61 €

♦ Contemporary ♦ Fashionable ♦

The business lunch is always packed in this stylish restaurant with a small terrace in front. You can fully enjoy classics and seasonal dishes thanks to the no-nonsense, relaxed atmosphere.

XX

Le Hollandais

Amsteldijk 41 ✉ 1074 HV – ✆ (0 20) 679 12 48 – www.lehollandais.nl – Closed Sunday and Monday **C2**

Rest – *(dinner only)* Menu 36/54 € – Carte approx. 50 €

♦ Contemporary ♦ Trendy ♦

The 1970s furniture and lighting, wooden floors and panelling create a charming setting. The menu features traditional simmered dishes, offal, blood sausage and homemade cold meats.

XX

Eau de Vie

Maasstraat 20 ✉ 1078 HK – ✆ (0 20) 662 95 88 – www.restaurant-eaudevie.nl – Closed 30 April, 25, 31 December-1 January and Saturday lunch

Rest – Menu 33 € (lunch), 38/58 € – Carte 45/60 € **C2**

♦ Contemporary ♦ Friendly ♦

This establishment run by a dynamic and motivated young team has lived up to its gastronomic promises. Surprise set menus, modern paintings on display and urban terrace.

XX

La Sirène - Hotel Apollo

Apollolaan 2 ✉ 1077 BA – ✆ (0 20) 673 59 22 – www.lasirene.nl – Closed mid July-mid August, Saturday lunch and Sunday **B2**

Rest – Menu 30 € (lunch), 33/53 € – Carte approx. 51 €

♦ Fish ♦ Formal ♦

Cuisine which comes in with the tide, served either in the large, bright dining room with views over the point where five canals meet or on the panoramic waterside terrace.

VandeMarkt

Schollenbrugstraat 8 ✉ 1091 EZ – ☎ (0 20) 468 69 58 – www.vandemarkt.nl – Closed 17 July-9 August, Sunday and Monday **C2**

Rest – *(dinner only)* Menu 35/40 € – Carte 47/58 €

◆ Contemporary ◆ Minimalist ◆

A gourmet establishment in a quiet neighbourhood with a discreet contemporary décor. Don't miss the "van de Schone Eenvoud" menu, which can also be adapted to suit vegetarians.

Chang-i

Jan Willem Brouwersstraat 7 (adjacent to the artists' entrance to the Concertgebouw) ✉ 1071 LH – ☎ (0 20) 470 17 00 – www.chang-i.nl – Closed 25-31 July and 25 December-1 January *Plan II* **E3**

Rest – *(booking advisable)* Menu 35/52 € – Carte 33/72 €

◆ Asian ◆ Trendy ◆

The 'i' in the name highlights the innovative nature of this chef's Asian cuisine. Trendy and intimate loungy atmosphere. Near a theatre.

Moerdijk

Willemsparkweg 155 ✉ 1071 GX – ☎ (0 20) 670 66 31 – www.restaurantmoerdijk.nl – Closed Saturday lunch and Sunday *Plan II* **E3**

Rest – Menu 45/60 € – Carte 52/66 €

◆ Contemporary ◆ Friendly ◆

In the modern setting of this pleasant restaurant renewed contemporary dishes are being served. Friendly staff and an elegant interior with culinary photographs.

A la Ferme

Govert Flinckstraat 251 ✉ 1073 BX – ☎ (0 20) 679 82 40 – www.alaferme.nl – Closed late July-early August, Sunday and Monday **C2**

Rest – *(dinner only)* Menu 32/44 € – Carte 37/65 €

◆ Classic ◆ Friendly ◆

Monthly menus featured in the contemporary dining room, in one of the smaller, more intimate rooms in the back, or under the grape arbour in summer.

The French Café

Gerard Doustraat 98 ✉ 1072 VX – ☎ (0 20) 470 03 01 – www.thefrenchcafe.nl – Closed late December, bank holidays and Sunday **C2**

Rest – *(dinner only)* Menu 36/63 € – Carte 40/65 €

◆ Traditional ◆ Friendly ◆

A tasteful modern setting with neo-retro wallpaper, a summer terrace overlooking the lively neighbourhood, and a French chef who cooks with Gallic flair. 2nd establishment with a simpler formula.

White Elephant

Van Woustraat 3 ✉ 1074 AA – ☎ (0 20) 679 55 56 – www.whiteelephant.nl *Plan II* **G3**

Rest – *(dinner only)* Menu 33/60 € – Carte 38/55 €

◆ Thai ◆ Exotic ◆

Thai restaurant with matching décor: panelling, orchids, bar in a traditional "hut", exotic terrace and friendly waiters in traditional costume. Authentic cuisine.

Elkaar

Alexanderplein 6 ✉ 1018 CG – ☎ (0 20) 330 75 59 – www.etenbijelkaar.nl – Closed 30 April, 25 and 31 December, 1 January and Saturday lunch

Rest – Menu 30 € (lunch), 36/55 € – Carte 41/55 € **C2**

◆ Contemporary ◆ Cosy ◆

Refined lunches and menus are offered at this restaurant in a large townhouse. Enthusiastic young team, bistro comforts, modern paintings and a teak terrace facing the Tropenmuseum.

George W.P.A.

Willemsparkweg 70 ✉ 1071 HK – ☎ (0 20) 470 25 30 – www.georgewpa.nl
Rest – Carte 33/53 € **B2**
♦ Brasserie ♦ Bistro ♦
This restaurant is made up out of three little buildings and a sunny outdoor seating area on a small square. A bistro-style interior with small tables, some art-nouveau details and an open kitchen give it an American atmosphere.

AT SCHIPHOL AIRPORT *Plan I*

Sheraton Airport

Schiphol bd 101 ✉ 1118 BG Schiphol – ☎ (0 20) 316 43 00 – www.sheraton.com/amsterdamair
405 rm – †159/399 € ††184/424 €, ☕ 29 € – 1 suite
Rest *Voyager* – *(closed lunch Saturday and Sunday) (open until 11 pm)*
Menu 40/48 € – Carte 48/70 €
♦ Chain hotel ♦ Business ♦ Modern ♦
Modern hotel complex near the airport, designed for a globe-trotting business clientèle. Guestrooms offer every comfort. Fine atrium. Full service. Modern brasserie with a bluish dome reminiscent of the Paris Zénith concert hall. International menu and buffets.

Hilton Schiphol without rest

Schiphol Bd 701 ✉ 1118 BN Schiphol – ☎ (0 20) 710 40 00 – www.hilton.com
278 rm – †135/349 € ††135/349 €, ☕ 27 € – 2 suites
♦ Chain hotel ♦ Business ♦ Functional ♦
A chain hotel, located near the airport and popular with business guests. Modern, well-equipped rooms and meeting facilities.

Radisson Blu Airport

Boeing Avenue 2 (Rijk) (South: 4 km via N201) ✉ 1119 PB Schiphol – ☎ (020) 655 31 31 – www.radissonblu.com/hotel-amsterdamairport
279 rm – †140/300 € ††140/300 €, ☕ 25 € – 2 suites
Rest – Menu 38 € – Carte 28/60 €
♦ Chain hotel ♦ Business ♦ Modern ♦
This hotel is ideal for business trips. It is spacious, close to the airport and motorway, with a cosy bar, meeting rooms and modern guestrooms lacking nothing in comfort. The restaurant menu offers international cuisine, dominated by Mediterranean dishes.

Crowne Plaza Amsterdam-Schiphol

Planeetbaan 2 ✉ 2132 HZ Hoofddorp – ☎ (0 23) 565 00 00 – www.crowneplaza.com/ams-schiphol
238 rm – †119/350 € ††119/350 €, ☕ 20 € – 4 suites
Rest – Carte 37/49 €
♦ Chain hotel ♦ Business ♦ Functional ♦
Establishment in a modern building, popular with business and conference clientele. Huge lobby, superb swimming pool, health club, large guestrooms and suites with lounges. "Sleep advantage" programme. Restaurant offering an international menu in several rooms.

Courtyard by Marriott - Amsterdam Airport

Bosweg 15 ✉ 2131 LX Hoofddorp – ☎ (0 23) 556 90 00 – www.claus.nl
140 rm – †99/189 € ††99/189 €, ☕ 19 € – 8 suites
Rest – Carte 26/40 €
♦ Chain hotel ♦ Business ♦ Modern ♦
A modern-style business hotel next to a wooded area and lake. Spacious and contemporary guestrooms with king-size beds. Designer fireside lounge. Brasserie serving intercontinental cuisine and pizzas.

Artemis

John M. Keynesplein 2 (exit ① Sloten) ✉ 1066 EP – ✆ (0 20) 714 10 00 – www.artemisamsterdam.com **A2**

247 rm – 79/295 € 79/295 €, 19 € – 9 suites

Rest – Menu 38 € – Carte 37/51 €

♦ Luxury ♦ Design ♦

This modern building of original design in the business district features Dutch designer-style décor. There is an art gallery to explore the subject in more detail. A large restaurant with ultra-modern décor and a big waterside terrace. Contemporary menu.

De Herbergh with rm

Sloterweg 259 ✉ 1171 CP Badhoevedorp – ✆ (0 20) 659 26 00 – www.herbergh.nl

24 rm – 80/120 € 85/125 €, 14 €

Rest – *(closed Sunday)* Menu 28 € – Carte 32/48 €

♦ Contemporary ♦ Cosy ♦

A new lease of life for this 100 year old, family-run inn: two generous, up-to-date menus delight food lovers in an airy and cosy setting. Trattoria formula also available. Attractive modern rooms. Facilities available for receptions and small executive seminars.

Marktzicht

Marktplein 31 ✉ 2132 DA Hoofddorp – ✆ (0 23) 561 24 11 – www.restaurant-marktzicht.nl – Closed 25 and 26 December, 1 January and Sunday

Rest – Menu 35/48 €

♦ Contemporary ♦ Rustic ♦

A wind of change is blowing through this old 19C inn on the Markt, built when the polder was erected. Up-to-date menu and welcoming terrace.

THE HAGUE

DEN HAAG – 'S GRAVENHAGE'

Population: 482 742 – Altitude: 3m

conotec/PHOTONONSTOP

The Hague appears to be a city of anomalies. Although the seat of Dutch government, it's not the capital of the Netherlands (which is Amsterdam); although a city of Europe wide importance, it's just as famous for its kiss-me-quick resort of Scheveningen; and although populated for hundreds of years by the well-to-do, its canal-side houses share little of Amsterdam's flamboyance.

The Hague earned its nickname 'the biggest village in Europe' because of its relatively small population sprawled about a large area: that 'village' is marked by an aristocratic charm, which is why it's rightly obtained another title – Holland's most elegant town. There are signs, though, that The Hague is doffing its neatly tailored cap to the 21C. Parts of the centre now shoot skywards courtesy of shiny government high-rises, while at ground level a rash of reasonably priced and buzzy restaurants and bars has brightened the streets. An outward-thinking city council has helped loosen the staid image with a lively programme of concerts and events, and there's an enticing range of museums clustered in the centre. A village, however large, wouldn't be a village without its sections of green and pleasant land, and The Hague doesn't disappoint with a kaleidoscope of leafy lanes and large parks.

LIVING THE CITY

Arrive at **Den Haag Centraal Station**, and you're only a five-minute walk from the centre of town (to your west). This is a compact quarter dominated by the **Binnenhof** parliament buildings. To the northeast of the centre are numerous green spaces and parks, while to the east and southeast lie the suburbs **Leidschendam, Voorburg** and **Rijswijk**. A couple of miles northwest of the centre is the **North Sea** and the popular beach resort of **Scheveningen**.

PRACTICAL INFORMATION

ARRIVAL-DEPARTURE

Rotterdam Airport is 16km southeast of The Hague which translates as a €45 taxi ride. Alternatively, there are shuttle and train services to Central Station which take 45 and 30min respectively.

TRANSPORT

A bus and tram system will whisk you around The Hague. Single tickets can be purchased from the bus driver but saver tickets must be bought in advance from the tourist information office, post offices, tobacconists, newsagents and hotels.

You can buy good value stripcards for your journeys. These are in two varieties; as a 15-stripcard or 45-stripcard and are valid throughout the country on buses, trams and metro. A one-day pass is also available for travel in The Hague, with price dependent on the amount of zones to be covered.

Once in The Hague, the only rail travel within the city is the line linking the two stations, Den Haag Centraal Station and Den Haag Hollands Spoor, which is a kilometre to the south of the centre, and is connected to it by frequent trams.

EXPLORING THE HAGUE

Although it gives the impression of being charmingly laid back and provincial, The Hague is a truly international city. It's home to over eighty embassies, as well as the International Court of Justice, and, of course, the Dutch Parliament. The Queen lives here too, albeit quite modestly. Not as modestly as the Crown Prince, though. His palace door opens on to the street. The air of gentle manners and 1950s calm is all-pervasive, as though the bureaucrats and bankers know that in a few minutes they can be sitting in a deckchair on the sandy beach.

→ LOUNGING ALONG THE LANGE

For all the new generation of eateries in the city, a stroll along **Lange Voorhout,** slap bang in the centre, even on a Saturday evening, can still be a serenely still experience. From here The Hague spreads through several square miles of art galleries and bistros. In the summer, the sun casts long shadows over leafy avenues and you can hear birds singing in the lime trees. A suitably bucolic spot to head for is the **Court Pond**, a dreamy lake which reflects the low-slung brick buildings of the Binnenhof – the Dutch Parliament. This is an impressive complex whose focal point is the thirteenth-century **Knights Hall**, a striking oak-roofed building in which the state opening of parliament takes place.

The tone is set for a visit to the adjacent **Mauritshuis**, not only The Hague's most important gallery, but one of the top art spaces in the world. What makes it so special is its size, or rather its lack of it. This is a compact and intimate gallery over just two floors, with around a hundred paintings on show. But what paintings! The core of the collection consists of masterpieces from the Dutch Golden Age, including works by Vermeer (yes, 'Girl With A Pearl Earring' is here), Rembrandt (the museum holds no less than twelve of his paintings), Hals and Potter. There are also stunning Flemish works from the sixteenth and seventeenth centuries by the likes of Rubens and van Dyck. Look out too for Holbein the Younger and some stark Flemish lowlife from the seventeenth century painter Brouwer, a man who knew his subject well, as he spent most of his short life in either a tavern or a prison.

→ PURE TORTURE

The feeling of cool sophistication continues as you regain Lange Voorhout. This is the main street in the city, a wide cobblestoned thoroughfare that becomes a leafy square. It boasts neoclassical mansions whose grand façades lead into foreign embassies and consulates. There's a museum on the square devoted to the vibrant works of the Dutch artist **M.C.Escher**, while two minutes' walk away yet more beautiful paintings are on offer at the **Museum Bredius**. These are packed tight like a splendid species in confinement, their setting enhanced by a sumptuous interior. The pick of the bunch are two works by Rembrandt. Just a short stroll west of the Museum Bredius, things take a darker turn as you arrive at a venue proud of its branding irons, execution swords and axes, elbow and thumb screws, racks and pillory boards: the **Prison Gate** museum, which occupies the old town prison, has a special section devoted to instruments of torture and interrogation. The tourist office people are quick to remind you that times have changed and the International Court of Justice really is based a few blocks from here.

→ LOOK AT THE VIEW!

If you head north past the **Noordeinde Palace**, home of the royals, you arrive, quite literally, at the Netherlands' biggest panorama. **Panorama Mesdag** was painted over the space of four months in 1880 by Hendrik Mesdag of the Hague School. It's a vast, cylindrical painting of Scheveningen, measuring 120m in circumference and standing 14m tall: it covers an amazing square mile of canvas (Mesdag did get assistance with his task!). From the viewing platform, the vista is endless in all directions: to the fishing village and its lighthouse, over the beach and the North Sea with its flat-bottomed fishing boats, to the fashionable seaside resort where bathing carriages are being rolled into the sea, over the dune landscape and on to The Hague. You can look three hundred and sixty degrees around you, and, to add to the illusion, the canvas itself blends into a 'virtual terrain' of seemingly abandoned objects on the floor. Real tufts of grass poke through the artificial beach that holds scraps of driftwood and a rusty anchor. Nearby, a weathered wooden chair lies next to a solitary clog. It all seems so real, you wonder why you can't sniff the seaweed or hear the swoosh of the waves.

→ A TRUE GEM

Heading inexorably towards the seaside, visitors are waylaid by another artistic gem – **The Gemeentemuseum**, the largest and most diverse of the city's exhibition spaces. Over seventy years old, it displays a rotated selection from a vast permanent collection. Nip down to the basement and you'll find eclectic sections on fashion and old musical instruments; upstairs the modern art section reflects changes from the early nineteenth century onwards. Many visitors are drawn to the impressive section on the De Stijl movement, which flourished between the two world wars, while others come because the museum boasts the world's largest collection of paintings by Holland's most famous twentieth century artist, Piet Mondrian. In his honour, an entire section is devoted to his early works. Trumping these, though, is his last (unfinished) painting 'Victory Boogie Woogie', a visual feast for the eye that's considered by many to be his best.

→ RATHER FRED THAN DEAD

Back in the centre of town, The Hague has some rather interesting shopping streets. First and foremost, hit the Fred, or, to be more precise, get along to **De Frederik Hendriklaan**, one of the city's most beautiful retail thoroughfares. It's lined with high-end boutiques and galleries, with a particular penchant for home furnishings and good food. There are charming streetside cafes here too. In **Hofweg,** right next to the Binnenhof, is **The Passage**, a restored covered arcade – the only one in the city – with a good selection of small boutiques and special interest shops. Meanwhile, Noordeinde is the place to go for elegant and imposing modern art galleries and boutiques, while the best antiques dealers can be found on **Denneweg**. The ideal way to round off your day is to take in a concert at the **Lucent Dans Theater**, a spankingly modern building near the Binnenhof, home to the National Dance Theatre. Their choreographed productions are of world renown and immense colour, a shimmering contrast to the coolly sedate charms of their home 'big village'.

CALENDAR HIGHLIGHTS

The Hague knows how to loosen its stays and flaunt itself when it comes to annual festivals. For instance, in April the Queen's Night Festival sees the city lighten up with five outdoor stages for a mammoth free music show…in honour of Beatrix. The focus turns seawards in May with the North Sea Regatta, which has sailing competitions between Scheveningen and Harwich in the UK. The sand stays in your eyes between April and June at the International Sand Sculpture Festival, as teams from around the

THE HAGUE IN…

→ ONE DAY

Binnenhof, Mauritshuis, Panorama Mesdag

→ TWO DAYS

Gemeentemuseum, 'The Fred', a stroll around Noordeinde, a show at Lucent Dans Theater

→ THREE DAYS

A day out at Scheveningen by the sea, Madurodam

world come up with magical creations made out of Scheveningen's shifting stuff. June's Music In My Head takes place at the Hague's Paard Van Troje over a couple of cutting-edge days: established rock acts line up alongside up-and-coming names. The city really throws off its ambassadorial trappings with July's De Parade, a travelling festival which alights in Westbroekpark with ten days of fairground rides, music, theatre, film, dance and opera. Tasty world cuisine's on offer too. Back at Scheveningen in August, the Van der Valk pier lights up twice every evening for the three nights of the International Fireworks Festival, while a month later the Todaysart Festival puts on a whole range of performing arts shows at twenty indoor and outdoor venues across the Hague. Fans of that event should also make a beeline for the Theater aan het Spui in November for the Crossing Border Festival which is, quite simply, Europe's biggest literature, music and visual arts all-in-one celebration, with over eighty acts taking part.

EATING OUT

Locals like to think that their 'biggest village in Europe' is the result of a lot made from a little. They call it the Hague Bluff. But what's that got to do with food? Well, the Hague Bluff is also a local pudding, made with eggs and sugar, representing the idea that something grand can be made from humble ingredients (in its finished state the Hague Bluff becomes a gooseberry fool). There's no bluff, though, about the city's restaurant scene. It's first rate in every respect, and although some are targeted full-on at the embassy army, many more are very affordable, with main courses set between fifteen and twenty euros. With the cuisine of more than twenty nationalities on offer, the choice is broad and pleasingly sophisticated: the number of exotic restaurants reflects the many cultures found here. Asian influences are everywhere, but in particular, the Indonesian connection is clear. There's a host of first-rate restaurants in the area just beyond Lange Voorhout around Denneweg and Frederikstraat. If you can't find what you want there, then head to Molenstraat, near the Noordeinde Palace, for another exciting cluster.

→ PEACE BE WITH YOU

The Peace Palace, to the north of the city, was the result of a donation by American millionaire Andrew Carnegie at the turn of the twentieth century. In turn, nations donated stained glass, marble, tapestries, urns, and a Swiss clock in the bell tower. Despite the onset of World War I, the Peace Palace's reputation went from strength to strength...today, this is where you'll find the International Court of Justice.

→ SCULPTURE BY THE SEA

If you decide to go to Scheveningen, you won't be alone. The resort is Holland's most popular seaside location and is visited by nine million a year. Its most fascinating attraction is the Museum Beelden-aan-Zee, which features modern sculptures in an old pavilion. Many leading sculptors are represented, including Fritz Koenig and Man Ray.

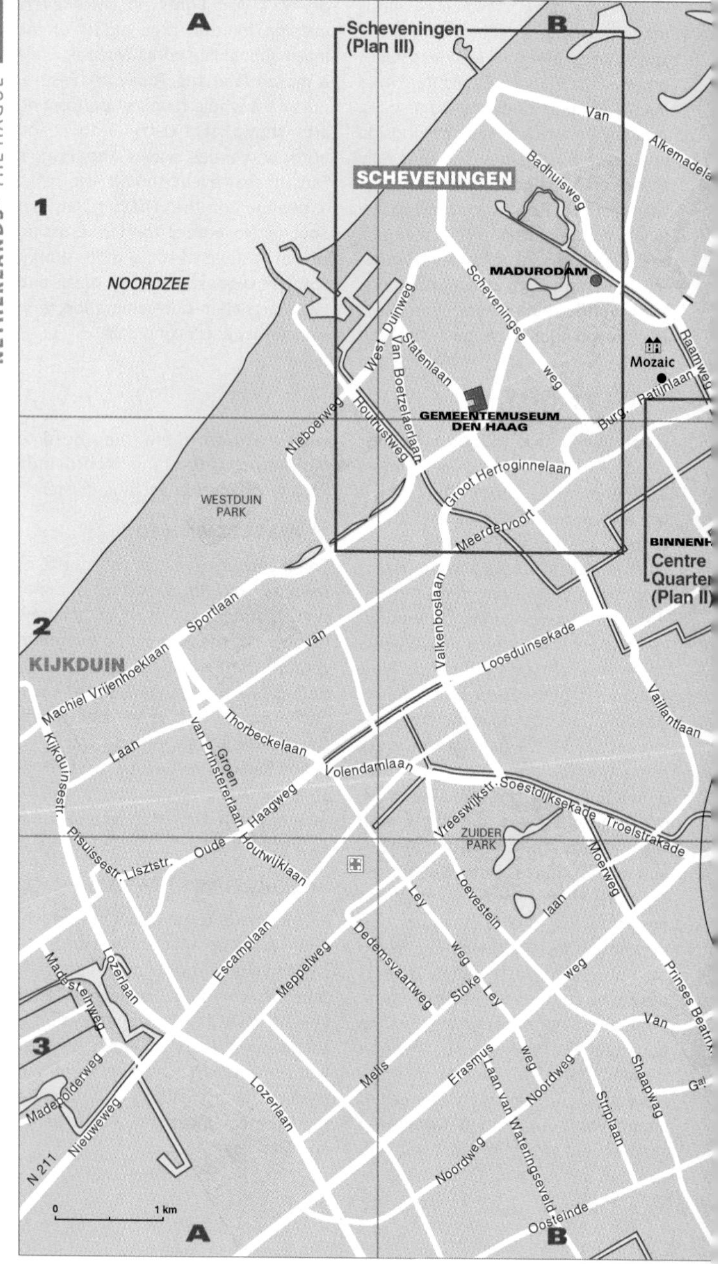
A
B
1
2
3
Scheveningen (Plan III)
SCHEVENINGEN
NOORDZEE
MADURODAM
Mozaic
GEMEENTEMUSEUM DEN HAAG
WESTDUIN PARK
BINNENH
Centre Quarter (Plan II)
KIJKDUIN
ZUIDER PARK
Van Alkemadelaan
Badhuisweg
Scheveningse weg
Raamweg
Burg. Patijnlaan
West Duinweg
Statenlaan
Van Boetzelaerlaan
Houtrustweg
Nieboerweg
Groot Hertoginnelaan
Meerdervoort
Valkenboslaan
Sportlaan
Machiel Vrijenhoeklaan
van
Laan
Loosduinsekade
Vaillantlaan
Thorbeckelaan
Groen van Prinstererlaan
Volendamlaan
Vreeswijkstr.
Soestdijksekade
Troelstrakade
Kijkduinsestr.
Haagweg
Oude Houtwijklaan
Pisuissestr.
Lisztstr.
Moerweg
Loevestein laan
Ley weg
Escamplaan
Meppelweg
Dedemsvaartweg
Stoke Ley weg
Madesteinweg
Lozerlaan
Madepolderweg
Nieuweweg
N 211
Mells
Erasmus weg
Laan van Wateringseveld
Noordweg
Striplaan
Shaapweg
Van
Prinses Beatrix
Oosteinde
0
1 km

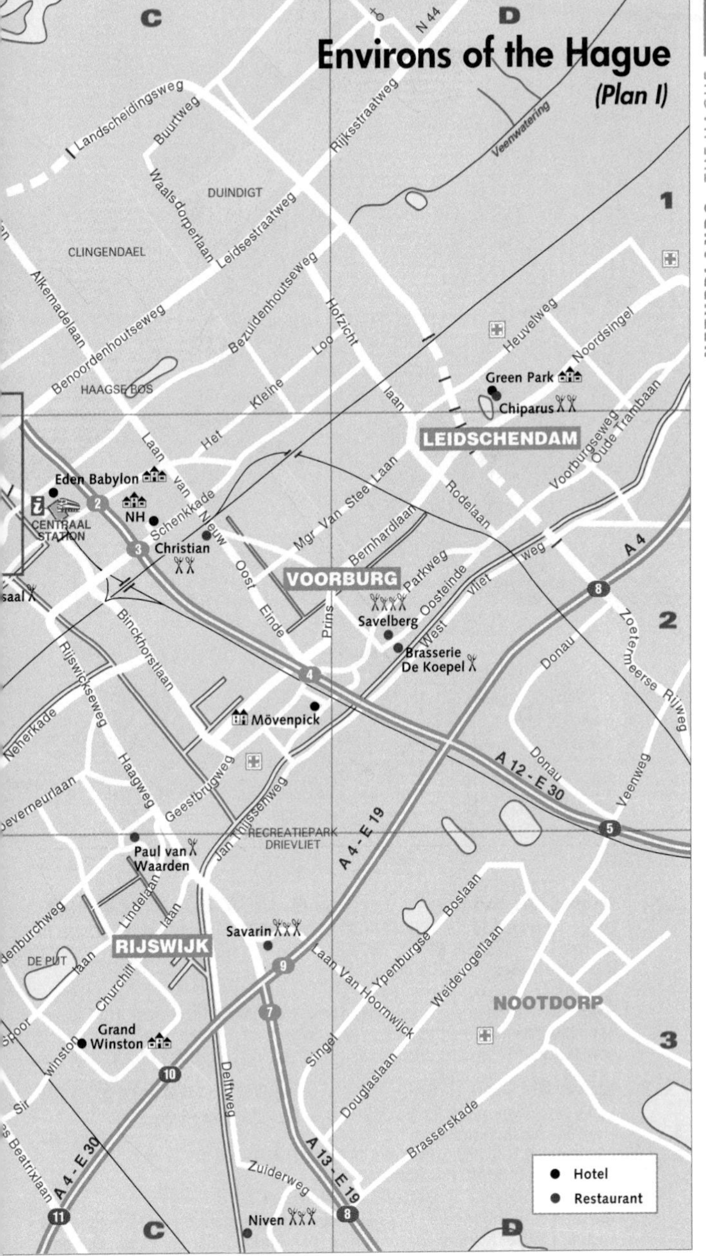
Environs of the Hague
(Plan I)
Hotel
Restaurant
LEIDSCHENDAM
VOORBURG
RIJSWIJK
NOOTDORP
DUINDIGT
CLINGENDAEL
HAAGSE BOS
CENTRAAL STATION
RECREATIEPARK DRIEVLIET
DE PUT
Eden Babylon
NH
Christian
Green Park
Chiparus
Savelberg
Brasserie De Koepel
Mövenpick
Paul van Waarden
Savarin
Grand Winston
Niven
A 12 - E 30
A 4 - E 19
A 13 - E 19
A 4 - E 30
A 4
N 44

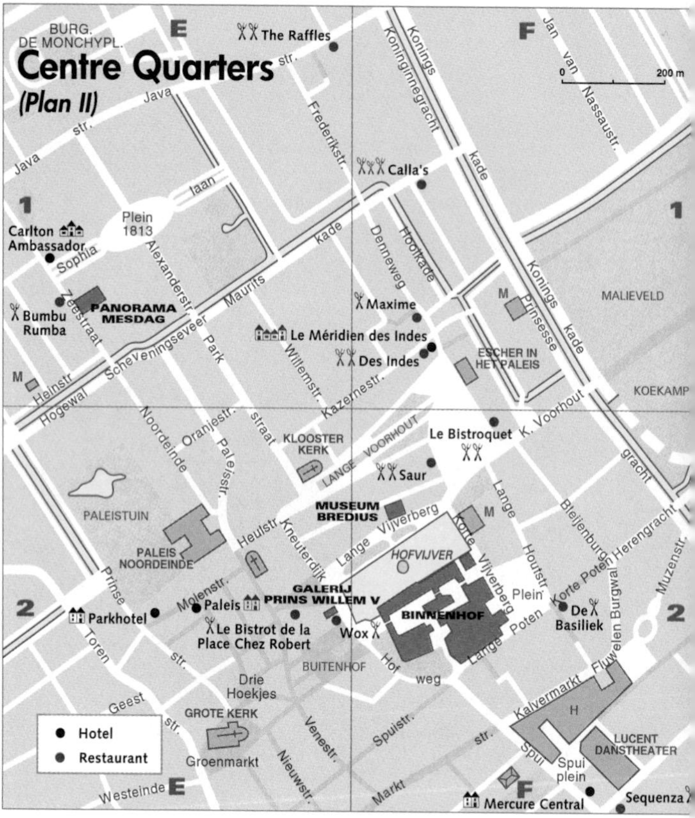

Centre Quarters
(Plan II)

● Hotel
● Restaurant

CENTRE — *Plan II*

Hotel des Indes

Lange Voorhout 54 ✉ 2514 EG – ✆ (0 70) 361 23 45 – www.hoteldesindes.nl
90 rm – 🚹175/350 € 🚹🚹175/350 €, ☕ 33 € – 2 suites **F1**
Rest ***Des Indes*** – see below
◆ Grand Luxury ◆ Design ◆
Following renovations by innovative French designer J. Garcia, this 1881 luxury hotel has been restored to its former glory in a refined style blending old and new. Luxury, full services, and a healing and relaxing spa. Famous for its high tea.

Eden Babylon

Koningin Julianaplein 35 ✉ 2595 AA – ✆ (0 70) 381 49 01 – www.edencityhotels.com *Plan I* **C2**
142 rm – 🚹100/275 € 🚹🚹100/275 €, ☕ 18 € – 1 suite
Rest – Menu 30/40 € – Carte 42/54 €
◆ Chain hotel ◆ Business ◆ Design ◆
The interior of this modern business hotel, near the station, was redesigned by Miguel Cancio Martins (decorator of the Buddha Bar in Paris). Designer bedrooms. Trendy lounge-bar and designer dining room overlooking a park. International menu, light portions, business clientele.

Bel Air

Johan de Wittlaan 30 ✉ 2517 JR – ✆ (0 70) 352 53 54 – www.belairhotel.nl *Plan III* **H3**

319 rm – 🛉105/235 € 🛉🛉105/235 €, ☕ 20 € – 8 suites

Rest – Menu 40/53 € – Carte approx. 50 €

♦ Chain hotel ♦ Classical ♦

Next to the Gemeentemuseum, Nederlands Congres Centrum and a park, Bel Air has one of the town's most extensive accommodation and conference facilities. New suites and studios. Contemporary brasserie with an airy, streamlined look. Jazzy lounge bar.

Crowne Plaza Promenade

van Stolkweg 1 ✉ 2585 JL – ✆ (0 70) 352 51 61 – www.crowneplazadenhaag.nl *Plan III* **H2**

92 rm – 🛉99/285 € 🛉🛉114/300 €, ☕ 23 € – 2 suites

Rest – Menu 39/45 € – Carte 46/62 €

♦ Chain hotel ♦ Functional ♦

Chain hotel overlooking a park that is home to the Madurodam (Miniature Holland). Modern artwork in the reception area, bedrooms from two periods, English bar. Convenient restaurant for those who don't feel like venturing into town.

NH

Prinses Margrietplantsoen 100 ✉ 2595 BR – ✆ (0 70) 381 23 45 – www.nh-hotels.com *Plan I* **C2**

205 rm – 🛉150/250 € 🛉🛉150/250 €, ☕ 19 €

Rest – Menu 22 € (lunch), 33/38 € – Carte approx. 45 €

♦ Chain hotel ♦ Business ♦ Modern ♦

NH chain unit in the heart of the local Manhattan. Glass-roofed atrium shopping centre, up-to-date identical bedrooms, conference rooms, nice breakfast buffet. Lounge restaurant with a trendy cafeteria concept. Perfect for a simple meal.

Carlton Ambassador

Sophialaan 2 ✉ 2514 JP – ✆ (0 70) 363 03 63 – www.carlton.nl/ambassador **E1**

77 rm – 🛉135/375 € 🛉🛉135/375 €, ☕ 24 € – 1 suite

Rest *Henricus* – Menu 33 € (lunch) – Carte 43/64 €

♦ Palace ♦ Classical ♦

Dozens of ancient chestnut trees surround this small luxury hotel in the Mesdag diplomatic district. Charming lobby, Dutch- and English-style bedrooms. À la carte menu at the Henricus restaurant, and Rubens brasserie in the cellar with a whiskey bar.

Parkhotel without rest

Molenstraat 53 ✉ 2513 BJ – ✆ (0 70) 362 43 71 – www.parkhoteldenhaag.nl **E2**

120 rm – 🛉79/150 € 🛉🛉89/250 €, ☕ 18 €

♦ Traditional ♦ Classical ♦

Contemporary dining room, dotted with 'neo-retro' influences in a hotel founded in 1912, which overlooks a park. Cosy lounge, Berlage staircase, modernised rooms and garden.

Paleis without rest

Molenstraat 26 ✉ 2513 BL – ✆ (0 70) 362 46 21 – www.paleishotel.nl

20 rm – 🛉145/285 € 🛉🛉165/295 €, ☕ 17 € **E2**

♦ Luxury ♦ Classical ♦

Plush boutique hotel noted for its personalised welcome. Louis XVI-style rooms adorned with rich fabrics by French designer Pierre Frey. Sumptuous breakfast room.

Mercure Central

Spui 180 ✉ 2511 BW – ✆ (0 70) 363 67 00 – www.mercure.com
156 rm – †99/214 € ††99/214 €, ☕ 20 € – 3 suites **F2**
Rest – *(closed Saturday and Sunday)* Menu 20 € (lunch) – Carte 27/41 €
◆ Chain hotel ◆ Business ◆ Design ◆
Newly renovated chain hotel catering to a business clientele. Centrally located (next to the theatre), modern architecture with a blue façade, smart up-to-date bedrooms and conference rooms. Restaurant in a friendly contemporary setting.

Mozaic without rest

Laan Copes van Cattenburgh 40 ✉ 2585 GB – ✆ (0 70) 352 23 35 – www.mozaic.nl *Plan I* **B1**
25 rm ☕ – †99 € ††125/149 €
◆ Family ◆ Design ◆
This manor house offers a friendly welcome with a personal touch and a cosy family atmosphere. Each room is its own special blend of design and comfort.

Calla's (Marcel van der Kleijn)

Laan van Roos en Doorn 51a ✉ 2514 BC – ✆ (0 70) 345 58 66 – www.restaurantcallas.nl – Closed 25 July-16 August, 25 December-4 January, Saturday lunch, Sunday and Monday **F1**
Rest – Menu 75/103 € bi – Carte 84/99 €
Spec. Tartelette van St.-Jacobsschelpen met parmezaankaas. Zeetong met dungesneden langoustines, crème van aardappel en schaaldierenjus. Crèpe soufflé met citroen, jasmijnthee en vanilleroomijs.
◆ Contemporary ◆ Elegant ◆
A former warehouse turned into a smart contemporary-style restaurant. Lounge, chef's table and a view of the kitchen below. Main room is upstairs.

Le Bistroquet

Lange Voorhout 98 ✉ 2514 EJ – ✆ (0 70) 360 11 70 – www.bistroquet.nl – Closed 24 December-2 January, Saturday lunch and Sunday **F2**
Rest – Menu 39/49 € – Carte 57/72 €
◆ Contemporary ◆ Cosy ◆
This plush bistro is popular with the diplomatic-parliamentary crowd. Up-to-date cuisine served in a warm, intimate atmosphere or outdoors in the shade of the square's trees.

Saur

Lange Voorhout 51 ✉ 2514 EC – ✆ (0 70) 361 70 70 – www.saur.nl – Closed Sunday **F2**
Rest – Menu 35 € (lunch), 39/99 € – Carte 55/87 €
◆ Traditional ◆ Brasserie ◆
This restaurant was recently reopened with professionalism, reviving its long and glorious past. French-style menu, good wine cellar, terrace on the square.

Rousseau

Van Boetzelaerlaan 134 ✉ 2581 AX – ✆ (0 70) 355 47 43 – www.restaurantrousseau.com – Closed 30 April-9 May, 24 July-15 August, 24 December-2 January, Saturday lunch, Sunday and Monday *Plan III* **G3**
Rest – Menu 28 € (lunch), 33/65 € – Carte approx. 60 €
◆ Traditional ◆ Friendly ◆
Seasonal French cuisine served in front of a Douanier Rousseau-style fresco (the chef-owner shares his surname) or under the courtyard pergola. Finely crafted menus. The dining room was renovated to celebrate 20 years of great meals!

XX **Christian**

Laan van Nieuw Oost Indië 1f ✉ 2593 BH – ✆ (0 70) 383 88 56 – www.restaurantchristian.nl – Closed 26 July-11 August, Tuesday and Wednesday Plan I **C2**

Rest – Menu 33 € (lunch), 38/75 € – Carte approx. 55 €

♦ Contemporary ♦ Friendly ♦

Christian grows most of the organic vegetables and condiments used in his dishes. Friendly setting, chef's table, patio with a terrace lounge.

XX **The Raffles**

Javastraat 63 ✉ 2585 AG – ✆ (0 70) 345 85 87 – www.restaurantraffles.com – Closed 1 week in February, last 2 weeks July-early August, Sunday and Monday

Rest – *(dinner only)* Menu 38/55 € – Carte 37/59 € **E1**

♦ Indonesian ♦ Friendly ♦

Located on the fittingly-named Javastraat, restaurant serving authentic, flavoursome Indonesian cooking, served in a suitably exotic setting, enhanced with Colonial touches.

XX **Des Indes** – Hotel des Indes

Lange Voorhout 54 ✉ 2514 EG – ✆ (0 70) 361 23 45 – www.hoteldesindes.nl – Closed last 2 weeks July-first 2 weeks August and Sunday dinner

Rest – Menu 50/63 € – Carte 61/75 € **F1**

♦ Contemporary ♦ Formal ♦

Tasty up-to-date cooking oozing with oriental spices and flavours; smart lounge ambience signed by J. Garcia. Cosmopolitan and affluent. Afternoon high teas.

X **Maxime**

Denneweg 10b ✉ 2514 CG – ✆ (0 70) 360 92 24 – www.restaurantmaxime.nl – Closed 25, 26 and 31 December **F1**

Rest – Menu 25 € (lunch)/33 €

♦ Contemporary ♦ Bistro ♦

Small hip bistro with a cosy décor offering two set menus and an à la carte lunch menu. Booking advised on weekends for both dinner sittings: (6-8pm) and (8-10pm).

X **Wox**

Buitenhof 36 ✉ 2513 AH – ✆ (0 70) 365 37 54 – www.wox.nl – Closed Tuesday lunch, Saturday lunch, Sunday and Monday **E2**

Rest – Carte 26/43 €

♦ Contemporary ♦ Trendy ♦

Fashionable brasserie between Buitenhof and Gevangenpoort serving French-Asian (wok) cuisine in a minimalist modern décor with mezzanine. Excellent wine list, particularly by the glass.

X **De Basiliek**

Korte Houtstraat 4a ✉ 2511 CD – ✆ (0 70) 360 61 44 – www.debasiliek.nl – Closed Saturday lunch and Sunday **F2**

Rest – Menu 29 € (lunch)/30 € – Carte approx. 50 €

♦ Contemporary ♦ Brasserie ♦

Trendy bistro on a pedestrian street near the Binnenhof. Cosy atmosphere with innovative lighting, and up-to-date cuisine with four choices on the menu at each sitting.

X **Bumbu Rumba**

Zeestraat 58 ✉ 2518 AB – ✆ (0 70) 360 06 50 – www.bumburumba.com – Closed Monday and Tuesday **E1**

Rest – *(dinner only)* Menu 40/53 € – Carte 40/57 €

♦ Indonesian ♦ Exotic ♦

Balinese cuisine served in an exotic setting (Buddhist statues, bamboo tables) brightened up with woks and spatulas recycled into wall lights and menu boards!

Basaal

Dunne Bierkade 3 ✉ 2512 BC – ☎ (0 70) 427 68 88 – www.basaal.net
– Closed 27 December-7 January, Monday and Tuesday *Plan I* **C2**
Rest – *(dinner only until 11 pm)* Menu 35 € – Carte 38/49 €
♦ Contemporary ♦ Bistro ♦
Up-to-the-minute menu served in a décor blending minimalist design and bistro comfort, or on a sidewalk terrace overlooking the canal and house barges. Charming owner.

Shirasagi

Stadhouderslaan 76 R ✉ 2517 JA – ☎ (0 70) 346 47 00 – www.shirasagi.nl
– Closed 31 December-3 January and Sunday *Plan III* **G3**
Rest – Menu 40 € (lunch), 50/80 € – Carte 31/63 €
♦ Japanese ♦ Minimalist ♦
Authentic Japanese restaurant in an attractive old house near the Gemeente-museum. Spacious but spare décor, open kitchen, sushi bar, teppanyaki, and rear terrace.

Le Bistrot de la Place Chez Norbert

Plaats 27 ✉ 2513 AD – ☎ (0 70) 364 33 27 – www.bistrotdelaplace.nl
– Closed first 2 weeks August, Saturday lunch and Sunday **E2**
Rest – Menu 35 € (lunch), 44/70 € bi – Carte 45/56 €
♦ French traditional ♦ Bistro ♦
From the décor to the dishes this bistro – next door to the centre of Dutch politics – is as French as it gets. Terrace on the square. Theme dinners featuring French songs on weekends.

Sequenza

Spui 224 ✉ 2511 BX – ☎ (0 70) 345 28 53
– Closed Sunday and Monday **F2**
Rest – *(dinner only until 11 pm) (set menu only)* Menu 43 €
♦ Contemporary ♦ Friendly ♦
Market-inspired, multi-choice menus made with the freshest ingredients. Calm and cosy atmosphere in the modernised dining room. Courtyard terrace.

SCHEVENINGEN *Plan III*

Steigenberger Kurhaus

Gevers Deynootplein 30 ✉ 2586 CK – ☎ (0 70) 416 26 36 – www.kurhaus.nl **G1**
245 rm – †145/300 € ††145/300 €, ☕ 25 € – 8 suites
Rest *Kandinsky* – see below
Rest *Kurzaal* – *☎ (0 70) 416 27 13* – Menu 33 €
♦ Palace ♦ Luxury ♦ Modern ♦
This beachside luxury hotel frequently hosts upmarket seminars. Extensive facilities, full spa service and sophisticated rooms equipped with modern comforts. Extensive modern menu served under the dome of a splendid period concert hall.

Carlton Beach

Gevers Deynootweg 201 ✉ 2586 HZ – ☎ (0 70) 354 14 14 – www.carlton.nl/beach **H1**
183 rm – †135/310 € ††150/325 €, ☕ 21 €
Rest – Menu 30 € – Carte 33/47 €
♦ Business ♦ Modern ♦
1980s building standing at the end of the dyke offering rooms that overlook the beach, dunes or street. Generous buffet and fine sea-view at breakfast time. A grillroom with a pirate-inspired décor, "beach brasserie" and summer "beach club".

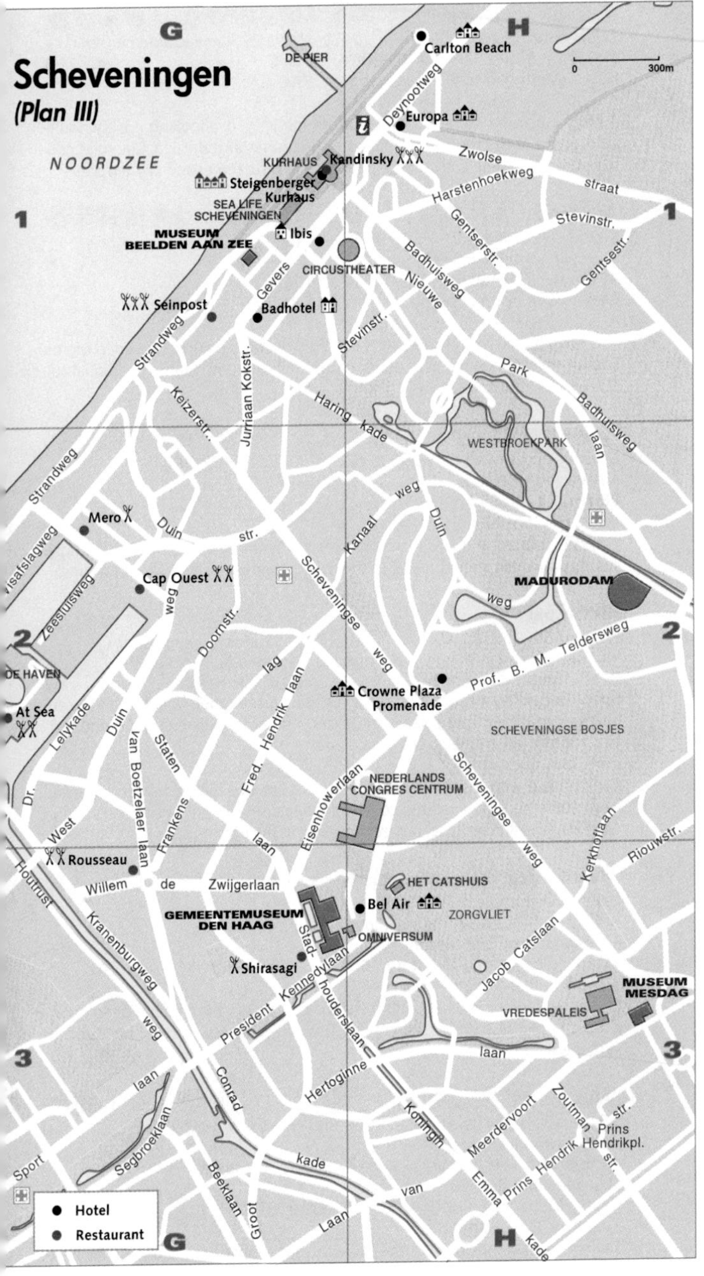

Scheveningen
(Plan III)
NOORDZEE
DE PIER
Carlton Beach
Europa
Kurhaus
Kandinsky
Steigenberger Kurhaus
SEA LIFE SCHEVENINGEN
MUSEUM BEELDEN AAN ZEE
Ibis
CIRCUSTHEATER
Seinpost
Badhotel
Deynootweg
Zwolse straat
Harstenhoekweg
Stevinstr.
Gentsestr.
Badhuisweg
Nieuwe
Gevers
Strandweg
Jurriaan Kokstr.
Keizerstr.
Haring kade
Park
WESTBROEKPARK
Badhuisweg laan
Mero
Duin str.
Kanaal weg
Duin weg
Visafslagweg
Zeesluisweg
Cap Ouest
Scheveningse weg
MADURODAM
DE HAVEN
At Sea
Doornstr.
Prof. B. M. Teldersweg
Crowne Plaza Promenade
SCHEVENINGSE BOSJES
Lelykade
Duin
Van Boetzelaer laan
Staten
Fred. Hendrik laan
NEDERLANDS CONGRES CENTRUM
Eisenhowerlaan
Dr.
West
Frankens
Rousseau
Willem de Zwijgerlaan
Houtrust
Kranenburgweg
HET CATSHUIS
Bel Air
ZORGVLIET
GEMEENTEMUSEUM DEN HAAG
OMNIVERSUM
Stadhouderslaan
Shirasagi
Kerkhoflaan
Riouwstr.
Jacob Catslaan
MUSEUM MESDAG
VREDESPALEIS
President Kennedylaan
laan
Hertoginne
Koningin
Conrad
Segbroeklaan
Sport laan
Meerdervoort
Zoutman str.
Prins Hendrikpl.
Prins Hendrik str.
Emma kade
Beeklaan
Groot
Laan van
0
300m
Hotel
Restaurant

Europa rest,

Zwolsestraat 2 ✉ 2587 VJ – ☎ (0 70) 416 95 95 – www.bilderberg.nl
174 rm – 109/209 € 109/209 €, 20 € **H1**
Rest – Menu 35/40 € – Carte approx. 37 €
♦ Chain hotel ♦ Functional ♦
A comfortable modern hotel, 300m from the jetty, overlooking a busy boulevard. Some of the rooms have views of the dunes and the sea. Colourful contemporary brasserie with an international à la carte menu and city terrace.

Badhotel

Gevers Deynootweg 15 ✉ 2586 BB – ☎ (0 70) 351 22 21 – www.badhotelscheveningen.nl **G1**
90 rm – 128/168 € 128/168 €, 16 €
Rest – *(dinner only)* Menu 33 € – Carte 31/39 €
♦ Traditional ♦ Classical ♦
This hotel on the main street offers tastefully decorated and maintained rooms. English-style lounge bar with a library. Conference rooms. Classic traditional cuisine in a tasteful and convivial dining room.

Ibis without rest

Gevers Deynootweg 63 ✉ 2586 BJ – ☎ (0 70) 354 33 00 – www.ibishotel.com **G1**
88 rm – 79/155 € 79/155 €, 13 €
♦ Chain hotel ♦ Functional ♦
Centrally located and close to all the resort's main amenities, this chain hotel stands on a main street parallel to the dyke (Strandweg). Two sizes of rooms.

Seinpost

Zeekant 60 ✉ 2586 AD – ☎ (0 70) 355 52 50 – www.seinpost.nl
– Closed Sunday in July-August, Saturday lunch and bank holidays
Rest – Menu 33 € (lunch), 45/65 € – Carte 63/93 € **G1**
Spec. Gebakken oesters met spek en vinaigrette met komkommer. Zeebaars in zoutkorst met seizoensgroenten en aardappelkrokant. Soufflé, sorbet, roomijs en cremeux van chocolade.
♦ Fish ♦ Design ♦
Book a table with a sea view in this modern rotunda, where fish and seafood reign supreme. Find a refined contemporary cuisine, interesting menus, astute wine list, plus an owner who is ever-present in the dining room.

Kandinsky – Hotel Steigenberger Kurhaus

Gevers Deynootplein 30 ✉ 2586 CK – ☎ (0 70) 416 26 34 – www.kurhaus.nl
– Closed Sunday and Monday **G1**
Rest – *(dinner only)* Menu 60/105 € bi – Carte 55/104 €
♦ Contemporary ♦ Formal ♦
Elegant restaurant in the resort's flagship hotel, where the chef has been effortlessly creating his classic cuisine since 1980. Seaside view and terrace overlooking the dyke.

Cap Ouest

Schokkerweg 37 (1st floor) ✉ 2583 BH – ☎ (0 70) 306 09 35 – www.capouest.nl
– Closed last week January-first week February, Sunday dinner October-May and lunch Saturday and Sunday **G2**
Rest – Menu 28 € (lunch), 38/55 € – Carte 53/71 €
♦ Fish ♦ Family ♦
Seafood restaurant opposite the harbour that supplies the kitchen with fresh North Sea produce. Modern décor, open kitchen, mezzanine and dockside terrace.

At Sea

Hellingweg 138 ✉ 2583 DX – ✆ (0 70) 331 74 45 – www.restaurantatsea.nl – Closed Saturday lunch, Sunday lunch and Wednesday **G2**

Rest – Menu 40/65 € – Carte 61/78 €

◆ Contemporary ◆ Fashionable ◆ Trendy ◆

Huge, trendy brasserie next to the harbour; watch the boats from the neat terrace. Stylish interior with a cosmopolitan atmosphere; a good time guaranteed by the professional team.

Mero

Vissershavenweg 61e ✉ 2583 DL – ✆ (0 70) 352 36 00 – www.merovis.nl – Closed Saturday lunch, Sunday lunch and Monday **G2**

Rest – Menu 29 € (lunch), 35/49 €

◆ Fish ◆ Brasserie ◆

Harbour-side fish restaurant in keeping with the times, both by its post-industrial loft-style, as by its cuisine, where the daily catch of fish and seafood takes pride of place.

ENVIRONS OF THE HAGUE

Plan I

Grand Winston

Generaal Eisenhowerplein 1 ✉ 2288 AE Rijswijk – ✆ (0 70) 414 15 00 – www.grandwinston.nl **C3**

245 rm – †89/229 € ††99/239 €, ☕ 20 € – 7 suites

Rest *Grand Canteen* – *(open until 11 pm)* Menu 28 € – Carte 31/66 €

◆ Business ◆ Modern ◆

A designer hotel next to the Rijswijk station with Winston Churchill watching over the lobby! Rooms in two modern blocks. Flamboyantly modern canteen; international menu.

Green Park

Weigelia 22 ✉ 2262 AB Leidschendam – ✆ (0 70) 320 92 80 – www.greenpark.nl **D1**

92 rm ☕ – †86/199 € ††96/225 € – 4 suites

◆ Chain hotel ◆ Business ◆ Classical ◆

Lakeside hotel built on piles not far from an immense shopping centre. The lobby is under the glass roof of an atrium and the best rooms enjoy a lake-view balcony.

Mövenpick

Stationsplein 8 ✉ 2275 AZ Voorburg – ✆ (0 70) 337 37 37 – www.moevenpick-voorburg.com **C2**

125 rm – †70/164 € ††70/164 €, ☕ 17 € **Rest** – Carte 28/41 €

◆ Chain hotel ◆ Functional ◆

Modern chain hotel, whose semicircular façade overlooks the station. Functional rooms, the best ones at the rear. Designer-style bar. Modern brasserie with an Italian-Asian focus: pasta and wok-cooked dishes. Front terrace.

Savelberg with rm

Oosteinde 14 ✉ 2271 EH Voorburg – ✆ (0 70) 387 20 81 – www.restauranthotelsavelberg.nl **D2**

14 rm – †150/350 € ††150/350 €, ☕ 19 €

Rest – *(closed Saturday lunch, Sunday and Monday)* Menu 58 € (lunch), 65/110 € – Carte 77/108 €

Spec. Salade van kreeft 'Savelberg'. Gegrilde tarbot met compote van uien en wintertruffel. Gebraden Bresse duif met ravioli van ui, groene linzen en jus van het karkas.

◆ Contemporary ◆ Formal ◆

This luxurious 18C abode (with a star since the late 20C) is a treat for the eyes and taste buds! Classic and innovative dishes, extensive wine cellar, well-informed sommelier and terrace overlooking the park. Elegant rooms and suites with balcony, all decorated with period furniture.

XXX

Savarin

Laan van Hoornwijck 29 ✉ 2289 DG Rijswijk – ✆ (0 70) 307 20 50 – www.savarin.nl – Closed Saturday lunch and Sunday **C3**

Rest – Menu 35/75 € – Carte 53/75 €

♦ Contemporary ♦ Formal ♦

Former farmhouse dating from 1916 where inventive cuisine is served in a contemporary setting with soft designer lighting. Colourful fireplace lounge, banquet space, conference room and terrace.

XXX ✿

Niven (Niven Kunz)

Delftweg 58a ✉ 2289 AL Rijswijk – ✆ (0 70) 307 79 70 – www.restaurantniven.nl – Closed last week July-first week August, late December-early January, Tuesday lunch, Saturday lunch, Sunday and Monday **C3**

Rest – Menu 35 € (lunch)/88 € – Carte 59/75 €

Spec. Gebakken rog in chorizopoeder met knolselderij, pistache, inktvis en jus van sjalotjes. Eendenlever candybar met salade van rode biet en sorbet van rode wijnazijn. Zeevruchten collectie met appel, aardappel en asperges.

♦ Contemporary ♦ Fashionable ♦ Elegant ♦

Taste the young chef's creative specialities in a spruce, up-to-the-minute decor (whitewashed rafters, modern artwork, upholstered benches, designer lighting) or on the terrace opposite the golf course. Smart ambience and stylish service.

XX

Chiparus – Hotel Green Park

Weigelia 22 ✉ 2262 AB Leidschendam – ✆ (0 70) 320 92 80 – www.greenpark.nl **D1**

Rest – Menu 33 € – Carte approx. 41 €

♦ Contemporary ♦ Fashionable ♦ Elegant ♦

This restaurant, treated to a smart, modern makeover, also boasts a lakeside terrace. Seasonal and à la carte menu. A glass of wine is suggested with each dish.

X ✿

Paul van Waarden

Tollensstraat 10 ✉ 2282 BM Rijswijk – ✆ (0 70) 414 08 12 – www.paulvanwaarden.nl – Closed 2 weeks in May, late December-early January, Saturday lunch, Sunday and Monday **C3**

Rest – Menu 38/53 € – Carte 54/75 €

Spec. Vier bereidingen met lever. Krokant gebakken kabeljauw met erwtensoep en gerookte paling. Tarte tatin van rabarber met gemberroomijs.

♦ Contemporary ♦ Brasserie ♦

A renovated house near the church tower offering tasty seasonal dishes at reasonable prices, served in three simple and airy dining rooms (bare tables, gastronomic photographs, cast iron basins) or on the patio in summer.

X

Brasserie De Koepel

Oosteinde 1 ✉ 2271 EA Voorburg – ✆ (0 70) 369 35 72 – www.brasseriedekoepel.nl – Closed 29 December-6 January **D2**

Rest – *(dinner only except Sunday; open until 11 pm)* Menu 35/44 € – Carte 40/46 €

♦ Contemporary ♦ Brasserie ♦

Former orangery in Vreugd en Rust park featuring a rotunda with columns, high bay windows, a cupola adorned with whimsical frescoes, red velvet padding, candlelight dinners, and a summer terrace.

ROTTERDAM

ROTTERDAM

Population: 584 107 – Altitude: sea level

ôme Dancette/Fotolia.com

Rotterdam trades on its earthy appeal, on a rough-and-ready grittiness tied in with its status as the largest seaport in the world, handling 350 million tonnes of goods a year, with over half of all goods that are heading into Europe passing through it. Flattened during the Second World War, Rotterdam was rebuilt on a grand scale, jettisoning the idea of streets full of terraced houses in favour of a modern cityscape of concrete and glass.

The city is located on the Nieuwe Maas, but is centred round a maze of other rivers - most importantly the Rhine and the Maas - and is only a few dozen kilometres inland from the North Sea. It spills over both banks of its river, and is linked by tunnels, bridges and the metro; the most stunning connection across the water is the modern Erasmusbridge, whose sleek design has come to embody the Rotterdam of the new millennium. It's mirrored on the southern banks by the development of the previously run-down Kop Van Zuid area into a zone of new build and sleek promise.

LIVING THE CITY

Rotterdam is a sprawling city that's eaten up both banks of the **Nieuwe Maas River**. Its northern extremity is bounded by the **Zestienhoven airport,** while to the south, over the water, shimmers the modernist, once industrialised, area of **Kop Van Zuid**. Central Rotterdam's main rail station, **Centraal**, is to the north of the river; immediately to its east is a complex array of modern high-rises with the focus on the pedestrianized **Lijnbaan**. The culture zone of **Museumpark** is close to the water, and it's bounded on either side by two old harbours, **Delfshaven** and **Oude Haven**. The latter is in the compact and interesting district of **Blaak**, another of the city's modernist shrines.

PRACTICAL INFORMATION

ARRIVAL-DEPARTURE

The Airport is 6km northwest of the city, with a taxi costing about €23. Shuttle buses no.33 and 43 run every 10min and take 20min to Central Railway Station.

TRANSPORT

Metro, bus, tram and train combine to delve into every little corner of the city. There are a variety of stripcards to ease your way around: from two-strip right up to forty-five strip tickets. That could entail a lot of fiddling about and franking. A better bet could be to invest in a one-day, two-day, or three-day card, which give you unlimited travel on any form of transport.

Another good idea is to buy a Rotterdam Card, which provides unlimited use of the transport network as well as free admission to most attractions. It's available for either 24 or 72 hours.

You can hire bicycles from the Centraal station cycle shop. These work out at good value, and can be hired for either a day or a week.

EXPLORING ROTTERDAM

Whatever else anyone may say about Rotterdam, no-one denies that it has edge. Pacy, big and brash, it barged its way into the European zeitgeist earlier this decade when it was European City of Culture. It lived – and still lives – easily with that term. Constructed anew after 1945, the bustling port city on the Nieuwe Maas introduced to Europe the concept of modern building, for good or bad. Walk down the Lijnbaan, and you're face to face with the continent's first pedestrianized shopping precinct. It's now fifty-five years old, and on no-one's list for an architecture award – but it's a fascinating prototype, all the same; back in 1953, this was very much the shape of things to come.

A different kind of modernity confronts you just a half mile to the east. The district of Blaak was a working-class stronghold until it was destroyed in World War II. The phoenix that arose took everyone by surprise. For starters, a space-age metro station rose from the ashes, alongside apartments that are shaped like cubes, up-ended on one corner and perched on tall stalks. They're called **Cube Houses**, and were built to the bemusement of locals a quarter of a century ago. One of them, the **Kijk-Kubus**, is open to visitors, but beware if you're unbalanced at the thought of an 'upside-down' house. The city's trademark melding of functional and eccentric is further enhanced just a bit to the southwest with the fabulous sounding **Boompjestorens**, three dice-shaped apartment blocks in a seventeenth century double row of lime trees turned into a modish boulevard.

➜ BUILDING SIGHTS

The more you wander the city, the more you realise that Blaak isn't the sole preserve of architectural innovation. Whatever your take on it all, there's no getting away from the fact that there are few places in the world that have such an eclectic range of buildings to keep you entertained (or bewildered). Try these for size: the **Euromast Space Tower** (which, at 185m, really is a size), a spire with super-fast automatic lifts which zoom you up for awesome views of the city; the **Groothandelsgebouw** (which translates as large business building) and is, well, a large business building with a stunning post-war design; the **Witte Huis**, a twelve-storey high-rise dating from 1897, making it Europe's first skyscraper; **Willemswerf**, the sparkling global HQ of shipping giant Nedlloyd; **Huis Sonnenfeld**, a modernist house from the 1930s that sets off the adjacent **Architectuur Instituut** a treat; the soaring **KPN Telekom Building**, built by Renzo Piano in 2000, and looking in its precarious way as if it's about to topple over; and the city's two iconic bridges, the **Willemsbrug**, and **Erasmusbrug,** whose graceful, angular lines of silver tubing have earned it the nickname 'The Swan'.

➜ HAVENS OF PEACE

If you're looking for a more picturesque aspect of Rotterdam – something that might give a clue to its long lost past – then bits of the Nieuwe Maas harbourside area can nudge you in the right direction. A couple of kilometres southwest of Centraal Station is Delfshaven, an antique harbour that managed to stay pretty much intact as the bombs fell. It has history: the Pilgrim Fathers set sail from here in 1620 en route to the New World, and its quiet waterways lend it a feel of decorous charm. Way off to the east at the other end of the central waterfront is Oude Haven, the city's oldest harbour dating from 1325, and sympathetically redeveloped after the War. A tiny inlet, it adds another dimension to the 'cube house'/Witte Huis area - it's lined with peaceful cafés and houses whose origins stretch back seven hundred years. The antique boats and barges that mill around just add to the feeling of a different city at a different time.

➜ DAM CULTURED

There's no problem locating the area where culture is the name of the game – the authorities found a wide, open area not far up from the waterfront and called it Museumpark. Chief amongst its glories is Rotterdam's number one attraction, The **Museum Boijmans Van Beuningen,** which covers a mighty span of art history and holds a continuing cycle of temporary exhibitions. The permanent collection ranges across all major schools of Dutch and continental art from old masters (Bosch, Breugel, Rembrandt) through the Impressionists (Van Gogh, Degas, Gaugin, Monet), to the modernists (Dali, Duchamp, Magritte). As a perfect foil, the nearby **Kunsthal** is a great place to look at premier league exhibitions of contemporary art, design and photography, while there's the **Natuurmuseum** next door, a pure joy for lovers of taxidermy. Outside, the nature's pretty good, too, as Museumpark gives you the chance for a good stroll, with a fountain, a lake and enough benches for you to sit and ruminate on the meaning of the giant rabbit sculptures that dot the lawn.

Finding out more about the history of Rotterdam itself is the preserve of two museums east of Museumpark near the old **Leuvehaven** harbour. The **Maritiem Museum** is a salty dog of a gallery, full of the sights and sounds of the city as seaport, and with an absorbing look at what it was like to be a seafarer in the seventeenth and eighteenth centuries. Up the road, past Churchillplein metro station, the **Museum het Schielandshuis** is housed in one of the city's few preserved seventeenth century mansions, and it paints a broader brush over Rotterdam's history, with original footage of World War II bombing, and, on a lighter note, social history in photographs.

The story of modern Rotterdam is embodied in the tale of the neighbourhood to the south of the river – Kop Van Zuid. Historically, a predominantly working class area with docks, a shipyard and a terminal for ocean-going liners, its stock plummeted in the 1960s and 70s when most of the heavy waterfront industry packed up and moved way out west to **Europoort** by the North Sea. Kop Van Zuid, poorly connected to the north bank, was abandoned. Then, in 1986, development started to turn the area around, and now fifteen thousand residents live in the hard-edged modern urban apartments that have helped earn the south bank its new reputation as a high quality zone with eye-catching architecture and smart cafés and bars. The icing on the cake for this, the city's most heralded up-and-coming quarter, came with the arrival of the **Luxor Theatre**, a stunning modern building that's brought a real touch of culture – through concerts, musicals and dance – to the 'other side' of the Nieuwe Maas.

CALENDAR HIGHLIGHTS

Holland's most prestigious jazz event, The North Sea Jazz Festival, has moved its base from The Hague to Rotterdam's Ahoy centre in Kop Van Zuid, a sure sign of the city's emergence on the cultural map. It attracts many of the world's top musicians and, held in mid-July, it's just part of a vibrant summer in the city. May's Dunya Festival presents a wealth of arts and culture from across the globe, with several stages around Euromast and Parklaan hosting music, storytelling and performance. The streets

ROTTERDAM IN...

→ ONE DAY
Blaak area, including Kijk-Kubus and Boompjestorens, Oude Haven, Museum Boijmans Van Beuningen

→ TWO DAYS
A fuller investigation of Museumpark, Delfshaven, the view from Euromast, a cruise along the Nieuwe Maas

→ THREE DAYS
Kop Van Zuid, including a meal at one of its restaurants, a show at the Luxor Theatre

come alive with colour at two spectacular events, one in July and one in August. The first – the Summer Carnival – matches the spirit of more exotic climes, a great street parade enlivened by ethnic groups from the likes of Cape Verde, the Antilles and Surinam. Then along comes Dance Parade, during which around forty decorated trucks wind their way through the centre, to the sound of pulsing drums, eventually arriving at Schiehaven's Lloydpier. As a complete contrast, the Municipal Theatre hosts the Poetry International Festival in June – the largest gathering of global poets in Europe; there are Dutch and English translations of their work. The action moves back outside again for September's World Port Festival, when, over three days, the secrets of the city's huge harbour are revealed: there are ship tours, rescue and aviation demos, boat cruises and bus trips. In the same month, The Kunsthal hosts Chocolad' Amour (can there *be* a more enticing name?), which does pretty much what it says on the label, with tasting sessions – surprise, surprise – a huge draw. Sticking to the food theme, the Kunsthal is also home base and kitchen for KunsthalCOOKING, a three-day food jamboree with tastings, again in September. January is the month for movie buffs with the twelve-day International Film Festival, renowned for its innovative aspect, while in March you can stay up late for Museum Night, when more than forty galleries and museums have extended opening hours – a great time for a guided tour.

EATING OUT

Rotterdam is a hot place for dining, in the literal and metaphorical sense. There are lots of places to tuck into the flavours of Holland's colonial past, in particular the spicy delicacies of Indonesia and Surinam. The long east/west stretch of Oude and Nieuwe Binnenweg is not only central and handy for many of the sights, it's also chock-full of good cafés, café-bars and restaurants. The recently smartened up canal district of Oudehaven has also introduced to the city a good selection of places to eat while taking in the relaxed vibe. Along the waterfront, various warehouses have been transformed into mega-restaurants, particularly around the Noordereiland isle in the middle of the river, while in Kop Van Zuid the Wilhelminapier quay is spot-on for a brand new area with good restaurants and tasty views to go with it. Many establishments in the city are closed at lunchtime, except business restaurants and those that set a high gastronomic standard and like to show it off in the middle of the day as well as in the evening. The bill includes service charge, and tipping is optional: round up the total if you're pleased with the service.

→ LIQUID REFRESHMENT

A satisfying – and speedy – way to get a duck's eye view of the intriguing architecture here is to take a water taxi. Introduced to the harbour just a few years ago, they whisk you along at nearly 30mph past the cranes, warehouses and giant cargo ships. They skim towards the harbour mouth, then spin round and bring you back, so that what you missed on the way out, you can catch on the return.

→ BINNEN THERE, BOUGHT IT

You may think you've *seen* a few oddities in Rotterdam, but the place to buy them is the massive Binnenrotte market, open three days of the week. It's not inconceivable to think you can get anything here, from antique dolls and Turkish bread to 1930s bikes and secondhand fishing rods.

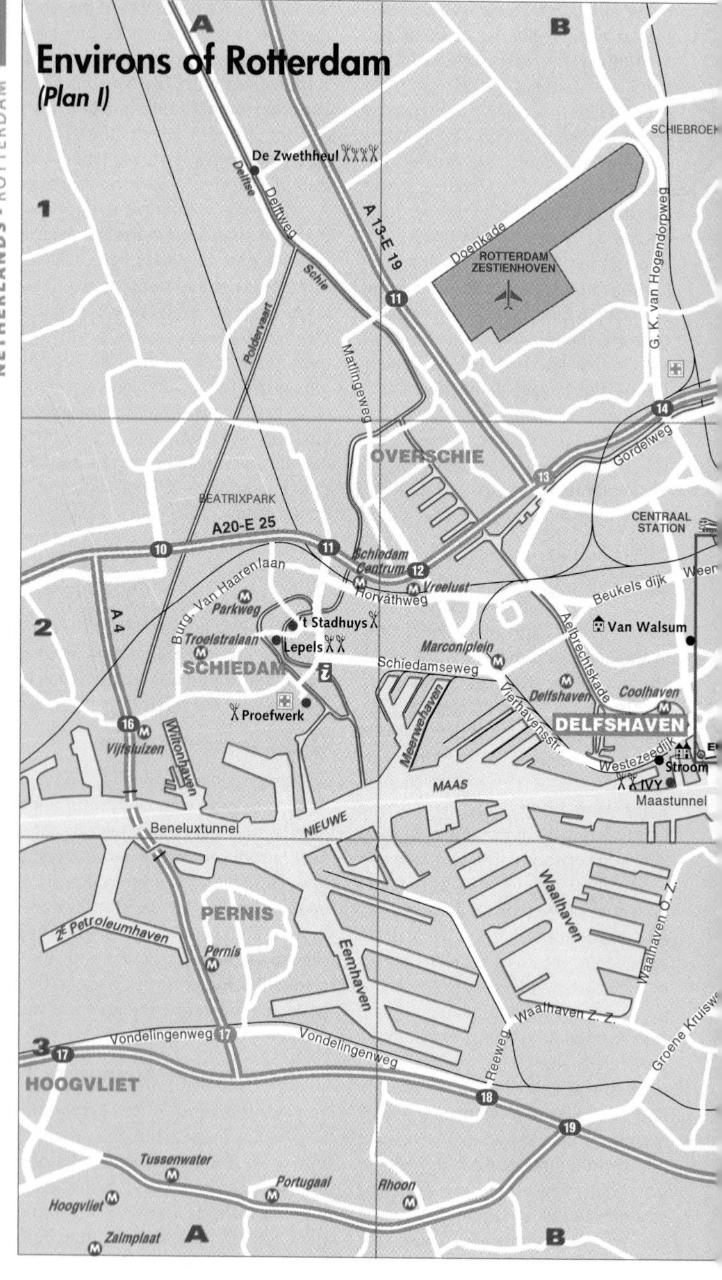
Environs of Rotterdam
(Plan I)
A
B
1
2
3
De Zwethheul
Delftse
Delftweg
Schie
A 13-E 19
Doenkade
ROTTERDAM ZESTIENHOVEN
SCHIEBROEK
G. K. van Hogendorpweg
Poldervaart
Matlingeweg
OVERSCHIE
Gordelweg
BEATRIXPARK
A20-E 25
CENTRAAL STATION
Schiedam Centrum
Vreelust
Horváthweg
Beukels dijk
Weena
Burg. Van Haarenlaan
Parkweg
't Stadhuys
Lepels
Troelstralaan
SCHIEDAM
Van Walsum
Marconiplein
Schiedamseweg
Aelbrechtskade
Delfshaven
Coolhaven
DELFSHAVEN
Vierhavensstr.
Meerwehaven
Proefwerk
A 4
Vijfsluizen
Wiltonhaven
Westezeedijk
Stroom
IVY
MAAS
Maastunnel
Beneluxtunnel
NIEUWE
PERNIS
2e Petroleumhaven
Pernis
Eemhaven
Waalhaven
Waalhaven O. Z.
Waalhaven Z. Z.
Vondelingenweg
Reeweg
Groene Kruisweg
HOOGVLIET
Tussenwater
Portugaal
Rhoon
Hoogvliet
Zalmplaat

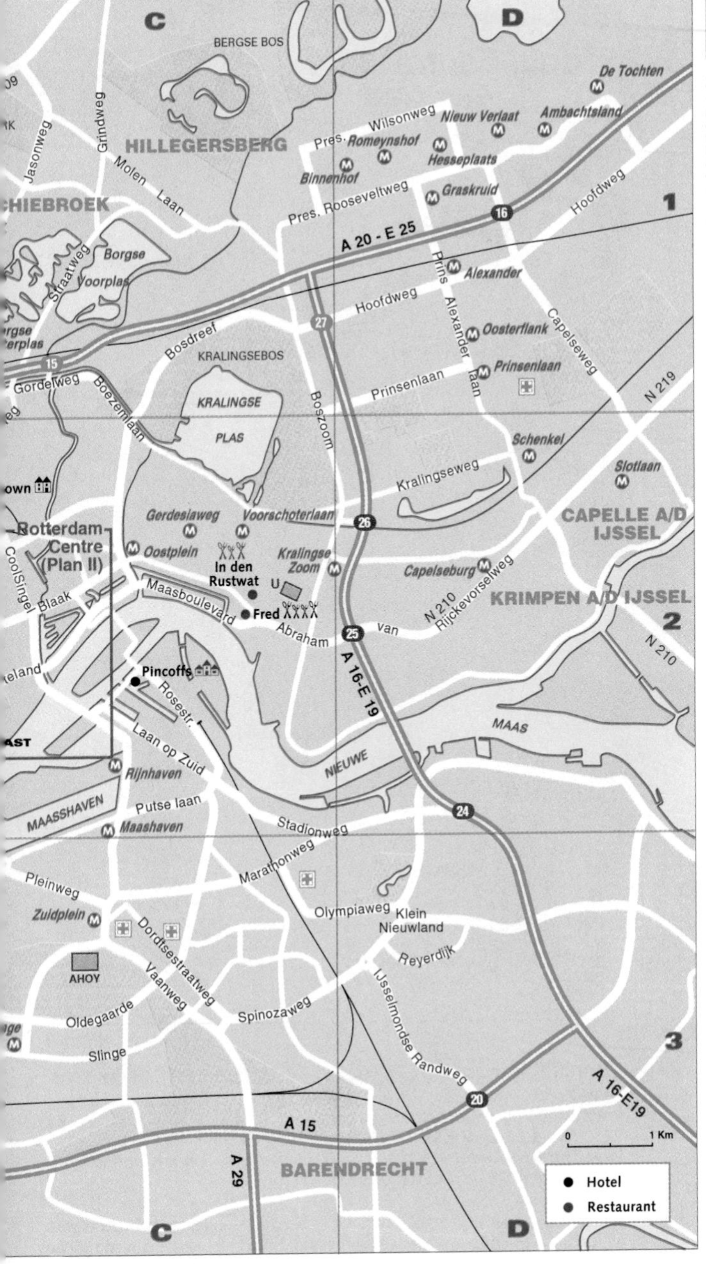
C
D
BERGSE BOS
De Tochten
Wilsonweg
Nieuw Verlaat
Ambachtsland
HILLEGERSBERG
Pres. Romeynshof
Hesseplaats
Binnenhof
Grindweg
Jasonweg
Molen Laan
Pres. Rooseveltweg
Graskruid
Hoofdweg
1
SCHIEBROEK
A 20 - E 25
16
Borgse Voorplas
Straatweg
Prins Alexander laan
Alexander
Hoofdweg
27
Oosterflank
Capelseweg
Bosdreef
KRALINGSEBOS
15
Gordelweg
Boezemlaan
Prinsenlaan
Prinsenlaan
N 219
KRALINGSE PLAS
Boszoom
Schenkel
Slotlaan
Kralingseweg
Gerdesiaweg
Voorschoterlaan
26
CAPELLE A/D IJSSEL
Rotterdam Centre (Plan II)
Oostplein
In den Rustwat
Kralingse Zoom
Capelseburg
CoolSingel
Blaak
Maasboulevard
U
Fred
KRIMPEN A/D IJSSEL
N 210
Rijckevorselweg
Abraham van
25
2
N 210
Pincoffs
Rosestr.
A 16-E 19
MAAS
Laan op Zuid
NIEUWE
Rijnhaven
MAASSHAVEN
Putse laan
Maashaven
Stadionweg
24
Marathonweg
Pleinweg
Zuidplein
Olympiaweg
Klein Nieuwland
Reyerdijk
Dordtsestraatweg
AHOY
Vaanweg
Oldegaarde
Spinozaweg
IJsselmondse Randweg
3
Slinge
A 16-E19
20
A 15
0
1 Km
A 29
BARENDRECHT
Hotel
Restaurant
C
D

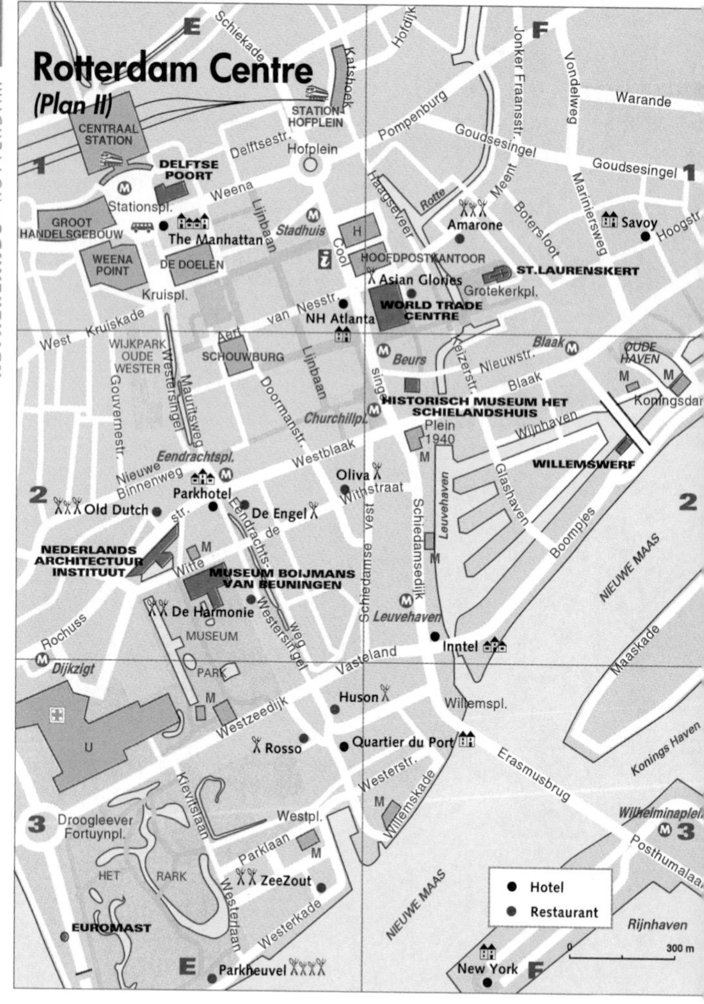

CENTRE

Plan II

The Manhattan

Weena 686 ✉ 3012 CN – ✆ (0 10) 430 20 00 – www.manhattanhotelrotterdam.com **E1**

211 rm – 109/359 € 134/384 €, ☕ 29 € – 3 suites

Rest *The Restaurant* – *(closed late December-early January and lunch Saturday and Sunday)* Carte 29/55 €

◆ Business ◆ Luxury ◆ Modern ◆

A huge skyscraper built across from the station, featuring large bedrooms with all modern comforts, conference rooms and a business centre. Striking urban view from the upper floors. Seasonal dishes served in a panoramic dining room with an airy contemporary décor.

Parkhotel

rest,

Westersingel 70 ✉ 3015 LB – ✆ (0 10) 436 36 11 – www.parkhotelrotterdam.nl **E2**

186 rm – 89/275 € 89/275 €, 24 € – 3 suites

Rest *Restaurant 70* – *(closed last 2 weeks July-first week August, late December-early January and Sunday) (dinner only)* Menu 35/40 € – Carte approx. 44 €

♦ Business ♦ Classic ♦

Hotel established in 1922 and modernised over the years, which explains the mixed architecture. Recently-renovated interior. Several types of guestroom. Cosy and comfortable hotel restaurant. Inner garden with terrace in summertime.

Inntel

rest,

Leuvehaven 80 ✉ 3011 EA – ✆ (0 10) 413 41 39 – www.inntelhotelsrotterdamcentre.nl **F2**

263 rm – 100/255 € 100/255 €, 24 €

Rest – *(closed Sunday dinner)* Menu 29 € – Carte 35/50 €

♦ Chain hotel ♦ Business ♦ Modern ♦

Excellent location for this chain hotel with all the modern conveniences, next to the harbour museum near the majestic Erasmus Bridge. Top-floor pool. Trendy brasserie-style establishment and panoramic bar with a blue, water-inspired décor.

Pincoffs without rest

Stieltjesstraat 34 ✉ 3071 JX – ✆ (0 10) 297 45 00 – www.hotelpincoffs.nl – Closed 1-16 August *Plan I* **C2**

16 rm – 125/165 € 165/185 €, 17 € – 1 suite

♦ Historic ♦ Modern ♦

A distinctive historic hotel and former customs house in the trendy Kop van Zuid district. Tastefully renovated. Guestrooms and hospitality with a personal touch.

NH Atlanta

Aert van Nesstraat 4 ✉ 3012 CA – ✆ (0 10) 206 78 00 – www.nh-hotels.com **E1**

215 rm – 69/200 € 69/200 €, 19 €

Rest – *(closed Saturday and Sunday) (dinner only)* Menu 29/45 € – Carte 32/52 €

♦ Chain hotel ♦ Business ♦ Functional ♦

A hotel across from the WTC with three buildings, the oldest dating from 1930. Rooms vary in size and age. Art deco elements in the communal and conference areas. Multiple-choice menu served in a welcoming 1900s setting.

Savoy without rest

Hoogstraat 81 ✉ 3011 PJ – ✆ (0 10) 413 92 80 – www.edencityhotels.com

94 rm – 80/275 € 80/275 €, 17 € **F1**

♦ Business ♦ Modern ♦

A seven-storey building, just a stone's throw from Blom's famous "cube houses". Modern rooms, the top ones have terraces. Lounge, bar, gym and conference rooms.

Stroom

rest, rm,

Lloydstraat 1 ✉ 3024 EA – ✆ (0 10) 221 40 60 – www.stroomrotterdam.nl

18 rm – 80/100 € 100/160 € – 3 suites *Plan I* **B2**

Rest – Menu 25 € (lunch), 30/45 € – Carte 30/68 €

♦ Business ♦ Modern ♦

In a newly-developed district near the docks, former power station now an ultra-trendy hotel. Remains of its industrial past displayed in the lobby. Bright minimalist-style designer rooms. An international menu served in a contemporary setting with an open kitchen.

New York

Koninginnenhoofd 1 (Wilhelminapier) ✉ *3072 AD – ✆ (0 10) 439 05 00 – www.hotelnewyork.nl* **F3**

72 rm – 110/280 € 110/280 €, ☕ 20 €

Rest – *(open until 11 pm)* Carte 29/58 €

♦ Traditional ♦ Retro ♦

The former HQ of the Holland-America shipping line is now a hotel with character. Rooms overlooking the port, town or river. Vintage New York-style barbershop. Spacious historic café in a "post-industrial" style with a modern menu that changes twice a year (summer and winter).

Crown

♿ rm, A/C rm,

Schiekade 658 ✉ *3032 AK – ✆ (0 10) 466 33 44 – www.crownrotterdam.nl*

116 rm ☕ – 69/109 € 89/129 € *Plan I* **C2**

Rest – *(closed Saturday and Sunday) (dinner only)* Carte approx. 36 €

♦ Chain hotel ♦ Traditional ♦ Functional ♦

On a busy main street, the hotel is made up of three old houses and a modern wing at the rear, where rooms are just as comfortable, but quieter. Restaurant offering an international menu in a contemporary setting.

Quartier du Port without rest

Van Vollenhovenstraat 48 ✉ *3016 BJ – ✆ (0 10) 240 04 25 – www.quartierduport.nl* **E3**

20 rm – 95/132 € 95/132 €, ☕ 13 €

♦ Inn ♦ Retro ♦

The maritime past of this period house (1900) can still be seen in some of the interior decoration. Three types of modern rooms; opt for one at the rear.

Van Walsum

Mathenesserlaan 199 ✉ *3014 HC – ✆ (0 10) 436 32 75 – www.hotelvanwalsum.nl – Closed 23 December-1 January* *Plan I* **B2**

28 rm ☕ – 85/110 € 110/145 € **Rest** – *(resident only)*

♦ Family ♦ Classic ♦

This 1895 abode has been run by the same family since 1955. Various kinds of rooms; ask for one of the cosier, renovated ones. Dining room-veranda opening onto a garden terrace.

Parkheuvel (Erik van Loo)

Heuvellaan 21 ✉ *3016 GL – ✆ (0 10) 436 07 66 – www.parkheuvel.nl – Closed 1-21 August, 27 December-9 January, Saturday lunch, Sunday and bank holidays* **E3**

Rest – Menu 50/135 € – Carte 80/118 €

Spec. Ravioli van zwarte Bresse kip met gebakken langoustines. Proeverij van lam met knoflookbeignets en basilicumjus (January-September). Frambozen gevuld met witte chocolademousse en frambozencoulis.

♦ Contemporary ♦ Formal ♦

A semicircular modern pavillion located on the Maas by a park with bay windows and a terrace overlooking the harbour. Lovely remodelled art deco interior, extensive menu and wine list, as well as impeccable service.

Fred (Fred Mustert)

A/C (dinner)

Honingerdijk 263 ✉ *3063 AM Kralingen – ✆ (0 10) 212 01 10 – www.restaurantfred.nl – Closed 25 July-14 August, 26 December-1 January, Saturday lunch and Sunday*

Rest – Menu 40 € (lunch), 60/75 € – Carte 72/81 € *Plan I* **C2**

Spec. Kalfstartaar met gebakken langoustines en gelei van tomaat. Gebraden barbarie-eend met lychees, tosti met gekonfijte eend en groene kerrie. Delice van karamel en chocolade met gepofte rijst en sorbet van espresso.

♦ Contemporary ♦ Design ♦

Creative meals produced by a talented chef in a cosy and original neo-baroque décor. It features a gilt-painted ceiling, LED lighting, and purple velvet Empire chairs.

XXX

Old Dutch

Rochussenstraat 20 ✉ 3015 EK – ✆ (0 10) 436 03 44 – www.olddutch.net – Closed bank holidays, Saturday and Sunday **E2**

Rest – Menu 38 € (lunch), 40/60 € – Carte 58/79 €

♦ Contemporary ♦ Formal ♦

This restaurant founded in 1932 serves up-to-date fare in a conventional classical décor with stained glass, beams, wood panelling and period furniture. Meat carved on the spot.

XXX ✿

Amarone (Gert Blom)

Meent 72a ✉ 3011 JN – ✆ (0 10) 414 84 87 – www.restaurantamarone.nl – Closed 18 July-7 August, 1-2 January, Saturday lunch, Sunday and bank holidays **F1**

Rest – Menu 35 € (lunch), 55/70 € – Carte 54/80 €

Spec. St.-Jacobsschelpen met truffel, hazelnoot en schuim van pecorino. Gebakken makreel met pata negra, polenta en vinaigrette van gember en kerrie. Barbarie-eend met stoofpotje van het pootje en de lever, groene kool en knolselderij.

♦ Contemporary ♦ Formal ♦

Close to the WTC, this restaurant offers a tasty updated menu and fashionable setting. It features large mirrors reflecting the open kitchen, striped chairs, grey benches and a fine glass-fronted wine cellar with delicious Amarones.

XXX

In den Rustwat

Honingerdijk 96 ✉ 3062 NX Kralingen – ✆ (0 10) 413 41 10 – www.idrw.nl – Closed 18 July-8 August, 25 December-9 January, Saturday lunch, Sunday and Monday *Plan I* **C2**

Rest – Menu 33 € (lunch), 43/58 € – Carte 53/62 €

♦ Contemporary ♦ Formal ♦

Near an arboretum, lovely old (1597) thatched-roof inn with a new wing. Old-fashioned, tastefully refreshed interior, up-to-date cuisine and terrace garden.

XX ✿

IVY (Francois Geurds)

Lloydstraat 204 ✉ 3024 EA – ✆ (0 10) 425 05 20 – www.restaurantivy.nl – Closed last week July-mid August, 25 and 26 December, first week January, Sunday and Monday *Plan I* **C2**

Rest – Menu 40 € (lunch), 79/139 € – Carte 57/96 €

Spec. Kreeft, kaviaar, pastinaak en gerookte boter. Bresse duif met amandelen. Kip dessert met pistache.

♦ Innovative ♦ Fashionable ♦

This recently opened restaurant in a new district near the port serves creative molecular cuisine that is spectacular in style. The chef here has been trained in some of Britain's finest restaurants, including the Fat Duck. Designer decor.

XX

De Harmonie

Westersingel 95 ✉ 3015 LC – ✆ (0 10) 436 36 10 – www.restaurantdeharmonie.nl – Closed 25 December-1st January, Saturday lunch and Sunday **E2**

Rest – Menu 35/60 € – Carte 53/75 €

♦ Contemporary ♦ Formal ♦

In a townhouse near the Museumpark, this modern restaurant serves contemporary flavours and is decorated with abstract paintings by the chef-owner. Luxuriant vegetation on the terrace.

XX

Zeezout

Westerkade 11b ✉ 3016 CL – ✆ (0 10) 436 50 49 – www.restaurantzeezout.nl – Closed Sunday lunch and Monday **E3**

Rest – Menu 33 € (lunch), 45/55 € – Carte 48/64 €

♦ Fish ♦ Formal ♦

The chic and trendy atmosphere, fish and seafood menu and waterside terrace are this modern brasserie's assets, whose name – "Sea Salt" – gives the game away.

X

Huson

Scheepstimmermanslaan 14 ✉ 3011 BS – ✆ (0 10) 413 03 71 – www.huson.info – Closed last week July-first 2 weeks August, 28 December-12 January, Saturday lunch and Sunday **E3**

Rest – Menu 32 € – Carte approx. 44 €

◆ Contemporary ◆ Brasserie ◆

At Huson find a trendy dining room in warm colours and an attentive welcome and service. There is a small seasonal menu with a variety of appetising dishes, luscious bouillabaisse year-round, and a tasting menu at the bar.

X

De Engel

(dinner)

Eendrachtsweg 19 ✉ 3012 LB – ✆ (0 10) 413 82 56 – www.engelgroep.com – Closed Saturday lunch and Sunday **E2**

Rest – Menu 35 € (lunch), 43/70 € bi – Carte 57/77 €

◆ Contemporary ◆ Friendly ◆

Opulent house set in a lively neighbourhood. Relaxed atmosphere, decorative mixture of old and new, French cuisine with a penchant for Mediterranean flavours.

X

Asian Glories

Leeuwenstraat 15 ✉ 3011 AL – ✆ (0 10) 411 71 07 – Closed Wednesday **F1**

Rest – Menu 30/47 € – Carte 24/53 €

◆ Chinese ◆ Family ◆

A distinctive establishment among Asian restaurants in Rotterdam, Asian Glories features fresh, authentic specialities from Canton (excellent dim sum) and Sichuan. New interior.

X

Oliva

Witte de Withstraat 15a ✉ 3012 BK – ✆ (0 10) 412 14 13 – www.restaurantoliva.nl **E2**

Rest – *(dinner only)* Menu 34/44 €

◆ Italian ◆ Bistro ◆

Lively Italian restaurant with a loft-inspired ambience. Open kitchen, simple menu and daily specials chalked on a board.

X

Rosso

Van Vollenhovenstraat 15 (access via Westerlijk Handelsterrein) ✉ 3016 BE – ✆ (0 10) 225 07 05 – www.rossorotterdam.nl – Closed last week July and Christmas **E3**

Rest – *(dinner only until 11 pm)* Menu 43/63 € – Carte 52/58 €

◆ Contemporary ◆ Fashionable ◆

Bar-restaurant in a renovated 19C warehouse with an up-to-date menu, clubbing atmosphere and designer décor in vibrant red tones. The lounge music really gets going after 11pm on weekends.

ENVIRONS OF ROTTERDAM

Plan I

XXXX

De Zwethheul (Mario Ridder)

Rotterdamseweg 480 (beside the canal in Zweth) ✉ 2636 KB Schipluiden – ✆ (0 10) 470 41 66 – www.zwethheul.nl – Closed 24 December-7 January, Saturday lunch and Monday **A1**

Rest – Menu 53 € (lunch), 105/140 € – Carte 82/129 €

Spec. Brioche gevuld met ganzenlever en truffel. Noordzeekrab, gemarineerde watermeloen en krokante suiker. Gepocheerde tong, paling, hollandaisesaus met gerookte knoflook.

◆ Innovative ◆ Design ◆

This remodelled former inn (1685) serves dazzling contemporary cuisine and select wines. Breathtaking views of the boats from the dining room and the shaded waterside terrace.

XX **Lepels**

Korte Haven 5 ✉ 3111 BH Schiedam – ✆ (0 10) 246 73 58
– www.lepels.net
– Closed 25 December-4 January, Saturday lunch, Sunday and Monday
Rest – Menu 30 € (lunch), 38/58 € – Carte 39/57 € **A2**

♦ Contemporary ♦ Brasserie ♦

Trendy restaurant between the covered market and the windmill. Central open kitchen, black and white designer décor, soft lighting, plates on display, lounge music and floating terrace on the canal.

X **'t Stadhuys**

Grote Markt 1a ✉ 3111 NG Schiedam – ✆ (0 10) 426 55 33
– www.restauranthetstadhuys.nl **A2**
Rest – Menu 29 € (lunch), 33/42 € – Carte 45/65 €

♦ Contemporary ♦ Brasserie ♦

A pretty baroque building, once Schiedam's town hall. Tavern-style meals at noon and gastronomic dishes for dinner. Terrace on the square. Popular "proeverij" menu (six small à la carte dishes).

X **Proefwerk**

Schoolstraat 1 ✉ 3116 HJ Schiedam – ✆ (0 10) 426 09 90
– www.restaurantproefwerk.nl
– Closed Monday **A2**
Rest – Menu 23 € (lunch)/25 € – Carte 39/52 €

♦ Contemporary ♦ Brasserie ♦

Set in an old juniper distillery. Trendy dining room with soft lighting revealing an open kitchen that produces up-to-date dishes. Enjoyable "surprise" menu.

NORWAY
NORGE

PROFILE

→ **Area:**
323 878 km^2 (125 049 sq mi).

→ **Population:**
4 801 100 inhabitants (est. 2006), density = 14 per km^2.

→ **Capital:**
Oslo (conurbation 876 391 inhabitants).

→ **Currency:**
Krone (kr or NOK) divided into 100 øre; rate of exchange: NOK 1 = € 0.12 = US$ 0.17 (Dec 2010).

→ **Government:**
Constitutional parliamentary monarchy with single-chamber Parliament (since 1945).

→ **Languages:**
Norwegian has two written variants: Bokmål (influenced by Danish) spoken by 80% of the population and Nynorsk (New Norwegian). Sami is the language of the Sami people in the far north. English is widely spoken.

→ **Specific public holidays:**
Maundy Thursday and Good Friday (Thursday and Friday before Easter); Constitution Day (17 May); Boxing Day (26 December).

→ **Local Time:**
GMT + 1 hour in winter and GMT + 2 hours in summer.

→ **Climate:**
Temperate northern maritime, with cold winters and mild summers (Oslo: January: -4°C, July: 16°C). Colder interior, fairly high precipitation in the coastal regions.

→ **International dialling Code:**
00 47 followed by full local number.

→ **Emergency:**
Police: ✆ **112**; Ambulance service: ✆ **113**; Fire Brigade: ✆ **110**.

→ **Electricity:**
220 volts AC, 50Hz; 2-pin round-shaped continental plugs.

→ **Formalities**
Travellers from the European Union (EU), Switzerland, Iceland and the main countries of North and South America need a national identity card or passport (America: passport required) to visit Norway for less than three months (tourism or business purpose). For visitors from other countries a visa may be required, in addition to a passport, especially for those wishing to stay for longer than three months. We advise you to check with your embassy before travelling.

OSLO

OSLO

Population: 580 229 (conurbation 876 391) – Altitude: 96m

ime/PHOTONONSTOP

Oslo has a lot going for it and one particularly striking downside. Let's get that out of the way first: it's currently the world's most expensive city, above even Tokyo, London and Paris. So don't expect the cheapest trip you've ever made. But it also rates as the city with the world's best standard of living, and its position, at the head of Oslofjord and surrounded by steep forested hills, is hard to match for drama and beauty. It's mellow and elegant, and though it can make as much of an impression on your wallet as on your memory, it's a charmingly compact place to stroll round, particularly in the summer, when the daylight hours practically abolish the night.

Oslo is rather underrated in that it lacks the urban cool of other Scandinavian cities like Copenhagen or Stockholm, but it boasts its fair share of trendy clubs and a raft of Michelin starred restaurants. Oh, and a real raft, too: Thor Hyerdahl's famous balsawood Kon-Tiki, which is one of the star turns in a city that loves its museums. You won't feel claustrophobic here; there's an uncluttered feel enhanced by parks and wide streets and, in the winter, there are times when you feel you have the whole place to yourself!

LIVING THE CITY

It's almost impossible for Oslo to live up to its lovely setting, but somehow it manages it. Drift into the city by boat down the Oslofjord and land at the smart harbour of **Aker Brygge**. To the west lies the charming **Bygdøy** peninsula, home, naturally enough, to museums permeated with the smell of the sea. North-west of your arrival point is **Frogner**, with its famous sculpture park, the place where locals hang out on long summer days. The centre of town, the commercial hub, is Karl Johans Gate, bounded at one end by the Royal Palace and at the other by the Cathedral, while further east lie two trendy multi-cultural areas, Grunerlokka and Grønland, which have taken on a vibrant edge over the last decade. This area is also home to the Edvard Munch Museum.

PRACTICAL INFORMATION

ARRIVAL-DEPARTURE

A taxi from Oslo International Airport, Gardermoen, which is 47km north of the city, will cost around NOK600. The train station is located beneath the terminal and the high speed Flytoget train takes 19 minutes to Oslo's central station. Alternatively, take the Express Bus to Galleri bus terminal – it leaves every 20min and takes 45min.

TRANSPORT

Serious sightseeing is enhanced with the Oslo Pass, which covers the transport system and entry to all those museums. It's valid for one to three days. Get it from the Information Centre next to Oslo Central Station.

Oslo is proud of its green credentials, and you'll have to pay a toll if you arrive by car. The integrated transport system within the city is efficient, comprising bus, tram or metro. You can obtain single or day tickets. For a small deposit, you can tap into the green-friendly Citybike scheme in Oslo. Go to a tourist information office, get your electronic 'Tourist Card', and hire one of the many free bicycles parked at different points around the city.

EXPLORING OSLO

Step ashore from your ferry at Akker Brygge - the swishly redeveloped harbour area of Oslo - in the summer months and it seems that the

population of Norway is your escort. Locals cherish this time of year, when the sun never apparently sets, and they spend long hours in the streets and parks of the city. This is when restaurants, bars and museums stay open that much longer, and concert halls and theatres move their productions outdoors; in mid-summer bonfires are lit and the clink of glasses rustles the still air in celebration of life al fresco.

Akker Brygge itself is a bustling waterfront area and a fine place to make the acquaintance of Oslo. It used to be a full-on shipyard, but has been re-born as a trendy glass-and-chrome shopping and entertainment quarter, more Fisherman's Wharf of San Francisco than Docklands of London. It's a lovely place to settle down with a glass of wine and look at the fishing boats, and there are some snazzy eating places, but be warned that lots of them weigh in with a hefty bill. Best bet is to stroll the waterfront down to one of the most striking buildings of the city, the **Akershus Fortress**, an imposing building that has acted as Oslo's guardian since the thirteenth century. In those seven hundred plus years, Akershus has been under siege nine times, but has never fallen except during World War II.

➜ OPEN GATE

Back up behind the harbour a coterie of colourful streets leads to the grand boulevard of Oslo: **Karl Johans Gate.** Aside from the shops, this is where many of Norway's most important buildings are based, including **Slottet** (the Royal Palace) and **Stortinget** (the Parliament building). Culture lovers need only pop round the corner to get a fix of Ibsen at the National Theatre, where his plays are a staple, and for good measure enjoy one of the country's finest art collections, which is included in the price of a ticket. It won't take long before you stumble on a museum. In this part of the capital alone, near the Royal Palace, are the Historical Museum, documenting Norwegian history, and the Stenersen Museum, named after the art collector who donated his entire collection to the city of Oslo. Wandering around further, you'll find museums dedicated to...well, you name it. Think architecture and zoology, and just about everything in between. Some of them have become especially well renowned. Modern art lovers, for instance, like to sniff out a couple in the streets behind Akershus, and with good reason. The Astrup Fearnley Museum of Modern Art is relatively new on the block (opened in 1993), housing recent works by Norwegian and critically acclaimed international artists in a strikingly modern building whose main entrance is two massive steel doors. Nearby is the National Museum for Art, Architecture and Design, full of disturbing works by post-war Norwegians in a rather eye-catching art nouveau building. Norway's largest cultural centre is the National Opera House. Opened in 2008 and designed by the Norwegian firm of architects Snøhetta, it allows visitors to walk across its striking, sloping structure which connects the bay with the waterfront.

➜ SCREAM OF THE CROP

Edvard Munch is a national institution in Norway. Though his fellow countrymen aren't particularly maudlin by nature, Munch revelled in despair, depression, disease and death. Or at least his paintings did. In the 1880s and 90s, when he was at his creative height, many people were outraged at his take on the national psyche, but now his work is lauded the length and breadth of the land, and features in two Oslo museums – The National Gallery, which contains a number of his most famous works, and the Munch Museum, out in Grunerlokka, an exhibition which is constantly changing, due to the huge amount of paintings, prints, drawings, plates and letters he produced. There are versions of The Scream in both galleries (dependent on the adroitness of thieves, of course…)

➜ MARITIME MUSEUMS

A short ferry trip across the Oslofjord takes you to the **Bygdøy** peninsula, a favoured summer retreat with its meadows, groves, beaches and watery views (you can take a bus here, too, but it's not quite as spectacular).

Bygdøy is home to some of the best attractions in the city (and yes, when we say attractions, we really mean – you've guessed it – museums). Being right alongside the fjord, these rightly take on a maritime quality. The **Kon-Tiki** Museum gives an evocatively vivid account of the exploits of the famed explorer Thor Heyerdahl, who sailed his balsawood raft across the South Pacific in 1947. It's there, looking remarkably flimsy, as is Ra II, in which he sailed the Atlantic in 1970. Next door, in the Fram Museum, proudly sits the Fram, 'the world's strongest ship' which sailed the North Pole and Antarctica a century ago: board her and see the preserved objects from those remarkable trips.

Hit land again and breathe in the fragrant pine before reaching the final piece of this triumvirate, the Viking Ship Museum, a church-like building containing three ancient oak ships (ancient here meaning the ninth century) whose sweeping lines are simple but elegant ; their ornate prows having been preserved in the clay of chieftains' graves. However, it's not all homage to derring-do in Bygdøy. Up the road from the Viking ships stands Europe's largest open-air museum, the **Norwegian Folk Museum** – more than 150 buildings from across Norway which you can wander around to your heart's content. Exhibits range from a twelfth century stave church to a petrol station from the 1920s.

➜ PARK AND GLIDE

Despite the user-friendly appeal of its other attractions, the two most popular places to visit in Oslo are a park and a ski jump. The park, in the Frogner quarter, is **Vigeland Park**, named after the sculptor Gustav Vigeland, and the thousands who flock here throughout the year add to the permanent numbers already present, resolutely naked and constructed from granite or weathered bronze. Inevitably, there's a museum on hand, with nearly 3000 sculptures and 10,000 drawings, all by Vigeland. Meanwhile, the ski jump is a metro ride away at Holmenkollen. If you visit in winter you might be lucky and catch a competition, but if you're here in the summer, go to the top of the jump and get the best view of Oslo imaginable. Yes, there's a ski museum too, located at the foot of the jump.

It *is* possible to stroll a part of Oslo without an exhibit in sight, unless you count the blond-highlighted cool cats of Grunerlokka and Grønland as exhibits. This is the east end part of the city which has evolved from worn-out working-class area to creative boho quarter and boasts a quirky range of cafés and restaurants frequented by local artists and photographers. It's by the Aker River, and the many small shops and delis are a febrile hunting ground, enhanced by many immigrant nationalities creating a buzzy, eclectic atmosphere.

OSLO IN…

➜ ONE DAY

Aker Brygge, Karl Johans Gate, a central museum, a meal in Grunerlokka

➜ TWO DAYS

Akershus, Astrup Fearnley Museum, ferry trip to Bygdøy, museum and picnic there

➜ THREE DAYS

Vigeland Park, Holmenkollen Ski Jump, a stroll round Grunerlokka, Munch Museum, supper in Akker Brygge

CALENDAR HIGHLIGHTS

Oslo's cultural highlights are obviously dependent on the time of year. If you're a ski fancier, then go in the winter months for competitions at Holmenkollen. At Christmas, the Folk Museum on Bygdøy and the seventeenth century former foundry at Baerums Verk with its workers' houses converted into small shops are magical places to be. February and March are the months for the Winter Night Festival, a classical music extravaganza, and the Oslo International Church Music Festival, held at the cathedral and other churches within the city. Summer is welcomed with St Hallvard's Day in May, when a host of concerts and theatre productions pronounce curtain-up; a month later, the Norwegian Wood rock festival is a three-day jamboree with mostly Norwegian bands. Bonfires are lit on Midsummer Night, and in July/August the Folk Museum has daily folk dancing and helpings of traditional food. Mid-August is given over to an International Jazz Festival, while the Oslo World Music Festival blasts out from various city venues in November. The Nobel Peace Prize, awarded in December, is celebrated with parades and festivities across town.

EATING OUT

Oslo has a very vibrant dining scene, albeit one that is somewhat expensive, particularly if you drink wine. The cooking is generally quite refined and classical, although some innovative menus are beginning to appear. France has always exerted the greatest influence on the cuisine but now younger chefs are looking also to Italy and Spain for inspiration and, these days, there is generally a broader choice of food styles. What is in no doubt is the quality of the produce used, whether that's the ever-popular game or the superlative shellfish which comes from very cold water, giving it a clean and fresh flavour. Classic Norwegian dishes often include fruit, such as lingonberries with venison. Lunch is not a particularly major affair ; most prefer just a snack or sandwich at midday while making dinner the main event of the day. You'll find most diners are seated by 7pm and are offered a 6, 7 or 8 course menu which they can reduce at their will, with a paired wine menu alongside. Service is another great strength of the restaurants ; staff are generally very polite, speak English and are fully versed in the menu.

It doesn't have to be expensive, though. Look out for konditoris (bakeries) where you can pick up sandwiches and pastries, while kafeterias serve substantial meals, traditional and simple, at reasonable prices.

→ TAKE THE TRAIN TO THE TRAIL

One of the reasons there aren't many people about in Oslo in the winter is that they're making use of the cross-country ski trails that encircle the city. There are 1,250 miles of them and they're floodlit at night. A local train ride gets you to them.

→ A FRIEND OF THE PEOPLE

Henrik Ibsen would walk every day from Oslo's Grand Café to the apartment in Arbiens Gate where he spent the last years of his life. He was so punctual with this sortie that the people of the city would set their watches by him.

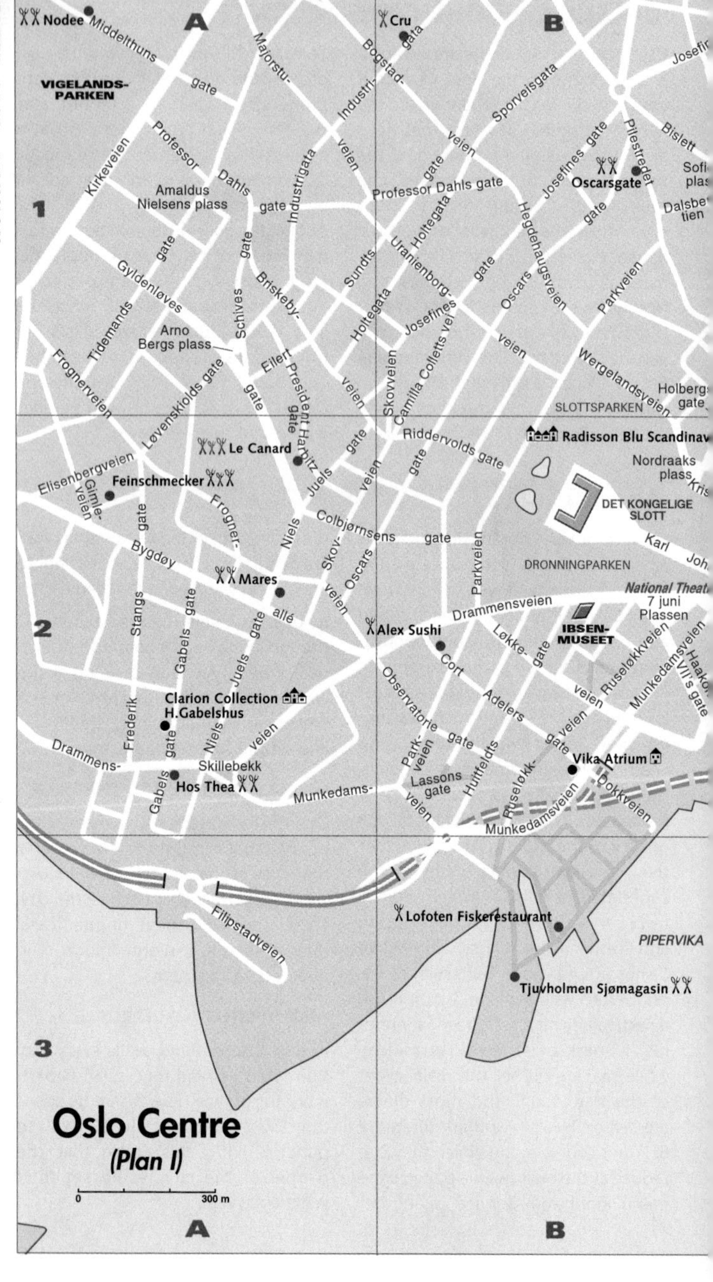
Oslo Centre
(Plan I)
Nodee
Cru
Oscarsgate
Le Canard
Feinschmecker
Mares
Alex Sushi
Radisson Blu Scandinav
Clarion Collection
H.Gabelshus
Hos Thea
Vika Atrium
Lofoten Fiskerestaurant
Tjuvholmen Sjømagasin
VIGELANDS-
PARKEN
DET KONGELIGE
SLOTT
SLOTTSPARKEN
DRONNINGPARKEN
IBSEN-
MUSEET
PIPERVIKA
National Theat
Amaldus
Nielsens plass
Arno
Bergs plass
Nordraaks
plass
7 juni
Plassen
Drammensveien
Munkedamsveien
Filipstadveien
Bygdøy allé
Frognerveien
Kirkeveien
Bogstadveien
Professor Dahls gate
Wergelandsveien
Parkveien
0
300 m

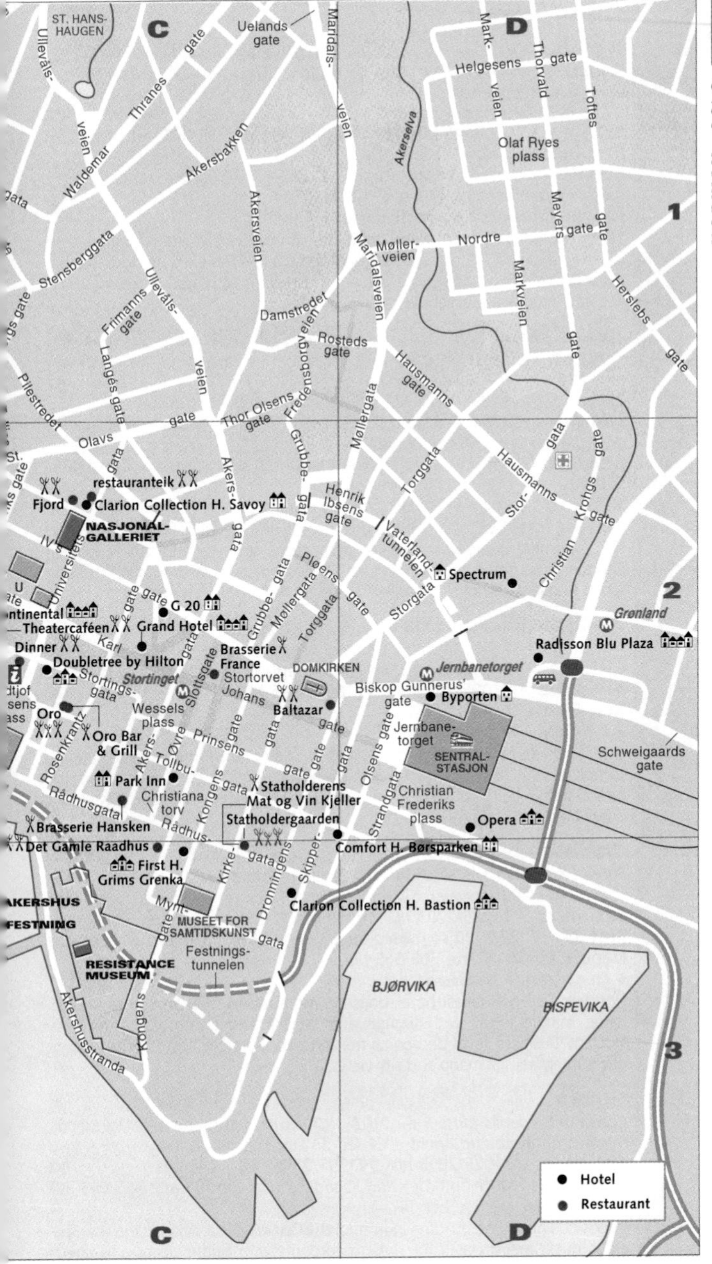

ST. HANS-HAUGEN
C
D
1
2
3
Uelands gate
Maridals-veien
Akerselva
Helgesens gate
Thorvald Meyers gate
Toftes gate
Mark-veien
Olaf Ryes plass
Nordre gate
Møller-veien
Maridalsveien
Markveien
Herslebs gate
Ullevåls-veien
Thranes gate
Waldemar
Akersbakken
Akersveien
Stensberggata
Frimanns gate
Langés gate
Pilestredet
Damstredet
Fredensborgveien
Rosteds gate
Hausmanns gate
Thor Olsens gate
Møllergata
Grubbe-gata
Olavs gate
Akers-gata
Torggata
Stor-gata
Christian Krohgs gate
Henrik Ibsens gate
Vaterland-tunnelen
Spectrum
restauranteik
Fjord
Clarion Collection H. Savoy
NASJONAL-GALLERIET
Universitets gate
Pløens gate
Storgata
Grønland
Radisson Blu Plaza
G 20
Continental
Theatercaféen
Grand Hotel
Karl Johans gate
Dinner
Doubletree by Hilton
Brasserie France
Stortorvet
DOMKIRKEN
Jernbanetorget
Stortinget
Stortings-gata
Slottsgate
Baltazar
Biskop Gunnerus' gate
Byporten
Oro
Oro Bar & Grill
Wessels plass
Rosenkrantz
Øvre Slottsgate
Prinsens gate
Jernbane-torget
SENTRAL-STASJON
Schweigaards gate
Park Inn
Tollbu-gata
Statholderens Mat og Vin Kjeller
Christiana torv
Kongens gate
Rådhusgata
Christian Frederiks plass
Olsens gate
Strandgata
Opera
Brasserie Hansken
Statholdergaarden
Comfort H. Børsparken
Det Gamle Raadhus
First H. Grims Grenka
Kirke-gata
Dronningens gata
Skipper-gata
Clarion Collection H. Bastion
AKERSHUS FESTNING
Mynt-gate
MUSEET FOR SAMTIDSKUNST
Festnings-tunnelen
RESISTANCE MUSEUM
BJØRVIKA
BISPEVIKA
Kongens
Akershusstranda
Hotel
Restaurant

CENTRE

Plan I

Continental

Stortingsgaten 24-26 ✉ 0117 – Ⓜ National Theatret – ✆ 22 82 40 00 – www.hotel-continental.no – Closed 23 December-2 January C2

152 rm – 1753/3545 NOK 2119/3545 NOK, 188 NOK – 3 suites

Rest *Theatercaféen* – see below

Rest *Restauranteik Annen Etage* – ✆ *22 54 79 70 (closed Sunday and Monday) (dinner only)* Menu 395 NOK

◆ Grand Luxury ◆ Traditional ◆ Classic ◆

Set by the National Theatre and run by the 4th generation of the family. Classical lounge-bar and bright, modern bedrooms; a few remain in a more traditional style. Very personal service. Spacious restaurant with opulent baroque styling and inventive set menu.

Grand Hotel

Karl Johans Gate 31 ✉ *0101* – Ⓜ *Stortinget* – ✆ *23 21 20 00* – *www.grand.no* C2

290 rm – 1395/2675 NOK 1895/2925 NOK – 9 suites

Rest *Julius Fritzner* – *(closed 23 December-3 January, Easter and Sunday) (dinner only)* Menu 595 NOK

Rest *Grand Café* – ✆ *23 21 20 18* – Menu 420 NOK (dinner) – Carte 485/570 NOK

◆ Grand Luxury ◆ Traditional ◆ Classic ◆

Imposing hotel built in 1874; the guest areas and grand ballrooms reflecting this. Charming bedrooms: some modern, some feminine and others in belle époque style. Smart wellness centre. Contemporary cuisine in stylish dining room. Brasserie dishes in characterful café.

Radisson Blu Scandinavia

Holbergsgate 30 ✉ *0166* – Ⓜ *National Theatret* – ✆ *23 29 30 00* – *www.radissonblu.com/scandinaviahotel-oslo*

479 rm – 1095/2695 NOK 1095/2995 NOK – 1 suite B2

Rest *Enzo* – Carte 385/565 NOK

◆ Luxury ◆ Modern ◆

One of Oslo's tallest buildings. Vast lobby filled with boutiques and lounge, complete with pianist. Pale wood furnished bedrooms have a Scandinavian feel. 21st floor bar boasts magnificent fjord and city views. Minimalist restaurant offers Mediterranean menu.

Radisson Blu Plaza

Sonja Henies Plass 3 ✉ *0134* – Ⓜ *Jernbanetorget* – ✆ *22 05 80 00* – *www.radissonblu.com* D2

673 rm – 1295/2795 NOK 1595/3095 NOK – 19 suites

Rest *34* – ✆ *22 05 80 34 (closed Sunday and bank holidays) (dinner only)* Menu 550 NOK – Carte 505/565 NOK

◆ Business ◆ Modern ◆

Northern Europe's tallest hotel, boasting more rooms than any other in Oslo. Large marble lobby with lounge and bar; extensive conference facilities. Modern 'Business' level bedrooms the most comfortable. Top floor restaurant offers international menu and city views.

Opera

Christian Frederiks plass 5 ✉ *0103* – Ⓜ *Jernbanetorget* – ✆ *24 10 30 00* – *www.thonhotels.no/opera* – *Closed 23 December-2 January*

432 rm – 1025/2095 NOK 1795/2395 NOK – 2 suites D2

Rest – *(closed lunch Saturday and Sunday) (buffet lunch)* Carte 495/605 NOK

◆ Business ◆ Modern ◆

Imposing light-stone building in front of the Opera House, close to the sea. Spacious guest areas; classically styled bedrooms with bright décor and cherry wood furnishings. Classical restaurant boasts huge windows, panoramic views and an international menu.

First H. Grims Grenka

Kongensgate 5 ✉ 0153 – Ⓜ Stortinget – ☎ 23 10 72 00 – www.grimsgrenka.no
50 rm – 1395/2395 NOK 1795/2595 NOK **C3**
Rest *Madu* – *(closed Sunday and Monday) (dinner only)* Menu 350 NOK – Carte 302/430 NOK
♦ Business ♦ Stylish ♦
Smart design hotel set between the main shopping street and the castle. Boutique interior with trendy bar and terrace. Well-equipped 'Summer' and 'Winter' bedrooms (atrium/outside views) with glass shower rooms. Innovative cuisine uses fine Nordic ingredients.

Clarion Collection H. Bastion without rest

Skippergaten 5 ✉ 0152 – Ⓜ Jernbanetorget – ☎ 22 47 77 00 – www.hotelbastion.no – Closed 22 December-3 January and Easter **C3**
94 rm – 780 NOK 980 NOK – 5 suites
♦ Business ♦ Modern ♦
On edge of city, close to the port. Charming English lobby and cosy lounge. Choice of bedrooms: classical or modern, the latter in silver and purple hues. Friendly staff and lots of regulars. Breakfast, snacks and evening buffet included.

Clarion Collection H. Gabelshus without rest

Gabelsgate 16 ✉ 0272 – ☎ 23 27 65 00 – www.choicehotels.no/no094 – Closed 22 December-2 January and Easter **A2**
113 rm – 1390/2090 NOK 1590/2190 NOK – 1 suite
♦ Traditional ♦ Classic ♦
Beautiful red-brick, ivy-covered house in smart, residential neighbourhood. Peaceful atmosphere with classical, wood-furnished lounge and library. Charming bedrooms offer pleasing contrast between the old and new. Evening buffet included.

Doubletree by Hilton

Stortingsgata 16 ✉ 0161 – Ⓜ National Theatret – ☎ 21 04 38 00 – www.doubletree.hilton.com/oslocitycentre **C2**
59 rm – 800/4137 NOK 1175/4324 NOK, 155 NOK
Rest – *(closed Sunday)* Carte 493/625 NOK
♦ Business ♦ Chain hotel ♦ Modern ♦
Smart hotel within historical building by the National Theatre. Impressive sculpted façade, marble hall and grand staircase. Modern lounge on mezzanine. Warm, luxurious bedrooms with design bathrooms. Italian restaurant overlooks trees and fountains in the square.

G 20

rm,

Grensen 20 ✉ 0180 – Ⓜ Stortinget – ☎ 22 01 64 00 – www.rica.no – Closed 22 December-3 January **C2**
96 rm – 745/1845 NOK 945/2095 NOK
Rest *Carls kokken* – *(closed Sunday and Monday) (dinner only)* Menu 495 NOK – Carte 495/595 NOK
♦ Business ♦ Chain hotel ♦ Modern ♦
Hip, new-build hotel with glass façade, set in the heart of the city. Compact, modern inner; pale wood bedrooms with desks, flat screens and iPod docks – rear rooms are quieter. Cellar restaurant with open ceiling crossed by a gangway; contemporary cooking.

Clarion Collection H. Savoy

Universitetsgata 11 ✉ 0164 – Ⓜ National Theatret – ☎ 23 35 42 00 – www.choice.no/hotels/no060 – Closed 22-29 December **C2**
93 rm – 770/2050 NOK 970/2050 NOK
Rest *restauranteik* – see below
♦ Business ♦ Classic ♦
Next to the national gallery, in a building dating back to 1850. Small, modern lobby; stylish, contemporary bedrooms where 'action photos' create focal points. Breakfast and evening buffet included.

Comfort H. Børsparken without rest

Tollbugata 4 ✉ 0152 – Ⓜ Jernbanetorget – ✆ 22 47 17 17 – www.choice.no **C/D2**

198 rm – 🚹680/1989 NOK 🚹🚹1989 NOK, ☕ 85 NOK

◆ Business ◆ Functional ◆

Centrally-located, with pleasant gardens in front. Modern guest areas. Uniformly decorated bedrooms with contemporary furnishings and designer lighting – front rooms have Opera House views.

Park Inn

Ovre Slottsgate 2c ✉ 0157 – ✆ 22 40 01 00 – www.oslo.parkinnhotell.no – Closed 23 December-3 January **C2**

118 rm ☕ – 🚹995/1395 NOK 🚹🚹995/1595 NOK

Rest – *(closed Sunday)* Carte 258/533 NOK

◆ Business ◆ Chain hotel ◆ Functional ◆

Converted apartment block near Karl Johans Gate. Modern lobby with red leather armchairs. Good-sized, functional bedrooms with pale wood furniture and modern lighting; top floor rooms have balconies. Red walls, black tables and typical grill menu in restaurant.

Byporten without rest

Jernbanetorget 6 ✉ 0154 – Ⓜ Jernbanetorget – ✆ 23 15 55 00 – www.scandichotels.com/byporten **D2**

235 rm ☕ – 🚹990/2590 NOK 🚹🚹1190/2790 NOK – 4 suites

◆ Business ◆ Modern ◆

Set inside a shopping arcade, with bus and train stops nearby. Small boutique and seating area in lobby. Smart Scandinavian-style bedrooms with modern furnishings and excellent soundproofing.

Vika Atrium without rest

Munkedamsveien 45 ✉ 0121 – Ⓜ National Theatret – ✆ 22 83 33 00 – www.thonhotels.no/vikaatrium **B2**

79 rm ☕ – 🚹895/1925 NOK 🚹🚹1095/2225 NOK

◆ Business ◆ Functional ◆

Located in a large office block by the harbour, in a redeveloped area. Bright lobby and glass-walled breakfast room. Bedrooms, over 7 floors, have smart, modern styling and marble bathrooms.

Spectrum without rest

Brugata 7 ✉ 0133 – Ⓜ Jernbanetorget – ✆ 23 36 27 00 – www.thonhotels.no/spectrum – Closed 17 December-3 January **D2**

151 rm ☕ – 🚹660/1110 NOK 🚹🚹925/1375 NOK

◆ Business ◆ Functional ◆

Budget hotel in a pedestrianised shopping street, close to the station. Unassuming exterior conceals a modern lobby and spacious breakfast room. Light-hued bedrooms offer basic comforts.

Le Canard

President Harbitz Gate 4 ✉ 0259 – ✆ 22 54 34 00 – www.lecanard.no – Closed Easter, 3 weeks July, Christmas-New Year, 22-26 February, Sunday and bank holidays **A2**

Rest – *(dinner only)* Menu 795/1110 NOK

Spec. Salmon mi-cuit with orange, fennel & dill. Venison with beetroot and celeriac, fig and Mole sauce. Mango parfait, coconut and banana, pineapple and chilli salsa.

◆ Contemporary ◆ Elegant ◆ Intimate ◆

Imposing red-brick villa with bar, lounge, stylish candlelit dining room and fabulous wine cellars for private dining. Seasonal menus feature well-judged, modern interpretations of classical combinations and are precisely executed, using fine Norwegian produce.

XXX ✿

Statholdergaarden (Bent Stiansen)

Rådhusgate 11, (entrance by Kirkegate) ✉ 0151 – Ⓜ Stortinget – ✆ 22 41 88 00 – www.statholdergaarden.no – Closed 18-25 April, 17 May, 13 June, 11 July-1 August, 23 December-2 January and Sunday **C2**

Rest *Statholderens Mat og Vin Kjeller* – see below

Rest – *(booking essential) (dinner only)* Menu 920/1095 NOK – Carte 755/799 NOK

Spec. Norwegian langoustine with smoked mackerel croquette and ginger beurre blanc. Fillet of lamb with caramelised onion, spinach and chevre tortellini, rosemary sauce.Vanilla bavaroise tart with raspberry sherbet, marinated peach and raspberry nougatine.

◆ Traditional ◆ Formal ◆ Elegant ◆

Attractive 17C house in the heart of the city, boasting an elegant interior, impressive stucco ceiling and chandeliers. Expertly rendered, traditional cooking, with fresh vegetables one of the chef's passions. Highly seasonal menu lists every ingredient used.

XXX ✿

Feinschmecker

Balchensgate 5 ✉ 0265 – ✆ 22 12 93 80 – www.feinschmecker.no – Closed Easter, 11 July-8 August and Sunday **A2**

Rest – *(dinner only)* Menu 695 NOK – Carte 685/850 NOK

Spec. Smoked Salma salmon with Aruga caviar. Roasted rack of lamb with wild mushrooms. Chocolate and passion fruit dessert.

◆ Traditional ◆ Formal ◆

Long-standing classical restaurant in smart residential suburb, with warm hues, semi-open kitchen, small lounge and loyal local following. Well-presented, unashamedly traditional dishes showcase good ingredients. Friendly, knowledgeable serving team.

XXX

Oro

Tordenskioldsgate 6A ✉ 0160 – Ⓜ Stortinget – ✆ 23 01 02 40 – www.ororestaurant.no – Closed Easter, 22 December-4 January and Sunday **C2**

Rest – *(booking essential) (dinner only and lunch November-December)* Menu 295/545 NOK – Carte 625/960 NOK

◆ International ◆ Cosy ◆

Warm, elegant restaurant in pale tones, with open kitchen to rear. Skilled team produce refined, flavoursome dishes crafted from well-sourced local produce. Modern, seasonal 5 course menus.

XX ✿

Oscarsgate (Bjorn Svensson)

Pilestredet 63 ✉ 0350 – ✆ 22 46 59 06 – www.restaurantoscarsgate.no – Closed July, 22 December-3 January, Sunday and Monday **B1**

Rest – *(booking essential) (dinner only)* Menu 995/1150 NOK – Carte 770/890 NOK

Spec. Ravioli with scallops and lobster, velouté sauce. French quail with chanterelle and truffle. Chocolate, Daim and sour cream ice cream.

◆ Innovative ◆ Formal ◆

Set at the city's edge, a small restaurant consisting of just seven tables. Passionate chef uses intricate techniques to produce modern, innovative dishes. Choice of 9 course tasting menu or à la carte featuring lobster, and market meat and fish of the day.

XX

Det Gamle Raadhus

Nedre Slottsgate 1 ✉ 0157 – Ⓜ Stortinget – ✆ 22 42 01 07 – www.gamleraadhus.no – Closed Easter, 3 weeks July, 22 December-4 January and Sunday

Rest – Menu 435 NOK (dinner) – Carte 404/658 NOK **C3**

◆ Traditional ◆ Rustic ◆

Brightly painted house dating from 1641. Charming, antique-filled inner with library, open-fired lounge and lovely terrace. Lunch in the bar; classical dinners in the traditional dining room.

XX

Fjord

Kristian Augusts Gt. 11 ✉ 0164 – Ⓜ National Theatret – ☎ 22 98 21 50 – www.restaurantfjord.no – Closed Easter, 4 weeks summer, Christmas, Sunday and Monday

Rest – *(dinner only)* Menu 445 NOK **C2**

♦ Seafood ♦ Design ♦ Fashionable ♦

Contemporary restaurant opposite the National Gallery. Dimly lit interior with open kitchen, blue glass walls and buffalo horns on the ceiling. Weekly set menu of flavoursome seafood dishes.

XX

Dinner

Stortingsgata 22 ✉ 0161 – Ⓜ National Theatret – ☎ 23 10 04 66 – www.dinner.no – Closed Easter, 24 December-1 January and Sunday lunch **C2**

Rest – Carte 424/551 NOK

♦ Chinese ♦ Design ♦

Set on the central square, close to the National Theatre. Black façade masks a modern, split-level inner. Cooking focuses on the Sichuan and Cantonese regions, with dim sum offered at lunch.

XX

Nodee

Middelthunsgt 25 ✉ 0368 – Ⓜ Majorstuen – ☎ 22 93 34 50 – www.nodee.no – Closed Easter, 23 December-1 January and Sunday lunch **A1**

Rest – Carte 436/559 NOK

♦ Asian ♦ Fashionable ♦

Smart, modern restaurant with lounge, sushi bar and large pavement terrace, set opposite Vigeland Sculpture Park. Extensive menu of Chinese, Japanese and Thai dishes. Knowledgeable service.

XX

Tjuvholmen Sjømagasin

Tjuvholmen Allé 14 ✉ 0252 – ☎ 23 89 77 77 – www.sjomagasinet.no – Closed Christmas-New Year, 10 days Easter and Sunday **B3**

Rest – Menu 465 NOK (dinner) – Carte 445/615 NOK

♦ Seafood ♦ Design ♦

Its name means 'island of the thieves' and 'sea store'. Vast, split-level interior with lounge, open kitchen and fish shop. 5 course seafood menu; lobster tank at entrance. Some fjord views.

XX

restauranteik – at Clarion Collection H. Savoy

Universitetsgata 11 ✉ 0164 – Ⓜ National Theatret – ☎ 22 36 07 10 – www.restauranteik.no – Closed Christmas, Easter, 4 weeks summer, Sunday and Monday

Rest – *(set menu only)(dinner only)* Menu 355/465 NOK **C2**

♦ Contemporary ♦ Fashionable ♦

Modern, minimalist dining room with open kitchen, glass-walled wine cellar and friendly atmosphere. Larger tables to the front, with more intimate banquette seating to the rear. Weekly set menu of inventive, international cuisine, which changes every Tuesday.

XX

Theatercaféen – at Continental Hotel

Stortingsgaten 24-26 ✉ 0117 – Ⓜ National Theatret – ☎ 22 82 40 50 – www.theatercafeen.no – Closed 25 December-2 January **C2**

Rest – *(light lunch)* Carte 334/755 NOK

♦ Traditional ♦ Brasserie ♦

Prestigious Oslo institution. Charming Viennese 'grand café' interior with pillars, black banquettes and art nouveau lighting. Elaborate lunchtime sandwiches make way for ambitious dinner menu.

XX

Mares

Skovveien 1 ✉ 0257 – ✆ 22 54 89 80 – www.mares.no
– closed 21-27 April, 5 July-3 August, 22 December-4 January and Sunday
Rest – *(booking essential)* Menu 429 NOK (dinner) – Carte 461/558 NOK **A2**

♦ Seafood ♦ Neighbourhood ♦

Bright, modern neighbourhood restaurant with fish shop and deli. Black ceiling and white seating, with glass wall looking into the kitchen. Contemporary seafood menu; foie gras also a speciality.

XX

Baltazar

Dronningensgt 27 ✉ 0154 – Ⓜ Jernbanetorget – ✆ 23 35 70 60
– www.baltazar.no
– Closed 1 and 17 May, July, Christmas and Sunday **C2**
Rest – *(dinner only)* Menu 645/895 NOK
Rest *Enoteca* – Carte 350/540 NOK

♦ Italian ♦ Friendly ♦

First-floor restaurant under the arches of a 19C brick market beside the cathedral. Smart interior with designer chairs and open kitchen. Two set menus of innovative, Italian dishes. Informal, ground floor eatery boasts a terrace and glass-covered wine cellar.

XX

Hos Thea

Gabelsgate 11 ✉ 0272 – ✆ 22 44 68 74 – www.hosthea.no
– Closed 4-25 July and Christmas **A2**
Rest – *(dinner only)* Menu 465 NOK – Carte 425/575 NOK

♦ Italian influences ♦ Family ♦

Small neighbourhood restaurant with black façade, set in a charming residential area. Beige colour scheme and views into the kitchen. Concise menu of Mediterranean dishes; good homemade bread.

X

Cru

Industrigaten 51 ✉ 0365 – ✆ 23 98 98 98 – www.cru.no
– Closed Sunday **B1**
Rest – *(dinner only)* Menu 395/595 NOK – Carte 447/497 NOK

♦ Traditional ♦ Wine bar ♦ Trendy ♦

Trendy, informal wine bar operation offering over 800 bins. Downstairs boasts an open fire and is great for one traditional dish or an aperitif. Upstairs displays light wood furniture and a daily blackboard menu of gutsy local dishes with the odd delicate touch.

X

Oro Bar & Grill

Tordenskioldsgate 6A ✉ 0160 – ✆ 23 01 02 40 – www.ororestaurant.no
– Closed Easter, 22 December-4 January and Sunday **C2**
Rest – Carte 327/537 NOK

♦ Modern ♦ Trendy ♦

Easy-going counterpart to adjoining Oro restaurant, featuring a central bar and polished wood tables. Lunch offers a set selection of earthy dishes. Grills feature in the evening, alongside daily specials – try the house dishes of gravadlax and Iberico pork.

X

Brasserie Hansken

Akersgate 2 ✉ 0158 – Ⓜ Stortinget – ✆ 22 42 60 88
– www.brasseriehansken.no
– Closed 2 weeks July, 1 week August and Sunday **C2**
Rest – Menu 445 NOK – Carte 490/605 NOK

♦ Brasserie ♦ Elegant ♦ Brasserie ♦

Traditional, wood-furnished brasserie with large terrace, not far from City Hall. Counter with bar stools to one side; tables set at black banquettes on the other. Contemporary brasserie menu.

Statholderens Mat og Vin Kjeller – at Statholdergaarden

Rådhusgate 11, 1st floor (entrance from Kirkengaten) ✉ 0151 – Ⓜ Stortinget – ✆ 22 41 88 00 – www.statholdergaarden.no
– Closed 18-25 April, 17 May, 13 June, 4 July-2 August, 23 December-3 January and Sunday **C2**

Rest – Menu 540 NOK (dinner) – Carte 513/573 NOK

♦ International ♦ Rustic ♦ Wine bar ♦

Three-roomed vaulted cellar set below, and run by the owner of, Statholdergaarden. Relaxed inner with large entrance wall filled with wine bottles. 10 course 'themed' set menu or à la carte.

Brasserie France 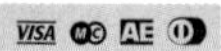

Øvre Slottsgate 16 ✉ 0157 – Ⓜ Stortinget – ✆ 23 10 01 65 – www.brasseriefrance.no
– Closed Easter, 23 December-7 January and Sunday **C2**

Rest – *(dinner only and light lunch Saturday)* Menu 395 NOK – Carte 405/505 NOK

♦ French ♦ Brasserie ♦

Lively French brasserie in pedestrianised shopping street. Main restaurant and terrace on ground floor; private rooms above. Brasserie classics and an 'eat-as-much-as-you-like' pastry trolley.

Alex Sushi

Cort Adelers Gate 2 ✉ 0254 – ✆ 22 43 99 99 – www.alexsushi.no
– Closed Easter, Christmas and New Year **B2**

Rest – *(dinner only)* Menu 361 NOK – Carte 360/579 NOK

♦ Japanese ♦ Design ♦

Glass-fronted Japanese restaurant in a busy, edge of city location. Bright inner made up of wood, steel and glass, with a unique, boat-shaped sushi bar. More tables and small lounge upstairs.

Lofoten Fiskerestaurant 

Stranden 75 ✉ 0250 – ✆ 22 83 08 08 – www.lofoten-fiskerestaurant.no
– Closed 23 December-5 January **B3**

Rest – Menu 450 NOK – Carte 487/875 NOK

♦ Seafood ♦ Brasserie ♦

Modern, fjord-side restaurant in bright, maritime colours, offering lovely views from its large windows and terrace. Traditional seafood menu. Semi-open kitchen and lobster tank on display.

ENVIRONS OF OSLO

AT GREFSEN North : 10 km by Ring 3

Grefsenkollen 

Grefsenkollveien 100 ✉ 0490 – ✆ 22 79 70 60 – www.grefsenkollen.no
– Closed 22 December-2 January and Monday

Rest – *(booking essential at dinner)* Menu 120 NOK (lunch), 645/875 NOK

♦ Modern ♦ Friendly ♦

Large wooden chalet with spacious terrace and lovely views over the city and fjord. Characterful, open-fired restaurant with dark wood furnishings, modern counter and open kitchen; smaller room at the end open for lunch. Evening set menu comes with wine pairings.

AT OSLO AIRPORT Northeast : 45 km by E 6 at Gardermoen

Clarion Oslo Airport

Hans Gaarderveg 15 (West : 6 km) ✉ 2060 – ✆ 63 94 94 94 – www.clarionosloairport.no
430 rm – 880/1890 NOK 1080/2090 NOK – 2 suites
Rest – *(buffet lunch)* Menu 265/365 NOK

♦ Business ♦ Functional ♦

Typical, two-storey Norwegian house, reached from the airport by a shuttle bus. Modern Scandinavian bedrooms in pale hues. One of the largest conference capacities in the country. Bar and open-fired lounges with live bands. Buffet meals in traditional restaurant.

AT HOLMENKOLLEN Northwest : 10 km by Bogstadveien, Sørkedalsveien and Holmenkollveien

Holmenkollen Park

Kongeveien 26 ✉ 0712 – Ⓜ Holmenkollen – ✆ 22 92 20 00 – www.holmenkollenparkhotel.no – Closed 22 December-3 January
325 rm – 795/2575 NOK 995/5395 NOK – 11 suites
Rest *De Fem Stuer* – *✆ 22 92 27 34 (buffet lunch)* Menu 565 NOK – Carte 425/565 NOK

♦ Traditional ♦ Personalised ♦

Impressive 1894 red wood building once used as a sanitorium for TB patients. Mix of classic and modern bedrooms with good comfort levels; some with city/fjord views. Extensive conference and wellness facilities. Buffet lunches followed by 2 evening set menus.

POLAND
POLSKA

PROFILE

→ **Area:**
312 677 km^2 (120 725 sq mi).

→ **Population:**
38 203 087 inhabitants (est. 2010), density = 124 per km^2.

→ **Capital:**
Warsaw (conurbation 2 785 000 inhabitants).

→ **Currency:**
Złoty (zl or PLN); rate of exchange: PLN 1 = € 0.25 = US$ 0.35 (Dec 2010).

→ **Government:**
Parliamentary republic (since 1990). Member of European Union since 2004.

→ **Language:**
Polish.

→ **Specific public holidays:**
National 3rd of May Holiday, Corpus Christi (9th Thursday after Easter), Independence Day (11 November).

→ **Local Time:**
GMT + 1 hour in winter and GMT + 2 hours in summer.

→ **Climate:**
Temperate continental with cold winters and warm summers (Warsaw: January: -2°C; July: 20°C).

→ **International dialling Code:**
00 48 followed by the area code and then the local number. Directory enquiries: ✆ **118 912**.

→ **Emergency:**
Ambulance: ✆ **999**; Fire Brigade: ✆ **998**; Police: ✆ **997**; Police from mobile: ✆ **112**.

→ **Electricity:**
230V AC, 50Hz; 2 pin round-shaped continental plugs.

→ **Formalities**
Travellers from the

European Union (EU), Switzerland, Iceland and the main countries of North and South America need a national identity card or passport (America: passport required) to visit Poland for less than three months (tourism or business purpose). For visitors from other countries a visa may be required, in addition to a passport, especially for those wishing to stay for longer than three months. We advise you to check with your embassy before travelling.

Warsaw

Warszawa

Population: 1 709 781 (conurbation 2 785 000) - Altitude: 106m.

Céline Lecardonnel/Fotolia.com

When UNESCO added Warsaw to its World Heritage list a few years ago, it was a fitting seal of approval for an inspired refit and rebuild: eighty per cent of the city had been destroyed during World War II, with over half the city's population either killed or displaced. Using plans of the old city, architects painstakingly rebuilt the shattered Polish capital throughout the 1950s until it became an admirable mirror image of its former self. Strolling around the renovated Old Town, it's hard to believe that most of it is just over sixty years old.

The city still has its grey communist era apartment blocks, and these pall desperately when up against the old-style buildings with their pastel prettiness and aristocratic swagger, their architecture spanning a whole range of movements from Gothic to Baroque, Rococo to Secession. It's a vibrant place to be, and the locals are well known for their exuberance and warmth: chat briefly to a Varsovian at bar or bus stop and you'll soon be given a phone number and an invitation to meet up and share a vodka. Throw in the charming river views, superb parkland, and hearty cuisine now on offer, and you have a city confidently reclaiming its glories of old.

LIVING THE CITY

Warsaw sidles up along the left bank of the River Vistula; its opposite side, the district of **Praga**, is mostly marshy banks fronting a district of tower blocks. The main area for visitors is the **Old Town**, nestling against the river, which was established at the end of the thirteenth century around what is now the Royal Castle. A century later the **New Town**, to the north, began to take shape. To the south of Old Town runs 'The Royal Route', so named because from the late middle ages wealthy citizens built summer residences with lush gardens along these rural thoroughfares. Continue southwards and you're in Lazienki Park with its palaces and pavilions. To the west lie the more commercial areas of Marshal Street and Solidarity Avenue, once the commercial heart of the city. The northwest of Warsaw was traditionally the Jewish district, destroyed during World War II, and today redeveloped with housing estates and the sobering Monument to the Ghetto Heroes.

PRACTICAL INFORMATION

ARRIVAL-DEPARTURE

Warsaw Frederic Chopin Airport in Okecie is 10km from the city. Bus 179 or 188 will take you to the centre in 20 mins. Ensure you take a taxi from the rank outside arrivals.

TRANSPORT

Warsaw's metro is under development, and the best way to get about town is bus or tram (beyond the centre) or on foot for the central attractions.

Buy a pack of ten tickets for travelling on Warsaw's public transport system. Most single tickets are bought from RUCH kiosks, but as these are often closed in the evenings and at weekends, it's best to get them in a pack. Ticket machines in the metro stations take credit cards and transactions can be carried out in English. A flat rate fare for all single journeys applies. One-day, seven-day and family tickets are also available.

It's well worth buying a Warsaw Tourist Card. Available from tourist information offices, it entitles you to free travel on public transport, free admission to 21 museums, and discounts in some shops, restaurants and leisure centres. Note that all museums offer free entry on a Sunday.

EXPLORING WARSAW

Warsaw is one of the youngest capital cities of Europe. It only assumed the mantle in 1596, after the royal castle in Cracow was destroyed by fire. It's been destroyed twice since then: by the Swedes in 1655 and the Germans in 1944. Visitors today are taken aback at how superbly the centre was rebuilt, using old documents and plans. The Old Town (Stare Miasto) is a masterclass of **Baroque** style in a smart geometric grid of little streets, swarming with delighted onlookers in summer.

➜ ROYAL FAMILIAR

The heartbeat of this quarter is **The Royal Castle**, the rebuild of which wasn't actually completed until 1988. It's now a museum and a focal point for formal ceremonies; it had once been the official residence of the Polish monarchs. Its interior is lavish, with many original furnishings and *objets d'art*: the Poles managed to hide many treasured statues and paintings from the Nazis. Check out the ballroom, Marble Room and Canaletto Room, each an opulent treat. Just north of Castle Square stands **Old Town Market Square**, which for centuries was the city's most important public meeting place. Here, everything from fairs to executions were carried out. The square's town hall was demolished nearly two hundred years ago, and its distinctive four sides are each named after parliamentarians of the eighteenth century; the houses grandly surrounding you were designed in the seventeenth. The Dekert side of the square is really worth discovering: all the houses are interconnected and form the Warsaw History Museum, which includes paintings, illustrations, archaeological finds, sculpture and photographs – a chronological odyssey through the city's troubled history. The cultural thrust of the square doesn't end here. On the Barss side stand two burghers' houses, a popular location for swarms of Varsovians, for this is the home of the Literature Museum, and in particular, first editions and original manuscripts of Poland's best-loved Romantic poet Adam Mickiewicz.

➜ NATIONAL TREASURE

Warsaw's real cultural gem is **The National Museum**: travel due south from Old Town Market Square for a mile to find it. Founded in 1862 with just 36 paintings, the museum now holds a mesmerising 780,000 exhibits. But you shouldn't suffer too much cultural overload: many are only on show at special exhibitions. Nevertheless, you might well feel like a park break when you stumble from the National's hallowed portals. You're in luck. A few minutes' walk and you're in **Lazienki Park,** Warsaw's green jewel, a luscious, peacock-strewn wonderland of old palaces and an orangery with an eighteenth century court theatre. There's a second theatre here, too, on an island with a moat separating the auditorium from the stage. And a neoclassical Temple based on ancient Greek design. Not forgetting the Chopin Monument, sculpted over one hundred years ago (1908) depicting the great man sitting under a willow tree in search of inspiration. In summer, the park is packed with visitors to the lakeside Palace on the Water, one of the finest examples of neoclassical architecture in Poland. There's another glorious park with palaces further south in Wilanow: again this is a lovely place to visit, with a stunning Baroque Park hiding behind the palace and, fascinatingly, a poster museum in a former stable: it includes posters by Picasso, Warhol and Mucha.

➜ GRAND TOUR

Warsaw has earned a reputation as a centre of cultural tourism thanks to numerous theatrical and musical venues. Top of the list is the grand sounding, grand looking...**Grand Theatre**, just south of Solidarity Avenue. Badly damaged during World War II, it was enlarged during reconstruction and its modern interiors have brought it bang up to date. This is where to go if you want to see top-class opera or ballet. Before going in, incidentally, you could stroll over to the nearby **Saxon Gardens**, Warsaw's first public park and another leafy oasis. Modelled on Versailles, it boasts statues, fountains, mature trees and, more sombrely, the Tomb of the

Unknown Soldier, a constant reminder of the city's anguished 20C history. Mozart lovers, meanwhile, often make a beeline for the Philharmonic Hall, near prestigious Marshal Street, where his music is a well-established attraction. And the Royal Castle is a great place to go for Renaissance and Baroque music (but remember it's only on a Sunday!)

Going shopping in Warsaw, as you might imagine, is a rather different experience than it was in 1989. From famine to feast might be putting it a bit strongly, but you get the picture. An expanding number of department stores and shopping arcades have arrived in the centre of the city with the Marshal Street area being the hub. For many locals, though, markets are what this city is really all about. Muffled up against the wind and snow, doing business with a street trader is part and parcel of Warsaw life. And for market lovers there's only one place to go – the '**Russian Market'**, across the river, in the Praga district. Quite simply, it's Europe's largest open-air market, a daily hotch-potch on a massive scale, the home of thousands of traders from Russia (hence the name) to the sub-Sahara, hawking everything from mobiles to counterfeit clothes, hunting knives to rifles. It encircles a vast disused stadium, and as you get off the number 12 tram, there are stalls as far as the eye can see. A bizarre bazaar, the like of which you won't have encountered before.

→ MOVING MEMORIALS

In the northwest of the city there are a lot of memorials: they tell the sombre story, in small part, of the many thousands of Jews who lived here before 1939, and who were murdered during World War II. One of the most affecting is the Monument to the Ghetto Heroes in **Zamenhofa**. It was erected in 1948, when the city was still in ruins, and powerfully commemorates the Ghetto Uprising of 1943, with men, women and children surrounded by the burning ghetto; the Warsaw Uprising Museum provides an excellent chronological overview of this defining moment in time. Other monuments in the area include the **Umschlagplatz** Monument, to denote an old railway siding where Jews were sent to concentration camps, and the Monument to 300 Victims, a small 'funeral pyre' at the location where the remains of 300 Jews and Poles were unearthed during building works. Both the last two monuments were completed just over twenty years ago.

CALENDAR HIGHLIGHTS

Warsaw is a hot spot for events, particularly in spring and autumn when the weather's at neither extreme. April kicks things off, with the Warsaw

WARSAW IN...

→ ONE DAY

Royal Castle, Warsaw History Museum, National Museum, Lazienki Park

→ TWO DAYS

Russian Market, Monument to the Ghetto Heroes, Saxon Gardens, top-class concert at Grand Theatre or Philharmonic Hall

→ THREE DAYS

The Royal Route, Marshal Street, Solidarity Avenue, Wilanow

Chamber Opera hosting the Polish Contemporary Opera Festival; then on the first day of May a historical communist holiday is celebrated throughout Poland, welcoming a colourful parade through the city streets. Music plays a special place in Varsovians' lives: in June, Chopin, their favourite son, is celebrated in concerts on Sunday afternoons in Lazienki Park, then in July and August the Warsaw Summer Jazz Days attract a variety of famous international jazz artists and musicians, and include many outdoor concerts, as well as performances at the Congress Hall. Another summer favourite is the Mozart Festival, where all of his operas are performed. Next, gaining in popularity, comes the Warsaw International Film Festival (WIFF), which takes place in October and is attended by directors and filmmakers from the world over. It's back to more music with the Baroque Opera Festival and the three-day Warsaw Jazz Jamboree at the end of the month – the latter spread across various venues, including the Kongresowa Hall on the Plac Defilad; while the Chopin International Piano Competition, held every five years, is one of the most important in the world. November rounds things off with the Warsaw Piano Festival, showcasing some of Poland's very best pianists at some truly spectacular venues, including the Philharmonic Hall and Royal Castle.

EATING OUT

There's an old Polish proverb that says: "Eat, drink and loosen your belt." It rather lost its edge during the communist era, but in the twenty years since democracy returned, the quality and quantity of Warsaw's restaurants has moved unerringly northwards. New venues seem to open weekly, and long gone are the days when a waiter would tell the hapless diner that none of the items on the menu were actually available. A visitor arriving for the first time since 1989 would be astonished at the proliferation of eateries, everything from veggie to Vietnamese, with fast food joints on most corners, as well as stalls selling falafel and noodles. A large Italian business community has encouraged a boom in the amount of good Italian restaurants. Asian food is also well represented, with Japanese restaurants particularly plentiful. What about Polish food? The centuries-old traditional cuisine of Warsaw was influenced by neighbouring countries, such as Russia, Ukraine and Germany, while Jewish dishes were also added to the mix. Over the years there has been a growing sophistication to the cooking and a lighter, more contemporary style is becoming evident, with time-honoured classics, such as the ubiquitous pierogi (turnovers with various fillings) and assorted pork dishes, having been updated with flair by Poland's finest chefs. Accompanied, of course, by Polish vodka, which covers a bewildering range of styles and brands, but tastes like no other vodka on earth: it has a distinct character, and should be served chilled. A good number of restaurants and cafés in central Warsaw provide stylised settings, such as a burgher's house, vaulted cellar, or Secessionist sophistication. Wherever you eat, check that VAT has been included with prices (it's not always) and add ten per cent for a tip, which is customary.

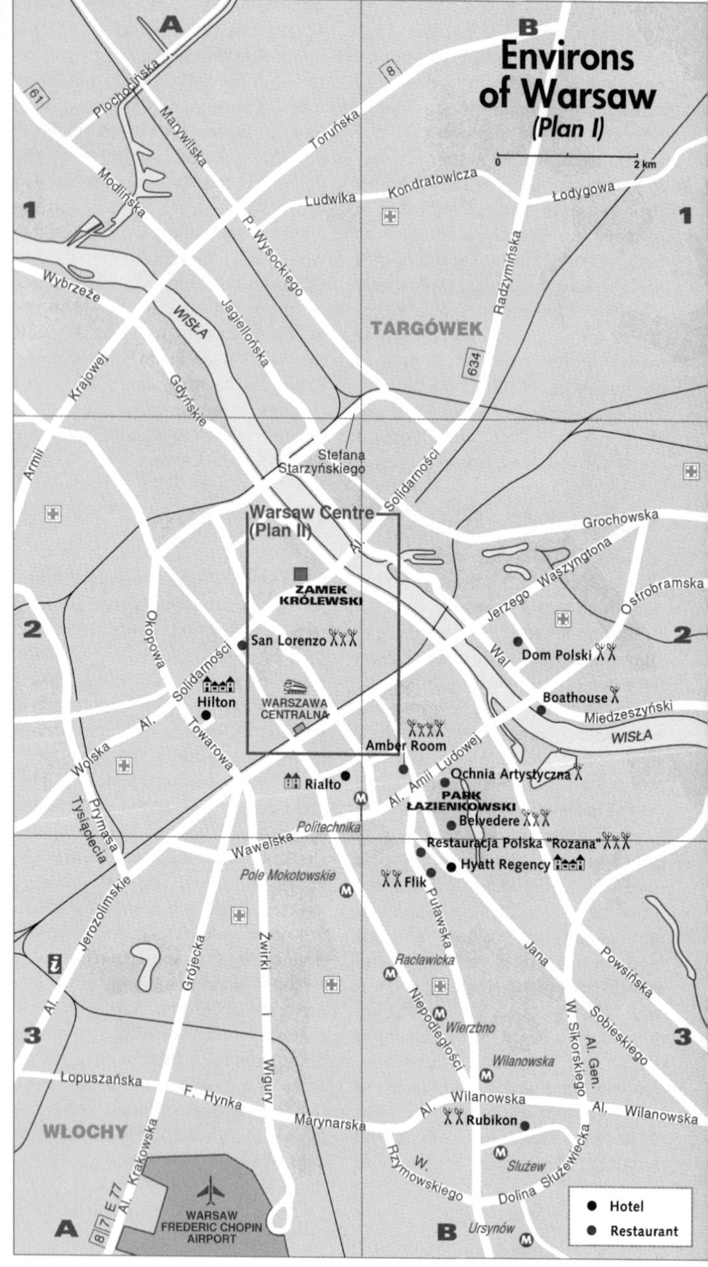
Environs of Warsaw
(Plan I)
0
2 km
A
B
1
2
3
Plochocińska
Marywilska
Modlińska
Toruńska
Ludwika
Kondratowicza
Łodygowa
Radzymińska
P. Wysockiego
Wybrzeże
WISŁA
Jagiellońska
TARGÓWEK
Krajowej
Gdyńskie
Armii
Stefana
Starzyńskiego
Solidarności
Al.
Warsaw Centre
(Plan II)
Grochowska
Jerzego Waszyngtona
Ostrobramska
ZAMEK
KRÓLEWSKI
San Lorenzo
Okopowa
Al. Solidarności
Hilton
WARSZAWA
CENTRALNA
Dom Polski
Wał
Boathouse
Miedzeszyński
WISŁA
Amber Room
Towarowa
Wolska
Rialto
Al. Armii Ludowej
Ochnia Artystyczna
PARK
ŁAZIENKOWSKI
Belvedere
Politechnika
Restauracja Polska "Rozana"
Hyatt Regency
Prymasa
Tysiąclecia
Wawelska
Pole Mokotowskie
Flik
Puławska
Jerozolimskie
Jana
Powsińska
Sobieskiego
Grójecka
Żwirki
Racławicka
Niepodległości
Wierzbno
Al.
W. Sikorskiego
Al. Gen.
Wilanowska
Łopuszańska
F. Hynka
Wigury
Marynarska
Al. Wilanowska
Rubikon
Al. Wilanowska
WŁOCHY
Al. Krakowska
Rzymowskiego
W.
Służew
Dolina Służewiecka
E 77
WARSAW
FREDERIC CHOPIN
AIRPORT
Ursynów
Hotel
Restaurant

Intercontinental

ul. Emilii Plater 49 ✉ 00 125 – Ⓜ Centrum – ✆ (022) 328 8888 – www.warsaw.intercontinental.com **C2**

328 rm – 🛉313/1080 PLN 🛉🛉313/1080 PLN, ☕ 91 PLN – 76 suites

Rest *Platter by Karol Okrasa* – see below

Rest *Downtown* – Menu 105 PLN

♦ Grand Luxury ♦ Business ♦ Modern ♦

Striking high-rise hotel in central location. Smart guest areas include a modern lobby, lounge and clubby bar. Impressive health and leisure club on 43rd and 44th floors boasts fantastic views. Comfy, contemporary bedrooms. Informal brasserie with accessible menu.

Hyatt Regency

ul. Belwederska 23 ✉ 00 761 – ✆ (022) 558 12 34 – www.warsaw.regency.hyatt.com *Plan I* **B3**

231 rm – 🛉400/800 PLN 🛉🛉500/850 PLN, ☕ 85 PLN – 19 suites

Rest *Venti Tre* – *✆ (022) 558 10 94* – Carte 109/149 PLN

♦ Luxury ♦ Business ♦ Modern ♦

Contemporary hotel with impressive open-plan lobby and glass-roofed lounge-bar. Spacious bedrooms boast top quality furniture, smart bathrooms and excellent facilities. Large, split-level restaurant offers extensive Mediterranean menu and wood-fired specialities.

Hilton

ul. Grzybowska 63 ✉ 00 844 – ✆ (022) 356 55 55 – www.hilton.com *Plan I* **A2**

314 rm – 🛉270/1100 PLN 🛉🛉270/1100 PLN, ☕ 88 PLN – 11 suites

Rest *Meza* – Carte 140/250 PLN

♦ Business ♦ Modern ♦

Large, modern hotel in the financial district. Bright atrium houses shops and lounge-bar; extensive business and leisure facilities include a casino. Well-equipped, contemporary bedrooms and smart club lounge. Informal restaurant serves Mediterranean cuisine.

Sheraton

ul. Bolesława Prusa 2 ✉ 00 493 – ✆ (022) 450 6100 – www.sheraton.com/warsaw **D2**

351 rm – 🛉343/1268 PLN 🛉🛉343/1268 PLN, ☕ 99 PLN – 14 suites

Rest *Oriental* – *✆ (022) 450 67 05 (closed Sunday dinner) (dinner only and Sunday lunch)* Carte 136/235 PLN

Rest *Olive* – *(lunch only)* Menu 78 PLN – Carte 84/179 PLN

♦ Luxury ♦ Business ♦ Classic ♦

Spacious corporate hotel on the historic Three Cross Square, with large, open-plan lobby and leather-furnished lounge-bar. Good conference and leisure facilities. Modern, well-equipped bedrooms. Asian dishes in Oriental. Mediterranean menu and buffet lunches in Olive.

Le Meridien Bristol

ul. Krakowskie Przedmieście 42-44 ✉ 00 325 – ✆ (022) 551 10 00 – www.lemeridien.pl **D1**

173 rm – 🛉500/1464 PLN 🛉🛉1464/1180 PLN, ☕ 110 PLN – 31 suites

Rest *Marconi* – *✆ (022) 551 11 832* – Carte 104/204 PLN

♦ Grand Luxury ♦ Classic ♦

Early 20C hotel next to the Presidential Palace, boasting an elegant, marble-floored reception and impressive columned bar. Good-sized, luxurious bedrooms with high level of facilities and marble bathrooms. Smart restaurant offers a Mediterranean-based menu.

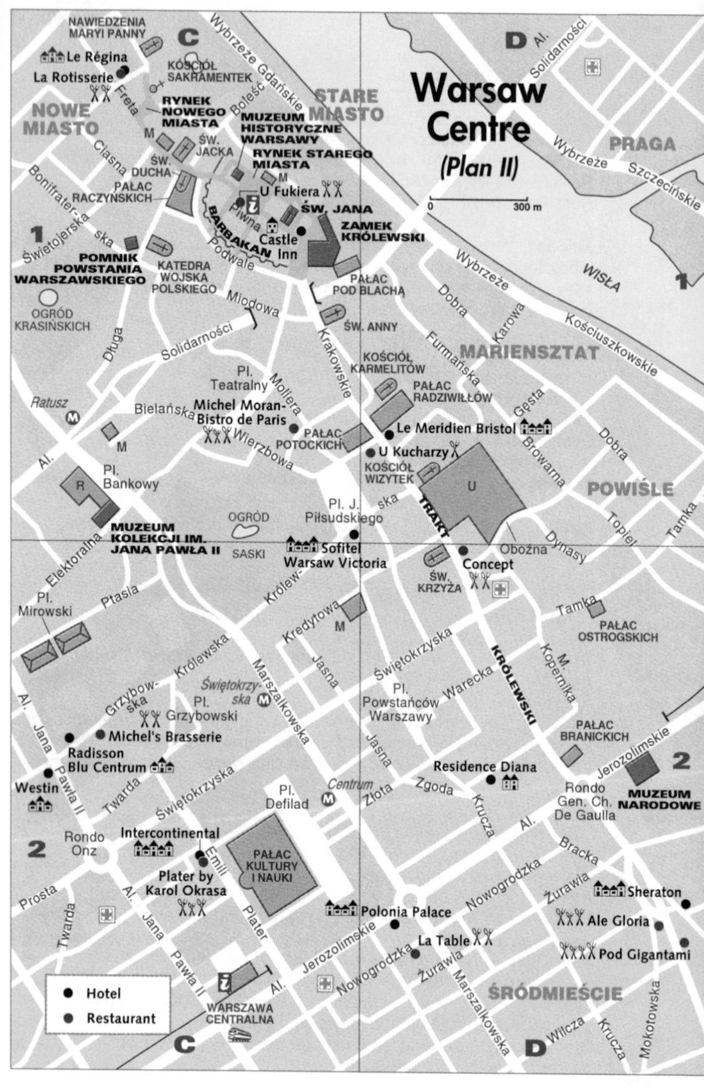

Warsaw Centre
(Plan II)
0
300 m
C
D
1
2
NOWE MIASTO
STARE MIASTO
PRAGA
MARIENSZTAT
POWIŚLE
ŚRÓDMIEŚCIE
NAWIEDZENIA MARYI PANNY
Le Régina
La Rotisserie
KOŚCIÓŁ SAKRAMENTEK
RYNEK NOWEGO MIASTA
MUZEUM HISTORYCZNE WARSAWY
ŚW. JACKA
ŚW. DUCHA
RYNEK STAREGO MIASTA
PAŁAC RACZYŃSKICH
U Fukiera
ŚW. JANA
ZAMEK KRÓLEWSKI
BARBAKAN
Castle Inn
POMNIK POWSTANIA WARSZAWSKIEGO
KATEDRA WOJSKA POLSKIEGO
PAŁAC POD BLACHĄ
OGRÓD KRASIŃSKICH
ŚW. ANNY
KOŚCIÓŁ KARMELITÓW
PAŁAC RADZIWIŁŁÓW
Pl. Teatralny
Ratusz
Michel Moran-Bistro de Paris
PAŁAC POTOCKICH
Le Meridien Bristol
U Kucharzy
KOŚCIÓŁ WIZYTEK
Pl. Bankowy
TRAKT
KRÓLEWSKI
Pl. J. Piłsudskiego
OGRÓD SASKI
MUZEUM KOLEKCJI IM. JANA PAWŁA II
Sofitel Warsaw Victoria
Concept
ŚW. KRZYŻA
Pl. Mirowski
PAŁAC OSTROGSKICH
Świętokrzyska
Pl. Grzybowski
Pl. Powstańców Warszawy
Michel's Brasserie
Radisson Blu Centrum
PAŁAC BRANICKICH
Residence Diana
Westin
Centrum
Pl. Defilad
Rondo Gen. Ch. De Gaulla
MUZEUM NARODOWE
Rondo Onz
Intercontinental
PAŁAC KULTURY I NAUKI
Plater by Karol Okrasa
Sheraton
Polonia Palace
Ale Gloria
La Table
Pod Gigantami
WARSZAWA CENTRALNA
Hotel
Restaurant
Wybrzeże Gdańskie
Wybrzeże Szczecińskie
Wybrzeże Kościuszkowskie
WISŁA
Al. Solidarności
Freta
Bolesć
Ciasna
Bonifraterska
Świętojerska
Piwna
Podwale
Miodowa
Długa
Solidarności
Krakowskie
Moliera
Bielańska
Wierzbowa
Dobra
Karowa
Furmańska
Gęsta
Browarna
Topiel
Tamka
Dynasy
Oboźna
Al. Elektoralna
Ptasia
Królewska
Kredytowa
Jasna
Marszałkowska
Grzybowska
Warecka
M. Kopernika
Al. Jana Pawła II
Twarda
Zgoda
Złota
Krucza
Al. Jerozolimskie
Bracka
Nowogrodzka
Żurawia
Emilii Plater
Prosta
Wilcza
Mokotowska

Polonia Palace

VISA AE

al. Jerozolimskie 45 ✉ *00 692* – Ⓜ *Centrum* – ✆ *(022) 318 2800*
– *www.poloniapalace.com* **D2**
206 rm – †260/915 PLN ††260/915 PLN, ☕ 80 PLN – 3 suites
Rest *Strauss* – ✆ *(022) 318 2834 (closed lunch Saturday and Sunday)*
Carte 69/175 PLN

♦ Business ♦ Classic ♦

Striking hotel dating from 1913, set on a busy central street. Elegant interior with lovely glass-roofed lobby, comfy lounge-bar and beautifully ornate, gilded ballroom. Modern, well-equipped bedrooms in browns and creams. International menu in formal restaurant.

Sofitel Warsaw Victoria

VISA AE

ul. Królewska 11 ✉ *00 065* – Ⓜ *Świętokrzyska*
– ✆ *(022) 657 80 11* – *www.sofitel.com* **C1/2**
291 rm – †950/1045 PLN ††1130 PLN, ☕ 95 PLN – 52 suites
Rest *Canaletto* – ✆ *(022) 657 8012 (dinner only)* Carte 125/235 PLN

♦ Business ♦ Classic ♦

Set next to Pilsudski Square, overlooking the Saxon Gardens. Spacious, contemporary guest areas feature lots of marble; bedrooms are comfy and well-equipped. Large conference centre and very pleasant leisure suite. Bright restaurant offers Italian-based menus.

Le Régina

VISA AE

ul. Kościelna 12 ✉ *00 218* – ✆ *(022) 531 60 00*
– *www.mamaison.com/leregina* **C1**
59 rm – †720/840 PLN ††720/840 PLN, ☕ 86 PLN – 2 suites
Rest *La Rotisserie* – see below

♦ Luxury ♦ Design ♦

Stylish boutique hotel housed in a neo-18C building, close to the Old Town. Comfortable, contemporary guest areas in natural hues. Understated bedrooms with smart bathrooms; 'Superior' boast balconies and hand-painted frescoes on the bed heads. Friendly service.

Radisson Blu Centrum

VISA AE

ul. Grzybowska 24 ✉ *00 132*
– Ⓜ *Świętokrzyska* – ✆ *(022) 321 88 88*
– *www.radissonblu.com/hotel-warsaw* **C2**
292 rm – †280/700 PLN ††280/700 PLN, ☕ 80 PLN – 19 suites
Rest *Brasserie at Ferdy's* – ✆ *(022) 321 88 22* – Carte 102/161 PLN

♦ Business ♦ Modern ♦

Glass-fronted hotel in the business district, boasting state-of-the-art conference facilities. Leather-furnished bar and well-equipped leisure centre. Smart Maritime, Scandinavian or Italian themed bedrooms. All-day brasserie offers Polish and Mediterranean fare.

Westin

VISA AE

al. Jana Pawła II 21 ✉ *00 854*
– Ⓜ *Świętokrzyska* – ✆ *(022) 450 80 00*
– *www.westin.com/warsaw* **C2**
348 rm – †332/1081 PLN ††332/1081 PLN, ☕ 99 PLN – 13 suites
Rest *Fusion* – Carte 131/180 PLN

♦ Luxury ♦ Business ♦ Modern ♦

Eye-catching modern building on a busy street, boasting an impressive glass atrium and glass lifts. Bright, open-plan lobby and lounge-bar; large conference capacity. Smart, contemporary bedrooms come with good facilities. East meets West in the restaurant.

Rialto

ul. Wilcza 73 ✉ *00 670 – Ⓜ Politechnika – ✆ (022) 584 87 00 – www.rialto.pl* *Plan I* **A2**

33 rm – 675/894 PLN 795/1073 PLN, 72 PLN – 11 suites

Rest – Menu 88 PLN – Carte 96/120 PLN

♦ Business ♦ Art Deco ♦

Attractive converted townhouse dating back to 1906. Elegant, sympathetically refurbished interior boasts original art deco and art nouveau features. Good-sized, classical bedrooms offer good facilities and have beautiful marble-floored bathrooms. Intimate cigar room and smart bar. Brasserie serves modern Polish menu.

Residence Diana

ul Chmiela 13a ✉ *00 021 – Ⓜ Centrum – ✆ (022) 505 9100 – www.residencediana.com* **D2**

12 rm – 270/392 PLN 392/588 PLN – **34 suites** – 588 PLN 981 PLN, 47 PLN

Rest *Amadera* – Carte 74/110 PLN

♦ Townhouse ♦ Cosy ♦

Set in a quiet courtyard off a busy central shopping street. Spacious reception and lounge. Large, modern bedrooms with small kitchen areas and good facilities. Smart, black wood furnished bar and restaurant; extensive Mediterranean menus and resident pianist.

Castle Inn without rest

Plac Zamkowy, ul Świętojańska 2 ✉ *00 288 – ✆ (022) 4250100 – www.castleinn.eu* **C1**

22 rm – 207/341 PLN 245/355 PLN, 29 PLN

♦ Family ♦ Historic ♦

Small 16C property on cobbled street in the heart of the Old Town – a stone's throw from the Castle. Very unique bedrooms: designed by local artists, they range from bohemian to contemporary.

Amber Room

al Ujazdowskie 13 ✉ *00 567 – ✆ (022) 523 6664 – www.kprb.pl/amber – Closed dinner 24 December, 31 December, Saturday lunch, Sunday and bank holidays* *Plan I* **B2**

Rest – Menu 79 PLN (lunch) – Carte 126/227 PLN

♦ Contemporary ♦ Formal ♦

Set in an attractive villa; home to the exclusive 'Round Table of Warsaw' club. Stylish dining room and pleasant summer terrace. Attentive, well-paced service. Refined, modern cooking relies on quality ingredients and displays original, sophisticated touches.

Pod Gigantami

al. Ujazdowskie 24 ✉ *00 478 – ✆ (022) 629 23 12 – www.podgigantami.pl*

Rest – Carte 110/157 PLN **D2**

♦ Contemporary ♦ Formal ♦

Elegant restaurant in grand property close to the embassies. Three beautifully styled dining rooms with large, well-spaced tables. Extensive classical menu of Polish and Mediterranean dishes.

Belvedere

ul. Agrykoli 1 (entry from ul Parkowa) ✉ *00 460 – ✆ (022) 55 86 700 – www.belvedere.com.pl – Closed 23 December-7 January* *Plan I* **B2**

Rest – *(booking essential)* Menu 65 PLN (lunch) – Carte 97/149 PLN

♦ Contemporary ♦ Formal ♦

Impressive Victorian orangery in Lazienki Park. Spacious, split-level dining room with large arched windows and tables hidden among the foliage. Light, refined Polish and international dishes.

XXX

Michel Moran - Bistro de Paris

pl. Piłsudskiego 9 ✉ 00 073 – Ⓜ Ratusz – ☎ (022) 826 01 07
– www.restaurantbistrodeparis.com
– Closed Sunday and bank holidays **C1**
Rest – Menu 103/125 PLN – Carte 112/194 PLN
◆ French ◆ Elegant ◆
Smart, marble-floored restaurant in striking columned building on the edge of the Old Town. Large menu of Polish and French dishes; the 'Classics' are a hit, with produce imported from France.

XXX

Platter by Karol Okrasa – at Intercontinental Hotel

ul. Emilii Plater 49 ✉ 00 125 – Ⓜ Centrum
– ☎ (022) 328 8730 – www.platter.pl
– Closed lunch Saturday and Sunday **C2**
Rest – Carte 157/430 PLN
◆ Contemporary ◆ Formal ◆
Modern hotel restaurant with smart red and black décor and open kitchen. Well-balanced menus change with the seasons and are classically based. Dishes are sophisticated, refined and flavoursome.

XXX

San Lorenzo

1st floor, al. Jana Pawla II 36 ✉ 00 141 – ☎ (022) 652 16 16
– www.sanlorenzo.pl
– Closed 24-26 December, 31 December, 1 January and 1-3 May
Rest – Carte 71/173 PLN *Plan I* **A2**
◆ Italian ◆ Formal ◆
Imposing classical building with ground floor bistro and wide marble staircase up to the elegant restaurant. Extensive menus of flavoursome Italian dishes, with Tuscan influences to the fore.

XXX

Polska "Rozana"

ul. Chocimska 7 ✉ 00 791 – ☎ (022) 848 12 25
– www.restauracjatradycja.pl *Plan I* **B3**
Rest – *(booking essential)* Carte 72/151 PLN
◆ Traditional ◆ Friendly ◆
Attractive villa with lovely enclosed terrace and early 20C Polish décor. Deceptively large inner with various rooms over 2 floors. Extensive menus of hearty Polish dishes; homemade desserts.

XXX

AleGloria

pl. Trzech Krzyzy 3 ✉ 00 535 – ☎ (022) 584 70 80
– www.alegloria.pl **D2**
Rest – Carte 106/229 PLN
◆ Polish ◆ Design ◆
Boutique shopping arcade with steep steps down to this spacious restaurant; formerly cellars and stables. Various charming, elegant dining rooms. Extensive menu of hearty Polish classics.

XX

Concept

ul Krakowskie Przedmieście 16-18 ✉ 00 325 – ☎ (022) 492 7409
– www.likusconceptstore.pl
– Closed Sunday and bank holidays **D1**
Rest – Menu 75 PLN (lunch) – Carte 147/189 PLN
◆ Contemporary ◆ Design ◆
Part of a small complex within the old Central Baths, consisting of a wine shop, a cigar room, and a fashion boutique set around a sunken pool. Characterful restaurant set in a columned, glass-roofed room. Good-sized menu of refined, modern Mediterranean dishes.

XX

Dom Polski

ul. Francuska 11 ✉ 03 906 – ✆ (022) 616 24 32
– www.restauracjadompolski.pl *Plan I* **B2**
Rest – *(Sunday brunch)* Menu 70 PLN (lunch) – Carte 68/171 PLN
♦ Traditional ♦ Friendly ♦
Mediterranean-style villa in a smart residential area, with lovely terrace to rear. Various small rooms are set over 2 floors. Extensive Polish menus offer weekly specials and a refined touch.

XX

La Rotisserie – at Le Régina Hotel

ul. Kościelna 12 ✉ 00 218 – ✆ (022) 531 60 00
– www.leregina.com
– Closed dinner 24 December **C1**
Rest – *(booking essential)* Menu 120 PLN – Carte 139/229 PLN
♦ Contemporary ♦ Modern ♦
Small but stylish hotel restaurant in neutral hues, with arched ceiling, enclosed courtyard terrace and Mediterranean villa styling. Refined, flavoursome modern dishes have Polish origins.

XX

Rubikon

ul. Wróbla 3-5 ✉ 02 736 – Ⓜ Służew – ✆ (022) 847 66 55
– www.rubikon.waw.pl
– Closed 25-26 December *Plan I* **B3**
Rest – Carte 84/123 PLN
♦ Italian ♦ Neighbourhood ♦
Attractive villa with smart, split-level restaurant and two large summer terraces. Marble flooring and wine racks on the walls. Extensive, authentic Italian menu features imported produce.

XX

La Table

ul. Nowogrodzka 38 ✉ 00 691 – Ⓜ Centrum – ✆ (22) 6229214
– www.latable.com.pl
– Closed 1 week July, Christmas, Saturday lunch, Sunday and bank holidays **D2**
Rest – Carte 63/122 PLN
♦ French ♦ Intimate ♦
Small, smoked glass fronted restaurant with purple mock flock wallpaper and matching table runners. Concise menu offers refined, flavoursome, classically based French dishes. Friendly service.

XX

Michel's Brasserie

ul. Gryzbowska 5a ✉ 00 132 – Ⓜ Świętokrzyska – ✆ (22) 564 5780
– www.michels-brasserie.com **C2**
Rest – Carte 80/127 PLN
♦ French ♦ Design ♦
Chic brasserie in orange, black and grey, with smart black wood tables, semi-circular booths, high bar stools and 2 terraces. Extensive, well-priced menus of classic French brasserie dishes.

XX

U Fukiera

Rynek Starego Miasta 27 ✉ 00 272 – ✆ (022) 831 10 13
– www.ufukiera.pl
– Closed 24-25 and 31 December **C1**
Rest – Menu 90/180 PLN – Carte 107/162 PLN
♦ Polish ♦ Rustic ♦
Traditional house with enclosed courtyard, on a historic cobbled square. Spacious inner made up of several intimate, homely rooms, including a 17C vaulted cellar. Hearty, classical cooking.

XX

Flik

ul. Puławska 43 ✉ 02 508 – ✆ (022) 849 44 34 – www.flik.com.pl
– Closed 25 December *Plan I* **B3**

Rest – Carte 67/89 PLN

♦ Traditional ♦ Neighbourhood ♦

Neat restaurant in a residential area near the park, displaying pretty floral décor, bamboo furniture and contemporary local art. Extensive, traditional menu; particularly friendly service.

X

Boathouse

Wal Miedzeszynski 389a ✉ 03-975 – ✆ (022) 616 32 23
– www.boathouse.pl *Plan 1* **B2**

Rest – *(brunch Saturday and Sunday)* Carte 88/199 PLN

♦ Mediterranean ♦ Rustic ♦

Wooden boathouse with lawns leading to the river. Rustic, two-floored inner complete with wine bar. Appealing Mediterranean menu. Seasonal themes often feature e.g. a dedicated shrimp menu.

X

Qchnia Artystyczna

Ujazdowski Castle, ul. Jazdow 2 ✉ 00 467 – ✆ (022) 625 76 27
– www.qchnia.pl *Plan I* **B2**

Rest – Carte 68/132 PLN

♦ Contemporary ♦ Fashionable ♦

Busy, two-roomed restaurant with simple furnishings, in a contemporary art gallery by the Royal Park. Short menus mix classical Polish and international influences; dishes are full of flavour.

X

U Kucharzy

ul. Ossolinskich 7 ✉ 00 087 – ✆ (022) 826 79 36 – www.gessler.pl
Rest – *(booking essential)* Menu 30 PLN (lunch) – Carte 82/124 PLN **D1**

♦ Polish ♦ Neighbourhood ♦

Large, lively restaurant in the old kitchens of a 19C former hotel. Tables overlook the chefs hard at work. Small, well-priced menus feature produce from the enthusiastic owner's nearby farm.

CRACOW

KRAKÓW

Population: 754 626 (conurbation 1 500 000) - Altitude: 219m

. Brillion/MICHELIN

Cracow has often been referred to as the 'new Prague', which is both good and bad news for the locals. They don't want the stag-party brigade who've recently been latching on to Poland's third biggest city as the place to go for cheap vodka. But they do want visitors who'll appreciate the superb cultural atmosphere and artistic treasures which abound here. Not for nothing was Cracow included in the very first UNESCO World Heritage List.

Unlike much of Poland, this beautiful old city - the country's capital from the eleventh to the seventeenth centuries - was spared Second World War destruction because the German Governor had his HQ here. So Cracow is still able to boast a hugely imposing market square that was the biggest in medieval Europe, and a hill that's crowned with not just a castle, but a cathedral too. And not far away there's even a glorious chapel made of salt one hundred metres underground! It's a city famous for its links with Judaism and its visitor-friendly Royal Route, but also for its cultural inheritance. During the Renaissance, Cracow became a centre of new ideas that drew the most outstanding writers, thinkers and musicians of the day. It has literally thousands of architectural monuments and millions of artefacts collected and displayed in its museums and churches. But it's very much a modern city, too, with an eye on the twenty first century.

LIVING THE CITY

The heart and soul of Cracow is its **old quarter**, which received its charter in 1257. This area is dominated by the imposing **Market Square**, and almost completely encircled by the restful green embrace of the **Planty** gardens. A short way to the south, briefly interrupted by the curving streets of **Okol** neighbourhood, is **Wawel Hill**, the second major tourist destination of the city. Further south from here is the characterful Jewish quarter of **Kazimierz.** The smartly residential areas of **Piasek** and **Nowy Swiat** are to the west of the old quarter.

PRACTICAL INFORMATION

ARRIVAL-DEPARTURE

John Paul II International Airport-Balice is 13km west of the city centre. A taxi will cost around 65PLN and take 20min. There's a free shuttle to the train station which is located 200m from the terminal building ; trains to the centre take 15min. Bus 192 goes to the central Bus station.

TRANSPORT

The historic centre of the city is a largely pedestrian precinct, so getting about on foot here is a traffic-free pleasure. The streets in the old quarter are laid out in a grid pattern, which makes orientation even easier.

The public transport system in Cracow is made up of an extensive network of buses and trams (there's no metro here). You can use your tickets on both bus or tram, and there are four different types available: timed (valid for one hour from the moment of punching), daily (from punching till midnight), weekly and family. Buy your tickets from MPK outlets or newspaper kiosks.

EXPLORING CRACOW

The sound of music has rasped out from Cracow's Market Square for centuries without a break. On the hour, every hour, for six hundred years a bugler has climbed one of the towers of **St Mary's Church**, and sounded a two-and-a-half minute bugle call across the square, day and night. It's just one of the quirks that gives this city its special appeal. The church itself, a Gothic basilica, is the proud owner of two towers, one taller than the other, making it the slightly uneven and easily distinguishable main landmark of Cracow. Inside, St Mary's is pretty impressive too, boasting Baroque and Renaissance finery (in the shape of the pulpit and the tombs), but most people who come here make for the **High Altar**, because this is the scene of daily theatre. At 11.45am, on the dot, a nun arrives and, in front of an expectant gallery, peels away the outer panels of Veit Stoss's 15C 39-ft. high, 36-ft long wood-carved polyptych. The inner cabinet is dazzling, a whole array of exquisite carvings tracing the death of Mary and her

Assumption in a blaze of golden sunbeams. Catch it if you can: the whole 'show' only lasts ten minutes each day.

→ CLOTHED IN HISTORY

Another notable – and ancient – building on the Market Square is the **Cloth Hall**, which dates back to the days of the original charter. Naturally enough, it once dealt in the trade of cloth, but now plays host to a colourful parade of souvenir stalls. More interestingly, inside its much remodelled walls is the impressive **Gallery of 19th Century Polish Painting.** Outside, in the huge arena of the square, there are churches, palaces, town houses, eye-catching modern sculptures, a sprinkling of designer clothes stores, and a whole al fresco jumble (at least in summer) of café tables and chairs. Near the Cloth Hall is one of the city's most beautiful palaces, **Christopher Palace**, which boasts a spectacular arcaded courtyard to dazzle the eye. You actually get double the value here, because it's also home to the **Museum of Cracow**, a fascinating treasure trove of goodies dug up from the city's rich history.

→ WAWEL

Jostling Market Square in the fame stakes is Wawel Hill. It's attached to the old quarter by the umbilical cord that is **Gródzska Street**, a lovely old cobbled thoroughfare with varying styles of architecture that are a delight to stroll past. Medieval kings made Wawel the seat of their political power, and a royal residence was built here, overlooking the city below. It went through much chopping and changing before evolving into the castle you see today, sprawling nonchalantly across the hill, its mishmash of styles representing Poland's turbulent history. Various captors have given it a style makeover down the centuries: in Renaissance times it was one of the most thrilling royal residences in Central Europe. Just to add more lustre, the 14C kings added a cathedral to the castle complex, and this is the final resting place of Poland's national heroes and royalty, making it the number one symbol of the country's statehood. There are beautifully carved tombs here, as well as important works of art, and the largest bell in Poland, weighing in at a mighty eleven tons.

→ KAZIMIERZ

The neighbourhood of Kazimierz is the most southerly quarter of Cracow. It feels like a different place, which isn't surprising because, until 1791, it was an independent town in its own right. It's a characterful area of narrow streets lined with low buildings, and has been a major centre of Jewish culture for over five hundred years. It's the ideal place to discover more about the story of the Jews in Poland and contains seven synagogues and a number of Jewish cemeteries. But it's also a magnet for Cracow's young, as many of the old buildings here have been reborn as cafés and bars. Steven Spielberg's epic drama *Schindler's List* was filmed around Kazimierz and the actors were regulars in the eating establishments around here, appreciating the blasts of live klezmer that periodically ring out from many of the neighbourhood's restaurants. Klezmer is Jewish folk music, and you'd have to have feet of clay for its infectious rhythms not to get you up and dancing.

→ SALT OF THE EARTH

The winters can get mighty cold in Cracow, and if you want to dive into a museum for cover, you'll find there are dozens hiding in all sorts of alleyways and corners. The main building of the **National Museum** takes some beating. A modern construction finished less than twenty years ago, it's west in Nowy Swiat. Suitably enough, it's full of 20C and contemporary Polish art; the Modernist section is a real stand out. Meanwhile, back in the old quarter, the **Czartoryski Museum** is for lovers of Western art. There are works by the likes of Leonardo Da Vinci and Rembrandt on display in three houses which exude a warm and homely feel. As a complete contrast, head out on a bus to the **Wieliczka salt mine** for a truly one-off experience. The mine has been operating for over nine hundred years, and has two hundred miles of underground corridors. Down the years miners have carved out hundreds of statues, and the most awe-inspiring is the **Chapel of St Kinga**. It took three miners sixty seven years to eke out this masterpiece, which lies over a hundred metres underground, and is fifty four metres long and twelve metres high. Everything in the chapel is made from rock salt, from the statue of Christ on the cross to the chandeliers, and it all makes for a spectacular experience. Should you get hungry down there, you can go for a meal at the deepest underground restaurant in the world.

→ DIG THE PLANTY

Very much back on terra firma, don't forget a stroll around the Planty, the 'green belt' that embraces the old quarter. It replaced the medieval walls of the city early in the nineteenth century, and its gardens were landscaped to make the most of the superb vistas on offer. The Planty has always been a popular venue for strolling and socialising, and for the last twenty years it's been getting lots of tender loving care, courtesy of period fencing and street lamps that give it the look it once knew two hundred years ago.

→ OVERWHELMING VISIT

An hour's journey from Cracow is Auschwitz, now a UNESCO World Heritage site. The grounds and buildings are open to visitors as a museum and poignant memorial; many of the inhabitants of Kazimierz were sent here by the Nazis. Remember that Auschwitz can be an emotionally draining experience.

CALENDAR HIGHLIGHTS

Cracow can get so cold in the winter that it pretty much shuts down on the festival front (though it looks beautiful under a blanket of snow). Things pick up in the spring with the arrival of the first crocuses and the first visitors drawing up chairs at al fresco tables in the old quarter. Two events in June highlight the city's love of myths: The Lajkonik Festival recalls an age-old victory for the citizens of Cracow over Tartar invaders. A procession of musicians and merrymakers takes three hours to pass from the 12C Convent of St Norbet to Market Square. Meanwhile, Wianki is based on a pagan festival, as wreaths of flowers are floated down

CRACOW IN...

→ ONE DAY

St Mary's Church, Cloth Hall, Wawel, main building of National Museum

→ TWO DAYS

Kazimierz, Czartoryski Museum, stroll round Planty

→ THREE DAYS

Trip either to Auschwitz or Wieliczka salt mine

the Vistula river, lit by huge bonfires as midsummer is celebrated to the sound of music and fireworks. The Kazimierz neighbourhood comes under the spotlight for the Cracow Jewish Culture Festival (June/July) when the quarter's lively streets, with their synagogues, cafés and pubs, celebrate Yiddish traditions with a whole range of concerts and recitals. The infectious sound of klezmer is a highlight. A month later, many of the beautiful buildings of the old quarter double as venues for Music in Old Cracow, a seventeen-day event featuring classical music from Baroque to Romantic to Modern. The sounds here will be familiar to most ears, but for those looking for something a bit different, October's intriguingly named International Festival of Forgotten Music is a treat. It features archaic songs from the Baltic region performed by country folk groups, and a good time is a cast-iron guarantee.

EATING OUT

Cracow has long had a reputation as a good place to go and eat. Even during the Communist era it kept its end up, with busy cafés serving good food unknown at the time in the rest of Poland. In the 1990s, hundreds of new restaurants opened their doors, often in pretty locations with medieval or Renaissance interiors. Other restaurateurs chose to go into ancient cellars, restored and furnished to give just the right intimate feel. As for the food itself, many Poles go misty-eyed at the thought of Bigos (Hunter's stew) on a cold winter's day. It's a game, sausage and cabbage stew that comes with sauerkraut, onion, potatoes, herbs and spices. It's reputed to get better with reheating on successive days, and lots of Cracow restaurants claim to serve the tastiest version. Pierogi is another local favourite: crescent-shaped dumplings which you can eat either in savoury or sweet style. Barszcz is a lemon and garlic flavoured beetroot soup that's invariably good value, while in Kazimierz, specialities include Jewish dumpling, filled with onion, cheese and potatoes, and Berdytchov soup, which imaginatively mixes honey and cinnamon with beef. Global grub is also on the menu here. Look around and you won't be short-changed on restaurants specialising in French, Greek, Vietnamese, Middle Eastern, Indian, Italian and Mexican food. You can eat quite late in Cracow: most restaurants don't close until around midnight, and there's no pressure on customers to rush their final drinks and leave. A tip of about ten per cent is the norm.

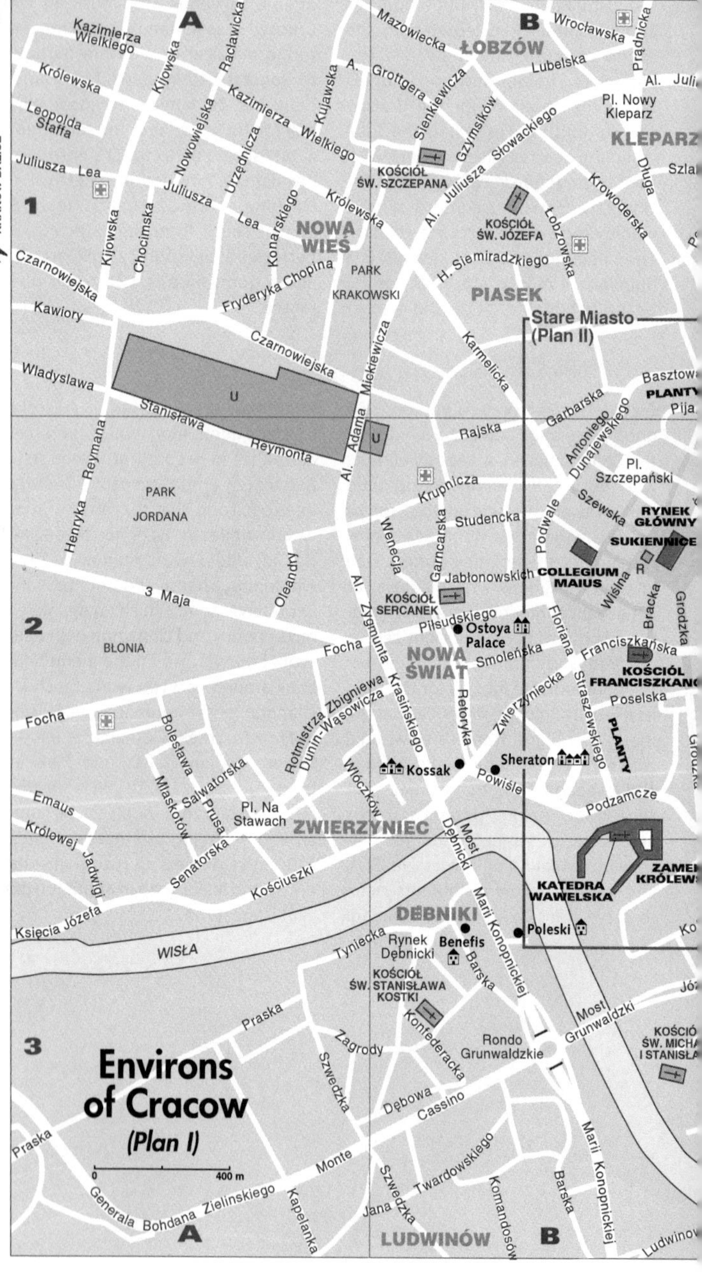
Environs of Cracow
(Plan I)
0
400 m
A
B
1
2
3
Kazimierza Wielkiego
Królewska
Leopolda Staffa
Juliusza Lea
Kijowska
Racławicka
Nowowiejska
Urzędnicza
Kujawska
Konarskiego
A. Grottgera
Mazowiecka
ŁOBZÓW
Wrocławska
Prądnicka
Lubelska
Sienkiewicza
Czymsików
KOŚCIÓŁ ŚW. SZCZEPANA
Al. Juliusza Słowackiego
Pl. Nowy Kleparz
KLEPARZ
Długa
Krowoderska
KOŚCIÓŁ ŚW. JÓZEFA
Łobzowska
NOWA WIEŚ
Chocimska
Czarnowiejska
Kawiory
Fryderyka Chopina
PARK KRAKOWSKI
H. Siemiradzkiego
PIASEK
Stare Miasto (Plan II)
Karmelicka
Wladyslawa Stanisława Reymonta
Al. Adama Mickiewicza
U
Garbarska
Rajska
Antoniego Dunajewskiego
Basztowa
PLANTY
Pl. Szczepański
Henryka Reymana
PARK JORDANA
Krupnicza
Studencka
Szewska
RYNEK GŁÓWNY
SUKIENNICE
Wenecja
Garncarska
Podwale
COLLEGIUM MAIUS
Jabłonowskich
Wiślna
Bracka
Grodzka
Oleandry
3 Maja
KOŚCIÓŁ SERCANEK
Al. Zygmunta Krasińskiego
Piłsudskiego
Ostoya Palace
BŁONIA
Focha
NOWA ŚWIAT
Smoleńska
Floriana Straszewskiego
Franciszkańska
KOŚCIÓŁ FRANCISZKAŃSKI
Poselska
Rotmistrza Zbigniewa Dunin-Wąsowicza
Reformacka
Zwierzyniecka
Bolesława
Salwatorska
Włóczków
Kossak
Sheraton
Powiśle
Emaus
Miaskotów
Prusa
Pl. Na Stawach
ZWIERZYNIEC
Podzamcze
Królowej Jadwigi
Senatorska
Most Dębnicki
KATEDRA WAWELSKA
Kościuszki
Księcia Józefa
WISŁA
DĘBNIKI
Marii Konopnickiej
Poleski
Tyniecka
Rynek Dębnicki
Benefis
Barska
KOŚCIÓŁ ŚW. STANISŁAWA KOSTKI
Praska
Zagrody
Konfederacka
Rondo Grunwaldzkie
Most Grunwaldzki
Szwedzka
Dębowa
Cassino
Monte
Twardowskiego
Komandosów
Generala Bohdana Zielinskiego
Kapelanka
Jana
LUDWINÓW

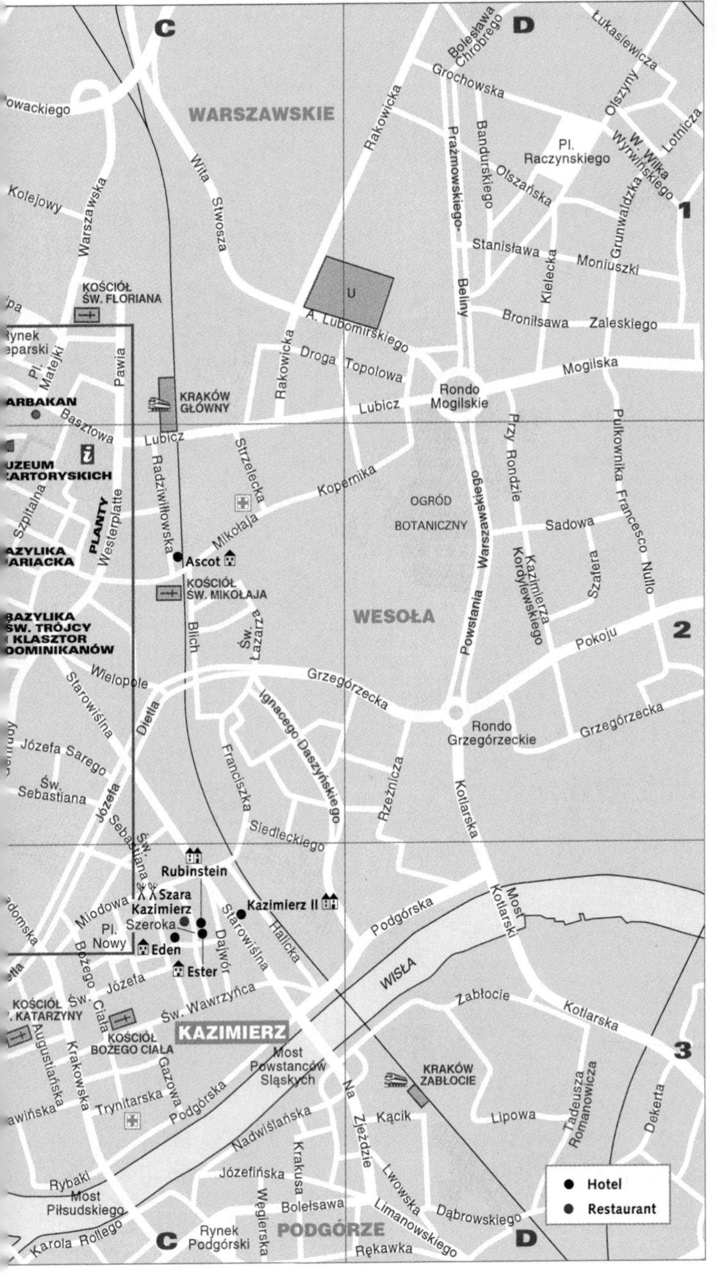

C
D
WARSZAWSKIE
WESOŁA
KAZIMIERZ
PODGÓRZE
OGRÓD BOTANICZNY
KRAKÓW GŁÓWNY
KRAKÓW ZABŁOCIE
KOŚCIÓŁ ŚW. FLORIANA
KOŚCIÓŁ ŚW. MIKOŁAJA
KOŚCIÓŁ BOŻEGO CIAŁA
Rondo Mogilskie
Rondo Grzegórzeckie
Pl. Raczynskiego
WISŁA
Ascot
Rubinstein
Szara Kazimierz
Kazimierz II
Eden
Ester
Hotel
Restaurant
1
2
3

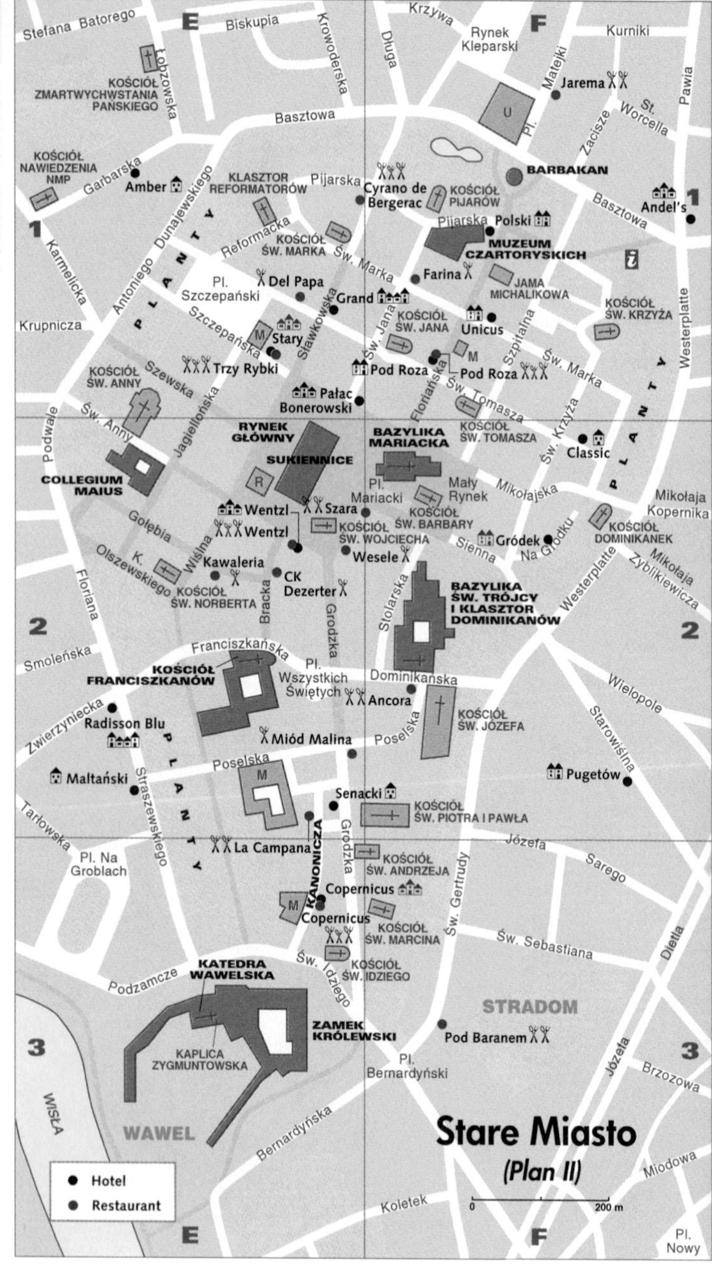
Stare Miasto
(Plan II)
Hotel
Restaurant
RYNEK GŁÓWNY
SUKIENNICE
BAZYLIKA MARIACKA
BARBAKAN
MUZEUM CZARTORYSKICH
COLLEGIUM MAIUS
KOŚCIÓŁ FRANCISZKANÓW
BAZYLIKA ŚW. TRÓJCY I KLASZTOR DOMINIKANÓW
KATEDRA WAWELSKA
ZAMEK KRÓLEWSKI
KAPLICA ZYGMUNTOWSKA
WAWEL
STRADOM
Wisła
Basztowa
Floriańska
Grodzka
Kanonicza
Wentzl
Copernicus
Pod Roza
Radisson Blu
Pod Baranem
Stefana Batorego
Biskupia
Krowoderska
Długa
Krzywa
Rynek Kleparski
Kurniki
Matejki
Jarema
Pawia
St. Worcella
Zacisze
Basztowa
Andel's
Pijarska
Cyrano de Bergerac
KOŚCIÓŁ PIJARÓW
Polski
JAMA MICHALIKOWA
Farina
KOŚCIÓŁ ŚW. KRZYŻA
Westerplatte
Unicus
KOŚCIÓŁ ŚW. JANA
Św. Jana
Grand
Del Papa
Pl. Szczepański
Szczepańska
Sławkowska
Stary
KOŚCIÓŁ ŚW. MARKA
Św. Marka
Reformacka
KLASZTOR REFORMATORÓW
KOŚCIÓŁ ZMARTWYCHWSTANIA PAŃSKIEGO
Łobzowska
KOŚCIÓŁ NAWIEDZENIA NMP
Garbarska
Amber
Antoniego Dunajewskiego
Karmelicka
Krupnicza
Trzy Rybki
Szewska
KOŚCIÓŁ ŚW. ANNY
Św. Anny
Jagiellońska
Podwale
Pałac Bonerowski
Szpitalna
Św. Tomasza
KOŚCIÓŁ ŚW. TOMASZA
Św. Krzyża
Classic
Mały Rynek
Pl. Mariacki
Mikołajska
Mikołaja Kopernika
KOŚCIÓŁ DOMINIKANEK
KOŚCIÓŁ ŚW. BARBARY
Szara
KOŚCIÓŁ ŚW. WOJCIECHA
Gołębia
Wiślna
K. Olszewskiego
KOŚCIÓŁ ŚW. NORBERTA
Kawaleria
CK Dezerter
Wesele
Bracka
Gródek
Na Gródku
Sienna
Mikołaja Zyblikiewicza
Stolarska
Floriana
Smoleńska
Franciszkańska
Pl. Wszystkich Świętych
Dominikańska
Ancora
Wielopole
KOŚCIÓŁ ŚW. JÓZEFA
Starowiślna
Poselska
Zwierzyniecka
Miód Malina
Maltański
Straszewskiego
Pugetów
Senacki
KOŚCIÓŁ ŚW. PIOTRA I PAWŁA
Tarłowska
Pl. Na Groblach
La Campana
KOŚCIÓŁ ŚW. ANDRZEJA
Józefa
Sarego
Św. Gertrudy
KOŚCIÓŁ ŚW. MARCINA
Św. Sebastiana
Dietla
Św. Idziego
KOŚCIÓŁ ŚW. IDZIEGO
Podzamcze
Pl. Bernardyński
Brzozowa
Bernardyńska
Koletek
Miodowa
Pl. Nowy
PLANTY
200 m

Sheraton

Ul. Powiśle 7 ✉ 31 101 – ✆ (12) 662 10 00 – www.sheraton.com/krakow *Plan I* **B2**

229 rm ☕ – 🚹995 PLN 🚹🚹1055 PLN – 3 suites

Rest *The Olive* – *✆ (12) 662 1660* – Carte 150/220 PLN

♦ Business ♦ Modern ♦

Near the castle, with views of the river; a purpose-built international hotel with vast glass-roofed atrium the centrepiece. Well-equipped bedrooms come with all mod cons. Mediterranean/international menu served in open-plan restaurant.

Radisson Blu

Ul. Straszewskiego 17 ✉ 31 101 – ✆ (12) 618 88 88 – www.radissonblu.com **E2**

177 rm – 🚹550/970 PLN 🚹🚹550/970 PLN, ☕ 95 PLN – 19 suites

Rest – *(buffet lunch)* Carte 85/150 PLN

♦ Business ♦ Modern ♦

Well-run chain hotel, five minutes from the square. Open-plan lobby and stylish bar. Generously proportioned, well-lit and warmly decorated bedrooms with a high level of facilities. Bright restaurant with regular buffets and themed evenings.

Grand

Ul. Slawkowska 5/7 ✉ 31 014 – ✆ (12) 424 08 00 – www.grand.pl **E1**

55 rm ☕ – 🚹390/1014 PLN 🚹🚹468/1092 PLN – 9 suites

Rest *Mirror Hall* – Menu 75/133 PLN – Carte 114/200 PLN

♦ Traditional ♦ Historic ♦ Classic ♦

Classical hotel, formerly the palace of Duke Czartoryski, restored to its former glory, with gold leaf, high ceilings and stained glass windows. Sumptuous suites; spotless bathrooms. Formal dining under chandeliers in the Mirror Hall.

Copernicus

Ul. Kanonicza 16 ✉ 31 002 – ✆ (12) 424 34 00 – www.hotel.com.pl

23 rm ☕ – 🚹800/900 PLN 🚹🚹900/980 PLN – 6 suites **E3**

Rest *Copernicus* – see below

♦ Historic ♦ Stylish ♦

Standing on one of the oldest streets in the city; restoration of this intimate, atmospheric and professionally run hotel revealed 15C ceiling inscriptions and ornaments. Stylish bedrooms boast handmade furniture, velvet bedspreads and silk drapes.

Stary

Ul. Szczepańska 5 ✉ 31 011 – ✆ (12) 384 08 08 – www.hotel.com.pl

46 rm ☕ – 🚹680/850 PLN 🚹🚹765/900 PLN – 7 suites **E1**

Rest *Trzy Rybki* – see below

♦ Townhouse ♦ Stylish ♦

Appealing and stylish hotel, its oldest part dating from the 15C, with original frescos on the walls. Atmospheric and very comfortable bedrooms with Polish oak furniture and luxury marble bathrooms. Strong level of service.

Wentzl

Rynek Główny 19 ✉ 31 008 – ✆ (12) 430 26 64 – www.wentzl.pl – Closed 25 December **E2**

18 rm ☕ – 🚹631/670 PLN 🚹🚹710/750 PLN

Rest *Wentzl* – see below

♦ Townhouse ♦ Historic ♦

15C house overlooking splendour of main square. Charming, antique-furnished bedrooms bedecked with art offer high level of facilities; those on top floor are contemporary in style, others more traditional.

Pałac Bonerowski

Ul. Św. Jana 1 ✉ 31 013 – ✆ (12) 374 13 00 – www.palacbonerowski.pl
8 rm – 952/1055 PLN 1071/1186 PLN – 6 suites **E1**
Rest *Milano* – Menu 80/110 PLN – Carte 86/126 PLN
♦ Palace ♦ Personalised ♦
Characterful hotel overlooking the main square, whose historic features include medieval portals and restored 17C polychrome and ceilings. Impressive suites; fashionable basement club. Classic Italian cuisine served in Milano.

Andel's

Ul. Pawia 3 ✉ 31 154 – ✆ (12) 660 01 00 – www.andelscracow.com
153 rm – 420/880 PLN 500/960 PLN – 6 suites **F1**
Rest – Menu 55 PLN (lunch) – Carte 65/113 PLN
♦ Business ♦ Modern ♦
Opposite main station, a purpose-built hotel boasting bright, open-plan public areas with original design features. Sharply decorated, modern and well-equipped bedrooms. Spacious restaurant opens out onto terrace and plaza, and serves international/Polish cuisine.

Kossak

Pl. Kossaka 1 ✉ 31 106 – ✆ (12) 379 5900 – www.hotelkossak.pl
55 rm – 525/683 PLN 584/743 PLN – 5 suites *Plan I* **B2**
Rest *Percheron* – *✆ (12) 379 5950 (dinner only)* Carte 62/94 PLN
Rest *Cafe Oranzeria* – *✆ (12) 379 5950* – Carte 60/104 PLN
♦ Business ♦ Modern ♦
The bigger sister to nearby Senacki. A contemporary business hotel whose lilac bedrooms are well-equipped and boast smart, modern bathrooms. Ground floor Percheron with international menu and Polish specialities. 7th floor Cafe Oranzeria affords castle views.

Gródek

Ul. Na Gródku 4 ✉ 31 028 – ✆ (12) 431 9030 – www.donimirski.com
21 rm – 390/450 PLN 510/670 PLN, 60 PLN – 2 suites **F2**
Rest *Restaurant* – *(dinner only)* Carte 63/119 PLN
♦ Townhouse ♦ Personalised ♦
Charming boutique hotel tucked away in an intimate location. Bright, comfortable guest areas include a cosy wood-panelled bar and pleasant roof terrace. Immaculately kept, characterful bedrooms display fine fabrics and good quality furniture. Sleek, stylish basement restaurant offers Polish cooking with some modern elements.

Pod Różą

Ul. Floriańska 14 ✉ 31 021 – ✆ (12) 424 33 00 – www.hotel.com.pl
53 rm – 552/720 PLN 612/720 PLN, 40 PLN – 4 suites **F1**
Rest *Pod Różą* – see below
Rest *Amarone* – *✆ (12) 424 33 81* – Carte 69/137 PLN
♦ Traditional ♦ Classic ♦
16C building – reputedly the oldest hotel in the city – whose past guests include such luminaries as Balzac and Liszt. Traditional rooms with antique furnishings. Atmospheric conference facilities in cellars. Amarone offers a wide selection of Italian dishes.

Unicus

Św. Marka 20 ✉ 31 020 – ✆ (12) 433 7111 – www.hotelunicus.pl
35 rm – 500/750 PLN 700/800 PLN **F1**
Rest – Carte 67/116 PLN
♦ Business ♦ Modern ♦
Stylish, centrally located hotel converted from tenement houses. Bedrooms colour coded, from olive green to pure white; iPod docking stations and spacious shower rooms. Cellar restaurant offers international menu with some Polish flavour.

Ostoya Palace

Ul. Pilsudskiego 24 ✉ 31 109 – ✆ (12) 430 90 00 – www.ostoyapalace.pl
24 rm – 350/400 PLN 420/480 PLN *Plan I* **B2**
Rest – Carte 58/113 PLN
♦ Historic ♦ Classic ♦
Discreet, comfortable and characterful hotel whose bedrooms reflect its 19C origins, with high ceilings and original stove heaters. Popular pub in basement. Restaurant boasts an original 15C feature ceiling and offers a Polish menu.

Pugetów without rest

Ul. Starowiślna 15a ✉ 31 038 – ✆ (12) 432 49 50 – www.donimirski.com
5 rm – 250/280 PLN 380/470 PLN, 60 PLN – 3 suites **F2**
♦ Traditional ♦ Historic ♦
Neat and cosy 19C house alongside Pugetów Palace, away from the main street, with the intimate feel of a private residence. Spacious rooms include huge antique-furnished suites.

Polski without rest

Ul.Pijarska 17 ✉ 31 015 – ✆ (12) 422 1144 – www.podorlem.com.pl
54 rm – 290/540 PLN 355/540 PLN – 3 suites **F1**
♦ Family ♦ Classic ♦
Traditional yet charming hotel, in a great spot next to the Czartoryski museum. Spotless bedrooms range from singles to triples; up-to-date bathrooms. In-house beauty therapist.

Maltański without rest

Ul. Straszewskiego 14 ✉ 31 101 – ✆ (12) 431 00 10 – www.donimirski.com
16 rm – 350/420 PLN 490/570 PLN, 60 PLN **E2**
♦ Traditional ♦ Personalised ♦
Charming little hotel set back from the road and run by a friendly team. Deceptively large bedrooms, all prettily decorated; those on the ground floor open onto small terraces.

Senacki without rest

Ul. Grodzka 51 ✉ 31 001 – ✆ (12) 422 76 86 – www.hotelsenacki.pl
18 rm – 377/584 PLN 504/643 PLN – 2 suites **E2**
♦ Townhouse ♦ Cosy ♦
Delightfully located hotel opposite the 17C Church of St Peter and Paul. Immaculate, homely and comfortable bedrooms are spread over four floors. Breakfast served in converted cellars.

Poleski

Ul. Sandomierska 6 ✉ 30 301 – ✆ (12) 260 54 15 – www.hotelpoleski.pl
20 rm – 265 PLN 305/345 PLN **B3**
Rest – Carte 48/100 PLN
♦ Modern ♦ Functional ♦
Simply decorated, affordable hotel, set in an enviable location over the river, just a 15 minute walk away from the city centre. Enjoy striking views of the castle from the rooftop terrace and corner bedrooms. First floor restaurant serves Polish cuisine.

Ascot without rest

Ul. Radziwillowska 3 ✉ 31 026 – ✆ (12) 384 06 06 – www.hotelascot.pl
49 rm – 290/370 PLN 350/460 PLN, 35 PLN *Plan I* **C2**
♦ Family ♦ Functional ♦
Feeling fresh and well-kept, this purpose-built hotel is a 5 minute walk from the centre. Small lobby with corner bar. Clean, compact, fairly priced bedrooms; some hold four beds.

Amber without rest

Ul. Garbarska 10 ✉ 31 131 – ✆ (12) 421 0606 – www.hotel-amber.pl **E1**

18 rm – 319/423 PLN 399/749 PLN

◆ Modern ◆ Functional ◆

Modern, tidy hotel with plenty of dark wood complemented with natural tones. All the spacious bedrooms have showers, some have sofas; the best are on the third floor. Helpful staff.

Benefis without rest

Ul. Barska 2 ✉ 30 307 – ✆ (12) 252 0710 – www.hotelbenefis.pl

12 rm – 230/280 PLN 250/330 PLN – 8 suites **B3**

◆ Modern ◆ Functional ◆

Stroll over the Most Dębnicki Bridge on the Wisła River to reach this small, purpose-built hotel. Uniform bedrooms with modern bathrooms; comfortable studio suites. Buffet breakfasts.

Classic without rest

Ul. Św. Tomasza 32 ✉ 31 014 – ✆ (12) 424 0303 – www.hotel-classic.pl **F2**

30 rm – 298/437 PLN 338/476 PLN

◆ Traditional ◆ Functional ◆

Simply styled but well-run hotel with keen staff and high standards of housekeeping. Central location yet quietly situated. Hot and cold buffet breakfast served in the basement.

Pod Różą – at Pod Różą Hotel

Ul. Floriańska 14 ✉ 31 021 – ✆ (12) 424 33 81 – www.hotel.com.pl

Rest – Carte 129/167 PLN **F1**

◆ International ◆ Design ◆

Artfully presented, carefully prepared and boldly flavoured cooking from an Italian menu; be sure to include a pasta course. Large room with glass roof and widely spaced tables.

Trzy Rybki – at Stary Hotel

Ul. Szczepańska 5 ✉ 31 011 – ✆ (12) 384 08 01 – www.hotel.com.pl

Rest – Carte 109/213 PLN **E1**

◆ Seafood ◆ Luxury ◆

Striking contemporary restaurant at the front of the Stary Hotel. European menu features Italian influences, with seafood the highlight. Polite, attentive service. Exclusively Italian wine list.

Copernicus – at Copernicus Hotel

Ul. Kanonicza 16 ✉ 31 002 – ✆ (12) 424 43421 – www.hotel.com.pl

Rest – *(booking essential at dinner)* Carte 147/167 PLN **E3**

◆ Polish ◆ Intimate ◆

Characterful and charming restaurant specialising in seasonal Polish cooking and European specialities. A table on the gallery allows one to fully appreciate the ornate Renaissance ceiling.

Wentzl – at Wentzl Hotel

Rynek Glówny 19 ✉ 31 008 – ✆ (12) 429 57 12 – www.wentzl.pl – Closed 24-25 December **E2**

Rest – Menu 70/110 PLN – Carte 110/160 PLN

◆ International ◆ Formal ◆

Charmingly run restaurant exuding palpable sense of history; impressive Renaissance interior includes original wood ceilings and 15C triptych. International notes added to Polish dishes.

XXX **Cyrano de Bergerac** with rm

Ul. Slawkowska 26 ✉ 31 014 – ✆ (12) 429 54 45 – www.cyranodebergerac.pl – Closed 24-26 December, 1-2 January, 24-25 April, 1 November and Sunday

4 rm – †280/320 PLN ††360/400 PLN, ☕ 25 PLN – 1 suite **E/F 1**

Rest – *(booking essential)* Menu 25/110 PLN – Carte 91/187 PLN

♦ French ♦ Romantic ♦

Characterful cellar restaurant where antiques, tapestries and candlelit tables create a wonderfully romantic atmosphere. Formal service lacks a little warmth. Expect robust, classical French cooking. Individually designed bedrooms each reflect a different era.

XX **Ancora**

Ul. Dominikánska 3 ✉ 31 043 – ✆ (12) 357 33 55 – www.ancora-restaurant.com – Closed 25 December and Easter Sunday **F2**

Rest – Carte 84/139 PLN

♦ International ♦ Fashionable ♦

Contemporary corner restaurant with open kitchen and photos of the chef in action; cavernous converted cellars downstairs. Regional produce appears in Polish dishes with a light modern edge.

XX **Szara**

Rynek Glówny 6 ✉ 31 042 – ✆ (12) 421 66 69 – www.szara.pl – Closed 24 December **E/F2**

Rest – Carte 86/140 PLN

♦ Polish ♦ Friendly ♦

Keenly run, family-owned brasserie-style restaurant on main square; both rooms with original Gothic vaulted ceilings. Flavourful European cuisine, with Polish and Swedish dishes to the fore.

XX **Jarema**

Pl. Matejki 5 ✉ 31 157 – ✆ (12) 429 3669 – www.jarema.pl – Closed 25 December **F1**

Rest – Menu 50/60 PLN – Carte 88/151 PLN

♦ Polish ♦ Family ♦

Enjoy authentic and carefully prepared home-style Eastern Polish cuisine in unpretentious, candlelit surroundings. Staff wear traditional dress and there is music every evening.

XX **Pod Baranem**

Św. Gertrudy 21 ✉ 31 049 – ✆ (12) 429 40 22 – www.podbaranem.com

Rest – Carte 47/112 PLN **F3**

♦ Polish ♦ Neighbourhood ♦ Family ♦

Family-run restaurant serving honest, seasonal Polish cooking with assured flavours. Staff, resplendent in waistcoats, share the owners' enthusiasm and offer keen and eager service.

X **Farina**

Ul. Św. Marka 16 ✉ 31 017 – ✆ (12) 422 16 80 – www.farina.com.pl – Closed 24-25 December and Easter **F1**

Rest – Carte 60/182 PLN

♦ Seafood ♦ Cosy ♦ Friendly ♦

Pretty, candlelit corner restaurant divided into three rooms, with warm and friendly service. Menu specialises in seafood, with a hint of Italian influence; fish trolley displays the day's catch.

X **Wesele**

Rynek Glówny 10 ✉ 31 042 – ✆ (12) 422 74 60 – www.weselerestauracja.pl – Closed 24-25 December and Easter **E2**

Rest – Carte 63/104 PLN

♦ Polish ♦ Intimate ♦

Proudly Polish restaurant set on the market square, boasting large windows, rustic wood panelling and summer terrace. Opt for the traditional Polish dishes and ask for a table upstairs.

Miód Malina

Ul. Grodzka 40 ✉ 31 044 – ✆ (12) 430 04 11 – www.miodmalina.pl
– Closed 24-25 December and Easter **E2**
Rest – *(booking essential at dinner)* Carte 68/98 PLN
♦ Italian ♦ Rustic ♦
Busy restaurant with pleasant atmosphere, serving a mix of Polish and Italian country dishes – some cooked in a wood-fired oven. Larger room with vaulted ceiling is the best place to sit.

La Campana

Ul. Kanonicza 7 ✉ 31 002 – ✆ (12) 430 2232 – www.lacampana.pl
– Closed 24-25 December and Easter **E1**
Rest – Carte 71/99 PLN
♦ Italian ♦ Cosy ♦
Cosy and candlelit in winter; walled garden full of olive trees for summer. Generous portions of flavoursome pastas and grilled meats – prosciutto a speciality. Menus available in braille.

Kawaleria

Ul. Gołębia 4 ✉ 31 007 – ✆ (12) 430 2432 – www.kawaleria.com.pl
– Closed 24-26 December **E2**
Rest – Carte 53/94 PLN
♦ Polish ♦ Family ♦ Bistro ♦
It's cosier than its size would suggest; its walls lovingly decorated with photos of the owner's great-grandfather, who was a cavalry commander. Polish cooking with a modern touch.

Del Papa

Ul. Św. Tomasza 6 ✉ 31 014 – ✆ (12) 421 83 43 – www.delpapa.pl
– Closed 24-26 December **E1**
Rest – Carte 46/96 PLN
♦ Italian ♦ Rustic ♦
Characterful, friendly and honest. Café-style front room; distressed brick walls in middle section; bright, glass-roofed rear room. Simple Italian food with home-made pasta and seasonal specials.

C. K. Dezerter

Ul. Bracka 6 ✉ 31 005 – ✆ (12) 422 79 31 – www.ckdezerter.pl
– Closed 25 December **E2**
Rest – Menu 25 PLN (weekday lunch) – Carte 40/80 PLN
♦ Polish ♦ Rustic ♦
A rustic farmhouse style, courtesy of the owner's own bric-a-brac, adds to the warm atmosphere. No frills home-style cooking, with pork specialities; apples often feature in desserts.

---

at KAZIMIERZ *Plan I*

Rubinstein

rm,

Ul. Szeroka 12 ✉ 31 053 – ✆ (12) 384 00 00
– www.hotelrubinstein.com **C3**
23 rm – †617/723 PLN ††702/787 PLN – 4 suites
Rest – Carte 119/187 PLN
♦ Historic ♦ Modern ♦
Characterful hotel converted from 15C tenement buildings and named after Helena, of cosmetics fame, who grew up in this street. Comfortable and individually designed bedrooms. Glass-roofed restaurant serves Polish and Italian dishes.

Kazimierz II without rest

Ul. Starowiślna 60 ✉ 31 035 – ✆ (12) 426 80 70 – www.hk.com.pl

23 rm – 260/380 PLN 320/380 PLN **C3**

◆ Family ◆ Functional ◆

Purpose-built hotel with decently sized uniform bedrooms in deep red or gold; those to the front are the largest, those at the rear the quietest. Basement room for breakfast buffet.

Ester

Ul. Szeroka 20 ✉ 31 053 – ✆ (12) 429 11 88 – www.hotel-ester.krakow.pl

32 rm – 440/650 PLN 500/700 PLN **C3**

Rest – Carte 63/92 PLN

◆ Townhouse ◆ Personalised ◆

Sweet and friendly hotel whose bedrooms are kept nicely up-to-date; they are spotlessly kept, decently sized and include five triple rooms. Café-style restaurant with summer terrace and live music at weekends.

Eden without rest

Ul. Ciemna 15 ✉ 31 053 – ✆ (12) 430 65 65 – www.hoteleden.pl

27 rm – 180/240 PLN 250/320 PLN **C3**

◆ Traditional ◆ Personalised ◆

Endearing hotel that's far nicer than the exterior suggests. Modest but clean and homely bedrooms; a characterful cellar pub and pleasant breakfast room. It also has its own mikveh.

Szara Kazimierz

Ul. Szeroka 39 ✉ 31 053 – ✆ (12) 429 12 19 – www.szarakazimierz.pl

Rest – Carte 59/86 PLN **C3**

◆ Polish ◆ Brasserie ◆

Sister to Szara in the old town; a friendly, brasserie-style restaurant with wood burning stoves and a secluded rear terrace. Polish classics prepared with care; fish soup a speciality.

PORTUGAL

PORTUGAL

PROFILE

→ **Area:**
92 391 km^2 .

→ **Population:**
10 637 713 (May 2010), density = 115,1 per km^2.

→ **Capital:**
Lisbon (conurbation 2 661 850 inhabitants).

→ **Currency:**
Euro (€); rate of exchange: € 1 = US$ 1.37 (Dec 2010).

→ **Government:**
Parliamentary republic (since 1976). Member of European Union since 1986.

→ **Language:**
Portuguese.

→ **Specific public holidays:**
Shrove Tuesday (February); Good Friday (Friday before Easter); Freedom Day (25 April), Corpus Christi (May or June); Portugal Day (10 June); Republic Day (5 October); Restoration of Independence Day (1 December); Immaculate Conception (8 December).

→ **Local Time:**
GMT in winter and GMT + 1 hour in summer.

→ **Climate:**
Temperate Mediterranean with warm winters and hot summers (Lisbon: January 15°C, July 26°C).

→ **International dialling Code:**
00 351 followed by a nine-digit number. National directory enquiries : ✆ **118**.

→ **Emergency:**
Dial ✆ **112**.

→ **Electricity:**
230-240 volts AC, 50 Hz; 2-pin round-shaped continental plugs.

→ **Formalities**
Travellers from the European Union

(EU), Switzerland, Iceland and the main countries of North and South America need a national identity card or passport (America: passport required) to visit Portugal for less than three months (tourism or business purpose). For visitors from other countries a visa may be required, in addition to a passport, especially for those wishing to stay for longer than three months. We advise you to check with your embassy before travelling.

LISBON
LISBOA

Population (est. 2010): 509 751 (conurbation 2 661 850) – Altitude: at sea level

'ain Rapoport/Fotolia.com

Lisbon wears a time-worn look of fading grandeur sitting as it does beneath huge open skies and within an amphitheatre of seven hills. Sited on the north bank of the River Tagus as it feeds into the Atlantic, it boasts an atmosphere that few cities can match; an enchanting walk around the streets of the Bairro Alto, Alfama, the Baixa or Graça has an old-time ambience all its own, matched only by a jaunt on the trams and funiculars that run up and down the steep hills.

At first sight Lisbon is all flaky palaces, meandering alleyways and castellated horizon quarried from medieval stone. But there's a 21C element to the city, kick-started with Expo 98 and carried on with the Euro 2004 football tournament. Slinky new developments line the riverside to east and west, linking the old and the new in a kind of glorious jumble spilling down the slopes to the water's edge. It's the views of that water from various vantage points all over Lisbon that continually draw the visitor: the vistas of the 'Straw Sea', so named because of the golden reflections of the sun on the Tagus, are an inspiration whatever time of year. So too are the sounds of fado, the city's alluring folk music. Fado conjures up a melancholic yearning, and can be heard in taverns and dives all over town. They are the songs of fate, and they add another layer of intrigue to Lisbon's absorbing patchwork.

LIVING THE CITY

Lisbon is strung out along the north bank of the curving **River Tagus**. The compact heart of the city is the **Baixa**, the flat eighteenth century grid of streets flanked by seven hills. Just to the west of the Baixa is the elegant commercial district of **Chiado** and the funky hilltop **Bairro Alto** , while immediately to the east is **Alfama**, a tightly packed former Moorish quarter with kasbah-like qualities. North of here is the working-class neighbourhood of **Graça**. Way out west lies the spacious riverside suburb of **Belém**, while up the river to the east can be found the ultra modern **Parque das Nações.**

PRACTICAL INFORMATION

ARRIVAL-DEPARTURE

The airport is just 7km from the city centre and a taxi will cost about €15. Alternatively, take the Aerobus which runs every 20min.

TRANSPORT

Lisbon's an easy city to get around. Four metro lines cover much of the central part of the city, with two different ticket types: single ticket or ten tickets.

There's also a good network of trams, buses and funiculars, with six main bus routes and three funiculars. Buses and trams operate every 11-15 minutes; tram routes 15 and 28 serve the main sights. Tickets for buses and trams can be bought as a single fare, a one-day or a three-day ticket. For buses, trams and funiculars: 4-day and 7-day passes are available.

The Lisboa Card is valid for unlimited travel on public transport and for free or reduced admission to most museums and cultural sites. Valid for 24, 48 or 72hr.

EXPLORING LISBON

Lisbon takes the best elements of other big cities and blends them together: the winding alleyways of Venice, the wide boulevards of Paris, the trams of Amsterdam, the cobbled streets of Brussels. And it doesn't end there: the **Ponte 25 de Abril**, slung out across the Tagus, looks just like San Francisco's Golden Gate, while the 80ft-high **statue of Christ**, on the river's far bank, is a spitting image of the original overlooking Rio. Despite all this, Lisbon is very much its own city with a distinct melancholy charm. Just wander up and down the slopes of its central core and you'll get the vibe.

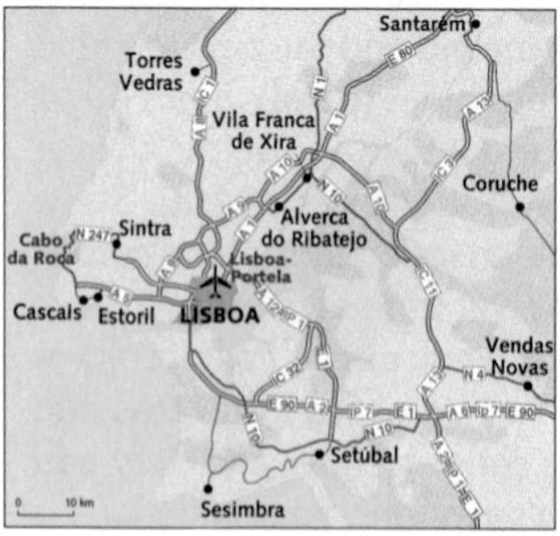

→ SO MOORISH

The Alfama district is the oldest bit of Lisbon still standing. It survived the 1755 earthquake which knocked out the rest of the city, but by then its Moorish population had moved further west. They left behind a myriad of tightly packed alleyways and steep streets lined with compact houses which exist to this day; the medieval layout has a humble allure, its alleys so narrow that the balconies on opposite sides of the street almost meet in greeting. There are local grocery stores hidden in corners, and cosy, cellar-like tavernas announcing themselves like a conspiratorial secret. Above Alfama is the city's most distinctive landmark: the **Castelo São Jorge**. The castle was built by the Moors on the site of a Roman fort, but was left in ruins for centuries until it was reconstructed in the Twentieth. Hang around the ramparts for gorgeous views of the Tagus estuary and the city lining its northern bank. Then head further north to the neighbourhood of Graça for more super views - mostly a panorama of rooftops - enjoyed best of all in the early evening at a café table beneath the swaying pines.

→ CENTRAL PLANNING

Looked down upon from the castle, bustling Baixa was totally destroyed in the earthquake, but, under the guidance of the Marquês de Pombal, this sea-level centre of town was reborn with neo-classical buildings and a symmetrically laid out grid of elegant, broad boulevards – it was one of Europe's first examples of town planning. This is the heart of the city, where the smart shops are. They're book-ended by two imposing squares, the buzzing **Praça do Comércio** down by the river, and the **Rossio** further north. A favourite way of coming into Lisbon is by ferry from the southern bank, alighting at the Praça do Comércio, and admiring the impressive triumphal arch which towers over the north side of the square. From here, you stroll into **Rua Augusta**, Lisbon's main tourist thoroughfare, lined with open-air cafés and smart boutiques. Handsomely adorned with mosaic pavements, it's lively, bustling and pedestrianized, and it's flanked on either side by **'Goldsmiths' Street'** and **'Silversmiths' Street'**, just to give you an idea of the kind of retail going on in this compact part of town. By day, it seems all of Lisbon is here, but as soon as darkness descends, Baixa becomes a ghost town.

Not so the adjacent quarter of Bairro Alto, high up the hill to the west of Baixa. It's a raffish, bohemian warren of streets that by day is peaceful enough, with hippie shops and sedate viewpoints. When the sun goes down, though, the shutters go up, hundreds of local restaurants open their doors, and the clubs and bars pulsate to the sounds of African and samba rhythms. This is a nightlife zone that doesn't let up till the dawn. When the day does come, shopping around Bairro Alto can be a very personalised and social occasion, where bars sell clothes, hairdressers flip open a beer bottle (for the customer, that is) and the cosy neighbourhood store boasts a DJ. The nearby district of Chiado exudes a different feel again: it's an area of elegant shops and old-style cafés, typified by the century-old **Café A Brasileira** with its carved and panelled wood interior set off by gleaming, gilded mirrors.

→ SEA THE PAST

Jump on a tram, head out west for half an hour, and you're in Belém, the riverside neighbourhood of Lisbon most in thrall to its seafaring past. When Vasco da Gama and Ferdinand Magellan were at the height of their medieval adventures, the city was celebrating their fame by building exuberant late-Gothic churches and monuments in Belem, from where they'd set sail. The real showstopper here is the **Jerónimos monastery**, an exotic structure with a richly carved cloister and portal. Vasco da Gama is buried here in a tomb of seafaring symbols; lying next to him is Portugal's most famous poet, Luis de Camões. Outside, Belém is a suburb of pocket-sized parks and gardens, a snazzy promenade with cafés and, when the sun's shining, a distinctly seaside vibe.

➜ PARQUE AND TIDE

You have to take a trip about eight kilometres east of the centre to find the glittering twenty first century face of Lisbon. You'll find it at Parque das Nações. Just two decades ago, this area was a wasteland, but it was developed for Expo 98, and is now a riot of modern attractions. Chief amongst these is the Portugal Pavilion, which boasts a stunning concrete canopy floating over its forecourt. There's also a science museum and an Oceanarium vying for your attention, but what might *really* grab it lies further along the riverside promenade: the **Vasco da Gama bridge** stretches for 10 miles across the wide river, making it the longest bridge in Europe.

➜ ACROSS THE RANGE

Not many art collections can claim to span 4,000 years of exhibits, but Lisbon boasts one, and it's not to be missed. The **Calouste Gulbenkian Museum**, north of the city centre, is a private collection that happens to be one of the finest in Europe. It ranges from ancient Egyptian statuettes to works by Turner, Rembrandt and Manet. There's also a stunning display of Oriental and Islamic pieces, as colourful as anything else on display here. The other hot museum of art to head for is down near the river at the western end of Bairro Alto. It's the **Museu Nacional de Arte Antiga**, which translates as the National Museum of Ancient Art. It houses a phenomenal range of Portuguese national art ranging from the twelfth to the nineteenth centuries, and it's the largest collection of paintings in the country, complemented by many works from other parts of Europe and the Orient. One look round here, taking in Portugal's historic links with so many other countries around the globe, gives another hint as to why Lisbon has bolted on all those parts of other world cities to create its magical whole.

CALENDAR HIGHLIGHTS

Despite their reputation as being more reserved than their Spanish neighbours, the Portuguese do love a party, particularly if there's a saint involved. Which means that Festas dos Santos Populares, (or Feast Days of the Popular Saints), in June, is Lisbon's biggest party. The city streets are decorated with paper lanterns, streamers and coloured lights, and balconies and railings are festooned, creating a magical sight. Another big celebration that month is Portugal's National Day, which marks the anniversary of the death of the country's greatest poet, Luis de Camões: when the city hosts various cultural events. On the theme of writing, June's Lisbon Book Fair, in Parque Eduardo VII, has been a great event since the 1930s, and you can browse old tomes, new books and comics at your leisure as

LISBON IN...

➜ ONE DAY

Alfama, Castelo São Jorge, Bairro Alto

➜ TWO DAYS

Baixa, Calouste Gulbenkian Museum, Parque das Nações

➜ THREE DAYS

Museu Nacional de Arte Antiga, Belém

you stroll amongst the trees. Also that month, the Alkantara Festival is a seventeen-day jamboree which includes theatre, dance and performance art, but which may be even more notable for its fascinating walk through Alfama, or its all-night marathon! The Parque do Tejo in Parque das Nações blasts to life in July when top names in rock give it their all at the Super Bock Super Rock Festival. Later that month, a slightly more refined air accompanies the Almada International Theatre Festival, during which various city venues host plays and exhibitions from across the globe. November's Arte Lisboa is an important event in the city's art world, with contemporary works filling sixty-six galleries at the FIL. In the spring, the Belém Cultural Centre hosts two important events: the Spring Festival (March), which puts on various shows, concerts and exhibitions, and then, in April, the CCB Music Festival: at this one, seven different stages are home to baroque orchestras, choirs and soloists in an intense three-day event. On the same theme, and running right through the winter and spring (November-May), Great Orchestras of the World, at the Coliseu dos Recreios, is presented by the influential Calouste Gulbenkian Foundation, and features various internationally renowned conductors and soloists.

EATING OUT

The cuisine of the Lisbon region can be characterised by its simplicity. *Lisboetas* love their local agricultural produce, prepared naturally, without the addition of a large number of extra ingredients. The city has an age-old maritime tradition and is open to the sea, so it's home to a range of dishes based on fish and seafood. There are a number of fishing ports nearby which supply it with ocean-fresh produce. Gastronomically, Lisbon doesn't disappoint, with all the country's regional cuisine represented: it might not be strikingly original, but there's a clear commitment to values such as simplicity and honesty. Having said that, the locals love *bacalhau* (cod), and it's said that there's a different way to prepare it each day for a year, while a Lisbon academy has identified over a thousand cod recipes. Eating in either a humble *tasca* (tavern with a few tables), *casa de pasto* (large dining room) or *restaurante*, there are some specialities to keep an eye open for. *Bacalhau* may come oven baked, slow cooked or cooked in milk, and served wrapped in cabbage, with tocino belly pork, a topping of mayonnaise or in a myriad of other ways. *Amêijoas à bulhão pato* (clams cooked with garlic and coriander), *cozido à Portuguesa* (traditional stew with beef, chicken and sausage cooked with vegetables and rice), *feijao à Portuguesa* (bean casserole with tocino belly pork), or *arroz de lamprea* (lamprey eel with rice) are all mainstays of the Lisbon menu. Enjoy them with a *vinho verde*, the wine of the region. A service charge will be included on your bill, but it's customary to leave a tip of about ten per cent.

→ A BAKER'S SECRET

Belém has always been famous for its tarts; in this case, they're warm, creamy, and dripping with custard. They're made at the legendary Antiga Confeitaria de Belém, and the secret recipe used in their production is known only to three bakers. Ten thousand *pastéis de Belém* are sold on an average weekday, and eaten, time permitting, in the café's rooms, which are famous far and wide for their colourful tiles depicting the area four hundred years ago.

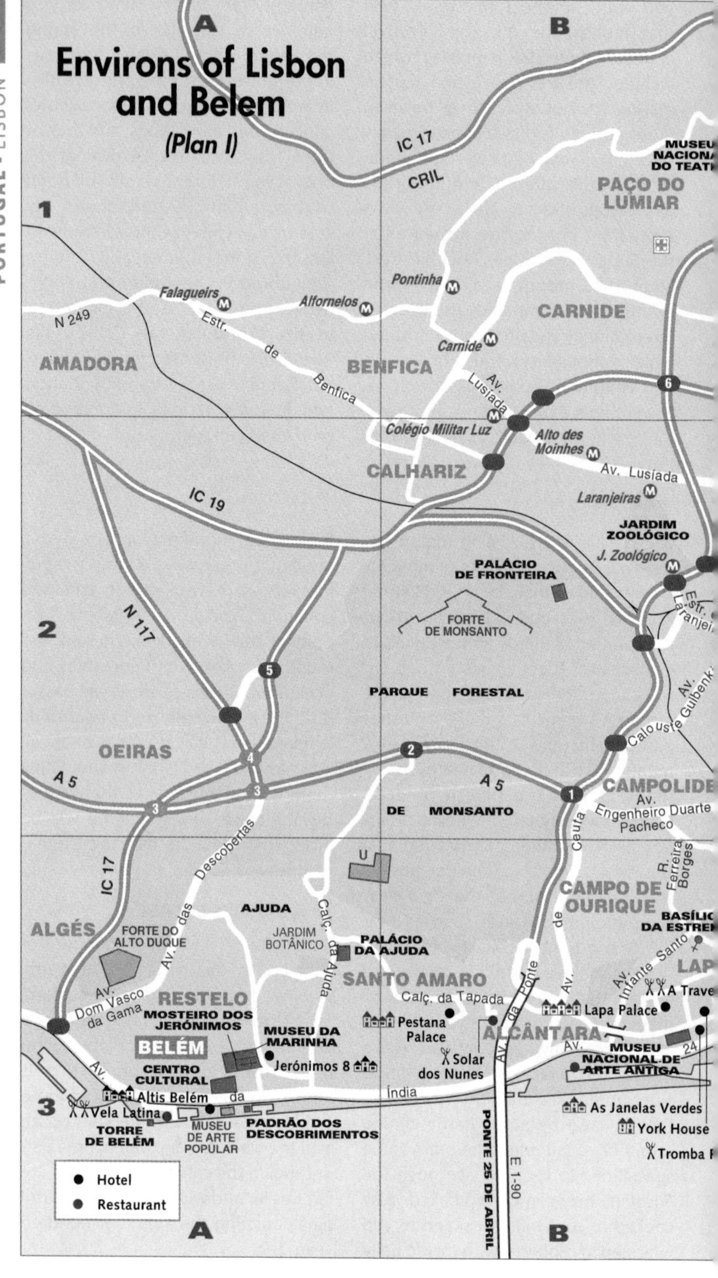
Environs of Lisbon and Belem
(Plan I)
A
B
1
2
3
IC 17
CRIL
PAÇO DO LUMIAR
CARNIDE
Pontinha
Falagueirs
Alfornelos
N 249
Estr. de Benfica
AMADORA
BENFICA
Carnide
Av. Lusíada
Colégio Militar Luz
Alto des Moinhes
CALHARIZ
Av. Lusíada
Laranjeiras
IC 19
JARDIM ZOOLÓGICO
J. Zoológico
PALÁCIO DE FRONTEIRA
FORTE DE MONSANTO
N 117
PARQUE FORESTAL
DE MONSANTO
OEIRAS
A 5
A 5
Av. Calouste Gulbenkian
CAMPOLIDE
Av. Engenheiro Duarte Pacheco
Av. das Descobertas
Av. de Ceuta
R. Ferreira Borges
CAMPO DE OURIQUE
AJUDA
ALGÉS
FORTE DO ALTO DUQUE
JARDIM BOTÂNICO
Calç. da Ajuda
PALÁCIO DA AJUDA
SANTO AMARO
Av. Infante Santo
A Travessa
Av. Dom Vasco da Gama
RESTELO
MOSTEIRO DOS JERÓNIMOS
MUSEU DA MARINHA
Calç. da Tapada
Pestana Palace
Av. da Ponte
Lapa Palace
ALCÂNTARA
BELÉM
Jerónimos 8
Solar dos Nunes
MUSEU NACIONAL DE ARTE ANTIGA
CENTRO CULTURAL
Altis Belém
Av. da Índia
Vela Latina
TORRE DE BELÉM
MUSEU DE ARTE POPULAR
PADRÃO DOS DESCOBRIMENTOS
PONTE 25 DE ABRIL
E 1-90
As Janelas Verdes
York House
Hotel
Restaurant

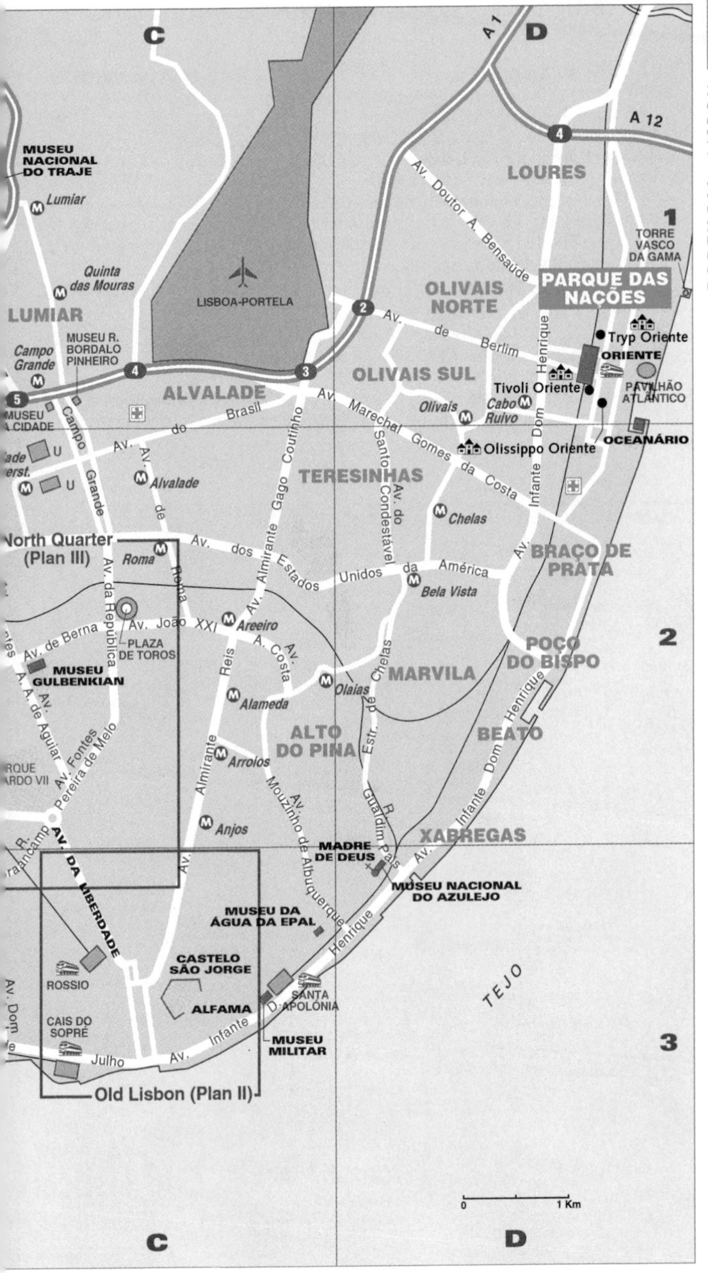

C
D
A 1
A 12
LOURES
MUSEU NACIONAL DO TRAJE
Lumiar
Quinta das Mouras
LUMIAR
LISBOA-PORTELA
MUSEU R. BORDALO PINHEIRO
Campo Grande
ALVALADE
OLIVAIS NORTE
OLIVAIS SUL
PARQUE DAS NAÇÕES
TORRE VASCO DA GAMA
Tryp Oriente
ORIENTE
Tivoli Oriente
PAVILHÃO ATLÂNTICO
OCEANÁRIO
Olissippo Oriente
Olivais
Cabo Ruivo
Av. Doutor A. Bensaúde
Av. de Berlim
Av. Marechal Gomes da Costa
Av. do Brasil
Av. Infante Dom Henrique
MUSEU DA CIDADE
TERESINHAS
Chelas
BRAÇO DE PRATA
Av. Almirante Gago Coutinho
Av. do Santo Condestável
Alvalade
Av. de Roma
North Quarter (Plan III)
Roma
Av. dos Estados Unidos da América
Bela Vista
Av. da República
Av. João XXI
Areeiro
Av. de Berna
PLAZA DE TOROS
MUSEU GULBENKIAN
Av. A. A. de Aguiar
Av. A. Costa
Almirante Reis
Olaias
Estr. de Chelas
MARVILA
POÇO DO BISPO
Alameda
ALTO DO PINA
BEATO
Arroios
Av. Fontes Pereira de Melo
Av. Mouzinho de Albuquerque
R. Gualdim Pais
Anjos
XABREGAS
MADRE DE DEUS
MUSEU NACIONAL DO AZULEJO
AV. DA LIBERDADE
MUSEU DA ÁGUA DA EPAL
CASTELO SÃO JORGE
ALFAMA
ROSSIO
SANTA APOLÓNIA
CAIS DO SOPRÉ
MUSEU MILITAR
Av. 24 de Julho
TEJO
Old Lisbon (Plan II)
0
1 Km
1
2
3

OLD LISBON (Alfama, Castelo de São Jorge, Rossio, Baixa, Chiado, Bairro Alto)

Plan II

Tivoli Lisboa

Av. da Liberdade 185 ✉ 1269-050 – Ⓜ Avenida – ✆ 213 19 89 00 – www.tivolihotels.com **E1**

260 rm – 🛉132/630 € 🛉🛉132/660 €, ☕ 15 € – 48 suites

Rest *Brasserie Flo Lisboa* – Carte 41/51 € **Rest *Terraço*** – Carte 45/58 €

♦ Business ♦ Modern ♦

This elegant, comfortable hotel has a delightful lounge area. The well-appointed guestrooms are cosy and stylish. Attractive swimming pool surrounded by trees. The Terraço restaurant has a dining room enclosed by large glass windows on the top floor, with stunning views of the city.

Avenida Palace without rest

Rua 1° de Dezembro 123 ✉ 1200-359 – Ⓜ Restauradores – ✆ 213 21 81 00 – www.hotelavenidapalace.pt **E1**

64 rm ☕ – 🛉350 € 🛉🛉400 € – 18 suites

♦ Historic ♦ Stylish ♦

An elegant, prestigious building dating from 1892. This hotel has a magnificent lounge area, delightful English-style bar and well-maintained, classical-style guestrooms.

Sofitel Lisbon Liberdade

Av. da Liberdade 127 ✉ 1269-038 – Ⓜ Avenida – ✆ 213 22 83 00 – www.sofitel.com **E1**

167 rm – ††145/350 € – 4 suites

Rest *Ad Lib* – see below

♦ Chain hotel ♦ Modern ♦

This hotel is decorated in contemporary-style with numerous designer details. It has fully equipped guestrooms furnished with top-quality materials.

Bairro Alto H.

Praça Luis de Camões 2 ✉ 1200-243 – Ⓜ Baixa-Chiado – ✆ 213 40 82 88 – www.bairroaltohotel.com **E2**

51 rm – †215/330 € ††250/650 € – 4 suites **Rest** – Carte 30/40 €

♦ Historic ♦ Modern ♦

An attractively restored building in the city's historic quarter. Contemporary decor with minimalist touches, and a roof terrace with views. A simple restaurant with large windows overlooking the square.

Lisboa Plaza

Travessa do Salitre 7 ✉ 1269-066 – Ⓜ Avenida – ✆ 213 21 82 18 – www.heritage.pt **E1**

94 rm – †120/226 € ††130/248 €, 14 € – 12 suites

Rest – Menu 35 €

♦ Business ♦ Classic ♦

Classic-style hotel with an attractive small lounge area and elegant guestrooms. Good facilities and high quality furnishings. The Lisboa Plaza's restaurant offers an attractive menu and a substantial buffet.

Do Chiado without rest

Rua Nova do Almada 114 ✉ 1200-290 – Ⓜ Baixa-Chiado – ✆ 213 25 61 00 – www.hoteldochiado.pt **E2**

40 rm – †184/294 € ††223/294 €

♦ Business ♦ Contemporary ♦

A hotel with well-appointed guestrooms in the heart of the Chiado district. Those on the seventh floor have private balconies with splendid views of the city.

Heritage Av Liberdade without rest

Av. da Liberdade 28 ✉ 1250-145 – Ⓜ Avenida – ✆ 213 40 40 40 – www.heritage.pt **E1**

42 rm – †150/295 € ††163/325 €, 14 €

♦ Business ♦ Contemporary ♦

The Heritage has a classic façade and a multipurpose public area, which also serves as the breakfast room. Well-appointed guestrooms that are contemporary in style.

NH Liberdade

Av. da Liberdade 180-B ✉ 1250-146 – Ⓜ Avenida – ✆ 213 51 40 60 – www.nh-hotels.com **E1**

58 rm – †118/193 € ††133/208 € – 25 suites **Rest** – Carte 30/35 €

♦ Chain hotel ♦ Modern ♦

Located in the city's main business district this comfortable, functional hotel is decorated in the typical style of this chain. Modern guestrooms in tones of grey. The restaurant menu features a combination of Spanish and Portuguese cuisine.

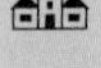

Internacional Design H. without rest

Rua da Betesga 3 ✉ 1100-090 – Ⓜ Rossio – ✆ 213 24 09 90 – www.idesignhotel.com **E2**

55 rm – ††90/500 €

♦ Business ♦ Design ♦

In keeping with the hotel name, the decor here is very much designer focused. The guestrooms are on four floors, each with its own style: urban, tribal, zen and pop.

Mundial rm,
Praça Martim Moniz 2 ✉ 1100-341 – Ⓜ Rossio – ✆ 218 84 20 00 – www.hotel-mundial.pt **F1**
345 rm – ††88/350 € – 5 suites
Rest *Varanda de Lisboa* – Carte 25/38 €
Rest *Jardim Mundial* – Carte approx. 25 €
◆ Business ◆ Classic ◆
This comfortable hotel is in the heart of the Baixa Pombalina district. It offers modern creature comforts and facilities, and pleasant, well-maintained and fully equipped guestrooms. This panoramic restaurant on the eighth floor boasts splendid views of the city.

Tivoli Jardim
Rua Julio Cesar Machado 7 ✉ 1250-135 – Ⓜ Avenida – ✆ 213 59 10 00 – www.tivolijardin.com **E1**
119 rm – ††115/270 €, 12.50 € **Rest** – Carte 36/55 €
◆ Business ◆ Functional ◆
Modern and functional facilities aimed at the business traveller. Large lobby and warmly decorated guestrooms in contemporary-style, half of which have their own terrace. This restaurant, with its bright, attractively lit dining room, specialises in traditional cuisine.

Britania without rest
Rua Rodrigues Sampaio 17 ✉ 1150-278 – Ⓜ Avenida – ✆ 213 15 50 16 – www.heritage.pt **E1**
33 rm – †130/230 € ††143/255 €, 14 €
◆ Business ◆ Classic ◆
The only public area in this hotel is the bar with its lovely wood floor and paintings of Portugal's former colonies. Spacious guestrooms with an Art Deco feel.

Olissippo Castelo without rest
Rua Costa do Castelo 126 ✉ 1100-179 – Ⓜ Rossio – ✆ 218 82 01 90 – www.olissippohotels.com **F2**
24 rm – †175 € ††195 €
◆ Business ◆ Classic ◆
Located on a hill next to the San Jorge castle, part of this hotel is built up against the castle ramparts. Very comfortable guestrooms, a dozen of which have their own garden terrace and magnificent views.

Veneza without rest
Av. da Liberdade 189 ✉ 1250-141 – Ⓜ Avenida – ✆ 213 52 26 18 – www.viphotels.com **E1**
37 rm – †55/62 € ††55/80 €, 8.50 €
◆ Palace ◆ Classic ◆
Housed in an elegant small mansion with limited public areas. Perfect blend of old-world charm and functional modern style in the lounge area and guestrooms.

Solar do Castelo without rest
Rua das Cozinhas 2 ✉ 1100-181 – Ⓜ Rossio – ✆ 218 80 60 50 – www.heritage.pt **F2**
14 rm – †162/310 € ††176/340 €, 14 €
◆ Palace ◆ Contemporary ◆
Small 18C mansion with a comfortable, completely renovated interior. The guestrooms here are modern and decorated with striking designer touches.

Metropole without rest
Praça Don Pedro IV-30 ✉ 1100-200 – Ⓜ Rossio – ✆ 213 21 90 30 – www.almeidahotels.com **E2**
36 rm – †137/195 € ††152/210 €
◆ Business ◆ Classic ◆
Early 20C building in the heart of old Lisbon. Traditional, comfortable guestrooms, the best of which have a balcony overlooking the Praça do Rossio.

Solar dos Mouros without rest

Rua do Milagre de Santo António 6 ✉ 1100-351 – Ⓜ Baixa-Chiado – ✆ 218 85 49 40 – www.solardosmouros.com **F2**

13 rm – ♦119/240 € ♦♦139/466 €, ☕ 14.80 €

♦ Business ♦ Contemporary ♦

A traditional-style hotel with an original decor, a somewhat irregular layout and a modern interior. Colourful guestrooms, some enjoying excellent views.

Albergaria Senhora do Monte without rest

Calçada do Monte 39 ✉ 1170-250 – Ⓜ Martim Moniz – ✆ 218 86 60 02 – www.senhoramonte.blogspot.com **F1**

28 rm ☕ – ♦65/99 € ♦♦75/150 €

♦ Business ♦ Classic ♦

This quiet hotel is in the Graça residential district. It has cosy, functional guestrooms that are classic in feel. There is a terrace-bar with splendid views of Lisbon.

Lisboa Tejo without rest

Rua dos Condes de Monsanto 2 ✉ 1100-159 – Ⓜ Rossio – ✆ 218 86 61 82 – www.evidenciahoteis.com **F2**

51 rm ☕ – ♦82/113 € ♦♦87/131 € – 7 suites

♦ Business ♦ Functional ♦

The Lisboa Tejo's overriding feature, both on the façade and inside, is the predominant use of the colour blue. Modernist-style lobby and well-appointed guestrooms.

Tavares (José Avillez)

Rua da Misericórdia 37 ✉ 1200-270 – Ⓜ Baixa-Chiado – ✆ 213 42 11 12 – www.restaurantetavares.pt – closed Sunday and Monday **E2**

Rest – Menu 90 € – Carte 68/95 €

Spec. A horta da "galinha dos ovos de ouro". Robalo escalfado a 54°. Pastel de nata em mil-folhas com gelado de canela.

♦ Inventive ♦ Formal ♦

Founded in 1784, this emblematic address is renowned for its history and elegance. It has an attractive entrance hall and majestic dining room with large mirrors, superb gilded work and chandeliers. Creative dishes with a solid base in traditional cuisine.

Gambrinus

Rua das Portas de Santo Antão 25 ✉ 1150-264 – Ⓜ Restauradores – ✆ 213 42 14 66 **E1**

Rest – Carte 50/70 €

♦ Traditional ♦ Formal ♦

This renowned Lisbon restaurant has an attractive bar and a dining room with a fireplace. Traditional Portuguese specialities, international cuisine and seafood.

Tágide

Largo da Academia Nacional de Belas Artes 18-20 ✉ 1200-005 – Ⓜ Baixa-Chiado – ✆ 21 340 40 10 – www.restaurantetagide.com – closed August, Sunday and Monday **E2**

Rest – Carte approx. 46 €

♦ Traditional ♦ Formal ♦

This very classic establishment has a stand-up bar and a private bar room that also functions as a tea room. The charming dining room is decorated with beautiful Portuguese tiles.

Casa do Leão

Castelo de São Jorge ✉ 1100-129 – Ⓜ Rossio – ✆ 218 87 59 62 – www.pousadas.pt **F2**

Rest – Carte 34/55 €

♦ Traditional ♦ Formal ♦

A unique location inside the defensive walls of the Castle of São Jorge. Typical Portuguese style dining room with a fireplace and vaulted roof, as well as a terrace with spectacular views.

Ad Lib – Hotel Sofitel Lisbon Liberdade
Av. da Liberdade 127 ✉ 1269-038 – Ⓜ Avenida – ✆ 213 22 83 50 – www.restauranteadlib.pt – closed Saturday lunch and Sunday lunch **E1**
Rest – Carte 30/50 €
♦ Traditional ♦ Trendy ♦
The entrance to the Ad Lib is separate from the hotel. Small reception area, and a glass-enclosed wine display. Modern decor with oriental touches in the dining room. Traditional cuisine.

Solar dos Presuntos
Rua das Portas de Santo Antão 150 ✉ 1150-269 – Ⓜ Avenida – ✆ 213 42 42 53 – www.solardospresuntos.com – closed August, Christmas, Sunday and Bank Holidays **E1**
Rest – Carte 39/45 €
♦ Traditional ♦ Trendy ♦
Run by its owners, this pleasant restaurant has an attractive counter of fresh produce on display. Large selection of traditional dishes and seafood specialities, as well as an excellent wine list.

La Paparrucha
Rua D. Pedro V 18-20 ✉ 1250-094 – Ⓜ Chiado – ✆ 213 42 53 33 – www.lapaparrucha.com **E1**
Rest – Carte approx. 32 €
♦ International ♦ Trendy ♦
A popular, functional Argentinean restaurant that specialises in top quality grilled meats. Good views, and a busy outdoor terrace.

NORTH QUARTER (Av. da Liberdade, Parque Eduardo VII, Museu Gulbenkian) *Plan III*

Four Seasons H. Ritz Lisbon
Rua Rodrigo da Fonseca 88 ✉ 1099-039 – Ⓜ Marquês de Pombal – ✆ 213 81 14 00 – www.fourseasons.com
262 rm – †295/500 € ††320/525 €, ☕ 30 € – 20 suites **G3**
Rest *Varanda* – Carte 70/85 €
♦ Grand Luxury ♦ Classic ♦
Luxurious, exquisite guestrooms, some of which are truly spectacular. Magnificent lounge areas and high quality furnishings. A wonderful place to stay! An attractive traditional restaurant. It offers à la carte options and a buffet at lunchtime, and more sophisticated dining in the evening.

Tiara Park Atlantic Lisboa
Rua Castilho 149 ✉ 1099-034 – Ⓜ Marquês de Pombal – ✆ 213 81 87 00 – www.tiara-hotels.com
314 rm – †100/450 € ††120/470 €, ☕ 23 € – 17 suites **G3**
Rest *L'Appart* – Carte 50/66 €
♦ Business ♦ Contemporary ♦
Excellent facilities and professional staff in this well-maintained hotel with modern guestrooms and suites. Marble bathrooms and quality furniture. An attractively decorated restaurant with four different dining areas. Options include a buffet, à la carte menu and daily specials.

Holiday Inn Lisbon Continental
Rua Laura Alves 9 ✉ 1069-169 – Ⓜ Campo Pequeno – ✆ 210 04 60 00 – www.holiday-inn.com
210 rm – †60/150 € ††70/180 €, ☕ 12.90 € – 10 suites **H1**
Rest – Menu 23 €
♦ Business ♦ Contemporary ♦
Popular with business travellers, the hotel has a contemporary façade and attractive public areas. The welcoming guestrooms are well appointed with good attention to detail. The hotel's dining room is somewhat lacking in charm.

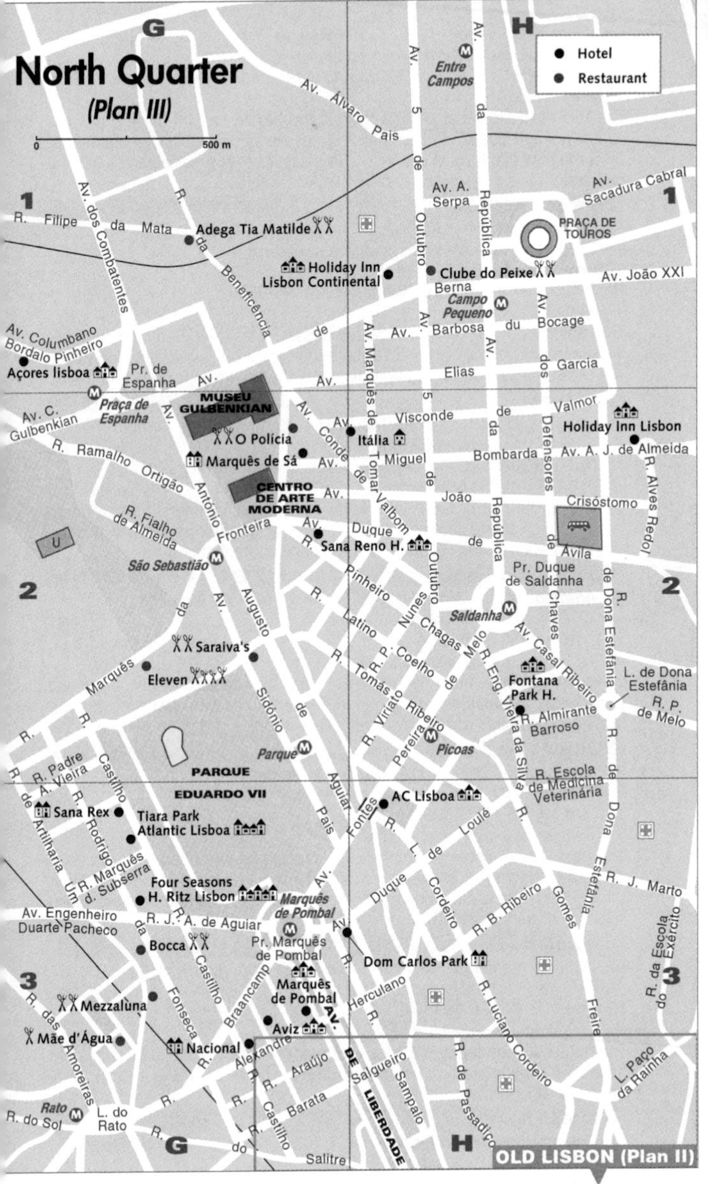
North Quarter
(Plan III)
0
500 m
Hotel
Restaurant
Adega Tia Matilde
Holiday Inn Lisbon Continental
Clube do Peixe
Açores lisboa
Museu Gulbenkian
O Polícia
Marquês de Sá
Itália
Holiday Inn Lisbon
Centro de Arte Moderna
Sana Reno H.
Saraiva's
Eleven
Fontana Park H.
AC Lisboa
Sana Rex
Tiara Park Atlantic Lisboa
Four Seasons H. Ritz Lisboa
Bocca
Dom Carlos Park
Marquês de Pombal
Mezzalùna
Aviz
Mãe d'Água
Nacional
Parque Eduardo VII
Praça de Touros
Entre Campos
Campo Pequeno
Praça de Espanha
São Sebastião
Saldanha
Picoas
Parque
Marquês de Pombal
Rato
Old Lisbon (Plan II)

Aviz rm,

Rua Duque de Palmela 32 ✉ 1250-098 – Ⓜ Marquês de Pombal – ☎ 210 40 20 00 – www.hotelaviz.com **G3**

56 rm – 120/150 € 150/350 € – 14 suites **Rest** – Carte 32/52 €

♦ Traditional ♦ Classic ♦

This hotel is designed along classic lines and has an elegant foyer. It features well-appointed guestrooms, some of which are dedicated to famous names from the past that have stayed here. This classic yet cosy restaurant is decorated with a variety of objects from the old Aviz hotel.

Fontana Park H. rm,

Rua Engenheiro Vieira da Silva 2 ✉ 1050-105 – Ⓜ Picoas – ☎ 210 41 06 00 – www.fontanaparkhotel.com **H2**

139 rm – 140/255 € 160/275 €

Rest – *(closed August and Sunday)* Carte 45/65 €

♦ Business ♦ Modern ♦

This designer hotel is very much geared to the 21C traveller. Find modern public areas, minimalist decor, comfortable guestrooms and a Zen inspired interior garden. This hotel boasts two restaurants: one Japanese, the other serving traditional cuisine.

AC Lisboa rm,

Rua Largo Andaluz 13 - B ✉ 1050-121 – Ⓜ Marquês de Pombal – ☎ 210 05 09 30 – www.ac-hotels.com **H3**

81 rm – 90/170 €, 10 € – 2 suites **Rest** – Menu 21 €

♦ Chain hotel ♦ Modern ♦

Occupying the rear of the Palacio Sottomayor, this chain hotel has a modern façade and extensive public areas. Fully equipped guestrooms, some with a terrace. A pleasant dining room offering à la carte and buffet choices.

Holiday Inn Lisbon rm,

Av. António José de Almeida 28-A ✉ 1000-044 – Ⓜ Alameda – ☎ 210 04 40 00 – www.holiday-inn.com **H2**

161 rm – 180 € 200 €, 13.50 € – 8 suites **Rest** – Menu 15 €

♦ Business ♦ Contemporary ♦

Contemporary-style hotel geared to business travellers. Pleasant lounge and public areas, in addition to well-appointed guestrooms with classic modern furnishings. The hotel's restaurant serves a varied choice of traditional dishes.

Marquês de Pombal rm,

Av. da Liberdade 243 ✉ 1250-143 – Ⓜ Marquês de Pombal – ☎ 213 19 79 00 – www.hotel-marquesdepombal.pt **G3**

120 rm – 138/172 € 150/184 € – 3 suites **Rest** – Carte 23/33 €

♦ Business ♦ Contemporary ♦

This hotel has a contemporary, functional feel. It features elegant furnishings, modern technology, a modular conference room and good levels of comfort throughout. The restaurant is connected to the cafeteria and serves a varied selection of traditional dishes.

Sana Reno H. without rest

Av. Duque d'Ávila 195-197 ✉ 1050-082 – Ⓜ São Sebastião – ☎ 213 13 50 00 – www.sanahotels.com **G2**

89 rm – 180 € 190 € – 3 suites

♦ Business ♦ Classic ♦

The hotel's elegant lobby provides a taste of the comfortable facilities on offer here. Well-appointed guestrooms with carpeted floors, as well as a small swimming pool and sauna.

Açores Lisboa rm,

Av. Columbano Bordalo Pinheiro 3 ✉ 1070-060 – Ⓜ Praça de Espanha – ☎ 217 22 29 20 – www.bensaude.pt **G1**

123 rm – 67/190 € 75/205 € – 5 suites **Rest** – Menu 15 €

♦ Chain hotel ♦ Business ♦ Contemporary ♦

A modern and functional chain hotel with friendly and enthusiastic staff. The limited space in its public areas is compensated by the well-appointed guestrooms and fully equipped bathrooms. The restaurant offers a buffet at midday, and a traditional menu at night.

Dom Carlos Park without rest
Av. Duque de Loulé 121 ✉ 1050-089 – Ⓜ Marquês de Pombal – ✆ 213 51 25 90 – www.domcarlospark.com **G-H3**
76 rm – 70/147 € 77/196 €
◆ Business ◆ Classic ◆
This classic, elegant hotel enjoys an excellent location, and provides the perfect setting for a relaxing break. Charming guestrooms with marble bathrooms. Limited public areas and lounges.

Marquês de Sá
rm,
Av. Miguel Bombarda 130 ✉ 1050-167 – Ⓜ São Sebastião – ✆ 217 91 10 14 – www.olissippohotels.com **G2**
163 rm – 150/180 € 170/200 € **Rest** – Menu 17 €
◆ Business ◆ Functional ◆
A functional hotel with an attractive lobby and spacious bar-lounge area. The guestrooms are well appointed, albeit relatively simple in style. The classic-style dining room offers a simple traditional menu.

Sana Rex H. without rest
Rua Castilho 169 ✉ 1070-051 – Ⓜ Marquês de Pombal – ✆ 213 88 21 61 – www.sanahotels.com **G3**
68 rm – 80/190 € 90/200 €
◆ Chain hotel ◆ Functional ◆
This hotel enjoys an attractive location opposite the Eduardo VII park, which is overlooked by many of the guestrooms. The lobby-bar, with its delightful paved floor, is particularly striking.

Nacional without rest
Rua Castilho 34 ✉ 1250-070 – Ⓜ Marquês de Pombal – ✆ 213 55 44 33 – www.hotel-nacional.com **G3**
61 rm – 64/90 € 75/106 €
◆ Business ◆ Classic ◆
Very professionally run with attentive service and a setting that is both functional and contemporary.

Itália without rest
Av. Visconde de Valmor 67 ✉ 1050-239 – Ⓜ Saldanha – ✆ 217 97 77 36 – www.residencial-italia.com **G-H2**
44 rm – 40/100 € 50/120 €
◆ Family ◆ Business ◆ Functional ◆
The attractive patio with its tables, lawn and orange trees comes as a pleasant surprise in the centre of the city. The guestrooms are modern, simple and functional.

Eleven
Rua Marquês de Fronteira ✉ 1070 – Ⓜ São Sebastião – ✆ 213 86 22 11 – www.restauranteleven.com – closed Sunday **G2**
Rest – Carte 60/76 €
◆ Inventive ◆ Trendy ◆
Attractive restaurant with a private bar/hall. The modern dining room has wonderful views of the park, the river and the city. Well-presented, creative cuisine.

Saraiva's
Rua Engenheiro Canto Resende 3 ✉ 1050-104 – Ⓜ São Sebastião – ✆ 213 54 06 09 – closed Friday dinner, Saturday and Bank Holidays **G2**
Rest – Carte 20/30 €
◆ Traditional ◆ Trendy ◆
Excellent, well-run restaurant decorated in a modern style reminiscent of the 1980s. Good choice of dishes on the menu, which features both traditional and international cuisine.

XX

Clube do Peixe

Av. 5 de Outubro 180 ✉ 1050-063 – Ⓜ Campo Pequeno – ✆ 217 97 34 34 – www.clube-do-peixe.com – closed Sunday **H1**

Rest – Carte 25/35 €

♦ Fish ♦ Formal ♦

A popular local restaurant with an attractive display of fish and seafood at the entrance. The dining room is classic-contemporary in style with the occasional maritime detail in the decor.

XX

Bocca

Rua Rodrigo da Fonseca 87 D ✉ 1250-190 – Ⓜ Marquês de Pombal – ✆ 213 80 83 83 – www.bocca.pt – closed Sunday and Monday

Rest – Carte 42/62 € **G3**

♦ Innovative ♦ Trendy ♦

The Bocca has two contemporary dining rooms with the first having views of the kitchen. There is also a gastro-bar area in the basement for tapas and raciones. Creative cuisine.

XX

Adega Tia Matilde

Rua da Beneficéncia 77 ✉ 1600-017 – Ⓜ Praça de Espanha – ✆ 217 97 21 72 – www.adegatiamatilde.com – closed Saturday dinner and Sunday

Rest – Carte 27/34 € **G1**

♦ Traditional ♦ Formal ♦

Family-run restaurant with a good local reputation. Spacious dining rooms and traditional cuisine. The large underground car park makes up for the poor location.

XX

Varanda da União

Rua Castilho 14 C-7° ✉ 1250-069 – Ⓜ Marquês de Pombal – ✆ 213 14 10 45 – www.varandadauniao.com – closed Saturday lunch, Sunday and Bank Holidays lunch *Plan II* **E1**

Rest – Carte 26/39 €

♦ Traditional ♦ Formal ♦

This successful restaurant on the seventh floor of an apartment building enjoys splendid views of the rooftops of Lisbon. High quality cuisine served by a plethora of waiters.

XX

O Polícia

Rua Marquês Sá da Bandeira 112 ✉ 1050-150 – Ⓜ São Sebastião – ✆ 217 96 35 05 – www.restauranteopolicia.com – closed Saturday dinner, Sunday and Bank Holidays **G2**

Rest – Carte 27/44 €

♦ Traditional ♦ Family ♦

This busy family-run restaurant is renowned for its fish. Display counter, attractive table settings and two entrances. Dining area divided into four rooms. Reservations recommended.

XX

Mezzaluna

Rua Artilharia Um 16 ✉ 1250-039 – Ⓜ Rato – ✆ 213 87 99 44 – www.chefguerrieri.com – closed Christmas, Saturday lunch and Sunday **G3**

Rest – Carte approx. 30 €

♦ Italian ♦ Formal ♦

The owner-chef runs this restaurant with a casual yet chic feel. The focus here is on traditional Italian cuisine with a few Italian-Portuguese variations.

X

Mãe d'Água

Travessa das Amoreiras 10 ✉ 1250-025 – Ⓜ Rato – ✆ 213 88 28 20 – closed 3 weeks in August, Saturday, Sunday and Bank Holidays

Rest – Carte 31/40 € **G3**

♦ Traditional ♦ Family ♦

The limited space in this restaurant adds to its cosy ambience. The dining room beyond the bar is decorated with bullfighting pictures and photos. Excellent service.

PARQUE DAS NAÇÕES

Plan I

Tivoli Oriente

Av. D. João II (Parque das Nações) ✉ 1990-083 – Ⓜ Oriente – ✆ 218 91 51 00 – www.tivolitejo.com **D1**

262 rm – 85/330 €, 10 € – 17 suites

Rest *VIII Colina* – Carte approx. 30 €

◆ Chain hotel ◆ Classic ◆

Attractive building next to the Oriente railway station. It offers contemporary guestrooms with small bathrooms. Pleasant public areas, albeit lacking in space. The VIII Colina restaurant enjoys superb panoramic views.

Olissippo Oriente

Rua. D. João II (Parque das Nações) ✉ 1990-083 – Ⓜ Oriente – ✆ 218 92 91 00 – www.olissippohotels.com **D1**

182 rm – 180/200 € 200/220 € **Rest** – Carte approx. 35 €

◆ Chain hotel ◆ Modern ◆

Situated on the Expo site, this hotel boasts modern facilities. It includes extensive public areas and lounges, meeting rooms and comfortable guestrooms. A refined dining room where guests can enjoy a full buffet or a menu featuring traditional cuisine.

Tryp Oriente

Av. D. João II (Parque das Nações) ✉ 1990-083 – Ⓜ Oriente – ✆ 218 93 00 00 – www.solmelia.com **D1**

206 rm – 130/165 € 145/185 € **Rest** – Menu 15 €

◆ Chain hotel ◆ Classic ◆

Situated on the Expo site, this functional hotel has a pleasant lounge-bar and spacious guestrooms - those on the upper floors enjoy lovely views. A bright restaurant with a limited menu. Separate entrance from the hotel.

AT WEST

Plan I

Lapa Palace

Rua do Pau de Bandeira 4 ✉ 1249-021 – Ⓜ Rato – ✆ 213 94 94 94 – www.olissippohotels.com **B3**

102 rm – 370/430 €, 28.50 € – 7 suites **Rest** – Carte 47/61 €

◆ Grand Luxury ◆ Classic ◆

On a hill, with the Tagus river in the distance, this 19C palace is a luxurious hideaway in a quiet and elegant part of the city. Intimate lounges, and delightful tree-lined gardens with a waterfall add to the overall charm. The restaurant serves fine cuisine with a focus on Italian and Portuguese specialities.

Pestana Palace

Rua Jau 54 ✉ 1300-314 – ✆ 213 61 56 00 – www.pestana.com **B3**

177 rm – 330/351 € 350/367 € – 17 suites

Rest *Valle Flor* – Carte 45/74 €

◆ Grand Luxury ◆ Palace ◆ Stylish ◆

Beautifully restored 19C palace with period decor, luxurious lounges and guestrooms filled with decorative detail. Well-maintained grounds with an abundance of flora. Magnificent restaurant both in terms of its cuisine and the beautiful and luxurious dining rooms.

As Janelas Verdes without rest

Rua das Janelas Verdes 47 ✉ 1200-690 – ✆ 213 96 81 43 – www.heritage.pt **B3**

29 rm – 143/280 € 157/298 €, 14 €

◆ Villa ◆ Classic ◆

Partially housed in an 18C mansion, this welcoming hotel has a delightful lounge-library and beautiful views. A romantic feel and classic style.

York House

Rua das Janelas Verdes 32 ✉ 1200-691 – Ⓜ Cais do Sodré – ✆ 213 96 24 35 – www.yorkhouselisboa.com **B3**

32 rm – †85/150 € ††95/220 €, ☕ 15 € **Rest** – Carte approx. 38 €

♦ Historic ♦ Contemporary ♦

Housed in a 17C convent, this hotel has a comfortable, contemporary interior. Its modern decor is furnished with period pieces. Classic-style restaurant adorned with an attractive frieze of old azulejo tiles.

A Travessa

Travessa do Convento das Bernardas 12 ✉ 1200-638 – Ⓜ Cais do Sodré – ✆ 213 90 20 34 – www.atravessa.com – closed Sunday **B3**

Rest – Carte 37/54 €

♦ French ♦ Cosy ♦

This restaurant occupies a 17C monastery. The dining room has a lovely vaulted ceiling, rustic-style flooring and an attractive terrace in the cloister.

Solar dos Nunes

Rua dos Lusíadas 68-72 ✉ 1300-372 – ✆ 213 64 73 59 – www.solardosnunes.pt – closed 7-31 August and Sunday **B3**

Rest – Carte approx. 30 €

♦ Traditional ♦ Friendly ♦

This restaurant has a friendly atmosphere, traditional-style dining rooms and a lovely paved floor. Wide choice of traditional Portuguese dishes and a good wine list.

Tromba Rija

Rua Cintura do Porto de Lisboa - edif 254 ✉ 1200-109 – Ⓜ Cais do Sodré – ✆ 213 97 15 07 – www.trombarija.com – closed Sunday dinner and Monday lunch **B3**

Rest – Menu 35 €

♦ Traditional ♦ Rustic ♦

Located in a former warehouse at the port. This restaurant offers a full buffet of traditional Portuguese cuisine featuring over 50 different dishes.

BELÉM

Plan I

Altis Belém

Doca do Bom Sucesso ✉ 1400-038 – ✆ 210 40 02 00 – www.altisbelemhotel.com **A3**

45 rm ☕ – †130/350 € ††150/570 € – 5 suites

Rest *Feitoria* – *(closed 7-23 August, Sunday and Monday)* Carte 34/52 €

♦ Luxury ♦ Business ♦ Modern ♦

This is an extremely luxurious and modern hotel. There is a complete spa, and the very large, personalised bedrooms all have views of the Tejo river. In this elegant and bright restaurant diners can enjoy cuisine that is both contemporary and creative.

Jerónimos 8 without rest

Rua dos Jerónimos 8 ✉ 1400-211 – ✆ 213 60 09 00 – www.jeronimos8.com

65 rm ☕ – †120/220 € ††140/240 € **A3**

♦ Business ♦ Modern ♦

This comfortable hotel is located next to the Monasterio de Los Jerónimos. It occupies an old building that has been completely renovated with a minimalist feel.

Vela Latina

Doca do Bom Sucesso ✉ 1400-038 – ✆ 213 01 71 18 – www.velalatina.pt – closed Sunday and Bank Holidays **A3**

Rest – Carte 35/50 €

♦ Traditional ♦ Formal ♦

Located near the Torre de Belém with an elegant private bar, splendid private dining room and a main lounge with typical maritime decor. Pleasant, glass-fronted terrace.

SPAIN
ESPAÑA

PROFILE

→ **Area:**
504 645 km².

→ **Population:**
46 122 169 inhabitants (est. 2010), density = 91,3 per km².

→ **Capital:**
Madrid (conurbation 6 360 388 inhabitants).

→ **Currency:**
Euro (€); rate of exchange: € 1 = US$ 1.37 (Dec. 2010).

→ **Government:**
Constitutional parliamentary monarchy (since 1978). Member of European Union since 1986.

→ **Languages:**
Spanish (Castilian) but also Catalan in Catalonia, Gallego in Galicia, Euskera in the Basque Country, Valencian in the Valencian Region and Mallorquin in the Balearic Isles.

→ **Specific public holidays:**
Epiphany (6 January); San Jose (19 March); Maundy Thursday (the day before Good Friday); Good Friday (Friday before Easter); National Day (12 October); Constitution Day (6 December); Immaculate Conception (8 December). Some public holidays may be replaced by the autonomous communities with another date.

→ **Local Time:**
GMT + 1 hour in winter and GMT + 2 hours in summer.

→ **Climate:**
Temperate Mediterranean with mild winters (colder in interior) and sunny, hot summers (Madrid: January: 6°C, July: 25°C).

→ **International dialling Code:**
00 34 followed by full 9-digit number. Directory enquiries: ✆ **11822**. International directory enquiries: ✆ **11825**. On-line telephone directory: www.blancas.paginasamarillas.es

→ **Emergency:**
Dial ✆ **112**; National Police: ✆ **091**.

→ **Electricity:**
220 or 225 volts AC (previously 110 V), 50 Hz; 2-pin round-shaped continental plugs.

→ **Formalities**
Travellers from the European Union (EU), Switzerland, Iceland and the main countries of North and South America need a national identity card or passport (America: passport required) to visit Spain for less than three months (tourism or business purpose). For visitors from other countries a visa may be required, in addition to a passport, especially for those wishing to stay for longer than three months. We advise you to check with your embassy before travelling.

MADRID

MADRID

Population (oct. 2010): 3 255 944 (conurbation 6 360 388) – Altitude: 655m

idas Zubkonis/Fotolia.com

Madrid is a city on the rise. The nightlife in Spain's proud capital is now second to none and the superb museums of art which make up the city's 'golden triangle' have all undergone thrilling reinvention in recent years.

The next big plan for Madrid is to have a square kilometre park near the river Manzanares, which runs just west of the city. In a big bid to give *madrileños* more clean air, the new park will be free of cars, and will boast bike lanes intermingled with eight thousand trees – and there'll be an artificial beach, too. The renaissance of Madrid has seen it develop as a big player on the world cultural stage, attracting more international music, theatre and dance than it would have dreamed of a decade ago. The new Royal Spanish Ballet will be based here, a testament to its rising cachet in the arts. This is a city that might think it has some catching up to do: it was only made the capital in 1561 on the whim of ruler, Felipe II. But its position was crucial: slap bang in the middle of the Iberian Peninsula. Ruled by Habsburgs and Bourbons, it soon made a mark in Europe.

The contemporary big wigs of Madrid are out to have the same effect with a 21C twist.

LIVING THE CITY

The central heart of Madrid is compact, defined by the teeming Habsburg hubs of **Puerta del Sol** and **Plaza Mayor**, and the mighty **Palacio Real**. East of here are the grand squares, fountains and fine museums of the Bourbon district with its easterly boundary, the **Retiro** park. West of the historical centre are the capacious green acres of **Casa de Campo**, while the affluent, regimented grid streets of **Salamanca** are to the east. Modern Madrid is just to the north, embodied in the grand north-south boulevard **Paseo de la Castellana**.

PRACTICAL INFORMATION

ARRIVAL-DEPARTURE

Madrid-Barajas Airport is approximately 13km east of the city. A taxi should cost around €25. Metro Line 8 runs every 4-7min, with a journey time of 50min. Chamartin Station is the railway station for services to the north of Spain and France ; Atocha Station for those to the south.

TRANSPORT

Madrid is covered by a bus and metro public transport system. You can buy single journey tickets, but a better bet for longer visits is a ten-trip Metrobus ticket, valid on both bus and metro networks, and better value than tickets bought individually. Get them from underground stations, bus ticket offices, newsstands and tobacconists.

Consider also the Tourist Travel Card, which is valid from one to seven days for unlimited travel on all public transport in Zone A or Zone T in the Madrid region. As well as usual outlets, it's also on sale at the city's two long-distance train stations, Chamartín and Atocha.

It's well worth forking out for a Madrid Card. You can get them for one, two, or three-day periods from a wide range of outlets. They entitle you to travel on all forms of public transport, and grant admission to more than forty museums. They're also valid for discounts in some nightclubs, shops and restaurants.

EXPLORING MADRID

All roads in Spain lead to the Puerta del Sol. This is not as fanciful as it sounds: the square - where it seems

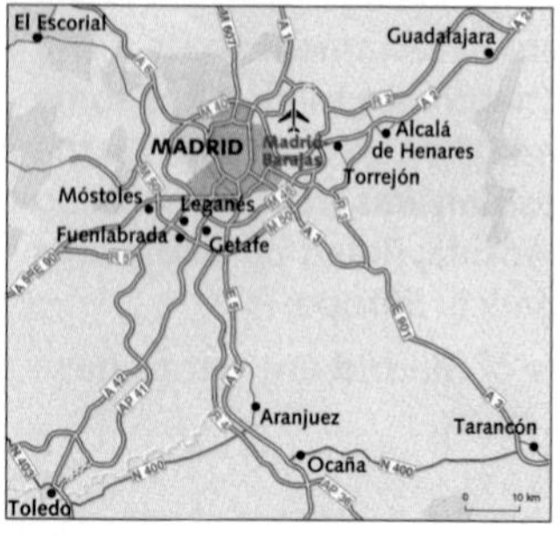

every tourist in Madrid has congregated for orientation guidelines - also bears a symbol on the ground marking Kilometre Zero, considered the centre of Spain's road network. This was once the eastern entrance to Madrid, with a castle and gatehouse. You'd never guess it now. With its iconic 'Tio Pepe' sherry sign leering overhead, the cafés and shops here are a non-stop buzz of activity as visitors plan their itineraries in the surrounding knot of narrow streets. The crescent shaped Puerta del Sol has its charms, but the area's finest square is a little way to the west.

Plaza Mayor is a beautifully arcaded rectangle which has been the focal point over the centuries of everything from bullfights to the trials of the Inquisition. It's still the ceremonial heart of the city, so one day you can expect a fiesta, the next a political rally. Despite all this, it can be surprisingly peaceful here during weekdays, and makes the perfect setting for a coffee or a meal at one of the many cafés whose tables spill out from the arcades. It boasts a distinctly Castilian character, and its theatrical face is best shown above the arcades of the Casa de la Panadería, which is decorated with eye-catching allegorical paintings. Just two hundred metres further west is the third of the old quarter's great squares, **Plaza de la Villa**, an atmospheric space surrounded by many historic buildings, such as the early fifteenth-century **Torre de los Lujanes**, which mixes Gothic embellishments with arches in a dramatic horse-shoe style.

→ REAL HEAD-TURNER

Head even further west, up a steep slope towards the river, and you come to Madrid's ultimate showpiece building: the **Palacio Real**. This is the biggest official royal residence in the world with a bewildering three thousand rooms. It took two 18C Bourbon monarchs twenty eight years to build themselves this cosy little number. You come to it across the huge semi-circular **Plaza de Oriente**, a theatrical concoction in itself. Inside, the show continues, with highlights left, right and centre. These include the superb Throne Room with its sculptures by Velázquez, the main staircase sculpted from Toledo marble, the lavishly decorated Garparini Rooms (all silk, stucco and chinoiserie), the magnificent State Dining Room, and the Royal Armoury, which includes the armour of El Cid and his horse.

Don't get the impression Madrid is all plaza and palaccio. You can come up for air at a number of imposing green spaces. Close to the Palaccio Real is the gracefully sloping **Campo del Moro**, while the western boundary of the city is the massive Casa de Campo, almost seven square miles of tennis courts, swimming pools, funfair, pines and scrubland. Madrid's favourite park, though, is on the eastern side of town. Retiro Park was once a three hundred acre royal palace garden. When it opened to the public in 1869 *madrileños* came in their thousands, and it's still the city's number one destination for chilling out. There's a large boating lake in the middle, and two elegant glasshouses useful for delving around as they house interesting free art exhibitions.

If you're at the Retiro, you're in the city's Bourbon quarter, named after the dynasty which developed it in the eighteenth century. Strolling around the park, there's every chance you've been to, or are heading towards, one of the three fabulous museums in the area: art lovers in this neck of the woods aren't just spoilt for choice, they can positively wallow in it. Top spot goes to the **Prado**, one of the world's great museums and the capital's top cultural attraction. It contains the world's richest assembly of Spanish painting, covering the 12C to 19C, with a magnificent range of works by Velázquez, Goya and El Greco. There's also a wealth of Italian Renaissance masterpieces and Flemish works. Ground floor highlights include Hieronymus Bosch's *The Garden of Earthly Delights*, and *The Annunciation* by Fra Angelico.

→ SEVEN CENTURIES OF ART

Cross the street and you're at another superb artistic offering. The **Museo Thyssen-Bornemisza** was bequeathed to Spain as recently as 1993, and is one of the most important private collections in the world. Installed in an 18C palace, its three floors cover seven centuries of Western art, from Van Eyck, Holbein, Titian, Durer and Rubens (top floor) to the Dutch Golden Age, German Expressionism and French Impressionism (first floor), and ending up with Picasso, Hopper and Freud at ground level. If you have the energy, saunter down the Paseo del Prado for less than half a mile and you'll reach the third of the triumvirate, the **Centro de Arte Reina Sofía**, the city's museum of modern art. Most people come here primarily to take in Picasso's haunting *Guernica*, but when they arrive they're knocked out by the whole place. It's an 18C former hospital, and its exhibition space is vast. The focus is on Spanish work (the 20C was a monumental century for Spanish art), and there are rooms devoted to Miró, Dalí and the surrealist film-maker Luis Buñuel.

→ GRAN TOUR

It's useful to have eyes not only in the back of your head but on top of it too when you're passing along the **Gran Vía**. This is Madrid's bustling main thoroughfare, whose construction started over one hundred years ago (1908) and was completed twenty years later. Sure, you have to watch out for the traffic streaming along it, but don't miss the fine 20C buildings towering above you, either. They represent a vivid panorama of modern architecture, from neo-classical to art deco. Gran Vía even has a structure straight out of a Jimmy Cagney movie: the 1920s **Telefónica** building is a slightly squashed version of a Manhattan skyscraper. A different style of street, and a different style of window gazing, can be found further east in the Salamanca district. Here you'll come across wide, sophisticated boulevards on a grid system where the shops and boutiques are of the smartly expensive variety.

Madrid is a hip and happening place wherever you turn at whatever time of day, and tourists from, say, northern Europe may have to adjust their body clocks to the city's late hour culture. However, even in this city, there are two areas just north of Gran Vía that are instantly recognisable for their extra cool vibe. **Chueca** and **Malasaña** have an arty, bohemian feel, defined by hip bars and sassy little shops. Chueca is the gay/lesbian quarter of the city; Malasaña's grungy ambience is, if anything, heightened by its charming cobbled streets, fountains and trees. Whichever quarter you hit on, you won't forget the nightlife in a hurry.

CALENDAR HIGHLIGHTS

The highlight of the year comes in May: the Fiesta de San Isidro, the feast of the region's patron saint. For a week either side of the fifteenth, the city pulsates with fiestas, music and dance; focal points are the Plaza Mayor and Jardines de las Vistillas. Just before this, on 2 May, Dos de Mayo

MADRID IN…

→ ONE DAY

Puerta del Sol, Plaza Mayor, Palacio Real, Prado

→ TWO DAYS

Museo Thyssen-Bornemisza, Retiro, Gran Vía, tapas at a traditional taberna

→ THREE DAYS

Chueca, Malasaña, Centro de Arte Reina Sofía

festivities in Malasaña commemorate a rebellion against French occupying forces. A more sedate air surrounds the Madrid Book Fair in Retiro Park at the end of the month. The summer's main festival is Los Veranos de la Villa, a series of concerts featuring international musicians in various city venues: for two months, Madrid is ablaze with opera, tango, flamenco, jazz, Spanish musicals, exhibitions and films. September sees Festival de Otoño, when drama, ballet and opera descend upon the city's concert venues. One of the most colourful sights of the Madrid winter is the Twelfth Night procession (5 January) which goes from Retiro to Plaza Mayor and is full of floats and accompanying animals. Art lovers don their coats and scarves and head for ARCO in February: this is the city's internationally renowned contemporary art fair, held in Parque Ferial Juan Carlos I. And then there's Carnaval, with fancy dress parties and a parade from Plaza de Colón to Plaza de Cibeles. Día de Cervantes (23 April) celebrates the great author's death with a book fair in Alcalá de Henares.

EATING OUT

Madrileños know how to pace themselves. Breakfast is around 8am, lunch 2pm or 3pm, 5pm is the beginning of the afternoon and dinner won't be until 10pm or 11pm. A late night? Until dawn the next day or later. Madrid is the European capital which has best managed to absorb the regional cuisine of the country, largely due to massive internal migration to the city. Spain has the highest bar-restaurant per inhabitant ratio in Europe, and Madrid clocks in with one bar-restaurant per 171 inhabitants. Strange as it may seem given its geography, the quality and range of fish available in Madrid is exceptional: it's the second largest central fish market in the world, after Tokyo. Two reasons: it's established a land port in the nearby town of Coslada, and ocean fresh seafood is transported to the capital on a daily basis from the Galician coast. If you want to tuck into local specialities, you'll find them everywhere around the city. But what to try? *Callos a la madrileña* is Madrid-style tripe, dating back to 1559, while *sopas de Ajo* (garlic soup) is a favourite on cold winter days. Another popular soup (also a main course) is *cocido madrileño*, hearty and aromatic and comprised of chick peas, meat, tocino belly pork, potatoes and vegetables, slowly cooked in a rich broth. Two top fish dishes are *besugo a la madrileña* (baked sea bream with white wine, parsley and potatoes), and *bacalao a la madrileña* (Madrid-style cod, with potatoes, onions, tomatoes, garlic and olive oil). Or, of course, there's always the ubiquitous *tortilla de patata* (potato omelette) found in any bar, taberna or cafetería. To experience the real Madrid dining ambience, get to a traditional taberna in the heart of the old neighbourhood: there are about one hundred remaining in the area, distinguished by large clock, carved wooden bar with zinc counter and wine flasks, marble table tops and ceramic tiles. At the end of a meal, the bill will include service, but tips in cash are commonplace: around five per cent of the total.

→ THE OLDEST

A taberna to make for when in the old town is Botín. The roast suckling pig on offer is renowned throughout Spain, and Ernest Hemingway was known to tuck in here. The establishment's real claim to fame, though, is its appearance in the Guinness Book of Records: it dates back to 1725, making it the oldest restaurant in the world.

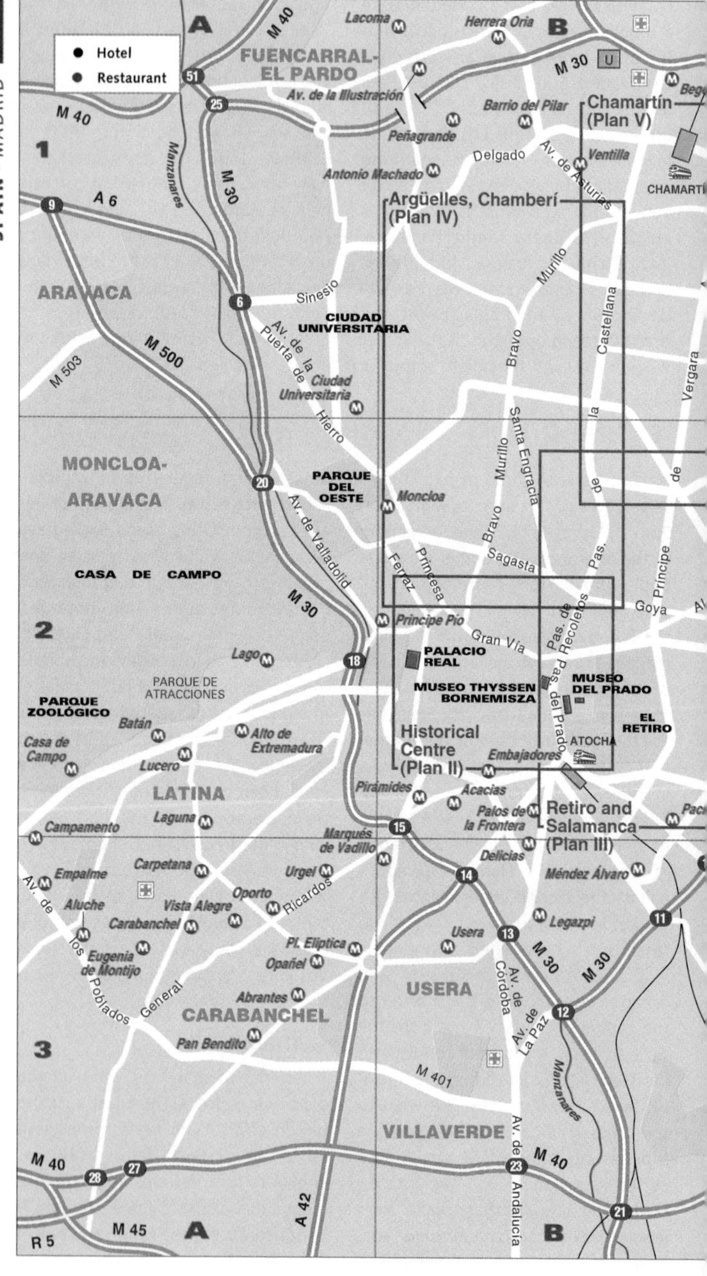
Hotel
Restaurant
FUENCARRAL-EL PARDO
ARAVACA
MONCLOA-ARAVACA
CASA DE CAMPO
CIUDAD UNIVERSITARIA
PARQUE DEL OESTE
PARQUE DE ATRACCIONES
PARQUE ZOOLÓGICO
LATINA
CARABANCHEL
USERA
VILLAVERDE
PALACIO REAL
MUSEO THYSSEN BORNEMISZA
MUSEO DEL PRADO
EL RETIRO
ATOCHA
CHAMARTÍ
Chamartín (Plan V)
Argüelles, Chamberí (Plan IV)
Historical Centre (Plan II)
Retiro and Salamanca (Plan III)
Av. de la Ilustración
Av. de la Puerta de Hierro
Av. de Valladolid
Av. de Asturias
Av. de los Poblados
Av. de Córdoba
Av. de La Paz
Av. de Andalucía
Gran Vía
Sagasta
Goya
Princesa
Ferraz
Santa Engracia
Bravo Murillo
Pas. de la Castellana
Pas. de Recoletos
Pas. del Prado
Príncipe de Vergara
Sinesio Delgado
General Ricardos
Manzanares
M 40
M 30
M 500
M 503
M 401
M 45
A 6
A 42
R 5
Lacoma
Herrera Oria
Peñagrande
Barrio del Pilar
Ventilla
Antonio Machado
Ciudad Universitaria
Moncloa
Príncipe Pío
Lago
Batán
Casa de Campo
Lucero
Alto de Extremadura
Campamento
Laguna
Empalme
Carpetana
Aluche
Vista Alegre
Carabanchel
Eugenia de Montijo
Urgel
Oporto
Marqués de Vadillo
Pirámides
Acacias
Embajadores
Palos de la Frontera
Delicias
Méndez Álvaro
Legazpi
Usera
Pl. Elíptica
Opañel
Abrantes
Pan Bendito
A
B
1
2
3

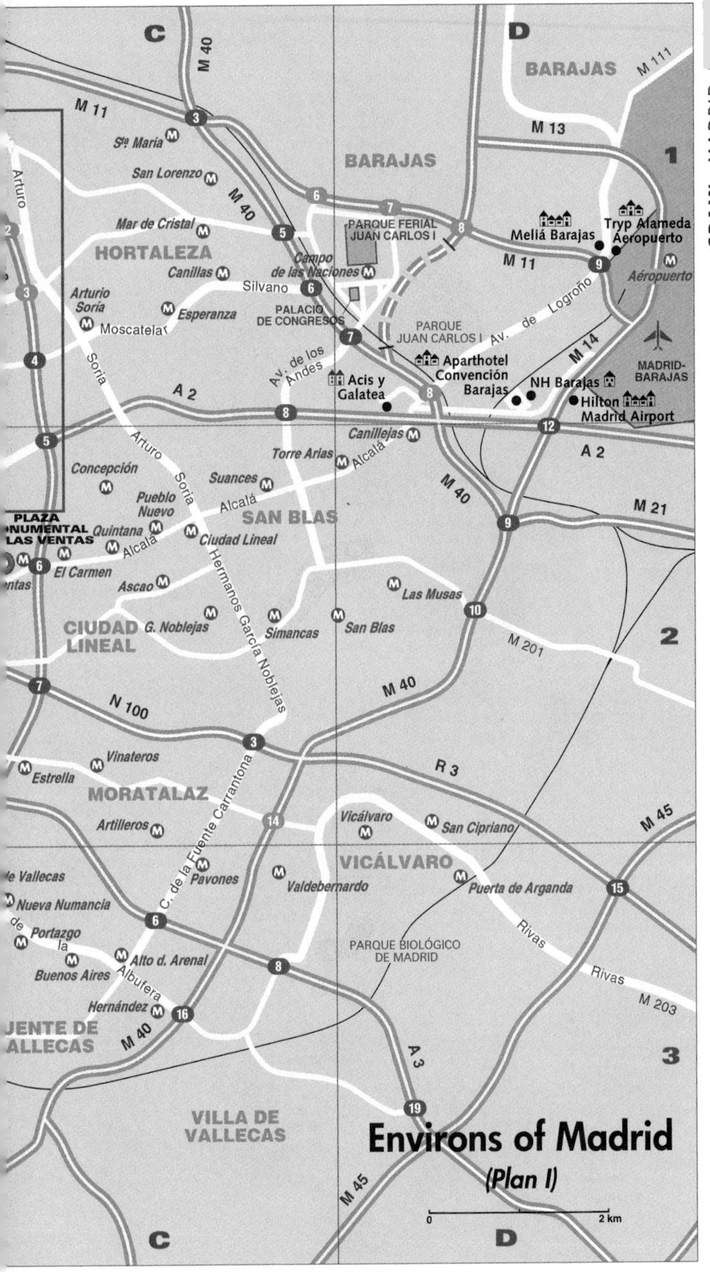

Environs of Madrid
(Plan I)

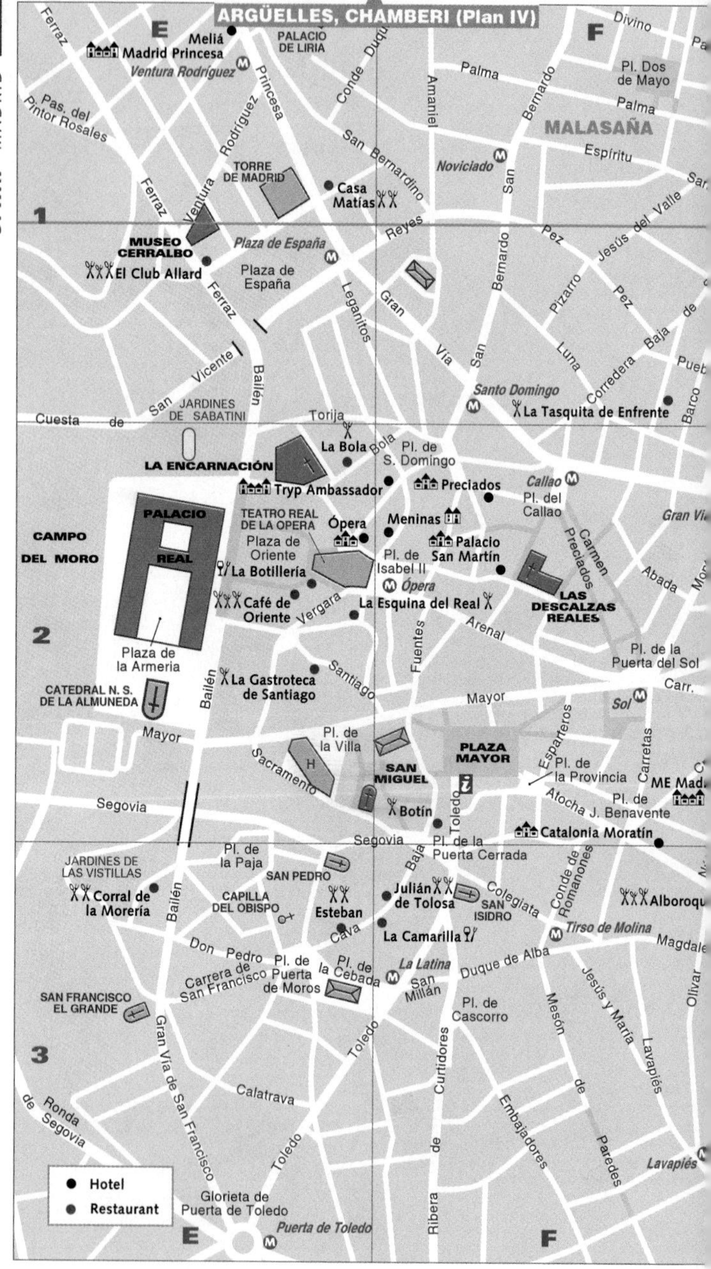
ARGÜELLES, CHAMBERI (Plan IV)
E
F
Meliá
Madrid Princesa
Ventura Rodríguez
PALACIO DE LIRIA
Princesa
Conde Duque
Amaniel
Palma
Bernardo
Pl. Dos de Mayo
Palma
MALASAÑA
Espíritu
Pas. del Pintor Rosales
Ventura Rodríguez
San Bernardino
Noviciado
San
TORRE DE MADRID
Casa Matías
Ferraz
MUSEO CERRALBO
El Club Allard
Plaza de España
Plaza de España
Reyes
San Bernardo
Pez
Jesús del Valle
Pizarro
Pez
Leganitos
Gran Vía
Luna
Baja de
Corredera
San Vicente
Bailén
Santo Domingo
La Tasquita de Enfrente
Barco
Cuesta de
JARDINES DE SABATINI
Torija
La Bola
Bola
Pl. de S. Domingo
LA ENCARNACIÓN
Tryp Ambassador
Preciados
Callao
Pl. del Callao
PALACIO REAL
CAMPO DEL MORO
TEATRO REAL DE LA OPERA
Ópera
Meninas
Plaza de Oriente
Palacio San Martín
Pl. de Isabel II
Ópera
Carmen
Preciados
La Botillería
Café de Oriente
Vergara
La Esquina del Real
LAS DESCALZAS REALES
Abada
Arenal
Plaza de la Armeria
Fuentes
Pl. de la Puerta del Sol
CATEDRAL N. S. DE LA ALMUNEDA
La Gastroteca de Santiago
Santiago
Mayor
Carr.
Sol
Mayor
Pl. de la Villa
Esparteros
Carretas
PLAZA MAYOR
Sacramento
SAN MIGUEL
Pl. de la Provincia
Pl. de J. Benavente
Atocha
Segovia
Botín
Toledo
Catalonia Moratín
Segovia
Pl. de la Puerta Cerrada
JARDINES DE LAS VISTILLAS
Pl. de la Paja
SAN PEDRO
Corral de la Morería
CAPILLA DEL OBISPO
Esteban
Julián de Tolosa
SAN ISIDRO
Colegiata
Conde de Romanones
Tirso de Molina
Cava
La Camarilla
Don Pedro
Carrera de San Francisco
Pl. de Puerta de Moros
Pl. de la Cebada
La Latina
San Millán
Duque de Alba
Magdale
SAN FRANCISCO EL GRANDE
Pl. de Cascorro
Mesón de Paredes
Jesús y María
Lavapiés
Olivar
Gran Vía de San Francisco
Toledo
Curtidores
Embajadores
3
Calatrava
Ronda de Segovia
Ribera de Curtidores
Lavapiés
Hotel
Restaurant
Glorieta de Puerta de Toledo
Puerta de Toledo
1
2

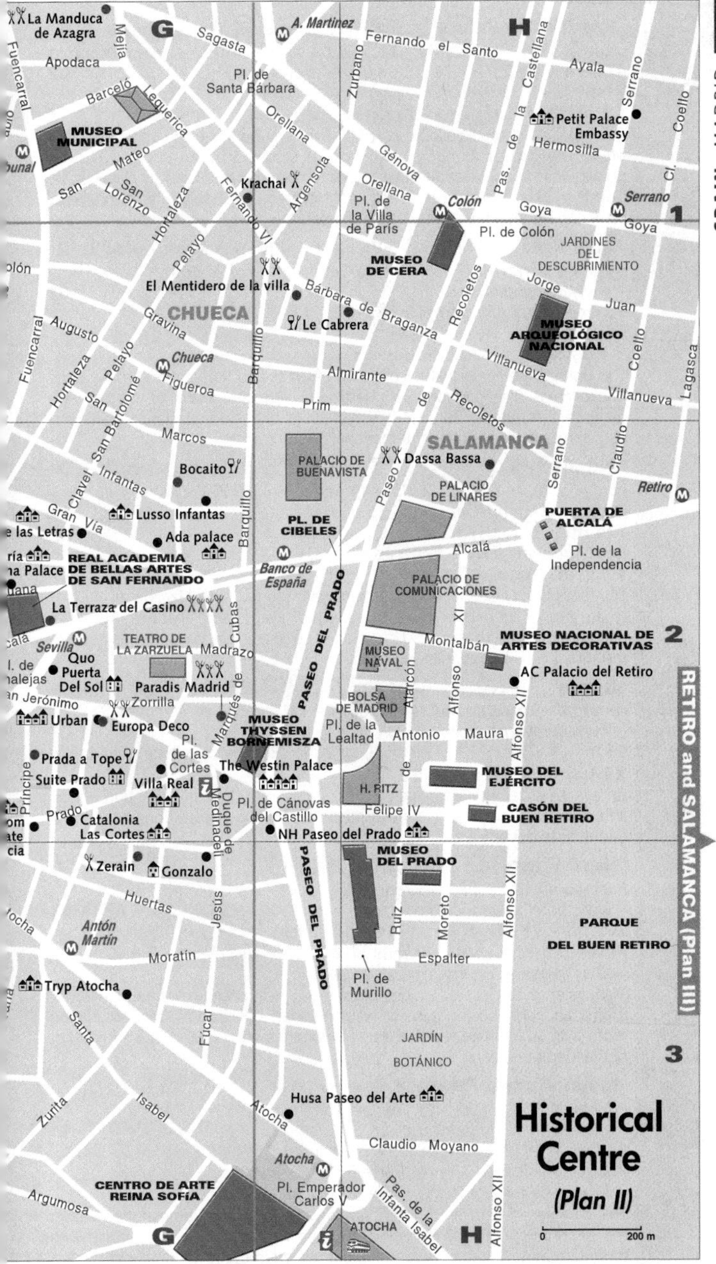
La Manduca de Azagra
Sagasta
A. Martinez
Fernando el Santo
Ayala
Pl. de Santa Bárbara
MUSEO MUNICIPAL
Petit Palace Embassy
Hermosilla
Krachai
Colón
Goya
Serrano
Pl. de Colón
JARDINES DEL DESCUBRIMIENTO
MUSEO DE CERA
El Mentidero de la villa
Le Cabrera
CHUECA
Chueca
MUSEO ARQUEOLÓGICO NACIONAL
SALAMANCA
Dassa Bassa
PALACIO DE BUENAVISTA
PALACIO DE LINARES
Bocaito
Lusso Infantas
Ada palace
PL. DE CIBELES
PUERTA DE ALCALÁ
Pl. de la Independencia
Retiro
REAL ACADEMIA DE BELLAS ARTES DE SAN FERNANDO
Banco de España
PALACIO DE COMUNICACIONES
La Terraza del Casino
Sevilla
TEATRO DE LA ZARZUELA
MUSEO NAVAL
MUSEO NACIONAL DE ARTES DECORATIVAS
Quo Puerta Del Sol
Paradis Madrid
AC Palacio del Retiro
BOLSA DE MADRID
Urban
Europa Deco
MUSEO THYSSEN BORNEMISZA
Pl. de la Lealtad
Prada a Tope
Suite Prado
Villa Real
The Westin Palace
H. RITZ
MUSEO DEL EJÉRCITO
CASÓN DEL BUEN RETIRO
Catalonia Las Cortes
NH Paseo del Prado
Pl. de Cánovas del Castillo
MUSEO DEL PRADO
Zerain
Gonzalo
PASEO DEL PRADO
Antón Martín
PARQUE DEL BUEN RETIRO
Tryp Atocha
Pl. de Murillo
JARDÍN BOTÁNICO
Husa Paseo del Arte
Atocha
CENTRO DE ARTE REINA SOFÍA
Pl. Emperador Carlos V
ATOCHA
Historical Centre (Plan II)
0
200 m
RETIRO and SALAMANCA (Plan III)

CENTRE

Plan II

The Westin Palace

pl. de las Cortes 7 ✉ 28014 – Ⓜ Sevilla – ✆ 913 60 80 00 – www.westin.com

421 rm – ††225/1740 €, ☕ 34 € – 47 suites **G2**

Rest – Carte 32/37 €

♦ Palace ♦ Luxury ♦ Classic ♦

This elegant, historic building is located directly opposite the Spanish parliament. The circular lounge/dining room is crowned by an impressive glass dome, while the superb guestrooms are furnished in an elegantly classic style. Guests in The Westin Palace's restaurant can enjoy suitably international à la carte choices along with a variety of themed menus.

Villa Real

pl. de las Cortes 10 ✉ 28014 – Ⓜ Sevilla – ✆ 914 20 37 67 – www.derbyhotels.com **G2**

96 rm – †145/385 € ††145/430 €, ☕ 21 € – 19 suites

Rest *East 47* – Menu 32 €

♦ Business ♦ Personalised ♦

This hotel displays a valuable collection of Greek and Roman art in many of its public areas. The comfortable guestrooms are attractively decorated with mahogany furniture. This informal restaurant with an abundance of natural light serves cuisine with an international flavour.

ME Madrid

pl. de Santa Ana 14 ✉ 28012 – Ⓜ Sevilla – ✆ 91 701 60 00 – www.memadrid.com **F2**

174 rm – ††165/369 €, ☕ 25 € – 18 suites

Rest *Midnight Rose* – Carte approx. 40 €

♦ Chain hotel ♦ Design ♦

The focus is very clearly on design here, with the traditional façade giving way to an interior embellished with a variety of avant-garde features. Attractive panoramic bar on the roof. Contemporary cuisine is the theme in this modern restaurant with an open-view kitchen.

Urban

carrera de San Jerónimo 34 ✉ 28014 – Ⓜ Sevilla – ✆ 917 87 77 70 – www.derbyhotels.com **G2**

96 rm – †175/425 € ††175/475 €, ☕ 21 € **Rest *Europa Decó*** – see below

♦ Business ♦ Design ♦

An avant-garde hotel with high quality furnishings, attractive lighting effects and numerous works of art on display. Well-equipped guestrooms with real attention to detail.

Husa Princesa

Princesa 40 ✉ 28008 – Ⓜ Argüelles – ✆ 915 42 21 00 – www.hotelhusaprincesa.com Plan IV **K3**

263 rm – ††160/350 €, ☕ 20 € – 12 suites

Rest – *(closed August, Sunday and Monday dinner)* Menu 55 €

♦ Business ♦ Chain hotel ♦ Classic ♦

Magnificent hotel located on one of the city's main avenues. It has large public rooms and spacious, extremely well-equipped guestrooms. Modern dining room with an intimate feel and a menu featuring traditional dishes with a hint of the Mediterranean.

Meliá Madrid Princesa

Princesa 27 ✉ 28008 – Ⓜ Ventura Rodríguez – ✆ 915 41 82 00 – www.meliamadridprincesa.com **E1**

237 rm – ††120/311 €, ☕ 25 € – 27 suites

Rest *Uno* – *(closed August)* Carte 35/53 €

♦ Business ♦ Modern ♦

This completely renovated hotel boasts a spacious lobby embellished with a mix of contemporary furniture and antiques. Well-appointed guestrooms with a modern feel. A contemporary menu is served in the restaurant, and there is a lounge area for tapas.

Tryp Ambassador

cuesta de Santo Domingo 5 28013 – Santo Domingo – 915 41 67 00 – www.solmelia.com **E-F2**

159 rm – 85/220 €, 18 € – 24 suites **Rest** – Carte 45/58 €

♦ Business ♦ Chain hotel ♦ Classic ♦

The Tryp Ambassador has a stately atmosphere with an attractive patio typical of this exclusive district of the city. Comfortable guestrooms with elegant, high quality furniture. Restaurant with a glass ceiling, in the style of a winter garden.

De las Letras

Gran Vía 11 28013 – Gran Vía – 915 23 79 80 – www.hoteldelasletras.com **G2**

108 rm – 119/415 €, 18 € **Rest** – Menu 20 €

♦ Business ♦ Design ♦

The restored exterior contrasts with a contemporary, colourful interior. The guestrooms are described as having a 'New York' style with intimate lighting and poems on the walls. The cuisine in this modern restaurant, which practically forms one room with the lounge-bar, is mainly focused around two menus.

María Elena Palace

Aduana 19 28013 – Sol – 913 60 49 30 – www.chh.es **G2**

87 rm – 100/250 € 120/450 €, 18 €

Rest – Menu 19 €

♦ Traditional ♦ Business ♦ Classic ♦

This hotel has an open lobby and a magnificent patio crowned by a glass dome. Classical-style bedrooms with quality furnishings, carpets and marble baths. The cuisine in this hotel's traditional yet welcoming restaurant is based on contemporary à la carte choices and a daily set menu.

NH Paseo del Prado

pl. Cánovas del Castillo 4 28014 – Banco de España – 913 30 24 00 – www.nh-hotels.com **G2**

114 rm – 89/514 €, 27 €

Rest *Estado Puro* – Carte approx. 25 €

♦ Chain hotel ♦ Business ♦ Classic ♦

This chain hotel enjoys an excellent location and as such is perfect for business and leisure travellers. Although a little on the small side, the guestrooms are of a high quality with modern furnishings. This lively restaurant offers a varied choice of raciones, classic tapas and main dishes.

Ópera

cuesta de Santo Domingo 2 28013 – Ópera – 91 541 28 00 – www.hotelopera.com **E2**

79 rm – 80/162 € 85/280 €, 15 €

Rest *El Café de La Ópera* – *(closed August)* Carte approx. 60 €

♦ Business ♦ Modern ♦

This hotel has a traditional bar with a lively ambience, one multi-purpose breakfast room and one room for meetings. Modern bedrooms with contemporary furnishings. One of the specific attractions of this restaurant is its live evening performances of opera and zarzuela.

Catalonia Las Cortes

Prado 6 28014 – Antón Martín – 913 89 60 51 – www.hoteles-catalonia.com **G2**

65 rm – 325/525 €, 16 € **Rest** – *(dinner only)* Menu 29 €

♦ Traditional ♦ Classic ♦

This 18C building once belonged to the Dukes of Noblejas. Fully-equipped guestrooms and a bright interior that combines the traditional and modern.

Lusso Infantas rm, AC SAT VISA MC AE

Infantas 29 ✉ 28004 – Ⓜ Chueca – ✆ 915 21 28 28 – www.hotelinfantas.com **G2**

40 rm – ††70/233 €, ☕ 15.15 €

Rest *Ex Libris* – Carte 31/47 €

♦ Business ♦ Modern ♦

The Infantas occupies an old building that has been completely renovated in contemporary-style. Well-appointed guestrooms and bathrooms. A minimalist-style restaurant serving creative cuisine, with the decor provided by ex libris on the walls.

Palacio San Martín without rest

pl. San Martín 5 ✉ 28013 – Ⓜ Callao – ✆ 917 01 50 00 – www.intur.com

93 rm – ††72/250 €, ☕ 12 € – 1 suite **F2**

♦ Business ♦ Stylish ♦

The hotel's lounge area occupies several corners of the hotel as well as the central patio, crowned by a glass roof. Varying sizes of guestrooms, all kitted out in classic furnishings.

Husa Paseo del Arte rm,

Atocha 123 ✉ 28012 – Ⓜ Atocha – ✆ 912 98 48 00 – www.husa.es

254 rm – ††90/220 €, ☕ 19.50 € – 6 suites **G3**

Rest – *(closed August)* Menu 22 €

♦ Business ♦ Functional ♦

As the name suggests, this hotel is extremely well placed for visiting Madrid's most famous museums. Bright and airy public areas and functional, high quality bedrooms. The restaurant occupies the interior patio with its glass ceiling and small garden.

Room Mate Alicia without rest

Prado 2 ✉ 28014 – Ⓜ Sevilla – ✆ 913 89 60 95 – www.room-matehotels.com **G2**

34 rm ☕ – †90/130 € ††100/170 €

♦ Business ♦ Modern ♦

The façade of this restored old building contrasts sharply with the modern interior. Contemporary guestrooms, some with a duplex layout, all of which are very urban in style.

Ada Palace rm,

Marqués de Valdeiglesias 1 ✉ 28004 – Ⓜ Banco de España – ✆ 91 701 19 19 – www.chh.es **G2**

80 rm – †90/260 € ††120/320 €, ☕ 15 €

Rest *Ágora* – Menu 22 €

♦ Historic ♦ Business ♦ Classic ♦

The Ada Palace occupies an historic building, which brings with it advantages and a few disadvantages, such as the small size of the reception area. Classic bedrooms offering acceptable levels of comfort. The restaurant is situated on the sixth floor, next to the cafeteria and the popular small terraces.

Preciados rm,

Preciados 37 ✉ 28013 – Ⓜ Callao – ✆ 914 54 44 00 – www.preciadoshotel.com **F2**

68 rm – †95/160 € ††105/300 €, ☕ 15 € – 5 suites **Rest** – Menu 18 €

♦ Business ♦ Modern ♦

The plain classic architectural style of this building, dating back to the 19C, contrasts with the modern, fully equipped interior. Smallish, cosy lounge area. This versatile restaurant offers a choice between traditional à la carte dining and two set menus.

Tryp Atocha without rest

Atocha 83 ✉ 28012 – Ⓜ Antón Martín – ☎ 913 30 05 00 – www.solmelia.com **G3**

150 rm – †210 € ††280 €, ☕ 16 €

♦ Business ♦ Chain hotel ♦ Functional ♦

Palace-like building from 1913 with modern, functional facilities. Spacious public areas, such as the ballroom with its large windows, and magnificent staircase.

Catalonia Moratín without rest

Atocha 23 ✉ 28012 – Ⓜ Sol – ☎ 913 69 71 71 – www.hoteles-catalonia.com **F2-3**

59 rm – †150/515 € ††190/515 €, ☕ 15 € – 4 suites

♦ Business ♦ Chain hotel ♦ Functional ♦

Housed in an 18C building, this hotel has retained some of its original decor, such as the staircase, and combined them with more modern features. Contemporary-style bedrooms, plus a lounge area occupying the carriage courtyard.

Husa Moncloa

Serrano Jover 1 ✉ 28015 – Ⓜ Argüelles – ☎ 915 42 45 85 – www.hotelhusamoncloa.com *Plan IV* **K3**

146 rm – ††125/230 €, ☕ 15 € – 2 suites

Rest – *(at Hotel Husa Princesa)*

♦ Business ♦ Chain hotel ♦ Functional ♦

This bed and breakfast is an annex to the Husa Princesa hotel, which provides the majority of its services. Spacious, well-equipped rooms.

Suite Prado without rest

Manuel Fernández y González 10 ✉ 28014 – Ⓜ Antón Martín – ☎ 914 20 23 18 – www.suiteprado.com **G2**

9 rm – †75/136 € ††75/195 €, ☕ 14 € – 9 suites

♦ Business ♦ Family ♦ Classic ♦

This hotel has a classic contemporary façade and a delightful old staircase. Family atmosphere and apartment-style bedrooms, each with their own lounge and kitchen.

Meninas without rest

Campomanes 7 ✉ 28005 – Ⓜ Ópera – ☎ 91 541 28 05 – www.hotelmeninas.com **F2**

37 rm – †99/165 € ††119/210 €, ☕ 15 €

♦ Family ♦ Cosy ♦

This hotel occupying a residential building is renowned for its friendly and personalised service. It has a welcoming public area with a library, in addition to modern guestrooms.

Quo Puerta del Sol without rest

Sevilla 4 ✉ 28014 – Ⓜ Sevilla – ☎ 915 32 90 49 – www.hotelesquo.com

61 rm – †80/245 € ††80/305 €, ☕ 17 € – 1 suite **G2**

♦ Business ♦ Design ♦

This hotel has small but well-appointed guestrooms decorated in attractive minimalist style. Limited lounge area.

Gonzalo without rest

Cervantes 34-3º ✉ 28014 – Ⓜ Antón Martín – ☎ 914 29 27 14 – www.hostalgonzalo.com **G3**

15 rm – †45 € ††55 €

♦ Business ♦ Family ♦ Functional ♦

This typical, family-run guesthouse occupies a residential building in the Las Letras district. Spacious guestrooms with simple, functional furnishings.

XXXX ✿✿ **La Terraza del Casino** (Paco Roncero)
Alcalá 15-3° ✉ 28014 – Ⓜ Sevilla – ☎ 91 532 12 75 – www.casinodemadrid.es – closed August, Saturday lunch, Sunday and Bank Holidays **G2**
Rest – Menu 120 € – Carte 70/85 €
Spec. Salmón marinado en miso con ensalada de piña, pepino e hinojo. Bogavante con arroz de aceite de oliva. Jarrete de ternera con papillote de verduras.
♦ Innovative ♦ Elegant ♦
This palatial 19C building is home to one of the most prestigious terraces in Madrid and has a decor that is more contemporary in style. The chef has created a modern, inventive à la carte menu that always showcases the very best ingredients and perfectly prepared dishes.

XXX ✿ **El Club Allard** (Diego Guerrero)
Ferraz 2 ✉ 28008 – Ⓜ Plaza España – ☎ 915 59 09 39 – www.elclub allard.com – Closed August, Saturday lunch, Sunday, Monday dinner and Bank Holidays
Rest – *(set menu only)* Menu 61/74 € **E1**
Spec. Mini babybell de Camembert trufado. Raviolis de alubias de Tolosa con infusión de berza. Rodaballo salvaje con cebolleta tierna al aroma de albahaca.
♦ Innovative ♦ Formal ♦
Located in a listed Modernist building, hence the lack of signage outside, this restaurant occupies an elegant dining room with a traditional atmosphere. The creative cuisine demonstrates a high level of technical expertise, including an interesting fusion of different products and delicate presentation.

XXX **Alboroque**
Atocha 34 ✉ 28012 – Ⓜ Antón Martín – ☎ 91 389 65 70 – www.alboroque.es – closed Sunday **F3**
Rest – Carte 40/45 €
♦ Modern ♦ Trendy ♦
Access to this restaurant, which occupies two of the building's wings, is via the carriage patio. Eating in one of the charming small dining rooms here is both a cultural and gastronomic experience with an emphasis on contemporary cuisine.

XXX **Paradis Madrid**
Marqués de Cubas 14 ✉ 28014 – Ⓜ Banco de España – ☎ 914 29 73 03 – www.paradis.es – closed Saturday lunch, Sunday and Bank Holidays **G2**
Rest – Carte 40/55 €
♦ Mediterranean ♦ Classic ♦
A modern restaurant next to the conference centre, with access via a delicatessen shop. Spacious dining room plus a tapas area.

XXX **Café de Oriente**
pl. de Oriente 2 ✉ 28013 – Ⓜ Ópera – ☎ 915 41 39 74 – www.grupolezama.es **E2**
Rest – Carte 40/57 €
♦ Traditional ♦ Formal ♦
This famous address opposite the royal palace offers its guests several different atmospheres including a luxurious cafeteria, an attractive wine bar-cum-dining room, and a number of elegant private rooms. The traditional à la carte menu shows the influence of the Basque country.

XXX **La Manduca de Azagra**
Sagasta 14 ✉ 28004 – Ⓜ Alonso Martínez – ☎ 915 91 01 12 – closed August, Sunday and Bank Holidays **G1**
Rest – Carte 45/50 €
♦ Traditional ♦ Minimalist ♦
This spacious, well-located restaurant is decorated in minimalist style with particular attention paid to the design and lighting. The menu focuses on high quality produce.

XX **El Mentidero de la Villa**

Santo Tomé 6 ✉ 28004 – Ⓜ Chueca – ☎ 913 08 12 85
– www.mentiderodelavilla.es
– closed August, Saturday lunch, Sunday, Monday dinner and Bank Holidays
Rest – Carte 43/55 € **G1**

♦ Modern ♦ Cosy ♦

A charming and intimate restaurant combining neat table settings and an original decor. The à la carte menu of traditional cuisine with a modern twist comes highly recommended.

XX **Casa Matías**

San Leonardo 12 ✉ 28015 – Ⓜ Plaza de España – ☎ 915 41 76 83
– www.casamatias.es – closed Sunday dinner **E1**
Rest – Carte 43/49 €

♦ Grills ♦ Rustic ♦

Decorated in the style of a Basque cider bar with large barrels from which customers can pour cider. Two spacious dining rooms in a rustic, modern style and a grill visible to diners.

XX **Julián de Tolosa**

Cava Baja 18 ✉ 28005 – Ⓜ La Latina – ☎ 913 65 82 10
– www.casajuliandetolosa.com – closed Sunday dinner **F3**
Rest – Carte 47/58 €

♦ Grills ♦ Rustic ♦

This famous carvery restaurant serves some of the best T-bone steaks in the city. The neo-rustic-style decor provides a backdrop for a concise menu based around high-quality ingredients.

XX **Europa Decó** – Hotel Urban

carrera de San Jerónimo 34 ✉ 28014 – Ⓜ Sevilla – ☎ 917 87 77 80
– www.derbyhotels.com
– closed August, Saturday lunch and Sunday **G2**
Rest – Carte approx. 50 €

♦ Innovative ♦ Fashionable ♦

Increasingly popular for its innovative design and excellent service. Mediterranean and ethnic cuisine prepared using fresh and exotic produce.

XX **Corral de la Morería**

Morería 17 ✉ 28005 – Ⓜ Ópera – ☎ 913 65 84 46
– www.corraldelamoreria.com **E3**
Rest – *(dinner only)* Carte 52/75 €

♦ Spanish ♦ Musical ♦

Restaurant with a high quality flamenco show. The closely packed tables are grouped around the stage. À la carte options, as well as various gastronomic menus.

XX **Esteban**

Cava Baja 36 ✉ 28005 – Ⓜ La Latina – ☎ 913 65 90 91
– www.rte-esteban.com
– closed 20 July-10 August, Sunday dinner, Monday dinner and Tuesday dinner
Rest – Carte 40/51 € **E3**

♦ Terroir ♦ Classic ♦

A welcoming hotel decorated in typical Castilian style with photos of famous characters on the walls. The restaurant serves traditional cuisine.

X **La Tasquita de Enfrente**

Ballesta 6 ✉ 28004 – Ⓜ Gran Vía – ☎ 91 532 54 49
– www.latasquitadeenfrente.com
– closed Holy Week, August, Sunday and Monday **F1**
Rest – *(booking essential)* Carte 56/68 €

♦ Traditional ♦ Family ♦

This small family-run restaurant continues to attract a loyal clientele. Enjoy the good, seasonal cuisine produced with simplicity, great care and intelligence.

X

La Esquina del Real

A/C VISA MC AE

Amnistía 4 ✉ 28013 – Ⓜ Ópera – ✆ 915 59 43 09
– closed 15 August-15 September, Saturday lunch, Sunday and Bank Holidays
Rest – Carte 40/50 € **E-F2**

♦ International ♦ Cosy ♦

A charming and intimate restaurant decorated in rustic style with stone and brick walls. Good service and an attractive menu with an emphasis on French cuisine.

X

Zerain

A/C VISA MC AE

Quevedo 3 ✉ 28014 – Ⓜ Antón Martín – ✆ 914 29 79 09
– www.restaurante-vasco-zerain-sidreria.es
– closed Sunday dinner **G3**
Rest – Carte 40/49 €

♦ Basque cuisine ♦ Rustic ♦

Typical Basque cider bar decorated with large barrels. Friendly atmosphere and cheerful decor with photographs of typical towns and villages. Affordable menu with an emphasis on roasted meats.

X

Krachai

A/C VISA MC AE

Fernando VI-11 ✉ 28004 – Ⓜ Alonso Martínez – ✆ 918 33 65 56
– www.krachai.es – closed August and Sunday dinner **G1**
Rest – Carte 25/35 €

♦ Thai ♦ Exotic ♦

The Krachai is split between two dining rooms, each with attractive lighting and a contemporary feel. The Thai cuisine on offer is listed on the menu according to the way it is prepared.

X

La Gastroteca de Santiago

A/C VISA MC AE

pl. Santiago 1 ✉ 28013 – Ⓜ Ópera – ✆ 915 48 07 07
– closed Holy Week, 15-31 August, Sunday dinner and Monday **E2**
Rest – Carte approx. 55 €

♦ Contemporary ♦ Cosy ♦

A small, cosy restaurant with two large French windows and a modern decor. Friendly staff, contemporary cuisine and a kitchen that is partially visible to diners.

X

La Bola

A/C

Bola 5 ✉ 28013 – Ⓜ Santo Domingo – ✆ 915 47 69 30 – www.labola.es
– closed Saturday dinner and Sunday in summer and Sunday dinner for rest of the year **E2**
Rest – Carte 30/35 €

♦ Spanish ♦ Traditional ♦

This family-run restaurant maintains the typical culinary traditions of old Madrid. The interior is traditional in character with old photos on the walls. If stews are your thing, make sure you order the cocido madrileño!

X

Botín

A/C VISA MC AE

Cuchilleros 17 ✉ 28005 – Ⓜ Sol – ✆ 913 66 42 17 – www.botin.es
Rest – Carte 35/45 € **F2**

♦ Spanish ♦ Rustic ♦

Founded in 1725, Botín has made it to the Guinness Book of Records as the oldest restaurant in the world. Its decor evokes the essence of old Madrid.

Le Cabrera

A/C VISA MC AE

Bárbara de Braganza 2 ✉ 28004 – Ⓜ Colón – ✆ 91 319 94 57
– www.lecabrera.com
– closed 8-23 August, Sunday and Monday **H1**
Ración approx. 8 €

♦ Modern ♦ Design ♦ Fashionable ♦

This original restaurant with its trendy decor is divided into two sections. One has access to the chef who prepares dishes behind a counter, and the other, in the basement, is designed primarily for drinks.

La Botillería del Café de Oriente

pl. de Oriente 4 ✉ 28013 – Ⓜ Ópera – ☏ 915 48 46 20 – www.grupolezama.es **E2**

Tapa 4 € **Ración** approx. 10 €

♦ Spanish ♦ Tapas bar ♦

Situated in a lively area of bars and restaurants. This Viennese-style café serves a wide variety of snacks and canapés, as well as excellent wines by the glass.

La Camarilla

Cava Baja 21 ✉ 28005 – Ⓜ Latina – ☏ 913 54 02 07 – www.lacamarillarestaurante.com – closed 4-22 July and Wednesday **F3**

Tapa 4 € **Ración** approx. 12 €

♦ Spanish ♦ Tapas bar ♦

La Camarilla is a good choice in the city for tapas and raciones. The large tapas-laden bar at the entrance leads to a modern and informal dining room.

Prada a Tope

Príncipe 11 ✉ 28012 – Ⓜ Sevilla – ☏ 914 29 59 21 – www.pradaatope.es – closed Sunday dinner and Monday **G2**

Tapa 6 € **Ración** approx. 10 €

♦ Spanish ♦ Tapas bar ♦

This restaurant follows the typical decor found throughout this chain. A bar, rustic-style tables and a plethora of wood in the dining room, which is adorned with old photos and typical products from the El Bierzo region.

Bocaito

Libertad 6 ✉ 28004 – Ⓜ Chueca – ☏ 915 32 12 19 – www.bocaito.com – closed August, Saturday lunch and Sunday **G2**

Tapa 2.80 € **Ración** approx. 11 €

♦ Spanish ♦ Tapas bar ♦

This restaurant is split between two premises which are connected to each other. Four dining rooms in total, each furnished in rustic Castilian style with a few bullfighting mementoes as part of the decor. Traditional cuisine.

Taberna de San Bernardo

San Bernardo 85 ✉ 28015 – Ⓜ San Bernardo – ☏ 914 45 41 70 – closed Monday *Plan IV* **K3**

Tapa 2 € **Ración** approx. 7 €

♦ Spanish ♦ Tapas bar ♦

A tavern-style bar with an authentic atmosphere. Large bar, a main dining room and two private rooms, the one in the basement surrounded by exposed brick walls. Popular dishes include papas con huevo (potatoes and eggs) and fritura de verduras (fried vegetables).

Kulto al Plato

Serrano Jover 1 ✉ 28015 – Ⓜ Argüelles – ☏ 91 758 59 46 – www.kultoalplato.com – closed Sunday *Plan IV* **K3**

Tapa 3.50 € **Ración** approx. 12.50 €

♦ Spanish ♦ Tapas bar ♦

This tapas bar is distributed over several levels. There are two table areas, one for the tapas tasting menus and the other, with higher tables, for nibbles.

RETIRO – SALAMANCA *Plan III*

Ritz

pl. de la Lealtad 5 ✉ 28014 – Ⓜ Banco de España – ☏ 917 01 67 67 – www.ritzmadrid.com **I2**

137 rm – ††350/700 €, ☕ 30 € – 30 suites **Rest** – Menu 61 €

♦ Grand Luxury ♦ Stylish ♦

This elegant, internationally renowned hotel occupies an early 20C mansion. Stunning lounge areas, with lavish decor in the guestrooms. The Ritz's restaurant boasts an elegant dining room and pleasant summer terrace.

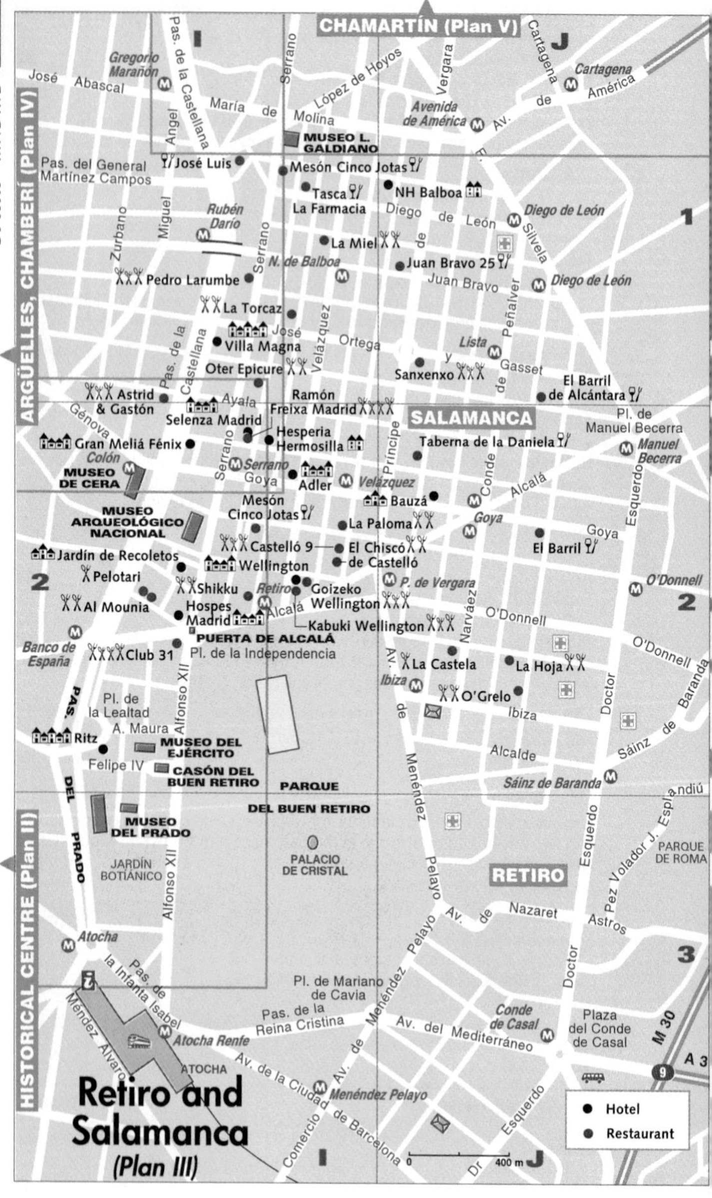
CHAMARTÍN (Plan V)
ARGÜELLES, CHAMBERÍ (Plan IV)
HISTORICAL CENTRE (Plan II)
SALAMANCA
RETIRO
MUSEO L. GALDIANO
MUSEO DE CERA
MUSEO ARQUEOLÓGICO NACIONAL
PUERTA DE ALCALÁ
MUSEO DEL EJÉRCITO
CASÓN DEL BUEN RETIRO
MUSEO DEL PRADO
PARQUE DEL BUEN RETIRO
PALACIO DE CRISTAL
JARDÍN BOTÁNICO
ATOCHA
José Luis
Mesón Cinco Jotas
Tasca La Farmacia
NH Balboa
La Miel
Juan Bravo 25
Pedro Larumbe
La Torcaz
Villa Magna
Oter Epicure
Sanxenxo
El Barril de Alcántara
Astrid & Gastón
Selenza Madrid
Freixa Madrid
Gran Meliá Fénix
Hesperia Hermosilla
Taberna de la Daniela
Adler
Bauzá
Mesón Cinco Jotas
La Paloma
Jardín de Recoletos
Castelló 9
El Chiscó de Castelló
El Barril
Wellington
Pelotari
Shikku
Goizeko Wellington
Al Mounia
Hospes Madrid
Kabuki Wellington
Club 31
La Castela
La Hoja
O'Grelo
Ritz
Plaza del Conde de Casal
PARQUE DE ROMA
Retiro and Salamanca (Plan III)
Hotel
Restaurant
0
400 m

Villa Magna

paseo de la Castellana 22 ✉ 28046 – Ⓜ Rubén Darío – ☎ 915 87 12 34 – www.hotelvillamagna.com **I1**

164 rm – 🛉300/550 € 🛉🛉300/610 €, ☕ 37 € – 17 suites

Rest *Villa Magna* – *(closed August, Sunday and Bank Holidays)* Carte approx. 75 €

Rest *Tsé Yang* – *(chinese restaurant)* Carte approx. 70 €

♦ Luxury ♦ Classic ♦

After a major renovation, this has a much brighter social area and contemporary-style bedrooms. Top floor suites boast stunning terraces. Enjoy delicious, innovative cuisine at the Villa Magna restaurant.

Hospes Madrid

pl. de la Independencia 3 ✉ 28001 – Ⓜ Retiro – ☎ 914 32 29 11 – www.hospes.es **I2**

40 rm – 🛉🛉162/589 €, ☕ 23.75 € – 1 suite

Rest – *(closed Sunday and Monday)* Menu 45 €

♦ Luxury ♦ Contemporary ♦

This establishment is set in a building dating from 1883, with the lobby occupying what was once the carriage entrance. Many of the modern bedrooms overlook the Puerta de Alcalá. There are two meeting rooms and a spa. This restaurant has a modern layout and serves a menu of contemporary cuisine.

Gran Meliá Fénix

Hermosilla 2 ✉ 28001 – Ⓜ Serrano – ☎ 914 31 67 00 – www.granmeliafenix.com **I2**

199 rm – 🛉165/395 € 🛉🛉175/405 €, ☕ 26 € – 16 suites

Rest – Menu 65 €

♦ Luxury ♦ Stylish ♦

This smart, distinctive hotel has bedrooms in an elegant, classical style equipped to a very high standard. Spacious public areas, including an impressive lounge crowned by a domed ceiling. This restaurant has a relaxed atmosphere and serves cuisine with Mediterranean overtones.

Wellington

Velázquez 8 ✉ 28001 – Ⓜ Retiro – ☎ 915 75 44 00 – www.hotel-wellington.com **I2**

233 rm – 🛉140/325 € 🛉🛉140/415 €, ☕ 22 € – 28 suites

Rest *Kabuki Wellington y Rest Goizeko Wellington* – see below

♦ Luxury ♦ Classic ♦

In an elegant district near the Retiro Park. Classic in style with recently modernised lounges and guestrooms. A popular haunt for bullfighting aficionados.

Adler

Velázquez 33 ✉ 28001 – Ⓜ Velázquez – ☎ 914 26 32 20 – www.hoteladler.es **I2**

44 rm – 🛉250/400 € 🛉🛉300/495 €, ☕ 27 € **Rest** – Carte 60/80 €

♦ Luxury ♦ Stylish ♦

This exclusive, select hotel has an elegant interior decorated with high quality furnishings. Comfortable guestrooms equipped to the highest standard. Restaurant with a charming atmosphere and impressive attention to detail in its decor.

AC Palacio del Retiro

Alfonso XII-14 ✉ 28014 – Ⓜ Retiro – ☎ 915 23 74 60 – www.ac-hotels.com *Plan II* **H2**

49 rm – 🛉210/305 € 🛉🛉220/340 €, ☕ 29 € – 1 suite

Rest – Carte approx. 47 €

♦ Business ♦ Classic ♦

Early-20C mansion with a reception area situated in what was once a passageway for horse-drawn carriages. Elegant public area and superb guestrooms. The restaurant, which is clearly focused towards the hotel's guests, serves a mix of traditional and contemporary dishes.

Selenza Madrid

Claudio Coello 67 ✉ *28001* – Ⓜ *Serrano* – ☎ *917 810 173 – www.selenzahoteles.es* **I2**

44 rm – ††175/230 €, ☕ 20 €

Rest *Ramón Freixa Madrid* – see below

◆ Business ◆ Contemporary ◆

Behind this establishment's attractive, classical façade is a designer reception hall and an elegant social area. The comfortable bedrooms all have classical, avant-garde elements.

Vincci Soma

Goya 79 ✉ *28001* – Ⓜ *Goya* – ☎ *914 35 75 45 – www.vinccihoteles.com*

169 rm – †57/464 € ††78/486 €, ☕ 17.30 € **J2**

Rest – *(closed August)* Menu 25 €

◆ Business ◆ Modern ◆

This centrally located hotel has modern facilities. It offers fully equipped guest-rooms, some of which have their own terrace. There is also an attractive lounge-library with a fireplace. This bright, modern restaurant is decorated in varying shades of white. It serves innovative, creative cuisine.

Petit Palace Embassy

Serrano 46 ✉ *28001* – Ⓜ *Serrano* – ☎ *914 31 30 60 – www.hthoteles.com*

75 rm – ††108/648 €, ☕ 17.30 € **H1**

Rest – *(closed August)* Menu 35 €

◆ Chain hotel ◆ Functional ◆

A combination of a beautiful 19C building with a designer interior, resulting in a bold but cosy atmosphere. Fully equipped bedrooms, each with a computer. This restaurant has the feel of a long and bright covered patio. One private dining room available.

Jardín de Recoletos

Gil de Santivañes 4 ✉ *28001* – Ⓜ *Serrano* – ☎ *917 81 16 40 – www.vphoteles.com* **I2**

43 rm ☕ – ††129/220 € **Rest** – Menu 25 €

◆ Traditional ◆ Classic ◆

Attractive façade with balustraded balconies. The hotel has an elegant reception hall with a glass ceiling, large studio-style guestrooms and an attractive patio-terrace. This small, classic-style dining room has a menu based around traditional cuisine.

NH Balboa without rest

Núñez de Balboa 112 ✉ *28006* – Ⓜ *Núñez de Balboa* – ☎ *915 63 03 24 – www.nh-hotels.com* **J1**

120 rm – †75/250 € ††90/300 €, ☕ 17 €

◆ Chain hotel ◆ Functional ◆

Beyond its compact foyer the Balboa has a multi-purpose area that acts as a breakfast room, reading room and bar. Most of the hotel's guestrooms have been renovated.

Hesperia Hermosilla without rest

Hermosilla 23 ✉ *28001* – Ⓜ *Serrano – ☎ 912 46 88 00 – www.hesperia-hermosilla.es* **I2**

67 rm – ††68/232 €, ☕ 16.15 €

◆ Chain hotel ◆ Business ◆ Functional ◆

This contemporary-style hotel is in a building from the early 20C. Find a cosy, glass-roofed patio, beautiful staircase, and comfortable bedrooms with fabrics covering the walls.

Club 31

Alcalá 58 ✉ *28014* – Ⓜ *Retiro* – ☎ *915 31 00 92 – www.club31.net – closed August* **I2**

Rest – Carte 50/65 €

◆ International ◆ Elegant ◆

This prestigious restaurant in the city has an interior decor combining the traditional and modern. Well-balanced menu based around international cuisine.

XXXX
✿✿

Ramón Freixa Madrid – Hotel Selenza Madrid

Claudio Coello 67 ✉ 28001 – Ⓜ Serrano – ✆ 917 81 82 62 – www.ramonfreixamadrid.com – closed Christmas, Holy Week, August, Sunday and Monday **I2**

Rest – Carte 71/88 €

Spec. Ostra a la plancha con corazones de lechuga, tartar de rubio sobre patata, torta de camarón y caldo de almejas. Salmonetes asados, habitas y guisantes, torrija al laurel, anchoa y piquillos con migas (primavera). Liebre a la royal (invierno).

♦ Inventive ♦ Design ♦

This modern restaurant has a few pleasantly arranged tables that are supplemented by an attractive terrace in summer. The cuisine is creative, well-balanced and beautifully presented, featuring ingredients of excellent quality.

XXX

Sanxenxo

José Ortega y Gasset 40 ✉ 28006 – Ⓜ Núñez de Balboa – ✆ 915 77 82 72 – www.sanxenxo.com.es – closed Holy Week, August and Sunday dinner **J1**

Rest – Carte 64/77 €

♦ Galician specialities ♦ Formal ♦

This restaurant serves traditional Galician cuisine based on quality fish and seafood. Covering two floors, the superb dining rooms are decorated with a profusion of granite and wood.

XXX

Pedro Larumbe

Serrano 61-2º ✉ 28006 – Ⓜ Rubén Darío – ✆ 915 75 11 12 – www.larumbe.com – closed Holy Week, 15 days in August, Sunday, Monday dinner in winter and Bank Holidays **I1**

Rest – Carte 43/50 €

♦ International ♦ Formal ♦

Housed on the top floor of a mansion, this restaurant has three elegant dining rooms with a unique and tasteful decor. International menu with a creative touch.

XXX

Goizeko Wellington – Hotel Wellington

Villanueva 34 ✉ 28001 – Ⓜ Retiro – ✆ 915 77 01 38 – www.goizekogaztelupe.com – closed Saturday lunch in July-August and Sunday **I2**

Rest – Carte 60/80 €

♦ Spanish ♦ Minimalist ♦

This elegant restaurant decorated in classic-modern style serves traditional, international cuisine with creative touches. Comprehensive wine list.

XXX
✿

Kabuki Wellington (Ricardo Sanz) – Hotel Wellington

Velázquez 6 ✉ 28001 – Ⓜ Retiro – ✆ 915 77 78 77 – www.restaurantekabuki.com – closed Holy Week, 1-21 August, Saturday lunch, Sunday and Bank Holidays

Rest – Menu 85 € – Carte 50/75 € **I2**

Spec. Sashimi de toro. Sushi. Carne de wagyu en salsa teriyaki.

♦ Japanese ♦ Design ♦

This restaurant is creating quite a stir in the Spanish capital. It has a large modern dining room on two levels with a sushi bar and designer-inspired decorative features. Well-prepared and beautifully presented Japanese cuisine with an emphasis on top quality ingredients.

XXX

Castelló 9

Castelló 9 ✉ 28001 – Ⓜ Príncipe de Vergara – ✆ 914 35 00 67 – www.castello9.es – closed Holy Week, August, Sunday and Bank Holidays **I2**

Rest – Carte 38/52 €

♦ International ♦ Formal ♦

An elegant, traditional restaurant in the Salamanca district. It has several intimate dining rooms, a classic international menu and a varied tasting menu.

XXX

Astrid & Gastón

paseo de la Castellana 13 ✉ 28046 – Ⓜ Serrano – ✆ 91 702 62 62 – www.astridygastonmadrid.com – closed Sunday **I1-2**

Rest – Carte 58/63 €

◆ International ◆ Friendly ◆

Extending over two floors, this restaurant has spacious dining areas decorated in contemporary-style. Bar for pre-dinner cocktails, and a menu specialising in Peruvian cuisine.

XX

La Paloma

Jorge Juan 39 ✉ 28001 – Ⓜ Príncipe de Vergara – ✆ 915 76 86 92 – www.rtelapaloma.com – closed Holy Week, August, Sunday and Bank Holidays **I2**

Rest – Carte 52/63 €

◆ International ◆ Fashionable ◆

A professionally run restaurant catering to a sophisticated clientele. Dining room on two levels, where the focus is on international and traditional cuisine. Excellent service.

XX

O'Grelo

Menorca 39 ✉ 28009 – Ⓜ Ibiza – ✆ 914 09 72 04 – www.restauranteogrelo.com – closed Sunday in July-August and Sunday dinner for rest of the year

Rest – Carte 55/61 € **J2**

◆ Galician specialities ◆ Rustic ◆

Enjoy excellent traditional Galician cuisine in this restaurant decorated in a neo-rustic style. Wide selection of fish and seafood and a tapas bar at the entrance.

XX

La Torcaz

Lagasca 81 ✉ 28006 – Ⓜ Núñez de Balboa – ✆ 915 75 41 30 – www.latorcaz.com – closed August and Sunday **I1**

Rest – Carte 45/58 €

◆ International ◆ Formal ◆

Friendly restaurant with an attractive wine display. The dining room, decorated in classical-contemporary style, is divided into three different ambiences. Excellent service and an extensive wine list.

XX

Dassa Bassa

Villalar 7 ✉ 28001 – Ⓜ Retiro – ✆ 915 76 73 97 – www.dassabassa.com – closed Holy Week, August, Sunday and Monday *Plan II* **H2**

Rest – Carte approx. 60 €

◆ Innovative ◆ Design ◆

This restaurant occupying what was once a coal cellar has an attractive foyer, and four modern dining rooms with designer detail. Creative cuisine with a particular focus on interesting flavours.

XX

Oter Epicure

Claudio Coello 71 ✉ 28001 – Ⓜ Serrano – ✆ 914 31 67 70 – www.oterepicure.com – closed Sunday and Bank Holidays dinner

Rest – Carte 42/48 € **I1**

◆ Terroir ◆ Classic ◆

The dining room of this restaurant is decorated in a contemporary-classical style in grey tones. Find a traditional menu, a well-stocked cellar, and a wide selection of cigars.

XX

Al Mounia

Recoletos 5 ✉ 28001 – Ⓜ Banco de España – ✆ 914 35 08 28 – www.almounia.es – closed 25 July-August and Sunday dinner **I2**

Rest – Carte approx. 50 €

◆ North African ◆ Exotic ◆

Exotically decorated restaurant near the National Archaeological Museum. Moroccan decoration with carved woodwork, stucco and typical low tables on carpeted floors. Traditional North African dishes.

Shikku

Lagasca 5 ✉ 28001 – Ⓜ Retiro – ✆ 91 431 93 08 – www.shikku.es – closed 8-22 August and Sunday **I2**

Rest – Carte approx. 55 €

◆ Japanese ◆ Trendy ◆

This restaurant has a bar at its entrance plus a dining room with a modern decor and carpeted floors. Japanese cuisine prepared with high quality ingredients.

La Miel

Maldonado 14 ✉ 28006 – Ⓜ Núñez de Balboa – ✆ 914 35 50 45 – www.restaurantelamiel.com – closed August and Sunday **I1**

Rest – Carte 38/48 €

◆ International ◆ Family ◆

Classic style restaurant with a husband and wife team in the kitchen and dining room. Comfortable dining room, attentive service and international cuisine. Good wine list.

El Chiscón de Castelló

Castelló 3 ✉ 28001 – Ⓜ Príncipe de Vergara – ✆ 915 75 56 62 – www.elchiscon.com – closed August, Sunday and Monday dinner **I2**

Rest – Carte 35/46 €

◆ Traditional ◆ Formal ◆

Behind the typical façade is a warmly decorated interior similar in style to a private home, especially in the first floor dining rooms. Reasonably priced traditional cuisine.

La Hoja

Doctor Castelo 48 ✉ 28009 – Ⓜ O'Donnell – ✆ 914 09 25 22 – www.lahoja.es – closed Sunday **J2**

Rest – Carte 35/50 €

◆ Asturian specialities ◆ Neighbourhood ◆

This restaurant has two classic-style dining rooms. Enjoy generous portions of traditional Asturian cooking, including bean dishes and chicken raised on the owner's farm. Delicatessen shop.

Pelotari

Recoletos 3 ✉ 28001 – Ⓜ Colón – ✆ 915 78 24 97 – www.pelotari-asador.com – closed Sunday **I2**

Rest – Carte 34/46 €

◆ Basque cuisine ◆ Rustic ◆

This typical Basque eatery specialising in roasted meats is run by its owners, with one in the kitchen and the other front of house. Four regional style dining rooms, two of which can be used as private rooms.

La Castela

Doctor Castelo 22 ✉ 28009 – Ⓜ Ibiza – ✆ 915 74 00 15 – www.lacastela.com – closed Holy Week, August and Sunday **J2**

Rest – Carte 35/50 €

◆ Traditional ◆ Classic ◆

A traditional Madrid style tavern with a tapas bar at the entrance. The menu in the traditional dining room is centred on international cuisine.

Juan Bravo 25

Juan Bravo 25 ✉ 28006 – Ⓜ Núñez de Balboa – ✆ 914 11 60 25 – www.juanbravo25.com – closed 15 days in August and Sunday

Tapa 3.50 € **Ración** approx. 18 € **J1**

◆ Traditional ◆ Tapas bar ◆

Large restaurant located on the mezzanine level with a central bar serving Basque style tapas and hors d'oeuvres. The adjoining dining room offers a traditional menu.

José Luis

General Oráa 5 ✉ 28006 – Ⓜ Rubén Darío – ✆ 915 61 64 13 – www.joseluis.es **I1**

Tapa 2.50 € **Ración** approx. 15 €

♦ Spanish ♦ Tapas bar ♦

This famous restaurant is located in a smart part of town. It serves a large choice of appetisers and tapas in an elegant setting with a classic decor.

Mesón Cinco Jotas

Puigcerdá ✉ 28001 – Ⓜ Serrano – ✆ 915 75 41 25 – www.mesoncincojotas.com **I2**

Tapa 3 € **Ración** approx. 15 €

♦ Spanish ♦ Tapas bar ♦

This mesón is renowned for its excellent hams and tapas. The restaurant has a splendid terrace, and three cosy dining rooms spread across three floors.

Tasca La Farmacia

Diego de León 9 ✉ 28006 – Ⓜ Diego de León – ✆ 915 64 86 52 – www.asadordearanda.com – closed 11 July-7 August and Sunday **I1**

Tapa 4.50 € **Ración** approx. 12 €

♦ Codfish specialities ♦ Tapas bar ♦

Traditional style tasca, with a beautifully tiled bar adorned with elegant motifs. House specialities include cod and 'zancarrón' (meat on the bone) tapas and snacks.

Mesón Cinco Jotas

Serrano 118 ✉ 28006 – Ⓜ Núñez de Balboa – ✆ 915 63 27 10 – www.mesoncincojotas.com **I1**

Tapa 5 € **Ración** approx. 12 €

♦ Spanish ♦ Tapas bar ♦

Contemporary-style mesón serving a varied array of tapas, snacks and sandwiches with an emphasis on Spanish hams and pork. Attractive dining room.

El Barril

Goya 86 ✉ 28009 – Ⓜ Goya – ✆ 915 78 39 98 – www.elbarrildegoya.com

Tapa 12 € **Ración** approx. 20 € **J2**

♦ Seafood ♦ Tapas bar ♦

Good seafood restaurant with an air-conditioned bar displaying an impressive range of high quality products. Dining room with a reasonable menu to the rear of the building.

Taberna de la Daniela

General Pardiñas 21 ✉ 28001 – Ⓜ Goya – ✆ 915 75 23 29 **J2**

Tapa 3 € **Ración** approx. 9 €

♦ Spanish ♦ Tapas bar ♦

Typical tavern in the Salamanca district, with a glass façade and several dining rooms. A good place to sample tapas, more substantial snacks, or to try the restaurant's famous stew, the cocido madrileño.

El Barril de Alcántara

Don Ramón de la Cruz 91 ✉ 28006 – Ⓜ Manuel Becerra – ✆ 914 01 33 05 – www.elbarrilalcantara.com **J1**

Tapa 7 € **Ración** approx. 15 €

♦ Seafood ♦ Tapas bar ♦

Renowned seafood restaurant with an excellent reputation for its cuisine and service. Enjoy seafood specialities and snacks either in the pub or in one of the two dining rooms.

ARGÜELLES — *Plan IV*

Mercure Madrid Plaza de España without rest

Tutor 1 ✉ 28008 – Ⓜ Ventura Rodríguez – ☎ 915 41 98 80 – www.mercure.com **K3**

96 rm – 85/330 € 85/355 €, ☕ 18 €

◆ Chain hotel ◆ Classic ◆

This classically designed hotel has pleasant public areas and cosy, elegant guestrooms. There is attention to detail and comfort in equal measure.

CHAMBERÍ — *Plan IV*

AC Santo Mauro

Zurbano 36 ✉ 28010 – Ⓜ Alonso Martínez – ☎ 913 19 69 00 – www.ac-hotels.com **L3**

43 rm – 200/300 € 240/360 €, ☕ 30 € – 8 suites

Rest *Santo Mauro* – *(closed August, Sunday and Monday)* Menu 90 €

◆ Palace ◆ Grand Luxury ◆ Contemporary ◆

This delightful, French-style mansion is located in the city's aristocratic and embassy district. Find luxurious features, and an elegant setting surrounded by an attractive garden. This highly distinguished restaurant occupies a stunning library-lounge.

Intercontinental Madrid

paseo de la Castellana 49 ✉ 28046 – Ⓜ Gregorio Marañón – ☎ 917 00 73 00 – www.madrid.intercontinental.com **L3**

279 rm – 159/259 €, ☕ 32 € – 33 suites **Rest** – Menu 42 €

◆ Chain hotel ◆ Classic ◆

This hotel has an elegant marble adorned lobby crowned with a cupola. Attractive inner terrace-patio and extremely comfortable guestrooms. The restaurant, located next to the bar, serves fine international cuisine.

Hesperia Madrid

paseo de la Castellana 57 ✉ 28046 – Ⓜ Gregorio Marañón – ☎ 912 10 88 00 – www.hesperia-madrid.com **L2**

139 rm – 122/411 € 157/421 €, ☕ 29 € – 32 suites

Rest *Santceloni* – see below

Rest – *(lunch only)* Menu 29 €

◆ Chain hotel ◆ Classic ◆

Conveniently located in a central business district, this hotel has a small lobby and a number of different lounge areas. Elegant, guestrooms that are in traditional in style. The restaurant in the internal patio also serves as the hotel's breakfast room.

Orfila

Orfila 6 ✉ 28010 – Ⓜ Alonso Martínez – ☎ 917 02 77 70 – www.hotelorfila.com – closed August **L3**

28 rm – 187/385 € 187/405 €, ☕ 30 € – 4 suites **Rest** – Menu 45 €

◆ Business ◆ Stylish ◆

A 19C mansion located in an exclusive residential area. A stately atmosphere pervades every room with furnishings that are classically elegant. À la carte dining in the Orfila's welcoming dining room or the indoor garden.

NH Abascal

José Abascal 47 ✉ 28003 – Ⓜ Gregorio Marañón – ☎ 914 41 00 15 – www.nh-hotels.com **L2**

180 rm – 59/224 €, ☕ 22 € – 3 suites

Rest – *(closed 15 July-August)* Carte 35/45 €

◆ Chain hotel ◆ Classic ◆ Functional ◆

An elegant building designed along classic lines and fronted by an attractive façade. Features include a delightful lobby embellished with marble columns, a patio-garden, a beautiful staircase and well-appointed guestrooms.

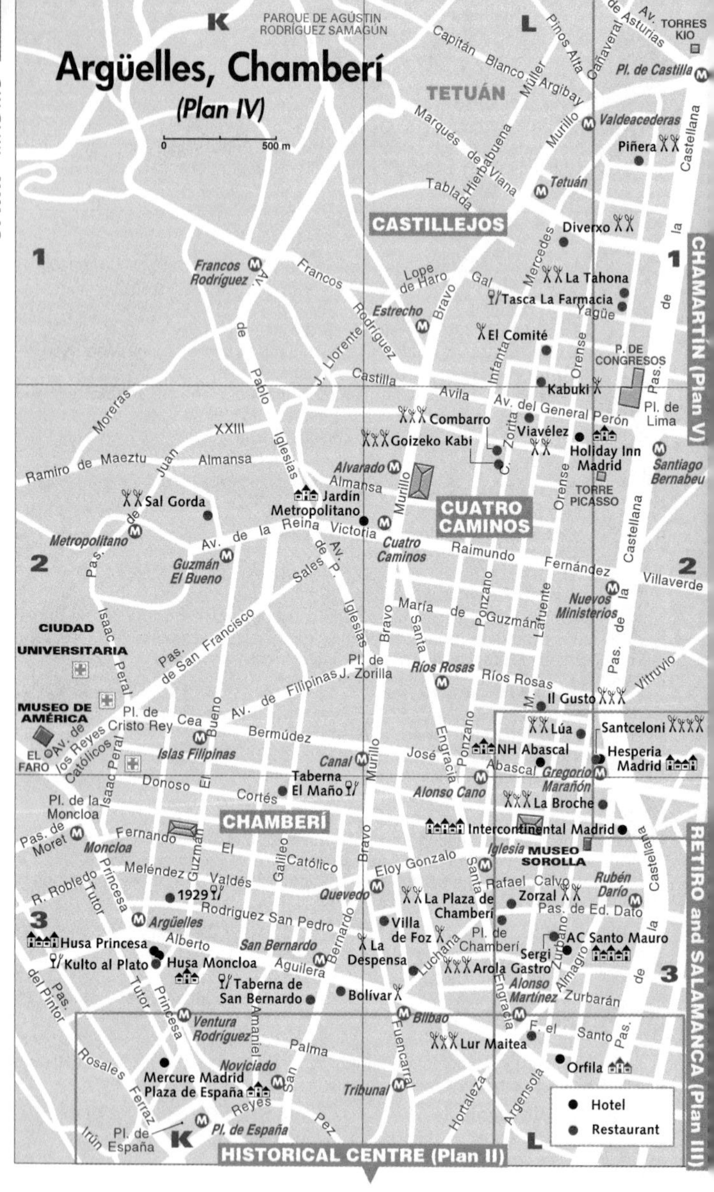

Argüelles, Chamberí
(Plan IV)
0
500 m
K
L
PARQUE DE AGÚSTIN RODRÍGUEZ SAMAGÚN
TETUÁN
CASTILLEJOS
CUATRO CAMINOS
CHAMBERÍ
CIUDAD UNIVERSITARIA
MUSEO DE AMÉRICA
MUSEO SOROLLA
TORRES KIO
TORRE PICASSO
P. DE CONGRESOS
CHAMARTÍN (Plan V)
RETIRO and SALAMANCA (Plan III)
HISTORICAL CENTRE (Plan II)
Piñera
Diverxo
La Tahona
Tasca La Farmacia
El Comité
Kabuki
Combarro
Goizeko Kabi
Viavélez
Holiday Inn Madrid
Sal Gorda
Jardín Metropolitano
Il Gusto
Lúa
Santceloni
NH Abascal
Hesperia Madrid
Taberna El Maño
La Broche
Intercontinental Madrid
1929
La Plaza de Chamberí
Zorzal
Villa de Foz
AC Santo Mauro
Sergi Arola Gastro
La Despensa
Husa Princesa
Kulto al Plato
Husa Moncloa
Taberna de San Bernardo
Bolívar
Lur Maitea
Orfila
Mercure Madrid Plaza de España
Hotel
Restaurant

XXXX ✿✿

Santceloni – Hotel Hesperia Madrid

paseo de la Castellana 57 ✉ 28046 – Ⓜ Gregorio Marañón – ✆ 912 10 88 40 – www.restaurantesantceloni.com – closed Holy Week, August, Saturday lunch, Sunday and Bank Holidays

Rest – Menu 120/195 € – Carte 111/138 € **L2**

Spec. Ostras en escabeche de cítricos, coliflor y rúcula. Carré de cochinillo asado al momento al aroma de tomillo. Crema de café con la mousse cocida de chocolate.

♦ Inventive ♦ Classic ♦

A magnificent gastronomic experience. The decor in this elegant restaurant is a combination of the traditional and contemporary in an attractive setting spilt between two floors. Superbly prepared classic cuisine with a modern slant, which incorporates extraordinary creative touches.

XXX ✿

La Broche

Miguel Ángel 29 ✉ 28010 – Ⓜ Gregorio Marañón – ✆ 913 99 34 37 – www.labroche.com – closed Holy Week, August, Sunday, Monday and Bank Holidays

Rest – Menu 70/100 € – Carte 66/89 € **L3**

Spec. Ajoblanco de almedras con langostino y aceite de argán. Rape a la parrilla con espárragos a la vainilla. Músico de frutos secos y queso.

♦ Contemporary ♦ Minimalist ♦

The open dining room, which looks onto the street via a large window, is minimalist in style with a predominance of varying tones of white. The chef's focus is on contemporary cuisine that takes classic combinations as a point of reference.

XXX

Il Gusto

Espronceda 27 ✉ 28003 – Ⓜ Canal – ✆ 915 35 39 02 – www.restauranteilgusto.com **L2**

Rest – Carte 35/45 €

♦ Italian ♦ Design ♦

Italian cuisine takes pride of place in this modern restaurant. It has an elegant dining room decorated with a profusion of marble and wood.

XXX ✿✿

Sergi Arola Gastro

Zurbano 31 ✉ 28010 – Ⓜ Rubén Darío – ✆ 91 310 21 69 – www.sergiarola.es – closed Christmas, Holy Week, 12-31 August, Saturday lunch and Sunday

Rest – *(set menu only)* Menu 95/160 € **L3**

Spec. Sardinas marinadas rellenas de huevas de arenque, pan y tomate. Lomo de mero negro en sopa de coco y curry. Coca de hígado de pato con verduras asadas al horno.

♦ Inventive ♦ Design ♦

This restaurant is home to a cocktail bar, a modern dining room and a unusual private room situated right by the kitchen. The chef's unique style and technical expertise are apparent in the delicate, perfectly balanced dishes on the menu.

XXX

Lur Maitea

Fernando el Santo 4 ✉ 28010 – Ⓜ Alonso Martínez – ✆ 913 08 03 50 – www.lurmaitearestaurante.com – closed August and Sunday

Rest – Carte 53/60 € **L3**

♦ Basque cuisine ♦ Formal ♦

Lur Maitea has become one of the city's best-known restaurants. It serves contemporary Basque cuisine in an elegant dining room with blue-inspired decor and wood flooring.

XX

Zorzal

paseo de Eduardo Dato 5 ✉ 28010 – Ⓜ Rubén Darío – ✆ 914 46 45 48 – www.restaurantezorzal.com – closed Holy Week, August, Sunday, Monday and Tuesday dinner

Rest – Carte approx. 35 € **L3**

♦ Innovative ♦ Trendy ♦

Behind the Zorzal's classic façade is a restaurant with a modern look with wood flooring and attractive table settings. The menu focuses on traditional cuisine enhanced by a few modern touches.

La Plaza de Chamberí

pl. de Chamberí 10 ✉ 28010 – Ⓜ Iglesia – ✆ 914 46 06 97 – www.restaurantelaplazadechamberi.com – closed Sunday dinner

Rest – Carte 37/44 € **L3**

♦ Traditional ♦ Formal ♦

A well-established and popular restaurant with an old-style dining room extending over two floors. The culinary focus here is on traditional cuisine.

Lúa

Zurbano 85 ✉ 28003 – Ⓜ Gregorio Marañón – ✆ 913 95 28 53 – www.restaurantelua.com – closed 15 days in August and Sunday **L2**

Rest – *(set menu only)* Menu 44 €

♦ Inventive ♦ Friendly ♦

This small, trendy restaurant has a lively atmosphere with the dining room separated into three sections. Creative, contemporary cuisine, including a tasting menu.

Bolívar

Manuela Malasaña 28 ✉ 28004 – Ⓜ San Bernardo – ✆ 914 45 12 74 – www.restaurantebolivar.com – closed August and Sunday **K3**

Rest – Carte 35/40 €

♦ Traditional ♦ Friendly ♦

This family-run restaurant in the traditional Malasaña district has excellent service and a reasonably priced, varied menu. Welcoming dining room with a modern feel.

Villa de Foz

Gonzálo de Córdoba 10 ✉ 28010 – Ⓜ Bilbao – ✆ 914 46 89 93 – www.villadefoz.com – closed August and Sunday **L3**

Rest – Carte 36/45 €

♦ Galician specialities ♦ Fashionable ♦

The Villa de Foz has two pleasant dining rooms, both decorated in a style that reflects traditional and contemporary influences. Its à la carte menu of traditional Galician cuisine is enhanced by a fine choice of raciones and home-made desserts.

Taberna El Maño

Vallehermoso 59 ✉ 28015 – Ⓜ Canal – ✆ 914 48 40 35 – closed Sunday dinner and Monday **K3**

Tapa 3 € **Ración** approx. 11.50 €

♦ Traditional ♦ Tapas bar ♦

Old, traditional restaurant decorated with a bullfighting theme. Tapas and snacks of a high quality.

1929

Rodríguez San Pedro 66 ✉ 28015 – Ⓜ Argüelles – ✆ 915 49 91 16 – www.taberna1929.com – closed August, Sunday and Bank Holidays

Tapa 2.20 € **Ración** approx. 10 € **K3**

♦ Traditional ♦ Tapas bar ♦

Rustic restaurant run by its owner. Well- stocked bar, barrels used as tables, and two dining rooms.

CASTILLEJOS – CUATRO CAMINOS *Plan IV*

Holiday Inn Madrid

pl. Carlos Trías Beltrán 4 (access by Orense 22) ✉ 28020 – Ⓜ Santiago Bernabeu – ✆ 914 56 80 00 – www.holidayinnmadrid.net **L2**

280 rm – ††90/450 €, ☕ 20 € – 33 suites **Rest** – Menu 28 €

♦ Chain hotel ♦ Contemporary ♦

Convenient location next to the Azca complex, a financial centre with a plethora of offices, shops and restaurants. Contemporary-style guestrooms, and an extensive range of additional services. The hotel's restaurant occupies a single, multi-purpose dining room.

Jardín Metropolitano

av. Reina Victoria 12 ✉ *28003* – Ⓜ *Cuatro Caminos* – ☎ *911 83 18 10*
– *www.vphoteles.com* **K-L2**
96 rm – 🛉95/300 € 🛉🛉115/320 €, ☕ 15 € – 6 suites
Rest – *(closed August)* Menu 25 €
♦ Traditional ♦ Classic ♦
This contemporary-style hotel occupies a building surrounding a central patio crowned by a skylight. Spacious, classical, and well-equipped bedrooms.

Combarro

Reina Mercedes 12 ✉ *28020* – Ⓜ *Nuevos Ministerios* – ☎ *915 54 77 84*
– *www.combarro.com*
– *closed Holy Week, August and Sunday dinner* **L2**
Rest – Carte 64/77 €
♦ Fish ♦ Formal ♦
Galician cuisine with an emphasis on fresh quality produce, including live fish tanks. Public bar, dining on the first floor and a number of rooms in the basement. Classic and elegant in style.

Goizeko Kabi

Comandante Zorita 37 ✉ *28020* – Ⓜ *Alvarado* – ☎ *915 33 01 85*
– *www.goizekogaztelupe.com*
– *closed Sunday* **L2**
Rest – Carte 53/61 €
♦ Basque cuisine ♦ Formal ♦
Prestigious address serving modern Basque cuisine. Although the tables are somewhat close together, the overall feel is one of refined elegance.

Piñera

Rosario Pino 12 ✉ *28012* – Ⓜ *Valdeacederas* – ☎ *914 25 14 25*
– *www.restaurantepinera.com*
– *closed 15 days in August* **L1**
Rest – Carte approx. 55 €
♦ Traditional ♦ Trendy ♦
The Piñera has an attractive entrance hall with a bar, in addition to two contemporary-style dining rooms and two private rooms. Traditional and international cuisine with a modern touch.

Diverxo (David Muñoz)

Pensamiento 28 ✉ *28020* – Ⓜ *Cuzco* – ☎ *91 570 07 66*
– *www.diverxo.com*
– *closed Christmas, Holy Week, 15 days in August, Sunday and Monday*
Rest – *(booking essential) (set menu only)* Menu 70/90 € **L1**
Spec. Mollete chino, bun de trompetas a la crema y piel de leche, tomate kumato cherry y cecina de buey. Rape chifa versión glaseado express. Canapé pekinés invertido con sésamo negro.
♦ Inventive ♦ Trendy ♦
This modern restaurant, accessed via a cocktail bar, has a bright, contemporary-style dining room. The tasting menus available feature inventive, fusion cuisine with more than a hint of Asian influence.

Viavélez

av. General Perón 10 ✉ *28020* – Ⓜ *Santiago Bernabeu* – ☎ *91 579 95 39*
– *www.restauranteviavelez.com*
– *closed Holy Week, August, Sunday dinner and Monday* **L2**
Rest – Carte 50/62 €
♦ Inventive ♦ Trendy ♦
This tavern-restaurant features a select tapas bar at the entrance and a modern and intimate dining room in the basement. Its creative cuisine is based on traditional Asturian recipes.

La Tahona

Capitán Haya 21 ✉ 28020 – Ⓜ Cuzco – ✆ 915 55 04 41 – www.asadordearanda.com – closed August and Sunday dinner

Rest – Carte 33/42 € **L1**

◆ Roast lamb ◆ Neighbourhood ◆

Bar in the entrance with a wood oven and wood panelling, followed by various dining rooms decorated in medieval Castilian style. Enjoy traditional roast dishes accompanied by the restaurant's own house red.

Sal Gorda

Beatriz de Bobadilla 9 ✉ 28040 – Ⓜ Guzmán El Bueno – ✆ 915 53 95 06 – www.restaurantesalgorda.es – closed Holy Week, August and Sunday **K2**

Rest – Carte 30/35 €

◆ International ◆ Formal ◆

Renowned professionals run this small restaurant. Find carefully prepared, classical cuisine based on traditional recipes, as well as some international dishes.

El Comité

pl. de San Amaro 8 ✉ 28020 – Ⓜ Nuevos Ministerios – ✆ 915 71 87 11 – closed Saturday lunch and Sunday **L1**

Rest – Carte 38/47 €

◆ French ◆ Bistro ◆

Cosy bistro-restaurant with café style furniture and a huge collection of old photographs. The menu here focuses on French cuisine.

Kabuki

av. Presidente Carmona 2 ✉ 28020 – Ⓜ Santiago Bernabeu – ✆ 914 17 64 15 – closed Holy Week, 8-31 August, Saturday lunch, Sunday and Bank Holidays

Rest – Menu 60 € – Carte 55/68 € **L1-2**

Spec. Atún tataki con purés de aceituna negra y manzana. Buey wagyu a la plancha. Daifuku y sorbete de maracuyá.

◆ Japanese ◆ Minimalist ◆

This intimate Japanese restaurant has a minimalist decor. There is a modern terrace and a kitchen-bar, where popular dishes such as sushi are prepared. The focus is on high quality ingredients, delicately prepared and adapted to a European palate.

Tasca La Farmacia

Capitán Haya 19 ✉ 28020 – Ⓜ Cuzco – ✆ 915 55 81 46 – www.asadordearanda.com – closed 10 August-6 September and Sunday **L1**

Tapa 4.50 € **Ración** approx. 12 €

◆ Codfish specialities ◆ Rustic ◆

Delightful restaurant decorated with azulejo tiles, stone arches, exposed brickwork, wrought iron lattice windows and an impressive glass ceiling. La Farmacia is famous for its cod dishes.

CHAMARTÍN *Plan V*

Puerta América

av. de América 41 ✉ 28002 – Ⓜ Cartagena – ✆ 917 44 54 00 – www.hotelpuertamerica.com **N3**

330 rm – ††150/486 €, ☕ 27 € – 33 suites

Rest *Lágrimas Negras* – *(closed Sunday and Monday dinner) (lunch only in August)* Carte 45/80 €

◆ Business ◆ Design ◆

Colourfully decorated and with numerous designer features, each of the floors of this hotel reflects the creativity of a renowned artist. The guestrooms are very original in style. This modern restaurant has a certain New York feel, with its bar area and high ceilings.

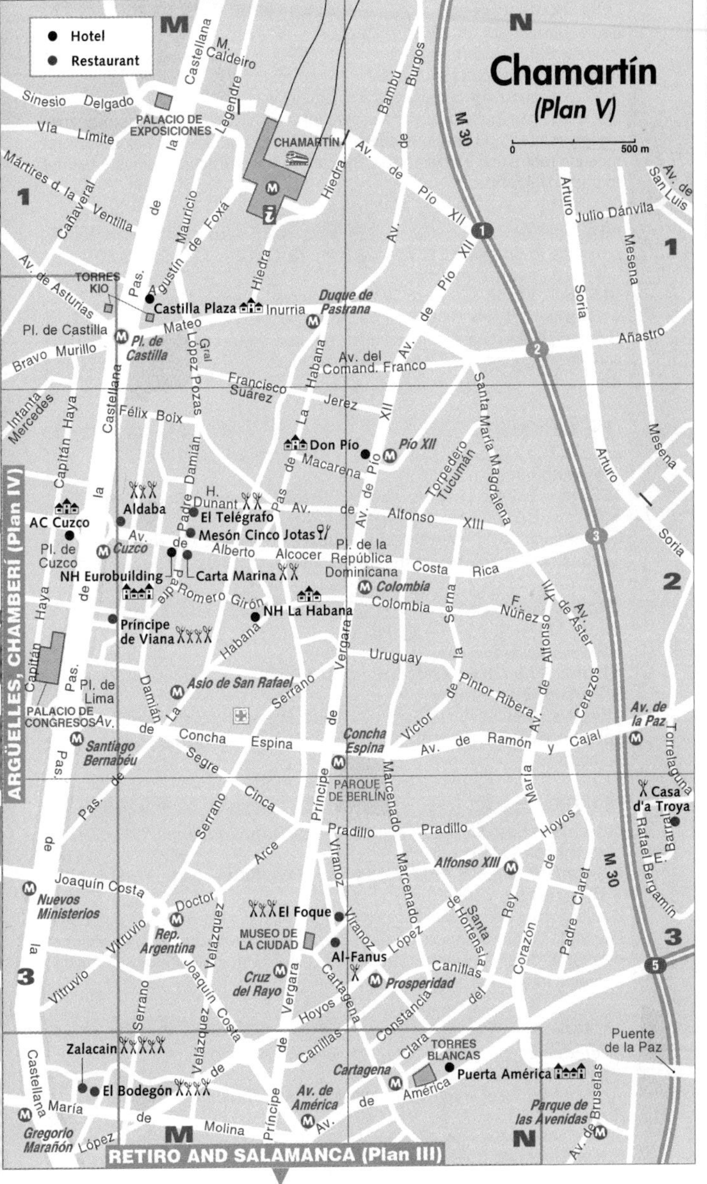
Chamartín
(Plan V)
Hotel
Restaurant
0
500 m
PALACIO DE EXPOSICIONES
CHAMARTÍN
TORRES KIO
Castilla Plaza
Don Pío
AC Cuzco
Aldaba
El Telégrafo
Mesón Cinco Jotas
Carta Marina
NH Eurobuilding
NH La Habana
Príncipe de Viana
PALACIO DE CONGRESOS
PARQUE DE BERLÍN
El Foque
MUSEO DE LA CIUDAD
Al-Fanus
Casa d'a Troya
TORRES BLANCAS
Puerta América
Zalacain
El Bodegón
Duque de Pastrana
Pl. de Castilla
Pío XII
Cuzco
Colombia
Asio de San Rafael
Santiago Bernabéu
Concha Espina
Av. de la Paz
Alfonso XIII
Nuevos Ministerios
Rep. Argentina
Cruz del Rayo
Prosperidad
Cartagena
Av. de América
Parque de las Avenidas
Gregorio Marañón
M 30
Puente de la Paz
ARGÜELLES, CHAMBERÍ (Plan IV)
RETIRO AND SALAMANCA (Plan III)

NH Eurobuilding

Padre Damián 23 ✉ 28036 – Ⓜ Cuzco – ☎ 913 53 73 00 – www.nh-hotels.com **M2**

455 rm – ††92/538 €, ☕ 23.80 € – 4 suites **Rest** – Menu 45 €

♦ Chain hotel ♦ Business ♦ Classic ♦

The decor here upholds the philosophy of this hotel chain, with comfortable, well-appointed and spacious guestrooms. Additional facilities include several meeting rooms and a modern spa. The cuisine in this restaurant remains faithful to traditional recipes.

AC Cuzco

paseo de la Castellana 133 ✉ 28046 – Ⓜ Cuzco – ☎ 915 56 06 00 – www.ac-hotels.com **M2**

315 rm – ††108/350 €, ☕ 22 € – 14 suites **Rest** – Menu 30 €

♦ Chain hotel ♦ Business ♦ Modern ♦

This completely renovated hotel offers guests a choice of modern, comfortable and well-designed rooms typical of the AC chain. Its restaurant is open 24hrs a day.

NH La Habana

paseo de La Habana 73 ✉ 28036 – Ⓜ Colombia – ☎ 914 43 07 20 – www.nh-hotels.com **M2**

155 rm – †204 € ††227 €, ☕ 19 € **Rest** – *(closed August)* Menu 30 €

♦ Chain hotel ♦ Functional ♦

Contemporary-style hotel aimed at a business clientele. The somewhat compact but comfortable bedrooms have modern furnishings and wood flooring.

Don Pío without rest

av. Pío XII-25 ✉ 28016 – Ⓜ Pio XII – ☎ 913 53 07 80 – www.hoteldonpio.com **N2**

41 rm – †72/128 € ††80/160 €, ☕ 14 €

♦ Family ♦ Classic ♦

Attractive patio-lobby crowned by a modern skylight overlooked by all the guestrooms. These are spacious and include features such as hydromassage bathtubs.

Castilla Plaza

paseo de la Castellana 220 ✉ 28046 – Ⓜ Plaza Castilla – ☎ 915 67 43 00 – www.abbahoteles.com **M1**

228 rm – †75/350 € ††125/350 €, ☕ 17 € **Rest** – Carte 37/43 €

♦ Business ♦ Classic ♦

Beautiful glass fronted building, which along with the Kio Towers, is part of the Puerta de Europa complex. Comfortable, contemporary-style with a wealth of decorative detail. This restaurant serves cuisine with a Mediterranean flavour, including interesting daily specials.

Zalacain

Álvarez de Baena 4 ✉ 28006 – Ⓜ Gregorio Marañón – ☎ 915 61 48 40 – www.restaurantezalacain.com – closed Holy Week, August, Saturday lunch, Sunday and Bank Holidays

Rest – Carte 67/83 € **M3**

Spec. Langostinos a la plancha sobre tomate, cebolla y aceitunas negras con vinagreta de trufas. Huevos trufados con hongos confitados y gambas. Entrecot de buey al vino tinto con tuétano de ternera jóven.

♦ Classic ♦ Elegant ♦

This building is one of the most prestigious and elegant in Spain. It boasts an attractive entrance hall, private bar, and various rooms with a refined classic atmosphere. The kitchen remains faithful to the highest standards of classic cuisine. Superb service.

XXXX

Príncipe de Viana

Manuel de Falla 5 ✉ 28036 – Ⓜ Santiago Bernabeu – ✆ 914 57 15 49 – closed Holy Week, August and Sunday **M2**

Rest – Carte 50/70 €

♦ Basque cuisine ♦ Formal ♦

This restaurant has a long-standing reputation for its excellent cuisine, which takes its inspiration from the Basque country and Navarra. Attractive decor and table settings.

XXXX

El Bodegón

Pinar 15 ✉ 28006 – Ⓜ Gregorio Marañón – ✆ 915 62 88 44 – www.grupovips.com – closed August, Saturday lunch and Sunday **M3**

Rest – Carte 57/81 €

♦ Traditional ♦ Formal ♦

Elegant restaurant in classical style with a private bar and dining rooms on various levels. The menu here focuses on traditional cuisine.

XXX

Aldaba

av. de Alberto Alcocer 5 ✉ 28036 – Ⓜ Cuzco – ✆ 913 59 73 86 – closed Holy Week, August, Saturday lunch, Sunday and Bank Holidays

Rest – Carte 56/69 € **M2**

♦ Classic ♦ Trendy ♦

This restaurant has a bar at the entrance, followed by an attractive dining room in classic-modern style and several small rooms for private dining. Excellent wine list.

XXX

El Foque

Suero de Quiñones 22 ✉ 28002 – Ⓜ Cruz del Rayo – ✆ 915 19 25 72 – www.elfoque.com – closed Sunday **M3**

Rest – Carte 38/47 €

♦ Codfish specialities ♦ Formal ♦

Conveniently located close to the Auditorio Nacional de Música, this restaurant on two levels has an attractive nautical decor with a mast and sails adorning the dining room. The house speciality is cod.

XX

El Telégrafo

Padre Damián 44 ✉ 28036 – Ⓜ Cuzco – ✆ 913 59 70 83 – www.eltelegrafomarisqueria.com **M2**

Rest – Carte approx. 50 €

♦ Fish ♦ Neighbourhood ♦

This seafood restaurant imitates the decor of the inside of a boat with dining rooms separated into different areas and levels. Attractive bar at the entrance with a seafood counter.

XX

Carta Marina

Padre Damián 40 ✉ 28036 – Ⓜ Cuzco – ✆ 914 58 68 26 – www.restaurantecartamarina.com – closed Holy Week, August and Sunday dinner **M2**

Rest – Carte 36/48 €

♦ Traditional ♦ Formal ♦

This restaurant has an attractive wood decor, private bar, and cosy dining rooms with a summer and winter terrace. Traditional Galician menu.

X

Al-Fanus

Pechuán 6 ✉ 28002 – Ⓜ Cruz del Rayo – ✆ 915 62 77 18 – www.alfanus.es – closed August and Sunday dinner **M3**

Rest – Carte 31/40 €

♦ International ♦ Formal ♦

Authentic Syrian cuisine is on offer in this restaurant with a bar at the entrance and a Moorish-style dining room. The intimate lighting is provided by hand-made metal wall lamps.

Casa d'a Troya

Emiliano Barral 14 ✉ 28043 – Ⓜ Avenida de la Paz – ✆ 914 16 44 55 – closed 24 December-2 January, Holy Week, 15 July-August, nights from Monday to Thursday, Sunday and Bank Holidays **N3**

Rest – Carte 45/58 €

◆ Galician specialities ◆ Family ◆

A family-run business offering simply prepared, traditional Galician cuisine. Lobby-bar and two comfortable dining rooms.

Mesón Cinco Jotas

Padre Damián 42 ✉ 28036 – Ⓜ Cuzco – ✆ 913 50 31 73 – www.mesoncincojotas.com **M2**

Tapa 3.20 € **Ración** approx. 13 €

◆ Spanish ◆ Tapas bar ◆

This chain restaurant specialises in top quality Iberian ham and chorizos. Varied tapas and à la carte menus served in two pleasant dining rooms.

PARQUE FERIAL *Plan I*

Acis y Galatea without rest

Galatea 6 ✉ 28042 – Ⓜ Canillejas – ✆ 917 43 49 01 – www.hotelesglobales.com **D1**

20 rm – 63/103 € 76/120 €

◆ Family ◆ Modern ◆

A friendly, family-run hotel with a certain charm. Modern decor with a contrasting light and dark colour scheme. Well-appointed guestrooms.

AT BARAJAS AIRPORT *Plan I*

Hilton Madrid Airport

av. de la Hispanidad 2-4 ✉ 28042 – Ⓜ Alameda de Osuna – ✆ 911 53 40 00 – www.madridairport.hilton.es **D1**

275 rm – 131/401 €, 26 € – 9 suites

Rest – Menu 35 €

◆ Business ◆ Design ◆

This modern-style hotel comprises of two cube-shaped buildings that are joined together. It is aimed at business customers and trade fair visitors due to proximity to the airport. This restaurant, in one of the patios, serves an international menu and buffet.

Meliá Barajas

av. de Logroño 305 (A 2 and turn to Barajas Town : 15 km) ✉ 28042 – Ⓜ Barajas – ✆ 917 47 77 00 – www.melia-barajas.com **D1**

220 rm – 235/255 €, 19.50 € – 8 suites **Rest** – Menu 32 €

◆ Business ◆ Classic ◆

Comfortable facilities and classical in style with fully equipped guestrooms and renovated bathrooms. A number of pleasant lounges are located around the garden and swimming pool area.

Tryp Alameda Aeropuerto

av. de Logroño 100 (A 2 and turn to Barajas Town : 15 km) ✉ 28042 – Ⓜ Barajas – ✆ 917 47 48 00 – www.solmelia.com **D1**

145 rm – 65/300 €, 15 € – 3 suites

Rest – Menu 15 €

◆ Business ◆ Functional ◆

Following extensive renovation, this hotel has a contemporary feel with a bright foyer, several lounge areas, and different categories of comfortable guestrooms. This spacious and functional restaurant combines the buffet with a set menu, as well as a traditional à la carte menu.

Aparthotel Convención Barajas without rest

Noray 10 (A 2 and turn to Barajas Town and Industrial Area : 10 km) ✉ 28042 – Ⓜ El Capricho – ☎ 913 71 74 10 – www.hotel-convencion.com

D1

95 suites – 51/225 €

♦ Business ♦ Classic ♦

Although the public areas in this twin tower hotel are limited, its apartment-style guestrooms are reasonably spacious, each with a small lounge and kitchen.

NH Barajas without rest

Catamarán 1 (A 2 and turn to Barajas Town and Industrial Area : 10 km) ✉ 28042 – Ⓜ El Capricho – ☎ 917 42 02 00 – www.nh-hotels.com

D1

173 rm – 49/163 €, 9.50 €

♦ Business ♦ Functional ♦

This airport hotel offers the usual comforts associated with the NH chain. Somewhat limited public areas but a good choice in its price range.

R

BARCELONA

BARCELONA

Population (oct. 2010): 1 621 537 (conurbation 5 380 050) – Altitude: sea level

It can't be overestimated how important Catalonia is to the locals of Barcelona. Pride in their autonomous region of Spain runs deep in the blood. Barcelona loves to mix the traditional with the avant-garde, and this exuberant opening of arms has seen it grow over the years into a pulsating city for visitors. Its rash of theatres, museums and concert halls is unmatched by most other European cities, and many artists and architects have chosen to live here. Testament to the creative zest of Barcelona lies in the fact that Picasso, Miró and Dalí, along with Gaudí and Subirachs, chose to make it their home.

The nineteenth century was a golden period in the city's artistic development, with the growth of the great Catalan Modernism movement. It was knocked back on its heels after the Spanish Civil War and the rise to power of the dictator Franco, who destroyed the hopes for an independent Catalonia. After his death, democracy came to Spain and in the last 30 years Barcelona has relished its position as capital of a restored autonomous region. Whether it's via fun-loving locals, record numbers of tourists thronging its streets, or the beloved Barça football team that reached the pinnacle of success with victories in the 2006 and 2009 European Champions League, this is a city that lives by the headlines it creates.

LIVING THE CITY

If you're up on **Montjuïc**, you get a great overview of the city below. Barcelona's atmospheric old town is near the harbour and reaches into the teeming streets of the **Gothic Quarter**, while the newer area is north of this, the elegant avenues in grid formation that make up Eixample. The coastal quarter of **Barça** has been transformed in recent times with the development of Barceloneta and its trendy informality. For many, though, the epicentre of this bubbling city is **The Ramblas**, scything through the centre of town.

PRACTICAL INFORMATION

ARRIVAL-DEPARTURE

Barcelona airport is located 13km southwest of the city. A taxi will cost around €25. Alternatively take the Renfe train (Line 2 suburban train) every 30min or Aerobus which runs approximately every 10min.

TRANSPORT

Barcelona Card – two to five days of unlimited travel, starting at 27 euros, on metro and buses; discounts on airport bus and cable cars; reduced entry to museums and attractions; discounts in several restaurants, bars and shops. It's sold at airport, tourist offices and various participating venues.

Articket – 22 euros: gives free entry to seven museums and galleries over six months and is available from tourist offices.

Look out for two tourist buses – Barcelona City Tour and Bus Turistic; both offer comprehensive tours of the city.

Walking tours include Modernisme, Picasso, Gothic and Gourmet – the latter includes stops in best cafés, food shops and markets.

EXPLORING BARCELONA

Has the vibrant and visceral Catalonian capital grown too popular for its own good? Some might say so but it's not hard to make the opposite case: Barcelona has always been a city that wears its heart on its sleeve, eager to show the world a love of eccentricity and affection for life after dark. No wonder the modernist master **Gaudí** flourished here: his ideals of creativity and vivacity fitted perfectly with those of the locals.

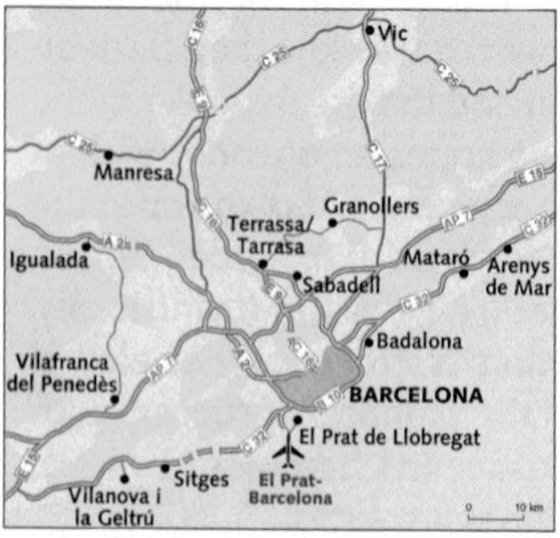

Following the 'grey years' of Franco, Barcelona really took off. It was awarded the 1992 Olympics, and the city fathers granted free reign to acclaimed architects and designers for a face-lifting blitz. From a virtual 'green-free' city, 19 new parks were created and nearly 30,000 new trees took root. Neglected squares were transformed with paved surfaces, shimmering mosaics and innovative sculptures, not to mention new seats from which to appreciate them. And the run-down seafront was spruced up, so that swathes of shiny new beach and bustling marina were created from wasteland. It's now possible to walk along five kilometres of waterfront or laze on a beach, though you might wish to avert your gaze from the señors of a certain vintage who have taken this late opportunity in life to stand naked at the water's edge.

➜ RAMBLING ON

Polls indicate that Barcelona is the European city best loved by visitors. Its beating heart, The **Ramblas**, runs straight up from the port, inexorably sucking in the world's tourists. Plane trees fan the way, and you can buy all manner of bird-life and flowers, or watch locals chatting at the news-stands. Along its three-quarter mile stretch, The Ramblas boasts numerous places to linger, from the exhibitions of the Centre d'Art Santa Mónica and waxwork likenesses at the Museu de Cera at one end, to the splendid 19C **Palau Moja** and famous Canaletes drinking fountain at the other. In between it's possible to get a feel for Gaudí's curves at the Palau Güell with its magnificently ornate chimneys, indulge in a treasure trove of musical paraphernalia at Casa Beethoven, or submerge into a feast of colourful fruit, fish and veg at the mighty Boquería market with its sturdy cast iron exterior and stained glass decorations.

You can retreat from the clamour of the Ramblas onto two of the city's most charming squares: **Plaça del Pi**, where buskers make the most of wonderful acoustics, or **Plaça Reial**, a harmonious spot with palm trees, fountains, classical buildings and lanterns designed by Gaudí.

In a city of churches, two stand out. The **Catedral de Santa Eulalia**, an imposing medieval giant that actually wasn't finished until 1913, is the star attraction of the Gothic quarter adjacent to the Ramblas. Its longevity of construction is being mirrored further across the city, where Gaudí's **Sagrada Familia**, Barcelona's most famously photographed landmark, remains unfinished, over 80 years after its creator was run down and killed by a trolley bus. Its circular towers, stretching conically to the heavens, look down eerily on a hollow interior, the project's completion date vaguely set for some time in the future. Gaudí spent the last 16 years of his life working on La Sagrada Familia. His name is entrenched in the city's recent history, his monuments to Modernism consigning design rulebooks to the scrap heap. No visitor should miss his work. La Pedrera ('The Stone Quarry' to natives) is an imposing apartment house with a fantastical, rippling façade and roof, while Casa Batlló's wonderfully sinister face depicts Sant Jordi and the Dragon: the cross on the top of the building is the knight's lance, the roof is the back of the beast, and the skeletal balconies are the skulls and bones of its wretched victims.

UNESCO has been busy in Barça. **Casa Batlló** is now one of its sites, as is the 100 year-old Palau de la Música Catalana, a richly ornate concert hall in the modernist style. Quirkiness pops up in all corners of the city with a wealth of offbeat museums dedicated to the likes of sewers, funeral carriages and shoes. The one most people head for, though, is the **Museu Picasso**, housed in five beautiful palaces, and containing over 3,600 of the great man's works, mostly from his early years and Blue Period. Picasso would have approved of the La Ribera district in which the museum is found: it's a bohemian, cutting edge area, and teems with boutiques, trendy cafés and snazzy restaurants.

➜ HEAD FOR THE HILL

For a different view of the city, then **Montjuïc** is the place to head for. The 700ft. hill, home of most events at the '92 Olympics, provides Barça's lungs.

You can reach the summit in style by cable car, and take in the views via new gardens and walkways. Don't miss out on a swim in the Olympic pool while you're there. Then soak up the glories of the world-renowned **Museu Nacional d'Art de Catalunya**, in the massive Palau Nacional. This contains a unique collection of Romanesque frescoes peeled carefully from the walls of churches in remote Pyrenean valleys.

Barcelona has changed much since George Orwell stayed in the city in the mid-thirties during the time of the Civil War. He wrote in Homage to Catalonia: "The working-class was in the saddle. Practically every building of any size had been seized by the workers." You could argue that artists and architects have now seized those very buildings. A former bullring in the city (bullfighting no longer exists now in Barcelona) is being transformed into an avant-garde shopping centre by Lord Rogers: an old infatuation being replaced by a very modern one.

CALENDAR HIGHLIGHTS

Think Barcelona and you think celebration. Unsurprisingly, the city enjoys a rich musical calendar. Maldades, in May, is a fiery flamenco festival which has strong similarities with the popular Rumba Catalana, while in the same month, the Barcelona Guitar Festival highlights international talent and emerging performers in locations around the city. From October through to July, the Gran Teatre del Liceu presents a wide-ranging programme of classical performances in luxurious surroundings. Also in October, the International Jazz Festival is one of Europe's longest-running and most well respected events, and the range of styles on offer is all-encompassing. Away from the music hall, you can get out and about on two wheels in the much-hyped Bicycle Week every June, and keep the midnight fires burning during the dramatic Fiesta de la Merce in September, when a spectacular late night train of dragons, eagles and devils haunts the streets to a sizzling backdrop of fireworks. There's another great knees-up in June in celebration of Saint John's Day when concerts, dances and bonfires come together in a dazzling explosion. For those in a quieter frame of mind, the Barcelona Book Market, every September, is a fine place to find a second hand book and appreciate charming Passeig de Grácia in Eixample.

BARCELONA IN...

→ ONE DAY

Catedral de Santa Eulalia, the Ramblas, La Pedrera, Museu Picasso, Sagrada Familia, chocolate shop

→ TWO DAYS

Montjuïc, Parc Güell, Nou Camp stadium, Barceloneta waterfront, Tibidabo (hill with 19C amusement park)

→ THREE DAYS

Barri Gotic and Palau de la Musica Catalana, Via Laietana (street with elegant façades and buzzy cafés), a trip to the resort of Sitges along the coast

EATING OUT

Barcelona has long had a good gastronomic tradition, not least because geographically it's been more influenced by France and Italy than other Spanish regions. But these days the sensual enjoyment of food has become something of a mainstream religion here. Not surprising, when you remember that Ferran Adriá's shrine-like El Bulli restaurant is along the Catalan coast, his reputation leading to an explosion of creative kitchens in the area. But if you want to stick with more traditional fare, the city has hundreds of tapas bars; a type of cuisine which is very refreshing knocked back with a draught beer. The city's location brings together produce from the land and the sea, with a firm emphasis on seasonality and quality produce. This explains why there are 39 markets in the city, all in great locations. Specialities to look out for include Pantumaca: slices of toasted bread with tomato and olive oil; Escalibada which is made with roasted vegetables; Esqueixada, a typically Catalan salad and Crema Catalana, a light custard. One little known facet of Barcelona life is its exquisite chocolate and sweet shops. Two stand out: Fargas, in the Barri Gothic, is the city's most famous chocolate shop, its 19C air giving it the status of a shrine, while Cacao Sampaka is the most elegant chocolate store you could ever wish to find and its creative concoctions, made with authentic cocoa, would make even Willie Wonka drool.

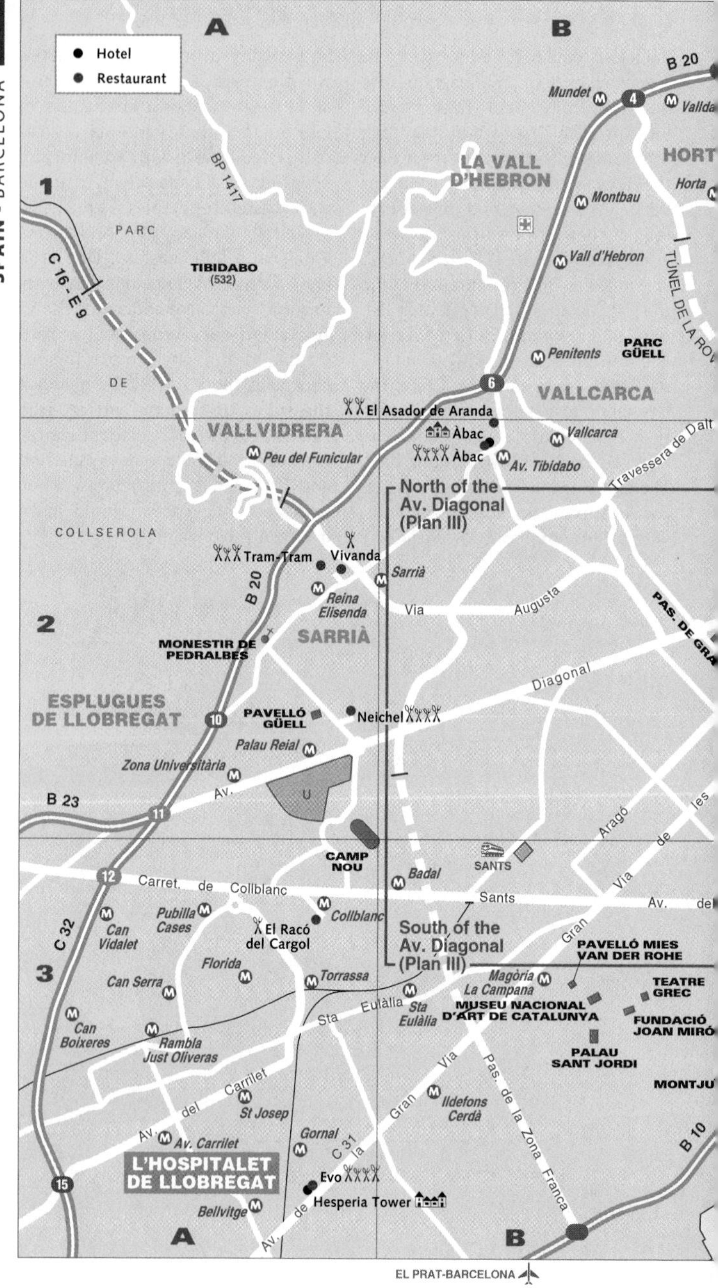
A
B
Hotel
Restaurant
B 20
Mundet
4
Vallda
HORT
LA VALL D'HEBRON
Horta
Montbau
BP 1417
1
PARC
TIBIDABO (532)
Vall d'Hebron
C 16 - E 9
TÚNEL DE LA RO
Penitents
PARC GÜELL
DE
6
VALLCARCA
El Asador de Aranda
VALLVIDRERA
Àbac
Àbac
Vallcarca
Peu del Funicular
Av. Tibidabo
Travessera de Dalt
North of the Av. Diagonal (Plan III)
COLLSEROLA
Tram-Tram
Vivanda
Sarrià
B 20
Reina Elisenda
Via Augusta
2
MONESTIR DE PEDRALBES
SARRIÀ
PAS. DE GRA
Diagonal
ESPLUGUES DE LLOBREGAT
10
PAVELLÓ GÜELL
Neichel
Palau Reial
Zona Universitària
B 23
Av.
U
11
Aragó
les
de
CAMP NOU
SANTS
12
Carret. de Collblanc
Badal
Via
Sants
Av.
de
Pubilla Cases
Collblanc
C 32
Can Vidalet
El Racó del Cargol
South of the Av. Diagonal (Plan III)
Gran
PAVELLÓ MIES VAN DER ROHE
3
Florida
Torrassa
Magòria La Campana
TEATRE GREC
Can Serra
Sta Eulàlia
Sta Eulàlia
MUSEU NACIONAL D'ART DE CATALUNYA
FUNDACIÓ JOAN MIRÓ
Can Boixeres
Rambla Just Oliveras
Gran Via
PALAU SANT JORDI
Pas. de la Zona Franca
MONTJU
Av. del Carrilet
St Josep
Ildefons Cerdà
Av. Carrilet
Gornal
C 31
la
B 10
L'HOSPITALET DE LLOBREGAT
Evo
15
Hesperia Tower
Bellvitge
Av. de
A
B
EL PRAT-BARCELONA

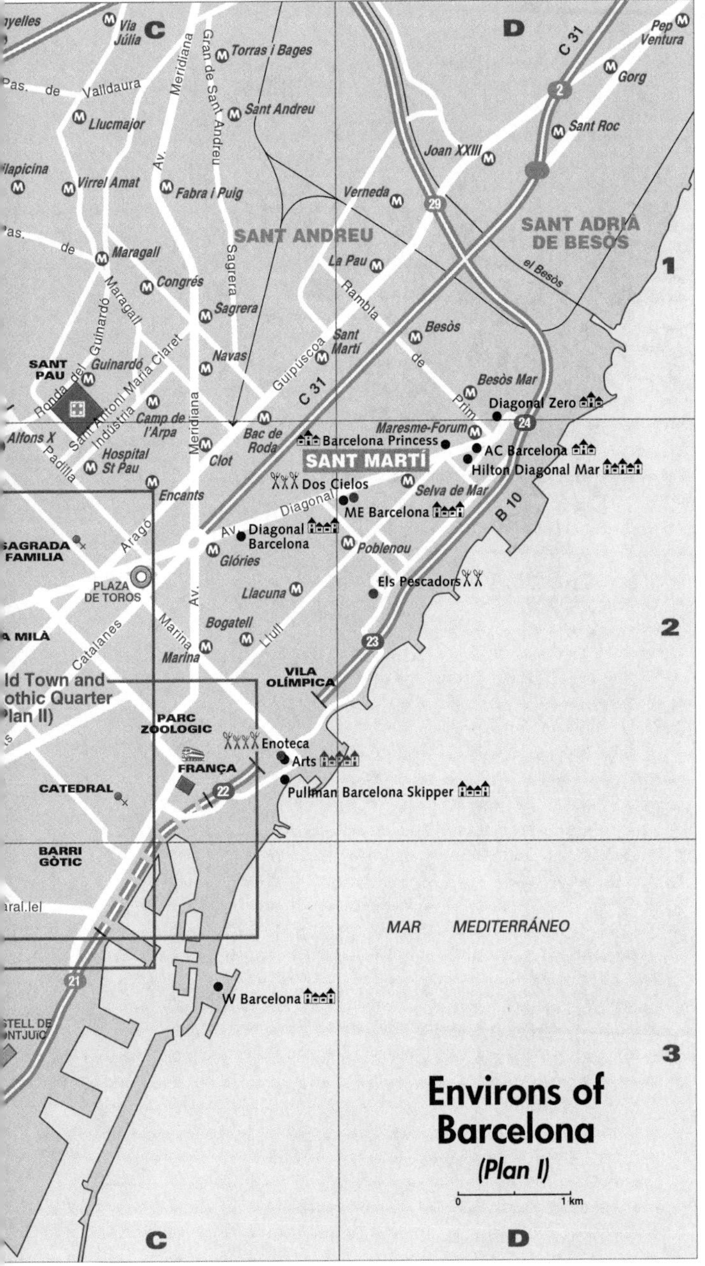
C
D
Via Júlia
Torras i Bages
Pep Ventura
Gorg
Pas. de Valldaura
Meridiana
Gran de Sant Andreu
Sant Andreu
Llucmajor
Sant Roc
Joan XXIII
Virrei Amat
Fabra i Puig
Verneda
SANT ANDREU
SANT ADRIÀ DE BESÒS
Maragall
La Pau
el Besòs
1
Congrés
Rambla de Prim
Sagrera
Besòs
Sant Martí
Guipúscoa
C 31
Navas
SANT PAU
Guinardó
Besòs Mar
Diagonal Zero
Camp de l'Arpa
Maresme-Forum
Alfons X
Bac de Roda
Barcelona Princess
AC Barcelona
Hospital St Pau
Clot
SANT MARTÍ
Hilton Diagonal Mar
Encants
Dos Cielos
Selva de Mar
Diagonal
ME Barcelona
B 10
SAGRADA FAMILIA
Av. Diagonal Barcelona
Glòries
Poblenou
PLAZA DE TOROS
Els Pescadors
Llacuna
Bogatell
Marina
2
Catalanes
Lull
VILA OLÍMPICA
Old Town and Gothic Quarter (Plan II)
PARC ZOOLOGIC
Enoteca
Arts
FRANÇA
CATEDRAL
Pullman Barcelona Skipper
BARRI GÒTIC
MAR MEDITERRÁNEO
W Barcelona
3
Environs of Barcelona
(Plan I)
0
1 km
C
D

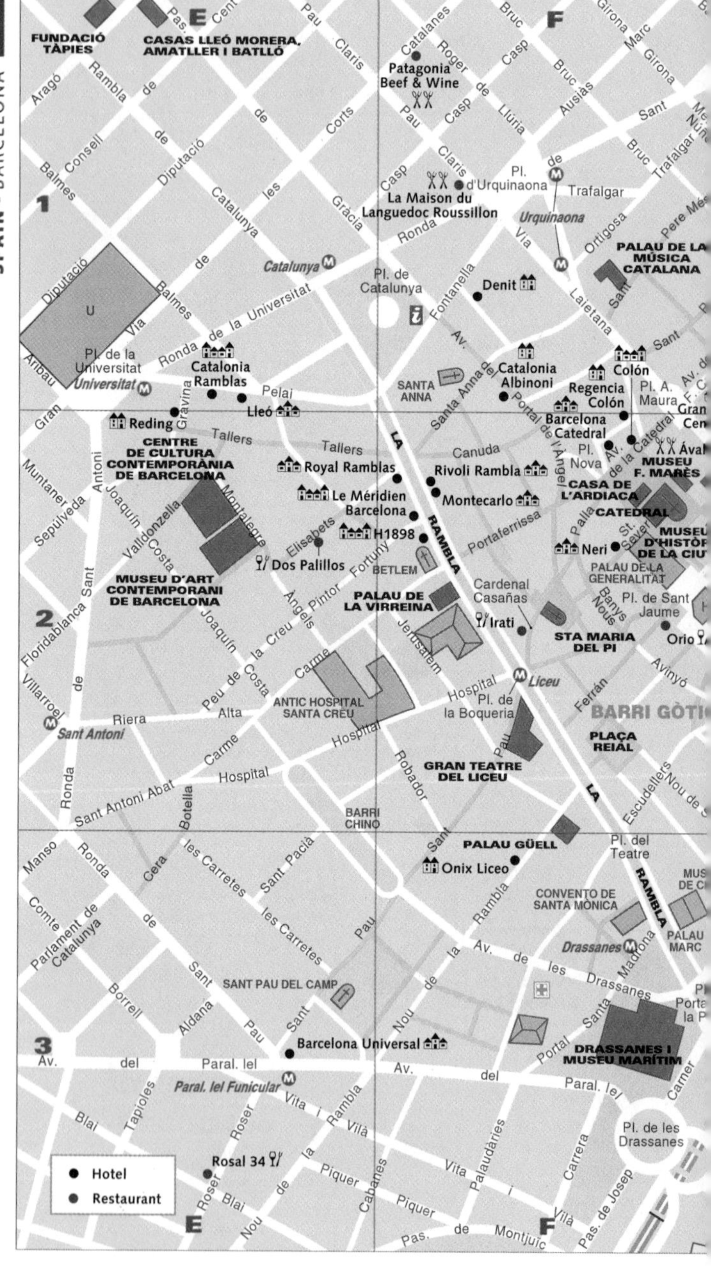

FUNDACIÓ TÀPIES
CASAS LLEÓ MORERA, AMATLLER I BATLLÓ
Patagonia Beef & Wine
La Maison du Languedoc Roussillon
Pl. d'Urquinaona
Urquinaona
Trafalgar
Catalunya
Pl. de Catalunya
PALAU DE LA MÚSICA CATALANA
Denit
Pl. de la Universitat
Universitat
Catalonia Ramblas
Lleó
Reding
Catalonia Albinoni
Colón
Regencia Colón
Pl. A. Maura
Barcelona Catedral
SANTA ANNA
CENTRE DE CULTURA CONTEMPORÀNIA DE BARCELONA
Royal Ramblas
Le Méridien Barcelona
H1898
Rivoli Rambla
Montecarlo
Pl. Nova
MUSEU F. MARÈS
CASA DE L'ARDIACA
CATEDRAL
Neri
PALAU DE LA GENERALITAT
Pl. de Sant Jaume
Orio
Dos Palillos
BETLEM
MUSEU D'ART CONTEMPORANI DE BARCELONA
PALAU DE LA VIRREINA
Irati
STA MARIA DEL PI
Liceu
Pl. de la Boqueria
ANTIC HOSPITAL SANTA CREU
BARRI GÒTIC
PLAÇA REIAL
Sant Antoni
GRAN TEATRE DEL LICEU
BARRI CHINO
PALAU GÜELL
Onix Liceo
Pl. del Teatre
CONVENTO DE SANTA MÒNICA
Drassanes
PALAU MARC
SANT PAU DEL CAMP
Barcelona Universal
DRASSANES I MUSEU MARÍTIM
Paral. lel Funicular
Pl. de les Drassanes
Rosal 34
LA RAMBLA
Hotel
Restaurant

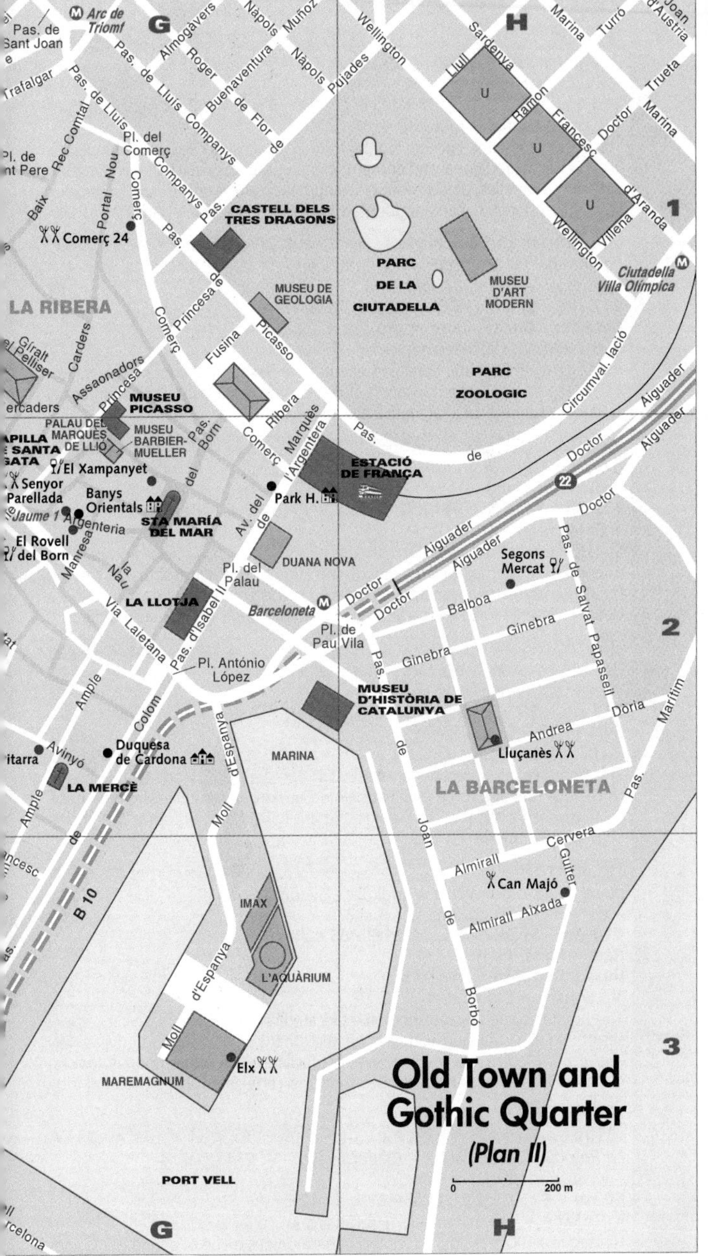
Old Town and Gothic Quarter
(Plan II)
Arc de Triomf
G
H
1
2
3
CASTELL DELS TRES DRAGONS
PARC DE LA CIUTADELLA
MUSEU DE GEOLOGIA
MUSEU D'ART MODERN
PARC ZOOLOGIC
Ciutadella Villa Olímpica
LA RIBERA
MUSEU PICASSO
PALAU DEL MARQUÈS DE LLIÓ
MUSEU BARBIER-MUELLER
El Xampanyet
Senyor Parellada
Banys Orientals
STA MARÍA DEL MAR
El Rovell del Born
Comerç 24
ESTACIÓ DE FRANÇA
Park H.
DUANA NOVA
LA LLOTJA
Barceloneta
Pl. del Palau
Pl. de Pau Vila
Pl. António López
Segons Mercat
MUSEU D'HISTÒRIA DE CATALUNYA
Duquesa de Cardona
LA MERCÈ
MARINA
Lluçanès
LA BARCELONETA
Can Majó
IMAX
L'AQUÀRIUM
Elx
MAREMAGNUM
PORT VELL
B 10
0
200 m

H1898

La Rambla 109 ✉ 08002 – Ⓜ Catalunya – ✆ 935 52 95 52 – www.hotel1898.com **F2**

166 rm – 180/350 € 265/405 €, 21 € – 3 suites **Rest** – Carte 36/59 €

♦ Chain hotel ♦ Classic ♦

The decor in this hotel occupying the former Tabacos de Filipinas headquarters is a mix of the traditional and contemporary. Spa area, guestrooms offering the very best amenities, plus a rooftop solarium with views of the city. This resolutely contemporary restaurant offers an à la carte menu of international dishes.

Le Méridien Barcelona

La Rambla 111 ✉ 08001 – Ⓜ Catalunya – ✆ 933 18 62 00 – www.lemeridiembarcelona.com **F2**

217 rm – 179/795 €, 25 € – 16 suites

Rest *Cent Onze* – Carte approx. 46 €

♦ Business ♦ Contemporary ♦

An elegant, emblematic hotel combining local flavour and contemporary, cosmopolitan style. Excellent location alongside the Ramblas. A bright, informal restaurant offering an imaginative à la carte menu.

Colón

av. de la Catedral 7 ✉ 08002 – Ⓜ Jaume I – ✆ 933 01 14 04 – www.hotelcolon.es **F2**

135 rm – 75/183 € 120/255 €, 18 € – 5 suites **Rest** – Menu 23 €

♦ Business ♦ Classic ♦

Superbly located opposite the cathedral. Classic bedrooms offering good levels of comfort, a third of which overlook the church. The guestrooms on the top floor have the added benefit of a terrace. In the Colón's dining room, choose between international à la carte dishes, a set daily menu, and a tasting menu.

Catalonia Ramblas

Pelai 28 ✉ 08001 – Ⓜ Universitat – ✆ 933 16 84 00 – www.restaurante-pelai.com **E1**

219 rm – 99/510 € 109/510 €, 16 € – 2 suites

Rest *Pelai* – Carte 29/40 €

♦ Business ♦ Design ♦

This hotel has an attractive façade linking two early 20C Modernist buildings. Numerous meeting rooms, well-appointed guestrooms and a swimming pool-solarium with a terrace. The Pelai restaurant has its own entrance. Traditional cuisine with a modern twist.

W Barcelona

pl. de la Rosa dels Vents 1 (Moll De Llevant) ✉ 08039 – ✆ 932 952 800 – www.w-barcelona.com *Plan I* **C3**

410 rm – 245/595 €, 25 € – 63 suites

Rest – Carte 35/49 €

Rest *Bravo 24* – Carte 40/58 €

♦ Luxury ♦ Design ♦

This hotel designed by Ricardo Bofill is located in the city's port area. It comprises of two glass buildings: one a cube, the other a huge sail rising impressively above the Mediterranean. Extensive spa facilities. This contemporary looking gastronomic restaurant offers guests an à la carte menu based around high quality products.

Montecarlo without rest

La Rambla 124 ✉ 08002 – Ⓜ Catalunya – ✆ 934 12 04 04 – www.montecarlobcn.com **F2**

50 rm – 110/157 € 168/421 €, 12 €

♦ Palace ♦ Townhouse ♦ Classic ♦

Housed in a 19C mansion, this hotel is a harmonious blend of period furnishings and modern comforts. Choose between classic bedrooms and those with a more modern look which have recently been renovated.

Neri

Sant Sever 5 ✉ *08002* – Ⓜ *Liceu* – ☎ *933 04 06 55* – *www.hotelneri.com*
21 rm – ††198/525 €, ☕ 21.50 € – 1 suite **F2**
Rest – Menu 22 €
♦ Townhouse ♦ Palace ♦ Design ♦
The modern interior of this hotel occupying an 18C mansion comes as something of a surprise. Library-lounge, designer-inspired guestrooms and a rooftop terrace. In the dining room, embellished with two 12C stone arches, diners can choose from a selection of contemporary Mediterranean cuisine.

Grand H. Central

Via Laietana 30 ✉ *08003* – Ⓜ *Jaume I* – ☎ *932 95 79 00*
– *www.grandhotelcentral.com* **F2**
141 rm – ††180/400 €, ☕ 20 € – 6 suites
Rest *Ávalon* – see below
♦ Townhouse ♦ Design ♦
This contemporary hotel emphasises modern design and functionality. Guestrooms feature great attention to detail. Terrace with a swimming pool and panoramic views.

Duquesa de Cardona

passeig de Colom 12 ✉ *08002* – Ⓜ *Drassanes* – ☎ *932 68 90 90*
– *www.hduquesadecardona.com* **G2**
40 rm – ††160/265 €, ☕ 14 €
Rest – *(closed August and Sunday)* Menu 18 €
♦ Historic ♦ Cosy ♦
This hotel occupies a charming 19C mansion that has retained many of its original features. Excellent guestrooms and an attractive terrace-solarium on the roof. A restaurant that is impressively classical in style with large arches and vaults.

Rivoli Ramblas

La Rambla 128 ✉ *08002* – Ⓜ *Catalunya* – ☎ *934 81 76 76*
– *www.rivolihotels.com* **F2**
119 rm – †110/290 € ††110/320 €, ☕ 15 € – 6 suites
Rest – Menu 14 €
♦ Business ♦ Classic ♦
This historical building has an attractive façade and a classic-contemporary décor with Art Deco features. Comfortable guestrooms and a pleasant interior terrace. In this restaurant guests can enjoy classic à la carte dishes with an international slant, alongside two set menus.

Royal Ramblas

La Rambla 117 ✉ *08002* – Ⓜ *Catalunya* – ☎ *933 01 94 00*
– *www.royalramblashotel.com* **F2**
119 rm – †110/190 € ††120/250 €, ☕ 10 €
Rest *La Poma* – Carte 34/51 €
♦ Business ♦ Classic ♦
Located in the heart of the city, this hotel's guestrooms are reasonably modern in appearance, with half overlooking the Ramblas; those on the first floor are superior in quality. This spacious restaurant, specialising in grilled meats and pizzas, has a separate entrance.

Barcelona Catedral

Dels Capellans 4 ✉ *08002* – Ⓜ *Catalunya* – ☎ *933 04 22 55*
– *www.barcelonacatedral.com* **F2**
80 rm – ††119/458 €, ☕ 18.50 €
Rest – *(closed August, Saturday, Sunday and Bank Holidays) (lunch only)* Menu 18.80 €
♦ Business ♦ Modern ♦
A hotel with a contemporary look enhanced by modern amenities and tasteful decor. Fully equipped guestrooms and an attractive terrace occupying an interior patio. This restaurant, located next to the bar, combines traditional à la carte choices with a set daily menu.

Barcelona Universal

av. del Paral.lel 80 ✉ 08001 – Ⓜ Paral.lel – ☎ 935 67 74 47 – www.nnhotels.com **E3**

164 rm – ††81/348 €, ☕ 15 €, 3 suites **Rest** – *(dinner only)* Menu 21.60 €

♦ Chain hotel ♦ Townhouse ♦ Contemporary ♦

This modern hotel offers spacious, well-appointed guestrooms and a lounge area with bar. Panoramic swimming pool with a solarium on the top floor. A simply furnished restaurant serving a buffet of grilled meats.

Lleó without rest

Pelai 22 ✉ 08001 – Ⓜ Universitat – ☎ 933 18 13 12 – www.hotel-lleo.com

89 rm – †135/160 € ††165/195 €, ☕ 14 € **E1**

♦ Business ♦ Functional ♦

A well-run hotel with an elegant façade and functional appearance. Comfortable guestrooms, spacious lounge area and a small rooftop pool.

Onix Liceo without rest

Nou de la Rambla 36 ✉ 08001 – Ⓜ Liceu – ☎ 93 481 64 41 – www.hotelonixliceo.com **F3**

45 rm – ††90/165 €, ☕ 8 €

♦ Business ♦ Contemporary ♦

This establishment occupies a 19C, renovated building, whose façade, light well and original marble staircase have been preserved. It has a modern social area and bedrooms in a functional style.

Catalonia Albinoni

av. Portal de l'Àngel 17 ✉ 08002 – Ⓜ Catalunya – ☎ 933 18 41 41 – www.hoteles-catalonia.com **F1**

83 rm – †90/215 € ††100/260 €, ☕ 16 € **Rest** – Menu 39 €

♦ Chain hotel ♦ Townhouse ♦ Functional ♦

This hotel occupies the former Rocamora palace, situated close to the Gothic quarter. Well-maintained lounge area and functional guestrooms, with those that have been renovated offering a more contemporary feel. The hotel's restaurant offers traditional à la carte choices and two daily menus.

Park H. without rest

av. Marqués de l'Argentera 11 ✉ 08003 – Ⓜ Barceloneta – ☎ 933 19 60 00 – www.parkhotelbarcelona.com **G2**

91 rm ☕ – †87/137 € ††104/191 €

♦ Business ♦ Modern ♦

A hotel occupying a listed building dating back to 1953. Delightful spiral staircase, lounge, and a majority of rooms which have been upgraded, some with a balcony.

Reding

Gravina 5-7 ✉ 08001 – Ⓜ Universitat – ☎ 934 12 10 97 – www.hotelreding.com **E1-2**

44 rm – †90/280 € ††100/300 €, ☕ 14 €

Rest – *(closed August, Saturday dinner, Sunday and Bank Holidays)* Menu 12 €

♦ Business ♦ Functional ♦

A hotel with a traditional façade located close to Plaça de Catalunya. Modern reception, a lounge area and attractively renovated guestrooms with functional furnishings. The simply designed dining room offers a menu featuring traditional and Catalan dishes.

Banys Orientals

L'Argenteria 37 ✉ 08003 – Ⓜ Jaume I – ☎ 932 68 84 60 – www.hotelbanysorientals.com **G2**

56 rm – †88 € ††100 €, ☕ 10 €

Rest *Senyor Parellada* – see below

♦ Business ♦ Design ♦

This hotel has comfortable, minimalist-style rooms. They feature plenty of design features, wooden floors and canopies above the beds. No lounge.

Regencia Colón without rest

Sagristans 13 ✉ 08002 – Ⓜ Jaume I – ✆ 933 18 98 58 – www.hotelregenciacolon.com **F1-2**

50 rm – †75/151 € ††75/183 €, ☕ 12 €

◆ Business ◆ Functional ◆

A good location in one of the most typical districts of the city. Functional rooms with wood floors and fully equipped bathrooms.

Denit without rest

Estruc 24 ✉ 08002 – Ⓜ Urquinaona – ✆ 935 45 40 00 – www.denit.com

36 rm – †79/189 € ††99/209 €, ☕ 6 € **F1**

◆ Business ◆ Functional ◆

This hotel with a classical façade is located in a back street of the city centre. Its bedrooms, all in a modern, urban and functional style, are distributed over five floors.

Lluçanès (Angel Pascual)

pl. de la Font ✉ 08003 – Ⓜ Barceloneta – ✆ 932 24 25 25 – www.restaurantllucanes.com – closed Sunday dinner and Monday **H2**

Rest – Menu 68/110 € – Carte 73/97 €

Spec. Canelón de pollo de pata negra del Penedès con bechamel de Idiazabal ahumado. Bacalao de Islandia, salsa holandesa de albaricoque ahumado y setas. Tartar de ternera de Galicia, mayonesa y trufa blanca de verano.

◆ Inventive ◆ Fashionable ◆

Lluçanès is located inside a former market in the old working class district of La Barceloneta. The bar with tables is for customers choosing the set menu, while the gastronomic restaurant on the first floor boasts designer furniture and views of the square. Contemporary Catalan cuisine.

Ávalon – Hotel Grand H. Central

Pare Gallifa 3 ✉ 08003 – Ⓜ Jaume I – ✆ 932 95 79 05 – www.avalonrestaurant.es **F2**

Rest – Carte approx. 35 €

◆ Inventive ◆ Formal ◆

This restaurant has its own distinctive personality, where young and friendly staff serve a creative set price menu. Modern facilities with many design elements.

La Maison du Languedoc Roussillon

Pau Claris 77 ✉ 08010 – Ⓜ Urquinaona – ✆ 933 01 04 98 – www.restaurantelanguedocroussillon.com **F1**

Rest – Carte 35/40 €

◆ French ◆ Classic ◆

With its warm lighting and contemporary decoration, this restaurant is the ideal setting in which to enjoy good regional French cuisine. Attentive service.

Comerç 24 (Carles Abellán)

Comerç 24 ✉ 08003 – Ⓜ Arc de Triomf – ✆ 933 19 21 02 – www.projectes24.com – closed Sunday and Monday **G1**

Rest – Menu 72/92 € – Carte 50/74 €

Spec. Guisantes de Llavaneres con calamar de potera (primavera). Ceviche de gambita de playa con melocotón de viña. Arroz de conejo y "espardenyes" con manzana y lima.

◆ Inventive ◆ Design ◆

This restaurant has a contemporary decor, including a kitchen visible to diners. It offers two tasting menus and a creative à la carte menu of delicious tapas, tostas and raciones. All of which are well prepared using the very best ingredients.

XX **Patagonia Beef & Wine**

Gran Via de les Corts Catalanes 660 ✉ 08010 – Ⓜ Passeig de Gràcia – ✆ 933 04 37 35 – www.patagoniabw.com **F1**

Rest – Carte 31/56 €

♦ Argentine ♦ Minimalist ♦

An attractive restaurant decorated in minimalist style. A comprehensive menu, with an emphasis on Argentinean red meat dishes.

XX **Senyor Parellada** – Hotel Banys Orientals

L'Argenteria 37 ✉ 08003 – Ⓜ Jaume I – ✆ 933 10 50 94 – www.senyorparellada.com **G2**

Rest – Carte 28/32 €

♦ Catalan cuisine ♦ Cosy ♦

Charming restaurant in a traditional-modern style. It features a bar, various dining rooms and an attractive small patio with a glass roof. Reasonably priced regional cuisine.

XX **Elx**

Moll d'Espanya-Maremagnum, Local 9 ✉ 08039 – Ⓜ Drassanes – ✆ 932 25 81 17 – www.restaurantelx.com **G3**

Rest – Carte 35/43 €

♦ Rice specialities ♦ Formal ♦

A restaurant graced with views of the fishing port. Modern dining room and an attractive terrace, where the focus is on fish and a good selection of savoury rice dishes.

X **Pitarra**

Avinyó 56 ✉ 08002 – Ⓜ Liceu – ✆ 933 01 16 47 – www.restaurantpitarra.cat – closed 13-28 August, Sunday and Bank Holidays dinner **G2**

Rest – Carte 28/45 €

♦ Traditional ♦ Cosy ♦

It was in these premises that Frederic Soler, a leading figure from the world of Catalan theatre, once had his watchmaker's shop. Dining rooms with an old-fashioned feel, including two rooms for private parties. Traditional cuisine.

X **Can Majó**

Almirall Aixada 23 ✉ 08003 – Ⓜ Barceloneta – ✆ 932 21 54 55 – www.canmajo.es – closed Sunday dinner and Monday **H3**

Rest – Carte approx. 44 €

♦ Fish ♦ Family ♦

Renowned, family-run restaurant serving an excellent menu focusing on seafood and rice dishes, hence the impressive seafood counter. Terrace.

El Rovell del Born

L'Argenteria 6 ✉ 08003 – Ⓜ Jaume I – ✆ 932 69 04 58 – www.elrovelldelborn.com – closed Monday except Bank Holidays **G2**

Tapa 9 € **Ración** approx. 15 €

♦ Traditional ♦ Tapas bar ♦

A tavern-style tapas bar with a contemporary design, a counter heaving with delicious raciones, along with a few high tables and wood-clad walls. Traditional à la carte menu with a modern twist.

Irati

Cardenal Casanyes 17 ✉ 08002 – Ⓜ Liceu – ✆ 933 02 30 84 – www.sagardi.com **F2**

Tapa 1.80 €

♦ Basque cuisine ♦ Tapas bar ♦

A typical Basque tavern close to the Gran Teatre del Liceu. Traditional carvery-style dining room where the menu focuses on innovative Basque cuisine. Good selection of tapas at the bar.

El Xampanyet

Montcada 22 ✉ 08003 – Ⓜ Jaume I – ✆ 933 19 70 03
– closed January, last 2 weeks August, Sunday dinner and Monday
Tapa 3.25 € **Ración** approx. 7.50 € **G2**

♦ Traditional ♦ Tapas bar ♦

This old tavern with a long-standing family tradition is decorated with typical azulejo tiles. Varied selection of tapas with an emphasis on cured meats and high-quality canned products.

Dos Palillos

Elisabets 9 ✉ 08001 – Ⓜ Catalunya – ✆ 93 304 05 13 – www.dospalillos.com
– closed 24 December-2 January, 1-29 August, Sunday and Monday (dinner only except Thursday, Friday and Saturday) **E2**
Tapa 4 € **Ración** approx. 10 €

♦ Inventive ♦ Fashionable ♦

Tapas bar serving Asian specialities in a pedestrian street. Classic bar at the entrance, and a second Japanese-style version inside with an open kitchen in the centre.

Rosal 34

Roser 34 ✉ 08004 – Ⓜ Paral.lel – ✆ 933 24 90 46 – www.rosal34.com
– closed 22-28 August, Sunday and Monday **E3**
Ración approx. 17 €

♦ Traditional ♦ Rustic ♦

Rosal 34 is located in an old family wine cellar, where the rustic stonework blends in with the contemporary decor. Seasonal dishes plus interesting tapas with a creative touch.

Orio

Ferran 38 ✉ 08002 – Ⓜ Jaume I – ✆ 933 179 407 – www.sagardi.com
Tapa 1.80 € **Ración** approx. 8 € **F2**

♦ Terroir ♦ Wine bar ♦

Well-located in a pedestrian street, the Orio has an appealing bar laden with tapas, an oyster section and a dining room with high tables in the basement.

Segons Mercat

Balboa 16 ✉ 08003 – Ⓜ Barceloneta – ✆ 933 10 78 80
– www.segonsmercat.com **H2**
Tapa 7 € **Ración** approx. 9 €

♦ Traditional ♦ Tapas bar ♦

This restaurant has a bar with an impressive display of fresh produce, in particular fish and seafood. A separate room is available for tapas, snacks and daily specials.

SOUTH of AV. DIAGONAL *Plan III*

El Palace

Gran Via de les Corts Catalanes 668 ✉ 08010 – Ⓜ Urquinaona
– ✆ 935 10 11 30 – www.hotelpalacebarcelona.com **L2**
119 rm – ††185/560 €, ☕ 28 € – 6 suites **Rest *Caelis*** – see below

♦ Grand Luxury ♦ Classic ♦

This emblematic hotel, occupying an old building that has recently been restored, is steeped in tradition. Refined public areas, and hugely comfortable guestrooms embellished with elegant wallpaper.

Majestic

passeig de Gràcia 68 ✉ 08007 – Ⓜ Passeig de Gràcia – ✆ 934 88 17 17
– www.hotelmajestic.es **K2**
271 rm – ††199/499 €, ☕ 25 € – 32 suites
Rest *Drolma* – see below **Rest** – Carte approx. 45 €

♦ Traditional ♦ Classic ♦

A renovated classic hotel on the Paseo de Gràcia. Superbly appointed guestrooms, although some are not particularly spacious. Impeccable service. Functional dining room offering both a set menu and buffet service.

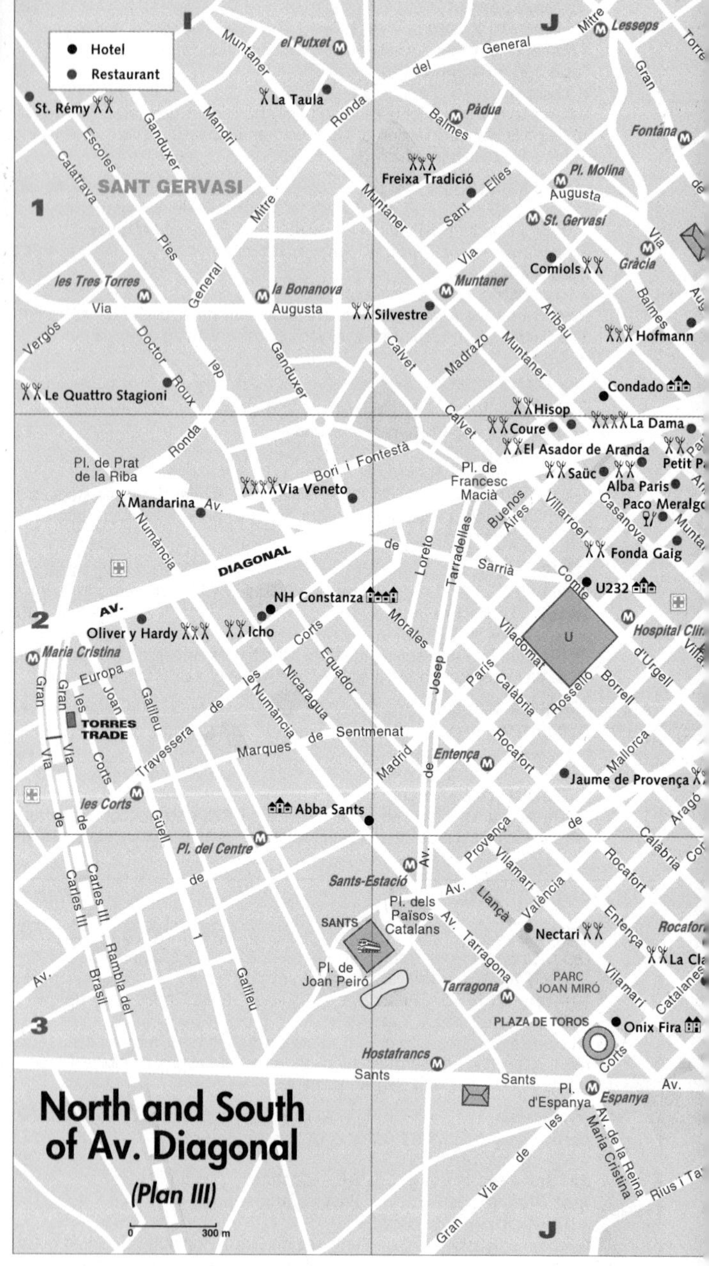
Hotel
Restaurant
I
J
1
2
3
SANT GERVASI
St. Rémy
La Taula
Freixa Tradició
Comiols
Silvestre
Hofmann
Le Quattro Stagioni
Condado
Hisop
Coure
La Dama
El Asador de Aranda
Petit P
Saüc
Alba Paris
Paco Meralgo
Mandarina
Via Veneto
Fonda Gaig
U232
NH Constanza
Oliver y Hardy
Icho
Jaume de Provença
Abba Sants
Nectari
La Cl
Onix Fira
el Putxet
Lesseps
Pàdua
Fontana
Pl. Molina
St. Gervasi
Gràcia
Muntaner
la Bonanova
les Tres Torres
Maria Cristina
Hospital Clí
Entença
les Corts
Pl. del Centre
Sants-Estació
Tarragona
Hostafrancs
Espanya
TORRES TRADE
SANTS
PARC JOAN MIRÓ
PLAZA DE TOROS
Pl. de Prat de la Riba
Pl. de Francesc Macià
Pl. dels Països Catalans
Pl. de Joan Peiró
Pl. d'Espanya
AV. DIAGONAL
North and South of Av. Diagonal
(Plan III)
0
300 m

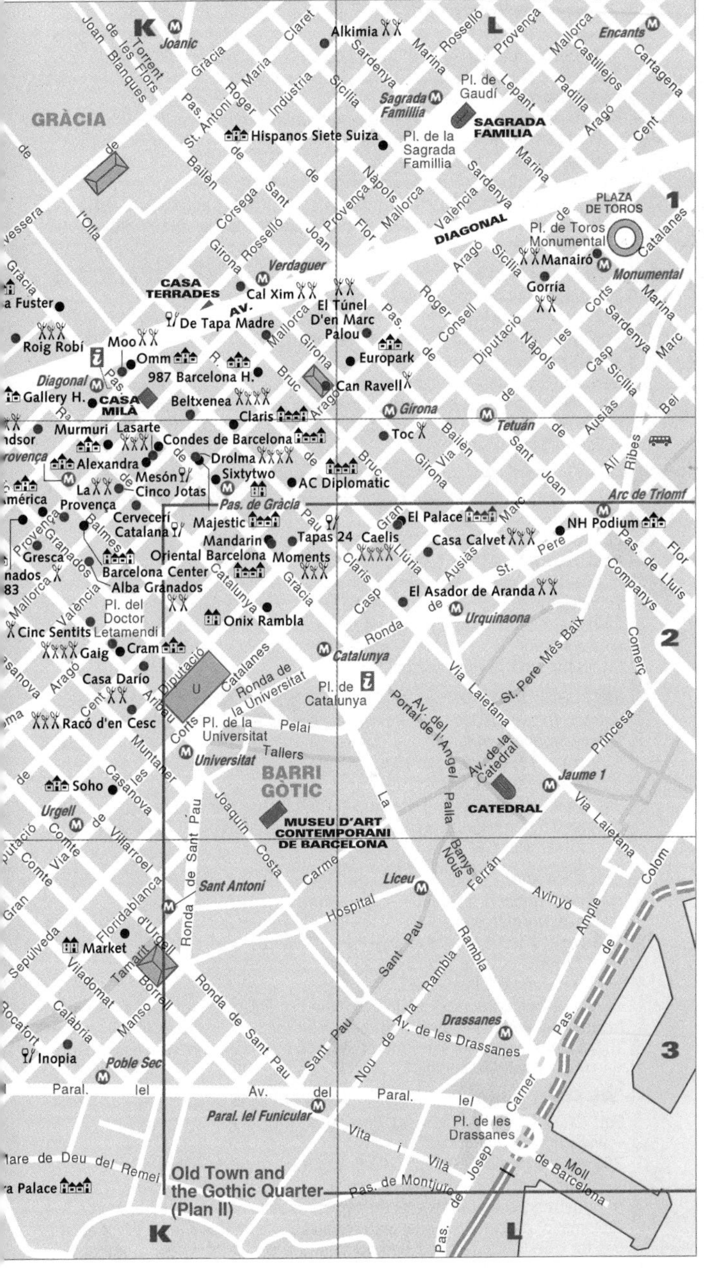
K
L
1
2
3
Joanic
Alkimia
Encants
GRÀCIA
Sagrada Familia
Pl. de Gaudí
SAGRADA FAMILIA
Hispanos Siete Suiza
Pl. de la Sagrada Famillia
PLAZA DE TOROS
Pl. de Toros Monumental
Manairó
Monumental
Gorría
DIAGONAL
Verdaguer
CASA TERRADES
Cal Xim
El Túnel D'en Marc Palou
AV. DIAGONAL
De Tapa Madre
Roig Robí
Moo
Omm
987 Barcelona H.
Europark
Diagonal
Can Ravell
Gallery H.
CASA MILÀ
Beltxenea
Girona
Tetuán
Murmuri
Lasarte
Claris
Condes de Barcelona
Toc
Alexandra
Drolma
Mesón Cinco Jotas
Sixtytwo
AC Diplomatic
La
Provença
Pas. de Gràcia
Arc de Triomf
Cerveceria Catalana
Majestic
El Palace
NH Podium
Mandarin
Tapas 24
Caelis
Casa Calvet
Gresca
Oriental Barcelona
Moments
Barcelona Center
Alba Granados
El Asador de Aranda
Urquinaona
Pl. del Doctor Letamendi
Onix Rambla
Cinc Sentits
Gaig
Cram
Catalunya
Casa Darío
Pl. de Catalunya
Racó d'en Cesc
Pl. de la Universitat
Universitat
BARRI GÒTIC
Jaume 1
Soho
CATEDRAL
Urgell
MUSEU D'ART CONTEMPORANI DE BARCELONA
Sant Antoni
Liceu
Market
Drassanes
Inopia
Poble Sec
Paral. lel Funicular
Pl. de les Drassanes
Palace
Old Town and the Gothic Quarter (Plan II)
Moll de Barcelona

Condes de Barcelona – (Monument i Center)
passeig de Gràcia 73-75 ✉ *08008*
– Ⓜ *Passeig de Gràcia* – ☏ *934 45 00 00* – *www.condesdebarcelona.com*
232 rm – ††135/315 €, ☕ 19 € – 3 suites **K2**
Rest *Lasarte* – see below
Rest *Loidi* – *(closed 2 weeks August, Sunday dinner and Bank Holidays dinner) (set menu only)* Menu 38 €
♦ Historic ♦ Classic ♦
This hotel occupies two of the city's most emblematic buildings, Casa Batlló and Casa Durella. A combination of modern comfort and period decor. Attractive sun terrace. Loidi has adopted a unique bistro concept based around two fixed price menus.

NH Constanza
Deu i Mata 69-99 ✉ *08029* – Ⓜ *Les Corts* – ☏ *932 81 15 00*
– *www.nh-hotels.com* **I2**
300 rm – ††115/290 €, ☕ 20 € – 8 suites **Rest** – Carte approx. 45 €
♦ Business ♦ Contemporary ♦
Designed by Rafael Moneo, the building makes full use of natural light and clean lines. Large lobby, modular meeting rooms and luxurious, functional bedrooms. The restaurant occupies a room decorated in varying tones of white. Traditional cuisine.

Claris
Pau Claris 150 ✉ *08009* – Ⓜ *Passeig de Gràcia* – ☏ *934 87 62 62*
– *www.derbyhotels.com* **K2**
80 rm – †157/425 € ††179/475 €, ☕ 21 € – 40 suites
Rest *East 47* – Menu 42 €
♦ Traditional ♦ Modern ♦
This elegant, stately hotel occupies the former Vedruna palace. It offers a perfect fusion of tradition, cutting-edge design and technology. Impressive archaeological collection. This attractively presented restaurant is decorated in a style that recalls the work of Andy Warhol.

Barcelona Center without rest
Balmes 103 ✉ *08008* – Ⓜ *Passeig de Gràcia* – ☏ *932 73 00 00*
– *www.hotelescenter.com* **K2**
129 rm – ††90/490 €, ☕ 13 € – 3 suites
♦ Chain hotel ♦ Classic ♦
Sheltered behind a striking, well-maintained façade, this hotel boasts superbly equipped modern guestrooms, impressive public areas and a huge solarium on the roof terrace.

Fira Palace
av. Rius i Taulet 1 ✉ *08004* – Ⓜ *Espanya* – ☏ *934 26 22 23*
– *www.fira-palace.com* **J-K3**
258 rm – †399 € ††425 €, ☕ 18 € – 18 suites
Rest *El Mall* – Carte 52/65 €
♦ Business ♦ Classic ♦
Traditional yet contemporary in style, the Fira Palace prides itself on its well-maintained amenities and high-quality furnishings. Well-appointed lounges and extremely spacious guestrooms. A rustic-style restaurant with a menu focusing on international cuisine.

AC Diplomatic
Pau Claris 122 ✉ *08009* – Ⓜ *Passeig de Gràcia* – ☏ *932 72 38 10*
– *www.hotelacdiplomatic.com* **K2**
209 rm – †100/280 € ††113/293 €, ☕ 19 € – 2 suites **Rest** – Menu 15 €
♦ Business ♦ Contemporary ♦
A modern hotel that replicates the typical appearance of an AC property. The Diplomatic combines designer features, creature comforts and excellent amenities for guests. Modernised bedrooms and a choice of meeting rooms. This chain hotel's first-floor restaurant offers a daily set menu alongside modern à la carte options.

Mandarin Oriental Barcelona

rm,

passeig de Gràcia 38-40 ✉ *08007* – Ⓜ *Passeig de Gràcia* – ☎ *93 151 88 88* – *www.mandarinoriental.com* **K2**

95 rm – ††325/540 €, ☕ 39 € – 3 suites

Rest *Moments* – see below

Rest – Menu 33 €

◆ Luxury ◆ Design ◆

This new luxury hotel occupies a former bank. The complete renovation of the building has resulted in a slick, designer-inspired interior, extensive spa facilities and guestrooms offering sumptuous levels of comfort. The restaurant in this luxury hotel is centred on fusion cuisine, including Asian and Mediterranean specialities.

Omm

Rosselló 265 ✉ *08008* – Ⓜ *Diagonal* – ☎ *934 45 40 00* – *www.hotelomm.es* **K1**

87 rm – ††215/475 €, ☕ 25 € – 4 suites

Rest *Moo* – see below

◆ Business ◆ Design ◆

Hidden behind the original façade is a highly contemporary hotel with spacious public areas divided into three sections. Extremely well-appointed guestrooms, and an attractive spa.

Cram

Aribau 54 ✉ *08011* – Ⓜ *Universitat* – ☎ *932 16 77 00* – *www.hotelcram.com* **K2**

67 rm – †100/495 € ††110/495 €, ☕ 22 €

Rest *Gaig* – see below

◆ Business ◆ Modern ◆

Although the guestrooms are on the small side, this is counter balanced by cutting-edge technology and the superb contemporary interior – the work of several famous designers.

Granados 83

rm,

Enric Granados 83 ✉ *08008* – Ⓜ *Provença* – ☎ *934 92 96 70* – *www.derbyhotels.com* **K2**

77 rm – †90/250 € ††100/350 €, ☕ 17 €

Rest – *(closed Saturday lunch and Sunday)* Carte approx. 37 €

◆ Business ◆ Design ◆

This cutting-edge hotel is characterised by its predominance of glass, steel and brick. The superbly appointed bedrooms are decorated with Asian antiques. This restaurant has a terrace and a simple fusion-style menu.

Murmuri

Rambla de Catalunya 104 ✉ *08008* – Ⓜ *Diagonal* – ☎ *93 550 06 00* – *www.murmuri.com* **K2**

53 rm – †149/449 € ††169/479 €, ☕ 16 € – 5 suites **Rest** – Menu 35 €

◆ Business ◆ Contemporary ◆

Building with a classical façade in the middle of Las Ramblas. The lobby is in a contemporary style, just like its simply decorated bedrooms. It features an attractive solarium-terrace. Taste carefully prepared Asian fusion cuisine in this restaurant.

Abba Sants

rm,

Numància 32 ✉ *08029* – Ⓜ *Sants-Estació* – ☎ *936 00 31 00* – *www.abbahoteles.com* **I2**

140 rm – †78/338 € ††78/349 €, ☕ 15.50 €

Rest *Amalur* – Carte approx. 35 €

◆ Business ◆ Functional ◆

This comfortable, modern and well-run hotel is popular with business travellers. Functional guestrooms and several multi-purpose meeting rooms. The Amalur offers attractive à la carte choices, although the daily set menu continues to be the restaurant's best seller.

Alexandra

Mallorca 251 ✉ 08008 – Ⓜ Passeig de Gràcia – ✆ 934 67 71 66 – www.hotel-alexandra.com **K2**

106 rm – ††115/300 € – 3 suites **Rest** – Menu 22.20 €

◆ Business ◆ Contemporary ◆

A welcoming hotel with contemporary public areas which include a cafeteria, and particularly comfortable guestrooms featuring parquet or stone flooring and modern furnishings. The simple à la carte menu in the functionally furnished dining is based around Italian cuisine.

U 232 without rest

Comte d'Urgell 232 ✉ 08036 – Ⓜ Hospital Clínic – ✆ 933 22 41 53 – www.nnhotels.com **J2**

102 rm – †90/200 € ††100/220 €, 13 €

◆ Business ◆ Classic ◆

This centrally located hotel combining traditional and more modern decor boasts welcoming public areas and comfortable guestrooms with open wardrobes and contemporary bathrooms.

Soho without rest

Gran Via de les Corts Catalanes 543-545 ✉ 08011 – Ⓜ Urgell – ✆ 935 52 96 10 – www.hotelsohobarcelona.com **K2**

51 rm – ††108/315 €, 14 €

◆ Business ◆ Design ◆

The Soho combines cutting-edge style with designer detail, the decorative use of light and the interplay of space. An interesting fusion of modern comfort and technology.

América without rest

Provença 195 ✉ 08008 – Ⓜ Provença – ✆ 934 87 62 92 – www.hotelamericabarcelona.com **K2**

60 rm – †80/196 € ††80/230 €, 15 €

◆ Business ◆ Contemporary ◆

Bright, contemporary hotel decorated in an attractive combination of red and white tones. Interior patio and functional, comfortable guestrooms.

Gallery H.

Rosselló 249 ✉ 08008 – Ⓜ Diagonal – ✆ 934 15 99 11 – www.galleryhotel.com **K1**

110 rm – ††100/350 €, 18 € – 5 suites **Rest** – Menu 23 €

◆ Business ◆ Functional ◆

Renovated, contemporary-style hotel with several meeting rooms and comfortable guestrooms. Fully equipped bathrooms showing careful attention to detail. The restaurant has large windows and a pleasant terrace in an interior courtyard.

Europark without rest

Aragó 325 ✉ 08009 – Ⓜ Girona – ✆ 93 457 92 05 – www.hoteleuropark.com

103 rm – ††86/354 €, 14 € – 2 suites **L1**

◆ Business ◆ Contemporary ◆

This contemporary hotel is in the very heart of town. Its small, social area is offset by well-equipped bedrooms. On the top floor are two suites with terraces and good views.

NH Podium

Bailén 4 ✉ 08010 – Ⓜ Arc de Triomf – ✆ 932 65 02 02 – www.nh-hotels.com

140 rm – †113/212 € ††115/235 €, 18.50 € – 5 suites **L2**

Rest *Corella* – *(closed August, Saturday and Sunday)* Carte 30/36 €

◆ Business ◆ Functional ◆

Located in the Modernist Ensanche district, the Podium has a classical façade with a contemporary interior and cosy guestrooms. Swimming pool and a fitness room with sauna on the top floor. A restaurant with a contemporary layout featuring quality furnishings, with an à la carte menu of international dishes.

987 Barcelona H. without rest

Mallorca 288 ✉ 08037 – Ⓜ Passeig de Gràcia – ✆ 93 476 33 96 – www.987hotels.com **K1**

88 rm – 🚹90/290 € 🚹🚹100/310 €, ☕ 14 €

♦ Business ♦ Design ♦

Designer decor is to the fore here, with coloured lights in the public areas, a pleasant internal patio and modern and functional guestrooms.

Sixtytwo without rest

passeig de Gràcia 62 ✉ 08007 – Ⓜ Passeig de Gràcia – ✆ 932 72 41 80 – www.sixtytwohotel.com **K2**

45 rm – 🚹129/279 € 🚹🚹149/662 €, ☕ 19.50 €

♦ Townhouse ♦ Modern ♦

This small hotel, with its attractive façade and modern interior, is situated along the Paseo de Gràcia. Well-equipped guestrooms, albeit a little on the small side.

Market

passatge Sant Antoni Abad 10 ✉ 08015 – Ⓜ Sant Antoni – ✆ 93 325 12 05 – www.markethotel.com.es **K3**

52 rm – 🚹60/130 € 🚹🚹65/145 €, ☕ 9.50 €

Rest – Menu 10 €

♦ Traditional ♦ Contemporary ♦

This establishment is in a good location next to the central Mercat de Sant Antoni, in an old residential building. A contemporary-colonial ambience is recreated in the bedrooms, all with wooden floors. This pleasant restaurant offers a set daily menu alongside traditional à la carte choices.

Onix Fira without rest

Llançà 30 ✉ 08015 – Ⓜ Espanya – ✆ 934 26 00 87 – www.hotelonixfira.com **J3**

80 rm – 🚹🚹60/119 €, ☕ 7.60 €

♦ Business ♦ Functional ♦

This simple, comfortable hotel is a good option for delegates attending the nearby 'Fira de Barcelona' complex. Spacious cafeteria and functional guest rooms.

Onix Rambla without rest

Rambla de Catalunya 24 ✉ 08007 – Ⓜ Catalunya – ✆ 933 42 79 80 – www.hotelonixrambla.com **K2**

40 rm – 🚹🚹92/152 €, ☕ 8.65 €

♦ Business ♦ Functional ♦

Simple, understated contemporary design with an emphasis on wood, white tones and concrete. The functional guestrooms are adorned with wooden laminate flooring.

XXXX ✿

Caelis – Hotel El Palace

Gran Via Corts Catalanes 668 ✉ 08010 – Ⓜ Urquinaona – ✆ 935 10 12 05 – www.caelis.com – closed Holy Week, August, Sunday and Monday **L2**

Rest – *(dinner only)* Menu 70/80 € – Carte 66/81 €

Spec. El té de colmenillas, pan de romero, chorizo y tripas de bacalao. Los macarrones rellenos como un "mar y montaña", bogavante y foie-gras. La vichyssoise en cubo de hielo, caviar Sturia y cucurucho de chantilly.

♦ Inventive ♦ Elegant ♦

Striking for its elegant atmosphere and contrasting decor, this restaurant has its own entrance, an attractive private room and a contemporary-style dining area. Beautifully presented, inventive cuisine made from only the best quality ingredients.

XXXX ✿

Drolma – Hotel Majestic

passeig de Gràcia 68 ✉ 08007
– Ⓜ Passeig de Gràcia – ☎ 934 96 77 10
– www.drolmarestaurant.cat
– closed Sunday **K2**

Rest – Menu 125 € – Carte 95/134 €

Spec. Canelones de faisana salvaje con trufas (diciembre-marzo). Gambas, crema fina de guisantes, menta y jamón. Bogavante con pasta y puerros.

♦ International ♦ Formal ♦

The impeccable furnishings and slick, classic-style decor with a predominance of wood combine to create a refined and elegant ambience. Cuisine with an international flavour with an emphasis on the finest ingredients.

XXXX ✿

Gaig (Carles Gaig) – Hotel Cram

Aragó 214 ✉ 08011 – Ⓜ Universitat – ☎ 934 29 10 17
– www.restaurantgaig.com
– closed Holy Week, 3 weeks in August, Sunday, Monday and Bank Holidays

Rest – Menu 90 € – Carte 58/83 € **K2**

Spec. Canelón tradicional a la crema de trufas. Tartar de lubina y gamba con caviar de arenque. Pies de cerdo guisados a la catalana.

♦ Inventive ♦ Design ♦

This restaurant boasts an attractive contemporary setting with superb attention to detail and magnificent service. The traditionally based cuisine reflects modern culinary tastes with an accent on market produce and presentation. Splendid wine cellar.

XXXX

La Dama

av. Diagonal 423 ✉ 08036
– Ⓜ Diagonal – ☎ 932 02 06 86
– www.ladama-restaurant.com **J2**

Rest – Carte 52/69 €

♦ International ♦ Retro ♦

La Dama has a classically elegant atmosphere with splendid Modernist detail both on the façade and within its walls. Excellent service.

XXXX

Beltxenea

Mallorca 275 ✉ 08008 – Ⓜ Diagonal – ☎ 932 15 30 24
– www.beltxenea.com
– closed August and Sunday **K1**

Rest – Carte 52/65 €

♦ Traditional ♦ Formal ♦

Located in an elegant mansion with a certain old world charm. Refined, classical cuisine with two dining rooms overlooking a small garden.

XXX ✿✿

Lasarte – Hotel Condes de Barcelona

Mallorca 259 ✉ 08008 – Ⓜ Passeig de Gràcia – ☎ 934 45 32 42
– www.restaurantlasarte.com
– closed Holy Week, August, Sunday, Monday and Bank Holiday **K2**

Rest – Menu 115 € – Carte 76/101 €

Spec. Ostras crujientes con ensaladilla de pomelo, nueces y caldo cítrico. Lenguado con aceite de moluscos, pulpo, cítricos y espolvoreado de nueces con mandarina. Pichón asado, oreja de cerdo, espinacas y crema de hongos.

♦ Inventive ♦ Trendy ♦

Lasarte bears the personal stamp of Martín Berasategui and his team. It features an attractive entrance hall and two delightfully laid-out dining rooms, both designed in a reasonably contemporary style. The menu is highly creative, featuring inventive dishes and traditional Basque specialities.

XXX

Casa Calvet

Casp 48 ✉ 08010 – Ⓜ Urquinaona – ☎ 934 12 40 12 – www.casacalvet.es – closed 20 days in August, Sunday and Bank Holidays **L2**

Rest – Carte 46/50 €

◆ Inventive ◆ Formal ◆

Housed in an attractive Modernist building designed by Gaudí. Well-presented traditional cuisine with a contemporary flavour, centred around the very best ingredients.

XXX

Windsor

Còrsega 286 ✉ 08008 – Ⓜ Diagonal – ☎ 932 37 75 88 – www.restaurantwindsor.com – closed 1-7 January, Holy Week, August and Sunday **K2**

Rest – Carte 42/54 €

◆ Catalan ◆ Formal ◆

Elegant, classical style restaurant with several private rooms and a main dining room that overlooks a garden. Good selection of contemporary Catalan dishes, as well as an excellent wine list.

XXX

Oliver y Hardy

av. Diagonal 593 ✉ 08014 – Ⓜ Maria Cristina – ☎ 934 19 31 81 – closed August, Saturday lunch, Sunday, Monday dinner and Tuesday dinner

Rest – Carte 39/48 € **I2**

◆ Traditional ◆ Formal ◆

A real classic of Barcelona nightlife, this venue has two sections: a night club on one side and a restaurant on the other serving traditional cuisine with a contemporary flair.

XXX

Jaume de Provença

Provença 88 ✉ 08029 – Ⓜ Entença – ☎ 934 30 00 29 – www.jaumeprovenza.com – closed Holy Week, August, Sunday dinner and Monday **J2**

Rest – Carte 42/63 €

◆ International ◆ Formal ◆

Run by its owner, this classical style restaurant has a bar, various wine cellars and a pleasant dining room with wood panelled walls.

XXX

Racó d'en Cesc

Diputació 201 ✉ 08011 – Ⓜ Universitat – ☎ 934 51 60 02 – Closed Holy Week, August, Sunday and Bank Holidays **K2**

Rest – Carte 44/52 €

◆ Inventive ◆ Classic ◆

This restaurant has an entrance hall, a resolutely traditional main dining room and various private rooms. Creative menu based on daily recommendations, accompanied by a comprehensive choice of wines.

XXX ✿

Moments – Hotel Mandarin Oriental Barcelona

passeig de Gràcia 38-40 ✉ 08007 – Ⓜ Passeig de Gràcia – ☎ 93 151 88 88 – www.mandarinoriental.com – closed Sunday and Monday **K2**

Rest – Menu 125 € – Carte 94/104 €

Spec. Arroz caldoso de gamba con picada de pescador. Pichón deshuesado relleno de papada de cerdo "Duroc" y hoja de cerezo japonés. Paisajes de Sant Pol en dos servicios.

◆ Inventive ◆ Fashionable ◆

Accessed via the hotel's reception area, this restaurant boasts a highly original decor with carpeting on the floor. The chef and his experienced team work together to create high quality, inventive cuisine with subtle combinations of flavours produced using the very best ingredients.

XX ✿

Cinc Sentits (Jordi Artal)

Aribau 58 ✉ 08011 – Ⓜ Universitat – ☎ 933 23 94 90
– www.cincsentits.com
– closed Holy Week, 15 days in August, Sunday and Monday **K2**

Rest – *(set menu only)* Menu 49/69 €

Spec. Salmonete de roca, chanfaina fresca y tomillo limón. Cochinillo ibérico con texturas de manzana. Chocolate con pan, aceite y sal.

♦ Inventive ♦ Minimalist ♦

This attractive restaurant has a minimalist style decor. No à la carte menu, just three tasting menus. Inventive cuisine that makes full use of high quality Catalan products.

XX ✿

Moo – Hotel Omm

Rosselló 265 ✉ 08008 – Ⓜ Diagonal – ☎ 934 45 40 00
– www.hotelomm.es – closed August and Sunday **K1**

Rest – Menu 69/100 € – Carte 62/79 €

Spec. Cigala con curry y rosas. Manzana caramelizada con foie-gras y aceite de vainilla. Pichón a la cuchara.

♦ Inventive ♦ Design ♦

This restaurant with a cosmopolitan feel incorporates a cafeteria and an open dining room with skylights and design-inspired decorative detail. Inventive cuisine featuring an astute combination of flavours, accompanied by a fine choice of original wines.

XX

Fonda Gaig

Còrsega 200 ✉ 08036 – Ⓜ Hospital Clinic – ☎ 934 53 20 20
– www.fondagaig.com
– closed Holy Week, 9-23 August, Sunday dinner and Monday **J2**

Rest – Carte approx. 50 €

♦ Catalan ♦ Trendy ♦

The name refers to the former family-run inn, now closed. It features a glass façade, lots of natural light in the two-floor dining room, and three private dining rooms. Catalan cuisine.

XX ✿

Saüc (Xavier Franco)

passatge Lluís Pellicer 12 ✉ 08036 – Ⓜ Hospital Clinic – ☎ 933 21 01 89
– www.saucrestaurant.com
– closed 7 days January, 21 days August, Sunday and Monday **J2**

Rest – Menu 60/85 € – Carte 58/70 €

Spec. Alubias de Santa Pau y gambas a la sal, pil-pil de ceps. Rodaballo, acelgas y espárragos silvestres, jugo de bogavante y azafrán (febrero-mayo). Jarrete de ternera lechal, "trinxat" de patata y perona.

♦ Inventive ♦ Family ♦

This restaurant designed along modern lines has a variety of avant-garde decorative features. It features two attractive dining rooms where the focus is on well-presented creative cuisine, which makes full use of high quality products.

XX

Petit París

París 196 ✉ 08036 – Ⓜ Diagonal – ☎ 932 18 26 78 **J2**

Rest – Carte 45/56 €

♦ Terroir ♦ Formal ♦

A charming restaurant decorated in a classical English style with a profusion of wood and wall paper. A regional menu featuring locally sourced products, in addition to daily specials.

XX

La Provença

Provença 242 ✉ 08008 – Ⓜ Diagonal – ☎ 933 23 23 67
– www.laprovenza.com **K2**

Rest – Carte 26/34 €

♦ Terroir ♦ Formal ♦

A cosy restaurant along classic-modern lines with numerous private dining areas. Popular with business clientele, the menu here is varied with a good choice of daily specials.

XX

El Túnel D'en Marc Palou

Bailén 91 ✉ 08009 – Ⓜ Girona – ✆ 932 65 86 58
– www.eltuneldenmarc.com
– closed August, Sunday and Monday dinner **L1**

Rest – Carte 36/43 €

♦ Inventive ♦ Trendy ♦

Located in a busy street, this restaurant has two contemporary-style dining rooms on two floors and a wine cellar which doubles as a private room. Traditional cuisine with a creative touch.

XX

Alba Granados

Enric Granados 34 ✉ 08036 – Ⓜ Diagonal – ✆ 934 54 61 16
– www.albagranados.com
– closed Sunday dinner **K2**

Rest – Carte 35/45 €

♦ Mediterranean ♦ Rustic ♦

Unusual decor, entirely centred around the world of wine. Dining rooms on two floors, where the traditional menu offers a good choice of grilled meats.

XX

El Asador de Aranda

Londres 94 ✉ 08036 – Ⓜ Hospital Clínic – ✆ 934 14 67 90
– www.asadordearanda.com
– closed Sunday dinner **L2**

Rest – Carte 33/37 €

♦ Roast lamb ♦ Rustic ♦

This spacious restaurant is decorated in Castilian style with a wood oven in full view of the dining room. Traditional cuisine with a particular focus on roast dishes.

XX

Gorría

Diputació 421 ✉ 08013 – Ⓜ Monumental – ✆ 932 45 11 64
– www.restaurantegorria.com
– closed Holy Week, August, Sunday, Monday dinner and Bank Holidays dinner **L1**

Rest – Carte 39/52 €

♦ Traditional ♦ Friendly ♦

A well-established Basque restaurant with rustic style decor. The excellent menu is complemented by an extensive wine list. Attentive service.

XX

Icho

Deu i Mata 69-95 ✉ 08029 – Ⓜ Les Corts – ✆ 934 44 33 70
– www.ichobcnjapones.com
– closed Holy Week, 2-23 August, Sunday and Monday dinner **I2**

Rest – Carte approx. 50 €

♦ Japanese ♦ Trendy ♦

The restaurant is named after a traditional Japanese tree. Its style is contemporary, service and cuisine are to a high standard, and the cuisine respects both technique and the product.

XX

Nectari

València 28 ✉ 08015 – Ⓜ Tarragona – ✆ 93 226 87 18 – www.nectari.es
– closed 15 days in August and Sunday **J3**

Rest – Carte 43/60 €

♦ Modern ♦ Trendy ♦

Occupying the lower floors of a residential building, this restaurant has two contemporary-style dining areas and one private dining room. Inventive Mediterranean cuisine from the owner-chef.

XX

El Asador de Aranda

Pau Clarís 70 ✉ 08010 – Ⓜ Urquinaona – ☏ 933 42 55 77 – www.asadordearanda.com – closed Sunday dinner **J2**

Rest – Carte 33/37 €

♦ Roast lamb ♦ Rustic ♦

Typical of this chain of carveries, this restaurant has a bar at the entrance, a rotisserie in full view of diners, as well as two welcoming dining rooms with elegant Castilian decor.

XX

Casa Darío

Consell de Cent 256 ✉ 08011 – Ⓜ Universitat – ☏ 934 53 31 35 – www.casadario.com – closed August and Sunday **K2**

Rest – Carte 44/57 €

♦ Galician specialities ♦ Formal ♦

A well-established restaurant with a good reputation for the quality of its ingredients. The restaurant has a private bar, three dining rooms and three private rooms. Galician dishes and seafood are the house specialities.

XX ✿

Manairó (Jordi Herrera)

Diputació 424 ✉ 08013 – Ⓜ Monumental – ☏ 932 31 00 57 – www.manairo.com – closed 16-22 August and Sunday **L1**

Rest – Menu 65/100 € – Carte 47/65 €

Spec. Calamares a la romana de huevos fritos con morcilla. Filete al clavo ardiendo. Huevos duros de coliflor y foie con verduras y trufa (diciembre-febrero).

♦ Inventive ♦ Trendy ♦

This small but extremely popular local restaurant is run by the owner-chef. The contemporary decor, embellished with works by various artists, serves as a backdrop for creative cuisine with a local flavour and impressive innovative touches.

XX

Alba París

París 168 ✉ 08036 – Ⓜ Hospital Clinic – ☏ 934 30 91 19 – www.albaparis.com – closed 1-15 August and Sunday **J2**

Rest – Carte approx. 40 €

♦ Traditional ♦ Formal ♦

The dining room in this family-run restaurant has a classical design with paintings on the walls that evoke the world of wine. Traditional cuisine, including chuletón a la piedra (stone-grilled T-bone steak), the house speciality.

XX

La Clara

Gran Via de les Corts Catalanes 442 ✉ 08015 – Ⓜ Rocafort – ☏ 932 89 34 60 – www.laclararestaurant.com **J3**

Rest – Carte 27/35 €

♦ Traditional ♦ Cosy ♦

Tapas bar and two modern dining rooms on different floors with the kitchen visible between the two. Traditional à la carte menu accompanied by an impressive wine list.

X

Gresca

Provença 230 ✉ 08036 – Ⓜ Diagonal – ☏ 93 451 61 93 – www.gresca.net – closed 15 August - 2 September, Saturday lunch and Sunday **K2**

Rest – Carte 32/44 €

♦ Modern ♦ Trendy ♦

The discreet façade leads to a spacious, minimalist-style dining room, decorated in contrasting shades of black and white. Contemporary cuisine from the conscientious chef.

Toc

Girona 59 ✉ 08009 – Ⓜ Girona – ☎ 934 88 11 48 – www.tocbcn.com – closed weekends in June-July, August, Saturday lunch and Sunday

Rest – Carte 37/53 € **L2**

♦ Catalan ♦ Trendy ♦

This restaurant extending over two floors has modern, 1970s inspired decor. Contemporary Catalan cuisine.

Can Ravell

Aragó 313 ✉ 08009 – Ⓜ Girona – ☎ 934 57 51 14 – www.ravell.com **K1**

Rest – Carte 33/50 €

♦ Traditional ♦ Family ♦

This unusual restaurant has a charcuterie at the entrance and a small kitchen which guests have to walk through to get to the dining room and private rooms. Traditional cuisine.

Mesón Cinco Jotas

Rambla de Catalunya 91-93 ✉ 08008 – Ⓜ Provença – ☎ 934 87 89 42 – www.mesoncincojotas.com **K2**

Tapa 5 € **Ración** approx. 20 €

♦ Traditional ♦ Tapas bar ♦

Spacious and rustic bar decorated with a profusion of wood. Enjoy the mouth-watering array of hams at a table by the entrance or in the rear dining room. Extensive tapas menu.

Cervecería Catalana

Mallorca 236 ✉ 08008 – Ⓜ Diagonal – ☎ 932 16 03 68 **K2**

Tapa 5 € **Ración** approx. 11 €

♦ Traditional ♦ Tapas bar ♦

This popular local pub, decorated with racks full of bottles, serves a comprehensive choice of top quality tapas.

De Tapa Madre

Mallorca 301 ✉ 08037 – Ⓜ Verdaguer – ☎ 934 59 31 34 – www.detapamadre.com **K1**

Tapa 5 € **Ración** approx. 15 €

♦ Traditional ♦ Rustic ♦

Rustic tapas bar with a small terrace, dining room and a private room on the upper floor. The tapas here are all produced from high quality ingredients.

Paco Meralgo

Muntaner 171 ✉ 08002 – Ⓜ Hospital Clínic – ☎ 934 30 90 27 – www.pacomeralgo.com **J2**

Tapa 6 € **Ración** approx. 20 €

♦ Modern ♦ Tapas bar ♦

The Paco Meralgo has two bars and two separate entrances. Although its most impressive features are its seafood display cabinets with a varied, fresh and top quality choice of options. A private room is also available.

Tapas 24

Diputació 269 ✉ 08007 – ☎ 93 488 09 77 – www.projectes24.com – closed Sunday **K2**

Tapa 5 € **Ración** approx. 8 €

♦ Traditional ♦ Tapas bar ♦

This bar is located in a half-basement. It creates a contemporary atmosphere with two bars and walls decorated with mosaics. Choose from its delicious menu of tapas and side dishes.

Inopia

Tamarit 104 ✉ *08015* – Ⓜ *Poble Sec* – ✆ *934 24 52 31*
– *www.barinopia.com*
– *close 15 days in Christmas, Holy Week, August, Sunday and Monday (dinner only except Saturday)* **K3**

Tapa 3 € **Ración** approx. 6 €

♦ Traditional ♦ Fashionable ♦

Situated close to the city's exhibition site, this restaurant stands out for its personalised decor. Traditional tapas created using top quality ingredients.

SANT MARTÍ *Plan I*

Arts

Marina 19 ✉ *08005* – Ⓜ *Ciutadella-Vila Olímpica* – ✆ *932 21 10 00*
– *www.hotelartsbarcelona.com* **C2**

397 rm – 385/1200 €, 37 € – 59 suites

Rest *Enoteca* – see below

Rest *Arola* – *(closed January)* Carte approx. 60 €

♦ Luxury ♦ Contemporary ♦

Splendid hotel occupying a glass tower overlooking the Olympic port. It has magnificent views of the city and rooms that combine luxury and ultramodern design. Arola is renowned for its top quality cuisine.

Hilton Diagonal Mar

passeig del Taulat 262-264 ✉ *08019*
– Ⓜ *El Maresme Fòrum* – ✆ *935 07 07 07*
– *www.hilton.com* **D2**

413 rm – 153/443 € 175/465 €, 24.50 € – 20 suites

Rest – Carte approx. 50 €

♦ Business ♦ Contemporary ♦

Located near the Fórum, the Hilton is a popular conference venue. The guestrooms have a clean, contemporary design, with high-quality modern furnishings ensuring a comfortable stay. The functional restaurant doubles as the breakfast buffet room and a dining room offering an international à la carte menu.

Diagonal Barcelona

av. Diagonal 205 ✉ *08018* – Ⓜ *Glòries* – ✆ *934 89 53 00*
– *www.hoteldiagonalbarcelona.com* **C2**

228 rm – 85/350 € 85/450 €, 17 € – 12 suites

Rest – *(closed August)* Menu 49 €

♦ Business ♦ Design ♦

Several well-known artists have given vent to their creativity in this designer hotel. Highly modern guestrooms with open bathrooms and a sun terrace on the top floor. This contemporary restaurant offers a traditional à la carte menu.

Pullman Barcelona Skipper

av. del Litoral 10 ✉ *08005*
– Ⓜ *Ciutadella-Vila Olímpica* – ✆ *932 21 65 65*
– *www.pullman-barcelona-skipper.com* **C2**

235 rm – 180/350 € 210/375 €, 25 € – 6 suites

Rest – Menu 36.50 €

♦ Business ♦ Modern ♦

This hotel combines designer detail and technology with a warm and welcoming setting. A varied lounge area, guestrooms offering modern creature comforts, a spa, plus an attractive rooftop terrace with a swimming pool. A bright, contemporary-style restaurant with views of the terrace. International cuisine.

ME Barcelona

Pere IV-272 ✉ 08005 – Ⓜ Poblenou – ✆ 93 367 20 50 – www.solmelia.com **D2**

236 rm – ††155/425 €, ☕ 22 € – 23 suites

Rest *Dos Cielos* – see below

Rest – Menu 30 €

◆ Business ◆ Design ◆

The hotel is set in a 30-floor glazed building. It has a modern lobby with designer details, a lounge-bar, and contemporary bedrooms all with views. The cuisine in the hotel's contemporary restaurant is firmly geared towards international tastebuds.

Diagonal Zero

pl. de Llevant ✉ 08019 – Ⓜ El Maresme Fòrum – ✆ 93 507 80 00 – www.hoteldiagonalzero.com **D1-2**

260 rm – †80/150 € ††90/180 €, ☕ 18 € – 2 suites

Rest – *(closed Sunday)* Menu 22 €

◆ Business ◆ Modern ◆

This hotel is well located next to the Barcelona Conference Centre. It offers guests bright and modern rooms equipped with the latest technology. Large gym and spa. The set menu and concise à la carte choices in this restaurant are based around Mediterranean cuisine.

Barcelona Princess

av. Diagonal 1 ✉ 08019 – Ⓜ El Maresme Fòrum – ✆ 93 356 10 00 – www.hotelbarcelonaprincess.com **D2**

322 rm – †79/315 € ††91/327 €, ☕ 19 € – 42 suites

Rest – Menu 14.95 €

◆ Business ◆ Contemporary ◆

The Princess occupies two modern tower blocks in the Fórum district of the city. Colourful lobby and contemporary-style guestrooms with good views and glass-enclosed bathrooms. Traditional à la carte choices are on offer in the bright and functional restaurant.

AC Barcelona

passeig del Taulat 278 ✉ 08019 – Ⓜ El Maresme Fòrum – ✆ 93 489 82 00 – www.ac-hotels.com **D2**

336 rm – ††100/330 €, ☕ 23 € – 32 suites **Rest** – Menu 25 €

◆ Business ◆ Contemporary ◆

Situated in the Fórum district of the city, this hotel offers the typical amenities associated with the AC chain, including a fully equipped spa. Modern, comfortable guestrooms with suites on the corners of the building. The hotel's modern dining room has a kitchen that remains open 24 hours a day.

Enoteca – Hotel Arts

Marina 19 ✉ 08005 – Ⓜ Ciutadella-Vila Olímpica – ✆ 932 21 10 00 – www.hotelartsbarcelona.com – closed August and Sunday **C2**

Rest – *(dinner only except Monday and Tuesday)* Menu 86 € – Carte 68/91 €

Spec. "Espardenyes" a la plancha. Rodaballo, espárragos silvestres, patata "aliña" y su jugo. Cordero de leche, polenta, tomate y trompetas de la muerte.

◆ Modern ◆ Classic ◆

The Enoteca's attractively designed dining room is a mix of the traditional and modern with a backdrop of display cabinets full of wine bottles. The cuisine is in keeping with the decor with perfectly prepared dishes of a consistently high quality.

XXX

Dos Cielos – Hotel ME Barcelona

Pere IV-272 ✉ *08005* – Ⓜ *Poblenou* – ☎ *93 367 20 70*
– *www.doscielos.com* **D2**

Rest – *(Closed 15 days is January, 15 days in August, Sunday and Monday)* Menu 85/110 € – Carte 76/96 €

Spec. San Pedro con alcachofas y huevo de codorniz. Civet de anguila con chalotas y ajos tiernos. Viaje amazónico.

◆ Modern ◆ Fashionable ◆

Situated on the 24th floor of the Me Barcelona hotel, this restaurant is unusual in that its kitchen is part of the dining room. It has elegantly laid tables and a stainless-steel bar where diners can also choose to eat. Enjoy stunning views of the city while sampling the unique, inventive cuisine on offer here.

XX

Els Pescadors

pl. Prim 1 ✉ *08005* – Ⓜ *Poblenou* – ☎ *932 25 20 18*
– *www.elspescadors.com* – *closed Holy Week* **D2**

Rest – Carte 39/51 €

◆ Regional ◆ Trendy ◆

This restaurant has three dining rooms, one in early-20C café style and two with a more modern decor. A generous menu based on fish and seafood with rice dishes and cod to the fore.

NORTH of AV. DIAGONAL *Plan III*

Casa Fuster

rm,

passeig de Gràcia 132 ✉ *08008* – Ⓜ *Diagonal* – ☎ *932 55 30 00*
– *www.hotelcasafuster.com* **K1**

66 rm – ††346/495 €, ☕ 25 € – 39 suites

Rest *Galaxó* – Carte 59/81 €

◆ Luxury ◆ Historic ◆ Contemporary ◆

This magnificent hotel occupies a beautiful Modernist building. Attractive lounge-café, top-quality guestrooms and a panoramic bar on the roof terrace. The culinary focus in this elegant restaurant is on traditional Catalan cuisine with a contemporary twist.

Àbac

av. del Tibidabo 1 ✉ *08022* – Ⓜ *Av. Tibidabo* – ☎ *93 319 66 00*
– *www.abacbarcelona.com* *Plan I* **B2**

15 rm – ††225/540 €, ☕ 30 €

Rest *Àbac* – see below

◆ Luxury ◆ Modern ◆

Spectacular guestrooms with a contemporary look, featuring top-quality furnishings, the latest technology and even colour therapy in the bathrooms. Modern spa.

Hispanos Siete Suiza

rm,

Sicilia 255 ✉ *08025* – Ⓜ *Sagrada Familia* – ☎ *932 08 20 51* – *www.h7s.es*

Rest *La Cúpula* – Carte 33/45 € **L1**

◆ Traditional ◆ Classic ◆

This comfortable, traditional property has apartments with two bedrooms, two bathrooms, a lounge and fully equipped kitchen. Most of the apartments have a terrace. The restaurant has two dining rooms, both exquisitely decorated in classical style with high-quality furniture.

Condado without rest

Aribau 201 ✉ *08021* – Ⓜ *Diagonal* – ☎ *932 00 23 11*
– *www.condadohotel.com* **J1**

75 rm – †85/255 € ††85/265 €, ☕ 12 € – 1 suite

◆ Business ◆ Classic ◆

A well-run hotel with a traditional yet contemporary look. Pleasant public areas with an Internet zone, plus pleasantly comfortable guestrooms, some with a terrace.

XXXX ✿

Via Veneto

A/C VISA MC AE

Ganduxer 10 ✉ 08021 – Ⓜ Hospital Clínic – ☎ 932 00 72 44
– www.viavenetorestaurant.com
– closed 1-20 August, Saturday lunch and Sunday **I2**

Rest – Menu 80/90 € – Carte 72/92 €

Spec. Tartar de cigalas con caviar de salmón y crema smitane. Pechuga de pichón asada con múrgulas, muslos rellenos a la royal y canelón de foie y manzana. Buñuelos de chocolate y avellana con velo de cacao y helado thai.

♦ International ♦ Retro ♦

This emblematic house recreates the delightful style of the Belle Époque period with its dining rooms laid out on various levels and impeccable service. It serves classic international cuisine embellished with a contemporary touch and accompanied by a superb selection of wines from the cellar, all of which attracts a well-heeled clientele.

XXXX ✿

Neichel (Jean Louis Neichel)

A/C VISA MC AE

Beltran i Rózpide 1 ✉ 08034 – Ⓜ Maria Cristina – ☎ 932 03 84 08
– www.neichel.es
– closed 7 days in January, 21 days in August, Sunday, Monday and Bank Holidays Plan I **A2**

Rest – Menu 73/90 € – Carte 66/80 €

Spec. Tartar de cangrejo real, bogavante, wakame y erizos de mar al jengibre fresco. Cochinillo crujiente con gambas y "espardenyes" a la naranja, jugo anisado como un mar y montaña. Papillote transparente templado tropical al ron, tonka y sorbete de maracuyá.

♦ Innovative ♦ Formal ♦

An elegant and traditional family-run restaurant with the father and son at the helm in the kitchen. It serves international cuisine that increasingly makes use of locally sourced products. Professionalism and high quality in equal measure.

XXXX ✿

Àbac – Hotel Àbac

A/C VISA MC AE

av. del Tibidabo 1 ✉ 08022 – Ⓜ Av. Tibidabo – ☎ 93 319 66 00
– www.abacbarcelona.com Plan I **B2**

Rest – *(closed Sunday and Monday)* Menu 125/140 €
– Carte 82/110 €

Spec. Ternera royale con concentrado destilado de Pedro Ximénez y texturas de manzana a la sidra. Lubina salvaje con escaloñas, reducción de cabernet, melocotón de viña al tomillo limonero y garnacha joven tratada a la naranja. Pintada con cigalas, tendón de ternera, tomate confitado y agua de verduras asadas.

♦ Inventive ♦ Trendy ♦

Àbac occupies an unusual villa in the upper part of the city. It features a terrace, a designer-inspired bar and an elegant and traditional dining room. The beautifully presented cuisine here is highly creative with delicate textures and flavours.

XXX

Freixa Tradició

A/C VISA MC AE

Sant Elíes 22 ✉ 08006 – Ⓜ Plaça Molina – ☎ 932 09 75 59
– www.freixatradicio.com
– closed Holy Week, 21 days in August, Sunday and Monday **J1**

Rest – Carte 37/43 €

♦ Traditional ♦ Trendy ♦

Modern restaurant with clean-cut, minimalist lines, designer details, and an excellent table service. Enjoy the 100% traditional cuisine of predominantly Catalan dishes.

XXX ✿

Hofmann (Mey Hofmann)

La Granada del Penedès 14-16 ✉ 08006 – Ⓜ Diagonal – ✆ 93 218 71 65 – www.hofmann-bcn.com
– closed Christmas, Holy Week, August, Saturday and Sunday **J1**

Rest – Carte 70/76 €

Spec. Tarta de sardinas con tomate y cebollitas nuevas en caliente. Ventresca de atún asada con pesto, salsa picante y alcaparrones. Pichón crujiente en dos texturas con chutney de cebolla especiada.

♦ Inventive ♦ Elegant ♦

The Hofmann reflects a contemporary gastronomic philosophy with its semi-private small rooms and an attractive main dining room with views of the kitchen via a large window. Creative cuisine that attracts a sizeable business clientele.

XXX

Roig Robí

Sèneca 20 ✉ 08006 – Ⓜ Diagonal – ✆ 932 18 92 22 – www.roigrobi.com
– Closed 7 days January, 21 days August, Saturday lunch and Sunday

Rest – Carte 58/73 € **k1**

♦ Terroir ♦ Formal ♦

A classic restaurant in a particularly pleasant setting, with a conservatory-style dining room arranged around a patio-garden. Traditional Catalan cuisine of a consistently high quality.

XXX

Tram-Tram

Major de Sarrià 121 ✉ 08017 – ✆ 932 04 85 18 – www.tram-tram.com
– Closed Chistmas, Holy Week, 15 days August, Sunday and Monday

Rest – Carte 38/45 € *Plan I* **A2**

♦ A la mode ♦ Family ♦

Located in the upper part of the city, Tram-Tram's dining room is classic in style and divided into two sections with two private rooms and a terrace-patio with a glass-fronted gallery. Creative cuisine.

XX

El Asador de Aranda

av. del Tibidabo 31 ✉ 08022 – ✆ 934 17 01 15
– www.asadordearanda.com
– closed on Sunday night *Plan I* **B1-2**

Rest – Carte 33/37 €

♦ Traditional ♦ Fashionable ♦

This restaurant occupies the incomparable Casa Roviralta, a Modernist building also known as El Frare Blanc. The culinary focus here is on typical Castilian cuisine, with a house speciality of roast lamb cooked in a clay oven.

XX ✿

Alkimia (Jordi Vilà)

Indústria 79 ✉ 08025 – Ⓜ Sagrada Familia – ✆ 932 07 61 15
– closed Holy Week, 21 days in August, Saturday and Sunday **K1**

Rest – Menu 58/74 € – Carte 66/75 €

Spec. San Pedro con verduras y láminas de panceta curada. Espaldita de lechazo churro con crema de tupinambo y salsifis. Flan de queso fresco con pera escalivada y regaliz.

♦ Inventive ♦ Minimalist ♦

This family-run business has a minimalist dining room where the service is of a high quality. The cuisine is centred around two tasting menus, one innovative in style, the other more traditional, from which à la carte choices are also available.

XX

Coure

passatge de Marimon 20 ✉ 08021 – Ⓜ Hospital Clínic – ✆ 932 00 75 32
– closed Holy Week, 21 days in August, Sunday and Monday **J2**

Rest – Carte 40/49 €

♦ Modern ♦ Trendy ♦

A modern restaurant with bright colours and a minimalist inspired decoration. Interesting and innovative cuisine from the owner-chef.

XX ✿

Hisop (Oriol Ivern)

passatge de Marimon 9 ✉ 08021 – Ⓜ Hospital Clínic – ✆ 932 41 32 33 – www.hisop.com – closed 7 days in January, Holy Week, 21 days in August, Saturday lunch, Sunday and Bank Holidays **J2**

Rest – Carte 50/58 €

Spec. Foie "after eight". Rape con colmenillas y wassabi. Pastelito de pistacho con rúcula y lima Keffir.

♦ Inventive ♦ Minimalist ♦

This small restaurant is both modern and intimate, crowned in one section by a high ceiling and in another by vaulted brickwork. It serves creative cuisine based around traditional dishes with an emphasis on quality ingredients.

XX

St. Rémy

Iradier 12 ✉ 08017 – ✆ 934 18 75 04 – www.stremyrestaurant.com – closed Sunday dinner **I1**

Rest – Carte 32/37 €

♦ Terroir ♦ Trendy ♦

The St Rémy occupies a small mansion with spacious dining rooms, modern furniture and elegant lighting. Catalan inspired cuisine.

XX

Comiols

Madrazo 68-70 ✉ 08006 – Ⓜ Pl. Molina – ✆ 932 09 07 91 – www.comiols.es – closed Holy Week, 15 days in August, Saturday lunch and Sunday dinner

Rest – Carte 44/58 € **J1**

♦ Modern ♦ Trendy ♦

Although at first glance it may come across as modern and somewhat informal, this restaurant is run with great professionalism. It features traditional dishes with a modern flair and a focus on light and healthy cuisine.

XX

Le Quattro Stagioni

Dr. Roux 37 ✉ 08017 – Ⓜ Les Tres Torres – ✆ 932 05 22 79 – www.4stagioni.com – closed Holy Week, Sunday and Monday lunch (July-August), Sunday dinner and Monday for rest of the year **I1**

Rest – Carte 33/39 €

♦ Italian ♦ Trendy ♦

Dining rooms on two floors with a glass-fronted terrace and outdoor patio. Mediterranean ambience, Italian cuisine and a wide selection of Italian wines.

XX

Silvestre

Santaló 101 ✉ 08021 – Ⓜ Muntaner – ✆ 932 41 40 31 – www.restaurantesilvestre.com – closed Holy Week, 15 days in August, Saturday lunch, Sunday and Bank Holidays **J1**

Rest – Carte approx. 37 €

♦ Traditional ♦ Formal ♦

The couple who own this restaurant have created a classical ambience with a number of separate dining areas providing a certain intimacy. Reasonably priced menu based around fresh market produce.

XX

Cal Xim

Girona 145 ✉ 08037 – Ⓜ Verdaguer – ✆ 934 59 20 30 – www.calxim.com – closed Holy Week, 15 days in August, Saturday and Sunday **K1**

Rest – Carte 25/42 €

♦ Grills ♦ Trendy ♦

The restaurant's dining room recreates a contemporary ambience with its half-visible, charcoal grill and one private dining room. Choose from the menu of traditional cuisine, chargrilled meats and an excellent wine cellar.

Mandarina

Caravel.la "La Niña" ✉ 08017 – Ⓜ María Cristina – ✆ 932 05 60 04 – www.mandarinarestaurant.com – closed 1-27 August, 1-8 January, Saturday and Sunday **I2**

Rest – *(lunch only)* Carte approx. 30 €

♦ Inventive ♦ Trendy ♦

The young and refreshing ambience of this restaurant enhances the feeling that you are eating light and healthy cuisine. There are two floors, a kitchen that is partially visible, plus a delicatessen shop.

La Taula

Sant Màrius 8-12 ✉ 08022 – Ⓜ El Putxet – ✆ 934 17 28 48 – www.lataula.com – closed Holy Week,August, Saturday lunch, Sunday and Bank Holidays

Rest – Carte 26/32 € **I1**

♦ International ♦ Formal ♦

A small and welcoming restaurant with interesting decorative detail. Two types of menu and a choice of daily specials are on offer in this busy and popular eatery.

Vivanda

Major de Sarrià 134 ✉ 08017 – Ⓜ Sarrià – ✆ 932 03 19 18 – closed Sunday dinner and Monday *Plan I* **A2**

Rest – Carte 22/33 €

♦ Traditional ♦ Trendy ♦

The atmosphere in Vivanda's dining room is modern, young and informal with a mix of normal tables and high tables with stools. Contemporary cooking, including a few stew dishes.

AT L'HOSPITALET de LLOBREGAT *Plan I*

Hesperia Tower

rm,

Gran Via 144 ✉ 08907 – Ⓜ Hospital de Bellvitge – ✆ 934 13 50 00 – www.hesperia-tower.com **A3**

248 rm – ††120/350 €, ☕ 24 € – 32 suites

Rest ***Evo*** – see below

Rest ***Bouquet*** – *(Closed August) (lunch only)* Carte approx. 65 €

♦ Chain hotel ♦ Business ♦ Modern ♦

This hotel occupying a tower block designed by the famous architect Richard Rogers boasts spacious public areas, a convention centre and contemporary guestrooms. The emphasis in this first-floor restaurant is on traditional cuisine prepared using seasonal products.

Evo – Hotel Hesperia Tower

Gran Via 144 ✉ 08907 – Ⓜ Hospital de Bellvitge – ✆ 934 13 50 00 – www.evorestaurante.com – closed August, Sunday and public holidays **A3**

Rest – *(dinner only except Saturday)* Menu 145/180 €

Spec. Ancas de rana crujientes con yogur griego aliñado. Anguila del delta del Ebro a la brasa con ragú de setas y pimientos asados. Bizcocho y crema de limón con hojaldre y helado de leche merengada.

♦ Innovative ♦ Design ♦

This restaurant stands at a height of 105m on top of a tower designed by the renowned architect Richard Rogers. Highlights include the modern panoramic dining room beneath a glass cupola, attractive design features and magnificent views. Innovative cuisine with a personalised touch.

El Racó del Cargol

Dr. Martí Julià 54 ✉ 08903 L'Hospitalet de Llobregat – Ⓜ Collblanc – ✆ 934 49 77 18 – www.rocxi.es
– closed Christmas, 21 days in August and Sunday **A3**

Rest – Carte 24/35 €

♦ Traditional ♦ Formal ♦

This restaurant has a bar, a traditional-style main dining room, as well as two further rooms upstairs. Typical Catalan cuisine and a choice of daily specials.

AT EL PRAT AIRPORT

Tryp Barcelona Aeropuerto

pl. del Pla de L'Estany 1-2 ✉ 08820
– ✆ 933 78 10 00 – www.trypbarcelonaaeropuerto.solmelia.com

196 rm – ††96/297 €, ☕ 15 € – 9 suites **Rest** – Carte approx. 42 €

♦ Business ♦ Contemporary ♦

A modern, functional hotel located in a business park near the airport. The large lobby, open to the ceiling several floors above, is enclosed by functional and well-appointed guestrooms.

VALENCIA

VALÈNCIA

Population (oct. 2010): 814 208 (Conurbation 2 509 547) - Altitude: 15m

lantide S.N.C./Age Fotostock

Spain's third largest city remained to all intents and purposes a tourist no-go destination for too many years, hidden beneath its sunny shell. Not any more. In 2007 the prestigious America's Cup set sail from its shores in the shadow of the most eye-catching leisure complex in Europe, a stunning twenty-first century addition to the city's skyline. Valencia has announced itself in a big way.

Why it was ever relegated in the visitor stakes is a mystery to all Valencians. Friendly and unpretentious, they're only too willing to tell you of the city's undeniable character and charm, its unspoilt beaches, museums, amazing nightlife and rip-roaring fiestas. And they have a point. The buildings of the city's beautiful old town are testament to its rich history: medieval churches, Renaissance halls of trade and baroque mansions are layered on top of an earlier Roman city. This is the home of paella, and a thriving café scene gives you ample opportunity to tuck into it. The sun shines most of the time here, but if you want shelter there are more than thirty museums on hand offering a cool escape.

LIVING THE CITY

Valencia sits in an enviable position on the Mediterranean coast; the city's port and its long golden beach are to the east. A mile or so inland is the heart of the city, its old town, a labyrinth of ancient cobbled streets. It's bounded to the north by the Turia River Park, created when the actual river was diverted after floods a half a century ago, and to the south by a semicircle of wide boulevards, which follow the line of the ancient city walls. The renowned nightlife district of Carmen is the northwest area of the old town.

PRACTICAL INFORMATION

ARRIVAL-DEPARTURE

Valencia-Manises Airport is 8km west of the city and a taxi to the centre will cost about €15. Alternatively take the Metro train (lines 3 and 5) or the Airport bus which runs every 20min and takes around 15min.

TRANSPORT

Valencia has an integrated transport system, with metro, buses and trams. Single tickets for the modern metro, which has five lines, are cheap and can be purchased from station machines or ticket offices. You can buy a one-day pass for the metro, trams and buses or, alternatively, a 10-trip pass for about twice the price.

Another useful investment is the Valencia Tourist Card, available from tourism offices, hotels, tobacconists and kiosks. It offers free travel on all forms of public transport, as well as discounts in museums, shops, restaurants and various leisure activities. The cards last for one, two, or three days.

EXPLORING VALENCIA

This is a city whose centre resembles a Gothic-Renaissance theme park. Valencia can trace two thousand years of history, and at times you might well believe there's a mazy little street or alleyway for each of those years. Certainly newcomers will get lost in the compact centre, but that's part of the charm of the place. Anyway, you'll always come to a hefty landmark before too long. The reason for all the cobbled warrens and hidden plazas, the grand mixture of architectural styles is simple: over time Valencia has seen many invaders come and go, from the Romans to the Visigoths, from the Aragonese to the Moors. Each has left behind a mark of its presence.

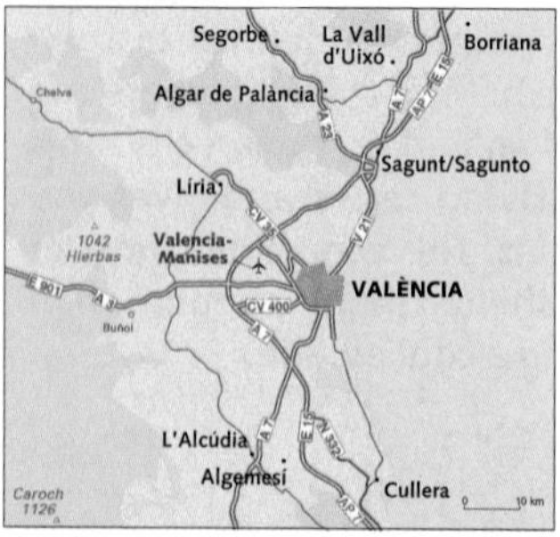

The city's focal point is the **Plaza de la Virgen**. This is at the hub of the old town, a square constructed of marble with central fountain and array of buzzy street cafés. What marks it out as special are the two mighty churches that dominate it. The **Cathedral** is the most important religious building in the city, a beguiling mishmash of Moorish, gothic and Baroque styles built between 1262 and 1426. Alabaster windows bathe the interior in a warm Mediterranean light, suitably mellow to appreciate two paintings by Goya in a private chapel instigated by the renowned Borgia family. Climb the octagonal bell tower, 165ft above the ground, for some spectacular vertiginous views across the old rooftops. Once you've stepped out from the Cathedral, you can step straight into the neighbouring **Basílica** and admire its seventeenth century baroque geography and gaze up at the dome for a beautiful fresco restored to its original glory. But don't look for candles to light: none are allowed in order to save the fresco from the effects of blackening.

➜ SILKY SMOOTH

A hop, skip and jump to the south west – so close you're unlikely even to get lost – stands the jewel in Valencia's gothic crown: **La Lonja**. This fabulous one-time Silk Exchange was constructed in the 15C in the days when Valencia was the Spanish capital of prosperity. These days it's a UNESCO World Heritage Site. The façade is impressive enough, but it's the interior that catches your breath with its elegant columns of white stone carved to resemble twisted bolts of silk. There are high vaulted ceilings, wrought-iron chandeliers, a hall with splendid carved figures and impish gargoyles, and a prison tower where disreputable silk merchants would be sent. There's also a hidden garden with orange trees where you can sit and contemplate all you've seen. La Lonja is still in use today – for stamp fairs…

➜ MARKET SHARES

Stamp lover or not, you'll come out of the Silk Exchange and face one of Valencia's most popular landmarks, the art nouveau **Central Market**, which has been a colourful centrepiece of local life for eighty years. It's a vast vaulted scrum of activity, one of the largest markets in Europe. The stalls, laden with gleaming tomatoes, hams, peppers and, above all, fish and shellfish, are an experience in themselves, set off by the wonderfully worn tiled and domed surroundings. If you counted the stalls here, you'd eventually reach an astronomical 959, so make sure you don't arrange to meet someone by the one that sells vegetables. They say that Valencians don't do things by halves, which is why there's a second great market to be found in the city: the **Mercado Colón**. This is a beautifully restored place with an ornate façade to the east of town. What it lacks in the fruit and veg stakes, it makes up for in cool cafés and boutiques which now populate most of the interior.

➜ FUTURISTIC CITY

Culturally, the city has been propelled into the major league in the last decade. What's taken it there is the exciting **City of Arts and Sciences** complex, which draws over four million visitors each year. Valencian authorities had the inspired notion to build it in the confines of the Turia River Park, the fabulous nine-mile green space created when the river was diverted after flooding in 1957. This futuristic 'city' is made up of four stunning buildings made of white concrete and glass; these are home to a science museum, an opera house, an aquarium and an Imax cinema with a planetarium and laserium. Whether you're planning to go in any of them, or come face-to-face with them on a stroll through the parkland, there's no way you can ignore these weirdly compelling, other-worldly domes and pods.

For the more conventionally-minded, there are two great art galleries in Valencia. Both are on the northern edge of the old town, one just to the south of the river park, the other just to its north. The first, the Valencian Institute of Modern Art (IVAM), was only twenty years old (as of 2009) but surprisingly it's Spain's oldest contemporary art museum. It boasts a brilliant display of sculpture by local artist Julio González, whose expressive iron masks and figures make him a true icon of modern sculpture. His work is backed up by a strong collection of international pop art and photography. Cross the Turia river bed and you'll soon arrive at the city's Museum of Fine Arts, one of the most important in Spain and generally regarded as a 'must see' by visitors. It's an easily identifiable place, with its blue-tiled dome jutting above the park; inside, it's a treasure trove of great works. There's much religious art from the 13C to 15C, mixed in with Bosch's breath-taking Triptych of the Passion. You'll also find works by most of Spain's greats such as Goya, El Greco and Velázquez, as well as plenty of modern art depicting the life of Valencia.

→ CLASSIC CARMEN

This part of town – between the hip and happening Calle Caballeros and the Turia River Park – is also the main area to hit for nightlife and bars. It's the district known as **Carmen**, and fittingly boasts its very own operatic style. Even for a late-night country like Spain, Valencia has a revered position in the good-time stakes, and Carmen is where it happens. At the weekends the smart clubs and bars are overflowing with locals and tourists alike: there's not much point in arriving before 11pm, while it's a sure-fire bet that the sunshine will be accompanying you on your way back to your hotel. If you're more interested in a quiet stroll than the bright lights, then a good walk in the old town is to the **Serranos Towers** on Plaza Fueros by the side of the park. It's a heavily fortified survivor from the city's medieval walls, and as it doesn't close till 8.30 in the evening, climb up to its battlements as the sun goes down. From here, take in the sparkling views as you look across the lights of the old town and down the length of the Turia River Park, where the spookily illuminated City of Arts and Sciences looks like a multi-pronged night-travelling space voyager.

CALENDAR HIGHLIGHTS

Valencia is a religious city, and nowhere is this more evident than in its festivals, which fill the streets throughout the year. These are not sombre affairs, and fireworks play a significant – and noisy – role on practically every occasion. It all gets underway on 5 January when the

VALENCIA IN…

→ ONE DAY

Plaza de la Virgen, La Lonja, Central Market, City of Arts and Sciences, a trip to the beach

→ TWO DAYS

IVAM (or Valencian Institute of Modern Art), another visit to City of Arts and Sciences, Carmen district nightlife

→ THREE DAYS

Long, slow stroll along the Turia River Park, followed by equally long, relaxing meal of paella at café on Plaza de la Virgen or along the beach promenade

Three Wise Men are lifted onto the City Hall balcony. Later that month the city's patron saint, St Vincent, is honoured in a procession from outside the cathedral. Easter sees Sailors' Holy Week and more rip-roaring processions, while kite-flying at the Turia River Park marks Easter Sunday and Monday. On the second Sunday of May all sorts of festivities coincide with the feast day of Our Lady of the Forsaken. Two months after Easter comes the feast of Corpus Christi (celebrated here for over 650 years), which sees a giant procession take to the streets led fittingly by eye-catching giant figures. As we say, a city of religion...Two festivals with a more secular tone are the Bienal de Valencia, an art-themed event from September to November (every second year, the next is in 2011) and the city's greatest extravaganza, Las Fallas. This is quite simply one of the greatest and craziest festivals in Europe; it always runs from 12-19 March and incorporates eardrum-shattering fireworks, brilliant parades, full-on parties and the ritual burning (on the last day) of satirical figures made from papier-mâché, some as tall as 25m. All this to celebrate the arrival of spring. And to add to its bizarre element, one of the giant figures is saved every year from conflagration, and stored in a special museum – the Guild of Fallas Artists Museum – way to the north of the city.

EATING OUT

Valencia is the city of paella. It was invented here, and this is the place to try it in infinite varieties. For a gargantuan helping, head off to the Las Arenas beach promenade, which is lined with a whole legion of seafood restaurants, anxious to send great platefuls your way. On a hot day (which is most days) the traditional liquid accompaniment is *agua de Valencia*, a potentially lethal combination of orange juice, Cava and vodka. Alternatively, if you're in town for Las Fallas, join a nomadic Fallas community group and eat it on the pavement amidst the firecrackers and parties. Generally speaking, food in Valencia is of the no-nonsense variety. Most restaurants remain very Spanish in character, and if you're not eating paella, then you'll probably be enjoying tapas, with an emphasis on the excellent local cured hams and cheeses. Slightly more 'off the wall' is the local delicacy of *all i pebre*, a mouth-watering meal of stewed eels from the local wetlands served in a garlic and red pepper sauce. The drink to cool down with is *horchata*. It's tigernut milk (a mixture of nuts, cinnamon, sugar and water) and is best enjoyed with a doughy cake. Meal times can throw the unwary visitor. Lunch is often not served until two in the afternoon, and dinner, in general, is never taken before nine at night. Adjust your eating habits accordingly. One thing that will be easy to get used to: service charge is always included in your bill, though if you wish to tip then five to ten per cent is ample.

➜ ON THE TILES

One of the best buildings in the city is home to the Ceramics Museum. It's the 15C Palacio del Marqués de Dos Aguas, just south of Plaza de la Virgen, and it's a baroque beauty (it was revamped in 1740). The over-the-top alabaster front door surround is something to behold, as is the sumptuous interior. Oh yes, and it has a superlative range of tiles, too.

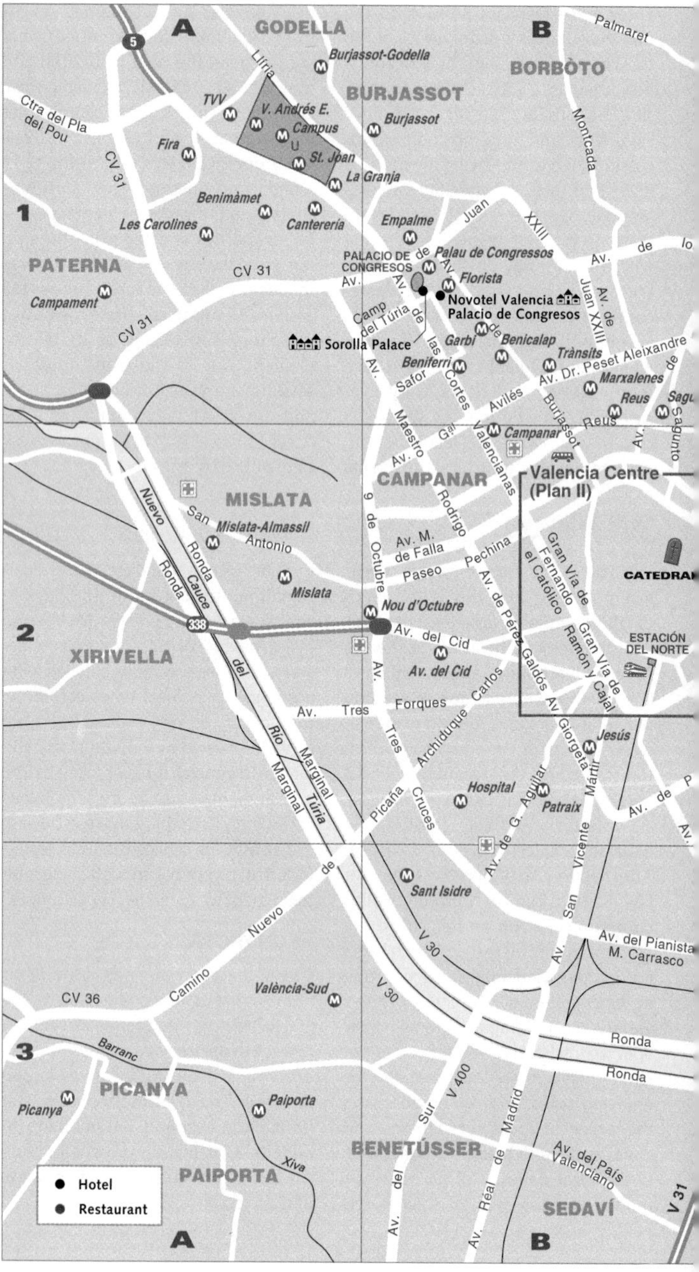

VALENCIA-MANISES

GODELLA
BURJASSOT
BORBÒTO
PATERNA
MISLATA
CAMPANAR
XIRIVELLA
PICANYA
PAIPORTA
BENETÚSSER
SEDAVÍ

Valencia Centre (Plan II)

Novotel Valencia Palacio de Congresos
Sorolla Palace
PALACIO DE CONGRESOS
CATEDRAL
ESTACIÓN DEL NORTE

Burjassot-Godella
TVV
V. Andrés E.
Campus
St. Joan
Burjassot
Fira
La Granja
Benimàmet
Les Carolines
Cantereria
Empalme
Palau de Congressos
Florista
Campament
Garbí
Benicalap
Beniferri
Trànsits
Marxalenes
Reus
Campanar
Mislata-Almassil
Mislata
Nou d'Octubre
Av. del Cid
Jesús
Hospital
Patraix
Sant Isidre
València-Sud
Paiporta
Picanya

Ctra del Pla del Pou
CV 31
CV 36
V 30
V 31
V 400
Llíria
Palmaret
Montcada
Av. de Juan XXIII
Av. Dr. Peset Aleixandre
Av. de las Cortes Valencianas
Av. Maestro Rodrigo
Av. Gral Avilés
Camp del Túria
Safor
Burjassot
Av. Saguntó
Nuevo Cauce del Río Túria
Ronda
Marginal
San Antonio
Av. M. de Falla
Paseo Pechina
Av. 9 de Octubre
Av. del Cid
Av. de Pérez Galdós
Gran Vía de Fernando el Católico
Gran Vía de Ramón y Cajal
Av. Tres Forques
Av. Tres Cruces
Archiduque Carlos
Av. Giorgeta
Av. de G. Aguilar
Av. San Vicente Mártir
Picaña
Camino Nuevo de Picaña
Av. del Pianista M. Carrasco
Av. del Sur
Av. Real de Madrid
Av. del País Valenciano
Barranc Xiva

A B 1 2 3

● Hotel
● Restaurant

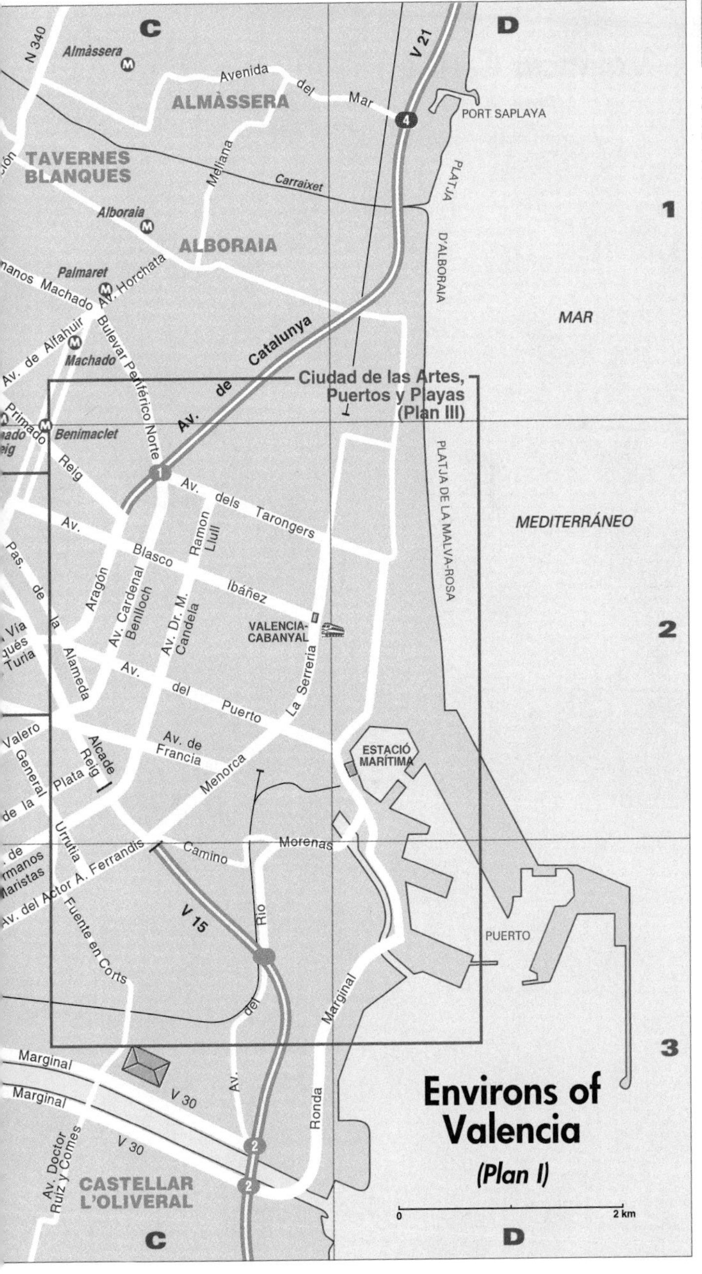

Environs of Valencia

(Plan I)

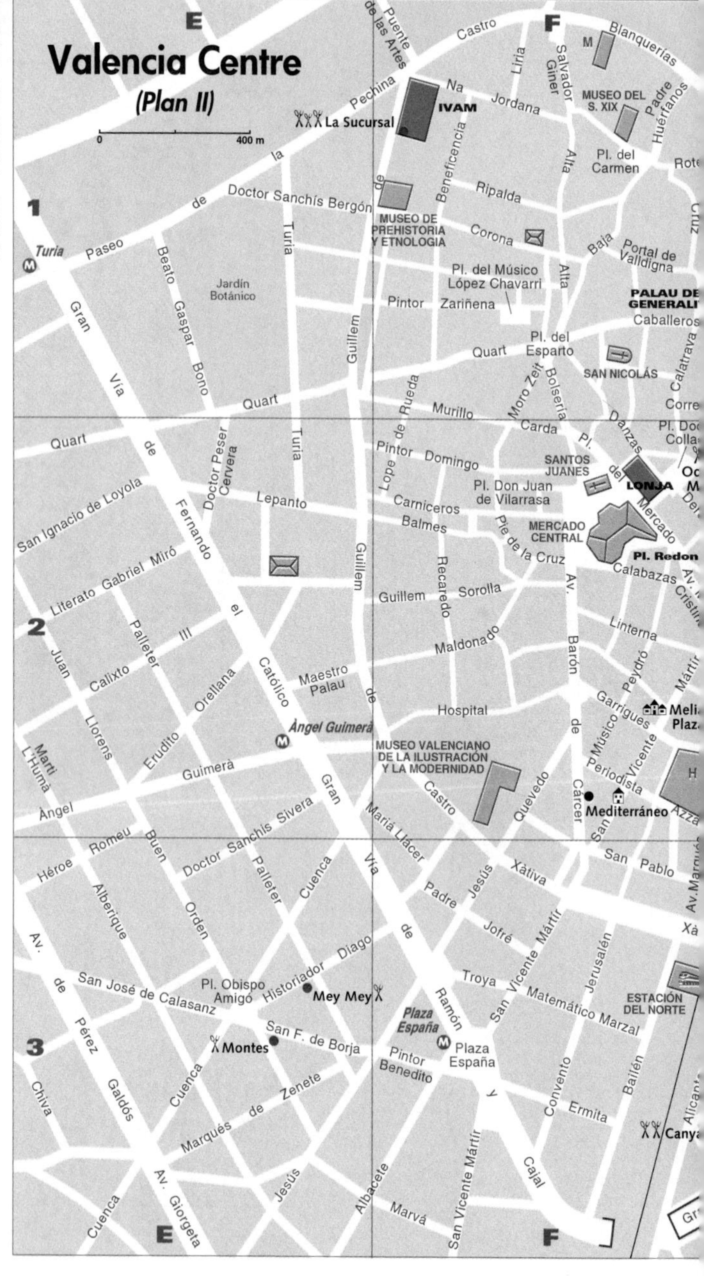
Valencia Centre
(Plan II)
0
400 m
La Sucursal
IVAM
MUSEO DEL S. XIX
Pl. del Carmen
MUSEO DE PREHISTORIA Y ETNOLOGIA
Jardín Botánico
Pl. del Músico López Chavarri
Pl. del Esparto
SAN NICOLÁS
SANTOS JUANES
Pl. Don Juan de Vilarrasa
LONJA
MERCADO CENTRAL
Pl. Redon
Turia
Àngel Guimerà
MUSEO VALENCIANO DE LA ILUSTRACIÓN Y LA MODERNIDAD
Mediterráneo
ESTACIÓN DEL NORTE
Pl. Obispo Amigó
Mey Mey
Montes
Plaza España
Plaza España
Gran Vía de Fernando el Católico
Gran Vía de Ramón y Cajal
Paseo de la Pechina
Doctor Sanchís Bergón
Quart
San Ignacio de Loyola
Literato Gabriel Miró
Juan Calixto III
Guillem de Castro
Pintor Domingo
Carniceros
Balmes
Maldonado
Hospital
Av. Barón de Cárcer
Xàtiva
San Pablo
San Vicente Mártir
Matemático Marzal
Troya
Jerusalén
Bailén
Convento
Ermita
Marvá
Albacete
Jesús
Cuenca
Marqués de Zenete
San F. de Borja
San José de Calasanz
Av. de Pérez Galdós
Av. Giorgeta
Chiva
Historiador Diago
Pintor Benedito
Canya

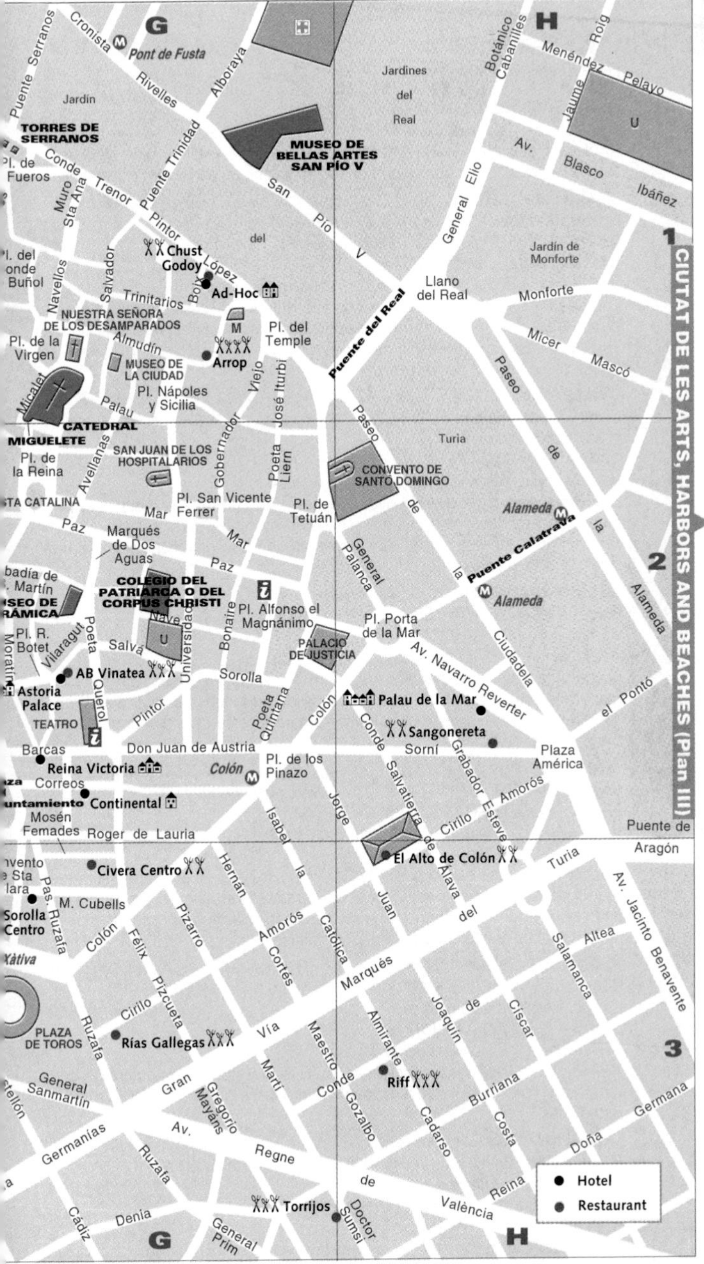

G
H
1
2
3
CIUTAT DE LES ARTS, HARBORS AND BEACHES (Plan III)
Cronista
Pont de Fusta
Rivelles
Alboraya
Puente Serranos
Jardín
TORRES DE SERRANOS
Pl. de Fueros
Conde Trenor
Muro Sta Ana
Puente Trinidad
MUSEO DE BELLAS ARTES SAN PÍO V
San Pío V
del
Jardines del Real
Botánico Cabanilles
Menéndez Pelayo
Jaume Roig
U
Av. Blasco Ibáñez
General Elío
Jardín de Monforte
Llano del Real
Monforte
Micer Mascó
Puente del Real
Pintor López
Chust Godoy
Ad-Hoc
Salvador
Navellos
Boix
Trinitarios
NUESTRA SEÑORA DE LOS DESAMPARADOS
M
Pl. del Temple
Pl. de la Virgen
Almudín
Arrop
MUSEO DE LA CIUDAD
Pl. Nápoles y Sicilia
Viejo
José Iturbi
Micalet
Palau
CATEDRAL
MIGUELETE
Pl. de la Reina
Avellanas
SAN JUAN DE LOS HOSPITALARIOS
Gobernador
Poeta Liern
Paseo de la Alameda
Turia
CONVENTO DE SANTO DOMINGO
Paseo de la Alameda
STA CATALINA
Mar
Pl. San Vicente Ferrer
Pl. de Tetuán
Alameda
Puente Calatrava
Paz
Marqués de Dos Aguas
Mar
General Palanca
Paz
Abadía de S. Martín
MUSEO DE CERÁMICA
COLEGIO DEL PATRIARCA O DEL CORPUS CHRISTI
Nave
Pl. Alfonso el Magnánimo
Alameda
Pl. R. Botet
Vilaragut
Poeta Querol
Salvá
U
Universidad
Bonaire
PALACIO DE JUSTICIA
Pl. Porta de la Mar
Av. Navarro Reverter
Ciudadela
Moratín
AB Vinatea
Sorolla
Astoria Palace
TEATRO
Pintor
Poeta Quintana
Colón
Palau de la Mar
Conde Salvatierra de Álava
Sangonereta
el Pontó
Barcas
Don Juan de Austria
Sorní
Plaza América
Reina Victoria
Colón
Pl. de los Pinazo
Grabador Esteve
Correos
Ayuntamiento
Continental
Jorge Juan
Cirilo Amorós
Mosén Femades
Roger de Lauria
Isabel la Católica
Puente de Aragón
El Alto de Colón
Turia
Convento de Sta Clara
Civera Centro
Hernán Cortés
Av. Jacinto Benavente
Pas. Ruzafa
M. Cubells
Sorolla Centro
Pizarro
Amorós
Marqués del Turia
Colón
Félix Pizcueta
Salamanca
Altea
Xàtiva
Joaquín Costa
Cirilo
Ciscar
PLAZA DE TOROS
Rías Gallegas
Vía
Maestro Gozalbo
Almirante Cadarso
Ruzafa
Gran Vía Marqués del Turia
Riff
Burriana
General Sanmartín
Gregorio Mayans
Conde
Germana
Castellón
Germanías
Av. Regne de València
Ruzafa
Doña
Reina
Hotel
Restaurant
Cádiz
Denia
Torrijos
General Prim
Doctor Sumsi

CENTRE

Plan II

Ayre Astoria Palace

pl. Rodrigo Botet 5 ✉ 46002 – Ⓜ Colón – ✆ 963 98 10 00 – www.ayrehoteles.com
197 rm – †70/316 € ††70/364 €, ☕ 15 € – 7 suites **G2**
Rest *AB Vinatea* – see below
◆ Business ◆ Classic ◆
An elegant, classical style and central location are the main selling points of the Ayre Astoria Palace. The executive rooms on the third floor are particularly comfortable.

Palau de la Mar

Navarro Reverter 14 ✉ *46004* – Ⓜ *Colón* – ✆ *963 16 28 84* – *www.hospes.es*
65 rm – ††110/180 €, ☕ 19 € **H2**
Rest *Senzone* – Carte 42/51 €
◆ Palace ◆ Townhouse ◆ Contemporary ◆
The 'Sea Palace' partially occupies two 19C mansions. These house the hotel's public areas and most of its fully equipped, minimalist-style rooms. Spa centre. This restaurant specialises in creative Mediterranean cuisine, including an impressive choice of rice dishes.

Meliá Plaza

pl. del Ayuntamiento 4 ✉ *46002* – Ⓜ *Xàtiva* – ✆ *963 52 06 12* – *www.solmelia.com* **F2**
100 rm – ††80/300 €, ☕ 15 € **Rest** – Menu 22 €
◆ Chain hotel ◆ Business ◆ Classic ◆
Following gradual renovation over the years, this comfortable hotel is known for its elegant decor and carefully chosen furnishings. Well-equipped guest-rooms. The restaurant serves Mediterranean and international cuisine, alongside a good selection of savoury rice dishes.

Reina Victoria

Barcas 4 ✉ *46002* – Ⓜ *Xàtiva* – ✆ *963 52 04 87* – *www.husa.es* **G2**
95 rm – †65/295 € ††65/350 €, ☕ 13 € **Rest** – Menu 21 €
◆ Chain hotel ◆ Business ◆ Classic ◆
Beautiful façade and an excellent location just a stone's throw from the city's main museums. Elegant facilities with an appealing lounge area and attractive contemporary-style guestrooms. Simple dining room on the first floor, next to the English style bar.

Ad-Hoc

Boix 4 ✉ *46003* – ✆ *963 91 91 40* – *www.adhochoteles.com*
28 rm – †70/180 € ††82/237 €, ☕ 13 € **G1**
Rest – *(closed Saturday lunch and Sunday)* Menu 19.50 €
◆ Business ◆ Cosy ◆
This hotel occupies an attractive 19C building. It has a small lounge area and rooms decorated in neo-rustic style with exposed brickwork, wooden beams and clay tiles. The restaurant has a pleasant and relaxing atmosphere, making it the perfect place for an after dinner cocktail.

Sorolla Centro without rest

Convento Santa Clara 5 ✉ *46002* – Ⓜ *Xàtiva* – ✆ *963 52 33 92* – *www.hotelsorollacentro.com* **G3**
58 rm – †64/160 € ††75/246 €, ☕ 10.70 €
◆ Business ◆ Functional ◆
The Sorolla boasts a glazed façade and fully refurbished reception area. A contemporary-style hotel with functional, comfortable guestrooms and modern bathrooms.

Mediterráneo without rest

Barón de Cárcer 45 ✉ *46001* – Ⓜ *Xàtiva* – ✆ *963 51 01 42* – *www.hotel-mediterraneo.es* **F2**
34 rm – †56/141 € ††56/195 €, ☕ 8 €
◆ Business ◆ Functional ◆
This centrally located hotel has a breakfast room on the first floor and classic bedrooms. Each of which has a fitted carpet and the full range of facilities you would expect of a hotel of this standard.

Continental without rest
Correos 8 ✉ 46002 – Ⓜ Colón – ✆ 963 53 52 82 – www.contitel.es **G2**
46 rm – 50/70 € 55/115 €
♦ Family ♦ Townhouse ♦ Functional ♦
A central hotel with a contemporary design and functional furniture. The lounge area is fairly small, but the bedrooms, half of which overlook an interior courtyard, are comfortable.

Arrop (Ricard Camarena)
Almirante 14 ✉ 46003 – ✆ 963 92 55 66 – www.arrop.com – closed Sunday and Monday **G1**
Rest – Menu 54/69 €
– Carte 52/70 €
Spec. Arroz de vaca gallega. Liebre a la royal, pera escalivada y rúcula. Mousse de galleta, fresa y coco.
♦ Inventive ♦ Design ♦
This restaurant occupies the lower section of a small palace. It has an elegant entrance hall and three dining rooms with a decor that combines archaeological remains and minimalist design. Creative cuisine featuring top quality ingredients presented in an exquisite manner.

Rías Gallegas
Cirilo Amorós 4 ✉ 46004 – Ⓜ Xàtiva – ✆ 963 52 51 11 – www.riasgallegas.es – closed Holy Week, 7-31 August, Sunday and Monday dinner **G3**
Rest – Carte 48/60 €
♦ Inventive ♦ Trendy ♦
This restaurant has undergone radical changes, both in terms of its decor and cuisine. The menu is now highly creative, featuring seafood specialities and a tasting menu.

Torrijos (Josep Quintana)
Dr. Sumsi 4 ✉ 46005 – Ⓜ Colón – ✆ 963 73 29 49 – www.restaurantetorrijos.com – closed 10-16 January, 25-30 April, 15-31 August, 5-11 September, Sunday and Monday **G-H3**
Rest – Menu 58/80 €
– Carte approx. 63 €
Spec. Langosta mediterránea con fideos y verduras, cocida con su propio coral al agua con gas. Cochinillo confitado con puré de patata, azafrán y mango. Arena de té verde con sorbete de "caipirinha" y espuma de coco.
♦ Inventive ♦ Trendy ♦
Once through the door of the Torrijos restaurant, guests can choose to dine in the elegant, modern dining room or in one of two private rooms, one of which is in the kitchen. Attractive glass-enclosed wine cellar, whose wines accompany creative cuisine with a high level of technical skill.

La Sucursal
Guillém de Castro 118 ✉ 46003 – Ⓜ Túria – ✆ 963 74 66 65 – www.restaurantelasucursal.com – closed 12-26 August, Saturday lunch and Sunday **F1**
Rest – Menu 70 € – Carte approx. 55 €
Spec. Steak tartar con encurtidos y velo de liliáceas. Salmonete de roca con verduras ecológicas y corales. Sorbete de melocolón de viña sanguina con esponja de vino dulce Monastrell.
♦ Inventive ♦ Trendy ♦
Located inside the Instituto Valenciano de Arte Moderno. It has a cafeteria for the general public on the ground floor and a minimalist dining room on the upper floor. The chef here perfectly combines traditional dishes with more inventive culinary creations.

XXX

AB Vinatea – Hotel Ayre Astoria Palace

Vilaragut 4 ✉ 46002 – Ⓜ Colón – ☎ 963 98 10 00 – www.ayrehoteles.com – closed Sunday, Monday and Tuesday dinner **G2**

Rest – Carte 35/50 €

♦ Traditional ♦ Trendy ♦

This restaurant has its own separate entrance. The modern dining room serves traditional and local cuisine with a modern touch, plus an excellent choice of rice dishes.

XXX ✿

Riff (Bernd Knöller)

Conde de Altea 18 ✉ 46005 – Ⓜ Colón – ☎ 963 33 53 53 – www.restaurante-riff.com – closed Holy Week, August, Sunday and Monday **H3**

Rest – Menu 55/89 € – Carte 56/67 €

Spec. Ensalada de puntillas, "all i oli" ligero, trompetas de la muerte y berros. Arroz "Brut". Sopa de piña, fresitas del bosque y helado de yogur.

♦ Inventive ♦ Trendy ♦

Hidden behind the small façade is an entrance hall and modern dining room with designer chairs and wood flooring. The cuisine here focuses on the latest culinary trends with creative dishes that hint at the origin of the chef, who hails from Germany.

XX

El Alto de Colón

Jorge Juan 19 ✉ 46004 – Ⓜ Colón – ☎ 963 53 09 00 – www.grupoelalto.com – closed Holy Week, August, Saturday lunch and Sunday **H3**

Rest – Carte 40/50 €

♦ Mediterranean ♦ Trendy ♦

This remarkable restaurant located in one of the towers of the Colón market is resolutely modern in style. Attractive tiled ceilings and contemporary Mediterranean cuisine.

XX

Ocho y Medio

pl. Lope de Vega 5 ✉ 46001 – ☎ 963 92 20 22 – www.elochoymedio.com

Rest – Carte 42/50 € **F2**

♦ Inventive ♦ Cosy ♦

This welcoming restaurant in a central location has a private bar, neo-rustic style decor, and two dining rooms on the first floor. Innovative, international menu.

XX

Civera Centro

Mosén Femades 10 ✉ 46002 – Ⓜ Colón – ☎ 963 52 97 64 – www.marisqueriascivera.com – closed 25 July-7 August **G3**

Rest – Carte approx. 45 €

♦ Seafood ♦ Friendly ♦

This restaurant specialising in fish, seafood and rice dishes has a tapas bar, maritime inspired dining rooms and several private rooms. The seafood platter here is particularly memorable.

XX

Canyar

Segorbe 5 ✉ 46004 – Ⓜ Bailén – ☎ 963 41 80 82 – www.canyarrestaurante.com – closed August, Saturday lunch and Sunday **F3**

Rest – *(set menu only)* Menu 73 €

♦ Traditional ♦ Formal ♦

This family-run restaurant is decorated in Art Deco-style with contemporary touches. The menu focuses uniquely on fish and seafood, with particular emphasis on local red prawns from Denia.

XX

Chust Godoy

Boix 6 ✉ 46003 – Ⓜ Colón – ☎ 963 91 38 15 – www.chustgodoy.com – closed Holy Week, August, Saturday lunch and Sunday **G1**

Rest – Carte 51/63 €

♦ Traditional ♦ Cosy ♦

Run by the chef and his wife, this reputable restaurant has a neo-rustic style dining room and two private rooms, one with a wine cellar atmosphere. Seasonal menu with a good selection of rice dishes.

Sangonereta

Sorni 31 ✉ 46004 – Ⓜ Colón – ☏ 963 73 81 70 – www.sangonereta.com – closed Holy Week, Saturday lunch and Sunday **H2**

Rest – Carte 44/59 €

♦ Inventive ♦ Trendy ♦

This restaurant has a contemporary feel, with four small rooms that can also be used as private dining areas. Creative cuisine, and a tasting menu.

Montes

pl. Obispo Amigó 5 ✉ 46007 – Ⓜ Pl. Espanya – ☏ 963 85 50 25 – closed Holy Week, August, Sunday dinner, Monday and Tuesday dinner

Rest – Carte 25/35 € **E3**

♦ Traditional ♦ Formal ♦

This restaurant serves traditional cuisine at reasonable prices. It has a small entrance hall, a long dining room, and at the back of the building, the main restaurant is decorated in classical style with regionally inspired decor.

Mey Mey

Historiador Diago 19 ✉ 46007 – Ⓜ Pl. Espanya – ☏ 963 84 07 47 – www.mey-mey.com **E3**

Rest – Carte 22/35 €

♦ Chinese ♦ Exotic ♦

Decorated in typical Chinese style, this well-run restaurant has an attractive circular fountain with colourful fish. Cantonese cuisine with an emphasis on steamed dishes.

CIUDAD DE LAS ARTES – HARBOURS – BEACHES *Plan III*

The Westin València

Amadeo de Saboya 16 ✉ 46010 – Ⓜ Alameda – ☏ 963 62 59 00 – www.westin.com **J1**

130 rm – ††120/510 €, ☕ 23 € – 5 suites

Rest *Oscar Torrijos* – Carte approx. 60 €

♦ Luxury ♦ Classic ♦

Housed in an attractive historic building with a large interior patio adorned with pergolas, the Westin offers spacious, well-appointed guestrooms decorated in an elegant, classical style. This gastronomic restaurant is run by a chef with an excellent reputation in the city.

Las Arenas

Eugenia Viñes 22 ✉ 46011 – Ⓜ Neptú – ☏ 963 12 06 00 – www.h-santos.es

243 rm – ††140/695 €, ☕ 22 € – 10 suites **K2**

Rest – Carte approx. 50 €

Rest *Sorolla* – Carte 40/60 €

♦ Luxury ♦ Business ♦ Classic ♦

A luxurious hotel located opposite the beach. Split between three buildings, the hotel boasts comfortable lounge areas, superb meeting rooms, and extremely well-equipped bedrooms. The elegant Sorolla restaurant serves a creative menu.

Neptuno

paseo de Neptuno 2 ✉ 46011 – Ⓜ Neptú – ☏ 963 56 77 77 – www.hotelneptunovalencia.com **K2**

50 rm ☕ – †115/205 € ††128/280 €

Rest *Tridente* – *(closed Monday)* Carte 40/50 €

♦ Townhouse ♦ Contemporary ♦

A contemporary-style hotel situated on the seafront. Well-equipped guestrooms designed in a minimalist style with quality materials and hydromassage bathtubs. The restaurant serves interesting, inventive cuisine, as well as savoury rice dishes.

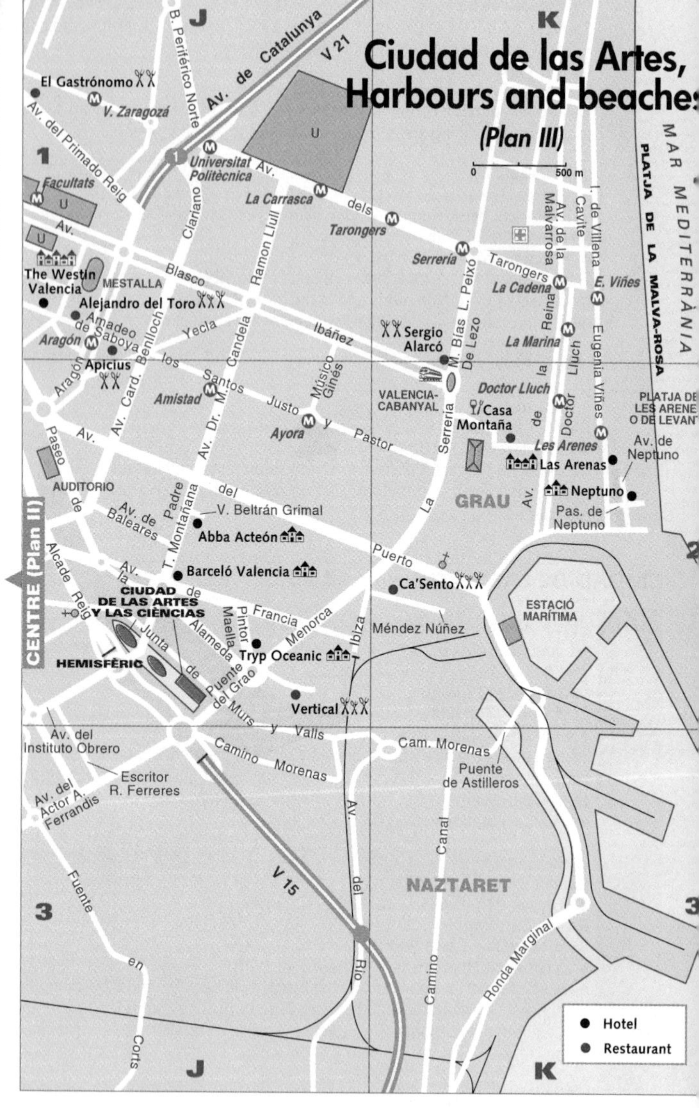
Ciudad de las Artes, Harbours and beaches
(Plan III)
J
K
1
3
0
500 m
El Gastrónomo
V. Zaragozá
Av. del Primado Reig
B. Periférico Norte
Av. de Catalunya
V 21
U
Universitat Politècnica
La Carrasca
Av. dels Tarongers
Facultats
The Westin Valencia
MESTALLA
Alejandro del Toro
Av. Blasco Ibáñez
Amadeo de Saboya
Aragón
Apicius
Clariano
Ramon Llull
Serrería
Tarongers
La Cadena
La Marina
Sergio Alarcó
M. Blas L. Peixó
De Lezo
VALENCIA-CABANYAL
Doctor Lluch
Casa Montaña
Les Arenes
Las Arenas
Neptuno
Av. de Neptuno
Pas. de Neptuno
GRAU
PLATJA DE LES ARENES O DE LEVANTE
PLATJA DE LA MALVA-ROSA
MAR MEDITERRÀNIA
Eugenia Viñes
E. Viñes
I. de Villena
Cavite
Av. de la Malvarrosa
Av. de la Reina
Yecla
Av. Card. Benlloch
Santos
Amistad
Av. Dr. M. Candela
Músico Ginés
Justo y Pastor
Ayora
Av. del Puerto
La Serrería
Paseo de Alcade Reig
AUDITORIO
Av. de Baleares
Padre T. Montañana
V. Beltrán Grimal
Abba Acteón
Barceló Valencia
Ca'Sento
Av. de la Francia
CIUDAD DE LAS ARTES Y LAS CIÈNCIAS
HEMISFÈRIC
Junta de Murs y Valls
Alameda
Pintor Maella
Puente del Grao
Menorca
Tryp Oceanic
Ibiza
Méndez Núñez
Vertical
ESTACIÓ MARÍTIMA
CENTRE (Plan II)
Av. del Instituto Obrero
Av. del Actor A. Ferrandis
Escritor R. Ferreres
Camino Morenas
Cam. Morenas
Puente de Astilleros
V 15
Av. del Río
Canal
Camino
NAZTARET
Ronda Marginal
Fuente en Corts
Hotel
Restaurant

Barceló València

av. de Francia 11 ✉ *46023* – Ⓜ *Amistat* – ✆ *963 30 63 44* – *www.barcelovalencia.com* **J2**

175 rm – ††65/450 €, ☕ 18 € – 12 suites

Rest – *(closed Sunday dinner)* Carte approx. 35 €

♦ Chain hotel ♦ Modern ♦

A superb location with beautiful views of the City of Arts and Sciences. Spacious, modern guestrooms, as well as a spa on the roof terrace. A contemporary-style restaurant serving traditional and international cuisine.

Abba Acteón

Vicente Beltrán Grimal 2 ✉ *46023* – Ⓜ *Ayora* – ✆ *963 31 07 07* – *www.abbahotels.com* **J2**

182 rm – †55/300 € ††55/320 €, ☕ 14.60 € – 5 suites

Rest *Amalur* – Carte approx. 42 €

♦ Chain hotel ♦ Contemporary ♦

A high quality, designer focused hotel. It offers spacious, carefully furnished guestrooms with excellent facilities and marble bathrooms. This bright, modern restaurant has an attractive layout and decor.

Tryp Oceanic

Pintor Maella 35 ✉ *46023* – Ⓜ *Serrería* – ✆ *963 35 03 00* – *www.solmelia.com* **J2**

195 rm – ††70/600 €, ☕ 15 € – 2 suites **Rest** – Carte 25/35 €

♦ Chain hotel ♦ Contemporary ♦

This hotel is located next to the City of Arts and Sciences. Pleasant lounge area, well-appointed rooms and a swimming pool surrounded by a garden. Modern, functional restaurant serving traditional cuisine.

Ca'Sento (Raúl Aleixandre)

Méndez Núñez 17 ✉ *46024* – Ⓜ *Ayora* – ✆ *963 30 17 75* – *www.casento.net* – *closed 15-31 March, 1-15 August, Sunday and Monday* **K2**

Rest – Menu 110 € – Carte 68/79 €

Spec. Ensalada de trufa de Benassal con alcachofa macerada (diciembre-marzo). All i pebre de anguilas. Ganache de chocolate con helado de caramelo y canela.

♦ Inventive ♦ Trendy ♦

A restaurant with a surprising modern style, including a designer-inspired decor and a kitchen that is semi-visible to customers. Dishes served here have a firm basis in the sea, and are all prepared using the best products to ensure superb textures and exquisite flavours.

Alejandro del Toro

Amadeo de Saboya 15 ✉ *46010* – Ⓜ *Aragón* – ✆ *963 93 40 46* – *www.restaurantealejandrodeltoro.com* – *closed Sunday* **J1**

Rest – Carte 55/68 €

♦ Inventive ♦ Trendy ♦

The owner-chef here serves creative cuisine in a spacious dining room with a minimalist aesthetic. Glazed wine cellar that leaves the kitchen visible to diners.

Vertical (Jorge De Andrés)

Luis Garcia Berlanga 19 ✉ *46013* – ✆ *963 30 38 00* – *www.restaurantevertical.com* – *closed 15-31 August and Sunday*

Rest – *(set menu only)* Menu 50/63 € **J2**

Spec. Cremoso de foie. Ciervo con frutos rojos y polenta. Soufflé de mascarpone, helado de leche de cabra y bizcocho de gorgonzola.

♦ Inventive ♦ Trendy ♦

This unique restaurant, occupying the top floor of the Confortel Aqua 4 hotel, boasts an impressive modern design and good views. The cuisine in the contemporary dining room is based around a single gastronomic menu.

Sergio Alarcó

Marino Blas de Lezo 23 ✉ 46022 – ✆ 963 55 22 80
– closed Sunday, Monday dinner and Tuesday dinner **K1-2**
Rest – Carte 35/44 €
◆ Traditional ◆ Trendy ◆
Run by the owner-chef, this restaurant has a minimalist style dining room that is striking with its glass-enclosed wine cellar. Menu based on traditional and international cuisine. Excellent service.

El Gastrónomo

av. Primado Reig 149 ✉ 46020 – Ⓜ Benimaclet – ✆ 963 69 70 36
– www.elgastronomorestaurante.com
– closed August, Sunday and Monday dinner **J1**
Rest – Carte 36/45 €
◆ International ◆ Formal ◆
An old-fashioned, highly professional restaurant with traditional decor. Good choice of dishes, including the house speciality, steak tartare.

Apicius

Eolo 7 ✉ 46021 – Ⓜ Aragón – ✆ 963 93 63 01 – www.restaurante-apicius.com
– closed Saturday lunch and Sunday **J1-2**
Rest – Carte 33/50 €
◆ Inventive ◆ Formal ◆
This restaurant is run with great enthusiasm and professionalism. There is a spacious single dining room that is both functional and contemporary. Concise yet imaginative à la carte choices, plus a tasting menu.

Casa Montaña

José Benlliure 69 ✉ 46011 – Ⓜ Marítim-Serrería – ✆ 963 67 23 14
– www.emilianobodega.com
– closed Sunday dinner **K2**
Tapa 3 € **Ración** approx. 12 €
◆ Traditional ◆ Wine bar ◆
This delightful old restaurant is decorated with traditional features and large wine barrels. It also has a number of dining rooms that can be used for private functions, a good tapas menu and an impressive wine cellar.

AT PALACIO DE CONGRESOS *Plan I*

Sorolla Palace

rm,

av. Cortes Valencianas 58 ✉ 46015 – Ⓜ Burjassot – ✆ 961 86 87 00
– www.hotelsorollapalace.com **B1**
246 rm – ††75/300 €, ☕ 15 € – 25 suites **Rest** – Carte 34/52 €
◆ Business ◆ Functional ◆
A hotel popular with business clientele due to its contemporary facilities and proximity to the Palacio de Congresos. Modern, functional guestrooms. An attractive restaurant with several private dining rooms.

Novotel València Palacio de Congresos

rm,

Valle de Ayora 1 ✉ 46015
– Ⓜ Beniferri – ✆ 963 99 74 00 – www.novotel.com **B1**
148 rm – ††69/210 €, ☕ 15 € – 3 suites **Rest** – Menu 18 €
◆ Chain hotel ◆ Business ◆ Functional ◆
This hotel has a decent sized lobby, a variety of lounge areas and pleasantly equipped guestrooms, all with desks and fully equipped bathrooms. The kitchen in this contemporary-style restaurant is in full view of the dining room.

SWEDEN
SVERIGE

PROFILE

→ **Area:**
449 964 km^2 (173 731 sq mi).

→ **Population:**
9 401 925 inhabitants (est. 2010), density = 21 per km^2.

→ **Capital:**
Stockholm 872 673 (conurbation 2 011 047 inhabitants).

→ **Currency:**
Swedish Kronor (Skr or SEK); rate of exchange: SEK 1 = € 0.10 = US$ 0.14 (Dec 2010).

→ **Government:**
Constitutional parliamentary monarchy (since 1950). Member of European Union since 1995.

→ **Language:**
Swedish; many Swedes also speak good English.

→ **Specific public holidays:**
Epiphany (6 January), Good Friday (Friday before Easter), National Day, 6 June, Midsummer's Day (Saturday between June 20-26), Halloween (Saturday between Oct 31-Nov 6), Christmas Day (25 December), Boxing Day (26 December).

→ **Local Time:**
GMT + 1 hour in winter and GMT + 2 hours in summer.

→ **Climate:**
Temperate continental with cold winters and mild summers (Stockholm: January: -3°C, July: 16°C).

→ **International dialling Code:**
00 46 followed by area code without the initial **0** and then the local number. International Directory Enquiries: ✆ **079 77**.

→ **Emergency:**
Dial ✆ **112** for Police, Fire Brigade, Ambulance, Poison hot-line, on-call doctors and 24hr Roadside breakdown service.

→ **Electricity:**
220 volts AC, 50 Hz; 2-pin round-shaped continental plugs.

→ **Formalities**
Travellers from the European Union (EU), Switzerland, Iceland and the main countries of North and South America need a national identity card or passport (America: passport required) to visit Sweden for less than three months (tourism or business purpose). For visitors from other countries a visa may be required, in addition to a passport, especially for those wishing to stay for longer than three months. We advise you to check with your embassy before travelling.

Stockholm

STOCKHOLM

Population: 825 057 (conurbation 2 011 047) – Altitude: sea level

nagepassion/Fotolia.com

Stockholm is the place to go for clean air, big skies and handsome architecture. And water. One of the great beauties of the city, possibly *the* great beauty, is the amount of water that runs through and around it. It's built on fourteen islands, and looks out on twenty four thousand of them. Ferries glide out to the larger ones, and some, such as Vaxholm and Grinda, are great for swimming, others for picnicking, cycling and walking. An astounding two-thirds of the area within the city limits is made up of water, parks and woodland, and there are dozens of little bridges to cross to get from one part of town to another. No wonder Swedes appear so calm and relaxed.

It's in Stockholm that the salty waters of the Baltic meet head-on the fresh waters of Lake Mälaren, reflecting the broad boulevards and elegant buildings that shimmer along their edge. Truly, this is 'The City That Floats On Water'. Chain stores that seem so unavoidable in other European cities seem to have given Stockholm a wide berth, while domes, spires and turrets dot a skyline that in the summertime never truly darkens. It wasn't too long ago that this was a city with practically no nightlife, but now it rivals other European capitals for its after dark attractions. Admirers call Stockholm the most beautiful city in the world – day or night, you can see their point.

LIVING THE CITY

The city of Stockholm is enough to give you double vision. Alongside the important looking buildings is an almost rural quality of open space and water. The heart of the city is the Old Town, **Gamla Stan**, full of alleyways and lanes little changed from their medieval origins. Just to the north is the modern centre, **Norrmalm**, the part of the city with the least pastoral appeal: a buzzing quarter of shopping malls, restaurants and bars. East of Gamla Stan you reach the small island of **Skeppsholmen**, which boasts fine views of the waterfront. Directly north from here is **Östermalm**, an area full of grand residences, while south-east is the lovely park island of Djurgården, where you can find two of the city's most popular attractions. South and west of Gamla Stan are the two areas where Stockholmers like to hang out, the trendy (and hilly) Södermalm, and Kungsholmen.

PRACTICAL INFORMATION

ARRIVAL-DEPARTURE

Stockholm Arlanda Airport is 40km northwest of the city. The Arlanda Express train takes 20min to Centralstation and departs every 15min. A single journey costs SEK 240. The airport bus (Flygbuss) to Cityterminalen takes 40min. A taxi will cost around SEK 500.

TRANSPORT

Invest in a Stockholm Card, available from tourist offices. It is valid for one, two or three days and offers free travel on public transport, including sightseeing boats, and free entry to over 70 attractions (museums, galleries and castles).

If you're using public transport, it's best to go by metro, as it offers a more direct route than the buses. The No 7 tram, which runs throughout the summer, takes in quite a few of the main attractions.

You can buy single tickets for the bus, tram and metro, but if you're planning to do lots of travelling about the city, you can also get passes which cover a whole day or three whole days.

EXPLORING STOCKHOLM

Stockholm's old town, Gamla Stan, is the focal point of any visit, and that's as true now as it was in the thirteenth century, when its naturally fortuitous

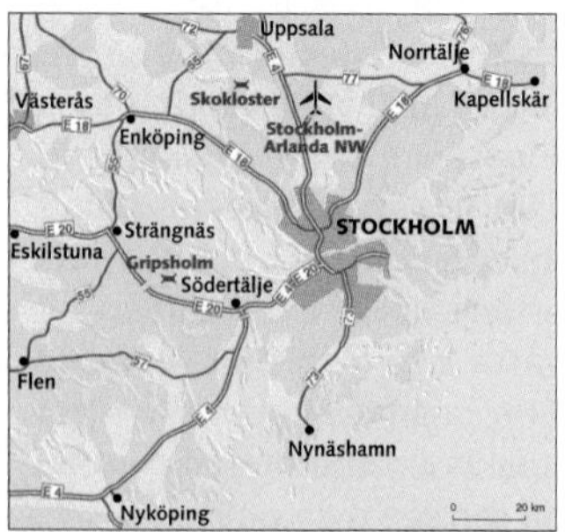

position between two channels of water made it the ideal setting for a fortress and the foundations of the city. It's a wonderfully enticing tangle of cobbled streets, small squares and gabled roofs. Remarkably, over eight hundred years it's been untouched by war or even the merest rumblings of local dissent. Its most imposing building is the Royal Palace, which has 600 rooms and good accessibility for the public. What it doesn't have is any royalty: they upped sticks and moved away to Drottningholm further along Lake Mälaren. What it retains is a museum dedicated to the Nobel Prize, art shops, galleries, antique shops, and the joyous feeling that although you might get lost in its maze of medieval stone streets, you'll reach water before too long. Near the opulent German Church (Tyska Kyrkan) try and find Marten Trotzigs Grand, the narrowest street in Stockholm. It's little more than a yard wide and has a beguiling lamp-lit atmosphere (it's also pretty steep).

→ QUAY MOMENTS

To escape any feelings of claustrophobia, head to the adjacent island of **Riddarholmen**, stand on its quay, breathe in its blasts of fresh air, and take in awesome views of **Lake Mälaren**, as well as the green heights of Southern Stockholm, and the vertical red-brick surprise of the City Hall, which seems to thrust straight out of the water. This is a graceful and imposing building, made up of eight million bricks, black granite reliefs and topped by three golden crowns; its first floor Golden Hall is decorated with nearly 20lb of gold leaf and eighteen million pieces of mosaic. If you're here in the summer, a great way of appreciating the visual splendour of the City Hall is to get to Riddarholmen at 3am (yes, three in the morning) and marvel at the changing hues of the early-hour light, from pastel blue to misty salmon, taking in the subtly changing shades of the brickwork. Catch up on your sleep later.

→ GET SKEPPTICAL

With all this light, shade and water, the last thing you might feel like doing is submerging yourself indoors, but if you miss the museums of Stockholm, you miss an essential part of the city's character. Actually, most of them are conveniently located on the city's 'museum island', **Skeppsholmen**. As you approach it, you see its most striking edifice, the **National Museum of Fine Arts**, over 200 years old, with a superb old masters collection, including works by Rembrandt, El Greco and Canaletto, and more recent paintings by Gauguin, Cézanne and Renoir. Further along the island are three more intriguing museums: the Museum of Modern Art, with works by Matisse, Klee and Modigliani; the Architecture Museum, which showcases one thousand years of Scandinavian design; and the Museum of Far Eastern Antiquities, a former stable with an enormous collection of Asian art. The two most popular attractions, though, are just to the east in the 'National City Park' of **Djurgården**. This unspoiled island of natural beauty contains miles of trails, grand oaks, handy restaurants and coffee shops, and two world-famous museums. The first of these, the **Vasa Museum**, is commonly considered the very best Stockholm has to offer, even though it only features one exhibit! The *Vasa* warship sank on its maiden voyage in Stockholm harbour in 1628, and was preserved for 300 years beneath the Baltic. Raised in 1961, it now stands magnificently complete in its vast 'hangar' by the water. See it, and prepare to gasp...

Inland from here is the world's most famous open-air museum, **Skansen**, located perfectly atop a hill and covering seventy-four wondrous acres. Skansen's over a hundred years old, and contains over a hundred and fifty reconstructed buildings depicting the lives of Swedes over different eras. You can see everything from windmills and farms to an entire township. It's beautifully put together, with not an ounce of tackiness, and even serves you delicious traditional food. In winter, warm up with a big bowl of soup.

→ DANCING QUEEN TO DRAMA QUEENS

Culture lovers can get a double hit in the smartly affluent area of **Östermalm**, 'over the water' northwest of Skansen. The Music Museum not only charts the history of music in

Sweden but also allows visitors to experiment with the different instruments they find there. And yes, there's a section given over to ABBA. Leave here, and just in front of you is the suitably dramatic looking Royal Theatre of Drama, the place where Garbo, both Bergmans and Von Sydow cut their teeth. It's a great place to get your own canines into a bit of Swedish angst, though obviously, if you haven't mastered the language, then actions may speak louder than words.

One part of the Swedish capital not so easy to negotiate for the cycling fraternity is the southern island of **Södermalm**, which has steeply craggy cliffs plunging down into the sea and the lake. Buildings look a bit perilous as they perch on the edge, but venture into their midst and come across a green and pleasant land. As in other European cities, this is a working class area that's been 'gentrified' to the extent that it contains some strikingly trendy bars, fashion boutiques and cafés, along with a number of charming small parks. And, of course, some of the views from these dizzy heights looking towards the city centre are spectacular.

→ WEST END IS NIGH

The western island of Stockholm, **Kungsholmen**, is where you'll find the previously mentioned City Hall; apart from that it has a rather sedate, neighbourhood feel, but one that's gradually acquiring a real buzz as swish little restaurants, bars and bistros start to pop up all over it. There was a bit of a 'big bang' around here a few years ago with the opening of a particularly smart boutique mall, and since then it's been rivalling Södermalm as the hippest place in town. It also boasts a promenade much loved by Stockholmers. The landscaped Norr Mälarstrand runs for a mile or so all the way along the water's edge from the City Hall, giving lovely lake views to the south, and proving once again that in this city the urban is always likely to play second fiddle to the pastoral.

CALENDAR HIGHLIGHTS

The Swedes may be modern in outlook, but culturally speaking they like to look to their past. Celebrations can tend towards the traditional, and they don't come much more traditional than the January Viking Run, a skiing race, starting in the town of Uppsala and finishing in Stockholm. Viking influence is to the fore again on Walpurgis Night, at the end of April, when bonfires light up the night sky in celebration of the arrival of Spring: various city venues reflect the night's activities. In June, the Stockholm Marathon begins and ends at the Olympic Stadium, while Gamla Stan provides a fitting backdrop for the Early Music Festival, featuring music

STOCKHOLM IN...

→ ONE DAY

Gamla Stan, City Hall, Vasa or Skansen museums, meal on Södermalm

→ TWO DAYS

Coffee in Kungsholmen, museums in Skeppsholmen, Djurgården stroll, another evening in Södermalm

→ THREE DAYS

Shopping in Norrmalm, boat trip round the archipelago

of pre-1750. Everyone heads over to Skansen Museum on Midsummer Eve to dance and drink the night (which looks like day, of course) away... there's no guarantee that the drinks are any cheaper than usual, though. July's Jazz Festival also includes blues, soul and reggae, while in the run-up to Christmas there's the world-famous Nobel Prize Day, around 10th December, and St Lucia Day (13th) when candles burn in coffee shops and restaurants, and young girls are crowned with wreaths of lighted candles: it's all to signify the light that will eventually break through winter's gloom.

EATING OUT

Everyone thinks that eating out in Stockholm is invariably expensive, but with a little forward planning it doesn't have to be. In the middle of the day, most restaurants and cafés offer very good value set menus. Keep in mind that, unlike in Southern Europe, the Swedes like to get their eating done early. Lunch is considered fair game from 11am (until 2pm), while dinner is on the go from 6pm, and they might want to start putting chairs on the tables sometime after 9pm. Don't nip out for breakfast: there are few places open in the early morning. Picking wild food is a birthright of Swedes, and there's no law to stop you going into forest or field to pick blueberries, cloudberries, cranberries, strawberries, mushrooms and the like. This love of outdoor, natural fare means that Stockholmers have a special bond with menus which relate to the seasons: keep your eyes open for restaurants that feature *husmanskost,* or traditional Swedish dishes. Try and find somewhere with a good **smörgåsbord**: if you're lucky, this should include soup, herring, warm potatoes and gravlax, followed by salads, cold meats, meatballs, beef and chicken, washed down with beer. As for tipping, well, the service charge is included in the bill, but charming service (common in Stockholm) might make you add on a bit more for the waiting staff.

➜ FULL STEAM AHEAD

More memorable than a trip on a motorised launch - why not head out from Stockholm's waterfront on a full-blown steamship? There are about ten plying the archipelago and Lake Mälaren. There used to be hundreds, but the introduction of car travel put paid to most of them. One blast from the funnel and you'll be smitten.

Apart from Södermalm, Stockholm's a pretty flat city that is ideal for cycling around. Alternatively, see its natural wonders from above – this is a rare example of a world capital that allows hot-air balloons to fly over.

Catching the metro (or tunnelbana, to be precise) in Stockholm is less of a chore than in other cities. That's because it's the world's longest art gallery! It displays artwork by the city's most creative talents along its underground system – so watch out for paintings, mosaics, sculptures and murals where you wouldn't normally expect to find them.

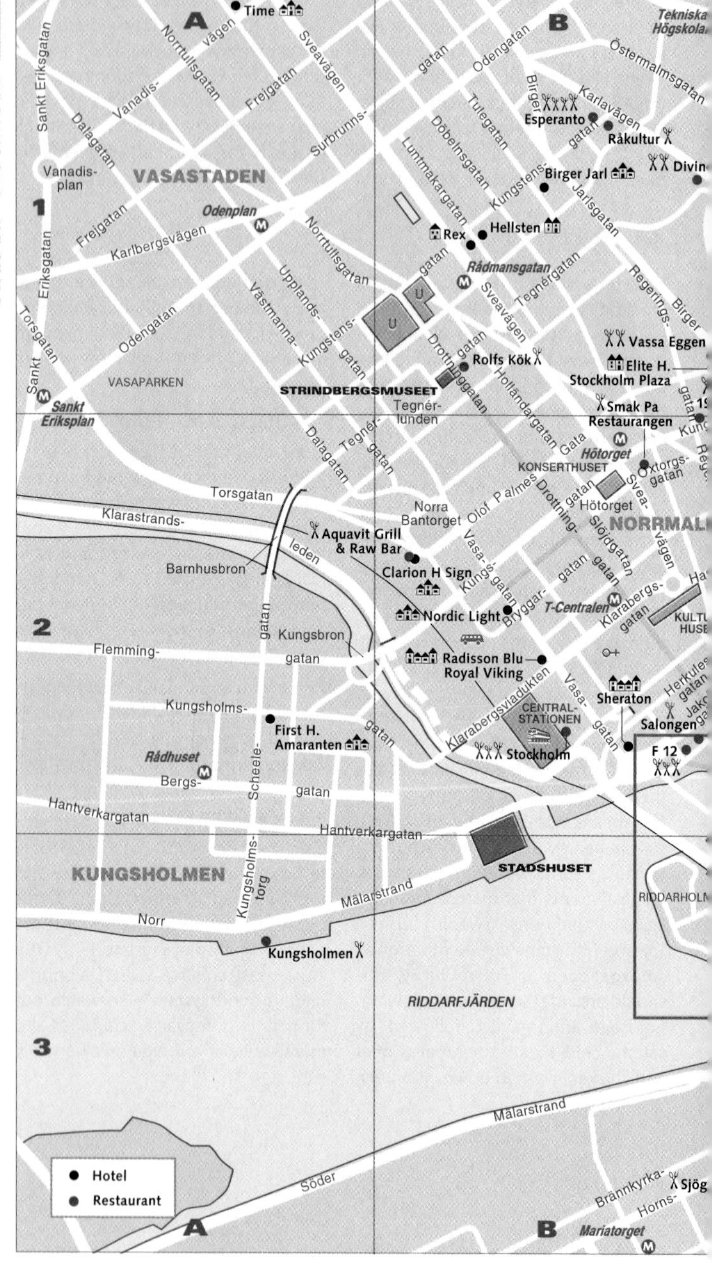
A
B
1
2
3
VASASTADEN
Odenplan
Vanadis-
plan
Sankt Eriksgatan
Dalagatan
Vanadis-
vägen
Norrtullsgatan
Frejgatan
Sveavägen
Surbrunns-
Karlbergsvägen
Odengatan
VASAPARKEN
Torsgatan
Sankt
Eriksplan
Upplands-
Västmanna-
Kungstens-
gatan
STRINDBERGSMUSEET
Tegnér-
lunden
Time
Rex
Hellsten
Rådmansgatan
Tulegatan
Döbelnsgatan
Luntmakargatan
Birger
Karlavägen
Esperanto
Råkultur
Birger Jarl
Divin
Jarlsgatan
Östermalmsgatan
Tekniska
Högskolan
Tegnérgatan
Regerings-
Vassa Eggen
Elite H.
Stockholm Plaza
Smak Pa
Restaurangen
Rolfs Kök
Drottninggatan
Holländargatan
Hötorget
KONSERTHUSET
Oxtorgs-
gatan
NORRMALM
Norra
Bantorget
Olof Palmes Gata
Klarastrands-
leden
Barnhusbron
Aquavit Grill
& Raw Bar
Clarion H Sign
Nordic Light
Kungsgatan
Vasagatan
Bryggar-
T-Centralen
Klarabergs-
gatan
Slöjdgatan
Kungsbron
Flemming-
gatan
Radisson Blu
Royal Viking
Sheraton
Salongen
Kungsholms-
First H.
Amaranten
Scheele-
gatan
Rådhuset
Bergs-
gatan
Hantverkargatan
Klarabergsviadukten
CENTRAL-
STATIONEN
Stockholm
F 12
STADSHUSET
KUNGSHOLMEN
Kungsholms-
torg
Norr
Mälarstrand
Kungsholmen
RIDDARFJÄRDEN
RIDDARHOLMEN
Mälarstrand
Söder
Brännkyrka-
Horns-
Sjög
Mariatorget
Hotel
Restaurant

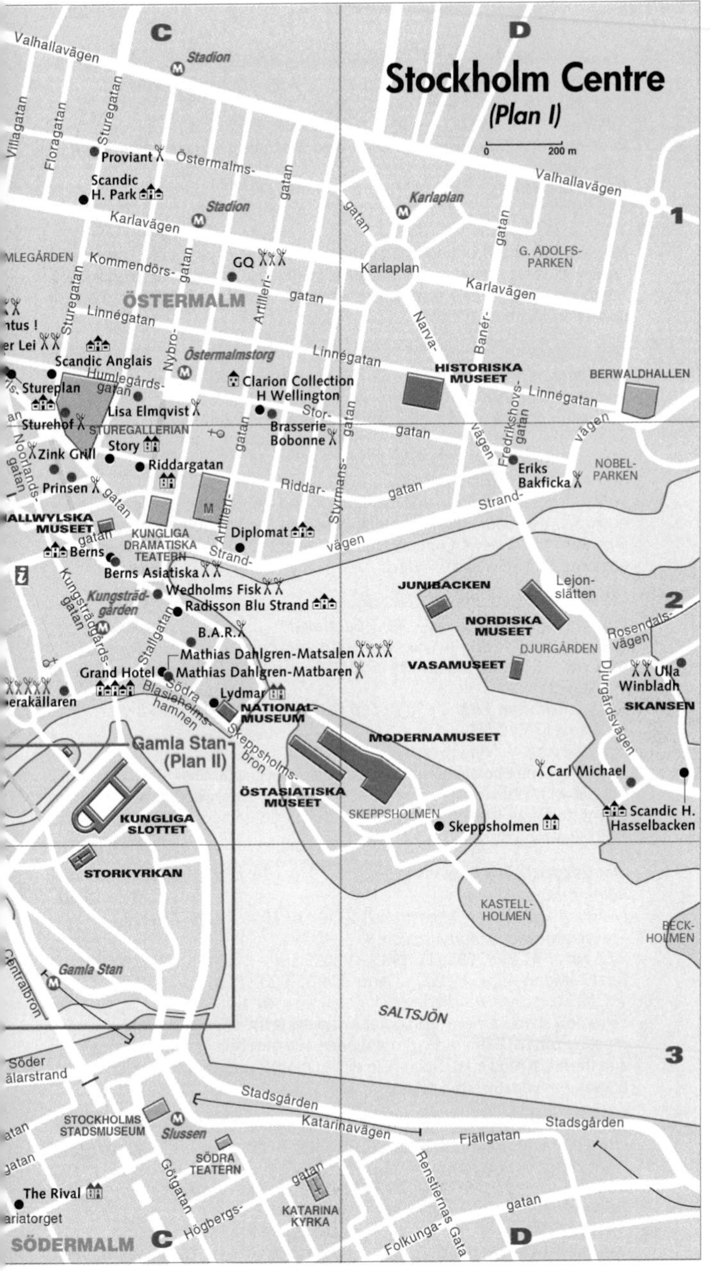

Stockholm Centre
(Plan I)
0
200 m
C
D
1
2
3
Valhallavägen
Stadion
Villagatan
Floragatan
Sturegatan
Proviant
Östermalms-
gatan
Scandic H. Park
Stadion
Karlavägen
Karlaplan
gatan
G. ADOLFS-PARKEN
Kommendörs-
gatan
GQ
Karlaplan
Karlavägen
Artilleri-
ÖSTERMALM
Linnégatan
Nybro-
Östermalmstorg
Linnégatan
Narva-
Banér-
HISTORISKA MUSEET
BERWALDHALLEN
Linnégatan
Scandic Anglais
Humlegårds-
gatan
Clarion Collection
H Wellington
Stureplan
Lisa Elmqvist
Stor-
gatan
Sturehof
STUREGALLERIAN
Brasserie
Bobonne
gatan
Fredrikshovs-
gatan
vägen
Story
Zink Grill
Riddargatan
Eriks Bakficka
NOBEL-PARKEN
Norrlands-
gatan
Prinsen
Riddar-
gatan
Strand-
Styrmans-
gatan
KUNGLIGA DRAMATISKA TEATERN
Diplomat
vägen
Berns
Strand-
Berns Asiatiska
JUNIBACKEN
Lejon-
slätten
Kungsträd-
gården
Wedholms Fisk
Radisson Blu Strand
NORDISKA MUSEET
Rosendals-
vägen
Kungsträdgårds-
gatan
B.A.R.
Stallgatan
DJURGÅRDEN
Mathias Dahlgren-Matsalen
VASAMUSEET
Ulla Winbladh
Grand Hotel
Mathias Dahlgren-Matbaren
Södra Blasieholms-
hamnen
SKANSEN
Lydmar
NATIONAL-MUSEUM
Djurgårdsvägen
Gamla Stan
(Plan II)
Skeppsholms-
bron
MODERNAMUSEET
Carl Michael
ÖSTASIATISKA MUSEET
KUNGLIGA SLOTTET
SKEPPSHOLMEN
Skeppsholmen
Scandic H. Hasselbacken
STORKYRKAN
KASTELL-HOLMEN
BECK-HOLMEN
Centralbron
Gamla Stan
SALTSJÖN
Söder
älarstrand
Stadsgården
Katarinavägen
Stadsgården
Fjällgatan
STOCKHOLMS STADSMUSEUM
Slussen
SÖDRA TEATERN
Götgatan
gatan
Renstiernas Gata
The Rival
KATARINA KYRKA
gatan
ariatorget
Högbergs-
Folkunga-
SÖDERMALM

Grand Hôtel
Södra Blasieholmshamnen 8 ✉ *S-103 27* – Ⓜ *Kungsträdgården* – ✆ *(08) 679 35 00* – *www.grandhotel.se* **C2**
331 rm – †1900/4600 SEK ††2500/4900 SEK, ☕ 265 SEK – 37 suites
Rest *Mathias Dahlgren-Matsalen and Mathias Dahlgren-Matbaren* – see below
Rest *Verandan* – ✆ *(08) 679 35 86* – Menu 590 SEK (dinner) – Carte 420/795 SEK
♦ Grand Luxury ♦ Classic ♦
Majestic 19C waterfront hotel; an integral part of the city's history. Large guest areas include a stylish bar, impressive conference room and splendid spa. Bedrooms range in style, some boast sea views. Verandan offers all day Swedish cuisine and harbour outlook.

Sheraton
Tegelbacken 6 ✉ *S-101 23* – Ⓜ *T-Centralen* – ✆ *(08) 412 34 00* – *www.sheratonstockholm.com* **B2**
458 rm – †3495 SEK ††3495 SEK, ☕ 259 SEK – 7 suites
Rest *360°* – ✆ *(08) 412 34 72 (closed lunch Saturday and Sunday)* Menu 495 SEK – Carte 385/585 SEK
♦ Business ♦ Modern ♦
Well-run hotel boasting large bar-lounge and good business facilities. Well-equipped bedrooms display neutral hues and modern furniture; ask for one with Gamla Stan views. Contemporary restaurant offers international buffet lunches and Italian/Swedish dinners.

Radisson Blu Royal Viking
Vasagatan 1 ✉ *S-101 24* – Ⓜ *T-Centralen* – ✆ *(08) 506 540 00* – *www.royalviking.stockholm.radissonsas.com*
456 rm – †1350/3195 SEK ††1550/3195 SEK, ☕ 125 SEK – 3 suites **B2**
Rest *Stockholm Fisk* – ✆ *(08) 506 541 10* – Menu 395 SEK (dinner) – Carte 417/820 SEK
♦ Business ♦ Modern ♦
Large city centre hotel boasting good leisure/meeting facilities and a panoramic sky bar with city views. Bedrooms vary greatly – from wood-furnished Viking rooms, to bright Italian rooms and cosy suites. Contemporary restaurant offers mainly seafood dishes.

Courtyard by Marriott
rm, rm,
Rålambshovsladen 50
(West : 4 km by Norr Malastrand) ✉ *S-112 19* – ✆ *(08) 441 3100* – *www.stockholmcourtyard.com*
277 rm – †1290/2095 SEK ††1290/2095 SEK – 1 suite
Rest – Menu 433/526 SEK – Carte 324/557 SEK
♦ Chain hotel ♦ Modern ♦ Functional ♦
Extremely spacious new-build hotel, just outside the city centre. Well-equipped meeting rooms. Generously proportioned, modern bedrooms with huge beds and the latest mod cons. Open-plan dining room is popular with the locals, offering menus with Swedish roots.

Clarion H. Sign
Östra Järnvägsgatan 35 ✉ *S-101 26* – Ⓜ *T-Centralen* – ✆ *(08) 676 98 00* – *www.clarionsign.com* **B2**
550 rm ☕ – †1345/1450 SEK ††1545/1870 SEK – 8 suites
Rest *Aquavit Grill & Raw Bar* – see below
♦ Business ♦ Chain hotel ♦ Modern ♦
Vast hotel boasting the city's largest conference facilities. Each floor of bright, modern bedrooms is styled after a different designer; top floor offers prime views. Smart spa and rooftop pool.

Radisson Blu Strand

Nybrokajen 9 ✉ S-103 27 – Ⓜ Kungsträdgården – ✆ (08) 506 640 00 – www.radissonblu.com/strand-hotel.stockholm **C2**

141 rm – 🚹1295/3695 SEK 🚹🚹1695/3995 SEK, ☕ 180 SEK – 11 suites

Rest – Menu 345 SEK – Carte 305/515 SEK

♦ Business ♦ Classic ♦

Well-run harbourside hotel. Red-brick 1920s building has a classical feel; 1930s extension is more contemporary. Many bedrooms have water views – impressive Tower Suite boasts a private roof terrace. Courtyard dining room mixes Swedish and international cuisine.

Diplomat

Strandvägen 7c ✉ S-104 40 – Ⓜ Kungsträdgården – ✆ (08) 459 68 00 – www.diplomathotel.com – Closed 22-27 December **C2**

126 rm – 🚹1750/2650 SEK 🚹🚹2750/3550 SEK, ☕ 195 SEK – 4 suites

Rest *T Bar* – *✆ (08) 459 68 02 (brunch Saturday and Sunday)* Carte 323/622 SEK

♦ Traditional ♦ Classic ♦

Attractive 1911 art nouveau building blending early 20C charm with contemporary furnishings and facilities. Cosy library-lounge; lovely preserved lift leads to elegant bedrooms – some with harbour views. Scandinavian-inspired brasserie dishes served in T Bar.

Berns

Näckströmsgatan 8, Berzelii Park ✉ S-111 47 – Ⓜ Kungsträdgården – ✆ (08) 566 322 00 – www.berns.se **C2**

79 rm ☕ – 🚹1295/2950 SEK 🚹🚹1770/4800 SEK – 3 suites

Rest *Berns Asiatiska* – see below

♦ Business ♦ Stylish ♦

Centrally located hotel built in 1863 by the Royal Family tailor, and very much part of local history. Modern, minimalist interior; newer, more contemporary bedrooms are largest and comfiest.

Stureplan

Birger Jarlsgatan 24 ✉ S-114 34 – Ⓜ Östermalmstorg – ✆ (08) 440 66 00 – www.hotelstureplan.se **C1**

101 rm ☕ – 🚹1300/3100 SEK 🚹🚹2650/3750 SEK

Rest *Per Lei* – see below

♦ Traditional ♦ Classic ♦

Ornate 19C building with earlier Gustavian-style interior. Modern amenities. Charming, individually styled bedrooms – choose from compact 'Cabin', modern 'Loft' or spacious 'Classic' styles.

Time without rest

Vanadisvägen 12 ✉ S-113 46 – Ⓜ Odenplan – ✆ (08) 54 54 73 00 – www.timehotel.se **A1**

144 rm ☕ – 🚹1490/2050 SEK 🚹🚹1590/2250 SEK

♦ Business ♦ Modern ♦

Spacious, purpose-built business hotel on edge of town, with high-ceilinged lobby and modern buffet breakfast room. Large, functional bedrooms and studios in light hues; some with balconies.

Scandic H. Park

Karlavägen 43 ✉ S-102 46 – Ⓜ Stadion – ✆ (08) 517 348 00 – www.scandichotels.com/park **C1**

193 rm ☕ – 🚹1390/2590 SEK 🚹🚹1490/2890 SEK – 8 suites

Rest *Park Village* – Menu 245/495 SEK – Carte 285/415 SEK

♦ Business ♦ Functional ♦

Set in a chic neighbourhood facing Humlegärden Park. Light walls contrast with dark furniture in large, well-kept bedrooms; warm, contemporary suites offer lovely park or avenue views. Restaurant boasts oversized windows and summer terrace with park outlooks.

Birger Jarl

Tulegatan 8 ✉ *S-104 32 –* Ⓜ *Rådmansgatan –* ☎ *(08) 674 18 00 – www.birgerjarl.se* **B1**

230 rm – 🚹890/2990 SEK 🚹🚹2490/3090 SEK – 5 suites

Rest – *(closed lunch Saturday and Sunday)* Carte 376/518 SEK

♦ Business ♦ Design ♦ Modern ♦

1970s building set in residential area, with unassuming façade that belies its interior. Art and sculpture displays in lobby; chic, stylish bedrooms – 17 designed by famous Swedish artists. Bright restaurant offers regional dishes and express business lunches.

Nordic Light

Vasaplan 7 ✉ *S-101 37 –* Ⓜ *T-Centralen –* ☎ *(08) 505 630 00 – www.nordiclighthotel.com* **B2**

175 rm – 🚹2450/4300 SEK 🚹🚹4300 SEK, 180 SEK

Rest – Carte 308/478 SEK

♦ Business ♦ Design ♦

Contemporary glass-walled building set in the city's heart. Spacious, open-plan interior with black and white décor and modern furnishings. Smart bedrooms with colourful lighting systems. Stylish round dining room furnished in white; exceptional American wine list.

Scandic Anglais

Humlegardsgatan 23 ✉ *S-102 44 –* Ⓜ *Östermalmstorg – ☎ (08) 517 340 00 – www.scandichotels.com* **C1**

217 rm – 🚹690/3590 SEK 🚹🚹1290/3590 SEK – 13 suites

Rest – *(closed Saturday lunch and Sunday) (buffet lunch)* Menu 145 SEK – Carte dinner approx. 620 SEK

♦ Chain hotel ♦ Modern ♦

Modern city centre hotel with stylish lobby, well-equipped conference rooms and choice of bars. Bedrooms range from tiny cabin rooms to spacious suites boasting balconies and park views. Open-plan restaurant offers buffet lunches and international dinners.

First H. Amaranten

rest,

Kungsholmsgatan 31 ✉ *S-104 20 –* Ⓜ *Rådhuset – ☎ (08) 692 52 00 – www.firsthotels.se/amaranten* **A2**

457 rm – 🚹1700/2190 SEK 🚹🚹1900/2390 SEK – 4 suites

Rest *Amaranten* – *(closed Saturday lunch and Sunday)* Carte 281/469 SEK

♦ Business ♦ Modern ♦

Large commercial hotel with modern open-plan lobby and contemporary décor. Compact, functional bedrooms are designed for business use; executive rooms and suites set on the 7th floor. Express business lunches in Amarenten, which serves modern Swedish cuisine.

Lydmar

Södra Blasieholmshamnen 2 ✉ *S-103 24 –* Ⓜ *Kungsträdgården – ☎ (08) 22 31 60 – www.lydmar.com* **C2**

40 rm – 🚹3200/3900 SEK 🚹🚹6200 SEK – 6 suites **Rest** – Carte 375/580 SEK

♦ Townhouse ♦ Stylish ♦ Design ♦

Charming, luxury townhouse, superbly located opposite the Palace. Gallery entrance sets the scene with its eclectic art and décor. Spacious, individually styled bedrooms boast a range of funky furnishings and smart, stylish bathrooms. Casual lounge and easy-going bar. Attractive restaurant offers comforting classics.

Story

Riddergatan 6 ✉ *S-114 35 –* Ⓜ *Östermalmstorg –* ☎ *(08) 545 039 40 – www.storyhotels.com* **B2**

83 rm – 🚹990/1990 SEK 🚹🚹1590/3090 SEK

Rest *Story Kitchen* – *(closed Saturday and Sunday lunch)* Carte 500/800 SEK

♦ Townhouse ♦ Personalised ♦ Design ♦

Collection of converted townhouses with stylish, bohemian feel. Modern bedrooms display interesting designer touches; delightful bathrooms boast monsoon showers. Funky café-bar. Laid-back restaurant with seasonal Swedish and Italian-influenced tapas dishes.

Hellsten without rest

Luntmakargatan 68 ✉ S-113 51 – Ⓜ Rådmannsgatan – ✆ (08) 661 86 00 – www.hellsten.se
– Closed 23-26 December **B1**

78 rm – 1290/2390 SEK 1690/2490 SEK

♦ Townhouse ♦ Personalised ♦ Cosy ♦

Set in a suburban street, displaying souvenirs and furnishings from the owner's globetrotting adventures. Choose between large, high-ceilinged bedrooms or smaller, more uniquely styled rooms.

Skeppsholmen

Gröna Gången 1 (Skeppsholmen Island) ✉ S-111 86 – ✆ (08) 407 23 00 – www.hotelskeppsholmen.se **D2**

78 rm – 1317/2595 SEK 1557/2595 SEK – 3 suites

Rest – Menu 645 SEK (dinner) – Carte 385/620 SEK

♦ Historic ♦ Design ♦

Passionately run 17C hotel, set by a beautiful park on a small, peaceful island. Modern Scandinavian art, décor and furnishings feature throughout; white bedrooms display minimalist influences and sea or park views. Dining room offers traditional Swedish cuisine.

Riddargatan without rest

Riddargatan 14 ✉ S-114 35 – Ⓜ Östermalmstorg – ✆ (08) 555 730 00 – www.profilhotels.se
– Closed 23-26 December **C2**

74 rm – 1250/2295 SEK 1450/2295 SEK – 4 suites

♦ Business ♦ Modern ♦

Close to the theatre, shops and restaurants. Nicely equipped, modern bedrooms – those in newer wing have bright bold designs; all have an exercise DVD and weights. Contemporary breakfast room.

Elite H. Stockholm Plaza

Birger Jarlsgatan 29 ✉ S-103 95 – Ⓜ Östermalmstorg – ✆ (08) 566 220 00 – www.elite.se **B1**

135 rm – 1000/2700 SEK 1500/2900 SEK – 8 suites

Rest *Vassa Eggen* – see below

♦ Business ♦ Functional ♦

Attractive building dating from 1884, with bright lobby, basement conference facilities and shops nearby. Modern, functional bedrooms in neutral hues; pleasant, contemporary suites.

Clarion Collection H. Wellington without rest

Storgatan 6 ✉ S-114 51 – Ⓜ Östermalmstorg – ✆ (08) 667 09 10 – www.wellington.se
– Closed 23 December-4 January **C1**

58 rm – 1095/2595 SEK 1895/2995 SEK – 2 suites

♦ Business ♦ Functional ♦

Well-located for shopping and tourism. Contemporary lounge and pleasant breakfast room. Compact but well-equipped bedrooms, many with balconies and city/courtyard views. Buffet dinners.

Rex without rest

Luntmakargatan 73 ✉ S-113 51 – Ⓜ Rådmannsgatan – ✆ (08) 16 00 40 – www.rexhotel.se
– Closed 23-26 December **B1**

55 rm – 1190/2190 SEK 1490/2290 SEK

♦ Townhouse ♦ Modern ♦

Suburban hotel dating back to 1866. Comfy, compact bedrooms; newer annexe rooms more contemporary in style, with interesting furnishings. Breakfast on pleasant veranda overlooking courtyard.

XXXXX

Operakällaren

Operahuset, Karl XII's Torg ✉ S-111 86 – Ⓜ Kungsträdgården – ✆ (08) 676 58 01 – www.operakallaren.se – Closed 11 July-8 August, 25 December-11 January, Sunday and Monday

Rest – *(dinner only)* Carte 765/1460 SEK **C2**

◆ Classic ◆ Formal ◆ Luxury ◆

Set in the historic Opera House, this is one of the most opulent restaurants in town. Stunning high-ceilinged room displays 19C wood carvings, original fresco paintings and elegant chandeliers. Seasonal cooking uses complex preparations in ambitious combinations.

XXXX ✿✿

Mathias Dahlgren-Matsalen – at Grand Hotel

Södra Blasieholmshamnen 6 ✉ S-103 27 – Ⓜ Kungsträdgården – ✆ (08) 679 35 84 – www.mdghs.com – Closed 14 July-9 August, 24 December-9 January, Sunday and Monday **C2**

Rest – *(booking essential) (dinner only)* Carte 1250/1500 SEK

Spec. Scandinavian sashimi. Seared roe deer with red and yellow beets. Goat's cheese cake with cherries.

◆ Modern ◆ Elegant ◆ Luxury ◆

Set in the city's top hotel, boasting contemporary décor, original features and waterfront views. Passionately prepared dishes rely on fine local ingredients, focusing on natural flavours and displaying the occasional creative element. Discreet, dedicated service.

XXXX ✿

Esperanto (Daniel Höglander/Sayan Isaksson)

Kungstensgatan 2, (1st floor) ✉ S-114 25 – Ⓜ Tekniska Högskolan – ✆ (08) 696 23 23 – www.esperantorestaurant.se – Closed July,18 December-7 January, Sunday, Monday and Tuesday

Rest – *(dinner only) (set menu only)* Menu 995/1175 SEK **B1**

Spec. Langoustine with porcini, foie gras and frozen hazelnut. Wild duck with pears and Jerusalem artichoke. Tangerine Jardin d'hiver.

◆ Innovative ◆ Formal ◆ Luxury ◆

Understated candlelit restaurant located on the first floor of a converted theatre – boasting an impressive curved ceiling and pleasant lounge-bar. Elaborate service. Creative, original cooking is light and flavours are well-defined. Choice of two set menus.

XXX ✿

F12 (Danyel Couet)

Rödbotorget 2 ✉ S-111 52 – Ⓜ T-Centralen – ✆ (08) 24 80 52 – www.f12.se – Closed 25 December and Sunday **B2**

Rest – *(booking essential) (dinner only)* Menu 395/795 SEK – Carte approx. 769 SEK

Spec. Foie gras 'bon bon'. Young reindeer with truffle in burnt hay. Comice pear 'After Eight' with wild mint and bitter chocolate.

◆ Innovative ◆ Fashionable ◆ Design ◆

Stylish restaurant set in the Academy of Arts, displaying warm green hues and a spacious bar. Well-balanced mix of traditional and innovative dishes, each crafted from quality ingredients; choice of tasting menu or monthly themed à la carte. Excellent service.

XXX

GQ

Kommendörsgatan 23 ✉ S-114 48 – Ⓜ Stadion – ✆ (08) 545 674 30 – www.gqrestaurang.se – Closed 22 December-10 January, Sunday, Monday and bank holidays

Rest – *(dinner only)* Menu 595 SEK – Carte 350/845 SEK **C1**

◆ Traditional ◆ Elegant ◆

Candlelit restaurant and wine bar run by passionate, knowledgeable team. Classical cooking with modern touches; set menus offer wine pairings. They also host cookery classes and wine evenings.

XXX **Stockholm**

Centralplan/Ingång från Vasagatan ✉ S-101 35 – Ⓜ T-Centralen – ✆ (08) 20 20 49 – www.restaurangstockholm.se – Closed July, Saturday lunch, Sunday and bank holidays **B2**

Rest – Menu 295/495 SEK – Carte 465/620 SEK

♦ Swedish ♦ Fashionable ♦

Contemporary glass-walled restaurant with comfy lounge-bar and modern Scandinavian furnishings. Swedish-inspired recipes feature fresh ingredients and modern French touches. Efficient service.

XX **Berns Asiatiska** – at Berns Hotel

Näckströmsgatan 8, Berzelii Park ✉ S-111 47 – Ⓜ Kungsträdgården – ✆ (08) 566 322 22 – www.berns.se **C2**

Rest – Menu 235 SEK (lunch) – Carte 320/655 SEK

♦ Asian influences ♦ Fashionable ♦ Romantic ♦

Stunningly restored rococo ballroom dating back to 1863 – set in the Berns hotel, close to the theatre – and boasting a pleasant terrace overlooking Berzeli Park. Offers plenty of choice, with an extensive 101 dish Asian fusion menu and wide-ranging sushi selection.

XX **Wedholms Fisk**

Nybrokajen 17 ✉ S-111 48 – Ⓜ Kungsträdgården – ✆ (08) 611 78 74 – www.wedholmsfisk.se – Closed 24 December-1 January, Saturday lunch, Sunday and bank holidays

Rest – *(dinner only July-August) (booking essential)* Carte 430/1080 SEK **C2**

♦ Seafood ♦ Formal ♦

Set on Stockholm's 'little Wall Street', a popular 19C harbourside townhouse with elegant interior and formal, friendly service. Menus display simply and accurately prepared seafood dishes.

XX **Pontus!**

Brunnsgatan 1 ✉ S-111 38 – Ⓜ Östermalmstorg – ✆ (08) 545 27300 – www.pontusfrithiof.com – Closed 1 January, mid summer, Christmas and Sunday **C1**

Rest – *(booking essential)* Menu 299 SEK (dinner) – Carte 490/865 SEK

♦ Inventive ♦ Fashionable ♦

Relaxed, 'three-in-one' eatery that's a hit with the locals. Choose between oysters at the counter, modern Asian dishes in the bar or contemporary Swedish cuisine in the library dining room.

XX **Divino**

Karlavägen 28 ✉ S-114 31 – Ⓜ Tekniska Högskolan – ✆ (08) 611 02 69 – www.divino.se – Closed Sunday **B1**

Rest – Menu 390/495 SEK – Carte 495/895 SEK

♦ Italian ♦ Elegant ♦

Italian restaurant, deli and wine cellar; in a chic neighbourhood next to Humlegården Park. Contemporary interior with chandeliers, design furniture and relaxed lounge. Seasonal set menus.

XX **Per Lei** – at Stureplan Hotel

Birger Jarlsgatan 26 ✉ S-114 34 – Ⓜ Östermalmstorg – ✆ (08) 411 38 11 – www.perlei.se – Closed Sunday **C1**

Rest – *(restricted lunch at weekends)* Menu 320/475 SEK – Carte 485/665 SEK

♦ Italian ♦ Cosy ♦

Cosy hotel dining room with velvet armchairs, attractive bar, small courtyard and summer roof terrace. Well-prepared, generously proportioned Italian dishes; some Swedish twists at lunch.

XX **1900**

Regeringsgatan 66 ✉ S-111 39 – Ⓜ Hötorget – ✆ (08) 20 60 10 – www.r1900.se – Closed Saturday lunch, Sunday and bank holidays

Rest – Menu 550 SEK (dinner) – Carte 365/645 SEK **B2**

♦ Swedish ♦ Fashionable ♦ Friendly ♦

Contemporary bistro offering a homely Swedish menu with modern twists. Cooking uses quality local and seasonal ingredients; additional casual seating area serves more gastropub-style dishes.

XX **Vassa Eggen** – at Elite H. Stockholm Plaza

Birger Jarlsgatan 29 ✉ S-103 25 – Ⓜ Östermalmstorg – ✆ (08) 21 61 69 – www.vassaeggen.com – Closed Saturday lunch and Sunday

Rest – Menu 355/595 SEK – Carte 480/725 SEK **B1**

♦ Steakhouse ♦ Fashionable ♦

Contemporary hotel dining room with open kitchen, vast modern paintings, relaxed atmosphere and sizeable bar. Up-to-the-minute steakhouse menu features tasty meat, seafood and fish dishes.

X **Mathias Dahlgren-Matbaren** – at Grand Hotel

Södra Blasieholmshamnen 6 ✉ S-103 27 – Ⓜ Kungsträdgården – ✆ (08) 679 35 84 – www.mdghs.com – Closed 14 July-9 August, 24 December-9 January, Saturday lunch and Sunday

Rest – Carte 415/750 SEK **C2**

Spec. Herring with sour cream, egg and chives. Pumpkin and broccoli. Baked chocolate with toffee ice cream.

♦ Modern ♦ Trendy ♦

Lively eatery displaying contemporary Swedish design furniture. Concise menu changes up to twice a day, featuring straightforward yet perfectly balanced recipes with a simple but playful modern style. Dishes are carefully crafted using top quality ingredients.

X **Salongen**

Fredsgatan 12 ✉ S-111 52 – Ⓜ T-Centralen – ✆ (08) 505 244 04 – www.f12salongen.se – Closed Saturday lunch and Sunday **B2**

Rest – Menu 495 SEK (dinner) – Carte approx. 421 SEK

♦ International ♦ Cosy ♦

Close to the F12 restaurant and run by the same team. Choice of two casual but elegant dining rooms filled with antiques and knick-knacks, or a summer terrace facing Gamla Stan. Menus mix French brasserie, traditional Swedish and Mediterranean influences.

X **Brasserie Bobonne**

Storgatan 12 ✉ S-114 44 – Ⓜ Östermalmstorg – ✆ (08) 660 03 18 – www.brasseriebobonne.se – Closed 5 weeks July-August, Christmas, Sunday and bank holidays **C1**

Rest – *(booking essential) (dinner only)* Menu 498 SEK – Carte 365/555 SEK

♦ French ♦ Cosy ♦

Small, cosy, two-roomed restaurant with open kitchen, comfy chairs and period floor tiles. Blackboard displays tasty, well-balanced dishes crafted from fresh ingredients – menus are largely French-inspired, with a few modern touches and the odd Swedish recipe.

X **Proviant**

Sturegatan 19 ✉ S-114 36 – Ⓜ Stadion – ✆ (08) 22 60 50 – www.proviant.se – Closed 4 weeks July-August, Christmas-New Year, Saturday and Sunday lunch

Rest – Carte 400/575 SEK **C1**

♦ Swedish ♦ Bistro ♦

Popular restaurant located in a chic residential area by Sture Park, with smart, new contemporary décor and a welcoming bistro feel. Choose from a simple weekly blackboard menu at lunch or traditional Swedish dishes at dinner. Set French menu Sunday nights.

Sturehof

Stureplan 2-4 ✉ S-114 46 – Ⓜ Östermalmstorg – ✆ (08) 440 57 30 – www.sturehof.com C1

Rest – Carte 387/718 SEK

♦ Seafood ♦ Brasserie ♦

Lively city centre café-brasserie, dating back to 1896. Long glass-walled dining room with two bars and pleasant drinks terrace. Fresh, tasty, unfussy seafood dishes. Open every day til late.

Aquavit Grill & Raw Bar – at Clarion H. Sign

Östra Järnvägsgatan 35 ✉ S-101 26 – Ⓜ T-Centralen – ✆ (08) 676 98 50 – www.aquavitgrillrawbar.se B2

Rest – Menu 355 SEK (lunch) – Carte 325/735 SEK

♦ International ♦ Minimalist ♦

Informal restaurant with summer terrace. Menus mix Scandinavian and American cuisine; portions are larger than most. Grill for strip steak and rib-eye; Raw Bar for oysters and catch of the day.

Kungsholmen

Norr Mälarstrand Kajplats 464 ✉ S-112 20 – Ⓜ Rådhuset – ✆ (08) 50 52 44 50 – www.kungsholmen.com A3

Rest – *(dinner only)* Carte approx. 410 SEK

♦ International ♦ Trendy ♦

Relaxed riverbank eatery with trendy cocktail bar. Modern food court layout, with seven themed open kitchens: bread, soup, salad, sushi, bistro dishes, grills and ice cream. Friendly team.

Eriks Bakficka

Fredrikshovsgatan 4 ✉ S-115 23 – ✆ (08) 660 15 99 – www.eriks.se – Closed Saturday lunch and Sunday D2

Rest – Carte 420/585 SEK

♦ Swedish ♦ Bistro ♦

Basement restaurant set in a residential area close to the attractive Djurgårdsbron Bridge. Two bistro-style rooms with marble tables. Simple, unpretentious Swedish cuisine. A local favourite.

Prinsen

Mäster Samuelsgatan 4 ✉ S-111 44 – Ⓜ Östermalmstorg – ✆ (08) 611 13 31 – www.restaurangprinsen.se – Closed 24 June, 24-25 December, 1 January and Sunday lunch

Rest – *(booking essential)* Menu 485 SEK – Carte 377/759 SEK C2

♦ Traditional ♦ Brasserie ♦ Retro ♦

Renowned brasserie with basement seafood bar. Frequented by literary/artistic figures since its opening in 1897 and only on its 3rd owner. Menus mix French, Swedish and Mediterranean influences.

B.A.R.

Blasieholmsgatan 4A ✉ S-111 48 – Ⓜ Kungsträdgården – ✆ (08) 611 53 35 – www.restaurangbar.se – Closed 23 December-3 January and lunch Saturday and Sunday

Rest – Carte 240/525 SEK C2

♦ Seafood ♦ Brasserie ♦ Trendy ♦

Spacious canteen restaurant with industrial feel. Choose a simply prepared small dish or create a custom-style grill by selecting your own meat/fish from the ice display in the open kitchen.

Råkultur

Kungstensgatan 2 ✉ S-114 25 – Ⓜ Tekniska Högskolan – ✆ (08) 696 23 25 – www.rakultur.se – Closed 2 weeks Christmas, Saturday and Sunday

Rest – Carte approx. 319 SEK B1

♦ Japanese ♦ Trendy ♦

By the same team as Esperanto. The name means 'Raw Culture' – the cuisine reflects this, focusing on sushi, sashimi and maki, plus some more contemporary recipes. Friendly, informal service.

Rolfs Kök

Tegnérgatan 41 ✉ S-111 61 – Ⓜ Rådmansgatan – ✆ (08) 10 16 96 – www.rolfskok.se – Closed July, 24-26, and 31 December, 1 January, lunch Saturday-Sunday and bank holidays **B1**

Rest – *(booking essential)* Carte 425/640 SEK

♦ Modern ♦ Bistro ♦

Small, buzzy gastropub in lively commercial district, with contemporary interior design by famous Swedish artists. Open kitchen involves guests in preparation of tasty, rustic dishes, which rely on fresh ingredients and follow simple recipes. 30 wines by the glass.

Smak På Restaurangen

Oxtorgsgatan 14 ✉ S-111 57 – Ⓜ Hötorget – ✆ (08) 22 09 52 – www.restaurangentm.com – Closed 1 week Christmas, 4 weeks summer, Saturday lunch and Sunday **B2**

Rest – *(booking essential)* Menu 250/550 SEK – Carte 350/550 SEK

♦ Innovative ♦ Trendy ♦

Large, contemporary restaurant from the same owners as F12, with summer terrace and ingredient-filled, glass-topped tables. Light lunches; interesting dinners consisting of small tasting plates.

Zink Grill

Biblioteksgatan 5 ✉ S-111 46 – Ⓜ Östermalmstorg – ✆ (08) 611 42 22 – www.zinkgrill.se **C2**

Rest – Carte approx. 440 SEK

♦ French ♦ Bistro ♦

Lively bistro with vintage furnishings, charcuterie stand and terrace. Simple bistro-style dishes mix Swedish and Mediterranean influences – fish and meat are cooked on a charcoal grill.

Lisa Elmqvist

Östermalms Saluhall ✉ S-114 39 – Ⓜ Östermalmstorg – ✆ (08) 553 40410 – www.lisaelmqvist.se – Closed 6 January, 9, 22 and 25 April, 2, 6 and 24-26 June, 5 November, 24-26 December, Sunday and bank holidays

Rest – *(booking essential midweek) (lunch only)* **C1**

Carte 490/1220 SEK

♦ Seafood ♦ Minimalist ♦

Family-run for over 80 years, a lively, informal operation in an impressive 19C red-brick market hall. Open kitchen, fish shop and deli. Menus based on catch of the day; mainly Swedish recipes.

AT GAMLA STAN (OLD STOCKHOLM) *Plan II*

First H. Reisen

rest,

Skeppsbron 12 ✉ S-111 30 – Ⓜ Gamla Stan – ✆ (08) 22 32 60 – www.firsthotels.com/reisen **F1**

138 rm – †1800/2290 SEK ††2000/2490 SEK – 6 suites

Rest *Reisen Bar and Dining Room* – *(dinner only)* Carte 445/630 SEK

♦ Business ♦ Classic ♦

19C waterfront hotel with contemporary black and white décor, library lounge and rustic bar. Comfortable, functional bedrooms; some with quayside views. Leisure facilities in 17C vaulted cellar. Bright, modern dining room mixes Swedish and international influences.

Rica H. Gamla Stan without rest

Lilla Nygatan 25 ✉ S-111 28 – Ⓜ Gamla Stan – ✆ (08) 723 72 50 – www.rica.se **F1**

50 rm – †795/2495 SEK ††1295/2995 SEK – 1 suite

♦ Historic ♦ Classic ♦

17C house in pleasant Old Town setting. Cosy, classically styled bedrooms are well-maintained and well-equipped; smart, compact bathrooms. Top-floor terrace offers superb rooftop and city views.

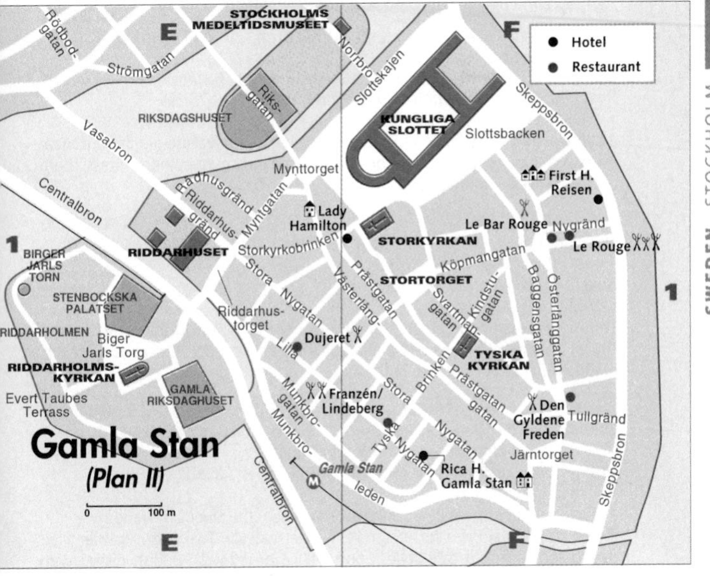

Lady Hamilton without rest

Storkyrkobrinken 5 ✉ S-111 28 – Ⓜ Gamla Stan – ✆ (08) 506 401 00 – www.ladyhamiltonhotel.se **E/F1**

34 rm – †990/3190 SEK ††1690/3690 SEK, ☕ 160 SEK

♦ Historic ♦ Cosy ♦

15C building, well-located near the Royal Palace, on the island of Gamla Stan. Charming classical breakfast room; pool and sauna in vaulted cellar. Compact bedrooms with functional furniture.

Le Rouge

Brunnsgränd 2-4 ✉ 111 30 – Ⓜ Gamla Stan – ✆ (08) 505 244 30 – www.lerouge.se – Closed Sunday **F1**

Rest – *(dinner only)* Carte 400/715 SEK

♦ French traditional ♦ Musical ♦ Exotic ♦

Richly decorated restaurant with exuberant atmosphere, extravagant burlesque theme and live piano evenings. Carefully prepared classical French dishes served by a professional team.

Frantzén/Lindeberg (Bjorn Frantzén/Daniel Lindeberg)

Lilla Nygatan 21 ✉ S-111 28 – Ⓜ Gamla Stan – ✆ (08) 20 85 80 – www.frantzen-lindeberg.com – Closed Sunday and Monday **F1**

Rest – *(set menu only) (booking essential) (dinner only)* Menu 1295/1495 SEK

Spec. Scallops cooked in their shell. Monkfish with home-grown vegetables. Oven-baked blueberry ice cream with honey cress.

♦ Innovative ♦ Romantic ♦ Fashionable ♦

Small, intimate, yet elegant restaurant. Daily menus are prepared according to the seasons, and are formed around the latest market produce and fruit/vegetables picked from the gardens that morning. Refined, creative cuisine employs some inventive techniques.

Djuret

Lilla Nygatan 3 ✉ S-111 28 – Ⓜ Gamla Stan – ✆ (08) 506 400 84 – www.djuret.se – Closed 18 December-10 January, Sunday and bank holidays **E1**

Rest – *(booking essential) (dinner only)* Carte 310/675 SEK

♦ Meat specialities ♦ Rustic ♦ Neighbourhood ♦

A carnivore's dream. The concise but appealing menu features a different meat every 2 weeks, be it lamb, beef or elk. Sit at the bar counter, in the 'Meat' room or trophy-filled 'Hunting' room.

Le Bar Rouge

Österlänggatan 17 ✉ S-111 30 – Ⓜ Gamla Stan – ✆ (08) 505 244 30 – www.lerouge.se/lebar **F1**

Rest – Carte approx. 388 SEK

♦ French ♦ Cosy ♦

The more casual counterpart to Le Rouge; boasting velvet fabrics, large armchairs, baroque furniture and a charming summer terrace. Dishes mix French, Mediterranean and Swedish influences.

Den Gyldene Freden

Österlånggatan 51 ✉ S-103 17 – Ⓜ Gamla Stan – ✆ (08) 24 97 60 – www.gyldenefreden.se – Closed Sunday **F1**

Rest – *(booking essential)* Menu 345/585 SEK – Carte 395/580 SEK

♦ Traditional ♦ Rustic ♦ Inn ♦

Attractive 1722 inn, set in a historical area, where the Swedish Academy – who award the Nobel Prize for literature – meet weekly. Two lively, candle-filled dining rooms in old café style. Good choice of refined Swedish dishes with some modern influences.

AT DJURGÅRDEN *Plan I*

Scandic H. Hasselbacken

Hazeliusbacken 20 ✉ S-100 55 – ✆ (08) 517 343 00 – www.scandichotels.com/hasselbacken

111 rm – †1290/3090 SEK ††1390/3190 SEK – 1 suite **D2**

Rest *Restaurang Hasselbacken* – *(closed Sunday dinner)* Menu 235/455 SEK – Carte dinner 235/530 SEK

♦ Business ♦ Functional ♦

Located just outside the city centre in Djurgården Park, close to the Vasa Museum. A popular place to hold conferences and events. Functional bedrooms have desks and partial park views. Large restaurant boasts ornate mirrored ceiling and pleasant summer terrace.

Ulla Winbladh

Rosendalsvägen 8 ✉ S-115 21 – ✆ (08) 534 897 01 – www.ullawinbladh.se **D2**

Rest – *(booking essential)* Carte 217/635 SEK

♦ Traditional Swedish ♦ Inn ♦

Set in a charming park location and popular with the locals; originally built as a steam bakery for the 1897 Stockholm World Fair. Several knick-knack filled rooms in old 'inn' style; pleasant summer terrace. Traditional Swedish cuisine includes herring buffets.

Carl Michael

Allmänna Gränd 6 ✉ S-115 21 – ✆ (08) 667 45 96 – www.carlmichael.se – Closed first 2 weeks January, 1 week Christmas and Monday in winter

Rest – Menu 555 SEK (dinner) – Carte 440/620 SEK **D2**

♦ Swedish ♦ Cosy ♦

Charming, rustic 18C house next to the amusement park. Choice of pleasant summer terrace or warm, bistro-style dining room with cosy farmhouse feel. Traditional Swedish cooking to the fore.

AT SÖDERMALM

Plan I

Clarion H. Stockholm

Ring Vägen 98 ✉ *S-104 60* – Ⓜ *Skanstull* – ✆ *(08) 462 1000*
– www.clarionstockholm.com
522 rm – 970/2470 SEK 1270/2670 SEK – 10 suites
Rest *Gretas Kok* – *(closed Sunday) (dinner only)* Carte 330/565 SEK
♦ Business ♦ Modern ♦

Purpose-built hotel with well-equipped conference facilities and modern, functional style. Spacious lobby and breakfast room; live music at weekends. Bedrooms vary from singles to sizeable suites. Named after Greta Garbo, the restaurant serves international cuisine.

The Rival

Mariatorget 3 ✉ *S-118 91* – Ⓜ *Mariatorget* – ✆ *(08) 545 789 00*
– www.rival.se **C3**
97 rm – 1195/2295 SEK 2295/3195 SEK, 175 SEK – 2 suites
Rest *The Bistro* – *(dinner only and Sunday Brunch)* Carte 286/520 SEK
♦ Business ♦ Stylish ♦

Owned by ABBA's Benny Andersson, a contemporary boutique hotel in a charming neighbourhood, with warm atmosphere, colourful, movie-themed bedrooms and designs by local artists. 700-seater 1937 art deco theatre hosts events and shows. Nicely furnished lounge, bar and restaurant offer a wide range of international dishes.

Sjögräs

Timmermansgatan 24 ✉ *S-118 55* – Ⓜ *Mariatorget* – ✆ *(08) 84 12 00*
– www.sjogras.com – Closed 18-31 July, 23 December-4 January and Sunday
Rest – *(booking essential) (dinner only)* Carte 436/659 SEK **B3**
♦ French ♦ Bistro ♦ Friendly ♦

Simple yet lively restaurant in pleasant residential neighbourhood by Mariatorget Park. Contemporary décor and furniture, open kitchen and charming service. French-inspired menus display generous, flavoursome dishes with some local influences. Over 300 choices of rum.

AT ARLANDA AIRPORT

Radisson Blu Sky City

at Terminals 4-5, 2nd floor above street level (Stockholm-Arlanda, Sky City)
✉ *S-190 45* – ✆ *(08) 50 67 4000*
– www.skycity.arlanda.stockholm.radissonblu.com
229 rm – 1350/1995 SEK 1350/1995 SEK, 145 SEK – 1 suite
Rest *Stockholm Fisk* – ✆ *(08) 506 740 25* – Carte 360/500 SEK
♦ Business ♦ Modern ♦

Clean, comfortable corporate hotel set between terminals 4 and 5, and offering good facilities. Fully soundproofed bedrooms come in four contemporary styles - Ocean, Urban, Business and Chilli. Open-plan bistro overlooks the airport and offers a seafood menu.

ENVIRONS OF STOCKHOLM

AT NORRTULL North : 2 km by Sveavägen (at beginning of E4)

Stallmästaregården

✉ *SE-113 47* – Ⓜ *Karlberg* – ✆ *(08) 610 13 00*
– www.stallmastaregarden.se – Closed Christmas
46 rm – 1295/2195 SEK 1295/2195 SEK – 3 suites
Rest – Menu 535 SEK (dinner) – Carte 550/585 SEK
♦ Inn ♦ Cosy ♦

17C inn set around a central courtyard, boasting park and water views. Swedish décor in guest areas; period Oriental-themed bedrooms with modern comforts. Function rooms in separate building. Large dining room with summer terrace offers traditional Swedish cuisine.

AT LADUGÅRDSGÄRDET East : 3 km by Strandvägen

Villa Källhagen

Djurgårdsbrunnsvägen 10 ✉ S-115 27 – ✆ (08) 665 03 00 – www.kallhagen.se

33 rm – 🛉2395 SEK 🛉🛉2395 SEK – 3 suites

Rest – *(closed Sunday lunch)* Menu 365 SEK (lunch)/698 SEK – Carte 458/790 SEK

♦ Inn ♦ Business ♦ Modern ♦

Well-run hotel in idyllic waterside location, surrounded by a park and walking trail. Comfy guest areas. Quiet bedrooms in 4 contemporary colour schemes inspired by the seasons. Great views from the restaurant and terrace; Swedish menu has a Mediterranean edge.

AT FJÄDERHOLMARNA ISLAND East: 25 minutes by boat from Sodlermalm, or 5 minutes from Nacka Strand

XX

Fjäderholmarnas Krog

Stora Fjäderholmen ✉ S-100 05 – ✆ (08) 718 33 55 – www.fjaderholmarnaskrog.se – Closed January-April, 12 September-23 November and 22-31 December

Rest – *(booking essential)* Carte 440/805 SEK

♦ Seafood ♦ Friendly ♦

Cosy, candlelit restaurant with large terrace; delightfully set on the harbourside of this lovely island. Menus offer traditional Swedish cuisine and include plenty of fish and seafood dishes. Delivered by boat, fresh produce arrives at the door each day.

AT ENSKEDEDALEN Southeast : 9 kms by Nynasvagen

X

Enskede Krog

Gamla Tyresovagen 326 ✉ S-121 33 – Ⓜ Sandsborg – ✆ (08) 394300 – www.enskedekrog.se – Closed 3 weeks July, 24 December-31 January and Monday dinner

Rest – *(booking advisable) (buffet lunch)* Carte 400/475 SEK

♦ Swedish ♦ Neighbourhood ♦ Cosy ♦

Popular neighbourhood restaurant with lovely garden. Buffet lunches offer four hot dishes alongside fresh salad. Traditional Swedish dinner menu relies on locally foraged, seasonal ingredients.

AT NACKA STRAND Southeast : 10 km by Stadsgården or 20 mins by boat from Nybrokajen

Hotel J without rest

Ellensviksvägen 1 ✉ S-131 28 – ✆ (08) 601 30 00 – www.hotelj.com – Closed 23-31 December

40 rm – 🛉1845/2145 SEK 🛉🛉2245/2545 SEK – 5 suites

♦ Historic ♦ Design ♦

20C red-brick hotel with more modern wing; located in a quiet park overlooking the sea. Charming guest areas display characterful maritime knick knacks. Bedrooms and duplex suites boast quirky, yacht-themed décor – many have balconies and/or sea views.

X

Restaurant J

Augustendalsvägen 52 ✉ S-131 28 – ✆ (08) 601 30 25 – www.restaurantj.com – Closed 23-31 December

Rest – Menu 475 SEK (dinner) – Carte 380/560 SEK

♦ Traditional ♦ Brasserie ♦

Located 100m from Hotel J, facing the marina. Large room with maritime décor, open kitchen and bar counter. Oversized windows and terrace provide great views. Simple Swedish and global dishes.

AT LILLA ESSINGEN West : 5.5 km by Norr Mälarstrand

XX ✿ **Lux Stockholm** (Henrik Norström)

Primusgatan 116 ✉ S-112 67 – ✆ (08) 619 01 90 – www.luxstockholm.com – Closed 22 December-7 January, 4 weeks July-August, Sunday and Monday

Rest – *(booking essential)* Menu 895/1175 SEK – Carte 800/850 SEK

Spec. Pepper-fried duck breast with creamy baked egg and truffle. Pike-perch with caviar, grilled vendace and cabbage. Apple with caramel, salted lavender and blackcurrants.

♦ Innovative ♦ Design ♦ Cosy ♦

Old waterside Electrolux factory building. Modern dining room and delightful terrace. Contemporary cooking uses local, seasonal produce. Bi-monthly menus offer light lunches, 4 or 9 course set dinners and lots of specials. Dishes finished off in the dining room. (Suffered a major fire as we went to print.)

AT BOCKHOLMEN ISLAND Northwest : 7 km by Sveavägen and E18

X **Bockholmen**

Bockholmsvägen ✉ S-170 78 Solna – Ⓜ Bergshamra – ✆ (08) 624 22 00 – www.bockholmen.com – Closed 25-27 June, 22 December-March and Monday October-April

Rest – *(booking essential) (dinner only and lunch in summer)* Menu 349 SEK bi/535 SEK – Carte 415/620 SEK

♦ Scandinavian ♦ Friendly ♦ Rustic ♦

Endearing eatery in idyllic setting, boasting lovely terrace and outside bar. Traditional cooking displays modern Mediterranean elements and well-sourced produce. Check opening hours carefully.

AT EDSVICKEN Northwest : 8 km by Sveavägen and E 18 towards Norrtälje

XX **Ulriksdals Wärdshus**

(take first junction for Ulriksdals Slott) ✉ 170 79 Solna – Ⓜ Bergshamra – ✆ (08) 85 08 15 – www.ulriksdalswardshus.se – Closed 8-29 July, Tuesday January-April and Monday

Rest – *(booking essential)* Menu 550 SEK – Carte 545/735 SEK

♦ Traditional ♦ Inn ♦

Delightful 19C inn with winter garden décor, charming private rooms, park/water views and lovely drinks terrace. Tasty, well-presented, modern Swedish dishes; traditional weekend smörgåsbord.

WE 58
FLAX

GOTHENBURG

GÖTEBORG

Population: 506 083 (conurbation 915 983) - Altitude: sea level

;jell Holmner/Göteborg & Co/www.imagebank.sweden.se

It's not everywhere you find a cook's face on a postage stamp, but Gothenburg's Leif Mannerström has achieved this curious honour, as good an indication as any that in this attractive west coast city, cuisine is a major priority, and seafood its *cause célèbre*. Gothenburg is universally considered to be Sweden's friendliest town, a throwback to its days as a leading trading centre and seaport, a cosmopolitan place where you're as likely to strike up a conversation with a local as come face-to-face with a restaurant – and there are over 650 of those.

This is a compact, pretty city whose roots go back four hundred years. It has trams, broad avenues and canals – the Dutch designed it all. Its centre is boisterous but never feels tourist heavy and overcrowded; Gothenburgers take life at a more leisurely pace than their Stockholm cousins over on the east coast. The mighty shipyards that once dominated the shoreline are now quiet. Go to the centre, though, and you find the good-time ambience of Avenyn, a vivacious thoroughfare full of places to eat and drink. But for those still itching for a feel of the heavy industry that once defined the place, there's a Volvo museum sparkling with chrome and shiny steel. Truly, a city for all comers.

LIVING THE CITY

Unless you really do fancy the visit to the Volvo museum (which is north of the Göta river) there's not much point in crossing from the southern side of Gothenburg. The Old Town is the historic heart: its tight grid of streets has grand façades and a fascinating waterfront. Southeast of here is the commercial and retail hub of **Avenyn**, where the pretty people like to be seen. Just west is the **Vasastan** quarter, full of fine National Romantic buildings. Further west again is **Haga**, an old working-class district which – you've guessed it – has been gentrified, its cobbled streets sprawling with cafes and boutiques. Adjacent to Haga is the district of **Linné**, a racy and vibrant area that has catapulted itself into the same league as Avenyn – its elegantly tall nineteenth-century Dutch-inspired buildings perhaps giving it the edge.

PRACTICAL INFORMATION

ARRIVAL-DEPARTURE

Landvetter Airport is 25km east of the city although City Airport in the northwest is increasingly popular. A taxi from either airport will cost approximately SEK350, although there are also bus connections, including FlyBussarna, which costs SEK 75. There are regular ferry services from Kiel.

TRANSPORT

The Gothenburg Card gives you unlimited bus, tram and boat travel within the city. It will also guarantee you a sightseeing tour, admission to the Liseberg amusement park, entry to most museums, and discounts in certain shops. They are valid for either one or two days, and are available from Tourist Information offices, the amusement park, newspaper kiosks, hotels and campsites.

Doing a fair amount of bus and tram travel? Then get a 24 or 72 hour credit card style pass for unlimited travel on trams, buses and boats. Single tickets are also available.

Punts – flat Paddan boats - are a pleasant way to explore this maritime city in summer, gliding past stately canalside buildings. They pass under 20 bridges; you're advised to duck on numerous occasions, as a lot of them were built for the vertically challenged.

EXPLORING GOTHENBURG

If you've been to San Francisco and liked what you saw, then you'll probably be partial to Gothenburg. It's often compared to the hip US city: it occupies a breezy west coast location, has plenty of bridges, hills, water and trams, and, as with Fisherman's Wharf, it boasts an abundance of seafood restaurants. Like San Francisco, there's a welcoming spirit about the place, and a true cosmopolitan air. Canals, silently ringing the city, bring the emphasis back to Europe, as does the grand Neoclassical architecture, a product of Gothenburg's spirited history of

trading, as merchants from around the continent stayed on and built grand houses in which to live.

→ CRANE SUPREME

As this is a maritime town, down along the quayside is as good a place to get your bearings as any. There is much character here, as the grandly decaying shipyards sadly eye your progress along the waterfront. Here, at Lilla Bommen harbour, the sombre glory of the rusting, arching cranes are juxtaposed against temples of modernism, such as the iconic **Utkiken Tower** from the late 1980s, better known as 'The Lipstick Tower' because of its lusty scarlet tip, offering a great viewing platform over Gothenburg. And just along the blustery waterfront, competing with it in the iconic stakes, is another relatively recent arrival, 1994's strikingly modern **Opera House,** designed with its location uppermost, to resemble a fine ship. It puts on not just opera, but ballet and musicals, too. The salty location meets its match two minutes' stroll further along at the **Maritiman**, a truly floating maritime museum which can rightly label itself the 'largest ship museum in the world'. It's a retirement home for twenty boats – a cross-section of Sweden's naval heritage. These include a lightship, a fire-fighting vessel, a vast destroyer and a submarine that should be avoided by claustrophobia sufferers at all costs.

→ MAKING HIS POINT

It won't take you long to turn inland and reach the heart of the Old Town. You'll know when you're there, because you'll see a big copper statue of Gustav II Adolf pointing down to the spot where he allegedly declared he would build his city. This is **Gustav Adolf's Torg**, the stately main square, and close by are two buildings worth visiting. The **Kronhuset** was built by the Dutch over 350 years ago and is the city's oldest secular building, while the **Stadsmuseum** is a cultural powerhouse, boasting exhibits of Gothenburg's rich history all the way back to the days of the Vikings and including a very impressive long-boat. All around this area are 17C streets, canals and buildings; and the Stadsmuseum itself is housed inside the former auction house of the Swedish East India Company, richly endowed with stone pillars, frescoes and stained glass.

Both these buildings are dwarfed by a monstrous interloper, one which owes its origins to twenty first century consumerism. The gigantic **Nordstan** is Sweden's biggest shopping centre and it has some eye-catching modern Nordic design amongst its sparkly boutiques and chain stores. It should satisfy any shopping itch you were waiting to scratch, but if not then head due south to the main thoroughfare of Kungsportsavenyn, more elegantly known as **Avenyn**, which, to be more accurate, is actually a place to be seen rather than to shop. It's adorned with grand nineteenth century houses, and their ground floors have been transformed into swish cafés, bars or restaurants, for this is the avenue with the highest density of places to eat in Sweden. In the summer, tables spill out, a chrome carnival shimmering along Avenyn's spacious, cobbled length, the young and the wish-they-were-still-young adding their own lustre. One of the city's abiding delights is that the centre, though lively, never feels over-crowded or in a rush: the sense of harmony and space is never strained.

→ NORTHERN LIGHT

At the southern end of Avenyn stands one of the city's best attractions, the **Art Museum**, housed in a massive building, which, rather impressively, claims the finest collection of Nordic art in Scandinavia. Head for the sixth floor where the Furstenberg Galleries are full of work by revered early 20C century artists which brings to life the landscapes, shades and nuances of the Nordic countries. On other floors there are also works by the French Impressionists, Munch, Van Gogh and Gauguin. Half-way down Avenyn, just over in the adjoining area of Vasastan, can be found the Röhsska Museum of Design and Applied Art, which takes you on an excellent trip through the centuries and continents, looking at aesthetic glories from ancient Asian ceramics to 21C mod cons.

Gothenburg boasts another 'biggest in Scandinavia' if you meander southeast from Avenyn. It's **Liseberg** - a magical name to those in the know, conjuring up roller coaster rides, shocking pink paintwork, fairy lights and sweet-scented waffles. Opened in 1923, it's Scandinavia's biggest amusement park, bigger even than Copenhagen's Tivoli, and reaches the parts of adults other amusement parks fail to reach, as it boasts trees, fountains and flowers to give it the authentic feel of a 'proper' park. There's another reason to go to Liseberg now: it's right next door to a museum, opened only in 2004, that's won a host of plaudits including Sweden's most prestigious architecture award, plus worldwide praise for its refreshing exhibitions. This is the **Museum of World Culture**, which apart from its startling four-storey glass atrium, also offers a clear-sighted angle on the diverse variety of world cultures through a series of changing exhibitions. The café/restaurant here is pretty good, too.

→ HAGA SAGA

Gothenburg's most remarkably transformed quarter is **Haga**, its south-western district. Not so long ago it was so run-down that it was on the verge of demolition, but the nineteenth-century artisan houses were replenished in the 1980s and now some of the coolest of the city's cool hang out here. During the daytime it can be a delightful place to visit with its village-like ambience – sip a coffee at an outside table on a cobbled street, or wander round the stylish boutiques. Carry on a bit further west and you're in **Linné**, the smart area named after famed Swedish scientist Carl von Linné (whose 300th birthday was celebrated in style in the country in 2007). Linné has a rash of trendy places to eat and drink, and is now considered a second Avenyn, but without the tourist gloss. There are nineteenth century buildings in the Dutch style and atmospheric antique shops all melding together to create a quarter very much with its own style and patina.

→ STOCK COMMENT

If you hear a Gothenburger making a dismissive remark about an 08-er, it's not some kind of Swedish rhyming slang. 08 is the telephone code for Stockholm, and saying something not so nice about Stockholm is par for the course in Gothenburg.

GOTHENBURG IN...

→ ONE DAY

The old town, the harbour, a meal in Haga, a stroll around Linné

→ TWO DAYS

Liseberg, The Museum of World Culture, Art Museum

→ THREE DAYS

A trip on a Paddan boat, a night at the Opera House (or a boat trip around the archipelago)

➜ STATUESQUE

At the southern end of Avenyn, in Götaplatsen square, stands the unmissable bronze statue of the nude Poseidon. In 1931, when he first appeared, the outlandish size of his male member caused outrage amongst the citizenry, so it was chopped painfully short, leaving modern onlookers to wonder at the somewhat out of proportion 7m high statue staring at them.

CALENDAR HIGHLIGHTS

Gothenburg is a serious party city, and the stress is on the serious side of things in April and May when the International Science Festival hits town. This is closely followed by the party element when, later in the month, the Gothenburg Jazz Festival explodes into life. A sporting and musical dimension is much to the fore in June and July: June's Oops Cup is a well-established yachting event, with spectators close to the action as the trimarans race near to shore; blues fans should head to Slottsparken zoo the same month for the Gothenburg Blues Party. Then in July, the Gothia Cup at the Ullevi Stadium is a massively important youth cup for footballers from around the world, established for over thirty years with representations from over a hundred countries, and, yes, boasting more wins for Swedish teams than any other. August's Gothenburg Cultural Party is the biggest city festival in Sweden, taking up every inch the town has to offer, with more than six hundred concerts and cultural events. Culture vultures can gorge themselves on the Art Biennial from September to November – a contemporary art smorgasbord with seminars and workshops at various city locations. As the nights get darker in October, Kulturnatta brings much light relief with events ranging from poetry readings to theatrical productions.

EATING OUT

No wonder Gothenburg's oldest food market is called Feskekörka or 'Fish Church'. Locals will always give thanks for the humble herring and the Fish Church does indeed look like a place of worship, but its pews are stalls of oysters, prawns and salmon, and where you might expect to find an organ loft, you'll find a restaurant instead. There are more than 650 of them in the city, a bewildering total for a population of around half a million. Food – and in particular the piscine variety - is a big reason for visiting Gothenburg. Its restaurants have earned a plethora of Michelin stars which are dotted all over the compact city. As is often the case in Scandinavia, best practice is to eat your main meal at lunchtime, when fixed price specials are such good value. Restaurants with a European base are worth trying out: there are a lot of them here and often they use a Swedish fishy staple as a starting point. If you're in town in the summer, don't miss out on the delicious local fruits for dessert: soft and juicy, they're a must. Gothenburgers also love the traditional food pairing 'SOS', where herring and cheese are washed down with schnapps. You're not expected to tip in Gothenburg's eateries, though it is customary to round the bill up to the nearest 10-20kr.

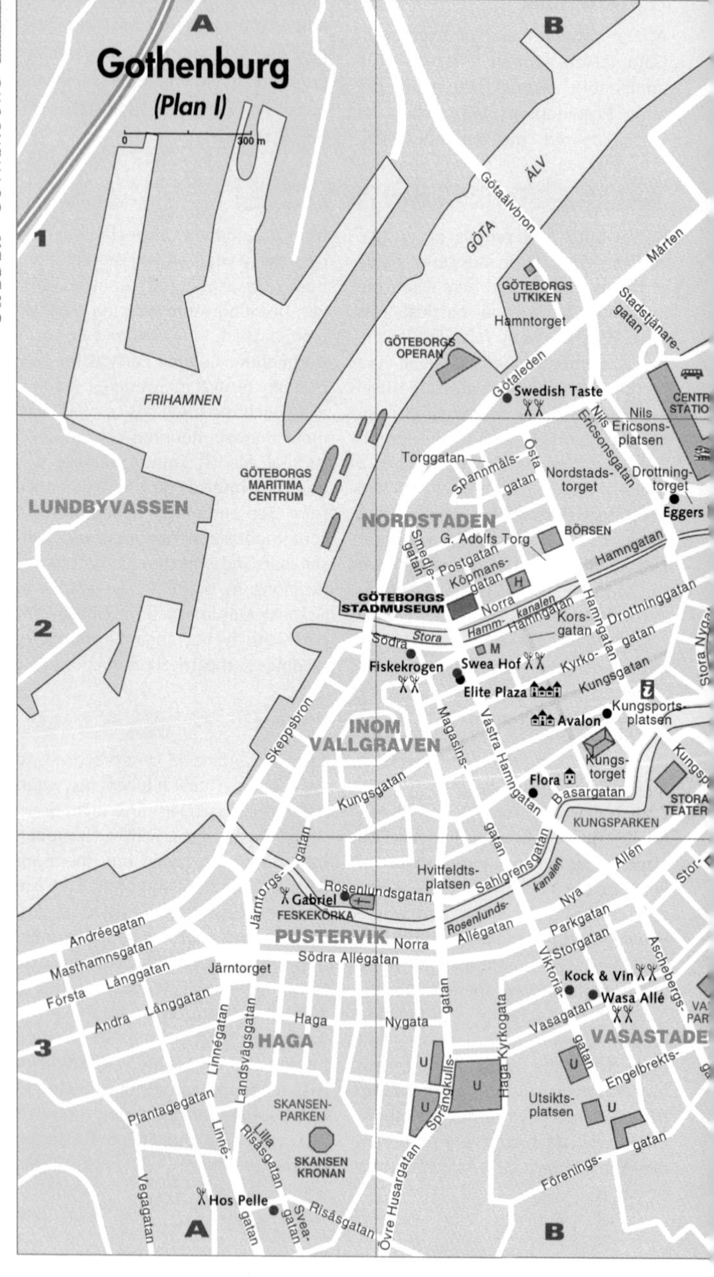

Gothenburg
(Plan I)
0
300 m
A
B
1
2
3
GÖTA ÄLV
Götaälvbron
Mårten
Stadstjänare-gatan
GÖTEBORGS UTKIKEN
Hamntorget
GÖTEBORGS OPERAN
Götaleden
Swedish Taste
CENTR STATIO
FRIHAMNEN
Nils Ericsons-platsen
Nils Ericsonsgatan
Torggatan
Spannmåls-gatan
Östa
Nordstads-torget
Drottning-torget
Eggers
GÖTEBORGS MARITIMA CENTRUM
LUNDBYVASSEN
NORDSTADEN
BÖRSEN
Smedie-gatan
G. Adolfs Torg
Postgatan
Köpmans-gatan
Hamngatan
GÖTEBORGS STADMUSEUM
Norra Hamngatan
Hamm-kanalen
Stora
Södra
Korsgatan
Hamngatan
Drottninggatan
Fiskekrogen
Swea Hof
M
Kyrkogatan
Elite Plaza
Kungsgatan
Stora Nygatan
Kungsports-platsen
Avalon
Skeppsbron
INOM VALLGRAVEN
Magasins-gatan
Västra Hamngatan
Kungs-torget
Flora
Basargatan
Kungsgatan
STORA TEATER
KUNGSPARKEN
Hvitfeldts-platsen
Sahlgrensgatan
kanalen
Allén
Stor-
Järntorgs-gatan
Rosenlundsgatan
Gabriel
FESKEKÖRKA
Nya
Rosenlunds-kanalen
Allégatan
Parkgatan
Andréegatan
PUSTERVIK
Norra
Storgatan
Masthamnsgatan
Södra Allégatan
Järntorget
Viktoria-gatan
Aschebergs-
Kock & Vin
Första Långgatan
Wasa Allé
Andra Långgatan
Haga
Nygata
Vasagatan
3
HAGA
Linnégatan
Landsvägsgatan
VASASTADE
U
Haga Kyrkogata
Engelbrekts-
Plantagegatan
Sprängkulls-
Utsikts-platsen
SKANSEN-PARKEN
Linné-gatan
Lilla Risåsgatan
SKANSEN KRONAN
Övre Husargatan
Förenings-gatan
Vegagatan
Hos Pelle
Svea-gatan
Risåsgatan
A
B

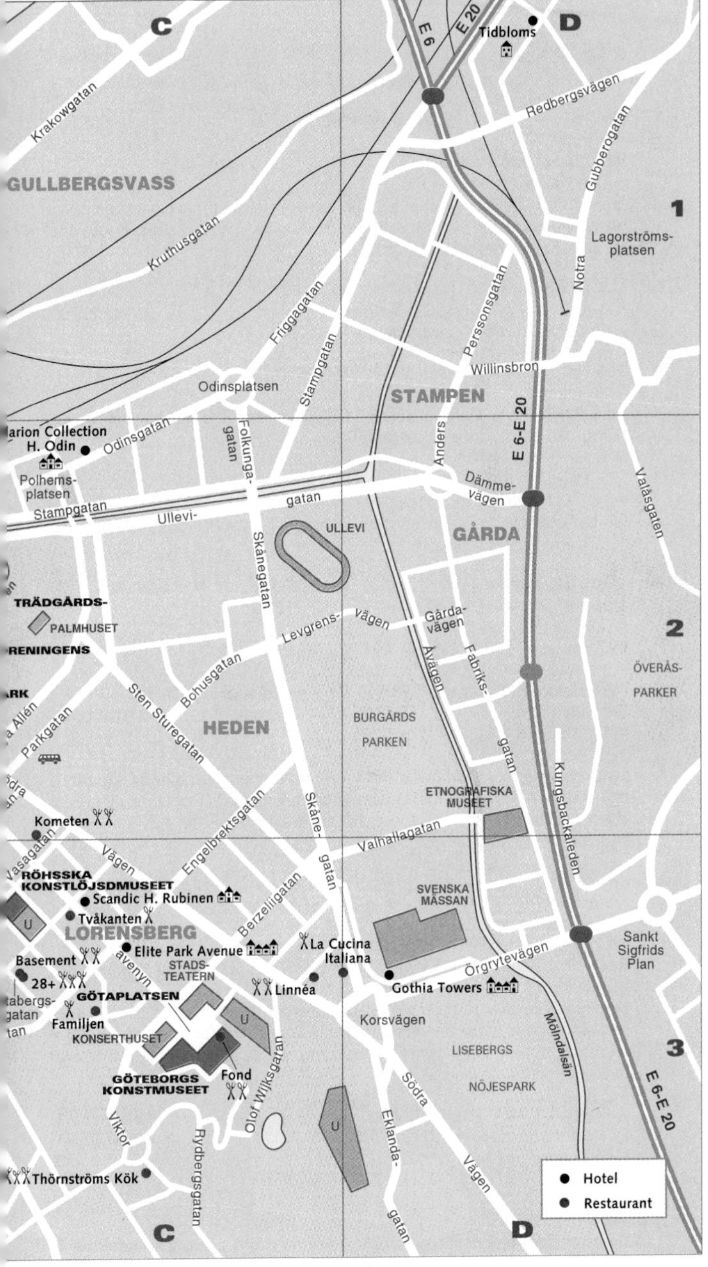
C
D
E 6
E 20
Tidbloms
Redbergsvägen
Krakowgatan
GULLBERGSVASS
Gubberogatan
Kruthusgatan
Lagorströms-
platsen
Notra
Friggagatan
Stampgatan
Perssonsgatan
Willinsbron
Odinsplatsen
STAMPEN
E 6-E 20
Marion Collection
H. Odin
Odinsgatan
Folkunga-
gatan
Anders
Polhems-
platsen
Dämme-
vägen
Valåsgaten
Stampgatan
Ullevi-
gatan
ULLEVI
GÅRDA
Skånegatan
TRÄDGÅRDS-
PALMHUSET
FÖRENINGENS
PARK
Levgrens-
vägen
Gårda-
vägen
Bohusgatan
Ävägen
Fabriks-
gatan
ÖVERÅS-
PARKER
Allén
Parkgatan
Sten Sturegatan
HEDEN
BURGÅRDS
PARKEN
Kungsbackaleden
Södra
Kometen
Engelbrektsgatan
Skåne-
gatan
ETNOGRAFISKA
MUSEET
Vasagatan
Vägen
Valhallagatan
RÖHSSKA
KONSTLÖJSDMUSEET
Scandic H. Rubinen
Berzeliigatan
SVENSKA
MÄSSAN
Tvåkanten
LORENSBERG
Elite Park Avenue
La Cucina
Italiana
Sankt
Sigfrids
Plan
Basement
avenyn
STADS-
TEATERN
Örgrytevägen
28+
Linnéa
Gothia Towers
GÖTAPLATSEN
Familjen
KONSERTHUSET
Korsvägen
Mölndalsån
LISEBERGS
NÖJESPARK
3
GÖTEBORGS
KONSTMUSEET
Fond
Olof Wijksgatan
Södra
Viktor
Eklanda-
gatan
Vägen
Rydbergsgatan
Thörnströms Kök
Hotel
Restaurant
1
2

CENTRE

Plan I

Elite Plaza

Västra Hamngatan 3 ✉ S-402 22 – ✆ (031) 720 40 40 – www.elite.se – Closed 23-26 December **B2**

136 rm – †1600/1800 SEK ††1900/2100 SEK – 6 suites

Rest *Swea Hof* – see below

♦ Luxury ♦ Modern ♦

Grand 19C building near the harbour, with smart, classical architectural style; many original features still remain. 5th floor bedrooms are most spacious and modern. Basement fitness and bar.

Elite Park Avenue

Kungsportsavenyn 36-38 ✉ S-400 15 – ✆ (031) 727 1000 – www.elite.se – Closed 24-26 December **C3**

306 rm – †1050/2350 SEK ††1450/2550 SEK – 11 suites

Rest *Park Aveny Cafe* – *(closed 24-27 December and Sunday dinner)* Menu 485 SEK (dinner) – Carte 410/595 SEK

♦ Business ♦ Modern ♦

1950s building with stylish, contemporary inner and smart spa. Spacious, well-equipped bedrooms with large bathrooms; rooftop suites have balconies. English bar and small Italian eatery-cum-nightclub. Formal bistro offers a blend of French and Swedish cooking.

Gothia Towers

Mässans Gata 24 ✉ S-402 26 – ✆ (031) 750 88 00 – www.gothiatowers.se **D3**

697 rm – †995/2195 SEK ††1195/2395 SEK – 8 suites

Rest *Heaven 23* – Menu 255/515 SEK – Carte approx. 530 SEK

Rest *Incontro* – *✆ (031) 750 88 05 (closed Sunday dinner) (buffet lunch)* Menu 495 SEK – Carte 445/565 SEK

♦ Business ♦ Modern ♦

Spacious, twin-towered hotel – the largest in Northern Scandinavia – run by a trust. Fresh, modern bedrooms with good business facilities. Light, airy guest areas. Spectacular views and local fish in Heaven 23. Piano bar, terrace and regional Italian fare in Incontro.

Avalon

Kungstorget 9 ✉ S-411 17 – ✆ (031) 751 02 00 – www.avalonhotel.se **B2**

98 rm – †1190/2790 SEK ††1690/2990 SEK – 3 suites

Rest – *(closed Sunday in winter)* Menu 325/495 SEK – Carte 555/755 SEK

♦ Business ♦ Modern ♦

Boutique hotel in a great central location near the shops, harbour and theatres. Modern, slightly funky bedrooms with the latest mod cons and stylish bathrooms; penthouse suites have small balcony terraces. All-day bistro-style restaurant opens onto the piazza.

Clarion Collection H. Odin without rest

Odinsgatan 6 ✉ S-411 03 – ✆ (031) 745 22 00 – www.hotelodin.se **C2**

171 rm – †780/2480 SEK ††1080/2680 SEK – 9 suites

♦ Business ♦ Modern ♦

Unassuming exterior conceals a light, airy atrium and smart, spacious, Scandic style apartments with small kitchens and seating areas. Breakfast and all-day snacks are included in the rate.

Scandic Rubinen

Kungsportsavenyn 24 ✉ S-400 14 – ☎ (031) 751 54 00
– www.scandichotels.com/rubinen **C3**
191 rm ☕ – 🚹850/2430 SEK 🚹🚹1150/2530 SEK
– 3 suites
Rest – *(Closed Sunday lunch)* Carte 219/435 SEK
♦ Business ♦ Modern ♦

Set on the main street, in the heart of town; the red interior paying homage to a late local resident who collected Ruby-coloured objects. Fresh, modern Scandic-style bedrooms. Rooftop bar affords great views. Lively Latino restaurant opens onto the pavement.

Eggers

Drottningtorget ✉ S-404 24
– ☎ (031) 333 44 40 – www.hoteleggers.se
– Closed 23-26 December **B2**
69 rm ☕ – 🚹995/1995 SEK 🚹🚹1450/2625 SEK
Rest – *(closed July, 22 December-9 January and bank holidays)*
Menu 395/515 SEK – Carte 405/530 SEK
♦ Traditional ♦ Classic ♦

1859 railway hotel that opened with electricity and telephones in every room. Warm, welcoming inner features original wrought iron and stained glass, period furnishings and some four-posters. Ornate restaurant offers Swedish classics and international favourites.

Novotel Göteborg

Klippan 1 (Southwest : 3.5 km by Andréeg taking Kiel-Klippan Ö exit, or boat from Rosenlund) ✉ SE-414 51 – ☎ (031) 720 22 00
– www.novotel.se
151 rm ☕ – 🚹1460/1720 SEK 🚹🚹1560/1820 SEK
– 1 suite
Rest *Carnegie Kaj* – Carte 269/515 SEK
♦ Chain hotel ♦ Business ♦ Functional ♦

Converted waterfront brewery, displaying a collection of vintage Porter beer. Clean, bright interior with attractive atrium affording views of the Göta Älv river. Spacious, Scandic-style bedrooms. Restaurant mixes Swedish classics and international favourites.

Flora without rest

Grönsakstorget 2 ✉ 411 17
– ☎ (031) 13 86 16 – www.hotelflora.se
– Closed 23 December-2 January **B2**
68 rm ☕ – 🚹1295/1695 SEK 🚹🚹1695/2045 SEK
♦ Family ♦ Functional ♦

Pleasantly located by the canal and the local market, and within easy walking distance of town. Funky all-day bar-cum-breakfast room. Clean, uncluttered bedrooms; ask for one at the front.

Tidbloms

Olskroksgatan 23 ✉ S-416 66 – ☎ (031) 707 50 00
– www.tidbloms.com **D1**
42 rm ☕ – 🚹825/1550 SEK 🚹🚹1025/1695 SEK
Rest – *(dinner only)* Menu 195/365 SEK
– Carte 335/446 SEK
♦ Business ♦ Traditional ♦ Functional ♦

Turreted red-brick hotel, originally built to accommodate Scottish engineers working in the city. Clean, tidy bedrooms with subtle contemporary touches and walk-in showers. Peaceful location. Pub-style restaurant with Scottish theme and good selection of whiskies.

XXX ✿

Thörnströms Kök (Hakan Thörnström)

Teknologgatan 3 ✉ S-41132 – ✆ (031) 16 20 66 – www.thornstromskok.com – Closed 2 July-16 August, 25 December-1 January, Sunday, Monday and bank holidays **C3**

Rest – *(booking essential) (dinner only)* Menu 560 SEK – Carte 515/650 SEK

Spec. Salmon and scallops with cucumber and horseradish. Terrine of veal tail with dill glazed tongue and chanterelles. Rosehips with rosemary and browned butter ice cream.

♦ Seasonal cuisine ♦ Neighbourhood ♦

Set in a quiet residential area, an elegant restaurant with stunning wine cave. Good choice of menus, including 3 tasting options. Classically based cooking follows the Scandic penchant for freshness, simplicity and fullness of flavour. Smart, knowledgeable team.

XXX ✿

28+

Götabergsgatan 28 ✉ S-411 34 – ✆ (031) 20 21 61 – www.28plus.se – Closed 3 July-25 August, 23-27 December, 6-9 January, 24-26 April and Sunday

Rest – *(dinner only)* Menu 610/635 SEK – Carte 605/635 SEK **C3**

Spec. Crayfish tails with fennel mayonnaise. Halibut with chanterelles, cauliflower and thyme jus. Blackberries with white chocolate and yoghurt sorbet.

♦ Modern ♦

Long-standing Gothenburg institution that celebrated 25 years in 2010. Very formally run, with an outstanding wine list; let the sommelier decide. Classical cooking blends French/Swedish influences and relies on quality ingredients. Cheese is taken seriously.

XX ✿

Kock & Vin

Viktoriagatan 12 ✉ S-411 25 – ✆ (031) 701 79 79 – www.kockvin.se – Closed 3-31 July, 23 December-3 January and Sunday **B3**

Rest – *(dinner only)* Menu 595/795 SEK – Carte 535/685 SEK

Spec. Lobster with salsify, sago and veal tongue. Char with rye bread, mushrooms and lingonberries. Sweetened potato cream with frozen pearls of fennel.

♦ Innovative ♦ Friendly ♦

Contemporary candlelit restaurant with ornate 19C ceiling. Basement bar serves light plates and a fine selection of cheeses; dining room focuses on modern, seasonal, Swedish-based dishes. Preparation is precise and presentation, pleasing. Service is clued-up.

XX ✿

Basement (Ulf Wagner)

Götabergsgatan 28 ✉ S-411 – ✆ (031) 28 27 29 – www.restbasement.com – Closed July, 23 December-6 January, Sunday and Monday **C3**

Rest – *(dinner only)* Menu 520/795 SEK

Spec. Lobster salad with sultana raisins and crispy bacon. Braised calf's leg with sweetbreads and truffle. Saffron marinated carpaccio of pineapple with vanilla and chilli ice cream.

♦ Innovative ♦ Fashionable ♦

Long-standing basement restaurant divided into a series of dining rooms and dominated by an open kitchen. Choose between the popular 'Classic' menu, where preparations remain traditional, or the 'Wagner' menu where more modern dishes come with original twists.

XX ✿

Fond (Stefan Karlsson)

Götaplatsen ✉ S 412 56 – ✆ (031) 81 25 80 – www.fondrestaurang.com – Closed 4 weeks summer, 2 weeks Christmas, Sunday, Saturday lunch and bank holidays **C3**

Rest – Carte 505/730 SEK

Spec. Smoked salmon with prawns, mushooms and horseradish. Lemon-salted cod with anchovies and wild oyster broth. Baked chocolate with raspberry vodka and cardamom.

♦ Modern ♦ Trendy ♦

Stylish, modern restaurant with large circular bar and floor to ceiling windows overlooking the piazza. Chef-owner's cooking moves with the seasons, offering clearly defined flavours and making good use of salting and curing. Service is professional and warm.

XX

Fiskekrogen

Lilla Torget 1 ✉ S-411 18 – ✆ (031) 10 10 05 – www.fiskekrogen.com – Closed July, Christmas-New Year and Sunday **B2**

Rest – *(buffet lunch)* Menu 308 SEK – Carte 570/770 SEK

◆ Seafood ◆ Brasserie ◆

Once a 1920s Grand Café, now a real city institution. Impressive room with smart columns, wood panelling and central bar. Quality seafood dishes and extensive buffet lunch. Formal service.

XX

Linnéa

Södra Vägen 32 ✉ S-412 54 – ✆ (031) 16 11 83 – www.linneaartestaurant.se – Closed 23-26 June, 15 July-20 August, 23 December-8 January, Sunday and bank holidays **C3**

Rest – *(dinner only)* Menu 395 SEK – Carte 315/595 SEK

◆ Innovative ◆ Design ◆

Striking 'Art Restaurant' and bar displaying modern glass sculptures and installations. Dine in the casual bistro or, on certain nights, from innovative set menus in the formal dining area.

XX

Wasa Allé

Vasagatan 24 ✉ 400 16 – ✆ (031) 13 13 70 – www.wasaalle.se – Closed 23 December-7 January, 20 June-15 August, lunch Saturday-Sunday and dinner Sunday-Monday **B3**

Rest – Menu 325/525 SEK – Carte (dinner) 610/685 SEK

◆ Modern ◆ Elegant ◆

Contemporary restaurant with pleasant bar, occupying an appealing corner spot on a tree-lined avenue. Traditional buffet lunches; more modern dinner menus that rely on indigenous ingredients.

XX

Swedish Taste

Sankt Eriksgatan 6 ✉ SE-411 05 – ✆ (031) 13 27 80 – www.swedishtaste.com – Closed 3 July-2 August, 25 December, Saturday lunch and Sunday

Rest – Menu 295 SEK (lunch) – Carte 380/700 SEK **B1**

◆ Modern ◆ Fashionable ◆

3-storey venture consisting of a restaurant, deli, café and cookery school. Traditional lunch menu; more elaborate, contemporary offerings at dinner. Top produce and authentic Swedish flavours.

XX

Swea Hof – at Elite Plaza Hotel

Västra Hamngatan 3 ✉ S-404 22 – ✆ (031) 720 40 40 – www.elite.se/sweahof – Closed 23-26 December **B2**

Rest – *(closed lunch Saturday and Sunday)* Menu 425/555 SEK – Carte 515/665 SEK

◆ Modern ◆ Formal ◆

Striking hotel restaurant with metal framework and glass roof. Concise business menu at lunch; greater choice at dinner. Fresh, clean cooking combines French and modern Scandinavian influences.

XX

Kometen

Vasagatan 58 ✉ 411 37 – ✆ (031) 137988 – www.restaurangkometen.se – Closed 24-26 December and 1 January **C2**

Rest – *(booking essential)* Carte 400/600 SEK

◆ Scandinavian ◆ Family ◆

Lively all-day bistro with local cult status, dating back to 1934. Classical, art deco inner matched by similarly honest, rustic cooking. Weinerschnitzel has been served here for over 75 years.

Hos Pelle

Djupedalsgatan 2 ✉ S-413 07 – ✆ (031) 12 10 31 – www.hospelle.com
– Closed 20 June-10 August, 23-30 December, Saturday lunch and Sunday
Rest – Menu 425 SEK (dinner) – Carte lunch approx. 395 SEK **A3**
◆ Traditional ◆ Neighbourhood ◆

Long-standing neighbourhood restaurant offering wholesome, traditional cooking. Eat in the wine bar or one of two cosy, rustic dining rooms. Simple blackboard lunch; concise set dinner option.

La Cucina Italiana

Skånegatan 33 ✉ S-412 52 – ✆ (031) 16 63 07 – www.lacucinaitaliana.nu
– Closed Christmas, mid summer and Sunday **C3**
Rest – *(booking essential) (dinner only)* Menu 500/900 SEK
◆ Italian ◆ Friendly ◆

Enthusiastically run restaurant consisting of just 6 intimate tables. Choose between a 4 or 7 course surprise tasting menu. Chef-owner regularly travels back to his homeland to source produce.

Tvåkanten

Kungsportsavenyn 27 ✉ S-411 36 – ✆ (031) 18 21 15 – www.tvakanten.se
– Closed 25 December and 1 January **C3**
Rest – Menu 220/695 SEK – Carte 345/645 SEK
◆ Traditional ◆ Brasserie ◆

Set in a prime corner position on one of the most famous streets. Busy ground floor bar with high level seating leads into cosy cellar dining room. Menus range from brunch and all-day snacks to a more ambitious à la carte. Classical cooking and great wine list.

Familjen

Arkivgatan 7 ✉ 411 34 – ✆ (031) 20 79 79 – www.restaurangfamiljen.se
– Closed 24-26 and 31 December and Sunday **C3**
Rest – *(dinner only) (booking essential)* Menu 295/405 SEK – Carte 299/425 SEK
◆ Scandinavian ◆ Retro ◆ Design ◆

Bright, funky eatery divided into two parts: a bright red room and characterful cellar with glass wine cave; and a bar with open-plan kitchen and bench seating. Good value daily 3 course set menu and tasting plate selection. Large terrace and great wine list.

Gabriel

Feskekorka ✉ S-411 20 – ✆ (031) 13 90 51 – www.restauranggabriel.se
– Closed Sunday and Monday **A3**
Rest – *(lunch only) (booking advisable)* Carte 295/415 SEK
◆ Seafood ◆ Minimalist ◆

Casual first floor restaurant located in the famous 'Fish Church' market and boasting an excellent selection of fresh seafood from local Scandic waters: try the tasty mussels and fried herring.

ENVIRONS OF GOTHENBURG

AT ERIKSBERG West : 6 km by Götaälvbron and Lundbyleden, or boat from Rosenlund

Quality Hotel 11

Maskingatan 11 ✉ S-417 64 – ✆ (031) 779 11 11 – www.hotel11.se
– Closed 21 December to 3 January
260 rm – †990/1890 SEK ††1190/2090 SEK
Rest *Kök & Bar 67* – *(closed lunch Saturday and Sunday)* Menu 457 SEK (dinner) – Carte 325/475 SEK
◆ Business ◆ Functional ◆

Striking former shipbuilding warehouse by the river. Its greatest strength is its huge meeting and events capacity. Good-sized, functional bedrooms; the 8th floor rooms boast city views from furnished balconies. Split-level lounge-bar offers traditional menu.

Villan without rest

Sjöportsgatan 2 ✉ S-417 64 – ✆ (31) 725 77 77 – www.hotelvillan.com
26 rm – 1100/1700 SEK 1200/1900 SEK
♦ Traditional ♦ Modern ♦
Characterful Swedish house; once home to a shipbuilding manager. Stylish interior with smart, clean lines. Contemporary bedrooms boast good mod cons – No 31 has a sauna and TV in the bathroom. Breakfast at River Café.

River Café

Dockepiren ✉ S-417 64 – ✆ (031) 51 00 00 – www.rivercafe.se
– Closed Saturday lunch and Sunday
Rest – *(booking advisable)* Menu 335/485 SEK – Carte 320/590 SEK
♦ Seasonal cuisine ♦ Friendly ♦
Delightfully set on the pier, overlooking the city and harbour. Elegant first-floor restaurant with open kitchen and bar. Seasonal à la carte of fresh, hearty, Scandic dishes; simple set lunch.

AT LANDVETTER AIRPORT East : 30 km by Rd 40

Landvetter Airport Hotel

Flygets Hotellväg ✉ S-438 13 – ✆ (031) 97 75 50
– www.landvetterairporthotel.se
133 rm – 1395/1695 SEK 1695/2095 SEK – 1 suite
Rest – *(buffet lunch)* Menu 198 SEK – Carte 225/510 SEK
♦ Business ♦ Modern ♦
Located just minutes from the airport terminal but in a pleasant, semi-rural setting. Light, open interior has a fresh Scandic style and calm air. Warm, welcoming bedrooms come in a mix of styles. Informal restaurant offers Swedish/global fare and buffet lunch.

SWITZERLAND
SUISSE, SCHWEIZ, SVIZZERA

PROFILE

→ **Area:**
41 284 km²
(15 940 sq mi).

→ **Population:**
7 460 000 (est. 2006), density = 181 per km².

→ **Capital:**
Bern (Berne) (conurbation 349 100 inhabitants).

→ **Currency:**
Swiss Franc (CHF); rate of exchange CHF 1 = € 0.79 = US$ 1.03 (Dec 2010).

→ **Government:**
Federation of 26 cantons with 2 assemblies (National Council and Council of State) forming the Federal Assembly.

→ **Languages:**
German (64% of population), French (20%), Italian (7%) are spoken in all administrative departments, shops, hotels and restaurants. Romansh (1%) in the Grisons canton.

→ **Specific public holidays:**
Berchtold's Day (2 January); Good Friday (Friday before Easter); Swiss National Holiday (1 August); St. Stephen's Day (26 December). Thanksgiving (Jeûne Fédéral in French; Bettag in German) is observed in all cantons, except Geneva, on the third Sunday in September; the Geneva canton holds Thanksgiving on the second Thursday in September.

→ **Local Time:**
GMT + 1 hour in winter, GMT+ 2 hours in summer.

→ **Climate**
Temperate continental, varies with altitude – most of the country has cold winters and warm summers (Bern: January: 0°C, July: 19°C).

→ **International dialling Code**
00 41 followed by the area or city code (Geneva: **22**, Bern: **31**, Zurich: **44** or **43**) and then the local number.

→ **Emergency**
Police: ✆ **117**; Medical emergencies: ✆ **144**; Fire Brigade: ✆ **118**. Anglo-Phone (24 hr

information and helpline in English): ✆ **0900 576 444**.

→ **Electricity:**
220 volts AC, 50 Hz; 2-pin round-shaped continental plugs.

→ **Formalities**
Travellers from the European Union (EU), Iceland and the main countries of North and South America need a national identity card or passport (America: passport required) to visit Switzerland for less than three months (tourism or business purpose). For visitors from other countries a visa may be required, in addition to a passport, especially for those wishing to stay for longer than three months. We advise you to check with your embassy before travelling.

Bern
BERNE

Population: 128 300 (conurbation 349 100) – Altitude: 548m

. Parneix/Fotolia.com

To look at Bern, you'd never believe it a capital city. Small and beautifully proportioned, its old town sits sedately on a spur overlooking the river Aare, at a point where the river bends back on itself, giving a graceful curve to the landscape. UNESCO was so impressed it gave Bern World Heritage status.

In fact, the little city is the best preserved medieval centre north of the Alps, and the layout of the streets has barely changed since the Duke of Zahringen chose the superbly defended site to found a city over eight hundred years ago. Most of the buildings date from the period between the 14 and 16C when Bern was at the height of its power – one good reason why it feels much more human than many other European cities. The cluster of cobbled lanes, surrounded by ornate sandstone arcaded buildings and numerous fountains and wells, give it the feel of a delightfully overgrown village. Albert Einstein felt so secure here that while ostensibly employed as a clerk in the Bern patent office he managed to find the time to work out his Theory of Relativity.

LIVING THE CITY

Bern is a wonderfully compact city. Its **Old Town** stretches eastwards over a narrow peninsula, and is surrounded by the curving **River Aare**. The eastern limit of the Old Town is the **Nydeggbrücke** (bridge); the western end is the **Käfigturm** tower, once a city gate and prison. On the southern side of the Aare lies the small **Kirchenfeld** quarter which houses some impressive museums. The capital's famous brown bears are over the river via the Nydeggbrücke.

PRACTICAL INFORMATION

ARRIVAL-DEPARTURE

Bern-Belp International Airport is 9km southeast of the city. There's a shuttle bus every 30 minutes which takes 20 minutes to the city centre. A taxi will cost around 50CHF.

TRANSPORT

The Bern Card is well worth investing in. It gives unlimited travel, free admission to museums and gardens, and various reductions around the city. It's available from the Tourist Office, museums and hotels, and is valid for 24hr, 48hr or 72hr.

As Bern is small enough to walk around, it requires no more than a super-efficient bus and tram network. A short cable-railway links the Marzili quarter to the Bundeshaus. You can buy your ticket at the bus or tram stop.

EXPLORING BERN

It might sound like a cliché, but Bern is the secret jewel of the Alps. Its spectacular setting takes newcomers aback. Perched aloft on its precipice, surrounded by steep, wooded hills and mountains, who could resist a visit to one of the city's fifty-foot high bridges to watch the gushing grey-green foaming glacier waters of the Aare below? It's not hard to see why UNESCO bestowed its seal of approval upon Bern in 1983. Its perfectly preserved ancient centre comprises superb five-storey red-roofed houses, many of which date back to the 15C, separated by broad, cobbled streets enlivened by equally ancient, brightly coloured fountains. From springtime onwards, the rich sandstone of the buildings is shocked into life by dazzlingly-hued hanging baskets and the heraldic pennants of the Swiss cantons. It's an easy place to explore on foot, and even easier to get your bearings. With dominant landmarks all around your eyes would have to be closed to miss either the river, the Prison Tower, the **Clock Tower**, or the spiralling splendour of the Gothic **Cathedral.**

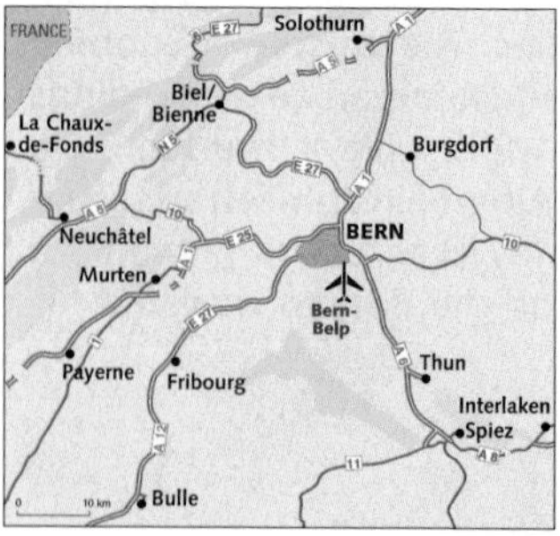

→ TOWERING ACHIEVEMENT

Bern's dramatic Cathedral is the tallest church in Switzerland. It was a long time in creation: over four hundred and fifty years, from 1421 until 1893, when the spire was finally added. The least you can do is pay it a visit, and when you do, don't miss the dramatic 15C stained glass windows in the choir. The tower is unusual in that it still has tower-keepers to look after it. If you're feeling energetic, you can climb to the top yourself, and take in a fine view of the city's curves. There's barely a straight line to be seen as cobbled streets wind every which way, forming fascinating parabolas. Back down at *gasse* level, a little way west from the Cathedral, is the central landmark of Bern, the Clock Tower. Its beautiful astronomical clockface has been keeping time here since 1530 and its elaborate chimes start at four minutes before the hour, when mechanical bears and a crowing cock start their regular procession in front of captivated visitors.

→ SHOPPING? IT'S COVERED

Appearances can deceive. On first acquaintance, the Swiss capital may hardly seem like a retail hot-spot. But rather surprisingly, this is a city beloved for its shopping opportunities. Not for Bern the antiseptic malls or cloned high streets of less fortunate towns. Instead, it boasts the longest covered shopping promenade in Europe. Sheltering underneath arcades with medieval vaulted roofs covering the pavement below, these dainty shops take the form of small boutiques selling a bewildering assortment of things. And they're entwined with charming cafés and restaurants, many within atmospheric vaulted cellars. Most of these arcades are along an east-west axis running from the Nydeggbrücke ; at its western end a sprinkling of colourful markets brings you back out into the open air.

→ FEAT OF KLEE

The world of art has a picture-perfect setting here. Until 2005, the main attraction was based at the **Museum of Fine Arts** (on the old town's north side), and with good reason: its globally renowned collection spans the 14C to 20C and includes everything from early Renaissance to Old Master to French Impressionist, not forgetting a broad representation of Switzerland's finest, including Albert Anker and Ferdinand Hodler. Since 2005, many visitors to Bern have been beating a path to the easterly **Schöngrün** quarter, to an audacious and extraordinary wave-shaped museum which emerges from a hillside: The **Zentrum Paul Klee**. This holds a mind-boggling amount of paintings (shown in rotation) by Bern's most famous artist, including four thousand works donated by a couple of collectors alone. The building was designed by Renzo Piano, creator of Paris's Pompidou Centre, and also includes a chamber concert hall.

Cross the **Kirchenfeldbrücke** to the southern side of the Aare, and you're in a museum wonderland. There's the **Bern Museum of History** in a building like a grand medieval castle; the **Art Gallery** with its rolling programme of modern art exhibitions; the **Swiss Alpine Museum**, which offers an engrossing look at environmental issues as well as the history, flora and fauna of the Alps; and three other museums with an eclectic focus ranging from human communications, to Swiss rifles to natural history.

Being out of doors is the real clue to getting the most out of Bern. A top walk is beside the Aare through the former artisans' quarter of **Matte**, or, in the eastern section of the main axis through the old town, the streets of **Postgasse** and **Gerechtigkeitsgasse**. Some of the oldest and most appealing of Bern's arcaded buildings are here: many were built as guild houses, and sport decorative motifs proudly pointing out the relevant trade.

➜ A FINE TOWN, RELATIVELY SPEAKING

Albert Einstein was a man who loved the outdoors: he would famously shuffle around the streets of Bern, often in green slippers, carrying a net bag for his shopping. He lived on **Kramgasse** for two years from 1903, and it was while here that he began to develop his Theory of Relativity. His small apartment is now a little museum, hung with documents and photos, and containing his writing desk. There's not much doubt the great man would have related strongly to the street in which he lived: in an earlier decade, the poet Goethe called Kramgasse "the most beautiful street in the world".

➜ FRINGE BENEFITS

Adding to the beauty and beguilement of Bern's streets are a warren of fringe theatres, many of them tucked comfortably away in the cellars of houses along the thoroughfares of the old town. More conventionally, performance lovers can head for the very visible Stadttheater on centrally located Kornhausplatz, to get a more mainstream dramatic fix. This is Bern's most beautiful theatre, the primary venue for the city's resident opera company and contemporary dance troupe. Another fine show is offered at the Bundesplatz, home of the Swiss Federal Parliament. The fountain in the square has twenty-six jets, each one representing a canton. In the summer months, these shoot skywards every thirty minutes, stopping passers-by in their tracks, and enhancing the centuries-old feeling that in its modest way Bern is just a delightful place to be.

CALENDAR HIGHLIGHTS

It's not often that deepest November plays host to a city's biggest annual bash; even less so when onions are involved. But Bern's November Onion Market takes pride of place in the events calendar. Taking over the old town between the railway station and the Bundesplatz, over fifty tons of onions from all over Switzerland guarantee a tear-jerking celebration. Incongruously, jazz is the other big-hitter in the city. There are four annual festivals, two of which take place in January and February (the Jazz Weekend and the Be-Jazz Winterfestival). The biggest is the week-long International Jazz Festival in May, which features top stars from the worlds of jazz, blues, gospel and Latin. Costumed parades light up the streets at the Fasnacht Carnival in February, while the summer's two top events are the Gurtenfestival (July), a high-powered rock music event in Gurtenpark, over the river to the south of the old town, and Altstadtsommer,

BERN IN...

➜ ONE DAY

River walk, Old Town (Cathedral, Clock Tower, arcades), Museum of Fine Arts, cellar fringe theatre

➜ TWO DAYS

Zentrum Paul Klee, Einstein's house, Stadttheater

➜ THREE DAYS

Repeat some of the delights of the first two days...but more slowly!

a series of concerts in the magical setting of the old town itself. There's also an absorbing Bern Dance Festival in June, in which people arrive from all over the world to give displays of their country's dance styles. You can check it out in bars, restaurants, concert halls and theatres.

EATING OUT

Bern is a great place to sit and enjoy a meal. Pride of place must go to the good range of al fresco venues in the squares of the old town, invariably popular spots to enjoy coffee and cake. Hiding away in the arcades are many delightful dining choices; some of the best for location alone are in vaulted cellars that breathe historic ambience. There's no shortage of international restaurants, either, but if you want to feel what a real Swiss restaurant is like, head for a traditional old-style rustic eatery complete with cow-bells, and sample local dishes like the Berner Platte - a heaving plate of hot and cold meats, served with beans and sauerkraut – or treberwurst, a sausage poached with fermented grape skins. Along with German restaurants, French and Italian Switzerland each have their own distinctive cuisine well represented here, so it's not difficult to go from rösti to risotto and gnocchi, raclette and fondue. And, of course, there's always cheese and chocolate waiting in the wings. A fifteen percent service charge is always added, but it's customary to round the bill up.

→ BEAR NECESSITIES

For good or bad, there are bears in Bern, in the bear pits, just across from the Nydeggbrücke. The city is named after bears, and they've been kept in the city since the early sixteenth century. Despite constant protests from animal rights activists, the bears are a very popular tourist attraction.

→ MOUNTAIN CLIMB

If you fancy a memorable day trip from Bern, the city is handily placed for excursions to the dramatic mountain ranges of the Bernese Oberland. It's only twenty minutes by train to Thun, where lake cruise boats leave from outside the station. You can easily get to Interlaken, but best of all, perhaps, is the unforgettable journey to Europe's highest railway station at Jungfraujoch, an easy day trip.

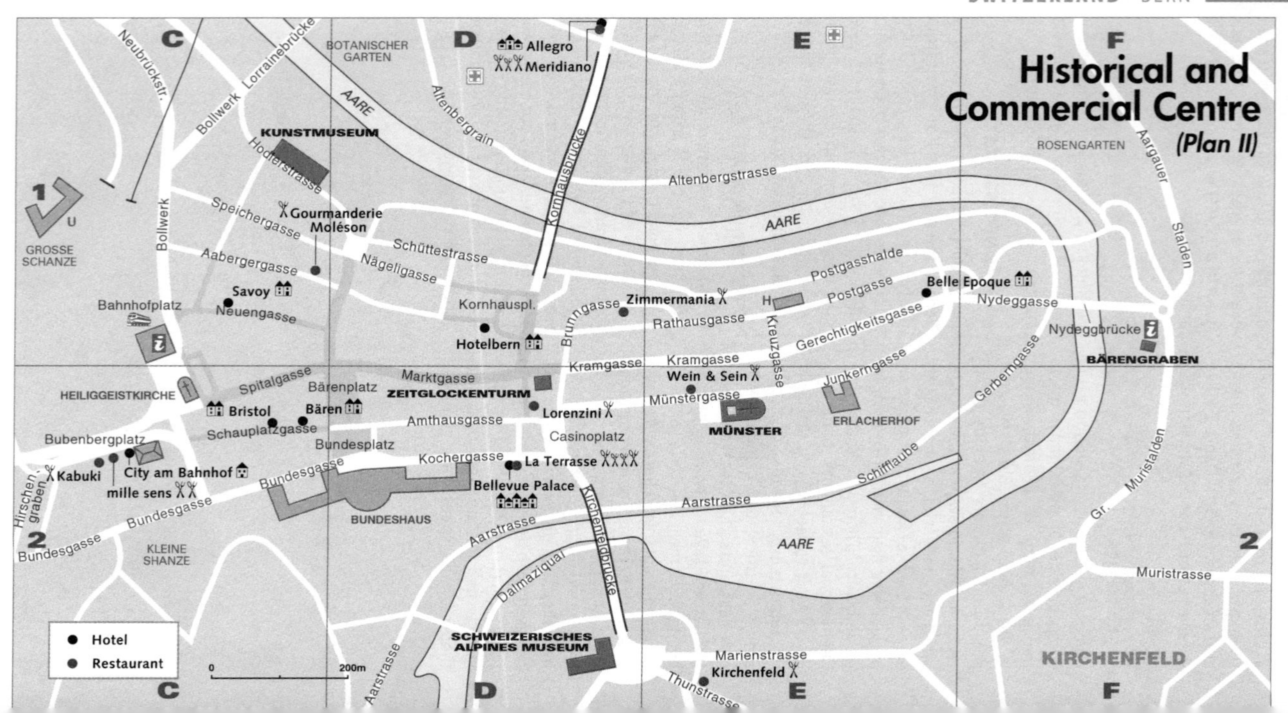
Historical and Commercial Centre
(Plan II)
C
D
E
F
1
2
BOTANISCHER GARTEN
ROSENGARTEN
KIRCHENFELD
GROSSE SCHANZE
KLEINE SHANZE
AARE
Allegro
Meridiano
KUNSTMUSEUM
Gourmanderie Moléson
Savoy
Hotelbern
Zimmermania
Belle Epoque
Wein & Sein
Lorenzini
La Terrasse
Bellevue Palace
Bristol
Bären
Kabuki
City am Bahnhof
mille sens
Kirchenfeld
ZEITGLOCKENTURM
MÜNSTER
ERLACHERHOF
BUNDESHAUS
HEILIGGEISTKIRCHE
BÄRENGRABEN
SCHWEIZERISCHES ALPINES MUSEUM
Neubrückstr.
Lorrainebrücke
Bollwerk
Hodlerstrasse
Speichergasse
Aabergergasse
Neuengasse
Bahnhofplatz
Schüttestrasse
Nägeligasse
Kornhauspl.
Kornhausbrücke
Altenbergrain
Altenbergstrasse
Aargauer
Stalden
Postgasshalde
Postgasse
Nydeggasse
Nydeggbrücke
Brunngasse
Rathausgasse
Kreuzgasse
Gerechtigkeitsgasse
Kramgasse
Junkerngasse
Münstergasse
Gerberngasse
Marktgasse
Spitalgasse
Bärenplatz
Amthausgasse
Casinoplatz
Schauplatzgasse
Bundesplatz
Bubenbergplatz
Kochergasse
Bundesgasse
Hirschengraben
Schifflaube
Aarstrasse
Kirchenfeldbrücke
Dalmaziquai
Gr. Muristalden
Muristrasse
Marienstrasse
Thunstrasse
Hotel
Restaurant
0
200m

Bellevue Palace

Kochergasse 3 ✉ 3000 – ✆ 031 320 45 45 – www.bellevue-palace.ch **D2**
126 rm – ♦389/495 CHF ♦♦510/608 CHF, ☕ 36 CHF – 15 suites
Rest *La Terrasse* – see below
Rest *Bellevue Bar* – Carte 55/103 CHF
♦ Palace ♦ Classic ♦

This exclusive hotel established in 1913 and sited in the heart of Bern offers first-class guestrooms and suites and elegant conference facilities in a truly unique atmosphere. Modern gym with sauna. The comfortable Bellevue Bar serves international cuisine.

Allegro

Kornhausstr. 3 ✉ 3000 – ✆ 031 339 55 00 – www.kursaal-bern.ch **D1**
171 rm – ♦250/350 CHF ♦♦310/410 CHF, ☕ 25 CHF – 2 suites
Rest *Meridiano* – see below
Rest *Yù* – *✆ 031 339 52 50 (closed 3 weeks August and Monday - Tuesday) (dinner only)* Menu 42/88 CHF – Carte 48/76 CHF
Rest *Giardino* – *✆ 031 339 51 80* – Carte 49/72 CHF
♦ Business ♦ Modern ♦

This trendy hotel has something to offer both conference organisers and individual travellers. It offers modern rooms in various categories including an attractive penthouse floor complete with its own lounge. The Yù restaurant serves Chinese cuisine. The Giardino serves Italian cuisine.

Hotelbern

Zeughausgasse 9 ✉ 3011 – ✆ 031 329 22 22 – www.hotelbern.ch
98 rm ☕ – ♦200/320 CHF ♦♦270/380 CHF **D1**
Rest *Kurierstube* – *(closed 3 July - 14 August and Sunday)* Menu 38 CHF (lunch)/82 CHF – Carte 51/106 CHF
Rest *7-Stube* – *✆ 031 329 22 33* – Carte 24/81 CHF
♦ Business ♦ Modern ♦

Located in a striking townhouse in the centre of Bern, this business hotel offers colourful, contemporary guestrooms and meeting rooms complete with the latest facilities. A high-quality, elegant restaurant. Rustic-style restaurant.

Savoy without rest

Neuengasse 26 ✉ 3011 – ✆ 031 311 44 05 – www.zghotels.ch
54 rm ☕ – ♦235/260 CHF ♦♦330 CHF **C1**
♦ Business ♦ Classic ♦

This hotel offers high-quality rooms with the latest technology and an attractive breakfast room with a generous buffet. Central location conveniently close to the railway station.

Belle Epoque

Gerechtigkeitsgasse 18 ✉ 3011 – ✆ 031 311 43 36 – www.belle-epoque.ch
17 rm – ♦250 CHF ♦♦350 CHF, ☕ 21 CHF **E1**
Rest – Carte 39/75 CHF
♦ Business ♦ Cosy ♦

This centuries-old city centre hotel is tastefully decorated with Art Nouveau paintings, fixtures and fittings. Highly individual rooms with a personal touch. The restaurant serves classical cuisine – steak tartare is a speciality.

Bristol without rest

Schauplatzgasse 10 ✉ 3011 – ✆ 031 311 01 01 – www.bristolbern.ch
92 rm ☕ – ♦203/298 CHF ♦♦246/376 CHF **C2**
♦ Business ♦ Modern ♦

This townhouse hotel offers contemporary rooms and a small sauna (additional charge payable) which is shared with the adjacent Hotel Bären.

Bären without rest

Schauplatzgasse 4 ✉ *3011 – ✆ 031 311 33 67 – www.baerenbern.ch*
57 rm – 203/298 CHF 276/376 CHF **C2**

◆ Business ◆ Modern ◆

Just a stone's throw from the Bundesplatz, this hotel located in a well-maintained townhouse offers individually furnished guestrooms in a contemporary style. A small sauna is available for an additional charge.

City am Bahnhof without rest

Bubenbergplatz 7 ✉ *3011 – ✆ 031 311 53 77 – www.fassbindhotels.ch*
58 rm – 154/250 CHF 198/290 CHF, 20 CHF **C2**

◆ Business ◆ Functional ◆

Conveniently located close to the pedestrian zone and opposite the railway station, this hotel offers well-equipped rooms.

La Terrasse – Hotel Bellevue Palace

Kochergasse 3 ✉ *3001 – ✆ 031 320 45 45 – www.bellevue-palace.ch*
Rest – Menu 72/135 CHF – Carte 86/152 CHF **D2**

◆ Seasonal cuisine ◆ Classic ◆

Ambitious, contemporary seasonal cuisine with traditional roots is served in this tastefully decorated setting. The terrace affords magnificent views over the Aare.

Meridiano – Hotel Allegro

Kornhausstr. 3 ✉ *3013 – ✆ 031 339 52 45 – www.kursaal-bern.ch*
– Closed 3 weeks July and Saturday lunch, Sunday - Monday **D1**
Rest – Menu 45 CHF (lunch)/165 CHF – Carte 103/145 CHF
Spec. Kalbskräuterhacktäschli auf gratinierten Büffelricotta-Basilikum-Cannelloni. Duett von der Taube am Tisch tranchiert. Limonentarte mit flambierten Erdbeeren.

◆ Modern ◆ Trendy ◆

This modern and elegant restaurant has wonderful views of Bern, which are no less impressive from the covered terrace. Very attentive service and fine cuisine by Markus Arnold.

mille sens

Bubenbergplatz 9 (at the Markthalle) ✉ *3011 – ✆ 031 329 29 29*
– www.millesens.ch – Closed 3 weeks July and Sunday **C2**
Rest – Menu 68 CHF (lunch)/86 CHF – Carte 49/94 CHF

◆ Modern ◆ Fashionable ◆

This restaurant in the market hall – with its numerous shops, eateries and bars – is vibrant and lively and offers tasty, modern food at fair prices. At noon: business lunch, "blackboard" and "Quick Tray".

Wein & Sein (Beat Blum)

Münstergasse 50 ✉ *3011 – ✆ 031 311 98 44 – www.weinundsein.ch*
– Closed 24 July - 16 August and Sunday - Monday **E2**
Rest – *(dinner only) (booking advisable)* Menu 92 CHF
Spec. Sommerwild (May - July). Wildgeflügel in den Federn. Schokoladensoufflé.

◆ Modern ◆ Trendy ◆

Beat Blum presents his daily changing menu on a board in a very pleasant and easy-going atmosphere. Enjoy contemporary cuisine with a personal touch, the friendly and informal service, and excellent wine recommendations.

Kirchenfeld

Thunstr. 5 ✉ *3005 – ✆ 031 351 02 78 – www.kirchenfeld.ch*
– Closed Sunday and Monday **E2**
Rest – *(booking advisable)* Menu 68 CHF – Carte 41/80 CHF

◆ Modern ◆ Brasserie ◆

This charming restaurant in a historic townhouse was established in 1885. The food is unfussy and tasty, and the smaller lunch menu is popular among business people in a hurry. Good tram links.

Lorenzini

Hotelgasse 10 ✉ 3011 – ☎ 031 318 50 67 – www.lorenzini.ch
Rest – Carte 51/91 CHF **D2**
♦ Italian ♦ Friendly ♦
This attractive Italian restaurant located in the pedestrian zone is tastefully decorated with original paintings. It boasts a formal restaurant on the first floor and a bar, bistro and attractive interior courtyard at ground level.

Zimmermania

Brunngasse 19 ✉ 3011 – ☎ 031 311 15 42 – www.zimmermania.ch
– Closed 10 July - 8 August, Sunday - Monday and Bank Holidays
Rest – Menu 56 CHF – Carte 40/90 CHF **D1**
♦ Traditional ♦ Bistro ♦
The atmosphere in this cosy, traditionally run restaurant located in a narrow alleyway in the old town is lively and informal.

Gourmanderie Moléson

Aarbergergasse 24 ✉ 3011 – ☎ 031 311 44 63 – www.moleson-bern.ch
– Closed over Christmas, 31 December - 3 January, over Easter and Saturday lunch, Sunday **C1**
Rest – Menu 69/79 CHF – Carte 52/91 CHF
♦ Traditional ♦ Brasserie ♦
Established in 1865, the Moléson is a lively restaurant located in the centre of Bern. It serves a range of traditional-style dishes from Alsace Flammkuchen to multi-course meals.

Kabuki

Bubenbergplatz 9 (at the Markthalle) ✉ 3011 – ☎ 031 329 29 19
– www.kabuki.ch
– Closed Sunday and Bank Holidays **C2**
Rest – Menu 68/89 CHF – Carte 42/97 CHF
♦ Japanese ♦ Exotic ♦
An unostentatiously modern restaurant serving Japanese cuisine and sushi in the basement of the lively market hall. The bar offers a fascinating glimpse of activities in the adjacent kitchen.

ENVIRONS OF BERN

Plan I

Innere Enge

Engestr. 54 ✉ 3012 – ☎ 031 309 61 11 – www.zghotels.ch **A1**
26 rm – †315/345 CHF ††370/420 CHF
Rest *Josephine* – *☎ 031 309 61 15* – Menu 50 CHF (lunch)/84 CHF
– Carte 43/92 CHF
♦ Business ♦ Classic ♦
Passionate about jazz, your hosts have created this unique hotel-cum-jazz venue. Many of the rooms are named after famous musicians and decorated with original artefacts. The basement houses a jazz club. Josephine's Brasserie and the historic Park Pavilion offer views over the city.

Sternen

Thunstr. 80 – ☎ 031 950 71 11 – www.sternenmuri.ch
– Closed Christmas - early January, 23 July - 7 August **B2**
44 rm – †203 CHF ††276 CHF **Rest** – Carte 41/120 CHF
♦ Traditional ♦ Functional ♦
This recently extended hotel offers contemporary rooms decorated in shades of yellow, green and blue in the annexe and more traditional rooms, some with exposed beams, in the main building. Good transport connections into the city. Both the Läubli restaurant and residents' dining room serve contemporary cuisine. Attractive private dining rooms are also available.

Ambassador

Seftigenstr. 99 ✉ *3007 – ✆ 031 370 99 99 – www.fassbindhotels.com*
97 rm – †202/330 CHF ††252/370 CHF, ☕ 24 CHF **A2**
Rest *Taishi* – *(closed early July - mid August and Saturday lunch, Sunday - Monday)* Menu 30/95 CHF – Carte 44/97 CHF
Rest *Pavillon* – Menu 89 CHF – Carte 35/90 CHF
♦ Business ♦ Contemporary ♦

This business hotel with modern guestrooms equipped with the latest technology and free parking is located on the edge of the city with good transport links. Japanese restaurant serving griddle-cooked teppanyaki dishes. This light and airy restaurant serves international cuisine.

Astoria

Zieglerstr. 66 ✉ *3007 – ✆ 031 378 66 66 – www.astoria-bern.ch*
– Closed Christmas - 2 January **A2**
63 rm ☕ – †160/180 CHF ††190/210 CHF
Rest – *(closed Christmas - 2 January, 2 weeks end July - early August and Saturday lunch, Sunday)* Carte 32/54 CHF
♦ Townhouse ♦ Business ♦ Contemporary ♦

Contemporary, functional rooms combine with a location on the edge of the city centre and good transport links to make this hotel ideal for business travellers or visitors on a short city break. Pleasant breakfast room with a small terrace. Bistro-style restaurant offering predominantly Mediterranean fare.

Ador without rest

Laupenstr. 15 ✉ *3001 – ✆ 031 388 01 11 – www.hotelador.ch*
– Closed Christmas - 3 January **A2**
57 rm ☕ – †155/308 CHF ††185/320 CHF
♦ Business ♦ Modern ♦

This hotel located close to the railway station offers small rooms equipped with the latest technology making it ideal for the business traveller.

Landhaus Liebefeld with rm

Schwarzenburgstr. 134 – ✆ 031 971 07 58 – www.landhaus-liebefeld.ch
– Closed Sunday **A2**
6 rm ☕ – †178 CHF ††280 CHF
Rest – *(booking advisable)* Menu 85/136 CHF – Carte 39/107 CHF
Rest *Gaststube* – *(closed Sunday)* Carte 34/84 CHF
♦ Seasonal cuisine ♦ Cosy ♦

Friendly, well-trained staff serve contemporary cuisine in this smart former sheriff's residence. The elegant restaurant boasts a charming garden terrace. Good value classics and seasonal dishes in the bar parlour. The attractive rooms in this hotel are individually furnished and decorated.

Schöngrün (Werner Rothen)

Monument im Fruchtland 1 (at Paul Klee Centre) ✉ *3006 – ✆ 031 359 02 90 – www.restaurants-schoengruen.ch – Closed Monday and Tuesday*
Rest – *(booking advisable)* Menu 59 CHF (lunch)/130 CHF – Carte 104/135 CHF **B1**
Spec. Lachsforelle mit Birne, Wasabi und Lotus-Chips. Taube mit Mandarine, Pastinaken-Mostarda und Polenta-Praline. Kaffee, Passionsfrucht und Cashewnuss.
♦ International ♦ Trendy ♦

Next door to the renowned Paul Klee Centre is this historical villa with a modern glass annexe. It houses a very stylish restaurant with friendly and competent service. The dishes are sumptuously and creatively prepared.

La Tavola Pronta

Laupenstr. 57 ✉ *3008 – ✆ 031 382 66 33 – www.latavolapronta.ch*
– Closed July - August and Saturday lunch, Sunday - Monday **A2**
Rest – *(booking advisable)* Menu 80/105 CHF
♦ Italian ♦ Cosy ♦

A pleasant little basement restaurant with modern decor where chef Beat Thomi creates flavoursome Piedmontese food in a number of set menus.

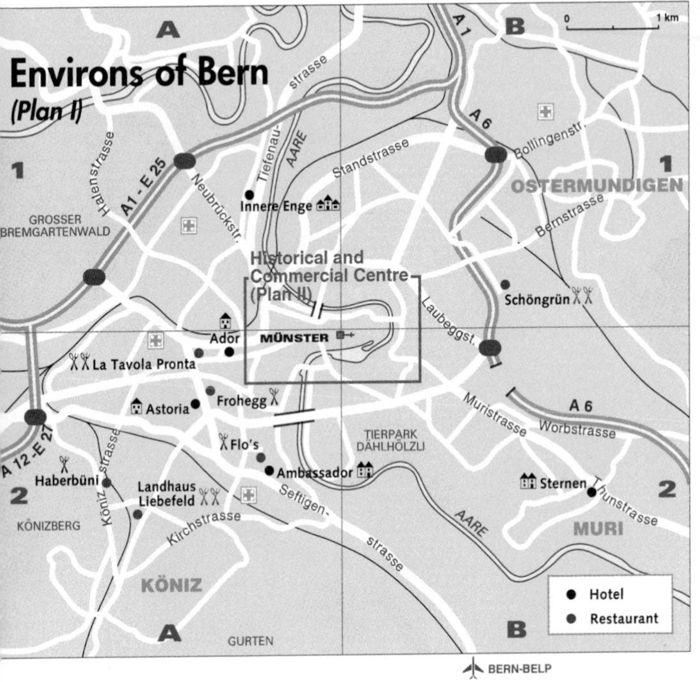

Flo's

Weissenbühlweg 40 ✉ 3007 – ✆ 031 372 05 55 – www.flos-restaurant.ch – Closed 20 December – 16 January, 17 April - 1 May, 25 June - 28 August, 24 September - 16 October and Sunday - Wednesday **A2**

Rest – *(dinner only) (booking advisable)* Menu 65/95 CHF – Carte 56/65 CHF

♦ Modern ♦ Fashionable ♦

Run by the dedicated Manz siblings, the atmosphere in this modern restaurant is lively and the service very friendly. Watch delicious international dishes being prepared in the open-view kitchen. The number nine tram stops right at the door.

Frohegg

Belpstr. 51 ✉ 3007 – ✆ 031 382 25 24 – www.frohegg.ch – Closed Sunday **A2**

Rest – *(booking advisable)* Carte 44/75 CHF

♦ Seasonal cuisine ♦ Cosy ♦

This cosy restaurant located in a 1898 townhouse and serving seasonal cuisine has been privately run for more than 20 years. It has a lovely winter garden and wisteria-covered terrace.

Haberbüni

Könizstr. 175 – ✆ 031 972 56 55 – www.haberbueni.ch – Closed Saturday lunch and Sunday **A2**

Rest – *(booking advisable) (in summer small lunchtime)* Menu 58 CHF (lunch)/110 CHF – Carte 52/85 CHF

♦ International ♦ Cosy ♦

This warm and welcoming restaurant set in the loft of a large renovated farmhouse or Büni offers ambitious contemporary cuisine and a fine selection of wines. Shorter midday menu and good business lunch options.

GENEVA
GENEVE

Population (est. 2005): 189 957 (conurbation 698 000) - Altitude: 375m

eng Guan Toh/Fotolia.com

In just about every detail except efficiency, Geneva exudes a distinctly Latin feel. It boasts a proud cosmopolitanism, with about one in three of its residents being non-Swiss, drawn here by the presence of the largest UN office outside New York, as well as a whole swathe of international organisations dealing with every human concern under the – frequently dazzling - sun. Its renowned ***savoir-vivre*** challenges that of equally swishy Zurich, while it also enjoys cultural ties with Paris, and is often called 'the twenty first arrondissement'.

It could hardly have a better setting. It's strung around the sparkling shores of Europe's largest alpine lake. Enter the city on that lake and you have mountains to either side – take your pick from Jura or Alps. There are manicured city parks and the world's tallest fountain, the bisecting River Rhône and the world's longest bench on which to sit and take it all in. Geneva is renowned for its orderliness: the Reformation was born here under the austere preachings of Calvin, and the city has been a place of refuge to Europeans for at least five centuries, providing sanctuary for religious dissidents, revolutionaries and elopers. Hell-raising poets, too, in the shape of Byron and Shelley. Nowadays, new arrivals tend to be of a more conservative persuasion, as they go their elegant way balancing international affairs alongside ***la belle vie.***

LIVING THE CITY

Geneva may be in Switzerland, but it's almost totally surrounded by France. The **River Rhône** snakes through the centre, dividing the city into **the right bank** (north side, the **'international quarter'**), and the **left bank** (south side, the **old town**). To the east of Geneva is **Lake Léman** (Lake Geneva in English), while the **Jura** mountains dominate the right bank, and the **Alps** form a backdrop to the left bank. Geneva's **international airport** is to the northwest of the city, while the popular suburb of **Carouge** is to the south.

PRACTICAL INFORMATION

ARRIVAL-DEPARTURE

Geneva International Airport is just 4km from the city centre and a taxi will cost around 35CHF. Trains depart every 15min and take just 6min. Bus 10 runs every 10min.

TRANSPORT

Geneva is served by an efficient public transport network which, true to the cliché, runs like clockwork. There are various timed cards depending on how much travelling you intend to do: for one hour, one day, or 9am-midnight. A useful alternative: if you're making several trips, pick up a 48- or 72-hour Geneva Transport Card from the tourist office for unlimited use of the city's trams, trains, buses and boats. It also offers free admission to many top museums and attractions, plus reductions in some restaurants and shops.

There's nothing better than a cycle ride along the long quaysides by the lake. The city encourages pedal power, and from May to October bikes can be borrowed for free. More information from Geneva Tourism on Rue du Mont-Blanc.

EXPLORING GENEVA

It may be one of the most famous cities in the world, in one of the world's most beautiful locations, but Geneva is actually pretty small, not much bigger than a medium-sized town. The fame that goes before it stems mostly from all those organisations based here whose tentacles embrace the world. And, of course, everyone knows about the Lake. This is what makes Geneva extra special, giving it that sense of a bygone seaside resort. The huge expanse of water is a perfect foil for the majesty of the surrounding mountains. Its mirror-like surface is as flat as a pancake, save for an iconic landmark that has first-time visitors drawing breath before the search for superlatives. The **Jet d'Eau** is a stirring sight from the aeroplane window coming in to land. The world's tallest fountain, it shoots water with incredible force 140m into the air, and when the sun shines creates a shimmering rainbow. Watch out, though: spectators on the adjacent pier get a regular spraying.

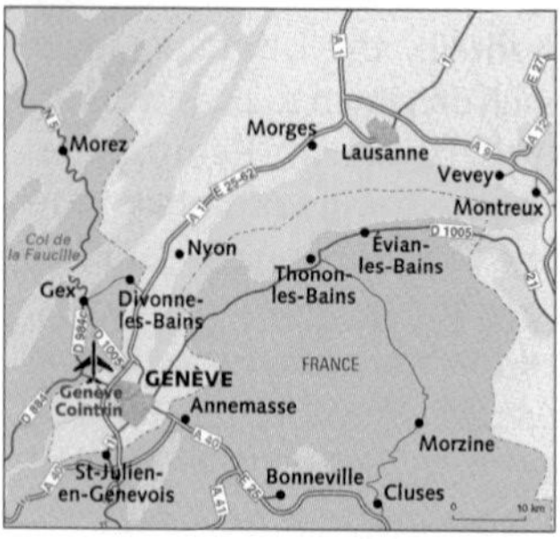

Its forceful presence is at odds with the quiet and measured calm of the medieval old town, which lies nearby along the left bank. Here, the cobbled streets invariably lead to the dominant **St Peter's Cathedral**, sitting proudly atop its hill. This medieval monolith has Romanesque and Gothic origins hidden behind a neoclassical façade; its huge rose window is a glowing gem in the sunlight. You can go from the highs (via steep spiral steps for a look at the bell tower and awesome views of the lake and mountains) to the subterranean lows (an underground archaeological site that traces the cathedral's early foundations).

→ SEEDS OF TIME

Back up at lake level, and standing in an enviable position close to the water's edge, is a permanent tribute to 'Swiss timing' - the **Floral Clock**. This is a favourite spot for clicking cameras. It's certainly colourful: over six thousand dazzling flowers and plants are arranged in new displays each spring and autumn in celebration of local watch-making. You won't need to check your timepiece to get to one of the old town's most fascinating attractions – **Maison Tavel** is just a short stroll south. This is the place to visit to get an idea of what Geneva looked like in the Middle Ages. Set in the city's oldest house, dating back to the fourteenth century, there are displays of antique furniture, silverware and tapestries spanning six hundred years. Highlight is a seven-metre-long model of Geneva pre-1850. It took the very patient Auguste Magnin eighteen years to make it out of zinc and copper.

→ WALL OF DEFIANCE

Magnin's honest endeavours would have met with the approval of Jean Calvin, the father of the 16C Protestant movement who lived and lectured in Geneva, and set in stone the city's 'work ethic' image that lives on to this day. There are two lasting memorials to him: one is the recently opened **International Museum of the Reformation,** near the Cathedral, which is chock-full of objects, books and paintings about the religious upheavals of the time; and then there's the breathtaking, hundred-yard long **Reformation Wall** in the **Parc des Bastions**, a dazzlingly white construction, a century old, with a fifteen-foot high statue of Calvin at its heart. If all this earnestness has left you feeling the need to chill out a bit, then the park itself is an ideal place. Its wide, tree-lined avenues are tailor-made for strolling, stopping off to watch chess being played on giant boards, while locals jog along trying to decide which of the thousand restaurants in town will play host to their expense account tonight.

For the ultimate Genevan chill-out, the coolest place in town in the summer months is **Bains des Paquis** on the Right Bank – just look for the soaring white lighthouse. Some forty years ago, this area had a bad boy reputation forged by its proximity to the dodgy Paquis district. Today, not only is Paquis the multicultural buzzword for boho chic, but the Bains itself is now a fun-filled pier and beach zone that entices a veritable league of nations to sample its charms. This is where, whether Rastafarian or restaurateur, the world comes to hang around, to graze on a lazy lunchtime picnic, read a paperback, swim in the lake, or just enjoy the sun. Beaches, boardwalk or rocks – take your pick of where you want to flop down. When it gets chilly, a big draw is the state-of-the-art spa complex on the pier, where you can steam in the hammams, sauna or solarium.

→ DRAWN AWAY

There comes a time when everyone has to forego the delights of the Lake, and Geneva has a sprinkling of top museums to investigate. Modernists should head for **MAMCO – the Museum of Contemporary Art** – which, suitably enough, is housed in a refitted industrial factory from the 1950s. It puts on a whole raft of fresh, cutting edge exhibitions that cover a range of mediums. Across town is the more conservative but equally riveting **Art & History Museum**, a cavernous place that makes the most of its space with paintings, sculpture, arty room interiors and medieval weaponry. Roman pottery and Egyptian antiquities are popular attractions, as are masterpieces from the likes of Van Gogh, Rembrandt and Monet, but the highlight is a fifteenth century altarpiece by Konrad Witz. Meanwhile, right in the centre of the old town, on **Place Neuve**, the **Rath Museum** is dedicated to fine arts and is well known for putting on excellent temporary exhibitions. For something completely different, the **International Red Cross Museum**, way up north on the right bank near the massive HQ of the United Nations, is a thought-provoking museum with multimedia displays that highlights the work through the decades of the world's largest humanitarian network, started by Genevan philanthropist Henri Dunant in 1864. The soundtracks, photos and films that accompany this sometimes-harrowing exhibition enhance the Red Cross's compelling story. That other Swiss speciality, timekeeping, is celebrated in a treasure trove of ticks and tocks at **Patek Philippe Museum**, next to the Museum of Contemporary Art. On show is everything from exquisite seventeenth century pocket watches to stylish art nouveau creations.

→ THE GENEVA UNCONVENTION

When Genevans seek a musical fix, their natural port of call is the **Grand Theatre**, in the heart of Place Neuve, which is internationally famous for its world-class theatre, ballet, dance and opera. Those looking for more edgy material have a pretty impressive choice: **Salle Centrale** puts on everything from art-house movies to improvised plays; **Theatre du Grütli** takes the term 'experimental' to new levels in its theatre and comedy productions; and **L'Usine** – an old gold-roughing factory – contributes art happenings, dance nights and weird cabaret to Geneva's cultural map.

CALENDAR HIGHLIGHTS

One event stands head and shoulders above any other here: the Escalade. This atmospheric procession through the old town over the weekend closest to 12 December commemorates the battle to defend the Protestant city against the Catholic House of Savoy. The attack, in 1602, was repulsed, and Geneva's celebratory costumed procession takes place by the light of

GENEVA IN...

→ ONE DAY

St Peter's Cathedral, Maison Tavel, Jet d'Eau. Reformation Wall

→ TWO DAYS

MAMCO (or Art & History Museum), a stroll along the edge of the lake, a trip to Carouge

→ THREE DAYS

A day in Paquis, with a lazy time at the Bains des Paquis

torches to the sound of drums, fifes, trumpets and musketeers opening fire on horseback. It can get quite noisy. The volume's pretty high in August, too, when another big event, The Geneva Fête, kicks off. Days of music, shows, dancing and gastronomy are concluded with a firework display that lights up the lakeside. Other summer highlights include June's Bol d'Or Race, when the peace of Lake Geneva succumbs to over six hundred boats and yachts contesting the Golden Cup; the Fête de la Musique, also in June, which sees open-air stages in many streets and squares for a riot of concerts featuring every kind of musical form; and August's Fêtes de Geneve, when the streets are again awash with colour for fireworks, parties and parades (and it's all free!). There's more of a 'Protestant friendly' air about the Antiques and Bric-A-Brac Fair (October) in the Plaine de Plainpalais, an immense showcase of dealers' stalls by the Rhône. But the temperature rises again in October for the Flamenco Festival, a week-long celebration that brings the spirit of Seville to the Swiss Alps.

EATING OUT

One thing's for sure: you won't be hard pressed to find an eating establishment in Geneva. All those big international organisations take a bit of feeding, and so you'll find over a thousand dining establishments in the city and its surrounds. If you're looking for elegance, then head to a restaurant overlooking the lake; if your tastes are more for the 'nonna' style of home-cooked Sardinian fare, make tracks for the charming Italianate suburb of Carouge just to the south, where little cafés serve up delicious antipasti, risotto and fresh fish. If you haven't an expense account to blow, but fancy something with an international accent, then Paquis has it all, and at a fair price. This trendy part of Geneva offers flavours on a truly global scale from Moroccan to Mexican, from Jordanian to Japanese. The old town is the place for Swiss staples, packed as it is with delightful brasseries and alpine-style chalets: you can't go wrong here if your fancy is for fondue, or a heartily rustic papet vaudois (cream-leek casserole). Longeole (pork sausage enlivened with cumin and fennel) is a popular choice for meat eaters. Rösti, of course, is ubiquitous. For a bit of extra atmosphere, head downstairs to dine in a vaulted cellar with flickering candles. Though restaurants include a service charge of fifteen per cent, it's customary to leave a tip if you were happy with the service – round up the bill or give the waiter a tip between five and ten per cent.

→ CAROUSE IN CAROUGE

For Geneva with a true Latin heart, take a tram to Carouge. From 1754 till 1816, this now hip suburb was part of the kingdom of Sardinia. Designed by Piedmontese architects, its chessboard pattern of blocks enclosing courtyard gardens provides a wonderfully understated charm, enhanced by funky bars, boutiques, Italian cafés and artists' workshops.

→ CHILLON OUT

Byron and Shelley visited Geneva in 1816, and the Lord wrote a poem afterwards about the four-year imprisonment of Prior Bonivard in the fabulous castle of Chillon overlooking Lake Geneva. You can see the castle, and others, on an idyllic lake cruise. Vessels – some of them paddlesteamers – serve forty-two piers, and are a delightfully relaxing way of getting to see many of the places around the lake.

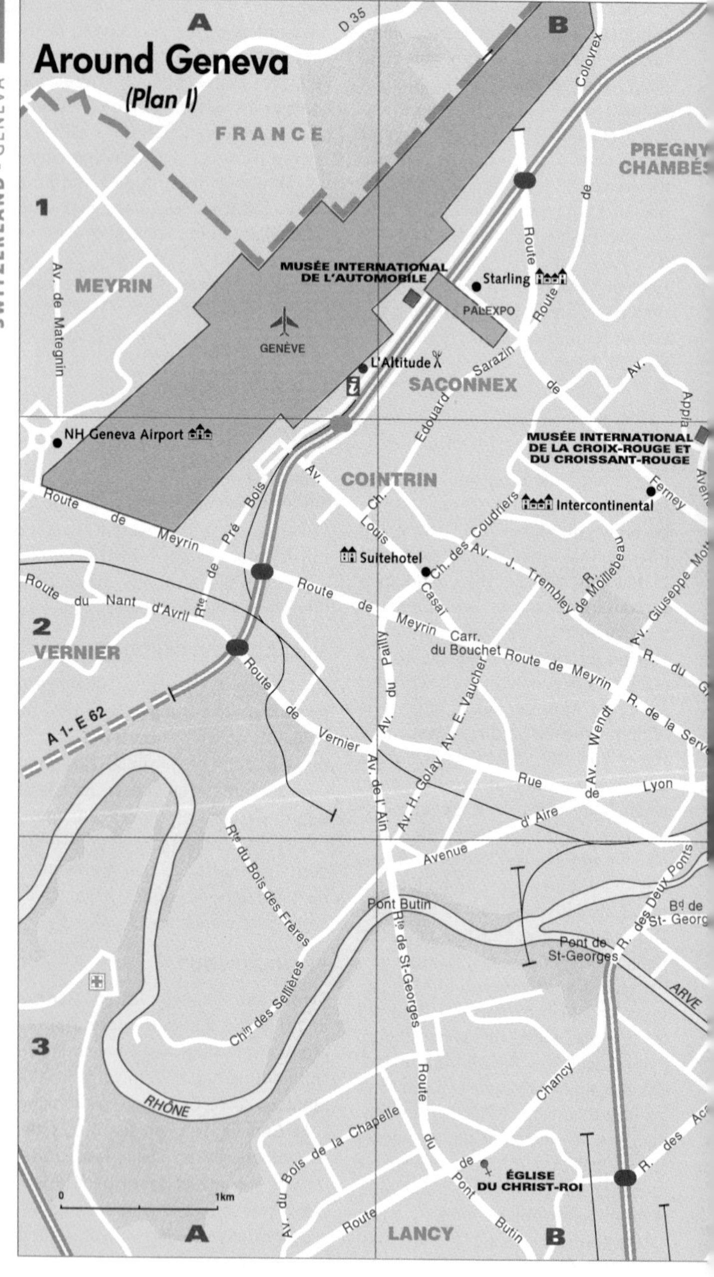
Around Geneva
(Plan I)
A
B
1
2
3
FRANCE
D 35
MEYRIN
Av. de Mategnin
MUSÉE INTERNATIONAL DE L'AUTOMOBILE
GENÈVE
PALEXPO
Starling
L'Altitude
SACONNEX
PREGNY CHAMBÉSY
Colovrex
Route de
Route de
Sarazin
Edouard
Av.
Appia
MUSÉE INTERNATIONAL DE LA CROIX-ROUGE ET DU CROISSANT-ROUGE
NH Geneva Airport
COINTRIN
Intercontinental
Ferney
Route de Meyrin
Rte de Pré Bois
Av. Louis Casaï
Ch. des Coudriers
Suitehotel
Av. J. Trembley
R. de Moillebeau
Av. Giuseppe Motta
Route du Nant d'Avril
VERNIER
Carr. du Bouchet
Route de Meyrin
R. du
Av. du Pailly
Av. E. Vaucher
Av. Wendt
R. de la Servette
A 1- E 62
Route de Vernier
Av. de l'Ain
Av. H. Golay
Rue de Lyon
Avenue d'Aire
Rte du Bois des Frères
Pont Butin
Rte de St-Georges
R. des Deux Ponts
Bd de St-Georges
Pont de St-Georges
ARVE
Chin des Sellières
RHÔNE
Route de Chancy
Av. du Bois de la Chapelle
Route du Pont Butin
ÉGLISE DU CHRIST-ROI
R. des Ac
0
1km
LANCY
Route

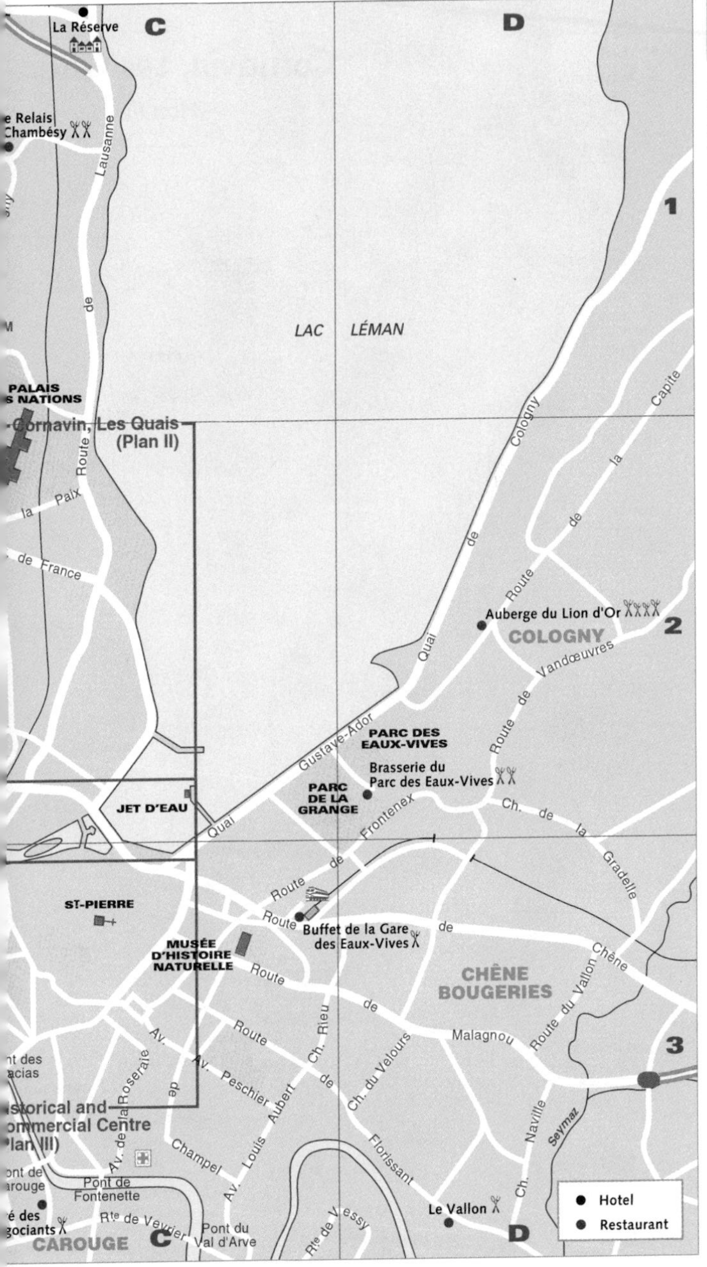

La Réserve
C
D
e Relais
Chambésy
Lausanne
de
LAC LÉMAN
1
PALAIS
S NATIONS
Cornavin, Les Quais
(Plan II)
Route
la Paix
de France
Quai de Cologny
Route de la Capite
Auberge du Lion d'Or
2
COLOGNY
Route de Vandœuvres
PARC DES
EAUX-VIVES
Brasserie du
Parc des Eaux-Vives
Quai Gustave-Ador
PARC
DE LA
GRANGE
JET D'EAU
Route de Frontenex
Ch. de la Gradelle
ST-PIERRE
Route de Chêne
Buffet de la Gare
des Eaux-Vives
MUSÉE
D'HISTOIRE
NATURELLE
CHÊNE
BOUGERIES
Route de Malagnou
Route du Vallon
Ch. Rieu
Ch. du Velours
Av. de la Roseraie
Av. Peschier
Route de Florissant
Av. Louis Aubert
Champel
3
Seymaz
Ch. Naville
Historical and
Commercial Centre
(Plan III)
Pont de
Fontenette
Pont de
Carouge
Le Vallon
Rte de Veyrier
Pont du
Val d'Arve
Rte de Vessy
CAROUGE
Hotel
Restaurant

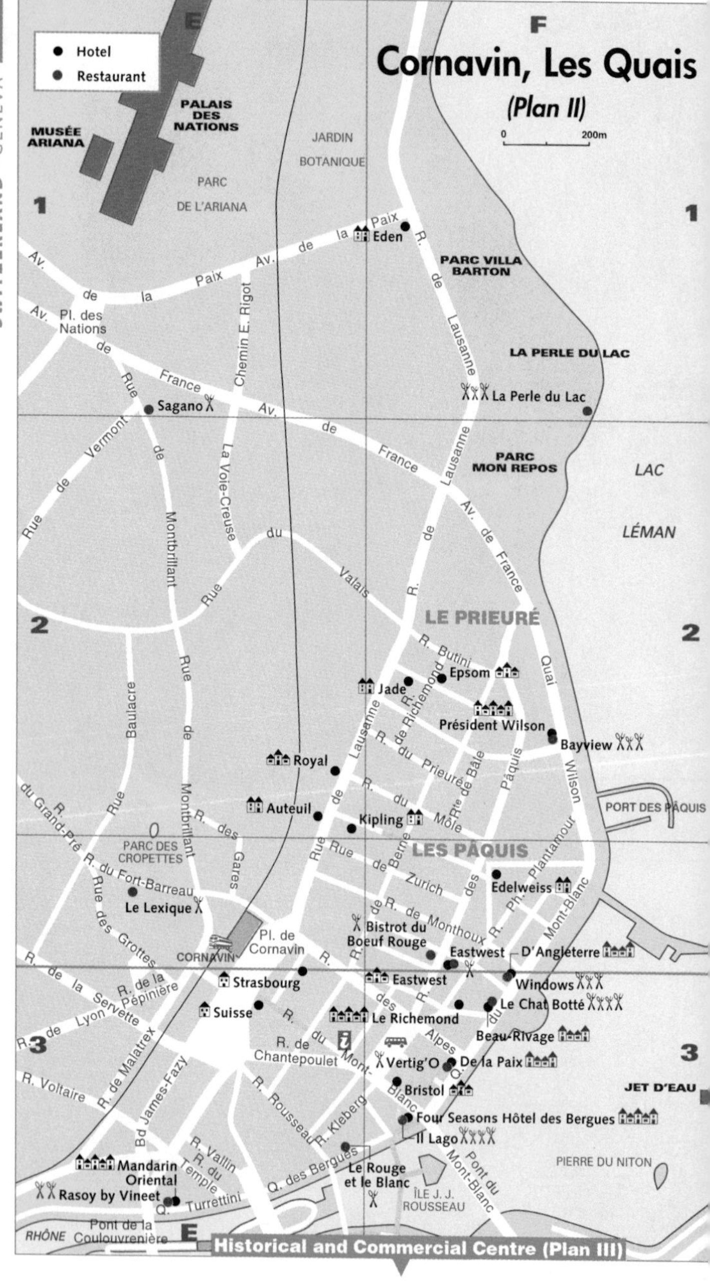
Cornavin, Les Quais
(Plan II)
Hotel
Restaurant
0
200m
PALAIS DES NATIONS
MUSÉE ARIANA
JARDIN BOTANIQUE
PARC DE L'ARIANA
Eden
PARC VILLA BARTON
Av. de la Paix
Pl. des Nations
Chemin E. Rigot
R. de Lausanne
LA PERLE DU LAC
La Perle du Lac
Sagano
Av. de France
Rue de Vermont
Rue de Montbrillant
La Voie-Creuse
PARC MON REPOS
LAC LÉMAN
Rue du Valais
LE PRIEURÉ
R. Butini
Epsom
Jade
R. de Richemond
Président Wilson
Bayview
Quai Wilson
Royal
R. du Prieuré
Rte de Bâle
Pâquis
Auteuil
Kipling
R. du Môle
PORT DES PÂQUIS
Rue Baulacre
R. du Grand-Pré
R. des Gares
PARC DES CROPETTES
LES PÂQUIS
Rue de Berne
Rue de Zurich
R. des Ph. Plantamour
Edelweiss
R. du Fort-Barreau
Rue des Grottes
Le Lexique
R. de Monthoux
Mont-Blanc
Bistrot du Boeuf Rouge
Pl. de Cornavin
CORNAVIN
Eastwest
D'Angleterre
Strasbourg
Windows
R. de la Servette
R. de la Pépinière
R. des Alpes
Le Chat Botté
Suisse
Le Richemond
R. de Lyon
Beau-Rivage
R. de Chantepoulet
Vertig'O
De la Paix
R. du Mont-Blanc
R. Voltaire
R. de Malatrex
Bd James-Fazy
R. Rousseau
Bristol
JET D'EAU
Four Seasons Hôtel des Bergues
R. Kleberg
Il Lago
R. Vallin
R. du Temple
Q. des Bergues
Le Rouge et le Blanc
Pont du Mont-Blanc
PIERRE DU NITON
Mandarin Oriental
Rasoy by Vineet
Q. Turrettini
ÎLE J. J. ROUSSEAU
RHÔNE
Pont de la Coulouvrenière
Historical and Commercial Centre (Plan III)

Four Seasons Hôtel des Bergues

33 quai des Bergues ✉ *1201 – ✆ 022 908 70 00 – www.fourseasons.com/geneva* F3

116 rm – †795/950 CHF ††845/1000 CHF, ☕ 55 CHF – 25 suites

Rest *Il Lago* – see below

♦ Palace ♦ Stylish ♦

The oldest and most luxurious of Geneva's luxury hotels (1834) has had a face-lift. The hotel boasts a superb lobby, lounges adorned with polished marble and magnificent flower displays, an elegant bar, Empire-style or contemporary guestrooms and suites, and impeccable service.

Mandarin Oriental

1 quai Turrettini ✉ *1201 – ✆ 022 909 00 00 – www.mandarinoriental.com/geneva* E3

182 rm – †935/1420 CHF ††995/1480 CHF, ☕ 49 CHF – 30 suites

Rest *Rasoi by Vineet* – see below

Rest *Le Sud* – *✆ 022 909 00 05* – Carte 66/135 CHF

♦ Grand Luxury ♦ Art Deco ♦

Sumptuous contemporary-style rooms with Art Deco furnishings, either overlooking the Rhône or a small courtyard. The best suites (with a terrace) are on the seventh floor. Le Sud offers both a Mediterranean atmosphere and menu.

Le Richemond

8 r. Adhémar - Fabri ✉ *1201 – ✆ 022 715 70 00 – www.roccofortecollection.com* F3

109 rm – †750/1450 CHF ††850/1550 CHF, ☕ 48 CHF – 10 suites

Rest *Le Jardin* – Menu 68 CHF (lunch)/115 CHF – Carte 96/155 CHF

♦ Grand Luxury ♦ Modern ♦

This hotel was opened in 1863 and has been recently renovated. It offers rooms and suites decorated in a chic, contemporary style, with a view of the lake and the Jet d'Eau from the upper floors. Beauty parlour, sauna and hammam. Italian cuisine is served in an elegant, modern dining room or on the attractive terrace facing the Brunswick gardens.

Président Wilson

47 quai Wilson ✉ *1201 – ✆ 022 906 66 66 – www.hotelpwilson.com* F2

228 rm – †490/1050 CHF ††490/1050 CHF, ☕ 45 CHF – 13 suites

Rest *Bayview* – see below

Rest *L'Arabesque* – Menu 48 CHF (lunch)/105 CHF – Carte 65/96 CHF

Rest *La Terrasse du Bayview* – *(closed mid September - mid April)* Menu 55 CHF (lunch)/68 CHF – Carte 91/138 CHF

♦ Grand Luxury ♦ Stylish ♦

Overlooking the lake, this hotel is adorned with marble decor, fine wood furnishings and attractive flower arrangements. There is a contemporary-style lobby, attractive pool and 40 modern guestrooms. Enjoy Lebanese delicacies in the magical atmosphere of this restaurant. La Terrasse du Bayview specialises in Mediterranean cuisine (open in season).

Beau-Rivage

13 quai du Mont-Blanc ✉ *1201 – ✆ 022 716 66 66 – www.beau-rivage.ch*

90 rm – †800/1200 CHF ††900/1400 CHF, ☕ 46 CHF – 11 suites F3

Rest *Le Chat Botté* – see below

Rest *Patara* – *✆ 022 731 55 66 (closed 21 December - 4 January)* Menu 95/125 CHF – Carte 75/113 CHF

♦ Grand Luxury ♦ Stylish ♦

The same family has run this hotel, facing the lake and the famous Jet d'Eau, since 1865. There is an impressive atrium adorned with colonnades and a fountain, as well as splendid views from the terrace. Elegant guestrooms. The Patara specialises in Thai cuisine.

D'Angleterre

17 quai du Mont-Blanc ✉ 1201 – ✆ 022 906 55 55 – www.hoteldangleterre.ch
45 rm – 690/990 CHF 690/990 CHF, ☕ 48 CHF **F1**
Rest *Windows* – see below
♦ Luxury ♦ Classic ♦
Built in 1872, this elegant luxury hotel overlooks Lake Geneva. Enjoy the excellent service, stylish rooms and an impressive presidential suite. There are also reception rooms and a retro-style bar with a lounge-library by the fire.

De la Paix

11 quai du Mont-Blanc ✉ 1201 – ✆ 022 909 60 00 – www.concorde-hotels.com/hoteldelapaix **F3**
84 rm – 750/1100 CHF 800/1100 CHF, ☕ 40 CHF – 2 suites
Rest *Vertig'O* – see below
♦ Luxury ♦ Classic ♦
This palatial, historic hotel built in 1865 faces the lake. Find a grandiose lobby, luxurious Grace Kelly suite and personalised guestrooms decorated according to two themes: water drops and rose petals. Warm, cosy atmosphere in the Nobel bar.

InterContinental

7 ch. du Petit-Saconnex ✉ 1209 – ✆ 022 919 39 39 – www.intercontinental-geneva.ch *Plan I* **B2**
334 rm ☕ – 765 CHF 815 CHF – 56 suites
Rest *Woods* – Menu 44 CHF (lunch) – Carte 75/92 CHF
♦ Chain hotel ♦ Design ♦
This hotel is housed in a 1960s building near the Palais des Nations. A designer from New York has refurbished the guestrooms. It also boasts modern public rooms, conference facilities, an attractive swimming pool and a spa. This spacious and comfortable restaurant serves modern cuisine in a contemporary atmosphere.

Bristol

10 r. du Mont-Blanc ✉ 1201 – ✆ 022 716 57 00 – www.bristol.ch
100 rm – 365/640 CHF 500/685 CHF, ☕ 36 CHF – 6 suites **F3**
Rest – Menu 52 CHF – Carte 70/115 CHF
♦ Business ♦ Classic ♦
This establishment has a British-style lobby and luxurious rooms (either overlooking the city or the garden). It also offers a cosy lounge-bar, relaxing well-being centre, and gentle harp music at breakfast. This restaurant has an elegant, hushed dining room. It is decorated with plush carpets, heavy curtains, Baccarat crystal lamps and chandeliers, and medallion chairs.

Royal

41 r. de Lausanne ✉ 1201 – ✆ 022 906 14 14 – www.manotel.com
202 rm – 360/615 CHF 360/615 CHF, ☕ 30 CHF – 6 suites **E2**
Rest *Le Duo* – Carte 47/101 CHF
♦ Business ♦ Classic ♦
Busy roadside and modern business hotel, set between the railway station and the lake. Some rooms have been renovated in warm shades (stone and wood). Conference centre. This restaurant offers two distinct dining experiences: a traditional menu in the bistro-style dining room, and more inventive cuisine in the restaurant. Terrace under the arcades.

Epsom

18 r. de Richemont ✉ 1202 – ✆ 022 544 66 66 – www.manotel.com
153 rm – 310/615 CHF 310/615 CHF, ☕ 30 CHF **F2**
Rest *Portobello & Co* – Menu 40 CHF (lunch)/61 CHF – Carte 50/93 CHF
♦ Business ♦ Classic ♦
This contemporary-style hotel is in a quiet road in the city centre. It offers pleasant guestrooms, some of which have a balcony overlooking the lake. There is also modern public rooms and conference facilities. With a focus on olive oil based Mediterranean cuisine, this restaurant has a delightful veranda with a real southern feel.

Eastwest

6 r. des Pâquis ✉ 1201 – ✆ 022 708 17 17 – www.eastwesthotel.ch
41 rm – 420/735 CHF 492/735 CHF, 35 CHF – 4 suites **F3**
Rest *Eastwest* – see below

◆ Townhouse ◆ Modern ◆

This centrally located hotel has a pleasant Japanese-style ambience. Find a warm, cosy lounge, minimalist meeting room, comfortable guestrooms, as well as a fitness area and sauna.

Auteuil without rest

33 r. de Lausanne ✉ 1201 – ✆ 022 544 22 22 – www.manotel.com
104 rm – 330/560 CHF 330/560 CHF, 28 CHF – 8 suites **E2**

◆ Business ◆ Classic ◆

This establishment has a designer style lobby adorned with portraits of stars. It offers modern, comfortable guestrooms and there is a bright breakfast area that catches the morning sun.

Kipling without rest

27 r. de la Navigation ✉ 1201 – ✆ 022 544 40 40 – www.manotel.com
62 rm – 270/430 CHF 270/430 CHF, 18 CHF **E-F2**

◆ Business ◆ Modern ◆

This hotel has created an exotic atmosphere, from the aroma of incense in the lobby to the cosy guestrooms. The 'executive' rooms are more spacious in size and have a balcony.

Jade without rest

55 r. Rothschild ✉ 1202 – ✆ 022 544 38 38 – www.manotel.com
47 rm – 180/430 CHF 180/530 CHF, 18 CHF **F2**

◆ Business ◆ Modern ◆

This pleasant hotel has been decorated according to the principles of Chinese philosophy and Feng Shui. Find harmony and serenity in a minimalist, modern environment. There is an attractive patio for summer dining.

Edelweiss

2 pl. de la Navigation ✉ 1201 – ✆ 022 544 51 51 – www.manotel.com
42 rm – 290/530 CHF 290/530 CHF, 18 CHF **F3**
Rest – *(closed 3 - 16 January) (dinner only)* Menu 40/75 CHF
– Carte 42/84 CHF

◆ Business ◆ Cosy ◆

This hotel is decorated inside and out in the style of a typical Swiss chalet. It offers cosy, comfortable guestrooms with light wood furnishings. Spacious executive rooms also available. Friendly service. This authentic Swiss restaurant serves regional specialities with a focus on cheese dishes.

Eden

135 r. de Lausanne ✉ 1202 – ✆ 022 716 37 00 – www.eden.ch
54 rm – 185/285 CHF 240/340 CHF **F1**
Rest – *(closed 24 December - 9 January, 25 July – 14 August and Saturday - Sunday)* Menu 28/33 CHF – Carte 44/61 CHF

◆ Business ◆ Classic ◆

Situated between the botanical gardens, the WTO and Barton park, this hotel was built in 1936, the same year as the nearby Palais des Nations. Find traditionally furnished guestrooms and a cosy lounge. The soft lighting gives this restaurant an intimate atmosphere.

Strasbourg without rest

10 r. Pradier ✉ 1201 – ✆ 022 906 58 00 – www.hotelstrasbourg.ch
51 rm – 170/210 CHF 230/270 CHF – 2 suites **E3**

◆ Business ◆ Functional ◆

This traditional hotel is a stone's throw from the station. It offers attractive, well-kept guestrooms and an elegant suite. There is also a pleasant lounge and small meeting room.

Suisse without rest

10 pl. de Cornavin ✉ 1201 – ✆ 022 732 66 30 – www.hotel-suisse.ch **F3**

62 rm – 210/260 CHF 270/295 CHF

♦ Business ♦ Functional ♦

This non-smoking hotel is conveniently located opposite the railway station. It offers guests a choice of standard or more contemporary luxury rooms with a predominantly red colour scheme. Rooms on the sixth floor have the benefit of a small balcony.

Il Lago – Four Seasons Hôtel des Bergues

33 quai des Bergues ✉ 1201 – ✆ 022 908 71 10 – www.fourseasons.com/geneva **F3**

Rest – *(booking advisable)* Menu 78 CHF (lunch)/130 CHF – Carte 110/158 CHF

♦ Italian ♦ Classic ♦

This restaurant specialising in fine Italian cuisine has a classical, opulent decor with exquisite hand-painted wallpaper in the dining room. Enjoy fine wines, excellent service, and a lovely terrace overlooking the Rhône.

Le Chat Botté – Hôtel Beau Rivage

13 quai du Mont-Blanc ✉ 1201 – ✆ 022 716 66 66 – www.beau-rivage.ch – Closed 22 April - 1 May, Saturday lunch and Sunday **F3**

Rest – Menu 70 CHF (lunch)/220 CHF – Carte 123/218 CHF

Spec. La langoustine, vinaigrette aux agrumes, chiffonade de basilic. La grenouille en gigotin et tempura, mousseline de pousse d'épinards, crème d'ail. Le foie gras de canard, olives noires confites.

♦ Classic ♦ Elegant ♦

This noteworthy restaurant in a luxury hotel is intimate and comfy. It offers elegant, classic cuisine based on excellent regional produce, as well as a prestigious wine list and impeccable service. Pretty summer terrace with lake view.

Bayview – Hôtel Président Wilson

47 quai Wilson ✉ 1201 – ✆ 022 906 66 66 – www.hotelpwilson.com – closed 2 - 12 January, 4 July – 17 August, Saturday lunch and Sunday

Rest – Menu 55 CHF (lunch)/140 CHF – Carte 115/154 CHF **F2**

♦ Euro-asiatic ♦ Fashionable ♦

Enjoy excellent fusion cuisine in a hushed, elegant atmosphere in this restaurant, where the decor is very much modern in style with leather, wood, and shades of beige and chocolate.

La Perle du Lac

126 r. de Lausanne ✉ 1202 – ✆ 022 909 10 20 – www.laperledulac.ch – Closed 24 December - 12 January and Monday **F1**

Rest – Menu 65 CHF (lunch)/130 CHF – Carte 83/134 CHF

♦ Traditional ♦ Classic ♦

This 100 year-old chalet stands in imposing grounds on the lakeshore. It boasts dining rooms full of character, an attractive terrace with fine views, a traditional menu, and a pianist in the dining room.

Windows – Hôtel D'Angleterre

17 quai du Mont-Blanc ✉ 1201 – ✆ 022 906 55 55 – www.hoteldangleterre.ch – Closed Sunday **F1**

Rest – Menu 51 CHF (lunch)/120 CHF – Carte 101/150 CHF

♦ French ♦ Classic ♦

Typical French cuisine, such as foie gras, snails, lobster and pigeon, is served in this restaurant which offers fine views of Lake Geneva.

Rasoi by Vineet – Hôtel Mandarin Oriental

1 quai Turrettini ✉ 1201 – ☎ 022 909 00 06 – www.rasoi.ch
– Closed Sunday and Monday **E3**
Rest – *(booking advisable)* Menu 65 CHF (lunch)/130 CHF
– Carte 102/160 CHF
Spec. Assiette Rasoi : Noix de Saint-Jacques au "Gunpowder", volaille tikka à la moutarde rouge, agneau "achari pasanda", chutney au crabe. Homard et cacao : Homard grillé aux épices, risotto khichdi au brocoli et gingembre, poudre d'épices et cacao. Biryani au poulet : Dum Parda biryani en croûte avec un riz parfumé aux épices et fruits secs, Kachumber raita.

♦ Indian ♦ Design ♦

Deliciously reworked Indian cuisine served in a very trendy setting. There is a winter garden and a designer tandoor where the naan are cooked. Attentive service and cosmopolitan atmosphere.

Vertig'O – Hôtel de la Paix

11 quai du Mont-Blanc ✉ 1201 – ☎ 022 909 60 73
– www.concorde-hotels.com/vertigo
– Closed 18 December - 6 January, 16 July – 23 August and Saturday lunch, Sunday - Monday **F3**
Rest – Menu 65 CHF (lunch)/155 CHF – Carte 116/140 CHF
Spec. Noix de ris de veau à l'écrasé de Belle de Fontenay et morilles. Bar de ligne et son cannelloni au chèvre frais. Aiguillettes de Saint-Pierre en barigoule d'artichaut.

♦ Traditional ♦ Fashionable ♦

Hotel restaurant with contemporary and fashionable decor where you can enjoy modern dishes of distinctive flavour based on selected produce. Pretty table settings. Attentive service.

Eastwest – Hôtel Eastwest

6 r. des Pâquis ✉ 1201 – ☎ 022 708 17 07
– www.eastwesthotel.ch **F3**
Rest – *(booking advisable)* Menu 68 CHF – Carte 61/98 CHF

♦ Modern ♦ Design ♦

This aptly named restaurant combines the influences of the East and West, with its Japanese-style decor, seasonal produce and traditional cuisine with just a hint of exotic flavour.

Le Lexique

14 r. de la Faucille ✉ 1201 – ☎ 022 733 31 31
– www.lelexique.ch
– Closed 23 December - 3 January, 30 July - 22 August and Saturday lunch, Sunday - Monday **E3**
Rest – *(booking advisable)* Menu 68 CHF – Carte 70/87 CHF

♦ Seasonal cuisine ♦ Simple ♦

This charming restaurant in the grotto district will delight with fresh, seasonal cuisine offering good quality for the price. Food is served in the dining room or on the pavement terrace in summer.

Bistrot du Boeuf Rouge

17 r. Dr. Alfred-Vincent ✉ 1201 – ☎ 022 732 75 37
– www.boeufrouge.ch
– Closed 24 December - 2 January, 16 July – 14 August and Saturday - Sunday
Rest – *(booking advisable)* Menu 38 CHF (lunch)/54 CHF **F3**
– Carte 50/81 CHF

♦ Bistro ♦ Brasserie ♦

For over 20 years, the Farina family have been lovingly running this typically French bistro (zinc, benches, old advertisements and sets of mirrors). Specialities from Lyon, local dishes and gourmet specials feature on the menu.

Sagano

86 r. de Montbrillant ✉ 1202 – ✆ 022 733 11 50
– Closed Saturday lunch and Sunday **E1**
Rest – *(booking advisable)* Menu 40 CHF (lunch)/90 CHF – Carte 52/95 CHF
♦ Japanese ♦ Exotic ♦
This attractive restaurant serves excellent Japanese food amid a minimalist decor of tatamis and low tables. Good wine list.

Le Rouge et le Blanc

27 quai des Bergues ✉ 1201 – ✆ 022 731 15 50 – www.lerougeblanc.ch
– Closed 23 December - 2 January and Sunday **E3**
Rest – *(booking advisable)* Menu 44 CHF (lunch) – Carte 65/75 CHF
♦ Modern ♦ Wine bar ♦
This friendly wine bar-cum-restaurant has an extensive wine list and a knowledgeable wine waiter. Sample the homemade charcuterie and traditional cuisine, which has lower prices at lunchtime.

LEFT BANK *Plan III*

Swissôtel Métropole

34 quai Général-Guisan ✉ 1204 – ✆ 022 318 32 00
– www.swissotel.com/geneva **H1**
118 rm – 🚹440/890 CHF 🚹🚹470/890 CHF, ☕ 42 CHF – 8 suites
Rest *Le Grand Quai* – *✆ 022 318 34 63* – Carte 88/126 CHF
♦ Luxury ♦ Classic ♦
Offering a combination of cosy elegance and modern luxury, this smart hotel dating from 1854 has views of the Jet d'Eau. Conference facilities and fitness suite. Attractive terraces. The Grand Quai serves creative, seasonal cuisine in an elegant, contemporary setting.

Les Armures

1 r. du Puits-Saint-Pierre ✉ 1204 – ✆ 022 310 91 72
– www.hotel-les-armures.ch **H2**
32 rm ☕ – 🚹445/535 CHF 🚹🚹695/720 CHF
Rest – *(closed Christmas and New Year)* Carte 40/83 CHF
♦ Traditional ♦ Historic ♦
This 17C building, nestled in the heart of old Geneva, has a welcoming interior that tastefully combines old and new. There is a choice of modern or more rustic rooms. Some of the world's most famous celebrities have stayed here! This restaurant has an authentic atmosphere, typical 'carnotzet' (wine cellar), and an outdoor terrace. Fondues and raclettes on the menu.

De la Cigogne

17 pl. Longemalle ✉ 1204 – ✆ 022 818 40 40 – www.cigogne.ch
52 rm ☕ – 🚹410 CHF 🚹🚹520 CHF – 6 suites **H1-2**
Rest – *(closed Christmas - New Year, 16 July - 21 August and Sunday lunch)* Menu 65 CHF (lunch)/125 CHF – Carte 84/106 CHF
♦ Traditional ♦ Historic ♦
This charming Belle Époque hotel has a chic, classical style. Find a cosy atmosphere with individually styled rooms, and suites embellished with antique furniture. The soft lighting in this restaurant gives it an intimate atmosphere. Traditional cuisine.

Tiffany

20 r. de l'Arquebuse ✉ 1204 – ✆ 022 708 16 16 – www.tiffanyhotel.ch
46 rm – 🚹340/450 CHF 🚹🚹460/525 CHF, ☕ 35 CHF – 2 suites **G2**
Rest – *(closed Christmas and New Year)* Carte 53/89 CHF
♦ Traditional ♦ Classic ♦
This elegant hotel is housed in a late-19C residence. It has fully renovated public rooms, and guestrooms decorated in a Belle Époque style. This charming retro-style brasserie has an Art Nouveau decor with Tiffany lamps. The menu bears the mark of the Pourcel brothers.

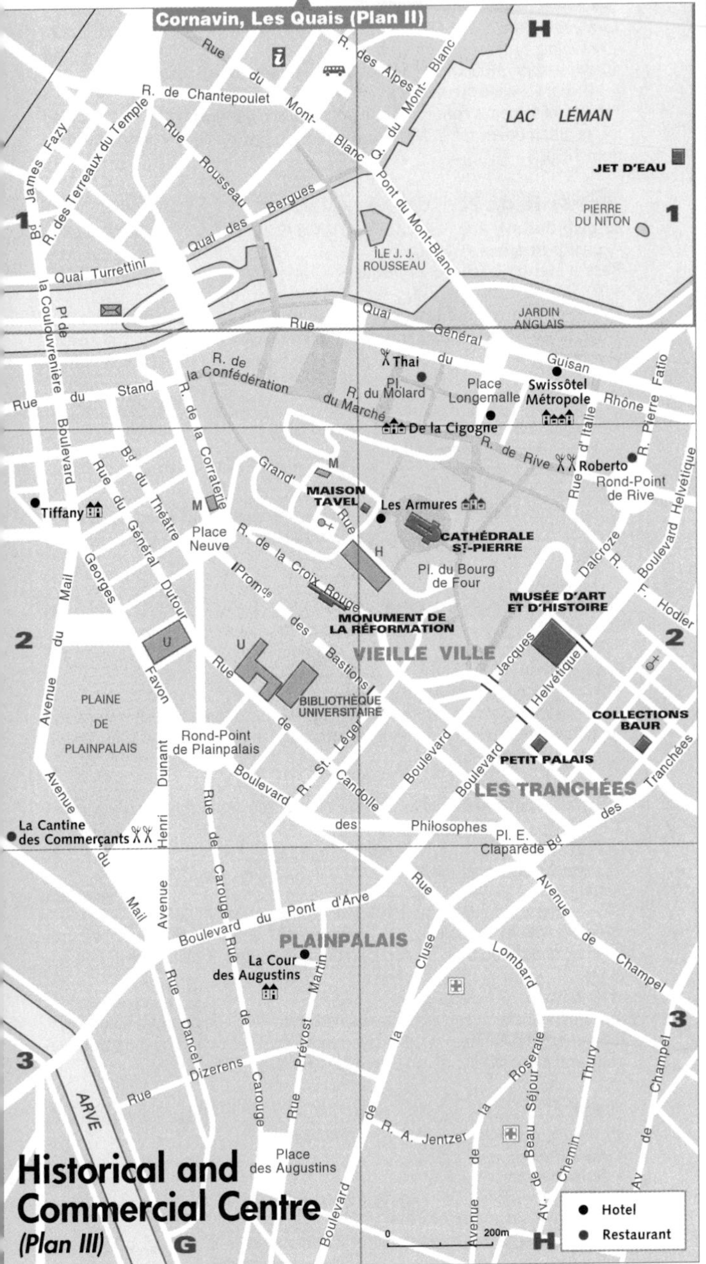

Cornavin, Les Quais (Plan II)
H
Rue du Mont-Blanc
R. des Alpes
Q. du Mont-Blanc
R. de Chantepoulet
Bd James Fazy
R. des Terreaux du Temple
Rue Rousseau
LAC LÉMAN
JET D'EAU
Quai des Bergues
Pont du Mont-Blanc
PIERRE DU NITON
1
1
ÎLE J. J. ROUSSEAU
Quai Turrettini
Pt de la Coulouvrenière
Quai Général Guisan
Rue du Rhône
JARDIN ANGLAIS
R. de la Confédération
Thai
Pl. du Molard
Place Longemalle
Swissôtel Métropole
R. Pierre Fatio
Rue du Stand
R. du Marché
De la Cigogne
R. de Rive
Roberto
Rue d' Italie
Rond-Point de Rive
Boulevard Helvétique
Boulevard
Rue du Général Dutour
Bd du Théâtre
R. de la Corraterie
Grand' Rue
M
MAISON TAVEL
Les Armures
Tiffany
M
Place Neuve
CATHÉDRALE ST-PIERRE
R. de la Croix Rouge
H
Pl. du Bourg de Four
R. Dalcroze
Georges Favon
Promde des Bastions
MONUMENT DE LA RÉFORMATION
MUSÉE D'ART ET D'HISTOIRE
F. Hodler
2
2
U
U
VIEILLE VILLE
Jacques
Helvétique
Avenue du Mail
PLAINE DE PLAINPALAIS
Rue de Candolle
BIBLIOTHÈQUE UNIVERSITAIRE
COLLECTIONS BAUR
Rond-Point de Plainpalais
R. St. Léger
Boulevard
PETIT PALAIS
Avenue Henri Dunant
Rue de Carouge
Boulevard des Philosophes
LES TRANCHÉES
Bd des Tranchées
La Cantine des Commerçants
Pl. E. Claparède
Avenue du Mail
Rue de la Cluse
Avenue de Champel
Boulevard du Pont d'Arve
PLAINPALAIS
Rue Martin
La Cour des Augustins
Lombard
Rue Dancet
3
3
Rue Dizerens
Rue Prévost
Roseraie
Thury
ARVE
Chemin
Av. de Champel
R. A. Jentzer
Avenue de la
Beau Séjour
Av. de
Place des Augustins
Historical and Commercial Centre (Plan III)
G
Boulevard
0
200m
H
Hotel
Restaurant

La Cour des Augustins without rest

15 r. Jean-Violette ✉ 1205 – ☎ 022 322 21 00
– www.lacourdesaugustins.com **G3**
40 rm – †295/400 CHF ††345/450 CHF, ☕ 24 CHF – 8 suites
♦ Historic ♦ Business ♦ Design ♦
This establishment's concept is "boutique, gallery, designer hotel". It is favoured for its ultramodern minimalist luxury (made in Switzerland), within a building from 1850!

Brasserie du Parc des Eaux-Vives

82 quai Gustave-Ador ✉ 1207 – ☎ 022 849 75 75
– www.parcdeseauxvives.ch *Plan I* **D2**
Rest – Menu 62 CHF (lunch)/98 CHF – Carte 68/98 CHF
♦ Modern ♦ Trendy ♦
This elegant, modern brasserie is on the ground floor of the Eaux-Vives park lodge. Enjoy the contemporary cuisine, a fine view of the lake and the inviting teak terrace.

Roberto

10 r. Pierre-Fatio ✉ 1204 – ☎ 022 311 80 33
– Closed Saturday dinner and Sunday **H2**
Rest – *(booking advisable)* Carte 67/95 CHF
♦ Italian ♦ Classic ♦
Enjoy a touch of the 'dolce vita' in this Italian restaurant renowned for its warm decor and authentic cuisine. It goes without saying that the pasta is home-made!

La Cantine des Commerçants

29 bd Carl Vogt ✉ 1205 – ☎ 022 328 16 70 – www.lacantine.ch
– Closed Christmas - early January, 1 - 15 August and Sunday **G3**
Rest – Menu 32 CHF (lunch) – Carte 52/110 CHF
♦ International ♦ Design ♦
A modern bistro serving up-to-date fare at reasonable prices. Fresh colours and contemporary or vintage furniture create a stylish interior. Large summer terrace on the pavement.

Buffet de la Gare des Eaux-Vives (Serge Labrosse)

7 av. de la Gare des Eaux-Vives ✉ 1207
– ☎ 022 840 44 30 – www.lebuffetdelagare.ch
– Closed 23 December - 9 January, 23 July – 15 August and Saturday - Sunday *Plan I* **C3**
Rest – Menu 55 CHF (lunch)/135 CHF – Carte 103/148 CHF
Spec. Raviole et médaillons de homard, petit pois, kumquat et céleri croquant. Cube de poitrine de cochon confit. Le rouget, rouille et croûtons safranés.
♦ Inventive ♦ Classic ♦
A charming location and a chef renowned on the Geneva gourmet scene. Light modern setting, terrace on the quay, creative cuisine inspired by the Mediterranean and a good cellar of wines from Switzerland and the Rhone.

Thai

3 r. Neuve-du-Molard ✉ 1204 – ☎ 022 310 12 54
– www.thai-geneve.com
– Closed Sunday **H1**
Rest – Menu 85/98 CHF – Carte 65/101 CHF
♦ Asian ♦ Fashionable ♦
This establishment is sensational in its oriental-style design, in perfect harmony with the chef's dishes. These offer a modern day twist to Thai culinary heritage.

ENVIRONS AND COINTRIN AIRPORT *Plan I*

La Réserve

301 rte de Lausanne – ✆ 022 959 59 59 – www.lareserve.ch **C1**
102 rm – ♦490/600 CHF ♦♦590/750 CHF, ☕ 45 CHF – 17 suites
Rest *Le Loti* – *✆ 022 959 59 79* – Carte 71/150 CHF
Rest *Tsé-Fung* – *✆ 022 959 58 88* – Carte 69/155 CHF
♦ Grand Luxury ♦ Design ♦

This luxury hotel boasts modern rooms and suites with terraces, most of which overlook the park and swimming pool. Magnificent decor designed by Garcia, plus a superb spa. Italian specialities and an exotic decor. Both the cuisine and the elegant decor at the Tsé-Fung have a Chinese flavour.

Starling

34 rte François-Peyrot – ✆ 022 747 02 02 – www.shgeneva.ch **B1**
496 rm – ♦295/600 CHF ♦♦295/600 CHF, ☕ 39 CHF
Rest *Starling Café* – *✆ 022 747 02 47 (closed Saturday - Sunday) (lunch only)* Menu 55 CHF (lunch) – Carte 65/103 CHF
Rest *L'Olivo* – *✆ 022 747 04 00 (closed 19 December - 1 January)* Menu 55 CHF (lunch)/95 CHF – Carte 70/99 CHF
♦ Business ♦ Contemporary ♦

This American-style hotel is near the airport and Palexpo. It focuses on business and conference tourism. There are modern or traditional-style guestrooms and some leisure facilities. Art-deco design and international cuisine feature at the Starling Café. The Olivo has a real Mediterranean feel with its Italian cuisine and attractive terrace.

NH Geneva Airport

21 av. de Mategnin – ✆ 022 989 90 00 – www.nh-hotels.com **A2**
190 rm – ♦160/400 CHF ♦♦160/400 CHF, ☕ 30 CHF
Rest *Le Pavillon* – Carte 53/90 CHF
♦ Chain hotel ♦ Design ♦

This red brick hotel has a distinctive circular shape in keeping with its modern-style interiors. Find well-maintained rooms and a designer lobby with an attractive bar. Enjoy up-to-date cuisine in a modern setting under the Pavillon's dome.

Suitehotel

28 av. Louis-Casaï – ✆ 022 710 46 46 – www.suite-hotel.com **B2**
86 rm – ♦212/270 CHF ♦♦212/270 CHF, ☕ 13 CHF
Rest *Swiss Bistro* – *(closed Saturday and Sunday)* Carte 44/70 CHF
♦ Chain hotel ♦ Modern ♦

This colourful business hotel is located between the airport and the town centre. It has modern rooms with multimedia systems, and an office-cum-lounge area separated by a sliding door. Self-service cafeteria. Brasserie with a modern setting. Its bistro-type menu has Swiss touches.

Auberge du Lion d'Or (Thomas Byrne et Gilles Dupont)

5 pl. Pierre-Gautier – ✆ 022 736 44 32 – www.liondor.ch
– Closed 24 December - 17 January and Saturday - Sunday **D2**
Rest – Menu 75 CHF (lunch)/220 CHF – Carte 149/192 CHF
Rest *Le Bistro de Cologny* – *(closed 24 December - 10 January and Saturday - Sunday)* Menu 49 CHF (lunch)/90 CHF – Carte 79/124 CHF
Spec. Ravioles de crabe royal du Kamtchatka. Loup de mer en croûte de sel marin. Filet mignon de veau à la poêle, crémée de morilles au vin jaune.
♦ Modern ♦ Elegant ♦

Selected products cooked with audacity and creativity by four hands! Also find: a sought after wine cellar, professional service, and a romantic view over the lake from the dining room, lounge/bar/smoking room and charming terrace. This modern bistro has an attractive outdoor terrace.

XXXX ✿✿

Domaine de Châteauvieux (Philippe Chevrier) with rm

16 ch. de Châteauvieux (Satigny, West: 10 km) – ✆ 022 753 15 11 – www.chateauvieux.ch – Closed 24 December - 10 January, 17 - 25 April, 24 July – 8 August and Sunday - Monday

13 rm – 340/480 CHF 340/480 CHF

Rest – *(booking advisable)* Menu 92 CHF (lunch)/290 CHF Carte 200/324 CHF

Spec. Les Cannellones au tartare de veau parfumés au basilic. La côte et filet d'agneau, confit d'épaule aux aubergines. Le Saint-Honoré à la crème chiboust, croustillant et glace caramel.

♦ Innovative ♦ Luxury ♦

In the heart of the Geneva vineyards, this old farm has high ceilings, stone walls and ancient beams. Philippe Chevrier puts his mark on it with sought-after French gastronomy and a prestigious wine list. Stylish rooms with excellent bedding and modern bathrooms. Carefully prepared breakfast.

XX ✿

Le Cigalon (Jean-Marc Bessire)

*39 rte d'Ambilly (South-East: 5 km by Route de Chêne **D3**) – ✆ 022 349 97 33 – www.le-cigalon.ch – Closed Christmas, 31 December - 10 January, 21 - 30 April, 24 July – 16 August and Sunday - Monday*

Rest – Menu 54 CHF (lunch)/140 CHF – Carte 84/118 CHF

Spec. Saumon d'Ecosse façon "Maki Sushi", saladine aux algues. Rouget barbet grillé sur peau croustillante, panisse à la farine de pois-chiche. Saint Pierre rôti, risotto au basilic Thaïlandais.

♦ Fish ♦ Family ♦

The best of the small catches from the Breton and Mediterranean coasts are transformed in ever-changing recipes. Find an ocean decor, chef's table in the kitchen and a rear terrace. Sound advice regarding the choice of wines.

XX

Le Relais de Chambésy

8 pl. de Chambésy – ✆ 022 758 11 05 – www.relaisdechambesy.ch – Closed 22 December - 9 January, 23 July - 8 August, Saturday lunch and Sunday

Rest – Menu 36 CHF (lunch)/108 CHF – Carte 63/105 CHF **C1**

♦ French ♦ Rustic ♦

This restaurant combines charm and tradition in the heart of Chambésy. French-style cuisine served in several dining rooms or on the attractive terrace in summer.

X

Le Vallon

182 rte de Florissant – ✆ 022 347 11 04 – www.restaurant-vallon.com – Closed Christmas - early January and Sunday - Monday **D3**

Rest – *(booking advisable)* Menu 52 CHF (lunch)/88 CHF – Carte 78/113 CHF

♦ Traditional ♦ Bistro ♦

This restaurant has a pink, wisteria-adorned façade, a cheerful, old-fashioned bistro decor, and a vine-covered pergola-terrace. Menu choices are highlighted on a slate board or on easels placed on the table.

X

Café des Négociants

29 r. de la Filature – ✆ 022 300 31 30 – www.negociants.ch – Closed 24 December - 2 January and Saturday - Sunday **C3**

Rest – *(booking advisable)* Menu 29 CHF (lunch)/88 CHF Carte 61/104 CHF

♦ Seasonal cuisine ♦ Brasserie ♦

Sample delicious seasonal cuisine served in a nostalgic bistro setting or on the summer terrace. Well-stocked and superbly compiled wine list.

X

L'Altitude

13 rte de l'Aeroport – ✆ 022 817 46 09 – www.altitude-geneva.ch

Rest – Menu 65 CHF (lunch) – Carte 86/103 CHF **A1**

♦ International ♦ Fashionable ♦

Restaurant located on level three of the airport (arrivals). Modern decor, cosmopolitan flavours, lounge-style bar, meeting rooms, and a view of the runway and the Alps. Buffet only on Saturday and Sunday lunchtimes.

Zurich

Zürich

Population (est.2010): 382 906 (conurbation 1 081 700) – Altitude: 409m

rubi/Fotolia.com

Zurich has a lot of things going for it. A lot of history (two thousand years' worth), a lot of water (two rivers and a huge lake), a lot of beauty (its old town is a visual feast), and, let's face it, a lot of wealth (it's Switzerland's richest city). It's an important financial and commercial centre, and has a well-earned reputation for good living with a rich cultural life, reflected in an abundance of smart restaurants and outdoor cafés.

The place strikes a nice balance – it's large enough to boast some world-class facilities but small enough to hold on to its charm and old-world ambience. The window-shopping here sets it apart from many other European cities – from tiny boutiques and specialist emporiums to a shopping boulevard that's famed across the globe. Although it's not Switzerland's political capital, it's the spiritual one because of its pulsing arts scene: for those who might think the Swiss a bit staid, think again – this is where the nihilistic, anti-art Dada movement began.

LIVING THE CITY

The attractive **Lake Zurich** flows northwards into the city, which forms a pleasingly symmetrical arc around it. From the lake, the river **Limmat** bisects Zurich, flowing north until it reaches another river, the narrower **Sihl.** On the Limmat's west bank lies the **Old Town**, the medieval hub, overlooked by two dominant churches. The stylishly vibrant **Bahnhofstrasse**, the smartest shopping street in town, follows the line of the former city walls. Across the Limmat on the east side, the unmissable landmark is the magnificent twin-towered **Grossmünster**, while just beyond is the charmingly historic district of **Niederdorf**. Way down south is the city's largest green space, the **Zürichhorn Park.**

PRACTICAL INFORMATION

ARRIVAL-DEPARTURE

Zurich International Airport (Kloten) is located 10km north of the city. Trains run every 10-15min and take 10min. A taxi will be about 50CHF. Zürich Hauptbahnhof is the main railway station for international and inter-city trains.

TRANSPORT

As this is Switzerland, you can guarantee that the public transport system runs like clockwork. The city operates an efficient system on bus, tram, metro, train and boat. You can buy a single ticket, day ticket, or 9 o'clock Pass. Tickets are available from ticket machines and tourist offices. Remember to validate your ticket at the ticket machine or special orange-coloured machine before boarding.

The Zurichcard grants unlimited travel on all public transport (including river and lake boats). It also gives you admission to more than forty museums and art collections. The card can be purchased for twenty-four or seventy-two hours.

Cycle riding is encouraged here. Hire bikes for free for the day from beside the main railway station. All you have to do is leave ID and a local currency deposit.

EXPLORING ZURICH

Mention Zurich and your first thoughts may turn to bankers and precision timing. But Zurich is a beautiful, medieval city that has been a respected base of European culture for centuries. To wander round and about the alleyways of its Old Town (the **Altstadt**) is to explore a fascinating labyrinth of cobbled streets, flower-filled squares and ancient pastel-shaded houses. Momentous events have happened here. In the cobbled **Münsterhof Square**, in the Old Town's heart, Winston Churchill delivered a famous speech after World War II, declaring "Europe Arise!" in praise of a postwar European union. These words are on a plaque set into the cobbles, a reminder that this city

has played a recognisable part in the continent's history. Further proof is just over the water at the imposing Grossmünster, where the zealous preaching of radical cleric Huldrych Zwingli set in motion the wheels of the sixteenth-century Reformation.

➔ BAHN-STORMER

The plaque to Churchill is no more than a cuckoo's call from the Bahnhofstrasse, a mile-long, tram-packed avenue stretching south to the edge of Lake Zurich. The city's commercial centre, Bahnhoffstrasse is lined with upmarket shops and chic restaurants, its gravitas enhanced by the headquarters of several major Swiss banks. Between it and the river lies a warren of medieval lanes full of small, individual shops selling a range of quirky things. Act like a smart local, and get some respite from the bustle by ducking into the lanes that head up to the **Lindenhof.** This tree-covered hill is where Zurich began: the Romans founded a customs post here as early as the first century BC. It's a delightful spot to take a rest; an observation platform gives you views of the surrounding rooftops and the Limmat gliding along below. There's a giant chessboard on the hill-top where old boys wreathed in concentration search for checkmate underneath the lime trees.

On this west side of the Limmat there are two distinctive churches, less than two hundred metres apart. The **Church of St Peter**, whose main body is exactly three hundred years old, seems to be an ideal landmark for the punctual Swiss: its clockface, at twenty-eight feet in diameter, is the largest in Europe, so you'll know if you have the time to nip south a little way and pay a visit to **Fraumünster**. This is a graceful building whose history stretches back over a thousand years, but its main claim to fame is more recent. The breathtaking stained glass windows were added in 1970, and were the inspiration of Marc Chagall. They're a delicious fusion of ethereal light and colour.

➔ SWISS ROLE

At the top end of Bahnhofstrasse, past the grand railway station, is the equally imposing **Swiss National Museum**. Ideal for a rainy day, this vast collection covers everything you'll need to know about Switzerland from prehistoric times to the 21C. Its main highlight is a beautifully preserved 18C Benedictine pharmacy. Head across the river, though, for the top cultural attraction of the city: if you go on past the Grossmünster, you'll reach the **Kunsthaus**, Switzerland's premier art gallery. It's easy to get round, and its permanent art collection is outstanding. You can admire thrilling paintings by Swiss artists such as Giacometti and Fussli, plus a broad range of work that takes in medieval religious paintings, Dutch Old Masters, Impressionists and Surrealists. Dadaists are there too, of course, but it might be fun to see their actual birthplace before encountering them at the Kunsthaus. For this, stroll up through the pretty eastern section of the Altstadt – Niederdorf – till you come to the near-mystical **Cabaret Voltaire** on the corner of **Niederdorfstrasse** and **Spiegelgasse**. This updated café-bar and arts centre is where artist Tristan Tzara and like-minded refugees from World War I founded an avant-garde artistic movement in 1916 as an anarchic reaction against all the horrifying carnage – Dada.

➔ LOOK WHO'S AT THE ODEON

At the same time as Tzara and his pals were in the process of revolutionising art, guess who was down the road killing time before the armistice ? None other than James Joyce and Vladimir Ilyich Lenin. They'd both become devotees of another legendary Zurich watering hole, the **Café Odeon** (although, unfortunately, there's no record of them ever having met). What would have captivated the great writer and the great revolutionary was the wonderful atmosphere of this Viennese-style coffee house. Looking out over bustling **Bellevueplatz**, the Café Odeon had, and still has, all the grand trimmings, including plate-glass windows, polished red marble and deep leather armchairs.

➜ GO WEST

The shock of the new has slammed into Zurich. Go north of the main station and you'll come to Zurich West. But this is no railway terminus; it's the evolutionary outcome of the city's vibrant cultural scene and its cutting-edge reputation in the worlds of fashion and design. Zurich West is set in a former industrial and red light area that's taken on a new life. It's now an arty warehouse zone with a funky, chic, up-and-coming feel. Full of clubs, cinemas and restaurants, it's centred round **Langstrasse**, a road crisscrossed by flyovers and railway bridges, and is the complete antithesis to the idea of Zurich as an icy financial centre.

➜ LAKE ARRIVAL

Search out a more peaceful, relaxing vibe at the other end of the city. If you head south from Grossmünster, there's a delightful narrow strip of parkland running parallel to the lake's eastern shore alongside the arrow-straight **Utoquai**. It's full of trees and flowerbeds and ends up at the idyllically set Zürichhorn Park, which rubs verdant shoulders with the wide expanses of Lake Zurich. From here, watch the boats in and out of the Limmat: catch one yourself from the city's landing stage at **Bürkliplatz**. A trip on the water is a must here. The lovely forty-kilometre lake stretches in an arc from Zurich to the foot of the Alps. There's a good choice of trips, from short sorties to cruises of half a day, taking in a range of lakeshore towns and villages. The water is crystal clear and unpolluted, so if you fancy, you can take a dip, too.

On your walk down Utoquai, you might like to take a little detour at **Falkenstrasse** and check out the glorious **Opera House**. Better still, try and get some tickets for a performance. This is one of Europe's leading opera and ballet theatres, a neo-Baroque beauty, designed by nineteenth century Viennese architects who knew a thing or two about this kind of opulence.

CALENDAR HIGHLIGHTS

Zurich's renown as a cultural leader reaches its annual highpoint at the Zurich Festival, every June and July, during which much of the city

ZURICH IN...

➜ ONE DAY
Old Town, Bahnhofstrasse, Zurich West, Grossmünster

➜ TWO DAYS
Watch the chessplayers on Lindenhof, see Chagall's glorious windows at Fraumünster, Kunsthaus, Cabaret Voltaire, Café Odeon

➜ THREE DAYS
Utoquai, Zürichhorn Park, a night at the Opera House

resounds to international music, opera, theatre and dance, and thousands pour in to visit the performances. Theatre lovers can indulge their habit for longer at August's Theatre Spectacle, where innovative productions take centre stage, while in September athletics fans flock to the Letzigrund Stadium – the 'magic track' – for the legendary Weltklasse, which in 2008 celebrated eighty years of the event. The Zurich International Art Fair at Kongresshaus in October features everything from painting to sculpture and photography to video, but by then many will be outdoors in training for December's Silvesterlauf, a festively decorated race through the Old Town in which ten thousand competitors select various distances to run. February's Art On Ice at Hallenstadium is a 'feelgood' mix of musical stars, ice skaters and dynamic lightshow, while the same month's Carnival Procession transforms the city centre into a garish float-fest, highlighted by guggen music, when groups of musicians and non-musicians bang out an impromptu blast of rhythms, culminating in the Guggen Monster Concert in Münsterhof Square.

EATING OUT

Zurich stands out in Switzerland (along with Geneva) for its top-class restaurants serving international cuisine. Zurich, though, takes the prize when it comes to trendy, cutting-edge places to dine, whether restaurant or bar, whether along the lakeside or in the converted loft of an old factory. In the middle of the day, most locals go for the cheaper daily lunchtime menus, saving themselves for the glories of the evening. The city is host to many traditional, longstanding Italian restaurants, but if you want to try something 'totally Zurcher', you can't do any better than tackle geschnetzeltes with rösti: sliced veal fried in butter, simmered with onions and mushrooms, with a dash of white wine and cream, served with hashed brown potatoes. A good place for simple restaurants and bars is Niederdorf, while Zurich West is coming on strong with its twenty first century zeitgeist diners. When you're happy with the service you usually round up a small bill or leave up to ten percent on a larger one.

➜ PANORAMA

Take a 15-minute train journey from the main station for quite simply the very best view of Zurich. Known to Zurchers as the 'top of Zurich', Uetliberg is an 871m mountain with a forested mountain ridge, lush green meadows, tinkling cowbells and, best of all, fantastic 360-degree views of the city, the lake and the Alps. The train will take you to the summit, or you can walk up yourself: it should take a fit person about one and a half hours.

➜ AN ARTY BREW

An old brewery is now the home of two of Zurich's very best contemporary art museums. The former home of Löwenbräu in Limmatstrasse has been converted into bright, white rooms which house the Migros Museum, with its huge permanent collection, and the Kunsthalle Zurich, which puts on temporary exhibitions for up-and-coming stars of the art world.

➜ AND FINALLY...

In case anyone still thinks of Zurich as a staid place for intrepid clockwatchers: it has the highest density of pavement cafés in the world; its opera house has staged more premieres than any other; and its river and lake are home to no less than eighteen sandy beaches.

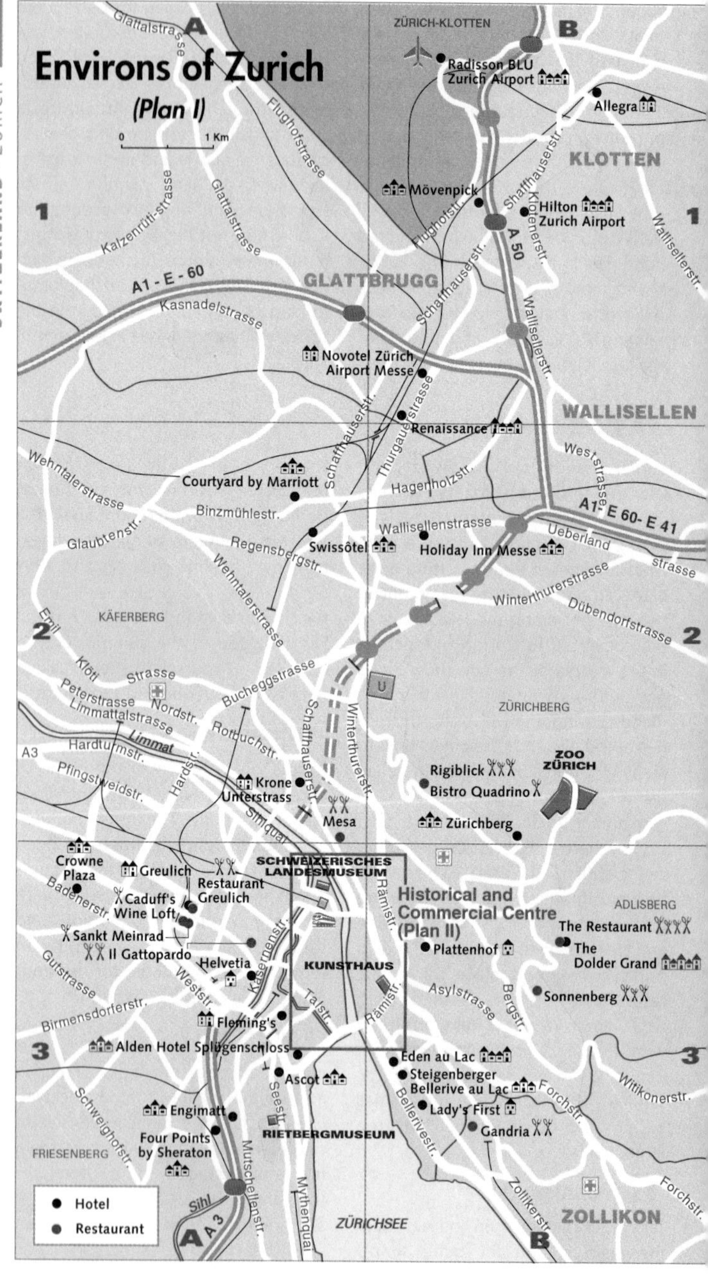
Environs of Zurich
(Plan I)
0
1 Km
ZÜRICH-KLOTTEN
Radisson BLU Zurich Airport
Allegra
KLOTTEN
Mövenpick
Hilton Zurich Airport
GLATTBRUGG
A1 - E - 60
Novotel Zürich Airport Messe
WALLISELLEN
Renaissance
Courtyard by Marriott
A1- E 60- E 41
Swissôtel
Holiday Inn Messe
KÄFERBERG
ZÜRICHBERG
ZOO ZÜRICH
Rigiblick
Bistro Quadrino
Krone Unterstrass
Mesa
Zürichberg
SCHWEIZERISCHES LANDESMUSEUM
Historical and Commercial Centre (Plan II)
ADLISBERG
The Restaurant
The Dolder Grand
Crowne Plaza
Greulich
Restaurant Greulich
Caduff's Wine Loft
Sankt Meinrad
Il Gattopardo
Helvetia
KUNSTHAUS
Plattenhof
Sonnenberg
Fleming's
Alden Hotel Splügenschloss
Eden au Lac
Ascot
Steigenberger Bellerive au Lac
Lady's First
Engimatt
Gandria
Four Points by Sheraton
RIETBERGMUSEUM
FRIESENBERG
ZÜRICHSEE
ZOLLIKON
Hotel
Restaurant
Glattalstrasse
Flughofstrasse
Kalzenrüti-strasse
Kasnadelstrasse
Schaffhauserstr.
Thurgauerstrasse
Wallisellerstr.
Klotenerstr.
Weststrasse
Wehntalerstrasse
Binzmühlestr.
Glaubtenstr.
Regensbergstr.
Hagenholzstr.
Wallisellenstrasse
Ueberlandstrasse
Winterthurerstrasse
Dübendorfstrasse
Bucheggstrasse
Rotbuchstr.
Peterstrasse
Limmattalstrasse
Nordstr.
Limmat
Hardturmstr.
Pfingstweidstr.
Hardstr.
Sihlquai
Rämistr.
Badenerstr.
Gutstrasse
Weststr.
Kasernenstr.
Talstr.
Asylstrasse
Bergstr.
Birmensdorferstr.
Witikonerstr.
Forchstr.
Seestr.
Bellerivestr.
Schweighofstr.
Mutschellenstr.
Mythenquai
Zollikerstr.
Sihl
A3
A 50
A
B
1
2
3

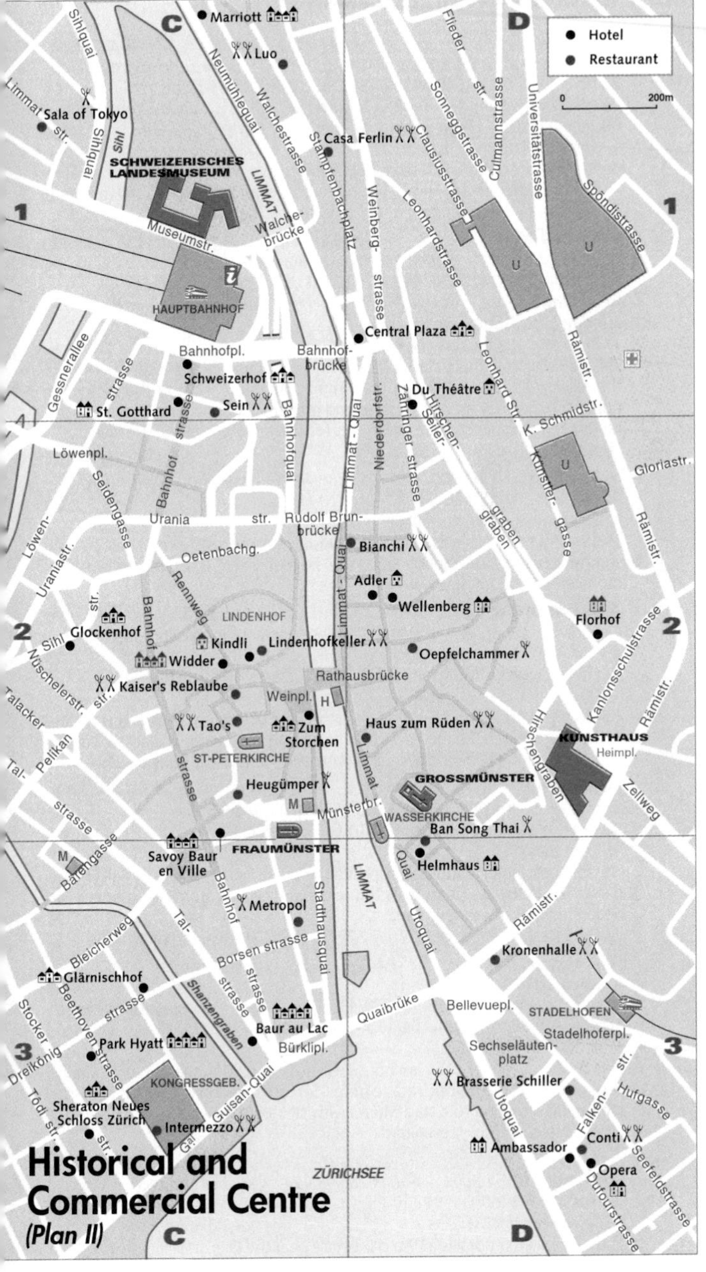

Historical and Commercial Centre
(Plan II)

Marriott

Neumühlequai 42 ✉ 8001 – ✆ 044 360 70 70 – www.zurichmarriott.com
264 rm – 380/435 CHF 380/435 CHF, 39 CHF – 9 suites **C1**
Rest *White Elephant* – *(closed Saturday lunch and Sunday lunch)* Carte 64/79 CHF **Rest *Echo*** – *(dinner only)* Carte 36/92 CHF
♦ Chain hotel ♦ Classic ♦
Beside the river, this multi-storey building has its own underground parking. The rooms differ in size and layout but are all comfortable and contemporary. This restaurant has a modern design and serves Thai food.

Central Plaza

Central 1 ✉ 8001 – ✆ 044 256 56 56 – www.central.ch **D1**
105 rm – 395/420 CHF 395/420 CHF, 18 CHF – 4 suites
Rest *King's Cave* – *✆ 044 256 55 55 (closed Saturday lunch and Sunday lunch)* Carte 61/85 CHF
♦ Business ♦ Modern ♦
This 1883 hotel with its classic façade and spacious lobby is located opposite the railway station and beside the Limmat. Although most of the rooms are not very large, they are comfortable and modern. Find the King's Cave grill restaurant in the vaulted cellar, which was formerly part of the UBS Treasury.

Wellenberg without rest

Niederdorfstr. 10 ✉ 8001 – ✆ 043 888 44 44 – www.hotel-wellenberg.ch
45 rm – 325/420 CHF 420/470 CHF **D2**
♦ Business ♦ Modern ♦
This well-run hotel is in the old town. Most of the rooms are cosy, modern and surprisingly spacious, though some are simpler. There is a pleasant breakfast room with a good buffet.

Ambassador

Falkenstr. 6 ✉ 8008 – ✆ 044 258 98 98 – www.ambassadorhotel.ch
45 rm – 265/480 CHF 395/580 CHF, 28 CHF **D3**
Rest *A l'Opera* – Menu 36 CHF (lunch) – Carte 45/110 CHF
♦ Townhouse ♦ Cosy ♦
This former patrician house is located on the edge of the city centre and very close to the opera house. The rooms have contemporary furnishings and are well-equipped. Restaurant A l'Opera is decorated with wall paintings and Opera scenes.

Opera without rest

Dufourstr. 5 ✉ 8008 – ✆ 044 258 99 99 – www.operahotel.ch
58 rm – 250/330 CHF 350/510 CHF, 26 CHF **D3**
♦ Business ♦ Cosy ♦
This business hotel is situated opposite the opera house, which has given it its name. The lobby area is stylishly laid out, and the guestrooms are modern and decorated in warm tones.

Florhof

Florhofgasse 4 ✉ 8001 – ✆ 044 250 26 26 – www.florhof.ch – Closed 24 - 30 December **D2**
35 rm – 250/315 CHF 370/415 CHF **Rest** – *(closed Saturday lunch, Sunday – Monday)* Menu 86/110 CHF – Carte 84/101 CHF
♦ Traditional ♦ Personalised ♦
This beautiful, former patrician house will not disappoint guests seeking individuality. Behind the historic façade from 1576 are hidden cosy rooms furnished with great attention to detail. More lavish still are the two junior suites in the attic. An elegant, cosy restaurant.

Helmhaus without rest

Schifflände 30 ✉ 8001 – ✆ 044 266 95 95 – www.helmhaus.ch
24 rm – 260 CHF 350 CHF **D3**
♦ Townhouse ♦ Cosy ♦
This carefully run hotel is in the city centre near the lake. It will impress with its cosy, good value and up-to-date furnishings. There is a friendly and modern breakfast room.

Du Théâtre without rest

Seilergraben 69 ✉ 8001 – ✆ 044 267 26 70 – www.hotel-du-theatre.ch

50 rm – 195/265 CHF 275/320 CHF, 19 CHF **D1**

◆ Townhouse ◆ Modern ◆

On the edge of the old city and just a short walk from the main railway station, this hotel offers modern guestrooms equipped with the latest technology. Enjoy a small range of international dishes in the La Suite lounge.

Adler

Rosengasse 10 (at Hirschenplatz) ✉ 8001 – ✆ 044 266 96 96 – www.hotel-adler.ch **D2**

52 rm – 155/240 CHF 195/310 CHF

Rest *Swiss Chuchi* – Carte 43/80 CHF

◆ Business ◆ Functional ◆

This hotel offers bright, modern guestrooms equipped with the latest technology and decorated with paintings depicting views of Zürich's old town by contemporary artist Heinz Blum. Enjoy the rustic atmosphere in the Swiss Chuchi, located on the street.

Conti

Dufourstr. 1 ✉ 8008 – ✆ 044 251 06 66 – www.bindella.ch **D3**

Rest – Carte 66/118 CHF

◆ Italian ◆ Formal ◆

This restaurant is immediately next to the opera. Find an interior of classical dignity with a lovely high stucco ceiling, an exhibition of paintings, and Italian cuisine.

Haus zum Rüden

Limmatquai 42 (1st floor) ✉ 8001 – ✆ 044 261 95 66 – www.hauszumrueden.ch – Closed Saturday and Sunday **D2**

Rest – Menu 63 CHF (lunch)/138 CHF – Carte 78/129 CHF

◆ Classic ◆ Formal ◆

Surprisingly, the restaurant ceiling in this lovely 13C Guildhall is made of wooden barrels. Pleasant historical ambience and a classic menu.

Bianchi

Limmatquai 82 ✉ 8001 – ✆ 044 262 98 44 – www.ristorante-bianchi.ch

Rest – Menu 45/98 CHF – Carte 50/114 CHF **D2**

◆ Fish ◆ Fashionable ◆

This friendly, contemporary restaurant is located in a traffic-free zone close to the River Limmat. You can select your own fish and seafood from the generous buffet.

Kronenhalle

Rämistr. 4 ✉ 8001 – ✆ 044 262 99 00 – www.kronenhalle.com

Rest – *(booking advisable)* Carte 81/126 CHF **D3**

◆ Traditional ◆ Formal ◆

This building, constructed in 1862, is a Zurich institution located on Bellevue Square. Be sure to take a look at the art collection put together over a period of decades. The atmosphere is traditional, as is the cooking.

Brasserie Schiller

Goethestr. 10 ✉ 8001 – ✆ 044 222 20 30 – www.brasserie-schiller.ch

Rest – Menu 40 CHF (lunch)/115 CHF – Carte 49/129 CHF **D3**

◆ Classic ◆ Brasserie ◆

This pleasant, modern restaurant serves classic cuisine in the Neue Zürcher Zeitung building. In the evening a special opera menu is served until midnight.

Casa Ferlin

Stampfenbachstr. 38 ✉ 8006 – ✆ 044 362 35 09 – www.casaferlin.ch – Closed mid July – mid August and Saturday - Sunday **C-D1**

Rest – *(booking advisable)* Menu 54 CHF (lunch)/105 CHF – Carte 64/122 CHF

◆ Italian ◆ Family ◆

A traditional, family-run establishment with a classic, countrified atmosphere. The restaurant was first opened in 1907 and offers Italian cooking.

Luo – Hotel Continental

Stampfenbachstr. 60 ✉ 8006 – ✆ 043 810 00 65
– Closed 25 July - 14 August, Saturday lunch and Sunday **C1**
Rest – Menu 65/95 CHF – Carte 46/93 CHF
♦ Chinese ♦ Friendly ♦
Brick walls and a beautiful wooden ceiling give this restaurant a cared for, rustic feel. Delicious Chinese cuisine is on offer.

Oepfelchammer

Rindermarkt 12 (1st floor) ✉ 8001 – ✆ 044 251 23 36 – www.oepfelchammer.ch
– Closed 24 December – 4 January, 2 - 5 April, 19 July - 16 August, Sunday – Monday and Bank Holidays **D2**
Rest – Carte 58/82 CHF
♦ Traditional ♦ Rustic ♦
The poet Gottfried Keller was a regular of the original wine bar. The restaurant serves modern and traditional cuisine in this 19C building.

Ban Song Thai

Kirchgasse 6 ✉ 8001 – ✆ 044 252 33 31 – www.bansongthai.ch
– Closed Christmas - early January, 18 July - 7 August, Saturday lunch and Sunday
Rest – *(booking advisable)* Carte 41/75 CHF **D2**
♦ Asian ♦ Friendly ♦
This restaurant is located near the Kunsthaus and Grossmünster. It offers authentic Thai cuisine made from fresh products - as a lunchtime buffet or from a more extensive evening menu.

LEFT BANK OF THE RIVER LIMMAT *Plan II*

Baur au Lac

rm,

Talstr. 1 ✉ 8001 – ✆ 044 220 50 20 – www.bauraulac.ch **C3**
120 rm – †540/870 CHF ††870/1050 CHF, ☕ 42 CHF – 18 suites
Rest *Le Pavillon* – *✆ 044 220 50 22* – Menu 98 CHF (lunch)/240 CHF – Carte 116/162 CHF
Rest *Rive Gauche* – *✆ 044 220 50 60 (closed mid July - mid August, Sunday and Bank Holidays)* Carte 71/116 CHF
♦ Grand Luxury ♦ Elegant ♦
This imposing 19C hotel is sublime. It has a spacious lobby, luxurious rooms, and a lovely garden area. Le Pavillon serves Mediterranean cuisine. The Rive Gauche is fashionable and endearing.

Park Hyatt

Beethovenstr. 21 ✉ 8002 – ✆ 043 883 12 34 – www.zurich.park.hyatt.ch
142 rm – †480/1550 CHF ††630/1700 CHF, ☕ 47 CHF – 4 suites **C3**
Rest *Parkhuus* – *✆ 043 883 10 75 (closed Saturday lunch and Sunday)* Menu 59 CHF (lunch)/92 CHF – Carte 61/120 CHF
♦ Grand Luxury ♦ Modern ♦
The Park Hyatt has a large, elegant hall and a lobby area with an entrance to the striking Onyx Bar. It features stylish and modern rooms with lots of space, and a tasteful little spa. The elegant Parkhuus has a show kitchen and a glazed wine cellar on two floors.

Savoy Baur en Ville

Poststr. 12 (at Paradeplatz) ✉ 8001 – ✆ 044 215 25 25 – www.savoy-zuerich.ch
113 rm ☕ – †530/800 CHF ††780/840 CHF – 8 suites **C3**
Rest *Baur* – *(closed Saturday and Sunday)* Menu 74 CHF (lunch) – Carte 98/150 CHF
Rest *Orsini* – *(booking advisable)* Menu 74 CHF (lunch) – Carte 98/144 CHF
♦ Grand Luxury ♦ Classic ♦
This hotel and its beautiful, classic structure from 1838, fulfils all expectations. Enjoy the tradition conscious, exemplary service and its luxurious high quality interiors. The Baur is a classic, elegant restaurant on the first-floor. The Italian alternative is the Orsini.

Widder

Rennweg 7 ✉ 8001 – ✆ 044 224 25 26 – www.widderhotel.ch
49 rm – 560/610 CHF 755/935 CHF, 48 CHF – 7 suites **C2**
Rest – *(closed Sunday)* Menu 48 CHF (lunch)/145 CHF – Carte 90/150 CHF
◆ Luxury ◆ Design ◆
With its central Zürich location, this exclusive and attentively run hotel provides first-class service. It comprises eight townhouses thoughtfully restored to create a successful combination of the historic and the contemporary. The Widder and Turm restaurants are both elegant, yet furnished in quite different styles. A shorter menu is available in the garden.

Schweizerhof

Bahnhofplatz 7 ✉ 8021 – ✆ 044 218 88 88 – www.hotelschweizerhof.com
115 rm – 470/580 CHF 580/770 CHF **C1**
Rest *La Soupière* – *✆ 044 218 88 40 (closed Saturday lunch and Sunday, July - August: Saturday and Sunday)* Carte 92/120 CHF
◆ Luxury ◆ Classic ◆
This classic, 19C city hotel has an imposing façade. It stands out because of its excellent service, cosy atmosphere, and central location at the start of the pedestrian zone. Particularly comfortable junior suites are available. This restaurant has an elegant style.

Glockenhof

Sihlstr. 31 ✉ 8022 – ✆ 044 225 91 91 – www.glockenhof.ch **C2**
91 rm – 330/380 CHF 440 CHF
Rest – Menu 55 CHF – Carte 40/93 CHF
◆ Business ◆ Stylish ◆
The rooms in this historic city centre hotel are all individually furnished to the latest design standards, some using local Swiss materials. The Conrad is a simple, elegant restaurant. The Glogge Egge is a simpler daytime restaurant.

Four Points by Sheraton

rest,

Kalandergasse 1 (Sihlcity) ✉ 8045
– ✆ 044 554 00 00 – www.fourpoints.com/zurich *Plan I* **A3**
132 rm – 280/490 CHF 280/490 CHF, 30 CHF – 4 suites
Rest *Rampe Süd* – *(closed Sunday)* Menu 64 CHF (dinner) – Carte 50/89 CHF
◆ Chain hotel ◆ Design ◆
This hotel is located in the Sihlcity with its large shopping centre. It has comfortable and technically well-equipped rooms with a first-class modern design. This fashionable restaurant offers international cuisine.

Zum Storchen

rm,

Weinplatz 2 ✉ 8001 – ✆ 044 227 27 27 – www.storchen.ch **C2**
67 rm – 430/560 CHF 600/760 CHF – 1 suite
Rest *Rôtisserie* – *✆ 044 227 21 13* – Menu 85/110 CHF – Carte 69/117 CHF
◆ Traditional ◆ Classic ◆
This traditional hotel, one of the oldest in town, is situated on the Limmat. The elegant yet comfortable rooms are decorated with material from Jouy. A beautiful terrace by the river extends the restaurant facilities and offers views of the old town.

Sheraton Neues Schloss Zürich

Stockerstr. 17 ✉ 8002 – ✆ 044 286 94 00
– www.sheraton.com/neuesschloss **C3**
60 rm – 360/620 CHF 360/620 CHF, 39 CHF – 1 suite
Rest *Le Jardin Suisse* – *(closed Saturday, Sunday and Bank Holidays)* Menu 45 CHF – Carte 63/88 CHF
◆ Business ◆ Classic ◆
This hotel is not far from the lake. It has modern, comfortable and technically well-equipped rooms decorated in warm colours. This restaurant offers traditional Swiss cuisine.

Glärnischhof

Claridenstr. 30 ✉ 8002 – ✆ 044 286 22 22 – www.hotelglaernischhof.ch
62 rm – 360/440 CHF 460/500 CHF **C3**
Rest *Le Poisson* – *(closed Saturday - Sunday and Bank Holidays)*
Menu 61 CHF (lunch)/119 CHF – Carte 66/100 CHF
Rest *Vivace* – Menu 61/119 CHF – Carte 48/80 CHF
♦ Business ♦ Classic ♦
This business hotel in the financial district has a tasteful lobby and contemporary, functional guestrooms equipped with the latest technology. As the name suggests: in Le Poisson you will eat fish!

St. Gotthard

Bahnhofstr. 87 ✉ 8021 – ✆ 044 227 77 00 – www.hotelstgotthard.ch
143 rm – 315/550 CHF 315/550 CHF, 33 CHF **C1**
Rest *Hummer- & Austernbar* – *✆ 044 211 76 21 (closed 17 July - 15 August and Sunday - Monday)* Menu 68 CHF (lunch)/145 CHF – Carte 90/172 CHF
Rest *Lobbybar-Bistro* – *✆ 044 211 76 25* – Menu 65 CHF – Carte 49/81 CHF
♦ Traditional ♦ Classic ♦
This hotel is rich in tradition, dates from 1889, and is just a stone's throw from the main station. It has a classical setting with guestrooms equipped in a predominantly modern style. The menu in this tastefully elegant restaurant features shellfish and French cuisine.

Kindli

Pfalzgasse 1 ✉ 8001 – ✆ 043 888 76 76 – www.kindli.ch **C2**
20 rm – 260/350 CHF 380/460 CHF
Rest *Zum Kindli* – *✆ 043 888 76 78 (closed Sunday)* Carte 69/102 CHF
♦ Traditional ♦ Cosy ♦
Steeped in tradition, this Zürich townhouse from 1474 is a unique family-run venture. It has attentive service and charming rooms. Good value, small, long-stay apartments are available in a neighbouring building. A subtle, elegant restaurant with modern cuisine.

Tao's

Augustinergasse 3 ✉ 8001 – ✆ 044 448 11 22 – www.taos-lounge.ch – Closed Sunday **C2**
Rest – Carte 63/109 CHF **Rest *Lounge*** – *(dinner only)* Carte 42/62 CHF
♦ Fusion ♦ Exotic ♦
The exotic, Far Eastern tone exhibited by this tasteful and elegant restaurant is reflected in its cuisine, which mixes traditional and Asian flavours. A less formal alternative is the beautiful lounge on the ground floor with its lovely terrace.

Sein (Martin Surbeck)

Schützengasse 5 ✉ 8001 – ✆ 044 221 10 65 – www.zuerichsein.ch – Closed 24 December - 3 January, 18 April - 1 May, 18 July - 7 August and Saturday - Sunday
Rest – Menu 80/160 CHF – Carte 78/132 CHF **C1**
Rest *Tapas Bar* – Carte 34/67 CHF
Spec. Störcarpaccio mit Kaviar. Geschmorte Kalbsbaggen mit gestossenem Kaffee auf Kartoffelstock und Eisbergsalat. Frisch gefrorene Glace mit Vanille und Fruchtsauce.
♦ Inventive ♦ Fashionable ♦
An appealing restaurant, reflected in the creative cuisine of the proprietor and the elegant, clean-lined, contemporary-style interior. The service is friendly and competent. The Tapas Bar serves bite-sized delicacies in a relaxed lounge atmosphere.

Lindenhofkeller

Pfalzgasse 4 ✉ 8001 – ✆ 044 211 70 71 – www.lindenhofkeller.ch – Closed 26 April - 1 May, 26 July - 13 August and Saturday - Sunday, November - December: Saturday lunch and Sunday **C2**
Rest – Menu 65 CHF (lunch)/135 CHF – Carte 67/130 CHF
♦ Classic ♦ Elegant ♦
With its homely romantic touch, this elegant cellar restaurant with wine lounge fits harmoniously into the contemplative old town scene. Classic cooking with modern elements.

XX **Kaiser's Reblaube**

Glockengasse 7 ✉ 8001 – ✆ 044 221 21 20 – www.kaisers-reblaube.ch – Closed 23 July - 16 August, Saturday lunch and Sunday, April - September: Saturday lunch, Sunday and Monday dinner **C2**

Rest – *(booking advisable)* Menu 58 CHF (lunch)/165 CHF – Carte 63/106 CHF

♦ Seasonal cuisine ♦ Rustic ♦

Enjoy modern cooking with a traditional influence in this house that was built in 1260 along a small, narrow alley. Comfortable little restaurant on the first-floor and a wine bar on the ground floor.

XX **Intermezzo**

Beethovenstr. 2 (at Kongresshaus) ✉ 8002 – ✆ 044 206 36 42 – www.kongresshaus.ch – Closed 16 July - 14 August, Saturday - Sunday and Bank Holidays

Rest – Menu 59 CHF (lunch)/99 CHF – Carte 81/127 CHF **C3**

♦ Modern ♦ Formal ♦

Dine in contemporary style at this bright, elegant restaurant in the lakeside Congress Centre. Friendly, attentive service at well-presented tables.

X **Metropol**

Fraumünsterstr. 12 ✉ 8001 – ✆ 044 200 59 00 – www.metropol-restaurant.ch – Closed Sunday and Bank Holidays

Rest – Carte 61/116 CHF **C3**

♦ International ♦ Fashionable ♦

This beautiful, neo-Baroque house in the banking quarter houses the cleanly-styled modern restaurant with café, bar and lounge. International cuisine includes sushi and sashimi.

X **Heugümper**

Waaggasse 4 ✉ 8001 – ✆ 044 211 16 60 – www.restaurantheuguemper.ch – Closed Christmas - 31 December, 12 July - 9 August and Saturday - Sunday, October – December: Saturday lunch and Sunday **C2**

Rest – Menu 147 CHF – Carte 60/112 CHF

♦ Euro-asiatic ♦ Fashionable ♦

This venerable townhouse establishment in the heart of Zürich serves international cuisine with an Asian touch. There is a fashionable modern bistro on the ground floor and an elegant restaurant above.

X **Sala of Tokyo**

Limmatstr. 29 ✉ 8005 – ✆ 044 271 52 90 – www.sala-of-tokyo.ch – Closed 18 July - 9 August and Saturday lunch, Sunday - Monday

Rest – Menu 72/130 CHF – Carte 51/111 CHF **C1**

♦ Japanese ♦ Friendly ♦

As well as the sushi bar and restaurant, the establishment also offers a down-to-earth, modern atmosphere and authentic Japanese dishes. The house specialities are prepared on the Sankaiyaki grill tables.

NEAR THE AIRPORT *Plan I*

Radisson BLU Zurich Airport

✉ 8058 – ✆ 044 800 40 40 – www.zurich.radissonblu.com **B1**

330 rm – †215/495 CHF ††215/495 CHF, ☕ 37 CHF

Rest *Angels' Wine Tower Grill* – *(closed Sunday - Monday) (dinner only)* Carte 63/140 CHF

Rest *filini* – Carte 43/95 CHF

♦ Business ♦ Conference hotel ♦ Modern ♦

This hotel focused on business travellers with the 'At Home', 'Chic' and 'Fresh' rooms designed by Matteo Thun. There is also an impressive atrium lobby with an imposing 16m high Wine Tower. The Angels' Wine Tower Grill offers grilled dishes. Find retro style and Italian cuisine in Filini.

Renaissance

Thurgauerstr. 101 (Glattpark) – ✆ 044 874 50 00 – www.renaissancezurich.com
204 rm – †295/395 CHF ††295/395 CHF, ☕ 37 CHF – 7 suites **B2**
Rest *Asian Place* – *✆ 044 874 57 21 (closed 19 July - 23 August, Saturday lunch and Sunday)* Carte 41/80 CHF
Rest *Brasserie* – *✆ 044 874 57 21* – Menu 59 CHF – Carte 55/86 CHF
♦ Business ♦ Chain hotel ♦ Classic ♦
This hotel offers extensive leisure facilities (also open to the public) in the basement and has spacious, comfortable guestrooms which are traditional in style. In the Asian Place, the cuisine ranges from Chinese and Thai through to Japanese and Indonesian. A traditional brasserie.

Hilton Zurich Airport

Hohenbühlstr. 10 – ✆ 044 828 50 50 – www.hilton.ch/zuerich
321 rm – †220/450 CHF ††220/450 CHF, ☕ 39 CHF – 2 suites **B1**
Rest *Market Place* – Menu 60 CHF (buffet) – Carte 48/111 CHF
♦ Chain hotel ♦ Conference hotel ♦ Modern ♦
This hotel provides modern, functional and technically up-to-date rooms near to the airport. The relaxation rooms are spacious. The conference area is more variable. Market Place is a restaurant open to the hall with a show kitchen.

Mövenpick

Walter Mittelholzerstr. 8 – ✆ 044 808 88 88 – www.moevenpick-zurich.com
333 rm – †235/385 CHF ††235/385 CHF, ☕ 33 CHF – 10 suites **B1**
Rest – Menu 40 CHF – Carte 48/88 CHF
Rest *Appenzeller Stube* – *✆ 044 808 85 55 (closed mid July - mid August and Saturday lunch)* Menu 30/70 CHF – Carte 64/104 CHF
Rest *Dim Sum* – *✆ 044 808 84 44 (closed mid July - mid August and Sunday)* Menu 30/75 CHF – Carte 34/81 CHF
♦ Chain hotel ♦ Modern ♦
This hotel is situated right next to the motorway, and has a stylish lobby and reception area. Some of the modern rooms have a particularly simple design with strongly impacting colours. The Appenzeller Stube has a traditional Swiss style. The Dim Sum serves Chinese cuisine.

Courtyard by Marriott

Max Bill-Platz 19 – ✆ 044 564 04 04 – www.courtyardzurich.com
152 rm – †209/399 CHF ††209/399 CHF, ☕ 30 CHF – 2 suites **A2**
Rest – Menu 38 CHF (lunch)/50 CHF – Carte 37/84 CHF
♦ Chain hotel ♦ Business ♦ Modern ♦
This hotel for the business traveller exhibits the typical style of an American chain. The decoration of the technically well-equipped rooms is modern and yet classic. This fashionable restaurant offers international dishes.

Swissôtel

Schulstr. 44 (at Marktplatz) – ✆ 044 317 31 11 – www.swissotel.com/zurich
347 rm – †260/470 CHF ††260/470 CHF, ☕ 35 CHF – 11 suites **A2**
Rest *Dialog* – *✆ 044 317 33 91 (closed 17 July - 21 August, over Christmas and Saturday - Sunday)* Menu 62 CHF – Carte 62/75 CHF
Rest *Szenario* – *✆ 044 317 33 91* – Carte 44/82 CHF
♦ Business ♦ Chain hotel ♦ Contemporary ♦
This multi-storey building is on the market place in the town centre. The rooms are furnished with functional, light and ageless furniture. The indoor swimming pool on the 32nd floor offers views over the entire town. This gastronomic area is divided into two sections: a simple dining room and a more elegant restaurant.

Holiday Inn Messe

rm,

Wallisellenstr. 48 – ✆ 044 316 11 00 – www.holidayinn.com/zurichmesse
164 rm – †208/299 CHF ††208/299 CHF, ☕ 26 CHF – 2 suites **B2**
Rest – Carte 32/70 CHF
♦ Business ♦ Modern ♦
The main attraction of this hotel is its position directly opposite the Exhibition Centre. The well-appointed guestrooms are fresh and modern in design. Nice casual bistro atmosphere in the restaurant.

Novotel Zürich Airport Messe
Lindbergh-Platz 1 (Glattpark)
– ✆ 044 829 90 00 – www.novotel-zurich-airport-messe.com **A-B1**
255 rm – 199/499 CHF 199/499 CHF, 26 CHF **Rest** – Carte 52/81 CHF
♦ Chain hotel ♦ Modern ♦
Tailor-made for business guests, this hotel in the Office and Trade Centre offers contemporary-style rooms and good transport connections. This restaurant offers international cuisine in a fashionable atmosphere.

ENVIRONS OF ZURICH *Plan I*

The Dolder Grand
Kurhausstr. 65 ✉ 8032 – ✆ 044 456 60 00
– www.thedoldergrand.com **B3**
173 rm – 540/970 CHF 870/1150 CHF, 32 CHF – 11 suites
Rest ***The Restaurant*** – see below
Rest ***Garden Restaurant*** – Menu 50 CHF (lunch)/75 CHF – Carte 79/117 CHF
♦ Grand Luxury ♦ Modern ♦
This luxury hotel above the city is the flagship of the Zürich hotel trade. With an old 'Curhaus' from 1899 at its heart, the hotel unites the historic and the modern. The exquisite Top Suites are unique (170-400m2). The spa has European and Japanese influences The Garden Restaurant has a large terrace and good views.

Eden au Lac
Utoquai 45 ✉ 8008 – ✆ 044 266 25 25 – www.edenaulac.ch
50 rm – 450/590 CHF 690/765 CHF, 40 CHF – 5 suites **B3**
Rest – *(closed Saturday lunch)* Menu 50 CHF (lunch)/145 CHF – Carte 64/127 CHF
♦ Luxury ♦ Classic ♦
This 'little grand hotel' on the lake has been accommodating guests since 1909 in its classic, stylish interior. The beautiful rooms are very differently laid out. The elegant Eden restaurant is decorated in shades of red and blue and offers ambitious, modern cooking.

Steigenberger Bellerive au Lac
Utoquai 47 ✉ 8008 – ✆ 044 254 40 00
– www.zuerich.steigenberger.ch **B3**
51 rm – 373/423 CHF 393/448 CHF, 30 CHF
Rest – Menu 48/55 CHF – Carte 70/106 CHF
♦ Business ♦ Classic ♦
This is a charming boutique hotel in a very beautiful location beside the lake. The decor combines a classic, elegant style with modern lines and Feng-Shui elements. This restaurant offers a balanced, five component cuisine made from regional produce.

Zürichberg
Orellistr. 21 ✉ 8044 – ✆ 044 268 35 35 – www.zuerichberg.ch
66 rm – 290/590 CHF 340/590 CHF **B2**
Rest – Menu 45 CHF (lunch) – Carte 63/103 CHF
♦ Traditional ♦ Design ♦
The hotel consists of the classic former spa house, built in 1900, and a wood-panelled, elliptically shaped annexe. It offers tasteful, designer-style rooms, as well as a modern lobby with a bar and lounge. This straightforward restaurant has an open kitchen and a magnificent terrace overlooking the town and lake.

Alden Hotel Splügenschloss
Splügenstr. 2 ✉ 8002 – ✆ 044 289 99 99 – www.alden.ch
21 suites – 595/1530 CHF 595/1530 CHF **A3**
Rest ***Alden per te*** – Carte 66/129 CHF
♦ Luxury ♦ Design ♦
This fine little hotel is accommodated in a typical, listed building from 1895. It is a unique location with special designer furnishings. The mini bar is included in the room price. The decor of this restaurant, where you are served Italian cuisine, has clear-cut, modern lines. A beautiful stucco ceiling highlights the room.

Crowne Plaza

Badenerstr. 420 ✉ 8040 – ✆ 044 404 44 44 – www.cpzurich.ch
364 rm – 175/345 CHF 175/375 CHF, 33 CHF – 11 suites **A3**
Rest *Relais des Arts* – Menu 45 CHF (lunch) – Carte 63/91 CHF
♦ Business ♦ Chain hotel ♦ Modern ♦
This comfortable hotel for the business traveller has good transport connections. It offers predominantly new, modern, functional rooms and a spacious fitness area. The Relais des Arts has a classic ambience.

Ascot

Tessinerplatz 9 ✉ 8002 – ✆ 044 208 14 14 – www.ascot.ch **A3**
74 rm – 195/650 CHF 250/740 CHF **Rest** – Carte 62/113 CHF
♦ Traditional ♦ Classic ♦
This stylish hotel in the business district is full of atmosphere. Alongside its comfortable, newly renovated guestrooms it also offers an English-style bar. The Ascot offers an international menu with a range of "surf and turf" dishes.

Engimatt

Engimattstr. 14 ✉ 8002 – ✆ 044 284 16 16 – www.engimatt.ch
73 rm – 265/395 CHF 320/470 CHF **A3**
Rest – Menu 48 CHF (lunch) – Carte 38/83 CHF
♦ Business ♦ Personalised ♦
This hotel is in the Enge quarter near the centre of town yet it is surrounded by greenery. The lobby area has modern furnishings and the rooms are individual and cosy, and each has a balcony. This light, airy restaurant in the conservatory style has a pleasant garden terrace.

Greulich

Herman-Greulich-Str. 56 ✉ 8004 – ✆ 043 243 42 43 – www.greulich.ch
18 rm – 196/330 CHF 264/410 CHF, 28 CHF **A3**
Rest *Greulich* – see below
♦ Business ♦ Modern ♦
This small designer hotel convinces with its materially simple rooms and more spacious and junior suites - all are bright friendly and clearly laid out. Interior court with birch trees.

Krone Unterstrass

Schaffhauserstr. 1 ✉ 8006 – ✆ 044 360 56 56 – www.hotel-krone.ch
76 rm – 185/320 CHF 260/320 CHF, 19 CHF **A2**
Rest – Menu 65 CHF (lunch)/115 CHF – Carte 52/74 CHF
♦ Business ♦ Contemporary ♦
Located just to the north of the city centre, this hotel provides guests with functional, modern rooms equipped with the latest technology, some in the main building and others in the new Townhouse annexe. As well as the simple daily restaurant, there is a more sophisticated restaurant with an open fireplace and bar.

Fleming's

Brandschenkestr. 10 ✉ 8001 – ✆ 044 563 00 00
– www.flemings-hotels.com **A3**
28 rm – 290/338 CHF 345/378 CHF **Rest** – Carte 40/89 CHF
♦ Business ♦ Modern ♦
This hotel, close to the stock exchange, contains modern, functional, good value rooms. The granite-glass baths integrated into the space are remarkable. W-LAN at no extra cost.

Lady's First without rest

Mainaustr. 24 ✉ 8008 – ✆ 044 380 80 10 – www.ladysfirst.ch
– Closed 23 December - 4 January **B3**
28 rm – 220/310 CHF 275/375 CHF
♦ Family ♦ Modern ♦
A rather special hotel designed for women with stylish modern rooms. The wellness area is exclusively for ladies, but men are also welcome guests in the hotel.

Plattenhof

Plattenstr. 26 ✉ 8032 – ✆ 044 251 19 10 – www.plattenhof.ch
37 rm – 205/355 CHF 255/395 CHF **B3**
Rest *Sento* – ✆ *044 251 16 15 (closed Christmas - early January and Saturday - Sunday)* Carte 47/83 CHF

◆ Business ◆ Design ◆

This hotel is in a residential quarter on the edge of the city centre. Find distinctly personal service and functional rooms in a modern, plain, designer style. Sento has a bistro atmosphere and serves Italian cuisine.

Helvetia

Stauffacherquai 1 ✉ 8004 – ✆ 044 297 99 99 – www.hotel-helvetia.ch
15 rm – 180/250 CHF 220/280 CHF, 10 CHF **A3**
Rest – *(closed Saturday lunch and Sunday lunch)* Carte 61/96 CHF

◆ Townhouse ◆ Cosy ◆

This small, attractive hotel in a historic townhouse close to one of the bridges over the River Limmat offers charming, comfortable rooms with bright, modern fixtures and fittings. A classic-style restaurant on the first floor.

The Restaurant – Hotel The Dolder Grand

Kurhausstr. 65 ✉ 8032 – ✆ 044 456 60 00 – www.thedoldergrand.com – Closed 15 - 24 February, 24 July - 15 August and Saturday lunch, Sunday - Monday **B3**
Rest – *(booking advisable)* Menu 98 CHF (lunch)/208 CHF – Carte 142/189 CHF
Spec. Languste mit Mais, Honigbrot und Kaviar. Taube mit Kapstachelbeeren, Kronsbeeren und Pinienkernen. Warmer Apfelsaft mit Ingwer und weissem Portwein.

◆ Innovative ◆ Fashionable ◆

With Heiko Nieder this modern, elegant restaurant has a very talented young chef who uses excellent produce to create puristic, innovative and delicate dishes in his own inimitable style. Terrace with terrific views of the lake and town.

Rigiblick - Spice (Christian Nickel) with rm

Germaniastr. 99 ✉ 8044 – ✆ 043 255 15 70 – www.restaurant-rigiblick.ch **B2**
7 rm – 490/800 CHF 490/800 CHF
Rest *Bistro Quadrino* – see below **Rest** – *(closed Sunday and Monday) (booking advisable)* Menu 62 CHF (lunch)/158 CHF – Carte 121/128 CHF
Spec. Thunfisch und Makrele mit Apfel-Ingwergelee und Kokosschaum. Gebratene Entenleber mit Rucola-Zitronengratiné und Pumpernickel. Langoustine im grünen Reismantel mit Kürbischutney und Currysuppe.

◆ Euro-asiatic ◆ Formal ◆

Proprietor Christan Nickel prepares modern dishes with an Asian influence that are full of finesse. The elegant restaurant has a purist touch and views of Zurich from the fabulous terrace. The junior suite has been decorated in a first-class, modern-style.

Sonnenberg

Hitzigweg 15 ✉ 8032 – ✆ 044 266 97 97 – www.sonnenberg-zh.ch **B3**
Rest – *(booking essential)* Menu 60 CHF (lunch) – Carte 70/162 CHF

◆ Classic ◆ Formal ◆

A bright, elegant restaurant with attentive table service and an impressive view over Zürich and the lake. The house specialities are veal and beef dishes.

Mesa

Weinbergstr. 75 ✉ 8006 – ✆ 043 321 75 75 – www.mesa-restaurant.ch – Closed Christmas - mid January, 3 weeks July - August and Saturday lunch, Sunday - Monday **A2**
Rest – *(booking advisable)* Menu 79 CHF (lunch)/221 CHF – Carte 122/154 CHF
Spec. Krebse, Speck, Radieschen und grüner Spargel. Kalbsbries mit Vanille, Entenleber und Sellerie. Rind, Spinat, Bohnen mit Sangiovesejus.

◆ Modern ◆ Minimalist ◆

Enjoy the contemporary cuisine of Marcus G. Lindner in a friendly, modern atmosphere. An attentive and skilled young team serves the dishes, which are prepared with an individual touch. There is a more inexpensive lunchtime menu.

XX

Gandria

Rudolfstr. 6 ✉ 8008 – ✆ 044 422 72 42 – www.restaurant-gandria.ch
– Closed Christmas - 9 January, 30 May - 19 June, 12 - 19 September and Saturday lunch, Sunday, January - October: Saturday and Sunday

Rest – Carte 56/102 CHF **B3**

♦ Mediterranean ♦ Family ♦

The atmosphere in this small restaurant set close to Lake Zurich is friendly and relaxed. It serves Mediterranean cuisine in two cheerfully decorated dining rooms.

XX

Il Gattopardo

Rotwandstr. 48 ✉ 8004 – ✆ 043 443 48 48 – www.ilgattopardo.ch
– Closed 15 July - 15 August, Saturday lunch, Sunday - Monday lunch

Rest – Carte 80/108 CHF **A3**

♦ Italian ♦ Trendy ♦

A quite special, stylish atmosphere reigns in this elegantly furnished restaurant in a lovely, corner townhouse. The cuisine is classic Italian and a comfortable wine cellar is available for groups.

XX

Greulich – Hotel Greulich

Herman-Greulich-Str. 56 ✉ 8004 – ✆ 043 243 42 43 – www.greulich.ch
– Closed Saturday lunch and Sunday **A3**

Rest – Menu 68 CHF (veg.)/96 CHF – Carte 75/100 CHF

♦ Inventive ♦ Trendy ♦

This simple yet elegant restaurant with friendly, attentive service offers regional cuisine with a Mediterranean touch using predominantly organic produce. Pleasant terrace.

X

Sankt Meinrad

Stauffacherstr. 163 ✉ 8004 – ✆ 043 534 82 77 – www.sanktmeinrad.ch
– Closed 24 December - 11 January, 24 July - 16 August and Saturday lunch, Sunday - Tuesday lunch **A3**

Rest – *(booking advisable)* Menu 54 CHF (lunch)/140 CHF – Carte 92/119 CHF

♦ Inventive ♦ Fashionable ♦

Friendly, attentive service in a light and airy setting await in this small bistro-style restaurant where chef Antonino Alampi cooks modern food with a Mediterranean twist.

X

Caduff's Wine Loft

Kanzleistr. 126 ✉ 8004 – ✆ 044 240 22 55 – www.wineloft.ch
– Closed Christmas – 3 January, Saturday lunch and Sunday **A3**

Rest – *(booking advisable)* Menu 52 CHF (lunch) – Carte 72/121 CHF

♦ Modern ♦ Trendy ♦

This fashionable venue has a modern loft atmosphere. As well as the delicious fresh cooking made from quality products, there is an impressive wine selection, with over 2,000 labels on offer.

X

Bistro Quadrino – Restaurant Rigiblick

Germaniastr. 99 ✉ 8044 – ✆ 043 255 15 70 – www.restaurantrigiblick.ch
– Closed Monday **B2**

Rest – Carte 55/78 CHF

♦ Seasonal cuisine ♦ Bistro ♦

The cooking at this pleasantly informal bistro above the town has a hint of the Mediterranean and Asia. It offers an inexpensive but delicious alternative to the Spice. Lounge, food bar and walk-in wine display.

UNITED KINGDOM

UNITED KINGDOM

PROFILE

→ **AREA:**
244 157 km² (94 269 sq mi).

→ **POPULATION:**
61 393 000 inhabitants (est. 2008), density = 251 per km².

→ **CAPITAL:**
London (conurbation 12 300 000 inhabitants).

→ **CURRENCY:**
Pound sterling (£); rate of exchange: £ 1 = € 1.17 = US$ 1.61 (Dec. 2010).

→ **GOVERNMENT:**
Constitutional parliamentary monarchy (since 1707). Member of European Union since 1973.

→ **LANGUAGE:**
English.

→ **SPECIFIC PUBLIC HOLIDAYS:**
Good Friday (Friday before Easter), Easter Monday first and last Monday in May, last Monday in August, Boxing Day (26 December).

→ **LOCAL TIME:**
GMT in winter and GMT + 1 hour in summer.

→ **CLIMATE:**
Temperate maritime with cool winters and mild summers (London: January: 3°C, July: 17°C), rainfall evenly distributed throughout the year.

→ **INTERNATIONAL DIALLING CODE:**
00 44 followed by area or city code (London: **20**, Glasgow: **141**, etc.) and then the local number.

→ **EMERGENCY:**
Police, Fire Brigade, Ambulance: ✆ **999**.

→ **ELECTRICITY:**
240 volts AC, 50 Hz. 3 flat pin plugs.

→ **FORMALITIES**
Travellers from the European Union (EU), Switzerland, Iceland, the main countries of North and South America and some Commonwealth countries need a national identity card or passport (except for Irish nationals; America: passport required) to visit the United Kingdom for less than three months (tourism or business purpose). For visitors from other countries a visa may be required, in addition to a passport, especially for those wishing to stay for longer than three months. We advise you to check with your embassy before travelling.

LONDON

LONDON

Population: 7 556 900 (conurbation 12 300 000) – Altitude: sea level

/arc Pinter/Fotolia.com

The term 'world city' could have been invented for London. Time zones radiate from Greenwich, and global finances zap round the Square Mile, while a phalanx of international restaurants is the equal of anywhere on earth. A stunning diversity of population is testament to the city's famed tolerance; different lifestyles and languages are as much a part of the London scene as cockneys and black cabs. This mesmerising blur of life lures long-term visitors from abroad; recently, for example, many thousands of French and Polish workers have laid down roots within the M25.

Whereas Paris evolved through a grand design of formal planning, London grew over time in a pretty haphazard way, swallowing up surrounding villages, but retaining an enviable acreage of green 'lungs': a comforting 30 per cent of London's area is made up of open space. The drama of the city is reflected in its history. From Roman settlement to banking centre to capital of a 19C empire, the city's pulse has never missed a beat; it's no surprise that a dazzling array of theatres, restaurants, museums, markets and art galleries populate its streets. Plus, of course, over 3,500 pubs, the like of which you won't find anywhere else in the world.

LIVING THE CITY

London's piecemeal character has endowed it with distinctly different areas, often breathing down each other's necks. North of Piccadilly lie the playgrounds of Soho and Mayfair, while south is the classier gentleman's clubland of St James's. On the other side of town are Clerkenwell and Southwark, historically artisan areas that have been scrubbed down, freshened up and populated with hip offices and trendy places to eat and drink. The cool sophistication of Kensington and Knightsbridge is to the west, while a more touristy aesthetic is found in the heaving piazza zone of Covent Garden further east along the river.

PRACTICAL INFORMATION

ARRIVAL-DEPARTURE

Heathrow Express to Paddington is the quickest way of getting into the city from Heathrow Airport which is 20 miles west of London. A black cab will cost about £55. There are also bus and underground connections. From Gatwick Airport, take the Gatwick Express to Victoria station. Stansted Airport is 34 miles northeast of London and Luton 35 miles north and both are served by rail links.

TRANSPORT

If you're in London for a short period, get a Travelcard, which will take you all over the city's transport system. If you're around for the longer haul, invest in an Oyster Card, much beloved by locals: these are smartcards with electronically stored pre-pay credit, and they offer good savings on fares.

Just when everyone had got used to calling Waterloo the home of their Eurostar journey to the likes of Paris and Brussels, lo and behold the London terminus changed, and these days you should head for St Pancras.

EXPLORING LONDON

In a city that grew organically without planning committee, is there anywhere you'd call the centre? Instinctively, most locals would probably say **Piccadilly Circus** if only

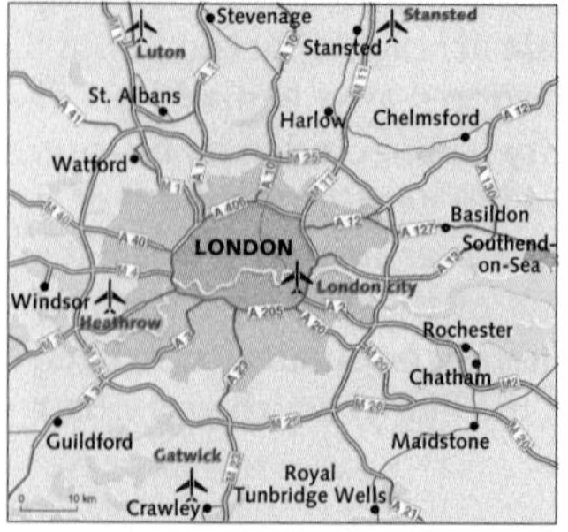

because all that neon advertising gives it the feel of a focal point. It can certainly make a claim as gateway to the West End: when you see the statue of Eros, you know you've 'arrived'. Along Piccadilly itself, the main attractions are a top end version of what draws people to London: culture (at the Royal Academy of Arts), retail (at Fortnum & Mason) and tradition (at The Ritz). From here, London sprawls out in all directions. To the south and west are the wide-open expanses of **Green Park** and **Hyde Park**. In the latter, riders trot their horses along Rotten Row and swimmers chill out in the cool waters of the snaking Serpentine. To the north, the habitués of **Mayfair** tend towards the monied, their dark suits flitting round the environs of Bond Street (with its Premier League shops), Grosvenor Square and the swanky Dorchester hotel. Go east, meanwhile, and you're in **Soho**, home to a lively gay culture and a dazzling array of little eateries and hip lounge bars in an equally bewildering maze of narrow streets.

➜ THE GHERKIN CLASSES

The engine-room of London is the **City**, where the bonus levels paid to bankers are almost as high as the vertiginous buildings in which they work. The skyline here is a blur of steel and glass, in recent years dominated by the highly distinctive Swiss Re building, affectionately known as The Gherkin. The City, and its upstream location, has been London's centre of commerce for nearly a thousand years. In the 11C, Edward The Confessor separated it from Westminster, where he concentrated royal power. But these days the area is not all about corporate finance. Flanking the City are Shoreditch, Hoxton, Finsbury and Clerkenwell, former run-down areas that have undergone a resurgence powered by a young(ish) and creatively-minded crowd.

➜ MARKET FRESH

For those who prefer their retail establishments of a more traditional kind, smart **Knightsbridge** is a perennial choice. Harrods and Harvey Nichols have stood proudly along the road from each other for many decades, the epitome of SW1 sophistication, but one of the great things about London is that street markets hold (nearly) as much cachet as the consumerist shrines. There are a great many of them, and they're dotted around all over the place. Food lovers should head for **Borough market**, under the railway arches at London Bridge. It's a gourmet's paradise, offering top quality produce from all over Britain. A grander setting is **Leadenhall market** in the City, which boasts cobbled walkways, glass roof and rare meats. **Portobello Road** in Notting Hill is world famous for its bric-à-brac, fruit and veg, and East End favourites **Brick Lane** and Ridley Road markets will keep you well stocked with everything from cheap perfume to blackened smoked fish heads! A top destination for plant lovers is **Columbia Road** market in the East End, while Old Spitalfields in the City is a great place to go for stylish handicrafts from the area's young artists.

Your Oyster card will take you far and wide sussing out the markets, but if a musical's your thing after a day battling for bargains, then you probably won't even need to take the Tube since the Leicester Square/Piccadilly area in the heart of town crams in enough board-treading venues to overwhelm even the most voracious addict of stage extravaganzas. Fringe theatre tends to play on the, well, fringes of town, so if you're looking for something a bit more thought-provoking than Abba, Queen or Andrew Lloyd Webber, then you might be better served looking to the likes of the Royal Court in Chelsea, the Old Vic at Waterloo or Islington's Kings Head or Almeida.

➜ POWER MAD

London's a great place to look at pictures. Who would have believed even a decade ago that the capital's leading tourist venue would be a disused old power station on the 'wrong' side of the Thames, but the **Tate Modern**, scrubbed up and, cocking a snook at St Paul's over the river, has proved itself a record-breaker and continues to draw the crowds. As ever, London's art galleries of an older vintage also attract visitors like bees to the honeypot, so prepare to stand a few tourists deep as you admire the world's greatest artists at the likes of The **National**

Gallery, The **National Portrait Gallery** and The **Royal Academy of Arts**. Museums – there are over 200 of them in London – are an institution here, and the Imperial War Museum in Lambeth is one of the best: first-rate exhibits on the First and Second World Wars offer fascinating and sobering perspectives on the realities of conflict.

➔ CAPITAL ACTION

Despite all its other claims to fame, you'd lay short odds that most of London's headlines around the world revolve around sport. On the football front, Chelsea FC's recent successes have doused the Royal Borough in even more glamorous gold-dust (getting a ticket for a home game, though, can be challenging); the brand new, wow-factor **Wembley** opened its doors in 2007 and looks set for an illustrious future; the London Marathon, run every April since 1981, was the first big-city 26 miler, and competitor numbers increase each year; there's the perennial newsworthiness of **Wimbledon** fortnight and the University boat race; and, of course, the city will remain in the sporting spotlight as the 2012 Olympics edges closer by the day.

It's not hard to see London as a melding together of its constituent parts, its 'villages': Kensington and Chelsea, Hampstead and Highgate, Bayswater and Maida Vale, Richmond and Twickenham. Each of these boasts its own community feel and its own areas of treasured green space. Don't be afraid to jump on a bus or dive onto a tube and find out for yourself what each has to offer. There are nearly 4,000 pubs around the city and each one offers a clue to the character of the area you're in. If you want to join the dots and link up lots of areas in one go, take a walk along the **Thames Path**, which covers the whole length of the river from source to sea – it's a stress-free way to take in some cracking views of a pulsating city.

CALENDAR HIGHLIGHTS

Some things never change. You can set your watch by some of London's calendar highlights: from the Boat Race in April to the Chelsea Flower Show in May, from Wimbledon Fortnight in June to the Great British Beer Festival in August, from the Notting Hill Carnival, also in August, to the London Film Festival in October. Other annual highlights are of more recent vintage. The New Year's Day Parade of extravagant floats starting from Parliament Square is settling in nicely, as is the St Patrick's Day Parade through Whitehall in March. The South Bank Beach, 'laid' in July to August, would have been considered a joke even 10 years ago, while ice rinks at the Natural History Museum, Hampton Court Palace, Tower of London, Somerset House and Kew Gardens now give an extra glow to Christmas revellers.

LONDON IN...

➔ ONE DAY

British Museum, Tower of London, St Paul's Cathedral, Tate Modern

➔ TWO DAYS

National Gallery, London Eye, Natural History Museum

➔ THREE DAYS

Science Museum, Victoria and Albert Museum, National Portrait Gallery

EATING OUT

Some years ago you could dine out in London on anything from a bacon and egg sandwich to its cucumber variant. Or so popular memory has it. These days it's one of the food capitals of the world, and you really can eat Malay to Mediterranean, Latin American to Lebanese right across zones one to five. But those wishing to sample classic British dishes also have more choice these days as more and more chefs are rediscovering home-grown ingredients, regional classics and traditional recipes. Eating in the capital can be pricey, so check out good value pre- and post-theatre menus, or tuck into lunch at one of the many eateries that drop their prices, but not their standards, in the middle of the day.

With over 6,000 restaurants in London (to say nothing of its cafés), it's possible to eat at any time. But central London restaurants can get very busy from about 7.30pm; if you haven't booked well in advance you might have more luck trying somewhere a bit further out.

"Would I were in an alehouse in London! I would give all my fame for a pot of ale and safety," says Shakespeare's Henry V. Samuel Johnson tended to agree, waxing lyrical upon the happiness produced by a good tavern or inn. Two examples of the dewy-eyed love the Londoner (albeit one a monarch) has for beer. Pubs are often open these days from 11am to 11pm (and beyond) so this particular love now knows no bounds, and any tourist is welcome to come along and enjoy the romance. It is not just the cooking that has improved in pubs - wine, too, has gained in popularity in recent years: woe betide any establishment in this city that can't distinguish its Chardonnay from its Pinot Grigio. And with more Champagne being quaffed in London than any city outside France, it's fair to say the taste for a tipple offers up a wide range of opportunities to anyone within the M25.

→ THERE'S NO RHYME OR REASON...

...when it comes to a formal tipping procedure. Some restaurants leave the amount open, while others add on anything up to 15%. Leaving a cash tip on the table guarantees the tip goes to the people it's meant for, the waiters. If you're not sure whether it's heading for their pockets then just ask them.

HOTELS - ALPHABETICAL LIST

RESTAURANTS - ALPHABETICAL LIST

N

O

P

Q

R

S

T

U

V

W

Y

Z

OPEN ON SATURDAY AND SUNDAY

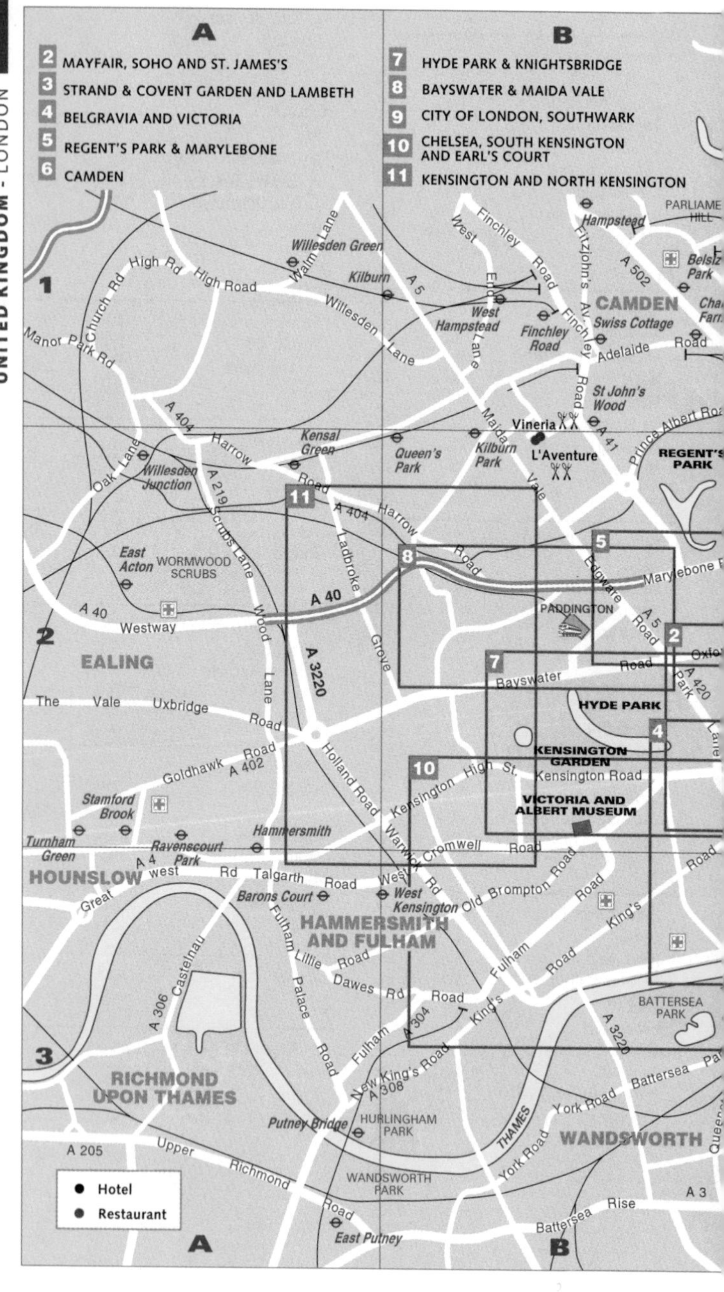
A
B
2 MAYFAIR, SOHO AND ST. JAMES'S
3 STRAND & COVENT GARDEN AND LAMBETH
4 BELGRAVIA AND VICTORIA
5 REGENT'S PARK & MARYLEBONE
6 CAMDEN
7 HYDE PARK & KNIGHTSBRIDGE
8 BAYSWATER & MAIDA VALE
9 CITY OF LONDON, SOUTHWARK
10 CHELSEA, SOUTH KENSINGTON AND EARL'S COURT
11 KENSINGTON AND NORTH KENSINGTON
Hampstead
Willesden Green
Kilburn
West Hampstead
Finchley Road
Swiss Cottage
CAMDEN
St John's Wood
Vineria
L'Aventure
Kensal Green
Queen's Park
Kilburn Park
REGENT'S PARK
Willesden Junction
East Acton
WORMWOOD SCRUBS
PADDINGTON
EALING
HYDE PARK
KENSINGTON GARDEN
VICTORIA AND ALBERT MUSEUM
Stamford Brook
Hammersmith
Turnham Green
Ravenscourt Park
HOUNSLOW
Barons Court
West Kensington
HAMMERSMITH AND FULHAM
BATTERSEA PARK
RICHMOND UPON THAMES
Putney Bridge
HURLINGHAM PARK
WANDSWORTH
WANDSWORTH PARK
East Putney
THAMES
Hotel
Restaurant

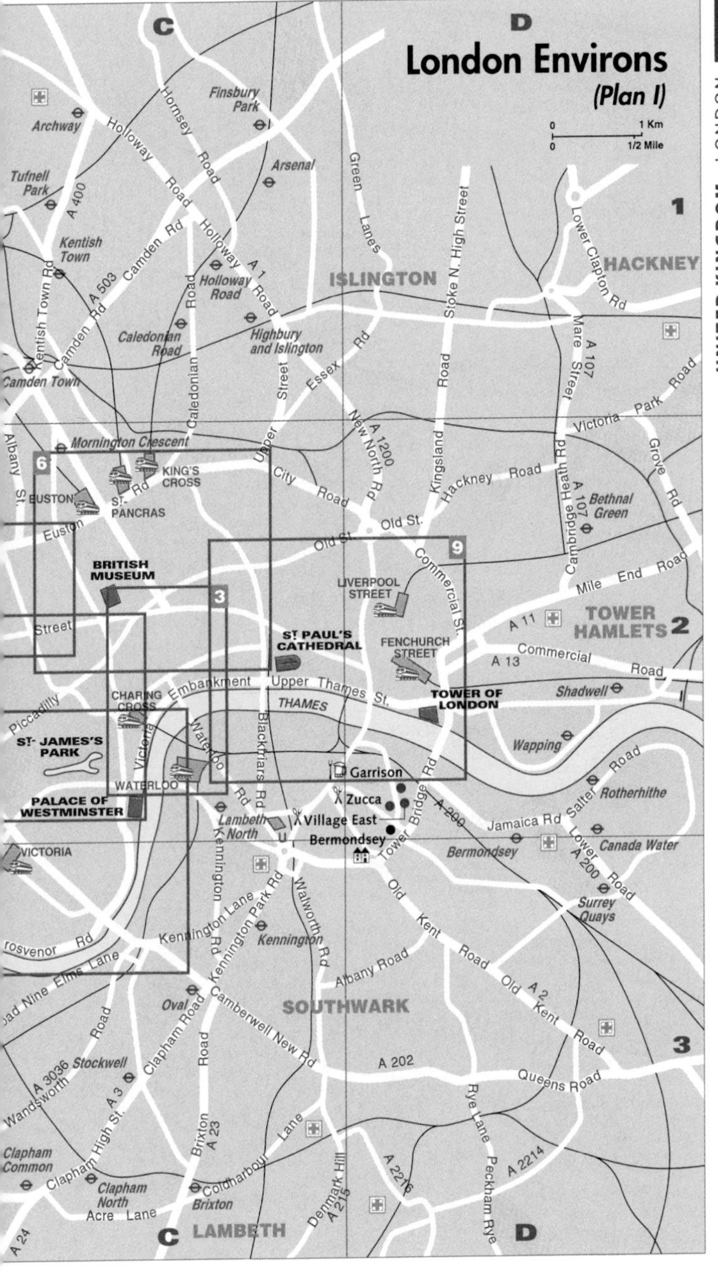

UNITED KINGDOM - LONDON

Mayfair, Soho and St. James's (Plan II)

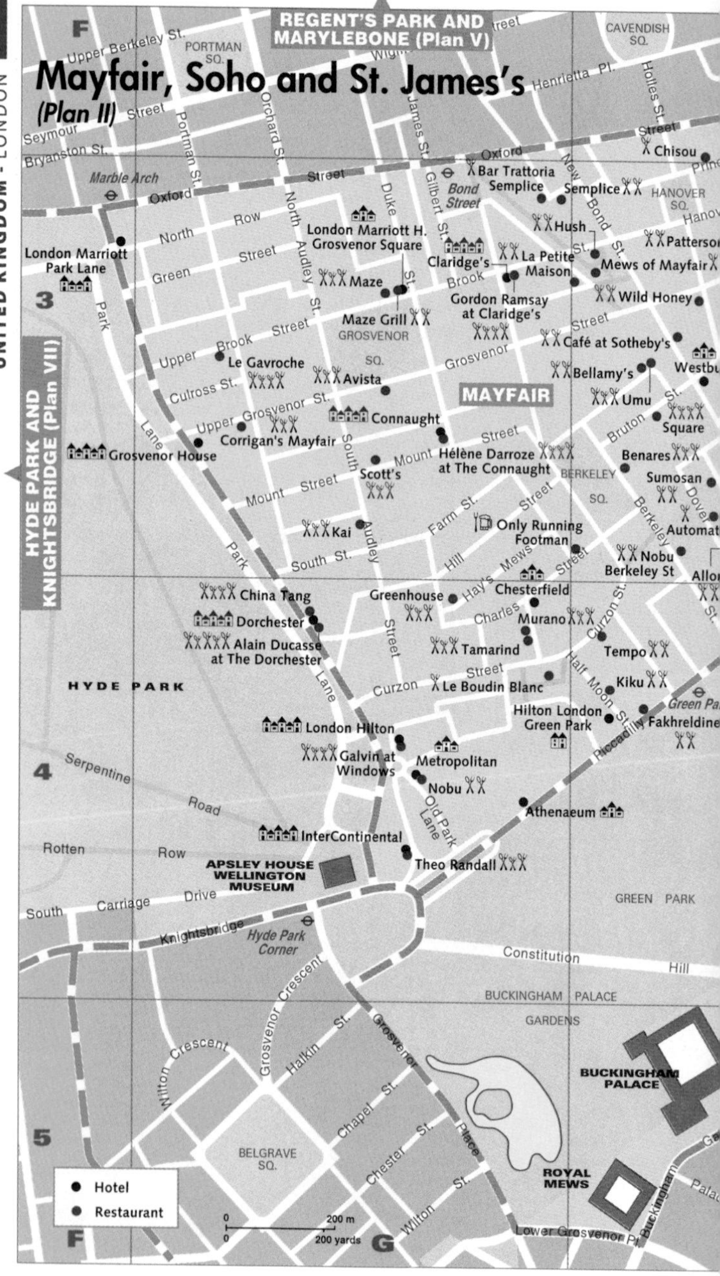

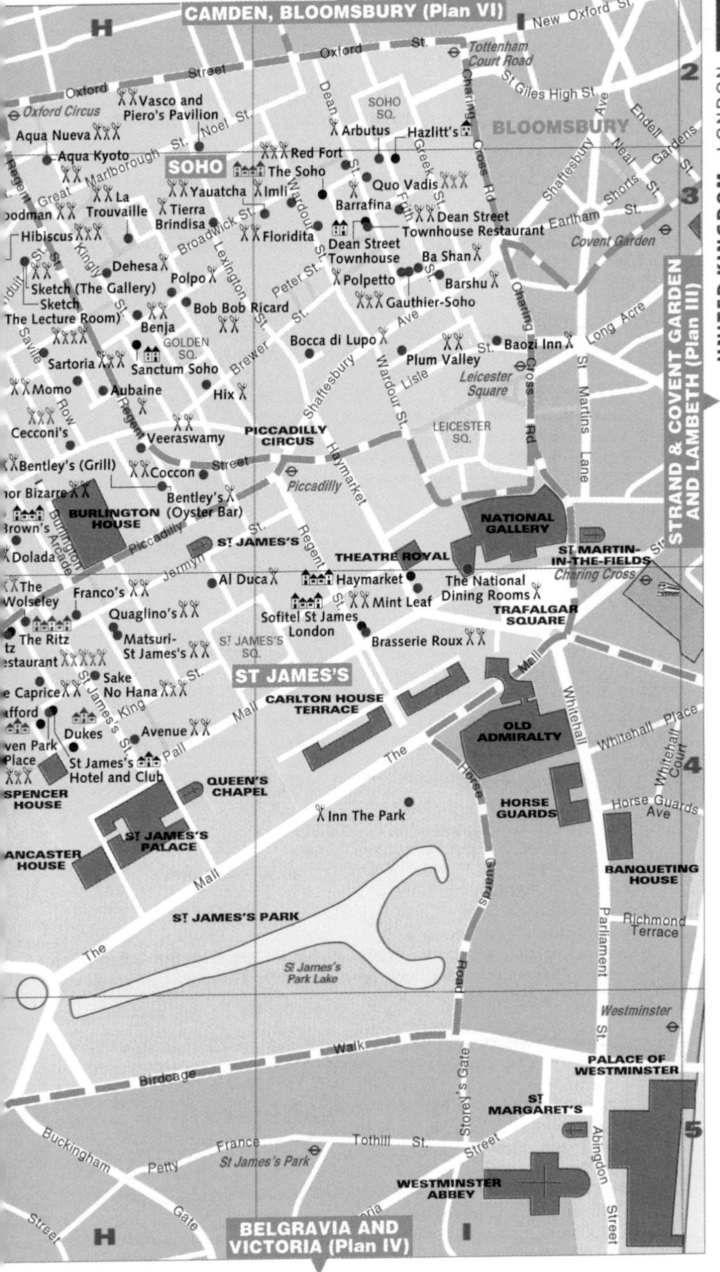
CAMDEN, BLOOMSBURY (Plan VI)
BELGRAVIA AND VICTORIA (Plan IV)
STRAND & COVENT GARDEN AND LAMBETH (Plan III)
SOHO
BLOOMSBURY
ST JAMES'S
PICCADILLY CIRCUS
GOLDEN SQ.
SOHO SQ.
LEICESTER SQ.
ST JAMES'S SQ.
BURLINGTON HOUSE
NATIONAL GALLERY
THEATRE ROYAL
ST MARTIN-IN-THE-FIELDS
TRAFALGAR SQUARE
CARLTON HOUSE TERRACE
OLD ADMIRALTY
HORSE GUARDS
BANQUETING HOUSE
QUEEN'S CHAPEL
ST JAMES'S PALACE
SPENCER HOUSE
LANCASTER HOUSE
ST JAMES'S PARK
St James's Park Lake
PALACE OF WESTMINSTER
ST MARGARET'S
WESTMINSTER ABBEY
Oxford Circus
Tottenham Court Road
Covent Garden
Leicester Square
Piccadilly
Charing Cross
Westminster
St James's Park
Vasco and Piero's Pavilion
Aqua Nueva
Aqua Kyoto
La Trouvaille
Hibiscus
Sketch (The Gallery)
Sketch The Lecture Room
Dehesa
Polpo
Bob Bob Ricard
Benja
Sartoria
Sanctum Soho
Momo
Aubaine
Cecconi's
Veeraswamy
Bentley's (Grill)
Coccon
Bentley's (Oyster Bar)
Yauatcha
Imli
Tierra Brindisa
Floridita
Arbutus
Red Fort
The Soho
Hazlitt's
Quo Vadis
Barrafina
Dean Street Townhouse Restaurant
Dean Street Townhouse
Ba Shan
Polpetto
Barshu
Gauthier-Soho
Bocca di Lupo
Plum Valley
Baozi Inn
Hix
Al Duca
Haymarket
Mint Leaf
Sofitel St James London
Brasserie Roux
The National Dining Rooms
The Wolseley
Franco's
Quaglino's
Matsuri-St James's
The Ritz
Sake No Hana
Dukes
Avenue
St James's Hotel and Club
Inn The Park
Oxford Street
New Oxford St.
St Giles High St.
Charing Cross Rd
Shaftesbury Ave
Long Acre
St Martins Lane
Whitehall
Whitehall Place
Horse Guards Ave
Horse Guards Road
Parliament St.
Richmond Terrace
Birdcage Walk
Tothill St.
Storey's Gate
Abingdon Street
Petty France
Buckingham Gate
The Mall
Pall Mall
Jermyn St.
Regent St.
Haymarket
Wardour St.
Dean St.
Greek St.
Frith St.
Lexington St.
Broadwick St.
Brewer St.
Great Marlborough St.
Kingly St.
Savile Row
King St.
St James's St.
Lisle St.
Peter St.
Noel St.
Earlham St.
Shorts Gardens
Neal St.
Endell St.
H
I
2
3
4
5

Mayfair

Dorchester

Park Ln. ✉ *W1K 1QA* – Ⓜ *Hyde Park Corner* – ✆ *(020) 7629 8888 – www.thedorchester.com* **G4**

196 rm – †£ 258/906 ††£ 318/906, ☐ £ 31.50 – 54 suites

Rest *Alain Ducasse at The Dorchester and China Tang* – see below

Rest *The Grill* – Menu £ 26/30 – Carte £ 44/90

♦ Grand Luxury ♦ Classic ♦

A sumptuously decorated, luxury hotel offering every possible facility. Impressive marbled and pillared promenade. Rooms quintessentially English in style. Exemplary levels of service. Exuberant tartan décor in The Grill.

Claridge's

Brook St ✉ *W1K 4HR* – Ⓜ *Bond Street* – ✆ *(020) 7629 8860 – www.claridges.co.uk* **G3**

143 rm – †£ 732 ††£ 732, ☐ £ 29 – 60 suites

Rest *Gordon Ramsay at Claridge's* – see below

♦ Grand Luxury ♦ Classic ♦

Rightly celebrated for its art deco and one of London's finest hotels. Exceptionally well-appointed and sumptuous bedrooms, all with butler service. Magnificent Foyer for afternoon tea.

Connaught

Carlos Pl. ✉ *W1K 2AL* – Ⓜ *Bond Street* – ✆ *(020) 7499 7070 – www.the-connaught.co.uk* **G3**

95 rm – †£ 660 ††£ 780, ☐ £ 30 – 26 suites

Rest *Hélène Darroze at The Connaught* – see below

Rest *Espelette* – ✆ *(020) 3147 7100* – Carte £ 39/77

♦ Grand Luxury ♦ Classic ♦

Restored and renovated but still retaining an elegant British feel. Now this famous London hotel offers a choice between contemporary and classic bedrooms. Two stylish bars. Espelette for all day, informal dining.

InterContinental

1 Hamilton Pl, Park Ln. ✉ *W1J 7QY – Ⓜ Hyde Park Corner* – ✆ *(020) 7409 3131 – www.london.intercontinental.com* **G4**

399 rm – †£ 275/475 ††£ 275/475, ☐ £ 26.50 – 48 suites

Rest *Theo Randall* – see below

Rest *Cookbook Café* – Carte £ 29/61

♦ Business ♦ Modern ♦

International hotel relaunched in 2007 after major refit. English-style bedrooms with hi-tech equipment and large, open-plan lobby. Cookbook Café invites visiting chefs to showcase their talents.

London Hilton

22 Park Ln. ✉ *W1K 1BE* – Ⓜ *Hyde Park Corner* – ✆ *(020) 7493 8000 – www.hilton.co.uk/londonparklane* **G4**

397 rm – †£ 246/660 ††£ 246/660, ☐ £ 26.50 – 56 suites

Rest *Galvin at Windows* – see below

Rest *Trader Vics* – ✆ *(020) 7208 4113 (closed 25-26 December)* Carte £ 33/53

Rest *Podium* – ✆ *(020) 72084022* – Menu £ 21 – Carte £ 28/50

♦ Business ♦ Classic ♦

This 28 storey tower is one of the city's tallest hotels, providing impressive views from the upper floors. Club floor bedrooms are particularly comfortable. Exotic Trader Vics with bamboo and plants. Modern European food in Podium.

Grosvenor House

Park Ln. ✉ *W1K 7TN* – Ⓜ *Marble Arch* – ✆ *(020) 7499 6363*
– *www.londongrosvenorhouse.co.uk* **G3**

378 rm – †£ 299/395 ††£ 299/395, ☕ £ 28 – 52 suites

Rest *JW Steakhouse* – ✆ *(020) 7399 8460* – Carte £ 35/70

♦ Business ♦ Classic ♦

Refurbished hotel in commanding position by Hyde Park. Uniform, comfortable bedrooms in classic Marriott styling. Boasts the largest ballroom in Europe. JW Steakhouse serves prime, hand-cut beef and fresh seafood.

Westbury

Bond St. ✉ *W1S 2YF* – Ⓜ *Bond Street* – ✆ *(020) 7629 7755*
– *www.westburymayfair.com* **H3**

232 rm – †£ 238/561 ††£ 298/618, ☕ £ 26 – 13 suites

Rest – *(closed Saturday lunch and Sunday dinner)* Menu £ 30/58

♦ Business ♦ Modern ♦

Caused a commotion with its New York styling when it opened in the 1950s; now fully refurbished. Smart, comfortable bedrooms; art deco suites. Elegant, well-known Polo bar. Bright, fresh restaurant; extensive private dining facilities.

Brown's

Albemarle St. ✉ *W1S 4BP* – Ⓜ *Green Park* – ✆ *(020) 7493 6020*
– *www.roccofortecollection.com* **H3**

105 rm – †£ 312/474 ††£ 354/540, ☕ £ 27 – 12 suites

Rest *HIX at The Albemarle* – ✆ *(020) 7518 4004* – Menu £ 30
– Carte £ 28/64

♦ Luxury ♦ Stylish ♦

This urbane hotel with an illustrious past offers a swish bar featuring Terence Donovan prints, up-to-the minute bedrooms and a quintessentially English sitting room for tea. Wood panelled dining room with traditional British cooking.

London Marriott H. Park Lane

140 Park Lane ✉ *W1K 7AA* – Ⓜ *Marble Arch*
– ✆ *(020) 7493 7000* – *www.londonmarriott.parklane.co.uk* **F3**

148 rm – †£ 419 ††£ 419, ☕ £ 25 – 9 suites

Rest *140 Park Lane* – Menu £ 22 – Carte £ 31/48

♦ Luxury ♦ Design ♦

This international hotel is usefully located close to the shops of Oxford Street and Hyde Park. Well-kept basement health club. Smart, generously sized bedrooms are well-equipped. Attractive restaurant overlooks Marble Arch.

Metropolitan

Old Park Ln ✉ *W1K 1LB* – Ⓜ *Hyde Park Corner* – ✆ *(020) 7447 1000*
– *www.metropolitan.como.bz*
– *Closed 25 December and 1 January* **G4**

147 rm – †£ 468 ††£ 468, ☕ £ 28 – 3 suites

Rest *Nobu* – see below

♦ Modern ♦ Design ♦

A minimalist interior and a voguish reputation have made this hotel and its Met Bar the favoured choice of pop stars and celebrities. Sleek design and fashionably attired staff set it apart.

Athenaeum

116 Piccadilly ✉ *W1J 7BJ* – Ⓜ *Hyde Park Corner* – ✆ *(020) 7499 3464*
– *www.athenaeumhotel.com* **G4**

145 rm – †£ 390 ††£ 516, ☕ £ 27 – 11 suites

Rest *Damask* – Menu £ 19/27 – Carte £ 43/63

♦ Luxury ♦ Classic ♦

A new look for this 1920s building, with its stylish bedrooms which come in cool pastel shades and have floor to ceiling windows. 'Living Wall' a striking feature, along with whisky-stocked bar. Bright restaurant offers plenty of classics.

Chesterfield

35 Charles St. ✉ *W1J 5EB – Ⓜ Green Park – ✆ (020) 7491 2622 – www.chesterfieldmayfair.com* **G4**

103 rm – 🚹£ 222/402 🚹🚹£ 246/402, ☕ £ 22.50 – 4 suites

Rest – Menu £ 30 (lunch) – Carte £ 37/59

◆ Townhouse ◆ Classic ◆

An assuredly English feel to this Georgian house. Discreet lobby leads to a clubby bar and wood panelled library. Individually decorated bedrooms, with some antique pieces. Intimate and pretty restaurant.

London Marriott H. Grosvenor Square

Grosvenor Sq. ✉ *W1K 6JP – Ⓜ Bond Street – ✆ (020) 7493 1232 – www.marriottgrosvenorsquare.com* **G3**

226 rm – 🚹£ 275/430 🚹🚹£ 275/430, ☕ £ 22 – 11 suites

Rest *Maze Grill* – see below

◆ Business ◆ Functional ◆

A well-appointed international group hotel that benefits from an excellent location in the heart of Mayfair. Many of the bedrooms specifically equipped for the business traveller.

Hilton London Green Park

Half Moon St. ✉ *W1J 7BN – Ⓜ Green Park – ✆ (020) 7629 7522 – www.hilton.co.uk/greenpark* **H4**

162 rm – 🚹£ 114/305 🚹🚹£ 137/317, ☕ £ 19.95

Rest – *(bar lunch Saturday and Sunday)* Menu £ 20 – Carte £ 31/36

◆ Business ◆ Functional ◆

A row of sympathetically adjoined townhouses in the heart of Mayfair, dating from the 1730s. Bedrooms vary in size and shape; those on the first and fifth floors have been refurbished in a bright, contemporary style. Modern menu served in airy restaurant.

Alain Ducasse at The Dorchester

✿✿✿

Park Ln. ✉ *W1K 1QA – Ⓜ Hyde Park Corner – ✆ (020) 7629 8866 – www.alainducasse-dorchester.com – Closed 25 December dinner until dinner 31 December, 22-25 April, 7-30 August, Saturday lunch, Sunday and Monday* **G4**

Rest – Menu £ 50/78

Spec. Roasted chicken and lobster with sweetbreads. Fillet of beef and foie gras Rossini with 'sacristain' potatoes. 'Baba like in Monte-Carlo'.

◆ French ◆ Fashionable ◆ Design ◆

Luxury and extravagance are the hallmarks of this Alain Ducasse outpost. Dining room is elegant without being staid; food is modern and refined yet satisfying and balanced. Service is formal and well-organised.

Hélène Darroze at The Connaught

✿✿

Carlos Pl. ✉ *W1K 2AL – Ⓜ Bond Street – ✆ (020) 3147 7200 – www.the-connaught.co.uk – Closed 2 weeks August, 1 week January, Saturday lunch, Sunday and Monday* **G3**

Rest – *(booking essential)* Menu £ 35/75

Spec. Foie gras with mild spices and dried fruit chutney. Scallops with tandoori spices and lemongrass. Strawberry and bay leaf panna cotta with lemon jelly.

◆ French ◆ Luxury ◆ Elegant ◆

Landes and the SW of France inform Hélène Darroze's exquisite cooking, although international influences also play a part. The dining room is elegant and comfortable, with original mahogany wood panelling. Service is courteous and professional.

XXXX ✿✿

Le Gavroche (Michel Roux Jnr)

43 Upper Brook St. ✉ W1K 7QR – Ⓜ Marble Arch – ✆ (020) 7408 0881 – www.le-gavroche.co.uk – Closed Christmas-New Year, Sunday and bank holidays **G3**

Rest – *(booking essential)* Menu £ 49 (lunch) – Carte £ 60/107

Spec. Soufflé Suissesse. Roast black-leg chicken with morels and madeira sauce. Chocolate and praline indulgence with gold leaf.

♦ French ♦ Formal ♦ Luxury ♦

Classic and indulgent French cuisine is the draw at Michel Roux's renowned London institution. The large, smart basement room has a clubby, masculine feel; service is formal and structured.

XXXX ✿✿

Square (Philip Howard)

6-10 Bruton St. ✉ W1J 6PU – Ⓜ Green Park – ✆ (020) 7495 7100 – www.squarerestaurant.com – Closed 25 December, 1 January and lunch Saturday, Sunday and bank holidays **H3**

Rest – Menu £ 35/75

Spec. Langoustine with Parmesan gnocchi and truffle. Saddle of hare with tarte fine of celeriac and pear. Brillat-Savarin cheesecake with passion fruit and mango.

♦ French ♦ Formal ♦

Confident and accomplished kitchen which understands the importance of sound techniques, prime ingredients and clarity of flavour. The room is comfortable and the buoyant atmosphere prevents things becoming too formal. Good cheeseboard.

XXXX ✿

Sketch (The Lecture Room & Library)

9 Conduit St. (First Floor) ✉ W1S 2XG – Ⓜ Oxford Street – ✆ (020) 76594500 – www.sketch.uk.com – Closed 25-30 December, last 2 weeks August, Saturday lunch, Sunday, Monday and bank holidays **H3**

Rest – *(booking essential)* Menu £ 35 (lunch) – Carte £ 70/129

Spec. Langoustines 'addressed in five ways'. Lamb with aubergine, tomato, ewe's milk cheese and spinach. Pierre Gagnaire's 'grand dessert'.

♦ French ♦ Luxury ♦ Elegant ♦

Pierre Gagnaire's London operation is found within a striking 18C townhouse which is full of colour, energy and vitality. The menus offer plenty of choice; cooking is ambitious and elaborate, and dishes arrive artfully presented.

XXXX ✿

Galvin at Windows – at London Hilton Hotel

22 Park Ln. ✉ W1K 1BE – Ⓜ Hyde Park Corner – ✆ (020) 7208 4021 – www.galvinatwindows.com – Closed 25 December, Saturday lunch, Sunday dinner and bank holidays **G4**

Rest – Menu £ 27/65

Spec. Scallop, cuttlefish and chorizo paella. Spiced pigeon with foie gras boudin and macaroni gratin. Rum baba with crème Chantilly.

♦ French ♦ Formal ♦

Spectacular views from the 28th floor of the Hilton are not the only draw: the room is contemporary and cleverly laid out, service is attentive and efficient and the cooking is confident, detailed, balanced and satisfying.

XXXX

Gordon Ramsay at Claridge's

Brook St. ✉ W1K 4HR – Ⓜ Bond Street – ✆ (020) 7499 0099 – www.gordonramsay.com/claridges **G3**

Rest – *(booking essential)* Menu £ 30/70

♦ Modern European ♦ Luxury ♦ Elegant ♦

Grand and impressive room within the elegant surroundings of Claridge's hotel. Service is ceremonial and structured and the cooking is classically based. Popular chef's table in the kitchen.

XXXX

China Tang – at Dorchester Hotel

AC VISA MC AE

Park Ln. ✉ W1A 2HJ – Ⓜ Hyde Park Corner – ✆ (020) 7629 9988 – www.thedorchester.com – Closed 25 December **G4**

Rest – Menu £ 15 (lunch) – Carte £ 40/70

◆ Chinese ◆ Fashionable ◆

Sir David Tang's atmospheric, art deco-inspired Chinese restaurant is always abuzz with activity. The kitchen is a model of conservatism and concentrates on traditional Cantonese specialities.

XXX ✿✿

Hibiscus (Claude Bosi)

AC VISA MC AE

29 Maddox St. ✉ W1S 2PA – Ⓜ Oxford Circus – ✆ (020) 7629 2999 – www.hibiscusrestaurant.co.uk – Closed 23 December-3 January, Sunday and Monday **H3**

Rest – Menu £ 30/75

Spec. Smoked sweetbreads with lettuce velouté and brown butter. Lobster with pork 'san choi bau' and hollandaise. Chocolate tart with basil ice cream.

◆ Innovative ◆ Elegant ◆

Claude Bosi's cooking is creative and bold, but with a sound, classical base; desserts are a real highlight. Attractive room combines French oak with Welsh slate as a reminder of his previous restaurant in Ludlow. Formal and conscientious service.

XXX ✿

Greenhouse

AC VISA MC AE

27a Hay's Mews ✉ W1J 5NY – Ⓜ Hyde Park Corner – ✆ (020) 7499 3331 – www.greenhouserestaurant.co.uk – Closed 24 December-4 January, Saturday lunch, Sunday and bank holidays

Rest – Menu £ 29/70 **G4**

Spec. Calves sweetbreads with wild garlic and leeks. Lamb with artichokes, quinoa and lemon cream. "Snix" - chocolate, salted caramel and peanuts.

◆ Innovative ◆ Fashionable ◆

Smart, elegant restaurant broken up into sections by glass screens. Innovative selection of elaborately presented dishes, underpinned with sound French culinary techniques.

XXX ✿

Murano (Angela Hartnett)

AC VISA MC AE

20 Queen St. ✉ W1J 5PP – Ⓜ Green Park – ✆ (020) 7495 1127 – www.angela-hartnett.com – Closed 24 December until dinner 31 December and Sunday **G4**

Rest – Menu £ 30/60

Spec. Apple, black pudding and octopus salad with chorizo oil. Lamb with celery and olive purée, artichokes and garlic. Chocolate mousse with raspberry sorbet.

◆ Italian influences ◆ Fashionable ◆ Elegant ◆

Now wholly owned by chef Angela Hartnett, this bright and stylishly decorated restaurant provides a luminous setting for her refined and balanced cooking, with its strong Italian influences. The best tables are at the front, by the window.

XXX ✿

Maze

AC VISA MC AE

10-13 Grosvenor Sq. ✉ W1K 6JP – Ⓜ Bond Street – ✆ (020) 7107 0000 – www.gordonramsay.com **G3**

Rest – Menu £ 23 (lunch) – Carte £ 29/33

Spec. Terrine of foie gras and smoked eel with apple and celery. Roast duck with pickled red endive and beetroot. Rice pudding with chocolate and an orange and thyme marmalade.

◆ Innovative ◆ Fashionable ◆

Choose a variety of small but expertly formed dishes at this sleek and stylish contemporary restaurant. The cooking is innovative, balanced and precise; service is well-organised.

XXX ✿

Kai

AC ⛭ VISA MC AE ①

65 South Audley St. ✉ W1K 2QU – Ⓜ Hyde Park Corner – ☎ (020) 7493 8988 – www.kaimayfair.co.uk
– Closed 25-26 December and 1 January **G3**

Rest – *(booking essential)* Menu £ 19 (lunch) – Carte £ 40/75

Spec. Wasabi prawns with mango and basil seeds. Sea bass with chickpeas, shallots and ginger. Rice dumplings with ginger and honey wafers.

♦ Chinese ♦ Intimate ♦ Formal ♦

Carefully prepared Chinese food, from a menu that mixes the classics with more innovative dishes; flavours are clean and assured. Spread over two floors, with sweet natured service and smart surroundings.

XXX ✿

Benares (Atul Kochhar)

AC ⛭ VISA MC AE ①

12a Berkeley Square House ✉ W1J 6BS – Ⓜ Green Park – ☎ (020) 7629 8886 – www.benaresrestaurant.com
– Closed 25 December and 1 January **H3**

Rest – Menu £ 25 (lunch) – Carte £ 45/83

Spec. Tandoor roasted pigeon with vanilla and beetroot. Tiger prawns with asparagus and spring onions. Strawberry jelly with black pepper and yoghurt parfait.

♦ Indian ♦ Formal ♦

Modern techniques are added to a classical base to create contemporary Indian cuisine that continues to evolve. The smart first-floor surroundings match the food in their sophistication. Popular and stylish Chef's Table.

XXX ✿

Tamarind

AC VISA MC AE ①

20 Queen St. ✉ W1J 5PR – Ⓜ Green Park – ☎ (020) 7629 3561 – www.tamarindrestaurant.com
– Closed 25-27 December, 1 January, lunch Saturday and bank holidays

Rest – Menu £ 19 (weekday lunch) – Carte £ 48/72 **G4**

Spec. Spiced chickpeas and whole-wheat crisps with mint chutney. Lamb cutlets marinated with garlic, papaya and fennel. Mango kulfi.

♦ Indian ♦ Formal ♦

Makes the best use of its basement location, with smoked mirrors, gilded columns and a somewhat exclusive feel. Appealing and balanced Indian cooking; kebabs and curries are the specialities, complemented by carefully prepared vegetable dishes.

XXX ✿

Umu

AC VISA MC AE ①

14-16 Bruton Pl. ✉ W1J 6LX – Ⓜ Bond Street – ☎ (020) 7499 8881 – www.umurestaurant.com
– Closed 24 December-6 January, Saturday lunch, Sunday and bank holidays

Rest – Menu £ 25 (lunch) – Carte £ 33/48 ✿ **H3**

Spec. Langoustine with amber tomato jelly, vinaigrette and caviar. Pigeon with radish and egg yolk sauce. Japanese tiramisu with macha tea and sake.

♦ Japanese ♦ Fashionable ♦

Stylish, discreet interior using natural materials, with central sushi bar. Extensive choice of Japanese dishes; choose one of the seasonal kaiseki menus for the full experience. Over 160 different labels of sake.

XXX

Scott's

AC ⛭ VISA MC AE ①

20 Mount St ✉ W1K 2HE – Ⓜ Bond Street – ☎ (020) 7495 7309 – www.scotts-restaurant.com
– Closed dinner 24, 25-26 December and 1 January **G3**

Rest – Carte £ 33/64

♦ Seafood ♦ Fashionable ♦

A landmark London institution reborn. Stylish yet traditional; oak panelling juxtaposed with vibrant artwork from young British artists. Top quality seafood, kept simple.

XXX

Cecconi's

5a Burlington Gdns ✉ W1S 3EP – Ⓜ Green Park – ✆ (020) 7434 1500 – www.cecconis.com – Closed 25 December **H3**

Rest – *(booking essential)* Carte £ 27/45

♦ Italian ♦ Fashionable ♦

Branches of this fashionable restaurant are now opening up around the world. Regulars pop in for a bite at the bar; the restaurant prepares the classic dishes with care. Open from breakfast onwards; popular for weekend brunches.

XXX

Corrigan's Mayfair

28 Upper Grosvenor St. ✉ W1K 7EH – Ⓜ Marble Arch – ✆ (020) 74999943 – www.corrigansmayfair.com – Closed 25-26 December, 1 January and Saturday lunch **G3**

Rest – Menu £ 27 (lunch) – Carte £ 43/73

♦ British ♦ Elegant ♦

Richard Corrigan's flagship celebrates British and Irish cooking, with game a speciality. The room is comfortable, clubby and quite glamorous and feels as though it has been around for years.

XXX

Bentley's (Grill)

11-15 Swallow St. ✉ W1B 4DG – Ⓜ Piccadilly Circus – ✆ (020) 7734 4756 – www.bentleys.org – Closed 25-26 December, 1 January, Saturday lunch and Sunday

Rest – Carte £ 35/90 **H3**

♦ British ♦ Elegant ♦

Entrance into striking bar; panelled staircase to richly decorated restaurant. Carefully sourced seafood or meat dishes enhanced by clean, crisp cooking. Unruffled service.

XXX

Theo Randall – at Intercontinental Hotel

1 Hamilton Pl, Park Ln. ✉ W1J 7QY – Ⓜ Hyde Park Corner – ✆ (020) 7318 8747 – www.theorandall.com – Closed Saturday lunch, Sunday and bank holidays **G4**

Rest – Menu £ 27 (lunch and early/late dinner) – Carte £ 45/55

♦ Italian ♦ Fashionable ♦

Daily changing seasonal menu of comforting Italian dishes, served in the smart and spacious surroundings of an international hotel. Wood oven a feature; produce imported directly from Italy.

XXX

Sartoria

20 Savile Row ✉ W1S 3PR – Ⓜ Green Park – ✆ (020) 7534 7000 – www.sartoriabar.com – Closed 24-25 December, Sunday, Saturday lunch and bank holidays

Rest – Menu £ 24 – Carte £ 34/44 **H3**

♦ Italian ♦ Formal ♦

In the street renowned for English tailoring, a coolly sophisticated restaurant to suit those looking for classic Italian cooking with modern touches.

XXX

Avista

Millennium Mayfair Hotel, 39 Grosvenor Sq ✉ W1K 2HP – Ⓜ Bond Street – ✆ (020) 7596 3399 – www.avistarestaurant.com – Closed Saturday lunch and Sunday **G3**

Rest – Menu £ 23 (lunch) – Carte £ 28/66

♦ Italian ♦ Luxury ♦

A large room, softened by neutral shades, within the Millennium Hotel. The menu traverses Italy and the cooking marries the rustic with the more refined. Pasta dishes are a highlight.

XX ✿

Wild Honey

12 St George St. ✉ *W1S 2FB – Ⓜ Oxford Circus – ✆ (020) 7758 9160 – www.wildhoneyrestaurant.co.uk – Closed 25-26 December and 1 January* **H3**

Rest – Menu £ 20 (lunch) – Carte £ 33/46

Spec. Belly pork with snails, garlic and parsley. Veal with gnocchi and young vegetables. Wild honey ice cream with crushed honeycomb.

◆ Modern European ◆ Design ◆

Skilled kitchen uses seasonal ingredients at their peak to create dishes full of flavour and free from ostentation. Attractive oak-panelled room, with booth seating for larger groups. Personable and unobtrusive service.

XX ✿

Semplice (Marco Torri)

9-10 Blenheim St. ✉ *W1S 1LJ – Ⓜ Bond Street – ✆ (020) 7495 1509 – www.ristorantesemplice.com – Closed 2 weeks Christmas, Easter, Saturday lunch and Sunday* **G3**

Rest – *(booking essential at dinner)* Menu £ 30 (lunch) – Carte £ 34/53

Spec. Veal served with tonnata sauce. Rabbit with glazed carrots and artichoke sauce. Domori chocolate fondant

◆ Italian ◆ Fashionable ◆

Plenty of regulars are always in evidence in this comfortable and stylish restaurant, decorated with ebony, leather and gold. The enthusiasm of the young owners is palpable; the kitchen uses small, specialist suppliers in unfussy, flavoursome dishes.

XX ✿

Nobu Berkeley St

15 Berkeley St. ✉ *W1J 8DY – Ⓜ Green Park – ✆ (020) 7290 9222 – www.noburestaurants.com/berkeley – Closed 25-26 December, Saturday, Sunday and bank holidays* **H3**

Rest – *(booking essential)* Carte £ 65/85

Spec. King crab claw tempura with butter ponzu. Black cod with miso. Chocolate tart with sake kasu ice cream and chocolate sauce.

◆ Japanese ◆ Fashionable ◆

Offers all the innovative Nobu favourites, along with specialities from the wood oven. Large, lively but smoothly run first floor operation with plenty of glamour; ground floor destination bar. Helpful, well-informed service.

XX

Maze Grill – at London Marriott H. Grosvenor Square

10-13 Grosvenor Sq. ✉ *W1K 6JP – Ⓜ Bond Street – ✆ (020) 7495 2211 – www.gordonramsay.com* **G3**

Rest – Menu £ 21 (lunch) – Carte £ 30/47

◆ Beef specialities ◆ Retro ◆

An addendum to Maze, with a menu specialising in steaks, from Hereford grass-fed to Wagyu 9th grade; all appealingly served on wooden boards, with a variety of sauces and side dishes.

XX

Bellamy's

18 Bruton Pl. ✉ *W1J 6LY – Ⓜ Bond Street – ✆ (020) 7491 2727 – www.bellamysrestaurant.co.uk – Closed Saturday lunch, Sunday and bank holidays,* **H3**

Rest – Menu £ 29 – Carte £ 43/57

◆ French ◆ Brasserie ◆

French deli/brasserie tucked down a smart mews. Go past the caviar and cheeses into the restaurant proper for a very traditional, but well-executed, range of Gallic classics.

XX

Patterson's

4 Mill St. ✉ *W1S 2AX – Ⓜ Oxford Street – ✆ (020) 7499 1308 – www.pattersonsrestaurant.com – Closed 25-26 December, Saturday lunch and Sunday* **H3**

Rest – Menu £ 23/45

◆ Modern European ◆ Intimate ◆

Stylish modern interior in black and white. Elegant tables and attentive service. Modern British cooking with concise wine list and sensible prices.

XX

Alloro

19-20 Dover St. ✉ W1S 4LU – Ⓜ Green Park – ☎ (020) 7495 4768
– www.alloro-restaurant.co.uk
– Closed Christmas-New Year, Saturday lunch and Sunday **H3**

Rest – Menu £ 33/35

♦ Italian ♦ Fashionable ♦

Confidently run and smartly dressed Italian with an appealing and sensibly priced menu of easy-to-eat dishes. All breads and pasta made in-house. Boisterous and busy adjacent baretto.

XX

Goodman

26 Maddox St. ✉ W1S 1QH – Ⓜ Oxford Circus – ☎ (020) 74993776
– www.goodmanrestaurants.com
– Closed Sunday and bank holidays **H3**

Rest – *(booking essential)* Menu £ 18 (lunch) – Carte £ 26/51

♦ Beef specialities ♦ Brasserie ♦

A worthy attempt at recreating a New York steakhouse; all leather and wood and macho swagger. Beef is dry or wet aged in house and comes with a choice of four sauces; rib-eye the speciality.

XX

Dolada

13 Albemarle St. ✉ W1S 4HJ – Ⓜ Green Park – ☎ (020) 7409 1011
– www.dolada.co.uk
– Closed 23 December-6 January, Saturday lunch and Sunday **H3**

Rest – Menu £ 23 (lunch) – Carte £ 22/46

♦ Italian ♦ Neighbourhood ♦

Smart basement restaurant lightened by confident and thoughtful service. Dishes from across Italy; the deconstructed spaghetti carbonara a speciality. Even more originality in the tasting menu.

XX

Hush

8 Lancashire Ct., Brook St. ✉ W1S 1EY – Ⓜ Bond Street – ☎ (020) 7659 1500 – www.hush.co.uk
– Closed 25-26 December, 1 January and Sunday **H3**

Rest – *(booking essential)* Carte £ 25/47

♦ Modern European ♦ Fashionable ♦

Accessible brasserie-style menu served in a large, busy room; smart destination bar upstairs and plenty of private dining. Tucked away in a charming courtyard, with a summer terrace.

XX

Fakhreldine

85 Piccadilly ✉ W1J 7NB – Ⓜ Green Park – ☎ (020) 7493 3424
– www.fakhreldine.co.uk **H4**

Rest – Menu £ 14/29 – Carte £ 28/42

♦ Lebanese ♦ Fashionable ♦

Long-standing restaurant with great view of Green Park. Large selection of classic meze dishes and more modern European-style menu of original Lebanese dishes.

XX ✿

Nobu – at The Metropolitan Hotel

19 Old Park Ln. ✉ W1Y 1LB – Ⓜ Hyde Park Corner – ☎ (020) 7447 4747
– www.noburestaurants.com
– Closed 25-26 December and 1 January **G4**

Rest – *(booking essential)* Carte £ 37/68

Spec. Tuna sashimi salad with matsuhisa dressing. Black cod with miso. Chocolate bento box with green tea ice cream.

♦ Japanese ♦ Fashionable ♦ Minimalist ♦

Its celebrity clientele ensure this remains one of the more glamorous spots. Staff are fully conversant in the innovative menu that adds South American influences to Japanese cooking. Has spawned many imitators.

XX

Tempo

54 Curzon St. ✉ W1J 8PG – Ⓜ Green Park – ☏ (020) 7629 2742 – www.tempomayfair.co.uk – Closed 24 December-3 January, Sunday and bank holidays **H4**

Rest – Menu £ 22 (lunch) – Carte £ 29/50

♦ Italian ♦ Neighbourhood ♦ Fashionable ♦

The hands-on owner is a reassuring presence in this cosy restaurant, which re-opened in 2010 after a full revamp. The menu covers all Italian regions and includes cicchetti, or small plates.

XX

Sumosan

26 Albemarle St. ✉ W1S 4HY – Ⓜ Green Park – ☏ (020) 7495 5999 – www.sumosan.com – Closed bank holidays, lunch Saturday and Sunday

Rest – Carte £ 53/97 **H3**

♦ Japanese ♦ Fashionable ♦

Aims to attract the smart set, with its cocktail list, modern interpretations of Japanese flavours and too-cool-to-smile service. Skilled kitchen deftly executes a wide-ranging menu.

XX

Mews of Mayfair

10-11 Lancashire Ct., Brook St. (first floor) ✉ W1S 1EY – Ⓜ Bond Street – ☏ (020) 7518 9388 – www.mewsofmayfair.com – Closed 25-26 December, Sunday dinner and bank holidays **H3**

Rest – Menu £ 19 (lunch) – Carte £ 29/47

♦ Modern European ♦ Friendly ♦

This pretty restaurant, bright in summer and warm in winter, is on the first floor of a mews house, once used as storage rooms for Savile Row. Seasonal menus offer something for everyone.

XX

Chor Bizarre

16 Albemarle St. ✉ W1S 4HW – Ⓜ Green Park – ☏ (020) 7629 9802 – www.chorbizarre.com **H3**

Rest – Carte £ 32/47

♦ Indian ♦ Exotic ♦

Eccentric and colourful décor of trinkets, curios and antiques; the name translates as 'thieves' market'. The menu is long and chatty; dishes from more northerly parts of India are the highlight.

XX

Sketch (The Gallery)

9 Conduit St. ✉ W1S 2XG – Ⓜ Oxford Street – ☏ (020) 7659 4500 – www.sketch.uk.com – Closed 25-26 December, Sunday and bank holidays

Rest – *(dinner only) (booking essential)* Carte £ 35/63 **H3**

♦ International ♦ Trendy ♦

Art gallery during the day morphs into a noisy brasserie at night, when aphorisms are projected onto the white walls. Menu is international in its scope; the cocktail list is equally popular.

XX

Cocoon

65 Regent St. ✉ W1B 4EA – Ⓜ Piccadilly Circus – ☏ (020) 7494 7600 – www.cocoon-restaurants.com **H3**

Rest – Menu £ 25/50 – Carte £ 31/44

♦ Asian ♦ Exotic ♦

Trendy restaurant, based on a prime Regent Street site. Silk nets cleverly divide long, winding room. Bold, eclectic menus cover a wide spectrum of Asian dishes.

XX

Momo

25 Heddon St. ✉ W1B 4BH – Ⓜ Oxford Circus – ☏ (020) 7434 4040 – www.momoresto.com – Closed 25 December and Sunday lunch

Rest – Menu £ 19 (lunch) – Carte £ 31/47 **H3**

♦ Moroccan ♦ Exotic ♦

Lanterns, rugs, trinkets and music contribute to the authentic Moroccan atmosphere; come in a group to better appreciate it. The more traditional dishes are the kitchen's strength.

XX

Veeraswamy

Victory House, 99 Regent St. (entrance on Swallow St.) ✉ W1B 4RS – Ⓜ Piccadilly Circus – ✆ (020) 7734 1401 – www.realindianfood.com – Closed dinner 25 December **H3**

Rest – Menu £ 21 (lunch and early dinner) – Carte £ 34/49

♦ Indian ♦ Design ♦

May have opened back in 1926 but feels fresh and is awash with vibrant colours and always full of bustle. Skilled kitchen cleverly mixes the traditional with more contemporary creations.

XX

La Petite Maison

54 Brooks Mews ✉ W1K 4EG – Ⓜ Bond Street – ✆ (020) 7495 4774 – www.lpmlondon.co.uk – Closed 25-26 December **H3**

Rest – Carte £ 32/65

♦ French ♦ Fashionable ♦

Open-plan restaurant; sister to the eponymous Nice original. Healthy French Mediterranean cooking with a seafood slant. 20 starters to choose from; sharing is encouraged.

XX

Cafe at Sotheby's

34-35 New Bond St. ✉ W1A 2AA – Ⓜ Bond Street – ✆ (020) 7293 5077 – www.sothebys.com – Closed 24 December-4 January, Saturday, Sunday and bank hoildays

Rest – *(lunch only) (booking essential)* Carte £ 26/35 **H3**

♦ Modern European ♦ Intimate ♦

Occupying a cosy space just off the foyer of the famous auction house. The appealing lunch menu changes weekly; the lobster sandwich is a perennial favourite. Service is discreet.

XX

Kiku

17 Half Moon St. ✉ W1J 7BE – Ⓜ Green Park – ✆ (020) 7499 4208 – www.kikurestaurant.co.uk – Closed 25 December, 1 January, lunch Sunday and bank holidays

Rest – Menu £ 20 (lunch) – Carte £ 29/55 **H4**

♦ Japanese ♦ Neighbourhood ♦ Friendly ♦

Bright and fresh feel thanks to minimalistic décor of stone and natural wood. A plethora of menus, a fierce adherence to seasonality and an authentic emphasis on presentation.

X

Bar Trattoria Semplice

22 Woodstock St. ✉ W1C 2AR – Ⓜ Bond Street – ✆ (020) 74918638 – www.bartrattoriasemplice.com – Closed 25-26 December, Easter and bank holidays **G3**

Rest – Menu £ 17 (lunch) – Carte £ 23/36

♦ Italian ♦ Friendly ♦

Baby sister to Semplice a few yards away, offering simpler, well-priced cooking in a relaxed and fun room. Specialities from a different region of Italy are featured each month. All-day menu in bar.

X

Chisou

4 Princes St. ✉ W1B 2LE – Ⓜ Oxford Circus – ✆ (020) 7629 3931 – www.chisou.co.uk – Closed Christmas-New Year, Sunday and bank holidays **H2/3**

Rest – Menu £ 15 (lunch) – Carte £ 25/43

♦ Japanese ♦ Cosy ♦ Minimalist ♦

In Mayfair's Japanese quarter; simple slate flooring and polished wood tables. Cosy sushi bar to rear. Elaborate menus of modern/classic Japanese dishes. Gets very busy.

Bentley's (Oyster Bar)

11-15 Swallow St. ✉ *W1B 4DG – Ⓜ Piccadilly Circus – ☎ (020) 7734 4756 – www.bentleys.org – Closed 25 December and 1 January* **H3**

Rest – Carte £ 29/85

◆ Seafood ◆ Bistro ◆

Sit at the counter to watch white-jacketed staff open oysters by the bucket load. Interesting seafood menus feature tasty fish pies; lots of daily specials on blackboard.

Aubaine

4 Heddon St. ✉ *W1B 4BS – Ⓜ Oxford Circus – ☎ (020) 7440 2510 – www.aubaine.co.uk – Closed Sunday dinner* **H3**

Rest – Menu £ 19 (lunch) – Carte approx. £ 28

◆ French ◆ Bistro ◆

Sister to the Chelsea original but this time without the boulangerie. The look is of a farmhouse as imagined by a townie; the accessible menu wouldn't look out of place in a bistro.

Automat

33 Dover St. ✉ *W1S 4NF – Ⓜ Green Park – ☎ (020) 7499 3033 – www.automat-london.com – Closed 25-26 December and 1 January* **H3**

Rest – Carte £ 39/50

◆ American ◆ Brasserie ◆

Buzzing New York style brasserie in three areas: a café, a 'dining car' with deep leather banquettes, and actual brasserie itself. Classic dishes from burgers to cheesecake.

Le Boudin Blanc

5 Trebeck St. ✉ *W1J 7LT – Ⓜ Green Park – ☎ (020) 7499 3292 – www.boudinblanc.co.uk – Closed 24-26 December* **G4**

Rest – Menu £ 15 (lunch and early dinner) – Carte £ 32/44

◆ French ◆ Rustic ◆

Appealing, lively French bistro in Shepherd Market, spread over two floors. Satisfying French classics and country cooking is the draw, along with authentic Gallic service. Good value lunch menu.

Only Running Footman

5 Charles St ✉ *W1J 5DF – Ⓜ Green Park. – ☎ (020) 7499 2988 – www.therunningfootmanmayfair.com* **H3**

Rest – Carte £ 26/35

◆ Pub ◆ Traditional ◆

Busy ground floor bar with its appealing menu of pub classics doesn't take bookings. By contrast, upstairs is formal and its menu more European and ambitious but simpler dishes still the best.

Soho

Soho

4 Richmond Mews ✉ *W1D 3DH – Ⓜ Tottenham Court Road – ☎ (020) 7559 3000 – www.sohohotel.com* **I3**

89 rm – †£ 348 ††£ 432, ☕ £ 19.50 – 2 suites

Rest *Refuel* – ☎ *(020) 7559 3007* – Menu £ 23 – Carte £ 32/48

◆ Luxury ◆ Stylish ◆

Stylish and very fashionable hotel boasts two screening rooms, comfy drawing room and up-to-the-minute bedrooms, some vivid, others more muted, all boasting hi-tech extras. Contemporary bar and restaurant.

Sanctum Soho

20 Warwick St ✉ W1B 5NF – Ⓜ Piccadilly Circus – ✆ (020) 7292 6100 – www.sanctumsoho.com **H3**

30 rm – †£ 276/516 ††£ 276/516, ☕ £ 15

Rest *No. 20* – *(Closed Sunday dinner)* Menu £ 20 – Carte £ 27/39

◆ Modern ◆ Classic ◆

Plenty of glitz and bling at this funky, self-styled rock 'n' roll hotel, with some innovative touches such as TVs behind mirrors. Rooftop lounge and hot tub. Relaxed and comfortable dining with plenty of classic dishes.

Dean Street Townhouse

69-71 Dean St. ✉ W1D 3SE – ✆ (0207) 4341775 – www.deanstreettownhouse.com **I3**

39 rm – †£ 120/270 ††£ 120/270, ☕ £ 15

Rest *Dean Street Townhouse Restaurant* – see below

◆ Townhouse ◆ Classic ◆

In the heart of Soho where bedrooms range from tiny to bigger; the latter have roll-top baths in the room. All are well designed and come with a good range of extras. Cosy ground floor lounge.

Hazlitt's without rest

6 Frith St ✉ W1D 3JA – Ⓜ Tottenham Court Road – ✆ (020) 7434 1771 – www.hazlittshotel.com **I3**

29 rm – †£ 149/230 ††£ 169/230 – 3 suites

◆ Townhouse ◆ Historic ◆

Three adjoining early 18C townhouses and former home of the eponymous essayist. Idiosyncratic bedrooms, many with antique furniture and Victorian baths; ask for one of the newer ones.

XXX ✿

Gauthier - Soho

21 Romilly St ✉ W1D 5AF – Ⓜ Leicester Square – ✆ (020) 7494 3111 – www.gauthiersoho.co.uk – Closed 21-30 August, Sunday, lunch Saturday and bank holidays

Rest – Menu £ 25/35 **I3**

Spec. Truffle risotto with brown butter and Parmesan. Roast red deer with pear and celeriac. Goose egg soufflé with chocolate custard.

◆ French ◆ Intimate ◆ Neighbourhood ◆

Professionally run restaurant with an intimate and somewhat secretive feel, spread over three floors of an 18C townhouse. The refined and elegant cooking emphasises the natural flavours of the quality ingredients.

XXX

Quo Vadis

26-29 Dean St. ✉ W1D 3LL – Ⓜ Tottenham Court Road – ✆ (020) 7437 9585 – www.quovadis.co.uk – Closed Sunday from 30 April-1 October and bank holidays **I3**

Rest – Menu £ 20 (lunch) – Carte £ 29/33

◆ British ◆ Fashionable ◆

Dating from the 1920s and renewed in 2008; a veritable Soho institution with an art deco feel. Instantly appealing menu of carefully prepared classics, from grilled Hereford beef to assorted seafood.

XXX

Aqua Nueva

240 Regent St. (entrance on Argyll St.) ✉ W1F 7EB – Ⓜ Oxford Circus – ✆ (020) 74780540 – www.aqua-london.com – Closed 25-26 December, 1 January and Sunday **H3**

Rest – Menu £ 20 (lunch) – Carte £ 30/52

◆ Spanish ◆ Design ◆ Fashionable ◆

Large operation on the 5th floor of a former department store. Choose between the elegant main dining room or the more buzzy but equally stylish tapas bar. Spanish food interpreted in a modern style.

XXX **Red Fort**

77 Dean St. ✉ *W1D 3SH* – Ⓜ *Tottenham Court Road – ☎ (020) 7437 2525 – www.redfort.co.uk – Closed 25 December, lunch Saturday, Sunday and bank holidays* **I3**

Rest – *(booking advisable at dinner)* Menu £ 20/40 – Carte £ 33/40

♦ Indian ♦ Fashionable ♦

Smart, stylish restaurant with modern water feature and glass ceiling to rear. Seasonally changing menus of authentic dishes handed down over generations.

XX **Dean Street Townhouse Restaurant**

69-71 Dean St. ✉ *W1D 3SE* – Ⓜ *Tottenham Court Road – ☎ (0207) 4341775 – www.deanstreettownhouse.com* **I3**

Rest – *(booking essential)* Carte £ 22/40

♦ British ♦ Brasserie ♦ Elegant ♦

Georgian house now home to a fashionable and very busy bar and restaurant; the Parlour is the less hectic area. Appealingly classic British food includes some retro dishes and satisfying puddings.

XX ✿ **Yauatcha**

15 Broadwick St ✉ *W1F 0DL* – Ⓜ *Tottenham Court Road – ☎ (020) 7494 8888 – www.yauatcha.com – Closed 24-25 December* **I3**

Rest – Carte £ 27/59

Spec. Scallop shu mai with tobiko caviar. Spicy king soya wagyu beef. Chocolate and raspberry delice with vanilla ice cream.

♦ Chinese ♦ Design ♦

Refined, delicate and delicious dim sum; ideal for sharing in a group. Stylish surroundings spread over two floors: the lighter, brighter ground floor or the darker, more atmospheric basement. Afternoon teas also a speciality.

XX **Aqua Kyoto**

240 Regent St. (entrance on Argyll St.) ✉ *W1F 7EB* – Ⓜ *Oxford Circus – ☎ (020) 7478 0540 – www.aqua-london.com – Closed 25-26 December, 1 January and Sunday* **H3**

Rest – Menu £ 17 (lunch) – Carte £ 34/54

♦ Japanese ♦ Trendy ♦

The more boisterous of the two large restaurants on the 5th floor of Aqua London, along with a busy bar. Ideally suited to larger groups, as the contemporary Japanese food is designed for sharing.

XX **Bob Bob Ricard**

1 Upper James St ✉ *W1F 9DF* – Ⓜ *Oxford Circus – ☎ (020) 3145 1000 – www.bobbobricard.com – Closed 25-26 December* **H3**

Rest – Carte £ 26/49

♦ Modern European ♦ Retro ♦

Enigmatically decorated and flamboyant grand café, with a menu that offers everything from caviar and jelly, to beef Wellington or a bowl of cornflakes. Open from early to very late.

XX **Floridita**

100 Wardour St ✉ *W1F 0TN* – Ⓜ *Tottenham Court Road – ☎ (020) 7314 4000 – www.floriditalondon.com – Closed 25-26 December, 1 January, Sunday, Monday and bank holidays* **I3**

Rest – *(dinner only and lunch in December)* Menu £ 39 – Carte £ 28/60

♦ Latin American ♦ Musical ♦

Mediterranean tapas on the ground floor; the huge downstairs for live music, dancing and Latin American specialities, from Cuban spice to Argentinean beef. Great cocktails and a party atmosphere.

XX

Benja

17 Beak St ✉ W1F 9RW – Ⓜ Oxford Circus – ✆ (020) 7287 0555 – www.benjarestaurant.com – Closed Sunday **H3**

Rest – Carte £ 25/39

♦ Thai ♦ Intimate ♦ Exotic ♦

Soho townhouse divided into three sleek and colourful floors including an intimate basement bar. Thai food is carefully prepared and full of punchy flavours. Service is very charming.

XX

Vasco and Piero's Pavilion

15 Poland St ✉ W1F 8QE – Ⓜ Oxford Circus – ✆ (020) 7437 8774 – www.vascosfood.com – Closed Saturday lunch, Sunday and bank holidays

Rest – *(booking essential at lunch)* Menu £ 20 – Carte lunch £ 27/38 **H2**

♦ Italian ♦ Friendly ♦

Celebrating forty years in 2011; its longevity down to its twice-daily changing menu and the simple but effective Umbrian-influenced cooking. The bright room attracts a high proportion of regulars.

XX

La Trouvaille

12A Newburgh St. ✉ W1F 7RR – Ⓜ Oxford Circus – ✆ (020) 7287 8488 – www.latrouvaille.co.uk – Closed Monday dinner, Sunday and bank holidays **H3**

Rest – Menu £ 21/35

♦ French ♦ Bistro ♦ Friendly ♦

In a charming cobbled street and keenly run by two northern Frenchmen. Ground floor for cheese, charcuterie and wine; upstairs for set menus of classic French cooking. Wines are largely organic.

XX

Plum Valley

20 Gerrard St ✉ W1D 6JQ – Ⓜ Leicester Square – ✆ (020) 7494 4366 – Closed 24-25 December **I3**

Rest – Menu £ 38 – Carte £ 19/30

♦ Chinese ♦ Design ♦

Its striking black façade make this modern Chinese restaurant easy to spot in Chinatown. Mostly Cantonese cooking, with occasional forays into Vietnam and Thailand; dim sum is the strength.

X

Arbutus

63-64 Frith St. ✉ W1D 3JW – Ⓜ Tottenham Court Road – ✆ (020) 7734 4545 – www.arbutusrestaurant.co.uk – Closed 25-26 December and 1 January **I3**

Rest – *(booking advisable)* Menu £ 17 (lunch) – Carte £ 28/37

Spec. Braised pigs head, ravioli of caramelised onions. Rabbit with braised celery and shoulder cottage pie. Crème caramel.

♦ Modern European ♦ Bistro ♦

It takes a lot of work and experience to make it all look so easy. Bubbly and enthusiastic service; relaxed, sociable surroundings and bistro-style dishes packed with flavour from a highly skilled kitchen. Terrific, affordable wine list.

X

Bocca di Lupo

12 Archer St. ✉ WID 7BB – Ⓜ Piccadilly Circus – ✆ (020) 7734 2223 – www.boccadilupo.com – Closed Christmas-New Year and Sunday dinner **I3**

Rest – *(booking essential)* Carte £ 19/39

♦ Italian ♦ Tapas bar ♦

Deservedly busy and great fun; but atmosphere, food and service are all best when sitting at the marble counter, watching the chefs. Specialities from across Italy are available in large or small sizes; they're full of flavour and vitality.

Polpo

41 Beak St. ✉ W1F 9SB – Ⓜ Oxford Circus – ✆ (0207) 734 4479 – www.polpo.co.uk – Closed 25 December-1 January, Sunday dinner and bank holidays

Rest – Carte £ 12/20 **H3**

♦ Italian ♦ Tapas bar ♦

A fun and lively Venetian bacaro, with a stripped-down, faux-industrial look. The small plates, from arancini and prosciutto to fritto misto and Cotechino sausage, are so well priced that waiting for a table is worth it.

Dehesa

25 Ganton St. ✉ W1F 9BP – Ⓜ Oxford Circus – ✆ (020) 7494 4170 – www.dehesa.co.uk – Closed Christmas and Sunday dinner **H3**

Rest – Carte £ 20/30

♦ Mediterranean ♦ Tapas bar ♦

Repeats the success of its sister restaurant, Salt Yard, by offering tasty, good value Spanish and Italian tapas. Unhurried atmosphere in appealing corner location. Terrific drinks list too.

Hix

66-70 Brewer St. ✉ WIF 9UP – Ⓜ Piccadilly Circus – ✆ (020) 72923518 – www.hixsoho.co.uk – Closed 25-26 December **H3**

Rest – Carte £ 27/55

♦ British ♦ Fashionable ♦

The exterior hints at exclusivity but the enormous interior is fun and sociable and comes decorated with the works of eminent British artists. Expect classic British dishes and ingredients.

Tierra Brindisa

46 Broadwick St. ✉ W1F 7AF – Ⓜ Tottenham Court Road – ✆ (020) 7534 1690 – www.brindisatapaskitchens.com – Closed Sunday

Rest – *(booking essential at dinner)* Carte £ 18/30 **H3**

♦ Spanish ♦ Tapas bar ♦

Sister to Tapas Brindisa in Borough Market; this is a slightly more structured affair but still as busy and enjoyable. Focus is on natural flavours, uncluttered plates and quality Spanish produce.

Barrafina

54 Frith St. ✉ W1D 3SL – Ⓜ Tottenham Court Road – ✆ (020) 7813 8016 – www.barrafina.co.uk – Closed bank holidays **I3**

Rest – *(bookings not accepted)* Carte £ 30/45

♦ Spanish ♦ Tapas bar ♦

Centred around a counter with seating for 20, come here if you want authentic Spanish tapas served in a buzzy atmosphere. Seafood is a speciality and the Jabugo ham a must.

Barshu

28 Frith St. ✉ W1D 5LF – Ⓜ Leicester Square – ✆ (020) 7287 8822 – www.bar-shu.co.uk – Closed 24-25 December **I3**

Rest – *(booking advisable)* Carte £ 24/35

♦ Chinese ♦ Exotic ♦

The fiery and authentic flavours of China's Sichuan Province are the draw here; help is at hand as menu has pictures. It's decorated with carved wood and lanterns; downstairs is better for groups.

Imli

167-169 Wardour St ✉ W1F 8WR – Ⓜ Tottenham Court Road – ✆ (020) 7287 4243 – www.imli.co.uk – Closed 25-26 December and 1 January

Rest – Menu £ 9 (weekday lunch)/13 – Carte £ 20/30 **I3**

♦ Indian ♦ Bistro ♦

Long, spacious interior is a busy, buzzy place. Good value, fresh and tasty Indian tapas-style dishes prove a popular currency. Same owners as Tamarind.

Polpetto

46 Dean St, (1st floor) ✉ W1D 5BG – Ⓜ Leicester Square – ☎ (020) 77341969 – www.polpetto.co.uk – Closed 25 December-1 January, Sunday and bank holidays **I3**

Rest – Carte £ 16/22

♦ Italian ♦ Tapas bar ♦ Friendly ♦

Baby sister to Polpo is located, incongruously, above the iconic French House pub. It's just one small but thoughtfully designed room; order a number of the small, keenly priced plates.

Ba Shan

24 Romilly St. ✉ W1D 5AH – Ⓜ Leicester Square – ☎ (020) 72873266 – Closed Christmas **I3**

Rest – *(booking advisable)* Carte £ 16/26

♦ Chinese ♦ Cosy ♦

3-4 tables in each of the five rooms. Open all day, serving a mix of 'snack' and 'home-style' dishes, some with Sichuan leanings, others from northern areas and Henan province.

Baozi Inn

25 Newport Court ✉ WC2H 7JS – Ⓜ Leicester Square – ☎ (020) 7287 6877 – Closed 24-25 December **I3**

Rest – Carte £ 19/25

♦ Chinese ♦ Exotic ♦

Baozi, or steamed filled buns, are a good way to start, followed by some fiery Sichuan specialities. Simple, honest and friendly restaurant, just off the main strip of Chinatown.

St James's

The Ritz

150 Piccadilly ✉ W1J 9BR – Ⓜ Green Park – ☎ (020) 7493 8181 – www.theritzlondon.com **H4**

116 rm – †£ 300/954 ††£ 420/954, ☕ £ 35 – 17 suites

Rest *The Ritz Restaurant* – see below

♦ Grand Luxury ♦ Stylish ♦

World famous hotel, opened 1906 as a fine example of Louis XVI architecture and decoration. Elegant Palm Court famed for its afternoon tea. Many of the lavishly appointed and luxurious rooms and suites overlook the park.

Sofitel St James London

6 Waterloo Pl. ✉ SW1Y 4AN – Ⓜ Piccadilly Circus – ☎ (020) 7747 2200 – www.sofitelstjames.com **I4**

180 rm ☕ – †£ 450/510 ††£ 528 – 6 suites

Rest *Brasserie Roux* – see below

♦ Luxury ♦ Classic ♦

Grade II listed building in smart Pall Mall location. Classically English interiors include floral Rose Lounge and clubby bar. Comfortable, well-fitted bedrooms and impressive spa.

Haymarket

1 Suffolk Pl. ✉ SW1Y 4HX – Ⓜ Piccadilly Circus – ☎ (020) 7470 4000 – www.firmdalehotels.com **I4**

47 rm – †£ 396 ††£ 396, ☕ £ 19.50 – 3 suites

Rest *Brumus* – Menu £ 22 – Carte £ 32/48

♦ Luxury ♦ Stylish ♦

Smart, spacious hotel in John Nash Regency building, with stylish blend of modern and antique furnishings. Large, comfortable bedrooms in soothing colours. Impressive pool. Brumus bar and restaurant puts focus on Italian cooking.

Dukes

35 St James's Pl. ✉ *SW1A 1NY* – Ⓜ *Green Park* – ✆ *(020) 7491 4840*
– *www.dukeshotel.com* **H4**

84 rm – †£ 234/530 ††£ 414/689, ☕ £ 22 – 6 suites

Rest – Menu £ 19/21 – Carte £ 30/44

♦ Traditional ♦ Luxury ♦ Classic ♦

The most recent redecoration retained the discreet, traditionally British feel of this hotel in a central but quiet location. Dukes bar famous for its martinis. Elegant bedrooms with country house feel. Discreet dining room.

Stafford

16-18 St James's Pl. ✉ *SW1A 1NJ* – Ⓜ *Green Park* – ✆ *(020) 7493 0111*
– *www.kempinski.com/london* **H4**

73 rm – †£ 492/528 ††£ 528, ☕ £ 25 – 15 suites

Rest – *(closed Saturday lunch and bank holidays)* Menu £ 30 (lunch) – Carte dinner £ 34/65

♦ Townhouse ♦ Stylish ♦

A genteel atmosphere prevails in this discreet 'country house in the city'. Bedrooms divided between main house, converted 18C stables and newer Mews. Traditional and intimate dining room.

St James's Hotel and Club

7-8 Park Pl. ✉ *SW1A 1LS* – Ⓜ *Green Park* – ✆ *(020) 7316 1600*
– *www.stjameshotelandclub.com* **H4**

50 rm – †£ 282/414 ††£ 282/522, ☕ £ 22 – 10 suites

Rest ***Seven Park Place*** – see below

♦ Business ♦ Modern ♦

1890s house in cul-de-sac, formerly a private club, reopened as a hotel in 2008. Modern, boutique–style interior with over 200 paintings. Fine finish to compact, but well-equipped bedrooms.

The Ritz Restaurant – at The Ritz Hotel

150 Piccadilly ✉ *W1J 9BR* – Ⓜ *Green Park* – ✆ *(020) 7493 8181*
– *www.theritzlondon.com* **H4**

Rest – Menu £ 39/48 – Carte £ 64/87

♦ Traditional ♦ Luxury ♦

Grand and lavish restaurant, with Louis XVI decoration, trompe l'oeil and ornate gilding. Delightful terrace over Green Park. Structured, formal service. Classic, traditional dishes are the highlight of the menu. Jacket and tie required.

The Wolseley

160 Piccadilly ✉ *W1J 9EB* – Ⓜ *Green Park* – ✆ *(020) 7499 6996*
– *www.thewolseley.com*
– *Closed dinner 24 and 31 December, 25 December and August bank holiday*

Rest – *(booking essential)* Carte £ 21/51 **H4**

♦ Modern European ♦ Fashionable ♦

Feels like a grand European coffee house, with pillars and high vaulted ceiling. Appealing menus range from caviar to a hot dog. Open from breakfast and boasts a celebrity following.

Seven Park Place – at St James's Hotel and Club

7-8 Park Pl. ✉ *SW1A 1LS* – Ⓜ *Green Park* – ✆ *(020) 7316 1614* – *www.stjameshotelandclub.com* – *Closed Sunday and Monday*

Rest – *(booking essential)* Menu £ 30/45 **H4**

Spec. Foie gras with roasted peaches and gingerbread. Lamb with garlic purée and rosemary jus. White chocolate parfait with cherries.

♦ Modern European ♦ Cosy ♦ Fashionable ♦

Small restaurant concealed somewhat within St. James's Hotel and divided between two rooms; ask for the gilded back room. The accomplished food has a French base, displays confidence and clarity and uses quality British ingredients.

XXX **Sake No Hana**

23 St James's St ✉ SW1A 1HA – Ⓜ Green Park – ☎ (020) 7925 8988 – www.sakenohana.com – Closed 24-25 December and Sunday lunch

Rest – Carte £ 20/60 **H4**

◆ Japanese ◆ Design ◆

Stylish first floor restaurant reached by elevator, where cedar wood décor goes some way to disguising an ugly '60s building. Mix of traditional and modern Japanese food; ground floor sushi bar.

XX **Brasserie Roux** – at Sofitel St James London

8 Pall Mall ✉ SW1Y 5NG – Ⓜ Piccadilly Circus – ☎ (020) 7968 2900 – www.brasserieroux.com **I4**

Rest – Menu £ 20 – Carte £ 21/45

◆ French ◆ Brasserie ◆

Informal, smart, classic brasserie style with large windows making the most of the location. Extensive choice of French classics. Restaurant concept to change mid 2011.

XX **Le Caprice**

Arlington House, Arlington St. ✉ SW1A 1RJ – Ⓜ Green Park – ☎ (020) 7629 2239 – www.le-caprice.co.uk – Closed 24-26 December and 1 January **H4**

Rest – Menu £ 20 (dinner) – Carte £ 29/53

◆ Modern European ◆ Fashionable ◆

Still attracting a fashionable clientele and as busy as ever. Dine at the bar or in the smoothly run restaurant. Food combines timeless classics with modern dishes.

XX **Franco's**

61 Jermyn St. ✉ SW1Y 6LX – Ⓜ Green Park – ☎ (020) 7499 2211 – www.francoslondon.com – Closed Sunday and bank holidays

Rest – *(booking essential)* Menu £ 26 (lunch) – Carte £ 37/52 **H4**

◆ Italian ◆ Formal ◆

Open from breakfast until late, with café at the front leading into smart, clubby restaurant. Menu covers all parts of Italy and includes popular grill section and plenty of classics.

XX **Avenue**

7-9 St James's St. ✉ SW1A 1EE – Ⓜ Green Park – ☎ (020) 7321 2111 – www.theavenue-restaurant.co.uk – Closed 25-26 December, Saturday lunch and Sunday **H4**

Rest – Menu £ 25 – Carte £ 28/57

◆ Modern European ◆ Brasserie ◆

Large, brash restaurant, with sheer white décor and a very popular bar. All-encompassing menu, with everything from caviar to burgers. Service comes with an urgency not always required.

XX **Matsuri - St James's**

15 Bury St. ✉ SW1Y 6AL – Ⓜ Green Park – ☎ (020) 7839 1101 – www.matsuri-restaurant.com – Closed 25 December and 1 January

Rest – Menu £ 25 (lunch and early dinner) – Carte £ 25/44 **H4**

◆ Japanese ◆ Friendly ◆

Sweet natured service at this traditional Japanese stalwart. Teppan-yaki is their speciality, with Scottish beef the highlight; sushi counter also available. Good value lunch menus.

XX **Quaglino's**

16 Bury St ✉ SW1Y 6AL – Ⓜ Green Park – ☎ (020) 7930 6767 – www.quaglinos.co.uk – Closed 25 December, Sunday and bank holidays

Rest – Menu £ 20 – Carte £ 33/46 **H4**

◆ Modern European ◆ Design ◆

This big, bold restaurant achieved iconic status on reopening in the early '90s. No longer quite so glamorous but it still offers a good night out and a easy menu, with fruits de mer the highlight.

XX

Mint Leaf

Suffolk Pl. ✉ SW1Y 4HX – Ⓜ Piccadilly Circus – ☎ (020) 7930 9020 – www.mintleafrestaurant.com – Closed 25-26 December, 1 January, lunch Saturday and Sunday

Rest – Menu £ 18/20 – Carte £ 29/37 **I4**

♦ Indian ♦ Design ♦

Cavernous and moodily lit basement restaurant incorporating trendy bar with lounge music and extensive cocktail list. Contemporary Indian cooking with curries the highlight.

X

Al Duca

4-5 Duke of York St. ✉ SW1Y 6LA – Ⓜ Piccadilly Circus – ☎ (020) 7839 3090 – www.alduca-restaurant.co.uk – Closed 24 December-4 January and Sunday

Rest – Menu £ 18/28 **H4**

♦ Italian ♦ Friendly ♦

Cooking which focuses on flavour continues to draw in the regulars at this warm and spirited Italian restaurant. Prices are keen when one considers the central location and service is brisk and confident.

X

Inn the Park

St James's Park ✉ SW1A 2BJ – Ⓜ Charing Cross – ☎ (020) 7451 9999 – www.innthepark.com – Closed 25 December **I4**

Rest – Carte £ 26/36

♦ British ♦ Design ♦

Oliver Peyton's eco-friendly restaurant in the middle of the park, with a terrific terrace. British menu uses many small suppliers. Cooking is straightforward and wholesome.

X

Portrait

National Portrait Gallery, St Martin's Pl (3rd Floor) ✉ WC2H 0HE – Ⓜ Charing Cross – ☎ (020) 7312 2490 – www.searcys.co.uk – Closed 24-26 December *Plan III* **I3**

Rest – *(lunch only and dinner Thursday-Saturday) (booking essential)* Menu £ 25 – Carte £ 29/37

♦ Modern European ♦ Design ♦

On the top floor of National Portrait Gallery with rooftop local landmark views: a charming spot for lunch. Modern British/European dishes; weekend brunch.

X

The National Dining Rooms

Sainsbury Wing, The National Gallery, Trafalgar Sq ✉ WC2N 5DN – Ⓜ Charing Cross – ☎ (020) 7747 2525 – www.thenationaldiningrooms.co.uk – Closed 25-26 December and 1 January **I4**

Rest – *(lunch only and dinner Friday)* Menu £ 28 – Carte approx. £ 25

♦ British ♦ Design ♦

Set on the East Wing's first floor, you can tuck into cakes in the bakery or grab a prime corner table in the restaurant for great views and proudly seasonal British menus.

STRAND – COVENT GARDEN – LAMBETH *Plan III*

Strand and Covent Garden

Savoy

Strand ✉ WC2R 0EU – Ⓜ Charing Cross – ☎ (020) 7836 4343 – www.fairmont.com/savoy **J3**

221 rm – †£ 654/714 ††£ 1074, ☐ £ 30 – 47 suites

Rest *River Room* – Menu £ 29 – Carte £ 44/56

♦ Grand Luxury ♦ Stylish ♦

The grande dame of London hotels dazzles once again! Reopened in 2010 following a 3 year restoration, its luxurious bedrooms and stunning suites come in an Edwardian or art deco style. Thames Foyer is the hotel's heart; choose the famous American Bar or new Beaufort Bar. River Room now has a more contemporary feel.

One Aldwych

1 Aldwych ✉ WC2B 4RH – Ⓜ Temple – ✆ (020) 7300 1000 – www.onealdwych.com J3

93 rm – †£ 468/583 ††£ 468/583, ☕ £ 23 – 12 suites

Rest *Axis* – see below

Rest *Indigo* – Menu £ 20 – Carte £ 31/43

◆ Grand Luxury ◆ Modern ◆

Former 19C bank, now a stylish hotel with lots of artwork; the lobby changes its look seasonally and doubles as a bar. Stylish, contemporary bedrooms with the latest mod cons; the deluxe rooms and suites are particularly desirable. Impressive leisure facilities. Light, accessible menu at Indigo.

Swissôtel The Howard

Temple Pl ✉ WC2R 2PR – Ⓜ Temple – ✆ (020) 7836 3555 – www.swissotel.com/london J3

187 rm – †£ 140/260 ††£ 180/280, ☕ £ 23.50 – 2 suites

Rest *12 Temple Place* – *✆ (020) 7300 1700 (Closed 1 January, dinner 24 December, 25, 31 December, Saturday lunch, Sunday and bank holidays)* Menu £ 21 (lunch) – Carte £ 32/45

◆ Luxury ◆ Modern ◆

Discreet elegance is the order of the day at this handsomely appointed hotel. Many of the comfortable rooms enjoy balcony views of the Thames. Attentive service. Large terrace to restaurant serving modern European dishes.

St Martins Lane

45 St Martin's Ln ✉ WC2N 3HX – Ⓜ Charing Cross – ✆ (020) 7300 5500 – www.morganshotelgroup.com I3

202 rm – †£ 246/594 ††£ 246/594, ☕ £ 25 – 2 suites

Rest *Asia de Cuba* – Menu £ 60 – Carte £ 50/118

◆ Luxury ◆ Design ◆

The unmistakable hand of Philippe Starck evident at this most contemporary of hotels. Unique and stylish, from the starkly modern lobby to the state-of-the-art rooms. 350 varieties of rum and tasty Asian dishes at fashionable Asia de Cuba.

The Ivy

1-5 West St ✉ WC2H 9NQ – Ⓜ Leicester Square – ✆ (020) 7836 4751 – www.the-ivy.co.uk – Closed 24-26 December and 1 January

Rest – Carte £ 27/52 I3

◆ International ◆ Fashionable ◆

One of the original celebrity hang-out restaurants; still pulling them in. Appealing menu, from shepherd's pie to fishcakes and nursery puddings. Staff go about their business with alacrity.

Axis – at One Aldwych Hotel

1 Aldwych ✉ WC2B 4RH – Ⓜ Temple – ✆ (020) 7300 0300 – www.onealdwych.com – Closed Sunday and Monday J3

Rest – Menu £ 20 – Carte £ 32/42

◆ Modern European ◆ Design ◆

A spiral marble staircase leading down to this impressively high-ceilinged restaurant adds to the expectation. The menu is a combination of British classics and lighter European choices.

J. Sheekey

28-32 St Martin's Ct. ✉ WC2 4AL – Ⓜ Leicester Square – ✆ (020) 7240 2565 – www.j-sheekey.co.uk – Closed 25-26 December and 1 January I3

Rest – *(booking essential)* Menu £ 26 (weekend lunch) – Carte £ 19/64

◆ Seafood ◆ Fashionable ◆

Festooned with photographs of actors and linked to the theatrical world since opening in 1890. Wood panels and alcove tables add famed intimacy. Accomplished seafood cooking.

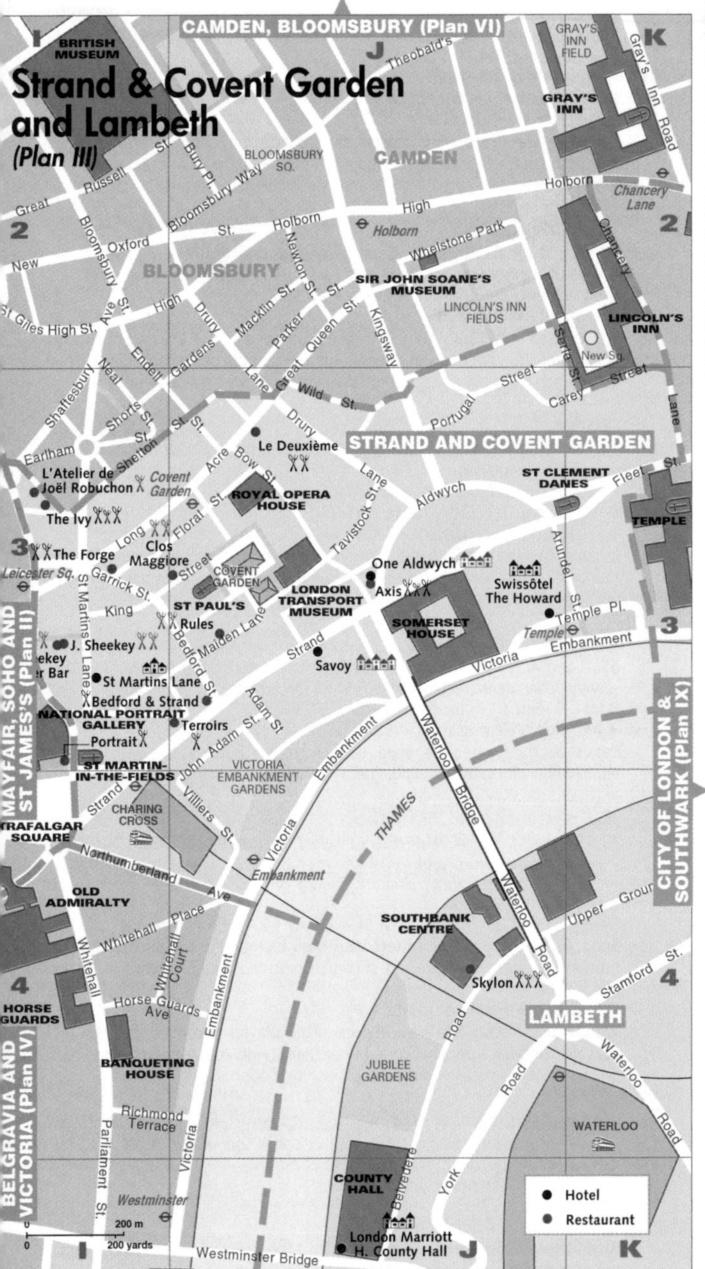

Strand & Covent Garden and Lambeth
(Plan III)
CAMDEN, BLOOMSBURY (Plan VI)
BRITISH MUSEUM
GRAY'S INN FIELD
GRAY'S INN
BLOOMSBURY SQ.
CAMDEN
Holborn
Chancery Lane
BLOOMSBURY
SIR JOHN SOANE'S MUSEUM
LINCOLN'S INN FIELDS
LINCOLN'S INN
STRAND AND COVENT GARDEN
Le Deuxième
ST CLEMENT DANES
L'Atelier de Joël Robuchon
Covent Garden
ROYAL OPERA HOUSE
The Ivy
TEMPLE
The Forge
Clos Maggiore
COVENT GARDEN
LONDON TRANSPORT MUSEUM
One Aldwych
Axis
Swissôtel The Howard
ST PAUL'S
Rules
SOMERSET HOUSE
Temple
J. Sheekey
Savoy
St Martins Lane
Bedford & Strand
NATIONAL PORTRAIT GALLERY
Portrait
Terroirs
ST MARTIN-IN-THE-FIELDS
VICTORIA EMBANKMENT GARDENS
CHARING CROSS
TRAFALGAR SQUARE
THAMES
OLD ADMIRALTY
SOUTHBANK CENTRE
Skylon
HORSE GUARDS
LAMBETH
BANQUETING HOUSE
JUBILEE GARDENS
WATERLOO
COUNTY HALL
Westminster
London Marriott H. County Hall
Hotel
Restaurant
MAYFAIR, SOHO AND ST JAMES'S (Plan II)
CITY OF LONDON & SOUTHWARK (Plan IX)
BELGRAVIA AND VICTORIA (Plan IV)
200 m
200 yards

XX

Rules

35 Maiden Ln. ✉ WC2E 7LB – Ⓜ Leicester Square – ☎ (020) 7836 5314 – www.rules.co.uk – Closed 4 days Christmas **J3**

Rest – *(booking essential)* Carte £ 34/58

♦ British ♦ Formal ♦

London's oldest restaurant boasts a fine collection of antique cartoons, drawings and paintings. Tradition continues in the menu, specialising in game from its own estate.

XX

Clos Maggiore

33 King St ✉ WC2E 8JD – Ⓜ Leicester Square – ☎ (020) 7379 9696 – www.closmaggiore.com – Closed lunch 24 December-26 December

Rest – Menu £ 20 (lunch) – Carte £ 29/34 **J3**

♦ French ♦ Formal ♦

Well-dressed restaurant with poised service; ask for a table in the enchanting little rear conservatory, whose roof opens in summer. Sophisticated cooking from a largely French repertoire. Exceptional value lunch and pre-theatre menus.

XX

Forge

14 Garrick St ✉ WC2E 9BJ – Ⓜ Leicester Square – ☎ (020) 73791432 – www.theforgerestaurant.co.uk – Closed 24 December and bank holidays **I3**

Rest – Menu £ 17/28 – Carte £ 31/38

♦ Modern European ♦ Trendy ♦

Décor mixes the old with the new; the front area is more intimate, the back more fun. Extensive menu offers something for everyone, from pasta to Dover Sole, tournedos Rossini to a hamburger.

XX

Le Deuxième

65a Long Acre ✉ WC2E 9JH – Ⓜ Covent Garden – ☎ (020) 7379 0033 – www.ledeuxieme.com – Closed 24-25 December **J3**

Rest – Menu £ 17 (lunch) – Carte £ 33/38

♦ Modern European ♦ Brasserie ♦

Caters well for theatregoers: opens early, closes late. Buzzy eatery, simply decorated in white with subtle lighting. International menu but emphasis within Europe.

X
✿✿

L'Atelier de Joël Robuchon

13-15 West St. ✉ WC2H 9NE – Ⓜ Leicester Square – ☎ (020) 7010 8600 – www.joelrobuchon.co.uk – Closed 25-26 December,1 January, Sunday and bank holidays **I3**

Rest – Carte £ 45/100

Rest *La Cuisine* – 13-15 West St – Menu £ 27 – Carte £ 43/85

Spec. Crispy langoustine fritters with basil pistou. Rib of veal with girolles, fondant potatoes and braised sucrine. Cointreau soufflé with milk chocolate ice cream.

♦ French ♦ Fashionable ♦

Wonderfully precise, creative and occasionally playful cooking; dishes may look delicate but pack a punch. Ground floor Atelier with counter seating and chefs on view. More structured La Cuisine. Cool top floor bar.

X

J. Sheekey Oyster Bar

33-34 St Martin's Ct. ✉ WC2 4AL – Ⓜ Leicester Square – ☎ (020) 7240 2565 – www.j-sheeky.co.uk – Closed 25-26 December and 1 January **I3**

Rest – Carte £ 23/35

♦ Seafood ♦ Intimate ♦

An addendum to J. Sheekey restaurant. Sit at the bar to watch the chefs prepare the same quality seafood as next door but at slightly lower prices; fish pie and fruits de mer are the popular choices. Open all day.

Terroirs

5 William IV St ✉ WC2N 4DW – Ⓜ Charing Cross – ☎ (020) 7036 0660
– www.terroirswinebar.com
– Closed 24-27, 31 December, 1 January, Sunday and bank holidays

Rest – Carte £ 20/33 J3

◆ French ◆ Bistro ◆

Eat in the ground floor bistro/wine bar or two floors below at 'Downstairs at Terroirs' where the menu is a little more substantial. Flavoursome French cooking, with extra Italian and Spanish influences. Thoughtfully compiled wine list.

Bedford & Strand

1a Bedford St ✉ WC2E 9HH – Ⓜ Charing Cross – ☎ (020) 7836 3033
– www.bedford-strand.com
– Closed 24 December-3 January, Sunday and bank holidays J3

Rest – *(booking essential)* Carte £ 27/38

◆ British ◆ Wine bar ◆

They call themselves a 'wine room and bistro' which neatly sums up both the philosophy and the style of the place – interesting wines, reassuringly familiar food and relaxed basement surroundings.

Lambeth

London Marriott H. County Hall

rm, AC

Westminster Bridge Rd ✉ SE1 7PB
– Ⓜ Westminster – ☎ (020) 7928 5200
– www.marriottcountyhall.com J5

195 rm – †£ 448 ††£ 448, ☐ £ 20.95 – 5 suites

Rest *County Hall* – ☎ (020) 7902 8000 *(closed 26 December)* Menu £ 28 – Carte £ 32/43

◆ Luxury ◆ Classic ◆

Occupying the historic County Hall building. Many of the spacious and comfortable bedrooms enjoy river and Parliament outlook. Impressive leisure facilities. World famous views from restaurant.

Skylon

1 Southbank Centre, Belvedere Rd ✉ SE1 8XX – Ⓜ Waterloo
– ☎ (020) 7654 7800 – www.skylonrestaurant.co.uk
– Closed 25 December and Sunday dinner J4

Rest – Menu £ 28/45

◆ Modern European ◆ Design ◆

Ask for a window table here at the Royal Festival Hall. Informal grill-style operation on one side, a more formal and expensive restaurant on the other, with a busy cocktail bar in the middle.

BELGRAVIA – VICTORIA

Plan IV

Belgravia

Berkeley

Wilton Pl. ✉ SW1X 7RL – Ⓜ Knightsbridge – ☎ (020) 7235 6000
– www.the-berkeley.co.uk G4

189 rm – †£ 588/708 ††£ 708, ☐ £ 29 – 25 suites

Rest *Marcus Wareing at The Berkeley and Koffmann's* – see below

◆ Grand Luxury ◆ Stylish ◆

Discreet and rejuvenated hotel with rooftop pool and opulently decorated bedrooms. Relax in the gilded and panelled Caramel Room or have a drink in the cool Blue Bar.

Belgravia and Victoria
(Plan IV)

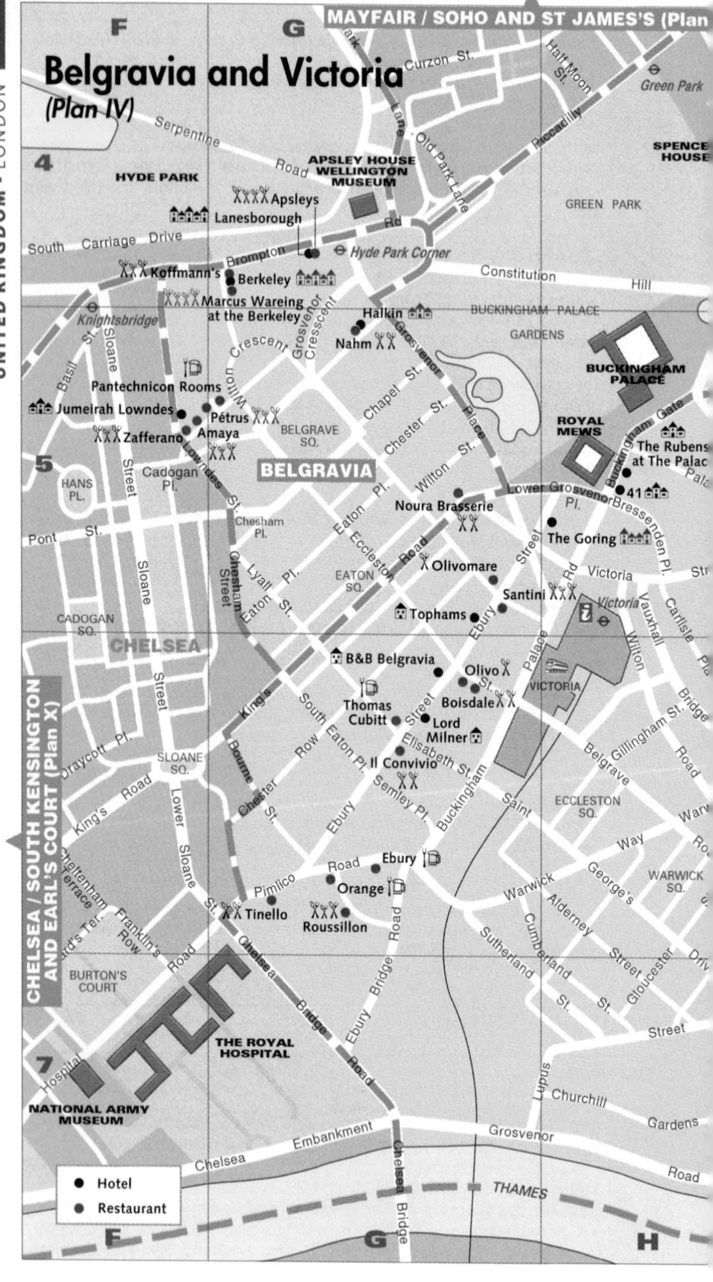

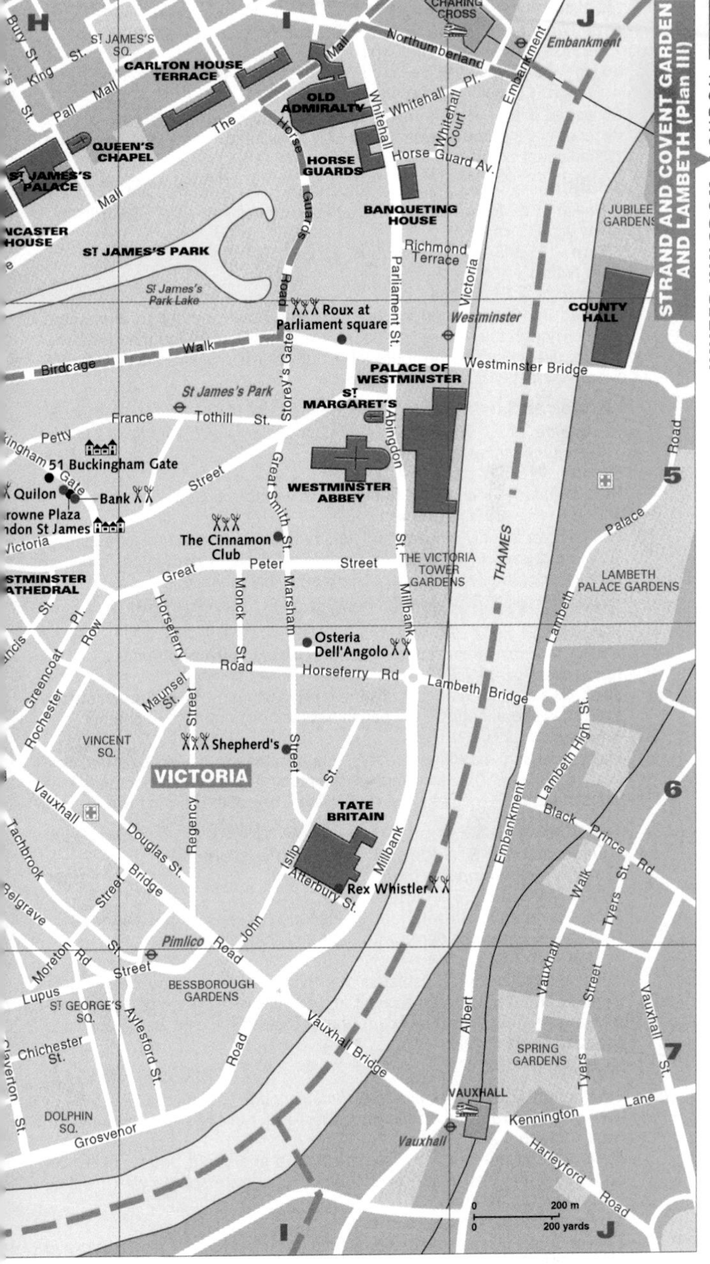
STRAND AND COVENT GARDEN AND LAMBETH (Plan III)
H
I
J
5
6
7
CHARING CROSS
Northumberland
Embankment
ST JAMES'S SQ.
CARLTON HOUSE TERRACE
King St.
Pall Mall
The Mall
OLD ADMIRALTY
Whitehall
Whitehall Pl.
Whitehall Court
Horse Guard Av.
QUEEN'S CHAPEL
ST JAMES'S PALACE
HORSE GUARDS
Horse Guards Road
BANQUETING HOUSE
JUBILEE GARDENS
ST JAMES'S PARK
St James's Park Lake
Richmond Terrace
Parliament St.
Victoria
Roux at Parliament square
Westminster
COUNTY HALL
Birdcage Walk
PALACE OF WESTMINSTER
Westminster Bridge
St James's Park
Storey's Gate
ST MARGARET'S
France
Tothill St.
Petty
51 Buckingham Gate
Quilon
Bank
Abingdon
Road
Great Smith St.
WESTMINSTER ABBEY
Street
Palace
The Cinnamon Club
St.
THE VICTORIA TOWER GARDENS
THAMES
LAMBETH PALACE GARDENS
Great Peter Street
Monck St.
Marsham
Millbank
Lambeth
Horseferry
Row
Greencoat Pl.
Osteria Dell'Angolo
Horseferry Rd
Lambeth Bridge
Rochester
Maunsel St.
Street
Shepherd's
Street
Lambeth High St.
VINCENT SQ.
VICTORIA
St.
Embankment
Black Prince Rd
Vauxhall
TATE BRITAIN
Tachbrook
Douglas St.
Regency
Millbank
Islip
Bridge
Street
Atterbury St.
Rex Whistler
Walk
Tyers St.
Belgrave
John
Pimlico Road
Moreton
Rd
St.
Street
Vauxhall
Street
Vauxhall St.
Lupus
BESSBOROUGH GARDENS
ST GEORGE'S SQ.
Vauxhall Bridge
Albert
Aylesford St.
Chichester St.
Road
SPRING GARDENS
Tyers
VAUXHALL
Lane
Kennington
Vauxhall
DOLPHIN SQ.
Grosvenor
Harleyford
Road
0 200 m
0 200 yards

Lanesborough

Hyde Park Corner ✉ *SW1X 7TA* – Ⓜ *Hyde Park Corner* – ✆ *(020) 7259 5599* – *www.lanesborough.com* **G4**

86 rm – †£ 450/594 ††£ 594, ☕ £ 30 – 10 suites **Rest *Apsleys*** – see below

♦ Grand Luxury ♦ Classic ♦

Converted in the 1990s from 18C St George's Hospital. Butler service offered. Regency-era inspired decoration; lavishly appointed rooms with impressive technological extras.

Halkin

5 Halkin St ✉ *SW1X 7DJ* – Ⓜ *Hyde Park Corner* – ✆ *(020) 7333 1000* – *www.halkin.como.bz* **G5**

35 rm – †£ 348/600 ††£ 348/600, ☕ £ 27.50 – 6 suites

Rest *Nahm* – see below

♦ Luxury ♦ Stylish ♦

Opened in 1991 as London's first boutique hotel and still looking sharp today. Thoughtfully conceived bedrooms with silk walls and marbled bathrooms; everything at the touch of a button. Abundant Armani-clad staff. Small, discreet bar.

Jumeirah Lowndes

rm,

21 Lowndes St ✉ *SW1X 9ES* – Ⓜ *Knightsbridge* – ✆ *(020) 7823 1234* – *www.jumeirahlowndeshotel.com* **F5**

87 rm – ††£ 598, ☕ £ 27 – 14 suites

Rest *Mimosa* – Menu £ 18 (lunch) – Carte approx. £ 33

♦ Business ♦ Modern ♦

Compact yet friendly modern corporate hotel within this exclusive residential area. Good levels of personal service offered. Close to the famous shops of Knightsbridge. Modern restaurant opens onto street terrace.

Marcus Wareing at The Berkeley

Wilton Pl. ✉ *SW1X 7RL* – Ⓜ *Knightsbridge* – ✆ *(020) 7235 1200* – *www.marcus-wareing.com* – *Closed Saturday lunch and Sunday*

Rest – Menu £ 38/75 **G4**

Spec. Sweetbread, ginger and pineapple gastrique. Halibut with lobster, asparagus and almonds. Basil parfait with lemon caramel and sherbet.

♦ French ♦ Formal ♦

Marcus Wareing's cooking is creative, sophisticated and backed by sound classical techniques. The restaurant is sumptuously appointed, and service is smooth and well-organised. The chef's table is one of the best in town.

Apsleys – at Lanesborough Hotel

Hyde Park Corner ✉ *SW1X 7TA* – Ⓜ *Hyde Park Corner* – ✆ *(020) 7333 7254* – *www.apsleys.co.uk* **G4**

Rest – Menu £ 28/35 – Carte £ 51/80

Spec. Potato agnolotti with lobster. Pigeon with pearl onions and mustard seed sauce. Chocolate dome with mint and sea salt ice cream.

♦ Italian ♦ Elegant ♦

Under the guidance of celebrated chef Heinz Beck from Rome's La Pergola. Exquisite and precise Italian cooking, in a grand, eye-catching but far from intimidating room, designed by Adam Tihany. The serving team are polished and the atmosphere upbeat.

Pétrus

1 Kinnerton St. ✉ *SW1X 8EA* – Ⓜ *Knightsbridge* – ✆ *(020) 7592 1609* – *www.gordonramsay.com/petrus* – *Closed 25 December and Sunday*

Rest – Menu £ 25/55 **G5**

Spec. Langoustine tail with watercress soup and confit potato. Beef fillet and shin with celeriac and Barolo sauce. Chocolate sphere with milk ice cream and honeycomb.

♦ Modern European ♦ Elegant ♦

Elegant Gordon Ramsay restaurant, opened in 2010, in tones of silver, oyster and – as a nod to the name – claret. Immaculately laid tables; experienced service team with personality. Elaborate French-based cooking uses top quality ingredients.

XXX ✿

Amaya

Halkin Arcade, 19 Motcomb St ✉ SW1X 8JT – Ⓜ Knightsbridge – ✆ (020) 7823 1166 – www.realindianfood.com
– Closed 25 December **F5**

Rest – Menu £ 25/39 – Carte £ 32/68

Spec. Tarragon and turmeric chicken tikka. Duck grilled wtih tamarind glaze. Rose petal crème brûlée.

♦ Indian ♦ Fashionable ♦

Order a selection of small dishes from the tawa griddle, tandoor or sigri grill and finish with a curry or biryani. Dishes are aromatic and satisfying and the cooking skilled and consistent. The busy restaurant is suitably bright and colourful.

XXX ✿

Zafferano

15 Lowndes St ✉ SW1X 9EY – Ⓜ Knightsbridge – ✆ (020) 7235 5800 – www.zafferanorestaurant.com
– Closed Christmas-New Year **F5**

Rest – *(booking essential)* Carte £ 36/65

Spec. Cured pork in figs, mozzarella in carrozza. Pappardelle with lamb ragu and pecorino cheese. Chocolate fondant with gianduia chocolate ice cream.

♦ Italian ♦ Fashionable ♦

Pasta is the star of the show at this perennially busy Italian restaurant. The cooking is reliable and assured and the menus balanced. The stylish surroundings are comfortable but also full of bustle; the bar is an appealing adjunct.

XXX

Koffmann's – at Berkeley Hotel

Wilton Pl. ✉ SW1X 7RL – Ⓜ Knightsbridge – ✆ (020) 7235 1010 – www.the-berkeley.co.uk **G4**

Rest – Menu £ 23 (lunch) – Carte £ 46/77

♦ French ♦ Design ♦ Fashionable ♦

Pierre Koffmann, one of London's most fêted chefs, was enticed out of retirement to open this smart, comfortable and spacious restaurant. Expect plenty of gutsy flavours true to his Gascon roots.

XX

Nahm – at Halkin Hotel

5 Halkin St. ✉ SW1X 7DJ – Ⓜ Hyde Park Corner – ✆ (020) 7333 1234 – www.halkin.como.bz
– Closed lunch Saturday and Sunday **G5**

Rest – *(booking advisable)* Menu £ 25/60 – Carte £ 40/50

♦ Thai ♦ Design ♦

An appealing mix of copper tones, wood and candlelight, along with an understated hint of Asian design, gives the room a warm feel. The Thai cuisine served here is based on Royal Thai traditions.

XX

Noura Brasserie

16 Hobart Pl. ✉ SW1W 0HH – Ⓜ Victoria – ✆ (020) 7235 9444 – www.noura.co.uk **G5**

Rest – Menu £ 18/45 – Carte £ 24/39

♦ Lebanese ♦ Brasserie ♦

Dine in either the bright bar or the comfortable, contemporary restaurant. Authentic, modern Lebanese cooking specialises in chargrilled meats and meze.

Pantechnicon Rooms

10 Motcomb St ✉ SW1X 8LA – Ⓜ Knightsbridge – ✆ (020) 7730 6074 – www.thepantechnicon.com **G5**

Rest – Carte £ 30/45

♦ Pub ♦ Neighbourhood ♦

Urbane, enthusiastically run pub with a busy ground floor and altogether more formal upstairs dining room. Traditional dishes are given a modern twist; oysters and Scottish steaks are perennials.

Victoria

The Goring

15 Beeston Pl, Grosvenor Gdns ✉ *SW1W 0JW*
– Ⓜ *Victoria* – ✆ *(020) 7396 9000*
– *www.thegoring.com* **H5**
65 rm – †£ 492/570 ††£ 550, ☕ £ 25 – 6 suites
Rest – *(Closed Saturday lunch)* Menu £ 35 (lunch)/48

◆ Traditional ◆ Luxury ◆ Classic ◆

Celebrated its centenary in 2010; this very English hotel is still owned and run by the Goring family who built it - the fourth generation is now at the helm. Many of the attractive rooms overlook a peaceful garden. Elegantly appointed restaurant with an appropriately British menu.

Crowne Plaza London - St James

rm,

45 Buckingham Gate ✉ *SW1E 6AF*
– Ⓜ *St James's Park* – ✆ *(020) 7834 6655*
– *www.london.crowneplaza.com* **H5**
321 rm – †£ 426 ††£ 426, ☕ £ 18.50 – 19 suites
Rest *Quilon and Bank* – see below
Rest *Bistro 51* – Carte £ 33/47

◆ Luxury ◆ Classic ◆

Built in 1897 as serviced accommodation for visiting aristocrats. Behind the impressive Edwardian façade lies an equally elegant interior. Quietest rooms overlook courtyard. Bright and informal café-style restaurant.

51 Buckingham Gate without rest

51 Buckingham Gate ✉ *SW1E 6AF*
– Ⓜ *St James's Park* – ✆ *(020) 7769 7766*
– *www.51-buckinghamgate.com* **H5**
89 suites – ††£ 702, ☕ £ 22.50

◆ Luxury ◆ Classic ◆

In the courtyard of the Crowne Plaza but offering greater levels of comfort and service. Contemporary in style, suites range from one to seven bedrooms. Butler service available. Restaurants located in adjacent hotel.

41 without rest

41 Buckingham Palace Rd. ✉ *SW1W 0PS* – Ⓜ *Victoria*
– ✆ *(020) 7300 0041* – *www.41hotel.com* **H5**
29 rm – †£ 275/395 ††£ 287/419, ☕ £ 25 – 1 suite

◆ Luxury ◆ Classic ◆

Smart and discreet addendum to The Rubens hotel next door. Attractively decorated and quiet lounge where breakfast is served; comfortable bedrooms boast fireplaces and plenty of extras.

The Rubens at The Palace

39 Buckingham Palace Rd ✉ *SW1W 0PS* – Ⓜ *Victoria*
– ✆ *(020) 7834 6600* – *www.rubenshotel.com* **H5**
160 rm – †£ 155/311 ††£ 167/311, ☕ £ 18.50 – 1 suite
Rest *Old Masters* – *(Closed lunch Saturday and Sunday)* Menu £ 28
Rest *Library* – *(dinner only)* Menu £ 35 – Carte £ 42/59
Rest *bbar* – ✆ *(020) 7958 7000 (Closed Saturday, Sunday and bank holidays)* Menu £ 21 – Carte £ 25/47

◆ Traditional ◆ Classic ◆

Discreet, comfortable hotel in great location for visitors to London. Constant reinvestment ensures bright and contemporary bedrooms. Old Masters for grills. Fine dining in cosy Library. Casual dining in bbar.

Tophams without rest

24-32 Ebury St ✉ SW1W 0LU – Ⓜ Victoria – ✆ (020) 7730 3313 – www.tophamshotel.com **G5**

48 rm – †£ 95/375 ††£ 109/375, ☕ £ 14.95

♦ Townhouse ♦ Personalised ♦

A row of five pretty terraced houses, in a good spot for tourists and recently refurbished. Neat bedrooms with large bathrooms and good mod cons. Comfortable breakfast room.

B + B Belgravia without rest

64-66 Ebury St ✉ SW1W 9QD – Ⓜ Victoria – ✆ (020) 7259 8570 – www.bb-belgravia.com **G6**

17 rm ☕ – †£ 99 ††£ 170

♦ Townhouse ♦ Personalised ♦

Two houses, three floors, and, considering the location, representing good value accommodation. Sleek, clean-lined bedrooms. Breakfast overlooking little garden terrace.

Lord Milner without rest

111 Ebury Street ✉ SW1W 9QU – Ⓜ Victoria – ✆ (020) 7881 9880 – www.lordmilner.com **G6**

10 rm – †£ 100/165 ††£ 115/165, ☕ £ 14 – 1 suite

♦ Townhouse ♦ Classic ♦

A four storey terraced house, with individually decorated bedrooms, three with four-poster beds and all with marble bathrooms. Garden Suite the best room, with its own patio. No public areas.

XXX ✿

Quilon – at Crowne Plaza London - St James Hotel

41 Buckingham Gate ✉ SW1E 6AF – Ⓜ St James's Park – ✆ (020) 7821 1899 – www.quilon.co.uk – Closed Saturday lunch

Rest – Menu £ 22/39 – Carte dinner £ 34/57 **H5**

Spec. Spiced oysters and lentils with onion relish. Koondapur halibut curry and tamarind gravy. Spiced dark chocolate and hazelnut mousse

♦ Indian ♦ Exotic ♦

Vibrant and well-balanced Indian dishes, many of which originate from the south west coast of India but are given a 'Western' twist . Skilled use of spices, appealing seafood specialities and well-organised service.

XXX

Roux at Parliament Square

RICS, Parliament Sq. ✉ SW1P 3AD – Ⓜ Westminster – ✆ (020) 7334 3737 – www.rouxatparliamentsquare.co.uk – Closed Christmas-New Year, Saturday and Sunday **I5**

Rest – Menu £ 30/55

♦ French ♦ Elegant ♦

Light floods through the Georgian windows of this comfortable Westminster restaurant, popular with MPs and surveyors. French base to the food, which is intricate but also light and contemporary.

XXX

Roussillon

16 St Barnabas St ✉ SW1W 8PE – Ⓜ Sloane Square – ✆ (020) 7730 5550 – www.roussillon.co.uk – Closed Christmas-New Year, Saturday lunch and Sunday **G6**

Rest – Menu £ 35/60

♦ French ♦ Neighbourhood ♦

A longstanding neighbourhood restaurant, with a comfortable, discreet and grown up feel. Expect quite formal service and a creative style of cooking.

XXX

The Cinnamon Club

30-32 Great Smith St ✉ SW1P 3BU – Ⓜ St James's Park – ✆ (020) 7222 2555 – www.cinnamonclub.com – Closed 1 January, Sunday and bank holidays

Rest – Menu £ 22 – Carte £ 29/45 **I5**

♦ Indian ♦ Fashionable ♦

Housed in former Westminster Library: exterior has ornate detail, interior is stylish and modern. Walls are lined with books. New Wave Indian cooking with plenty of choice.

XXX **Santini**

29 Ebury St ✉ SW1W 0NZ – Ⓜ Victoria – ☎ (020) 7730 4094 – www.santini-restaurant.com – Closed 1 January, Easter, 23-27 December, lunch Saturday and Sunday

Rest – Menu £ 25 (dinner) – Carte £ 29/54 **G5**

◆ Italian ◆ Formal ◆

Smart, crisp and cool Italian restaurant, with a large, impressive terrace and old-school service. Menu has subtle Venetian accent but is not inexpensive; pastas and desserts are good.

XXX **Shepherd's**

Marsham Ct., Marsham St. ✉ SW1P 4LA – Ⓜ Pimlico – ☎ (020) 7834 9552 – www.langansrestaurants.co.uk – Closed bank holidays

Rest – *(booking essential)* Menu £ 38 **I6**

◆ British ◆ Formal ◆

A truly English restaurant where game and traditional puddings are a highlight. Popular with those from Westminster – the booths offer a degree of privacy.

XX **Il Convivio**

143 Ebury St ✉ SW1W 9QN – Ⓜ Sloane Square – ☎ (020) 7730 4099 – www.etruscarestaurants.com – Closed Christmas-New Year, Sunday and bank holidays **G6**

Rest – Carte £ 34/50

◆ Italian ◆ Intimate ◆

Handsome Georgian house, with a retractable roof and Dante's poetry embossed on the walls. All pasta is made on the top floor of the house. Dishes are artfully presented and flavoursome.

XX **Tinello**

87 Pimlico Rd ✉ SW1W 8PH – Ⓜ Sloane Square – ☎ (020) 7730 3663 – www.tinello.co.uk – Closed 24 December-2 January and Sunday

Rest – *(booking essential at dinner)* Carte £ 32/37 **G6**

◆ Italian ◆ Design ◆ Friendly ◆

Sleekly designed Italian restaurant run by two brothers, both alumni of Locanda Locatelli. Their native Tuscany informs the cooking; the antipasti or 'small eats' section is very appealing.

XX **Boisdale**

15 Eccleston St ✉ SW1W 9LX – Ⓜ Victoria – ☎ (020) 7730 6922 – www.boisdale.co.uk – Closed 1 week Christmas, Saturday lunch and Sunday

Rest – Menu £ 20 – Carte £ 30/64 **G6**

◆ Scottish ◆ Cosy ◆

A proudly Scottish restaurant with acres of tartan and a charmingly higgledy-piggledy layout. Stand-outs are the smoked salmon and the 28-day aged Aberdeenshire cuts of beef. Live nightly jazz.

XX **Rex Whistler**

Tate Britain, Millbank ✉ SW1P 4RG – Ⓜ Pimlico – ☎ (020) 7887 8825 – www.tate.org.uk/britain/eatanddrink – Closed 24-26 December **I6**

Rest – *(lunch only) (booking essential)* Menu £ 20 – Carte £ 33/40

◆ British ◆ Friendly ◆

As with upstairs, it celebrates Britain, with a daily catch from Newlyn and fruity desserts the specialities. Comfortable room, with striking Rex Whistler mural. Terrific wine list.

XX **Bank** – at Crowne Plaza London-St James Hotel

45 Buckingham Gate ✉ SW1E 6BS – Ⓜ St James's Park – ☎ (020) 7630 6644 – www.bankrestaurants.com – Closed Saturday lunch, Sunday and bank holidays **H5**

Rest – *(booking essential at lunch)* Carte £ 34/49

◆ Modern European ◆ Brasserie ◆

Behind the understated entrance lies a vibrant and busy interior. Pass through one of Europe's longest bars to reach the conservatory restaurant, where you'll find a varied, accessible menu.

Osteria Dell' Angolo

47 Marsham St. ✉ SW1P 3DR – Ⓜ St. James's Park – ✆ (020) 32681077
– www.osteriadellangolo.co.uk
– Closed 24-31 December, Saturday lunch, Sunday and bank holidays
Rest – Menu £ 15/20 – Carte £ 29/42 **I6**
◆ Italian ◆ Neighbourhood ◆

Expert restaurateur Claudio Pulze opened this sunny Italian restaurant opposite the Home Office in 2009. Tuscan element to the cooking, along with some creativity; service is keen and friendly.

Olivo

21 Eccleston St ✉ SW1W 9LX – Ⓜ Victoria – ✆ (020) 7730 2505
– www.olivorestaurant.com
– Closed lunch Saturday and Sunday and bank holidays **G6**
Rest – Menu £ 25 (lunch) – Carte dinner £ 33/38
◆ Italian ◆ Neighbourhood ◆

Carefully prepared, authentic Sardinian specialities are the highlight at this popular Italian restaurant. Simply decorated in blues and yellows, with an atmosphere of bonhomie.

Olivomare

10 Lower Belgrave St ✉ SW1W 0LJ – Ⓜ Victoria – ✆ (020) 7730 9022
– www.olivorestaurants.com
– Closed bank holidays **G5**
Rest – Carte £ 36/39
◆ Seafood ◆ Design ◆ Neighbourhood ◆

Expect understated and stylish piscatorial decoration and seafood with a Sardinian base. Fortnightly changing menu, with high quality produce, much of which is available in shop next door.

Ebury

11 Pimlico Rd ✉ SW1W 8NA – Ⓜ Sloane Square. – ✆ (020) 7730 6784
– www.theebury.co.uk
– Closed 25-26 December **G6**
Rest – Menu £ 20 – Carte £ 30/45
◆ Pub ◆ Trendy ◆

Smart and stylish room, with an appealing menu ranging from burgers to black bream. Low-slung tables around popular central bar; efficient service. Upstairs is used for private parties.

Thomas Cubitt

44 Elizabeth St ✉ SW1W 9PA – Ⓜ Sloane Square. – ✆ (020) 7730 6060
– www.thethomascubitt.co.uk **G6**
Rest – *(booking essential)* Carte £ 30/45
◆ Pub ◆ Fashionable ◆

A pub of two halves: choose the busy ground floor bar with its accessible menu or upstairs for more ambitious, quite elaborate cooking with courteous service and a less frenetic environment.

Orange with rm

37-39 Pimlico Rd ✉ SW1W 8NE – Ⓜ Sloane Square. – ✆ (020) 7881 9844
– www.theorange.co.uk **G6**
4 rm – †£ 189/212 ††£ 189/212
Rest – Carte £ 23/26
◆ Friendly ◆ Family ◆

Family-friendly pub with laid-back atmosphere and slight colonial feel. Pizza from the wood-fired oven in the bar or rustic cooking in the upstairs dining room. Film nights on Monday. Bedrooms named after local streets.

The Landmark London

222 Marylebone Rd ✉ *NW1 6JQ* – Ⓜ *Edgware Rd* – ✆ *(020) 7631 8000* – *www.landmarklondon.co.uk* **F1**

291 rm – †£ 312/660 ††£ 312/660, ☕ £ 28 – 9 suites

Rest *Winter Garden* – Carte £ 35/74

♦ Grand Luxury ♦ Classic ♦

Imposing Victorian Gothic building with a vast glass-enclosed atrium, overlooked by many of the modern, well-equipped bedrooms. Winter Garden popular for afternoon tea.

Hyatt Regency London-The Churchill

30 Portman Sq. ✉ *W1H 7BH* – Ⓜ *Marble Arch* – ✆ *(020) 7486 5800* – *www.london.churchill.hyatt.com* **G2**

404 rm – †£ 240/480 ††£ 240/480, ☕ £ 27.50 – 40 suites

Rest *The Montagu* – ✆ *(020) 7299 2037* – Menu £ 26 – Carte £ 37/53

♦ Luxury ♦ Classic ♦

Smart property overlooking attractive square. Elegant marbled lobby. Well-appointed and refurbished rooms have the international traveller in mind. Restaurant provides popular Sunday brunch entertainment.

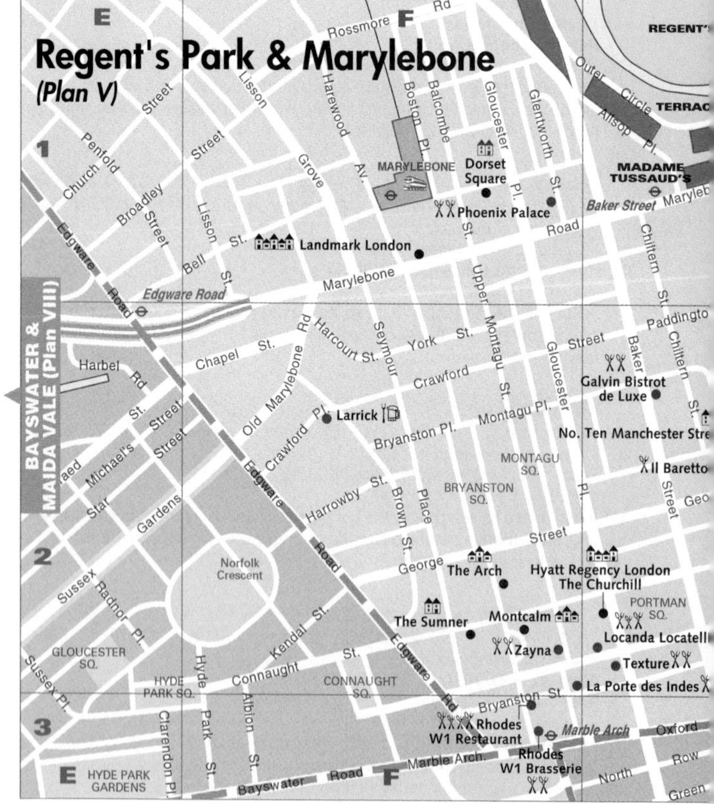

Langham

1c Portland Pl., Regent St. ✉ W1B 1JA – Ⓜ Oxford Circus – ✆ (020) 7636 1000 – www.langhamhotels.com **H2**

359 rm – †£ 192/225 ††£ 446/675, ☕ £ 30 – 21 suites

Rest *Landau* – ✆ (020) 7965 0165 (Closed Saturday lunch and Sunday) Menu £ 29 (lunch) – Carte £ 51/60

◆ Luxury ◆ Classic ◆

Opened in 1865 and relaunched in 2009 following a major refurbishment. Impressive art deco Palm Court; comfortable bedrooms and notable leisure facilities. The Landau is an eye-catching and ornate room, with a wide-ranging menu.

Montcalm

34-40 Great Cumberland Pl. ✉ W1H 7TW – Ⓜ Marble Arch – ✆ (020) 7402 4288 – www.montcalm.co.uk **F2**

126 rm – †£ 420 ††£ 420/1020, ☕ £ 19.95 – 17 suites

Rest *Vetro* – (closed Sunday dinner) Carte £ 29/45

◆ Business ◆ Stylish ◆

Named after an 18C French general, The Montcalm forms part of a crescent of townhouses with a Georgian façade. A top-to-toe refurbishment has created smart and contemporary bedrooms in lively colours. Classic Italian dishes in Vetro.

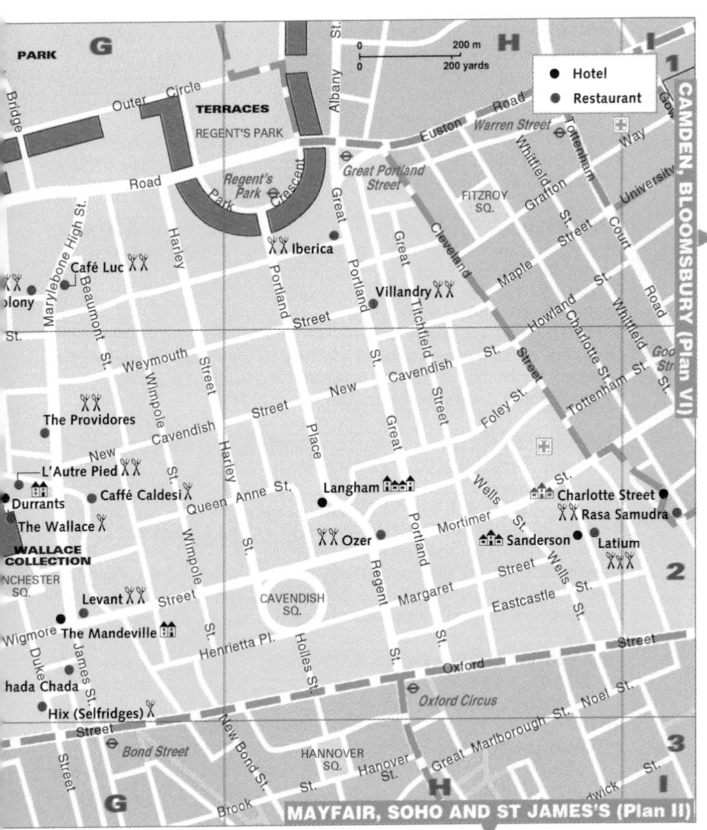

The Arch

rm,

50 Great Cumberland Pl. ✉ *W1H 7FD – Ⓜ Marble Arch – ✆ (020) 77244700 – www.thearchlondon.com* **F2**

80 rm – £ 294 £ 360/540, £ 18.95 – 2 suites

Rest *Hunter 486* – *✆ (020) 7725 4825* – Menu £ 20 (lunch) – Carte £ 23/53

♦ Traditional ♦ Stylish ♦

Fashioned out of a row of seven terrace houses and two mews cottages. Plenty of extras and thoughtful touches are found in the comfortable bedrooms. Interesting pieces of art throughout. Relaxed restaurant doubles as a champagne bar.

Sanderson

50 Berners St ✉ *W1T 3NG – Ⓜ Oxford Circus – ✆ (020) 7300 1400 – www.morganshotelgroup.com* **H2**

150 rm – £ 414/627 £ 414/627, £ 25

Rest *Suka* – Carte £ 35/45

♦ Luxury ♦ Minimalist ♦

Designed by Philipe Starck and still attracting a suitably fashionable crowd. Purple Bar dark and moody; Long Bar bright and stylish. Pure white bedrooms with idiosyncratic design touches. Malaysian dishes designed for sharing in Suka.

Dorset Square without rest

39 Dorset Sq ✉ *NW1 6QN – Ⓜ Marylebone – ✆ (020) 7723 7874 – www.dorsetsquare.co.uk* **F1**

37 rm – £ 120/240 £ 174/336, £ 15

♦ Townhouse ♦ Classic ♦

Converted Regency townhouses in a charming square which was the site of the original Lord's cricket ground. A warm and welcoming country house in the city with individually decorated rooms.

Durrants

rest,

26-32 George St. ✉ *W1H 5BJ – Ⓜ Bond Street – ✆ (020) 7935 8131 – www.durrantshotel.co.uk* **G2**

92 rm – £ 125 £ 175, £ 18 – 4 suites

Rest – *(Closed dinner 25 December)* Carte £ 31/41

♦ Traditional ♦ Classic ♦

Traditional, privately owned hotel with friendly, long-standing staff. Refurbished bedrooms are brighter in style but still English in character. Clubby dining room for mix of British classics and lighter, European dishes.

Mandeville

rm,

Mandeville Pl. ✉ *W1U 2BE – Ⓜ Bond Street – ✆ (020) 7935 5599 – www.mandeville.co.uk* **G2**

140 rm – £ 383 £ 407, £ 22.50 – 2 suites

Rest *de Ville* – *(closed Sunday)* Menu £ 30 – Carte £ 27/36

♦ Chain hotel ♦ Design ♦

Usefully located hotel with marbled reception leading into a very colourful and comfortable bar. Stylish rooms have flatscreen TVs and make good use of the space available. Modern British cuisine served in bright de Ville restaurant.

No.Ten Manchester Street without rest

✉ *W1U 4DG – Ⓜ Baker Street – ✆ (020) 7317 5900 – www.tenmanchesterstreethotel.com* **G2**

44 rm – £ 167 £ 263, £ 15.50 – 1 suite

♦ Townhouse ♦ Modern ♦

Converted Edwardian house in an appealing, central location. Discreet entrance leads into stylish little lounge; semi-enclosed cigar bar also a feature. Neat and well-kept bedrooms.

The Sumner without rest

54 Upper Berkeley St ✉ W1H 7QR – Ⓜ Marble Arch – ☎ (020) 7723 2244 – www.thesumner.com **F2**

20 rm ☕ – 🚹£ 200 🚹🚹£ 200

◆ Townhouse ◆ Personalised ◆

Two Georgian terrace houses in central location. Comfy, stylish sitting room; basement breakfast room. Largest bedrooms, 101 and 201, benefit from having full-length windows.

Hart House without rest

51 Gloucester Pl. ✉ W1U 8JF – Ⓜ Marble Arch – ☎ (020) 7935 2288 – www.harthouse.co.uk **F2**

15 rm ☕ – 🚹£ 89/135 🚹🚹£ 125/150

◆ Traditional ◆ Functional ◆

Within an attractive Georgian terrace and run by the same family for over 35 years. Warm and welcoming service; well-kept, competitively priced bedrooms over three floors.

St George without rest

49 Gloucester Pl. ✉ W1U 8JE – Ⓜ Marble Arch – ☎ (020) 7486 8586 – www.stgeorge-hotel.net **F2**

18 rm – 🚹£ 85/145 🚹🚹£ 110/195, ☕ £ 5

◆ Traditional ◆ Cosy ◆

Terraced house on a busy street, usefully located within walking distance of many attractions. Offers a warm welcome and comfortable bedrooms which are spotlessly maintained.

Rhodes W1 (Restaurant)

Cumberland Hotel, Great Cumberland Pl. ✉ W1H 7DL – Ⓜ Marble Arch – ☎ (020) 7616 5930 – www.rhodesw1.com – Closed 2 weeks in summer, Saturday lunch, Sunday and Monday

Rest – *(booking advisable)* Menu £ 25/50 **F3**

Spec. Scallops with braised oxtail and blood orange. Pigeon with foie gras, chicory and pickled blackberries. Pistachio cake with apricot and tarragon ice cream.

◆ French ◆ Luxury ◆

Just 12 tables in a warm and textured room designed by Kelly Hoppen. Influences are more European than usual for a Gary Rhodes restaurant but with the same emphasis on clear, uncluttered flavours.

Locanda Locatelli

8 Seymour St. ✉ W1H 7JZ – Ⓜ Marble Arch – ☎ (020) 7935 9088 – www.locandalocatelli.com – Closed 25-26 December **G2**

Rest – Carte £ 41/60

Spec. Chestnut tagliatelle with wild mushrooms. Veal saltimbocca. Degustation of Amedei chocolate.

◆ Italian ◆ Fashionable ◆

Slick and dapper-looking Italian with a celebrity following and a sophisticated atmosphere. Plenty of interest on the extensive menu, with cooking that is confident, balanced and expertly rendered; pastas and desserts are the stand-out courses.

Latium

21 Berners St. ✉ W1T 3LP – Ⓜ Oxford Circus – ☎ (020) 7323 9123 – www.latiumrestaurant.com – Closed 10 days Christmas, Saturday lunch, Sunday and bank holidays

Rest – Menu £ 20/33 **H2**

◆ Italian ◆ Neighbourhood ◆

Bright and contemporary surroundings but with warm and welcoming service. Owner-chef from Lazio but dishes come from across Italy, often using British produce. Ravioli is the house speciality.

XX ✿

Texture (Agnar Sverrisson) A/C VISA MC AE

34 Portman St. ✉ W1H 7BY – Ⓜ Marble Arch – ✆ (020) 7224 0028 – www.texture-restaurant.co.uk – Closed Christmas-New Year, 2 weeks August, Sunday and Monday

Rest – Menu £ 22 (lunch) – Carte £ 43/51 **G2**

Spec. Salmon graflax with horseradish and rye bread. Icelandic salted cod with barley and shellfish jus. White chocolate mousse with cucumber and dill.

♦ Innovative ♦ Design ♦

Technically skilled but light and invigorating cooking from Icelandic chef-owner, who uses ingredients from home. Bright restaurant with high ceiling and popular adjoining champagne bar. Pleasant service from keen staff, ready with a smile.

XX ✿

L'Autre Pied (Marcus Eaves) A/C VISA MC AE

5-7 Blandford St. ✉ W1U 3DB – Ⓜ Bond Street – ✆ (020) 74869696 – www.lautrepied.co.uk **G2**

Rest – Menu £ 21 (lunch) – Carte £ 39/60

Spec. Raviolo of veal and chorizo with shellfish bisque. Roast pork with croquette of spiced pig's head. Baked Alaska, elderflower and vanilla ice cream

♦ Modern European ♦ Neighbourhood ♦

A more informal sibling to Pied à Terre, with red leather seating, closely set tables and relaxed atmosphere. But cooking is just as ambitious: it is original, creative and technically adroit.

XX

Galvin Bistrot de Luxe A/C VISA MC AE

66 Baker St. ✉ W1U 7DJ – Ⓜ Baker Street – ✆ (020) 7935 4007 – www.galvinrestaurants.com – Closed 25-26 December and 1 January **G2**

Rest – Menu £ 18/20 – Carte £ 32/51

♦ French ♦ Bistro ♦

Firmly established modern Gallic bistro with ceiling fans, globe lights and wood panelled walls. Satisfying and precisely cooked classic French dishes from the Galvin brothers.

XX

Zayna A/C VISA MC AE

25 New Quebec St. ✉ W1H 7SF – Ⓜ Marble Arch – ✆ (020) 77232229 – www.zaynarestaurant.co.uk **F2**

Rest – Menu £ 25/30 – Carte £ 30/40

♦ Indian ♦ Elegant ♦ Intimate ♦

Enthusiastically run, elegant restaurant spread over two floors, with keen owner. Interesting north Indian and Pakistani delicacies; kitchen only uses halal meat and free-range chicken.

XX

Ozer A/C VISA MC AE

5 Langham Pl., Regent St. ✉ W1B 3DG – Ⓜ Oxford Circus – ✆ (020) 7323 0505 – www.ozer.co.uk **H2**

Rest – Menu £ 19/23 – Carte £ 21/42

♦ Turkish ♦ Design ♦

The large front bar is always busy but go through to the equally popular but comfortable restaurant to enjoy authentic Turkish food. Wide range of appealing hot and cold meze is the draw.

XX

Rhodes W1 Brasserie A/C VISA MC AE

Great Cumberland Pl. ✉ W1H 7DL – Ⓜ Marble Arch – ✆ (020) 7616 5930 – www.rhodesw1.com **F3**

Rest – Menu £ 21 (lunch) – Carte £ 27/44

♦ Modern European ♦ Brasserie ♦

Large brasserie on the ground floor of the Cumberland hotel, with keen, helpful service and equally big bar. Expect Gary Rhodes' signature dishes, alongside others of a more European persuasion.

XX

Colony

8 Paddington St ✉ W1U 5QH – Ⓜ Baker Street – ✆ (020) 7935 3353 – www.colonybarandgrill.com G1

Rest – Menu £ 20 – Carte £ 26/42

◆ Indian ◆ Wine bar ◆ Trendy ◆

Courtesy of Atul Kochhar, of Benares fame: small tasting plates, lunchtime thalis and grazing menus with mostly Indian influences are served at this relaxed lounge bar with a dining area.

XX

Iberica

195 Great Portland St ✉ W1W 5PS – Ⓜ Great Portland Street – ✆ (020) 7636 8650 – www.ibericalondon.co.uk – Closed Sunday dinner H1

Rest – *(booking advisable at dinner)* Menu £ 22 (weekday lunch) – Carte £ 15/32

◆ Spanish ◆ Tapas bar ◆

These large premises pay homage to Spain's food and culture. Punchy flavoured tapas in the ground floor bar; more intimate upstairs. Wander through the deli to appreciate the quality of ingredients.

XX

The Providores

109 Marylebone High St. ✉ W1U 4RX – Ⓜ Bond Street – ✆ (020) 7935 6175 – www.theprovidores.co.uk – Closed Christmas-New Year G2

Rest – Carte £ 36/57

◆ Innovative ◆ Trendy ◆

Packed ground floor for tapas; upstairs for innovative fusion cooking, with spices and ingredients from around the world, including Australasia. Starter-sized dishes at dinner allow for greater choice.

XX

Cafe Luc

50 Marylebone High St ✉ W1U 5HN – Ⓜ Regent's Park – ✆ (020) 7258 8595 – www.cafeluc.com G1

Rest – Menu £ 16 – Carte £ 24/35

◆ Modern European ◆ Brasserie ◆ Friendly ◆

Spacious, grand and keenly run brasserie with smart leather banquette seating and clusters of lights. The menu offers a host of brasserie and continental classics to suit all tastes.

XX

La Porte des Indes

32 Bryanston St ✉ W1H 7EG – Ⓜ Marble Arch – ✆ (020) 7224 0055 – www.laportedesindes.com – Closed 25-26 December and 1 January F2

Rest – Menu £ 36 – Carte £ 36/56

◆ Indian ◆ Exotic ◆

Don't be fooled by the discreet entrance: inside there is a spectacularly unrestrained display of palm trees, murals and waterfalls. French-influenced Indian cuisine.

XX

Levant

Jason Ct., 76 Wigmore St. ✉ W1U 2SJ – Ⓜ Bond Street – ✆ (020) 7224 1111 – www.levant.co.uk – Closed 23-29 December and 1 January G2

Rest – *(dinner only and lunch Saturday-Sunday)* Menu £ 28 – Carte £ 20/40

◆ Lebanese ◆ Exotic ◆

Belly dancing, lanterns and a low-slung bar all add up to an exotic dining experience. The Lebanese food is satisfying and authentic, carefully prepared and ideal for sharing in groups.

XX

Villandry

170 Great Portland St ✉ W1W 5QB – Ⓜ Regent's Park – ✆ (020) 7631 3131 – www.villandry.com – Closed Christmas, New Year and Sunday dinner

Rest – Carte £ 25/47 **H1**

♦ French ♦ Brasserie ♦

The senses are heightened by passing through the well-stocked deli to the dining room behind. Bare walls, wooden tables and a menu offering simple, tasty dishes.

XX

L'Aventure

3 Blenheim Ter ✉ NW8 0EH – Ⓜ St John's Wood – ✆ (020) 7624 6232 – Closed first week January, last 2 weeks August, Saturday lunch and Sunday

Rest – Menu £ 20/40 *Plan I* **B2**

♦ French ♦ Neighbourhood ♦

Behind the pretty tree-lined entrance you'll find a charming neighbourhood restaurant. Relaxed atmosphere and service by personable owner. Authentic French cuisine.

XX

Phoenix Palace

5 Glentworth St. ✉ NW1 5PG – Ⓜ Baker Street – ✆ (020) 7486 3515 – www.phoenixpalace.co.uk **F1**

Rest – *(booking advisable at dinner)* Menu £ 25 – Carte approx. £ 28

♦ Chinese ♦ Friendly ♦

Huge restaurant offering a plethora of menus but the cooking is still good. Dim sum during the day and Cantonese dishes and rotisserie meats at night draw in the groups of families and friends.

XX

Vineria

1 Blenheim Ter. ✉ NW8 0EH – Ⓜ St John's Wood – ✆ (020) 7328 5014 – www.vineria.it – Closed Monday *Plan I* **B2**

Rest – Menu £ 20 (lunch) – Carte £ 27/37

♦ Italian ♦ Neighbourhood ♦

Pleasant enclosed front terrace; conservatory section and white walls ensure a bright interior. Undemanding menu covers all parts of Italy, with pasta dishes the kitchen's strength.

X

Trishna

15-17 Blandford St. ✉ W1U 3DG – Ⓜ Baker Street – ✆ (020) 79355624 – www.trishnalondon.com – Closed 25-29 December and 1-4 January **G2**

Rest – Menu £ 16/35 – Carte £ 29/39

♦ Indian ♦ Neighbourhood ♦

A franchise of the celebrated Mumbai restaurant. Specialises in fish and seafood dishes, the brown crab with butter garlic being a highlight. Bright surroundings allow the focus to be the food.

X

Hix (Selfridges)

Mezzanine Fl, Selfridges, 400 Oxford St ✉ W1A 1AB – Ⓜ Bond Street – ✆ (020) 7499 5400 – www.hixatselfridges.co.uk **G2**

Rest – Carte £ 25/40

♦ Modern European ♦ Brasserie ♦

On the mezzanine floor of the famous store; open from breakfast onwards, with a popular champagne bar to refuel shoppers. Menu is lighter and more European than at the other Hix restaurants.

X

The Wallace

Hertford House, Manchester Sq ✉ W1U 3BN – Ⓜ Bond Street – ✆ (020) 7563 9505 – www.thewallacerestaurant.com – Closed 24-27 December

Rest – *(lunch only and dinner Friday-Saturday)* Carte £ 26/35 **G2**

♦ French ♦ Friendly ♦

Large glass-roofed courtyard on the ground floor of Hertford House, home of the splendid Wallace Collection. French-influenced menu, with fruits de mer section; terrines are the house speciality.

Caffé Caldesi

118 Marylebone Ln. (1st floor) ✉ W1U 2QF – Ⓜ Bond Street – ☎ (020) 7487 0754 – www.caldesi.com – Closed 25-26 December and 1 January **G2**

Rest – Menu £ 17 (lunch) – Carte £ 26/40

◆ Italian ◆ Neighbourhood ◆

Converted pub with a simple modern interior in which to enjoy tasty, uncomplicated Italian dishes. Downstairs is a lively bar with a deli counter serving pizzas and pastas.

Dinings

22 Harcourt St. ✉ W1H 4HH – Ⓜ Marylebone – ☎ (020) 7723 0666 – www.dinings.co.uk – Closed lunch Saturday and Sunday **F2**

Rest – *(booking essential)* Carte £ 31/43

◆ Japanese ◆ Cosy ◆ Minimalist ◆

Resembles an after-work Japanese izakaya, or pub, with chummy atmosphere and loud music. Food is a mix of small plates of delicate dishes, a blend of modern and the more traditional.

Il Baretto

43 Blandford St. ✉ W1U 7HF – Ⓜ Baker Street – ☎ (020) 74867340 – www.ilbaretto.co.uk – Closed 24-26 December **G2**

Rest – Carte £ 21/46

◆ Italian ◆ Neighbourhood ◆

The wood-fired oven is the star of the show at this neighbourhood Italian. The extensive menu has something for everyone, although prices vary a lot. The basement room has a lively atmosphere.

Chada Chada

16-17 Picton Pl. ✉ W1U 1BP – Ⓜ Bond Street – ☎ (020) 7935 8212 – www.chadathai.com – Closed Sunday and bank holidays **G2**

Rest – Carte £ 19/47

◆ Thai ◆ Minimalist ◆

Authentic and fragrant Thai cooking; the good value menu offers some interesting departures from the norm. Service is eager to please in the compact and cosy rooms.

Larrik

32 Crawford Pl ✉ W1H 5NN – Ⓜ Edgware Road. – ☎ (020) 7723 0066 – www.thelarrik.com – Closed 25 December **F2**

Rest – Carte £ 20/27

◆ Pub ◆ Friendly ◆

The front section of this traditional looking pub is brighter and more fun. The kitchen is well-grounded in the basics and reliable, whether making a salad or burger. Regularly changing real ales.

CAMDEN *Plan VI*

Bloomsbury

Covent Garden

10 Monmouth St. ✉ WC2H 9HB – Ⓜ Covent Garden – ☎ (020) 7806 1000 – www.firmdalehotels.com **I3**

56 rm – †£ 288 ††£ 408, ☕ £ 21 – 2 suites

Rest *Brasserie Max* – *(booking essential)* Menu £ 25 – Carte £ 34/54

◆ Luxury ◆ Stylish ◆

Individually designed and stylish bedrooms, with CDs and DVDs discreetly concealed. Boasts a very comfortable first floor oak-panelled drawing room with its own honesty bar. Busy, warm and relaxed restaurant also offers afternoon tea.

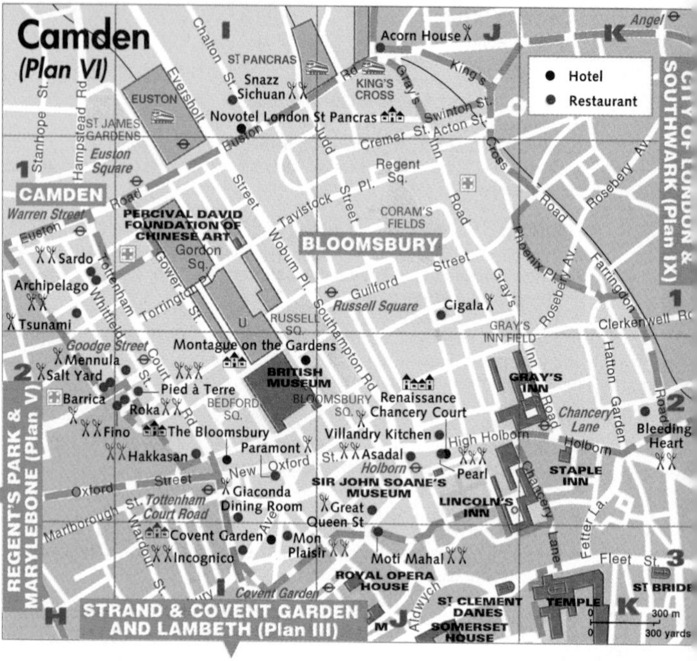

Camden (Plan VI)

● Hotel
● Restaurant

Charlotte Street

rm,

15 Charlotte St. ✉ *W1T 1RJ* – Ⓜ *Goodge Street* – ✆ *(020) 7806 2000 – www.firmdalehotels.com* I2

48 rm – †£ 276 ††£ 384, ☕ £ 20 – 4 suites

Rest *Oscar* – ✆ *(020) 7907 4005* – Menu £ 25 – Carte £ 33/50

◆ Luxury ◆ Stylish ◆

Interior designed with a charming and understated English feel. Impeccably kept and individually decorated bedrooms. In-house screening room. Bright restaurant with large bar and European menu.

Montague on the Gardens

rm,

15 Montague St. ✉ *WC1B 5BJ* – Ⓜ *Holborn* – ✆ *(020) 7637 1001 – www.montaguehotel.com* I2

94 rm – †£ 145/230 ††£ 165/230, ☕ £ 16.50 – 6 suites

Rest *The Blue Door Bistro* – Menu £ 25 – Carte £ 29/51

◆ Townhouse ◆ Classic ◆

Cosy British feel to this period townhouse. Clubby bar and conservatory overlooking a secluded garden. Individually decorated bedrooms. Bistro divided into two small, pretty rooms.

The Bloomsbury

rm,

16-22 Gt Russell St ✉ *WC1B 3NN* – Ⓜ *Tottenham Court Road* – ✆ *(020) 7347 1000 – www.doylecollection.com/bloomsbury* I2

153 rm – †£ 138/334 ††£ 138/334, ☕ £ 21

Rest *Landseer* – *(bar lunch)* Carte £ 30/42

◆ Chain hotel ◆ Stylish ◆

Refurbished in 2009. Neo-Georgian building by Edward Lutyens, built for YMCA in 1929. Smart comfortable interior, from the lobby to the bedrooms. Restaurant with mostly British menu.

XXX ✿✿

Pied à Terre (Shane Osborn)

34 Charlotte St ✉ W1T 2NH – Ⓜ Goodge Street – ✆ (020) 7636 1178 – www.pied-a-terre.co.uk
– Closed last week December, first week January, Saturday lunch, Sunday and bank holidays I2

Rest – Menu £ 30/72

Spec. Foie gras in Sauternes consommé, smoked bacon and red onion. Pigeon with liquorice purée, caramelised endive and caramel. Honey poached apricot, almond financier and vanilla ice cream.

◆ Innovative ◆ Fashionable ◆

David Moore made the best of limited space to create a stylish and intimate restaurant that is very well established and professionally run. Shane Osborn's cooking is expertly rendered and elaborate in style but with clear flavours.

XX ✿

Hakkasan

8 Hanway Pl. ✉ W1T 1HD – Ⓜ Tottenham Court Road – ✆ (020) 7927 7000 – www.hakkasan.com
– Closed 24-25 December I2

Rest – Carte £ 43/95

Spec. Crispy duck salad with pine nuts and shallots. Grilled sea bass with honey. 'Chocolate textures'.

◆ Chinese ◆ Trendy ◆

Cool and seductive subterranean restaurant, with an air of exclusivity. Innovation and originality have been added to the Cantonese base to create dishes with zip and depth. Lunchtime dim sum is a highlight.

XX

Mon Plaisir

19-21 Monmouth St. ✉ WC2H 9DD – Ⓜ Covent Garden – ✆ (020) 7836 7243 – www.monplaisir.co.uk
– Closed Christmas and New Year, Sunday and bank holidays I3

Rest – Menu £ 17 (lunch) – Carte £ 29/38

◆ French ◆ Family ◆

This proud French institution opened in the 1940s. Enjoy satisfyingly authentic classics in any of the four contrasting rooms, full of Gallic charm; the bar was salvaged from a Lyonnais brothel.

XX

Incognico

117 Shaftesbury Ave. ✉ WC2H 8AD – Ⓜ Tottenham Court Road – ✆ (020) 7836 8866 – www.incognico.com I3

Rest – Menu £ 20/25 – Carte £ 31/38

◆ Modern European ◆ Brasserie ◆

Comfortable, smartly dressed restaurant with dark wood and brown leather lending a masculine, clubby feel. Influences from France and Italy inform the cooking from a capable kitchen.

XX

Roka

37 Charlotte St ✉ W1T 1RR – Ⓜ Goodge Street – ✆ (020) 7580 6464 – www.rokarestaurant.com
– Closed 24- 26 December and 1 January I2

Rest – Carte approx. £ 38

◆ Japanese ◆ Fashionable ◆

Bright, atmospheric interior of teak and oak; bustling and trendy feel. Contemporary touches added to Japanese dishes; try specialities from the on-view Robata grill. Capable and chatty service.

XX

Fino

VISA MC AE

33 Charlotte St. (entrance on Rathbone St.) ✉ W1T 1RR – Ⓜ Goodge Street – ☎ (020) 7813 8010 – www.finorestaurant.com – Closed Saturday lunch and Sunday **I2**

Rest – Menu £ 18 (lunch) – Carte £ 28/44

◆ Spanish ◆ Fashionable ◆

Seafood is handled especially well in this lively, quite smart and smoothly run basement tapas restaurant. Sensibly divided menu, with dishes designed for sharing. Youthful, helpful service.

XX

Sardo

A/C VISA MC AE ⓓ

45 Grafton Way ✉ W1T 5DQ – Ⓜ Warren Street – ☎ (020) 7387 2521 – www.sardo-restaurant.com – Closed Christmas, Saturday lunch and Sunday **H1**

Rest – Carte £ 26/34

◆ Italian ◆ Family ◆

Expect a warm and welcoming atmosphere at this simply decorated Italian restaurant, with plenty of regulars and friendly service. Sardinian specialities and seasonal specials are the highlights.

XX

Archipelago

VISA MC AE ⓓ

110 Whitfield St. ✉ W1T 5ED – Ⓜ Goodge Street – ☎ (020) 7383 3346 – www.archipelago-restaurant.co.uk – Closed Saturday lunch, Sunday and bank holidays **H1**

Rest – Carte £ 27/40

◆ Innovative ◆ Exotic ◆

Eccentrically decorated in the style of an overflowing bazaar. Asian influence to the equally exotic and highly unusual menu which could include crocodile, zebra, wildebeest and even scorpion.

XX

Rasa Samudra

VISA MC AE

5 Charlotte St. ✉ W1T 1RE – Ⓜ Goodge Street – ☎ (020) 7637 0222 – www.rasarestaurants.com – Closed 25 December, 1 January and Sunday lunch **I2**

Rest – Menu £ 23/30 – Carte £ 18/29

◆ Indian ◆ Exotic ◆

Its bright pink hue makes it easy to spot. Specialises in the southwest region of Kerala so expect fish, vegetarian dishes and plenty of coconut and have the pre-meal snacks. Well meaning service.

X

Mennula

A/C ⇔ VISA MC AE ⓓ

10 Charlotte St. ✉ W1T 2LT – Ⓜ Goodge Street – ☎ (020) 7363 2833 – www.mennula.com – Closed Saturday lunch and bank holidays **I2**

Rest – Menu £ 20 (lunch) – Carte £ 27/43

◆ Italian ◆ Intimate ◆

Sicilian specialities provide the highlights at this enthusiastically run Italian restaurant, whose name means 'almond'. Compact but bright, crisply decorated room; ask for one of the booths.

X

Paramount

≤ A/C ⇔ VISA MC AE ⓓ

Centre Point, 101-103 New Oxford St. (31st Floor) ✉ WC1A 1DD – Ⓜ Tottenham Court Road – ☎ (020) 7420 2900 – www.paramount.uk.net – Closed 25 December and Sunday **I2**

Rest – Menu £ 24 (lunch) – Carte £ 35/51

◆ Modern European ◆

Worth the palaver of getting into this Grade II listed building: the views are terrific and this is a fun, keenly run restaurant. Ambitious and quite elaborate cooking; champagne bar one floor up.

Giaconda Dining Room

9 Denmark St. ✉ WC2H 8LS – Ⓜ Tottenham Court Road – ✆ (020) 7240 3334 – www.giacondadining.com
– Closed 2 weeks August, Easter, Saturday, Sunday and bank holidays

Rest – *(booking essential)* Carte £ 24/28 **I2**

◆ Modern European ◆ Minimalist ◆

Aussie owners run a small, fun and very busy place in an unpromising location. The very well priced menu offers an appealing mix of gutsy, confident, no-nonsense food, with French and Italian influences.

Salt Yard

54 Goodge St. ✉ W1T 4NA – Ⓜ Goodge Street – ✆ (020) 7637 0657 – www.saltyard.co.uk
– Closed Christmas and New Year, Saturday lunch, Sunday and bank holidays

Rest – Carte £ 25/35 **H2**

◆ Mediterranean ◆ Tapas bar ◆

Ground floor bar and buzzy basement restaurant specialising in good value plates of tasty Italian and Spanish dishes, ideal for sharing; charcuterie a speciality. Super wine list.

Cigala

54 Lamb's Conduit St. ✉ WC1N 3LW – Ⓜ Russell Square – ✆ (020) 7405 1717 – www.cigala.co.uk
– Closed 24-26 December and Easter **J1**

Rest – *(booking essential)* Menu £ 18 (lunch) – Carte £ 21/43

◆ Spanish ◆ Neighbourhood ◆ Bistro ◆

Spanish restaurant on corner of attractive street. Simply furnished; open-plan kitchen. Robust Iberian cooking, with some dishes designed for sharing; interesting drinks list.

Tsunami

93 Charlotte St. ✉ W1T 4PY – Ⓜ Goodge Street – ✆ (020) 76370050 – www.tsunamirestaurant.co.uk
– Closed 24-26 December, 1 January, Saturday lunch and Sunday

Rest – Menu £ 15 (lunch) – Carte £ 21/40 **H1**

◆ Japanese ◆ Cosy ◆ Trendy ◆

Sister to the original in Clapham. Sweet, pretty place, with lacquered walls, floral motif and moody lighting. Contemporary Japanese cuisine is carefully prepared and sensibly priced.

Acorn House

69 Swinton St. ✉ WC1X 9NT – Ⓜ King's Cross – ✆ (020) 7812 1842 – www.acornhouserestaurant.com
– Closed Saturday lunch and bank holidays **J0**

Rest – Menu £ 25 (dinner) – Carte £ 22/32

◆ Modern European ◆ Bistro ◆

Eco-friendly training restaurant with a bright and appealing café-style feel and helpful service. Dishes are healthy, seasonal and generously proportioned, using organic ingredients.

Barrica

62 Goodge St ✉ W1T 4NE – Ⓜ Goodge Street – ✆ (020) 74369448 – www.barrica.co.uk
– Closed Sunday and bank holidays **H2**

Rest – *(booking essential)* Carte £ 20/23

◆ Spanish ◆ Tapas bar ◆

Lively, noisy and warmly decorated tapas bar. Authentic dishes come with plenty of flavour and are complemented by a thoughtfully compiled Spanish wine list. Busy front bar.

EUSTON

Novotel London St. Pancras

100-110 Euston Rd. ✉ *NW1 2AJ*
– Ⓜ Euston – ✆ (020) 7666 9000
– www.novotel.com **I0**
309 rm – †£ 295 ††£ 295, ☕ £ 14.95 – 3 suites
Rest – *(bar lunch Saturday, Sunday and bank holidays)* Menu £ 19/23 – Carte £ 26/42
♦ Business ♦ Modern ♦
Halfway between Euston and Kings Cross, this hotel has good-sized bedrooms for London and those on the higher floors enjoy views over the city. Good business amenities. International menu and buffet breakfast.

Snazz Sichuan

37 Chalton St ✉ *NW1 1JD – Ⓜ Euston – ✆ (020) 7388 0808*
– www.newchinaclub.co.uk **I0**
Rest – Carte £ 10/40
♦ Chinese ♦ Fashionable ♦
Authentic Sichuan atmosphere and cooking, with gallery and traditional tea room. Menu split into hot and cold dishes; the fiery Sichuan pepper helps heat you from inside out.

HATTON GARDEN

Bleeding Heart

Bleeding Heart Yard (off Greville St.) ✉ *EC1N 8SJ*
– Ⓜ Farringdon – ✆ (020) 7242 8238
– www.bleedingheart.co.uk
– Closed 24 December-4 January, Saturday and Sunday **K2**
Rest – *(booking essential)* Carte £ 26/41
♦ French ♦ Romantic ♦
Dickensian Yard plays host to this atmospheric, candlelit restaurant; popular with those from The City. Classic French cuisine is the draw, with service that's formal but has personality.

HOLBORN

Renaissance Chancery Court

252 High Holborn ✉ *WC1V 7EN*
– Ⓜ Holborn – ✆ (020) 7829 9888
– www.renaissancechancerycourt.com **J2**
354 rm – †£ 264/366 ††£ 264/366, ☕ £ 24.50 – 2 suites
Rest *Pearl* – see below
♦ Business ♦ Stylish ♦
Striking building built in 1914, now an imposing place to stay. Impressive marbled lobby and grand central courtyard. Very large bedrooms with comprehensive modern facilities.

Pearl – at Renaissance Chancery Court Hotel

252 High Holborn ✉ *WC1V 7EN*
– Ⓜ Holborn – ✆ (020) 7829 7000
– www.pearl-restaurant.com
– Closed last 2 weeks August, Christmas, Saturday lunch, Sunday and bank holidays **J2**
Rest – Menu £ 29/58
♦ French ♦ Elegant ♦
Impressive former banking hall, with walls clad in Italian marble and Corinthian columns. Waiters provide efficient service at well-spaced tables; cooking shows originality.

XX

Asadal

A/C VISA MC AE

227 High Holborn ✉ WC1V 7DA – Ⓜ Holborn – ✆ (020) 7430 9006 – www.asadal.co.uk – Closed 25-26 December, 1 January and Sunday lunch J2

Rest – Menu £ 12 (lunch) – Carte £ 13/20

♦ Korean ♦ Friendly ♦

Sharing is the key in this busy basement, where you'll be oblivious to its unprepossessing location. Hotpots and barbecues the highlights from the easy-to-follow menu. Swift service.

XX

Moti Mahal

A/C VISA MC AE

45 Great Queen St. ✉ WC2B 5AA – Ⓜ Holborn – ✆ (020) 7240 9329 – www.motimahal-uk.com – Closed 25-27 December, 1-2 January, Saturday lunch and Sunday

Rest – Carte £ 43/58 J3

♦ Indian ♦ Elegant ♦

Restaurant is split between a bright, busy ground floor and more intimate basement. Specialities follow the Grand Trunk Road, stretching from Bengal to the North West and the Pakistan border.

X

Great Queen Street

VISA MC

32 Great Queen St ✉ WC2B 5AA – Ⓜ Holborn – ✆ (020) 7242 0622 – Closed Christmas, New Year, Sunday dinner and bank holidays

Rest – *(booking essential)* Carte £ 25/32 J2

♦ British ♦ Rustic ♦

The menu is a model of British understatement; the cooking, confident and satisfying with laudable prices and generous portions. Lively atmosphere and enthusiastic service.

X

Villandry Kitchen

A/C MC AE

95-97 High Holborn ✉ WC1V 6LF – Ⓜ Holborn – ✆ (020) 72424580 – www.villandry.com – Closed 25-26 December and 1 January

Rest – Carte £ 21/34 J2

♦ French ♦ Bistro ♦ Rustic ♦

Open all day and offering everything from breakfast and afternoon tea to pizza, charcuterie and comforting French classics. Large, animated room with rustic feel and friendly service.

HYDE PARK – KNIGHTSBRIDGE

Plan VII

Mandarin Oriental Hyde Park

A/C VISA MC AE

66 Knightsbridge ✉ SW1X 7LA – Ⓜ Knightsbridge – ✆ (020) 7235 2000 – www.mandarinoriental.com/london F4

173 rm – †£ 666/750 ††£ 666/750, ☕ £ 29 – 25 suites

Rest *Bar Boulud* – see below

♦ Grand Luxury ♦ Classic ♦

Built in 1889 this classic hotel, with striking façade, remains one of London's grandest. Many of the luxurious and impeccably kept bedrooms enjoy views of Hyde Park. Heston Blumenthal due to open as we went to print.

XX

Zuma

A/C VISA MC AE

5 Raphael St ✉ SW7 1DL – Ⓜ Knightsbridge – ✆ (020) 7584 1010 – www.zumarestaurant.com – Closed 25-26 December-1 January

Rest – Carte £ 60/90 F5

♦ Japanese ♦ Fashionable ♦

Eye-catching design that blends East with West. Bustling atmosphere; fashionable clientele; popular sushi bar. Varied and interesting contemporary Japanese food.

Hyde Park & Knightsbridge

(Plan VII)

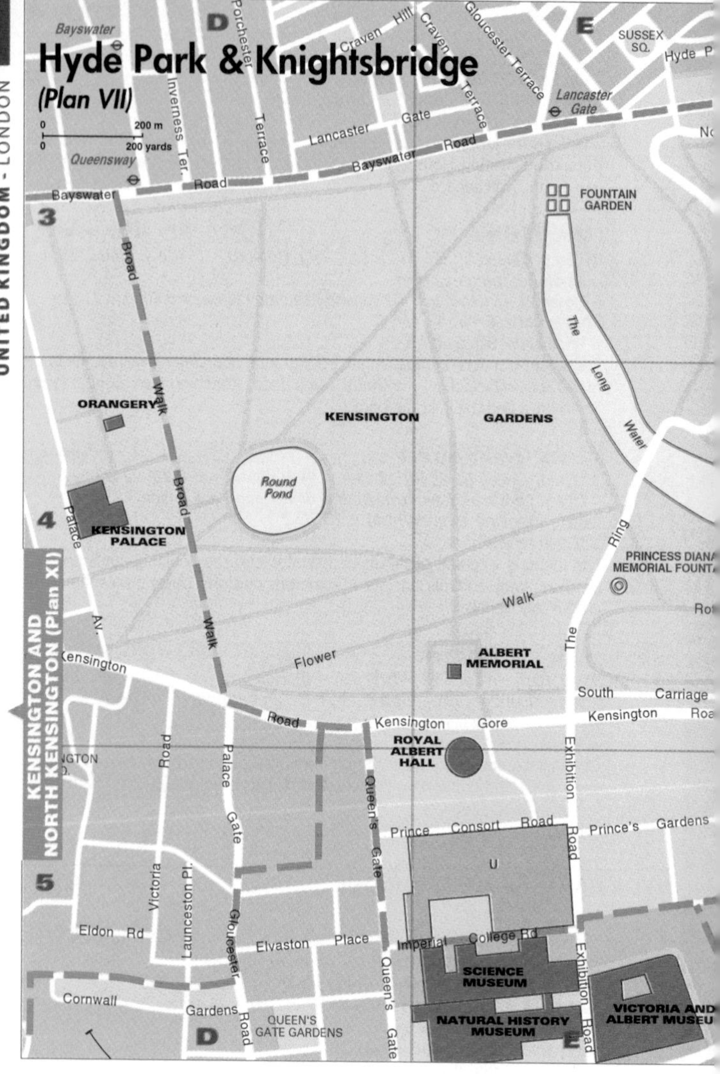

KENSINGTON AND NORTH KENSINGTON (Plan XI)

Bar Boulud – at Mandarin Oriental Hyde Park Hotel

66 Knightsbridge ✉ SW1X 7LA – Ⓜ Knightsbridge
– ✆ (020) 72013899 – www.barboulud.com/barbouludlondon

Rest – Menu £ 20 (lunch and early dinner) – Carte £ 29/48 **F4**

♦ French ♦ Design ♦

Daniel Boulud's London outpost is fashionable, fun and frantic. His hometown is Lyon but he built his considerable reputation in New York, so charcuterie, sausages and burgers are the highlights.

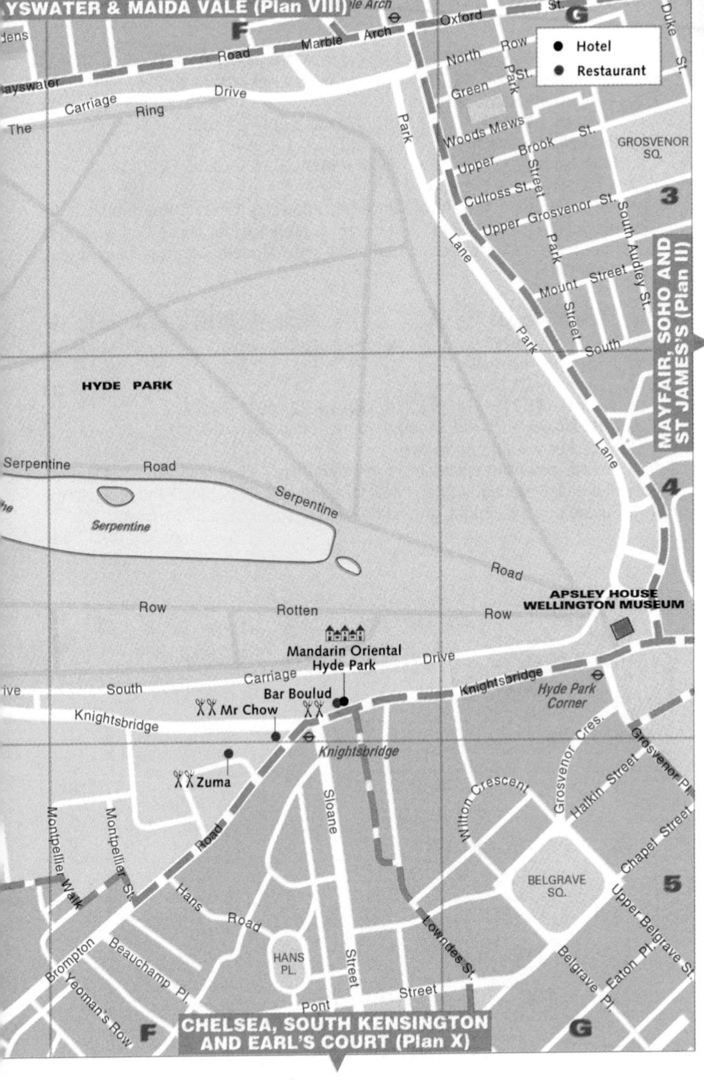

Mr Chow

151 Knightsbridge ✉ *SW1X 7PA – Ⓜ Knightsbridge – ✆ (020) 7589 7347 – www.mrchow.com – Closed 24-26 December, 1 January and Monday lunch*

Rest – Carte £ 39/63 **F4**

♦ Chinese ♦ Friendly ♦

Long-standing Chinese restaurant, opened in 1968. Smart clientele, stylish and comfortable surroundings and prompt service from Italian waiters. Carefully prepared and satisfying food.

Lancaster London

Lancaster Ter. ✉ W2 2TY – Ⓜ Lancaster Gate – ✆ (020) 7262 6737 – www.lancasterlondon.com **E3**

394 rm – †£ 191/372 ††£ 191/372, ☕ £ 20 – 22 suites

Rest *Nipa* – see below

Rest *Island* – ✆ (020) 7551 6070 – Menu £ 19 – Carte £ 24/48

♦ Business ♦ Classic ♦

Formerly called the Royal Lancaster. Imposing 1960s purpose-built hotel overlooking Hyde Park. Extensive conference facilities. Well-equipped bedrooms are decorated in traditional style. Modern, bright restaurant with open kitchen.

The Hempel

31-35 Craven Hill Gdns. ✉ W2 3EA – Ⓜ Queensway – ✆ (020) 7298 9000 – www.the-hempel.co.uk – Closed 24-28 December **D3**

44 rm – †£ 219/334 ††£ 219/334, ☕ £ 21.50 – 6 suites

Rest *No.35* – *(closed Sunday) (dinner only)* Carte £ 32/47

♦ Luxury ♦ Minimalist ♦

A crisp, minimalist environment in a blizzard of white; room 110 has a suspended bed. Basement art gallery also used for private parties. Zen garden in the Square opposite. Bright, ground floor dining room has a British menu.

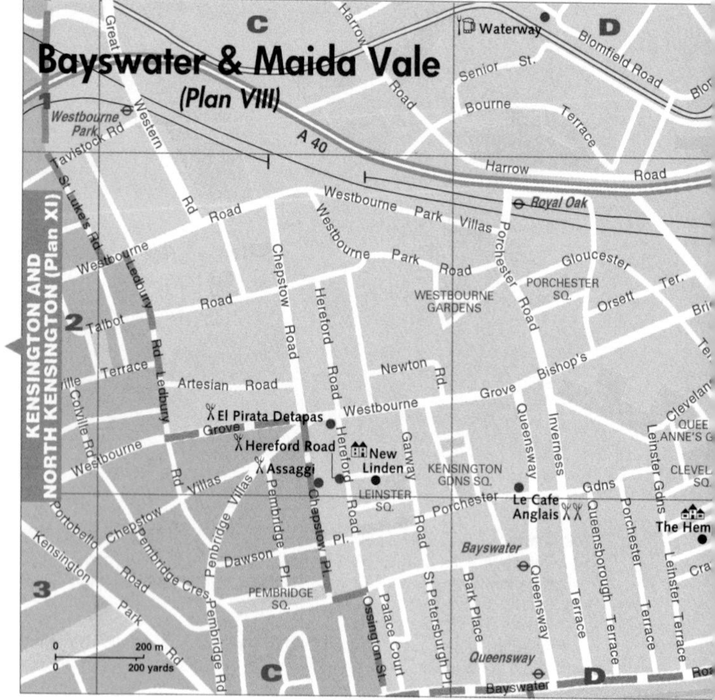

New Linden without rest

59 Leinster Sq. ✉ W2 4PS – Ⓜ Bayswater – ✆ (020) 7221 4321 – www.mayflower-group.co.uk **C2**

50 rm – †£ 110/144 ††£ 156/180

♦ Family ♦ Functional ♦

Smart four storey white stucco façade. Basement breakfast room with sunny aspect. Bedrooms are its strength: flat screen TVs and wooden floors; two split-level family rooms.

Le Café Anglais

8 Porchester Gdns. ✉ W2 4BD – Ⓜ Bayswater – ✆ (020) 72211415 – www.lecafeanglais.co.uk – Closed 25-26 December and 1 January

Rest – Menu £ 22/25 – Carte £ 26/46 **D2**

♦ Modern European ♦ Brasserie ♦

Big, bustling and contemporary brasserie with art deco styling, within Whiteley's shopping centre. Large and very appealing selection of classic brasserie food; the rotisserie is the centrepiece.

Angelus

4 Bathurst St. ✉ W2 2SD – Ⓜ Lancaster Gate – ✆ (020) 7402 0083 – www.angelusrestaurant.co.uk – Closed 24 December-2 January

Rest – Menu £ 30 (lunch) – Carte £ 34/56 **E3**

♦ French ♦ Brasserie ♦

Hospitable owner has created an attractive French brasserie within a 19C former pub, with a warm and inclusive feel. Satisfying and honest French cooking uses seasonal British ingredients.

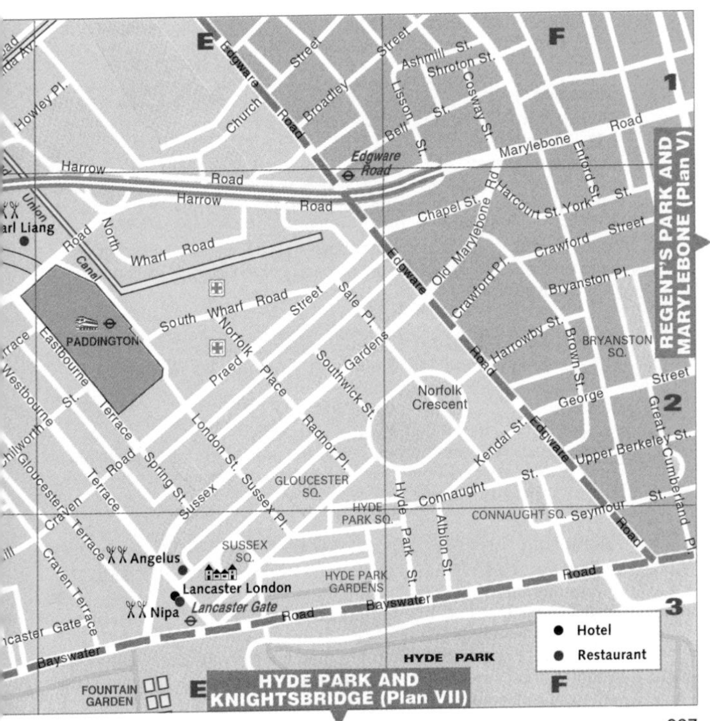

XX

Nipa – at Lancaster London Hotel

Lancaster Ter. ✉ *W2 2TY* – Ⓜ *Lancaster Gate* – ✆ *(020) 7551 6039*
– *www.niparestaurant.co.uk*
– *Closed Saturday lunch and Sunday* **E3**

Rest – Menu £ 29/32 – Carte £ 26/37

♦ Thai ♦ Exotic ♦

On the 1st floor and overlooking Hyde Park. Authentic and ornately decorated restaurant offers subtly spiced Thai cuisine. Keen to please staff in traditional silk costumes.

XX

Pearl Liang

8 Sheldon Sq., Paddington Central ✉ *W2 6EZ*
– Ⓜ *Paddington* – ✆ *(020) 7289 7000*
– *www.pearlliang.co.uk* **D2**

Rest – Menu £ 25 – Carte £ 25/44

♦ Chinese ♦ Minimalist ♦

Spacious, business-orientated Chinese restaurant within a corporate development. Extensive choice from a variety of set menus; try the more unusual dishes like jellyfish or pig's trotter.

X

Hereford Road

3 Hereford Rd. ✉ *W2 4AB* – Ⓜ *Bayswater* – ✆ *(020) 77271144*
– *www.herefordroad.org*
– *Closed 25-26 December and 1 January* **C2**

Rest – *(booking essential)* Menu £ 16 (weekday lunch) – Carte £ 23/29

♦ British ♦ Neighbourhood ♦

Converted butcher's shop specialising in tasty British dishes without frills, using first rate, seasonal ingredients; offal a highlight. Booths for six people are the prized seats. Friendly and relaxed feel.

X

Assaggi

39 Chepstow Pl., (above Chepstow pub) ✉ *W2 4TS*
– Ⓜ *Bayswater* – ✆ *(020) 7792 5501*
– *www.assaggi.com*
– *Closed 2 weeks Christmas, Sunday and bank holidays* **C2**

Rest – *(booking essential)* Carte approx. £ 47

♦ Italian ♦ Rustic ♦

Pared-down simplicity to this room above a pub, where regulars are given fulsome welcomes. Cooking relies on the quality of the ingredients and the wine list is exclusively Italian.

X

El Pirata De Tapas

115 Westbourne Grove ✉ *W2 4UP* – Ⓜ *Bayswater* – ✆ *(020) 77275000*
– *www.elpiratadetapas.co.uk* **C2**

Rest – Menu £ 10 (lunch) – Carte approx. £ 25

♦ Spanish ♦ Tapas Bar ♦

Contemporary yet warm Spanish restaurant with a genuine neighbourhood feel. Authentic flavours from a well-priced and appealing selection of tapas, ideal for sharing with friends.

Waterway

54 Formosa St ✉ *W9 2JU* – Ⓜ *Warwick Avenue.* – ✆ *(020) 7266 3557*
– *www.thewaterway.co.uk* **D1**

Rest – Menu £ 17 (lunch) – Carte £ 30/45

♦ Pub ♦ Trendy ♦

Terrific decked terrace by the canal its most appealing feature. Contemporary interior with busy cocktail bar; menu in separate dining room mixes the classics with more ambitious dishes.

City of London

Andaz Liverpool Street

Liverpool St. ✉ EC2M 7QN – Ⓜ Liverpool Street – ✆ (020) 7961 1234 – www.andaz.com M2
264 rm – †£ 270/378 ††£ 300/408, ☕ £ 20 – 3 suites
Rest *1901* – see below
Rest *Catch* – ✆ (020) 7618 7200 (closed Saturday and Sunday) Carte £ 34/81
Rest *Miyako* – ✆ (020) 7618 7100 (closed Saturday lunch and Sunday) (booking essential) Carte £ 15/46

♦ Grand Luxury ♦ Design ♦

A contemporary and stylish interior hides behind the classic Victorian façade; part of the Hyatt group. Bright and spacious bedrooms with state-of-the-art facilities. Seafood at Catch, based within original hotel lobby. Miyako is a compact Japanese restaurant.

Threadneedles

5 Threadneedle St. ✉ EC2R 8AY – Ⓜ Bank – ✆ (020) 7657 8080 – www.theetoncollection.com M3
68 rm – †£ 414 ††£ 546, ☕ £ 19.50 – 1 suite
Rest *Bonds* – see below

♦ Business ♦ Modern ♦

A converted bank, dating from 1856, with a stunning stained-glass cupola in the lounge. Bedrooms are very stylish and individual featuring CD players and Egyptian cotton sheets.

Apex City of London

No 1, Seething Ln. ✉ EC3N 4AX – Ⓜ Tower Hill – ✆ (020) 7702 2020 – www.apexhotels.co.uk N3
179 rm – †£ 384 ††£ 384, ☕ £ 18
Rest *Addendum* – ✆ (020) 7977 9500 – Menu £ 20 (dinner) – Carte £ 24/41

♦ Business ♦ Modern ♦

Tucked away behind Tower of London, overlooking leafy square. Smart meeting facilities and well-equipped gym. Comfortable bedrooms and sleek bathrooms. Easy-going style in Addendum.

Rhodes Twenty Four

24th floor, Tower 42, 25 Old Broad St. ✉ EC2N 1HQ – Ⓜ Liverpool Street – ✆ (020) 7877 7703 – www.rhodes24.co.uk
– Closed 24 December-4 January, Saturday, Sunday and bank holidays
Rest – Carte £ 37/61 M3
Spec. Sardines on toast with tomato and cucumber dressing. Steamed mutton and onion suet pudding with carrots. Bread and butter pudding.

♦ British ♦ Formal ♦ Intimate ♦

Prepare for security checks at Tower 42 before taking the lift up to its 24th floor; the views will be worth it. The unmistakeable signature of Gary Rhodes is writ large on the menu: seasonal dishes of a pleasingly British persuasion.

Coq d'Argent

1 Poultry ✉ EC2R 8EJ – Ⓜ Bank – ✆ (020) 7395 5000 – www.coqdargent.co.uk
– Closed Christmas, bank holidays, Saturday lunch and Sunday dinner
Rest – (booking essential) Menu £ 28 (lunch) – Carte £ 44/58 M3

♦ French ♦ Design ♦

Resembling the bow of a ship; with a busy bar, terrace and formal garden providing commanding views over the Square Mile. Slick, well run, modern restaurant; appealing shellfish counter.

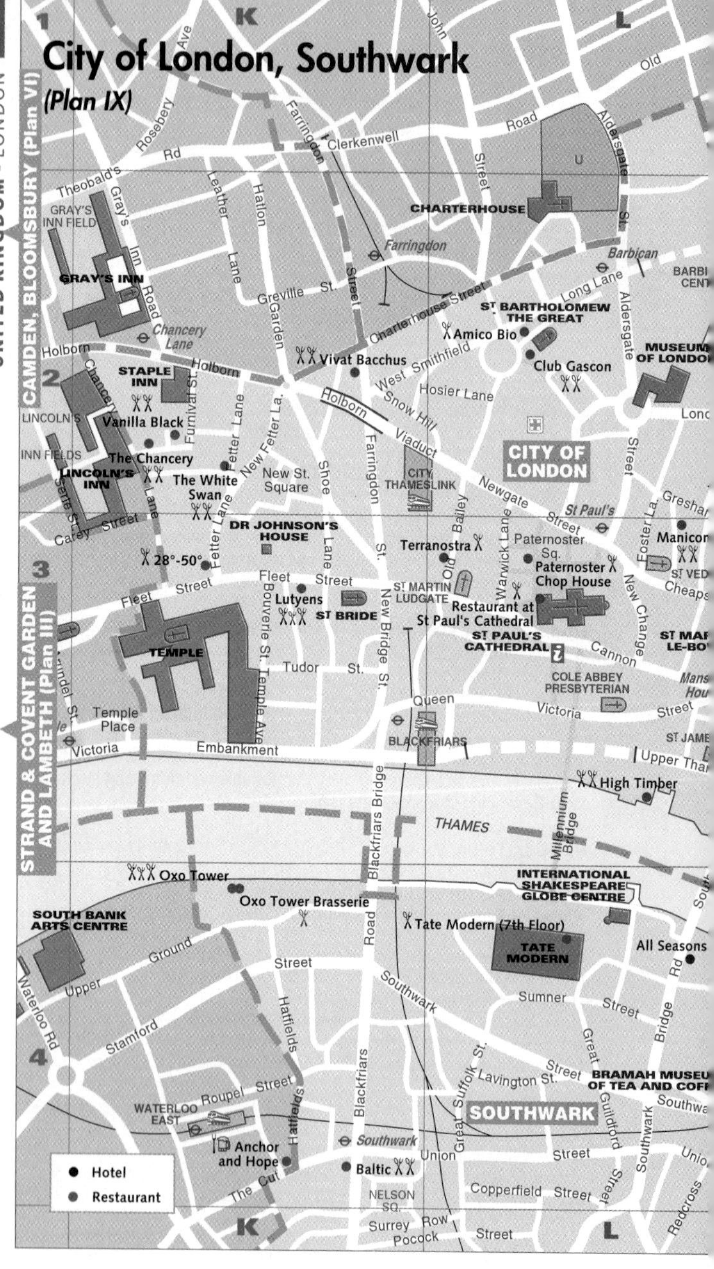
City of London, Southwark
(Plan IX)
CAMDEN, BLOOMSBURY (Plan VI)
STRAND & COVENT GARDEN AND LAMBETH (Plan III)
K
L
1
2
3
4
Hotel
Restaurant
CHARTERHOUSE
GRAY'S INN FIELD
GRAY'S INN
STAPLE INN
LINCOLN'S INN FIELDS
LINCOLN'S INN
DR JOHNSON'S HOUSE
TEMPLE
ST BRIDE
ST MARTIN LUDGATE
ST BARTHOLOMEW THE GREAT
MUSEUM OF LONDON
CITY OF LONDON
CITY THAMESLINK
ST PAUL'S CATHEDRAL
COLE ABBEY PRESBYTERIAN
BLACKFRIARS
THAMES
INTERNATIONAL SHAKESPEARE GLOBE CENTRE
TATE MODERN
SOUTH BANK ARTS CENTRE
WATERLOO EAST
SOUTHWARK
NELSON SQ.
BRAMAH MUSEU OF TEA AND COFF
Farringdon
Barbican
Chancery Lane
St Paul's
Southwark
Vivat Bacchus
Amico Bio
Club Gascon
Vanilla Black
The Chancery
The White Swan
28°-50°
Terranostra
Paternoster Chop House
Restaurant at St Paul's Cathedral
Lutyens
High Timber
Oxo Tower
Oxo Tower Brasserie
Tate Modern (7th Floor)
All Seasons
Anchor and Hope
Baltic
Clerkenwell Road
Farringdon Street
Holborn
Holborn Viaduct
Fleet Street
Victoria Embankment
Blackfriars Bridge
Millennium Bridge
Southwark Street
Union Street
The Cut
Copperfield Street
Surrey Row
Pocock Street
Stamford Street
Upper Ground
Waterloo Rd
Roupel Street
Hatfields
Blackfriars Road
Great Suffolk St.
Lavington St.
Sumner Street
Great Guildford Street
Southwark Bridge Rd
Redcross
Newgate Street
Cannon
Queen Victoria Street
Upper Thames
Long Lane
Aldersgate Street
Charterhouse Street
West Smithfield
Hosier Lane
Snow Hill
Old Bailey
Warwick Lane
Paternoster Sq.
New Change
Foster La.
Cheapside
Gresham
Greville St.
Hatton Garden
Leather Lane
Rosebery Ave
Theobald's Rd
Gray's Inn Road
Chancery Lane
Furnival St.
Fetter Lane
New Fetter La.
New St. Square
Shoe Lane
Farringdon St.
New Bridge St.
Bouverie St.
Temple Ave
Tudor St.
Temple Place
Carey Street
Serle St.
Arundel St.
St John Street
Old
Aldersgate St.

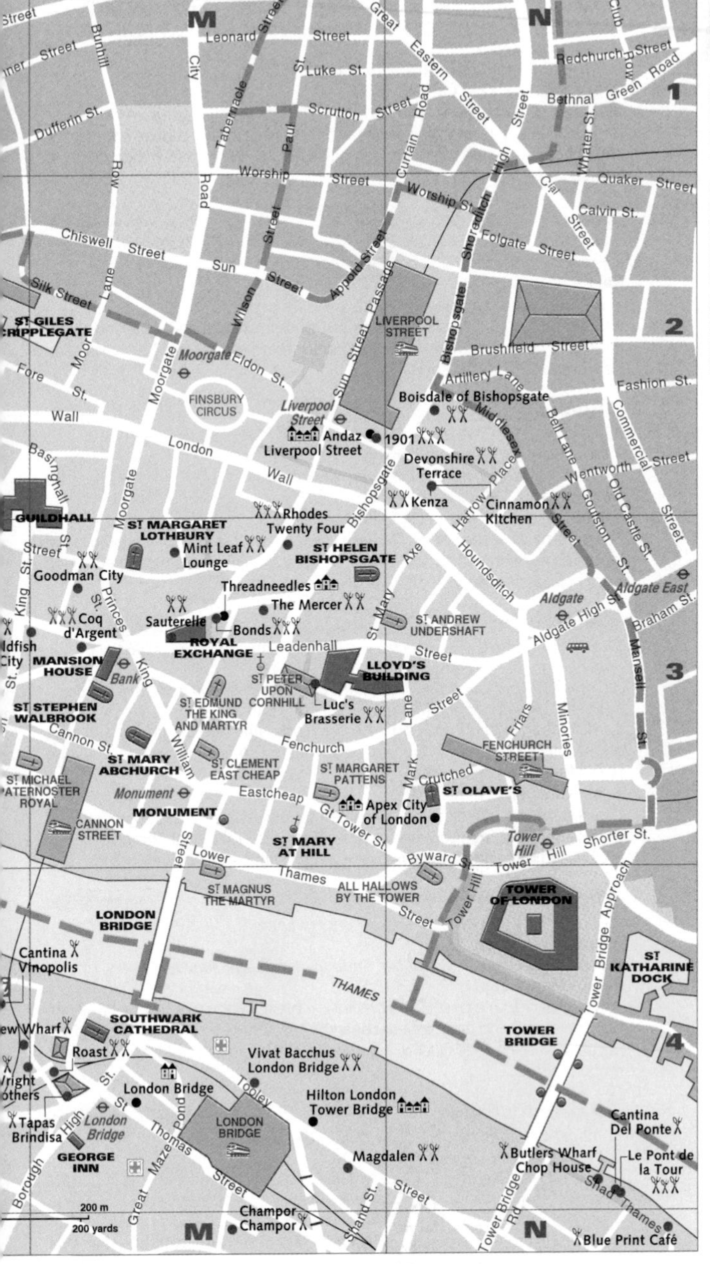

M
N
1
2
3
4
Leonard Street
Great Eastern Street
Redchurch Street
Bethnal Green Road
St. Luke St.
Scrutton Street
Curtain Road
Tabernacle Street
Paul Street
City Road
Bunhill Row
Dufferin St.
Worship Street
Worship St.
Shoreditch High Street
Quaker Street
Calvin St.
Chiswell Street
Sun Street
Folgate Street
Appold Street
Wilson Street
Silk Street
Moor Lane
ST GILES CRIPPLEGATE
LIVERPOOL STREET
Sun Street Passage
Bishopsgate
Brushfield Street
Moorgate
Eldon St.
Fore St.
FINSBURY CIRCUS
Liverpool Street
Artillery Lane
Fashion St.
Wall
London Wall
Boisdale of Bishopsgate
Andaz Liverpool Street
1901
Devonshire Terrace
Middlesex Street
Bell Lane
Commercial Street
Wentworth Street
Basinghall Street
Kenza
Harrow Place
Cinnamon Kitchen
Goulston St.
Old Castle St.
GUILDHALL
Rhodes Twenty Four
ST MARGARET LOTHBURY
Mint Leaf Lounge
ST HELEN BISHOPSGATE
Houndsditch
Goodman City
Threadneedles
Aldgate
Aldgate East
Braham St.
King St.
Princes St.
The Mercer
St Mary Axe
Sauterelle
Bonds
Coq d'Argent
ST ANDREW UNDERSHAFT
Aldgate High St.
ROYAL EXCHANGE
Leadenhall Street
MANSION HOUSE
Bank
King William
LLOYD'S BUILDING
ST PETER UPON CORNHILL
Luc's Brasserie
Mansell St.
ST STEPHEN WALBROOK
ST EDMUND THE KING AND MARTYR
Lime Street
Cannon St.
Fenchurch Street
Minories
Jewry Street
FENCHURCH STREET
ST MARY ABCHURCH
ST CLEMENT EAST CHEAP
ST MARGARET PATTENS
Mark Lane
Crutched Friars
ST MICHAEL PATERNOSTER ROYAL
Monument
Eastcheap
ST OLAVE'S
Apex City of London
MONUMENT
Gt Tower St.
CANNON STREET
ST MARY AT HILL
Tower Hill
Shorter St.
Lower Thames Street
Byward St.
ST MAGNUS THE MARTYR
ALL HALLOWS BY THE TOWER
TOWER OF LONDON
Tower Bridge Approach
LONDON BRIDGE
Cantina Vinopolis
THAMES
ST KATHARINE DOCK
New Wharf
SOUTHWARK CATHEDRAL
TOWER BRIDGE
Roast
Vivat Bacchus London Bridge
Wright Brothers
London Bridge
Tooley Street
Hilton London Tower Bridge
Tapas Brindisa
Borough High St.
St Thomas Street
Cantina Del Ponte
GEORGE INN
Magdalen
Butlers Wharf Chop House
Le Pont de la Tour
Shad Thames
Maze Pond
Great Maze Pond
Shand St.
Tower Bridge Rd
200 m
200 yards
Champor Champor
Blue Print Café

XXX

1901 – at Andaz Liverpool Street Hotel

Liverpool St. ✉ EC2M 7QN – Ⓜ Liverpool Street – ✆ (020) 7618 7000 – www.andaz.com – Closed Saturday lunch, Sunday and bank holidays **M2**

Rest – Menu £ 22 – Carte £ 36/47

♦ French ♦ Elegant ♦

An impressive and imposing room, with an eye-catching cupola, cocktail bar and cheese and wine room. Kitchen makes proud use of British ingredients in refined and skilled cooking.

XXX

Bonds – at Threadneedles Hotel

5 Threadneedle St. ✉ EC2R 8AY – Ⓜ Bank – ✆ (020) 7657 8088 – www.theetoncollection.com – Closed Saturday and Sunday

Rest – Menu £ 18/20 – Carte £ 27/53 **M3**

♦ Modern European ♦ Retro ♦ Luxury ♦

Former banking hall from the 1850s, with pillars, marble and panelling. Experienced kitchen produces dishes with bold flavours; fish from Newhaven and slow-cooked meats the specialities.

XXX

Lutyens

85 Fleet St. ✉ EC4Y 1AE – Ⓜ St Paul's – ✆ (020) 75838385 – www.lutyens-restaurant.com – Closed 24 December-4 January and bank holidays **K3**

Rest – Menu £ 40 (dinner) – Carte £ 38/57

♦ Modern European ♦ Fashionable ♦

The unmistakable hand of Sir Terence Conran: timeless and understated good looks mixed with functionality and an appealing Anglo-French menu with plenty of classics that include fruits de mer.

XX ✿

Club Gascon (Pascal Aussignac)

57 West Smithfield ✉ EC1A 9DS – Ⓜ Barbican – ✆ (020) 7796 0600 – www.clubgascon.com – Closed Christmas and New Year, Saturday lunch, Sunday and bank holidays

Rest – *(booking essential)* Menu £ 28 (lunch) – Carte £ 37/57 **L2**

Spec. White pudding gnocchi with asparagus and sea urchin jus. Coconut glazed black cod with white port and winkle risotto. Rhubarb and custard sweet foie gras with vanilla.

♦ French ♦ Intimate ♦

The gastronomy of Gascony and France's southwest are the starting points but the assured and intensely flavoured cooking also pushes at the boundaries. Marble and huge floral displays create suitably atmospheric surroundings.

XX

The Chancery

9 Cursitor St ✉ EC4A 1LL – Ⓜ Chancery Lane – ✆ (020) 7831 4000 – www.thechancery.co.uk – Closed 24-27 and 31 December, Saturday lunch and Sunday **K2**

Rest – Menu £ 35

♦ Modern European ♦ Formal ♦ Neighbourhood ♦

Cosy restaurant and basement bar near the Law Courts with contemporary interior and intimate feel. Quality ingredients put to good use in accomplished, modern dishes.

XX

Mint Leaf Lounge

12 Angel Ct., Lothbury ✉ EC2R 7HB – Ⓜ Bank – ✆ (020) 76000992 – www.mintleaflounge.com – Closed 25-26 December, Saturday, Sunday and bank holidays **M3**

Rest – Menu £ 18 (lunch) – Carte £ 30/45

♦ Indian ♦ Design ♦ Fashionable ♦

Sister branch to the original in St James's. Slick and stylish, with busy bar. Well paced service of carefully prepared contemporary Indian food, with many of the influences from the south.

XX **Vivat Bacchus**

(basement) 47 Farringdon St ✉ EC4A 4LL – Ⓜ Farringdon – ☎ (020) 7353 2648 – www.vivatbacchus.co.uk
– Closed 24 December-5 January, Saturday and Sunday **K2**

Rest – Menu £ 15/18 – Carte £ 20/42

◆ Traditional ◆ Wine bar ◆ Friendly ◆

Platters and tapas served in the large bar; more intimate basement restaurant for meat dishes and South African specialities. Hugely impressive wine list with five cellars of wine.

XX **Vanilla Black**

17-18 Tooks Ct. ✉ EC4A 1LB – Ⓜ Chancery Lane – ☎ (020) 72422622 – www.vanillablack.co.uk
– Closed Christmas and New Year, Saturday lunch, Sunday and bank holidays except Good Friday **K2**

Rest – Menu £ 23/30

◆ Vegetarian ◆ Minimalist ◆

Proving that vegetarian food can be flavoursome and satisfying, with a menu that is varied and imaginative. This is a well run, friendly restaurant with understated décor, run by a husband and wife team.

XX **Cinnamon Kitchen**

9 Devonshire Sq. ✉ EC2M 4YL – Ⓜ Liverpool Street – ☎ (020) 7626 5000 – www.cinnamon-kitchen.com
– Closed 1 January, Saturday lunch, Sunday and bank holidays **N2**

Rest – Menu £ 18/19 – Carte £ 23/33

◆ Indian ◆ Friendly ◆ Wine bar ◆

Sister to The Cinnamon Club. Contemporary Indian cooking, with punchy flavours and arresting presentation. Sprightly service in large, modern surroundings. Watch the action from the Tandoor Bar.

XX **Kenza**

10 Devonshire Sq. ✉ EC2M 4YP – Ⓜ Liverpool Street – ☎ (020) 79295533 – www.kenza-restaurant.com
– Closed Saturday lunch, Sunday and bank holidays **N2**

Rest – Menu £ 12 – Carte £ 26/37

◆ Lebanese ◆ Exotic ◆

Exotic basement restaurant, with lamps, carvings, pumping music and nightly belly dancing. Lebanese and Moroccan cooking are the menu influences and the cooking is authentic and accurate.

XX **Devonshire Terrace**

Devonshire Sq. ✉ EC2M 4WY – Ⓜ Liverpool Street – ☎ (020) 72563233 – www.devonshireterrace.co.uk
– Closed Saturday, Sunday and bank holidays **N2**

Rest – Carte £ 28/41

◆ Modern European ◆ Brasserie ◆

Brasserie-style cooking, where you choose the sauce and side dish to accompany your main course. Bright and busy restaurant with open kitchen and choice of two terraces, one within large atrium.

XX **Sauterelle**

The Royal Exchange ✉ EC3V 3LR – Ⓜ Bank – ☎ (020) 7618 2483 – www.restaurantsauterelle.com
– Closed Christmas-New Year, Saturday, Sunday and bank holidays **M3**

Rest – Menu £ 24 – Carte £ 31/54

◆ French ◆ Design ◆

Impressive location on the mezzanine floor of The Royal Exchange; ask for a table looking down over the Grand Café. A largely French inspired contemporary menu makes good use of luxury ingredients.

XX

The Mercer

A/C VISA MC AE

34 Threadneedle St ✉ EC2R 8AY – Ⓜ Bank – ☎ (020) 7628 0001
– www.themercer.co.uk
– Closed 24 December-2 January, Saturday, Sunday and bank bolidays

Rest – Carte £ 28/42 M3

◆ Modern European ◆ Brasserie ◆

Converted bank, with airy feel thanks to high ceilings and large windows. Brasserie style menu with appealing mix of classics and comfort food. Huge choice of wines available by glass or carafe.

XX

Boisdale of Bishopsgate

A/C VISA MC AE

Swedeland Crt., 202 Bishopsgate ✉ EC2M 4NR
– Ⓜ Liverpool Street – ☎ (020) 7283 1763
– www.boisdale.co.uk
– Closed 23 December-2 January, Saturday, Sunday and bank holidays

Rest – Carte £ 27/55 N2

◆ Scottish ◆ Intimate ◆ Cosy ◆

Through ground floor bar, serving oysters and champagne, to brick vaulted basement with red and tartan décor. Menu featuring Scottish produce. Live jazz most evenings.

XX

The White Swan

A/C VISA MC AE

108 Fetter Lane ✉ EC4A 1ES – Ⓜ Chancery Lane – ☎ (020) 7242 9696
– www.thewhiteswanlondon.com
– Closed 25-26 December K2

Rest – Carte £ 30/40

◆ Modern European ◆ Pub ◆ Neighbourhood ◆

Smart dining room above pub just off Fleet Street: mirrored ceilings, colourful paintings on walls. Modern, daily changing menus, are good value for the heart of London.

XX

Manicomio

A/C VISA MC AE

6 Gutter Ln. ✉ EC2V 8AS – Ⓜ St Paul's – ☎ (020) 77265010
– www.manicomio.co.uk
– Closed 24 December-3 January, Saturday, Sunday and bank holidays

Rest – Menu £ 20 – Carte £ 33/51 L3

◆ Italian ◆ Brasserie ◆

Second branch to follow the first in Chelsea. Regional Italian fare, with top-notch ingredients. Bright and fresh first floor restaurant, with deli-café on the ground floor and bar on top floor.

XX

Luc's Brasserie

VISA MC AE

17-22 Leadenhall Market ✉ EC3V 1LR – Ⓜ Bank – ☎ (020) 7621 0666
– www.lucsbrasserie.com
– Closed 25 December-4 January, Saturday, Sunday, bank holidays, dinner Friday and Monday M3

Rest – *(booking essential at lunch)* Menu £ 19 – Carte £ 29/41

◆ French ◆ Brasserie ◆

Looks down on the Victorian splendour of Leadenhall Market. First appeared in 1890 but re-invigorated this century. The menu is a paean to all things French and every classic dish is there.

XX

High Timber

A/C VISA MC AE

8 High Timber St. ✉ EC4V 3PA – Ⓜ Mansion House – ☎ (020) 72481777
– www.hightimber.com
– Closed 25-26 December, Saturday, Sunday and bank holidays L3

Rest – Menu £ 19 (lunch) – Carte £ 24/51

◆ Modern European ◆ Rustic ◆

Rustic look to the room, despite being in a modern block, offering river views. Great wine cellar, with large choice from South Africa, the owners' homeland. Cumbrian steaks the speciality.

Goodman City

11 Old Jewry ✉ EC2R 8DU – Ⓜ Bank – ✆ (020) 7600 8220 – www.goodmanrestaurants.com – Closed Saturday and Sunday **M3**

Rest – Menu £ 18 (lunch) – Carte £ 26/63

♦ Beef specialities ♦ Design ♦ Bistro ♦

Steaks, cut to order, are the stars of the show at this sister to the Mayfair original. Choose corn-fed, wet-matured USDA beef or Scottish and Irish grass-fed; plenty of side dishes available too.

Amico Bio

44 Cloth Fair ✉ EC1A 7JQ – Ⓜ Barbican – ✆ (0207) 6007778 – www.amicobio.co.uk – Closed 25 December, Saturday lunch, Sunday and bank holidays

Rest – Carte £ 17/21 **L2**

♦ Italian vegetarian ♦ Friendly ♦ Neighbourhood ♦

Simple little place owned by an experienced chef and his cousin; the organic produce comes from the family farm in Capua and the combination of flavours remain true to their upbringing in Campania.

Terranostra

27 Old Bailey ✉ EC4M 7HS – Ⓜ St Paul's – ✆ (020) 3201 0077 – www.terranostrafood.co.uk – Closed Saturday lunch and Sunday **L3**

Rest – *(booking advisable at lunch)* Carte £ 23/30

♦ Italian ♦ Rustic ♦

Its informal, relaxed feel and sweet-natured service provides the ideal respite from the bustle of The City and the trauma of the Old Bailey. Light, fresh food, with Sardinian leanings.

Paternoster Chop House

Warwick Ct., Paternoster Sq. ✉ EC4M 7DX – Ⓜ St Paul's – ✆ (020) 7029 9400 – www.paternosterchophouse.com – Closed 24 December-1 January, Saturday, Sunday dinner and bank holidays

Rest – Menu £ 27 – Carte £ 29/45 **L3**

♦ British ♦ Brasserie ♦ Trendy ♦

Appropriately British menu in a restaurant lying in the shadow of St Paul's Cathedral. Large, open room with full-length windows; busy bar attached. Kitchen uses thoughtfully sourced produce.

28°-50°

140 Fetter Ln ✉ EC4A 1BT – Ⓜ Temple – ✆ (020) 72428877 – www.2850.co.uk – Closed Christmas-New Year, Saturday and Sunday **K3**

Rest – Menu £ 22 (lunch) – Carte £ 28/35

♦ French ♦ Wine Bar ♦

Subterranean wine bar and informal restaurant, from the same owners as Texture. Robust, mostly French dishes accompany a thoughtfully assembled wine list, with much choice by the glass.

Restaurant at St Paul's Cathedral

St Paul's Churchyard ✉ EC4M 8AD – Ⓜ St. Paul's – ✆ (020) 7248 2469 – www.restaurantatstpauls.co.uk **L3**

Rest – *(lunch only) (booking advisable)* Menu £ 24

♦ British ♦ Bistro ♦

Tucked away in a corner of the crypt of Sir Christopher Wren's 17C masterpiece. The kitchen prepares everything from scratch and celebrates all things British, including drinks.

Goldfish City

46 Gresham St ✉ EC2V 7AY – Ⓜ Bank – ✆ (020) 7726 0308
– www.goldfish-resaturant.co.uk
– Closed Saturday, Sunday and bank holidays **M3**

Rest – *(booking advisable)* Menu £ 23/30 – Carte £ 23/37

◆ Asian ◆ Intimate ◆ Neighbourhood ◆

Busy at lunch thanks to the selection of well-priced steamed dim sum. Balanced main menu mixes the classic with the modern. Spread over three floors, with discreet décor and helpful service.

Bermondsey

Hilton London Tower Bridge

5 More London, Tooley St. ✉ SE1 2BY
– Ⓜ London Bridge – ✆ (020) 3002 4300 – www.hilton.co.uk/towerbridge

245 rm – †£ 418 ††£ 418, ☐ £ 19.95 **M4**

Rest – Menu £ 22 (dinner) – Carte £ 32/35

◆ Business ◆ Modern ◆

Usefully located new-style Hilton hotel with boldly decorated open-plan lobby. Contemporary bedrooms boast well-designed features; 4 floors of executive rooms. Dine on classics and comfort food in restaurant with outdoor seating.

Bermondsey Square

Bermondsey Sq, Tower Bridge Rd ✉ SE1 3UN – Ⓜ London Bridge
– ✆ (0207) 378 2450 – www.bermondseysquarehotel.co.uk *Plan I* **D2**

79 rm – †£ 129/219 ††£ 139/219, ☐ £ 10.95

Rest *Alfie's* – ✆ (0870) 111 2525 – Menu £ 15/17 – Carte approx. £ 26

◆ Business ◆ Modern ◆

Opened in 2009 in hip, regenerated square. Cleverly designed hotel, with subtle '60s influence and fun feel. Well-equipped rooms, including four loft suites. English menu in Alfie's makes good use of local food markets.

London Bridge

8-18 London Bridge St. ✉ SE1 9SG – Ⓜ London Bridge – ✆ (020) 7855 2200 – www.londonbridgehotel.com **M4**

138 rm – †£ 344 ††£ 344, ☐ £ 16.95 – 3 suites

Rest *Londinium* – *(dinner only)* Carte £ 26/40

◆ Business ◆ Classic ◆

In one of the oldest parts of London, independently owned with an ornate façade dating from 1915. Modern interior with classically decorated bedrooms and an impressive gym. Londinium for brasserie dining.

Le Pont de la Tour

36d Shad Thames, Butlers Wharf ✉ SE1 2YE – Ⓜ London Bridge
– ✆ (020) 7403 8403 – www.lepontdelatour.co.uk **N4**

Rest – Menu £ 32/43

◆ French ◆ Elegant ◆

Elegant and stylish room commanding spectacular views of the Thames and Tower Bridge, with more informal bar attached. Expect professional, detailed service and a modern menu.

Vivat Bacchus London Bridge

4 Hays Ln. ✉ SE1 2HB – Ⓜ London Bridge – ✆ (0207) 234 0891
– www.vivatbacchus.co.uk
– Closed 24 December-3 January, bank holidays and Sunday **M4**

Rest – Menu £ 12/20 – Carte £ 26/36

◆ Traditional ◆ Wine bar ◆ Friendly ◆

South African element to both the menu and the very impressive wine list. International platters in ground floor wine bar; robust cooking in the basement restaurant, with its great cheese room.

Magdalen

152 Tooley St. ✉ SE1 2TU – Ⓜ London Bridge – ✆ (020) 7403 1342 – www.magdalenrestaurant.co.uk
– Closed Christmas and New Year, 2 weeks August, Saturday lunch, Sunday and bank holidays **M4**

Rest – Menu £ 19 (lunch) – Carte £ 28/36

♦ British ♦ Neighbourhood ♦

Confident and satisfying British cooking with big flavours, using carefully sourced ingredients. Divided between two floors; upstairs is more convivial, downstairs more intimate.

Zucca

184 Bermondsey St ✉ SE1 3TQ – Ⓜ Borough – ✆ (020) 7378 6809 – www.zuccalondon.com
– Closed 24 December-10 January, Sunday dinner and Monday *Plan I* **D2**

Rest – *(booking essential at dinner)* Carte £ 18/24

♦ Italian ♦ Friendly ♦

Bright and buzzy modern room, where the informed Italian cooking is driven by the fresh ingredients, the prices are more than generous and the service is sweet and responsive. The appealing antipasti is great for sharing.

Blueprint Café

Design Museum, Shad Thames, Butlers Wharf ✉ SE1 2YD – Ⓜ London Bridge – ✆ (020) 7378 7031 – www.danddlondon.com
– Closed Sunday dinner **N5**

Rest – Menu £ 20 – Carte £ 22/36

♦ Modern European ♦ Brasserie ♦

Champions British produce in dishes using simple, but informed, techniques. Bright, retro feel; located above the Design Museum, with retractable windows and binoculars on each table.

Village East

171-173 Bermondsey St. ✉ SE1 3UW – Ⓜ London Bridge – ✆ (020) 7357 6082 – www.villageeast.co.uk
– Closed 25-26 December *Plan I* **D2**

Rest – Carte £ 29/37

♦ Modern European ♦ Trendy ♦ Neighbourhood ♦

In a glass-fronted block sandwiched by Georgian townhouses, this trendy restaurant has two loud, buzzy bars and dining areas serving ample portions of modern British fare.

Cantina Del Ponte

36c Shad Thames, Butlers Wharf ✉ SE1 2YE – Ⓜ London Bridge – ✆ (020) 7403 5403 – www.cantina.co.uk
– Closed 25-27 December **N4**

Rest – Menu £ 15/19 – Carte £ 27/38

♦ Italian ♦ Rustic ♦

An Italian stalwart, refurbished late in 2007. Simple menu offers an appealing mix of classic dishes, with a good value set menu until 7pm. Riverside setting with pleasant terrace.

Butlers Wharf Chop House

36e Shad Thames, Butlers Wharf ✉ SE1 2YE – Ⓜ London Bridge – ✆ (020) 7403 3403 – www.chophouse.co.uk
– Closed 1-2 January **N4**

Rest – Menu £ 22 (lunch) – Carte £ 28/43

♦ British ♦ Design ♦

Grab a table on the terrace in summer and dine in the shadow of Tower Bridge. Rustic feel to the interior; noisy and fun. The menu focuses on traditional English ingredients and dishes.

Champor-Champor

62-64 Weston St. ✉ SE1 3QJ – Ⓜ London Bridge – ✆ (020) 7403 4600 – www.champor-champor.com
– Closed 1 week Christmas, 1 week Easter, Sunday and bank holidays
Rest – *(dinner only)* Menu £ 32 **M5**

♦ Asian ♦ Exotic ♦

Choice of two beguiling and colourful rooms: ask for the second as it has even more character, better lighting and a mezzanine. Food is rooted in Malay traditions with a hint of modernity.

Garrison

99-101 Bermondsey St ✉ SE1 3XB – Ⓜ London Bridge. – ✆ (020) 7089 9355 – www.thegarrison.co.uk *Plan I* **D2**
Rest – *(booking essential at dinner)* Menu £ 14 – Carte £ 30/40

♦ Pub ♦ Friendly ♦

Known for its vintage look, booths and sweet-natured service, The Garrison boasts a warm, relaxed vibe. Open from breakfast until dinner where a Mediterranean-led menu pulls in the crowd.

SOUTHWARK

All Seasons

47 Southwark Bridge Rd ✉ SE1 9HH – Ⓜ London Bridge – ✆ (020) 7015 1480 – www.all-seasons-hotels.com **L4**
78 rm – †£ 195 ††£ 195, ☐ £ 5 – 6 suites
Rest – *(dinner only)* Carte £ 18/28

♦ Business ♦ Functional ♦

Purpose-built budget hotel south of the City, near the Globe Theatre. Uniform style, reasonably spacious bedrooms with writing desks. Top floor dining room with bar.

Oxo Tower

Oxo Tower Wharf (8th floor), Barge House St. ✉ SE1 9PH – Ⓜ Southwark – ✆ (020) 7803 3888 – www.harveynichols.com **K4**
Rest *Oxo Tower Brasserie* – see below
Rest – Menu £ 35 (lunch) – Carte £ 46/64

♦ Modern European ♦

Top of a converted factory, providing stunning views of the Thames and beyond. Stylish, minimalist interior with huge windows. Modern, mostly European, cuisine.

Roast

The Floral Hall, Borough Mkt. ✉ SE1 1TL – Ⓜ London Bridge – ✆ (0845) 034 7300 – www.roast-restaurant.com
– Closed 26 and 31 December, 1 January and Sunday dinner **M4**
Rest – *(booking essential)* Menu £ 26 (lunch) – Carte £ 39/54

♦ British ♦ Fashionable ♦

Set into the roof of Borough Market's Floral Hall. Extensive cocktail list in bar; split-level restaurant has views to St Paul's. Robust English cooking uses market produce.

Baltic

74 Blackfriars Rd ✉ SE1 8HA – Ⓜ Southwark – ✆ (020) 7928 1111 – www.balticrestaurant.co.uk
– Closed 24-26 December **K4**
Rest – *(booking advisable at dinner)* Menu £ 15/18 – Carte £ 22/34

♦ Eastern European ♦ Brasserie ♦

Celebrates 10 years in 2011. Set in a Grade II listed 18C former coach house. Enjoy big portions of authentic and hearty east European food. Interesting vodkas; live jazz on Sundays.

Oxo Tower Brasserie

Oxo Tower Wharf (8th floor), Barge House St. ✉ *SE1 9PH – Ⓜ Southwark – ✆ (020) 7803 3888 – www.harveynichols.com*

Rest – Carte £ 37/57 **K4**

♦ Modern European ♦ Design ♦

Same views but less formal and more fun than the restaurant. Open-plan kitchen produces a modern, easy to eat and quite light menu. In summer, try to secure a table on the terrace.

Cantina Vinopolis

No.1 Bank End ✉ *SE1 9BU – Ⓜ London Bridge – ✆ (020) 7940 8333 – www.cantinavinopolis.com – Closed 25-26 December* **L4**

Rest – Menu £ 30 – Carte £ 23/39

♦ International ♦ Bistro ♦

Large, solid brick vaulted room under Victorian railway arches, with an adjacent wine museum. Modern menu with a huge selection of wines by the glass.

Tate Modern (Restaurant)

Tate Modern (7th floor), Bankside ✉ *SE1 9TG – Ⓜ Southwark – ✆ (020) 7887 8888 – www.tate.org.uk/modern/eatanddrink – Closed 24-26 December* **L4**

Rest – *(lunch only and dinner Friday-Saturday)* Carte £ 30/36

♦ British ♦ Friendly ♦

7th floor restaurant with floor to ceilings windows on two sides and large mural. Appealing mix of light and zesty dishes, with seasonal produce. Good choice of wines and non-alcoholic drinks.

Tapas Brindisa

18-20 Southwark St., Borough Market ✉ *SE1 1TJ – Ⓜ London Bridge – ✆ (020) 7357 8880 – www.brindisatapaskitchens.com – Closed 25-28 December and 1 January* **M4**

Rest – *(bookings not accepted)* Carte £ 19/27

♦ Spanish ♦

Prime quality Spanish produce sold in owner's shops and this bustling eatery on edge of Borough Market. Freshly prepared, tasty tapas: waiters will assist with your choice.

Wright Brothers

11 Stoney St., Borough Market ✉ *SE1 9AD – Ⓜ London Bridge – ✆ (020) 7403 9554 – www.wrightbrothers.co.uk – Closed Christmas-New Year and bank holidays* **L4**

Rest – *(booking advisable)* Carte £ 23/40

♦ Seafood ♦ Wine bar ♦

Originally an oyster wholesaler; now offers a wide range of oysters along with porter, as well as fruits de mer, daily specials and assorted pies. It fills quickly and an air of contentment reigns.

Brew Wharf

Brew Wharf Yard, Stoney St ✉ *SE1 9AD – Ⓜ London Bridge – ✆ (020) 7378 6601 – www.brewwharf.com – Closed Christmas-New Year, Sunday* and bank holidays **L4**

Rest – Menu £ 24 – Carte £ 22/33

♦ Traditional ♦ Pub ♦

A busy bar, microbrewery and restaurant; come in a group to enjoy the sports screen and vast selection of beers and ales. The gutsy food and shared platters are the perfect match for the beer.

Anchor & Hope

36 The Cut ✉ SE1 8LP – Ⓜ Southwark. – ✆ (020) 7928 9898
– Closed 2 weeks at Christmas, Easter, May and August bank holidays, Sunday dinner and Monday lunch **K4**
Rest – *(bookings not accepted)* Menu £ 30 (lunch) – Carte £ 22/35
♦ British ♦ Pub ♦
As popular as ever thanks to its congenial feel and lived-in looks but mostly because of the appealingly seasonal menu and the gutsy, bold cooking that delivers on flavour. No reservations so be prepared to wait at the bar.

CHELSEA – SOUTH KENSINGTON – EARL'S COURT *Plan X*

Chelsea

Jumeirah Carlton Tower

Cadogan Pl. ✉ SW1X 9PY
– Ⓜ Knightsbridge – ✆ (020) 7235 1234
– www.jumeirah.com **F5**
190 rm – †£ 264/750 ††£ 264/750, ☕ £ 37 – 30 suites
Rest *Rib Room* – Menu £ 30 (lunch) – Carte approx. £ 63
♦ Grand Luxury ♦ Classic ♦
Imposing international hotel overlooking a leafy square. Well-equipped rooftop health club has great views. Generously proportioned bedrooms boast every conceivable facility. Rib Room restaurant has a clubby atmosphere.

Sheraton Park Tower

101 Knightsbridge ✉ SW1X 7RN
– Ⓜ Knightsbridge – ✆ (020) 7235 8050
– www.luxurycollection.com/parktowerlondon
– Closed 25-26 December and 1 January **F4**
275 rm – †£ 570 ††£ 570, ☕ £ 25 – 5 suites
Rest *One-O-One* – see below
♦ Luxury ♦ Business ♦
Built in the 1970s in a unique cylindrical shape. Well-equipped bedrooms are all identical in size. Top floor executive rooms have commanding views of Hyde Park and City.

The Capital

22-24 Basil St. ✉ SW3 1AT – Ⓜ Knightsbridge – ✆ (020) 7589 5171
– www.capitalhotel.co.uk **F5**
49 rm – †£ 276/366 ††£ 366, ☕ £ 19.50 – 8 suites
Rest – *(booking essential)* Menu £ 35 (lunch)
– Carte £ 48/66
♦ Luxury ♦ Traditional ♦ Classic ♦
In 2011, this thoroughly British hotel celebrates 40 years under the same private ownership. Immaculately kept bedrooms, a discreet atmosphere and conscientious, attentive service are the hallmarks. Elegant and formal dining offers a menu of classic British dishes.

Draycott without rest

26 Cadogan Gdns ✉ SW3 2RP – Ⓜ Sloane Square – ✆ (020) 7730 6466
– www.draycotthotel.com **F6**
35 rm – †£ 156/312 ††£ 251/312, ☕ £ 20.95 – 11 suites
♦ Townhouse ♦ Stylish ♦
Charming, discreet 19C house with elegant sitting room overlooking tranquil garden for afternoon tea. Bedrooms are individually decorated in a country house style and are named after writers or actors.

The Cadogan

75 Sloane St ✉ SW1X 9SG – Ⓜ Knightsbridge – ✆ (020) 7235 7141 – www.cadogan.com **F5**

63 rm – †£ 275/325 ††£ 325, ☕ £ 22.50

Rest *Langtry's* – *(closed Sunday dinner)* Menu £ 20 – Carte £ 31/46

♦ Luxury ♦ Cosy ♦

An Edwardian townhouse, made famous by two former residents – Oscar Wilde and Lillie Langtry. Quiet drawing room for afternoon tea; bedrooms are varied and comfortable. Discreet restaurant; traditional menu.

Knightsbridge

10 Beaufort Gdns ✉ SW3 1PT – Ⓜ Knightsbridge – ✆ (020) 7584 6300 – www.knightsbridgehotel.com **F5**

44 rm – †£ 204 ††£ 372, ☕ £ 17.50

Rest – *(room service only)*

♦ Luxury ♦ Townhouse ♦ Stylish ♦

Attractively furnished townhouse with a very stylish, discreet feel. Every bedroom is immaculately appointed and has an individuality of its own; fine detailing throughout.

Egerton House

17-19 Egerton Ter. ✉ SW3 2BX – Ⓜ South Kensington – ✆ (020) 7589 2412 – www.egertonhousehotel.com **F5**

27 rm – †£ 282/318 ††£ 306/390, ☕ £ 25 – 1 suite

Rest – *(room service only)* Carte £ 35/55

♦ Townhouse ♦ Classic ♦

Discreet, compact but comfortable townhouse in a good location, well-maintained throughout and owned by Red Carnation group. High levels of personal service make the hotel stand out.

The Levin

28 Basil St. ✉ SW3 1AS – Ⓜ Knightsbridge – ✆ (020) 7589 6286 – www.thelevinhotel.co.uk **F5**

12 rm ☕ – †£ 342 ††£ 438

Rest *Le Metro* – *(closed Sunday dinner)* Menu £ 20 – Carte £ 22/35

♦ Townhouse ♦ Classic ♦

Impressive façade, contemporary interior and comfortable bedrooms in subtle art deco style, boasting marvellous champagne mini bars. Sister to The Capital hotel. Informal brasserie includes blackboard menu and pies of the week.

Beaufort without rest

33 Beaufort Gdns ✉ SW3 1PP – Ⓜ Knightsbridge – ✆ (020) 7584 5252 – www.thebeaufort.co.uk **F5**

29 rm – †£ 173/253 ††£ 322/334, ☕ £ 19.50

♦ Traditional ♦ Classic ♦

A vast collection of English floral watercolours adorn this 19C townhouse in a useful location. Modern and co-ordinated rooms. Tariff includes all drinks and afternoon tea.

Sydney House without rest

9-11 Sydney St. ✉ SW3 6PU – Ⓜ South Kensington – ✆ (020) 7376 7711 – www.sydneyhousechelsea.com – Closed 25-29 December **E6**

21 rm – †£ 145/215 ††£ 175/295, ☕ £ 10.95

♦ Townhouse ♦ Modern ♦

Stylish, discreet and compact Georgian townhouse made brighter through mirrors and light wood. Thoughtfully designed bedrooms; Room 43 has its own terrace. Part of Abode group.

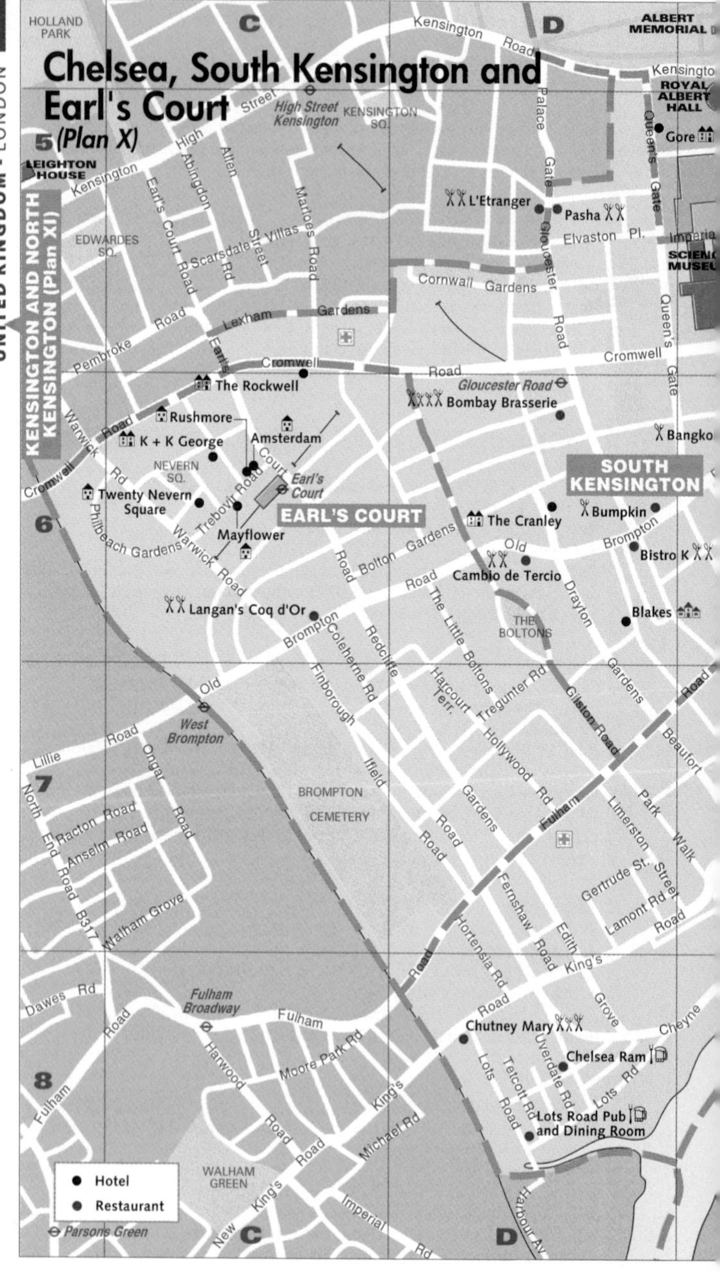

Chelsea, South Kensington and Earl's Court
(Plan X)
HOLLAND PARK
C
D
ALBERT MEMORIAL
Kensington Road
ROYAL ALBERT HALL
Gore
High Street Kensington
KENSINGTON SQ.
5
LEIGHTON HOUSE
Kensington High Street
Abingdon
Allen
Marloes Road
Palace Gate
Queen's Gate
L'Etranger
Pasha
Elvaston Pl.
Imperial
SCIENCE MUSEUM
KENSINGTON AND NORTH KENSINGTON (Plan XI)
EDWARDES SQ.
Earl's Court Road
Scarsdale Villas
Rd
Street
Gloucester Road
Cornwall Gardens
Lexham Gardens
Pembroke Road
Cromwell Road
The Rockwell
Gloucester Road
Bombay Brasserie
Rushmore
K + K George
Amsterdam
NEVERN SQ.
Earl's Court
Bangkok
SOUTH KENSINGTON
Twenty Nevern Square
EARL'S COURT
Bumpkin
Warwick Rd
Trebovir Road
The Cranley
Brompton
6
Philbeach Gardens
Mayflower
Warwick Road
Bolton Gardens
Old Brompton Road
Bistro K
Cambio de Tercio
Langan's Coq d'Or
The Little Boltons
THE BOLTONS
Drayton Gardens
Blakes
Coleherne Rd
Redcliffe
Finborough
Harcourt Terr.
Tregunter Rd
Gilston Road
West Brompton
Lillie Road
Ongar Road
Iffield
Hollywood Rd
Beaufort
7
BROMPTON CEMETERY
Gardens
Road
Fulham Road
Limerston Street
Park Walk
North End Road B317
Racton Road
Anselm Road
Fernshaw Road
Gertrude St.
Lamont Rd
Walham Grove
Hortensia Rd
Edith Grove
King's Road
Dawes Rd
Fulham Broadway
Chutney Mary
Cheyne
Harwood
Moore Park Rd
Chelsea Ram
8
Fulham Road
Lots Road
Tetcott Rd
Uverdale Rd
Lots Road Pub and Dining Room
King's Road
Michael Rd
WALHAM GREEN
Hotel
Restaurant
Parsons Green
New King's Road
Imperial Rd
Harbour Av

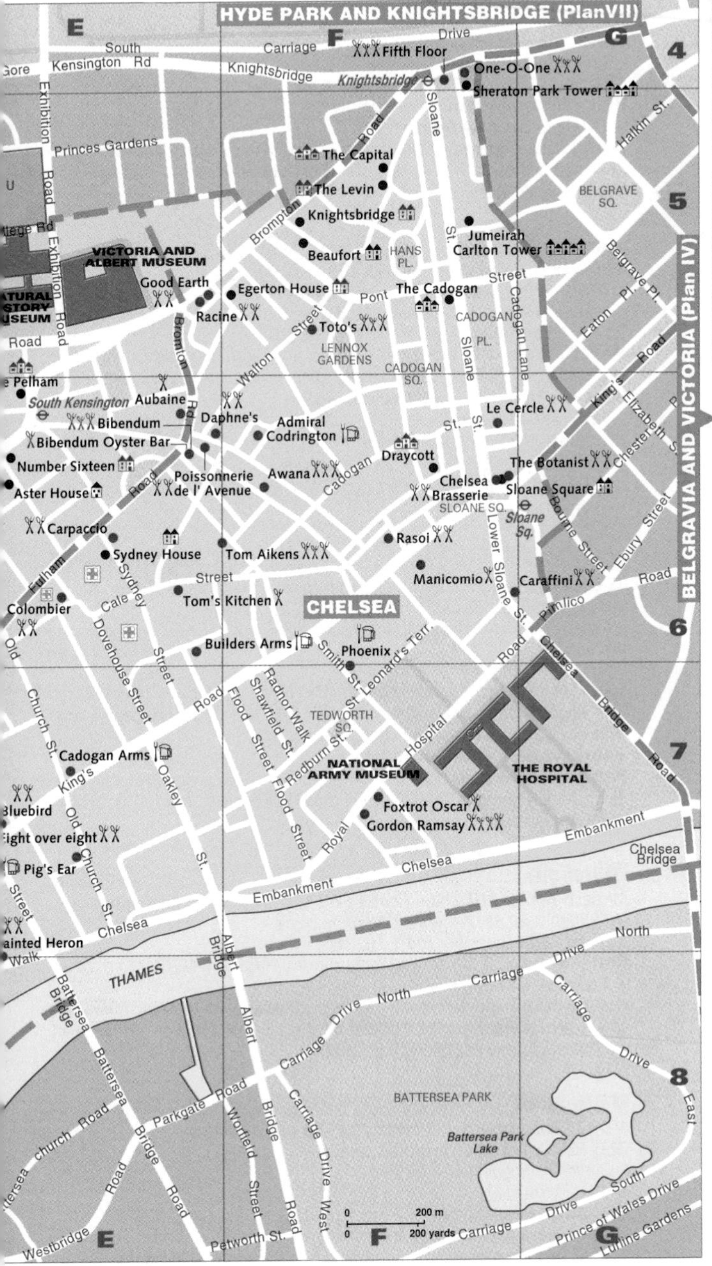
HYDE PARK AND KNIGHTSBRIDGE (PlanVII)
BELGRAVIA AND VICTORIA (Plan IV)
Fifth Floor
One-O-One
Sheraton Park Tower
The Capital
The Levin
Knightsbridge
Beaufort
Jumeirah Carlton Tower
Egerton House
The Cadogan
Good Earth
Racine
Toto's
VICTORIA AND ALBERT MUSEUM
Pelham
Aubaine
Bibendum
Bibendum Oyster Bar
Daphne's
Admiral Codrington
Le Cercle
Number Sixteen
Draycott
Awana
Poissonnerie de l' Avenue
The Botanist
Aster House
Chelsea Brasserie
Sloane Square
Carpaccio
Rasoi
Sydney House
Tom Aikens
Manicomio
Caraffini
Colombier
Tom's Kitchen
CHELSEA
Builders Arms
Phoenix
Cadogan Arms
NATIONAL ARMY MUSEUM
THE ROYAL HOSPITAL
Bluebird
Eight over eight
Foxtrot Oscar
Gordon Ramsay
Pig's Ear
Painted Heron
THAMES
BATTERSEA PARK
Battersea Park Lake
South Kensington
Sloane Sq.
HANS PL.
CADOGAN PL.
LENNOX GARDENS
CADOGAN SQ.
SLOANE SQ.
BELGRAVE SQ.
TEDWORTH SQ.
0 200 m
0 200 yards

The Sloane Square

7-12 Sloane Sq. ✉ *SW1W 8EG* – Ⓜ *Sloane Square* – ✆ *(020) 7896 9988* – *www.sloanesquarehotel.co.uk*
– *Closed Christmas* **F6**

102 rm – †£ 187/310 ††£ 332, ☕ £ 6.50

Rest *Chelsea Brasserie* – see below

◆ Business ◆ Modern ◆

Red-brick hotel opened in 2007, boasts bright, contemporary décor. Stylish, co-ordinated bedrooms, with laptops; library of DVDs and games available. Rooms at back slightly quieter.

Gordon Ramsay

68-69 Royal Hospital Rd. ✉ *SW3 4HP* – Ⓜ *Sloane Square* – ✆ *(020) 7352 4441* – *www.gordonramsay.com*
– *Closed Christmas, Saturday and Sunday* **F7**

Rest – *(booking essential)* Menu £ 45/90

Spec. Butter poached lobster with morels, asparagus and wild garlic. Pigeon with polenta, shallots, beetroot and date sauce. Strawberry and lemon balm Eton mess with vanilla ice cream wafer.

◆ French ◆ Formal ◆

Head Chef Clare Smyth has brought a lighter, more instinctive style to the cooking while still delivering on the Gordon Ramsay classics. The elegant simplicity of the room exudes calmness; service is equally composed and well-organised.

Tom Aikens

43 Elystan St. ✉ *SW3 3NT* – Ⓜ *South Kensington* – ✆ *(020) 7584 2003* – *www.tomaikens.co.uk*
– *Closed 24-29 December, 1-3 January, Saturday lunch, Sunday and bank holidays* **E6**

Rest – Carte £ 53/89

Spec. Sheep's cheese gazpacho with chervil cannelloni and honey. Lamb with aligot potato and anchovy beignet. Truffle and vanilla panna cotta with black pepper and white chocolate.

◆ Innovative ◆ Fashionable ◆

Neat and elegant dining room, with well co-ordinated service. Seasonal ingredients, largely from the British Isles, are used in dishes that show plenty of originality and skill, with fish the kitchen's strength.

Bibendum

Michelin House, 81 Fulham Rd. ✉ *SW3 6RD* – Ⓜ *South Kensington* – ✆ *(020) 7581 5817* – *www.bibendum.co.uk*
– *Closed 24-26 December and 1 January* **E6**

Rest – Menu £ 30 (lunch and early dinner) – Carte £ 40/61

◆ French ◆ Design ◆

Has maintained a loyal following for over 20 years, with its French food that comes with a British accent. Located on the 1st floor of a London landmark – Michelin's former HQ, dating from 1911.

Fifth Floor – at Harvey Nichols

109-125 Knightsbridge ✉ *SW1X 7RJ* – Ⓜ *Knightsbridge* – ✆ *(020) 7235 5250* – *www.harveynichols.com*
– *Closed Sunday dinner* **F4**

Rest – Menu £ 25/40

◆ Modern European ◆ Fashionable ◆

Modern cooking with influences kept mostly from within Europe. Stylish and elegant, tent-like room with sophisticated bar attached; reached via its own elevator. Prompt service.

XXX

Toto's

Walton House, Walton St ✉ SW3 2JH
– Ⓜ Knightsbridge – ✆ (020) 7589 0075
– Closed 25-27 December **F5**
Rest – *(booking essential at dinner)* Menu £ 27 (lunch) – Carte £ 33/51
♦ Italian ♦ Formal ♦
A long standing Chelsea institution, with old school service and plenty of local regulars who add to the discreet atmosphere. Familiar and satisfying dishes, with homemade pasta the highlight.

XXX

Awana

85 Sloane Ave. ✉ SW3 3DX – Ⓜ South Kensington – ✆ (020) 7584 8880
– www.awana.co.uk
– Closed 25 December and 1 January **F6**
Rest – *(booking essential)* Menu £ 15 (lunch) – Carte £ 27/54
♦ Malaysian ♦ Exotic ♦
Smart and stylish restaurant showcasing Malaysia's rich culinary diversity. The 'Malaysian Journey' menu provides a good introduction. If without a booking, consider sitting at the Satay Bar.

XXX

Chutney Mary

535 King's Rd. ✉ SW10 0SZ – Ⓜ Fulham Broadway – ✆ (020) 7351 3113
– www.realindianfood.com
– Closed dinner 25 December **D8**
Rest – *(dinner only and lunch Saturday-Sunday)* Menu £ 22 – Carte £ 37/47
♦ Indian ♦ Exotic ♦
Soft lighting and sepia etchings hold sway at this forever popular restaurant. Extensive menu of specialities from all corners of India. Complementary wine list.

XXX

One-O-One – at Sheraton Park Tower Hotel

101 Knightsbridge ✉ SW1X 7RN – Ⓜ Knightsbridge – ✆ (020) 7290 7101
– www.oneoonerestaurant.com **F4**
Rest – Menu £ 19/42 – Carte £ 50/66
♦ Seafood ♦ Design ♦
Smart ground floor restaurant; lacking a little in atmosphere but the seafood is good. Much of the produce from Brittany and Norway; don't miss the King crab legs. Small tasting plates also offered.

XX ✿

Rasoi (Vineet Bhatia)

10 Lincoln St. ✉ SW3 2TS – Ⓜ Sloane Square – ✆ (020) 7225 1881
– www.rasoirestaurant.co.uk
– Closed Saturday lunch **F6**
Rest – Menu £ 26 (lunch) – Carte £ 58/83
Spec. Seafood medley with soft-shell crab chutney and gun powder prawn. Charcoal roasted lamb chops with chilli and roasted peanut khichdi. Spiced caramelised pineapple.
♦ Indian ♦ Intimate ♦
Innovative and creative Indian cuisine in the incongruous setting of a typical Chelsea townhouse. Ring the doorbell and you'll be greeted by an exotic aroma that hints of what's to follow.

XX

Le Colombier

145 Dovehouse St. ✉ SW3 6LB – Ⓜ South Kensington – ✆ (020) 7351 1155 – www.le-colombier-restaurant.co.uk **E6**
Rest – Menu £ 26 (lunch) – Carte £ 31/50
♦ French ♦ Neighbourhood ♦
Proudly Gallic corner restaurant in an affluent residential area. Attractive enclosed terrace. Bright and cheerful surroundings and service of traditional French cooking.

XX **Racine** A/C VISA MC AE

239 Brompton Rd ✉ SW3 2EP – Ⓜ South Kensington – ✆ (020) 7584 4477 – www.racine-restaurant.com – Closed 25 December **E5**

Rest – Menu £ 18/20 (lunch and early dinner) – Carte £ 28/44

◆ French ◆ Brasserie ◆

An authentic feel to this French brasserie, with dark leather seats, wood floors and mirrors. The menu provides a roll-call of classic regional specialities, from steak tartare to fruits de mer.

XX **Daphne's** A/C VISA MC AE

112 Draycott Ave. ✉ SW3 3AE – Ⓜ South Kensington – ✆ (020) 7589 4257 – www.daphnes-restaurant.co.uk – Closed 25-26 December and 1 January **E6**

Rest – *(booking essential)* Menu £ 19 (lunch and early dinner) – Carte £ 29/48

◆ Italian ◆ Fashionable ◆

Established over 40 years ago and a Chelsea institution with 'celebrity' following. Reliable formula of tired and tested Italian classics in a room with a warm, Tuscan feel.

XX **Poissonnerie de l'Avenue** A/C VISA MC AE

82 Sloane Ave. ✉ SW3 3DZ – Ⓜ South Kensington – ✆ (020) 7589 2457 – www.poissonneriedelavenue.com – Closed 24-26 December **E6**

Rest – Menu £ 28 (lunch) – Carte £ 25/39

◆ Seafood ◆ Formal ◆

A smart, personally run, wood-panelled Chelsea institution since 1946. Its extensive choice of carefully prepared, traditional seafood dishes attracts a smart and loyal following.

XX **Caraffini** A/C VISA MC AE

61-63 Lower Sloane St. ✉ SW1W 8DH – Ⓜ Sloane Square – ✆ (020) 7259 0235 – www.caraffini.co.uk – Closed 25 December, Easter, Sunday and bank holidays **F6**

Rest – *(booking essential)* Carte £ 23/41

◆ Italian ◆ Friendly ◆

The omnipresent and ebullient owner oversees the friendly service in this attractive neighbourhood restaurant. Authentic and robust Italian cooking; informal atmosphere.

XX **Eight over Eight** A/C VISA MC AE

392 King's Rd ✉ SW3 5UZ – Ⓜ Gloucester Road – ✆ (020) 7349 9934 – www.rickerrestaurants.com – Closed Sunday lunch **E7**

Rest – Menu £ 17 – Carte £ 28/39

◆ Asian ◆ Fashionable ◆

Reopened in 2010 after a fire, with a slightly plusher feel; still as popular as ever with the fashionable crowds. Influences stretch across South East Asia and dishes are designed for sharing.

XX **Bluebird** A/C VISA MC AE

350 King's Rd. ✉ SW3 5UU – Ⓜ Sloane Square – ✆ (020) 7559 1000 – www.bluebirdchelsea.com **E7**

Rest – Menu £ 21 – Carte £ 26/73

◆ British ◆ Design ◆

Former industrial space incorporates everything from a wine store to a private members club. Large, buzzy restaurant champions British produce in an appealing menu that has something for everyone.

XX **Le Cercle**

1 Wilbraham Pl ✉ SW1X 9AE – Ⓜ Sloane Square – ✆ (020) 7901 9999 – www.lecercle.co.uk – Closed Christmas - New Year, Sunday and Monday **F6**

Rest – Carte £ 20/35

◆ French ◆ Fashionable ◆

Deep basement location made into a fashionable spot, with drapes and high ceilings; comes alive more at dinner. Order three or four small plates of the delicate French cooking per person.

XX **Painted Heron**

112 Cheyne Walk ✉ SW10 0DJ – Ⓜ Gloucester Road – ✆ (020) 7351 5232 – www.thepaintedheron.com – Closed 25 December, 1 January

Rest – *(dinner only and lunch Saturday-Sunday)* Menu £ 35 (dinner) – Carte £ 31/42 **E7/8**

◆ Indian ◆ Formal ◆ Neighbourhood ◆

Well-supported locally and quite formally run Indian restaurant. Nooks and crannies create an intimate atmosphere. Fish and game dishes are the highlight of the contemporary cooking.

XX **Carpaccio**

4 Sydney St. ✉ SW3 6PP – Ⓜ South Kensington – ✆ (020) 7352 3435 – www.carpacciorestaurant.co.uk – Closed Christmas, Sunday, Monday lunch and bank holidays **E6**

Rest – Carte £ 26/42

◆ Italian ◆ Neighbourhood ◆

Lively local Italian with an animated service crew; blokey decoration courtesy of stills from Bond movies and Ayrton Senna's cockpit. All-encompassing menu ranges from pizza to carpaccio.

XX **Good Earth**

233 Brompton Rd. ✉ SW3 2EP – Ⓜ Knightsbridge – ✆ (020) 7584 3658 – www.goodearthgroup.co.uk – Closed 23-31 December **E5**

Rest – Menu £ 14/30 – Carte £ 28/37

◆ Chinese ◆ Formal ◆

The basement is busier and more popular than the ground floor. Extensive menu makes good use of quality ingredients and offers appealing choice between classic and more unusual dishes.

XX **The Botanist**

7 Sloane Sq ✉ SW1W 8EE – Ⓜ Sloane Square – ✆ (020) 7730 0077 – www.thebotanistonsloanesquare.com – Closed 25-26 December, Saturday, Sunday and bank holidays **F6**

Rest – Menu £ 29 – Carte £ 26/33

◆ Modern European ◆ Wine bar ◆ Neighbourhood ◆

Pass through the busy bar to get to the stylish and comfortable restaurant with its warm and vibrant atmosphere. Appealing and accessible menu delivers unfussy and satisfying dishes.

XX **Chelsea Brasserie** – at The Sloane Square Hotel

7-12 Sloane Sq. ✉ SW1W 8EG – Ⓜ Sloane Square – ✆ (020) 7896 9988 – www.sloanesquarehotel.co.uk – Closed Christmas and Sunday dinner **F6**

Rest – Menu £ 25 (weekday dinner) – Carte £ 34/40

◆ French ◆ Brasserie ◆

You pass through the busy bar to get to the smartly lit brasserie, with exposed brick, mirrors and tiles. Cooking has a strong French base. Good value theatre menu and brisk service.

Bibendum Oyster Bar

Michelin House, 81 Fulham Rd. ✉ SW3 6RD – Ⓜ South Kensington – ☎ (020) 7589 1480 – www.bibendum.co.uk – Closed 24-26 December and 1 January **E6**

Rest – *(bookings not accepted)* Carte £ 20/33

♦ Seafood ♦ Rustic ♦

Oysters, potted shrimps and a shared plateau de fruits de mer are the highlights at this continental-style café, with its mosaic floor and colourful ceramic tiles. Wine list includes 460ml pots.

Foxtrot Oscar

79 Royal Hospital Rd. ✉ SW3 4HN – Ⓜ Sloane Square – ☎ (020) 7352 4448 – www.gordonramsay.com – Closed 25 December

Rest – *(booking essential)* Menu £ 22 (lunch) – Carte £ 25/37 **F7**

♦ Traditional ♦ Cosy ♦ Neighbourhood ♦

Gordon Ramsay's least known restaurant has a relaxed, local feel, with celebrity photographs adorning its burgundy walls. Bistro cooking, with the Foxtrot Burger being a highlight.

Manicomio

85 Duke of York Sq., King's Rd. ✉ SW3 4LY – Ⓜ Sloane Square – ☎ (020) 7730 3366 – www.manicomio.co.uk – Closed 25-26 December and 1 January

Rest – Carte £ 34/40 **F6**

♦ Italian ♦ Rustic ♦ Neighbourhood ♦

Modern, busy Italian, popular with shoppers and visitors to the Saatchi Gallery; the simplest dishes are the best ones. The terrific terrace fills quickly. Next door is their café and deli.

Aubaine

260-262 Brompton Rd. ✉ SW3 2AS – Ⓜ South Kensington – ☎ (020) 7052 0100 – www.aubaine.co.uk – Closed 25 December **E6**

Rest – Carte £ 22/44

♦ French ♦ Friendly ♦

'Boulangerie, patisserie, restaurant'. Pass the bakery aromas to an all-day eatery with 'distressed' country feel. Well-judged menus range from croque monsieur to coq au vin.

Tom's Kitchen

27 Cale St. ✉ SW3 3QP – Ⓜ South Kensington – ☎ (020) 7349 0202 – www.tomskitchen.co.uk – Closed 25-26 December **E6**

Rest – Carte £ 34/60

♦ French ♦ Neighbourhood ♦

A converted pub, whose white tiles and mirrors help to give it an industrial feel. Appealing and wholesome dishes come in man-sized portions. The eponymous Tom is Tom Aikens.

Admiral Codrington

17 Mossop St ✉ SW3 2LY – Ⓜ South Kensington. – ☎ (020) 7581 0005 – www.theadmiralcodrington.com **F6**

Rest – Carte £ 24/30

♦ Pub ♦ British ♦

A Chelsea institution, with popular bar in the evenings and a separate, smart restaurant with retractable roof. The menu covers all bases and mixes British classics with European influences.

Chelsea Ram

32 Burnaby St ✉ SW10 0PL – Ⓜ Fulham Broadway. – ☎ (020) 7351 4008 – Closed Sunday dinner **D8**

Rest – Carte £ 18/30

♦ Pub ♦ Friendly ♦

A warm, welcoming and relaxed pub surrounded by residential streets, with a loyal local following. Expect proper 'pub grub' where the portions are generous and the prices fair.

Cadogan Arms

298 King's Rd ✉ SW3 5UG – Ⓜ South Kensington. – ☎ (020) 7352 6500
– www.thecadoganarmschelsea.com
– Closed 25-26 December **E7**

Rest – *(booking advisable at dinner)* Carte £ 24/37

♦ Pub ♦ Friendly ♦

Part of the Martin Brothers bourgeoning pub group. This is a proper pub, with billiard tables upstairs and a gusty, full-on menu. Stuffed and mounted animals stare down as you eat.

Builders Arms

13 Britten St ✉ SW3 3TY – Ⓜ South Kensington. – ☎ (020) 7349 9040
– www.geronimo-inns.co.uk
– Closed 25-26 December **E6**

Rest – *(bookings not accepted)* Carte £ 25/30

♦ Pub ♦ Rustic ♦

Lively and busy pub, popular with the locals. Rustic and satisfying cooking, with blackboard daily specials; the popular peri-peri chicken dish is for sharing. Regular wine promotions.

Pig's Ear

35 Old Church St ✉ SW3 5BS – Ⓜ Sloane Square. – ☎ (020) 7352 2908
– www.thepigsear.com
– Closed 2 weeks at Christmas and Sunday dinner **E7**

Rest – Carte £ 22/35

♦ Pub ♦ Friendly ♦

Honest pub, with rough-and-ready ground floor bar for lunch; more intimate, wood-panelled upstairs dining room for dinner. Robust, confident and satisfying cooking with a classical bent.

Phoenix

23 Smith St ✉ SW3 4EE – Ⓜ Sloane Square. – ☎ (020) 7730 9182
– www.geronimo-inns.co.uk – Closed 25-26 December **F6/7**

Rest – Carte £ 23/30

♦ Pub ♦ Friendly ♦

Friendly, conscientiously run Chelsea local, where satisfying and carefully prepared pub classics are served in the roomy, civilised bar or in the warm, comfortable dining room at the back.

Lots Road Pub & Dining Room

114 Lots Rd ✉ SW10 0RJ – Ⓜ Fulham Broadway. – ☎ (020) 7352 6645
– www.lotsroadpub.com **D8**

Rest – Carte £ 20/31

♦ Pub ♦ Friendly ♦

Lively semicircular shaped pub, close to Chelsea Harbour. Hearty and satisfying classics, from mussels to Perthshire côte de boeuf and a tart of the day. Service keeps it bright and cheery.

South Kensington

The Pelham

15 Cromwell Pl ✉ SW7 2LA – Ⓜ South Kensington – ☎ (020) 7589 8288
– www.pelhamhotel.co.uk **E6**

51 rm – †£ 182 ††£ 299/322, ☕ £ 17.50 – 1 suite

Rest ***Bistro Fifteen*** – *(Closed 25 December)* Menu £ 19/23
– Carte £ 35/46

♦ Luxury ♦ Stylish ♦

Immaculately kept, with willing staff and a discreet atmosphere. A mix of English country house and city town house, with panelled sitting room and library. Colourful all day bistro, candlelit at dinner, with European menu.

Blakes
rest, VISA AE

33 Roland Gdns. ✉ *SW7 3PF* – Ⓜ *Gloucester Road* – ✆ *(020) 7370 6701* – *www.blakeshotels.com* **D6**

33 rm – †£ 180/318 ††£ 390/450, ☕ £ 25 – 8 suites

Rest – Carte £ 40/76

♦ Luxury ♦ Design ♦

Behind the Victorian façade lies one of London's first 'boutique' hotels. Dramatic, bold and eclectic décor, with oriental influences and antiques from around the globe. Fashionable restaurant with bamboo and black walls.

Number Sixteen without rest

16 Sumner Pl ✉ *SW7 3EG* – Ⓜ *South Kensington* – ✆ *(020) 7589 5232* – *www.numbersixteenhotel.co.uk* **E6**

42 rm – †£ 144 ††£ 336, ☕ £ 17.50

♦ Townhouse ♦ Luxury ♦ Stylish ♦

Enticingly refurbished 19C town houses in smart area. Discreet entrance, comfy sitting room and charming breakfast terrace. Bedrooms in English country house style.

The Cranley without rest

10 Bina Gardens ✉ *SW5 0LA* – Ⓜ *Gloucester Road* – ✆ *(020) 7373 0123* – *www.cranley.franklynhotels.com* **D6**

38 rm – †£ 138/276 ††£ 161/305, ☕ £ 25 – 1 suite

♦ Townhouse ♦ Stylish ♦

Delightful Regency townhouse combines charm and period details with modern comforts and technology. Individually styled bedrooms; some with four-posters. Room service available.

The Rockwell

181-183 Cromwell Rd. ✉ *SW5 0SF* – Ⓜ *Earl's Court* – ✆ *(020) 7244 2000* – *www.therockwell.com* **C5/6**

40 rm – †£ 120/165 ††£ 180/190, ☕ £ 12.50

Rest – Menu £ 35 – Carte £ 30/39

♦ Townhouse ♦ Design ♦

Two Victorian houses with open, modern lobby and secluded, south-facing garden terrace. Bedrooms come in bold warm colours; 'Garden rooms' come with their own patios. Small dining room offers easy menu of modern European staples.

The Gore

190 Queen's Gate ✉ *SW7 5EX* – Ⓜ *Gloucester Road* – ✆ *(020) 7584 6601* – *www.gorehotel.com* **D5**

50 rm – †£ 207 ††£ 242, ☕ £ 16.95

Rest *190 Queensgate* – *(booking essential)* Menu £ 20/24 – Carte £ 26/42

♦ Traditional ♦ Classic ♦

Idiosyncratic Victorian house, with lobby covered with pictures and prints. Individually styled bedrooms have discreet mod cons and charming bathrooms. Informal bistro with European menu.

Aster House without rest

3 Sumner Pl. ✉ *SW7 3EE* – Ⓜ *South Kensington* – ✆ *(020) 7581 5888* – *www.asterhouse.com* **E6**

13 rm ☕ – †£ 96/216 ††£ 240/300

♦ Townhouse ♦ Cosy ♦

End of terrace Victorian house with a pretty little rear garden and first floor conservatory. Ground floor rooms available. Useful location for visiting many tourist attractions.

XXXX

Bombay Brasserie

Courtfield Rd. ✉ SW7 4QH – Ⓜ Gloucester Road – ✆ (020) 7370 4040 – www.bombaybrasserielondon.com – Closed 25-26 December **D6**

Rest – *(booking advisable at dinner)* Menu £ 22 (weekday lunch buffet) – Carte £ 31/43

♦ Indian ♦ Exotic ♦

Plush new look for this well-run, well-known and comfortable Indian restaurant; very smart bar and conservatory with a show kitchen. More creative dishes now sit alongside the more traditional.

XX

L'Etranger

36 Gloucester Rd. ✉ SW7 4QT – Ⓜ Gloucester Road – ✆ (020) 7584 1118 – www.circagroupltd.co.uk – Closed Saturday lunch **D5**

Rest – *(booking essential)* Menu £ 20 (lunch) – Carte £ 32/101

♦ Innovative ♦ Neighbourhood ♦ Romantic ♦

Silks and lilacs create a stylish, atmospheric feel; ask for a corner table. Interesting menus incorporate techniques and flavours from Japanese cooking. Impressive wine and sake lists.

XX

Pasha

1 Gloucester Rd ✉ SW7 4PP – Ⓜ Gloucester Road – ✆ (020) 7589 7969 – www.pasha-restaurant.co.uk – Closed 24-25 December **D5**

Rest – Menu £ 15/30 – Carte £ 26/32

♦ Moroccan ♦ Exotic ♦

Relax over ground floor cocktails, then descend to mosaic floored restaurant where the rose-petal strewn tables are the ideal accompaniment to tasty Moroccan home cooking.

XX

Bistro K

117-119 Old Brompton Rd. ✉ SW7 3RN – Ⓜ Gloucester Road – ✆ (020) 73737774 – www.bistro-k.co.uk – Closed Christmas and New Year, 2 weeks August, Monday and bank holidays

Rest – Menu £ 15/25 – Carte £ 29/44 **D6**

♦ French ♦ Design ♦ Neighbourhood ♦

More formal than the name would suggest and the cooking is more delicate and sophisticated. The surroundings are bright and contemporary and the front terrace is an appealing spot.

XX

Cambio de Tercio

163 Old Brompton Rd ✉ SW5 0LJ – Ⓜ Gloucester Road – ✆ (020) 7244 8970 – www.cambiodetercio.co.uk **D6**

Rest – Carte £ 30/54

♦ Spanish ♦ Cosy ♦

Good ingredients and authentic Spanish flavours; desserts are more contemporary. Choose tapas or regular menu. Service improves the more you visit. Owner also has tapas bar across the road.

X

Bumpkin

102 Old Brompton Rd ✉ SW7 3RD – Ⓜ Gloucester Road – ✆ (020) 73410802 – www.bumpkinuk.com **D6**

Rest – Carte £ 28/40

♦ British ♦ Neighbourhood ♦

Sister to the Notting Hill original with the same pub-like informality and friendly service. The kitchen champions British seasonal produce; the simpler dishes are the best ones.

X

Bangkok

9 Bute St ✉ SW7 3EY – Ⓜ South Kensington – ✆ (020) 7584 8529 – www.bankokrestaurant.co.uk – Closed Christmas-New Year and Sunday
Rest – Carte £ 22/29 **E6**

◆ Thai ◆ Neighbourhood ◆

This simple Thai bistro has been a popular local haunt for nearly 40 years. Guests can watch the chefs at work, preparing inexpensive and authentic dishes from the succinct menu.

Earl's Court

K + K George

1-15 Templeton Pl. ✉ SW5 9NB – Ⓜ Earl's Court – ✆ (020) 7598 8700 – www.kkhotels.com **C6**
154 rm ☕ – †£ 264 ††£ 264/336 **Rest** – Carte £ 23/34

◆ Business ◆ Modern ◆

Five converted 19C houses overlooking large rear garden. Scandinavian-style rooms with low beds, white walls and light wood furniture. Breakfast room has the garden view. Informal dining in the bar.

Twenty Nevern Square without rest

20 Nevern Sq. ✉ SW5 9PD – Ⓜ Earl's Court – ✆ (020) 7565 9555 – www.twentynevernsquare.co.uk **C6**
20 rm – †£ 119/156 ††£ 167/215, ☕ £ 10

◆ Townhouse ◆ Functional ◆

In an attractive Victorian garden square, an individually designed, privately owned townhouse. Original pieces of furniture and some rooms with their own terrace.

Mayflower without rest

26-28 Trebovir Rd. ✉ SW5 9NJ – Ⓜ Earl's Court – ✆ (020) 7370 0991 – www.mayflowerhotel.co.uk **C6**
43 rm – †£ 107/144 ††£ 138/180, ☕ £ 10 – 4 suites

◆ Modern ◆ Functional ◆

Conveniently placed, friendly establishment with a secluded rear breakfast terrace and basement breakfast room. Individually styled rooms with Asian influence.

Amsterdam without rest

7-9 Trebovir Rd. ✉ SW5 9LS – Ⓜ Earl's Court – ✆ (020) 7370 2814 – www.amsterdam-hotel.com **C6**
19 rm – †£ 96/125 ††£ 118/128 – 8 suites

◆ Townhouse ◆ Cosy ◆

Basement breakfast room and a small secluded garden. The brightly decorated bedrooms are light and airy. Some have smart wood floors; some boast their own balcony.

Rushmore without rest

11 Trebovir Rd. ✉ SW5 9LS – Ⓜ Earl's Court – ✆ (020) 7370 3839 – www.rushmore-hotel.co.uk **C6**
22 rm – †£ 71/96 ††£ 90/152

◆ Townhouse ◆ Retro ◆

Behind its Victorian façade lies a hotel popular with tourists. Individually decorated bedrooms in a variety of shapes and sizes. Piazza-style conservatory breakfast room.

XX

Langan's Coq d'Or

254-260 Old Brompton Rd. ✉ SW5 9HR – Ⓜ Earl's Court – ✆ (020) 7259 2599 – www.langansrestaurants.co.uk – Closed 25-26 December
Rest – Menu £ 27 **C6**

◆ Traditional ◆ Brasserie ◆

Sit in the glass-enclosed front section which opens onto the street in summer or in the warm main room whose walls are covered with pictures and photos. A menu of satisfying brasserie classics.

Kensington

Royal Garden

2-24 Kensington High St. ✉ *W8 4PT*
– Ⓜ High Street Kensington – ✆ (020) 7937 8000
– www.royalgardenhotel.co.uk **D4**
374 rm – †£ 215/310 ††£ 263/335, ☕ £ 21.50 – 22 suites
Rest *Park Terrace* – *✆ (020) 7361 0602* – Menu £ 20/31 – Carte £ 22/33
♦ Business ♦ Functional ♦
A tall, modern hotel with many of its rooms enjoying enviable views over the adjacent Kensington Gardens. All the modern amenities and services, with well-drilled staff. Bright, spacious Park Terrace offers British, Asian and modern European cuisine.

The Milestone

1-2 Kensington Ct. ✉ *W8 5DL*
– Ⓜ High Street Kensington – ✆ (020) 7917 1000
– www.milestonehotel.com **D4**
57 rm – †£ 282/336 ††£ 318/372, ☕ £ 29 – 6 suites
Rest – *(booking essential for non-residents)* Menu £ 27 – Carte £ 29/78
♦ Luxury ♦ Stylish ♦
Elegant hotel with decorative Victorian façade and English feel. Charming oak-panelled lounge and snug bar. Meticulously decorated bedrooms with period detail. Panelled dining room with charming little oratory for privacy seekers.

Baglioni

60 Hyde Park Gate ✉ *SW7 5BB*
– Ⓜ High Street Kensington – ✆ (020) 7368 5700
– www.baglionihotels.com **D4**
52 rm – †£ 335/474 ††£ 384/474, ☕ £ 28 – 15 suites
Rest *Brunello* – *✆ (020) 7368 5900* – Menu £ 22/27 – Carte £ 46/61
♦ Luxury ♦ Stylish ♦
Opposite Kensington Palace, this hotel boasts an ornate interior and a trendy basement bar. Small gym/sauna. Stylish bedrooms come in cool shades and boast impressive facilities. Restaurant specialises in rustic Italian cooking.

Launceston Place

1a Launceston Pl. ✉ *W8 5RL – Ⓜ Gloucester Road – ✆ (020) 7937 6912*
– www.launcestonplace-restaurant.co.uk
– Closed 25 December, 1 January, Monday lunch and bank holidays
Rest – Menu £ 20/48 **D5**
♦ Modern European ♦ Neighbourhood ♦
Its most recent reincarnation with dark walls and moody lighting, still attracts plenty of locals. Cooking is original and deftly executed and uses ingredients largely from the British Isles.

Belvedere

Holland House, off Abbotsbury Rd. ✉ *W8 6LU – Ⓜ Holland Park*
– ✆ (020) 7602 1238 – www.belvedererestaurant.co.uk
– Closed 1 January **B4**
Rest – Menu £ 20 (lunch) – Carte £ 28/44
♦ French ♦ Romantic ♦
Former 19C orangery in a delightful position in the middle of the park. On two floors with a bar and balcony terrace. Huge vases of flowers. Modern take on classic dishes.

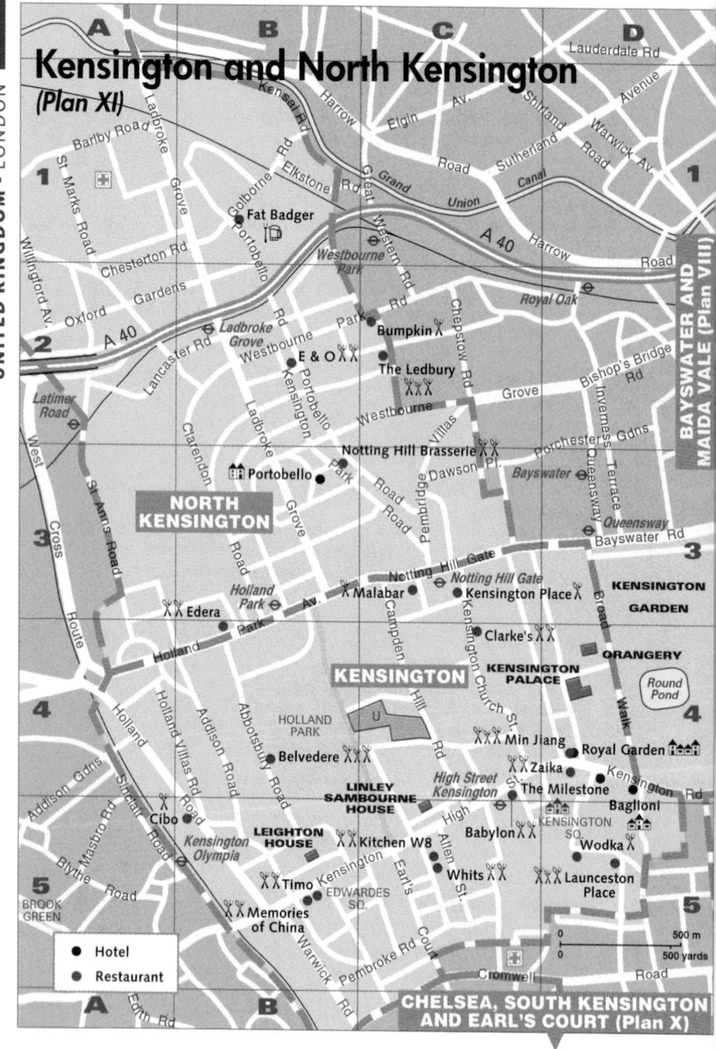

Min Jiang – at Royal Garden Hotel

Royal Garden Hotel, 10th Floor, 2-24 Kensington High St. ✉ W8 4PT – Ⓜ High Street Kensington – ✆ (020) 7361 1988 – www.minjiang.co.uk

D4

Rest – Menu £ 15/48 – Carte £ 34/119

♦ Chinese ♦ Elegant ♦

A comfortable Chinese restaurant looking down over Kensington Gardens from its 10th floor location. Most provinces of China are represented on the menu but the main speciality is the Beijing duck.

Kitchen W8

11-13 Abingdon Rd. ✉ W8 6AH – Ⓜ High Street Kensington – ✆ (020) 7937 0120 – www.kitchenw8.com
– Closed bank holidays **C5**

Rest – Menu £ 20 (lunch) – Carte £ 32/41

Spec. Smoked eel and mackerel with sweet mustard dressing. Cod with Parmesan gnocchi and girolles. Salted chocolate parfait with honeycomb ice cream.

♦ Modern European ♦ Neighbourhood ♦

Smart, comfortable restaurant which is not as casual as its name implies, but which does have a pleasant, neighbourhood feel. Skilled kitchen produces balanced dishes free of showiness, with the emphasis on flavour.

Babylon – at The Roof Gardens

99 Kensington High St (entrance on Derry St) ✉ W8 5SA – Ⓜ High Street Kensington – ✆ (020) 7368 3993 – www.roofgardens.virgin.com
– Closed 25-30 December and Sunday dinner **C4**

Rest – Menu £ 22 (lunch) – Carte £ 44/56

♦ Modern European ♦ Fashionable ♦

Situated on the roof of this pleasant London building affording attractive views of the London skyline. Stylish modern décor in keeping with the contemporary, British cooking.

Clarke's

124 Kensington Church St. ✉ W8 4BH – Ⓜ Notting Hill Gate – ✆ (020) 7221 9225 – www.sallyclarke.com
– Closed Christmas, Sunday dinner and bank holidays **C4**

Rest – Menu £ 40 (dinner) – Carte £ 37/41

♦ Modern European ♦ Neighbourhood ♦

Forever popular restaurant, serving a choice of dishes boasting trademark fresh, seasonal ingredients and famed lightness of touch. Loyal following for over 20 years.

Zaika

1 Kensington High St ✉ W8 5NP – Ⓜ High Street Kensington – ✆ (020) 7795 6533 – www.zaika-restaurant.co.uk
– Closed 25-26 December, 1-2 January and Monday lunch **D4**

Rest – Menu £ 25 (lunch) – Carte £ 31/48

♦ Indian ♦ Exotic ♦

A converted bank, sympathetically restored, with original features and Indian artefacts adding plenty of colour. Well-organised service of modern and quite innovative Indian dishes.

Whits

21 Abingdon Rd. ✉ W8 6AH – Ⓜ High Street Kensington – ✆ (020) 7938 1122 – www.whits.co.uk
– Closed Christmas, New Year, Sunday and Monday **C5**

Rest – Menu £ 19/24 – Carte dinner £ 31/39

♦ Modern European ♦ Neighbourhood ♦

Run by friendly owner. Bar runs length of lower level. Most diners migrate upstairs with its modish artwork and intimate tables. Modern cooking with generous portions.

Memories of China

353 Kensington High St ✉ W8 6NW – Ⓜ High Street Kensington – ✆ (020) 7603 6951 – www.memoriesofchinaken.co.uk
– Closed 25-26 December and 1 January **B5**

Rest – *(booking essential)* Menu £ 20 – Carte £ 32/59

♦ Chinese ♦ Neighbourhood ♦

Subtle lighting and brightly coloured high-back chairs add to the modern feel of this Chinese restaurant. Screens separate the tables. Plenty of choice from extensive menu.

Timo

343 Kensington High St. ✉ W8 6NW – Ⓜ High Street Kensington – ☎ (020) 7603 3888 – www.timorestaurant.net – Closed Christmas, Sunday and bank holidays **B5**

Rest – Menu £ 14 (lunch and early dinner) – Carte £ 30/44

♦ Italian ♦ Neighbourhood ♦

Modern, personally run restaurant with unadorned walls and comfortable seating in brown suede banquettes. Italian menus of contemporary dishes and daily changing specials.

Kensington Place

201-209 Kensington Church St. ✉ W8 7LX – Ⓜ Notting Hill Gate – ☎ (020) 7727 3184 – www.kensingtonplace-restaurant.co.uk

Rest – Menu £ 19/23 **C3**

♦ Modern European ♦ Neighbourhood ♦ Brasserie ♦

Opened in 1987 as a big, boisterous, brasserie; these days a little less noisy but it remains well run. Competitively priced set menu offers a wide choice of modern European dishes.

Cibo

3 Russell Gdns ✉ W14 8EZ – Ⓜ Kensington Olympia – ☎ (020) 7371 6271 – www.ciborestaurant.net – Closed 1 week Christmas, Sunday dinner and bank holidays **B5**

Rest – Carte £ 23/37

♦ Italian ♦ Neighbourhood ♦

Long-standing neighbourhood Italian with local following. More space at the back of the room. Robust, satisfying cooking; the huge grilled shellfish and seafood platter a speciality.

Malabar

27 Uxbridge St. ✉ W8 7TQ – Ⓜ Notting Hill Gate – ☎ (020) 7727 8800 – www.malabar-restaurant.co.uk – Closed 24-27 December **C3**

Rest – *(buffet lunch Sunday)* Menu £ 23 – Carte £ 19/33

♦ Indian ♦ Neighbourhood ♦

Opened in 1983 in a residential street, but keeps up its appearance, remaining fresh and good-looking. Balanced menu of carefully prepared and well-priced Indian dishes, including excellent breads. Courteous service.

Wódka

12 St Albans Grove ✉ W8 5PN – Ⓜ High Street Kensington – ☎ (020) 7937 6513 – www.wodka.co.uk **D5**

Rest – *(dinner only and lunch Wednesday-Friday)* Menu £ 18 (lunch and early dinner) – Carte £ 23/33

♦ Polish ♦ Friendly ♦ Neighbourhood ♦

Warmly run, long-standing neighbourhood Polish restaurant. Robust and satisfying dishes, with plenty of game, alongside heartening soups; but desserts also reveal a lightness of touch.

North Kensington

The Portobello without rest

22 Stanley Gdns. ✉ W11 2NG – Ⓜ Notting Hill Gate – ☎ (020) 7727 2777 – www.portobellohotel.co.uk – Closed Christmas **B3**

21 rm – †£ 168 ††£ 228, ☐ £ 17

♦ Townhouse ♦ Personalised ♦

An attractive Victorian townhouse in an elegant terrace. Original and theatrical décor. Circular beds, half-testers, Victorian baths: no two bedrooms are the same.

XXX ✿✿

The Ledbury

127 Ledbury Rd. ✉ W11 2AQ – Ⓜ Notting Hill Gate – ✆ (020) 7792 9090 – www.theledbury.com
– Closed 24-26 December, August bank holiday and Monday lunch
Rest – Menu £ 28 (lunch £ 40 Sunday)/65 (dinner) **C2**
Spec. Scallop ceviche with seaweed and horseradish. Roe deer baked in Douglas Fir with beetroot and bone marrow. Honey and gingerbread soufflé with thyme ice cream.
♦ French ♦ Neighbourhood ♦
Elegant, understated surroundings with professional, well-organised service but it still has a neighbourhood feel. Highly skilled kitchen with an inherent understanding of flavour; great ingredients, especially game in season.

XX

Notting Hill Brasserie

92 Kensington Park Rd ✉ W11 2PN – Ⓜ Notting Hill Gate – ✆ (020) 7229 4481 – www.nottinghillbrasserie.com **B3**
Rest – Menu £ 24/27 (lunch) – Carte £ 40/53
♦ French ♦ Neighbourhood ♦
Modern, comfortable restaurant with quiet, formal atmosphere, set over four small rooms. Authentic African artwork on walls. Contemporary dishes with European influence.

XX

Edera

148 Holland Park Ave. ✉ W11 4UE – Ⓜ Holland Park – ✆ (020) 7221 6090 – www.londonfinediningroup.com
– Closed Christmas and Easter **B4**
Rest – Carte £ 36/46
♦ Italian ♦ Neighbourhood ♦
Warm and comfortable neighbourhood restaurant with plenty of local regulars and efficient, well-marshalled service. Robust cooking has a subtle Sardinian accent and comes in generous portions.

XX

E&O

14 Blenheim Cres. ✉ W11 1NN – Ⓜ Ladbroke Grove – ✆ (020) 7229 5454 – www.rickerrestaurants.com
– Closed 25-26 December and August bank holiday **B2**
Rest – Menu £ 19 (weekday lunch) – Carte £ 27/50
♦ Asian ♦ Minimalist ♦
Mean, moody and cool: does that describe the surroundings or the A-list diners? Minimalist chic meets high sound levels. Menus scour Far East, with dishes meant for sharing.

X

Bumpkin

209 Westbourne Park Rd ✉ W11 1EA – Ⓜ Westbourne Park – ✆ (020) 7243 9818 – www.bumpkinuk.com
– Closed 1 January, 29 August and 25-26 December **C2**
Rest – Carte £ 28/40
Rest *Brasserie* – Carte £ 29/40
♦ British ♦ Family ♦
Converted pea-green pub with casual, clubby feel and wholesome philosophy of cooking seasonal, carefully sourced and organic food. Whisky tasting and private dining on top floors. First floor restaurant offers modern Mediterranean menu.

Fat Badger

310 Portobello Rd ✉ W10 5TA – Ⓜ Ladbroke Grove. – ✆ (020) 8969 4500 – www.thefatbadger.com **B1**
Rest – Menu £ 25 (lunch) – Carte £ 20/29
♦ British ♦ Pub ♦
Large rustic pub with old sofas, chandeliers and upstairs dining room with intriguing wallpaper. Seasonal and earthy British food, with whole beasts delivered to the kitchen.

LONDON HEATHROW AIRPORT

Sofitel

Terminal 5, Heathrow Airport ✉ TW6 2GD – ✆ (020) 8757 7777 – www.sofitel.com
578 rm – †£ 114/396 ††£ 114/396, ☕ £ 21.50 – 27 suites
Rest *Brasserie Roux* – Menu £ 20 – Carte £ 27/39
Rest *Vivre* – Menu £ 25 (dinner) – Carte £ 25/38
◆ Chain hotel ◆ Functional ◆
Smart and well-run contemporary hotel, opened in 2008. Designed around a series of atriums, with direct access to T5. Crisply decorated, comfortable bedrooms with luxurious bathrooms. French classics in Brasserie. International menu in large Vivre.

Hilton London Heathrow Airport

Terminal 4 ✉ TW6 3AF – ✆ (020) 8759 7755 – www.hilton.co.uk/heathrow
355 rm – †£ 153/377 ††£ 153/377, ☕ £ 21.95 – 5 suites
Rest *Aromi* – *(Closed lunch Saturday, Sunday and bank holidays) (buffet lunch)* Menu £ 33 – Carte £ 29/38
Rest *Zen Oriental* – *✆ (020) 8564 9609* – Menu £ 33 – Carte £ 34/63
◆ Chain hotel ◆ Business ◆ Functional ◆
Group hotel with a striking modern exterior and linked to Terminal 4 by a covered walkway. Good-sized bedrooms, with contemporary styled suites. Spacious Aromi in vast atrium. Zen Oriental offers formal Chinese experience.

London Heathrow Marriott

Bath Rd, Hayes ✉ UB3 5AN – ✆ (020) 8990 1100 – www.londonheathrowmarriott.co.uk
391 rm – †£ 227 ††£ 227, ☕ £ 16.95 – 2 suites
Rest *Tuscany* – *(closed Sunday) (dinner only)* Menu £ 39 – Carte £ 32/45
Rest *Allie's grille* – Carte £ 25/38
◆ Chain hotel ◆ Business ◆ Functional ◆
Built at the end of 20C, this modern, comfortable hotel is centred around a large atrium, with comprehensive business facilities: there is an exclusive Executive floor. Italian cuisine in bright and convivial Tuscany. Grill favourites in Allie's.

BIRMINGHAM

BIRMINGHAM

Population: 1 016 800 (conurbation 2 284 093) – Altitude: 98m

Duclerc/COLORISE

It takes a pretty big backwards leap of the imagination to visualise Birmingham as an insignificant market town, but England's second city was just such a place through much of its history. Then came the boom times of the Industrial Revolution, the town fattening up on the back of the local iron and coal trades. In many people's minds that legacy lives on, the city seen as a rather dour place with shoddy Victorian housing, but 21C Brum has swept away much of its factory grime and polished up its civic face.

Its first 'makeover' was nearly a century ago when Neville Chamberlain's dad Joseph, the then mayor, enlarged the city's boundaries to make it the second largest in the country. Today it's feeling the benefits of a second modernist surge - a multi-million pound regeneration, typified by a fusion of appealing squares and modern shopping arcades: the 'armadillo' shaped Selfridges store became a fashion icon and city symbol when it opened a few years ago. Being pretty much in the centre of England, Birmingham is easily accessible from all areas and is within a curtain call of Shakespeare's Stratford while the charming Cotswolds are practically in its southern suburbs (if you stretch the imagination a bit more). To add to its impressive credentials, it can boast more canal miles than Venice and more trees than it has inhabitants.

LIVING THE CITY

Birmingham is surrounded by towns of all shapes and sizes, from the glories of Stratford-on-Avon in the south and Bridgnorth and Ironbridge in the west, to the more 'subtle' attractions of Wolverhampton and Coventry in its hinterland. Birmingham's landscape inspired a certain resident, JRR Tolkien, to write 'Lord of the Rings', but he'd be lost nowadays, what with the undulating contours of the flyovers, the self-important muscle of the adjoining National Indoor Arena and International Convention Centre, and the nearby trendy makeover of the Gas Street Basin. To say nothing with what they've done to the Bullring ... he wouldn't know where he was in the Balti Triangle (south of the centre) but perhaps would feel more at home in the elegant Jewellery Quarter further north.

PRACTICAL INFORMATION

ARRIVAL-DEPARTURE

Birmingham International Airport is 8 miles east of the city. There's free Air-Rail connection to Birmingham International Station every 2mins. From there, frequent trains to New St Station take 20min.

TRANSPORT

Three miles an hour might seem like a slow way to get round the city, but canal travel by narrowboat is stress-free and relaxing. Alternatively, take a cycle ride or walk along the towpaths. Stop off at Brindleyplace's floating café, or take a short summer trip from there.

Birmingham has eight local rail lines for travel to anywhere in the country. A recent addition, Midland Metro, is a light railway linking Snow Hill station with Wolverhampton.

Centro provides a regular service around the city. Give the exact fare to your driver as you board or purchase day or off-peak weekly Centrocards.

EXPLORING BIRMINGHAM

A sassy blend of refined arcades, stylish malls, well-stocked markets and the world-famous Jewellery Quarter just up the road, not to mention miles of canal pathways and impressive galleries... strolling round Brum has a lot going for it. In the past, you'd have thought 'coal' or 'cars', even 'great key locks' when you thought of this city, but now a more likely reaction would be "Oh, let's go there for our shopping." Historically, there's no reason why this shouldn't be the case. Many world famous British brands were created here, ranging from Bakelite to Cadbury's, HP Sauce and Typhoo Tea to Brylcreem.

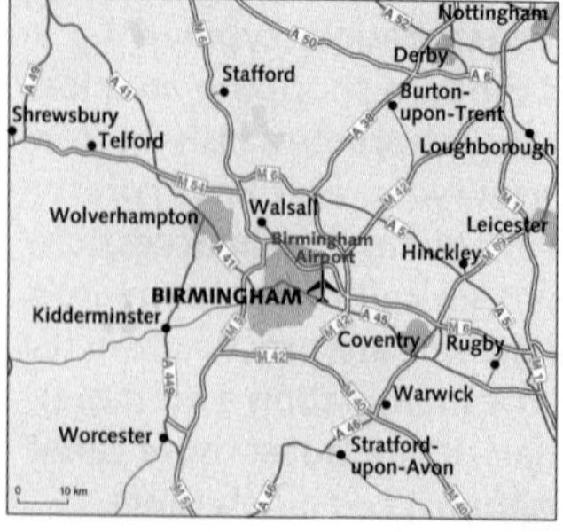

→ RAG TO A BULL (RING)

Much of the action takes place in the **Bullring** mega-complex, overseen by the shimmering ego of the Selfridges building, less a department store, more a self-assured statement of intent from Future

Systems, who designed it. Slightly more down-to-earth, and a mere stone's throw from the Bullring, is the flea market in Saint Martin's Market, known affectionately for 50 years as The Rag. Its 350 stalls complement the Bullring's grandeur rather well, and the antiques' and collectors' fairs it puts on are renowned amongst in-the-know locals. One less salubrious claim to fame... it also has a bit of a risqué reputation for early morning 'business transactions' before the stallholders arrive.

On the other side of the city, in the northern area of Hockley, is the **Jewellery Quarter**, the place to head for if you're after a quality piece of body adornment or silverware. Also known as 'The Golden Triangle', it's an area of smart Victorian buildings between Warstone Lane and Vyse Street, and it's steeped in 19C folklore: it democratized writing by supplying the world with cheap pen nibs for 130 years; it was where Joseph Hudson invented the police whistle, borrowing £20 from the Metropolitan Police so that he could get his hands on enough brass for 21,000 of them to be produced; and it's where the same man made the doomed whistles for the Titanic lifeboats (Kate Winslet used a 'rescued' one in the movie!). There are fascinating museums in the area too, such as the Jewellery Quarter Discovery Centre, which does pretty much what it says on the label.

→ A POSTING TO THE MAILBOX

You feel like you've moved forward a century or two when you step into the **Mailbox** area, not a half-mile from the main New Street railway station. It has a distinct 21st Century feel to it, proudly referring to itself as the UK's 'largest mixed use building'. What that actually means is that it incorporates penthouse style apartments, health clubs, office space, hotels, restaurants and shops... not a bad refit for a former mail sorting office. It's the West Midlands' answer to Bond Street, and it's where you'll find Britain's biggest Malmaison Hotel. But it's not the only area laying claim to being Brum's coolest. Just a waterbus ride away along the quaintly named Gas Street Basin sits **Brindleyplace**, an impressive and vibrant canalside destination, boasting tree-lined streets, eye-catching water features, striking architecture and a good few clear open spaces. It's got the Sea Life Centre, too, complete with a fully transparent underwater tube letting you walk, suspended in mid-'ocean', completely surrounded by sharks, skate, rays and all manner of marine life. One final conversion that's of interest: about 700 paces from the Bullring, southeast in the area of Digbeth, stands another icon of Birmingham's branded past: the Bird's custard factory. They don't make yellow gooey stuff there anymore though: The **Custard Factory** is now an arts and media quarter with a trendy pub, The Medicine Bar, and a host of urban style shops, green spaces, fountains and sculpture. It's in a smart square too.

→ ART ATTACK

Not everything in England's second city is rebranded, spruced up or brand new. There's still a reverence for old-fashioned style and taste embodied in a variety of esteemed establishments around the city. Take the **Barber Institute of Fine Art,** on the University of Birmingham campus in Edgbaston. This impressive art deco building, opened by Queen Mary in 1939, contains one of the finest small collections of European art in the UK, including Botticelli, Holbein, Rembrandt, Rubens, Van Gogh, Turner and Monet. Go up to the central Chamberlain Square to be equally impressed by the **Museum & Art Gallery**, which boasts a renowned collection of Pre-Raphaelite paintings, as well as works by Degas, Renoir and Canaletto. It also houses popular natural and local history sections, and the archaeology department is highly acclaimed. The Edwardian tearoom's not a bad place to relax for a spot of cultural reflection. Further north is Aston Hall, a fine Jacobean mansion built between 1618 and 1635 with friezes and plaster ceilings, a 40m long panelled gallery, gables and turrets, and with a collection that features textiles, furniture and paintings from the Birmingham Museum.

The world of science comes to life at **Millennium Point**, 10 minutes walk from the centre, its public areas dominated by an awesome central Hub with soaring atrium. This is where you'll find two visitor attractions, Thinktank, the city's science museum, and IMAX cinema. If you're more at home outdoors, then The Birmingham Botanical Gardens and Glasshouses is probably more your style. Based in Edgbaston, they opened in 1832, and today their 15 acres are an ideal place to wind down and find tranquility.

Of course, the city is only some 20 miles from the birthplace of William Shakespeare, **Stratford-upon-Avon**, and it's not unknown for visitors to forego even the delights of Birmingham in order to breathe in a bit of the Bard's magic. If you're lucky enough to be around on a summer Sunday (between July and September) there's really only one way to do the trip, and that's on the Shakespeare Express, a wonderful steam locomotive which starts from Snow Hill station, picks up passengers at Moor Street, and chugs its way through leafy Warwickshire countryside to Stratford. There's Pullman class dining if you're feeling extravagant: you can take breakfast on the way out, and high tea on the return journey.

CALENDAR HIGHLIGHTS

They like a party in Birmingham. There's a St George's Day Celebration every April, while in Handsworth the Caribbean-style Birmingham International Carnival takes place in August every second year, and winds its way to Perry Barr Park. Birmingham Pride attracts 100,000 visitors each year to the Hurst Street 'gay village' location. The largest single-day event, though, is the St. Patrick's Day Parade, which can claim to be the second biggest in Europe, after the one held in Dublin.

BIRMINGHAM IN...

→ ONE DAY

The Rag, The Bullring, a museum

→ TWO DAYS

Brindleyplace, a trip on the waterbus to The Mailbox, and a cycle ride round the canals.

→ THREE DAYS

If you're around on a summer Sunday, take the Shakespeare Express to Stratford. Or visit Bridgnorth and Ironbridge, cradle of the Industrial Revolution. Venture south to the idyllic Cotswolds.

EATING OUT

Temptation isn't far away from students at the city's main centre of learning, the University of Birmingham, to the south-west of the city, and not a million miles away from Cadbury World, the UK's only purpose-built visitor centre devoted entirely to chocolate. Located in the evocative sounding Bourneville area, staff are on hand to tell visitors the history of chocolate and how it's made, but, let's face it, most people go along to get a face full of the stuff in fresh liquid form straight from the vat.

More conventionally, many people who come to Birmingham make for the now legendary area of Sparkbrook, Balsall Heath and Moseley. In itself that may not sound too funky, but over the last 30 years it's become the area known as the Balti Triangle. The balti was 'officially' discovered in Birmingham in 1976, a full-on dish of aromatic spices, fresh herbs and rich curries, and The Triangle now boasts over 50 establishments dedicated to the dish.

For those after something a little more subtle, the city offers a growing number of lively and fashionable restaurants, offering assured and contemporary cuisine.

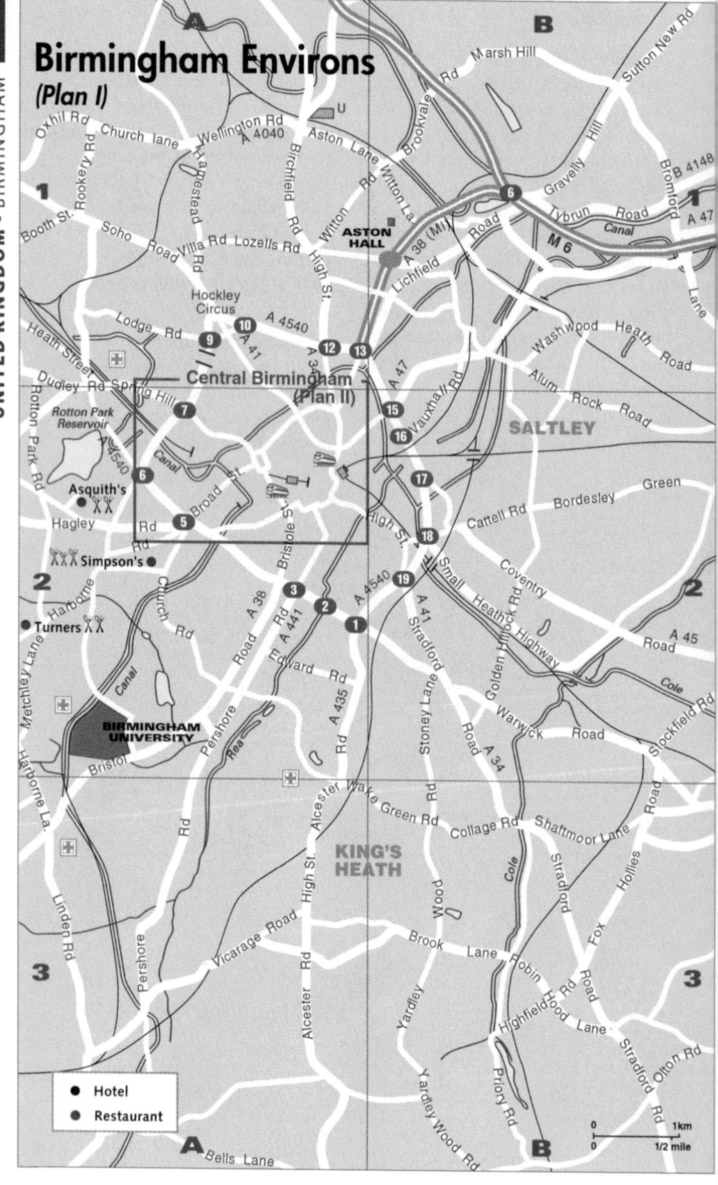
Birmingham Environs
(Plan I)
Central Birmingham
(Plan II)
ASTON HALL
SALTLEY
KING'S HEATH
BIRMINGHAM UNIVERSITY
Rotton Park Reservoir
Hockley Circus
Asquith's
Simpson's
Turners
Hotel
Restaurant
0 1km
0 1/2 mile

Hyatt Regency

2 Bridge St B1 2JZ – (0121) 643 1234
– www.birmingham.regency.hyatt.com D2
315 rm – £ 209 £ 209, £ 15.75 – 4 suites
Rest *Aria* – Menu £ 15 – Carte £ 27/42
♦ Luxury ♦ Modern ♦
Striking mirrored exterior. Glass enclosed lifts offer panoramic views. Sizeable rooms with floor to ceiling windows. Covered link with International Convention Centre. Contemporary style restaurant in central atrium; modish cooking.

Malmaison

Mailbox, 1 Wharfside St B1 1RD – (0121) 246 5000
– www.malmaison.com E2
184 rm – £ 170 £ 170/350, £ 13.95 – 1 suite
Rest *Brasserie* – Menu £ 16 (dinner) – Carte £ 26/33
♦ Luxury ♦ Stylish ♦
Stylish, modern boutique hotel, forms centrepiece of Mailbox development. Chic bar. Spacious, contemporary bedrooms with every modern facility; superb petit spa. Brasserie serving contemporary French-influenced cooking at reasonable prices.

Hotel Du Vin

25 Church St B3 2NR – (0121) 200 0600
– www.hotelduvin.com E2
66 rm – £ 160 £ 175/205, £ 14.50
Rest *Bistro* – Carte £ 35/45
♦ Business ♦ Design ♦
Former 19C eye hospital in heart of shopping centre; has relaxed, individual, boutique style. Low lighting in rooms of muted tones: Egyptian cotton and superb bathrooms. Champagne in "bubble lounge"; Parisian style brasserie.

City Inn

1 Brunswick Sq, Brindley Pl B1 2HW – (0121) 643 1003
– www.cityinn.com D2
238 rm – £ 79/225 £ 89/235
Rest *City Café* – (0121) 633 6300 – Menu £ 15/17 – Carte £ 24/31
♦ Chain hotel ♦ Business ♦ Functional ♦
In heart of vibrant Brindley Place; the spacious atrium with bright rugs and blond wood sets the tone for equally stylish bedrooms. Corporate friendly with many meeting rooms. Eat in restaurant, terrace or bar.

Simpsons (Andreas Antona) with rm

rest,

20 Highfield Rd, Edgbaston B15 3DU – (0121) 454 3434 – www.simpsonsrestaurant.co.uk
– Closed bank holidays Plan I **A2**
4 rm – £ 225 £ 225
Rest – *(closed Sunday dinner)* Menu £ 30/33 – Carte £ 40/53
Spec. Scallops with chorizo, tomato and squid. Aberdeenshire beef with braised cheek ravioli and toasted peanuts. Turrón parfait with raspberries.
♦ Contemporary ♦ Fashionable ♦
Smart Georgian mansion with stylish lounges, pleasant garden terrace and summer house. Tables are well-spaced; service is formal and efficient. Classical menu displays Mediterranean influences, contemporary twists and excellent produce. Spacious bedrooms boast French country styling.

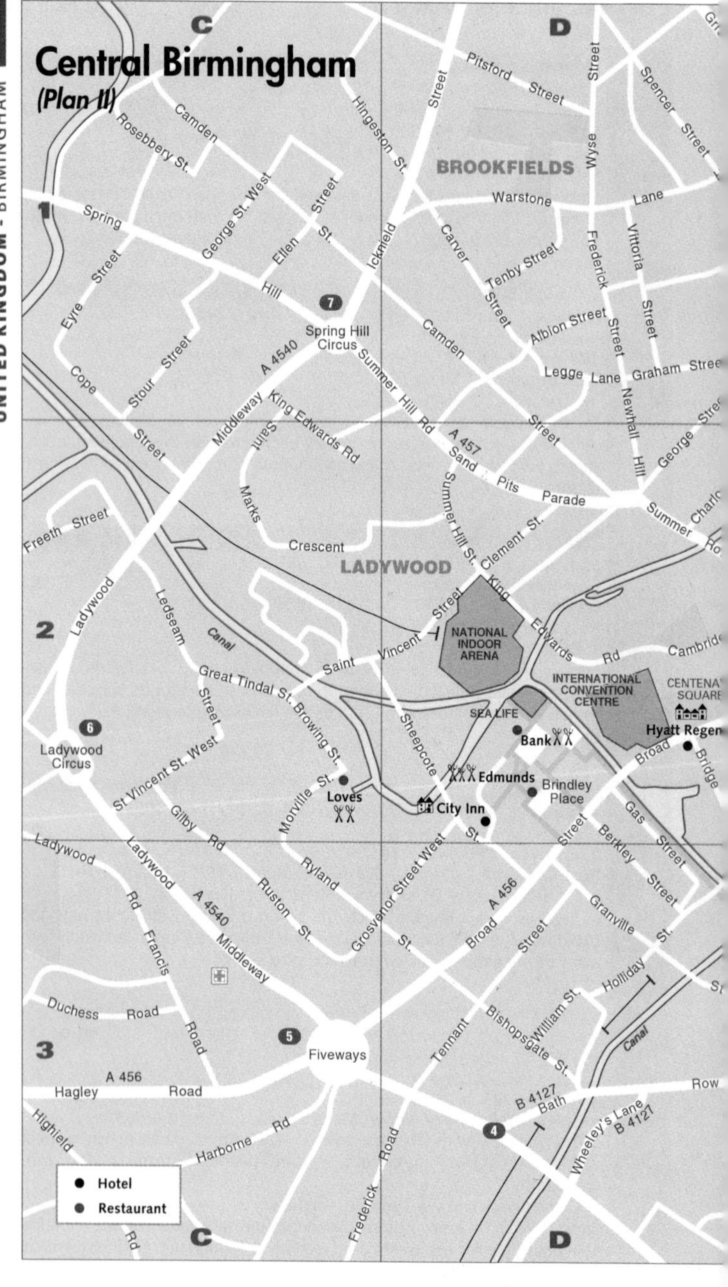
Central Birmingham
(Plan II)
BROOKFIELDS
LADYWOOD
NATIONAL INDOOR ARENA
INTERNATIONAL CONVENTION CENTRE
CENTENARY SQUARE
SEA LIFE
Bank
Hyatt Regency
Edmunds
Brindley Place
Loves
City Inn
Spring Hill Circus
Ladywood Circus
Fiveways
Hotel
Restaurant

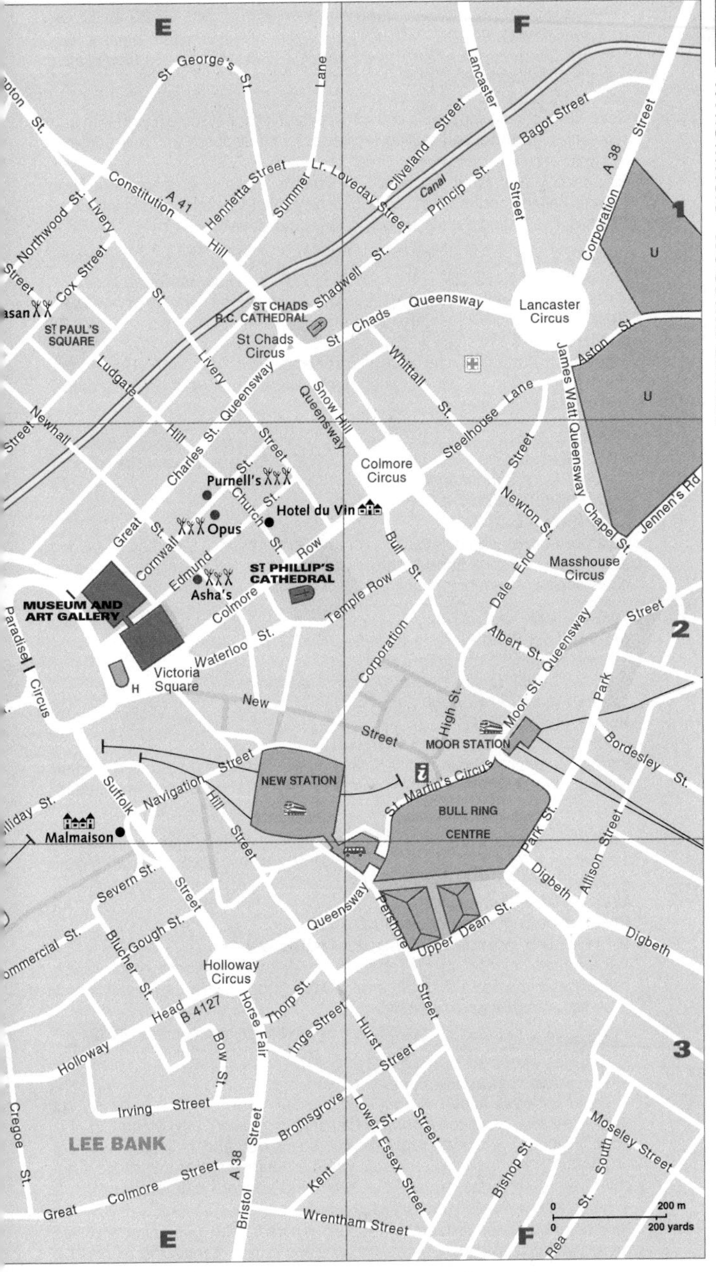
E
F
1
2
3
St. George's St.
Lane
Lancaster
Street
Bagot Street
Street
A 38
Corporation
Constitution
A 41
Hill
Henrietta Street
Summer
Lr. Loveday
Street
Cliveland
Street
Canal
Princip St.
Northwood St.
Livery
Street
Cox Street
St.
Shadwell
St.
ST CHADS
R.C. CATHEDRAL
Queensway
Lancaster
Circus
U
ST PAUL'S
SQUARE
St Chads
Circus
St Chads
Aston St.
James Watt Queensway
Ludgate
Livery
Queensway
Snow Hill
Queensway
Whittall
St.
Steelhouse Lane
Newhall
Street
Hill
Charles St.
Street
Colmore
Circus
Street
Newton St.
Chapel St.
Jennen's Rd
Purnell's
St.
Church
St.
Hotel du Vin
Opus
Great
St.
Cornwall
Row
Bull
St.
Edmund
St.
Asha's
ST PHILLIP'S
CATHEDRAL
Dale End
Masshouse
Circus
MUSEUM AND
ART GALLERY
Colmore
Temple Row
Paradise
Circus
Waterloo St.
Corporation
Albert St.
Queensway
Street
Victoria
Square
H
New
Street
High St.
Moor St.
Park
MOOR STATION
Bordesley
St.
Street
NEW STATION
Navigation
Hill
Street
St. Martin's Circus
BULL RING
CENTRE
Suffolk
Malmaison
Park St.
Allison Street
Digbeth
Severn St.
Street
Queensway
Pershore
Commercial St.
Blucher
St.
Gough St.
Upper Dean St.
Digbeth
Holloway
Circus
Street
Head
B 4127
Horse Fair
Thorp St.
Inge Street
Hurst
Street
Holloway
Bow
St.
Irving
Street
Cregoe
St.
LEE BANK
Bristol
A 38
Street
Bromsgrove
Lower
St.
Essex
Street
Street
Kent
St.
Moseley Street
South
St.
Bishop St.
Great
Colmore
Street
Wrentham Street
Rea
0
200 m
0
200 yards

XXX
✿

Purnell's (Glynn Purnell)

55 Cornwall St ✉ B3 2DH – ✆ (0121) 212 9799 – www.purnellsrestaurant.com – Closed Christmas-New Year, 1 week Easter, 2 weeks summer, Saturday lunch, Sunday and Monday **E2**

Rest – Menu £ 25/45

Spec. Salad of crab with apple and smoked paprika honeycomb. Lamb with butterbeans, pigs trotter and cauliflower. Pavlova with raspberry and mint sorbet.

♦ Modern ♦ Design ♦

Passionately run, stylish restaurant in sizeable red-brick property with large lounge. Refined and modern cooking displays plenty of original and individual touches. The tasting menus are particularly innovative in style.

XXX

Opus

54 Cornwall St ✉ B3 2DE – ✆ (0121) 200 2323 – www.opusrestaurant.co.uk – Closed 24 December-6 January, Saturday lunch, Sunday and bank holidays

Rest – Menu £ 19/28 – Carte £ 33/46 **E2**

♦ Modern ♦ Design ♦

Set in the heart of the financial district; its name means 'hard work'. Floor-to-ceiling windows, cocktail bar and chef's table. Modern menus of precisely prepared, wholesome dishes.

XXX

Asha's

12-22 Newhall St ✉ B3 3LX – ✆ (0121) 2002767 – www.ashasuk.co.uk – Closed Saturday and Sunday lunch **E2**

Rest – Menu £ 13/25 – Carte £ 26/39

♦ Indian ♦ Exotic ♦

Smart restaurant with delightful décor and vivid artwork. Owned by renowned artiste/gourmet Asha Bhosle. Authentic North West Indian cuisine cooked by chefs originally from that region.

XXX

Edmunds

6 Central Sq, Brindley Pl ✉ B1 2JB – ✆ (0121) 633 4944 – www.edmundsbirmingham.com – Closed 1 week spring, 1 week summer, 1 week autumn, 1 week winter, Saturday lunch, Sunday and bank holidays **D2**

Rest – Menu £ 19/40

♦ Modern European ♦ Formal ♦

Formal restaurant in heart of city. Smart interior with neutral décor and modern lighting. Immaculately laid tables boast fine china and glassware. Smart, attentive staff.

XX

Asquiths

1 Montague Rd ✉ B16 9HN – ✆ (0121) 455 0999 – www.theasquith.com – Closed Christmas-New Year, Easter, 2 weeks summer, Sunday dinner and lunch Monday-Wednesday *Plan 1* **A2**

Rest – *(booking essential)* Menu £ 20/35

♦ French ♦ Formal ♦ Neighbourhood ♦

Two-roomed neighbourhood restaurant in extended red-brick coach house; conservatory overlooks a small garden. Daily changing menu of skilful French cooking; smooth, assured flavours.

XX
✿

Turners (Richard Turner)

69 High St, Harborne ✉ B17 9NS – ✆ (0121) 426 4440 – www.turnersofharborne.com – Closed last week August, Sunday and Monday *Plan I* **A2**

Rest – *(booking essential) (Saturday dinner tasting menu only)* Menu £ 25/49

Spec. Scallops with peas, broad beans, quails egg and belly pork. Loin of veal with caramelised sweetbreads, white asparagus and truffle sauce. Chocolate tart with salted caramel ice cream and popcorn panna cotta.

♦ Modern ♦ Neighbourhood ♦

Neat neighbourhood restaurant in suburban parade, with wood panels, etched mirrors and velvet chairs. Concise à la carte and tasting menus offer refined, flavoursome dishes of accomplished, classical cooking with modern touches. Formal, structured service.

XX

Loves

VISA MC

The Glasshouse, Canal Sq ✉ B16 8FL – ✆ (0121) 454 5151
– www.loves-restaurant.co.uk
– Closed 2 weeks August, 2 weeks Christmas, Sunday and Monday

Rest – Menu £ 25/40 **C2**

♦ Inventive ♦ Fashionable ♦

Situated on the ground floor of an apartment block on the canal basin, with spacious, contemporary interior and smartly laid tables. Cooking uses modern techniques and presentation.

XX

Lasan

VISA MC AE

3-4 Dakota Buildings, James St, St Pauls Sq ✉ B3 1SD – ✆ (0121) 212 3664 – www.lasangroup.com
– Closed 25 December and Saturday lunch **E1**

Rest – Carte £ 30/51

♦ Indian ♦ Design ♦

Jewellery quarter restaurant of sophistication and style; good quality ingredients allow the clarity of the spices to shine through in this well-run Indian establishment.

XX

Bank

A/C VISA MC AE

4 Brindley Pl. ✉ B1 2JB – ✆ (0121) 633 4466 – www.bankrestaurants.com
– Closed 1 January and 26 December **D2**

Rest – Menu £ 15 (lunch and early dinner) – Carte £ 20/38

♦ Modern ♦ Brasserie ♦

Capacious, modern and busy bar-restaurant where chefs can be watched through a glass wall preparing the tasty modern dishes. Pleasant terrace area.

EDINBURGH

EDINBURGH

Population: 471 650 (conurbation 772 400) – Altitude: 50m

oug Pearson/Agency Jon Arnold Images/Age Fotostock

Edinburgh is often called 'the Athens of the North', but the beautiful Scottish capital can also bear comparison with Rome: like the Italian capital, it's laid out on seven hills. These were once of a volcanic nature, in contrast to the modern city, which is elegant, cool and sophisticated. It's essentially two cities in one, the medieval Old Town, huddled around and beneath the crags and battlements of the castle, and the smart Georgian terraces of the New Town, overseen by the eighteenth century architect Robert Adam. You could say there's a third element to the equation: the port of Leith, two miles from the centre, which has undergone a revamp over the last decade to take its place as Edinburgh's proud little relative.

This is a city that's been attracting tourists since the nineteenth century. You could even make a claim for Edinburgh being one of the places where the tourist industry came of age. That's why it sits so easily with the annual August invasion of the Edinburgh Festival. Since 1999 it's also been the home of the Scottish Parliament, adding a new dimension to its worldwide reputation. It accepts its plaudits with the same ease that it accepts an extra half million visitors at the height of summer. Its status as a UNESCO World Heritage site confirms it as a city that knows how to be both ancient and modern.

LIVING THE CITY

In the middle is the **castle**; to the south is the **old town;** to the north is the **new town**. There, in a nutshell, you have Edinburgh. But within that briefest of outlines lies so much life and colour you could find a new facet to interest you each day for a week. There's a natural boundary to the north at the Firth of Forth, while to the south lie the rolling Pentland Hills. Unless you've had a few too many drams, it's just about impossible to get lost here, as prominent landmarks like the Castle, Arthur's Seat and Calton Hill access all areas. Filleting the centre of town is the main artery of Princes Street, one side of which invites you to shop, the other to sit and relax in your own space.

PRACTICAL INFORMATION

ARRIVAL-DEPARTURE

8 miles to the west of the city is Edinburgh International Airport. There is an Airlink Bus Service to Waveley Bridge every 10min. A taxi to the city centre will cost around £17.

TRANSPORT

A great way of gaining access to many of Edinburgh's top sights is by getting an Edinburgh Pass. It gives you free entry to over 30 of the city's attractions and includes loads of great offers.

There's no underground or tram system in the city, so it might be wise to invest in a Daysaver ticket for the buses. For £2.50 you'll have the freedom of Edinburgh for 24 hours.

There are plenty of guided options for showing you around. Choose from an open-top bus, a walking or cycling tour, or, slightly more off the wall, a ghost tour of the old town. All city bus tours leave from Waverley Bridge and the hop-on, hop-off nature of the ticket will last you 24 hours.

EXPLORING EDINBURGH

The Castle Rock, epicentre of the Scottish capital, has been an elevated and indomitable refuge for over a thousand years, and it's from here that the city grew, abetted by Stuart kings who favoured Edinburgh as their royal residence. Breathe in its air and pick up its scent. Wherever you are, its ancient geography seeps into your pores. Whether it's from the extinct volcanic mound of Arthur's Seat in Holyrood Park, or the pivotal lump of rock upon which the castle hovers; whether you're atop the craggy splendour of Calton Hill or down in the mysterious dank of a medieval wynd, this is a city scraped from the work of primeval forces.

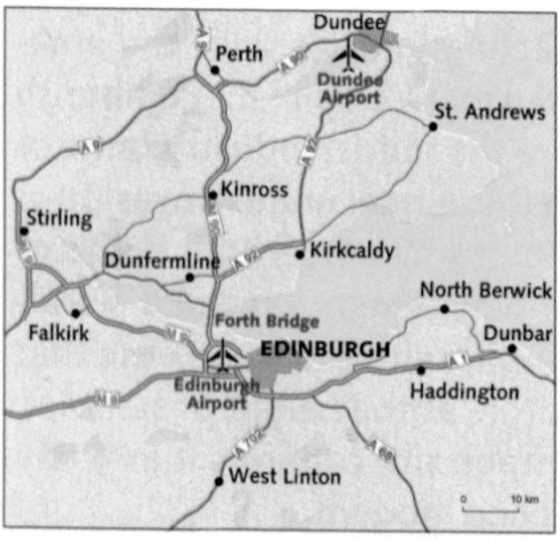

The old town is hued from stone, with tightly packed, granite grey houses, each having their own story to tell. **The Royal Mile** is the main spine of the area, running downhill from the castle through Lawnmarket past St Giles' Cathedral, through Canongate to Holyroodhouse and the Scottish Parliament building. The bottom section is far quieter than the tourist-oriented upper part, but all the way down, every narrow wynd (stone staircase) and (nearly) every building withholds ancient secrets, bound up in wondrous gables, turrets and towering chimneys. Two places to seek out in this vicinity: one is the **Writers' Museum** in Lady Stair's Close off Lawnmarket. This is full of the paraphernalia of three of Scotland's most famous writers – Robert Burns, Sir Walter Scott and Robert Louis Stevenson. The latter got his inspiration for Dr. Jekyll and Mr. Hyde from a notorious local schizophrenic who was a respectable councillor and cabinet-maker by day, burglar and thief by night. The man was eventually caught and hanged, but his name lives on at Deacon Brodie's Tavern further along Lawnmarket.

Try and avoid the crowds for a while by wandering off into a charming little close, or exploring the tunnels and wynds that connect streets on different levels - these can be the most fascinating elements of the Royal Mile. Gladstone's Land in Lawnmarket will enhance this feel for the sixteenth century: it's a six-storey former merchant's home and shop, and it's been restored to its former glory. You can actually partake in this yourself, as four of the apartments are available to rent. Any stroll down the Royal Mile wouldn't be complete without coming under the lowering glare of **St Giles' Cathedral**, or to give it its proper Scottish name, The High Kirk. It's a magnificently sombre place dating from 1120, but don't expect the interior to be too ornate: Calvinist zealots during the Reformation saw to that. This deep, dark landmark acts as a kind of focal point for Festival revellers, but of more relevance it's where ghost-tour companies pitch up and lead you off to spooky cellars and shabby arches.

→ SO WHAT'S NEW?

A different feel pervades the New Town, which you reach via a pleasant walk over the Waverley railway bridge and across Princes Street. 'New' in this case is a relative term. This part of town was pastureland known as The Long Dikes and architect Robert Adam transformed it in the latter part of the 18C, when union with England was bringing the city new prosperity. It's an area with wide, spacious streets, open grassy squares and classical lines: essentially it's the diametric opposite of the Old Town. Its rectangle of streets and terraces is one of the first and finest examples of town planning in Europe. The elegant Georgian architecture you find here now acts as the backdrop to a yummy collection of equally stylish shops, restaurants and bars; rather out of the ordinary in a stylistic sense is the distinctive neo-Gothic **Scottish National Portrait Gallery**, a great place to spend a wet afternoon, taking in the visual history of the country's rebels, philosophers, heroes and villains. Contemporary portraits include the likes of novelist Irvine Welsh, actor Sean Connery and ex-footballer Danny McGrain, possibly a surprise inclusion since he made his name playing for a Glasgow club...

Edinburgh never really takes on an 'industrial' aspect; with the likes of **Princes Street Gardens** right there in the heart of things, it's easy to feel green here. Nevertheless, there's a wonderful place to go if you want to take things to a more rural plane. It's The Water of Leith, a short bus ride out of the centre; it starts close to the entrance to Murrayfield Rugby

Stadium and meanders along a walkway for all of 21 miles, taking in the delightful Dean Village, a former grain-milling centre dating from the twelfth century, plunged down a valley 30 metres deep. The village's old buildings have been restored and converted into apartments and houses: there's a famous view here looking downstream beneath the thrusting arches of Thomas Telford's Dean Bridge (close by you can get a cultural hit at the Scottish National Gallery of Modern Art, which includes works by Vuillard, Matisse, Lichtenstein and Giacometti, as well as Scottish painters of the vibrant Colourist school).

The Water of Leith Walkway is one of the city's most tranquil strolls, with a pleasant mix of village and woodland along the way. An ideal end point for many is the **Royal Botanic Garden**, which boasts the world's largest collection of rhododendrons, plus rock gardens with a waterfall and redwoods in a mini-forest.

→ KEEPING YOU PAGED

Per capita head, Edinburgh boasts more booksellers than any other city in Britain. In 2004 it became the first city in the world to be named City of Literature by UNESCO.

→ TAKE IT OR LEITH IT

At the end of the engaging Walkway, **Leith** is a very agreeable place to pitch up. The former dockland area staring out onto the Firth of Forth was a typical run-down port of aching infrastructure and rough-and-ready seamen's bars until the late 80s, when it experienced a renaissance. Nineteenth century warehouses were converted into loft apartments and a coterie of stylish bars and restaurants opened their doors. Proof of their impact came when two eating establishments in the area earned Michelin stars: Martin Wishart and The Kitchin. Both are located in old dockside conversions. There's also the smart Ocean Terminal shopping complex adding a retail landmark to the serene waterfront ambience.

Edinburgh is a superb city to explore. Its topography and its architecture give it varied nuance and colour. It can also be a pretty cool city, and not just in the cultural sense. Summer temperatures are unlikely to climb much above 18 Celsius, but in a place as fascinating as this, wrap up warm and you'll hardly notice.

→ REEL LIFE

Edinburgh's a popular place with film-makers. Movies shot in and around the city include Trainspotting, The Prime of Miss Jean Brodie, The Da Vinci Code, The 39 Steps, and Mary Reilly.

EDINBURGH IN...

→ ONE DAY

Calton Hill, Royal Mile, Edinburgh Castle, New Town café, Old town pub

→ TWO DAYS

Water of Leith, Scottish National Gallery of Modern Art, Leith and one of its smart restaurants, Forth Rail Bridge

→ THREE DAYS

Arthur's Seat, National Museum of Scotland, Holyrood Park, a trip to the Pentland Hills

CALENDAR HIGHLIGHTS

Festivals are a part and parcel of Edinburgh life, and not just the famous jamboree every August. In the spring, the Ceilidh Culture Festival highlights local performers as well as others from around the world, and takes place over three weeks in 30 different venues. Mary King's Ghost Fest is a 10-day bonanza for anyone interested in the city's haunted sites, and includes overnight vigils and experiments. December is a special time of year here. There are all kinds of markets and fun fairs at Christmas, while Hogmanay is a four day sporrans-up with a torchlight procession on the 29th, a carnival on George Street on the 30th, a street party (to end all street parties) on New Year's Eve, plus a host of events to detox and energise on the first day of the year. The Summer Festival, the one that the world not only knows about but appears to attend en masse, is in fact an umbrella term for many distinct cultural events taking place, including an international festival and others for film, fringe, art, books, jazz and blues.

EATING OUT

Food and drink in Edinburgh takes on many forms. It can range from the 'tartan menus' fodder for tourists to the very best, via the smart conversions of Leith or the exquisite central hotels, as in the case of the landmark Balmoral, at the head of Princes Street with its immaculate basement restaurant, Number One. Edinburgh is said to have more restaurants per head of population than anywhere else in the UK, and you can admire the city from a rooftop table, or dine with ghosts in a basement eatery. There are some good pubs in the old town, such as the tiny but hip Black Bo's in Blackfriars Street, or the authentically atmospheric Ensign Ewart on Lawnmarket. Drinking dens also abound in Cowgate and Grassmarket. Further away, in West End, you'll find enticing late-night bars, while the stylish variety, serving cocktails, are more in order in the George Street area of new town. What to drink in Scotland's capital? Any beer by Deuchar's gets the thumbs-up, or a pint of Dark Island from Orkney. Peaty flavoured Laphroaig is a highly recommended dram of whisky. For those who might want to buy their grub and take it away to eat, then a visit to Valvona & Crolla is a must. It's in Elm Row near Calton Hill, and is a great Italian deli: a weekly van from Italy brings wonderful cheeses, olive oils, wine and salamis, and if the temptation's too strong, you can try them at once in the café at the back. The nineteenth century Cadenhead's on the Royal Mile is the place to go for whiskies: it sells a mind-boggling range of rare distillations.

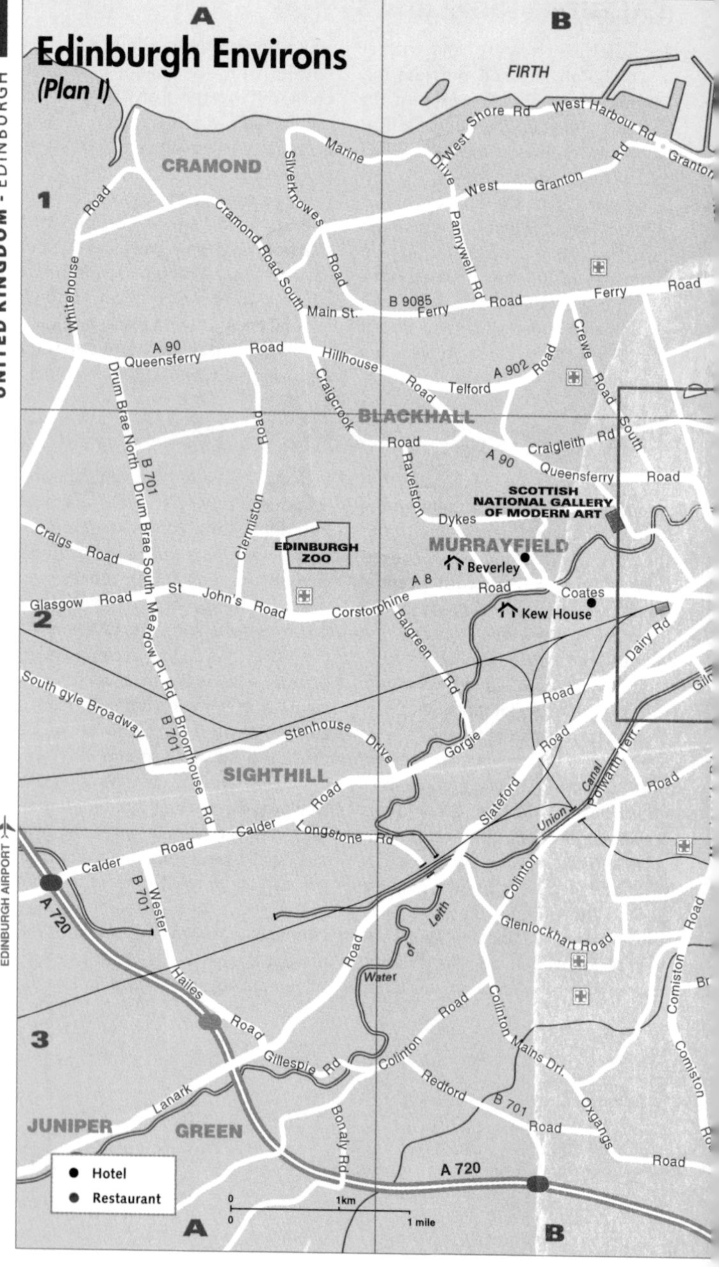
Edinburgh Environs
(Plan I)
A
B
1
2
3
FIRTH
CRAMOND
BLACKHALL
MURRAYFIELD
SIGHTHILL
JUNIPER
GREEN
EDINBURGH ZOO
SCOTTISH NATIONAL GALLERY OF MODERN ART
Beverley
Kew House
Coates
West Shore Rd
West Harbour Rd
Granton
Marine Drive
West Granton Rd
Silverknowes Road
Cramond Road South
Whitehouse Road
Pannywell Rd
B 9085 Ferry Road
Ferry Road
Main St.
A 90 Queensferry Road
Hillhouse Road
Telford Road
A 902
Craigcrook Road
Crewe Road South
Craigleith Rd
A 90 Queensferry Road
Ravelston Dykes
Drum Brae North
B 701
Drum Brae South
Clermiston Road
Craigs Road
Glasgow Road
St John's Road
A 8
Corstorphine Road
Balgreen Rd
Dairy Rd
Meadow Pl. Rd
B 701
Broomhouse Rd
South gyle Broadway
Stenhouse Drive
Gorgie Road
Slateford Road
Union Canal
Polwarth Terr.
Calder Road
Longstone Rd
B 701
Wester Hailes Road
A 720
Water of Leith
Colinton Road
Gleniockhart Road
Colinton Mains Dri.
Comiston Road
Gillespie Rd
Lanark Road
Bonaly Rd
Redford Road
B 701
Oxgangs Road
A 720
Hotel
Restaurant
0
1km
1 mile
EDINBURGH AIRPORT

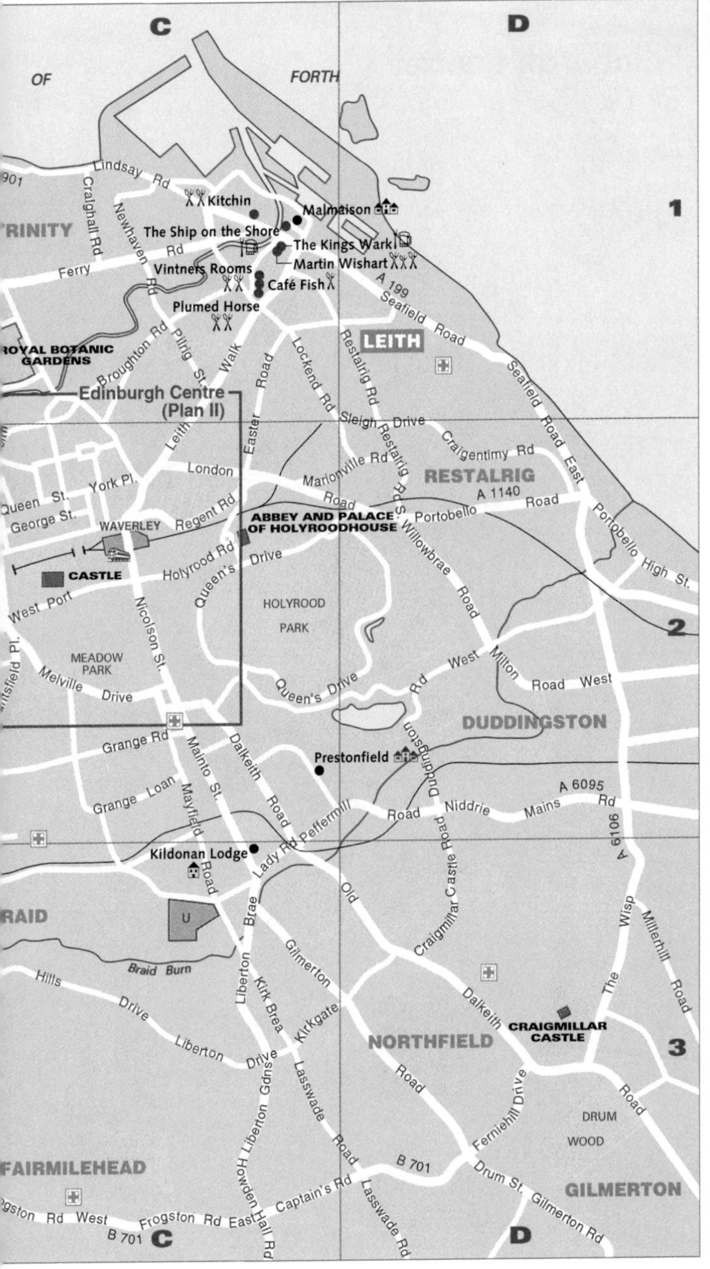
C
D
OF
FORTH
1
2
3
Lindsay Rd
TRINITY
Craighall Rd
Newhaven Rd
Kitchin
Malmaison
The Ship on the Shore
The Kings Wark
Martin Wishart
Ferry Rd
Vintners Rooms
Café Fish
Plumed Horse
A 199
Seafield Road
LEITH
ROYAL BOTANIC GARDENS
Broughton Rd
Pilrig St.
Leith Walk
Easter Road
Lochend Rd
Restalrig Rd
Edinburgh Centre (Plan II)
Sleigh Drive
Restalrig Rd
Craigentinny Rd
Seafield Road East
London Road
Marionville Rd
RESTALRIG
York Pl.
Queen St.
George St.
A 1140
Road
Portobello Road
Regent Rd
ABBEY AND PALACE OF HOLYROODHOUSE
WAVERLEY
Willowbrae Road
Portobello High St.
Holyrood Rd
Queen's Drive
CASTLE
West Port
HOLYROOD PARK
Nicolson St.
MEADOW PARK
Melville Drive
West Rd
Milton Road West
Queen's Drive
DUDDINGSTON
Grange Rd
Mainto St.
Dalkeith Road
Prestonfield
Duddingston
A 6095
Grange Loan
Mayfield Road
Peffermill Road
Niddrie Mains Rd
Kildonan Lodge
Lady Rd
A 6106
Old Dalkeith Road
Craigmillar Castle Road
BRAID
U
Brae
Gilmerton
The Wisp
Millerhill Road
Braid Burn
Hills Drive
Liberton
Kirk Brea
CRAIGMILLAR CASTLE
Liberton Drive
Kirkgate
NORTHFIELD
Road
Liberton Gdns
Lasswade Road
Ferniehill Drive
DRUM WOOD
FAIRMILEHEAD
B 701
Drum St.
GILMERTON
Captain's Rd
Gilmerton Rd
Frogston Rd West
Frogston Rd East
Howden Hall Rd
Lasswade Rd
B 701

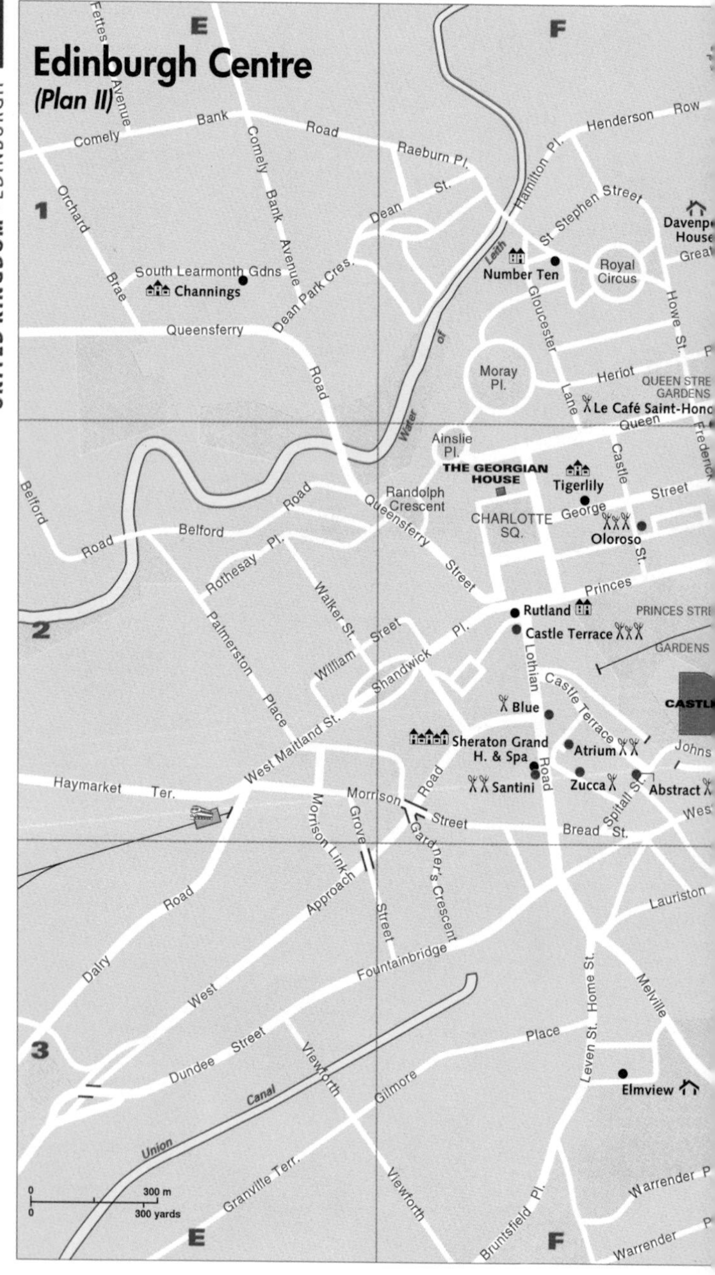
Edinburgh Centre
(Plan II)
E
F
1
2
3
Fettes Avenue
Comely Bank Road
Raeburn Pl.
Henderson Row
Orchard Brae
Comely Bank Avenue
Dean St.
Hamilton Pl.
St Stephen Street
Davenport House
South Learmonth Gdns
Channings
Dean Park Cres.
Number Ten
Royal Circus
Great
Queensferry Road
Water of Leith
Gloucester Lane
Howe St.
Moray Pl.
Heriot
QUEEN STREET GARDENS
Le Café Saint-Honoré
Queen
Ainslie Pl.
THE GEORGIAN HOUSE
Tigerlily
Castle
Frederick
Belford Road
Randolph Crescent
Street
George
CHARLOTTE SQ.
Oloroso
St.
Queensferry Street
Rothesay Pl.
Walker St.
Princes
Rutland
PRINCES STREET GARDENS
Castle Terrace
Palmerston Place
William Street
Shandwick Pl.
Lothian Road
Castle Terrace
CASTLE
Blue
Sheraton Grand H. & Spa
Atrium
Johnston
West Maitland St.
Santini
Zucca
Spittal St.
Abstract
Haymarket Ter.
Morrison Street
Bread St.
West
Morrison Link
Grove Street
Gardner's Crescent
Road
Approach
Dalry Road
Lauriston
Fountainbridge
West
Leven St.
Home St.
Melville
Dundee Street
Place
Viewforth
Gilmore
Elmview
Union Canal
Granville Terr.
Viewforth
Bruntsfield Pl.
Warrender P
Warrender
300 m
300 yards

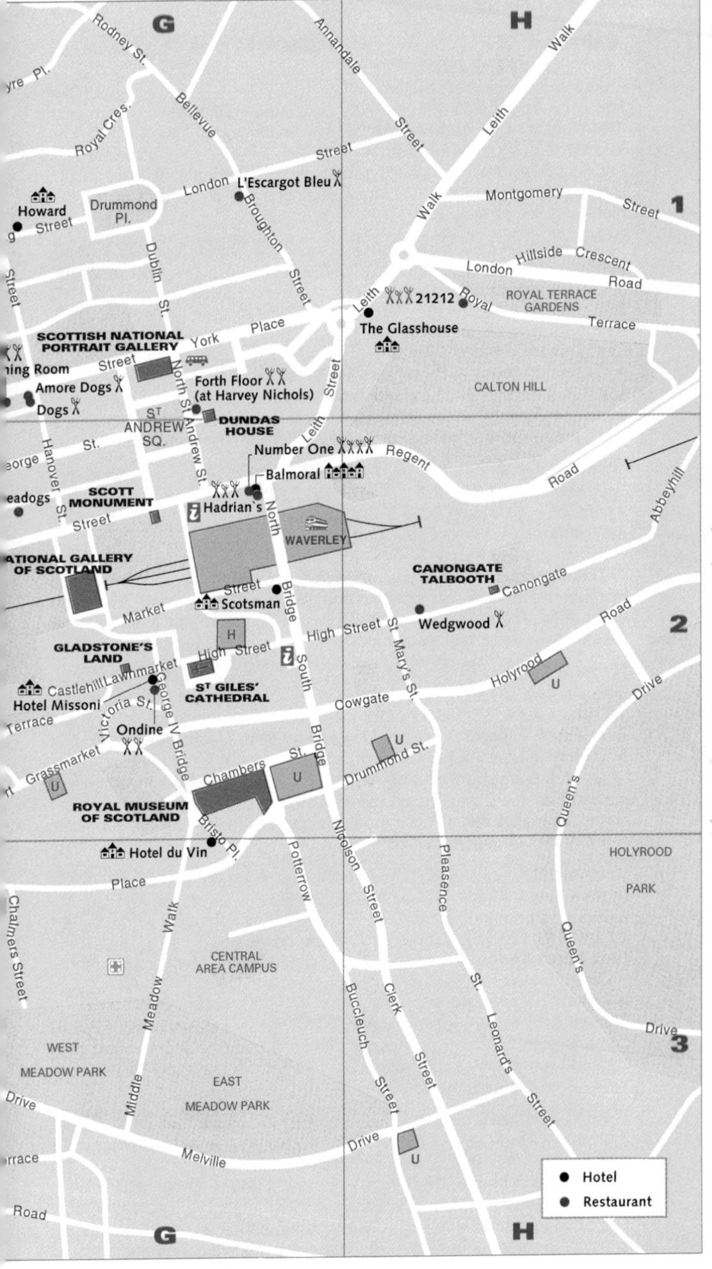

G
H
1
2
3
Rodney St.
Annandale Street
Leith Walk
Bellevue
Royal Cres.
London Street
L'Escargot Bleu
Broughton Street
Howard
Drummond Pl.
Dublin St.
Montgomery Street
Hillside Crescent
London Road
21212
Royal Terrace
ROYAL TERRACE GARDENS
The Glasshouse
York Place
SCOTTISH NATIONAL PORTRAIT GALLERY
Forth Floor (at Harvey Nichols)
Amore Dogs
Dogs
CALTON HILL
ST ANDREW SQ.
DUNDAS HOUSE
North St Andrew St.
Number One
Regent Road
Balmoral
Hanover St.
SCOTT MONUMENT
Hadrian's
North Bridge
WAVERLEY
Abbeyhill
NATIONAL GALLERY OF SCOTLAND
CANONGATE TALBOOTH
Canongate
Scotsman
Market Street
Wedgwood
High Street
St Mary's St.
GLADSTONE'S LAND
Lawnmarket
Castlehill
Hotel Missoni
ST GILES' CATHEDRAL
South Bridge
Holyrood Road
Cowgate
Victoria St.
George IV Bridge
Ondine
Grassmarket
Chambers St.
Drummond St.
Queen's Drive
ROYAL MUSEUM OF SCOTLAND
Bristo Pl.
Hotel du Vin
Potterrow
Nicolson Street
Pleasance
HOLYROOD PARK
Chalmers Street
Place
Meadow Walk
CENTRAL AREA CAMPUS
Buccleuch Street
Clerk Street
St. Leonard's Street
WEST MEADOW PARK
EAST MEADOW PARK
Middle Meadow Walk
Melville Drive
Road
Hotel
Restaurant

Balmoral

1 Princes St ✉ *EH2 2EQ – ☎ (0131) 556 2414 – www.roccofortecollection.com* **G2**

168 rm – ♦£ 320/335 ♦♦£ 380/400, ☕ £ 20.50 – 20 suites

Rest *Number One and Hadrian's* – see below

♦ Grand Luxury ♦ Classic ♦

Luxurious Edwardian hotel boasting classically styled bedrooms with rich fabrics and grand furnishings. Try traditional afternoon tea, or cocktails in the bar. Highly detailed service.

Sheraton Grand H. & Spa

1 Festival Sq ✉ *EH3 9SR – ☎ (0131) 229 9131 – www.sheratonedinburgh.co.uk* **F2**

253 rm – ♦£ 379/399 ♦♦£ 399/419, ☕ £ 19 – 16 suites

Rest *Santini* – see below

Rest *Terrace* – Menu £ 21/22

♦ Grand Luxury ♦ Business ♦ Classic ♦

Spacious, classically styled hotel with two entrances. Smart bedrooms boast strong comforts and latest mod cons. Impressive four storey glass cube houses restaurants and stunning spa. Overlooking Festival Square, Terrace offers a buffet menu.

Prestonfield

Priestfield Rd ✉ *EH16 5UT – ☎ (0131) 225 7800 – www.prestonfield.com*

23 rm ☕ – ♦£ 295 ♦♦£ 295 – 5 suites *Plan I* **C2**

Rest *Rhubarb* – Menu £ 30 – Carte £ 35/56

♦ Luxury ♦ Stylish ♦

17C country house with opulent interior, where warm colours and dim lighting mix with fine furniture, old tapestries and paintings – very romantic. Bedrooms are luxurious and uniquely appointed. Lavish dining room with intimate atmosphere serves classic and modern dishes.

Howard

34 Great King St ✉ *EH3 6QH – ☎ (0131) 557 3500 – www.thehoward.com*

14 rm ☕ – ♦£ 155/285 ♦♦£ 295 – 4 suites **G1**

Rest *Atholl* – *(booking essential for non-residents)* Menu £ 32

♦ Townhouse ♦ Classic ♦

Series of 3 Georgian townhouses displaying characterful original features and plenty of charm. Comfy period lounges. Spacious, luxurious bedrooms with classic furnishings and a contemporary edge; each room is assigned a butler. Fine dining in elegant restaurant.

Scotsman

20 North Bridge ✉ *EH1 1TR – ☎ (0131) 556 5565 – www.thescotsmanhotel.co.uk* **EY**

47 rm – ♦£ 120 ♦♦£ 300, ☕ £ 15 – 12 suites

Rest *North Bridge Brasserie* – *☎ (0131) 622 2900* – Menu £ 16 (lunch) – Carte £ 24/36

♦ Luxury ♦ Classic ♦

Characterful Victorian hotel with marble staircase and stained glass; formerly home to The Scotsman newspaper. Comfy, classical bedrooms boast mod cons and some views. Impressive leisure facilities. Contemporary brasserie serves modern European menu.

Hotel Missoni

1 George IV Bridge ✉ *EH1 1AD – ☎ (0131) 2206666 – www.hotelmissoni.com*

134 rm ☕ – ♦£ 180/250 ♦♦£ 190/260 – 2 suites **G2**

Rest *Cucina* – Menu £ 15 (lunch) – Carte £ 23/40

♦ Luxury ♦ Design ♦

First hotel in the world from this Milan fashion house; set in striking modern building on corner of The Royal Mile. Impressive modern design. Bedrooms on upper floors have rooftop views. Vibrant bar. Classic Italian cooking eaten at huge sharing tables in Cucina.

Channings

15 South Learmonth Gdns ✉ EH4 1EZ – ✆ (0131) 274 7401 – www.channings.co.uk **E1**

38 rm – ♦£ 95/250 ♦♦£ 125/250 – 3 suites **Rest** – Carte £ 14/30

♦ Townhouse ♦ Stylish ♦

Cosy Edwardian townhouse, tastefully furnished and run by friendly team. Individually appointed bedrooms: newer rooms are spacious, contemporary and themed after Shackleton, who lived nearby. Formal basement restaurant serves Gallic dishes.

Hotel du Vin

11 Bristo Pl ✉ EH1 1EZ – ✆ (0131) 2474900 – www.hotelduvin.com/edinburgh **G3**

47 rm – ♦£ 115/250 ♦♦£ 115/250, £ 14.50

Rest *Bistro* – Carte £ 22/36

♦ Luxury ♦ Design ♦

Boutique hotel located in city's former asylum, with contemporary, wine-themed bedrooms. Search out the murals featuring a caricature of Burke and Hare, and the whisky snug with its 300 spirits. Bistro offers superb wine list and a classic European menu.

Tigerlily

125 George St ✉ EH2 4JN – ✆ (0131) 225 5005 – www.tigerlilyedinburgh.co.uk – Closed 25 December **F2**

33 rm – ♦£ 195/225 ♦♦£ 195/225

Rest – Menu £ 23/33 – Carte £ 27/41

♦ Townhouse ♦ Design ♦

Classic Georgian townhouse concealing a funky, boutique interior. Large, individually designed bedrooms are luxurious, boasting seductive lighting, quality furnishings and superb wet rooms. Busy open-plan bar and dining room have similarly stylish, modern décor.

The Glasshouse without rest

2 Greenside Pl ✉ EH1 3AA – ✆ (0131) 525 8200 – www.theetoncollection.com – Closed 23-26 December **H1**

65 rm – ♦£ 295 ♦♦£ 295/450, £ 16.50

♦ Business ♦ Modern ♦

Contemporary glass hotel with 150 year old church façade. Stylish bedrooms have floor to ceiling windows and some balconies. Impressive two acre roof garden; honesty bar and 3 course room service.

Number Ten without rest

6-10 Gloucester Pl. ✉ EH3 6EF – ✆ (0131) 225 2720 – www.numbertenhotel.com **F1**

30 rm – ♦£ 128/168 ♦♦£ 148/198

♦ Townhouse ♦ Stylish ♦

Luxurious adjoining townhouses with romantic interiors and stunning restored staircases. Decorated in gold, black and silver colour schemes, bedrooms boast top class furnishings and jacuzzis.

Rutland

1-3 Rutland St. ✉ EH1 2AE – ✆ (0131) 2293402 – www.therutland.com – Closed 25 December **F2**

12 rm – ♦£ 250/350 ♦♦£ 250/350, £ 8

Rest – Menu £ 14 (lunch) – Carte £ 25/44

♦ Design ♦ Modern ♦

Boutique hotel with commanding position at top of Princes Street. Stylish, modern bedrooms have bold décor, flat screen TVs and large, slate-floored shower rooms. Intimate basement lounge. Contemporary restaurant uses plenty of Scottish produce in its classic dishes.

Kildonan Lodge
27 Craigmillar Park ✉ *EH16 5PE – ☎ (0131) 667 2793*
– www.kildonanlodgehotel.co.uk *Plan I* **C3**
12 rm – †£ 65/118 ††£ 98/159
Rest ***Mathew's*** – *(dinner only, booking essential)* Menu £ 19
– Carte £ 25/34
♦ Townhouse ♦ Cosy ♦
Well-managed detached Victorian house on main road into city. Spacious and traditionally furnished, with cosy fire-lit drawing room and comfy bedrooms; some with four-posters and jacuzzis. Mathew's offers classical dining and plenty of Scottish produce.

Davenport House without rest
58 Great King St ✉ *EH3 6QY – ☎ (0131) 558 8495*
– www.davenport-house.com – Closed 1 week Christmas **F1**
6 rm – †£ 65/110 ††£ 75/110
♦ Townhouse ♦ Classic ♦
Luxurious Georgian townhouse restored to its former glory. Cosy sitting room and spacious breakfast room. Bedrooms are at the top of the house and are decorated to a very high standard, with bathrooms to match.

Kew House without rest
1 Kew Terrace, Murrayfield ✉ *EH12 5JE – ☎ (0131) 313 0700*
– www.kewhouse.com – Closed 4-31 January *Plan I* **B2**
7 rm – †£ 78/145 ††£ 90/170
♦ Townhouse ♦ Personalised ♦
Personally run stone-built terraced house; larger than it looks from outside. Bedrooms are immaculately kept and up-to-date. Comfortable sitting room with free use of computer.

Elmview without rest
✉ *EH3 9LN – ☎ (0131) 228 1973 – www.elmview.co.uk*
– April-November **F3**
5 rm – †£ 90/110 ††£ 100/130
♦ Townhouse ♦ Modern ♦
Occupies the basement of a Victorian house in pretty terrace overlooking The Meadows. Bedrooms are spotlessly kept and are very large, with modern bathrooms. Owners are very welcoming.

Beverley without rest
40 Murrayfield Ave ✉ *EH12 6AY – ☎ (0131) 337 1128*
– www.thebeverley.com – Closed 23-26 December *Plan I* **B2**
8 rm – †£ 45/85 ††£ 70/100
♦ Townhouse ♦ Personalised ♦
Family-run, bay-windowed Victorian house in a peaceful tree-lined avenue, close to town. Elegant, individually furnished bedrooms display a classical style, boasting co-ordinating fabrics and matching bathrooms. Choice of cooked or continental buffet breakfast.

Number One – at The Balmoral Hotel
1 Princes St ✉ *EH2 2EQ – ☎ (0131) 557 6727*
– www.restaurantnumberone.com **G2**
Rest – *(dinner only)* Menu £ 59
Spec. Scallops with sweetcorn purée, pak choi, peanut and lime juice. Rump of lamb with aubergine purée and smoked tomato pepper stew. Peach and strawberry beignet with lemon verbena parfait.
♦ Modern ♦ Formal ♦
Stylish restaurant in a grand hotel, displaying bold red walls hung with fine art, well-spaced tables and deep corner banquettes. Ambitious cooking uses quality Scottish produce to create elaborate, precisely executed dishes. Assured, attentive service.

XXX ✿

21212 (Paul Kitching) with rm — AC rest, VISA MC AE

3 Royal Ter ✉ EH7 5AB – ✆ (0845) 2221212 – www.21212restaurant.co.uk – Closed 10 days January and 10 days July **H1**

4 rm – †£ 325 ††£ 325

Rest – *(closed Sunday and Monday)* Menu £ 35 (lunch)/65

Spec. Fillet of Cumbrian Old Spot pork with an assiette of Cumberland sausage, ham and black pudding. Pink trout fillet with globe artichokes, confit of leeks, crumpets and ginger butter sauce. Summer trifle with milk and white chocolate custard, vanilla cinnamon and apple

♦ Inventive ♦ Elegant ♦ Design ♦

Smart Georgian townhouse with high-ceilinged dining room, contemporary décor and an open kitchen. The restaurant's name reflects the number of dishes per course; skilful and innovative cooking offers some quirky combinations. Opulent 1st floor sitting room and luxurious bedrooms.

XXX

Castle Terrace — AC VISA MC AE

33-35 Castle Ter. ✉ EH1 2EL – ✆ (0131) 229 1222 – www.castleterracerestaurant.com – Closed 1-24 January, Sunday and Monday **F2**

Rest – Menu £ 20 (lunch) – Carte £ 37/51

♦ Modern European ♦ Design ♦

Set in the shadows of the castle, an understatedly elegant restaurant with gilded ceiling and lovely bar. Refined cooking showcases seasonal, local produce in an assured, unfussy manner, following a 'nature to plate' philosophy.

XXX

Oloroso — AC VISA MC AE

33 Castle St ✉ EH2 3DN – ✆ (0131) 226 7614 – www.oloroso.co.uk – Closed 25-26 December **F2**

Rest – Menu £ 25/40 – Carte £ 30/52

♦ Innovative ♦ Design ♦

Contemporary rooftop restaurant with buzzy atmosphere and good service. Huge glass windows and superb terrace boast city, river and castle views. Bar and grill menus display modern cooking.

XXX

Hadrian's – at Balmoral Hotel — AC VISA MC AE

2 North Bridge ✉ EH1 1TR – ✆ (0131) 557 5000 – www.roccofortecollection.com **G2**

Rest – Menu £ 23/25 – Carte £ 28/41

♦ Brasserie ♦ Brasserie ♦

Delightful restaurant where lime green colour scheme offsets dark floors and brown leather chairs. Brasserie classics display plenty of Scottish produce; excellent value 3 course set menu.

XX

Atrium — AC VISA MC AE

10 Cambridge St ✉ EH1 2ED – ✆ (0131) 228 8882 – www.atriumrestaurant.co.uk – Closed 1 January, 24-26 December, Saturday lunch and Sunday except August **F2**

Rest – Menu £ 20/25 – Carte £ 28/42

♦ Modern European ♦ Design ♦

Seductively lit restaurant with tables made out of old railway sleepers. Great value set selection, interesting à la carte and more ambitious tasting menu. Modern cooking uses local ingredients.

XX

Ondine — AC VISA MC AE

2 George IV Bridge (first floor) ✉ EH1 1AD – ✆ (0131) 226 1888 – www.ondinerestaurant.co.uk – Closed 2-10 January and Christmas **G2**

Rest – Menu £ 18 (lunch and early dinner) – Carte £ 27/42

♦ Seafood ♦ Design ♦ Friendly ♦

Smart, lively restaurant dominated by granite-topped bar and crustacean counter. Classic menus showcase prime Scottish seafood. Straightforward, tasty cooking. Well-structured service.

XX

Dining Room

VISA MC AE

The Scotch Malt Whisky Society, 28 Queen St ✉ EH2 1JX – ✆ (0131) 2202044 – www.thediningroomedinburgh.co.uk – Closed Sunday and dinner Monday

Rest – *(booking essential)* Menu £ 19 (lunch) – Carte £ 20/41 **F2**

♦ Modern European ♦ Elegant ♦

Set in fine Georgian building. Informal bistro by day, offering classic menu; linen and lights by night, with accomplished, modern dishes. Unsurprisingly superb range of whiskies.

XX

Forth Floor - Restaurant (at Harvey Nichols)

A/C VISA MC AE

30-34 St Andrew Sq ✉ EH2 2AD – ✆ (0131) 524 8350 – www.harveynichols.com – Closed 1 January, 25 December, dinner Sunday and Monday **G1**

Rest – Menu £ 25 (weekdays)/34 – Carte dinner Friday and Saturday approx. £ 40

♦ Modern European ♦ Fashionable ♦

Wonderful skyline views from huge room-length window; great sunsets. Bar divides it into formal area with pricier modern European menu, and more causal brasserie; good Scottish ingredients.

XX

Santini – at Sheraton Grand H. & Spa.

A/C P VISA MC AE

8 Conference Sq ✉ EH3 8AN – ✆ (0131) 221 7788 – www.santiniedinburgh.co.uk – Closed 1 January, Saturday lunch and Sunday

Rest – Menu £ 19 – Carte £ 21/45 **F2**

♦ Italian ♦ Fashionable ♦

Smart restaurant in huge glass cube. Dining room split in two: the right side more relaxed with piazza views and pleasant terrace. Wide-ranging menu of Italian classics; good value set selection.

X

Wedgwood

VISA MC AE

267 Canongate ✉ EH8 8BQ – ✆ (0131) 5588737 – www.wedgwoodtherestaurant.co.uk – Closed 3-21 January and 25-26 December **H2**

Rest – Menu £ 14 (lunch) – Carte £ 30/41

♦ Modern European ♦ Friendly ♦

Neat restaurant with bold white and crimson décor, hidden away at bottom of Royal Mile. Personally run, with friendly staff. Well presented, seasonal dishes; generous portions.

X

Dogs

VISA MC AE

110 Hanover St. ✉ EH2 1DR – ✆ (0131) 220 1208 – www.thedogsonline.co.uk

Rest – Carte £ 15/22 **G1**

♦ British ♦ Minimalist ♦ Brasserie ♦

Simple eatery set on the first floor of a classic Georgian mid-terraced property; where an impressive staircase leads up to a small but high-ceilinged dining room and appealing bar. Robust, good value comfort food is crafted from fresh, local, seasonal produce.

X

Blue

A/C VISA MC AE

10 Cambridge St ✉ EH1 2ED – ✆ (0131) 221 1222 – www.bluescotland.co.uk – Closed 1 January, 24-26 December and Sunday except during Edinburgh festival

Rest – Menu £ 20 – Carte £ 19/33 **F2**

♦ Modern European ♦ Fashionable ♦

Strikes a modern note with bright, curving walls, glass and simple settings. A café-bar with a light, concise and affordable menu drawing a young clientele. Bustling feel.

X

Zucca

A/C VISA MC AE

15-17 Grindlay St ✉ EH3 9AX – ✆ (0131) 2219323 – www.zuccarestaurant.co.uk **F2**

Rest – *(booking essential)* Menu £ 11/19 – Carte £ 22/36

♦ Italian ♦

Friendly, well-run restaurant adjacent to Lyceum Theatre. Head upstairs for classic Italian dishes and all-Italian wine list, with great value pre-theatre menus. Book or come after 8pm.

Amore Dogs

104 Hanover St ✉ EH2 1DR – ✆ (0131) 2205155 – www.amoredogs.co.uk – Closed 25 December **G1**

Rest – Carte £ 17/21

◆ Italian ◆ Wine bar ◆

Sister to 'The Dogs' next door, with similar canine-themed décor. Simple, spacious and open-plan, with a buzzy atmosphere and friendly service. Good value, rustic Italian dishes.

L'Escargot Bleu

56-56a Broughton St ✉ EH1 3SA – ✆ (0131) 557 1600 – www.lescargotbleu.co.uk – Closed Christmas **G1**

Rest – Carte £ 24/33

◆ French ◆ Bistro ◆

Authentic French bistro with basement épicerie; sit in the front room, with its large windows, gingham tablecloths and buzzy atmosphere. Keenly priced menus offer classic French dishes.

Le Café Saint-Honoré

34 North West Thistle Street Ln. ✉ EH2 1EA – ✆ (0131) 226 2211 – www.cafesthonore.com – Closed 1 January and 25-26 December

Rest – *(booking essential)* Menu £ 23 – Carte £ 27/43 **G2**

◆ French ◆ Bistro ◆

Long-standing classical French bistro, hidden away down a side street. Simple interior crammed full of mirrors and bric-a-brac. Affordable daily menu with Gallic touch. Friendly service.

Seadogs

43 Rose St ✉ EH2 2NH – ✆ (0131) 225 8028 – www.seadogsonline.co.uk – Closed 1 January and 25 December **G2**

Rest – *(booking advisable)* Carte £ 16/20

◆ Seafood ◆ Design ◆

Lively seafood restaurant with canine motif, funky wallpaper and fast, friendly service. Well-priced menus offer sustainable fish and chips, plus a choice of tasty lighter dishes.

LEITH

Plan I

Malmaison

rm,

1 Tower Pl ✉ EH6 7DB – ✆ (0131) 468 5000 – www.malmaison-edinburgh.com **C1**

100 rm – †£ 99/205 ††£ 99/205, ☐ £ 14.95

Rest *Brasserie* – Menu £ 16 (lunch) – Carte £ 28/50

◆ Business ◆ Stylish ◆

Elegantly styled converted sailors' mission, located on the quayside. Comfortable, well-equipped bedrooms; superiors/suites are stylish, luxurious and boast attractive harbour views. Large, bustling bar. Busy brasserie offering menu of classically based dishes.

Martin Wishart

54 The Shore ✉ EH6 6RA – ✆ (0131) 553 3557 – www.martin-wishart.co.uk – Closed 25-26 and 31 December, 1-15 January, Sunday and Monday

Rest – *(booking essential)* Menu £ 25 (weekday lunch)/60 **C1**

Spec. Roasted Kilbrannan scallops with Bellotta ham and parmesan velouté. Loin of Borders roe deer with goat's cheese gnocchi. Jivara milk chocolate mousse with Earl Grey ice cream.

◆ Innovative ◆ Formal ◆ Elegant ◆

Discrete façade leads to tastefully decorated room with bold, modern designs. Underpinned by a classical base, well presented dishes display carefully judged modern touches and excellent ingredients. Two tasting menus available.

Kitchin (Tom Kitchin)

78 Commercial Quay ✉ EH6 6LX – ✆ (0131) 555 1755 – www.thekitchin.com – Closed 1-14 January, Sunday and Monday
Rest – Menu £ 25 (lunch) – Carte £ 55/61 **C1**
Spec. Razor clams with chorizo and lemon confit. Lobster thermidor with buttered samphire, sea spinach and sautéed squid. Gooseberry panna cotta with a chilled gooseberry consommé and crème fraîche ice cream.
◆ French ◆ Design ◆
Converted dockside warehouse overlooking the quay. Expect refreshingly honest, very flavoursome and unfussy cooking from menus offering considerable choice. Seasonality, freshness and provenance are at the heart of the chef's philosophy.

Plumed Horse (Tony Borthwick)

50-54 Henderson St ✉ EH6 6DE – ✆ (0131) 554 5556 – www.plumedhorse.co.uk – Closed 2 weeks July, 1 week November, Christmas, 1-2 January, Sunday and Monday **C1**
Rest – Menu £ 26/48
Spec. Millefeuille of crab and langoustines, passion fruit mayonnaise, sweet and sour pineapple. Fillets of sea bream and red mullet with fennel gnocchi. Peach and raspberry baked Alaska with candied pistachios.
◆ Modern ◆ Neighbourhood ◆
Personally run restaurant with ornate ceiling, vivid paintings, an intimate feel and formal service. Well-crafted, classical cooking with strong, bold flavours and good use of Scottish ingredients.

Vintners Rooms

The Vaults, 87 Giles St ✉ EH6 6BZ – ✆ (0131) 554 6767 – www.vintersrooms.com – Closed 23 December-7 January, Sunday and Monday **C1**
Rest – Menu £ 23 (lunch) – Carte £ 40/48
◆ Mediterranean ◆ Rustic ◆
Hugely atmospheric: one characterful, flag-floored room and another more intimate, candlelit room with superb 1739 stucco ceiling. Wide-ranging Mediterranean menu. Over 1,200 single malts.

Cafe Fish

60 Henderson St ✉ EH6 6DE – ✆ (0131) 538 6131 – www.cafefish.net – Closed 3 weeks January, 25-26 December, Sunday dinner and Monday
Rest – Menu £ 14/24 – Carte approx. £ 26 **C1**
◆ Seafood ◆ Rustic ◆ Brasserie ◆
Light, modern, quasi-industrial style, with brushed aluminium bar and open-plan kitchen. Short menus of simply cooked seafood; good value fresh fish from sustainable Scottish sources.

The Ship on the Shore

24-26 The Shore ✉ EH6 6QN – ✆ (0131) 555 0409 – www.theshipontheshore.co.uk **C1**
Rest – Menu £ 15 – Carte £ 30/45
◆ Seafood ◆ Pub ◆
Smart period building on the quayside, modelled on the Royal Yacht Britannia and filled with nautical memorabilia. Seafood menu offers fresh, simply prepared, classical dishes.

The Kings Wark

36 The Shore ✉ EH6 6QU – ✆ (0131) 554 9260 – www.kingswark.com – Closed 25-26 December **C1**
Rest – Carte £ 13/30
◆ Traditional ◆ Pub ◆
Brightly coloured pub with old-fashioned interior, set on the quayside. Handwritten menus offer hearty, classical dishes; blackboard displays freshly prepared, locally sourced specials.

GLASGOW

GLASGOW

Population: 616 000 (conurbation 1 228 000) – Altitude: 8m

idler Steve/Prisma/Age Fotostock

Rising like the proverbial phoenix from the ashes, Glasgow can claim to be one of the great urban success stories of the past 20 years. Like a punch-drunk boxer, Scotland's second city was slumped against the ropes throughout much of the post-World War II era, its shipbuilding industry in tatters, its troubled, drink-fuelled reputation a byword for the poverty endemic to its inner areas. But the place that Daniel Defoe once called "the cleanest and beautifullest and best built city in Britain, London excepted" had an ace up its sleeve: the 1990 City of Culture award that turned its PR image upside down. From that time on, Glasgow has grown immensely as an arts, business and retail centre, and tourists have discovered for themselves its grand Victorian façade and eye-catching riverside milieu.

The Clyde played a pivotal role in the original growth of Glasgow: in the 18C as a source of trade with the Americas, and in the 19th as the centre for one of the world's major shipbuilding industries. During this period many of the imposing buildings on show today were constructed, a testament to the wealth of the city. Enlightened patrons held sway, and the world of art benefited handsomely from their endowments. Now Glasgow reaps a rich cultural harvest, a dynamic image hard to imagine in the debris of a generation ago.

LIVING THE CITY

Look at a map of Glasgow and see just how the centre is laid out, Manhattan style, in a neat grid system that makes getting around town a piece of cake. Cocooned within the curving arm of the M8 motorway, the area is home to most of Glasgow's main cultural venues. "Old Glasgow", just to the east, was the original medieval centre, but is now a thriving arts quarter, and also incorporates a large part of the city's gay scene. The West End, in a kind of hinterland away from the grid system, has practically invented itself as a town in its own right. It's a bohemian district filled with cafés, bars and restaurants, a million miles from the old image of a rough, tough city, and it's where you'll also find the main art gallery and museum at Kelvingrove. Go across the Clyde, to the south, and amongst the sprawling suburbs you come across gems like The Burrell Collection and Charles Rennie Mackintosh's Scotland Street School Museum and House for an Art Lover.

PRACTICAL INFORMATION

ARRIVAL-DEPARTURE

Glasgow International Airport is 8 miles west. A taxi costs approximately £20 or there are buses that stop close to Central Station.

TRANSPORT

Glasgow has a circular underground system covering the centre and west of the city – to go right round it only takes 24 minutes! Adult single fares are £1, returns £2. 10 and 20 multi-journey tickets are available, as are seven-day passes and day passes (the Discovery ticket).

Black cabs are easy to hail all over the city: expect your driver to have a smile on his face as Glasgow cabbies are some of the friendliest in the world.

A good idea on the buses is to buy a FirstDay ticket from your driver; this will let you hop on or off buses all day until midnight.

EXPLORING GLASGOW

If you'd been bold enough to take a walk around Glasgow in its days of great industrial output, you'd have been forgiven for thinking the buildings had been constructed of black slate, such was the soot and pollutant grime that attached itself to them. Actually, many of those buildings were things of beauty constructed with red or blond sandstone, and in more recent times they've been restored to their striking original appearance. **George Square** - the heart of the city - typifies all this. It's an inspiring place to stand, its splendidly ornate nineteenth century buildings confidently reflecting the era in which they were built; in the City Chambers to this day sits the City Council. But Glasgow wouldn't be Glasgow if there weren't a temple of culture nearby, and round the corner in Queen Street stands the **Gallery**

of Modern Art, housed in a stunning neo-classical building. Outside London, it's the UK's second most visited contemporary art gallery; this is a city that knows how to put on a show.

➜ BIG MACK

In the relentless days of heavy industry around the Clyde, one man's aesthetic vision helped raise people's sights above the back-breaking level of the shipyard and steel furnace. Charles Rennie Mackintosh kept alive the idea of architectural creativity with his stunning Art Nouveau 'Glasgow Style' designs. Go to Renfrew Street at the northern end of the central grid to find his elegant and unmistakable masterpiece, the **Glasgow School of Art**, started in 1899 and finished a decade later. Its stunning façade has been compared in scale and majesty to Michelangelo. On a slightly lesser scale, Mackintosh's distinctive lines are also evident at The Willow Tea Rooms in Sauchiehall Street and Buchanan Street (they're a great place to admire his work over a cuppa). Across the river, House For an Art Lover pretty much sums up its appeal. The legacy of CRM lives on: in 1999 Glasgow was the UK's City of Architecture and Design, and one of Mackintosh's buildings, the Glasgow Herald newspaper office, began a new life as **The Lighthouse**, Scotland's national centre for architecture and design. Since it opened its doors, The Lighthouse has attracted over three quarters of a million visitors making the most of attractions such as the Mackintosh Centre and The Mackintosh Tower with its spectacular views of the city.

➜ WE NEED TO TALK ABOUT KELVIN

It's quite handy that it rains so much in Glasgow. It's a very good excuse for visiting any of the thirteen museums and galleries that scatter themselves around the city, which, through its teeming industrial and cultural heritage, owns one of the richest collections in Europe. There's the **People's Palace** on Glasgow Green, for instance, which lives up to its name by telling the social history of the city from 1750 to the present day, including the rise of the tobacco lords, the poverty of the 'single end' tenement house families of the 1930s...and the eye-catching banana boots Billy Connolly wore on stage in the 1970s. A trip down to the Clyde brings you to the Science Centre and IMAX theatre, a state-of-the-art attraction setting a benchmark for scientific discovery, and most definitely not the place for visitors with a creationist slant on life. Carry on down into the depths of the southern suburbs for **The Burrell Collection**, quite simply a magnificent display of works of art from all periods and all continents, or head eastwards to the eerie shadow of the Necropolis (where Glasgow's industrial barons keep silent watch over their one-time nest-egg) where you'll find Provand's Lordship, the medieval city's only surviving house, now extensively restored to give a real fifteenth century feel. It's in the West End of the city, though, that arguably Glasgow's favourite landmark can be found: **The Kelvingrove** Art Gallery and Museum was reopened in 2006 after renovations, and it houses one of the finest civic collections in Europe, including fine art, archaeology and exhibits from the natural world. And if that's not enough to sate your appetite, the impressive Hunterian Museum and Art Gallery is just across Kelvingrove Park.

➜ TOPS FOR SHOPS

You might not be surprised to find that the shopping's rather good in Glasgow; in fact it's second only to London for retail power in the UK. In the central grid are no fewer than three precincts, in Argyle, Sauchiehall and Buchanan Streets. There are shopping malls (Buchanan Galleries and St. Enoch Centre), and boutique designer malls (Princes Square and the Italian Centre). Out in the slightly more rarefied air of the West End, you'll find a treasure trove of antiques and rare books, while back in the heart of town, the art galleries of West Regent Street highlight the contemporary works of both up-and-coming and established artists.

→ CLYDE VIBES

If you want to have a good time in this city it's almost impossible to fail in your quest. There's a vibrant music scene: in fact, Time Magazine not so long ago likened Glasgow to Detroit during its 1960s Motown heyday. Certainly the city has a happy knack of throwing up talented bands – of recent vintage are, for example, Franz Ferdinand, Belle & Sebastian and The Fratellis. And it was at the now legendary venue King Tut's Wah Wah Hut that Oasis were discovered by Glasgow's most famous record mogul Alan McGee. There are lots of venues to watch live music, from small pubs to landmark spaces such as the Glasgow Royal Concert Hall, the Scottish Exhibition Centre (impressively modernistic next to the Clyde), and the Barrowlands, a byword for musical excellence in the east end of the city.

Glasgow's legendary drinking culture does still live on, albeit in a noticeably more laidback 'European' style than of old, and nowhere more so than the cobbled Ashton Lane off trendy Byres Road in the West End. Jinty McGinty's bar is a favourite here, along with the locally renowned Chip. Beware strolling here on weekend evenings, as the cobbles disappear beneath the ever-burgeoning wave of humanity. Another establishment that will impress is Babbity Bowster, set in a carefully renovated townhouse in Blackfriars Street in the city centre, where the ale is invariably top-notch and the surroundings impressively informal.

If you should tire of this endlessly inspiring city, you'd be amazed at how close you are to the rugged Scottish countryside. Grab a seat on a West Highland line train out of Queen Street and you're staring at the wondrous hills within minutes…

CALENDAR HIGHLIGHTS

Glasgow's never short of a festival or two, and Glaswegians flock to them in their thousands. Celtic Connections, in January, is a widely acclaimed celebration of international roots music, while the Comedy Festival, each March, is the biggest in Europe, with the likes of Russell Brand and Joan Rivers doing a turn. Each June, The West End Festival, around Byres Road, is the city's biggest, featuring a wide range of street bands and cos-

GLASGOW IN…

→ ONE DAY

Kelvingrove Art Gallery, the West End, Glasgow School of Art

→ TWO DAYS

Sauchiehall Street (including Willow Tea Rooms), Provand's Lordship and Necropolis, Glasgow Green, a trip on the Clyde, Science Centre

→ THREE DAYS

A train journey to the rolling hills of the Clyde Valley, a concert at one of Glasgow's top ranking venues

tume groups. The same month, the International Jazz Festival does exactly what it says on the label. There's a Merchant City Festival in September, in which that part of Glasgow plays host to a wide variety of cultural shows, but it's the event in chilly November that many locals keep a weather eye open for. Whisky Live, at the Exhibition Centre, is, quite simply, the world's greatest celebration of Scotland's (arguably) finest export.

EATING OUT

The dreaded legend of the deep-fried Mars bar did no favours for the reputation of the Scottish diet. Don't mention it in Glasgow, though. In the last decade, the place has undergone a gourmet revolution, and these days you can enjoy good food in restaurants from all areas of the world. There are now many establishments specializing in modern Scottish cooking and fish menus have come of age. Go to the trendy West End or Merchant City quarters to find bistros and brasseries that wouldn't be out of place in France or Italy. Glasgow has made the most of the glorious natural larder on its doorstep: spring lamb from the Borders, Perthshire venison, fresh fish and shellfish from the Western Highlands and Aberdeen Angus beef. It's always had a lot of respect for its liquid refreshment: if you want beer, you can't go far wrong with a pint of Deuchar's, the award-winning Bitter & Twisted, or an 'imported' Dark Island from the Orkneys: locals have taken to real ale from the Scottish regions in a big way.

Blythswood Square

✉ G2 4AD – ✆ (0141) 248 8888 – www.blythswoodsquare.com
99 rm – 🛉£ 195 🛉🛉£ 285 – 1 suite **D2**
Rest *Restaurant* – see below
◆ Historic ◆ Townhouse ◆ Design ◆
Stunning property – former home of the Scottish RAC – set on delightful Georgian square; original features include beautifully ornate tiled entrance. Good-sized, modern bedrooms.

Hotel du Vin at One Devonshire Gardens

1 Devonshire Gardens ✉ G12 OUX – ✆ (0141) 339 2001 – www.hotelduvin.com rm, Plan I **A1**
45 rm – 🛉£ 150 🛉🛉£ 325, ☕ £ 17 – 4 suites
Rest *Bistro* – *(Closed Saturday lunch and dinner 25 December)*
Menu £ 18 (weekday lunch) – Carte dinner £ 31/51
◆ Townhouse ◆ Stylish ◆
Collection of adjoining 19C houses in terrace, refurbished with attention to detail. Warm, intimate and comfortable bedrooms are named after wines. High levels of service. Smart Bistro offers a classic grill menu, alongside a more innovative à la carte.

Radisson Blu Glasgow

rm,
301 Argyle St ✉ G2 8DL – ✆ (0141) 204 3333
246 rm – 🛉£ 135 🛉🛉£ 145, ☕ £ 16 – 1 suite **D2**
Rest *Collage* – Menu £ 20 – Carte £ 20/35
◆ Business ◆ Modern ◆
Stylish, modern, commercial hotel with impressive open-plan interior; set in central location close to the station. Three styles of bedroom – all offering good levels of comfort. Spacious dining room with central buffet area and all-encompassing menu.

Malmaison

rm,
278 West George St ✉ G2 4LL – ✆ (0141) 572 1000 – www.malmaison.com **C2**
68 rm – 🛉£ 150 🛉🛉£ 150, ☕ £ 13.95 – 4 suites
Rest *The Brasserie* – Menu £ 16 – Carte £ 29/41
◆ Business ◆ Stylish ◆
Visually arresting former Masonic chapel. Comfortable, well-proportioned rooms seem effortlessly stylish with bold patterns and colours and thoughtful extra attentions. Informal Brasserie with French themed menu and Champagne bar.

Abode Glasgow

rm,
129 Bath St ✉ G2 2SZ – ✆ (0141) 221 6789 – www.abodehotels.co.uk
59 rm – 🛉£ 130/175 🛉🛉£ 130/175, ☕ £ 13.50 **D2**
Rest *Michael Caines* – see below
Rest *Bar MC & Grill* – *(Closed Sunday and Monday)* Menu £ 13 (lunch) – Carte £ 37/44
◆ Business ◆ Stylish ◆
Near Mackintosh's School of Art, an early 20C building decorated with a daring modern palette. Striking colour schemes and lighting in the spacious, elegantly fitted bedrooms. All-day dining in stylish bar and grill.

Sherbrooke Castle

rm, rest,
11 Sherbrooke Ave, Pollokshields ✉ G41 4PG – ✆ (0141) 427 4227 – www.sherbrooke.co.uk Plan I **A2**
16 rm ☕ – 🛉£ 75/105 🛉🛉£ 75/175 – 1 suite
Rest *Morrisons* – Menu £ 14 (lunch) – Carte dinner £ 26/38
◆ Castle ◆ Classic ◆
Late 19C baronial Romanticism given free rein inside and out. The hall is richly furnished and imposing; rooms in the old castle have a comfortable country house refinement. Panelled Victorian dining room with open fire.

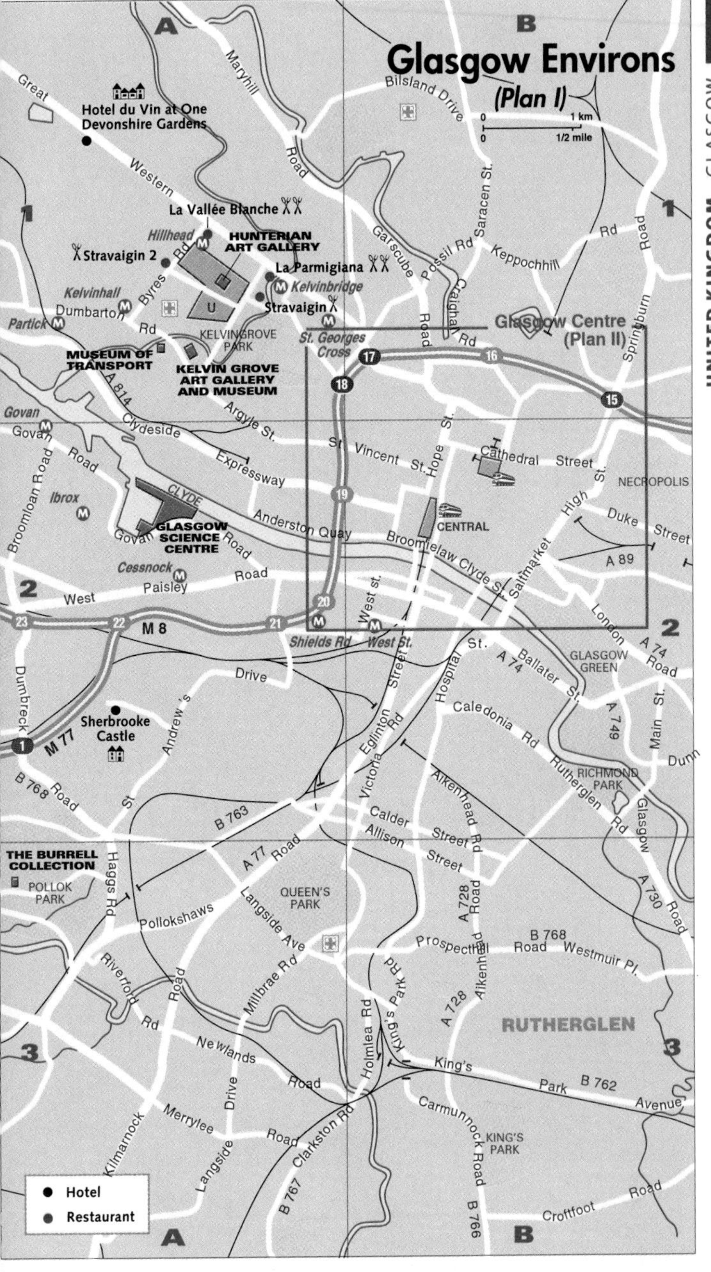
Glasgow Environs
(Plan I)
Hotel du Vin at One Devonshire Gardens
La Vallée Blanche
Stravaigin 2
HUNTERIAN ART GALLERY
La Parmigiana
Stravaigin
MUSEUM OF TRANSPORT
KELVIN GROVE ART GALLERY AND MUSEUM
GLASGOW SCIENCE CENTRE
CENTRAL
NECROPOLIS
Glasgow Centre (Plan II)
GLASGOW GREEN
RICHMOND PARK
Sherbrooke Castle
THE BURRELL COLLECTION
POLLOK PARK
QUEEN'S PARK
RUTHERGLEN
KING'S PARK
Hotel
Restaurant

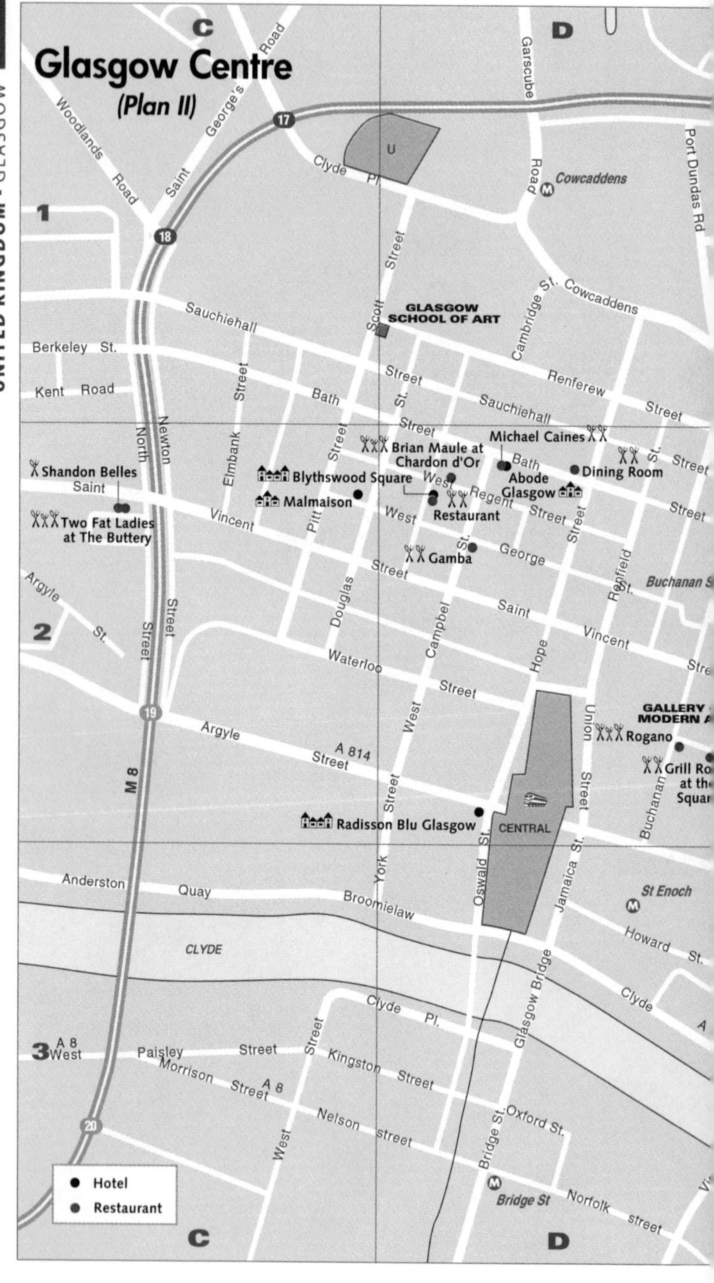
Glasgow Centre
(Plan II)
C
D
1
2
3
Woodlands Road
Saint George's Road
Clyde Pl.
Garscube Road
Cowcaddens
Port Dundas Rd
Scott Street
GLASGOW SCHOOL OF ART
Cambridge St.
Cowcaddens
Sauchiehall Street
Berkeley St.
Kent Road
Elmbank Street
Bath Street
Renferew Street
North Street
Newton Street
Shandon Belles
Saint Vincent Street
Two Fat Ladies at The Buttery
Blythswood Square
Malmaison
Brian Maule at Chardon d'Or
Michael Caines
Abode Glasgow
Dining Room
West Regent Street
Restaurant
Pitt Street
Douglas St.
West George Street
Gamba
Hope Street
Renfield St.
Buchanan St.
Argyle St.
Waterloo Street
Campbel St.
West Street
Argyle Street
A 814
M 8
Union Street
GALLERY OF MODERN ART
Rogano
Grill Room at the Square
Radisson Blu Glasgow
CENTRAL
Buchanan St.
York Street
Oswald St.
Jamaica St.
Anderston Quay
Broomielaw
St Enoch
Howard St.
CLYDE
Clyde Pl.
Glasgow Bridge
Clyde
A 8 West
Paisley Street
Kingston Street
Morrison Street
A 8
Nelson street
Oxford St.
West Street
Bridge St.
Bridge St
Norfolk street
17
18
19
20
Hotel
Restaurant

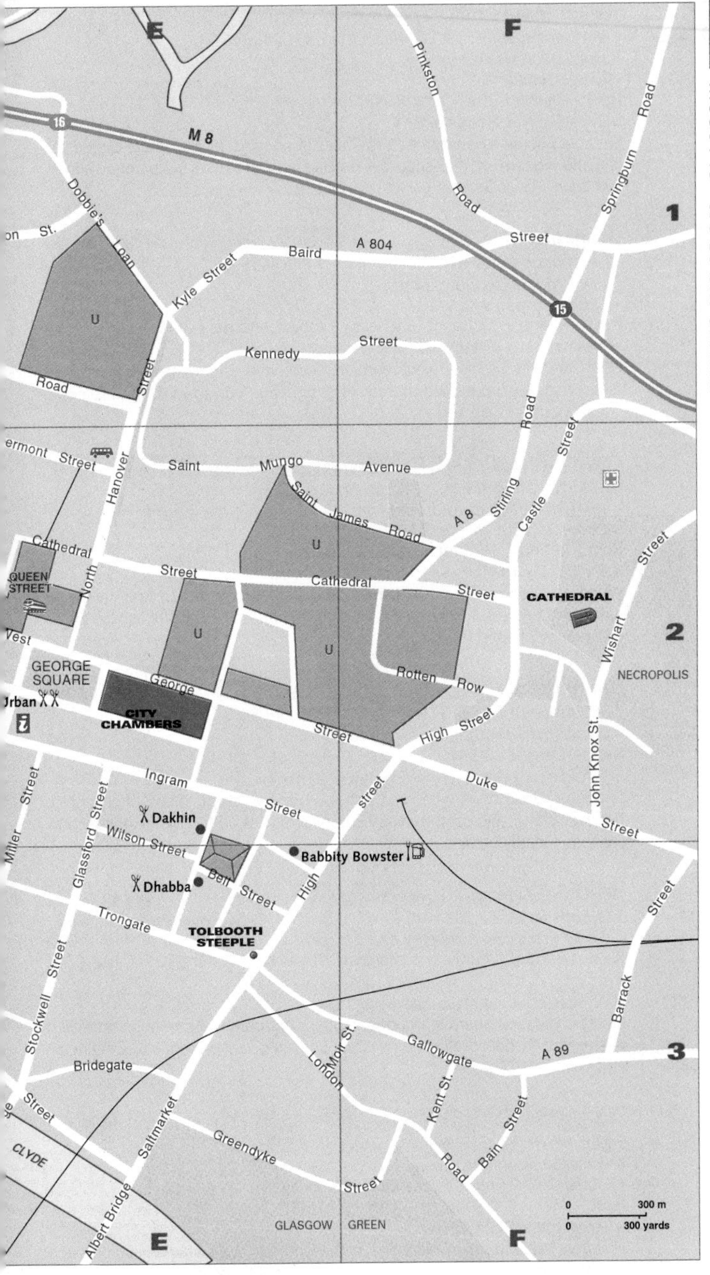
E
F
Pinkston
Road
Springburn
Road
M 8
16
15
Dobbie's
Loan
St.
Baird
A 804
Street
Kyle Street
Kennedy
Street
Road
Street
Hanover
Saint
Mungo
Avenue
Saint
James
Road
A 8
Stirling
Road
Castle
Street
Cathedral
Street
Cathedral
Street
QUEEN
STREET
North
CATHEDRAL
Wishart
Street
NECROPOLIS
GEORGE
SQUARE
George
Rotten
Row
CITY
CHAMBERS
Street
High
Street
Ingram
Street
Duke
Street
John Knox St.
Dakhin
Wilson Street
Babbity Bowster
Dhabba
Bell
Street
High
Miller
Street
Glassford
Street
Trongate
TOLBOOTH
STEEPLE
Street
Barrack
Stockwell
Street
Gallowgate
A 89
Bridegate
London
Moir St.
Kent St.
Street
Bain
Street
Saltmarket
Greendyke
Road
CLYDE
Street
Albert Bridge
GLASGOW
GREEN
E
F
1
2
3
0
300 m
0
300 yards

XXX

Brian Maule at Chardon d'Or

176 West Regent St ✉ G2 4RL – ✆ (0141) 248 3801
– www.brianmaule.com
– Closed Sunday **D2**
Rest – Menu £ 20 – Carte £ 34/52
♦ Modern ♦ Brasserie ♦
Sizeable Georgian house in suburbs, boasting original pillars, ornate carved ceiling and modern art. Well-spaced linen-clad tables; formal service from well-versed team. Classic Scottish cooking.

XXX

Rogano

11 Exchange Pl ✉ G1 3AN – ✆ (0141) 248 4055
– www.roganoglasgow.com
– Closed 1 January **D2**
Rest – Menu £ 22 (lunch and early dinner) – Carte £ 35/57
♦ Seafood ♦ Retro ♦
Long-standing Glasgow institution; art deco, with original panelling, stained glass windows and etched mirrors. Classic menus lean towards local seafood. The langoustines are a must.

XXX

Two Fat Ladies at The Buttery

652 Argyle St ✉ G3 8UF – ✆ (0141) 221 8188
– www.twofatladiesrestaurant.com
– Closed 26 December and 1-2 January **C2**
Rest – Menu £ 19 (lunch) – Carte £ 31/45
♦ British ♦ Rustic ♦
Wood-panelled restaurant with banquette seating and tartan furnishings; an old classic revived. Tasty, seasonal cooking; charming, attentive service and a great range of whiskies.

XX

Restaurant – at Blythswood Square Hotel

11 Blythswood Sq ✉ G2 4AD – ✆ (0141) 248 8888
– www.blythswoodsquare.com **D2**
Rest – Carte £ 33/54
♦ Modern ♦ Trendy ♦ Fashionable ♦
Spacious, stylish salon with large bar and booths. Eclectic menu offers choice between classic and contemporary European dishes, with separate grill section. Smooth, friendly service.

XX

Michael Caines – at Abode Glasgow Hotel

129 Bath St ✉ G2 2SZ – ✆ (0141) 221 6789 – www.michaelcaines.co.uk
– Closed first 2 weeks January and 2 weeks July **D2**
Rest – *(Closed Sunday and Monday)* Menu £ 16 (lunch)/19 – Carte £ 38/47
♦ Modern ♦ Fashionable ♦
Smart, stylish restaurant in boutique hotel, a mirrored wall creating impression of size. Quality décor matched by clean, unfussy cooking prepared with finesse and skill.

XX

La Vallée Blanche

360 Byres Rd ✉ G12 8AY – ✆ (0141) 334 3333
– www.lavalleeblanche.com
– Closed 25 December, 1 January and Monday Plan I **A1**
Rest – Menu £ 17 (lunch) – Carte £ 21/39
♦ French ♦ Formal ♦
First floor restaurant-cum-ski-lodge, with wood-clad walls, stag antler lights and myriad candles. Classical cooking with a seasonal French base. Formal service from a jolly team.

XX

Grill Room at The Square

VISA MC AE D

Second Floor, 29 Royal Exchange Sq ✉ G1 3AJ – ✆ (0141) 225 5615 – www.grillroomglasgow.com – Closed 1 January **D2**

Rest – *(booking advisable)* Menu £ 20 (lunch) – Carte £ 30/58

♦ Steakhouse ♦ Elegant ♦

Second floor of impressive Georgian building on Royal Exchange Square. Appealing menu focuses on seafood and 28-day hung Scottish steak, with choice of sauce and chunky chips.

XX

Urban

A/C VISA MC AE D

23-25 St Vincent Pl ✉ G1 2DT – ✆ (0141) 248 5636 – www.urbanbrasserie.co.uk – Closed 1-2 January and 25-26 December **E2**

Rest – Menu £ 20 – Carte £ 24/45

♦ Modern ♦ Brasserie ♦

Imposing 19C building in heart of city centre. Stylish, modern interior with individual booths and illuminated glass ceiling. Modern English cooking. Live piano at weekends.

XX

Dining Room

VISA MC AE

104 Bath St ✉ G2 2EN – ✆ (0141) 332 6678 – www.diningroomglasgow.co.uk – Closed 25-26 December, 1-2 January and Sunday **D2**

Rest – Menu £ 18 – Carte £ 29/38

♦ Mediterranean ♦ Neighbourhood ♦

Parrot motifs recur everywhere, even on the door handles. Well-spaced tables and mirrored walls add a sense of space to the basement. A free-ranging fusion style prevails.

XX

Gamba

VISA MC AE

225a West George St ✉ G2 2ND – ✆ (0141) 572 0899 – www.gamba.co.uk – Closed 1-2 January, 25-26 December and Sunday lunch **D2**

Rest – Menu £ 20 (lunch)/25 – Carte £ 35/48

♦ Seafood ♦ Rustic ♦

Extensive and appealing seafood menu; simple and effective cooking from chef-owner, with lemon sole a speciality. Comfortable dining room with good service from well-versed team.

XX

La Parmigiana

A/C VISA MC AE D

447 Great Western Rd, Kelvinbridge ✉ G12 8HH – ✆ (0141) 334 0686 – www.laparmigiana.co.uk – Closed 1 January, 25 December and Sunday dinner *Plan I* **A1**

Rest – *(booking essential)* Menu £ 17 (lunch)/19 – Carte £ 27/40

♦ Italian ♦ Neighbourhood ♦

Compact, pleasantly decorated traditional eatery with a lively atmosphere and good local reputation. Obliging, professional service and a sound, authentic Italian repertoire.

X

Dhabba

VISA MC AE

44 Candleriggs ✉ G1 1LE – ✆ (0141) 553 1249 – www.thedhabba.com – Closed 1 January **E3**

Rest – Menu £ 10 (lunch) – Carte £ 22/43

♦ Indian ♦ Exotic ♦

In the heart of the Merchant City, this large, modern restaurant boasts bold colours and huge wall photos. Concentrates on authentic, accomplished North Indian cooking.

Stravaigin

28 Gibson St, (basement) ✉ G12 8NX – ☎ (0141) 334 2665
– www.stravaigin.com
– Closed 25 December and 1 January *Plan I* **A1**
Rest – *(dinner only and lunch Saturday-Sunday)* Carte £ 24/32
♦ Modern ♦ Bistro ♦
Well-run, long-standing eatery with relaxed, informal feel. Bustling bar and welcoming basement dining room with soft, low lighting. Interesting modern menus display worldwide influences.

Stravaigin 2

8 Ruthven Lane (off Byres Rd) ✉ G12 9BG – ☎ (0141) 334 7165
– www.stravaigin.com
– Closed 1 January, lunch 2 January and 25-26 December *Plan I* **A1**
Rest – Menu £ 13 (lunch)/15 – Carte £ 18/30
♦ Modern ♦ Friendly ♦
Lilac painted cottage tucked away in an alley off Byres Road. Simple, unfussy, modern bistro-style interior, spread over two floors. Eclectic menu offers something for everyone.

Dakhin

First Floor, 89 Candleriggs ✉ G1 1NP – ☎ (0141) 553 2585
– www.dakhin.com
– Closed 1 January **E2**
Rest – Menu £ 10 (lunch) – Carte £ 22/43
♦ South Indian ♦ Cosy ♦
Large open-plan first floor restaurant in redeveloped area of city, serving authentic, flavoursome south Indian cooking. Friendly, informal atmosphere; knowledgeable service.

Shandon Belles

652 Argyle St ✉ G3 8UF – ☎ (0141) 221 8188
– www.twofatladiesrestaurant.com
– Closed 1-2 January, 26 December and Sunday **C2**
Rest – *(booking advisable)* Menu £ 16 (lunch and early dinner) – Carte £ 18/23
♦ Scottish ♦ Neighbourhood ♦ Cosy ♦
Rustic restaurant in the basement of The Buttery, with exposed brick walls, church pews and simply laid tables. Tasty, unfussy dishes with a hearty base. Friendly service.

Babbity Bowster

16-18 Blackfriars St ✉ G1 1PE – ☎ (0141) 552 5055
– Closed 25 December and 1 January **E3**
Rest – Carte £ 15/21
♦ Traditional ♦ Pub ♦
Double-fronted Georgian pub with fiercely Scottish interior; close to the Merchant City. Honest, seasonal cooking features traditional Scottish favourites; restaurant menu is more elaborate.

Eurozone : €

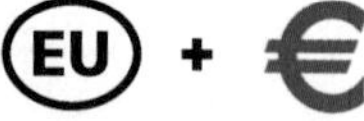

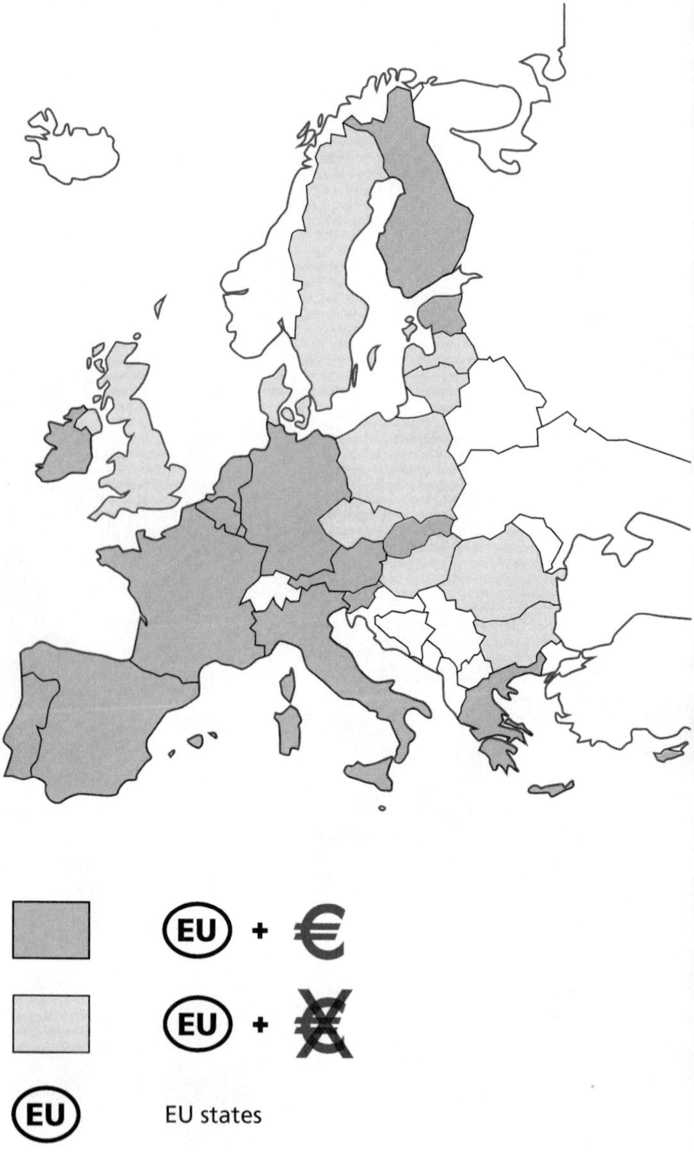

EU states

Schengen Countries

Area of free movement between member states

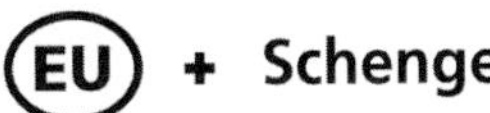

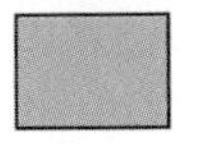
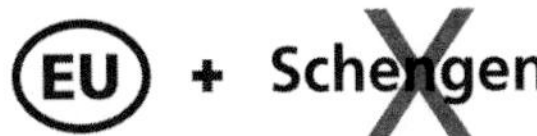

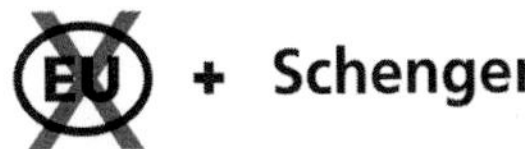

Driving in Europe

KEY

The information panels which follow give the principal motoring regulations in force when this guide was prepared for press; an explanation of the symbols is given below, together with some additional notes.

Speed restrictions in kilometres per hour applying to:

 motorways

 dual carriageways

 single carriageways

 urban areas

 Maximum permitted level of alcohol in the bloodstream. This should not be taken as an acceptable level - it is NEVER sensible to drink and drive.

 Whether tolls are payable on motorways and/or other parts of the road network.

 Whether seatbelts are compulsory for the driver and all passengers in both front and back seats.

 Whether headlights must be on at all times.

Driving in Europe

AUSTRIA	A	130		100	50	0,05	●	●	
BELGIUM	B	120	120	90	50	0,05		●	
CZECH REPUBLIC	CZ	130		90	50	**0,00**	●	●	31/10 -31/3
DENMARK	DK	130		80	50	0,05		●	●
FINLAND	FIN	120		80	50	0,05		●	●
FRANCE	F	130	110	90	50	0,05	●	●	
GERMANY	D			100	50	0,05		●	
GREECE	GR	120		90	50	0,05	●	●	
HUNGARY	H	130	110	90	50	**0,00**	●	●	●
IRELAND	IRL	120		80	50	0,08		●	
ITALY	I	130		90	50	0,05	●	●	●
LUXEMBOURG	L	130		90	50	0,08		●	
NETHERLANDS	NL	120	100	80	50	0,05		●	
NORWAY	N	90		80	50	0,02	●	●	●
POLAND	PL	130	120	90	50	0,02	●	●	1/10 -28/2
PORTUGAL	P	120	100	90	50	0,05	●	●	
SPAIN	E	120		90	50	0,05	●	●	
SWEDEN	S	110		70	50	0,02		●	●
SWITZERLAND	CH	120	100	80	50	0,05	●	●	
UNITED KINGDOM	GB	112		96	48	0,08		●	

● Compulsory

1/11-30/4 Period of regulation enforcement

Distances

A AUSTRIA
AL ALBANIA
B BELGIUM
BG BULGARIA
BIH BOSNIA-HERZEGOVINA
BY BELARUS
CZ CZECH REPUBLIC
CH SWITZERLAND
D GERMANY
DK DENMARK
E SPAIN
EST ESTONIA
F FRANCE
FIN FINLAND
GB UNITED KINGDOM
GR GREECE
H HUNGARY
HR CROATIA
I ITALY
IRL IRELAND
L LUXEMBOURG
LT LITHUANIA
LV LATVIA
M MALTA
MD MOLDAVIA
MK MACEDONIA (F.Y.R.O.M.)
MNE MONTENEGRO
N NORWAY
NL NETHERLANDS
P PORTUGAL
PL POLAND
S SWEDEN
RO ROMANIA
RUS RUSSIA
SRB SERBIA
SK SLOVAK REPUBLIC
SLO SLOVENIA
TR TURKEY
UA UKRAINE
123 : distances by road in kilometers
Glasgow
76
Edinburgh
IRL
673
DUBLIN
462
GB
Birmingham
202
LONDON
401
PARIS
127
Orléans
F
554
648
Toulouse
242
293
390
513
619
P
LISBON
MADRID
627
E

N
S
FIN
386
St.Petersburg
HELSINKI
316
OSLO
529
EST
RUS
1163
STOCKHOLM
292
LV
Gothenburg
668
323
LT
DK
COPENHAGEN
RUS
BY
322
PL
Hamburg
NL
286
BERLIN
594
471
WARSAW
AMSTERDAM
699
616
297
UA
Köln
428
D
340
535
Kraków
401
193
Frankfurt on Main
PRAGUE
L
CZ
284
SK
395
MD
128
494
LUXEMBOURG
VIENNA
360
682
Munich
BUDAPEST
225
Strasbourg
400
A
248
RO
245
311
503
H
121
Zurich
156
CH
SLO
HR
BERN
151
282
366
Lyon
317
Milan
BIH
1481
497
333
1857
SRB
BG
314
378
219
Firenze
MNE
Marseille
275
I
MK
ROME
AL
TR
GR
ATHENS
M

Time zones

MID-
NIGHT
180°
150°
120°
90°
60°
30°
+13
60°
-3.30
-3.30
International Date Line
30°
0°
-10
-9.30
+13
-6
30°
+12.45
Meridian
Greenwich
Standard Times ahead of or behind Greenwich Mean Time (+4.30 variation)
+ 12 -
- 11
- 10
- 9
- 8
- 7
- 6
- 5
- 4
- 3
- 2
- 1

Time zones

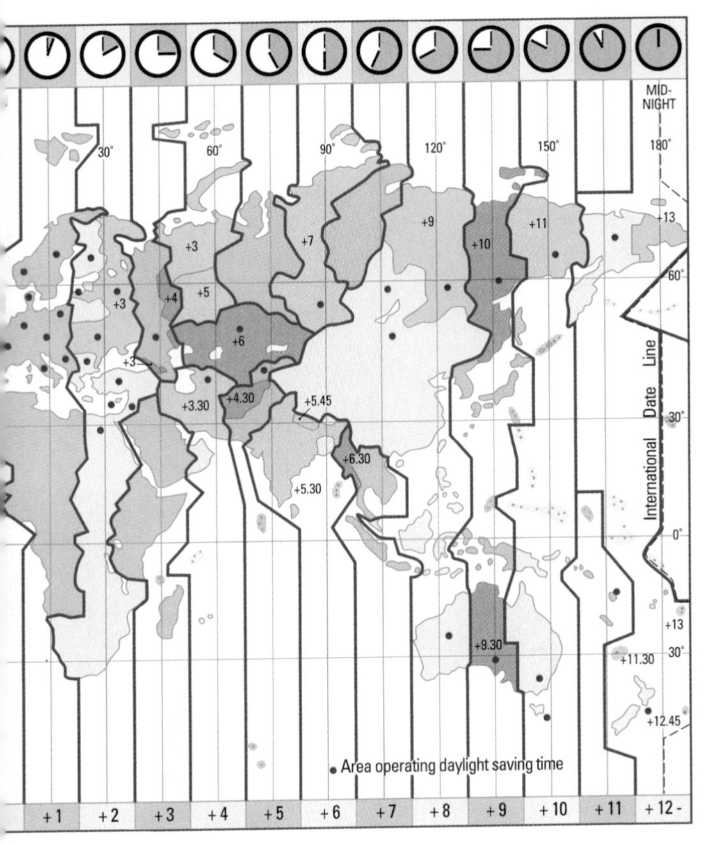

MID-
NIGHT
30°
60°
90°
120°
150°
180°
+13
+9
+11
+7
+10
+3
60°
+3
+4
+5
+6
+3
Line
Date
International
+3.30
+4.30
+5.45
30°
+6.30
+5.30
0°
+13
+9.30
30°
+11.30
+12.45
Area operating daylight saving time
+ 1
+ 2
+ 3
+ 4
+ 5
+ 6
+ 7
+ 8
+ 9
+ 10
+ 11
+ 12 -

Town plans

MAIN CONVENTIONAL SIGNS

●	Hotels	●	Restaurants

Sights

	Place of interest		Interesting place of worship

Roads

	Motorway	1	Junctions: complete
	Dual carriageway	1	Junctions: limited
	Pedestrian street		Station and railway

Various Signs

	Tourist Information Centre		Hospital
	Mosque		Covered market
	Synagogue		Public buildings:
	Ruins	H	Town Hall
	Garden, Park, Wood	R	Town Hall (Germany)
	Coach station	M	Museum
	Airport	U	University
M	Metro station		

Manufacture française des pneumatiques Michelin

Société en commandite par actions au capital de 304 000 000 EUR
Place des Carmes-Déchaux – 63 Clermont-Ferrand (France)
R.C.S. Clermond-Fd B 855 200 507

Michelin et Cie, Propriétaires-éditeurs, 2011

Dépôt légal : mars 2011

Printed in France : 02-2011/6-1

Compogravure : Jouve, Saran

Impression-Reliure : LA TIPOGRAFICA VARESE, Varese (Italia)

Cover photograph : Nikoner/Fotolia.com